Understand more, learn more, and get a better grade!

www.thomsonedu.com/criminaljustice

This text-specific companion website includes resources that will help you study! Visit today, and for every chapter of the book you'll find:

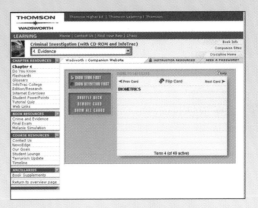

- **Tutorial Quizzes** that give you anytime, anywhere ability to test yourself, as well as feedback for each answer choice.
- **Chapter Outlines** to help focus your reading and study time, and **Chapter Reviews** to ensure that you understand the most essential concepts.

- **Flashcards** that test your knowledge of key terms, as well as a Glossary of key definitions.
- **Web links** to current websites that will enrich your understanding of every important topic!
- A sample **Final Exam** to help you better prepare for "the real thing."

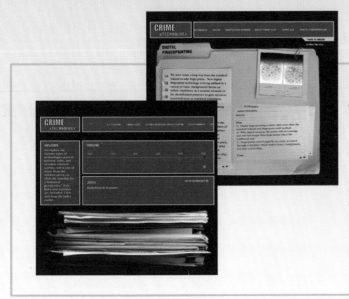

Plus, the Book Companion Website gives you access to Wadsworth's **Criminal Justice Resource Center**. This information-packed resource center includes an interactive *Crime and Technology* module, a *CJ Timeline* covering legal landmarks, a *Terrorism Update*, *Supreme Court* updates, the *Criminal Justice Library* (featuring online journals, news sources, graphs, and statistics), links to careers (in policing, the federal arena, academia, and protective services), a *Student Lounge* (offering study and career tips), and links to fun sites, such as *Disorder in the Courts* and *Help Locate a Fugitive*.

LOG ON TODAY!
The Criminal Investigation Book Companion Website
www.thomsonedu.com/criminaljustice

EIGHTH EDITION

CRIMINAL

INVESTIGATION

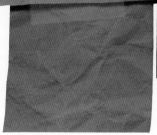

Wayne W. Bennett, LL.B.

Former Chief of Police, Edina, Minnesota, and Boulder City, Nevada

Kären M. Hess, PH.D.

President, Institute of Professional Development
Instructor, Normandale Community College

with contributions by
Christine Hess Orthmann, M. S.

WADSWORTH ™

THOMSON LEARNING

Australia • Canada • Mexico • Singapore
Spain • United Kingdom • United States

THOMSON

WADSWORTH

Criminal Investigation, **Eighth Edition**
Wayne W. Bennett and Kären M. Hess
with contributions by Christine Hess Orthmann

Acquisitions Editor: *Carolyn Henderson Meier*
Assistant Editor: *Jana Davis*
Editorial Assistant: *Rebecca Johnson*
Technology Project Manager: *Amanda Kaufmann*
Marketing Manager: *Terra Schultz*
Marketing Assistant: *Jaren Boland*
Marketing Communications Manager: *Linda Yip*
Project Manager, Editorial Production: *Matt Ballantyne*
Creative Director: *Rob Hugel*
Art Director: *Vernon Boes*

Print Buyer: *Barbara Britton*
Permissions Editor: *Roberta Broyer*
Production Service: *Graphic World Inc.*
Text Designer: *Lisa Delgado*
Photo Researcher: *Terri Wright*
Copy Editor: *Graphic World Inc.*
Cover Designer: *Yvo*
Cover Image: *Copyright © SHOUT/Alamy Images*
Compositor: *Graphic World Inc.*
Text and Cover Printer: *Transcontinental–Interglobe*

Printed in Canada
1 2 3 4 5 6 7 10 09 08 07 06 05

Library of Congress Control Number: 2005936157

Student Edition: ISBN 0-495-09340-8

For more information about our products,
contact us at:
Thomson Learning Academic Resource Center
1-800-423-0563
For permission to use material from this text or product, submit a request online at **http://www.thomsonrights.com**.
Any additional questions about permissions can be submitted by email to **thomsonrights@thomson.com**.

Thomson Higher Education
10 Davis Drive
Belmont, CA 94002-3098
USA

Credits appear on pages 659–660, which constitute a continuation of the copyright page.

Brief Contents

Contents

SECTION 3
INVESTIGATING VIOLENT CRIMES 228

8 Death Investigations 232

9 Assault, Domestic Violence, Stalking, and Elder Abuse 268

APPENDIXES

Preface

elcome to *Criminal Investigation*, Eighth Edition. Designed to be one of the most practical, hands-on, reliable textbooks you will ever purchase, *Criminal Investigation* presents the procedures, techniques, and applications of private and public investigation. The book seamlessly integrates coverage of modern investigative tools alongside discussion of established investigation procedures and techniques. The Eighth Edition features updated, enhanced coverage of such important topics as terrorism and homeland security, cybercrime, forensics and physical evidence, federal law enforcement investigations, report writing, crimes against children, investigative photography and sketching, preparing and presenting cases in court, identity theft, white-collar crime, and much more.

Forensics and crime-scene investigation are increasingly popular components of criminal investigation courses today and are correspondingly emphasized in this text, which features complete coverage of digital fingerprinting, DNA evidence and databases, ballistics, body-fluid collection and examination, contamination of evidence, new technologies, exhibiting evidence in court, and new technologies that are changing the way crime scenes are documented through photography, sketching, and so on.

Opportunities in investigations have altered since the terrorist attacks of 9-11. New careers have opened up in federal law enforcement, and interest in working with federal agencies has grown amongst job seekers. This new edition increases its focus on federal investigations. It also delves more deeply into the fight against terrorism and the ways in which law enforcement, whether federal, state, or local, must be involved and must work collaboratively with other agencies to be effective.

Criminal Investigation can serve as an overview of the entire field or as a solid foundation for specialized coursework. Although the content of each chapter could easily be expanded into an entire book or course, this text provides the basic concepts of each area of investigation and will prove to be an invaluable reference long after students move on from the classroom.

Organization of the Text

In Section 1, the student is introduced to the broad field of criminal investigation; to the elements of an effective, efficient investigation; and to the equipment, technology, and procedures that facilitate investigation (Chapter 1). Important court cases and decisions are cited and explained throughout the text.

Section 2 is designed to acquaint readers with various investigative responsibilities: documenting the scene by note taking, photographing, and sketching (Chapter 2); writing reports (Chapter 3); searching crime scenes and suspects (Chapter 4); identifying and collecting physical evidence for forensic examination (Chapter 5); obtaining information (Chapter 6); and identifying and arresting suspects (Chapter 7).

Sections 3, 4, and 5 illustrate how these responsibilities are carried out in specific types of investigations. Section 3 discusses the basics in investigating violent crimes: death investigations (Chapter 8); assault, domestic violence, stalking, and elder abuse (Chapter 9); sex offenses (Chapter 10); crimes against children (Chapter 11); and robbery (Chapter 12). Section 4 discusses crimes against property: burglary (Chapter 13); larceny/theft, fraud, and white-collar crime (Chapter 14); motor vehicle theft (Chapter 15); and arson (Chapter 16). Section 5 discusses other investigative challenges: computer crimes and their evolution into cybercrimes (Chapter 17); the dual threats of drug-related crime and organized crime (Chapter 18); the illegal activities of gangs, hate groups, and cults (Chapter 19); terrorism and homeland security (Chapter 20); and the culmination of investigations: preparing and presenting cases in court (Chapter 21).

New to This Edition

The Eighth Edition of *Criminal Investigation* has been completely updated with over 800 new references, most of which were published between 2003 and 2005. In addition to this freshness of the material, the text now appears in full color for the first time. Through the use of color we can better capture the details of technical photographs and other instructional images, which facilitates more complete student understanding of the material. A new chapter on terrorism and homeland security represents the most crucial content change made to the Eighth Edition and will be discussed in much greater detail later. Finally, a new design draws attention to the text's proven pedagogy, including *Do You Know?, Can You Define?, Technology Innovations*, and end-of-chapter *Checklists,* as well as the highlighted key points within the body of each chapter.

A truly exhaustive revision, the Eighth Edition features the following chapter-by-chapter enhancements:

- **Chapter 1: Criminal Investigation: An Overview**—This chapter now covers the dramatic change in the role of the detective, intuitive policing, the investigative process, the "CSI effect," the Case Investigative Life Cycle (CILC), data mining, and federal law enforcement resources for investigators.

- **Chapter 2: Documenting the Crime Scene: Note Taking, Photographing, and Sketching**—New topics include the intuitive pen, common mistakes made by untrained videographers, immersive imaging, the crime scene virtual tour (CSVT), advances in digital cameras, forensic photogrammetry, advances in GIS technology, authenticating digital images, using laser technology for measuring the crime scene, creating virtual crime scenes, and advances in computer-assisted crime-scene sketching.

- **Chapter 3: Writing Effective Reports**—Moved forward for emphasis and greatly expanded in this edition, report writing is now covered alongside other key investigative responsibilities such as documenting the crime scene and gathering information. New additions include an exercise comparing a bad report with a good report, a discussion of how reports are used, the various audiences of reports, the typical path of an investigative report, how a well-written report is created from start to finish, law enforcement report forms, an expanded discussion of the characteristics of effective reports, an expanded discussion of conclusionary language, some common problems with investigative reports, the differences between content and form, an evaluation checklist for reports, and citizen online report writing.

- **Chapter 4: Searches** (formerly Chapter 3)—Coverage of nearly 20 new Supreme Court decisions and a wealth of updated topics including the *United States v. Banks* (2003) Supreme Court ruling establishing the amount of time to wait before forcing entry to execute a search warrant; the peculiarity requirement; consent once removed; the *Hiibel* (2004) Supreme Court ruling requiring individuals to identify themselves during a *Terry* stop; the *Thorton v. United States* (2004) Supreme Court ruling that police can search a vehicle incident to arrest even if the arrestee has left the vehicle; *Illinois v. Lidster* (2004), in which the Supreme Court upheld the constitutionality of informational checkpoints; the *United States v. Flores-Montano* (2004) ruling that privacy interests *do* apply to vehicles crossing our borders; underwater searches; and the *Illinois v. Caballes* (2005) Supreme Court confirmation that a K-9 sniff does not constitute a search.

- **Chapter 5: Forensics/Physical Evidence** (formerly Chapter 4)—This chapter has been substantially expanded and updated because of growing interest in forensics techniques. It is also one of the best illustrated chapters of this new text; the full-color format brings numerous new photographs and illustrations to life. New coverage includes innovations in storing and tracking evidence, on-scene scanning of fingerprints, language analysis, automating DNA analysis, scent evidence, advances in examining firearms evidence, the 4R rule for examining glass evidence, new technology for detecting and identifying drug evidence, detecting bioterror agents, and product identification coding.

- **Chapter 6: Obtaining Information** (formerly Chapter 5)—New topics include using the Internet in investigations, the questioning process, avoiding contamination of an interview, the *Crawford v. Washington* (2004) Supreme Court ruling regarding testimonial hearsay, the *Fellers v. United States* (2004) Supreme Court ruling clarifying the Fifth and Sixth Amendments' right to counsel, the *Yarborough v. Alvarado* (2004) Supreme Court ruling that the *Miranda* custody standard applies to juveniles, the *United States v. Patane* (2004) Supreme Court ruling regarding the "fruit of the poisonous tree" doctrine, the "question first" or "beach-heading" interrogation technique and the Supreme Court ruling that the technique is unconstitutional (*Missouri v. Seibert*, 2004), research on "reading faces," the Four-Domain Model for detecting deception, statement analysis, emerging technologies to analyze brain waves to determine truthfulness, and innovations in sharing information across agencies.

- **Chapter 7: Identifying and Arresting Suspects** (formerly Chapter 6)—This chapter now includes advances in facial recognition; integrated biometric identification systems (IBISs), the Integrated Law Enforcement Face-Identification System (ILEFIS), age-progression fugitive portraits, geographic profiling, pretextual traffic stops, sequential vs. "six-pack" identification, biometric identification, undercover officers posing as inmates and online, the *Devenpeck et al. v. Alford* (2004) Supreme Court ruling on probable cause for arrest, *de facto* arrest, the Seizure Scale, avoiding civil liability, research findings on when force is most likely to be used, linear use-of-force continuums, circular use-of-force continuums, advances in less-than-lethal weapons, biometric gun holsters, the New Force Science™ Center, death by indifference, and use-of-force reports.

- **Chapter 8: Death Investigations** (formerly Chapter 7)—New discussions have been included on equivocal deaths, in-custody deaths, staged death scenes, a checklist for entomological evidence, drug-related deaths, expressive violence, instrumental violence, the "beltway snipers," lethal predators, cold cases, and protocol for death notifications.

- **Chapter 9: Assault, Domestic Violence, Stalking, and Elder Abuse** (formerly Chapter 8)—This chapter is crucial to future law enforcement professionals, who continue to be called on to respond to domestic and family violence calls. It now includes guidelines for responding to a domestic violence call, recent research on alternatives to arrest, effectiveness of various interventions, typologies of stalkers, cyberstalking, steps in investigating stalking, and financial abuse and exploitation of the elderly.

- **Chapter 10: Sex Offenses** (formerly Chapter 9)—New coverage includes human trafficking, the Trafficking Victims Protection Act, investigating cold cases, the significance of fantasy in sexual assault, expanded discussion of investigating date rape, detecting beverages that have been tampered with, and the national online registry of sex offenders.

- **Chapter 11: Crimes against Children and Youths** (formerly Chapter 10)—This chapter has been greatly expanded to incorporate new developments and give future investigators a thorough grasp on working cases that involve children. New topics include the Unborn Victims of Violence Act (Laci and Connor's Law), dangers of meth labs for children, special measures for drug-endangered children, considerations during an investigation of a sudden unexplained infant death (SUID), checklist of potential witnesses to child abuse, checklist of potential information sources, tips and reminders for law enforcement investigators, child pornography and sexual exploitation, special child exploitation task forces, federal agencies working against child pornography, international initiatives, investigating cybercrime offenders, the Innocent Images National Initiative, prostitution of juveniles, new software programs to find missing children, investigating a missing child report, going beyond Amber Alerts, child abduction homicides, an update on mass murders in our schools, and a four-pronged threat-assessment model.

- **Chapter 12: Robbery** (formerly Chapter 11)—New topics covered include bank surveillance cameras connected to local police departments and mapping robberies.

- **Chapter 13: Burglary** (formerly Chapter 12)—New coverage includes verified response policy to burglary alarms, DNA evidence in burglaries, and burglary prevention techniques.

- **Chapter 14: Larceny/Theft, Fraud, and White-Collar Crime** (formerly Chapter 13)—Coverage of white-collar crime in particular has been expanded to capture recent high-profile cases and new investigative tactics.

Topics added include the FBI's Financial Crime Section (FCS); radio frequency identification (RFID); terrorist and organized crime thefts; vendor fraud; cactus theft; livestock theft and reading brands; expanded discussion of cargo theft and supply-chain integrity; mortgage fraud; insurance fraud; Ponzi schemes; healthcare fraud; expanded discussion of identity theft; corporate fraud, including recent corporate scandals; money laundering, including smurfing, layering, structuring, and integration; and the FBI's two-pronged approach to investigating money laundering.

- **Chapter 15: Motor Vehicle Theft** (formerly Chapter 14)—New topics include telematic technology, vehicle cloning, a license-plate reading system, bait cars, border-area auto theft, theft of patrol cars, red flag indicators of stolen heavy equipment, theft of jet skis, Boat Watch USA, and deterring aircraft theft.

- **Chapter 16: Arson, Bombs, and Explosives** (formerly Chapter 15)—New topics include juvenile firesetting, disrupters, advances in technology to detect explosives, and raising awareness of the threat.

- **Chapter 17: Computer Crime and Its Evolution into Cybercrime** (formerly Chapter 16)—The latest techniques for investigating cybercrime are addressed in this chapter, along with key information on new crimes and criminal strategies online. New topics include the cost of computer crime; types of electronic crimes committed in 2005; the "Net" versus the "Web"; live chat and instant messaging; computer worms; denial-of-service attacks; Internet fraud, including reshipper schemes, spam, identity theft, phishing, spoofing, pharming, theft of intellectual property, and piracy of copyrighted material; cyberterrorism; types of investigative tools and equipment; detailed explanation of how a first responder should approach a computer-crime scene; recognizing and collecting traditional and digital evidence; reading an e-mail header; forensic examination of computer evidence; legal considerations in collecting computer evidence; organized cybercrime groups; and the current status of legislation addressing computer crimes.

- **Chapter 18: A Dual Threat: Drug-Related Crime and Organized Crime** (material formerly appeared in Chapters 17 and 19)—This heavily updated chapter now includes coverage of a relatively new illicit drug—Khat; a threat matrix (cocaine, heroin, marijuana, meth, and MDMA); major cocaine trafficking corridors in the United States; indicators of residential drug trafficking; imitation marijuana for undercover officers; drug paraphernalia stores; online drug dealers; identifying clandestine drug labs; indoor marijuana-growing operations; specific types of organized crime; and the enterprise theory of investigation.

- **Chapter 19: Criminal Activities of Gangs and Other Dangerous Groups** (material formerly appeared in Chapters 17 and 18)—New topics include ethnic gangs; gangs, organized crime, and terrorism; recognizing a gang problem; developing conspiracy cases against gangs; warning signs; reading graffiti; retailing; gang units and gang impact teams; civil gang injunctions and ordinances; gangs and community policing; federal efforts to combat the gang problem; hate crimes against the homeless; and investigating hate crimes on the Internet.

- **Chapter 20: Terrorism and Homeland Security** (formerly part of Chapter 19)—Terrorism and homeland security have been expanded into their own chapter to help equip future law enforcement professionals to hit the ground running in the fight against new threats to national security. This thoroughly expanded and updated chapter now includes international terrorism; the London bombings; international terrorist groups such as Hezbollah, Hamas, Palestinian Islamic Jihad, Al Aqsa Martyrs' Brigade, and al Qaeda; domestic terrorist groups in the United States such as white and black supremacists and right- and left-wing extremists, as well as pro-life, animal rights, and environmental extremists; terrorists as criminals; methods terrorists may use; WMD teams; terrorist threats from most likely to least likely; level of impact by weapon used; suspicious mail; detecting radiation and other bioterrorism agents; technological terrorism; funding terrorism; expanded discussion of the USA PATRIOT Act; hometown security and homeland security; investigating possible terrorist activities; the link between terrorism and white-collar crime; typical stages in a terrorist attack; the intelligence cycle; the National Criminal Intelligence Sharing Plan; initiatives in the fight against terrorism; increased border security; community vulnerability assessment; joint terrorism task forces; the role of the media, including the contagion effect; major concerns related to efforts to combat terrorism; and the *Hamdi v. Rumsfeld* (2004) and *Rasul v. Bush* (2004) Supreme Court rulings regarding detainees' rights.

- **Chapter 21: Preparing for and Presenting Cases in Court** (formerly Chapter 20)—This key chapter has been expanded and updated to prepare future investigators to defend their cases in a court of law. New coverage includes eradicating fear of testifying in court, the final report, relative importance of the prosecutor, the use of evidence in the stages of the criminal process, the Brady rule, impeaching testimony, knowing what is expected and the rules of the court, the witness sequestration rule, the American adversary system, expert testimony, a key to testifying during cross examination, and advice on testifying from a seasoned "Officer of the Year" investigator.

How to Use This Text

Criminal Investigation is a carefully structured learning experience. The more actively you participate in it, the more you will learn. You will learn and remember more if you first familiarize yourself with the total scope of the subject. Read and think about the table of contents, which provides an outline of the many facets of criminal investigation.

Then follow these steps for *quadruple-strength learning* as you study each chapter.

1. Read the objectives at the beginning of the chapter. These are stated as *Do You Know?* questions and are designed to help you assess your current knowledge of the subject of each question. Consider any preconceptions you may hold. Also, look at the key terms in the *Can You Define?* section, and watch for them when they are used.

2. Read the chapter while underlining, highlighting, or taking notes—whatever is your preferred study method. Pay special attention to all highlighted information or words that appear in boldface type. The former represent the answers to the chapter-opening *Do You Know?* questions, while the latter comprise the key terms identified in the chapter-opening *Can You Define?* section.

3. When you have finished reading the chapter, read the summary—your third exposure to the chapter's key information. Then return to the beginning of the chapter and quiz yourself. Can you answer the *Do You Know?* questions? *Can You Define?* the key terms?

4. Finally, in Sections 3, 4, and 5, complete the *Application* exercises at the end of each chapter. These exercises ask you to apply the chapter concepts in actual or hypothetical cases. Then read the *Discussion Questions* and be prepared to contribute to a class discussion of the ideas presented in the chapter.

By following these steps, you will learn more information, understand it more fully, and remember it longer.

Note: The material selected to highlight using the quadruple-strength learning instructional design includes only the chapter's key concepts. While this information is certainly important in that it provides a structural foundation for understanding the topic(s) discussed, you cannot simply glance over the *Do You Know?* highlighted boxes and summaries and expect to master the chapter. You are also responsible for reading and understanding the material that surrounds these boxed features.

Exploring Further

The text also provides an opportunity for you to apply what you have learned or to go into specific areas in greater depth through discussions and Internet assignments. Explore each of these areas as directed by the text or by your instructor. Be prepared to share your findings with the class. Good learning!

Ancillaries

To further enhance your study of criminal investigation, the following supplements are available to qualified adopters. Please consult your local sales representative for details.

For the Student

STUDENT STUDY GUIDE (Hal Nees, Metropolitan State College)—This helpful study tool contains chapter summaries, lists of key terms and concepts, and additional exercises to help you master the material, including numerous self-test questions with an answer keys. ISBN: 0-495-17013-5.

CRIME AND EVIDENCE IN ACTION CD-ROM—This engaging simulation provides an interactive discovery of criminal investigations. This CD-ROM features three in-depth crime-scene scenario cases that will allow students to analyze crime-scene evidence and then make decisions that will affect the outcome of the case. Each case allows the student to take on various roles—from scene investigation (including forensics) to arrest, the trial, incarceration, and even parole of the convicted felon. Students are encouraged to make choices as the case unfolds and conduct interactive investigative research in a simulated setting. This CD-ROM may be bundled with the text for a discount. ISBN: 0-534-61531-7.

CRIME SCENES 2.0: AN INTERACTIVE CRIMINAL JUSTICE CD-ROM—Recipient of several *New Media Magazine Invision Awards*, this interactive CD-ROM allows students to take on the roles of investigating officer, lawyer, parole officer, and judge in exciting and realistic scenarios! This CD-ROM may be bundled with the text for a discount. An *Instructor's Manual* is also available. ISBN: 0-534-56831-9.

MIND OF A KILLER CD-ROM—*Mind of a Killer* explores the psyche of a serial killer. The CD-ROM contains over 80 minutes of video, 3D simulations, three textbooks, an extensive mapping system, a library, and much more. ISBN: 0-534-50706-9.

CAREERS IN CRIMINAL JUSTICE 3.0 INTERACTIVE CD-ROM—This engaging self-exploration provides an interactive discovery of careers in criminal justice. The CD-ROM provides personalized results from a self-assessment of interests to help steer students to careers based on their profiles. Students gather information on various careers, from job descriptions and salaries to employment requirements and sample tests. Actual video profiles of criminal justice professionals bring the experience of working in the system to life. ISBN: 0-534-58571-X.

CAREERS IN CRIMINAL JUSTICE: FROM INTERNSHIP TO PROMOTION, FIFTH EDITION (J. Scott Harr and Kären M. Hess)—This supplemental book helps students develop a job-search strategy through resumes, cover letters, and interview techniques. It also provides students with extensive information on various criminal justice professions, including job descriptions, job salary suggestions, and contact information. Also included free is a copy of the *Careers in Criminal Justice 2.0 Interactive CD-ROM*. ISBN: 0-534-62620-3.

WADSWORTH'S GUIDE TO CAREERS IN CRIMINAL JUSTICE, THIRD EDITION (Carol Mathews, Century College)—This 96-page booklet helps students review the wide variety of careers in the criminal justice field. Included are job descriptions, salary suggestions, and contact information. ISBN: 0-495-13038-9.

INFOTRAC® COLLEGE EDITION STUDENT GUIDE FOR CRIMINAL JUSTICE—This 24-page booklet provides detailed user guides for students that illustrate how to use the InfoTrac College Edition database. Special features include login help, a complete search tips cheat-sheet, and a topic list of suggested keyword search terms for criminal justice. ISBN: 0-534-24719-9.

For the Instructor

INSTRUCTOR'S RESOURCE MANUAL WITH TEST BANK (Hal Nees, Metropolitan State College)—This manual offers you learning objectives, key terms, lecture outlines, discussion questions, active learning suggestions, supplemental lecture ideas, student activities and projects, and additional resources for instructors. Also included is a test bank of over 1200 questions in multiple-choice, true/false, fill-in-the-blank, and essay formats, along with a full answer key. ISBN: 0-495-17014-3.

EXAM VIEW®—Create, deliver, and customize tests and study guides (both print and online) in minutes with this easy-to-use assessment and tutorial system. Exam View offers both a Quick Test Wizard and an Online Test Wizard that guide you step-by-step through the process of creating tests, while the unique WYSIWYG capability allows you to see the test you are creating on the screen exactly as it will print or display online. You can build tests of up to 250 questions using up to 12 question types. Using Exam View's complete word-processing capabilities, you can enter an unlimited number of new questions or edit existing questions. ISBN: 0-495-17015-1.

The Wadsworth Criminal Justice Video Library

THE WADSWORTH CRIMINAL JUSTICE VIDEO LIBRARY—So many exciting, new videos . . . so many great ways to enrich your lectures and spark discussion of the material in this text. Please see our current offerings and review/use policies at **cj.wadsworth.com/videos.** The Wadsworth Video Library includes selections from a variety of sources and programs, including:

ABC NEWS VIDEO—Whatever you're looking for in the way of video support—short, high-interest clips from current news events or classic, historic raw footage going back 40 years—you can find it in our ABC News videos! Perfect for use as discussion starters or to enrich your lectures and spark interest in the text material, these videos provide students with a new lens through which to view the past and present, one that will greatly enhance their knowledge and understanding of significant events and open up to them new dimensions in learning. Clips are drawn from such programs as *World News Tonight*, *Good Morning America*, *This Week*, *PrimeTime Live*, *20/20*, and *Nightline*, as well as numerous ABC News specials and material from the Associated Press Television News and British Movietone News collections. Your Thomson Wadsworth representative will be happy to provide a complete listing of videos and policies.

COURT TV VIDEOS—One-hour videos featuring provocative, high-profile, and seminal court cases as well as key topics that affect our legal system. Available videos include Police Force: What Killed Malice Green; Cyber Crime; *Florida v. Wuornos*; Punishment: Cruel and Unusual; and many others. Over 30 videos are available, each of which follows a case from start to finish.

60 MINUTES VIDEO CLIPS—This video contains clips from CBS' acclaimed *60 Minutes* series that focus on the criminal justice system. Each segment is 12 minutes long and highlights a recent high-profile case or high-interest topic such as racial profiling, the impact of Megan's Law, investment fraud, etc.

Plus videos from the *A & E American Justice Series*, *Films for the Humanities*, and more. The A&E videos focus on high-interest topics and cases and feature episodes from A&E's *American Justice* series. Topics include life as a public defender, the challenges facing homicide detectives, juvenile justice, and unusual defenses criminals have tried to use. Or choose from hundreds of *Films for the Humanities* videos of varying length on such current topics as domestic violence, terrorism, juvenile courts, victim issues, white-collar crime, life after prison, and more. Some videos are less than ten minutes in length and provide ideal lecture launchers. Other videos are longer (up to 100 minutes) and can be used to start a deeper classroom discussion.

Your Thomson Wadsworth representative will be happy to provide details on our video policy by adoption size.

Acknowledgments

A number of professionals from academia and the field have reviewed the previous editions of *Criminal Investigation* and provided valuable suggestions. We thank them all: Joel J. Allen, Western Illinois University; Thomas Allen, University of South Dakota; Frank Anzelmi; Greg Arnold, Manatee Community College; John Ballard, Rochester Institute of Technology; Robert Barthol, Chabot College; Alison McKenney Brown, Wichita State University; Joseph Bunce, Montgomery College; William Castleberry, University of Tennessee at Martin; Walt Copley, Metropolitan State College of Denver; Edward Creekmore, Northland Community College; Elmer Criswell, Harrisburg Area Community College; Tom Cuda, Bunker Hill Community College; Stanley Cunningham, Western Illinois University; Andrew Dantschich, St. Petersburg Junior College; Wayne Dunning, Wichita State University; Cass Gaska, Henry Ford Community College; Bruce Gordon, University of Cincinnati; Edmund Grosskopf, Indiana State University; Keith Haley, University of Cincinnati; George Henthorn, Central Missouri State University; Robert Hewitt, Edison Community College; John Hicks, Hocking Technical College; Robert R. Ives, Rock Valley College; George Keefer, Southern Illinois at Carbondale; Richard Kurek, Erie Community College North; Robert A. Lorinskas, Southern Illinois at Carbondale; Stan Malm, University of Maryland; Jane E. McClellan; Gayle Mericle, Western Illinois University; Michael Meyer, University of North Dakota; Jane Kravits Munley, Luzerne County Community College; Robert Neville, College of the Siskiyous; James F. Newman, Rio Hondo Community College; Thomas O'Connor, North Carolina Wesleyan College; William L. Pelkey, Eastern Kentucky University; Ronald A. Pricom, New Mexico State University; Charles Quarles, University of Mississippi; Walter F. Ruger, Nassau Community College; Joseph R. Terrill,

Hartford Community College; Charles A. Tracy, Portland State University; Bob Walker, Trinity Valley Community College; and Richard Weber, Jamestown Community College.

The following reviewers contributed numerous suggestions to the Eighth Edition: Jeffrey Bumgarner, Minnesota State University; Chris DeLay, University of Louisiana at Lafayette; Robert E. Grubb, Jr., Marshall University; Ron Holt, Mercer University; Charles Thomas Kelly, Jr., Northwestern State University; and Jo Ann Short, Northern Virginia Community College, Annandale.

We greatly appreciate the input of these reviewers. Sole responsibility for all content, however, is our own.

The authors also wish to thank the following individuals for adding valuable insight to the discussions concerning their respective areas of expertise: Jeffrey Liroff, Ray Fernandez, Timothy Kennedy, and Captain Tommy Bibb for their contributions on cargo theft investigations; Richard Scott for his review of and input concerning computer crime and cyber crime investigations; and retired investigator Richard Gautsch for his careful review of the manuscript and for lending his exceptional personal experiences for inclusion in the text.

A special thank you to Christine Hess Orthmann for her extensive research and invaluable assistance with writing the revised manuscript. Additional special thanks go to Carolyn Henderson-Meier, executive editor; Jana Davis, assistant editor and development editor; Matt Ballantyne, production project manager; Bobbi Peacock, photo consultant; and Mike Ederer, our production editor at Graphic World Publishing Services.

Finally, thank you to our families and colleagues for their continuing support and encouragement throughout the development of *Criminal Investigation*, Eighth Edition.

About the Authors

his text is based on the practical experience of the late Wayne W. Bennett, who spent 45 years in law enforcement and had taught various aspects of criminal investigation for over 30 years, as well as the expertise of Kären M. Hess, who has been developing instructional programs for 30 years.

Wayne W. Bennett (d. 2004) was a graduate of the FBI National Police Academy, held an LL.B. degree in law and had served as the Director of Public Safety for the Edina, Minnesota, Police Department and as Chief of Police of the Boulder City, Nevada, Police Department. He was also coauthor of *Management and Supervision in Law Enforcement,* Fourth Edition.

Kären M. Hess holds a Ph.D. in instructional design from the University of Minnesota and a Ph.D. in criminal justice from Pacific Western University. Other Wadsworth texts Dr. Hess has coauthored are *Criminal Procedure, Corrections in the Twenty-First Century: A Practical Approach; Introduction to Law Enforcement and Criminal Justice* (Eighth Edition); *Introduction to Private Security* (Fourth Edition); *Juvenile Justice* (Fifth Edition); *Management and Supervision in Law Enforcement* (Fourth Edition); *Community Policing: Partnerships for Problem Solving* (Fourth Edition); *Police Operations* (Fourth Edition); and *Careers in Criminal Justice: From Internship to Promotion* (Fifth Edition). Dr. Hess is a member of the Academy of Criminal Justice Sciences (ACJS), the American Society for Law Enforcement Trainers (ASLET), the International Association of Chiefs of Police (IACP), the Police Executive Research Forum (PERF), and the Textbook and Academic Author's Association (TAA), of which she is a Fellow.

Section 1

INTRODUCTION

1. CRIMINAL INVESTIGATION: AN OVERVIEW

elcome to criminal investigation. What are you in for? Here's a glimpse . . .

New to law enforcement, Officer Richard Gautsch found himself standing over the bullet-ridden corpse of a 15-year-old gas station attendant. The boy had been robbed, kidnapped, and brutally executed, all for the 48 bucks in his pocket, and Gautsch's view of the world was forever changed. The 24-year-old detective (the youngest in Minnesota) had had little time to transition from life as a college jock to the violent world of murder investigations. And although naïve and inexperienced, he played a lead role in the pursuit, arrest, and conviction of the two murder suspects.

During the next five years with a suburban metro police department, Gautsch worked a variety of major cases throughout the metropolitan area, including numerous undercover assignments. His youthful appearance quickly landed him in the middle of a major angel dust investigation, and it didn't take long for him to realize that the glitz and glamour of *Miami Vice* was pure fiction. Detective Gautsch unexpectedly found himself in a car with two dealers, his informant, and a lit pipe full of the pungent chemical. As the pipe was being passed around, the dealers demanded to know why Gautsch wasn't inhaling. The informant (who was inhaling deeply) asked the same question. With no weapon or backup, Gautsch suddenly felt a sensation he'd never seen portrayed by the heroes of those one-hour cop shows—fear and the urge to flee. After a sprint to safety, Gautsch wondered if he'd chosen the right career.

As the young detective gained experience, he learned that successful investigations rely on communication skills and attention to tedious tasks. Searching filthy attics and sifting through the rotting contents of a dumpster are more common than are excitement and intrigue. Investigators' abilities to interview and to write reports are far more important than how accurately they shoot or how fast they can drive.

Gautsch was promoted to detective supervisor and placed in charge of the Investigation Unit. That same year, he investigated the murder of a young police officer answering a burglary call. The case was his most difficult—the officer was one of his best friends.

Left Hand

Five years later, Gautsch pinned on his captain's bars, his command expanding to include the Investigative Unit and a special multijurisdictional undercover task force. In 1988 he led a highly publicized murder investigation that stunned the entire community. After an argument with her boyfriend, a young mother was brutally stabbed to death in her apartment. The evidence against the boyfriend was so overwhelming that no one doubted his guilt, yet he remained uncharged. The community was outraged. Gautsch and his detectives doggedly pursued the suspect for three years, only to learn they had the wrong guy.

This thumbnail sketch of one detective's career offers a glimpse into the world of the criminal investigator. Criminal investigation is a complex, sophisticated field, each aspect of which could constitute a book. This text includes the most basic aspects of criminal investigation. Section 1 presents an overview of criminal investigation and general guidelines to follow or adapt in specific circumstances, as well as basic con-

siderations in the preliminary investigation, the most critical phase in the majority of investigations.

Investigators must be thoroughly familiar with crimes and their elements, modus operandi (MO) information, the major goals of investigation, the basic functions of investigating officers, and the investigators' relationships with other individuals and agencies.

Investigators do not operate in a vacuum but must relate to constitutional safeguards. They must also understand case law determining the parameters within which they perform the investigative process. How these constitutional safeguards and case law specifically affect investigations is emphasized throughout the text.

Criminal Investigation: An Overview

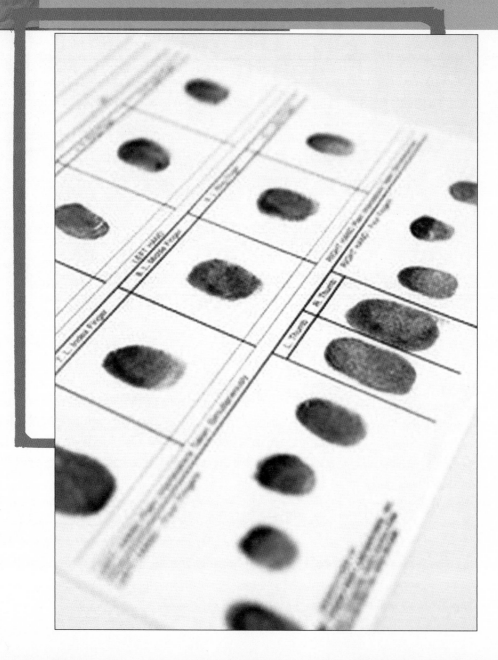

Can You Define?

Do You Know?

- What criminal investigation is?
- What the major goals of criminal investigation are?
- What basic functions investigators perform?
- What characteristics are important in investigators?
- Who usually arrives at a crime scene first?
- What should be done initially?
- What to do if a suspect is still at a crime scene? Has recently fled the scene?
- How the crime scene and evidence are protected and for how long?
- What responsibilities are included in the preliminary investigation?
- What the meaning and importance of *res gestae* statements are?
- How to determine whether a crime has been committed?
- Who is responsible for solving crimes?
- With whom investigators must relate?
- How to avoid civil lawsuits?

Outline

On April 19, 1995, Trooper Charlie Hanger of the Oklahoma Highway Patrol was traveling north on Interstate 35 when he saw a 1977 Mercury Marquis with no license plate. Hanger pulled the car over, and the only occupant, a white male, got out. While Hanger was questioning the driver about the license plate, the trooper noticed a bulge in the man's clothing. When asked, the man admitted he had a gun and was arrested. The driver—Timothy McVeigh—was later found responsible for the bombing of a federal building in Oklahoma City that killed 168 people and left hundreds injured. Some would say that the arrest was just plain luck. However, experience and alertness often play important roles.

An observant police officer can initiate an important criminal investigation, sometimes without realizing it at first. Criminal investigation combines art and science and requires extraordinary preparation and training. And in today's high-tech society, where information flows faster than ever and citizens expect results more quickly, investigators need to step up their technology and teamwork skills—they need an edge. The International Association of Chiefs of Police (IACP) declares:

> It's a new world and the role of the detective has changed dramatically. In the old world, shoe leather was the detective's primary tool. Luck and persistence were cornerstones of success. The key to managing a detective bureau was motivating the investigators.
>
> Now, in the information age, where technology advances daily, shoe leather is still important—as are luck and persistence—but aggressive detectives and their supervisors are constantly looking for a new edge. That edge might be a new method or approach to criminal investigations, or it may be the result of taking advantage of new developments in the forensic and management sciences. ("Recognizing Innovation," p.140)

Because no two crimes are identical, even if they are committed by the same person, each investigation is unique. The great range of variables in individual crimes makes it impossible to establish fixed rules for conducting an investigation. Nevertheless, some general guidelines help to ensure that investigations are thorough and effective. Investigators modify and adapt these guidelines to fit each case.

Investigators need not have superhuman reasoning ability. They must, however, proceed in an orderly, systematic way, gathering facts to analyze and evaluate. This chapter introduces decisions to be made and the actions to be taken. Subsequent chapters explain each step of the preliminary investigation more fully.

The chapter begins with important definitions and a discussion of the goals and basic functions of criminal investigation, followed by an examination of the characteristics of an effective investigator. Next, an overview of the investigative process is presented, as is that of the preliminary investigation, including the initial response, point of arrival, setting priorities, handling emergency situations, protecting the crime scene, and actually conducting the preliminary investigation. The chapter then discusses the role of the crime scene investigator (CSI), the follow-up investigation, computer-aided investigation, crime analysis, mapping, geographic information systems (GIS), problem-oriented policing, and investigative productivity. Next is an explanation of the numerous individuals and agencies with which investigators must interact and the importance of major-case task forces. The chapter concludes with discussions of federal law enforcement resources for investigators and ways to avoid civil liability.

Criminal Investigation Definitions

A **criminal investigation** is the process of discovering, collecting, preparing, identifying, and presenting evidence to determine what happened and who is responsible.

An investigation is a patient, step-by-step inquiry or observation, a careful examination, a recording of evidence, or a legal inquiry. The word **investigate** is derived from the Latin word *vestigare*, meaning to track or trace, a derivation easily related to police investigation. Williams (p.169) notes that an "investigator" can mean "any police employee (whether a detective, patrol officer, evidence technician, clerk, or other person) who contributes to an investigation."

Criminal investigation is a reconstructive process that uses **deductive reasoning,** a logical process in which a conclusion follows from specific facts. Based on specific pieces of evidence, investigators establish proof that a suspect is guilty of an offense. For example, finding the suspect's watch at the scene of a burglary is one piece of evidence that supports the premise that the suspect was at the scene. An issue that might arise is whether the watch could have been planted there. Investigators need to anticipate what issues might arise and what evidence is needed to support the prosecutor's case. All issues in dispute must be supported by evidence. The more evidence an investigation yields, the stronger the proof of guilt. Equally important, however, is evidence establishing innocence, as Williams (p.187) stresses: "Justice also requires the police to work to prevent innocent people from being accused of crimes."

Other Terms Defined

The first determination in a criminal investigation is whether a crime has, in fact, been committed. Does the evidence support a specific offense? A legal arrest cannot be made for an act that is not defined by statute or ordinance as a crime. Although everyone has a notion of what crime is, investigators must have a very precise understanding of what it means. Specific definitions of such terms as *crime, felony, misdemeanor, criminal statute,* and *ordinance* are found in case law:

- A **crime** is an act in violation of penal law and an offense against the state. The broader use of the term includes both felonies and misdemeanors. A crime is a violation of a public right or law. It is an act or omission forbidden by law and punishable by a fine, imprisonment, or even death. This is in contrast to torts, or private harms.
- A **felony** is a serious crime, graver than a misdemeanor; it is generally punishable by death or imprisonment of more than one year in a penitentiary.
- A **misdemeanor** is a crime or offense that is less serious than a felony and is punishable by a fine or imprisonment of up to one year in an institution other than a penitentiary.
- A **criminal statute** is a legislative act relating to a crime and its punishment.
- An **ordinance** is an act of the legislative body of a municipality or county relating to all the rules governing the municipality or county, including misdemeanors.

Crimes and their penalties are established and defined by state and federal statutes and local ordinances.[1] An act that is not declared a crime by statute or ordinance is not a chargeable offense, no matter how wrong it may seem. Designated crimes and their punishments change as society's attitudes change. In the past, for example, behavior associated with alcoholism was considered criminal, but today many states regard alcoholism as an illness. However, driving while intoxicated is now considered a much more serious offense than it was previously. Conversely, our society has designated as crimes certain acts, such as computer fraud, that were unknown in earlier times.

Crimes fall into two general categories—felonies and misdemeanors—depending on the severity of an act and its recommended punishment. The more serious society considers a crime, the more severe the penalty. Investigations involve both types of crimes. Misdemeanors are sometimes further subdivided into gross and petty misdemeanors, based on the value of the property involved.

Because definitions of crimes and their penalties vary considerably depending on whether they occur at the municipal, county, state, or federal level, investigators must be familiar with their area's criminal statutes and ordinances. For example, in some states, such as Michigan, shoplifting is a felony. Otherwise, in most states, the value of the shoplifted property determines whether the crime is a misdemeanor or a felony.

Statutes and ordinances list specific conditions, called the **elements of the crime,** that must occur for an act to be called a specific kind of crime. For example, a state statute might define burglary as occurring when (1) an accused enters a building (2) without the consent of the rightful owner (3) with the intent to commit a crime. An investigation must prove each element, even if the suspect has confessed. Many crimes have as an element **criminal intent,** that is, purposely performing an unlawful act or knowing an act to be illegal. Sections 3 and 4 of this text discuss the elements of major crimes. Knowing these elements is essential to gathering evidence to prove that a crime has been committed.

In addition to proving a crime has been committed, investigators must determine who committed it. Investigation is often aided by knowing how criminals usually operate, that is, their **modus operandi,** or **MO.** For example, it was relatively easy to recognize the "work" of Jack the Ripper or the D.C.-area snipers. The peculiarities of each crime scene may be entered into an MO file and matched with characteristics of known perpetrators of previous crimes. However, investigators must always be vigilant of the potential for "copycat" offenders.

MO information can provide clues in numerous cases. For example, if several burglaries are committed between 11 A.M. and 1 P.M. in one area of a community and all involve broken glass in a door, one may infer that the same individual committed the crimes. The probability of the burglaries being unrelated is low. One may further assume that the burglar would not commit armed robbery or other crimes unless surprised while committing a burglary.

Such assumptions are *not certainties,* however. Some criminals commit several types of crimes and may change the type according to need, opportunity, inability to repeat certain types of crimes, or greater sophistication. For example, a narcotics user may commit

---

[1] Some states, such as Illinois, do not consider violations of city ordinances to be crimes.

larceny, burglary, or robbery to obtain money for drugs. A burglar may age out and turn to shoplifting or may first steal checks and a check writer and then turn to forgery to cash the checks. Suspects should never be eliminated simply because their known MO does not fit the crime being investigated.

Goals of Criminal Investigations

 he goal of criminal investigation would obviously seem to be to solve cases, to discover "whodunit." In reality, the *goals* of criminal investigation are not quite so simple. To hold offenders to account, criminal investigation has several important goals.

The goals of criminal investigation are to:
- Determine whether a crime has been committed.
- Legally obtain information and evidence to identify the responsible person.
- Arrest the suspect.
- Recover stolen property.
- Present the best possible case to the prosecutor.

Williams (p.171) offers three more generalized goals of the investigative function: controlling criminals, pursuing justice, and addressing problems.

While committing crimes, people may make mistakes. They almost always leave some type of evidence. They may overlook tangible evidence such as a jacket, pen, purse, piece of paper, or card that connects them with a crime scene. Such evidence may be left for any number of reasons: carelessness, panic, underestimation of police capabilities, emotional or mental instability, or the influence of drugs or alcohol. More often, however, criminals leave *trace evidence,* less visible evidence such as fingerprints, small particles of glass or dirt, a faint footprint, body hairs, or clothing fibers.

Investigators search for evidence using methods discussed fully in Chapter 4. Sometimes, however, little or no evidence exists. Thus, not all crimes are solvable. For example, a theft committed by a transient who enters a house through an open door, takes food (larceny), eats it, and then leaves the area unseen is a crime not likely to be solved. A burglary committed by a person wearing gloves and whose footprints are washed away by a hard rain before police arrive will be more difficult to solve than if it had not rained. Often fingerprints are found but cannot be matched with any prints on file. Many cases have insufficient evidence, no witnesses, and no informants to provide leads.

Investigators learn to recognize when a case is unsolvable, but only after all **leads** (avenues bearing clues or potential sources of information relevant to solving the crime) have been exhausted. An FBI agent once remarked, "Any average person with training can pursue 'hot' leads. It is the investigator who can develop leads when the trail grows cold who is the superior investigator." A successful investigation is one in which:

- A logical sequence is followed.
- All physical evidence is legally obtained.
- All witnesses are effectively interviewed.
- All suspects are legally and effectively interrogated.
- All leads are thoroughly developed.
- All details of the case are accurately and completely recorded and reported.

Investigators systematically seek evidence to identify the individual who committed a crime, locate the individual, and obtain sufficient evidence to prove in court that the suspect is guilty beyond a reasonable doubt. Procedures to accomplish these goals are the focus of the remainder of this text. However, determining the truth is more important than obtaining a conviction or closing a case.

Basic Functions

uccessful investigation involves a balance between scientific knowledge acquired by study and experience and the skills acquired by the artful application of learned techniques. Police portrayals in mystery stories and on radio and television (Figure 1.1) seldom depict police investigations accurately.

Police investigations involve great attention to detail, an exceptionally suspicious nature at the appropriate time, considerable training in the classroom and the field, an unusual ability to obtain information from diverse types of personalities under adverse circumstances, and endless patience and perseverance.

Investigators perform the following functions:
- Provide emergency assistance.
- Secure the crime scene.
- Photograph, videotape, and sketch.
- Take notes and write reports.
- Search for, obtain, and process physical evidence.
- Obtain information from witnesses and suspects.
- Identify suspects.
- Conduct raids, surveillances, stakeouts, and undercover assignments.
- Testify in court.

Figure 1.1
Popular television series such as *CSI* have brought the role of the investigator into the public eye, perhaps raising expectations that a case can be solved within an hour, with time out for commercials.

© CBS Photo Archive.

Most of these basic functions are discussed in Section 2. What is important at this point is to realize the complexity of and interrelationships among the various functions performed by investigators and the skills they must develop.

Criminal investigation has become more scientific since 1750, when Henry Fielding's Bow Street Runners became the first paid detectives, as shown in Table 1.1. Despite these advances, investigators are frequently required to practice the "art" of investigation, that is, to rely on skill acquired by experience, study, and observation rather than on scientific principles. They must develop the ability to see relationships between and among apparently unrelated facts and to question the apparently unquestionable.

Characteristics of an Effective Investigator

A good investigator is knowledgeable, creative, patient, and persistent. A good investigator also reads a lot about a variety of subjects. Regardless of title, pay, or rank, investigative officers are more effective when they possess specific intellectual, psychological, and physical characteristics.

Intellectual Characteristics

Investigators must absorb training and apply it to their work. They must know the elements of the crime,

understand and be able to apply investigative techniques, and be able to work with many different types of people. Exceptional intelligence is not a requisite trait of an effective investigator; objectivity, logic, and common sense are more important.

> Effective investigators obtain and retain information; apply technical knowledge; and remain open-minded, objective, and logical. They are also **culturally adroit,** that is, skilled in interacting across gender, ethnic, generational, social, and political group lines.

Investigators obtain vast amounts of information. They meet and talk with people from all walks of life—blue-collar workers and professionals, males and females, adults and juveniles—and must adjust their approach to each. In addition, each crime scene must be absorbed and recalled, sometimes months or years later. Thus, accurate, complete, well-organized reports and records are essential.

Investigators also develop knowledge of and skill in investigative techniques such as interviewing and interrogating, photographing and sketching, searching, note taking, and numerous other areas discussed in Section 2. Knowledge of and skill in investigative techniques are acquired through continuous training and experience, including academic classroom experiences, personal experiences, street learning, and learning from others in the field.

The abilities to obtain and retain information and to use investigative techniques effectively are worth little without the ability to reason through a case. The mental process involved in investigation is extremely complex. Logic is indispensable and often involves reverse thinking, that is, working the case backward. Why did an event

Table 1.1 / **Major Advances in Criminal Investigation**

1868	DNA discovered.
1893	First major book on investigation, *Criminal Investigation* by Austrian Hans Gross, published.
Late 1800s	Alphonse Bertillon, the "Father of Personal Identification," used each person's unique physical body measurements as a means of identification.
	Edward Henry developed a fingerprinting system, which was adopted throughout England in 1900.
1909	Dr. Karl Landsteiner discovered the different human blood types and classified them into the A, B, AB, and O groups.
1910	Dr. Edmond Locard, a French criminologist, set forth his "exchange principle" stating that a criminal always removes something from a crime scene or leaves incriminating evidence behind.
1913	Professor Balthazard published his classic article on firearms identification.
1920s	Calvin Goddard raised firearms identification to a science and perfected the bullet comparison microscope.
1923	August Vollmer established the first full forensic laboratory, in Los Angeles.
Early 1950s	James Watson and Francis Crick identified the structure of DNA.
1985	Alec Jeffreys discovered the parts of the DNA structure that were unique in each person, making positive identification possible.
1986	First use of DNA typing in a criminal case, in England: DNA was used to clear a suspect in a murder. (A detective in the East Midlands read of the case and sought Jeffreys' help in solving the vicious murder and rape of two British schoolgirls. The police held a prime suspect in the case, a kitchen porter at an insane asylum who had confessed to one of the murders. They brought Jeffreys semen samples from the murder scenes and a blood sample from the suspect. Jeffreys confirmed that the same person committed both crimes, but it was not the suspect the police held. On November 21, 1986, the kitchen porter became the first person in the world to have his innocence proven by DNA testing.)
1988	First use of DNA typing in a criminal case, in the United States, in which a criminal was identified by DNA (*Florida v. Tommy Lee Andrews*). (Lifecodes Corporation [Stamford, CT] performed the tests in the first case in the United States in which a criminal was identified by DNA. The trial of accused rapist Tommy Lee Andrews began in Orlando, Florida, on November 3, 1987. A scientist from Lifecodes and an MIT biologist testified that semen from the victim matched Andrews' DNA, and that Andrews' print would be found in only 1 in 10 billion individuals. On November 6, 1987, the jury returned a guilty verdict and Andrews was subsequently sentenced to 22 years in prison.)

happen? When? How? Who is culpable? Investigators must examine all possible cause-and-effect relations, find links, and draw conclusions—but only after they thoroughly explore all alternatives.

Decision making is continual and, to be effective, must be based on facts. When investigators review information and evidence, they concentrate on what is known (facts) rather than on what is only probable (inferences), and they eliminate personal opinions as much as possible. With sufficient facts, investigators can make valid inferences, from which they can logically draw definite conclusions.

A **fact** is an action, an event, a circumstance, or an actual thing done. In contrast, an **inference** is a process of reasoning by which a fact may be deduced (deductive reasoning). An **opinion** is a personal belief. For example, an investigator called to the scene of a shooting finds a dead man with a revolver in his hand (fact) and a suicide note on the table (fact). The officer might infer that the man committed suicide. He or she might also hold the opinion that people who commit suicide are cowards. This opinion is irrelevant to the investigation. The inference, however, is critical. If the officer formulates a theory about the death based on suicide and sets out to prove the theory correct, much information and evidence may be ignored. This is known as **inductive reasoning,** going from the generalization and establishing it by gathering specific facts. (Recall from page 6 that criminal investigation is a reconstructive process that uses deductive reasoning.) Often both types of reasoning are required in an investigation.

Although investigators must draw inferences and form theories, they must also remain open-minded and willing to consider alternatives. Effective investigators guard against the tendency to become sold on a suspect or theory early in an investigation, because such a mindset creates an investigative myopia or shortsightedness, fostering the subconscious shaping of evidence or interpreting of information so as to support their premature theory. Preconceived ideas hinder good investigation;

objectivity is essential. Whenever an inference is drawn, its validity should be tested by examining the facts on which it is based. All alternatives should be considered; otherwise, valuable time may be lost, evidence may disappear, or the case may simply remain unsolved.

The hazards of drawing premature conclusions are illustrated by a homicide case in which lie-detection tests were given to two main suspects. Suspect A was given two polygraph tests by separate operators. Both tests indicated that he was deceptive on critical questions concerning the case. Suspect B was given a lie-detection voice-stress test that indicated he was truthful on the same questions. Based on these results, the investigators concentrated on discovering evidence to link Suspect A to the crime and ignored Suspect B. After six months of following up leads that turned into dead ends, the investigators resumed their investigation of Suspect B and discovered enough evidence to persuade him to confess to the crime.

The point of this illustration is not that lie-detection tests are invalid. In fact, correlation between positive test results and suspect involvement or guilt is very high. The point is that no one fact should dominate an entire investigation. All alternatives should be considered. In our illustrative case, Suspect B had taken six tranquilizers before taking the test, which made interpretation more difficult. Suspect A may have been involved in an unrelated homicide or may simply have been extremely nervous because he was a prime suspect. Perseverance eventually revealed the truth despite evidence apparently to the contrary.

Psychological Characteristics

Certain psychological characteristics are indispensable to effective investigation.

 Effective investigators are emotionally well balanced, detached, inquisitive, suspecting, discerning, self-disciplined, and persevering.

Investigation is highly stressful and involves many decisions. Therefore, it requires emotional stability. Officers who are overly defensive or overly sensitive may fall victim to stress. Investigators must also absorb abuse and at the same time show kindness and empathy. Further, they must remain detached and uninvolved; otherwise the problems of those with whom they are in contact will decrease their objectivity. Personal involvement with individuals associated with a case under investigation not only hinders the investigation but also poses a direct threat to the investigator's emotional well-being.

Although remaining detached and objective, effective investigators are intimately involved with every aspect of the case. They do not accept things at face value; rather, they question what they hear and see. They use their knowledge of human nature to determine the truth of what is said. People often lie or tell half-truths, but this does not necessarily mean that they are criminals. With experience, investigators develop a sense for who is telling the truth, who has important information, and who is acting suspiciously. The ability to distinguish the ordinary from the extraordinary and the normal from the suspicious is a hallmark of an effective investigator.

In addition, investigators must be self-disciplined and able to organize their time. Success often depends on an investigator developing efficient work habits, setting priorities, and using time wisely. Closely related to self-discipline is the willingness to persevere, to "stick with it" as long as is reasonable. Investigation often involves hours, days, or months of waiting and watching, of performing tedious, boring assignments that may or may not yield information or evidence helpful to the case. Thus, patience and perseverance are often the key to successful investigation. And although perseverance is desirable, it should not be confused with a stubborn refusal to admit a case is not likely to be solved.

Investigators often experience cases in which facts, reason, and logic seem to lead nowhere. Yet, when the case is about to be closed, by chance, additional clues surface. An obscure newspaper item, an anonymous phone tip, an overheard remark at a social function, or even a series of events having no apparent connection with the case may provide leads for further investigation. Many cases are solved when investigators develop leads and pursue both relevant and seemingly irrelevant information. This is where the art of investigation supersedes the science of investigation.

Perseverance, coupled with inquisitiveness and intuition, are indispensable in difficult cases. Although some deny the existence or worth of intuition, hundreds of experienced investigators attest to its value. **Intuition** is a "sudden knowing" without conscious reasoning or apparent logic. Based on knowledge and experience, it is commonly referred to as *street sense*. It is the urge to proceed with no apparent valid reason, a "gut feeling" developed through experience. Pinizzotto, Davis, and Miller (pp.1–2) have studied intuitive policing and provide, as an example, the following account:

> On a warm summer evening in a large American city, narcotics officers working the 4 P.M. to midnight shift began a "buy-bust" operation at an intersection known as an open-air drug market where approximately 50 to 60 persons, many presumably involved in narcotics trafficking, had congregated on the sidewalk. Five minutes earlier, two undercover officers had walked into the area and purchased illicit narcotic substances from several street dealers. The undercover officers then walked away from the intersection and broadcast the physical descriptions of the sellers to arrest teams, consisting of three unmarked vehicles containing three officers each. . . .

When the unmarked cars approached the street corner, the crowd immediately began dispersing. At this time, one officer observed a subject matching the description of one of the sellers provided by the undercover team and instructed the driver to stop. . . . As the officer who spotted the alleged dealer began yelling to the other officers to identify which of the suspects he intended to stop, another officer simultaneously exited the vehicle and pointed to a different individual approximately 30 feet farther down the sidewalk. The second officer began calling out to the others . . . to "get the one in the red shirt; he's got a gun." The man in the red shirt started to run down the sidewalk after he observed plainclothes officers approaching from both sides with their weapons drawn. The male surrendered, and the officers removed a .357-caliber revolver from his waistband and placed him under arrest. . . .

While the officers were in the station house processing the prisoners and completing the necessary paperwork, the officer who originally identified the seller turned to the officer who spotted the gunman and asked, "How did you know he had a gun?" The officer who noticed the gunman hesitated for a moment and stated, "I'm not sure why. I just knew." . . . [However,] as he began to recall the details and circumstances of the incident, he had to make a conscious effort to remember the observations that led him to conclude that the suspect possessed a handgun. First, the officer recalled that when pulling up to the scene, he saw the suspect sitting on the curb. As the officers approached and the crowd began to scatter, the man stood up and adjusted his waistband. Next, the officer remembered that although the weather was extremely warm, the suspect had on a long-sleeved dress shirt with the shirttails hanging out. Finally, he recalled that immediately after the male stood up, he turned the right side of his body away from the officer and began to walk in another direction, grabbing the right side of his waistband as if securing some type of object. The combination of these factors led the officer to correctly believe that the individual in the red shirt was armed.

The officer made these observations so rapidly that he experienced an "instantaneous recognition" of danger. However, he could not articulate these reasons to his fellow officers until after the incident was resolved.

Physical Characteristics

Age, height, and weight, unless they are extreme, are not important characteristics for investigators. However, some physical characteristics are important.

> Effective investigators are physically fit and have good vision and hearing.

Good health and a high energy level are beneficial because the hours spent performing investigative duties can be long and demanding. In addition to being physically fit, investigators are aided by keen vision and hearing. If uncorrected, color blindness, nearsightedness, night blindness, and farsightedness may impair investigative effectiveness. Hearing is especially important when darkness limits vision. Keen hearing helps to estimate the nearness of a suspect, the movement of animals or people, the direction of gunfire or other detonations, and the direction of foot sounds. In addition, investigators may have to listen to words during sobbing, moans, and hysteria; hear a very weak voice from a seriously wounded or dying person; listen to more than one person talking at a time; or conduct an interview while a plane is flying overhead, machinery is operating, or heavy traffic is passing by. All these intellectual, psychological, and physical characteristics may be needed in the preliminary investigation of a crime.

An Overview of the Investigative Process

A criminal investigation is usually initiated by personal observation or information from a citizen. Patrol officers may see a suspicious action or person, or a citizen may report suspicious actions or people. Such information is received at police headquarters by telephone, fax, e-mail, radio, or direct report when a person steps up to a police complaint desk. A police dispatcher relays the information to a patrol officer by radio or phone, and the officer responds. However the incident becomes known to police, this reporting of a crime sets the investigative wheels in motion and is the first stage in a criminal investigation. The various stages of the investigative process, as well as the personnel involved, the official reports generated, and the victim's role, are described in Table 1.2.

Thus an investigation starts with a direction to proceed to a scene. Department policy defines not only who is to respond but also the duties of these individuals, as well as those of evidence technicians, investigators, supervisors, and command personnel.

Fuller (p.35) observes: "One of the enduring myths of police work is the notion that the uniformed patrol officer, who is almost always the first responder to a criminal incident or emergency event, is only required to stand by the crime scene, write the offense report, and await the arrival of the detectives who will take over and continue the criminal investigation." He continues:

> While it is understandable that a trained and experienced detective or criminal investigator should be primarily responsible for conducting a major criminal inquiry, the patrol officer can and should play a critical role in the investigation by conducting a quality preliminary investigation concurrent with, and complementary to, the investigation by the specialist criminal investigator. (p.36)

Table 1.2 / **An Overview of the Investigative Process**

Stage	Police Personnel	Official Reports	Victim's Role
Reporting crime to the police	Operators, dispatchers	Tape of initial communication	Reporting the crime
Initial investigation: determining basic facts of the case and arresting suspects, if present	Patrol officers (sometimes an evidence technician and detectives)	Crime reports (sometimes physical-evidence reports or arrest report)	Providing information
Case screening: deciding whether to continue with the investigation	Investigations supervisor (sometimes a patrol supervisor)	Note on crime report, or screening form (some departments notify victims)	Sometimes notified about decisions
Follow-up investigation: pursuing leads developed earlier	Detective (sometimes a patrol officer for some crimes)	Supplemental report and perhaps an arrest report	Verifying information
Case preparation: presenting case to the prosecutor	Detective (sometimes a patrol officer)	Arrest report	No role (some departments may notify victim of an arrest)
Prosecution: attempting to get a conviction	Patrol officers and detectives to present evidence in court	Prosecutor's reports, court records	Providing testimony, if the case goes to trial; otherwise, little role

Source: Williams, Gerald L. "Criminal Investigations." In *Local Government Police Management*, 4th ed. Edited by William A. Geller and Darrel W. Stephens. Washington, DC: International City/County Management Association, 2003, p.181. Reprinted by permission.

The Preliminary Investigation: Basic Considerations

The first officer who responds is in charge until relieved by another officer. The same basic procedures are followed regardless of whether the first officer at the scene is a patrol officer, an investigator, or the chief of police.

The initial response is usually by a patrol officer assigned to the area where a crime has occurred.

The initial response is crucial to the success of an investigation. Although it is popularly believed that cases are won or lost in court, more cases actually are lost during the first hour of an investigation—the initial response period—than in court.

The Initial Response

After notification, either through direct observation or departmental communications, officers go to the scene as rapidly and safely as circumstances permit (Figure 1.2). A crime-response survey conducted by the Law Enforcement Assistance Administration (LEAA) revealed that a response time of one minute or less is necessary to increase the probability of arrest at the scene. Most police departments, however, cannot assure their citizens of such a short response time, even for emergencies. To provide a one-minute response time, police agencies would need much smaller patrol areas, much larger staffs, computer-dispatched vehicles and personnel, and, thus, much larger budgets.

It is important to arrive at a crime scene rapidly because:

- The suspect may still be at or near the scene.
- Injured persons may need emergency care.
- Witnesses may still be at the scene.
- A dying person may have a confession or other pertinent information to give.
- Weather conditions may change or destroy evidence.
- Someone may attempt to alter the crime scene.

The responding officers proceed to the scene as quickly as safety allows. Officers who injure themselves or someone else on the way to a call may create more serious problems than exist at the crime scene. They may, in fact, open themselves, their department, and even their city to a civil lawsuit.

The seriousness of a crime and whether it is in progress are important factors in the rapidity of response. The driving speed and use of emergency lights and siren depend on the information furnished. A siren speeds arrival, but it also prompts the criminal to flee the scene. On the other hand, in a violent crime against a person, a siren alerts the offender but may prevent further violence. Sometimes the victim, to avoid attracting attention, requests that no sirens and red lights be used.

Figure 1.2
Preplanning routes to high-crime areas can be critical to rapid response time. Even if no immediate arrest is made, the amount of information that can be obtained is directly related to the speed of the response.

The route taken is also discretionary. Officers should know which streets are under construction in their areas and avoid them. They must also choose between the fastest route and the route the suspect might use to leave the scene. When approaching a scene, officers should observe people leaving the scene and make mental notes of their descriptions. If two officers are in the patrol vehicle, one may write descriptions of people and vehicles observed leaving the scene. Many officers use tape recorders for such observations. This equipment permits either a single officer or the second person in a two-officer car to record while proceeding to the scene.

If other officers are available, they are alerted to cover escape routes rather than go directly to the scene. While driving to the scene, officers formulate a plan of action based on the type of crime and its location.

An immediate response may be crucial because, even if no immediate arrest is made, the amount of information that can be obtained is directly related to the speed of response.

Initial information is often the most important and accurate. Many departments are developing necessary guidelines for rapid responses, replacing the assumption that all calls for service should be responded to as rapidly as possible.

Other departments are finding that sending several vehicles to a crime scene may not be the most effective approach. Instead, they implement a "bull's-eye," or target, approach, dispatching only a few vehicles directly to the crime scene (the bull's-eye). Other units are sent to observe traffic at major intersections radiating away from the crime scene in an attempt to intercept fleeing suspects. Success depends on broadcasting the suspects' descriptions rapidly and getting to the major intersections quickly. In many cases, such a response is more effective in catching the suspects than focusing all resources directly on the crime scene itself.

The Point of Arrival

When the first officers arrive, the scene may be either utter confusion or deserted. Regardless of the situation, the officers must take charge immediately and form a plan for proceeding.

People at a crime scene are usually excited, apprehensive, and perplexed. They may be cooperative or uncooperative, confused or lucid. Therefore, officers must be flexible and understanding. Discretion and good judgment are essential because the greatest potential for solving the case lies with those present at the scene, even though many details of the crime may not be known at this stage. More decisions are made in less time at the point of arrival than at any other stage in the investigation, and this is when officers obtain the majority of leads for subsequent action.

Setting Priorities

Circumstances at the scene often dictate what is done first.

The priorities are as follows:
- **Handle emergencies first.**
- **Secure the scene.**
- **Investigate.**

The following guidelines can be adapted to fit specific circumstances.

Handling Emergency Situations

Sometimes emergencies dictate procedure. An **emergency** may include a dangerous suspect at or near the scene or a gravely injured person. For example, if you arrive at a crime scene and the suspect begins to shoot at you, apprehending the suspect obviously becomes your first priority. In other instances, a person may be so seriously injured that without immediate care, death is probable. Such emergencies take precedence over all other procedures.

Good judgment and the number of available officers dictate what should occur first if more than one emergency exists. Sometimes the decision is difficult. For example, if a victim is drowning, a suspect is running away, and only one officer is at the scene, the officer must make a split-second decision. Usually, saving life takes precedence. However, if the officer can do nothing to save the victim, the best alternative is to pursue the suspect. Apprehending the suspect may save other victims.

Responding to emergency situations causes the adrenaline to flow. At the same time, officers must plan their approach. One officer facing a life-or-death situation said he thought of a quotation: "Death must be a beautiful moment; otherwise they wouldn't save it until last." Holding this thought, he carried out his immediate responsibilities without hesitation.

Officers should also attempt to think like the suspect. They should decide which escape routes are probable and block them. Available information about the situation helps officers decide whether using lights and siren is advantageous to them or to the suspect. Officers should think what they would do if they were the suspect and were cornered at the crime scene. If it is daytime, officers may be visible and the suspect not. If it is nighttime, officers may be able to take advantage of a darker area for their approach.

Flexibility is essential. The situation must be carefully assessed because each incident is different and requires different approaches and techniques. Officers should be cognizant that more than one suspect may be present. They should check their equipment on the way to the scene and provide the dispatcher with all pertinent information. Maintaining some distance can facilitate observation and give officers time to make decisions that will enhance their safety.

A Suspect At or Near the Scene   If a call is made rapidly enough and officers can respond quickly, they may observe the crime in progress and arrest the suspect at the scene.

 Any suspect at the scene should be detained, questioned, and then released or arrested, depending on circumstances.

Departmental policy determines whether the first officer at the scene thoroughly interrogates a suspect. Before any in-custody interrogation, an officer must read the Miranda warning to the suspect (a legality discussed in Chapter 6). Even if the policy is that officers

do not interrogate suspects, officers often use discretion. For example, they may have to take a dying declaration or a suspect's spontaneous confession. If this occurs, a statement is taken immediately because the suspect may refuse, or be unable, to cooperate later. A more formal interrogation and written confession can be obtained later at the police department.

The suspect is removed from the scene as soon as possible to minimize the destruction of evidence and to facilitate questioning. The sooner suspects are removed, the less they can observe of the crime scene and possible evidence against them.

If the Suspect Has Recently Fled   If the suspect has just left the scene, immediate action is required. If the information is provided early enough, other units en route to the scene may make an arrest.

If a suspect has recently left the scene, officers obtain descriptions of the suspect, any vehicles, direction of travel, and any items taken. The information is dispatched to headquarters immediately.

As soon as practical, officers obtain more detailed information about the suspect's possible whereabouts, friends, descriptions of stolen items, and other relevant information regarding past criminal records and MOs.

If a Person Is Seriously Injured   Emergency first aid to victims, witnesses, and suspects is often a top priority of arriving officers. Officers should call for medical assistance and then do whatever possible until help arrives. They should observe and record the injured person's condition. When medical help arrives, officers should assist and instruct medical personnel during the care and removal of those injured to diminish the risk of contaminating the scene and losing evidence.

If a person is injured so severely that he or she must be removed from the scene, attending medical personnel should be instructed to listen to any statements or utterances the victim makes and to save all clothing for evidence. If the injured person is a suspect, a police officer almost always accompanies the suspect to the hospital. The humanitarian priority of administering first aid may have to become second priority if a dangerous suspect is still at or near the scene, because others may be injured or killed.

If a Dead Body Is at the Scene   A body at the crime scene may immediately become the center of attention, and even a suspect may be overlooked. If the victim is obviously dead, the body should be left just as it was found but it and its surroundings protected. Identifying the body is not an immediate concern. Preserving the scene is more important because it may later yield clues about the dead person's identity, the cause of death, and the individual responsible, as discussed in Chapter 8.

Protecting the Crime Scene

Securing the crime scene is a major responsibility of the first officers to arrive. Everything of a nonemergency nature is delayed until the scene is protected. The critical importance of securing the crime scene is better understood when one considers **Locard's principle of exchange,** a basic forensic theory which holds that objects that come in contact with each other always transfer material, however minute, to each other. This evidence can easily be lost if the crime scene goes unprotected. At outdoor scenes, weather conditions such as heat, wind, rain, snow, or sleet can alter or destroy physical evidence. In addition, people may accidentally or intentionally disturb the scene. Additions to the scene can be as disconcerting to later investigation as the removal of evidence.

Officers should explain to bystanders that protecting the crime scene is critical and that the public must be excluded. Bystanders should be treated courteously but firmly. A delicate part of public relations is dealing with the family of someone who has been killed. Officers should explain what they are doing and why and help family members to understand that certain steps must be taken to discover what happened and who is responsible.

Crime scene protection can be as simple as locking a door to a room or building, or it can involve roping off a large area outdoors. Within a room, chairs or boxes can be used to cordon off an area. Many officers carry rope in their vehicle for this purpose and attach a sign that says, "CRIME SCENE—DO NOT ENTER."

A guard should be stationed to maintain security. If all officers are busy with emergency matters, a citizen may be asked to help protect the area temporarily. In such cases, the citizen's name, address, and phone number should be recorded. The citizen should be given specific instructions and minimal duties. The citizen's main duty is to protect the crime scene by barring entrance and to keep passersby moving along. He or she should not let any person into the area except police who identify themselves with a badge. The citizen should be relieved from guard duty as soon as possible and thanked for the assistance.

Sometimes other officers arriving at the scene can cause problems by ignoring posted warnings and barriers. *Ironically, police officers with no assigned responsibilities at a scene are often the worst offenders.* Arriving officers and everyone present at the scene should be told what has happened and what they need to do. Other officers can be asked to help preserve the scene, interview witnesses, or search for evidence.

Evidence should be protected from destruction or alteration from the elements by being covered until photographing and measuring can be done. Sometimes investigators must move evidence before they can examine it. For example, a vehicle covered with snow, dust, or other materials can be moved into a garage. In one case a car used in a kidnapping was found four days later in a parking lot. Snow that had fallen since the kidnapping covered the car. To process the car's exterior for fingerprints, investigators took the car to a garage to let the snow melt and the surface dry. Evidence is discussed in depth in Chapter 5.

Conducting the Preliminary Investigation

After all emergency matters have been handled and the crime scene has been secured, the actual preliminary investigation can begin. This includes several steps whose order depends on the specific crime and the types of evidence and witnesses available.

Responsibilities during the preliminary investigation include:

- Questioning victims, witnesses, and suspects.
- Conducting a neighborhood canvass.
- Measuring, photographing, videotaping, and sketching the scene.
- Searching for evidence.
- Identifying, collecting, examining, and processing physical evidence.
- Recording all statements and observations in notes.

Each of these procedures is explained in Section 2. At this point what is important is the total picture, the overview. In simple cases one officer may perform all these procedures; in complex cases responsibilities may be divided among several officers. Everything that occurs at a crime scene is recorded with photographs, videotape, sketches, and complete, accurate notes. This record is the basis not only of future reports but also for future investigation and prosecution of the case.

Information may be volunteered by victims, witnesses, or suspects at or very near to the time of the criminal actions. Unplanned statements about what happened by people present are called *res gestae* ("things done") statements.

***Res gestae* statements** are spontaneous statements made at the time of a crime concerning and closely related to actions involved in the crime. They are often considered more truthful than later, planned responses.

Res gestae statements are generally an exception to the hearsay rule because they are usually very closely

All necessary measures to secure the crime scene must be taken—including locking, roping, barricading, and guarding—until the preliminary investigation is completed.

related to facts and are therefore admissible in court. *Res gestae* statements should be recorded in the field notes, and the person making the statements should sign or initial them so that there is no question of misunderstanding or of the person later denying having made the statement.

In addition to receiving and recording voluntary statements by victims and witnesses, investigators must go looking for information by conducting a neighborhood canvass. Fuller (p.36) stresses:

> [The neighborhood canvass] is the nuts and bolts of most preliminary investigations, and should be done on every criminal offense that is reported to your officers—no exceptions; this should be a procedural must! Basically, the neighborhood canvass is just what the name implies: going house-to-house and knocking on doors in the immediate vicinity of the offense, and along any known escape route to determine if anyone observed the offense and/or the suspect.
>
> This is a tiresome, labor-intensive process . . . , yet an efficient neighborhood canvass has probably solved more crimes than any other investigative technique, traditional or modern.

Determining Whether a Crime Has Been Committed and When

As soon as possible during the preliminary investigation, it is necessary to determine whether a crime has, in fact, been committed.

> Determining whether a crime has been committed involves knowing the elements of each major offense and the evidence that supports them and ascertaining whether they are present. Officers also try to determine when the event occurred.

Individual elements of various offenses are discussed in Sections 3 and 4.

Officers should observe the condition of the scene and talk to the complainant as soon as possible. After discussing the offense with the victim or complainant, the officers should determine whether a specific crime has been committed. It is common for crime victims to misclassify what has occurred. For example, they may report a burglary as a robbery. In addition, state statutes differ in their definitions of the elements of certain crimes. For example, in some states, entering a motor vehicle with intent to steal is larceny. In other states, it is burglary. Determining when the event occurred is critical for checking alibis and reconstructing the MO.

If no crime has been committed—for example, the matter is a civil rather than a criminal situation—the victim should be told how to obtain assistance.

Field Tests

Investigators often want to know whether evidence discovered is what they think it is—for example, a bloodstain or an illegal substance. Field-test kits help in this determination.

Field tests save investigators' time by identifying evidence that may have little chance of yielding positive results in the laboratory, and they are less expensive than full lab examinations. However, they are used on only a small number of specific items of evidence located at crime scenes. If a field test is affirmative, the evidence is submitted to a laboratory for a more detailed, expert examination whose results can then be presented in court.

Investigators can use field tests to develop and lift fingerprints; discover flammable substances through vapor and fluid examination; detect drugs, explosive substances on hands or clothing, imprints of firearms on hands, or bullet-hole residue; and conduct many other tests. Local, state, and federal police laboratories can furnish information on currently available field-test kits and may also provide training in their use.

Establishing a Command Center

In complex cases involving many officers, a command center may be set up where information about the crime is gathered and reviewed. This center receives summaries of communications, police reports, autopsy results, laboratory reports, results of interviews, updates on discovered evidence, and tips. Personnel at the center keep files of news releases and news articles and prepare an orderly, chronological progress report of the case for police command, staff, and field personnel. If the investigation becomes lengthy, the command center can be moved to police headquarters.

Dealing with the News Media

A close, almost symbiotic relationship exists between the police and the news media. They depend upon each other. Thus, it is important that the media and the police understand and respect each other's roles and responsibilities.

The media serve the public's right to know within legal and reasonable standards, a right protected by the First Amendment. The public is always hungry for news about crime. The police, on the other hand, are responsible for upholding the Sixth- and Fourteenth-Amendment guarantees of the right to a fair trial, the protection of a suspect's rights, and an individual's right to privacy. This often necessitates confidentiality. Further, making some information public would impair or even destroy many investigations. On the other hand, the police rely on the media to disseminate news about wanted suspects or to seek witnesses from the community. Many cases are solved because of information from citizens.

Some departments use public information officers (PIOs) to interface with the media. Other departments assign the highest-ranking officer at the time of an incident or use written information releases. Still others allow virtually any officer involved in a case to address the media. For example, as Gary (p.25) notes: "The Baltimore City Police Department has recently eliminated a layer in its media strategy, giving district commanders, lead investigators, and arresting officers latitude to speak directly to the press at a crime scene."

Media access to police information is neither comprehensive nor absolute. In general, the media have no right to enter any area to which the public does not have access, and all rules at cordoned-off crime scenes are as applicable to the media as they are to the general public (Figure 1.3). On the other hand, police may not construct a "cocoon" of secrecy. Neither should regard the other as the enemy.

Despite the need for cooperation, complaints from both sides are prevalent. News reporters complain that police withhold important information and are uncooperative. The police, on the other hand, may complain that reporters interfere with cases, lack sensitivity, frequently report inaccurately, and tend to sensationalize. Nonetheless, investigators must be cognizant of the national and even global reach of statements made to the media. The post-9/11 public is hungry for information about major criminal investigations, and tenacious journalists vie to be the first to break the story. Faced with the challenge of doing a job surrounded by a swarm of microphones and cameras, it is imperative that investigators resist any urge to respond sarcastically or rudely, as a hostile tone, while directed at the reporters, will ultimately be received by the viewing public (Buice, p.26).

Most members of the media understand the restrictions at a crime scene and cooperate. It is necessary to exercise firmness with those who do not follow instructions and even to exclude them if they jeopardize the investigation. Only facts—not opinions—should be given to reporters. The name of someone who has been killed should be given only after a careful identity check and notification of relatives. No information on the cause of death should be released; the medical examiner determines this. Likewise, no legal opinions about the specific crime or the perpetrator should be released. If officers do not know certain information, they can simply state that they do not know. The phrase "no comment" should be avoided. Buice (p.26) observes: "A number of public information officers from around the country have suggested that 'No comment' is more palatable with just a word or two of explanation as to why something cannot be discussed." He also states:

> Many police academies teach their police officers Verbal Judo: redirecting an opponent's negative energy to achieve a positive goal. Exactly the same concept can be used in media relations. Message management allows you to redirect the negative force of others toward positive outcomes.

Figure 1.3

Photographers watch as investigators collect evidence at a mass grave site. The media have no right to enter any area to which the public does not have access. However, the police may not construct a cocoon of secrecy around a case either.

© AP / Wide World Images.

Crime Scene Investigators

The popular television series *CSI* has brought the role of the crime scene investigator to the public, raising its interest in forensic science. Police, prosecutors and crime laboratories are finding themselves in the increasingly awkward position of imitating this program's artful, greatly exaggerated depiction of how a top-rate forensic science unit operates. Experts have named this the "CSI effect," a phenomenon in which the public has begun to demand that police and prosecutors conduct the high-tech forensic tests they see television characters doing each week ("Life Imitates Art," p.1).

The increased attention to the job of the crime scene investigator (CSI) can be seen in some colleges offering a degree in crime scene technology. According to Koivisto (2004):

A crime scene investigator is a forensic specialist whose specialty is the organized scientific collection and processing of evidence. Crime scene investigation requires years of training and experience, and a crime scene investigator must have both a general knowledge of lab analysis and a deep understanding in the areas of evidence recognition, documentation and recovery in order to be successful in his or her job.

A CSI is responsible for developing, processing, and packaging all physical evidence found at the crime scene and transporting it to the lab for forensic evaluation; attending and documenting autopsies; writing evidence reports to aid the ongoing criminal investigation; and testifying in court about the recovery and processing of crime scene evidence (Koivisto, 2004).

The Follow-Up Investigation

Preliminary investigations that satisfy all the investigative criteria do not necessarily yield enough information to prosecute a case. Despite a thorough preliminary investigation, many cases require a follow-up investigation. A need for a follow-up investigation does not necessarily reflect poorly on those who conducted the preliminary investigation. Often factors exist that are beyond the officers' control. Weather can destroy evidence before officers arrive at a scene; witnesses can be uncooperative; and evidence may be weak or nonexistent, even after a very thorough preliminary investigation.

The follow-up phase builds on what was learned during the preliminary investigation. It can be conducted by the officers who responded to the original call or, most often, by detectives or investigators, depending on the seriousness and complexity of the crime and the size of the department. If investigators take over a case begun by patrol officers, coordination is essential.

Investigative leads that may need to be pursued include checking the victim's background; talking to informants; determining who would benefit from the crime and who had sufficient knowledge to plan the crime; tracing weapons and stolen property; and searching MO, mug shot, and fingerprint files. Specific follow-up procedures for the major offenses are discussed in Sections 3, 4, and 5.

Computer-Aided Investigation

Computers have significantly affected police operations. As Douglas (p.42) remarks: "It seems that every time a new widget comes down the pike, the marketers come up with some way of making it adaptable to law enforcement." In addition to their obvious contribution to record keeping and statistical analysis, computers are becoming increasingly important in criminal investigations. Dees (2003, p.22) contends: "There is possibly no better investigative tool than information. Information, gathered through legitimate and illegitimate sources, has always been the cornerstone of investigation. In the days when most officers were walking neighborhood beats and didn't have global concerns, the information necessary to their jobs was kept mostly in their heads." Today, however, law enforcement would be hard pressed to do business, including conducting investigations, without the aid of computers.

Computers can help investigators efficiently access existing information such as fingerprint records and DNA tests, record new information and store it compactly for instant transmission anywhere, analyze the information for patterns (mapping), link crimes and criminals, manipulate digital representations to enhance the images, and re-create and visually track a series of events. Computers are also increasingly being used for electronic document management, allowing investigators to scan evidence captured from paper and attach audio and video clips to the case file. Furthermore, software is available to help investigators develop an analytical time line and manage the scheduling of tasks related to the investigation, such as follow-up interviews and evidence handling and analysis. As an example, Miller (pp.75–76) explains the capabilities of the Case Investigative Life Cycle (CILC) software (IRP Solutions, Colorado Springs, CO):

> [It] organizes major investigations by the three common investigative phases: initial, follow-up and prosecution. . . . The software meets standards described in the National Institute of Justice tract, "Crime Scene Investigation: A Guide for Law Enforcement," which has best practices guidelines that include handling evidence, interviews, searches and crime scene security.
>
> Starting with an initial investigation, CILC lets investigators organize incident, crime scene, witness, evidence and responder information. It then follows investigators through follow-up stages, including evidence analysis, a case-related calendar and "categorized suspect and non-suspect interview tracking." Finally, CILC's prosecution phase helps both investigators and prosecutors prepare for court using its calendar, witness and jury information, and discovery log.
>
> At all stages of the investigation, CILC allows investigators to generate, waiver, press release and search warrant forms.

The ability to share data across jurisdictional lines is one of the most valuable benefits computers provide to investigators. In addition, the Internet has become an invaluable tool to criminal investigators. And although some agencies have yet to realize the full potential of Internet access, many others are already capitalizing on the multiple benefits of being online. The Internet offers hundreds of thousands of websites to aid informed investigators.

Crime Analysis, Mapping, and Geographical Information Systems

Using crime mapping, spreadsheet software, and advanced data analysis, crime analysis units have become integral partners in today's policing. Prior to the computer revolution, the traditional crime map consisted of a large representation of a jurisdiction glued onto a bulletin board with colored pins stuck into it. These maps suffered many limitations—they lost previous crime patterns when they were updated, could not be manipulated or queried, and were difficult to read when several types of crimes represented by different colored pins were mixed together.

In addition to pushpin maps, investigators routinely used link charts to keep track of the people and places involved in a case, connecting index cards and photos with a maze of strings as relationships became established and details of an investigation emerged. The cumbersome pin maps and link charts have since given way to computerized crime maps and crime analysis programs. **Crime mapping** changes the focus from the criminal to the location of crimes—the **hot spots** where most crimes occur (Figure 1.4).

Diamond (p.42) notes: "Crime mapping grabbed the public's attention when the New York Police Department launched its COMPSTAT initiative under former Mayor Rudy Giuliani and former Police Commissioner William Bratton." CompStat, short for "computer statistics" or "comparison statistics," is a strategic crime-control technique based on four crime-reduction principles: "accurate and timely intelligence, effective tactics, rapid deployment of personnel and resources, and relentless follow-up and assessment" (Shane, p.13).

Geographic information systems (GIS) and geographic profiling are other powerful tools for investigators. Geographic profiling is based on the theory that all people, including criminals, have a pattern to their lives. This pattern involves, among other things, a limited geographical area that encompasses the bulk of a person's daily activities. Citing the "least effort" principle of human behavior, Weiss and Davis (p.24) note: "People travel only as far as they need to accomplish their goals and not much further. . . . The most probable area for a crime [is] near where the offender's desire to remain anonymous met with his desire to stay within his comfort zone." Gore and Pattavina (pp.471–472) add that hot-spot analysis can help investigators prioritize lists of suspects generated from descriptive and MO information or determine the order of mug shots for witness examination.

In addition to location, computer programs can help investigators uncover patterns in the timing of criminal events. Helms (p.144) asserts: "The spacial component of a crime forecast is only half the answer. In order to be useful, when an event will occur also must be approximately known." Unfortunately, time analysis methods have lagged behind spatial analysis techniques, thus far having proved more difficult to develop

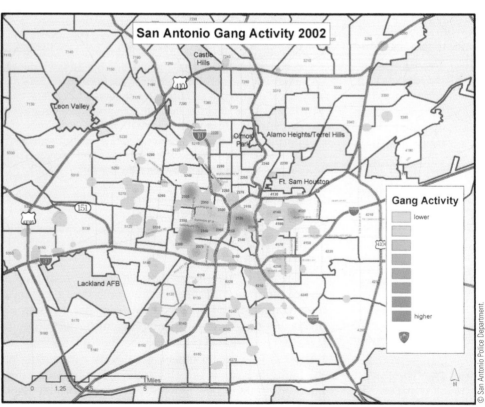

Figure 1.4

Computerized crime analysis programs have changed the focus of crime mapping from the criminal to the location of crimes—the hot spots where most crimes occur. This map shows several hot spots in San Antonio, Texas, where gang activity occurs more often.

© San Antonio Police Department.

and implement. The improvement of technology and the corresponding expansion of information now accessible to investigators has created a new set of challenges.

Data Mining

While information is, indeed, the cornerstone of investigation, the plethora of information being generated can easily overwhelm an investigator. To be effective, investigators must know how to sift through the mountains of available information to find the data that pertain to their case, a process known as **data mining.** McCue and Parker (p.115) state:

> Data mining can be used in law enforcement to discover new patterns or confirm suspected patterns or trends. One of the strengths of data mining, as opposed to more traditional statistical methods, is that it is not necessary to know exactly what you are looking for before you start. Data mining uses powerful analytical tools to quickly and thoroughly explore mountains of data and pull out the valuable, useable information. The primary use of data mining is to find something new in the data—to discover a new piece of information that no one knew previously.

For example, data mining applied in a homicide case might allow investigators to more quickly develop a possible motive and thus expedite the identification of a suspect or help narrow the field of possible suspects. McCue and Parker (p.122) conclude: "Intelligent, timely and complete analysis of the thousands of incident reports, crime tips, and other pieces of information that law enforcement professionals confront everyday is critical to fighting crime. The massive volume of data law enforcement organizations work with on a daily basis requires a different approach to analysis. . . . The successful exploitation of data mining and predictive analytics in law enforcement and intelligence analysis truly represents a powerful new tool, as well as a significant paradigm shift."

Problem-Oriented Policing

Data collected during criminal investigations can be extremely valuable to the problem-oriented policing that many departments are adopting. Investigators can analyze data to determine groups of problems rather than isolated incidents. According to Bichler and Gaines (p.57):

> A variety of techniques are used to identify police problems. The primary techniques used include observation and experience, crime analysis, police reports, calls for service analysis, crime mapping, community groups,

and surveys. When engaging in problem solving departments sometimes use multiple techniques. For example, a crime analysis unit may map crime and calls for service to determine the overlap and where hot spots exist. This information may then be supplemented with citizen surveys or officer input relative to the hot spots.

Once specific underlying problems are identified, departments can seek alternative approaches to reduce or eliminate the incidence of particular crimes.

In addition, although criminal investigations are, by nature, reactive, they can use the technology just described to become proactive in solving crimes. Criminal investigations are mainly about solving crimes that have occurred. Unsolved crimes are problems that usually depend for a solution more on whether the victims and witnesses identify the offenders than on keen deductive reasoning or cutting-edge forensic analysis.

The subject of problem-solving policing is beyond the scope of this text, but problem-oriented strategies can be used in criminal investigations in many ways. One way is to expand collaborations by having investigators work more effectively with patrol officers and with other law enforcement agencies. Another way is to improve the quality of information in existing data systems, especially MO files. The likelihood that an offender in a new case has been arrested previously (and should be in the MO file) is greater than often thought. Combining problem-oriented strategies with traditional investigative techniques can help investigators improve their ability to solve crimes and to help prevent them as well.

Investigative Productivity

Productivity has been of interest in the police field for some time. Major opposition to a focus on productivity in police work may arise because of alleged "quota systems" in issuing traffic citations. Productivity involves considerably more than issuing citations, however. Nearly all jobs have some standard of productivity, even though the job may not involve a production line.

A screening process to eliminate criminal investigations with low potential for being solved can often increase productivity. Many police departments screen investigations with a form that asks specific questions. If the answers to these questions are negative, the department either gives the case low priority for assignment or does not assign it at all.

Criminal investigation personnel have traditionally been evaluated by the number and type of cases assigned to them, the number of cases they bring to a successful conclusion, and the number of arrests they make and the amount of property they recover. The evaluations should also assess how well the officers use investigative resources and how well they perform overall within the department and in the community.

An advantage of continuous evaluation of productivity is that updating case status is possible at any time. Such information is useful not only for investigating but also for developing budgets, making additional case assignments, identifying MO similarities among cases, and responding to public inquiries.

The Investigative Function: The Responsibility of All Police Personnel

 arly police organizations were one-unit/ one-purpose departments with everyone performing generalized functions. However, over time, departments perceived a need for specialization. The first detective bureaus in the United States were established in Detroit in 1866 and then in New York in 1882. Investigation became specialized because of the following factors:

- The need to know about criminals and their MOs
- The amount of training necessary for learning and developing investigative techniques
- The frequency with which investigators had to leave their assigned shifts and areas during an investigation
- Patrol forces' heavy workloads
- A general administrative philosophy that supported specialization as a means of increasing efficiency and therefore solving more crimes

In larger police departments, specialization developed first in investigative functions before it did in other areas such as traffic, crime prevention, juveniles, and community relations. In departments with specialized investigative units, the investigative and patrol functions often experienced difficulty separating their respective duties. Duties often overlapped, decreasing efficient coordination.

Many of these difficulties have been overcome, but many others remain. Regardless of whether departments have specialists or generalists, their goal is the same: solving crimes.

 The ultimate responsibility for solving crimes lies with all police personnel. It must be a cooperative, coordinated departmental effort.

All levels of police administration and operations contribute to successful investigations. Administrative decisions affect the selection and assignment of personnel as well as the policies regulating their performance.

In most larger departments, the investigative division remains a separate unit under its own command and supervisory personnel. The officer in charge reports directly to the chief of police or a chief of operations. Department policy specifies the roles of and the relationships among the administrative, uniformed patrol, and investigative divisions. When these roles are clearly defined, the department can better achieve its common goals, with the investigative division fulfilling its assigned responsibilities in coordination with all other departments.

Today, however, researchers are studying the extent to which specialization should remain, its effectiveness, the number of personnel that should be assigned to specialized investigative functions, and the selection and training required for such specialization. The following factors appear to support the training of all officers to perform investigative duties:

- Increasing competition for tax monies
- Possession of highly sophisticated equipment by some criminals
- More criminals using multiple MOs
- "Withdrawal syndrome" within the general public (i.e., the desire to remain uninvolved necessitates specialized training in interviewing techniques)
- Overwhelming workload of cases assigned to investigative personnel
- More intelligent, better-educated police recruits
- More police training available

In addition, most police officers' daily activities are investigative, even though the matters they investigate may not involve crimes (Figure 1.5). Therefore, the trend is for a few specialists to direct an investigation and for all officers to assume a more active role in investigating crimes. This role gives patrol officers more responsibility when responding to a call to proceed to a crime scene. It also enables them to conduct as much of the follow-up investigation as their shift and assigned areas of patrol permit. The importance of the patrol officer's investigative role cannot be overemphasized.

Traditionally, uniformed patrol has been considered the backbone of the police department and has been responsible for the initial response to a crime. Because they are the first to arrive, patrol officers are in an ideal position to do more than conduct the preliminary investigation. Experiments have shown that initial investigations by patrol officers can be as effective as those conducted by specialists. This is partly because the officers deal with the entire case.

This new challenge for patrol officers—involvement in the entire investigative process—creates interest in crime prevention as well as investigation. In addition, giving patrol officers increased responsibility for investigating crimes frees up detectives to concentrate on offenses that require detailed investigations as well as on cases that require them to leave the community to conduct special interviews or to pursue leads. The result is better investigation by the patrol officer of the more frequent, less severe crimes.

Interrelationships with Others—Community Policing

Figure 1.5
Successful investigations often depend on information gathered from citizens, sometimes through a door-to-door canvass of a neighborhood.

Investigators do not work in a vacuum but rely heavily on assistance from numerous other individuals and agencies. They can benefit greatly from the trend toward departments adopting a **community policing** philosophy. In 1829 in England, Sir Robert Peel stated: "The police are the public and the public are the police." Scholars have pointed to this philosophy as the modern-day roots of community policing. Miller and Hess (p.xvii) note:

> Community policing . . . is a philosophy, a belief that working together, the police and the community can accomplish what neither can accomplish alone. The synergy that results from community policing can be powerful. It is like the power of a finely tuned athletic team, with each member contributing to the total effort.

> Using a community policing orientation, investigators interrelate with uniformed patrol officers, dispatchers, the prosecutor's staff, the defense counsel, supervisors, physicians, the coroner or medical examiner, laboratories, and citizens, including witnesses and victims.

Uniformed Patrol

As noted, patrol officers are a vital part of the investigative process because they are usually the first to arrive at a crime scene. What patrol officers do or fail to do at the scene greatly influences the outcome of an investigation. The patrol officer, as the person daily in the field, is closest to potential crime and has probably developed contacts who can provide information.

A potential pitfall is lack of direct, personal communication between uniformed and investigative personnel, which can result in attitudinal differences and divisiveness. Communication problems can be substantially reduced by using a simple checklist describing the

current investigative status of any cases jointly involving patrol and investigators. The form should include information such as that illustrated in Figure 1.6.

Patrol officers want to know what happens to the cases they begin. Officers who have been informed of the status of "their" cases report a feeling of work satisfaction not previously realized, increased rapport with investigative personnel, and a greater desire to make good initial reports on future cases.

Dispatchers

In most cases, a police dispatcher is the initial contact between a citizen and a police agency. Most citizens call a police agency only a few times during their lives, and their permanent impression of the police may hinge on this contact and the citizens' perceptions of the police agency's subsequent actions.

In addition, the information obtained by the dispatcher is often critical to the officer, the victim, other citizens, and the success of the investigation. The accuracy of the information dispatched to the field officer or investigator may determine the success or failure of the case. In critical incidents, contends Nowicki (p.42): "Dispatchers can literally make the difference between life and death for officers, innocent civilians and even assailants." The responding officer needs to know the exact nature and location of the incident. A direct radio, computer, or phone line should be cleared until the officer arrives at the scene. All pertinent descriptions and information should be dispatched directly to the responding officer.

Prosecutor's Staff

Cooperation between investigators and the prosecutor's staff depends on the personalities involved, the time available, a recognition that it is in everyone's best

```
┌─────────────────────────────────────────────────────────────────┐
│                          STATUS REPORT                          │
│                                                                 │
│   To:                                                           │
│   From:                                                         │
│   Case #:                                                       │
│   Date:                                                         │
│                                                                 │
│   _____ Offense sent to prosecution   _____ Added offenses        │
│   _____ Cleared by arrest             _____ Not cleared by arrest  │
│   _____ Refused prosecution           _____ Unfounded             │
│   _____ Suspect developed             _____ Suspect released      │
│   _____ Suspect in custody            _____ Suspect known         │
│   _____ Property recovered            _____ No property recovered │
│   _____ Case still open               _____ Case closed           │
│   _____ Good patrol report            _____ Incomplete patrol report │
│   _____ Need further information; please call: _____ │
└─────────────────────────────────────────────────────────────────┘
```

Figure 1.6
Sample checklist for case status report

interest to work together, and an acceptance of everyone's investigative roles and responsibilities. Given sufficient time and a willingness to work together, better investigations and prosecutions result. When investigators have concluded an investigation, they should seek the advice of the prosecutor's office. At this point the case may be prosecuted, new leads may be developed, or the case may be dropped, with both the investigator and the prosecutor's office agreeing that it would be inefficient to pursue it further.

The prosecutor's staff can give legal advice on statements, confessions, evidence, the search, and necessary legal papers and may also provide new perspectives on the facts in the case. The prosecutor's office can review investigative reports and evidence that relates to the elements of the offense, advise whether the proof is sufficient to proceed, and assist in further case preparation.

Defense Counsel

Our legal system is based on the adversary system: the accused against the accusor. Although both sides seek the same goal—determining truth and obtaining justice—the adversarial nature of the system requires that contacts between the defense counsel and investigators occur only on the advice of the prosecutor's office. Inquiries from the defense counsel should be referred to the prosecutor's office. If the court orders specific documents to be provided to the defense counsel, investigators must surrender the material, but they should seek the advice of the prosecution staff before releasing any documents or information.

Physicians, Coroners, and Medical Examiners

If a victim at a crime scene is obviously injured and a doctor is called to the scene, saving life takes precedence over all aspects of the investigation. However, the physician is there for emergency treatment, not to protect the crime scene, so investigators must take every possible precaution to protect the scene during the treatment of the victim.

Physicians and medical personnel should be directed to the victim by the route through the crime scene that is least destructive of evidence. They should be asked to listen carefully to anything the victim says and to hold all clothing as evidence for the police.

The coroner or medical examiner is called if the victim has died. Coroners or medical examiners have the authority to investigate deaths to determine whether they were natural, accidental, or the result of a criminal act. They can also provide information on the time of death and the type of weapon that might have caused it.

Depending on the individual case, investigators and the medical examiner or coroner may work as a team, with an investigator present at the autopsy. The medical examiner or coroner may obtain samples of hair, clothing, fibers, blood, and body organs or fluids as needed for later laboratory examination.

Forensic Crime Laboratories

Many criminal investigations involve the processing of physical evidence through a crime lab. Peterson and Hickman (p.1) report the existence of 351 publicly funded forensic crime laboratories throughout the United States at year-end 2002. These laboratories examine many types of evidence, including documents, computers, paints, hairs, fibers, blood and other body fluids, safe insulation, and various types of impressions.

Crime labs employ specialists trained in **criminalistics,** the recording, identification, and interpretation of the *minutiae* (minute details) of physical evidence. O'Connor (2004) explains: "A **criminalist** (aka crime scene technician, examiner, or investigator) is a person who searches for, collects, and preserves physical evidence in the investigation of crime and suspected criminals. . . . They are expected to be on call 24 hours a day to go out to crime scenes. . . . Some jurisdictions require the presence of a criminalist at all major crime scenes."

Criminalistics is a branch of **forensic science,** which is a broader field encompassing the application of science to the law. *Forensic* is an adjective defined as: "Relating to the use of science or technology in the investigation and establishment of facts or evidence in a court of law" (*American Heritage Dictionary,* 2000). Thus, forensic science covers a wide array of disciplines, including pathology, entomology, odontology, anthropology, photography, serology, toxicology, and the list goes on and on. O'Connor offers a succinct differentiation: "The services of a criminalist are used at the beginning of a case. By contrast, the services of a forensic scientist are primarily used at the end, or courtroom testimony phase, of a case."

All law enforcement agencies now have access to highly sophisticated criminalistic examinations through local, state, federal, and private laboratories. According to O'Connor: "At least 80% of [U.S. crime labs] are affiliated with a police agency (where they typically hold bureau status in the organization). The rest are located in the private sector and some of these are exemplary and known for a particular specialty: Cellmark Diagnostics (for DNA), Battelle Corp. (for arson cases), and Sirchie Corp. (for fingerprinting and trace evidence collection), to name a few."

The state crime laboratory is usually located either in the state's largest city or in the state capital and can be used by all police agencies of the state. The FBI Laboratory in Washington, D.C., is also available to all federal, state, and local law enforcement agencies, with personnel available to provide forensic examinations, technical support, expert witness testimony, and training.

Many public crime labs are currently overwhelmed with cases. According to Peterson and Hickman (p.1): "A typical laboratory in 2002 started the year with a backlog of about 390 requests, received 4,900 requests, and completed 4,600 requests." They also note: "Forty-one percent of publicly funded labs in 2002 reported outsourcing one or more types of forensic services to private labs. Overall, labs outsourced nearly 240,000 requests for forensic services" (p.1).

Citizens

Investigators are only as good as their sources of information. They seldom solve crimes without citizen assistance. In fact, citizens frequently provide the most important information in a case. Witnesses to a crime should be contacted immediately to minimize their time involved and inconvenience. Information about the general progress of the case should be relayed to those who have assisted. This will maintain their interest and increase their desire to cooperate at another time.

Citizens can help or hinder an investigation. Frequently, citizens who have been arrested in the past have information about crimes and the people who commit them. The manner and attitude with which such citizens are contacted will increase or decrease their cooperation with the police, as discussed in Chapter 6.

Witnesses

Witnesses are often the key to solving crimes. They can provide eyewitness accounts, or they can provide leads that would be otherwise unavailable. However, as Danaher (p.133) cautions: "Too many officers as well as civilians feel that eyewitness testimony is the most trusted form of evidence. The problem is, that this most trusted of evidence is all too often the least reliable." Danaher contends that this steadfast belief in the veracity of eyewitness accounts may cause officers to fall victim to the investigative paradigm: "Officers will either ignore evidence, or try to fit the evidence into their paradigm. In this paradigm officers fail to follow basic investigative fundamentals. That is, the officer must be completely objective."

Despite such criticism and controversy over the value of eyewitness testimony, the fact remains that judges and juries accord significant weight to eyewitness evidence. Hart (p.vi) asserts: "Cases in which DNA testing has exonerated individuals convicted on the basis of eyewitness testimony tend to make the headlines, but in actuality, the frequency of mistaken eyewitness identifications is quite small. The vast majority of eyewitness identifications are accurate and provide trustworthy evidence for the trier of fact."

Key witnesses should be kept informed of the progress of the case and of their role in the prosecution, if any. If they are to be called to testify in court, their testimony should be reviewed with them, and they should be given assurances that their participation is important in achieving justice.

Victims

Almost every crime has a victim. Catalano (p.1) reports:

> In 2003 U.S. residents age 12 or older experienced an estimated 24.2 million violent and property victimizations, according to the National Crime Victimization Survey (NCVS). These criminal victimizations included an estimated 18.6 million property crimes (burglary, motor vehicle theft, and theft), 5.4 million violent crimes (rape, sexual assault, robbery, aggravated assault, and simple assault), and 185,000 personal thefts (pocket picking and purse snatching).

Even so-called victimless crimes often have innocent victims who are not directly involved in a specific incident. The victim is often the reporting person (complainant) and often has the most valuable information. Yet, in many instances, the victim receives the least attention and assistance. Herman (p.34) observes: "Victims who receive the support they need—from law enforcement's first responders and others—recover more quickly and are more likely to participate in the investigation and prosecution of the crime."

Police should keep victims informed of investigative progress unless releasing the information would jeopardize prosecution of the case or unless the information is confidential. The Federal Victimization Bill provides matching-fund assistance to states for victims of some crimes. Numerous states also have victimization funds that can be used for funeral or other expenses according to predetermined criteria. Police agencies should maintain a list of federal, state, and local agencies, foundations, and support groups that provide assistance to victims. Police should tell victims how to contact community support groups. For example, most communities have support groups for victims of sexual offenses—if not locally, then at the county or state level.

In larger departments, psychological response teams are available. In smaller agencies, a chaplains' corps or clergy from the community may assist with death notifications and the immediate needs of victims.

Investigating officers should also give victims information on future crime prevention techniques and temporary safety precautions. They should help victims understand any court procedures that involve them. Officers should tell victims whether local counseling services are available and whether there is a safe place they can stay if this is an immediate concern.

Victims need to feel safe, to express their emotions, and to know what happens next.

Witnesses, Victims, and the Media

At any major crime scene or during any major criminal investigation, the media will be seeking all the human interest stories they can find. Their primary targets will be victims and witnesses. In some instances victims are taken by surprise when the media shows up without enough safeguards to protect their identity. And in some cases, victims inadvertently reveal information being withheld to preserve the integrity of an investigation.

Some police departments have tried to protect the privacy of victims and witnesses by providing them with a card telling them how to deal with the media (Figure 1.7). The back of the card lists telephone numbers for the public information office and the victim services section.

of 20 or more municipalities surrounding a core city. In a number of metropolitan areas, multijurisdictional major-case squads or metro crime teams have been formed, drawing the most talented investigative personnel from all jurisdictions. In addition, the services of federal, state, or county police agency personnel may be used.

Many agencies are developing special investigation units, focusing resources and training efforts on specific local crime problems. Other areas commonly investigated by special units include drug trafficking and gaming enforcement. In some major cases—for example, homicides involving multijurisdictional problems, serial killers, police officer killings, or multiple sex offenses—it is advisable to form a major-case task force from the jurisdictions that have vested interests in the case. All evidence from the joint case is normally sent to the same laboratory to maintain continuity and consistency. Murphy, Wexler, Davies, and Plotkin (p.13) observe:

> Local law enforcement have long been scrutinized for how they handle large-scale, complex criminal investigations—often those involving serial, spree or mass murderers or violence against national leaders or celebrities. Many of these notorious crimes were investigated within a task force structure, involving multiple agencies, jurisdiction or levels of government. These crimes shared a number of characteristics that called for complicated, demanding investigations that challenged the agencies tasked with solving them in unprecedented ways.

In examining the lessons learned from the D.C. sniper investigation, Murphy et al. (p.15) were able to

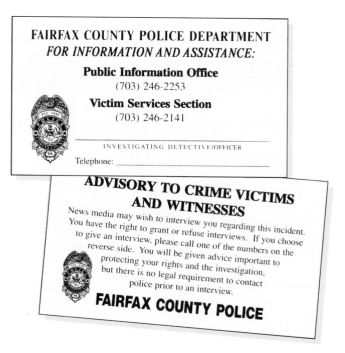

Figure 1.7

Media advisory to crime victims and witnesses

Source: Rick Rosenthal. "Victims, Witnesses and the Media." *Law and Order,* March 2000, p.21. Reprinted by permission of the Fairfax County (Virginia) Police Department.

Major-Case Task Forces

A *multidisciplinary* approach to case investigation uses specialists in various fields from within a particular jurisdiction. A *multijurisdictional* investigation, in contrast, uses personnel from different police agencies. Many metropolitan areas consist

identify some critical aspects of a successful investigation, including thorough planning and preparation, advanced role definition and delineation of responsibilities, efficient information management, and a focus on effective communication.

On the federal level, the Violent Criminal Apprehension Program (VICAP) has been created within the FBI to study and coordinate investigation of crimes of interstate and national interest. Murphy et al. (p.41) explain: "VICAP's mission is to facilitate cooperation, communication and coordination among law enforcement agencies and provide support in their efforts to investigate, identify, track, apprehend and prosecute violent serial offenders."

Interpol is an organization that coordinates information on international cases. Through Interpol all evidence concerning cases of mutual interest is collected, analyzed, and provided to the member jurisdictions.

Federal Law Enforcement Resources

F ederal law enforcement agencies can provide numerous resources to aid local and state agencies involved in high-profile investigations. Federal agencies may have forensic experts that a local or state law enforcement agency does not employ in-house. The ATF, FBI, and Secret Service are available for such forensic expertise. Specialized response units, such as the FBI's Critical Incident Response Group (CIRG), the Rapid Deployment Logistics Unit (RDLU), and the Hostage Rescue Team (HRT) are also accessible to local and state law enforcement. In addition, the National Center for the Analysis of Violent Crime (NCAVC) Behavioral Analysis Unit (BAU) provides behavioral-based investigative and operational support, as described by Murphy et al. (p.41):

> BAU . . . provides assistance to law enforcement through "criminal investigative analysis," a process of reviewing crimes from behavioral and investigative perspectives. BAU staff—commonly called profilers—assess the criminal act, interpret offender behavior and/or interact with the victim for the purposes of providing crime analysis, investigative suggestions, profiles of unknown offenders, threat analysis, critical incident analysis, interview strategies, major case management, search warrant assistance, prosecution and trial strategies, and expert testimony.

Before concluding this overview of criminal investigation, it is worth briefly considering what can happen if investigators step outside their legal boundaries during the course of an investigation. Some might think the worst-case scenario is that the suspect walks, but that

would be only part of the bad news. The other part: The investigator finds that the shoe is on the other foot, as he or she has now become the defendant in a civil liability suit.

Avoiding Civil Liability

C ivil liability refers to a person's degree of risk of being sued. Officers must face the unfortunate reality that being sued goes with wearing the uniform. Most civil lawsuits brought against law enforcement officers are based on Statute 42 of the U.S. Code, Section 1983, also called the Civil Rights Act. This act, passed in 1871, was designed to prevent the abuse of constitutional rights by officers who "under color of state law" denied defendants those rights, and states:

> Every person who, under color of any statute, ordinance, regulation, custom, or usage, of any State or Territory, subjects, or causes to be subjected any citizen of the United States or other person within the jurisdiction thereof to the deprivation of any rights, privileges, or immunities secured by the Constitution and laws, shall be liable to the party injured in an action at law, suit in equity, or other proper proceeding for redress.

Basically, Section 1983 states that anyone who acts under the authority of law and who violates another person's constitutional rights can be sued. Of particular relevance to criminal investigations are those constitutional protections involving searches and seizures, interrogations, and custody situations. Rutledge (p.66) stresses:

> Officers receive comprehensive indoctrination on the basics of arrest, search, and seizure during academies and in-service training, but there is a career-long need to continue to update that information. And the reason for this need is easy to understand: the law is constantly changing.
> . . . An officer who has no ongoing plan for keeping current with these changes is at greater risk for civil liability because he or she is more likely to be basing actions on outdated concepts of law.

Wrobleski and Hess (p.389) observe: "Investigative procedure is [one] area of police work commonly brought up in lawsuits. Almost every investigation gives officers discretion to decide what evidence should be included in prosecutor reports and warrant applications, and what evidence should be omitted." If investigators withhold **exculpatory evidence,** which is evidence favorable to the accused, the courts have deemed this to be a violation of a defendant's due process rights:

> Leaving out exculpatory evidence may lead to liability for false arrest, malicious prosecution, and illegal search

and seizure claims. To support such liability claims, a plaintiff must show that the affiant knowingly and deliberately, or with reckless disregard for the truth, omitted facts that are material or necessary to a finding of probable cause [*Franks v. Delaware*, 1978].

Investigators also face civil liability for filing false affidavits. As Lemons (p.8) explains:

> Before a search or arrest warrant is issued, the Fourth Amendment requires a truthful factual showing in the affidavit used to establish probable cause. Because "the Constitution prohibits an officer from making perjurious or recklessly false statements in support of a warrant,"[2] a complaint that an officer knowingly filed a false affidavit to secure a search or arrest warrant states a claim under section 1983.[3] Further, "where an officer knows, or has reason to know, that he has materially misled a mag-

istrate on the basis for a finding of probable cause . . . the shield of qualified immunity is lost."[4]

One of the best ways to avoid lawsuits or to defend yourself if sued is to keep complete, accurate records of all official actions you take. Hess and Wrobleski (p.467) offer suggestions to avoid lawsuits.

Protection against lawsuits includes:
- **Effective policies and procedures clearly communicated to all.**
- **Thorough and continuous training.**
- **Proper supervision and discipline.**
- **Accurate, thorough police reports.**

---

[2]*Kelly v. Curtis*, 21 F.3d 1544, 1554 (11th Cir. 1994)
[3]*United States v. Basham*, 286 F.3d 1199, 1204 (10th Cir. 2001)

[4]*Golino v. City of New Haven*, 950 F.2d 864, 871 (2d Cir. 1991), cert. denied, 505 U.S. 1221 (1992)

SUMMARY

A criminal investigation is the process of discovering, collecting, preparing, identifying, and presenting evidence to determine what happened and who is responsible. The goals of police investigation vary from department to department, but most investigations aim to:

- Determine whether a crime has been committed.
- Legally obtain sufficient information and evidence to identify the responsible person.
- Locate and arrest the suspect.
- Recover stolen property.
- Present the best possible case to the prosecutor.

Among the numerous functions performed by investigators are those of providing emergency assistance; securing the crime scene; photographing, videotaping, and sketching; taking notes and writing reports; searching for, obtaining, and processing physical evidence; obtaining information from witnesses and suspects; identifying suspects; conducting raids, surveillances, stakeouts, and undercover assignments; and testifying in court.

All investigators—whether patrol officers or detectives—are more effective when they possess certain intellectual, psychological, and physical characteristics. Effective investigators obtain and retain information, apply technical knowledge, and remain open-minded, objective, and logical. They are emotionally well balanced, detached, inquisitive, suspecting, discerning, self-disciplined, and persevering. Further, they are physically fit and have good vision and hearing.

The first officer to arrive at a crime scene is usually a patrol officer assigned to the area. In any preliminary investigation, it is critical to establish priorities. Emergencies are handled first, and then the crime scene is secured. Any suspect at the scene should be detained, questioned, and then either released or arrested, depending on circumstances. If a suspect has recently left the scene, general descriptions of the suspect, any vehicles, direction of travel, and any items taken should be obtained and dispatched to headquarters immediately.

After emergencies are dealt with, the first and most important function is to protect the crime scene and evidence. All necessary measures to secure the crime scene should be taken—including locking, roping, barricading, and guarding—until the preliminary investigation is completed.

Once the scene is secured, the preliminary investigation is conducted, which includes measuring, photographing, videotaping, and sketching the scene; searching for evidence; identifying, collecting, examining, and processing physical evidence; questioning victims, witnesses, and suspects; and recording all statements and observations in notes. *Res gestae* statements are spontaneous statements made at the time of a crime, concerning and closely related to actions involved in the crime. They are often considered more truthful than later, planned responses. The crime scene is preserved through these records.

As soon as possible, officers should determine whether a crime has been committed by knowing the elements of each major offense and the evidence that supports them and then ascertaining whether they are present. They should also try to determine when the event occurred.

Even in police departments that have highly specialized investigation departments, the ultimate responsibility for solving crimes lies with all police personnel. It must be a cooperative, coordinated departmental effort. Cooperation and coordination of efforts are also required outside the police department. Investigators must interrelate not only with uniformed patrol officers but also with dispatchers, the prosecutor's staff, the defense counsel, physicians, the coroner or medical examiner, laboratories, and citizens, including victims. Criminal investigation is, indeed, a mutual effort.

Protection against lawsuits includes (1) effective policies and procedures clearly communicated to all, (2) thorough and continuous training, (3) proper supervision and discipline, and (4) accurate, thorough police reports.

CHECKLIST

Preliminary Investigation

- Was a log kept of all actions taken by officers?
- Were all emergencies attended to first? (First aid; detaining suspects; broadcasting information regarding suspects)
- Was the crime scene secured and the evidence protected?
- Were photographs or videotapes taken?
- Were measurements and sketches made?
- Was all evidence preserved?
- Were witnesses interviewed as soon as possible and statements taken?

Questions

- How was the complaint received?
- What were the date and time it was received?
- What was the initial message received? (State the offense and location.)
- Where was the message received?
- Who was present at the time?
- Were any suspicious persons or vehicles observed while en route to the scene?
- What time did officers arrive at the scene?
- How light or dark was it?
- What were the weather conditions? Temperature?
- Were there other notable crime-scene conditions?

- How did officers first enter the scene? Describe in detail the exact position of doors or windows—open, closed, locked, glass broken, ajar, pried, or smashed. Were the lights on or off? Shades up or down?
- Was the heating or air conditioning on or off? Was a television, radio, or stereo on?
- Were dead or injured persons at the scene?
- What injuries to persons were observed? Was first aid administered?
- What type of crime was committed?
- Was the time the crime occurred estimated?
- Who was the first contact at the scene? (Name, address, telephone number)
- Who was the victim? (Name, address, telephone number) Was the victim able to give an account of the crime?
- What witnesses were at the scene? (Names, addresses, telephone numbers)
- Were unusual noises heard—shots, cars, screams, loud language, prying, or breaking noises?
- Had clocks stopped?
- Were animals at the scene?
- Was an exact description of the suspect obtained? (Physical description, jewelry worn, unusual voice or body odors; unusual marks, wounds, scratches, scars; nicknames used; clothing; cigarettes or cigars smoked; weapon used or carried; direction of leaving the scene)
- Was a vehicle involved? Make, model, color, direction, unusual marks?
- Were items taken from the scene? Exact description?
- What was done to protect the crime scene physically?
- What officers were present during the preliminary investigation?
- Were specialists called to assist? Who?
- Was the coroner or medical examiner notified?
- What evidence was discovered at the scene? How was it collected, identified, preserved? Were field tests used?

DISCUSSION QUESTIONS

1. What are the advantages of assigning all investigations to specialists? What disadvantages does this pose? Which approach do you support?
2. Of all the suggested characteristics required for an effective investigator, which three are the most critical? Are these qualifications more stringent than those required for a patrol officer?
3. What is the role of the victim in investigating crime?
4. What misconceptions regarding investigation are conveyed by television shows and movies?

5. What do you believe is the most important goal of a criminal investigation?
6. What major factors must responding officers consider while proceeding to a crime scene?
7. How important is response time to the investigation of a crime? How is the importance affected by the type of crime?
8. What determines who is in charge at a crime scene? What authority does this officer have?
9. Controversy exists over which emergency takes precedence: an armed suspect at or near the scene or a severely injured person. Which do you think should take priority? Why?
10. What balance should be maintained between freedom of the media to obtain information during a crime investigation and the right to privacy of the individuals involved?

MEDIA EXPLORATIONS

Internet

Complete one of the following assignments and be prepared to share your findings with the class.

- Go to the website of the National Institute of Justice (NIJ) "Mapping Crime: Principle and Practice" at http://www.ncjrs.org/html/nij/mapping/pdf.html and outline the chapters in this research guide. Then select one chapter and outline it.

- Go to the website of the Bureau of Justice Statistics at http://www.ojp.usdoj.gov/bjs/abstract/cvusst.htm and summarize what the site says about crimes reported and not reported to the police.

- Go to the Mapping and Analysis for Public Safety website at http://www.ojp.usdoj.gov/nij/maps/ or the National Center for Geographic Information and Analysis at http://www.ncgia.ucsb.edu/ and summarize the information you feel is important and informative for you and the rest of the class.

Crime and Evidence in Action

Select one of three criminal case scenarios and sign in for your shift. Your Mobile Data Terminal (MDT) will get you started and update you throughout the case. During the course of the case you'll become a patrol officer, detective, prosecutor, defense attorney, judge, corrections officer, or parole officer to conduct interactive investigative research. Each case unfolds as you respond to key decision points. Feedback for each possible answer choice is packed full of information, including term definitions, web links and important documentation. The sergeant is available at certain times to help mentor you, the Online

Resources website offers a variety of information, and be sure to take notes in your e-notebook during the suspect video statements and at key points throughout (these notes can be saved, printed, or e-mailed).

The interactive Forensics Tool Kit will test your ability to collect, transport, and analyze evidence from the crime scene. At the end of the case you can track how well you responded to each decision point and join the Discussion Forum for a postmortem. **Go to the CD and use the skills you've learned to solve a case.**

REFERENCES

American Heritage Dictionary of the English Language, 4th ed. Houghton Mifflin Company, 2000.

Bichler, Gisela, and Gaines, Larry. "An Examination of Police Officers' Insights Into Problem Identification and Problem Solving." *Crime and Delinquency*, January 2005, pp. 53–74.

Buice, Ed. "Media Relations: When the World is Watching." *Law and Order*, January 2003, pp. 24–26.

Catalano, Shannan M. *Criminal Victimization, 2003.* Washington, DC: Bureau of Justice Statistics National Crime Victimization Survey, September 2004. (NCJ 205455)

Danaher, Larry. "The Investigative Paradigm." *Law and Order*, June 2003, pp. 133–134.

Dees, Tim. "Computers in Law Enforcement." *Law and Order*, Fiftieth Anniversary Issue 1953–2003, pp. 22–25.

Diamond, Joe. "Connecting the Dots." *Police*, April 2004, pp. 42–47.

Douglas, Dave. "PDAs on Patrol." *Police*, February 2003, pp. 42–45.

Fuller, John. "A Training Dilemma: The Patrol Officer and the Preliminary Investigation." *The Law Enforcement Trainer*, May/June 2003, pp. 34–37.

Gary, Charles. "How to . . . Cope with the Press." *Police*, December 2003, pp. 24–29.

Gore, Richard Z., and Pattavina, April. "Applications for Examining the Journey-to-Crime Using Incident-Based Offender Residence Probability Surfaces." *Police Quarterly*, December 2004, pp. 457–474.

Hart, Sarah V. Foreword. In *Eyewitness Evidence: A Trainer's Manual for Law Enforcement*. Washington, DC: National Institute of Justice Special Report, September 2003, pp. v–vi.

Helms, Dan. "Whendunnit: Unraveling the Hidden Patterns in the Timing of Serial Crime." *Law Enforcement Technology*, July 2003, pp. 144–147.

Herman, Susan. "Law Enforcement and Victim Services: Rebuilding Lives, Together." *The Police Chief*, May 2002, pp. 34–37.

Hess, Kären M., and Wrobleski, Henry M. *Police Operations*, 4th ed. Belmont, CA: Wadsworth Publishing Company, 2006.

Koivisto, Anais. "Career Advice: How to Become a Crime Scene Investigator." WebGuru, Inc., 2004. www.webguru.com/crime-scene-investigator.htm

Lemons, Bryan R. "Civil Liability for False Affidavits." *The Police Chief*, November 2004, pp. 8–9.

"Life Imitates Art with 'CSI Effect.'" *Law Enforcement News*, June 2005, pp.1, 11.

McCue, Colleen, and Parker, André. "Connecting the Dots." *Law Enforcement Technology*, October 2003, pp. 115–122.

Miller, Christa. "From Crime Scene to Courtroom." *Law Enforcement Technology*, January 2003, pp. 70–77.

Miller, Linda S., and Hess, Kären M. *The Police in the Community: Strategies for the 21st Century*, 4th ed. Belmont, CA: Wadsworth Publishing Company, 2005.

Murphy, Gerard R.; Wexler, Chuck; Davies, Heather J.; and Plotkin, Martha. *Managing a Multijurisdictional Case: Identifying the Lessons Learned from the Sniper Investigation*. Washington, DC: Police Executive Research Forum, October 2004.

Nowicki, Ed. "Dispatchers and Officer Safety." *Law and Order*, April 2004, p. 42.

O'Connor, Thomas R. "An Introduction to Criminalistics and Physical Evidence." Online: http://faculty.ncwc .edu/toconnor/315/315lect02.htm. Updated January 6, 2004.

Peterson, Joseph L., and Hickman, Matthew J. *Census of Publicly Funded Forensic Crime Laboratories, 2002.* Washington, DC: Bureau of Justice Statistics Bulletin, February 2005. (NCJ 207205)

Pinizzotto, Anthony J., Davis, Edward F., and Miller, Charles E., III. "Intuitive Policing: Emotional/Rational Decision Making in Law Enforcement." *FBI Law Enforcement Bulletin*, February 2004, pp. 1–6.

"Recognizing Innovation in the Art and Science of Criminal Investigations." *The Police Chief*, April 2003, p. 140.

Rutledge, Devallis. "Controlling Lawsuit Risks." *Police*, February 2005, pp. 66–67.

Shane, Jon M. "Compstat Process." *FBI Law Enforcement Bulletin*, April 2004, pp. 12–21.

Weiss, Jim, and Davis, Mickey. "Geographic Profiling Finds Serial Criminals." *Law and Order*, December 2004, pp. 32–38.

Williams, Gerald L. "Criminal Investigations." In *Local Government Police Management*, 4th ed. Edited by William A. Geller and Darrel W. Stephens. Washington, DC: International City/County Management Association, 2003, pp. 169–205.

Wrobleski, Henry M. and Hess, Kären M. *Introduction to Law Enforcement and Criminal Justice*, 8th ed. Belmont, CA: Wadsworth Publishing Company, 2006.

CASES CITED

Franks v. Delaware, 438 U.S. 154, 165-166 (1978)

Golino v. City of New Haven, 950 F.2d 864, 871 (2d Cir. 1991), cert. denied, 505 U.S. 1221 (1992)

Kelly v. Curtis, 21 F.3d 1544, 1554 (11th Cir. 1994)

United States v. Basham, 286 F.3d 1199, 1204 (10th Cir. 2001)

Section 2

BASIC INVESTIGATIVE RESPONSIBILITIES

s Berg[1] points out: "Police can learn a few lessons from legendary basketball coach John Wooden," who believed that constantly practicing, mastering, and executing the basics were the keys to a team's success. Berg contends:

Officers, detectives, and sergeants should constantly evaluate their fundamentals. Are reported crimes being thoroughly investigated or merely reported? Are neighborhoods being canvassed for that one witness who may give us the little piece of information we need to identify the suspect? Have we searched thoroughly for evidence, including fingerprints, and have we protected evidence and gathered it in an expert manner? Are we completing well written reports that contain all of the information that will make a subsequent follow-up successful? Are we doing a comprehensive job investigating at a crime scene or do we always expect the experts and the specialists to "figure it out"?

Essentially, how well do our front-line patrol investigators, detectives, and sergeants execute the fundamentals of high-quality police work at the scene of a crime? As John Wooden taught us so many years ago, you don't get to cut the net down

[1] Gregory R. Berg. "Crime Scene Investigations—Time to Get Back to the Basics." *Law Enforcement News*, March 31, 1999, p.8.

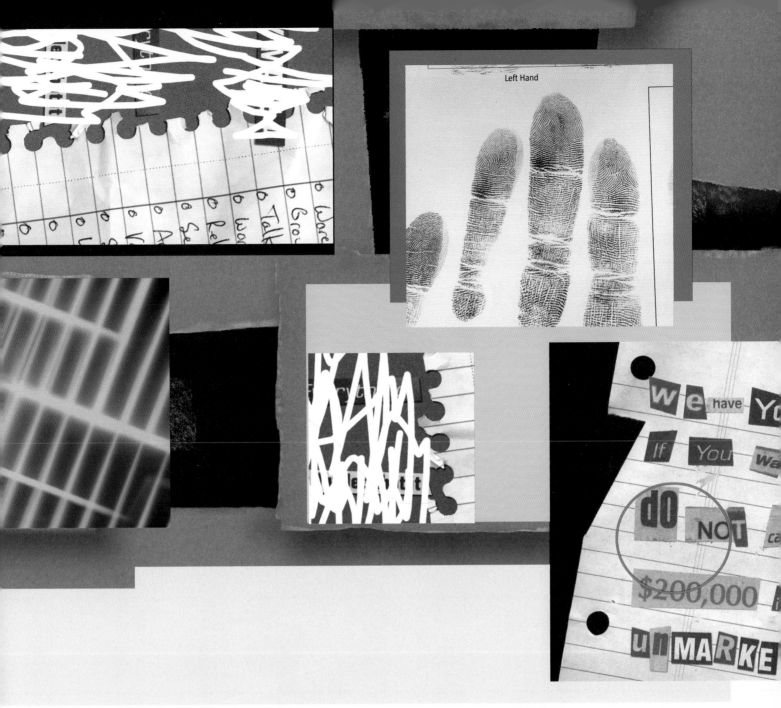

after the final game if you don't understand the most basic fundamentals of the game and perform them consistently well. So it is with front-line police work.

The basic investigative techniques introduced in Chapter 1 are central to the successful resolution of a crime. Investigators must be skilled in documenting the crime scene and any continuing investigation, including taking notes and photographs or videotaping and sketching (Chapter 2), and then casting this information into an effective report (Chapter 3). They must also be skilled in searching (Chapter 4); obtaining and processing physical evidence (Chapter 5); obtaining information through interviews and interrogation (Chapter 6); and identifying and arresting suspects and conducting raids, surveillances, stake-outs, and undercover assignments (Chapter 7).

Although these techniques are discussed separately, they actually overlap and often occur simultaneously. For example, note taking occurs at almost every phase of the investigation, as does obtaining information. Further, the techniques require modification to suit specific crimes, as discussed in Sections 3, 4, and 5. Nonetheless, investigation of specific crimes must proceed from a base of significant responsibilities applicable to most investigations. This section provides that base.

CHAPTER 2

Documenting the Crime Scene: Note Taking, Photographing, and Sketching

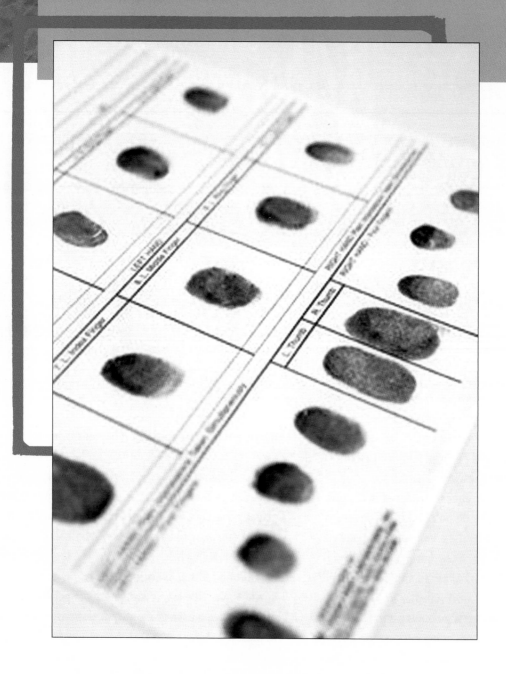

Can You Define?

Do You Know?

- Why notes are important in an investigation?
- When to take notes?
- What to record in investigative notes?
- How to record the notes?
- What the characteristics of effective notes are?
- Where to file notes if they are retained?
- What purposes are served by crime scene photography?
- What the advantages and disadvantages of using photography and videography are?
- What the minimum photographic equipment for an investigator is?
- What to photograph at a crime scene and in what sequence?
- What errors in technique to avoid?
- What types of photography are used in criminal investigations?
- What basic rules of evidence photographs must adhere to?
- What purposes are served by the crime scene sketch?
- What should be sketched?
- What materials are needed to make a rough sketch?
- What steps to take in making a rough sketch?
- How plotting methods are used in sketches?
- When a sketch or a scale drawing is admissible in court?

Outline

ocumentation is vital throughout an investigation. Smith (p.57) asserts: "While tools of the crime scene investigator vary, the most fundamental gear is the camera and notebook." Baldwin (2004) adds: "Documentation is made by notes, sketches and photographs. If you observe something in the crime scene then DOCUMENT IT! How are you going to convince the judge or jury of your interpretations if you can't prove the facts as you observed them? This is where most mistakes are made by the crime scene technician testifying in court hearings. They know what they saw but failed to properly document their observations."

Most people who go into law enforcement are amazed at the amount of paperwork and writing that is required—up to 70 percent of an investigator's job is consumed by these functions. In addition, photography plays an important role in documenting evidence and presenting cases in court. Some larger departments have a photographic unit. Other departments rely on their investigators to perform this function. Often both photographs and sketches must accompany written notes to provide a clear picture of the crime scene.

This chapter begins with a discussion of field notes: when to take them, what to record, and where to record. Next is a discussion of various methods of taking notes, the characteristics of effective notes, and filing notes, followed by an explanation of the admissibility of notes in court. The second major

discussion is investigative photography, beginning with a discussion of the advantages and disadvantages of photographs, the basic photographic equipment needed, training in and using investigative photography, and errors to avoid. This is followed by a description of other types of investigative photography and suggestions on how to identify, file, and maintain continuity of the photographs or videos. The discussion concludes with an explanation of the admissibility of photographic evidence in court.

The third portion of the chapter—crime scene sketching—begins with an overview of sketching and a description of a rough crime scene sketch and the steps involved in creating it. This is followed by an explanation of how to file the sketch and how it is used in creating the finished scale drawing as well as computer-assisted drawing. The discussion of crime scene sketching concludes with a discussion of the admissibility of sketches and drawings.

Field Notes: The Basics

Note taking is not unique to the police profession. News reporters take notes to prepare stories; physicians record information furnished by patients to follow the progress of a case; lawyers and judges take notes to assist in interviewing witnesses and making decisions; students take notes in class and as they read. Quite simply, notes are brief records of what is seen and/or heard.

Investigative notes are a permanent written record of the facts of a case to be used in further investigation, in writing reports, and in prosecuting the case.

Note taking and report writing are often regarded as unpleasant, boring tasks. Yet no duty is more important, as many officers have found, much to their embarrassment, when they did not take notes or took incomplete notes. Detailed notes can make or break a case. For example, when a defense attorney challenges in court the reliability or validity of various breath or blood measurements of alcohol content, the case often hinges on the thoroughness of an officer's written report. Accurate notes not only aid later recall but also are used for preparing sketches and reports. Notes are important throughout an entire investigation.

When to Take Notes

Start taking notes as soon as possible after receiving a call to respond and continue recording information as it is received throughout the investigation.

Sometimes it is physically impossible to take notes immediately—for example, while driving a vehicle or in complete darkness. At other times, taking notes immediately could hinder obtaining information if it intimidates a witness or suspect. Whether to take out a notebook immediately in the presence of a person being questioned is a matter of personal insight and experience.

When people are excited, want to get their name in the newspaper, or want to get your attention, you can usually record information immediately. Most people are willing to give information if you are friendly and courteous and you explain the importance of the information. In such cases no delay in taking notes is required (Figure 2.1).

On the other hand, reluctant witnesses and suspects may not talk if you record what they say. In such cases, obtain the information first and record it later. You must sense when it is best to delay writing notes. Specific methods of obtaining information from willing and unwilling people are discussed in Chapter 6.

Figure 2.1
Witnesses are important sources of information regarding crimes committed in their neighborhoods.

If someone gives you an exact wording of what was said by a person committing a crime, have the witness initial that portion of your notes after reading it to help ensure its accuracy. If possible, have people who give you information take time to write a statement in their own handwriting. This avoids the possibility that they may later claim that they did not make the statement or were misunderstood or misquoted.

What to Record

Take notes on everything you do in an official investigative capacity. Record all facts, regardless of where they may lead. Information establishing a suspect's innocence is as important as that establishing guilt.

Enter general information first: the time and date of the call, location, officer assigned, and arrival time at the scene. Police departments using centrally dispatched message centers may automatically record date, time, and case numbers. Even if this is done, make written notes of this initial information, because recorded tapes may not be kept for extended periods or may become unusable. The tapes and notes corroborate each other.

 Record all information that helps to answer the questions Who? What? Where? When? How? and Why?

As you take notes, ask yourself specific questions such as these:

- When: did the incident happen? was it discovered? was it reported? did the police arrive on the scene?

were suspects arrested? will the case be heard in court?

- Where: did the incident happen? was evidence found? stored? do victims, witnesses, and suspects live? do suspects frequent most often? were suspects arrested?

- Who: are suspects? accomplices? Complete descriptions would include gender, race, coloring, age, height, weight, hair (color, style, condition), eyes (color, size, glasses), nose (size, shape), ears (close to head or protruding), distinctive features (birthmarks, tattoos, scars, beard), clothing, voice (high or low, accent), and other distinctive characteristics such as walk.

- Who: were the victims? associates? was talked to? were witnesses? saw or heard something of importance? discovered the crime? reported the incident? made the complaint? investigated the incident? worked on the case? marked and received evidence? was notified? had a motive?

- What: type of crime was committed? was the amount of damage or value of the property involved? happened (narrative of the actions of suspects, victims, and witnesses; combines information included under "How")? evidence was found? preventive measures had been taken (safes, locks, alarms, etc.)? knowledge, skill, or strength was needed to commit the crime? was said? did the police officers do? further information is needed? further action is needed?

- How: was the crime discovered? does this crime relate to other crimes? did the crime occur? was evidence found? was information obtained?

● Why: was the crime committed (was there intent? consent? motive?)? was certain property stolen? was a particular time selected?

Make notes that describe the physical scene, including general weather and lighting conditions. Witnesses may testify to observations that would have been impossible given the existing weather or lighting. Accurate notes on such conditions will refute false or incorrect testimony.

Record everything you observe in the overall scene: all services rendered, including first aid; description of the injured; location of wounds; who transported the victim and how. Record complete and accurate information regarding all photographs taken at the scene. As the search is conducted, record the location and description of evidence and its preservation. Record information to identify the type of crime and what was said and by whom. Include the name, address, and phone number of every person present at the scene and all witnesses.

The amount of notes taken depends on the type of offense, the conditions of the case, your attitude and ability, and the number of other officers assigned to the case. Make sure you take enough notes to completely describe what you observe and do during an investigation. This will provide a solid foundation for a detailed report and for court testimony. If in doubt about whether to include a specific detail, record it. As noted succinctly in the Federal Bureau of Investigation's (2003) *Handbook of Forensic Services:* "Nothing is insignificant to record if it catches one's attention."

Do *not* jot down information unrelated to the investigation—for example, the phone number of a friend, an idea for a poem, or a doodle. If the defense attorney, judge, or jury sees your notes, such irrelevant material will reflect poorly on your professionalism.

Where to Record Notes

Use a notebook to record all facts observed and learned during an investigation. Despite the availability of sophisticated recorders and computers, the notebook remains one of the simplest, most economical, and most basic investigative tools. Notes taken on scraps of paper, on the backs of envelopes, or on napkins are apt to be lost, and they also reflect poorly on an officer's professionalism.

Divide the notebook into sections for easy reference. One section might contain frequently used telephone numbers. Another section might contain frequently needed addresses. This information can be a permanent part of the notebook. Identify the notebook with your name, address, and telephone number, and the address and telephone number of your police department.

Opinions vary as to whether it is better to use a loose-leaf notebook or separate spiral-bound notebooks for each case. If you use a loose-leaf notebook, you can easi-

ly add paper for each case you are working on as the need arises, and you can keep it well organized. Most investigators favor the loose-leaf notebook because of its flexibility in arranging notes for reports and for testifying in court. However, use of a loose-leaf notebook opens the opportunity of challenge from the defense attorney that the officer has fabricated the notes, adding or deleting relevant pages. This can be countered by numbering each page, followed by the date and case number, or by using a separate spiral notebook for each case.

Disadvantages of the latter approach are that the spiral notebook is often only partially used and therefore expensive and may be bulky for storage. Further, if other notes are kept in the same notebook, they also will be subject to the scrutiny of the defense. A final disadvantage is that if you need a blank sheet of paper for some reason, you should not take it from a spiral notebook because most of these notebooks indicate on the cover how many pages they contain. The defense can only conjecture about loose-leaf pages that might have been removed, but missing pages from a spiral notebook can be construed as evidence that something has been removed.

The decision to use a loose-leaf or spiral-bound notebook is sometimes a matter of department policy. In addition to the notebook, always carry pens and pencils. Use a pen for most notes, because ink is permanent. You may want to use pencil for rough sketches that require minor corrections as you sketch.

How to Take Notes

Note taking is an acquired skill. Time does not permit a verbatim transcript. Learn to select key facts and record them in abbreviated form.

Write brief, legible, abbreviated notes that others can understand.

Do not include words such as *a, and,* and *the* in your notes. Omit all other unnecessary words. For example, if a witness said, "I arrived here after having lunch at Harry's Cafe, a delightful little place over on the west side, at about 1:30, and I found my boss had been shot," you would record: "Witness arrived scene 1:30 (after lunch at Harry's Cafe) to find boss shot." You would not know at the time if the fact that she had lunch at Harry's Cafe was important, but it might be, so you would include it.

Write or print legibly, especially when recording names, addresses, telephone numbers, license numbers, distances, and other specific facts. If you make an error, cross it out, make the correction, and initial it. Do *not* erase. Whether intentional or accidental, erasures raise credibility questions.

Whenever possible, use standard abbreviations such as *mph, DWI, Ave.* Do *not,* however, devise your own shorthand. For example, if you wrote, "Body removed by A. K.," the initials *A. K.* would be meaningless to others. If you become ill, injured, or deceased, others must be able to read and understand your notes. This is necessary to further the investigation, even though some question regarding admissibility in court may arise.

Using a Tape Recorder Some police departments use tape recorders extensively because of the definite advantage of recording exactly what was stated with no danger of misinterpreting, slanting, or misquoting. However, tape recorders do not replace the notebook. Despite their advantages, they also have serious disadvantages. The most serious is that they can malfunction and fail to record valuable information. Weak batteries or background noise can also distort the information recorded. In addition, transcribing tapes is time consuming, expensive, and subject to error. Finally, the tapes themselves, not the transcription, are the original evidence and thus must be retained and filed.

If information is taped, check the recorder before using it, record the appropriate heading before beginning the questioning, and always play the tape back to ensure that the information is recorded satisfactorily. Supplement the tape with notes of the key points.

Technology Innovations

Dees (2005, p.310) reports:

Anoto is a system of specialized papers and an electronic pen that serves to capture handwritten information directly into an electronic document or database.

Users write freehand or fill out forms printed on special Anoto paper, using a fat pen...that reads a faint grid printed on the paper and thus "knows" where the writing is going. The user then sticks the pen into a cradle, where the written data transfers onto a host computer, which converts it into readable text...

Officers using the IS2Be "Intuitive Pen" system can hand-write information on their own agency's paper forms (printed on the special Anoto paper), and then have the information transferred into a computer-based document without the intervention of a data entry clerk or optical character recognition system. This is an excellent and innovative method for departments that want to keep all of their report files in electronic form, but don't want to force officers to enter data directly into a computer.

Characteristics of Effective Notes

ffective notes describe the scene and the events well enough to enable a prosecutor, judge, or jury to visualize them.

 Effective notes are complete, accurate, specific, factual, clear, well organized, and legible.

The basic purpose of notes is to record the *facts* of a case. Recall the discussion of the importance of objectivity in an investigation. Use this same objectivity in note taking. For example, you might include in your notes the *fact* that a suspect reached inside his jacket and your *inference* that he was reaching for a gun. Your *opinion* on the merits of gun-control laws, however, has no place in your notes. If you have a specific reason for including an opinion, clearly label the statement as an opinion. Normally, however, restrict your notes to the facts you observe and learn and the inferences you draw. If, for example, you see a person you consider to be nervous and you make a note to that effect, you are recording an

inference. If, on the other hand, you record specific observations such as: "The man kept looking over his shoulder, checking his watch, and wiping perspiration from his forehead," then you are recording facts on which you based your inference. You may not remember six months or a year later why you inferred that the man was nervous.

Record facts accurately. An inaccurately recorded name can result in the loss of a witness or suspect. Inaccurate measurements can lead to wrong conclusions. Have people spell their names for you. Repeat spellings and numbers for verification. Recheck measurements.

Be as specific as possible. Rather than writing *tall, fast,* or *far*, write *6'8"*, *80 mph,* or *50 feet.* Little agreement may exist on what is tall, fast, or far.

Notes are usually taken rapidly, increasing the chance of errors. Take enough time to write legibly and clearly. Legibility and clarity are not synonymous. *Legibility* refers to the distinctness of your letters and numbers. *Clarity* refers to the distinctness of your statements. For example, lack of clarity is seen in a note that states, "When victim saw suspect he pulled gun." *Who* pulled the gun: the victim or the suspect? The same lack of clarity is seen in the statements "When suspect turned quickly I fired" (Did the suspect turn quickly, or did the officer fire quickly?) and "When the suspect came out of the house, I hit him with the spotlight." Make certain your notes are clear and can be interpreted only one way.

Effective notes are also well organized. Make entries from each case on separate pages and number the pages. Keep the pages for each case together and record the case number on each page.

Filing Notes

Some officers destroy all their field notes after they have written their reports. They believe that notes simply duplicate what is in the report and may in fact contain information no longer pertinent when the report is written. Some police departments also have this as a policy.

If department policy is to keep the notes, place them in a location and under a filing system that makes them available months or even years later. Department policy usually determines where and how notes are filed.

If notes are retained, file them in a secure location readily accessible to investigators.

Store notes in an official police department case file or any secure location where they are available on short demand. Some departments file notes with the original file in the official records department. Others permit an officer to keep the original notes and file only the report made from the notes. Wherever notes are filed, they must be secure.

No one filing system is best. Notes may be filed alphabetically by the victim's name, by case number, or in chronological order. As long as the system is logical, the notes will be retrievable. Appeals have been granted as long as 20 years after convictions, with the defendant being granted a new trial. Because of this, many officers retain their notes indefinitely.

Admissibility of Notes in Court

The use of notes in court is probably their most important legal application. They can help discredit a suspect's or a defense witness's testimony; support evidence already given by a prosecution witness, strengthening that testimony; and defend against false allegations by the suspect or defense witnesses. Notes give you an advantage because others rarely make written notes and, therefore, must testify from memory.

All officers who are present at the scene while the notes are being taken and who witness the writing and initial the notes at that time may use the notes during courtroom testimony. If you anticipate the need to have other investigators testify from a specific set of notes, be sure they do in fact witness the original note taking at the crime scene and provide their initials on the original notes. The admissibility of notes in court is presented in greater detail in the final chapter of this text.

In addition to accurate notes, photographs provide vital and necessary means of documenting a crime scene.

Investigative Photography: An Overview

A picture is, indeed, worth a thousand words, and investigative photographs and videotapes are essential to proper crime scene documentation. The basic purpose of crime scene photography is to record the scene permanently. Photos and video taken immediately, using proper techniques to reproduce the entire crime scene, provide a factual record of high evidentiary value. The time that elapses between the commission of a crime and when a suspect in that crime is brought to trial can stretch into months or years, with the condition of the crime scene and physical evidence deteriorating along the way. Photos and videos preserve the scene. Do not touch or move any evidence until pictures and video have been taken of the general area and all evidence.

Photographs and videotapes reproduce the crime scene in detail for presentation to the prosecution, defense, witnesses, judge, and jury in court. They are used in investigating, prosecuting, and police training.

Although most crime scene photographs are taken by investigators, they may also be acquired from commercial or amateur photographers, attorneys, news media personnel, or the coroner's staff. For example, in an arson case at a church, photographs came from three outside sources. The pastor hired a photographer to take pictures for historical purposes and to assess damage; an insurance-company photographer took pictures; and a television news crew had taken live footage in-progress. These pictures, along with those taken by police personnel, provided an excellent record of the fire in-progress, its point of origin, and the resulting damage.

Videotape is now well established as an investigative tool. In fact, as noted by Senn (p.8): "Today's juries not only assume video evidence will be used, they're more demanding when it comes to quality." Lightweight, handheld video camcorders are easy to use at a crime scene. Videotapes can also be made of witness testimony, depositions, evidence, lineups, and even trials.

Advantages and Disadvantages of Photographs

One advantage of photographs is that they can be taken immediately, an important factor in bad weather or when many people are present. For example, a picture of a footprint in the dirt outside a window broken during a burglary can be important if it rains before a casting can be made. The same is true when a large number of people present might alter the scene.

Another obvious advantage of crime scene photographs is that they accurately represent the crime scene in court. The effect of pictures on a jury cannot be overestimated. Photographs are highly effective visual aids that corroborate the facts presented.

 Advantages of photographs: They can be taken immediately, accurately represent the crime scene and evidence, create interest, and increase attention to testimony.

Although photographs of a crime scene accurately represent what was present, they include everything at the scene, both relevant and irrelevant. So much detail may distract viewers of photographs.

 Disadvantages of photographs: They are not selective, do not show actual distances, and may be distorted and damaged by mechanical errors in shooting or processing.

Despite these disadvantages, photography is a valuable investigative technique. The introduction of video technology (analogue videocassettes or digital video discs [DVDs]) into crime scene investigation has allowed investigators to compensate for some of the shortcomings of still photography.

Advantages and Disadvantages of Video

A videocassette or DVD, played before a jury, can bring a crime scene to life in ways other evidence cannot and offers some distinct advantages over photographs, such as being able to show distance (Senn, p.8). Other advantages of video include its cost-effectiveness and the ability to view the crime scene immediately. While taping, the videographer can use the camera's audio function to describe the procedure being used to make the video and to explain what is being taped. Furthermore, a slow pan of a crime scene is more likely than a series of photographs to capture all evidence, including that in the periphery of view, which might seem rather inconsequential at the time.

 Advantages of videos: They can be viewed immediately, accurately represent the crime scene and evidence, are able to show distance more clearly than photos, have sound capability to more fully document what is being seen, and are cost-effective.

Regrettably, many agencies fail to provide adequate training to those tasked with videotaping a crime scene, assuming that if officers are able to tape their cousin's wedding or their daughter's soccer game, they should be able to handle a camcorder in any venue. Yet, as Jan Garvin, training vice president for the Law Enforcement and Emergency Services Video Association (LEVA), a nonprofit video training organization, states: "The decision to hand a camera to an untrained person is just as unfortunate as asking someone to make a tactical entry with a shotgun when all they've fired is a pistol" (Senn, p.12). The negative consequences of poor video can damage a case, as Senn (p.12) explains: "When videotaping efforts go bad, it can undermine the value and impact of the evidence—and can tee off a jury in the process."

Art Garrett, audiovisual specialist for the video unit of the Alameda County, California, DA's office, lists some common mistakes made by untrained crime scene videographers (Senn, pp.12, 14):

- Shooting too soon—unlike photos, which can be rearranged after the fact to show the crime scene in a logical sequence, videos must be thought out ahead of time if a logical progression is to occur
- Erratic camera movements and failure to use a tripod
- Inappropriate length—videos that are long and repetitive bore the jury; videos that are too short don't show enough
- Poor camera technique in general—poor focusing, overzealous use of the zoom button, bad composition, improper lighting
- Inadvertent audio—a camera's microphone (mic) is quite sensitive and can pick up sounds a distance away from the camera, including distracting background noises and embarrassing or inappropriate statements. The audio-record capability can be disabled by inserting a "dummy plug" into the camera's mic input.

Proper training can help eliminate most, if not all, of these common videotaping errors and increase the documentation value of crime scene videos.

 Disadvantages of videos: Many people mistakenly believe that no training in videotaping is necessary, which leads to poor video quality and a diminished value in the video's documentation of the crime scene.

A vast array of modern equipment has greatly enhanced the investigative usefulness of photography and videography.

Basic Photographic Equipment

Crime scene photography uses both common and special-function cameras and equipment, depending on the crime investigated and the investigator's preferences.

 At a minimum, have available and be skilled in operating a 35-mm single-lens reflex (SLR) camera (film or digital), a Polaroid-type instant-print camera, a press camera, a fingerprint camera, and video record/playback equipment.

Investigators commonly have individual preferences about the equipment to use in a given situation. Some have switched from 35-mm and press cameras to professional roll-film cameras. Generally, equipment should meet several photographic needs.

Versatile *35-mm film cameras* provide negatives for enlargements. Many models have an automatic built-in flash (which can be turned off) and can imprint the date directly on the photo. Many also allow the film to be rewound before the entire roll is shot.

Single-use cameras are another option for the first officer on a crime scene, regardless of photographic training or skill. These fixed-focus flash cameras come preloaded with both film and battery. The photographer simply points and shoots the photo.

Instant-print cameras such as those made by Polaroid and Impulse provide pictures at low cost per image. Instant-print photography provides immediate confirmation of the quality and accuracy of the picture at a time when it is possible to take another shot. The cameras are simple to operate, which lessens the need for training. Every officer on the force can use an instant-print camera. These cameras have good optics, resolu-

tion, and color and can document small evidence such as bullet holes. The greatest advantage, however, is that the photographer can tell immediately whether the photo is good.

Digital cameras (Figure 2.2) also provide instant verification of a photo's quality. One advantage of digital cameras is elimination of the time and expense involved in processing photographic film, while ensuring strict confidentiality. In addition, digital photos are quickly adaptable as e-mail attachments, as additions to electronic databases, and as inserts on written reports. Another advantage is that most digital cameras record technical information about each photograph, such as the date and time and specific camera settings, in a text file associated with the image. A significant advantage of digital over film photos is consistency. Digital photography, which suffers from none of the image degradation of analogue copies, changes the definition of what was once vaunted as the original master. Now every copy is, in effect, an original. All of the advantages of digital still photography apply to digital video recording.

Press cameras provide excellent photographs of a general scene as well as of smaller areas or small pieces of evidence. The ground glass of their lenses permits perfect focusing and shows exactly what portion of the scene will appear in the photograph. The 4″ × 5″ negative allows enlargement for detailed court presentation.

Fingerprint cameras are specially constructed to take pictures of fingerprints without distortion. They provide their own light through four bulbs, one in each corner. Removing a bulb from any corner provides slanted lighting to show fingerprint ridge detail. This camera can also photograph trace evidence such as bloodstains and tool marks.

© Stockdisc / Getty Images.

Figure 2.2
Digital technology is being used more often in documenting crime scenes. Digital cameras allow instant verification of a photo's quality, and most automatically stamp the date and time of the image capture on an attached text file.

Technology Innovations

A major advance is the ability of computer software to stitch together digital photos of 180 degrees or more to create one 360-degree photo—a panoramic view of a crime scene that is interactive, allowing viewers, including jury members, to walk through it as though they were there (Figure 2.3). This type of 360-degree photographic view is called **immersive imaging.** Against a backdrop of conventional photography's limitations, Davis (2005, p.68) describes the advantages of Crime Scene Virtual Tour (CSVT) software, which lets jurors virtually step into a crime scene:

> With conventional photography you'd need dozens of overlapping shots to achieve a 360-degree panorama of a crime scene, and you would still have confusing perspectives and limited range both horizontally and vertically. But CSVT lets you look at a panoramic scene from any angle. You can even zoom, pan, tilt, and rotate while considering the facts of the crime.
>
> If a suspect says she was standing at a certain place, you can virtually put yourself there and see her perspective. If a witness claims he saw the whole thing, a couple of shots and you'll know what he could and more importantly could not have seen.

Figure 2.3

The Crime Scene Virtual Tour software program allows investigators to recreate the crime scene and to piece together better the events that occurred. These programs may also be presented during trial to help a jury visualize the crime scene.

Video cameras are used to record alleged bribery, payoffs, and narcotics buys. Permanently installed units frequently photograph crimes actually being committed, such as bank robberies or shoplifting. Videotaping crime scenes is now commonplace. The cameras have become much less expensive, much more portable, and much easier to operate. They have the advantage of immediacy and elimination of a middle processing step in the chain of evidence. In addition, most can operate in quite limited light.

Camcorders and videotaping equipment have for some time been used for in-station recording of bookings and for testing of suspects in driving-while-intoxicated stops. Use of video cameras for crime scene investigations is now prevalent (Figure 2.4). Many police departments have purchased video equipment to record crime scenes and criminal acts such as vandalism, drug deals, and thefts, increasing convictions.

Many police departments have mounted video cameras on their patrol vehicles' dashboards, an application that offers many benefits. *Specialized cameras* such as binocular cameras and trip cameras (cameras that set themselves off) are helpful in surveillance.

Film for the various cameras may be black-and-white or color. Although more expensive, color film is often preferred because it is more realistic and accurate. Film can also be special-purpose, such as infrared film. Literature furnished with the camera gives detailed information about the type of film to use.

It is difficult to describe color and sometimes impossible to describe varying shades of color accurately. Therefore, color film has a clear advantage. Officers and witnesses can more easily recognize objects in color photographs. Color photographs can bring out faintly visible stains and preserve the original colors of objects that fade because of weather or age. Color photographs are especially helpful in showing the nature and extent of physical injuries. More extensive uses of color photography in police work are being developed each year, and improved film and processing are assisting in the admissibility of color photographs in court.[2]

Accessories, depending on the camera(s) used, include an exposure meter, flash attachments, and flood lamps and high-intensity spotlights. Lighting equipment can also assist in illuminating the scene as officers search for minute evidence. An adjustable tripod for mounting the camera at any angle makes for better photographs in most instances.

Lenses and filters are available for different purposes. Normal lenses are best for evidence, but sometimes special lenses are needed. For example, a telephoto lens can capture a distant subject, whereas a wide-angle lens can cover an entire room in a single frame. Various filters can eliminate certain colors from a photograph.

Selection of a camera and accessories is determined by budget, local needs, and investigator preference.

---

[2] Defense attorneys sometimes object to color photographs on the grounds that they are inflammatory. This concern is discussed later in the chapter.

Figure 2.4
Officer John Weaver of the Tyler (Texas) Police Department uses the Coban digital video camera system to review a traffic stop he made earlier in the day. The system, which records video and audio to a computer hard drive, is being installed in 60 Tyler police cruisers. Eventually, police headquarters will be able to see a live video transmission from the cameras through a wireless network. In addition to traffic stops, these video recorders can be used for taping evidence of driving under the influence and drug arrests. The tapes can also be used for training.

© AP / World Wide Photos

Sometimes investigators can borrow equipment from local schools or community organizations or share it with other agencies. In some communities, citizens lend special-purpose equipment to the police department.

Darkroom facilities are an additional consideration. Smaller departments often share a darkroom with another agency, such as a fire department. Larger departments usually have their own darkrooms. If a commercial developer is used, it may take too long to get pictures back, confidential information may be revealed, and the commercial developer may be required to testify in court. For these reasons, a police department may find it advantageous to have its own darkroom facilities or to share them with another agency.

Training in and Using Investigative Photography

Investigators can master most photographic equipment by reading the accompanying manuals and practicing. Some equipment, however, requires special training. Photographic training includes instruction in the operation of all available photographic equipment; shooting techniques; anticipated problems; and identifying, filing, and maintaining continuity of photographic evidence. Learn the nomenclature and operation of your available photo-

graphic equipment. Sometimes camera and equipment manufacturers or outlets provide such training.[3]

Professional commercial photographers in the community can sometimes assist in training or serve as consultants. They can provide information on photographic techniques and special problems such as lighting, close-ups, exposures, and use of filters. Training programs also include instructions on identifying and filing photographs and on establishing and maintaining the continuity of the chain of evidence.

Digital Cameras

As with other types of crime scene processing techniques, proper training in the use of digital equipment is essential. Digital technology brings with it a new language and application skill set for investigators to learn. While an in-depth discussion of digital technology, capabilities, and applications is beyond the scope of this text, a few examples should make clear the critical need for investigators to be thoroughly educated about and trained in the use of digital equipment.

One of the most basic terms used when discussing digital photography is **resolution,** which refers to the fineness of image detail either captured with a camera, displayed on a monitor, or printed on paper. High resolution produces a sharp image; low resolution, a blurrier

---

[3] The Polaroid Corporation provides training on law enforcement photography and publishes a photography newsletter for law enforcement called *Instant Evidence!* (Back issues are available online at www.polaroid.com/instantevidence) In addition, Polaroid has a technical assistance hotline: 1-800-225-1618. Their hotline for digital cameras is 1-800-432-5355.

image. Resolution is commonly quantified in terms of pixels. A **pixel** is the smallest unit of a digital image, generally a dot within the image (just as traditional newsprint photos are made up of tiny dots); one **megapixel** is about a million dots. The more dots, the larger the image can be made without losing resolution quality. Digital cameras or other capture devices range in resolution from 2 megapixels to 24 megapixels. However, resolution of computer monitors and printers, referred to as *output devices,* are given in terms of **PPI**, or pixels per inch. Both types of resolution must be factored in when taking digital photographs, as both affect the final size and quality of the image. An image photographed with a high-resolution camera (the capture device), if printed on a low-resolution printer (the output device), will not show fine detail clearly. A low-resolution image, if enlarged too much, will also lose quality.

An understanding of resolution is critical for investigators who use digital cameras to document a crime scene because resolution affects every aspect of digital imaging. Improper choice of equipment or incorrect settings on it will produce low-quality results, which may have damaging consequences in the courtroom. Witzke (p.40) explains:

> Agencies may buy inexpensive digital cameras just because they are affordable and use the argument that they are good enough. A concern is that image quality degradation has a serious side effect in a forensic environment. A department should ask itself how well it defends image quality and integrity in the courtroom because of color interpolation and image compression. Defense attorneys are learning to challenge the integrity of digital images because the image format used at the point of capture creates artifacts within the final image.

The importance of understanding resolution, and the plethora of other digital terms and concepts too detailed to explore here, is brought into focus when one considers evidentiary standards and requirements surrounding this technology. For example, an investigator photographing latent prints at a crime scene must know that "[t]o comply with FBI IAFIS [Integrated Automated Fingerprint Identification System] requirements, a latent print must be captured with a minimum resolution of 1,000 PPI, but also be printed as life size" (Witzke, p.45). In other words, for digital images to have any value in the courtroom, investigators had better thoroughly understand their equipment and apply the technology properly. (Admissibility of photographs is examined shortly.)

What to Photograph or Videotape

Take sufficient photographs and/or videotape to reconstruct the entire scene. This usually requires a series of shots, notably of the entrance point, the crime commission area, and the exit point. If possible, show the entire scene of the crime in a pictorial sequence. This helps relate the crime to other crimes.

Move the camera to cover the entire crime scene area, but plan a sequence of shots that least disturb the scene. The initial photographs showing the entire crime scene should use a technique called **overlapping.** Photograph the scene clockwise and take the first picture with a specific object on the right. For the second photo, make sure that the same object is on the left side of the photograph. Continue in this way until you have covered the entire scene.

First photograph the general area, then specific areas, and finally specific objects of evidence. Take exterior shots first because they are the most subject to alteration by weather and security violations.

This progression of shots or video will reconstruct the commission of a crime:

1. Take *long-range* shots of the locality, points of ingress and egress, normal entry to the property and buildings, exterior of the buildings and grounds, and street signs or other identifiable structures that will establish location.

2. Take *medium-range* shots of the immediate crime scene and the location of objects of evidence within the area or room.

3. Take *close-range* shots of specific evidence such as hairs, fibers, footprints, and bloodstains. The entire surface of some objects may be photographed to show all the evidence; for example, a table surface may contain bloodstains, fingerprints, hairs, and fibers.

Zoom lenses allow close shots without disturbing the crime scene, and close-ups are possible with macro lenses. Such close-range shots usually should include a marker, sometimes called a scale. A **marker** is anything used in a picture to show accurate or relative size. It is usually a ruler, but it can be some other object of a known size. An important point: Using a marker introduces something foreign to the crime scene. The same is true of chalk marks drawn around a body or placed on walls to illustrate bullet direction. Therefore, first take a picture of the scene or object without the marker; then add the marker and take a second photograph.

Photogrammetry can be used at most crime scenes. However, different crimes require different types of photographs. In arson cases, photograph the point of origin and any incendiary devices. In burglaries, photograph the points of entry and exit, tool marks, fingerprints, and other trace evidence. In assaults, photograph injuries and do so in color if possible. In homicides or suicides, photograph the deceased, including pictures of

Technology Innovations

Forensic photogrammetry is the technique of extrapolating three-dimensional (3-D) measurements from two-dimensional photographs. Photogrammetry can also automatically orient photographs taken from awkward angles and can correct for camera misalignment. Furthermore, this technique can cut in half the amount of time investigators spend performing on-site mapping of a crime scene. To the question "Why should law enforcement agencies consider photogrammetry?" Galvin (2005, p.37) answers:

> The primary benefit is that images can be recorded quickly on-scene, minimizing time spent at the incident scene. The scene and resulting 3D measurements are permanently archived using a modestly priced digital camera in combination with a special photogrammetry software program. Measurements can be made months or even years after an incident.
>
> The images create an irrefutable recording of the three-dimensional measurements of scene evidence for CAD [computer-aided design] diagramming, particularly useful for litigation.

the clothing worn; take a full-length picture showing height, position of the body and all extremities, and evidence near the body. Photograph injured parts of the body to show the location and extent of injuries and any postmortem lividity (discussed in Chapter 8).

Errors to Avoid

To obtain effective photographs and videos, be familiar with your equipment and check it before you use it.

> Take photographs and/or videos before anything is disturbed. Avoid inaccuracies and distortions.

If something has been moved, do *not* put it back. It is legally impossible to return an object to its original position. To minimize distortion or misrepresentation, maintain proper perspective and attempt to show the objects in a crime scene in their relative size and position. Take pictures from eye level, the height from which people normally observe objects.

Types of Investigative Photography

I n addition to crime scene photography, certain other types of photography play vital roles in investigation.

> Types of investigative photography include crime scene, surveillance, aerial, night, laboratory, lineup, and mug shot.

Surveillance Photography

Surveillance photography establishes the identity of a subject or records criminal behavior without the photographer's presence being known to the subject. The photographs or videotapes can help identify a suspect's associates, destroy an alibi, plan a raid, or develop a surveillance plan. Banks and stores frequently use surveillance cameras to help identify robbers and burglars. Numerous bank robbers have been identified through photographs taken by surveillance cameras installed in the bank.

Photographs during a stakeout are usually taken with an SLR camera with several telephoto lenses. Sometimes infrared film is used. It may be necessary to use a van—preferably borrowed because it is best to use a vehicle only once for such purposes. An appliance repair van or any van that would commonly be seen in the area is desirable.

Concealing a camera can be a problem. You might use a bag, briefcase, suitcase, or coat pocket with an opening. You can also conceal the camera by using rooftops or windows of buildings or vehicles in the area. A camera kept away from a vehicle window is rarely seen by people outside the vehicle. Keep the camera loaded and adjusted to the required light so you can take pictures instantly.

Surveillance photography is often called **trap photography,** because the photos prove that an incident occurred and can help identify suspects and weapons. These photos corroborate witness testimony and identification. The fact that the photos exist often induces guilty pleas without court appearances, thus saving investigators' time.

Battery-operated cameras can be moved to different locations. You can reduce the amount of film needed by using triggering devices such as bait-money pull switches or by placing activation buttons in several locations where employees can reach them easily. Lighting conditions determine whether color or black-and-white film is appropriate. Hidden camcorders can be used at drug-buy scenes.

Surveillance photography can also be a crime prevention/detection tool. For example, the Newark Police Department has video cameras mounted in six different areas of the 2-square-mile downtown area. An officer observes what is taking place in each area from a central location. Burglaries and street robberies have decreased, and the police have successfully presented the videos as evidence in court.

Aerial Photography

Investigators often use aerial photography to cover extensive areas. For example, it can be used following a bank robbery to show roads leading to and from the bank. It is also useful when police know that a crime is going to be committed but not when. Aerial photography shows routes to the scene as well as how to block escape routes and avoid detours during pursuit and where to set up roadblocks. It is essential in locating dead-end streets—information that can be very important if a chase ensues. Aerial pictures can also help establish the location of a crime scene, especially in large rural areas or mountainous sectors. Geographical Information Systems (GIS) technology is now enhancing the aerial views of crimes scenes, as Quail (p.100) explains: "GIS technology is capable in assisting in an investigation by providing relevant background information about specific investigation scenes to the investigator. Aerial and topographical maps provide useable detail to orient investigators of routes, buildings, streets and other terrain with reasonable clarity."

Aerial photographs are often available in commercial photographers' files, engineering offices, or highway-planning agencies. The vast areas covered by highways and engineering projects usually require aerial mapping. Federal, state, county, and municipal agencies also may have aerial photos. If none are available, a local photographer can be hired to provide them. Many larger departments and county sheriff's offices have helicopters that may be available.

Aerial photos can be enlarged or presented on slides to show the relationships of streets and roads. For example, in the John F. Kennedy assassination investigation, the entire area was photographed, including all points from which shots might have been fired. More recently, software based on aerial photography was used by multiple jurisdictions involved in the D.C. sniper investigation.

A new high-tech application of aerial photography involves **pictometry,** computer technology that integrates various aerial shots of a land-based artifact taken straight down (orthogonal) and from numerous angles (oblique). The result is a high-resolution 3-D image of the object, whether it be a landmark, a neighborhood, a bridge, a river, a house, or any other structure or geological feature, which investigators may view from multiple perspectives with the simple click of a mouse (Figure 2.5). The software also features extreme zooming capabilities, allowing investigators to rotate and zoom in on a particular structure.

Night Photography

Taking pictures at night presents special problems, particularly that of illuminating a scene. Adequate light can be obtained by increasing exposure time, using a photoflash for small areas and a flash series for larger areas, or using floodlights. Floodlights also aid in locating evidence and decrease the chance of evidence being accidentally destroyed.

Kramer (p.42) suggests that investigators can make the camera see as the photographer sees through camera position, time exposure, and supplemental lighting. To accomplish this, the following equipment is needed: a manual camera with "bulb" setting, normal lens, tripod, high-power flash, and an external battery pack. State-of-the-art night-vision devices/cameras are dramatically better than earlier ones. Their range extends up to a mile. Because they are quite expensive and used infrequently, they are often shared with other federal, state, or county law enforcement agencies. Night-vision devices use image intensification and can be binoculars, weapon mounted, camera mounted, or head mounted.

Laboratory Photography

Not all investigative photography is done in the field. Sometimes objects are photographed in a laboratory with special equipment that is too large, delicate, or expensive to use in the field. For example, infrared film photographs can reveal the contents of unopened envelopes, bloodstains, alterations to documents, variations in types of ink, and residue near where a bullet has passed through clothing. X-ray cameras can detect loaded dice.

Microphotography takes pictures through a microscope and can help identify minute particles of evidence such as hairs or fibers. In contrast, **macrophotography** enlarges a subject. For example, a fingerprint or a tool mark can be greatly enlarged to show the details of ridges or striations.

Laser-beam photography can reveal evidence indiscernible to the naked eye. For example, it can reveal the outline of a footprint in a carpet, even though the fibers have returned to normal position.

Ultraviolet-light photography uses the low end of the color spectrum, which is invisible to human sight, to make visible impressions of bruises and injuries long

Figure 2.5A

Pictometry software with GIS overlays allows investigators to see up to 12 different views of this geographic area.

Images courtesy of Pictometry International

Figure 2.5B

This screen capture highlights some of the different functions available with pictometry software, such as measuring distances and heights, and determining a precise geographic location with latitude/longitude coordinates.

© Will Smith / Pictometry

after their actual occurrence. Bite marks, injuries due to beatings, cigarette burns, neck strangulation marks, and other impressions left from intentional injuries can be reproduced and used as evidence in criminal cases by scanning the presumed area of injury with a fluorescent or blue light. The damage impression left by the injury is then photographed. In addition, the type of weapon used in committing a crime can often be determined by examining its impression, developed by using ultraviolet light.

Mug Shots

Although investigators seldom take **mug shots** themselves, these photographs are often significant in criminal investigations. Mug shots originated in nineteenth-century France when Alphonse Bertillon developed a method of identification that used an extensive system of measurements to describe people. The Bertillon identification system included a written description, the complete measurements of the person, and a photograph.

© Joel Gordon.

Figure 2.6
A video-imaging system allows officers to sort a database using specific char-acteristics–race, sex, hair color, height, age, distinguishing marks–in fact, any feature that can be visually described.

The pictures of people in police custody were kept in department files for identification and became known as *mug shots.* Gathered in files and displayed in groups, they were called a **rogues' gallery.**

Opinions differ regarding the preferred poses for mug shots. Some agencies believe the front and profile of the head are sufficient; others prefer full-length, stand-up pictures. No matter what the pose, mug shots should include the facial features and the clothing worn at the time of arrest, because a defendant's appearance may change between the time of arrest and trial. Mug shots can be filed by age, sex, and height to make them more readily accessible for viewing. Mug shots can be carried in the field to identify suspicious persons or to show to crime victims to assist in identifying their attacker. They are also used for "wanted" circulars dis-tributed to other police agencies and the public. The use of mug shots in suspect identification is discussed in Chapter 7.

Lineup Photographs

The computer's capacity to sort through a database of mug shots and bring up all the "hits" within specific categories can assist in generating photographic line-ups. After entering characteristics of a known suspect, an officer can select six to twelve other "hits" to be used for presentation with the suspect's photo (Figure 2.6). In addition, videotapes or photographs of people included in lineups may be taken to establish the fairness of the lineup.

Identifying, Filing, and Maintaining Security of Evidence

Photographs must be properly identified, filed, and kept secure to be admissible as evidence.

Identifying

In the field notes, the photographs taken should be dat-ed and numbered in sequence. Include the case number, type of offense, and subject of the picture. To further identify the photograph with the crime scene and the subject, record the photographer's name, location and direction of the camera, lens type, approximate distance in feet to the subject, film and shutter speed, lighting, weather conditions, and a brief description of the scene in the picture.

The photos should also be marked like any other evidence relating to the crime scene using a procedure called **backing.** This includes writing on the back of the photo your initials, the date the photo was taken, what the photo depicts, and the direction of north.

Filing

File the picture and negatives for easy reference. Pictures in the case file are available to others. There-fore, it is usually best to put them in a special photo-graph file, cross-referenced by case number.

Maintaining Security

Record the chain of custody of the film and pho-tographs in the field notes or in a special file. Mark and identify the film as it is removed from the camera. Each time the film changes possession, record the name of the person accepting it. If a commercial firm develops the film, take it to the company in person or send it by reg-istered mail with a return receipt.

Admissibility of Photographs in Court

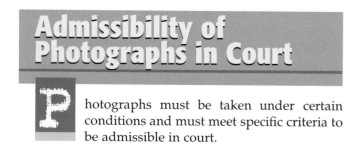

Photographs must be taken under certain conditions and must meet specific criteria to be admissible in court.

> Photographs must be material, relevant, competent, accurate, free of distortion, and noninflammatory.

A **material photograph** relates to a specific case and subject. Material evidence is relevant and forms a substantive part of the case presented or has a legitimate and effective influence on the decision of the case. A **relevant photograph** helps explain testimony. A **competent photograph** accurately represents what it purports to represent, is properly identified, and is properly placed in the chain of evidence and secured until court presentation.

Testimony reports the exact conditions under which the photographs were taken, the equipment and type of film used, and where the film was processed. Photographs must be accurate and free of distortion. If nothing has been removed from or added to the scene, the photograph will be accurate. Inaccuracies do not necessarily render the photograph inadmissible as evidence as long as they are fully explained and the court is not misled about what the picture represents.

Likewise, distortion will not necessarily disqualify a photograph as evidence if no attempt is made to misrepresent the photograph and if the distortion is adequately explained. For example, an amateur photographer may have taken the picture from an unusual camera height to produce a dramatic effect, not knowing the picture would later be useful as evidence in a criminal investigation.

Color distortion is a frequent objection. Because most objects have color, black-and-white photographs are technically distorted. Therefore, color photographs usually constitute better evidence. However, color can also be distorted by inadequate lighting or faulty processing. Nevertheless, the photograph can still be useful, especially if the object's shape is more important than its color.

Although color photographs are less distorted and are usually better evidence than black-and-white photographs, they have often been objected to as being inflammatory—for example, showing in gruesome, vivid color a badly beaten body. To be ruled inadmissible, color photographs must be judged by the court to be so inflammatory that they will unduly influence the jury. Sometimes taking both color and black-and-white pictures is advisable. The black-and-white pictures can be introduced as evidence; the color pictures can be used for investigatory purposes only.

Objections to enlargements have also been raised. Such objections can be nullified by producing the original negative along with the enlargement to prove that no alterations have been made.

Authenticating Digital Images

The availability of software, such as Adobe Photoshop, that modifies, enhances, or otherwise alters digital images raises authenticity issues and concerns over such digital photographs' originality and integrity. To overcome defense challenges that a digital image was altered or otherwise tampered with, investigators must rigorously maintain the chain of custody and use techniques that safeguard the authenticity of their photographs. Several software programs have been developed that "watermark" or authenticate the original image, either at the point of capture (within the camera) or as it is downloaded from the camera to a computer. The programs then store the original image in a secure location and write-protect it, making it impossible to alter the original, yet still allowing copies to be manipulated for investigative purposes.

In addition to admissible photographs and videotapes, investigators usually must prepare a crime scene sketch.

Crime Scene Sketches: An Overview

An investigator's scene sketch can be more descriptive than hundreds of words and is often an extremely important investigative aid. The crime scene **sketch** accomplishes the following:

- Accurately portrays the physical facts
- Relates to the sequence of events at the scene
- Establishes the precise location and relationship of objects and evidence at the scene
- Helps to create a mental picture of the scene for those not present
- Is a permanent record of the scene
- Is usually admissible in court

> A crime scene sketch assists in (1) interviewing and interrogating people, (2) preparing the investigative report, and (3) presenting the case in court.

The sketch supplements photographs, notes, plaster casts, and other investigative techniques. Artistic ability is helpful but not essential in making crime scene sketches. Still, many police officers avoid making sketches. To overcome this hesitance, practice by drawing familiar scenes such as your home, office, or police station. Use graph paper to make sketching easier.

The most common types of sketches are those drawn at the crime scene, called *rough sketches,* and those completed later by an investigator or a drafter, called *scale* (or *finished*) *drawings.* Both describe the crime scene pictorially and show the precise location of objects and evidence.

The Rough Sketch

 rough sketch is the first pencil-drawn outline of a scene and the location of objects and evidence within this outline. It is not usually drawn to scale, although distances are measured and entered in the appropriate locations.

Sketch all serious crime and crash scenes after photographs are taken and before anything is moved. Sketch the entire scene, the objects, and the evidence.

It is better to include too much rather than too little, but do not include irrelevant objects that clutter and confuse the sketch.

The area to be sketched depends on the crime scene. If it involves a large area, make a sketch of nearby streets, vegetation, and entrance and exit paths. If the scene is inside a house or apartment building, show the scene's location in relation to the larger structure. If the scene involves only a single room, sketch only the immediate crime scene, including an outline of the room, objects, and the evidence within it.

Do not overlook the possible availability of architectural drawings of the house or building. These are often on file with local engineering, assessing, or building departments or with the architect who drew the original plans.

Sketching Materials

Materials needed for rough sketches should be assembled and placed in their own kit or in the crime scene investigation kit.

 Materials for the rough sketch include paper, pencil, long steel measuring tape, carpenter-type ruler, straightedge, clipboard, eraser, compass, protractor, and thumbtacks.

Paper of any type will do, but plain white or graph paper is best. No lines interfere if you use plain white. On the other hand, graph paper provides distance ratios and allows for more accurate depictions of the relationships between objects and evidence at the scene. When sketching, use a hard lead pencil to avoid smudges. Keep two or three pencils on hand.

Use a 50- to 150-foot steel measuring tape for measuring long distances. Steel is preferable because it does not stretch and therefore is more accurate than cloth tape. Use a carpenter-type ruler to take short and close-quarter measurements and a straightedge to draw straight lines. A clipboard will give a firm, level drawing surface.

Use a compass to determine true north, especially in areas and buildings laid out in other than true directions. Use a protractor to find the proper angles when determining coordinates.

Thumbtacks are helpful to hold down one end of the tape when you measure. You can also use them to fasten paper to a drawing surface if no clipboard is available.

Steps in Sketching the Crime Scene

 nce photographs have been taken and other priority steps in the preliminary investigation performed, you can begin sketching the crime scene. First, make an overall judgment of the scene. Remember not to move, remove, touch, or pick up anything until it has been photographed, located on the rough sketch, and described in detail in your notes. Then handle objects only in accordance with the techniques for preserving evidence.

To sketch a crime scene:
- Observe and plan.
- Measure distances.
- Outline the area.
- Locate objects and evidence within the outline.
- Record details.
- Make notes.
- Identify the sketch with a legend and a scale.
- Reassess the sketch.

Step One: Observe and Plan

Before starting to sketch, observe the scene as many times as you need to feel comfortable with it. Take in the entire scene mentally so you can recall it later. Plan in

Figure 2.7
Accuracy is vital when making crime scene measurements. Here, New York Police measure off the distance of the crime scene by the yellow markers where spent shell cases lay on 35th street off 8th Ave. in New York, Wednesday, March 6, 2002, following a shooting.

advance how to proceed in an organized way to avoid destruction of evidence. Ask yourself, "What is relevant to the crime? What should be included in the sketch?"

The size of the area determines how many sketches you make. For example, part of the crime may have taken place indoors and another part outdoors a considerable distance away. To include the entire area would make the scale too small. Therefore, make two sketches.

Decide Where to Start The overview also helps you determine where to start sketching and measuring. If the scene is a room, stand in the doorway and start the sketch there. Then continue clockwise or counterclockwise. The photographs, sketch, and search are all made in the same direction. Usually it does not matter which direction is selected, but try to use the one that is least disturbing to evidence.

Step Two: Measure and Outline the Area

All measurements must be accurate. Do not estimate distances or use paces or shoe length measurement. Use conventional units of measurements such as inches, feet, or yards. Do not move any objects while measuring (Figure 2.7).

If another officer is helping you take measurements, reverse the ends of the tape so both of you can observe the actual distance on the tape. Legally, it is *hearsay* for officers to testify to what they did not actually observe. If a third officer is taking notes, that officer can testify to only the measurements given to him or her unless he or

she actually saw the tape measurement. However, all officers may testify from the same notes if they review and initial them as they are made.

Do not measure from movable objects. Use *fixed locations* such as walls, trees, telephone poles, building corners, curbs, and so on. Measure from wall to wall, not baseboard to baseboard.

Once the outside measurements have been made, sketch the outline, maintaining some distance ratio. Use the longest measurement first and orient the sketch paper to this distance, positioning the sketch so *north is toward the top of the paper.* Place the outside limits in the sketch using dimension lines such as this:

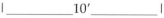

Determine the **scale** by taking the longest measurement at the scene and dividing it by the longest measurement of the paper used for sketching. For example, if your paper is 10 inches and the longest measurement at the scene is 100 feet, let 1 inch equal 10 feet. Use the largest, simplest scale possible. Table 2.1 presents suggested scales for sketches.

Graph paper makes it easier to draw to scale. Each square can equal one square foot or one square inch, depending on the size of the scene. The outline sketch of a room might look like Figure 2.8, whereas the outline sketch of an outdoor scene might look like Figure 2.9.

Next, measure and sketch the doors and windows. Record their measurements and indicate whether the doors open in or out. To measure windows, use the width and height of the actual window opening; do not include the window frame. The outline of a room with doors and windows added might look like Figure 2.10.

Table 2.1 / **Suggested Scales for Sketches**

Indoor Areas	Outdoor Areas
1/2'' = 1' (small rooms)	1/2'' = 10' (large buildings and grounds)
1/4'' = 1' (large rooms)	1/8'' = 10' (large land areas)
1/8'' = 1' (very large rooms)	

Sketch the location of physical objects within the perimeter. Use approximate shapes for large objects and symbols for small ones. Place items of evidence in the sketch at the same time you place objects. Use numbers to designate objects and letters to designate evidence. Include such items as bullet entry or exit points, body, hair, gun, fibers, bloodstains, and so on. Use exact measurements to show the location of evidence within the room and in relation to all other objects.

Opinions differ on whether to include the location of evidence in this sketch. If evidence is placed within the sketch, some courts have withheld introduction of the sketch until the evidence has been approved. If the evidence is placed only in the finished scale drawing, the sketch can be introduced and used by witnesses to corroborate their testimony.

While sketching, check measurements frequently. Make corrections if needed, but make no changes after leaving the scene. Measurements may or may not be placed in the sketch itself, depending on how many objects are located in the available space. Measurements can be placed in your notes and later entered in the scale drawing.

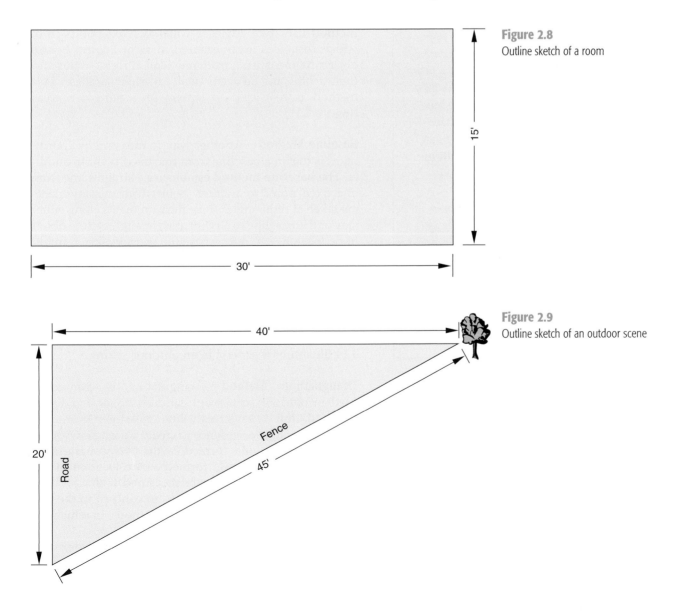

Figure 2.8
Outline sketch of a room

Figure 2.9
Outline sketch of an outdoor scene

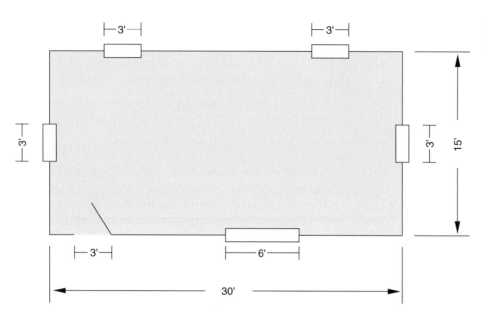

Figure 2.10
Outline sketch of room with door and windows

Technology Innovations

As with many other aspects of crime scene processing, technology is making the measuring process faster and more accurate. Siuru (p.52) describes a new tool called SceneVision-3D, which can reduce the time it takes to measure a crime scene from hours to minutes: "At the heart of the system is the DeltaSphere-3000 3D Scene Digitizer that features a time-of-flight, modulated beam, laser rangefinder to produce three-dimensional measurements at the rate of approximately 25,000 measurements-per-second."

Numerous software products allow these laser measurements to be coupled with digital photographs of the area to create a virtual scene that, like those generated by pictometry, can be rotated and zoomed in on. "Investigators and jurors can view the room just like when the police first arrived or see a crime scene as if they actually walked into a room through a particular door" (Siuru, p.54).

Step Three: Plot Objects and Evidence

 Plotting methods are used to locate objects and evidence on the sketch. They include the use of rectangular coordinates, a baseline, triangulation, and compass points.

To plot objects and evidence accurately, determine fixed points from which to measure.

Rectangular-Coordinate Method The rectangular-coordinate method is a common way to locate objects and evidence in a room. The **rectangular-coordinate method** uses two adjacent walls as fixed points from which distances are measured at right angles. Locate objects by measuring from one wall at right angles and then from the adjacent wall at right angles. This method is restricted to square or rectangular areas (Figure 2.11).

Baseline Method Another way to measure by coordinates is to run a baseline from one fixed point to another. The **baseline method** establishes a straight line from one fixed point to another, from which measurements are taken at right angles. Take measurements along either side of the baseline to a point at right angles to the object to be located. An indoor baseline method sketch might look like Figure 2.12 or Figure 2.13. Outdoors, it might look like Figure 2.14.

Sometimes the distance between two locations is important. For example, the distance from the normal route to a door might be very important if evidence is found in a room. The 34-foot measurement in Figure 2.14 illustrates this need in an outdoor setting.

Triangulation Method Triangulation is commonly used in outdoor scenes but can also be used indoors. **Triangulation** uses straight-line measures from two fixed objects to the evidence to create a triangle with the evidence in the angle formed by the two straight lines. The degree of the angle formed at the location of the object or evidence can then be measured with a protractor. The angle can be any degree, in contrast to the rectangular-coordinate and baseline methods, in which the angle is always a right angle (90 degrees).

Always select the best fixed points possible, with emphasis on their permanence. Fixed points may be closet doors, electrical outlets, door jambs, or corners of a

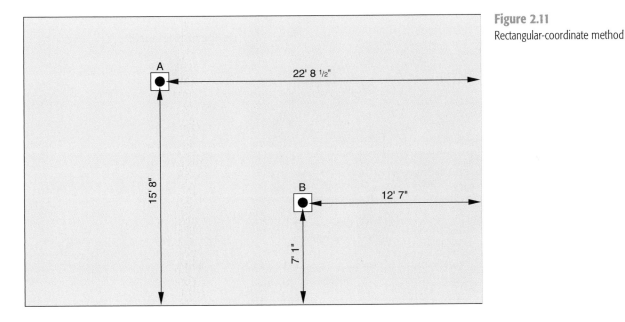

Figure 2.11
Rectangular-coordinate method

structure. It is sometimes impossible to get to the corners of a room for accurate measurements due to obstacles. Triangulation is illustrated in Figure 2.15.

Compass-Point Method The **compass-point method** uses a protractor to measure the angle formed by two lines. In Figure 2.16, for example, Object A is located 10'7'' from origin C and at an angle of 59 degrees from the vertical line through point C. Object B is 16'7'' from origin C at an angle of 47 degrees from the vertical.

Cross-Projection Method For some interior crime scenes, it is useful to show the relationship between evidence on the floors and the walls. This can be done by sketching the room as though the viewer is straight

above it, looking down. In effect, the room is flattened out much like a box cut down at the four corners and opened out flat. A **cross-projection sketch** presents the floor and walls as though they were one surface. Objects of evidence on both the floor and the walls can be measured to show their relationship on a single plane, as shown in Figure 2.17.

Step Four: Take Notes

After you have completed your sketch, take careful notes regarding all relevant factors associated with the scene that are not sketchable, such as lighting conditions, colors, and people present.

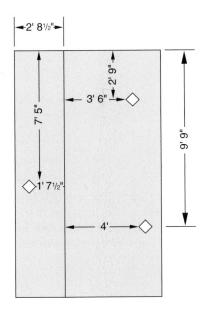

Figure 2.12
Center baseline method

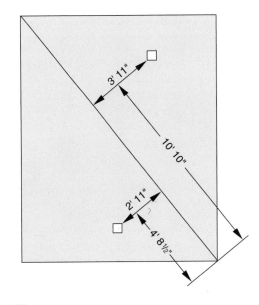

Figure 2.13
Diagonal baseline method

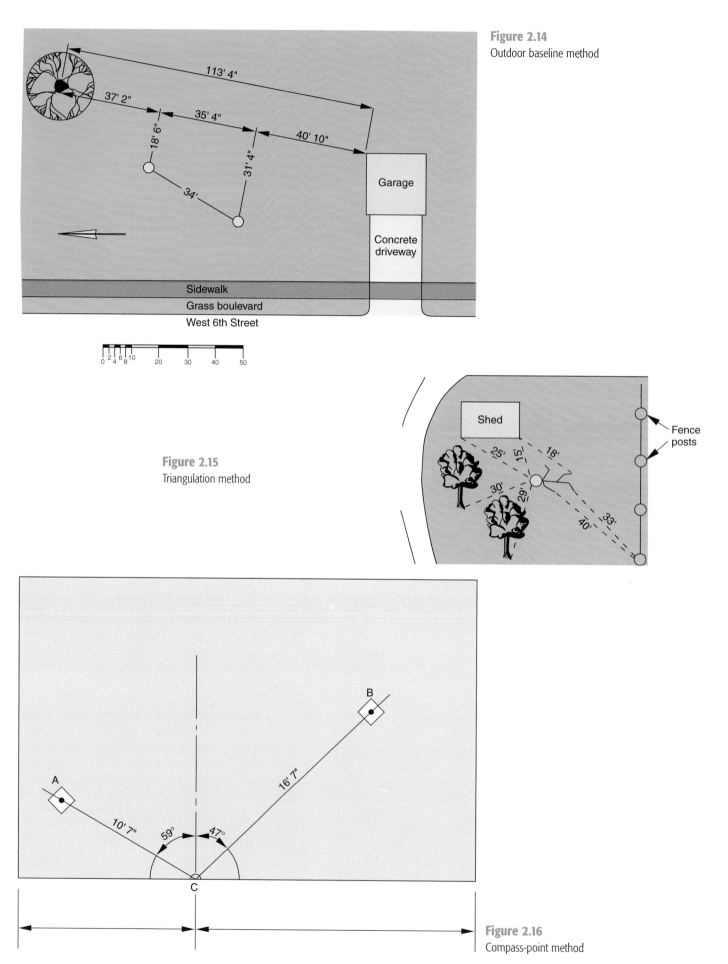

Figure 2.14
Outdoor baseline method

113' 4"

37' 2"

35' 4"

40' 10"

18' 6"

31' 4"

34'

Garage

Concrete
driveway

Sidewalk

Grass boulevard

West 6th Street

0 2 4 6 8 10   20   30   40   50

Figure 2.15
Triangulation method

Shed

Fence
posts

25'   15'   18'

30'   29'

40'   33'

Figure 2.16
Compass-point method

B

A

16' 7"

10' 7"

59°   47°

C

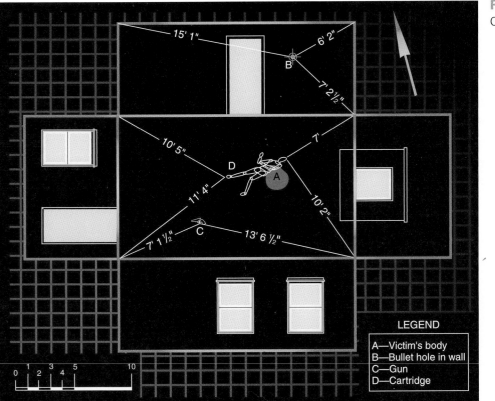

Figure 2.17
Cross-projection sketch

LEGEND
A—Victim's body
B—Bullet hole in wall
C—Gun
D—Cartridge

Step Five: Identify the Scene

Prepare a **legend** containing the case number, type of crime, name of the victim or complainant, location, date, time, investigator, anyone assisting, scale of the sketch, direction of north, and name of the person making the sketch (Figure 2.18).

Step Six: Reassess the Sketch

Before leaving the scene, make sure you have recorded everything you need on the sketch. Make sure nothing has been overlooked or incorrectly diagrammed. Once you have left, nothing should be added to the sketch. Compare the scene with the sketch. Are all measurements included? Have all relevant notations been made? Have you missed anything? Figure 2.19 is a completed rough sketch of a crime scene.

File the Sketch

Place the rough sketch in a secure file. It is a permanent record for all future investigations of the crime. It may be used later to question witnesses or suspects and is the foundation for the finished scale drawing. The better the rough sketch is, the better the finished drawing will be.

Keep the rough sketch in its original form even after the scale drawing is completed because it may be

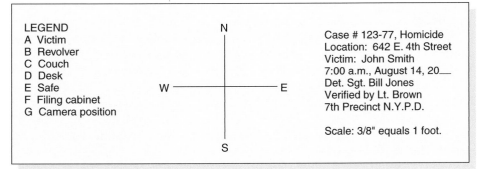

LEGEND
A Victim
B Revolver
C Couch
D Desk
E Safe
F Filing cabinet
G Camera position

N
W —— E
S

Case # 123-77, Homicide
Location: 642 E. 4th Street
Victim: John Smith
7:00 a.m., August 14, 20___
Det. Sgt. Bill Jones
Verified by Lt. Brown
7th Precinct N.Y.P.D.

Scale: 3/8" equals 1 foot.

Figure 2.18
Sample legend

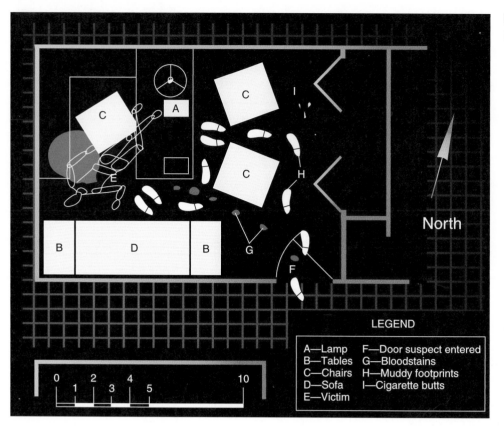

Figure 2.19
Completed crime scene sketch

LEGEND

A—Lamp   F—Door suspect entered
B—Tables   G—Bloodstains
C—Chairs   H—Muddy footprints
D—Sofa   I—Cigarette butts
E—Victim

North

needed for testifying. Otherwise the defense may claim that changes were made in preparing the scale drawings.

The Finished Scale Drawing

Given a well-drawn rough sketch, the finished scale drawing can be completed. The **finished scale drawing** is done in ink on a good grade of paper and is drawn to scale, using exact measurements. The materials used for making scale drawings are listed in Table 2.2.

The artistic refinements of the scale drawing do not permit it to be made at the crime scene. Instead it is made at the police station by the investigator or by a drafter. If anyone other than the investigator prepares the finished scale drawing, the investigator must review it carefully and sign it along with the drafter.

The finished drawing can be simple or complex, but it must represent the actual distances, objects, and evidence contained in the rough sketch. Color designations and plastic overlays to illustrate other phases of the investigation are often added. The drawing can be duplicated for other investigators and distributed to the prosecuting attorney. It is usually placed on white mounting board for display in court. A finished scale drawing is illustrated in Figure 2.20.

Computer-Assisted Drawing

As evidenced throughout this entire chapter, computer technology has enhanced many of the processes and procedures involved in crime scene documentation. In the fourth edition of this text (1990), computer-aided design (CAD) was highlighted as a Technological Advance, a cutting edge tool for criminal investigators. Back then, cumbersome, confusing, and complicated CAD software made it challenging for even the most computer-savvy investigators to fully implement this technology. However, drawing software for investigators has improved significantly over the past decade, and today a plethora of user-friendly CAD programs are available: Crime Zone, Quick Scene, DeltaSphere 3000, iWitness, Linear Systems, MapScenes, ScenePD, SmartDraw, SmartRoads, PanoScan, Vista FX, HawkEye, VS Investigator Suite . . . and the list is sure to grow.

Table 2.2 / **Materials for Making Scale Drawings**

Materials	Uses
Drawing kit	Contains tools for finer drawing
Triangular scale rule	Accurate scaling
Templates (assorted shapes, sizes)	Curves, oddly shaped objects
Indelible ink	For permanency of finished drawing
Drafting table	Ease, perfection in drawing
T-square	Accurate, straight lines, right angles
Drafting paper	Higher-quality absorption of inks, better display
Colors	Show areas of comparison

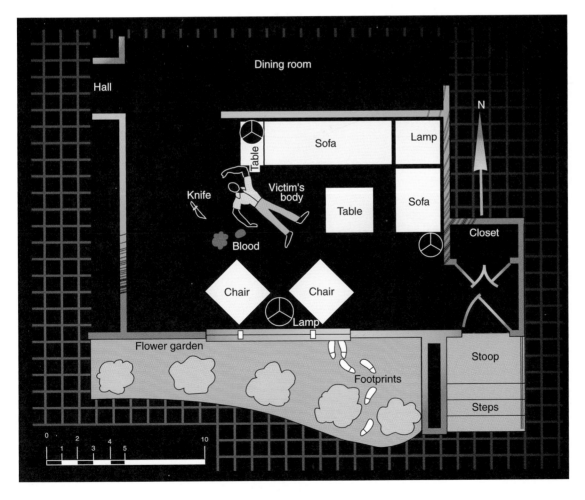

Figure 2.20
Finished scale drawing

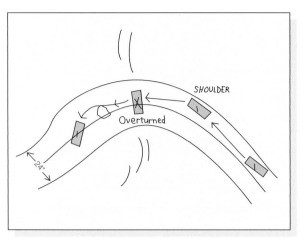

Typical Hand-Drawn Diagram

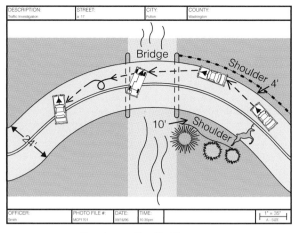

Courtroom-Quality Diagrams
Drawn with the Crime Zone

Figure 2.21

Comparison of a hand-drawn and computer-generated crime scene "sketch"

Reprinted by permission of the CAD Zone, Inc.

Benefits of CAD programs, alternately called computer-assisted drafting programs, include their accuracy, repeatability, and simplicity. In addition, the diagram files can be inserted into other documents, including final crime reports. Figure 2.21 compares a typical hand-drawn diagram with one drawn with a CAD software program.

In describing Crime Zone, one of the most popular forensic diagramming applications currently available, Davis (2004, p.86) remarks that the easy-to-use drawing

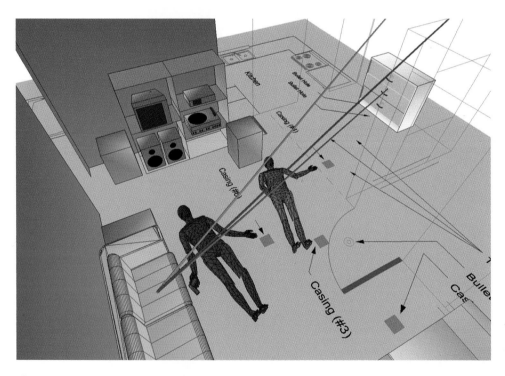

Figure 2.22

This is a 3D recreation of a homicide shooting, showing in detail the bullet trajectories and the final resting positions of the fatalities. The diagram contains both solid and "see-through" walls to display a more correct perspective. The diagram was created with The Crime Zone diagramming software, available from the CAD Zone, Inc. (Image created by CAD Zone, Inc.)

[Au/Pub: Sourceline to come with photo.]

Figure 2.23

A screen capture of the VistaFX CAD program in use. Officers can enter measurements and ballistic data to create a recreation of a crime scene and then manipulate the images to view the scene from various angles.

Created by VS Visual Statement, Inc., using Vista FX software.

program is great for novice users such as street cops but that it "also includes all the bells and whistles necessary for the work of more seasoned investigators." Crime Zone's 3-D graphics have also been used to diagram the trajectory of bullets, to document the scene of a carjacking, and to help a jury visualize the locations of witnesses, police officers, victims, and suspects at the scene of a drug-related shooting (Spraggs, p.38). Furthermore, investigators using Crime Zone are able to create diagrams with great precision and attention to detail, giving the drawing greater credibility in the courtroom, for, as Spraggs (p.39) contends: "Small details count, like articulated joints on the figures that allow the user to ensure the body is accurately portrayed in the diagram" (Figure 2.22).

The Vista FX drawing program, like many software packages, contains several versions, each with features geared toward different applications (Figure 2.23). For example, crash reconstruction programs would likely include a linear momentum analysis feature, calculators for deriving acceleration/deceleration rates, and pre-drawn symbols of intersections and other driving- and road-related icons. In contrast, a crime scene investigation edition of the same general CAD package might offer a bloodstain-pattern analysis feature, ballistics data, and predrawn symbols of bodies or various weapons. In touting the many features available with the MapScenes software package, including the more than 7,000 predrawn shapes and symbols, Dees ("MapScenes," p.45) states: "The program is capable of generating 3-D animations from actual data, in case you want to make one of those nifty computer movies like they have in *CSI*." A 3-D crime scene is illustrated in Figure 2.24.

Speed and portability are two other features investigators desire when selecting a CAD program. For those wanting to generate a rapid 2-D diagram, Kanable (p.114) notes: "SmartRoads is the fastest option, allowing a crash, crime or fire scene to be created in under 30 seconds." Portable data collection software is also becoming more popular: "A law enforcement professional's work, of course, is highly mobile, so any way to make technology portable is a huge benefit. Some drawing companies, in fact, offer drawing program software that fits right into a Pocket PC" (*Law and Order* Staff, p.42).

Portable data collection and drawing units save investigators' time by rapidly generating accurate, scaled diagrams at crime scenes, thus reducing time spent measuring and diagramming and allowing more time to actually investigate. According to Galvin (2004, p.44): "Perhaps the bottom line of today's portable data collection technology is the ability to allow the real evidence that has been collected, verified and protected to speak for itself in a finished diagram, inside a courtroom." Indeed, all the bells, whistles, and portable time-saving features of a CAD program are meaningless if the drawing does not hold up in court. As to the ability of one such program to meet this standard, the *Law and Order* staff (p.43) observe: "Naturally, the ultimate test of any diagram's value, regardless of its manufacturer's claims, is the courtroom. The Vista FX has had its day in court, [and its diagrams] have proven to be highly accurate and have never been rejected."

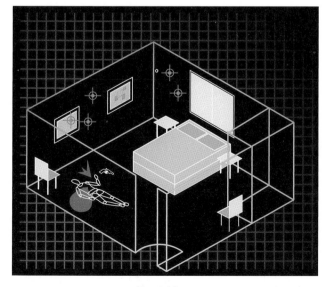

Homicide

Figure 2.24

"3-D" crime scene

Reprinted by permission of the CAD Zone, Inc.

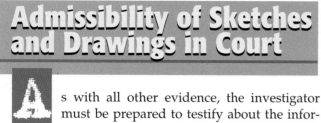

Admissibility of Sketches and Drawings in Court

s with all other evidence, the investigator must be prepared to testify about the information contained in the sketch, the conditions under which it was made, and the process used to construct it.

 An *admissible sketch* is drawn or personally witnessed by an investigator and accurately portrays a crime scene.

A scale drawing also is admissible if the investigating officer drew it or approved it after it was drawn and if it accurately represents the rough sketch. The rough sketch must remain available as evidence.

Well-prepared sketches and drawings help judges, juries, witnesses, and other people to visualize crime scenes. The responsibilities of an investigator in court are the focus of Chapter 21.

SUMMARY

Investigative notes and reports are critical parts of a criminal investigation. Notes are a permanent written record of the facts of a case to be used in further investigation, in writing reports and in prosecuting the case. Start to take notes as soon as possible after receiving an initial call to respond, and continue recording information as it is received throughout the investigation.

Record all relevant information concerning the crime, the crime scene, and the investigation, including information that helps answer the questions Who? What? Where? When? How? and Why? Write brief, abbreviated notes that others can understand. Make them complete, accurate, specific, factual, clear, well organized, and legible. After you have written your report, file your notes in a secure location readily accessible to you or destroy them according to department policy. Original notes are legally admissible in court and may be used to testify from or to refresh your memory. Take to court only those notes that pertain to the case.

Photography, one of the first investigative techniques to be used at a crime scene, helps to establish that a crime was committed and to trace the occurrence of the crime. Photographs and videotapes reproduce the crime scene in detail for presentation to the prosecution, defense, witnesses, judge, and jury in court. They are used in investigation, prosecution, and police training.

Photography has become increasingly important in criminal investigation because it can immediately preserve evidence, accurately represent the crime scene and evidence, create interest, and increase attention to testimony. However, photographs also have disadvantages: They are not selective, do not show actual distances, and may be distorted and damaged by mechanical errors in shooting or processing. At a minimum, have available and be skilled in operating a 35-mm SLR camera (film or digital), an instant-print camera, a press camera, a fingerprint camera, and video equipment.

Videos (videocassettes and DVDs) are now well established as an investigative tool. Videos can be viewed immediately, accurately represent the crime scene and evidence, are able to show distance more clearly than photos, have sound capability to more fully document what is being seen, and are cost-effective. The disadvantages of videos, however, center around the mistaken belief that no training in videotaping is necessary, which leads to poor video quality and a diminishing of the video's value in documenting the crime scene.

Take photographs and video of the entire crime scene before anything is disturbed, and avoid inaccuracies and distortions. First photograph the general area, then specific areas, and finally specific objects of evidence. Take exterior shots first. Categories of investigative photography include crime scene surveillance, aerial, night, laboratory, mug shot, and lineup.

After photographs are taken, they must be properly identified, filed, and kept secure to be admissible as evidence. In addition, rules of evidence dictate that photographs be material, relevant, competent, accurate, free of distortion, and noninflammatory.

In addition to photographs, crime scene sketches are often used. A crime scene sketch assists in (1) interviewing and interrogating people, (2) preparing the investigative report, and (3) presenting the case in court. Photographs, sketches, and written notes are often needed to provide a clear picture of the scene.

Sketch the scene of a serious crime or crash after photographing it and before moving anything. Include all relevant objects and evidence. Materials needed for making the rough sketch include paper, pencil, long steel measuring tape, carpenter-type ruler, straightedge, clipboard, eraser, compass, protractor, and thumbtacks. The steps involved in sketching include (1) observing and planning; (2) measuring distances and outlining the general area; (3) locating, measuring, and recording objects and evidence within the outline; (4) taking notes; (5) identifying the scene; and (6) reassessing the sketch.

Plotting methods useful in locating objects and evidence include rectangular-coordinate, baseline, triangulation, and compass-point. A cross-projection sketch shows the floor and walls in the same plane.

After completing the sketch, record in your notes the lighting conditions, colors, people present at the scene, and all other information that cannot be sketched. Then place a legend in the lower corner of the sketch, outside the room or area outline. Identify the scene completely—the location, type of crime, and case number. Include the scale and an arrow indicating north pointing to the top of the sketch. Include the name of the person making the sketch. Before leaving the scene, make sure nothing has been overlooked. Keep the sketch secure, because it is the basis for the finished scale drawing and may be needed as evidence in court.

The finished scale drawing is done in ink on a good grade of paper and is drawn to scale using exact measurements. Both the rough sketch and the scale drawing are admissible in court if they are made or personally witnessed by the investigator and accurately portray the crime scene. The original rough sketch must remain available as evidence.

CHECKLISTS

Note Taking

- Is my notebook readily available?
- Does it contain an adequate supply of blank paper?
- Is it logically organized?
- Have I recorded all relevant information legibly?

- Have I identified each page of notes with case number and page number?
- Have I included sketches and diagrams where appropriate?
- Have I filed the notes securely?

Police Photography

- Have I photographed the entire scene and specific objects before moving anything?
- Have I included markers where needed to indicate size of evidence?
- Have I recorded equipment and techniques used, lighting conditions, and so on, in notes?
- Have I checked for other sources of available photographs?

Questions

- Do the photographs taken at the crime scene depict the scene as you saw it?
- Do they show the exact appearance and condition of the scene as it appeared on your arrival?
- Have exterior pictures been taken to show entrances to the scene and the outside appearance of the crime scene?
- Have close-up shots been taken of the entry and exit points?
- Were aerial photos taken of the crime scene that show routes into and out of the scene area?
- Were interior pictures taken showing the entire layout of the facility in which the crime occurred?
- Do the photographs show the criminal act itself; for example, in a burglary, do the pictures show pry marks on the door, a broken window, or shattered glass on the ground or floor?
- Were detailed pictures taken of how the crime was committed? the tools with which it was committed? any weapon used?
- Do photographs show the victim? injuries? Were wounds, scratches, bruises, or other marks recorded in color as soon as possible after the commission of the crime? a day or two later as well?
- Were pictures taken of the deceased at the scene, including exact position, clothing worn, wounds?
- Were pictures taken at the autopsy?
- Do photographs show the property attacked?
- Were detailed pictures taken of all items of evidence before they were collected, showing exact condition and position at the scene?
- Was anything moved before the picture was taken? (If so, was it recorded in your notes?)
- Were photographs true and accurate representations of relevant material?

- Are laboratory photos available for scientific tests conducted?
- Were photographs taken of the suspect to show appearance and condition at the time of the crime, including close-ups of clothing worn?
- Were all pictures used for identifying suspects placed in special envelopes for later court testimony?
- If a lineup was conducted, were pictures taken of the lineup to show the people selected and their appearance in relation to each other?
- If a motor vehicle was involved, were detailed pictures taken of the vehicle's exterior and interior, color, license plate, and any damaged areas?
- What types of photographs are available: moving pictures, black-and-white, color, videotapes?
- Are there crime-in-progress pictures from on-the-scene cameras such as bank surveillance cameras, or were pictures taken by media photographers?
- Have photographs been suitably mounted for presentation in court?
- Have all relevant notes been recorded in the notebook?

Sketches

- Is your sketching kit readily available?
- Is the kit completely equipped?
- Have you formed a plan for making the sketch?
- Have you selected the simplest, largest scale?
- Have you sketched the outline of the room or area first?
- Have you used the appropriate plotting method to locate objects and evidence?
- Have you then added objects and evidence, including measurements?
- Have you recorded in your notes information that cannot be sketched?
- Have you prepared a legend for the sketch that includes identifying information, the scale, and the direction of north?
- Have you reassessed the sketch and compared it with the scene?
- Have you kept the sketch secure?
- Have you prepared or had someone else prepare a finished scale drawing if needed?

DISCUSSION QUESTIONS

1. When else do you take notes in your life? How do these notes differ from those taken during an investigation?

2. What is the *most* important use of notes?

3. Critics of the policy of instructing witnesses to read and then initial investigative notes contend that witnesses may not be able to read them, that it takes too much time to discuss the notes with witnesses, and that the practice inhibits officers from recording all observations. How would you counter such arguments, or do you agree with them?

4. Do you think notes should be retained or destroyed after a report has been written?

5. Have you ever found yourself in a position where you realized that you did not take sufficient notes? Explain.

6. When should notes be taken? not taken?

7. In what types of crimes are photographs likely to be important to the investigation?

8. How are investigative photographs developed and filed in your police department?

9. What basic sketching materials would you want in an investigative kit?

10. By which plotting method could you best locate your precise position in your surroundings at this moment?

MEDIA EXPLORATIONS

Internet

Go to the following websites and take notes comparing and contrasting the cameras of the three companies:

- www.kodak.com
- www.usa.canon.com
- www.fujifilm.com

Crime and Evidence in Action

Select one of the three criminal case scenarios and sign in for your shift. Your Mobile Data Terminal (MDT) will get you started and update you throughout the case. During the course of the case you'll become a patrol officer, detective, prosecutor, defense attorney, judge, corrections officer, or parole officer to conduct interactive investigative research. Each case unfolds as you respond to key decision points. Feedback for each possible answer choice is packed full of information, including term definitions, web links and important documentation. The sergeant is available at certain times to help mentor you, the Online Resources website offers a variety of informa-

tion, and be sure to take notes in your e-notebook during the suspect video statements and at key points throughout (these notes can be saved, printed, or e-mailed). The interactive Forensics Tool Kit will test your ability to collect, transport, and analyze evidence from the crime scene. At the end of the case you can track how well you responded to each decision point and join the Discussion Forum for a postmortem. **Go to the CD and use the skills you've learned to solve a case.**

REFERENCES

Baldwin, Hayden B. "Crime Scene Interpretation." http://www.feinc.net/cs-int.htm. Updated December 2004; accessed May 31, 2005.

Davis, Bob. "The CAD Zone Law Enforcement Drawing Software." *Police*, March 2004, pp. 86–87.

Davis, Bob. "Easypano Crime Scene Virtual Tour and Publisher." *Police*, April 2005, pp. 68–70.

Dees, Tim. "MapScenes." *Law and Order*, December 2004, p. 45.

Dees, Tim. "New Technology at IACP 2004." *Law and Order*, February 2005, pp. 308–314.

Federal Bureau of Investigation. *Handbook of Forensic Services*. 2003. http://www.fbi.gov/hq/lab/handbook/intro16.htm

Galvin, Bob. "Police Agencies Adopt Portable Technology to Capture Data." *Law and Order*, December 2004, pp. 40–44.

Galvin, Bob. "Photogrammetry Mapping for Crime Scenes." *Law and Order*, March 2005, pp. 36–41.

Kanable, Rebecca. "2D Today and Tomorrow." *Law Enforcement Technology*, July 2004, pp. 106–115.

Kramer, Robert. ""Painting with Light." *Law Enforcement Technology*, June 2005, pp. 38–46.

Law and Order Staff. "Visual Statement's Vista FX and HawkEye." *Law and Order*, March 2005, pp. 42–44.

Quail, Thomas. "GIS Technology Provides Aerial Views of Crime Scene." *Law Enforcement Technology*, February 2005, p. 100.

Senn, Pamela Mills. "Bringing a Crime Scene to Life." *Law Enforcement Technology*, February 2005, pp. 8–19.

Siuru, Bill. "Laser Technology Helps Preserve Crimes Scenes." *Law and Order*, May 2004, pp. 52–56.

Smith, Jeff. "Instant Photography for Crime Scene Investigators." *Law and Order*, November 2003, pp. 56–59.

Spraggs, David. "The Next Dimension." *Police*, November 2004, pp. 36–41.

Witzke, David. "The New Digital Mantra: Resolution, Resolution, Resolution." *Law Enforcement Technology*, June 2004, pp. 38–48.

Writing Effective Reports

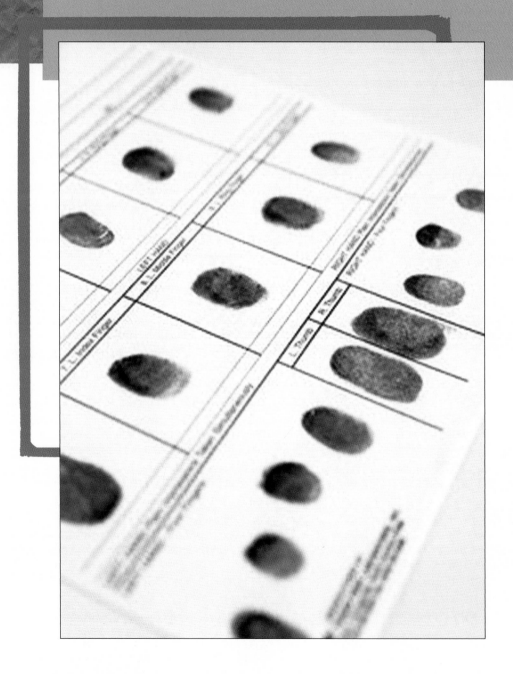

Can You Define?

Do You Know?

- Why reports are important to an investigation?
- How reports are used?
- Who reads your reports?
- What common problems occur in many police reports?
- Which is more important: content or form?
- What the characteristics of effective investigative reports are?
- How to differentiate among facts, inferences, and opinions?
- Why your reports should be well written?

Outline

One of the most important skills investigators must develop is report writing. The remainder of this volume discusses in detail how evidence is located and processed; how witnesses, victims, suspects, and others are questioned; and how specific cases are investigated. Report writing is included here because the report captures the essentials of an investigation.

This chapter begins with a discussion of the importance of investigative reports. This is followed by a look at how reports are used, the various audiences of investigative reports, how a well-written report is created from start to finish, and some common problems with many police reports. Next the differences between content and form are reviewed, followed by a brief description of organizing and structuring the narrative portion of the report and a description of the characteristics of effective reports. Then taping and dictating reports and computerized report writing (Figure 3.1) are discussed, as well as evaluating reports. The chapter concludes with a discussion of a new trend, online reporting by citizens, and a final look at why reports are so important.

The Importance of Reports

 rlando W. Wilson and Roy C. McLaren wrote in *Police Administration* nearly 30 years ago:

Almost everything that a police officer does must be reduced to writing. What is written is often the determining factor in whether a suspect is arrested in the first place and, if he is arrested, whether he is convicted and sentenced. The contents of written reports, in fact, often have great bearing in life-and-death situations. To say that officers need to be proficient in report writing is an understatement.

Nelson (p.226) notes: "Paperwork has never been fun. It is the drudgery of law enforcement. However, . . . what officers do not often recognize is that their reports are part of the arsenal with which they put criminals behind bars. A well-crafted report is as important as the investigation, for without the former the latter is meaningless." According to Scoville (p.37): "Faced with a well-documented police report, defendants are more apt to cop a plea than go to trial, in hope of a more lenient sentence. Indeed, it's not unfair to say that plea bargaining is often a trial by police report."

Calling the task of writing reports "unglamorous but critically important," Dees (p.18) observes: "Of all the ills that complicate the lives of police recruits and the people who train them, report writing has long been at the top of the list." The importance of well-written reports becomes obvious when you realize that your reports are *used,* not simply filed away. If investigative reports were not required for efficient law enforcement, you would not have to write them.

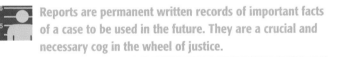

Reports are permanent written records of important facts of a case to be used in the future. They are a crucial and necessary cog in the wheel of justice.

Miller (p.6) points out: "The fact that police reports help make the criminal justice system function correctly should be reason enough to devote the time and energy necessary to write a good report." Miller (p.7) also

Figure 3.1
Laptop computers in squad cars make writing reports much more efficient. In addition, the reports can be sent via wireless connection directly to headquarters without delay.

© A. Ramey / Photoedit.

points out: "Good investigations and well-written reports have a positive and beneficial effect on the victims of crime and on the private citizens who will later appear as witnesses in court."

Well-written reports not only further the cause of justice, but also reflect positively on your education, your competence, and your professionalism. Indeed, as Sievert (p.35) contends: "Good or bad, the language, style and tone of our investigative reports [tell] the reader about the writer. . . . Juries and even District Attorneys equate sloppy police writing with sloppy thinking and careless investigative methods." Figure 3.2 shows the typical path of an investigative report. The number of times the report loops between the supervisor and the officer, or between the prosecutor and the officer, depends on how carefully (or carelessly) the officer constructs the report to begin with.

Most law enforcement officers submit their reports for prosecution with concern over the outcome but without much thought about the wheels they've started in motion. This is understandable, for they've done their jobs, and many more cases wait to be investigated. But what happens when they haven't really done their jobs? when their reports are distorted or incomplete (as many are) because of poor writing? The results not only cost the taxpayers in wasted personnel-hours, but they also breed disaster in the courtroom, if the case even makes it that far. For example, a study conducted for the City of San Francisco found that poor police report writing was jeopardizing effective criminal prosecution, with less than 4 percent of all felony arrest cases each year making it to prosecution (Sievert, p.35).

The little things in a report can have major consequences for the disposition of a case. Consider this all-too-common example: In one criminal case the reporting officer, using the passive voice, wrote, "The weapon was found in the bushes where the suspect had thrown it." He did not clarify this statement elsewhere in his report. Expectedly, the prosecuting attorney subpoenaed the reporting officer to testify at the preliminary hearing. Unfortunately, the reporting officer's testimony revealed that his partner, not he, had observed the suspect's action and had retrieved the weapon. The partner was unavailable to testify on short notice. Without her testimony, the necessary elements of the crime could not be established and the case was dismissed, having to be refiled. The personnel-hours expended at the time of the dismissal, by witnesses, secretaries, clerks, attorneys, and the judge, were virtually wasted because the whole process had to be repeated. The reporting officer could have avoided the problem at the onset through use of the active voice, which would have provided clarification. Sadly, this basic writing error is not an isolated example; it, and others like it, slip through the system daily, causing delays in the judicial process and depleting dwindling budgets.

To better understand how to write effective reports, consider first how they may be used.

Uses of Reports

 eports are permanent records of all important facts in a case. They are a stockpile of information to be drawn upon by all individuals on a law enforcement team. They are an aid to individual law enforcement officers and investigators, supervisors, administrators, the courts, other governmental agencies, reporters, and private individuals. Further, the efficiency of a department is directly related to the quality of its reports and reporting procedures.

Consider the case of an officer called to the scene of a hit-and-run. The initial accident report would be used to continue the investigation of the offense. If the offender were apprehended, the report would be used by the prosecuting attorneys in preparing the case, by the responding police officer when testifying in court, by the judge in determining the facts of the case, and by the jury if a trial resulted. The report might also be used by the department in determining where dangerous intersections exist and in making future plans. Additionally, an officer's supervisor could use the report to evaluate the performance of the investigating officer. If the officer failed to conduct a thorough investigation, this lack of thoroughness would show in the report.

Reports are used to:

- Examine the past.
- Keep other police officers informed.
- Continue investigations.
- Prepare court cases.
- Provide the courts with relevant facts.
- Coordinate law enforcement activities.
- Plan for future law enforcement services.
- Evaluate individual officer and department performance.
- Refresh a witness's memory as to what he or she said occurred.
- Refresh the investigating officer's memory during the trial.
- Compile statistics on crime in a given jurisdiction.
- Provide information to insurance investigators.

Reports are critical in examining police performance and investigating potentially illegal police practices. For example, Levenson ("State on Hunt") notes that 247 police departments throughout Massachusetts have been urged to voluntarily augment their traffic stop reports in an effort to shed light on allegations of racial profiling. Although many agencies are embracing the initiative as a way to seize control of their traffic data and build confidence in the fairness of their policing, other departments are opting out of the program,

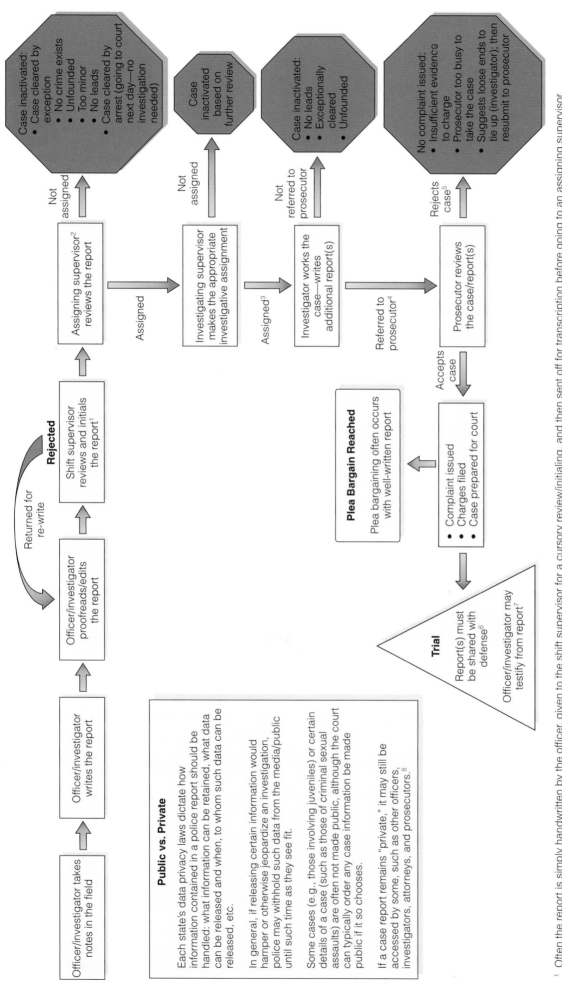

Public vs. Private

Each state's data privacy laws dictate how information contained in a police report should be handled: what information can be retained, what data can be released and when, to whom such data can be released, etc.

In general, if releasing certain information would hamper or otherwise jeopardize an investigation, police may withhold such data from the media/public until such time as they see fit.

Some cases (e.g., those involving juveniles) or certain details of a case (such as those of criminal sexual assaults) are often not made public, although the court can typically order any case information be made public if it so chooses.

If a case report remains "private," it may still be accessed by some, such as other officers, investigators, attorneys, and prosecutors.[8]

---

1 Often the report is simply handwritten by the officer, given to the shift supervisor for a cursory review/initialing, and then sent off for transcription before going to an assigning supervisor.
2 Assigning supervisor is typically of higher rank (lieutenant, captain, etc.).
3 In smaller departments, the case may go to a generalized investigator. In larger departments, several investigative units may exist (homicide, arson, motor vehicle theft, etc.).
4 Case can proceed to prosecutor with or without an arrest having been made.
5 A rejection does not necessarily mean case is not prosecutable at a later date. It means only that a complaint is not issued at that time.
6 Who has access to the report(s) at trial varies by state. For example, in Minnesota, the judge and jury do not automatically receive the report(s).
7 The report itself is not evidence, but any testimony the officer/investigator provides becomes part of the trial record (testimonial evidence).
8 Check with your state's data privacy law. Laws vary from state to state regarding what can be retained, what must be released, and when information must be released. Consideration must also be given to whether or not release of information would hamper any ongoing investigations.

Figure 3.2

Typical path of an investigative report. *Note: Because this process varies from department to department, this flowchart illustrates a generalized oversimplification of one way an investigative report might travel from origination to final disposition.*

claiming that the more extensive reports add to their already excessive paperwork load. Some critics of the program believe officers might be dissuaded from making legitimate traffic stops because of the undue amount of paperwork these will generate.

The various uses of reports make obvious the fact that they will be read by many different people for many different reasons. These people make up your audience.

The Audience

hat you write may be read by other officers, your supervisor, lawyers, judges, jurors, social workers, city officials, insurance adjusters and investigators, citizens, and reporters—people from different backgrounds and fields who have varying degrees of familiarity with legal terms and police jargon. Certainly the vast majority of your audience will not have been present at the crime scene. Therefore, you must communicate clearly to these numerous readers *what* happened, *when,* and *how.*

Reports are read by:
- Other officers.
- Supervisors.
- Attorneys and judges.
- Jurors.
- City officials.
- Insurance adjusters and investigators.
- Citizens.
- Reporters.

You should neither talk down to your audience nor try to make your report appear "more professional" by using bureaucratic, complicated language. Keep your reports straightforward and reader friendly, focusing on the need to *express* the facts of the case rather than trying to *impress* the audience with your expansive vocabulary. Writing to impress rather than express is a common problem with many investigative reports.

Common Problems with Many Police Reports

riting effective investigation reports is a skill that must be learned and practiced just as any other skill necessary in police work, such as firearms use, self-defense techniques, and interview methods. Unfortunately, some departments have yet to develop a full appreciation of the benefits of well-written reports. In these agencies, reports are viewed as tedious time wasters that keep investigators from more significant tasks. Field training officers encourage new recruits to take report shortcuts, while administrators look the other way, happy to avoid the overtime that can occur with thorough, accurate, complex reports. Amid such an environment, effective report writing skills are neither taught nor recognized as important, and problems in the department's police reports abound.

Among the common problems in police reports are:
- Confusing or unclear sentences.
- Conclusions, assumptions, and opinions.
- Extreme wordiness and overuse of police jargon and abbreviations.
- Missing or incomplete information.
- Misspelled words and grammatical/mechanical errors.
- Referring to "above" information.

Having briefly looked at the "don'ts" of report writing, the discussion now turns to the "do's" and how to craft a well-written report.

The Well-Written Report: From Start to Finish

eport writing is a skill that takes time and practice to develop. It is *not* a talent—you are not expected to write entertaining literary masterpieces, full of insight and originality. Instead, to write an effective, successful report, you must organize your notes and adhere to some basic standards of written English regarding content and form.

Organizing Information

A cornerstone of good report writing is organization. Good reports do not just happen. The writer plans in advance in what order the information should be written. Too many officers simply sit down and start writing without giving any thought to how the report should flow, which results in more time spent rewriting and revising later. To use your time most efficiently, first make an informal outline. Next, list what you want to include under each heading in the outline. Review your notes and number each statement to match a heading in your outline. For example, if Section III.C of the outline is headed "Description of Suspect #2," write *III.C* in the margin wherever Suspect #2 is described in your notes. List the facts of the investigation in **chronological order** beginning with the response to the call and concluding with the end of the investigation. If the report is long (more than four pages), use headings to guide the reader—for example, "Initial Response," "Crime-Scene Conditions," "Photographs Taken," "Evidence," "Witnesses," "Suspects," and so on. After you complete the outline and determine where each note fits, you are ready to begin writing.

Structuring the Narrative

Usually the **narrative,** the "story" of the case in chronological order, is structured as follows:

1. The opening paragraph of a police report states the time, date, type of incident, and how you became involved.
2. The next paragraph contains what you were told by the victim or witness. For each person talked to, use a separate paragraph.
3. Next record what you did based on the information you received.
4. The final paragraph states the disposition of the case.

Steps 2 and 3 may be repeated several times in a report on a case where you talk to several witnesses/victims.

A Brief Look at Law Enforcement Report Forms While this chapter focuses on writing narrative reports, many departments use box-style law enforcement report forms for certain offenses and incidents. Law enforcement report forms vary greatly in format, and the examples shown in Figure 3.3 are only a few of the types of forms in use.

Hess and Wrobleski (p.iv) state: "Report forms such as those shown [in Figure 3.3] contain boxes or separate category sections, e.g., property loss section, for placement of descriptive information, addresses and phone numbers of the persons involved. It is unnecessary to repeat this information in the narrative *unless it is needed for clarity* because it tends to interrupt the flow of words and clutter the narrative." In contrast, narrative reports that do *not* use the box-style format include descriptive information, addresses, and phone numbers within the body of the narrative, since no separate section exists for those data.

Read the following excerpt from a narrative report, noting the underlined descriptive information.

> I talked to the victim, Betty Jones, <u>355 Rose St., Albany, New York, phone 555-9002.</u> Jones told me that her diamond ring was taken during the burglary. The ring was a <u>2-carat diamond stone, platinum setting, with the initials B.A.J. inside the band, valued at $11,500.00.</u>

If these data were, instead, to be formatted into a box-style report, the underlined descriptive information, address, and phone number would be deleted from the narrative *unless that information was needed for clarity*, as shown in the following excerpt:

> The victim, Betty Jones, told me that her diamond ring was taken during the burglary.

Brown and Cox (p.84) note that formerly many agencies used a three-part report: the blanks at the beginning of the report, a synopsis or summary, and the narrative. They contend that many agencies have moved away from the use of synopses recently. However, if your department does use a synopsis format, include the *who, what, when,* and *where,* but not the *why:* "Concentrate on making the synopsis as brief and clear as possible."

Characteristics of Effective Reports: Content and Form

In addition to a well-structured narrative, an effective report exhibits several other characteristics, which generally fall into one of two areas: **content,** or *what* is said, and **form,** or *how* it is written.

 The effective report writer attends to both content and form, as they are equally important in a well-written report.

The *content* of an effective report is factual, accurate, objective, and complete. The *form* of a well-written report is concise, clear, grammatically and mechanically correct, and written in standard English. An effective report is also organized into paragraphs and written in the past tense, using the first person and active voice. Finally, a well-written report is audience focused, legible, and submitted on time. Table 3.1 illustrates the differences between content and form as they relate to investigative reports.

An effective report is factual, accurate, objective, complete, concise, clear, grammatically and mechanically correct, written in standard English, organized into paragraphs, written in the past tense, uses the first person and active voice, and is audience focused and legible, leaving the reader with a positive impression of the writer's competence. It is also submitted on time.

Factual The basic purpose of any investigation report is to record the facts. A **fact** is a statement that can be proven. (It may be proven false, but it is still classified as a factual statement.) The truthfulness or accuracy of facts will be discussed shortly. First consider how to clearly distinguish among three basic types of statements.

Fact: A statement that can be proven.
Example: The man has a bulge in his black leather jacket pocket.
Inference: A conclusion based on reasoning.
Example: The man is probably carrying a gun.
Opinion: A personal belief.
Example: Black leather jackets are cool.

Table 3.1 / **Investigative Reports: Content and Form Compared**

Content—*what* is said	Form—*how* it is said
The elements of the crime	Word choice
Descriptions of suspects, victims, etc.	Sentence and paragraph length
Evidence collected	Spelling
Actions of victim, witnesses, suspects	Punctuation
Observations: weather, road conditions, smells, sounds, oddities, etc.	Grammar
	Mechanics

A well-written report is factual. It does *not* contain opinions. You can discuss and debate facts and inferences logically and reasonably and come to some agreement on them. An **opinion**, however, reflects personal beliefs, on which there is seldom agreement. For example, how do you resolve the differences between two people arguing over whether pie tastes better than cake? You can't. It's simply a matter of personal preference.

Inferences (conclusions) can prove valuable in a report, provided they are based on sufficient evidence. Sometimes it is hard to distinguish between facts and inferences. One way to tell them apart is to ask the question "Can the statement be simply proven true or false, or do I need other facts to make it reasonable?" For example, if you wanted to verify the statement "The driver of the truck was drunk," you would need to supply several facts to support your inference. One such fact might be that he had a blood alcohol content over .10. Other facts might include your observations, such as his slurred speech, his red and watery eyes, five empty beer cans behind the driver's seat, and the strong odor of an alcoholic beverage on the driver's breath.

An **inference** is not really true or false; it is sound or unsound (believable or not believable). And the only way to make an inference sound (believable) is to provide facts to support it. One way to ensure that your inference is clearly an inference, instead of a fact, would be to use the word *apparently* or *appeared* (e.g., "The driver appeared to be under the influence of alcohol").

Inferences are also referred to as **conclusionary language**. Avoid conclusionary language by *showing*, not *telling*. For example, do not write, "The man *could not* walk a straight line." You do not know what another person can or cannot do. A more factual way to report this would be "The man *did* not walk a straight line." Even better would be, "The man stepped 18 inches to the right of the line twice and 12 inches to the left of the line three times." Consider this account by Rutledge (pp.110-111):

I once got into a drunk driving trial where, according to the arresting officer, the defendant had "repeatedly refused" to take a chemical test. The defendant was named Sanchez, and at trial he insisted, through a court interpreter, that he neither spoke nor understood any

English. His defense that he couldn't possibly refuse an English-language request when he couldn't even understand it sold well with the jury, especially after the officer had to admit that he didn't recall exactly how or in what specific words the defendant had "refused" a test. The cop couldn't live with his conclusionary report. Neither could I. The defendant lived with it very comfortably, and he owed his acquittal directly to the same officer who had arrested him. Ironic?

We would have been much better off if the cop had never used the conclusionary word "refused," but had instead married the defendant to his own words! The report could have helped the prosecution, instead of the defense, if it had been written like this:

After I explained the need to take a chemical test, Sanchez said, in Spanish-accented English, "Screw you, cop. . . . I ain't taking no test, man. Why don't you take it yourself?" I told him he had to take a test or his license would be suspended. He said, "I don't need no license to drive, man. I know lots of people drive without a license. You ain't scared me, man, and I ain't taking no stupid test. I'll beat this thing."

See the difference? Not a single conclusion or interpretation. The reader gets to "hear" the same things the writer heard. The officer could have lived with something like that—the defendant couldn't.

The following conclusionary statements can also jeopardize the effectiveness and value of investigative reports:

- "They denied any involvement in the crime."
- "She confessed to seven more arsons."
- "He admitted breaking into the warehouse."
- "He consented to a search of the trunk."
- "She waived her rights per Miranda."

Table 3.2 presents alternatives to conclusionary words and phrases that will make reports more factual and, thus, more effective and valuable.

Conclusionary language may also lead to inaccuracies in your report.

Accurate   To be useful, facts must be accurate. An effective report accurately records the correct time and date, correct names of all persons involved, correct phone numbers and addresses, and exact descriptions of the crime scene, property, vehicles, and suspects involved.

Plymouth Police Department

3400 Plymouth Blvd. • Plymouth, MN 55447

(763) 509-5160

fax: (763) 509-5167

Type	MOC

No.

Reported	Date
	call	asn	arr	clr

Location

Occurred	date	time	SAA

Badge no.	report	assist

Person 1 ☐ Complainant ☐ Victim ☐ Witness ☐ Mentioned

Name (last, first, middle)	DOB	☐ M ☐ F Sex
Address	home phone	work phone
City, state, zip	school	misc/insurance
Driver's license	race ☐ White ☐ African Am ☐ Am Indian ☐ Hispanic ☐ Asian ☐ Other	
misc/parents/work		

Person 2 ☐ Complainant ☐ Victim ☐ Witness ☐ Mentioned

Name (last, first, middle)	DOB	☐ M ☐ F Sex
address	home phone	work phone
city, state, zip	school	misc/insurance
driver's license	race ☐ White ☐ African Am ☐ Am Indian ☐ Hispanic ☐ Asian ☐ Other	
misc/parents/work		

☐ **Additional names/vehicle supplement attached**

Patrol Investigation ☐ video tape ☐ audio tape (statement or evidence)

☐ solvability factors ☐ photos taken ☐ forced entry ☐ domestic/vic info **victim will prosecute** **SFD**

☐ written statement ☐ prints lifted ☐ attached garage ☐ none ☐ yes ☐ no ☐

Narrative

_____

_____

_____

_____

_____

_____

_____

☐ Continued

Disposition ☐ pending ☐ clear arrest

☐ assist and advised ☐ clear exceptionally

☐ unfounded

Patrol supervisor	Inv Supervisor	Inv assigned	Entry

Figure 3.3

Types of law enforcement report forms.

Source: Adapted from Kären M. Hess and Henry M. Wrobleski. *For the Record: Report Writing in Law Enforcement*, 5th Edition. Bloomington, MN: Innovative Systems–Publishers, Inc., 2002, p.iv. Reprinted by permission.

SUSPECT 1: (last, first, middle)			DOB		☐ M ☐ F Sex
address		home phone		work phone	
city, state, zip		ht	wt	hair	eye	school/grade

SUSPECT 1: (last, first, middle) — DOB — ☐ M ☐ F Sex

address — home phone — work phone

city, state, zip

| ht | wt | hair | eye | school/grade |

driver's license — race: ☐ White ☐ African Am ☐ Am Indian ☐ Hispanic ☐ Asian ☐ Other

parents & work phone — misc

misc/work

Patrol Action

☐ suspect	☐ juvenile arrest	☐ no contact	☐ booked Plymouth	**Miranda**
☐ adult arrest	☐ juvenile blue	☐ warn & release	☐ booked Hennepin	☐ Yes ☐ No
☐ missing person	☐ school alcohol report	☐ bail release	☐ booked JC	**Attorney requested**
☐ runaway	☐ parents notified	☐ citation	☐ PFC	☐ Yes ☐ No

SUSPECT 2 (last, first, middle) — DOB — ☐ M ☐ F Sex

Address — home phone — work phone

city, state, zip

| ht | wt | hair | eye | school/grade |

driver's license — race: ☐ White ☐ African Am ☐ Am Indian ☐ Hispanic ☐ Asian ☐ Other

parents & work phone — misc

misc/work

Patrol Action

☐ suspect	☐ juvenile arrest	☐ no contact	☐ booked Plymouth	**Miranda**
☐ adult arrest	☐ juvenile blue	☐ warn & release	☐ booked Hennepin	☐ Yes ☐ No
☐ missing person	☐ school alcohol report	☐ bail release	☐ booked JC	**Attorney requested**
☐ runaway	☐ parents notified	☐ citation	☐ PFC	☐ Yes ☐ No

Property   S=stolen   D=damaged   L=lost   THIS SECTION NOT FOR IMPOUNDED PROPERTY   ☐ Inventory report attached

Victim	Code	Qty	Item	Brand/description/model	Serial #	Value	NCIC

Vehicle #1   ☐ victim's   ☐ stolen   ☐ recovered   ☐ impounded   ☐ bicycle   ☐ mentioned   ☐ suspect

Plate #	State	Plate year	Owner	
Make	Model	Year	Color	Style

Vehicle #2   ☐ victim's   ☐ stolen   ☐ recovered   ☐ impounded   ☐ bicycle   ☐ mentioned   ☐ suspect

Plate #	State	Plate year	Owner	
Make	Model	Year	Color	Style

By my signature I release all duly authorized peace officers from any legal claim for any damages, loss or expense incurred in the recovery, holding, storage, or conveyance OR verify I am the guardian of a missing juvenile listed in this report.   Signature_____

Figure 3.3
continued

Have people spell their names. Repeat spellings and numbers for verification. Recheck measurements. Be sure of the accuracy of your facts. An inaccurately recorded license number may result in losing a witness or suspect. Inaccurate measurement or recording of the distance and location of skid marks, bullet holes, or bodies may lead to wrong conclusions.

To be accurate, you must be specific. For example, it is better to say, "The car was traveling in excess of 90 mph" than to say, "The car was traveling fast." It is more accurate to describe a suspect as "approximately six-foot-six" than to describe him as "tall."

You must have the facts in the case correct. If your report says four men were involved in a robbery and in reality, three men and a woman were involved, your report would be inaccurate. If you are unsure of the gender of the individuals involved in an incident, identify them as "people," "suspects," "witnesses," or whatever the case may be. If your facts come from the statement of a witness rather than from your own observation, say so in your report.

Phrases such as "He saw what happened" or "He heard what happened" are conclusionary and may also lead to inaccuracies in your report. People can be looking directly at something and not see it, either because they are simply not paying attention or because they have terrible vision. The same is true of hearing. Again, you do not know what another person sees or hears. Your report should say, "He *said* he saw what happened" or "He looked directly at the man committing the crime."

Another common conclusionary statement found in police reports is, "The check was signed by John Doe." Unless you saw John Doe sign the check, the correct (accurate) statement would be, "The check was signed John Doe." The little two-letter word *by* can create tremendous problems for you on the witness stand.

Vague, imprecise words have no place in police reports. The following words and phrases should *not* be used because they are not specific: *a few, several, many, frequently, often.* Finally, instead of writing *contacted,* be specific by using *telephoned, visited, e-mailed,* or whatever particular mode of communication was involved.

Objective   You have seen that reports must be factual. It is possible, however, to include only factual statements in a report and still not be objective. Being **objective** means being nonopinionated, fair, and impartial. Lack of objectivity can result from either of two things: poor word choice or omission of facts.

Word choice is an often overlooked—yet very important—aspect of report writing. Consider, for example, the difference in effect achieved by these three sentences:

> The man cried.
> The man wept.
> The man blubbered.

Although you want to be specific, you must also be aware of the effect of the words you use. Words that have little emotional effect, e.g., *cried*, are called **denotative** words. The denotative meaning of a word is its *objective* meaning. In contrast, words that do have an emotional effect are called **connotative** words, e.g., *wept, blubbered.* The connotative meaning of a word comprises its positive or negative overtones. In the three sentences above, only the first sentence is truly objective. The second sentence makes the reader feel sympathetic toward the man. The third makes the reader unsympathetic.

Likewise, derogatory, biased terms referring to a person's race, ethnicity, religion, or sexual preference have no place in police reports. A defense attorney will certainly capitalize on words with emotional overtones and attempt to show bias. Even the use of *claimed* rather than *stated* can be used to advantage by a defense attorney, who might suggest that the officer's use of *claimed* implies that the officer did not believe the statement.

Also, use the correct word. Do not confuse words that are similar, or you can be made to appear ridiculous. For example, this sentence in an officer's report would probably cast suspicion on the officer's intelligence: "During our training we spent four hours learning to resemble a firearm and the remainder of the time learning defective driving."

Keep to the facts. Include all facts, even those that may appear to be damaging to your case. Objectivity is

Table 3.2 / **Avoiding Conclusionary Language**

You Can't Live with These	So Use	You Can't Live with These	So Use
Indicated, refused, admitted, confessed, denied, consented, identified, waived, profanity, threatening, obscene, evasive, deceptive	A verbatim or approximate quotation of what was said	Angry, upset, nervous, excited, happy, unhappy, intentional, accidental, heard, saw, knew, thought	The source of your conclusions (when you're attributing them to someone else)
Assaulted, attacked, accosted, confrontation, escalated, struggle ensued, resisted, battered, intimidated, bullied, forced	A factual account of who did what	Matching the description, suspicious, furtive, strange, abnormal, typical, uncooperative, belligerent, combative, obnoxious, abusive, exigent	The reasons for your belief that these apply

Source: Devallis Rutledge. *The New Police Report Manual*, 2nd ed. Belmont, CA: Wadsworth Publishing Company, 2000, pp.135-136. Reprinted by permission.

attained by including both sides of the account. **Slanting,** that is, including only one side of a story or only facts that tend to prove or support the officer's theory, can also make a report nonobjective. A good report includes both sides of an incident when possible. Even when facts tend to go against your theory about what happened, you are obligated to include them. Omitting important facts is *not* objective.

Complete Information kept in the reporting officer's head is of no value to anyone else involved in the case. An effective report contains answers to at least six basic questions: Who? What? When? Where? How? and Why? The *who, what, when,* and *where* questions should be answered by factual statements. The *how* and *why* statements may require inferences. When this is the case, clearly label the statements as inferences. This is especially true when answering the question of cause. To avoid slanting the report, record all possible causes no matter how implausible they may seem at the time.

If a form is used for your reports, all applicable blanks at the top of the form should be filled in. Certain agencies require a slash mark, the abbreviation N.A. (not applicable), or the abbreviation UNK (unknown) to be placed in any box that does not contain information.

Each specific type of crime requires different information. Sections 3, 4, and 5 discuss specific offenses and contain checklists outlining information that should be included in your report.

Concise Being **concise** means making every word count without leaving out important facts. Avoid wordiness; length alone does not ensure quality. Some reports can be written in half a page; others require 12 or even 20 pages. No specific length can be prescribed, but strive to include all relevant information in as few words as possible.

You can reduce wordiness in two basic ways: (1) Leave out unnecessary information and (2) use as few words as possible to record the necessary facts. For example, do not write, "The car was blue in color"; write "The car was blue." A phrase such as "information which is of a confidential nature" should be recognized as a wordy way of saying "confidential information."

Do not make the mistake of equating conciseness with brevity. Being brief is not the same as being concise. For example, compare:

Brief: She drove a car.
Concise: She drove a maroon 1992 Chevrolet Caprice.
Wordy: She drove a car that was a 1992 Chevrolet Caprice and was maroon in color.

Avoiding wordiness does not mean eliminating details; it means eliminating empty words and phrases. Consider these examples of how to make wordy phrases more concise:

Wordy	Concise
made a note of the fact that	noted
square in shape	square
in the amount of	for
despite the fact that	although
for the purpose of determining	to determine

Table 3.3 lists more natural-sounding alternatives for wordy, artificial phrases.

Clear An investigation report should have only one interpretation. Two people should be able to read the report and come up with the same word-picture and understanding of the events. Make certain your sentences can be read only one way. For example, consider the following unclear sentences:

- When completely plastered, officers who volunteer will paint the locker room.
- Miami police kill a man with a machete.
- Three cars were reported stolen by the Los Angeles police yesterday.
- Police begin campaign to run down jaywalkers.
- Squad helps dog bite victim.

Rewrite such sentences so that only one interpretation is possible. For example, the first sentence in the previous list might read: "Officers who volunteer will paint the locker room after it is completely plastered." The third sentence might read: "According to the Los Angeles police, three cars were reported stolen yesterday."

Follow these guidelines to make your reports clearer:

- *Use specific, concrete facts and details.* Compare the following statements and determine which is clearer:
  1. The car sped away and turned the corner.
  2. The gold 1996 Cadillac Fleetwood pulled away from the curb, accelerated to approximately 65 mph, and then turned off First Street onto Brooklyn Boulevard.

  The second statement is clearer because it contains concrete facts and details.

- *Keep descriptive words and phrases as close as possible to the words they describe.* Compare the following statements and determine which is clearer.
  1. He replaced the gun into the holster which he had just fired.
  2. He replaced the gun, which he had just fired, into the holster.

  The second statement is clearer because the phrase "which he had just fired" is placed close to the word it modifies (*gun*).

Table 3.3 / **Artificial-Sounding vs. Natural-Sounding Words and Phrases**

Artificial	Natural	Artificial	Natural
initiated		altercation	
commenced		mutual combat	
inaugurated	began	physical confrontation	fight
originated		exchange of physical blows	
presently		in reference to	
currently		reference	
at the present	now	in regard to	about
at the present time		regarding	
at this time		on the subject of	
due to the fact that		visually perceived	
considering that		visually noticed	
as a result of the fact that	because, since	observed	saw
in view of the fact that		viewed	
in light of the fact that			
made an effort		related	
made an attempt	tried	stated	said
endeavored		verbalized	
attempted		articulated	

continued

Source: Devallis Rutledge. *The New Police Report Manual*, 2nd ed. Belmont, CA Wadsworth Publishing Company, 2000, pp.75-78. Reprinted by permission.

- *Use diagrams and sketches when a description is complex.* This is especially true in reports of crashes, homicides, and burglaries. The diagrams do not have to be artistic masterpieces. They should, however, be in approximate proportion and should help the reader follow the narrative portion of the report. As noted in Chapter 2, software for computer-assisted diagrams are now readily available.

- *Do not use uncommon abbreviations.* Some abbreviations (such as *Mr., Dr., Ave., St., Feb., Aug., NY, CA*) are so commonly used that they require no explanation. Other abbreviations, however, are commonly used only in law enforcement. Do not use these in your reports, since not all readers will understand them. Confusion can result if two people have different interpretations of an abbreviation. For example, what does S.O.B. mean to you? To most people it has a negative meaning. But for people in the health field, it means "short of breath." Meier and Adams (p.102) provide this example as something that can be used in your notes but should not appear, as such, in a report:

Unk/B/M/, nfd, driving unk/Chry/4DBlu, nfd

Instead, write out:

Unknown black male (no further description available) was seen driving a blue Chrysler 4-door (no further description available).

Use only abbreviations common to everyone.

- *Use short sentences, well organized into short paragraphs.* Short sentences are easier to read. Likewise, paragraphs should be relatively short, usually five to ten sentences. Each question to be answered in the report should have its own paragraph. The report should be organized logically. Most commonly it begins with *when* and *where* and then tells *who* and *what*. The *what* should be in chronological order—that is, going from beginning to end without skipping back and forth.

Grammatically and Mechanically Correct If you were to *hear* the words "Your chances of being promoted are good if you can write effective reports," you would probably feel differently than if you were to *read* the

Table 3.3 / *continued*

Artificial	Natural	Artificial	Natural
maintained surveillance over		informed	
kept under observation	watched	advised	told
visually monitored		indicated	
		communicated verbally	
at this point		6' in height	6' tall/high
at this time	then	2' in width	2' wide
at which time		3' in length	3' long
at which point in time		8" in depth	8" deep
as of this date		telephonically contacted	
as of this time	yet	reached via landline	phoned
as of the present time		contacted by telephone	
alighted from		verbal altercation	
exited	got out	verbal dispute	argument
dismounted		verbal confrontation	
requested		prior to	
inquired	asked	previous to	before
queried		in advance of	
in order to		for the reason that	
with the intention of	to	in order that	so
with the objective to			

same words written like this: "yur chances of bein pro-mottid are gud. if you kin rite afectiv riports." The **mechanics**—spelling, capitalization, and punctuation—involved in translating ideas and spoken words into written words are important. Yet, as Clark (p.56) observes: "Probably the most common writing error police officers make is misspelled words." Mistakes in spelling, punctuation, capitalization, and grammar give the impression that the writer is careless, uneducated, or stupid—maybe all three!

Use a dictionary and a grammar book if in doubt about how to write something. The dictionary can tell you not only how to spell a word but also whether it should be capitalized and how it should be abbreviated. To make spelling less difficult, consider using a *speller/divider*. These little reference books contain thousands of the most commonly used words, showing their spelling and how they are divided. The reader is not distracted by definitions, information on the history of

the word, synonyms, and so on. The most important advantage is that one speller/divider page has as many words on it as 15 to 20 dictionary pages.

Use caution when relying on grammar- and spell-checker programs to find mistakes in computerized documents. Sievert (p.37) observes:

> In what is probably the ultimate irony, one of the solutions to improved report writing is also one of the causes of imprecise writing. Studies indicate word processor Grammar Check functions will catch about 60% of the errors. This is a benefit to the average writer, yet reliance on Grammar Check reduces the skill set of the writer and leaves almost half the errors unflagged. Even worse, the Spell Checker provides an accurate spelling, but it does not check meaning—resulting, at times, in the grotesque misuse of a word.

For example, if an investigator wrote that a victim of an assault was unable to be interviewed because "she had lapsed into a *comma,*" or that a suspect had been restrained because "he was acting *erotically*," when what the writer meant to say was "coma" and "*erratically*," respectively, the reader might question the investigator's intelligence and/or attention to detail.

Written in Standard English People often disagree about what standard English is. And the standards between spoken and written English differ. For example, if you were to *say*, "I'm gonna go walkin' in the mornin'," it would probably sound all right. People often drop the "g" when they speak. In writing, however, this is not acceptable.

Just as there are rules for spelling, capitalization, and punctuation, there are rules for *what* words are used *when*. For example, it is standard to say "he doesn't" rather than "he don't"; "I don't have any" rather than "I ain't got none"; "he and I are partners" rather than "him and me are partners."

Your experience with English will often tell you what is standard and what is not—especially if you have lived in surroundings in which standard English is used. If you speak standard English, you will probably also write in standard English. But that is not always true.

Paragraphs As discussed earlier, in structuring the narrative and making your report clear, effective writers use paragraphs to guide the reader. Keep the paragraphs short (usually 100 words or less). Skip a line to indicate the beginning of a new paragraph. Discuss only one subject in each paragraph. Start a new paragraph when you change speakers, locations, time, or ideas—for example, when you go from observations to descriptions to statements.

Paragraphs are reader friendly, guiding the reader through your report. Most paragraphs should be 5 to 6 sentences, although they may be a single sentence or up to 10 or 15 sentences on occasion.

Past Tense Write in the **past tense** throughout the report. Past-tense writing uses verbs that show that events have already occurred. Your report contains what *was* true at the time you took your notes. Use of present tense can cause tremendous problems later. For example, suppose you wrote, "John Doe *lives* at 100 South Street and *works* for Ace Trucking Company." One year later you find yourself on the witness stand with a defense attorney asking you: "Now, Officer, your report says that John Doe lives at 100 South Street. Is that correct?" You may not know, and you would have to say so. The next question: "Now, Officer, your report says John Doe works for Ace Trucking Company. Is *that* correct?" Again, you may be uncertain and be forced into an "I don't know" response. Use of the past tense in your report avoids this problem.

First Person Use the first person to refer to yourself. **First person** in English uses the words *I, me, my, we, us,* and *our.* The sentence "*I* responded to the call" is written in the first person. This is in contrast to "*This officer* responded to the call," which uses the third person.

Whether you remember your English classes and discussions of first-, second-, and third-person singular and plural is irrelevant. Simply remember to refer to yourself as *I* rather than as *this officer.*

Active Voice A sentence may be either active or passive. This is an easy distinction to make if you think about what the words *active* and *passive* mean. (Forget about the term *voice;* it is a technical grammatical term you do not need to understand to write well.) In the **active voice** the subject of the sentence performs the actions—for example, "I wrote the report." This is in contrast to the *passive* voice, in which the subject does nothing—for example, "The report was written by me." The report did not do anything. The problem with the passive voice is that often the *by* is left off—for example, "The report was written." Later, no one knows who did the writing. Passive voice results in a "whodunit" that can have serious consequences in court.

Statements are usually clearer in the active voice. Although most sentences should be in the active voice, a *passive* sentence is acceptable in the following situations:

1. If the doer of the action is unknown, unimportant, or obvious.

   Example: The gun had been fired three times.

   We don't know who fired it. This is better than "Someone had fired the gun three times."

   Example: The woman has been arrested four times.

   Who arrested her each time is not important.

   Example: Felix Umburger was paroled in April.

   Who is obviously the parole board.

2. When you want to call special attention to the receiver of the action rather than the doer.

   Example: Officer Morris was promoted after the examination.

   Not only is it unimportant who promoted him, you want to call attention to Officer Morris.

3. When it would be unfair or embarrassing to be mentioned by name.

   Example: The program was postponed because the wrong film was sent.

   Better than: The program was postponed because Sergeant Fairchild sent the wrong film.

   Example: Insufficient evidence was gathered at the crime scene.

   Better than: Investigator Hanks gathered insufficient evidence at the crime scene.

Audience Focused Always consider who your audience is. Recall the diversity of possible readers of police reports. Given these varied backgrounds and individuals with limited familiarity with law enforcement terminology, the necessity for audience-focused reports becomes obvious. By keeping in mind this diverse audience, you will construct a report that is reader friendly.

One way to be reader friendly is to be certain that the narrative portion of your report can stand alone. That calls for eliminating such phrases as *the above*. A reader-friendly report does not begin, "On the above date at the above time, I responded to the above address to investigate a burglary in progress."

Using such phrases presents two problems. First, if readers take time to look "above" to find the information, their train of thought is broken. It is difficult to find where to resume reading, and time is wasted. Second, if readers do *not* take time to look "above," important information is not conveyed, and it is very likely that the reader, perhaps subconsciously, will be wondering what would have been found "above." If information is important enough to refer to in your report, include it in the narrative. Do not take the lazy approach and ask your reader to search for the information "above."

Another way to write a reader-friendly report is to steer clear of police lingo and other bureaucratic language and use plain English. Meier and Adams (p.99) point out that officers tend to speak and write in a dialect of English they call "Cop Speak," which the majority of the public often does not understand. In explaining why investigators and other law enforcement officers should avoid jargon and other "insider" terminology when communicating with those outside the field, Moore (p.266) notes: "This type of language makes it seem as if you don't share the same language as the public you serve. It goes against the basic principles of community policing and sets criminal justice agencies and their personnel apart from the very people they rely on for information, funding and authority."

Legible and On Time   It does little good to learn to write well if no one can read it or if the report is turned in after it was needed. Ideally, reports should be typed; and in today's computer-driven world, most reports are generated this way. Sometimes, however, this is not practical or possible. In fact, a poorly typed report is often as difficult to read as an illegible one. If you do not type your reports, and if you know that you have poor handwriting, you may want to print your reports by hand. Granted, this is slower than cursive, but a report that cannot be read is of little use to anyone. Whether your reports are typed, written, or printed, make certain that others can read them easily and that they are submitted on time.

Taping and Dictating Reports

ape-recording or dictating reports is common in some departments. Reports that need quick attention may be red-tagged, and records personnel type all red-tagged cases first.

In effect, tape-recording or dictating reports shifts the bulk of writing/transcribing time to the records

---

Technology Innovations

A new technology called the Intuitive Pen recognizes handwriting, taking what an officer has written and converting it into an electronic form, thereby reducing redundancies and increasing the efficiency and accuracy of the report generating process. Simon (p.96) explains:

> This pen can save officers time since data collected in the field will not need to be retyped. Every stroke created by this pen is saved. . . . To retrieve the information, the pen is inserted into the docking station, which is connected to a computer through a USB cable. This information is then transferred to the computer and the software converts it into typed text within the form.
>
> While many investigators carry PDAs [personal digital assistants] or tablet PCs [personal computers] to record information, such devices are not configured to allow a fast, easy switch between the various preloaded forms officers use to enter important data, as is often needed in a rapidly unfolding or emergency situation. The Intuitive Pen, however, is able to effectively and accurately capture information that is not collected sequentially.
>
> The pen can be interfaced with a report management system that automatically converts the data into an appropriate format for use in a department's reports. Furthermore, it can be used as part of an evidence tracking program, creating an evidence receipt copy in the field and then being docked at the station, with the data retrieved and used to print barcode labels for all evidence collected (p.99).

Another advance is computer-assisted report entry (CARE). This live-entry system centers around a CARE operator who leads officers through preformatted screens and questions, allowing them to complete reports in a matter of minutes. The CARE system has reduced report-writing times and improved the quality, accuracy, and timeliness of police reports. In addition, Uniform Crime Reporting information is automatically aggregated.

Although computerized report writing has greatly increased officers' efficiency, it cannot correct sloppy data entry. Officers are responsible for the accuracy and clarity of the data. The accuracy and clarity of a report are often deciding factors in whether a case is prosecuted. Preparing for and presenting cases in court are discussed in Chapter 21.

division. Even with taping or dictating, however, officers must still take final responsibility for what is contained in the report. Do not assume that what you think you spoke into a dictation machine is what will end up on paper. Following are some humorous illustrations of how some dictated sentences can be misinterpreted:

- He called for a toe truck.
- Smith was arrested for a mister meaner.
- Jones was a drug attic.
- The victim was over rot.
- Johnson died of a harder tack.

Computerized Report Writing

Computers have made significant contributions to efficiency in report writing. The hardware available for word processing has become smaller and faster (Figure 3.4). It is easier to use and much more portable. Software too has kept pace. In addition to sophisticated spell- and grammar-checker programs (to be used with the caveats noted above under "Grammatically and Mechanically Correct"), other programs have been developed to help in the actual preparation of police reports. Pen-based computers also make report writing easier. Pen computing uses a special "pen" to write on a computer screen.

How many times have you heard, "Great job. Now do it again"? Simon (p.94) notes that this phrase can deflate the morale of anyone who has gone to great lengths to ensure accuracy and completeness the first time a task is completed. Yet police officers encounter this "do it again" hurdle every time they fill out a report. The task of report writing is filled with redundancies—turning handwritten

notes into typed reports, sometimes filling out numerous forms along the way, all involving the same basic information garnered from the initial note-taking event. Each transfer of data not only takes time from an investigator but also introduces an opportunity for error—a transposed number or two, a misspelled name, a detail that gets overlooked and never makes it to the final report.

Evaluating Your Report

Once you have written your report, evaluate it. Do not simply add the final period, staple the pages together, and turn it in. Reread it. Make certain it says what you want it to and contains no content or composition errors. Ask yourself if the report is factual, accurate, objective, complete, concise, clear, grammatically and mechanically correct, written in standard English, organized into paragraphs, written in the past tense, uses the first person and active voice, and is audience focused and legible. Table 3.4 provides an evaluation checklist for investigative reports.

Citizen Online Report Writing

A new trend allows citizens to file crime reports online, which has the potential of easing reporting delays for those jurisdictions suffering from staffing shortages and/or unmanageable caseloads. Necessarily, online reporting is used only for discovery crimes, not involvement crimes, and is most appropriate for property crimes where no suspect information is available (Smith, p.41). In accessing

Figure 3.4
Law enforcement officers rely heavily on computers to generate reports quickly. Attention to detail is still necessary for reports to be accurate.

© Robert E. Daemmrich / Getty Images.

Table 3.4 / **Evaluation Checklist for Reports**

Is the Report:
Factual?
Accurate?
Objective?
Complete?
Chronological?
Concise?
Clear?
Mechanically correct?
Grammatically correct?
Written in standard English?
Organized into paragraphs?
Does the Report Use:
First person?
Active voice?
Past tense?
Are the Sentences Mechanically Correct in Terms of:
Spelling?
Capitalization?
Punctuation?
Abbreviations?
Is the Report Audience Focused and Legible?
Does the Report Allow the Reader to Visualize What Happened?

Source: Adapted from Kären M. Hess and Henry M. Wrobleski. *For the Record: Report Writing in Law Enforcement,* 5th ed. Bloomington, MN: Innovative Systems-Publishers, Inc., 2002, p.196. Used with permission.

the local department's website and pulling up the page with the crime report form, citizens are able to complete an online report with such required fields as name, address, type of incident, or loss experienced, etc. Before the citizen can submit the report, a warning appears stating the penalties for filing a false report.

Once submitted, the report can be retrieved and proofed by a records clerk in the police department, who determines whether the report is valid and assigns a case number to those meeting the predetermined criteria. Some systems allow the report to be directly downloaded into the department's records management system, and some generate a confirmation postcard containing the case number, which is sent to the person who submitted the report. An increasing number of departments are switching to e-mail confirmation.

Smith (p.41) notes, however, that limitations exist as to which crimes can or should be reported via the Internet: "It is important that any crimes in which the victim knows, or can identify, the suspect are not reported online. Cases with known suspects should be reported through normal procedures to ensure that the proper information is collected for follow-up investigation."

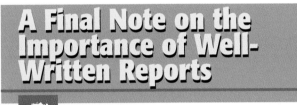

The Final Report

The culmination of the preceding steps is the final, or prosecution, report, containing all essential information for bringing a case to trial. The final report will be examined more closely in Chapter 21, as part of preparing a case for court.

A Final Note on the Importance of Well-Written Reports

Given the many uses of reports and the number of individuals who rely on them, the importance of reports should now be clear. What is key here is to make these necessary documents as well written as possible, thus maximizing the benefits they can provide. A report written well the first time means less time spent rewriting it. A well-written report also keeps everyone involved in the case up-to-speed and clear on the facts, which can lead to higher prosecution rates, more plea bargains, fewer trials, and an easing of caseloads on the court system. A well-written report can also save an investigator from spending an inordinate amount of time on the witness stand, attempting to explain any omissions, errors, or points of confusion found in poorly written reports. All of these benefits ultimately save the department time and expense.

In today's litigious society, where anyone can sue anyone else for practically anything, law enforcement is not immune to becoming the target of a lawsuit. For this reason, well-written reports can reduce legal liability for both the officer and the department by clearly documenting the actions taken throughout the investigation.

A final benefit of well-written reports is to the writer, in that they can greatly enhance an officer's career by reflecting positively on the investigator's education, competence, and professionalism.

A well-written report helps the criminal justice system operate more efficiently and effectively, saves the department time and expense, reduces liability for the department and the officer, and reflects positively on the investigator who wrote it.

Figures 3.5 and 3.6 (provided, along with the accompanying narrative, by Detective Richard Gautsch) are examples of a poorly written and a well-written report, respectively.

You are the Police Chief. It's a busy Monday morning, and Mayor Brown calls you in a panic. A dozen reporters are outside her office wanting information about the robbery at Helen's Liquor Store. She wants you to come to her office to answer these questions. You have five minutes to review the report submitted by Officer Clueless, who is off for three days picking blueberries in Wisconsin. You grab the report and your cold cup of coffee and start down the hall, reading . . .

Figure 3.5

Example of a bad police report.

Courtesy of Detective Richard Gautsch. Reprinted with permission.

Report of Officer Iam Clueless

This officer was working the middle shift to cover for Officer Johnson who had called in sick. While on routine patrol in the north shopping center at the above listed time I responded with lights and siren in accordance with our policy to a report of a robbery at Helen's Liquor Store. The perp had been arrested by officer Andrews driving northbound several blocks from the scene. When this officer arrived at the above listed address their were two men standing near the front door. The clerk was frightened bad and nearly out of control as he walked back into the store. He said he'd been ripped off by a man wearing orange colored coveralls, a blue baseball cap about 40 years old, 6', with big ears weighing about 200 pounds who pushed him against the wall and grabbed money from the till and a gun had been fired as he exited the front door. No one was hurt and this officer decided not to request an ambulance. The other witness followed us into the store and was obviously drunk and also adorned in coveralls orange in color and two sizes too big, which made him look sloppy. This witness proceeded to the main door and a piece was pointed out a short distance from the sidewalk where the perp must have thrown it. The clerk indicated that he new the guy and that there regular customers. This officer asked the clerk if he could make a positive identification of the party and he acknowledged in the affirmative. I new Officer Andrews was 10–12 with one and I asked him his ETA. He said he was waiting for a CSO to stand by for the hook, but there always late and we needed a new system for tows. He snapped your just gonna have to wait, I'll get there ASAP. He said he thought we were close enough in time to do a one on one showup and this officer concurred. When I first arrived at the scene, this officer was of the opinion that the man in the orange colored coveralls was acting strange and may have been thinking about booking on me. I contemplated cuffing him, but the PC was a little weak. I engaged the party in further conversation to ascertain weather he'd offer additional incriminating evidence or make a damaging utterance. Having recently attended training in the latest Miranda rulings, this officers surmised he was within his rights to converse with the subject since he wasn't in custody and he hadn't lawyered up. As I asked him questions, he became defensive and moved in a suspicious manner. It became evident that he had drug and alcohol problems and this officer made the decision to render the firearm safe and secure it in the trunk of my squad. On the arrival of Officer Andrews, the clerk shouted out the door that their brothers and of course he can identify him. Officer Andrews then rolled up and lowered his window. The clerk went hysterical and screamed that he owed him a hundred bucks. Both witnesses positively identified the suspect sitting in the back seat with a sour look. Officer Andrews gave the clerk back a hundred dollars and transported the suspect who was wearing orange colored coveralls and a blue hat to the PD for booking. He identified the defendant as Bart Jennings, 5-11-65. The suspect confessed in front of us and totally exonerated his brother. The clerk calmed down and asked when he'd get the gun back. I said that was up to the detectives and cleared the scene at 5624 Forest Street. This officer identified the witnesses as Stanley Jennings and Thomas Benson. See above for addresses and DOB's. END OF REPORT

End of report, and you're scratching your head, thinking, *"Huh?"* You've just finished 626 words of confusion when you arrive at the mayor's office to brief the media. No sooner have you finished providing the few facts of the case you were actually able to glean from this report when reporters start shooting questions at you:

- Who fired the gun? (passive sentence—don't know)
- Whose gun was it? (pronoun reference—don't know)
- How much money was taken? (doesn't say)
- Who owed the clerk $100? (pronoun reference)
- How much did the suspect's ears weigh? (misplaced modifier)

"Where's Helen's Liquor Store?" one reporter asks. You scan the report but can't find the address easily because it's buried near the end, out of chronological order.

Abbreviations and acronyms, jargon and slang, opinions and conclusions, ears that weigh 200 pounds. This report is a disaster! you think to yourself as the pack of reporters disperses and you head back to your office. If only the case had been handled by Officer Gotta Clue. It would have read something like . . .

Figure 3.6

Example of a good police report.

Courtesy of Detective Richard Gautsch. Reprinted with permission.

Report of Officer Gotta Clue

On 10-20-04 at 1900 hours, I was dispatched to Helen's Liquor Store (5624 Forest Street) regarding a robbery. I arrived at 1905 and saw the victim, Thomas Benson, and a witness, Stanley Jennings, standing outside the front door. Both men identified themselves with Minnesota driver's licenses. I followed Benson into the store.

Benson paced and his hands trembled as he spoke. He told me that at 1845 hours a customer pushed him against the wall, grabbed about $100 from the cash register, and ran from the store. The robber dropped a handgun outside the door as he left, and it fired. Benson described the man as white, about 40 years old, 6 feet tall, 200 pounds, with big ears. He wore orange coveralls and a blue baseball hat. Benson said he knew the man and could identify him.

As I spoke with Benson, S. Jennings came into the store and stood by the front door. He was wearing orange coveralls, swayed from side to side, and repeatedly moved his hands in and out of his pockets. His eyes were red and watery, and I smelled the odor of an alcoholic beverage on his breath. S. Jennings opened the door and pointed at a Colt 38 caliber revolver in the grass about 6 feet west of the sidewalk.

After marking the location of the revolver with an evidence tag, I placed the gun in the trunk of my squad for safety reasons.

At 1910 hours Officer Andrews contacted me by radio. He had detained Bart Jennings (5-11-65) several blocks north of Helen's Liquor Store. Andrews brought B. Jennings back to the liquor store at 1925 hours. B. Jennings was wearing orange coveralls, a blue baseball cap, and had big ears. He stayed in the back seat of the squad. (Please see Officer Andrews' arrest report.)

Benson ran toward the squad and shouted, "That's him, that's the creep. He owes me 100 bucks." He also told me that Stanley and Bart Jennings were brothers.

S. Jennings leaned against the front door of the store and said, "Yup, that's him."

B. Jennings shifted forward in his seat and stated, "I done it, but I didn't use no gun. It just fell out of my pocket. And Stan didn't know I was going to do it."

Officer Andrews transported B. Jennings to the Police Department. I told Benson and S. Jennings that a detective would contact them. I logged the gun into evidence.

Case referred to Investigations.

Compare Clueless's report with Clue's. No contest. Clue's report attends to both content and form and is:

- Factual—numerous examples such as description of S. Jennings' actions and appearance: "swayed from side to side," "eyes were red and watery," and "odor of an alcoholic beverage on his breath," as opposed to Clueless's description: "obviously drunk" (conclusionary)
- Accurate—again, many examples, such as "revolver in the grass about six feet west of the sidewalk" instead of 'a piece was pointed out a short distance from the sidewalk'
- Objective—"Benson ran toward the squad and shouted" versus "the clerk went hysterical and screamed"
- Complete—answers the six questions, Who? What? Where? When? How? and Why? In contrast, Clueless's report is filled with off-topic, extraneous information that clutters the report: It does not matter that Clueless was covering for Johnson, who had called in sick, or that Clueless had recently attended training in the latest Miranda rulings.
- Chronological—starts with the dispatch, ends with disposition
- Concise—431 words, compared with 626
- Clear—"Benson described the man as . . . 200 pounds, with big ears," compared with "with big ears weighing about 200 pounds." Officer Clue's report contained no uncommon abbreviations or acronyms
- Mechanically correct—no errors in spelling, punctuation, or capitalization
- Grammatically correct—proper word usage
- Written in standard English—no jargon ("lawyered up") or slang ("piece" instead of revolver)
- Organized into paragraphs—Clueless's is one long, disorganized paragraph
- Written in the past tense
- Written in first person, not "this officer"
- Written using the active voice

Officer Gotta Clue's report is audience focused and allows the reader to visualize what happened. It leaves the reader with a positive impression of the writer's competence.

SUMMARY

Reports are permanent written records of important facts of a case to be used in the future. They are a crucial and necessary cog in the wheel of justice.

Reports are used to examine the past, keep other police officers informed, continue investigations, prepare court cases, provide the courts with relevant facts, coordinate law enforcement activities, plan for future law enforcement services, evaluate individual officer and department performance, refresh a witness's memory as to what he or she said occurred, refresh the investigating officer's memory during the trial, compile statistics on crime in a given jurisdiction, and provide information to insurance investigators. Reports are read by other officers, supervisors, attorneys and judges, jurors, city officials, insurance adjusters and investigators, citizens, and reporters.

Among the common problems in police reports are:

- Confusing or unclear sentences.
- Conclusions, assumptions, and opinions.
- Extreme wordiness and overuse of police jargon and abbreviations.
- Missing or incomplete information.
- Misspelled words and grammatical/mechanical errors.
- Referring to "above" information.

The effective report writer attends to both content and form, as they are equally important in a well-written report. An effective report is factual. A fact is a statement that can be proven; an inference is a conclusion based on reasoning; and an opinion is a personal belief. A well-written report is also accurate, objective, complete, concise, clear, grammatically and mechanically correct, written in standard English, organized into paragraphs, written in the past tense, uses the first person and active voice, and is audience focused and legible, leaving the reader with a positive impression of the writer's competence. It is also submitted on time.

A well-written report helps the criminal justice system operate more efficiently and effectively, saves the department time and expense, reduces liability for the department and the officer, and reflects positively on the investigator who wrote it.

CHECKLIST

Report Writing

- Have I made a rough outline and organized my notes?
- Have I included all relevant information?
- Have I included headings?

- Have I proofread the paper to spot content and composition errors?
- Have I submitted all required reports on time?
- Have both negative and positive information been submitted to the prosecuting attorney?

DISCUSSION QUESTIONS

1. What is the *most* important use of reports?
2. Do you think notes should be retained or destroyed after a report has been written?
3. How important are reports for prosecution of a case?
4. Is time a factor in the quality of reports?
5. Can the content and form of a report actually be separated?
6. What gives you the most difficulty in writing reports?
7. What are your strengths in report writing?
8. Are you familiar with any report-writing software? If so, what is your opinion of the program(s)?
9. What are the advantages and disadvantages of having citizens use online reporting?
10. How do you feel about having to submit both positive and negative information to the prosecuting attorney?

MEDIA EXPLORATIONS

Internet

Search for *report writing in law enforcement*. Find one article relevant to writing offense reports, outline it, and share your outline with the class.

Crime and Evidence in Action

Go to the CD and choose the drug bust/gang homicide/sexual assault case. During the course of the case you'll become patrol officer, detective, defense attorney, and corrections officer to conduct interactive investigative research. Each case unfolds as you respond to key decision points. Feedback for each possible answer choice is packed full of information, including term definitions, Web links, and important documentation. The sergeant is available at certain times to help mentor you, the Online Resources website offers a variety of information, and be sure to take notes in your e-notebook during the suspect video statements and at key points throughout (these notes can be saved, printed, or e-mailed). The Forensics Exercise will test your ability to collect, transport, and analyze evidence from the crime scene. At the end of the case, you can track how well you responded to each decision point and join the Discussion Forum for a postmortem. **Go to the CD and use the skills you've learned in this chapter to solve a case.**

REFERENCES

Brown, Jerrold G., and Cox, Clarice R. *Report Writing for Criminal Justice Professionals.* Cincinnati, OH: Anderson Publishing Co., 1998.

Clark, Kimberly. *How to Really, Really Write Those Boring Police Reports!* Flushing, NY: Looseleaf Law Publications, 2001.

Dees, Tim. "Report Writing Aids." *Law and Order,* December 2003, pp. 18-20.

Hess, Kären M., and Wrobleski, Henry M. *For the Record: Report Writing in Law Enforcement,* 5th ed. Bloomington, MN: Innovative Systems-Publishers, Inc., 2002.

Levenson, Michael. "State on Hunt for Racial Profiling: Police Report Adds Context to Road Stops." *The Boston Globe* online, July 5, 2005. Retrieved August 31, 2005, from http://www.boston.com/news/local/massachusetts/articles/2005/07/05/state_on_hunt_for_racial_profiling

Meier, Nicholas, and Adams, R. J. *Plain English for Cops.* Durham, NC: Carolina Academic Press, 1999.

Miller, S. Dennis. *How to Write a Police Report.* Albany, NY: Delmar Publishers, Inc., 1993.

Moore, Carole. "Plain English." *Law Enforcement Technology,* December 2004, p. 266.

Nelson, Kurt R. "The Police Report in the Officer's Arsenal." *Law and Order,* September 2002, pp. 226-228.

Rutledge, Devallis. *The New Police Report Manual,* 2nd ed. Belmont, CA: Wadsworth Publishing Company, 2000.

Scoville, Dean. "The Dreaded Report: We Must Do It, So Why Not Get It Write?" *Police,* March 2000, pp. 36-38.

Sievert, Gordon. "The Essence of Quality: Writing Successful Reports." *The Law Enforcement Trainer,* Fourth Quarter 2004, pp. 35-39.

Simon, Sam. "Reducing Redundancy in Report Writing." *Law Enforcement Technology,* April 2005, pp. 94-99.

Smith, Eric. "Online Reporting." *Law and Order,* May 2004, pp. 40-42.

CHAPTER 4

Searches

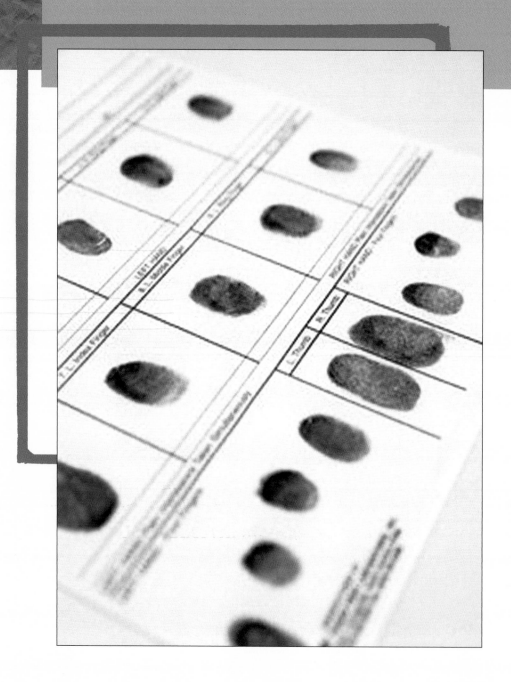

Can You Define?

Do You Know?

- Which constitutional amendment restricts investigative searches?
- What is required for an effective search?
- What the preconditions and limitations of a legal search are?
- When a warrantless search is justified?
- What precedents are established by the *Carroll, Chambers, Chimel, Mapp, Terry,* and *Weeks* decisions?
- What basic restriction is placed on all searches?
- What the exclusionary rule is and how it affects investigators?
- What a successful crime scene search accomplishes?
- What is included in organizing a crime scene search?
- What physical evidence is?
- What search patterns are used in exterior searches? interior searches?
- How to search a vehicle, a suspect, and a dead body?
- How dogs can be used in searches?

Outline

Searching is a vital task in most criminal investigations because through searching, evidence of crime and against criminals is obtained. Equally vital, however, is an investigator's understanding of the laws relating to searches. Every search must be firmly based on an understanding of the restrictions under which police officers must operate.

To **search** is to go over or look through for the purpose of finding something. *State v. Woodall* (1989) legally defines a search as "an examination of a man's house or other buildings or premises, or of his person, or of his vehicle, aircraft, etc., with a view to the discovery of contraband or illicit or stolen property, or some evidence of guilt to be used in the prosecution of a criminal action or offense with which he is charged."

Investigators make many kinds of searches. They search crime scenes, suspects, dead bodies, vehicles, hotel rooms, apartments, homes, and offices. The same basic principles apply to most searches. This chapter

begins with a discussion of legal searches, the Fourth Amendment, and the consequences imposed by the exclusionary rule if the legal requirements are not met. This is followed by a description of the crime scene search and specific search patterns that may be used. Next is a description of the other types of investigative searches, including searches of buildings, trash or garbage cans, vehicles, suspects, and dead bodies. The chapter concludes with a discussion of the use of dogs in searches.

Legal Searches and the Fourth Amendment

An understanding of the Fourth Amendment to the U.S. Constitution and its relevance for searches and seizures is critical for any investigator. The Fourth Amendment states:

> The right of the people to be secure in their persons, houses, papers, and effects, against unreasonable searches and seizures, shall not be violated, and no warrants shall issue, but upon probable cause, supported by oath or affirmation, and particularly describing the place to be searched, and the persons or things to be seized.

The Fourth Amendment to the U.S. Constitution forbids unreasonable searches and seizures.

The Fourth Amendment strikes a balance between individual liberties and the rights of society. It is an outgrowth of the desire of the founders of the United States to eliminate the offensive British practices that existed before the Revolutionary War, such as forcing the colonists to provide British soldiers housing and indiscriminately searching the homes of those suspected of disloyalty to the king. The Fourth Amendment meant to assure that the new government would respect the dignity and privacy of its citizens.

The courts are bound by rules and can admit evidence only if it is obtained constitutionally. Thus the legality of a search must always be kept in mind during an investigation.

To conduct an effective search, know the legal requirements for searching, the items being searched for, and the elements of the crime being investigated; be organized, systematic, and thorough.

The courts have adopted guidelines to assure law enforcement personnel that if they adhere to certain rules, their searches or seizures will be reasonable, and thus legal.

A search can be justified and therefore considered legal if any of the following conditions are met:
- **A search warrant has been issued.**
- **Consent is given.**
- **An officer stops a suspicious person and believes the person may be armed.**
- **The search is incidental to a lawful arrest.**
- **An emergency exists.**

If any *one* of these *preconditions* exists, a search will be considered "reasonable" and therefore legal. However, as Shinder (p.38) cautions: "States can impose further restrictions on police powers within their boundaries, so understanding federal guidelines is only the starting point."

Search with a Warrant

Technically—according to the Fourth Amendment—all searches are to be conducted under the authority of a warrant. In 1948 the Supreme Court ruled in *Johnson v. United States* that without exigent circumstances, searches are presumptively unconstitutional if not authorized by a search warrant. According to Hatch (p.11): "Search warrants are important instruments. . . . Sometimes, especially in drug investigations, the entire case rides on evidence discovered during the execution of a search warrant. By carefully drafting applications for search warrants, officers can help to ensure successful prosecution."

To obtain a valid search warrant, officers must appear before a judge and establish probable cause to believe that the location contains evidence of a crime and specifically describe that evidence. **Probable cause** is more than reasonable suspicion. Probable cause to search requires that a combination of facts makes it more likely than not that items sought are where the police believe them to be. Probable cause is what would lead a person of "reasonable caution" to believe that something connected with a crime is on the premises or person to be searched. Hatch (p.13) cautions that when using information from a civilian on a search warrant application, officers should state whether the civilian is an informant from the "criminal culture" or a "first-time citizen informant" providing information as a civic duty.

The Supreme Court has established requirements for using informants in establishing probable cause. In *Aguilar v. Texas* (1964) the Court adopted a two-pronged test: (1) Is the informant reliable/credible? and (2) is the information believable? This two-pronged approach was upheld in *Spinelli v. United States* (1969) when the Court ruled that the affidavit of the Federal Bureau of Investigation (FBI) for a warrant was insufficient to establish probable cause because there was not enough information to adequately assess the informant's reliability.

The Court abandoned this two-pronged approach in *Illinois v. Gates* (1983), where the Court ruled that probable cause is a practical concept that should not be weighed by scholars using tests, such as the *Aguilar-Spinelli* two-pronged test. Rather, the test for probable cause under the Fourth Amendment should be a **totality-of-the-circumstances test.** This is a principle upon which a number of legal assessments are made; it refers to the sum total of factors leading a reasonable person to a course of action. However, federal courts are still guided by the two-pronged *Aguilar-Spinelli* test, and several states also adhere to this more stringent requirement for establishing probable cause.

In addition to establishing probable cause for a search, the warrant must contain the reasons for requesting it, the names of the people presenting affidavits, what specifically is being sought, and the signature of the judge issuing it. The warrant must be based on facts and sworn to by the officer requesting the warrant. An address and description of the location must be given—for example, "100 S. Main Street," "the ABC Liquor Store," or "1234 Forest Drive, a private home." Figure 4.1 is an example of a search warrant.

Figure 4.1
Search warrant

```
                    SEARCH WARRANT                           2-1
STATE OF MINNESOTA, COUNTY OF _____Hennepin_____  Justice ____ COURT
TO:__Edina Police Department any officer_____
_____ (A) PEACE OFFICER(S) OF THE STATE OF MINNESOTA.
    WHEREAS, _____Patrick Olson_____ has this day on oath, made application to the said Court
applying for issuance of a search warrant to search the following described (premises) (motor vehicle) (person):
__716 Sunshine Avenue, a private residence,_____

_____
located in the city of ____Edina____,county of ____Hennepin____ STATE OF MINN.
for the following described property and things: (attach and identify additional sheet if necessary)

    One brown, 21" Panasonic Television,
    Serial Number, 63412X


    WHEREAS, the application and supporting affidavit of ____Patrick Olson____
(was) (were) duly presented and read by the Court, and being fully advised in the premises.
    NOW, THEREFORE, the Court finds that probable cause exists for the issuance of a search warrant upon
the following grounds: (Strike inapplicable paragraphs)
    1. The property above-described was stolen or embezzled.
    2. The property above-described was used as a means of committing a crime.
    3. The possession of the property above-described constitutes a crime.
    4. The property above described is in the possession of a person with intent to use such property as a
means of committing a crime.
    5. The property above described constitutes evidence which tends to show a crime has been committed,
or tends to show that a particular person has committed a crime.
    The Court further finds that probable cause exists to believe that the above-described property and things
(are) (will be) (at the above-described premises) (in the above-described motor vehicle) (on the person of _____ ).
    The Court further finds that a nighttime search is necessary to prevent the loss, destruction or removal
of the objects of said search.
    The Court further finds that entry without announcement of authority or purpose is necessary (to prevent
the loss, destruction or removal of the objects of said search) (and) (to protect the safety of the peace officers).
    NOW, THEREFORE, YOU, __a peace officer of the Edina Police__
Department_____
THE PEACE OFFICERS(S) AFORESAID, ARE HEREBY COMMANDED (TO ENTER WITHOUT ANNOUNCEMENT OF
AUTHORITY AND PURPOSE) (IN THE DAYTIME ONLY) (IN THE DAYTIME OR NIGHTTIME)      TO SEARCH
(THE DESCRIBED PREMISES) (THE DESCRIBED MOTOR VEHICLE) (THE PERSON OF
_____) FOR THE ABOVE DESCRIBED PROPERTY AND THINGS.   AND TO SEIZE SAID
PROPERTY AND THINGS AND  (TO RETAIN THEM IN CUSTODY SUBJECT TO COURT ORDER AND ACCORDING
TO LAW) (DELIVER CUSTODY OF SAID PROPERTY AND THINGS TO _____
                              ).
                    BY THE COURT:

                    Oscar Kuntson
Dated____4-14____, 20_06    JUDGE OF                          COURT
                    Justice Court
COURT - WHITE COPY • PROS. ATTY. - YELLOW COPY • PEACE OFFICER - PINK COPY • PREMISES/PERSON - GOLD COPY
```

A search warrant can be issued to search for and seize the following:

- Stolen or embezzled property
- Property designed or intended for use in committing a crime
- Property that indicates a crime has been committed or a particular person has committed a crime

Once a warrant is obtained, it should be executed promptly. In many states, the warrant is good for 10 days between 6 A.M. And 9 P.M. unless endorsed otherwise. Usually the officer serving the warrant knocks on the particular door, states the purpose of the search, and gives a copy of the warrant to the person who has answered the knock. This "knock-and-announce" rule is based in English common law and ensures the right to privacy in one's home.

In *Wilson v. Arkansas* (1995) the Court made this centuries-old rule a constitutional mandate: "The underlying command of the Fourth Amendment is always that searches and seizures be reasonable, and that the common-law requirement that officers announce their identity and purpose before entering a house forms a part of the Fourth Amendment inquiry into the reasonableness of the officers' entry." As Spector (p.66) contends: "If [residents have] knowledge of the police presence and intent, they should have an opportunity to comply by opening their door and consenting to entry before officers break the door down."

Noting that the knock-and-announce rule predates the Constitution, Devanney and Devanney (2003, p.72) suggest three reasons for this rule: (1) to protect citizens' right to privacy, (2) to reduce risk of possible violence to both police and residence occupants, and (3) to prevent needless destruction of private property.

In a unanimous ruling in *United States v. Banks* (2003), the Supreme Court upheld the forced entry into a suspected drug dealer's apartment 15 to 20 seconds after police knocked and announced themselves. Lane (p.A19) explains that the ruling overturned a federal appeal court's attempt to list conditions governing how long officers must wait and strengthened police powers in cases where loss of evidence or physical danger were crucial factors.

Makholm (2004, p.64) notes: "This ruling provides much needed guidance to law enforcement officers/entry teams, heretofore wondering just how long they need to wait before forcing entry into a residence." According to Hopper (2004, p.24): "The Court seems to appreciate the difficult challenges that law enforcement faces." However, as Cerullo and Means (p.10) suggest: "After *Banks*, an officer executing a search warrant must still balance the knock, announce and wait requirements against both officer safety and evidence destruction concerns, and the entry must still conform to a reasonableness standard."

Rutledge (2004b, p.75) advises videotaping knock-notice announcement and entry to provide evidence of compliance with the rule as well as the exact amount of time officers waited before forced entry. He suggests that officers keep repeating the announcement until someone responds or a forced entry is made.

The courts have recognized that there are some instances in which safe and effective law enforcement requires that certain exceptions be made to the knock-and-announce rule. A **no-knock warrant** may be issued if evidence may be easily destroyed or if there is advance knowledge of explosives or other specific danger to an officer (*Richards v. Wisconsin*, 1997). Hopper (2003, p.171) suggests that a no-knock warrant might be granted, for instance, if a suspect has a prior history of being armed, combative, and/or resistant to arrest. Further, officers may enter by force to execute a search warrant if no one is there to admit them. The Court has also ruled (*Illinois v. McArthur*, 2001) that officers may detain residents outside their homes until a search warrant can be obtained if necessary.

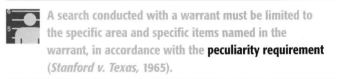

A search conducted with a warrant must be limited to the specific area and specific items named in the warrant, in accordance with the **peculiarity requirement** (*Stanford v. Texas*, 1965).

During a search conducted with a warrant, items not specified in the warrant may be seized if they are similar to the items described, if they are related to the particular crime described, or if they are contraband.

Search with Consent

Searching without a warrant is allowed if consent is given by a person having authority to do so. This might be a spouse or roommate, a business partner if the search is at a place of business, the owner of a car, and the like. Stephen (p.64) cautions that consent to enter a home does not "automatically equal the right to search it." As with a search warrant, however, searches conducted with consent have limitations.

Consent to search must be voluntary, and the search must be limited to the area for which consent is given.

The consent must not be in response to an officer's claim of lawful authority or phrased as a command or threat. It must be a genuine request for permission to search. A genuine affirmative reply must also be given; a simple nodding of the head or opening of a door is not sufficient. Silence is *not* consent. The Supreme Court ruled in *Schneckloth v. Bustamonte* (1973) that it would use the totality-of-the-circumstances test to determine whether the consent was voluntary. This includes the characteristics of the subject, the environment (location, number of people and officers present, and time of day), the subject's actions or statements, and the officer's actions or statements. Holcomb (2004, p.30) advises that officers carefully document everything they say and do while asking for consent and while conducting the search.

Some officers use a prepared consent form to be signed by the person giving consent. Holcomb (2003, p.26) points out that the government has the burden of proving a person voluntarily consented to a search and that a signed statement of consent has been found to be a "clear indication of voluntariness." If consent is given, the person granting it must be legally competent to do so. Further, the person may revoke the consent at any time during the search. Holcomb (2005a, p.26) asserts: "The prevailing view is that an individual may revoke a previously given consent to search at any time prior to the discovery of the items sought." If this occurs, officers are obligated to discontinue the search.

If the police believe the person giving consent has authority, they may act on this belief, even though it later turns out the person did not have authority. Any of several people occupying a location may usually give consent for the entire premises.

A form of consent with which officers should be familiar is the *consent once removed* exception to the search warrant requirement. Hendrie (p.24) explains that under this exception, officers can make a warrantless entry to arrest a suspect if consent to enter was given earlier to an undercover officer or informant.

Patdown or Frisk during a "Stop"

One duty of police officers is to investigate suspicious circumstances, including stopping and questioning people who are acting suspiciously. The procedures for stopping and questioning suspects are regulated by the same justifications and limitations associated with lawful searches and seizures. If you suspect that a person you have stopped for questioning may be armed, conduct a through-the-clothes patdown for weapons. If you feel what may be a weapon, you may seize it.

Two situations require police officers to stop and question individuals: (1) to investigate suspicious circumstances and (2) to identify someone who looks like a suspect named in an arrest warrant or whose description has been broadcast in an all-points bulletin (APB).

The landmark decision in *Terry v. Ohio* (1968) established police officers' right to **patdown** or **frisk** a person they have stopped to question if they believe the person might be armed and dangerous (Figure 4.2). The prime requisite for stopping, questioning, and possibly frisking someone is *reasonable suspicion,* a lesser standard than probable cause but equally difficult to define. Connor (p.41) cautions that the stop and the frisk are two separate actions and that each must be separately justified.

The *Terry* decision established that a patdown or frisk is a "protective search for weapons" and as such must be "confined to a scope reasonably designed to discover guns, knives, clubs and other hidden instruments for the assault of a police officer or others."

The Court warned that such a search is "a serious intrusion upon the sanctity of the person which may inflict great indignity and arouse strong resentment, and it is not to be undertaken lightly."

Terry has been further expanded in other cases. *Adams v. Williams* (1972) established that officers may stop and question individuals based on information received from informants. *United States v. Hensley* (1985) established that police officers may stop and question suspects when they believe they recognize them from "wanted" flyers issued by another police department.

Stop-and-frisk has been validated on the basis of furtive movements; inappropriate attire; carrying suspicious objects such as a television or a pillowcase; vague, nonspecific answers to routine questions; refusal to identify oneself; and appearing to be out of place. As established in *Alabama v. White* (1990), such a stop-and-frisk can also be made based on an anonymous tip, provided the tip predicts future activities the officer can corroborate, making it reasonable to think the informant has reliable knowledge about the suspect. However, in *Florida v. J. L.* (2000) the Court held that police could not stop and frisk someone based solely on an anonymous tip.

Usually during a *Terry* **stop**, law enforcement officers ask those they detain to identify themselves. *Hiibel v. Sixth Judicial District Court of Nevada, Humboldt County* (2004) ruled that state statutes requiring individuals to identify themselves as part of an investigative stop do not violate the Fourth or Fifth Amendments. Such statutes are constitutional. Grasso (p.27) points out that until this ruling, whether a suspect could be arrested and prosecuted for refusing to answer an officer's

Figure 4.2

As established by the *Terry* decision, this officer is restricted to a patdown for weapons because no arrest has been made at this point.

demand for identification was an "open question." He suggests that the ruling makes such statutes a "useful tool to keep in your duty bag." Concurring, Rutledge (2004c, p.74) explains that in most circumstances, willful failure to produce identification can amount to "unlawful obstruction or delay of official duty," an arrestable offense in most jurisdictions. Ginn (p.10) notes that the ruling in *Hiibel* is "very narrow" and that it applies only if a state law requires that a person provide his or her name to law enforcement officers.

In *United States v. Drayton* (2002) the Supreme Court ruled that law enforcement officers do not need to advise bus passengers of their right not to cooperate during a consensual bus interdiction. Vehicle stops as well as checkpoints for various purposes are discussed shortly.

Search Following an Arrest

Every lawful arrest is accompanied by a search of the arrested person to protect the arresting officers and others and to prevent destruction of evidence. Any weapon or dangerous substance or evidence discovered in the search may be seized. Limitations on a search incidental to arrest are found in *Chimel v. California* (1969).

The **Chimel decision** established that a search incidental to a lawful arrest must be made simultaneously with the arrest and must be confined to the area within the suspect's immediate control.

A person's **immediate control** encompasses the area within the person's reach. The Court noted that using an arrest to justify a thorough search would give police the power to conduct "general searches," which were declared unconstitutional nearly 200 years ago.

If law enforcement officers take luggage or other personal property into their exclusive control and there is no longer any danger that the arrestee might gain access to the property to seize a weapon or destroy evidence, a search of that property is no longer an incident of the arrest and a search warrant should be obtained.

Maryland v. Buie (1990) expanded the area of a premises search following a lawful arrest to ensure officers' safety. In this case the Supreme Court added authority for the police to search areas immediately adjoining the place of arrest. Such a **protective sweep,** or *Buie* **sweep,** is justified when reasonable suspicion exists that another person might be present who poses a danger to the arresting officers. The search must be confined to areas where a person might be hiding.

New York v. Belton (1981) established that the vehicle of a person who has been arrested can be searched without a warrant:

When a policeman has made a lawful custodial arrest of the occupant of an automobile, he may, as a contempora-

neous incident of that arrest, search the passenger compartment of that automobile. It follows from this conclusion that the police may also examine the contents of any containers found within the passenger compartment, for if the passenger compartment is within reach of the arrestee, so also will containers in it be within his reach.

Search in an Emergency Situation

In situations where police officers believe there is probable cause but have no time to secure a warrant—for example, if shots are being fired or a person is screaming—they may act on their own discretion.

A warrantless search in the absence of a lawful arrest or consent is justified only in emergencies or **exigent circumstances** where probable cause exists and the search must be conducted immediately (*New York v. Quarles,* 1984).

Holtz (2003b, p.110) notes that most courts recognize three elements that must be met to support a warrantless entry under the exigent circumstances exception:

1. There must be reason to believe a *real* emergency exists requiring *immediate action* to protect or preserve life or to prevent serious injury.

2. Any entry or search must not be motivated primarily by a wish to find evidence.

3. There must be a connection between the emergency and the area entered or searched.

In *Mincey v. Arizona* (1978), the Supreme Court stated that the Fourth Amendment does not require police officers to delay a search in the course of an investigation if to do so would gravely endanger their lives or the lives of others. Once the danger has been eliminated, however, any further search should be conducted only after obtaining a search warrant.

Warrantless Searches of Vehicles

Holtz (2003a, p.146) notes: "A motor vehicle stop is a 'seizure' within the meaning of the Fourth Amendment. As such, it must, as a general rule, be supported by a reasonable suspicion of wrongdoing." Warrantless searches are often justified because of a vehicle's **mobility,** that is, the vehicle can be easily moved. The precedent for a warrantless search of an automobile was established in *Carroll v. United States* (1925).

The *Carroll* decision established that automobiles may be searched without a warrant if (1) there is probable cause for the search and (2) the vehicle would be gone before a search warrant could be obtained.

During a stop of a moving vehicle, if officers have probable cause, they may search the vehicle and any closed containers in it. If probable cause does not exist, officers may be able to obtain voluntary consent to search the vehicle, including any closed containers (*Florida v. Jimeno*, 1990). The driver must be competent to give such consent, and silence is not consent. Further, if at any time the driver rescinds consent, the search must cease.

Officers must also know their state's laws regarding full searches of automobiles pursuant to the issuance of a traffic citation, which may often seem contradictory. Although several states have statutes that authorize searches of vehicles following the issuance of a traffic citation, the policy in most states is to allow searches only after a driver has been arrested and is in custody. In *Knowles v. Iowa* (1998), the Supreme Court ruled that when an officer issues a citation instead of making an arrest, a full search of the driver's car violates the Fourth Amendment.

However, the Court has also ruled in *Wyoming v. Houghton* (1999) that an officer may search the belongings of an automobile passenger simply because the officer suspects the driver has done something wrong. This "passenger property exception" ruling was intended to prevent drivers from claiming that illegal drugs or other contraband belonged to passengers, not themselves.

Limitations on warrantless automobile searches were set in *United States v. Henry* (1958). In this case the Court said: "Once these items [for which a search warrant would be sought] are located, the search must terminate. If, however, while legitimately looking for such articles, the officer unexpectedly discovers evidence of another crime, he can seize that evidence as well."

Searches of Vehicles Incident to and Contemporaneous with Lawful Arrests

In *New York v. Belton* (1981) the Supreme Court ruled that searches of vehicles incident to and contemporaneous with a lawful arrest are valid: "Once an officer determines that there is probable cause to make an arrest, it is reasonable to allow officers to ensure their safety and to preserve evidence by searching the entire passenger compartment."

Rutledge (2004a, p.140) suggests that *Belton* sought to establish a "bright-line rule" (a definitive, unequivocal judicial decision), but it left in doubt whether the rule applied if the driver or a passenger got out of the vehicle before being contacted by the police. This was established in *Thornton v. United States* (2004), in which the Supreme Court ruled that police can search the passenger compartment of a vehicle incident to arrest when the arrestee was approached after recently occupying that vehicle.

Vehicle Searches at Roadblocks and Checkpoints

A quarter-century ago, in *United States v. Martinez-Fuerte* (1976), the Supreme Court ruled that checkpoints at the country's borders were constitutional because they served the national interest and that this interest outweighed the checkpoint's minimal intrusion on driver privacy. According to Clark (p.22): "A true border search can be made without probable cause, without a warrant and, indeed, without any articulable suspicion at all." He says that the only limitation on a border search is the Fourth Amendment requirement that it be conducted reasonably. Clark (p.25) also explains the *functional equivalent doctrine,* which establishes that routine border searches are constitutional at places other than actual borders where travelers frequently enter or leave the country, including international airports.

Three years later in *Brown v. Texas* (1979), the Supreme Court created a *balancing test* (an evaluation of interests and factors) to determine the constitutionality of roadblocks. The *Brown* balancing test requires that courts evaluating the lawfulness of roadblocks consider three factors:

1. The gravity of the public concerns served by establishing the roadblock.
2. The degree to which the roadblock is likely to succeed in serving the public interest.
3. The severity with which the roadblock interferes with individual liberty.

Michigan v. Sitz (1990) established that *sobriety* checkpoints to combat drunken driving were reasonable under the *Brown* balancing test if they met certain guidelines. However, the Court ruled in *City of Indianapolis v. Edmond* (2000) that checkpoints for *drugs* are unconstitutional: "We cannot sanction stops justified only by the generalized and ever-present possibility that interrogation and inspection may reveal that any given motorist has committed some crime." Risher (p.12) explains that "*Edmond* made it clear that vehicle checkpoints for general crime control are constitutionally unreasonable."

In *Illinois v. Lidster* (2004) the Court upheld the constitutionality of *informational checkpoints*. Justice Breyer explained:

> The stop's primary law enforcement purpose was not to determine whether a vehicle's occupants were committing a crime, but to ask vehicle occupants, as members of the public, for their help in providing information about a crime in all likelihood committed by others. The police expected the information elicited to help them apprehend, not the vehicle's occupants, but other individuals.

Devanney and Devanney (2004, p.20) contend: "The Supreme Court decision in *Illinois v. Lidster* represents a victory for the police and legitimizes an important investigative method." Another victory for law enforcement came in 2004 in *United States v. Flores-Montano*, in which the Supreme Court unanimously overturned a decision by a circuit court of appeals, ruling that privacy interests do not apply to vehicles crossing the border ("Court Allows Routine Search of Vehicle Fuel Tank at Border," p.6). Chief Justice Rehnquist wrote:

> Complex balancing tests to determine what is a "routine" search of a vehicle . . . have no place in border searches of vehicles. The government's interest in preventing the entry of unwanted persons and effects is at its zenith at the international border. Time and again, we have stated that searches made at the border . . . are reasonable simply by virtue of the fact that they occur at the border.

Inventory Searches Unlike a search incidental to an arrest, a vehicle search need not be made immediately.

Chambers v. Maroney (1970) established that a vehicle may be taken to headquarters to be searched.

When police take custody of a vehicle (or other property), the courts have upheld their right to inventory such property for the following reasons:

- To protect the owner's property. This obligation may be legal or moral, but the courts have supported the police's responsibility to protect property taken into custody from unauthorized interference.
- To protect the police from disputes and claims that the property was stolen or damaged. Proper inventory at the time of custody provides an accurate record of the condition of the property at the time it was seized.
- To protect the police and the public from danger. Custody of an automobile or a person subjects the police to conditions that require searching the person or the vehicle for objects such as bombs, chemicals, razor blades, weapons, and so on that may harm the officers or the premises where the vehicle or person is taken.
- To determine the owner's identity. Identifying the owner may be associated with identifying the person under arrest, or it may help the police know to whom the property should be released.

The courts have held that each of these factors outweighs the privacy interests of property and therefore justifies an inventory search. The search must be reasonable. To be correct in the inventory procedure, the police must show legal seizure and make an inventory according to approved procedures.

Although inventory and search are technically two different processes, in practice they may take place simultaneously. If property found during such an inventory is evidence of a crime, it is admissible in court. It is advisable, however, where a vehicle is no longer mobile or is in the custody of the police, to obtain a search warrant so as not to jeopardize an otherwise perfectly valid case.

While the major cases governing warrantless searches of a vehicle have just been discussed, there are others you may encounter during the course of an investigation. Table 4.1 summarizes the relevant court rulings related to automobile searches.

Basic Limitation on Searches

All searches have one limitation.

The most important limitation on any search is that the scope must be narrow. General searches are unconstitutional.

Laws regulating how and when searches may be legally conducted are numerous and complex. It is critical, however, that officers who are responsible for criminal investigations know these laws and operate within them. The penalty for not doing so is extreme— no evidence obtained during an illegal search will be allowed at a trial, as established by the exclusionary rule.

The Exclusionary Rule

hrough the exclusionary rule, the courts enforce the prohibition against unreasonable searches set forth in the Fourth Amendment. In the early 1900s the federal courts declared that "they would require that evidence be obtained in compliance with constitutional standards" contained in the Fourth Amendment.

The **exclusionary rule** established that courts may not accept evidence obtained by unreasonable search and seizure, regardless of its relevance to a case. *Weeks v. United States* (1914) made the rule applicable at the federal level; *Mapp v. Ohio* (1961) made it applicable to *all* courts.

The exclusionary rule affects not only illegally seized evidence but also evidence obtained as a result of the illegally seized evidence, referred to as *fruit of the poisonous tree*. The **"fruit-of-the-poisonous-tree"**

Table 4.1 / **Summary of Major Court Rulings Regarding Vehicle Searches**

Case Decision	Holding
New York v. Belton (1981)	After a custodial arrest of an occupant of the vehicle, officers may conduct an immediate search of the vehicle, following the rule that the search is incident to arrest. The search must be limited to the passenger compartment and may be a general search without a specific object in mind. The search may include closed containers.
Florida v. Jimeno (1990)	A warrantless search may be made when consent is obtained from the owner or person in possession of the vehicle. The entire vehicle may be searched, including closed containers, unless the consentor has expressed limitation.
Florida v. Wells (1990)	The contents of a lawfully impounded vehicle may be inventoried for purposes of property accountability, public safety, and protection against later claims of damage or loss of property.
Texas v. Brown (1983)	Contraband or evidence in plain view may be confiscated. Two conditions must exist: (1) The officer must be legally present and (2) there must be probable cause to believe that the object in plain view is contraband or the instrumentality of a crime.
United States v. Bowhay (1993)	Because a department policy required officers to search everything, the officers had no discretion. Therefore, the presence of an investigative motive did not prohibit the inventory search.
United States v. Ibarra (1992)	If there is no statutory authority to impound, the vehicle cannot be taken into custody legally; therefore, an inventory search under these circumstances would be inadmissible.
United States v. Ross (1982)	A search may be made when probable cause exists to believe that contraband or evidence is within the vehicle. This includes the trunk or closed containers in the vehicle.
United States v. Williams (1991)	An on-site inventory of property is legally permissible, even though done in advance of impounding, if there is authority and circumstances to justify impound.

doctrine established that evidence obtained as a result of an earlier illegality must be excluded from trial.

The exclusionary rule may seem to favor criminals at the expense of law enforcement, but this was not the Court's intent. The Court recognized that important exceptions to this rule might occur. Two of the most important exceptions are the inevitable-discovery doctrine and the good-faith doctrine.

In *Nix v. Williams* (1984), a defendant's right to counsel under the Sixth Amendment was violated, resulting in his making incriminating statements and leading the police to the body of his murder victim. Searchers who had been conducting an extensive, systematic search of the area then terminated their search. If the search had continued, the search party would inevitably have discovered the victim's body. The **inevitable-discovery doctrine** established that if illegally obtained evidence would in all likelihood eventually have been discovered legally, it may be used.

The intent of the exclusionary rule, the Court said, was to deter police from violating citizens' constitutional rights. In the majority opinion, Chief Justice Warren E. Burger wrote: "Exclusion of physical evidence that would inevitably have been discovered adds nothing to either the integrity or fairness of a criminal trial."

In *United States v. Leon* (1984), police in Burbank, California, were investigating a drug-trafficking operation and, following up on a tip from an unreliable informant, applied for and were issued an apparently valid search warrant. Their searches revealed large quantities of drugs and other evidence at various locations. The defendants challenged the sufficiency of the warrant and moved to suppress the evidence seized on the basis of the search warrant. The district court held that the affidavit was insufficient to establish probable cause because of the informant's unreliability. The U.S. Court of Appeals affirmed the action of the district court. Then the U.S. Supreme Court reviewed whether the exclusionary rule should be modified to allow the admission of evidence seized in *reasonably good faith*. The Court noted that the exclusionary rule is a *judicially created remedy* intended to serve as a deterrent rather than a guaranteed constitutional right. The **good-faith doctrine** established that illegally obtained evidence may be admissible if the police were truly not aware they were violating a suspect's Fourth Amendment rights.

Having looked at the legal restrictions on searching, now consider the searches themselves, beginning with the search of a crime scene. Although each crime scene is unique, certain general guidelines apply.

The Crime Scene Search

A basic function of investigators is to conduct a thorough, legal search at the scene of a crime. Geberth (p.46) points out: "The search of the crime scene is the most important phase of the investigation conducted at the scene." He suggests that physical evidence is the "unimpeachable witness" that is not influenced by faulty memories, prejudices, poor vision, or a desire to stay uninvolved.

Even though not initially visible, evidence in some form is present at most crime scenes. The goal of any search during an investigation, at the crime scene or elsewhere, is to discover evidence that helps to

- Establish that a crime _was_ committed and _what_ the specific crime was.
- Establish _when_ the crime was committed.
- Identify _who_ committed the crime.
- Explain _how_ the crime was committed.
- Suggest _why_ the crime was committed.

 A successful crime scene search locates, identifies, and preserves all evidence present.

Evidence found at a scene assists in re-creating a crime in much the same way that bricks, properly placed, result in the construction of a building. A meticulous, properly conducted search usually results in the discovery of evidence. The security measures taken by the first officer at the scene determine whether evidence is discovered intact or after it has been altered or destroyed. During a search, do not change or contaminate physical evidence in any way, or it will be declared inadmissible. Maintain the chain of custody of evidence from the initial discovery to the time of the trial as discussed in the next chapter.

Organizing the Crime Scene Search

After emergencies have been attended to, the scene has been secured, witnesses have been located and separated for interviewing, and photographing and sketching have been completed, a search plan must be formulated. Also, a search headquarters needs to be established away from the scene to prevent destruction of evidence.

 Organizing a search includes dividing the duties, selecting a search pattern, assigning personnel and equipment, and giving instructions.

Proper organization results in a thorough search with no accidental destruction of evidence. However, even the best-organized search may not yield evidence. Evidence may have been destroyed before the search or removed by the criminal. In a few, rare instances, evidence is simply nonexistent.

In a single-investigator search, one officer conducts the physical search and describes, identifies, and preserves the evidence found. If two or more officers conduct the search, the highest-ranking officer on the scene usually assumes command. In accordance with department policy, the officer in charge assigns personnel based on their training. For example, if one officer has specialized training in photography, another in sketching, and a third in fingerprinting, they are assigned to their respective specialties. Someone is assigned to each function required in the search. Often two officers are assigned to take measurements to ensure accuracy. These same two officers can collect, identify, and preserve evidence as it is found. Evidence should never be removed from the scene without the permission of the search leader.

The search leader also determines the number of personnel needed, the type of search best suited for the area, and the items most likely to be found. Personnel are assigned according to the selected search pattern. Members of the search party are given all known details of the crime and instructed on the type of evidence to seek and the members' specific responsibilities.

The search leader also determines whether anyone other than the person who committed the crime has entered the scene. If so, the person is asked to explain in detail any contacts with the scene that might have contaminated evidence. If no one has entered the scene between the time the crime was committed and when the police arrived, and if the scene was immediately secured, the scene is considered to be a **true,** or **uncontaminated, scene;** that is, no evidence has been introduced into it or taken from it except by the person who committed the crime.

Physical Evidence

Physical evidence ranges in size from very large objects to minute substances. Understanding what types of evidence can be found at various types of crime scenes is important to the search. Obviously not everything found at a scene is evidence.

 Knowing what to search for is indispensable to an effective crime scene search. _Physical evidence_ is anything material and relevant to the crime being investigated.

The elements of the crime help to determine what will be useful as evidence. For example, a burglary requires an illegal entry; therefore, toolmarks and broken glass in a door or window are evidence that assist in proving burglary.

A forcible rape requires a sexual act against a victim's will. Therefore, bruises, semen stains, or witnesses hearing screams would help to establish evidence of that crime. Specific types of evidence to seek are discussed in Chapter 5 and throughout Sections Three, Four, and Five.

Besides knowing what types of evidence to search for, investigators must know where evidence is most likely to be found. For example, evidence is often found on or near the route used to and from a crime. A suspect may drop items used to commit a crime or leave shoe or tire prints. Evidence is also frequently found on or near a dead body.

The **"elephant-in-a-matchbox" doctrine** requires that searchers consider the probable size and shape of evidence they seek because, for example, large objects cannot be concealed in tiny areas. Ignoring this doctrine can result in a search that wastes resources, destroys potential evidence, and leaves a place in shambles. It may also result in violating the Fourth Amendment requirements on reasonable searches.

Search Patterns

All **search patterns** have a common denominator: They are designed to locate systematically any evidence at a crime scene or any other area where evidence might be found. Most patterns involve partitioning search areas into workable sizes. The search pattern should be adapted to the area involved, the personnel available, the time limits imposed by weather and light conditions, and the circumstances of the individual crime scene. Such patterns ensure thoroughness.

Exterior Searches

Exterior searches can cover small, large, or vast areas. Regardless of the dimensions, the area to be searched can be divided into subareas and diagrammed on paper. As each area is searched, check it off. Be certain sufficient light is available. A search conducted with inadequate light can destroy more evidence than it yields. If weather conditions are favorable, delay nighttime searches until daylight if feasible.

Exterior search patterns divide an area into lanes, concentric circles, or zones.

Lane-Search Pattern The **lane-search pattern** partitions the area into lanes, using stakes and string, as

illustrated in Figure 4.3. A **lane** is a narrow strip. An officer is assigned to each lane. Therefore, the number of lanes to use depends on the number of officers available to search.

These lanes can be imaginary. Officers' search widths vary from arm's length to shoulder-to-shoulder, either on foot or on their knees. Such searches use no string or cord to mark the lanes.

If only one officer is available for the search, the lane pattern can be adapted to what is commonly called the **strip-search pattern**, illustrated in Figure 4.4.

For an extensive search, the lane pattern is often modified to form a **grid**, and the area is crisscrossed, as illustrated in Figure 4.5.

Circle-Search Pattern Another commonly used pattern is the **circle search**, which begins at the center of an area to be searched and spreads out in ever-widening concentric circles (Figure 4.6).

A wooden stake with a long rope is driven into the ground at the center of the area to be searched. Knots are tied in the rope at selected regular intervals. The searcher circles around the stake in the area delineated by the first knot, searching the area within the first circle. When this area is completed, the searcher moves to the second knot and repeats the procedure. The search is continued in ever-widening circles until the entire area is covered.

Zone- or Sector-Search Pattern In the **zone** or **sector** search, an area is divided into equal squares on a map of the area, and each square is numbered. Search personnel are assigned to specific squares (Figure 4.7).

Interior Searches

The foregoing exterior search patterns can be adapted to an interior crime scene. Of prime concern is to search thoroughly without destroying evidence.

Interior searches go from the general to the specific, usually in a circular pattern, covering all surfaces of a search area. The floor should be searched first.

In making an interior search, look closely at all room surfaces, including the floor, ceiling, walls, and all objects on the floor and walls. Evidence can be found on any surface.

The floor usually produces the most evidence, followed by doors and windows. Although the ceiling is often missed in a search, it too can contain evidence such as stains or bullet holes. It can even contain such unlikely evidence as footprints. Footprints were found on the ceiling by an alert officer during the investigation of a bank burglary. Paperhangers had left wallpaper on the bank's floor during the night and had hung it on the

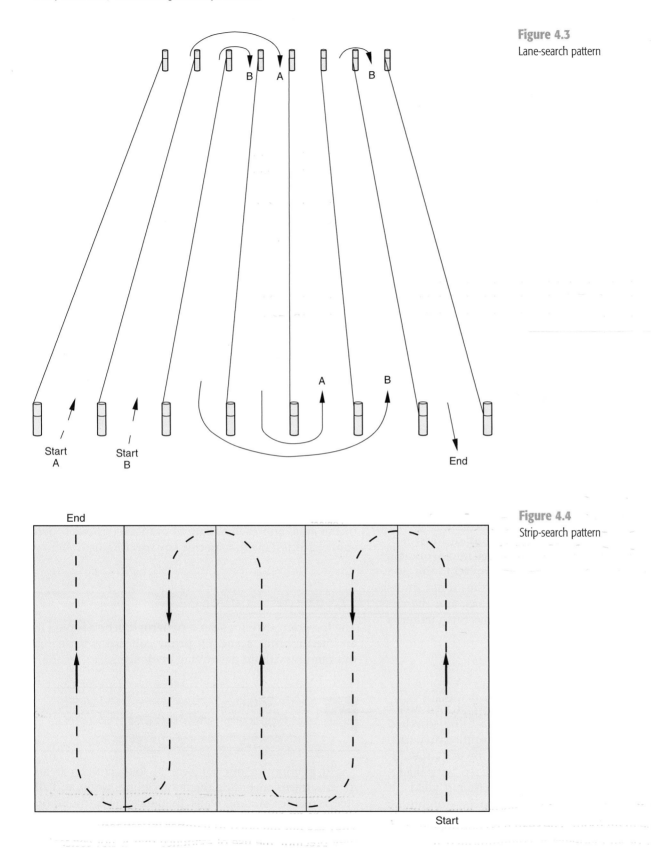

Figure 4.3
Lane-search pattern

Start
A

Start
B

A

B

End

Figure 4.4
Strip-search pattern

End

Start

ceiling early the next morning before the burglary was discovered. During the night, one of the burglars had stepped on the wallpaper, leaving a footprint that was transferred in a faint outline to the ceiling.

An interior room search usually starts at the point of entry. The floor is searched first so that no evidence is inadvertently destroyed during the remainder of the search. The lane- or zone-search patterns are adaptable to an interior floor search.

After the floor search, the walls—including doors and windows—and then the ceiling are searched, normally using a clockwise or counterclockwise pattern

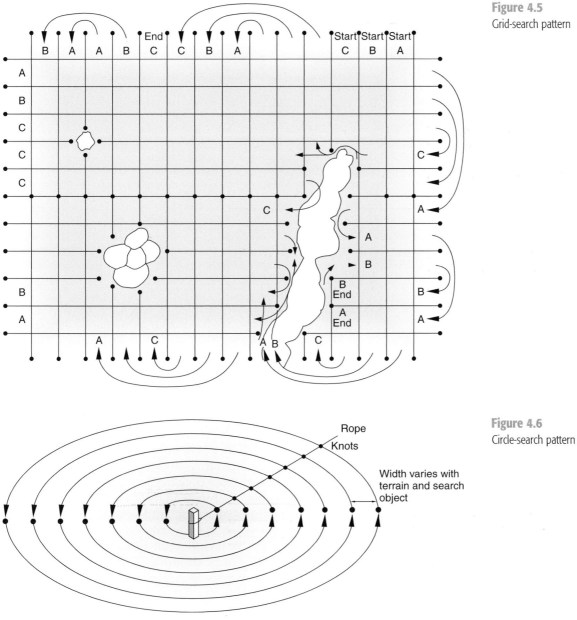

Figure 4.5
Grid-search pattern

Figure 4.6
Circle-search pattern

around the room. Because doors and windows are points of entry and exit, soil, fingerprints, glass fragments, and other evidence are often found there. Walls may contain marks, bloodstains, or trace evidence such as hairs or fibers.

After a room is searched in one direction, it is often searched in the opposite direction because lighting is different from different angles. The same general procedures are followed in searching closets, halls, or other rooms off the main room. The search is coordinated, and the location of all evidence is communicated to members of the search team.

General Guidelines

The precise search pattern used is immaterial as long as the search is systematic and covers the entire area.

Assigning two officers to search the same area greatly increases the probability of discovering evidence. Finding evidence is no reason to stop a search. Continue searching until the entire area is covered.

Plain-View Evidence

The limitations on searches are intended to protect the rights of all citizens and to ensure due process of law. They are not intended to hamper investigations, nor do they preclude the use of evidence that is not concealed and that is accidentally found.

 Plain-view evidence—unconcealed evidence seen by an officer engaged in a lawful activity—is admissible in court (*United States v. Henry*, 1958).

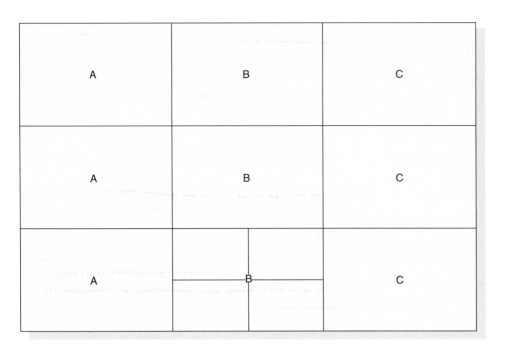

Figure 4.7
Zone- or sector-search pattern

Although the Fourth Amendment prohibits unreasonable intrusions into a person's privacy, the precedent for plain-view evidence was established in *Katz v. United States* (1967) when the Supreme Court held: "The Fourth Amendment protects people, not places. What a person knowingly exposes to the public, even in his own home or office, is not a subject of Fourth Amendment protection. But what he seeks to preserve as private, even in an area accessible to the public, may be constitutionally protected." In both *Michigan v. Tyler* (1978) and *Mincey v. Arizona* (1978), the Court ruled that while officers are on the premises pursuing their legitimate emergency activities, any evidence in plain view may be seized.

An officer cannot obtain a warrant and fail to mention a particular object and then use "plain view" to justify its seizure. If the officer is looking for it initially, it must be mentioned in the warrant. Plain-view evidence itself is not sufficient to justify a warrantless seizure of evidence; probable cause must also exist.

Evidence may also be seized if an officer relies on a sense other than sight. For example, a customs officer who smells marijuana coming from a package has probable cause to make an arrest under a "plain-smell" rationale (*United States v. Lueck*, 1982).

Officers may seize any contraband they discover during a legal search. In *Boyd v. United States* (1886), Justice Bradley stated: "The search for and seizure of stolen or forfeited goods or goods liable to duties and concealed to avoid payment thereof, are totally different things from a search or a seizure of a man's private books and papers. In one case the government is entitled to the property, and in the other it is not."

Plain Feel/Touch

The "plain-feel/touch" exception is an extension of the plain-view exception. As Hunsucker (p.10) so aptly states: "Anywhere a law enforcement officer has a right to be, he has a right to see—through the use of any of his unaided senses." If a police officer lawfully pats down a suspect's outer clothing and feels an object that he *immediately* identifies as contraband—in other words, **plain feel/touch evidence**—a warrantless seizure is justified because there is no invasion of the suspect's privacy beyond that already authorized by the officer's search for weapons (*Minnesota v. Dickerson*, 1993).

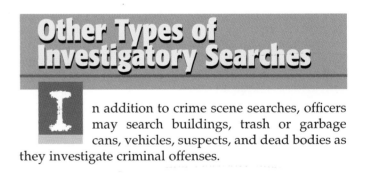

Other Types of Investigatory Searches

In addition to crime scene searches, officers may search buildings, trash or garbage cans, vehicles, suspects, and dead bodies as they investigate criminal offenses.

Building Searches

When executing a warrant to search a building, officers should first familiarize themselves with the location and the past record of the person living there. Check records for any previous police actions at that location. Garner (2003b, p.62) cautions: "When it comes to searching buildings, there's no such thing as a 'safe' house." Decide on the least dangerous time of day for the suspect, the police, and the neighborhood. For example, the time of day when children come home from school would not be a good time to execute a warrant.

Do not treat the execution of a search warrant as routine. Plan for the worst-case scenario. Think *safety* first and last. Arrive safely. Turn off your vehicle's dome light as you approach the building. Stay away from the headlights or turn them off. Use any available cover as you approach the building.

Have a plan before entering the building. Secure the outside perimeter and as many exits as possible—at a minimum, the front and rear doors. If possible, call for a backup before entering and search with a partner. Once inside, wait for your vision to adjust to interior light conditions.

Keep light and weapons away from your body. Reduce the audio level of your radio, and turn off your beeper. Go quickly through doors into dark areas. When moving around objects, take quick peeks before proceeding. Avoid windows. Use light and cover to your advantage. Know where you are at all times and how to get back to where you were. Look for exits. If the entire building is to be searched, use a systematic approach. Secure each area as it is searched.

Rutledge (2005, p.72) explains that when police conduct a search of a suspect's home under authority of a search warrant, it is common to find several people present. Sometimes those present outnumber the officers on the scene, posing problems of safety and control. Guidelines for this situation were established in *Michigan v. Summers* (1981) when the Supreme Court stated: "We hold that a warrant to search for contraband founded on probable cause carries with it the limited authority to detain the occupants of the premises while a proper search is conducted." The Court did not say whether detained individuals could be handcuffed or for how long they could be detained.

Law enforcement officers may also require residents to remain outside of their home until a search warrant can be obtained if the officers have probable cause to believe that the home contains evidence of illegal activity (*Illinois v. McArthur*, 2001).

Officers should be aware of the ruling in *Kyllo v. United States* (2001), which held that thermal scanning of a private residence from outside the residence is a search under the Fourth Amendment and requires a search warrant. Woessner and Sims (p.229) note: "Far from creating an innovative constitutional guarantee, the *Kyllo* decision represents a narrowly defined respite from the ever-encroaching powers of government-sponsored surveillance." They point out that a key argument in *Kyllo* was that thermal imaging was not in "general public use." Worrall (p.205) suggests that *Kyllo* did not establish a bright-line rule and is flawed because there is no agreement on the general-public-use

standard. It would appear that thermal imaging, which uses infrared technology, might be considered in general public use based on information provided by Freeborg (p.51), who reports that an infrared news journal, *Maxtec*, estimates the commercial potential with all infrared products to be more than $1 billion this year, with an expected annual growth of 20 percent.

Trash or Garbage Can Searches

Trash and garbage cans in alleys and on public sidewalks are often the depository for evidence of thefts, drug possession, and even homicides. In *California v. Greenwood* (1988), the Supreme Court ruled that containers left on public property are open to search by police without a warrant. The Supreme Court ruled that such a search does not constitute a violation of the Fourth Amendment or a reasonable expectation of privacy: "It is common knowledge that plastic garbage bags left on a public street are readily accessible to animals, children, scavengers, snoops, and other members of the public," and therefore "no reasonable expectation of privacy" is violated by such a search. Trash or garbage containers on private property may not be searched without a warrant.

The most important factor in determining the legality of a warrantless trash inspection is the physical location of the retrieved trash. Police cannot trespass to gain access to the trash location, and the trash must not be located within the curtilage, which the Supreme Court has described as "the area to which extends the intimate activity associated with the sanctity of a man's home and the privacies of life." In other words, curtilage is that portion of a residence that is not open to the public. It is reserved for private owner or family use, and an expectation of privacy exists. This is in contrast to sidewalks and alleys that are used by the public. In *United States v. Dunn* (1987), the Court ruled:

> We believe that curtilage questions should be resolved with particular reference to four factors: the proximity of the area claimed to be curtilage to the home, whether the area is included within an enclosure surrounding the home, the nature of the uses to which the area is put, and the steps taken by the resident to protect the area from observation by people passing by.

Searches of trash may also extend to the local landfill.

Vehicle Searches

Cars, aircraft, boats, motorcycles, buses, trucks, and vans can contain evidence of a crime. Again, the type of crime determines the area to be searched and the evidence to be sought. In a hit-and-run accident, the car's undercarriage can have hairs and fibers, or the interior may reveal a hidden liquor bottle. In narcotics arrests, various types of drugs are often found in cars, planes, and boats. An ordinary vehicle has hundreds of places to hide drugs. In some cases, vehicles may have specially constructed compartments.

As with other types of searches, a vehicle search must be systematic and thorough. Evidence is more likely to be found if two officers conduct the search.

> Remove occupants from the car. First search the area around the vehicle and then the exterior. Finally, search the interior along one side from front to back, and then return along the other side to the front.

Before entering a vehicle, search the area around it for evidence related to the crime. Next examine the vehicle's exterior for fingerprints, dents, scratches, or hairs and fibers. Examine the grill, front bumper, fender areas, and license plates. Open the hood and check the numerous recesses of the motor, radiator, battery, battery case, engine block, clutch and starter housings, ventilating ducts, air filter, body frame, and supports. Open the trunk and examine any clothing, rags, containers, tools, the spare-tire well, and the interior of the trunk lid.

Finally, search the vehicle's interior, following the same procedures used in searching a room. Vacuum the car before getting into it. Package collections from different areas of the car separately. Then systematically examine ashtrays, the glove compartment, areas under the seats, and the window areas. Remove the seats and vacuum the floor. Hairs and fibers or traces of soil may be discovered that will connect a suspect with soil samples from the crime scene.

Use a flashlight and a mirror to examine the area behind the dashboard. Feeling by hand is not effective because of the numerous wires located there. Look for fingerprints in the obvious places: window and door handles, underside of the steering wheel, radio buttons,

ashtrays, distributor cap, jack, rearview mirror, hood latches, and seat adjustment levers.

Figure 4.8 illustrates the areas of vehicles that should be searched. The vehicle is divided into specific search areas to ensure order and thoroughness.

As in any other search, take precautions to prevent contaminating evidence. Be alert to what is an original part of the vehicle and what has been added. For example, compartments for concealing illegal drugs or other contraband are sometimes added. The systems and equipment of the vehicle should be validated. Is the exhaust real or phony? Check recesses and cup holders for sneaker flip panels that may contain contraband or weapons. Check the headliner. In convertibles, check the boot.

Some officers use a wheeled platform that has dual periscopic mirrors and fluorescent lights and rolls easily under a vehicle, allowing them to view its underside. A handheld model is also available, allowing viewing of vehicle interiors, engine compartments, and tops of high-profile vehicles (Figure 4.9).

Suspect Searches

How a suspect should be searched depends on whether an arrest has been made. If you have reasonable suspicion to stop or probable cause to arrest a person, be cautious. Many officers are injured or killed because they fail to search a suspect. If a suspect is in a car, have him or her step out of the car, and be careful to protect yourself from a suddenly opened door.

> If the suspect has not been arrested, confine your search to a patdown or frisk for weapons. If the suspect has been arrested, make a complete body search for weapons and evidence. In either event, always be on your guard.

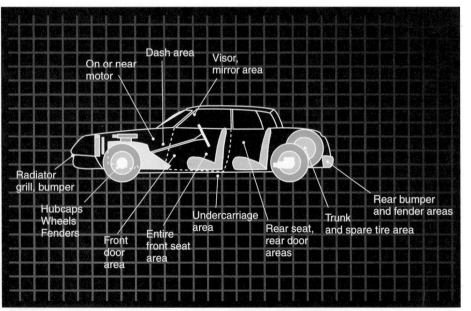

Figure 4.8
Vehicle areas that should be searched

Dash area
On or near motor
Visor, mirror area
Radiator grill, bumper
Hubcaps Wheels Fenders
Front door area
Entire front seat area
Undercarriage area
Rear seat, rear door areas
Trunk and spare tire area
Rear bumper and fender areas

James Shaffer/Photoedit

Figure 4.9

As established by the *Carroll* decision, an officer may search a vehicle without a warrant if he or she has probable cause to believe it contains evidence of a crime. Evidence is more likely to be found if two officers conduct the search. Here, two Dubuque, Iowa, police officers search the front seat of an SUV.

Garner (2003a, p.44) suggests several "cardinal rules." First, if possible, search a person while a cover officer observes the search. Second, if taking a person into custody, handcuff first and then search. Third, even patdown searches should be done only while wearing protective gloves. Fourth, before conducting any search, ask the suspect if he has anything on him that could get the officer into trouble, asking specifically about needles and blades. Fifth, not everything that looks innocent is. Garner (2003a, p.45) notes that survivalist magazines and catalogs contain many ads for cutting instruments and firearms disguised as pagers, pens, belt buckles, and credit cards.

Thorough Search If you arrest a suspect, conduct a complete body search for both weapons and evidence. Whether you use an against-the-wall spread-eagle search or a simple stand-up search, follow a methodical, exact procedure. The complete body search often includes taking samples of hair and fingernail scrapings as well as testing for firearm residue when appropriate. Regardless of whether an arrest has been made, respect the dignity of the suspect while you conduct the patdown or search, but do not let your guard down.

Strip searches may be conducted only after an arrest and when the prisoner is in a secure facility. Such searches should be conducted by individuals of the same gender as the suspect and in private and should follow written guidelines. Considerations in deciding when a strip search is necessary include the individual's past behavior, the possibility that the person is concealing dangerous drugs or weapons, whether the person will be alone or with others in a cell, and how long the person will be in custody. Cavity searches go beyond the normal strip search and must follow very strict

departmental guidelines. Normally such searches should be conducted by medical personnel.

Inhibitors to a Thorough Search A variety of factors may inhibit an officer's ability or desire to conduct a thorough search of a suspect. The presence of bodily fluids is one factor that may interfere with a complete search. The threat of contracting AIDS or hepatitis infections in the line of duty has led police to consider using special equipment when searching suspects. Goggles or face masks are other pieces of equipment that reduce personal contact with blood and other body fluids, the main carriers of these viruses. Officers must also be alert to suspects who may spit on or bite them.

Another inhibitor to thorough searches is a fear of needles. When searching, officers should avoid putting their hands into suspects' pockets. They should use patting, rather than grabbing, motions to avoid being stuck by sharp objects such as hypodermic needles. Techniques for collecting evidence that may be contaminated with the AIDS virus are discussed in the next chapter.

Weather can be another factor that compromises the thoroughness of a search. Driving rains, freezing or sweltering temperatures, blowing snow—all may entice an officer to hurry through a search.

Dead Body Searches

Searching a dead body should be done only *after* the coroner or medical examiner has arrived or given permission. In one case a well-meaning officer turned a body over to search for identification before the medical examiner arrived. This caused major problems in documenting the position of the body.

Searching a dead body is unpleasant, even when the person has died recently. It is extremely unpleasant if the person has been dead for a long period. In some such cases, the body can be searched only in the coroner's examination room, where effective exhaust ventilation is available.

> Search a dead body systematically and completely. Include the immediate area around and under the body.

The search usually begins with the clothing, which is likely to reveal a wallet or personal identification papers as well as trace evidence. If the body is not fingerprinted at the scene, tie paper bags securely on the hands so that fingerprinting can be done at the coroner's laboratory. If possible, place the body in a body bag to ensure that no physical evidence is lost while it is being transported.

Search the area around and beneath where the body lay immediately after it is removed. A bullet may have passed through part of the body and lodged in the floor or the dirt beneath it. Trace evidence may have fallen from the body or clothing as the body was removed. Inventory and describe all items removed from the deceased.

Department policy determines the extent of a search at the scene. Normally a complete examination is delayed until the body is received by the coroner's office. The coroner may take fingernail scrapings, blood and semen samples, and possibly some body organs to establish poisoning or the path of a bullet or knife.

Once the body is taken to a funeral home, its organs and fluids will be contaminated by burial preparation. Once the body is buried, it is a long, difficult legal process to exhume it for further examination. If the body is cremated, obviously no further examination is possible.

Underwater Searches

Underwater searches might involve victim, aircraft, firearm, or vehicle recovery. Keeton (2003a, pp.22–23) observes that underwater investigations demand extensive equipment and highly skilled personnel, noting that the risk to personnel increases "dramatically."

According to Keeton (2003b, p.103), the time frame for underwater investigations may be dictated by depth as well as limited visibility, extreme water temperature, swift currents, and hazardous material conditions. He notes that when investigators locate a victim, their first observations must be concerned with whether they are at a crime scene or an accident scene. Keeton (2003b, p.104) describes the normal body position of a drowning victim as face down and in a semi-fetal position. If divers find a victim underwater whose limbs and fists are straight, this indicates the person may have been killed on land and rigor mortis had set in before the body was submerged.

Keeton (2003c, p.109) describes the Trident Foundation as a valuable resource for underwater searches. This nonprofit organization was created specifically to assist public safety agencies with aquatic investigations and recoveries. The staff includes law enforcement, fire service and military personnel, and industry representatives.

Technology Innovations

Nielsen (p.79) stresses that metal detectors are a necessity in underwater searches—particularly pulse induction metal detectors. These detectors are known for their deep seeking capabilities. Advances in the technology have reduced power requirements, resulting in longer battery life and decreased weight.

Use of Dogs in a Search

"A K9 can be an invaluable resource to a patrol officer," says Petrocelli (p.126). Because of their acute sense of smell, dogs can be trained to track and locate suspects as well as detect certain evidence such as explosives and narcotics. Moore (p.78) reports that humans have about 5 million cells devoted to their sense of smell, compared with a dog's 220 million cells. She says that a dog's sense of smell is so acute that it can detect one drop of blood in 5 quarts of water. Hamilton (p.18) also comments on the value of canines, noting that a dog's sense of smell is 700 times greater than that of humans and that a dog can search a building in 10 minutes, whereas it takes two or three officers an hour to conduct the same search.

Dogs are ideally suited to assist in searching large areas; areas with poor visibility, such as warehouses that may contain thousands of items; or any area with numerous hiding places. According to Moore (p.76): "Dogs can do the work of three people. If you pit machine against dog, the dog can do five times the work of the machine." Moore (p.79) reports that between fiscal years 1993 and 2002, border patrol canine teams found 244,965 concealed people, 3,407,464 pounds of narcotics and other drugs worth more than $2.7 trillion, and more than $42 million in U.S. currency. In addition, using dogs for such purposes lessens the physical risk to investigating officers.

> Dogs can be trained to locate suspects, narcotics, explosives, cadavers, and more.

The use of dogs to sniff out narcotics has been widely publicized. Because narcotics can be concealed in so many different ways, using dogs to locate them has greatly assisted law enforcement officers (Figure 4.10). Attempts to mask drug odors from dogs trained to sniff out drugs are futile because dogs can smell more than one odor simultaneously.

In *Illinois v. Caballes* (2005) the Supreme Court confirmed that a dog sniff was not a search under the Fourth Amendment (Holcomb, 2005b, p.8). A *New York Times* headline declared: "Justices Uphold Use of Drug-Sniffing Dogs in Traffic Stops" (Greenhouse, 2005). Makholm (2005, p.54) explains that in *Cabelles,* the Supreme Court reinforced law enforcement's ability to identify narcotics traffickers and users by using police K-9s and walk-around searches of vehicles stopped for traffic offenses. Devanney (p.12) cautions that although *Cabelles* allows "major new legal freedoms" for law enforcement officers in stop situations, use of a drug-sniffing canine cannot prolong a stop. If this occurs, the dog sniff will become an illegal search.

Paul J. Richards/AFP/Getty Images

Figure 4.10
Specially trained K-9s can
searching for drugs or exp
U.S. Capitol Police dog team searches
motorists passing near the U.S. Capitol
in Washington, DC.

Dogs have also been trained to detect explosives both before and after detonation. Their ability to detect explosives before detonation lessens the risk to officers and can help prevent crimes. A study by the Law Enforcement Assistance Administration and the Federal Aviation Authority demonstrated that dogs can locate explosives twice as often as humans can. In the case of detonated explosives, dogs have helped locate bomb fragments hidden under piles of debris and at considerable distances from the detonation point.

As agents of the police, dogs are subject to the same legal limitations on searches that officers are. Court rulings appear to highlight the benefits of using K-9s to build probable cause to seize and arrest. In *United States v. Place* (1983), the Supreme Court ruled that exposure of luggage located in a public place to a police K-9 sniff was not a search within the meaning of the Fourth Amendment. In essence, such a ruling concedes that the use of dogs may lead to the same end via less intrusive means, thus sparing law enforcement other time-consuming steps required to effect a legal search.

K-9s have also been used to seek out and detain suspects. Courts have ruled that using K-9s can enhance the safety of officers, bystanders, and suspects. Smith (p.18) contends that K-9s should be considered as less-lethal alternatives to the use of deadly force. Guidelines for deploying K-9s are found in *Graham v. Connor* (1989). Before deploying a K-9, a handler should consider the totality of the circumstances and the available information, including the severity of the crime, whether the suspect poses an immediate threat to the safety of officers or others, and whether the suspect is actively resisting arrest or attempting to evade arrest by flight (Smith, p.18). Green (p.39) advises that administrators and trainers should be familiar with case law pertaining to canines and suggests as a resource the website of Terry Fleck (www.k9fleck.org), an expert in canine legalities.

If a police department is not large enough to have or lacks sufficient need for a search dog and trained handler, learn where the nearest trained search dogs are and how they can be obtained if needed. Many major airports have dogs trained to locate explosives and may make these dogs available to police upon request.

SUMMARY

The Fourth Amendment to the Constitution forbids unreasonable searches and seizures. Therefore, investigators must know what constitutes a reasonable, legal search. To search effectively, know the legal requirements for searching, the items you are searching for, and the elements of the crime. Be organized, systematic, and thorough.

A search can be justified if (1) a search warrant has been issued, (2) consent is given, (3) an officer stops a suspicious person and believes the person may be armed, (4) the search is incidental to a lawful arrest, or (5) an emergency exists. Each of these situations has limitations. A search conducted with a warrant must be limited to the area and items specified in the warrant, in accordance with the peculiarity requirement. A search conducted with consent requires that the consent be voluntary and that the search be limited to the area for which the consent was given. The "search" in a stop-and-frisk situation must be limited to a patdown for weapons. The *Terry* decision established that a patdown or frisk is a "protective search for weapons" and as such must be "confined to a scope reasonably designed to discover guns, knives, clubs, and other hidden instruments for the assault of a police officer or others." A search incidental to a lawful arrest must be made simultaneously with the arrest and be confined to the area within the suspect's immediate control (*Chimel*). A warrantless search in the absence of a lawful arrest or consent is justified only in emergencies where probable cause exists, and the search must be conducted immediately.

The most important limitation on any search is that the scope must be narrow; general searches are unconstitutional. If a search is *not* conducted legally, the evidence obtained is worthless. According to the exclusionary rule, evidence obtained in unreasonable search and seizure, regardless of how relevant the evidence may be, is inadmissible in court. *Weeks v. United States* established the exclusionary rule at the federal level; *Mapp v. Ohio* made it applicable to all courts.

A successful crime scene search locates, identifies, and preserves all evidence present. For maximum effectiveness, a search must be well organized. This entails dividing the duties, selecting a search pattern, assigning personnel and equipment, and giving instructions. Knowing what to search for is indispensable to an effective search. Anything material and relevant to the crime might be evidence.

Search patterns have been developed that help to ensure a thorough search. Exterior search patterns divide an area into lanes, strips, concentric circles, or zones. Interior searches go from the general to the specific, usually in a circular pattern that covers all surfaces of the area being searched. The floor is searched first.

In addition to crime scenes, investigators frequently search vehicles, suspects, and dead bodies. When searching a vehicle, remove the occupants from the car. First search the area around the vehicle, then the vehicle's exterior. Finally, search the interior along one side from front to back and then return along the other side to the front. Vehicles may be searched without a warrant if there is probable cause and if the vehicle would be gone before a search warrant could be obtained (*Carroll*). *Chambers v. Maroney* established that a vehicle may be taken to headquarters to be searched in certain circumstances.

When searching a suspect who has not been arrested, confine the search to a patdown for weapons (*Terry*). If the suspect has been arrested, conduct a complete body search for weapons and evidence. Always be on your guard. Search a dead body systematically and completely; include the immediate area around and under the body. Specially trained dogs can be very helpful in locating suspects, narcotics, or explosives.

CHECKLIST

The Search

- Is the search legal?
- Was a pattern followed?
- Was all evidence photographed, recorded in the notes, identified, and packaged properly?
- Was the search completed even if evidence was found early in the search?
- Were all suspects searched?
- Did more than one investigator search?
- Was plain-view evidence seized? If so, were the circumstances recorded?

DISCUSSION QUESTIONS

1. Why do you suppose the Fourth Amendment was written?
2. What are the advantages of having several officers search a crime scene? What are the disadvantages?
3. What are the steps in obtaining a search warrant?
4. What procedure is best for searching a suspect?
5. Many court decisions regarding police involve the question of legal searches. What factors are considered in the legal search of a person, a private

dwelling, abandoned property, a business building, a car, or corporate offices?

6. What basic steps constitute a thorough search of a dwelling?

7. Should there be legal provisions for an officer to seize evidence without a warrant if the evidence may be destroyed or removed before a warrant can be obtained?

8. Under what circumstances are police authorized to conduct no-knock searches?

9. Imagine that you are assigned to search a tavern at 10 A.M. for illegal gambling devices. Twenty patrons plus the bartender are in the tavern, but the owner is not present. How would you execute the search warrant?

10. Police officers frequently stop vehicles for traffic violations. Under the plain-view doctrine, what evidence may be taken during such a stop? May the officers search the vehicle? the driver? the occupants?

MEDIA EXPLORATIONS

Internet

Select one assignment to complete.

1. Using Google, search for one of these key terms: *exclusionary rule, fruit-of-the-poisonous-tree doctrine, inevitable-discovery doctrine,* or *plain-view evidence.* Select one article and outline it to share with the class.

2. Using Google, search for *Terry v. Ohio.* Select one article and outline it to share with the class.

3. Go to the FBI website at www.fbi.gov/programs/lab/handbook/intro.htm to view the *Handbook of Forensic Services.* Outline the chapter on the crime scene search.

Crime and Evidence in Action

Select one of three criminal case scenarios and sign in for your shift. Your Mobile Data Terminal (MDT) will get you started and update you throughout the case. During the course of the case you'll become a patrol officer, detective, prosecutor, defense attorney, judge, corrections officer, or parole officer to conduct interactive investigative research. Each case unfolds as you respond to key decision points. Feedback for each possible answer choice is packed full of information, including term definitions, web links, and important documentation. The sergeant is available at certain times to help mentor you, the Online Resources website offers a variety of information, and be sure to take notes in your e-notebook during the suspect video statements and at key points throughout (these notes can be saved, printed, or e-mailed). The interactive Forensics Tool Kit will test your ability to collect, transport, and analyze evidence from the crime scene. At the end of the case you can track how well you responded to each decision point and join the Discussion Forum for a postmortem. **Go to the CD and use the skills you've learned to solve a case.**

REFERENCES

Cerullo, Rob, and Means, Randy. "U.S. Supreme Court Sharpens Police Drug-Fighting Tools." *The Police Chief,* February 2004, pp. 10–12.

Clark, M. Wesley. "U.S. Land Border Search Authority." *FBI Law Enforcement Bulletin,* August 2004, pp. 22–32.

Connor, Gregory. "Street Critique: Investigative Detentions." *The Law Enforcement Trainer,* Jan/Feb/March 2005, pp. 40–41.

"Court Allows Routine Search of Vehicle Fuel Tank at Border." *Criminal Justice Newsletter,* April 15, 2004, pp. 6–7.

Devanney, Joe. "Supreme Court: 'Sniff Search' Permissible." *Law and Order,* April 2005, pp. 12–14.

Devanney, Joe, and Devanney, Diane. "An Analysis of the Knock and Announce Rule." *Tactical Response,* Spring 2003, pp. 72–74.

Devanney, Joe, and Devanney, Diane. "Supreme Court Rules in Roadblock Case." *Law and Order,* May 2004, p. 20.

Freeborg, Stacy. "Heat Seekers." *Minnesota Business,* October 2003, pp. 28–75.

Garner, Gerald W. "Search Patterns." *Police,* May 2003a, pp. 44–50.

Garner, Gerald W. "Structure Searches." *Police,* September 2003b, pp. 62–64.

Geberth, Vernon. "Considerations for Crime Scene Investigation." *Law and Order,* May 2003, pp. 46–51.

Ginn, Beverly A. "Stop-and-Identify Laws." *The Police Chief,* September 2004, pp. 10–11.

Grasso, John. "Failure to Identify to Police." *Law and Order,* January 2005, pp. 27–28.

Green, Bernie. "Well Trained and Reliable Canine." *Law and Order,* April 2004, pp. 38–40.

Greenhouse, Linda. "Justices Uphold Use of Drug-Sniffing Dogs in Traffic Stops." *New York Times,* January 25, 2005.

Hamilton, Melanie. "How to . . . Start a Canine Unit." *Police,* 2003, pp. 18–23.

Hatch, Mike. "Drafting Search Warrants." *Minnesota Police Chief,* Spring 2003, pp. 11–15.

Hendrie, Edward M. "Consent Once Removed." *FBI Law Enforcement Bulletin*, February 2003, pp. 24–32.

Holcomb, Jayme Walker. "Obtaining Written Consent to Search." *FBI Law Enforcement Bulletin*, March 2003, pp. 26–32.

Holcomb, Jayme Walker. "Consent Searches Scope." *FBI Law Enforcement Bulletin*, February 2004, pp. 22–32.

Holcomb, Jayme Walker. "Revoking Consent to Search." *FBI Law Enforcement Bulletin*, February 2005a, pp. 25–32.

Holcomb, Jayme Walker. "Supreme Court Confirms Drug Sniff of Car During a Traffic Stop Is Not a Fourth Amendment Search." *The Police Chief*, March 2005b, pp. 8–9.

Holtz, Larry E. "Roadside Checkpoints and Crime Control." *Law Enforcement Technology*, September 2003a, p. 146.

Holtz, Larry E. "Warrantless Entries." *Law Enforcement Technology*, February 2003b, p. 110.

Hopper, Joan. "Waiting. . . The Knock and Announce Statute." *Law and Order*, October 2003, pp. 169–173.

Hopper, Joan. "Every Second Counts to the U.S. Supreme Court." *Law and Order*, January 2004, pp. 22–24.

Hunsucker, Keith. "Right to Be, Right to See: Practical Fourth Amendment Application for Law Enforcement Officers." *The Police Chief*, September 2003, pp. 10–13.

Keeton, Doyle. "Diving In." *Law Enforcement Technology*, June 2003a, pp. 22–30.

Keeton, Doyle. "Human Remains Underwater." *Law Enforcement Technology*, July 2003b, pp. 102–108.

Keeton, Doyle. "A Partnership for Investigative Success." *Law and Order*, June 2003c, pp. 109–112.

Lane, Charles. "Supreme Court Backs Speedy Forced Entry in Drug Investigations." *Washington Post* as reported in the (Minneapolis/St. Paul) *Star Tribune*, December 3, 2003, p. A19.

Makholm, John A. "Legal Lights." *The Law Enforcement Trainer*, January/February 2004, pp. 64–65.

Makholm, John A. "Legal Lights." *The Law Enforcement Trainer*, Jan/Feb/March 2005, pp. 54–55.

Moore, Carole. "Who Let the Dogs Out?" *Law Enforcement Technology*, September 2004, pp. 74–80.

Nielsen, Eugene. "Metal Detectors at the Crime Scene." *Law and Order*, December 2003, pp. 78–81.

Petrocelli, Joseph. "Patrol Response to a K9 Deployment." *Law and Order*, November 2004, p. 126.

Risher, Julie A. "New U.S. Supreme Court Decision Approves 'Informational' Checkpoint." *The Police Chief*, March 2004, pp. 10–12.

Rutledge, Devallis. "Incident to Arrest." *Police*, July 2004a, pp. 140–142.

Rutledge, Devallis. "Knock before Entry." *Police*, February 2004b, pp. 74–75.

Rutledge, Devallis. "Stop and Identify." *Police*, October 2004c, pp. 74–76.

Rutledge, Devallis. "Holding Back Home Occupants." *Police*, May 2005, pp. 72–75.

Shinder, Deborah Littlejohn. "Understanding Legal Issues." *Law and Order*, December 2003, pp. 38–44.

Smith, Brad. "K9 Use of Force Case Law." *Tactical Response*, Summer 2004, pp. 18–21.

Spector, Elliot B. "How Long to Wait?" *Tactical Response*, Fall 2004, pp. 66–72.

Stephen, John A. "Knock and Talk." *Police*, January 2003, pp. 64–67.

Woessner, Matthew C., and Sims, Barbara. "Technological Innovation and the Application of the Fourth Amendment." *Journal of Contemporary Criminal Justice*, May 2003, pp. 224–238.

Worrall, John L. "Why the Supreme Court Has Not Laid the Thermal-Imaging Debate to Rest." May 2003, pp. 203–223.

CASES CITED

Adams v. Williams, 407 U.S. 143 (1972)

Aguilar v. Texas, 378 U.S. 108 (1964)

Alabama v. White, 496 U.S. 235,329 (1990)

Boyd v. United States, 116 U.S. 616 (1886)

Brown v. Texas, 443 U.S. 47, 99 (1979)

California v. Greenwood, 486 U.S. 35 (1988)

Carroll v. United States, 267 U.S. 132 (1925)

Chambers v. Maroney, 399 U.S. 42 (1970)

Chimel v. California, 395 U.S. 752 (1969)

City of Indianapolis v. Edmond, 531 U.S. 32, 41 (2000)

Florida v. Jimeno, 499 U.S. 934 (1990)

Florida v. J. L., 529 U.S. 266 (2000)

Graham v. Connor, 109 S.Ct. 1865 (1989)

Hiibel v. Sixth Judicial District Court of Nevada, Humboldt County, 124 S.Ct. 2451 (2004)

Illinois v. Caballes, 2005 W: 123826 (2005)

Illinois v. Gates, 462 U.S. 213 (1983)

Illinois v. Lidster, 124 S.Ct. 885 (2004)

Illinois v. McArthur, 121 S.Ct. 946 (2001)

Johnson v. United States, 333 U.S. 10 (1948)

Katz v. United States, 389 U.S. 347, 351 (1967)

Knowles v. Iowa, 525 U.S. 113 (1998)

Kyllo v. United States, 121 S.Ct. 2038 (2001)

Mapp v. Ohio, 367 U.S. 643 (1961)

Maryland v. Buie, 494 U.S. 325 (1990)

Michigan v. Sitz, 496 U.S. 444, 455 (1990)

Michigan v. Summers, 452 U.S. 692 (1981)

Michigan v. Tyler, 436 U.S. 499 (1978)

Mincey v. Arizona, 437 U.S. 385 (1978)

Minnesota v. Dickerson, 508 U.S. 336 (1993)

New York v. Belton, 453 U.S. 454 (1981)

New York v. Quarles, 467 U.S. 649 (1984)

Nix v. Williams, 467 U.S. 431 (1984)

Richards v. Wisconsin, 520 U.S. 385 (1997)

Schneckloth v. Bustamonte, 412 U.S. 218 (1973)

Spinelli v. United States, 393 U.S. 410 (1969)

Stanford v. Texas, 380 U.S. 926 (1965)

State v. Woodall, 385 S.E.2d 253, W.Va. (1989)

Terry v. Ohio, 392 U.S. 1 (1968)

Thornton v. United States, 124 S.Ct. 2127 (2004)

United States v. Banks, 124 S.Ct. 521 (2003)

United States v. Drayton, 2002 WL 1305729 (June 17, 2002)

United States v. Dunn, 818 F.2d 742 (10th Cir. 1987)

United States v. Flores-Montano, No. 02-1793 (2004)

United States v. Henry, 447 U.S. 264 (1958)

United States v. Hensley, 469 U.S. 221 (1985)

United States v. Leon, 468 U.S. 897 (1984)

United States v. Lueck, 678 F.2d 895, 903 (11th Cir. 1982)

United States v. Martinez-Fuerte, 428 U.S. 543 (1976)

United States v. Place, 462 U.S. 696 (1983)

Weeks v. United States, 232 U.S. 383 (1914)

Wilson v. Arkansas, 514 U.S. 927 (1995)

Wyoming v. Houghton, 526 U.S. 295 (1999)

CHAPTER 5

Forensics/Physical Evidence

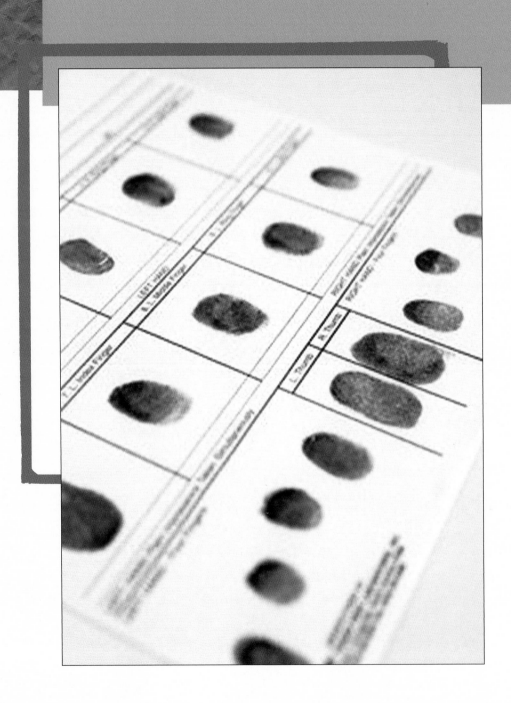

Can You Define?

Do You Know?

- What is involved in processing physical evidence?
- How to determine what is evidence?
- What the common errors in collecting evidence are?
- How to identify evidence?
- What to record in your notes?
- How to package evidence?
- How to convey evidence to a department or a laboratory?
- How and where evidence is stored?
- How to ensure admissibility of physical evidence in court?
- How physical evidence is finally disposed of?
- What types of evidence are most commonly found in criminal investigations and how to collect, identify, and package each?
- What can and cannot be determined from fingerprints, DNA, bloodstains, and hairs?
- What DNA profiling is?

Outline

M odern forensic science dates back to 1910 and the "exchange principle" set forth by French criminologist Edmond Locard. As explained in Chapter 1, *Locard's exchange principle* states that whenever two objects come in contact with each other (e.g., a criminal and an object or objects at a crime scene), there is always a transfer of information, however minute, between them. In other words, a criminal always removes something from the crime scene and leaves behind incriminating evidence. The remnants of this transfer are called **proxy data,** the evidence analyzed by forensic scientists to uncover the relationships between people, places, and objects.

A primary purpose of an investigation is to locate, identify, and preserve **evidence**—data on which a judgment or conclusion may be based. Evidence is used for determining the facts in a case, for later laboratory examination, and for direct presentation in court. **Best evidence,** in the legal sense, is the original evidence or highest available degree of proof that can be produced. Investigators should be cognizant throughout an investigation of the best-evidence rule, which stipulates that the original evidence is to be presented in court whenever possible. Other factors pertaining to admissibility of evidence will be discussed later in the chapter.

This chapter begins with some basic definitions, followed by a discussion of investigative equipment. Next the chapter describes how to avoid contaminating the crime scene as well as how to process evidence, beginning with discovering or recognizing evidence; collecting, identifying, and recording it; packaging, conveying, and storing it; exhibiting it in court; and disposing of it when it is no longer needed. This is followed by a discussion of frequently examined evidence including fingerprints; voiceprints; language; DNA; blood and other body fluids; scent; hairs and fibers; shoe and tire impressions; bite marks; tools and tool marks; firearms and ammunition; glass; soils and minerals; safe insulation; ropes, strings, and tapes; drugs; bioterror agents; documents; laundry and dry-cleaning marks; paint; skeletal remains; and wood. The chapter concludes with a look at handling evidence while avoiding exposure to infectious disease.

Definitions

Evidence is generally categorized as one of four types: testimonial, documentary, demonstrative, or physical. *Testimonial evidence* is information obtained through interviewing and interrogating individuals about what they saw (eyewitness evidence), heard (hearsay evidence), or know (character evidence). Testimonial evidence is the subject of Chapter 6. *Documentary evidence* typically includes written material, audio recordings, and videos. *Demonstrative evidence* includes mockups and scale models of objects or places related to the crime scene and helps juries visualize more clearly what they are unable to view personally. Occasionally, however, juries are taken to the crime scene if the judge deems it vital to the fair processing of the case, but this is expensive and time-consuming. Most commonly, investigators deal with physical evidence. **Physical evidence** is anything real—i.e., which has substance—that helps to establish the facts of a case. It can be seen, touched, smelled, or tasted; is solid, semisolid, or liquid; and can be large or tiny (Figure 5.1). It may be at an immediate crime scene or miles away; it may also be on a suspect or a victim.

Some evidence ties one crime to a similar crime or connects one suspect with another. Evidence can also provide new leads when a case appears to be unsolvable. Further, evidence corroborates statements from witnesses to or victims of a crime. Convictions are not achieved from statements, admissions, or confessions alone. A crime must be proven by independent investigation and physical evidence (Figure 5.2).

For example, in a small western town, a 6-year-old girl and her parents told police the girl had been sexually molested. The girl told police that a man had taken her to the desert, had shown her some "naughty" pictures that he burned, and had then molested her. Because it was difficult for the police to rely on the girl's statement, they needed physical evidence to corroborate her story. Fortunately, the girl remembered where the man had taken her and led the police there. They found remains of the burned pictures and confiscated them as evidence. The remains of one picture, showing the suspect with a naked young girl on his lap, were sufficient to identify

Figure 5.1
A forensic laboratory technician prepares a blood sample for DNA analysis.

AP/Wide World Photos

Figure 5.2
David Coffman of the Florida Department of Law Enforcement shows how the agency's high-tech DNA database allows investigators to search for DNA matches.

him by the rings on his fingers. This physical evidence supporting the girl's testimony resulted in a charge of lewdness with a minor.

Physical evidence can be classified in different ways. One common classification is direct and indirect evidence. **Direct evidence** establishes proof of a fact without any other evidence. **Indirect evidence** merely *tends* to incriminate a person—for instance, a suspect's footprints found near the crime scene. Indirect evidence is also called **circumstantial evidence,** or evidence from which inferences are drawn. A popular myth is that circumstantial evidence will not stand alone without other facts to support it, but many convictions have been obtained primarily on circumstantial evidence.

Extremely small items, such as hair or fibers, are a subset of direct evidence called **trace evidence.** Evidence established by law is called *prima facie* **evidence.** For example, 0.8 percent ethanol in the blood is direct or *prima facie* evidence of intoxication in some states. **Associative evidence** links a suspect with a crime. Associative evidence includes fingerprints, footprints, bloodstains, hairs, and fibers.

Corpus delicti evidence establishes that a crime has been committed. Contrary to popular belief, the **corpus delicti** ("body of the crime") in a murder case is not the dead body but the fact that death resulted from a criminal act. Corpus delicti evidence supports the elements of the crime. Pry marks on an entry door are corpus delicti evidence in a burglary.

Probative evidence is vital to the investigation or prosecution of a case, tending to prove or actually proving guilt or innocence. Also of extreme importance to the investigator is *exculpatory evidence,* discussed in Chapter 1, which is physical evidence that clears one of blame—for example, having a blood type different from that of blood found at a murder scene.

Material evidence forms a substantive part of the case or has a legitimate and effective influence on the decision of the case. **Relevant evidence** applies to the matter in question. **Competent evidence** has been properly collected, identified, filed, and continuously secured.

To locate and properly process evidence at a crime scene, investigators must have the necessary tools and equipment.

Investigative Equipment

Frontline police personnel who conduct a preliminary investigation need specific equipment to accomplish their assigned tasks. Although not all crime scenes require all items of equipment, you cannot predict the nature of the next committed crime or the equipment you will need. Therefore, you should have available at all times a crime scene investigation kit containing basic equipment. Check the kit's equipment after each use, replacing items as required.

Investigations can be simple or complex and can reveal little or much physical evidence. Consequently, the equipment needs of each investigation are different. Table 5.1, alphabetized for easy reference, contains the investigative equipment most often used.

Although the list may seem extensive, numerous other items are also often used in investigations: bags, binoculars, blankets, brushes, bullhorns, cable, capsules, chains, checklists, chemicals, chisels, coat hangers (to hang up wet or bloodstained clothing), combs, cotton, cutters, directories, drug kits, eyedroppers, files, fixatives, flares or fuses, floodlamps, forceps, forms, gas masks, generators, gloves, guns, hammers, hatchets, levels, lights, magnets, manuals, maps, matches, metal detectors, moulages (for making impressions or casts), nails, padlocks, pails, plastic sheets, punches, putty, rags, receipts, rubber, saws, scrapers, shovels, sidecutters, solvent, sponges, sprays, stamps, swabs, syringes, tape, tape recorders, thermometers, tin snips, towels, transceivers (to communicate in large buildings, warehouses, apartment complexes, or open areas), vacuums, wax, wire, and wrenches. The blood-test kits, gun-residue kits, and other field-test kits described in Chapter 1 are also used.

Newer, more specialized equipment for investigation may also include pagers, cellular phones, latex gloves, goggles, metal detectors, electronic tracking systems, digital voice recorders, camcorders, and much more, discussed throughout this section. Many departments are able to use forfeiture assets confiscated during drug busts and other law enforcement efforts to purchase specialized investigative equipment. Additional heavy-duty, less-portable equipment such as large pry bars or long ladders are frequently found on fire and

Table 5.1 / **Equipment for Processing Evidence**

Item	Uses
Cameras and film*	(Whatever type is available; perhaps several types) To photograph scene and evidence
Chalk and chalk line	To mark off search areas; to outline bodies or objects removed from the scene
Compass*	To obtain directions for report orientation and searches
Containers	(Boxes, bags of all sizes and shapes; lightweight plastic or paper; telescoping or collapsible glass bottles and new paint containers) To contain all types of evidence
Crayon or magic marker	To mark evidence
Envelopes, all sizes	To collect evidence
Fingerprint kit	(Various developing powders, fingerprint camera, fingerprint cards, ink pads, spoons, iodine fumer tube, lifting tape) To develop latent fingerprints
First-aid kit	To treat injured persons at the crime scene
Flashlight and batteries	To search dark areas, such as tunnels, holes, wells, windowless rooms; to search for latent fingerprints
Knife	To cut ropes, string, stakes, etc.
Labels, all sizes	(Evidence labels; labels such as "do not touch," "do not open," "handle with care," "fragile") To label evidence and to provide directions
Magnifier	To locate fingerprints and minute evidence
Measuring tape, steel	To measure long distances
Mirror with collapsible handle	To look in out-of-the-way locations for evidence
Money	To pay fares in case of vehicle failure, to tip, to purchase small amounts of needed supplies
Notebook*	To record information
Paper*	(Notebook, graph, scratch pads, wrapping) To take notes, sketch scene, wrap evidence
Pencils*	(At least two; sharpened) To make sketches
Pens*	(At least two; nonsmudge type) To take notes, make sketches

rescue vehicles and can be used jointly by the police and fire departments.

Selecting Equipment

Survey the types of crimes and evidence most frequently found at crime scenes in your jurisdiction. Select equipment to process and preserve the evidence you are most likely to encounter. For example, because fingerprints are often found at crime scenes, fingerprint-processing equipment should be included in the basic kit. However, you would probably not need to take a shovel along to investigate a rape.

After the basic equipment needs are identified, select specific equipment that is frequently needed, lightweight, compact, high quality, versatile, and reasonably priced. For example, boxes should either nest or be collapsible. Containers should be lightweight and plastic. The lighter and smaller the equipment, the more items can be carried in the kit. Consider miniaturized electronic equipment rather than heavier, battery-operated items. Select equipment that accomplishes more than one function, such as a knife with many features or other multipurpose tools.

Equipment Containers

The equipment can be put into one container or divided into several containers, based on frequency of use. This is an administrative decision determined by each department's needs. Dividing equipment results in a compact, lightweight kit suitable for most crime scenes while ensuring availability of other equipment needed to investigate less common cases.

Carriers or containers come in all shapes, sizes, colors, and designs. Briefcases, attaché cases, and transparent plastic bags are convenient to use. Some commercially produced kits include basic equipment. However, many departments prefer to design their own kits, adapted to their specific needs. The container should look professional, and a list of its contents should be attached to the outside or inside the cover.

Table 5.1 / *continued*

Item	Uses
Picks	(Door lock picks and ice picks) To use as thumbtacks; to hold one end of a rope or tape
Plaster	To make casts of tire treads and footprints
Pliers	To pry and twist; to obtain evidence
Protractor	To measure angles
Rope	(Fluorescent, lightweight, approximately 300 feet) To protect the crime scene
Ruler, carpenter-type*	To measure short distances
Ruler, straightedge*	To measure small items/distances
Scissors	To cut tapes, reproduce size of objects in paper, cut first-aid gauze
Screwdrivers, standard and Phillips	To turn and pry
Scribe	To mark metal objects for evidence
Sketching supplies*	(Ruler, pencil, graph paper, etc.) To make sketches
Spatula	To dig; to stir
String	To tie objects and boxes containing evidence; to protect the crime scene; to mark off search areas
Tags	To attach to items of evidence
Templates	To aid in sketching
Tongue depressors, wooden	To stir; to add reinforcements to plaster casts; to make side forms for casting; to lift objects without touching them
Tubes, glass, with stoppers	To contain evidence
Tweezers	To pick up evidence without contamination
Wrecking bar	To pry open doors, windows, entryways, or exits

*The use of these items has been discussed earlier in the text (see Chapter 2).

continued

Transporting Equipment

Crime scene investigative equipment is transported in a police vehicle, an investigator's vehicle, or a crime van. The equipment can be transported in the trunk of a car, or a vehicle can be modified to carry it. For example, special racks can be put in the trunk, or the rear seat can be removed and special racks installed. Investigators are advised, when storing equipment in a car trunk, to organize items laterally (side to side) instead of longitudinally (front to back), for if the car is involved in a high-speed rear-end collision, equipment oriented front-to-back can puncture through the back seat of the car or rupture the fuel tank (*Law and Order* Staff, p.52).

A mobile crime lab is usually a commercially customized van that provides compartments to hold equipment and countertops for processing evidence. However, a van cannot go directly to some crime scenes, so the equipment must be transported from the van in other containers. The most frequently used equipment should be in the most accessible locations in the vehicle.

Substances that freeze or change consistency in temperature extremes should be protected (Figure 5.3).

All selected vehicles should be equipped with radio communication and be capable of conveying equipment to disaster scenes as well as to crime scenes—to make them cost-effective. Cost-effectiveness can be further enhanced if the vehicles are available as command posts, for stakeouts, and as personnel carriers.

Regardless of whether you work with a fully equipped mobile crime laboratory or a small, portable crime scene investigation kit, your knowledge and skills as an investigator are indispensable to a successful investigation. The most sophisticated, expensive investigative equipment available is only as effective as you are in using it.

Training in Equipment Use

The largest failure in gathering evidence is not the equipment available but lack of training in using it effectively. Each officer should understand the use and

Figure 5.3
This all-purpose investigation kit was designed for general crime investigation. It contains materials for lifting and developing fingerprints, along with a variety of specialized tools for gathering and storing evidence.

operation of each item of equipment in the kit. Expertise comes with training and experience. Periodic refresher sessions should be held to update personnel on new techniques, equipment, and administrative decisions.

Once investigators have the proper equipment and are competent in using it, they are ready to begin finding and processing evidence. Before actually stepping into the crime scene to process evidence, however, it is vitally important that investigators protect the integrity of the scene to keep it from becoming contaminated.

Crime Scene Integrity and Contamination of Evidence

The value of evidence is directly affected by what happens to it immediately following the crime. Evidence in an unprotected crime scene will degrade, diminish, or disappear over time unless collected and preserved. Recalling Locard's principle of exchange, Houck (p.128) observes: "Once criminal activity has stopped, any transfers that take place may be considered contamination, that is, an undesired transfer of information between items of evidence." In fact, the very act of collecting evidence, no matter how

carefully done, will result in a postcrime transfer of material—**contamination.**

To minimize contamination of a crime scene and the evidence within, cordon off the area and keep all unnecessary people, including police officers, outside the scene perimeter. Regarding those law enforcement officers who cruise through a scene out of curiosity, Moore (p.130) states:

> All those feet trampling through the room or the field, obliterating clues, adding to the trace evidence at a scene and distracting the officers who are working it from their jobs, combine to add an unnecessary challenge to your investigation.
>
> One way to discourage "rubbernecking cops" is to station a couple of patrol officers at the point of entry on a scene and hand them clipboards. Tell them to write down the names of every person who enters and exits, and note the times. Have them let the offending officers know that the information will be sent to the district attorney's office when and if the case goes to trial. Everyone who walks through the crime scene can be added to the list of witnesses subpoenaed to court.

Make sure that evidence does not lose its value— its integrity—because of a contaminated crime scene. **Integrity of evidence** refers to the requirement that any item introduced in court must be in the same condition as when it was found at the crime scene. This is documented by the **chain of evidence,** also called the **chain of custody:** documentation of what has happened to the evidence from the time it was discovered until it is needed in court, including every person who has had custody of the evidence and why.

The value of evidence may also be compromised by improper collection, handling, or identification. Therefore, investigators' evidence processing skills are extremely important.

Processing Evidence: From Discovery to Disposal

 imply collecting physical evidence is not enough. To be of value, the evidence must be legally seized and properly and legally processed. Of importance at this point is **processing evidence** correctly. This includes discovering or recognizing evidence; collecting, recording, and identifying it; packaging, conveying, and storing it; examining it; exhibiting it in court; and disposing of it when the case is closed (Figure 5.4).

Figure 5.4
Evidence at a crime scene must be properly identified, collected, and preserved to be of value. Crime scene tape helps protect the area from contamination or the destruction or removal of evidence. Here, investigators walk between police lines January 17, 2001, in front of the wreakage of a tractor-trailer truck that burned after crashing into the southern entrance of the California State Capitol building late January 16. The driver of the truck was killed in the crash. Although not entirely sure, police officials believe the crash was intentional and are treating the area as a crime scene.

 Processing physical evidence includes discovering or recognizing it; collecting, recording, and identifying it; packaging, conveying, and storing it; examining it; exhibiting it in court; and disposing of it when the case is closed.

Discovering or Recognizing Evidence

During the search of a crime scene, it is often difficult to determine immediately what is or might be evidence. Numerous objects are present, and obviously not all are evidence.

 To determine what is evidence, first consider the apparent crime. Then look for any objects unrelated or foreign to the scene, unusual in location or number, or damaged or broken or whose relation to other objects suggests a pattern that fits the crime.

The importance of physical evidence depends on its ability to establish that a crime was committed and to show how, when, and by whom. Logic and experience help investigators determine the relative value of physical evidence. Evidence in its original state is more valuable than altered or damaged evidence.

Probabilities play a large role in determining the value of evidence. Fingerprints and DNA, for example, provide positive identification. In contrast, blood type

does *not* provide positive identification, but it can help eliminate a person as a suspect.

An object's individuality is also important. For example, a heel mark's value is directly proportional to the number of its specific features, such as brand name, number of nails, and individual wear patterns that can be identified. Some objects have identification marks on them. Other evidence requires a *comparison* to be of value—a tire impression matching a tire, a bullet matching a specific revolver, a torn piece of clothing matching a shirt.

A **standard of comparison** is an object, measure, or model with which evidence is compared to determine whether both came from the same source. Fingerprints are the most familiar example of evidence requiring a standard of comparison. A fingerprint found at a crime scene must be matched with a known print to be of value. Likewise, a piece of glass found in a suspect's coat pocket can be compared with glass collected from a window pane broken during a burglary.

Sometimes how an object fits with the surroundings determines whether it is likely to be evidence. For example, a man's handkerchief found in a women's locker room does not fit. The same handkerchief in a men's locker room is less likely to be evidence.

Sometimes, to detect evidence, the human eye needs assistance. Tools and techniques available to enhance evidence detection include forensic light sources and three-dimensional (3-D) technology.

Forensic Light Sources Forensic light sources (FLSs), also called alternative light sources (ALSs), are becoming

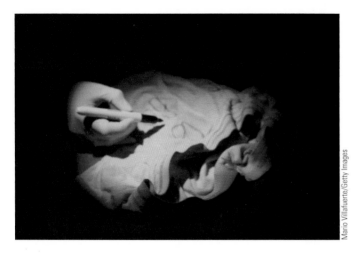

Mario Villafuerte/Getty Images

Figure 5.5

Forensic light sources help investigators find hard-to-see crime scene evidence. Here, an alternative light source is used to detect samples of semen and vaginal fluid on a piece of men's underwear. Forensic DNA investigation contributed to the identification, capture, and conviction of Derrick Todd Lee, who is currently on Louisiana's death row for one of the seven murders he has been linked to through DNA. Lee is also suspected in several other unsolved homicides.

increasingly popular and easier to use (Figure 5.5). An FLS that works on the principle of ultraviolet fluorescence, infrared luminescence, or laser light can make evidence visible that is not otherwise detectable to the naked eye, such as latent prints, body fluids, and even altered signatures.

Ultraviolet (UV) light is the invisible energy at the violet end of the color spectrum that causes substances to emit visible light, commonly called *fluorescence.* Evidence that fluoresces, or glows, is easier to see—sometimes thousands of times easier. For some kinds of hard-to-see evidence—small amounts of semen, for instance, or fibers—an FLS is the only practical way to make the invisible visible. An inexpensive tool for investigators projects a filtered light beam onto evidence dusted with fluorescent powder, and a luminescent print appears immediately. A portable long-wave UV-light source can illuminate latent prints on several types of objects. Evidence is then exposed to superglue (cyanoacrylate), then stained or dusted. After this it can be viewed under the UV light source.

Thermal imaging is another common forensic light technique. In one case a motorcyclist driving along a highway had shot a trucker. The crime scene was 1.5 miles long, and officers had 14 shell casings to locate. Using a thermal imager, they were able to recover all 14 casings.

The Law Enforcement Thermographers Association (LETA) has approved thermal imaging for search and rescue missions, fugitive searches, perimeter surveillance, vehicle pursuits, flight safety, marine and ground surveillance, structure profiles, disturbed surfaces, and hidden compartments. Thermal imaging is often used

by police to detect heat generated by indoor marijuana-growing operations. However, recall from Chapter 4 that the Supreme Court has ruled that using thermal imaging to view inside a residence is a search under the Fourth Amendment and requires a search warrant.

Forensic 3-D Technology One of the newest tools available to forensic evidence analysts is 3-D technology. Scarborough (2004, pp.80–81) explains: "The unaided human eye perceives approximately 32 of a possible 256 grayscale values. Normal human vision is also unable to distinguish subtle variations in image intensities. . . . Using 3D technology, humans can view the full range of image intensity values contained in the evidence image. With the data visually displayed as topography, all 256 possible values are discernible to the human eye."

Three-dimensional analysis software allows investigators to examine in greater detail bullet and shell casings, fingerprints, bite marks, tool marks, and documents. Hypothesizing on the future of this technology, Scarborough (2004, p.87) states: "3D visualization may be part of the forensic software combination that allows evidence digitally captured at the crime scene to be analyzed in real time from the scene."

Collecting, Marking, and Identifying Evidence

Once evidence is discovered, photograph and sketch it before collecting it. Then, collect and identify all objects that are or may be evidence, leaving the final decision regarding relevance to the prosecutor.

Collecting evidence requires judgment and care. Put liquids in bottles. Protect cartridges and spent bullets with cotton, and put them in small containers. Put other items in appropriate containers to preserve them for later packaging and transporting. The scene of a violent crime should be vacuumed with a machine that has a filter attachment. The vacuumed material can then be placed in an evidence bag and submitted to a crime laboratory.

Be sure to collect an adequate amount of the sample and to obtain standards of comparison, if necessary. Take extreme care to avoid **cross-contamination,** that is, allowing items of evidence to touch one another and thus exchange matter. When using the same tool for several tasks, be certain it is thoroughly cleaned after each use to prevent the transfer of material from one piece of evidence to another.

 Common errors in collecting evidence are (1) not collecting enough of the sample, (2) not obtaining standards of comparison, and (3) not maintaining the integrity of the evidence.

To simplify testimony in court, one officer usually collects evidence and another officer takes notes on the location, description, and condition of each item. The officer collecting evidence enters this information in personal notes or witnesses and initials the notes of the officer assigned to record information. All evidence is identified by the officer who collects it and by any other officer who takes initial custody of it.

 Mark or identify each item of evidence in a way that can be recognized later. Indicate the date and case number as well as your personal identifying mark or initials.

Make your marking easily recognizable and as small as possible—to reduce the possibility of destroying part of the evidence. Mark all evidence as it is collected or received. Do not alter, change, or destroy evidence or reduce its value by the identification marking. Where and how to mark depends on the item. A pen is suitable for some objects. A stylus is used for those that require a more permanent mark that cannot be done with a pen, such as metal boxes, motor parts, and furniture. Other objects can be tagged, labeled, or placed in containers that are then marked and sealed.

 Record in your notes the date and time of collection, where the evidence was found and by whom, the case number, a description of the item, and who took custody.

Evidence descriptions can be computer entered and cross-referenced to current cases in the local jurisdiction and the surrounding area.

Packaging and Preserving Evidence

Careful packaging maintains the evidence in its original state, preventing damage or contamination. Do not mix, or cross-contaminate, evidence. Package each item separately, keeping in mind the specific requirements for that type of evidence. Some evidence is placed in sterile containers. Other types, such as firing-pin impressions or markings on a fatal bullet, are packed to prevent breakage or wrapped in cotton to prevent damage to individual characteristics. Hairs, fibers, and other trace evidence are often placed in paper that is folded so that the evidence cannot fall out. This is called a *druggist fold* (Figure 5.6).

 Package each item separately in a durable container to maintain the integrity of evidence.

Packaging is extremely important. Although sometimes plastic bags are used, few large departments use

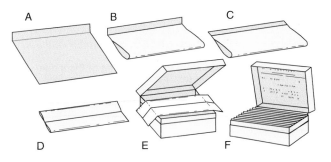

Figure 5.6
The druggist fold

plastic because it does not "breathe" and hence may cause condensation to form. This can impede laboratory examination of the evidence. Many departments use new brown-paper grocery bags, especially for clothing. Although boxes may be better in some respects, they can be impractical to carry and difficult to find. You can usually find a supermarket open somewhere if you run out of bags. Be sure to provide a means of sealing whatever type of container is used to maintain the integrity of the evidence.

Preserve evidence on immovable items at the scene. Often some reproduction of the evidence is made. Fingerprints are developed, photographed, lifted, and later compared. Tool marks are reproduced through photography, modeling clay, moulage, silicone, and other impression-making materials. (These methods are acceptable in accordance with the best-evidence rule.) Specific requirements for the most frequently found evidence and best evidence are discussed later.

Submit movable items directly into evidence or send them to a laboratory for analysis. Sometimes an object is both evidence and a container of evidence. For example, a stolen radio found in a suspect's car is evidence of theft, and the fingerprints of a second suspect found on the radio are evidence that links that person to the theft.

Before packaging evidence for mailing to a laboratory, make sure it was legally obtained and has been properly identified and recorded in your notes. Submitting inadmissible evidence is costly and inefficient. Pack any bulky item in a sturdy box, seal the box with tape, and mark it "evidence." If any latent evidence such as a fingerprint is on the surface of the object (Figure 5.7), be sure to state this clearly.

Place a transmittal letter to the laboratory in an envelope attached to the outside of the box. This letter should contain the name of the suspect and the victim, if any; indicate what examinations are desired and which tests, if any, have already been done; and refer to any other pertinent correspondence or reports. Include a copy of the letter with the evidence, and mail the original separately. Retain a copy for your files. Figure 5.8 shows a sample letter.

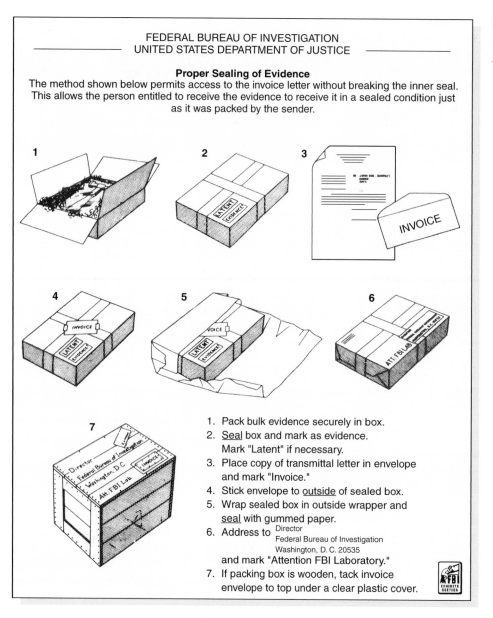

Transporting Evidence

If the crime laboratory is nearby, an officer can deliver the evidence personally. However, even if the evidence is personally delivered, include with it a written request on department letterhead or a department form.

> Personal delivery, registered mail, insured parcel post, air express, Federal Express (FedEx), and United Parcel Service (UPS) are legal ways to transport evidence. Always specify that the person receiving the evidence is to sign for it.

How evidence should be transported depends on its size and type and the distance involved. Use the fastest method available. If the package is mailed, request a return receipt.

Protecting and Storing Evidence

Before, during, and after its examination, evidence must be securely protected and properly stored. Physical evidence is subject to chemical change, negligence, accident, intentional damage, theft, and alteration during handling. With proper storage, however, theft, loss, tampering, contamination, and deterioration may be prevented. Protecting and storing evidence is often the weakest link in the chain of evidence. All too often defendants are found not guilty because evidence in the chain of custody is not documented and cannot be determined.

In addition to being secure, the storage area must be well organized and free from pests, insects, and excessive heat or moisture. A proper storage area has ample space and is climate controlled, typically kept at 65° to

Figure 5.8
Sample letter to the FBI lab
Source: Courtesy of the FBI.

┌─────────────────────────────────┐
│   USE OFFICIAL LETTERHEAD   │
└─────────────────────────────────┘

(Police Headquarters
  Right City, State zip code
  March 17, 20_ _)

Director
Federal Bureau of Investigation
U. S. Department of Justice
Washington, D. C. 20535

ATTENTION: FBI LABORATORY

Dear Director:

RE: GUY PIDGIN, SUSPECT
       EMPALL MERCHANDISE MART
       BURGLARY

Sometime during the early morning of March 16, 20_ _, someone entered the Empall Merchandise Mart through an unlocked side window and made an unsuccessful attempt to rip open the safe. The outer layer of metal on the safe door had been pried loose from the upper right corner and bent outward, ripping the metal along the top and down the side of the safe about 12" each way. The burglar may have been scared away because the job was not completed. Investigation led us to Guy Pidgin, who denies complicity. He voluntarily let us take his shoes and trousers and a crowbar that was under his bed in his rooming house.

I am sending by Federal Express a package containing the following evidence in this case:

1.   One pair of shoes obtained from Guy Pidgin
2.   A pair of grey flannel trousers obtained from Guy Pidgin
3.   One 28" crowbar obtained from Guy Pidgin
4.   Safe insulation taken from door of safe at Empall Merchandise Mart
5.   Piece of bent metal approximately 12" x 12" taken from door of safe at Empall Merchandise Mart. In order to differentiate the two sides cut by us, we have placed adhesive tape on them.
6.   Chips of paint taken from the side of safe
7.   Fingerprint card for Guy Pidgin
8.   Ten transparent lifts

Please examine the shoes and trousers for safe insulation or any paint chips that match the paint taken from the safe. Also, we would be interested to know if you can determine if the crowbar was used to open the safe. Examine items 5 and 8 to determine if latent fingerprints are present. If present, compare with item 7.

This evidence, which should be returned to us, has not been examined by any other expert.

Very truly yours,

James T. Wixling
Chief of Police

75° Fahrenheit. Evidence is stored in vaults, property rooms, evidence rooms, evidence lockers, garages, or morgues or under special conditions such as refrigeration. At a crime scene, an officer's vehicle trunk can provide temporary storage.

Some evidence requires more care than others. Improperly sealed containers can allow liquid evidence to evaporate or moisture to enter. Envelopes can split open. Tags can fall off.

Writing on labels can become smudged, blurred, or faded to the point of illegibility. Therefore, take care to handle evidence gently, keeping it away from moisture and heat sources. Be sure to keep electronic evidence, such as computers and disks, away from strong magnets and other forces that may corrupt the data.

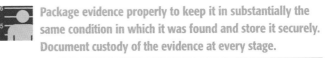

Package evidence properly to keep it in substantially the same condition in which it was found and store it securely. Document custody of the evidence at every stage.

All evidence received is recorded in a register, properly marked, and put in an appropriate place. An evidence custodian checks each piece of evidence to ensure that all forms are properly completed and that the evidence is the same as described in the forms. Figure 5.9 shows a sample evidence card.

Strict checkout procedures ensure that the evidence is always accounted for. Everyone who takes evidence signs for it, giving the date, time, place it is to be taken, and purpose. When the evidence is returned, it is again signed for, dated, and examined to ensure it is in the same condition as when taken. Any change in condition is noted and explained.

Property Management   Barbeau (p.96) stresses: "Evidence is the means to determine the truth about a question of fact during a trial. For effective prosecution, physical evidence can be the most important means to support the basis for a decision by a judge or jury. It is critical, therefore, to have an effective evidence [management] operation." But securing, storing, and tracking evidence is no small task, as Weiss and Davis (p.92) observe: "The evidence room has everything from drugs, money and firearms to bicycles, lawn mowers and clothing. Each article must be accounted for; nothing can be lost or misplaced." Some evidence, such as explosives or biohazardous material, may pose a danger to property room managers, require special training in how to handle, and necessitate specialized facilities and features for safe storage.

Managing the growing mass of evidence is becoming increasingly challenging. For example, a major crime scene investigation might generate 200 or more individual pieces of evidence (Robin and Smith, p.46). The amount of property that must be tracked and stored in metropolitan departments is typically 100,000 to 400,000 or more items. The Palm Beach County (Florida) Sheriff's Office, which operates the thirteenth largest jail facility in the nation, takes in more than 1,700 evidence submissions a month and then must track and store that evidence for a long time, in some cases for five generations, even though only 1 to 2 percent of the evidence ever goes to court (Glass, pp.36–37). Nonetheless, the consequences of mishandling such property can range from public embarrassment to financial liability, criminal charges against the department, and the inadmissibility of key evidence (Kinman, p.28).

To account for so many items accurately and to maintain the chain of custody, each item must be categorized and described, including ownership (rightful, seized, found, etc.). Its location should be documented, as should its disposition (returned, auctioned, burned, etc.).

Automated evidence storage can prevent many problems. Computer programs are available to help manage the property/evidence room. Many property control systems are using bar codes, which are extremely efficient and effective. At the time property is "booked," it is entered into a computer and given a bar code, which is affixed to the item. During any subsequent signing in/out of the property, the chain of custody is updated by scanning the item's evidence bar code into the log. Such a system provides an audit trail, helps with the inventory process, and prints management and audit reports and disposition logs.

BOULDER CITY	EVIDENCE		POLICE DEPT.
DATE 3-12-20_ _		DR. NUMBER #97-1640	
SUSPECT William Vellum		JUV ☐ ADULT ☒	
CHARGE Rape			
LOCATION 1162 Maple Avenue, Boulder City, Nevada			
BOOKED BY (FINDING OFFICER'S SIGNATURE) Alfred Culp		DATE AND TIME	
INITIALS & P. NUMBER OF BOOKING OFFICER			

ARTICLES BOOKED

ITEM a pair of shorts	ITEM NO. 623
ITEM one womens slacks and panties	ITEM NO. 624
ITEM one bed sheet	ITEM NO. 625

INITIALS USED ON ITEMS BOOKED AC	THIS PACKAGE NO.	TOTAL NO. PACKAGES 3
CO-DEFENDANT none		JUV ☐ ADULT ☐
CO-DEFENDANT		JUV ☐ ADULT ☐

CHAIN OF CUSTODY

SIGNATURE	DATE 3-12-20_ _	TIME 1940
SIGNATURE	DATE	TIME
SIGNATURE	DATE	TIME
SIGNATURE	DATE	TIME
SIGNATURE	DATE	TIME
SIGNATURE	DATE	TIME

Figure 5.9
Evidence card

Source: Courtesy of the Boulder City Police Department.

Exhibiting Evidence in Court

Evidence is of little value to a criminal case if it is inadmissible in court. Therefore, adherence to a strict protocol is essential to ensure that evidence may be used during a trial.

> To ensure admissibility of evidence in court, be able to (1) identify the evidence as that found at the crime scene, (2) describe exactly where it was found, (3) establish its custody from discovery to the present, and (4) voluntarily explain any changes that have occurred in the evidence.

Typically, the officer who will identify the evidence in court obtains it from the evidence custodian and delivers it to the prosecuting attorney, who takes it to the courtroom and introduces it at the proper time. The identifying officer uses the notes he or she made at the scene to lay the proper foundation for identifying the evidence.

In addition to the integrity of the evidence itself, consideration should be given to *how* evidence is presented in court. Colwell (p.64) contends: "If the evidence comes to court in a battered cardboard box with the label of a national athletic wear chain on it, the jury draws one conclusion. If, instead, the evidence is transported and sits in the courtroom in a clean, neatly labeled banker's box, quite another conclusion is drawn." Simple details like this can make a difference in jury perception, which, right or wrong, influences the credibility of the prosecution's case.

Frye* and *Daubert Scientific evidence is commonly presented in court as part of either the prosecutor's or the defense's case and is frequently accompanied by expert testimony. When assessing the admissibility of expert opinions based on scientific evidence or knowledge, courts look to the rulings of the *Frye* and *Daubert* cases for guidance. The opinion in *Frye v. United States* (1923) reads, in part:

> Just when a scientific principle or discovery crosses the line between the experimental and demonstrable stages is difficult to define. Somewhere in this twilight zone the evidential force of the principle must be recognized, and while courts will go a long way in admitting expert testimony deduced from a well-recognized scientific principle or discovery, the thing from which the deduction is made must be *sufficiently established to have gained general acceptance in the particular field* in which it belongs [emphasis added].

The merits of *Frye* faced much debate, and the *Frye* test was effectively displaced when the Supreme Court, in *Daubert v. Merrell Dow Pharmaceuticals* (1993), held that the Federal Rules of Evidence, not *Frye*, provide the standard for admitting expert scientific testimony. Within the Rules is specifically R.702, which speaks directly to expert testimony:

> If scientific, technical, or other specialized knowledge will assist the trier of fact to understand the evidence or to determine a fact in issue, a witness qualified as an expert by knowledge, skill, experience, training, or education, may testify thereto in the form of an opinion or otherwise.

In their opinion summary, the Supreme Court stated:

> "General acceptance" is not a necessary precondition to the admissibility of scientific evidence under the Federal Rules of Evidence, but the Rules—especially R.702—do assign to the trial judge the task of ensuring that an expert's testimony both rests on a reliable foundation and is relevant to the task at hand. Pertinent evidence based on scientifically valid principles will satisfy those demands.

This requirement that an expert's testimony be both *reliable* and *relevant* is known as the two-pronged **Daubert standard.**

Final Disposition of Evidence

Evidence must be legally disposed of to prevent major storage problems as well as pilferage or unauthorized conversion to personal use. While state statutes and city ordinances specify *how* to dispose of evidence, most do not specify *when* this should occur. Therefore, departments typically go by the statute of limitations for the type of case when deciding how long to hold items of evidence before disposing of them. Every criminal offense has a statute of limitations except homicide, and these statutes vary from state to state.

In cases involving suspects, arrests, plea bargains, or trials, evidence is held until the case is cleared, at which time personal property may be returned to the rightful owner. In cases in which prosecution is not anticipated, contraband items can be released at any time. In misdemeanor cases where there are no suspects or arrests after one year, the property can generally be returned to the owner, sold, or destroyed. Items of evidence may also be returned or otherwise disposed of because the cases have exceeded the statute of limitations. As a general rule, evidence for felony cases is held three to five years, and evidence in sexual assault cases is retained for five to six years (Glass, p.36). However, when an appeal occurs or is anticipated or the case is a homicide, evidence must be maintained indefinitely.

Furthermore, guidelines for disposing of evidence are changing because of advancing forensic technologies, which are allowing cases to be solved many years after the commission of a crime. For example, Illinois expanded its statute of limitations for sexual assault cases to 25 years because of improvements in DNA analysis technology (Glass, p.36).

> Evidence is either returned to the owner, auctioned, or destroyed.

Evidence is either disposed of continuously, annually, or on a special date. Departments using computerized evidence management programs can generate routine inventory reports that show the status of each case and whether the related evidence must be maintained or can be disposed of. Departments without such a system must manually review the status of items and then either return them as evidence to storage or dispose of them. Witnessed affidavits of disposal list all items sold, destroyed, or returned. The affidavits include the date, type of disposition, location, and names of all witnesses to the disposition.

Having explored the path evidence generally takes during the course of an investigation, the discussion now turns to the most common types of evidence encountered and how they are examined.

Frequently Examined Evidence

The laboratory analyzes evidence associated with the physical characteristics of suspects using biometrics. **Biometrics** is the statisti-

cal study of biological data, which allows for positive identification of individuals. Biometric identification technology ranges from fingerprints to techniques that recognize voices, hand geometry, facial characteristics, and even blood vessels in the iris of an eye. In terms of relative error rates, fingerprints and iris recognition are considered most reliable, followed by facial and hand, with voice the least reliable.

The lab also analyzes the class and individual characteristics of objects providing evidence. **Class characteristics** are the features that place an item into a specific category. For example, the size and shape of a tool mark may indicate that the tool used was a screwdriver rather than a pry bar. **Individual characteristics** are the features that distinguish one item from another of the same type. For example, chips and wear patterns in the blade of a screwdriver may leave marks that are distinguishable from those of any other screwdriver.

> Frequently examined physical evidence includes fingerprints; voiceprints; language; DNA; blood and other body fluids; scent; hairs and fibers; shoe and tire impressions; bite marks; tools and tool marks; firearms and ammunition; glass; soils and minerals; safe insulation; rope, strings, and tapes; drugs; bioterror agents; documents; laundry and dry-cleaning marks; paint; skeletal remains; and wood.

Fingerprints

At the end of each human finger, on the palm side, exists a unique arrangement of small lines called *friction ridges,* which provide just enough roughness to give fingers "traction" when holding or otherwise manipulating objects. Within these friction ridges lie sweat pores. When the sweat they produce mixes with body oils, dirt, or other matter, that substance will rub off on any surface the finger touches, leaving behind a print if the surface is relatively smooth.

These prints are useful in criminal investigations because a person's friction-ridge patterns are formed before birth and remain the same throughout that person's life. The lines in the thumbprint raindrops made by a second grader in art class will be the same pattern years later the person's thumb will leave on the newspaper she reads every morning before going to work. Besides remaining consistent over time, prints are useful because they are unique—no two people have the same friction-ridge pattern. Therefore, fingerprints are a positive way to prove that a suspect was at a crime scene. The implications of finding identifiable prints at the scene vary with each case. For example, prints may not be important if the suspect had a legitimate reason for being there. Often, however, this is not the case.

Although many laypeople assume that identifiable fingerprints are almost always found at a crime scene, in many cases none are found. Even when they are, it is

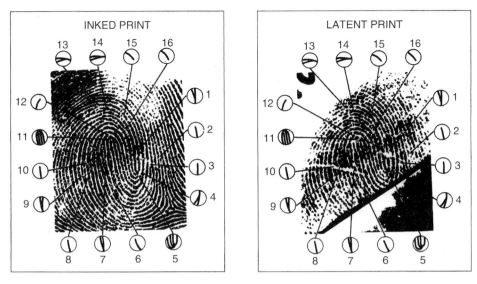

Figure 5.10

Three men checked into a motel at 11:00 p.m. Shortly after midnight, when a new desk clerk came on duty, the men went to the office and committed an armed robbery. Police investigating the scene went to the room occupied by the three men and found a latent fingerprint on an ashtray. The print was later matched to one of the suspects whose fingerprints were on file with the police department.

often difficult to locate the person who matches the prints. If a person's prints are not on file and there are no suspects, fingerprints are virtually worthless. Other times, however, fingerprints are the most important physical evidence in a case (Figure 5.10). Finding fingerprints at a crime scene requires training and experience. Some surfaces retain prints more easily than others.

Fingerprints are of various types:

- **Latent fingerprints** are impressions transferred to a surface, either by sweat on the ridges of the fingers or because the fingers carry residue of oil, dirt, blood, or other substance. Latent fingerprints can be visible or invisible.

- **Visible fingerprints** are made when fingers are dirty or stained. They occur primarily on glossy or light-colored surfaces and can be dusted and lifted.

- **Plastic fingerprints,** one form of visible print, are impressions left in soft substances such as putty, grease, tar, butter, or soft soap. These prints are photographed, not dusted.

- **Invisible fingerprints** are not readily seen but can be developed through powders or chemicals. They are normally left on nonporous surfaces.

 Any hard, smooth, nonporous surface can contain latent fingerprints.

Nonporous surfaces include light switches; window frames and moldings; enameled surfaces of walls, doors, and painted or varnished objects; wood; lamps; polished silver surfaces; and glass. Fingerprints often occur on documents, glass, metals, tools, and weapons used in a crime as well as on any objects picked up or touched by a suspect. Objects such as firearms, tools, small metal objects, bottles, glassware, documents, and other transportable items are submitted to a laboratory, where the prints are developed by experts.

Some porous materials also produce latent prints. For example, paper and cloth surfaces have developed excellent prints. Passing a flashlight at an oblique angle over a surface helps to locate possible prints. Latent prints have even been collected from human skin.

Begin the search for fingerprints by determining the entry and exit points and the route through a crime scene. Look in the obvious places as well as less-obvious places such as the underside of toilet seats and the back of car rearview mirrors. Examine objects that appear to have been moved. Consider the nature of the crime and how it was probably committed. Prints found on large, immovable objects are processed at the scene by photographing or dusting with powder or chemicals.

Dusting Latent Fingerprints Fingerprint dusting powders are available in various colors and chemical compositions to provide maximum development and contrasts. When dusting for fingerprints, use a powder that contrasts in color to the surface.

 Do not powder a print unless it is necessary, and do not powder a visible print until after you photograph it.

To dust for fingerprints, follow these steps (Figure 5.11):

1. Make sure the brush is clean. Roll the handle of the brush between your palms to separate the bristles.

2. Shake the powder can to loosen the powder. Apply the powder *lightly* to the print, following the contour lines of the ridges to bring out details.

3. Remove all excess powder.

4. Photograph.

Use a camel-hair brush for most surfaces. Use an aspirator for dusting ceilings and slanted or difficult areas. If in doubt about which powder or brush to use, test them on a similar area first.

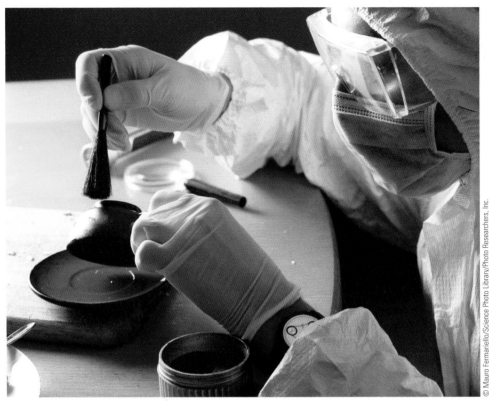

Figure 5.11

A forensic investigator uses a fine brush to apply fingerprinting dust to a cup. The dust adheres to the oil of a fingerprint, revealing a distinctive ridged pattern which can be used to identify the person who held the cup, thereby linking them to this crime scene.

Learn to use the various materials by watching an experienced investigator demonstrate the correct powders, brushes, and techniques. Then practice placing latent prints on various surfaces and using different-colored powders to determine how well each adheres and how much color contrast it provides. Practice until you can recognize surfaces and select the appropriate powder.

When photographing developed latent prints, record the color of the powder used, the color of the surface, and the location of the prints. Place your identification, date, and case number on the back of the photograph and submit it to the crime laboratory. The laboratory will determine whether it is an identifiable print and whether it matches a known suspect or other people whose prints were submitted for elimination.

Lifting Prints To lift fingerprints, use a commercially prepared lifter that has both a black-and-white background and a wide transparent lift tape. Use black lifters for light powders and light lifters for black powders.

To lift prints on doorknobs or rounded surfaces, use transparent tape so you can see any spots where the tape is not sticking. Put the tape over the dusted print. Do not use too much pressure. Work out any bubbles that appear under the tape by applying extra pressure. When you have lifted the print, transfer it to a fingerprint card. Figure 5.12 illustrates this procedure.

Common errors in lifting prints include removing too much or too little powder from the ridges, allowing bubbles to develop under the tape, and failing to make two lifts when a second lift would be better than the first.

Chemical Development of Latent Fingerprints Although powders are used to develop latent fingerprints on many surfaces, they are not recommended for unpainted wood, paper, cardboard, or other absorbent surfaces. Using powder on such surfaces will smudge any prints, destroying their value as evidence. For such surfaces, use a special chemical such as iodine, ninhydrin, or silver nitrate.

Use gloves and a holding device to avoid contaminating the evidence by inadvertently adding your own fingerprints. The chemicals can all be applied to the same specimen because each reacts differently with various types of materials. However, if *all* are used, the order must be iodine first, then ninhydrin, and finally silver nitrate.

In the *iodine method,* iodine crystals are placed in a fuming cabinet or a specially prepared fuming gun. The crystals are heated and vaporized, producing a violet fume that is absorbed by the oil in the fingerprints. The fingerprint ridges appear yellow-brown and must be photographed immediately because they fade quickly. Fuming cabinets and guns can be made or purchased from police supply houses.

The *ninhydrin method* develops amino acids. Ninhydrin (highly flammable) is available in spray cans or in a powder form from which a solution of the powder and acetone or ethyl alcohol is made. The evidence is then either sprayed or brushed with or dipped into the ninhydrin. Development of prints can be speeded up by applying heat from a fan, pressing iron, or oven. At room temperature, prints develop in a minimum of two hours; with a pressing iron, they develop almost immediately.

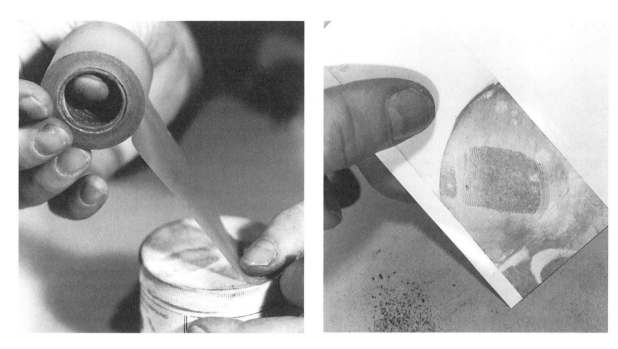

Figure 5.12
Lifting Prints. The photos above show the proper method of applying fingerprint tape (*left*) and transferring the lifted print to a fingerprint card (*right*).

Ninhydrin-developed prints do not fade immediately, but they eventually lose contrast. Therefore, photograph them soon after development.

The *silver nitrate method* develops sodium chloride in the fingerprint ridges into silver chloride that appears as a red-brown print. Because silver nitrate destroys oils and amino acids, it must be used *after* the iodine and ninhydrin methods. Immerse the specimen in a solution of 3 to 10 percent silver nitrate and distilled water. Remove it immediately and hang it to dry. The prints can be developed more rapidly by applying light until they start to develop. They should be photographed immediately because they disappear after several hours.

Other Methods of Lifting Prints Fingerprints may also be located and developed by using Magnabrush techniques, laser technology, gelatin lifters, and cyanoacrylate (superglue). Superglue fuming involves heating three or four drops of glue to generate fumes that adhere to fingerprints. The process can effectively develop prints on plastic, bank checks, counterfeit money, metal, and skin. Portable lasers are used to find and highlight fingerprints. They can detect fingerprints on the skin of a murder victim and trace a gunshot path.

Investigators can also use gelatin lifters to lift dusted prints or dust marks (footprints) from a wide variety of surfaces. Used in Europe for decades, the lifters are flexible and easily cut to suit specific needs. They can lift dust prints from any smooth surface—from tile floors to cardboard boxes. The high contrast of the black lifters allows investigators to see dust prints not visible to the naked eye, and the lifted prints photograph extremely well. In addition, the lifters can pick up

particle samples such as hair or paint chips. In the laboratory, tweezers or a scalpel can remove the samples from the lifter without damaging the sampled material.

Elimination Prints If fingerprint evidence is found, it is important to know whose prints "belong" at the scene. Prints of persons with reason to be at the scene are taken and used as **elimination prints.** For example, family members in a home where a crime has occurred or employees of a business that has been robbed should be fingerprinted so that their fingerprints at the scene can be eliminated from suspicion.

Inked Prints Most police departments have equipment for taking fingerprints. Standard procedure is to fingerprint all adults who have been arrested, either at the time of booking or at the time of release. These fingerprint records help ensure that the person arrested is identified correctly. Some departments have portable fingerprint kits in patrol vehicles that allow them to take inked prints and develop latent prints at crime scenes.

To take inked prints, start by rolling the right thumb and fingers in the order stated on the card. Then roll the left thumb and fingers in order. Use a complete roll; that is, go from one side to the other. Next, *press* the fingers and then the thumb of each hand on the spaces provided on the card. The card also has spaces for information about the person and the classification made by the fingerprint examiner. Learn to take inked fingerprints by having someone demonstrate.

Digital Fingerprinting Advances in computer technology are allowing digital fingerprinting to replace inked

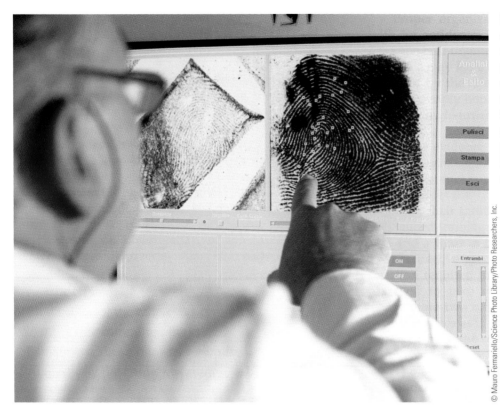

Figure 5.13

An automated fingerprint identification system matches fingerprints recovered at crime scenes with the millions of prints stored in its database. Here a forensic scientist points at fingerprints being compared by characteristic features (square yellow markers). Computer analysis enables very large numbers of fingerprints to be compared with great speed, allowing suspects to be linked to any unsolved crime on record.

© Mauro Fermariello/Science Photo Library/Photo Researchers, Inc.

printing. An **automated fingerprint identification system (AFIS)** (Figure 5.13) can digitize fingerprint information to produce **inkless fingerprints.** Latent fingerprints are scanned and converted into an electronic image that is stored in a database for rapid retrieval.

In this method, a suspect's hand is placed onto a glass platen, where a laser optically scans the prints and transfers them onto a fingerprint card. Stored fingerprint information includes the person's gender, date of birth, and classification formula and each finger's ridge count. AFIS technology maps fingerprints and creates a spatial geometry of the minutiae of the print, which is changed into a binary code for the computer's searching algorithm. When queried, the system selects the cards within the range limitations for the entered classification formula. The capability of registering thousands of details makes it possible for the computer to complete a search in minutes that would take days manually. The search success rate has been up to 98 percent in some departments with files under one million. Once the computer search finds a hit, a fingerprint expert then visually compares the prints.

If no match is found in local or state files, prints are submitted to the FBI Identification Division for a further search. This division has on file fingerprints of arrested people as well as of nearly 100 million other people such as aliens and individuals in government services, including the military. Given that approximately 35 to 40 percent of crime scenes have latent prints, AFIS is a tremendous advance in crime fighting.

The value of AFIS technology was first seen when it was used to solve the "Night Stalker" serial killer case

Technology Innovations

According to Scarborough (2005, p.42): "The first 24 hours after a homicide are important in order to develop the necessary evidence to determine the perpetrator." Combine this time-critical element of a homicide investigation with the estimate that up to 40 percent of individuals questioned in the field by law enforcement lack proper identification, and the benefits of mobile AFIS become clear. Scarborough (2005, p.49) notes:

The potential exists to adapt mobile AFIS systems to quickly identify fingerprints at crime scenes. The units will need to be modified to accommodate the scanning of crime scene prints, but this process could greatly reduce the . . . important time frame [of] the first 24 hours in which a suspect is identified after the commission of a crime.

in 1985. AFIS systems are constantly being augmented with the introduction of new services and features and recently went mobile, allowing investigators in the field to take a live scan of a person's prints.

In 1999 the FBI introduced its Integrated Automated Fingerprint Identification System (IAFIS), which provides five major services to local, state, and federal law enforcement and criminal justice agencies:

- Ten-print–based identification services (i.e., ten rolled fingerprint impressions and ten flat fingerprint impressions)
- Latent fingerprint services
- Subject search and criminal history services
- Document and image services
- Remote search services

One benefit of electronic fingerprinting systems is their increased speed and accuracy. Another major benefit of this technology is the ability to transmit the print image over telephone or cable lines from one AFIS system to another or to computerized criminal records centers. This feature also allows international sharing of databases to help capture criminals who move from one country to another. Casey (p.108) reports: "Today, there are nearly 49 million tenprint database records in IAFIS; and over 82 percent of daily submissions to FBI/IAFIS are now digital." Kanable (2003b, pp.51–52) notes: "A latent fingerprint entered into IAFIS led to Lee Boyd Malvo, one of the two suspects in the Washington area sniper case. The fingerprints were in IAFIS because Malvo had been previously arrested by the INS."

Despite the many benefits provided by AFIS and IAFIS, these programs simply search the databases for possible matches. In the end, a human fingerprint examiner must determine the match.

Fingerprint Patterns, Analysis, and Identification   Once a print has been captured, whether chemically devel-

oped, rolled in ink, or digitally scanned, the fingerprint patterns are analyzed for unique features that will, hopefully, lead to the identification of one individual. Fingerprint patterns are classified as *arched*, *looped*, or *whorled*. Variations of these configurations result in the nine basic fingerprint patterns illustrated in Figure 5.14. Normally, twelve matchable characteristics on a single fingerprint are required for positive identification.

When using digital fingerprint images, the quality of the image becomes a critical factor in whether the analyst can clearly discern and compare the minutiae. As with rolled (inked) prints, smudges and distortions reduce the usefulness of the print. Digital programs, if not up to standard, might also create artifacts or false minutiae in the image, which will obviously impair an examiner's ability to analyze and match a print. Casey (p.113) states: "Latent examiners . . . have long understood the importance of image quality in making positive identifications from partial latent fingerprints. This has led to the establishment of minimum standards known today as Appendix F." By adhering to these standards, and future amendments, investigators and their departments can ensure maximum usefulness of the prints they scan.

Usefulness of Fingerprints   Fingerprints are of extreme evidentiary value in criminal investigations.

 Fingerprints are *positive* evidence of a person's identity. They cannot, however, indicate a person's age, sex, or race.

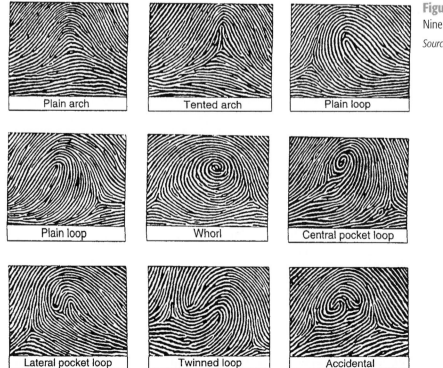

Figure 5.14

Nine basic fingerprint patterns

Source: Courtesy of the *FBI Law Enforcement Bulletin*

Plain arch   Tented arch   Plain loop

Plain loop   Whorl   Central pocket loop

Lateral pocket loop   Twinned loop   Accidental

Fingerprinting is increasingly being applied to homeland security efforts, as fingerprints can be sent via communications systems across the country and around the globe and visually reproduced. Crime victims are identified by their prints to prove the corpus delicti. Courts, parole and probation officers, and prosecutors use fingerprints to positively identify people with multiple criminal records.

Fingerprints also aid in noncriminal investigations by helping to identify victims of mass disasters, missing persons, amnesia victims, and unconscious persons. Military agencies use fingerprints recorded at enlistment to identify those killed in combat. Hospitals use fingerprints or footprints to identify newborn babies. Furthermore, fingerprints are becoming widely used as identification for cashing checks and processing legal documents.

Admissibility in Court   To ensure admissibility in court, investigators should establish the probative value of the print; that is, either the defendant had claimed never being at the scene, or even if the defendant had legitimate access to the scene, he or she did not have legitimate access to the object on which the print was found, or the print was found on the instrumentality of the crime. Investigators should also ensure admissibility by the testimony of the investigator who lifted the latent print, by the level of expertise used by the fingerprint examiner, and by the testimony of the file supervisor who maintained the print.

As with digital photography, digital fingerprinting has faced authenticity and admissibility challenges in court. Nislow (p.1) explains: "When police technicians enhance digital prints with software such as the widely popular Adobe Photoshop, additions and subtractions from the image are made which can change the print's characteristics without the program creating a log of those modifications." Despite attempts to create tracking software, such as MoreHits, to overcome such challenges, thus far no tool has been designed that will offer a secure chain of custody for digital prints.

Other Types of Prints   Suspects may leave palmprints, footprints, or even prints of lips. These impressions can be photographed and developed just as fingerprints are.

Palmprints contain many more friction-ridge landmarks than fingerprints, thus giving print examiners more points of comparison to use when determining matches. Biometric databases are also beginning to store prints from the part of the hand called the *writer's edge,* the side of the hand, from the wrist up to the curled fifth, or "pinkie," finger, that rests on the table or paper when someone is writing. According to Taylor and Knapp (p.154): "Experts in the forensic identification field know that a significant portion of latent lifts obtained from actual crime scenes turn out to be from parts of the hand other than the fingertips. The consensus is that 30 percent of crimes go unsolved because of

this and that up to 50 percent of crime scene prints are not from fingertips, but from other parts of the hand."

In one interesting case a burglar shattered a restaurant's plate glass window. The police found no fingerprints around the window but did find footprints and a toe print on a piece of the broken glass. These were developed and lifted. Later a 17 year old was arrested for vagrancy. Learning that he often went barefoot, police also took his footprints and forwarded them to the FBI. They were identical to those on the plate glass window fragment. It was learned that the youth had taken off his shoes and put his socks on his hands to avoid leaving fingerprints at the crime scene. He was found guilty.

In another case, a string of peeping-tom cases was solved because of three lip impressions left by the suspect on a windowpane. And in a case in Illinois, authorities matched lip prints on a piece of duct tape the suspect had held in his mouth while binding a victim.

Voiceprints

A **voiceprint** is a graphic record made by a sound spectrograph of the energy patterns emitted by speech. Like fingerprints, no two voiceprints are alike. Voiceprints can assist in identifying bomb hoaxers, obscene phone callers, and others who use the phone illegally. A voiceprint made during a phone call can be retained until a suspect is in custody.

As with many other investigative techniques, advances in forensic audio analysis are giving investigators higher-quality data despite efforts of those being surveilled to distort their voices or conceal them with high levels of background noise. Hanson (2004c, p.96) states: "Modern forensic audio analysis uses adaptive digital filters that significantly increase the ability to remove background noise and enhancement of speech and data from tapes." This technology can also analyze sounds other than voices, thus converting annoying background noise into isolated, distinguishable sounds that give clues as to where the calls are originating.

The use of voiceprints in criminal trials is controversial. In a number of cases, convictions obtained through voiceprints have been reversed because the voiceprints were not regarded as sufficiently reliable.

Language Analysis

A useful and often overlooked type of evidence is the actual language used by victims, witnesses, and suspects. To capture this type of evidence, many officers and investigators carry lightweight digital voice recorders with date- and time-stamp features. In explaining the value of voice recordings in court proceedings, one officer states: "You can't put state-of-mind on paper, but you can certainly hear it in their voices. . . . We've had some very successful prosecutions that have relied on those recordings.

Sometimes witnesses will change their stories half-way through a case, and it's known that the first statement is almost always the best" (Estersohn, p.60).

One area of language analysis involves **psycholinguistics,** the study of the mental processes involved in the comprehension, production, and acquisition of language ("Psycholinguistics," 2005). Van Nostrand and Auletta (2005) define forensic psycholinguistics as the "art (and science) of determining as much as possible about . . . potential criminal[s], such as . . . kidnapper[s] or terrorist[s], using as source any communication, either written or oral, received from them, but prior to being able to establish their identity." According to Hanson (2004c, p.99): "Changes in emotional state alter voice patterns and sometimes reveal a lot about a person." An individual's communication, whether written or spoken, may provide clues as to his or her gender, age, race, or ethnicity or what part of the country (or world) the person grew up in or has spent recent time in. Language analysis may also provide insight into a person's educational level, political views, and religious orientation, which may in turn provide further evidence regarding a criminal motive.

Human DNA Profiling

Human cells contain discrete packs of information known as chromosomes, which are made of DNA. **DNA,** or *deoxyribonucleic acid,* is an organic substance contained in a cell's nucleus. The DNA double-helix strand is composed of building blocks called *nucleotides,* which consist of a base molecule connected to a molecule of sugar and a molecule of phosphoric acid. The four bases are adenine (A), guanine (G), cytosine (C), and thymine (T), which link to each other to form a chain millions of nucleotides long. Within this DNA

chain are areas of *conserved regions,* where the A-T-C-G pattern is the same for every human, and *variable regions,* where the nucleotide sequence is distinct and different for every person, thereby determining a person's individual characteristics. This unique *genetic code* can be used to create a **genetic fingerprint** to positively identify a person. Except for identical twins, no two individuals have the same DNA structure.

DNA profiling uses material from which chromosomes are made to identify individuals positively.

DNA can tell investigators the sample donor's gender, race, eye color, and hair color. DNA profiling can be done on cells from almost any part of the body. The FBI's *Handbook of Forensic Services* (p.34) explains: "There are two sources of DNA used in forensic analyses. Nuclear DNA (nDNA) is typically analyzed in evidence containing blood, semen, saliva, body tissues, and hairs that have tissue at their root ends. Mitochondrial DNA (mtDNA) is typically analyzed in evidence containing naturally shed hairs, hair fragments, bones, and teeth." Table 5.2 lists possible items of crime scene evidence on which DNA might be located.

DNA technology is used in paternity testing, immigration disputes, missing persons and unidentified-body cases, and criminal and assailant identification. DNA analysis was used to identify many of the 9/11 World Trade Center victims. DNA keeps its integrity in dried specimens for long periods and consequently can help toward the resolution of unsolved cases.

Collecting and Preserving DNA Evidence Considering the potential value of DNA evidence in a criminal case, it is important that investigators understand and be

Table 5.2 / **Identifying DNA Evidence**

Evidence	Possible Location of DNA on the Evidence	Source of DNA
Baseball bat	Handle, end	Sweat, skin, blood, tissue
Hat, bandanna, or mask	Inside	Sweat, hair, dandruff
Eyeglasses	Nose or ear pieces, lens	Sweat, skin
Toothpick	Tips	Saliva
Tape or ligature	Inside/outside surface	Skin, sweat
Bottle, can, or glass	Sides, mouthpiece	Saliva, sweat
"Through and through" bullet	Outside surface	Blood, tissue
Bite mark	Individual's skin or clothing	Saliva
Fingernail, partial fingernail	Scrapings	Blood, sweat, tissue
Used cigarette	Cigarette butt	Saliva

Source: U.S. Department of Justice, National Institute of Justice, National Commission on the Future of DNA Evidence,
What Every Law Enforcement Officer Should Know about DNA Evidence, Washington, DC, 1999.

trained in proper collection and preservation procedures for this type of evidence. Gahn (p.73) stresses:

> Investigators should always use clean disposable gloves when collecting or examining evidence and gloves should be changed when new items are handled to avoid potential contamination of DNA. Similarly, officials should avoid coughing or sneezing near evidence since their own DNA may contaminate evidence.
>
> Since DNA may be found almost anywhere at a crime scene, take precaution when relocating evidence to different areas of the scene, because if DNA evidence is located in those areas, contamination of the original evidence may occur.

The National Institute of Justice (NIJ) offers additional guidelines to help investigators avoid contaminating DNA evidence:

- Use disposable instruments or clean them thoroughly before and after handling each sample.
- Avoid talking, sneezing, and coughing over evidence.
- Air-dry evidence thoroughly before packaging.
- Put evidence into new paper bags or envelopes, not into plastic bags; and never use staples.

Regarding the storage and preservation of DNA evidence, Gahn (p.73) notes: "Environmental conditions also have a direct impact on the integrity of DNA evidence. As a result, it is imperative that evidence be stored properly from the point of collection. Heat, humidity, bacteria and mold, and sunlight can quickly degrade DNA. Therefore all DNA evidence should be kept cool and dry and away from direct sunlight." Page (2004b, p.108) adds: "Blood products from a paper cut, skin follicles dropped from scratching one's nose, and saliva from an innocent sneeze [by a law officer] can all contaminate a crime scene." To prevent such inadvertent DNA contamination, investigators should wear protective clothing, including face masks, body suits, and shoe coverings (Page, 2004b, p.112). Additional precautions include double gloving and using disposable tweezers, scalpels, and other collection tools (Page, 2004b, p.113).

Suggestions for collecting and preserving DNA evidence are offered by Lifecodes Corporation in Table 5.3.

An innovative two-day course called "DNA from Crime Scene to Courtroom" is offered by the NIJ's National Law Enforcement and Corrections Technology Center (NLECTC)–Rocky Mountain, in Denver, Colorado. The course teaches investigators, crime scene personnel, and prosecutors about the powers and pitfalls of DNA evidence. Students are walked through a mock crime scene to learn where to search for DNA evidence and how to collect and preserve it. Then they are shown how a forensic scientist analyzes the sample. Kanable (2005, p.44) explains: "By seeing the process used by the scientist to produce results, students have a better understanding of what happens in the lab and why results take time to produce."

DNA Testing   Because of the expense and time involved, three criteria must usually be met for a lab to accept DNA samples:

- Sufficient material must be submitted.
- Samples (exemplars) must be submitted from both the suspect and the victim.
- The evidence must be probative.

Different methods of DNA analysis are available, but as Jones (p.93) notes: "Today, most crime labs use a DNA typing system that takes advantage of the polymerase chain reaction (PCR), a technique that duplicates short segments of DNA." The short pieces of DNA that PCR targets are areas where the genetic code repeats, called short tandem repeats (STRs). Each human chromosome contains hundreds of different types of STRs, with the number of repeats on each chromosome varying greatly among individuals. This variation creates a genetic uniqueness for every person that DNA analysts are able to profile (Figure 5.15).

Prior to PCR, the dominant technique for DNA analysis was restriction fragment length polymorphism (RFLP, pronounced *riff-lip*). While many labs still use this method, a significant shortcoming is that it requires a large amount of intact DNA, while PCR needs only a tiny amount, even if degraded, of DNA.

Another extremely useful forensic DNA analysis method examines a genetic marker called a single nucleotide polymorphism (SNP, pronounced *snip*) (Figure 5.16). A SNP is a one-base difference in the DNA sequence between individuals, which researchers have discovered can reveal measurable genetic differences among various racial populations.

Advancements continue to be made in DNA testing. The National Institute of Standards and Technology has developed a quality assurance standards kit for DNA typing that laboratories can use to assess the accuracy of their DNA testing procedures within a narrow margin of error.

DNA Databases   In October 1998, under the authority of the DNA Identification Act of 1994, the FBI activated a database called the National DNA Index System (NDIS) in an effort to establish a national DNA index for law enforcement purposes. In 1990 the FBI Laboratory launched a pilot project called CODIS (Combined DNA Index System), which blended forensic science and computer technology to help solve violent crimes. CODIS created a distributed database with three hierarchical tiers—local, state, and national—enabling participating laboratories to exchange and compare DNA profiles electronically. DNA profiles are generated at the local level (LDIS) and then flow to the state (SDIS) and national (NDIS) levels. NDIS is at the top of the CODIS hierarchy. When CODIS was first implemented, it served 14 state and local laboratories. As of May 2005, 49 states, the District of Columbia, and Puerto Rico were

Table 5.3 / **Collecting Evidence for DNA Analysis**

Types of Evidence and Minimal Amounts to Collect

Blood

Fresh liquid blood: 3 drops
Stains: Quarter size
Drawn specimens (exemplars): 1 cc or 1 mL

Semen

Fresh liquid semen: 3 drops
Stains: Dime size
Swabs: 2 swabs

Other types

Tissues/Bones/Teeth: Although small amounts of evidence have provided enough DNA for analysis, the amount that will be needed is unpredictable and depends on many factors, including age and concentration of sample.

How to Collect Biological Evidence

Specimens should be collected and dried as soon as possible to avoid bacterial contamination.

Wet specimens

Quick-dry using a hair dryer on the cool setting.
For large amounts of material, use a large floor fan.
Absorb wet specimen onto sterile gauze, 100% cotton, or Q-Tips and then dry.

Dry specimens

Scrape dried specimen from permanent surfaces.
Cut dried specimen out from large areas.
Package whole items if manageable.

Packaging Specimens

Drying specimens isn't enough. They must be kept as free from moisture as possible. Therefore:

Small items

Place the collected specimen in a zip-lock bag.
Squeeze the air out of the bag.

Larger items

Use paper bags for large items and tape them closed.

Storing Collected Evidence

Heat can destroy DNA. Therefore, if the evidence is not sent for DNA analysis within a few days, store the packaged evidence as directed.

Short-term storage (less than 30 days)

Store in freezer.
If freezer is not available, refrigerate evidence.
Store at room temperature for only 1–2 days.

Extended storage (more than 30 days)

Call Lifecodes for recommendations. When it has been collected and stored properly, evidence as old as 10 years has been successfully analyzed.

Sending Evidence for DNA Analysis

Send evidence and exemplar samples, from the victim and suspect(s), properly labeled, together with a written description of the specimens. Include any other important or relevant facts concerning the case and origin of the sample(s) for the forensic scientist. Send samples via an overnight carrier. The sender is responsible for following the chain of custody.

Source: Lifecodes Corporation, Saw Mill River Road, Valhalla, NY 10595 © 1990. By permission.

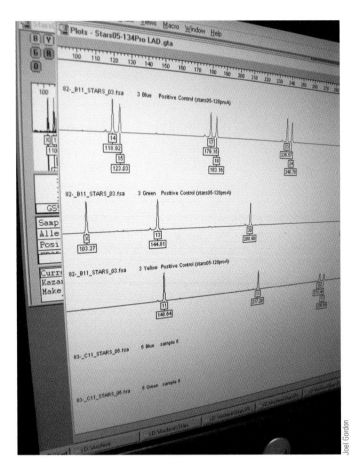

Joel Gordon

Figure 5.15

The polymerase chain reaction (PCR) technique known as the short tandem repeat (STR) DNA method. STRs are genetic markers that vary in size among individuals and are very discriminating for single-source samples, meaning they can be used to determine with 99.999% certainty that a specific DNA sample came from a particular individual.

Technology Innovations

Spraggs (pp.36,38) describes a new and controversial technology developed by DNAPrint Genomics called DNAWitness, which uses SNPs to help investigators eliminate entire populations of potential suspects:

DNA Witness lets you include or exclude certain persons from an investigation based on their ancestry. . . . The latest version . . . analyzes 176 SNPs that are Ancestry Information Markers (AIMs), determined by testing hundreds of individuals with deep genealogical histories in the four population groups [European, East Asian, Native American, and Sub-Saharan African].

The results can provide a profile of a person's physical appearance based on the person's genetic percentages of these four population groups. Spraggs (p.38) notes that DNAWitness can also help in victim identification:

In November 2003 a woman's dismembered body was found in a wooded area of Frederick County, Virginia. The woman's head was missing and investigators were having a difficult time identifying the victim.

Police submitted her genetic material to DNAPrint. The results showed the victim was 85 percent East Asian, not Hispanic, as investigators previously believed.

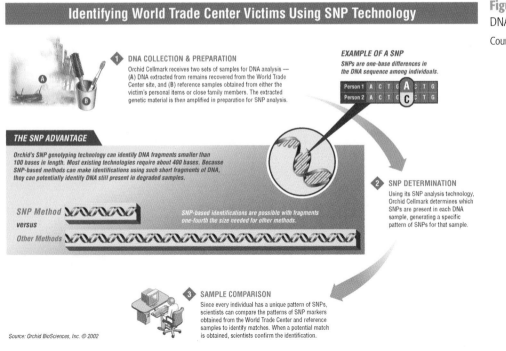

Figure 5.16
DNA profiling process
Courtesy of Orchid Cellmark Inc.

NDIS participants, with Mississippi the only non-NDIS state (Federal Bureau of Investigation, "CODIS").

The CODIS database is organized into two indexes: the forensic and offender indexes. The *forensic index* contains DNA profiles from crime scene evidence where the offender's identity is unknown. The *offender index* contains DNA profiles of individuals convicted of sex offenses and other violent crimes. Investigators can submit biological evidence from a crime scene to CODIS and cross-check it against existing profiles, generating investigative leads and making links between crimes and offenders (Figure 5.17). As with IAFIS and fingerprint searches, all DNA hits identified by CODIS must be subsequently validated as a match by a qualified DNA analyst.

As of May 2005, the NDIS forensic index contained 108,976 profiles, and the convicted offender index contained 2,390,740 profiles (FBI CODIS website). However, many more profiles could, and should, be added to CODIS if the enormous backlog of untested DNA evidence were addressed. According to Lovrich et al. (2004), more than 540,000 cases with biological evidence still await DNA testing, including 52,000 homicide cases, 169,000 sexual assault cases, and 264,000 property cases. Of these backlogged cases, only 10 percent are at crime labs, meaning that the bulk of untested DNA evidence is still in possession of local law enforcement agencies, which, unfortunately, rarely possess the stringent protection and preservation protocol common at crime laboratories. One reason for the large backlog in DNA evidence testing is the length of time needed to process a typical sample, with state labs averaging 23.9 weeks for an unnamed suspect rape kit and local labs averaging 30 weeks (Lovrich et al.).

Several suggestions have been made to expedite the processing of DNA evidence and reduce the number of backlogged cases. President Bush's 2004 paper, "Advancing Justice Through DNA Technology," set forth a number of initiatives to help crime labs better achieve their mission, including automation tools such as robotic DNA extraction units.

Figure 5.17
A scientist holds a DNA microarray slide, while the computer monitor behind her displays another microarray. An array is an orderly arrangement of samples and provides a medium for matching known and unknown DNA samples.

The potential for human error and contamination is a critical factor in determining DNA evidence's admissibility in court.

Admissibility in Court Cases involving DNA are being decided by courts case by case. In the first appeal from a finding of guilty, the Virginia State Supreme Court upheld the conviction and death sentence of Timothy Spencer in the rape and murder of two women, holding that DNA test results were reliable. In other cases, however, DNA analysis has been rendered worthless by the defense's successful attack on the methods used to collect and store the evidence on which DNA analysis was performed. In the O. J. Simpson double-murder trial, DNA matches were disregarded by jurors after questions were raised about how blood samples were collected, preserved, and examined.

Blood and Other Body Fluids

Blood and other body fluids such as semen and urine can provide valuable information. Blood assists in establishing that a violent crime was committed, in recreating the movements of a suspect or victim, and in eliminating suspects. Body fluids can be found on a suspect's or victim's clothing, on the floor or walls, on furniture, and on other objects. Some body fluids, such as semen and saliva, may be difficult to detect but, given their natural fluorescent property, will become visible under a variety of FLSs.

Blood is important as evidence in crimes of violence. Heelprints of shoes in blood splashes may be identifiable apart from the blood analysis. It is important to test the stain or sample to determine whether it

Technology Innovations

Automating the DNA analysis process can reduce the critical labor- and time-intensive aspects that contribute to the backlog, thereby increasing analyst productivity, limiting human error, and reducing contamination. Wilson (p.90) states: "There is a system available that fully combines robotics and computer software to process DNA from convicted offender samples. These samples can then be matched by CODIS with record speed and accuracy."

is, in fact, human blood. In addition, because blood is so highly visible and recognizable, those who commit violent crimes usually attempt to remove blood from items. A number of reagents—including luminol, tetramethyl benzedrine, and phenolphthalein—can identify blood at a crime scene, and because crime laboratories are swamped with evidence to examine, such preliminary on-scene testing is important.

Luminol, for example, is an easy-to-apply water-based solution sprayed from a pump bottle over an area where blood traces are suspected (Figure 5.18). Luminol causes blood to fluoresce a pale blue color and can detect blood that has been diluted up to 10,000 times. Another benefit to using luminol is that it does not harm DNA in blood, thus allowing the blood to be collected for further analysis. However, as noted by LeMay (p.140), investigators must be aware that luminol can give false positive reactions and therefore is only a presumptive positive test for blood. Luminol also reacts with bleach products and some metals or strong oxidiz-

ing agents. Consequently, if a surface was cleaned with bleach, it might react when sprayed with luminol.

Bloodstains and spatter patterns are also useful evidence, as they are characteristics of certain physical forces and can help investigators determine how a criminal event played out. According to Hanson (2004a, p.84): "Bloodstain patterns occur in several distinct categories, each revealing a piece of the crime scene puzzle." But as Akin (p.21) contends: "Blood spatter analysis requires the same expert interpretation as fingerprints." Therefore, investigators or technicians must accurately measure, record, and photograph blood spatters at a crime scene so that expert bloodstain analysts can properly interpret the spatter data.

Computer programs make bloodstain analysis faster, easier, and more accurate. Some programs can calculate bloodstain measurements for point of origin, letting investigators know, for example, where a gunshot victim stood. Computer software is also available that takes bloodstain pattern data and converts them into a 3-D model of the crime scene, helping investigators reconstruct specific spatial and sequential events that occurred before and during the act of bloodshed.

Blood-spatter patterns can help to determine a suspect's truthfulness (Figure 5.19). In many cases suspects have claimed a death was accidental, but the location and angle of blood-spatter patterns refuted their statements.

Collect *liquid* blood with an eyedropper and put it in a test tube. Write the subject's name and other pertinent information on medical tape applied to the outside. Send by air express, priority mail, or registered mail. Scrape *dry* blood flakes into a pillbox or envelope, identified in the same way. Mark bloodstained clothing with a string tag or directly on the clothing. If the bloodstain is moist, air-dry the clothing before packing (Figure 5.20).

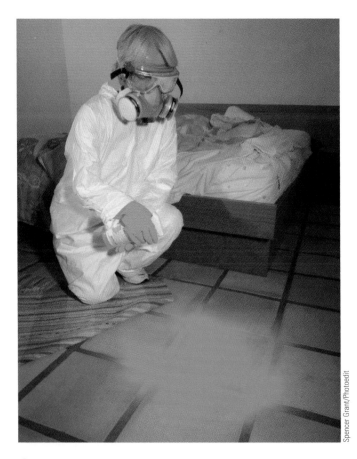

 Blood can be identified as animal or human and is most useful in eliminating suspects. Age or race cannot be determined from blood samples, but DNA analysis can provide positive identification.

In some cases blood, without DNA analysis having been performed on it, can help to infer race; for example, sickle-shaped red blood cells occur primarily in African Americans.

Scent

A type of evidence that does not receive much attention is scent evidence. Yet, as Kanable (2003a, p.130) asserts: "Scent evidence is valuable because it can establish probable cause for arrest or provide positive identification in some cases—even long after the crime scene has disappeared." Every person has a unique scent, which cannot be masked or eliminated, not even by the most potent perfume.

Figure 5.18
Investigators use luminol to look for the possible presence of blood at a crime scene. Even if blood has been cleaned up, enough can remain that when the chemicals in luminol come into contact with the hemoglobin in the blood traces, a light-producing chemical reaction takes place. Investigators using luminol will try to make the crime scene as dark as possible so that the glow of the reaction can illuminate patterns, footprints, or possibly traces of blood in unsuspected places. This crime-scene investigator is wearing specialized gear recommended for when luminol is used.

Spencer Grant/Photoedit

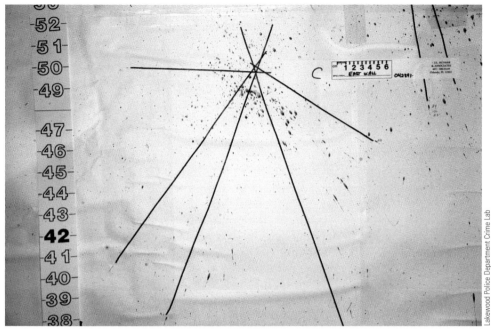

Lakewood Police Department Crime Lab

Figure 5.19
Blood pattern analysis can help investigators determine where the blood originated, the distance from there to where the blood came to rest, the type and direction of impact creating the bloodstains, the type of object producing them, and the position of the victim and the assailant during and after the bloodshed. Generally, the smaller the size of the bloodspatters, the greater the energy used to create them. This bloodspatter was the result of a beating and is an example of a medium-velocity event. The various measurements made by the investigators show the technique of examining the pattern to determine the area of convergence before calculating the area of origin.

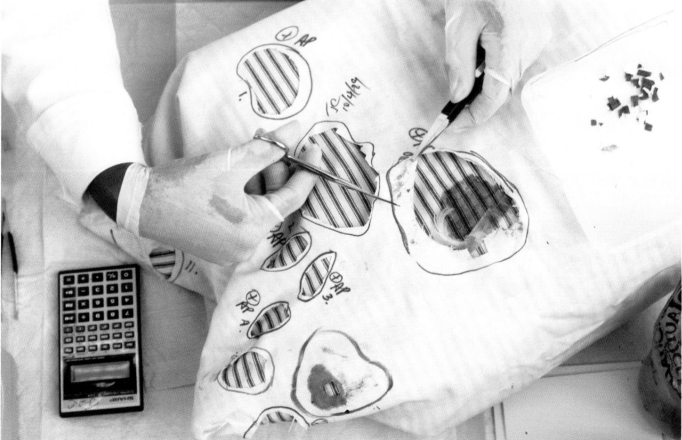

Getty Images/Gamma Liaison/Stephen Ferry

Figure 5.20
A laboratory technician recovers samples from a blood-stained pillow found at a crime scene. These samples can be used for DNA testing against blood drawn from a suspect. Good conservation of samples is the only condition required for DNA tests to be reliable, even after a long period of time.

A person's scent profile is the combination of sweat, oils, and gases his or her body produces. These smells, along with the skin cells every body constantly sheds, are detectable to specially trained scent-discriminating dogs (Kanable, 2003a, p.130). Scents can also be categorized as primary and secondary. For example, in a child abduction case, a dog was given a shirt of the missing girl as the scent article and tracked this primary scent to the location of her body in a field. At this point, the investigators held off going to her body right away in order to allow the dog to refocus on the secondary scent of the abductor. However, if officers, search volunteers, parents, or any other person comes in contact with the victim, the scene becomes scent contaminated and a valuable opportunity to track the secondary scent of the perpetrator is lost.

Scent evidence can also be collected by placing a sterile gauze pad on another item of evidence. A Scent Transfer Unit uses a vacuum system to trap the scent on the gauze. If there is no scent article available, the unit can be placed in a closed room and allowed to vacuum the air for five minutes in an effort to capture a scent (Kanable, 2003a, p.133). These scent pads can be presented to a tracking dog or placed in a freezer for preservation.

Hairs and Fibers

Hairs and fibers are often difficult to locate without a careful search and strong lighting. FLSs are commonly used to locate hair and fiber evidence in carpets and bedding or on other surfaces. They are valuable evidence because they can place a suspect at a crime scene, especially in violent crimes in which interchange of hairs and fibers is likely to occur. Hairs and fibers can also be taken from the scene by the suspect.

Place hairs and fibers found at the crime scene in paper, using a druggist fold, or in a small box. Seal all edges and openings, and identify on the outside. If hairs and fibers are found on an object small enough to send to a laboratory, leave them on the object. Hairs and fibers often adhere to blood, flesh, or other materials. If the hairs are visible but are not adhering firmly to the object, record their location in your notes. Then place them in a pillbox or glass vial to send to a laboratory. Do not use plastic.

If you suspect that hairs are on an object, carefully wrap the object and send it intact to a laboratory. Attempt to obtain 25 to 50 full hairs from the appropriate part of the suspect's body for comparison, using a forceps or comb. Document the hair and fiber evidence using special filters, light sources, and photomicrographs to reproduce the specimens in black-and-white or color.

Examining Hair A hair shaft has a *cuticle* on the outside consisting of overlapping scales that always point toward the tip, a *cortex* consisting of elongated cells, and the *medulla*—the center of the hair—consisting of vari-

ably shaped cells. Variations in these structures make comparisons and identifications possible.

> Microscopic examination determines whether hair is animal or human. Many characteristics can be determined from human hair: the part of the body it came from; whether it was bleached or dyed, freshly cut, pulled out or burned; and whether there is blood or semen on it. Race, sex, and age cannot be determined.

As with blood samples, it is extremely difficult to state that a hair came from a certain person, but it can usually be determined that a hair did *not* come from a certain person. Hair evidence is important because it does not deteriorate and is commonly left at a crime scene without a subject's knowledge. Laboratory examination does not destroy hair evidence as it does many other types of evidence. Hair evidence may be subjected to microscopic examination to determine type (e.g., facial or pubic), to biological examination to determine blood-type group, and to toxicological examination to determine the presence of drugs or poisons (Figure 5.21).

According to the National Institute of Justice (p.5), instruments used in *secondary ion mass spectrometry*, or SIMS, can distinguish trace hair samples using consumer chemicals as identifiers: "Chemicals found in hair conditioning products produce distinctive chemical signatures, allowing the identification of hair samples based on the product used." While chemical colorants and other products commonly applied to human hair can thwart microscopic analysis, SIMS is not only unaffected

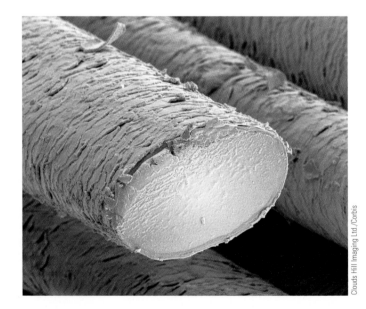

Clouds Hill Imaging Ltd./Corbis

Figure 5.21

A micrograph of a hair sample showing a recent cut. This cross-section lets investigators view the three basic layers of a hair shaft: the cuticle, the outer layer of protective scales; the cortex, a second, thicker layer that provides strength to the hair shaft and determines the color and texture of hair; and the medulla, a third, inner layer that is present only in thick, large hairs.

by these substances but can actually take advantage of their presence to enhance identification (National Institute of Justice, p.5).

Examining Fibers Fibers fall into four general groups: mineral, vegetable, animal, and synthetic. Mineral fibers most frequently submitted are glass and asbestos. Vegetable fibers include cotton, jute, manila, kapok, hemp, and many others. Animal fibers are primarily wool and silk. Synthetics include rayons, polyesters, nylons, and others. Each fiber has individual characteristics that can be analyzed chemically.

Fibers are actually more distinguishable than hairs. Fiber examination can determine a fiber's thickness, the number of fibers per strand, and other characteristics that help identify clothing. Fibers can be tested for origin and color. Although often overlooked, fibers are the most frequently located microscopic evidence. They are often found in assaults, homicides, and rapes, where personal contact results in an exchange of clothing fibers. Fibers can be found under a suspect's or victim's fingernails. Burglaries can yield fibers at narrow entrance or exit points where clothing gets snagged. Hit-and-run accidents often yield fibers adhering to vehicles' door handles, grilles, fenders, or undercarriages.

Advances in FLSs used to examine evidence have been particularly beneficial in the area of fiber evidence, where often only a strand or two is found. Hanson (2004b, p.139) notes: "In the past, to perform adequate chemical analysis of fiber evidence usually meant destroying a part or all of the evidence to get useable results. ALS [alternative light source] combined with microscopic equipment now provides a powerful tool to analyze the color makeup of a fiber, and most importantly the analysis does not destroy the original evidence."

Shoe and Tire Impressions

Shoe and tire prints are fairly common evidence at crime scenes and, if collected, recorded, and analyzed properly, can yield valuable investigative data. Shoe footprints, in addition to providing unique wear patterns that can be compared with a suspect's shoes, can indicate whether a person was walking or running, was carrying something heavy, or was unfamiliar with the area or unsure of the terrain. Tire marks can show the approximate speed and direction of travel and the manufacturer and year the tires were made. Bodziak (2003b, p. 82) adds: "To the trained forensic tire expert, the tire is actually a complicated piece of engineering . . . [consisting] of more than a dozen components." In the July 1999 slaying of a Yosemite Park naturalist, the killer left behind footprints and the distinctive tracks of his vehicle, which had a different brand of tire on every wheel.

If shoe or tire prints are found on paper or cardboard, photograph them and then submit the originals for laboratory examination (Figure 5.22). Use latent fin-

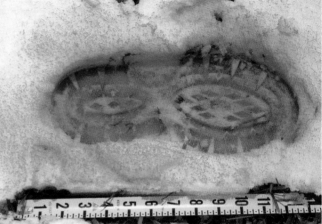

Figure 5.22

Shoes and boots can leave distinctive impressions that can be traced to an individual's personal possessions. Manufacturers can provide photographs of their specific lines of shoes and boots that can be compared with photographs taken at the scene.

gerprint lifters to lift shoe and tire tread impressions from smooth surfaces. Photograph with and without a marker before lifting the impression. Do not attempt to fit your shoe into the suspect's shoe print to determine size. This can destroy the shoe print. Regarding two-dimensional tire prints, unless the actual impression occurs on material small enough to be submitted to the lab, the only other way to collect or recover the evidence is to photograph the length of the impression with a long scale adjacent to it (Bodziak, 2003b, p.89).

Shoe and tire impressions generally have unique wear patterns that should be cast when possible. Three-dimensional impressions should always be cast.

 After photographing, cast shoe or tire tread impressions found in dirt, sand, or snow.

To **cast** is to make an impression. The word also refers to the impression that results. Some departments use plaster, whereas others prefer dental casting material because of its strength and durability and because it needs no reinforcement. Premeasured mix kits are also available. The steps in making a plaster cast of an impression are these (Figure 5.23):

1. Build a retaining frame around the impression about 2 inches from its edges.

2. Coat the impression with five or six layers of alcohol and shellac or inexpensive hairspray, allowing each coat to dry before applying the next. Apply talcum powder to the last layer so the spray can easily be removed from the cast.

3. Rapidly mix the plaster following directions on the box.

Figure 5.23
Making a plaster cast of a shoe impression

4. Pour the plaster into the impression, using a spatula to cushion its fall and guide it into all areas of the impression. Fill the impression halfway.

5. Add wire or gauze to reinforce the impression.

6. Pour in more plaster until it overflows to the retaining frame.

7. Before the cast hardens, use a pencil or other pointed instrument to incise your initials, the case number, and the date on the back of the impression.

8. After the cast hardens, remove it and the retaining frame. Do not wash the cast; the laboratory does this.

9. Carefully wrap the cast in protective material to avoid breakage, and place it in a strong box to ship to the laboratory.

The laboratory compares the cast with manufacturers' shoe and tire tread files.

A relatively new technique in preserving shoe impression evidence involves a device called an electrostatic dust print lifter (EDPL). EDPL is used on dry-origin shoe impressions, which involve the transfer of dry residue on a shoe tread to another dry surface, such as a carpet or seat cushion. These impressions are very fragile and among the most difficult to locate. As Bodziak (2003a, p.96) explains: "The EDPL lifts the dry origin impression and transfers it to a black film that makes it very visible. It is important to note that using the EDPL is harmless to any other original impression evidence." The lift must then be photographed before it can be analyzed, as the lift itself is extremely fragile.

Bite Marks

Bites may occur during commission of a violent crime, inflicted by either the victim or the perpetrator, and the marks left behind can be collected as evidence. Bite marks may also be found in partially eaten food or other objects that had been placed inside a person's mouth. If the impression is visible, photograph it and then swab the bite area for saliva, blood residue, DNA, and micro-organisms. Then cast it in the same way as shoe and tire tread impressions. Dental impression material is again preferred because of its fine texture.

If a bite mark is too shallow to cast, photograph it and then "lift" it by placing tape over it and then transferring the tape to plastic to see the outline of the mark. FLSs help locate bite marks that are not visible. Again, once illuminated, photograph the bite marks.

Tools and Tool Marks

Common tools such as hammers and screwdrivers are often used in crimes and cause little suspicion if found in someone's possession. Such tools are often found in a suspect's vehicle, on the person, or at the residence. If a tool is found at a crime scene, determine whether it belongs to the property owner. Broken tool pieces may be found at a crime scene, on a suspect, or on a suspect's property (Figure 5.24).

 Identify each suspect tool with a string tag. Wrap it separately and pack it in a strong box for transport to the laboratory.

A **tool mark** is an impression left by a tool on a surface. For example, a screwdriver forced between a window and a sill may leave a mark the same depth and width as the screwdriver. The resiliency of the surface

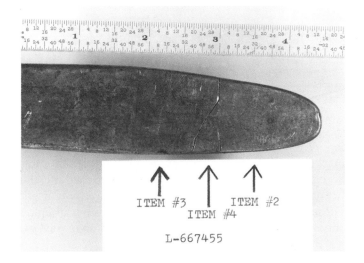

Figure 5.24
Broken tool comparison. Pry tool used to pry open the rear door of a hardware store. Items 2 and 4 were found at the scene of the burglary. Item 3 was found in a toolbox in the suspect's car. This evidence led to the suspect's conviction for burglary.

may cause explainable differences in mark dimensions and tool dimensions. If the screwdriver has a chipped head or other imperfections, it will leave impressions for later comparison. Tool marks are often found in burglaries, auto thefts, and larcenies in which objects are forced open.

A tool mark provides leads as to the size and type of tool that made it. Examining a suspect tool determines, within limits, whether it could have made the mark in question. Even if you find a suspect tool, it is not always possible to match it to the tool mark, especially if the tool was damaged when the mark was made. However, residue from the forced surface may adhere to the tool, making a comparison possible.

Do not attempt to fit a suspected tool into a mark to see if it matches. This disturbs the mark, as well as any paint or other trace evidence on the suspect tool, making the tool inadmissible as evidence.

 Photograph tool marks and then either cast them or send the object on which they appear to a laboratory.

Photographing Tool Marks First photograph the location of the tool or tool mark within the general crime scene. Then take close-ups first without and then with a marker to show actual size and detail.

Casting Tool Marks Casting of tool marks presents special problems because they often are not on a horizontal surface. In such cases, construct a platform or bridge around the mark by taping tin or other pliable material to the surface. Plaster of Paris, plasticine, and waxes do not provide the detail necessary for tool striation marks. Better results are obtained from moulage, silicone, and other thermosetting materials.

Comparing Tool Marks Tool marks are easy to compare if a suspect tool has not been altered or damaged since it made the mark. If the tool is found, send it to the laboratory for several comparison standards.

 A tool mark is compared with a standard-of-comparison impression rather than with the tool itself.

The material used for the standard is as close as possible to the original material. Ideally, a portion of the original material is used.

The tool mark found at the scene and the standard of comparison are placed under a microscope to make the striation marks appear as light and dark lines. The lines are then adjusted to see whether they match. Variations of approximately 10 degrees in angle are permissible. Roughly 60 percent of the lines should match in the comparison (Figure 5.25).

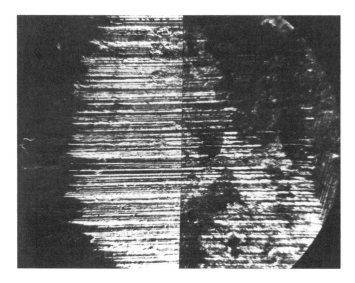

Figure 5.25
Comparison of tool marks. Striation pattern of a sledgehammer used to open a safe. The white marks are safe insulation. The left half of the photograph is evidence obtained at the scene of the crime; the right half shows the actual hammer seized from the suspect. The marks were matched up under a comparison microscope and magnified. The result was a positive match.

Value of Tool Marks A specific mark may be similar to or found in the same relative location as tool marks found at other crimes. Evidence of the way a tool is applied—the angle, amount of pressure, and general use—can tie one crime to another. A tool mark also makes it easier to look for a specific type of tool. Possession of, or fingerprints on, such a tool can implicate a suspect.

Firearms and Ammunition

Many violent crimes are committed with a firearm: a revolver, a pistol, a rifle, or a shotgun. Each firearm imparts a distinctive fingerprint, or ballistic signature, to every bullet and casing fired through it, which provides useful evidence to investigators. The broad definition of **ballistics** is that it is the study of the dynamics of projectiles, from propulsion through flight to impact; a narrower definition is that it is the study of the functioning of firearms.

The **bore** refers to the inside portion of a weapon's barrel, which is surrounded by raised ridges called **lands** and recessed areas called grooves. These lands and grooves make up the **rifling** and grip and spin the bullet as it passes through the bore, providing greater projectile control and accuracy. **Caliber** refers to the diameter of the bore as measured between lands, as well as the size of bullet intended to be used with a specific weapon. As the bullet rotates through the barrel, it receives highly individualized and characteristic **striations,** or scratches, from the rifling, which provide valuable comparison evidence on recovered bullets. A fired bullet is marked only by the barrel, but a fired cartridge

case is marked by several parts of the weapon when it is loaded, fired, and extracted.

Several factors can affect a bullet's path. Intervening objects, especially the contents of pockets, can deflect bullets. A raised arm can produce the illusion that a bullet pierced the clothing and went sideways before entering the body. It may also suggest that the point of impact was lower than it actually was. This phenomenon gave rise to the controversy regarding the first bullet that struck President John F. Kennedy, which hit him in the neck. Because he had his arm raised to wave at the moment of impact, the hole in his jacket suggested that the bullet hit him between his shoulder blades when draped normally. Bullets can also veer within the body after striking a bone or upon leaving the body.

Collecting and Identifying Firearms and Ammunition
Use extreme caution when handling firearms found at a crime scene. Tools used to manufacture weapons and defects in weapons acquired through use or neglect often permit positive identification. A bullet or cartridge case can often be linked with the weapon from which it was fired. When handling a weapon found at a crime scene, do NOT put an object inside the barrel to pick it up. The object may scratch the inside of the barrel, affecting a ballistics test. Include in your notes the firearm's make, caliber, model, type, serial number, and finish, along with any unusual characteristics.

Examine weapons for latent fingerprints. Photograph weapons and then identify them with a string tag. Unload firearms. Record the serial number on the string tag and in your notes. Label the packing container "Firearms." Identify bullets on the base, cartridges on the outside of the case near the bullet end, and cartridge cases on the inside near the open end. Put ammunition in cotton or soft paper and ship to a laboratory. Never send live ammunition through the mail; use a common carrier.

Evidence from Firearms and Ammunition Gunpowder tests, shot pattern tests, and functional tests of a weapon can be made and compared. The rifling of a gun barrel, the gun's ejection and extraction mechanisms, and markings made by these mechanisms can also be compared. Class characteristics of a bullet caused by the firearm's barrel can help identify the weapon used. These class characteristics include the number of lands and grooves in the firearm's barrel and their height, width, and depth (Figure 5.26).

Evidence bullets are compared to determine whether a specific bullet was fired from a specific comparison weapon. Figure 5.27 shows how bullets and casings receive a signature. Firearms examiners linked 11 sniper shootings around Washington, DC, in October 2002 using the same methods to analyze bullets and casings. Shot patterns determine the distance from which

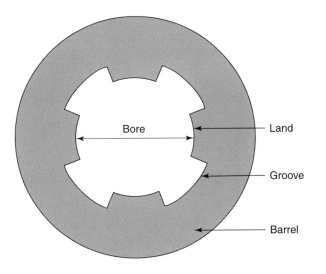

Figure 5.26
Features of a rifled firearm's barrel

the victim was shot and may disclose the type of choke on the gun and its barrel length. Gun parts found at a crime scene are compared with a weapon, and the trigger pull is tested and measured.

Forensic criminologists can use firearms evidence smaller than a fingernail to build a case strong enough to put people in prison. However, crime labs have faced increasingly difficult identification challenges with certain types of bullets and projectiles. As Wallace (p.36) states: "Crimes are committed with every weapon imaginable, but for crime labs the most difficult rounds for forensic identification are the soft point, hollow point, shotgun or high caliber rifle." The problem lies in the fact that the water tank has been the standard tool for such testing, and the types of rounds Wallace identifies are likely to either rupture these tanks, distort to such a degree that they are rendered useless for examination, or fragment into tiny pieces also unsuitable for analysis.

How bullets and casings receive a signature
When a weapon is fired, it leaves unique markings—much like fingerprints—on bullets and casings.

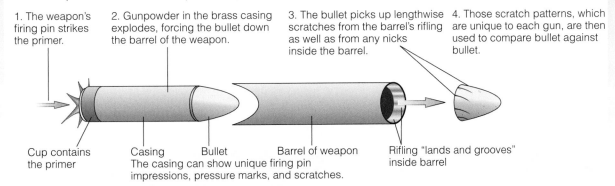

1. The weapon's firing pin strikes the primer.

2. Gunpowder in the brass casing explodes, forcing the bullet down the barrel of the weapon.

3. The bullet picks up lengthwise scratches from the barrel's rifling as well as from any nicks inside the barrel.

4. Those scratch patterns, which are unique to each gun, are then used to compare bullet against bullet.

Cup contains the primer

Casing
The casing can show unique firing pin impressions, pressure marks, and scratches.

Bullet

Barrel of weapon

Rifling "lands and grooves" inside barrel

Linking weapons to shootings
Here are two ways the FBI's DrugFire system and the ATF's Integrated Ballistics Identification System (IBIS) databases can use the markings to link weapons to shootings.

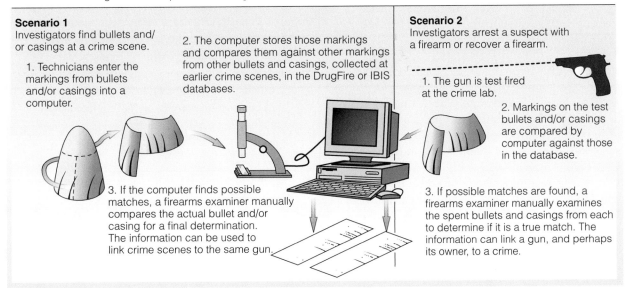

Scenario 1
Investigators find bullets and/or casings at a crime scene.

1. Technicians enter the markings from bullets and/or casings into a computer.

2. The computer stores those markings and compares them against other markings from other bullets and casings, collected in earlier crime scenes, in the DrugFire or IBIS databases.

3. If the computer finds possible matches, a firearms examiner manually compares the actual bullet and/or casing for a final determination. The information can be used to link crime scenes to the same gun.

Scenario 2
Investigators arrest a suspect with a firearm or recover a firearm.

1. The gun is test fired at the crime lab.

2. Markings on the test bullets and/or casings are compared by computer against those in the database.

3. If possible matches are found, a firearms examiner manually examines the spent bullets and casings from each to determine if it is a true match. The information can link a gun, and perhaps its owner, to a crime.

Figure 5.27
Bullets and casings

Source: Chris Graves, "Linking Guns, Crime Is No Longer a Shot in the Dark." (Minneapolis/St.Paul) *Star Tribune,* February 19, 1996, p.A8. Data from Minneapolis Police. Minnesota Bureau of Criminal Apprehension.

Technology Innovations

Wallace (p.38) reports:

The Duke Projectile Recovery System (DPRS) . . . is the answer to all of the flaws that exist in current water tank technology. . . . .The DPRS is capable of capturing any type of round undamaged. It will capture any round, fully intact, including powder residue. The importance of this sentence cannot be overstated. "Any round" includes hollow points, soft points, high caliber rifles, and shotgun slugs. Previously, shotguns were believed to be untraceable. . . . As a bullet is fired into the DPRS, it is immediately encased in a specific blend of fibers selected because of their behavior when subjected to high velocity kinetic energy. The bullet, protected during the encapsulation process, is then subjected to a process that rapidly decelerates the bullet and safely brings it to a stop. The bullet can then be retrieved in "as fired" condition . . . completely intact, without distortion, and with all markings in place. The powder residue can still be seen and can be used for chemical matching.

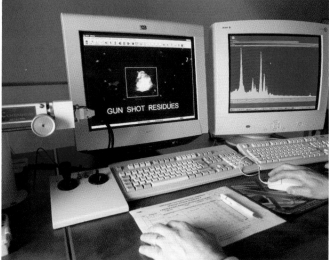

Figure 5.28

Analysis of gunshot residue (GSR). These two screens display the results of GSR analysis with a scanning electron microscope (SEM, left) and an x-ray beam (right).

Gunshot residue (GSR) is another type of evidence investigators may seek in crimes involving firearms. Whenever a firearm is discharged, the gunpowder and primer combine to form a gaseous cloud or residue, sometimes referred to as a plume, that can reach up to 5 feet from the weapon. This residue may settle on the hands, sleeves, face, and other parts of the shooter, as well as any other object or person within the residue fallout radius. Through various techniques, this residue may be detected and used as evidence.

Laboratory examination of GSR under a scanning electron microscope (SEM) is considered the most reliable analysis method (Figure 5.28). Adhesive tapes are applied to a person's hands and then placed under an SEM, which the technician uses to locate and identify specific residue particles and their composition.

Shooter ID kits are also available for conducting GSR tests in the field. These kits allow officers to quickly test multiple suspects and may also be used by investigators in distinguishing between a suicide and a homicide, with the absence of GSR on a victim indicating homicide and an abundance of GSR suggesting suicide. According to Nielsen (p.113), however, one of the biggest advantages of the field kits is their ability to collect and preserve data for subsequent evidentiary testing and confirmation by a forensic lab using SEM. While laboratory SEM analysis is the preferred method for verifying GSR, it is also time-consuming and, as such, fairly inefficient.

Technology Innovations

Lundrigan (p.68) describes the cutting-edge GSR technology developed by ASPEX:

Its system is able to analyze up to 30 adhesive stubs simultaneously, and offers the fastest and most accurate detection on the market. It can be used around the clock, can handle a high volume, and can be "brought into the field." Also, as this system is automated, the skill of the [SEM] operator no longer influences the quality of the results.

Using the adhesive sampling stubs, specimens can be taken from either skin or fabric. The ASPEX GRS system is able to detect individual residue particles, and determine the dimensions as well as the chemical structure of each particle. Essentially, it is able to create a unique residue profile or "fingerprint," and identify the presence of GSR particles beyond a shadow of a doubt.

As with fingerprints and DNA, a national database of ballistic information has helped investigators link firearms with offenders. Prior to 2002, the ATF, with IBIS, and the FBI, with DrugFire, each collected ballistic data but kept their systems separate, due to incompatibility issues. Realizing the value in and need for a unified ballistic evidence system, the ATF created the National Integrated Ballistic Information Network (NIBIN).

Glass

Glass can have great evidentiary value. Tiny pieces of glass can adhere to a suspect's shoes and clothing. Larger glass fragments are processed for fingerprints and can be fit back together to indicate the direction from which the glass was broken. The source of broken glass fragments also can often be determined.

 Label glass fragments using adhesive tape on each piece. Wrap each piece separately in cotton to avoid chipping, and place them in a strong box marked "fragile" to send to the laboratory.

Microscopic, spectrographic, and physical comparisons are made of the glass fragments. Microscopic examination of the edges of two pieces of glass can prove they were one piece at one time. **Spectrographic analysis** can determine the elements of the glass, even extremely small fragments. Submit for comparison pieces of glass at least the size of a half-dollar.

In general, high-velocity impacts are less likely to shatter glass than low-velocity impacts. A bullet that does not shatter glass will generally leave a small, round entry hole and a larger, cone-shaped exit hole (Figure 5.29). The faster a bullet travels, the smaller the cracks and/or the tighter the entry point will be.

The sequence of bullets fired through a piece of glass can be determined from the pattern of cracks. The direction and angle of a bullet or bullets through glass can also be determined by assembling the fragments. The resulting pattern of cracks indicates the bullet's direction. Steck-Flynn (2005b, p.56) explains: "When a projectile hits a glass surface the glass bends and energy dissipating from the point of impact causes 'radial' fractures to occur on the side of the glass opposite the point of impact. . . . Concentric rings known as 'concentric fractures' will surround the hole left by the projectile."

This allows investigators to determine which side of a piece of glass has received an impact, because a blow causes the glass to compress on that side and to stretch on the opposite side. As the impact occurs, concentric

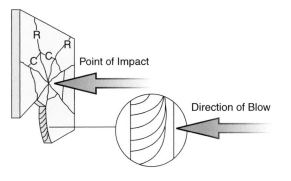

Figure 5.30
Glass cracks caused by a blow. C = circle cracks; R = radical cracks

fractures form around the point of impact and interconnect with radial cracks to form triangular pieces. The edge of each triangular piece has visible stress lines that tell the direction of the blow. The lines on the side that was struck have almost parallel stress lines that tend to curve downward on the side of the glass opposite the blow (see Figure 5.30). Such an examination can establish whether a burglar broke out of or into a building.

In addition to concentric and radial fractures, investigators should look for *Wallner lines*, also called ridges, which are rib-shaped marks with a wavelike pattern and are almost always concave in the direction from which the crack was propagating (Federal Bureau of Investigation, 2005). In low-velocity impact fractures, the ridges or Wallner lines on radial cracks nearest the point of impact are at right angles to the side opposite, or to the rear, of the impact, a phenomenon referred to as the "4R Rule" (*R*idges on *r*adial cracks are at *r*ight angles to the *r*ear) (Federal Bureau of Investigation, 2005). It should be noted, however, that tempered glass, laminated glass, and small pieces of glass tightly held in a frame or window case do not reliably demonstrate the fracture patterns just described.

Because larger glass fragments can be matched by fitting the pieces together, a slight mark put on the side of the glass that was facing out helps to reconstruct stress lines. To protect glass as evidence, put sharp points in putty, modeling clay, or some other soft substance.

Soils and Minerals

Forensic geologists examine soils and minerals—substances such as mud, cement, plaster, ceramics, and insulation—found at a crime scene or on a victim, a suspect, clothing, vehicles, or other items. This circumstantial evidence can place a suspect at a crime scene or destroy an alibi.

Although most soil evidence is found outdoors, suspects can bring soil into structures from the outside. Soils found inside a structure are most valuable if brought there on a suspect's shoes or clothing from his or her area of residence. Steck-Flynn (2005a, p.34)

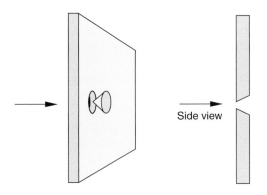

Figure 5.29
Bullet entry and exit holes

asserts: "'Double transfer' is even more convincing. If soil from a suspect's home territory is found on a victim or in [the victim's] home, and soil from the victim's home territory is found on the suspect's clothing or footwear, this is considered double transfer and the mathematical probability of the suspect having been at the crime scene increases dramatically." Because soils found in the victim's residence may have been brought there by the victim or by other persons not suspected in the crime, collect elimination samples of soil from the area around the scene.

> Put one pound of comparison soil into a container identified on the outside. Collect evidence soil the same way. Seal both containers to prevent loss, wrap them, and send them to a laboratory.

Soils vary greatly in color, particle size, mineral content, and chemical composition. Some comparisons are visual; others are made through laboratory analysis. Both differences and similarities have value because soils separated by only a few inches can be very different. Therefore, take sufficient samples directly from and around the suspected area at perhaps 5- to 100-foot intervals, depending on the scene. Finley (p.4) advises: "Most analyses require approximately 1 cup of soil. If considerable gravel or other coarse material is present, investigators should increase the size of the sample." In addition, soil samples should be packaged in only glass vials or plastic locking bags, never envelopes (Figure 5.31).

If soil evidence is in or on a suspect's clothing, send the entire article with the soil intact to the laboratory. If an object containing soil cannot be moved, use a spatula to gather the soil. Then place the soil in a can or paper bag, properly marked and identified.

Chemical analysis of soil is expensive and not always satisfactory. Soil is generally examined by density, by **X-ray diffraction** (to determine mineral content), and by microscope.

Because varied species of plants grow in different sections of the country, examination of dirt evidence that contains pollen and spores (palynology) is useful. It can refute the alibi of a suspect who is arrested at a distance from a crime scene and denies having been there. Electron microscope detection of pollen and spores found at the crime scene and on the suspect's clothing or vehicle will refute the alibi.

Safe Insulation

Most safes are fire-resistant, sheet-steel boxes with thick insulation. If safes are pried, ripped, punched, drilled, or blown open, the insulation breaks apart and falls or disseminates into the room. Burglars often carry some of this insulation in their clothing. People with safe insulation in or on their clothing must be considered

Figure 5.31
An investigator collecting soil evidence at a crime scene.

suspects, because few people normally come into contact with safe insulation. Tools used to open a safe can also have insulation on them, as may the floor of a vehicle in which the tools were placed after a burglary. Investigating burglary is the focus of Chapter 13.

> Put samples of safe insulation in paper containers identified on the outside.

Finley (p.5) notes: "If the safe is present at the scene, investigators should take samples of all walls because replacement of one or more walls with different safe insulation is common. Investigators should keep the sample dry and intact to prevent destroying any of the unique physical characteristics of the insulation." Safe insulation can be compared with particles found on a suspect or on the tools or vehicle used during a crime. Comparison tests can show what type of safe the insulation came from and whether it is the same insulation found at other burglaries. Insulation is also found on paint chips from safes. Always take standards of comparison if safe insulation is found at a crime scene.

The FBI and other laboratories maintain files on safe insulations used by major safe companies. Home and building insulation materials are also on file. This information is available to all law enforcement agencies.

© AP/Wide World Photo

Ropes, Strings, and Tapes

Ropes, twines, strings, and tapes are frequently used in crimes and can provide leads in identifying and linking suspects with a crime.

 Put labeled rope, twine, and string into a container. Put tapes on waxed paper or cellophane and then place them in a container.

Laboratories have various comparison standards for ropes, twines, and tapes. If a suspect sample matches a known sample, the laboratory can determine the manufacturer of the item and its most common uses. Cordage can be compared for composition, construction, color, and diameter. Rope ends can be matched if they are frayed. Likewise, pieces of torn tape can be compared with a suspect roll of tape.

Fingerprints can occur on either side of a tape. The smooth side is developed by the normal powder method or by using cyanoacrylate (superglue) if the surface is extremely slick. The sticky-side prints will be visible and are either photographed or retained intact.

Drugs

Drug-identification kits can be used to make a preliminary analysis of a suspicious substance, but a full analysis must be done at a laboratory.

 Put liquid drugs in a bottle and attach a label. Put powdered and solid drugs in a pillbox or powder box and identify in the same way.

If a drug is a prescription drug, verify the contents with the issuing pharmacist. Determine how much of the original prescription has been consumed.

Bioterror Agents

In the post-9/11 world, the entire law enforcement profession has a heightened awareness of terrorism and the tools employed by those seeking to paralyze our citizens, not only psychologically through fear, but also perhaps physically through chemical agents. Unfortunately, the methods to analyze and fingerprint the source of these weapons are currently insufficient.

However, as Page (2004a, p.68) posits: "Forensics may get some help from a novel 'fingerprinting' technique under development by government researchers. With this technology, law enforcement agencies could have a new way to trace the origin of anthrax and other chemical or biological agents" (Figure 5.32). The technique is based on the existence of stable, naturally occurring isotopes that exist in virtually every element

but that possess extremely subtle differences from source to source. Page (2004a, p.69) explains: "By looking at the isotope ratios of carbon and nitrogen, researchers could tell, for example, if two batches of anthrax were made in the same lab or perhaps by the same person."

Technology Innovations

A new device called the "Hound" is offering law enforcement officers and investigators a new tool for detecting and identifying drugs:

The "Hound" is a toolbox-sized sniffer that can detect drug residue in concentrations so small that the skin oil left behind on a doorknob may be enough to trigger the device's alarm. . . . It works by drawing several cubic feet of air through a filter and concentrating the compounds extracted into a smaller air sample. The substances contained in the smaller sample are then analyzed by an ion mobility spectrometer that is part of the device. (Dees, p.113)

The device can also be calibrated to detect explosives. A prototype of the Hound is being used in field trials by a specialized crimes and narcotics task force involved in ongoing narcotics investigations in southern Texas (Dees, p.113).

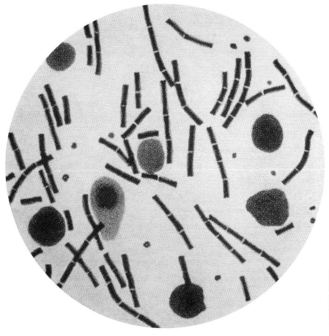

Figure 5.32
This Hiss Capsule strain of Anthrax under a microscope shows both spores (the circular globs) and the bacteria in its vegetative state (rod-shaped links).

Documents

Typing, handwriting, and printing can be examined. Typewriters and printers can be compared and paper identification attempted. Different types of writing instruments—pens, crayons, and pencils—and various types of inks can also be compared. Indented writings, obliterated or altered writings, used carbon paper, burned or charred paper, and shoeprint or tire tread impressions made on paper surfaces can all be examined in a laboratory. A document's age can also be determined.

 Do not touch documents with your bare hands. Place documents in a cellophane envelope and then in a manila envelope identified on the outside.

Standards of comparison are required for many document examinations. To obtain handwriting standards from a suspect, take samples until you believe he or she is writing normally. The suspect should not see the original document or copy. Tell the suspect what to write and remove each sample from sight after it is completed. Provide no instructions on spelling, punctuation, or wording. Use the same size and type of paper and writing materials as the original. Obtain right-handed and left-handed samples as well as samples written at different speeds. Samples of undictated writings, such as letters, are also helpful as standards. In forgery cases, include the genuine signatures as well as the forged ones. As in other areas of evidence examination, computer programs have also been developed to analyze handwriting.

People often type anonymous or threatening letters, believing that typewritten materials are not as traceable as handwritten ones. However, some courts have held that typewriting can be compared more accurately than handwriting and almost as accurately as fingerprints. To collect typewriting standards, remove the ribbon from the suspected typewriter and send the ribbon to a laboratory. Use a different ribbon to take each sample. Take samples using light, medium, and heavy pressure. Submit one carbon-copy sample with the typewriter on stencil position. Do not send the typewriter to a laboratory, but hold it as evidence.

Given enough typing samples, it is often possible to determine the make and model of a machine. Typewriter standard files are available for this purpose at the FBI laboratory. The information can greatly narrow the search for the actual machine. The most important comparison is between the suspect document and a specific typewriter.

As word processing replaces typewriters, the word-processing software program and the printer used become important evidence. Computer scanners and desktop publishing programs make producing fraudulent documents much easier. Collect as evidence the computer hard drive, printer, copier, scanner, or whichever devices were used to generate the document.

Computer-related document evidence may be contained on tapes or disks, not readily discernible and highly susceptible to destruction. In addition to information on tapes and disks, evidence may take the form of data reports, programming, or other printed materials based on information from computer files. Investigators who handle computer tapes and disks should avoid contact with the recording surfaces. They should never write on computer disk labels with a ballpoint pen or pencil and should never use paper clips on or rubber bands around computer disks. To do so may destroy the data they contain. Computer tapes and disks taken as evidence should be stored vertically, at approximately 70°F and away from bright light, dust, and magnetic fields.

Photographs frequently are also valuable evidence, whether taken by an officer or by someone outside the department. Some researchers are focusing their efforts on techniques to enhance grainy, blurred, or poorly contrasted photographs by digitally converting them and subjecting them to software programs. Photographic images of injuries on human skin can be enhanced using reflective and fluorescent UV imaging.

Recall that the best-evidence rule stipulates that the original evidence is to be presented whenever possible. For example, a photograph or photocopy of a forged check is not admissible in court; the check itself is required.

The FBI also maintains a national fraudulent check file, an anonymous letter file, a bank robbery note file, paper watermarks, safety paper, and checkwriter standards. When submitting any document evidence to a laboratory, clearly indicate which documents are original and which are comparison standards. Also indicate whether latent fingerprints are requested. Although original documents are needed for laboratory examinations and court exhibits, copies can be used for file searches. A photograph is superior to a photocopy.

Laundry and Dry-Cleaning Marks

Many launderers and dry cleaners use specific marking systems. The Laundry and Dry Cleaning National Association has files on such marking systems. Many police laboratories also maintain a file of visible and invisible laundry marks used by local establishments. Military clothing is marked with the wearer's serial number, name, and organization.

 Use UV light to detect invisible laundry marks. Submit the entire garment to a laboratory, identified with a string tag or a marking directly on the garment.

Laundry and dry-cleaning marks are used to identify the dead and injured in mass disasters such as airplane crashes, fires, and floods and in other circumstances as well. For example, a dead baby was traced by its sheet's laundry marks. Clothing labels can also assist in locating the possible source of the clothing.

Paint

Police laboratories and the FBI maintain files of automobile paints. These standards can help identify the year, make, and/or color of a motor vehicle from a chip of paint left at the scene. Paints are complex and are individual in color, composition, texture, and layer composition.

 In hit-and-run cases, collect paint samples from any area of the vehicle that had contact with the victim. Take paint samples down to the original metal to show the layer composition.

Use small boxes for submitting paint samples to the crime lab, putting samples from different parts of the vehicle in separate small boxes. If paint chips are on the clothing of the victim or suspect, send the entire article of clothing in a paper bag to the laboratory, properly labeled and identified.

Skeletal Remains

Laboratory examination can determine whether skeletal remains are animal or human.

 If adequate human skeletal remains are available, the sex, race, approximate age at death, approximate height, and approximate time since death can be determined.

Dental comparisons and X-rays of old fractures are other important **identifying features** or individual characteristics.

Forensic anthropology uses standard scientific techniques developed by physical anthropologists and archaeologists to identify human skeletal remains as they relate to a criminal case (Figure 5.33). Ongoing research at the Body Farm in Knoxville, Tennessee, is helping scientists observe the decomposition process of the human body following death and how exposure to various environmental conditions impacts this process. The data from the Body Farm provides a sort of "standard" for investigators to compare their crime scene evidence with (Mertens, p.32).

Figure 5.33
A forensic anthropologist examines a cranium exhumed from a mass grave. DNA samples from victims' remains are compared with the DNA samples taken from living family members in an effort to identify each victim.

Wood

Wood comparisons are made from items on a suspect, in a vehicle, or in or on clothing found at a crime scene. The origin is determined by the size or the fit of the fracture with an original piece of wood or by matching the sides or ends of pieces of wood. The type of wood is determined from its cellular elements. When handling wood evidence, if it is found wet, keep it wet; if it is dry, keep it dry.

Other Types of Evidence

Prescription eyeglasses, broken buttons, glove prints, and other personal evidence found at a crime scene can also be examined and compared. Nyberg (p.41) urges investigators to learn to read "product DNA," the printed code that appears on nearly every manufactured, mass-produced item:

> Product Identification Coding (PIC) offers a veritable universe of information, rich with potential leads for the investigator who doesn't overlook the possibilities. . . .
>
> Pick the nearest mass-produced item. It might be a soda can, a pack of cigarettes, or a CD. Somewhere on that item is at least one set of alphanumeric codes. When it comes to items like beer and soda, the numbers on the can contain volumes of information and, with a little persistence, an investigator can find out when that can was made, packaged, shipped, and delivered, and to what store.

Nyberg (pp.44–45) provides a partial list of items an investigator may find discarded at a crime scene that may yield useful information, including store and restaurant receipts, beverage containers, cigarette packages and even individual cigarettes, membership and check-cashing cards, clothing manufacturer labels and laundry tags, and footwear. He suggests:

> Look at the . . . list and think about how each piece of information can branch out. What kind of case are you working? Maybe it's a narcotics case and the smugglers ate at a certain restaurant together. With that restaurant receipt, you can learn who their server was and where they sat. Did the server overhear anything? Can he or she make IDs from photos? If necessary, could you get the names of people from neighboring tables (from credit card receipts), find them and interview them to see if they overheard anything? (p.45)

If there is a problem processing any evidence, a laboratory can provide specific collecting and packaging instructions.

Evidence Handling and Infectious Disease

Throughout this chapter you have looked at ways to collect evidence and keep it secure from contamination. As a final discussion in handling physical evidence, consider how to protect yourself from contamination. "One of the risks you face as a law enforcement officer is potential exposure to bloodborne pathogens such as the hepatitis B virus, the hepatitis C virus and the human immunodeficiency virus (HIV)" (*Bloodborne Pathogens*, p.2). Investigators are likely to encounter crimes of violence involving the blood and other body fluids of people with infectious diseases. Police officers are likely to encounter these infectious body fluids during the search of crime scenes

involving violence. Therefore it is important to know the facts about these infectious agents (Figure 5.34).

AIDS is not spread through casual contact such as touching an infected person or sharing equipment. Nor is it spread through the air by coughing or sneezing. An important issue related to HIV/AIDS is a person's confidentiality rights concerning his or her HIV status, including disclosure of such information in police reports. Investigators should be familiar with their jurisdiction's basic medical information confidentiality laws as well as any other specific laws pertaining to HIV/AIDS.

Chances are less than 1 percent that an officer will contract the AIDS virus on the job. Tuberculosis (TB), meningitis, and hepatitis pose greater threats. TB is transmitted through the air by coughing, hacking, and wheezing. TB can also be transmitted through saliva, urine, blood, and other body fluids. Meningitis, spread through the air, causes inflammation of the membranes that surround the brain. The hepatitis B virus, known today as HBV, is a bloodborne pathogen that can live outside the body longer than HIV. HBV is found in human blood, urine, semen, cerebrospinal fluid, vaginal secretions, and saliva. A safe, effective vaccine to prevent HBV is available.

Use precautions when collecting blood evidence and other body fluids. *Consider all body secretions as potential health hazards.* If there are body fluids at a crime scene, even if dried, wear latex gloves, goggles, and a face mask. Secure evidence in glass, metal, or plastic containers. Seal evidence bags with tape rather than staples. Do not allow hand-to-mouth or hand-to-face contact during collection. Do not eat, smoke, apply makeup, or drink at crime scenes, because these activities may transfer contaminated body fluids to you. When finished, wash your hands thoroughly (20 to 30 seconds) with soap and water.

Figure 5.34
Investigators in hazmat suits get decontaminated between the Longworth and Rayburn House Office Buildings on Capital Hill in Washington, DC, on October 24, 2001. The buildings were being swept for anthrax.

©Reuters/William Philpott/CORBIS

While processing the crime scene, constantly be alert for sharp objects, such as hypodermic needles and syringes. If practical, use disposable items where blood is present so the items can be incinerated. All nondisposable items, such as cameras, tools, and notebooks, must be decontaminated using a bleach solution or rubbing alcohol. Even evidence that has been properly dried and packaged is still potentially infectious. Therefore, place appropriate warnings on all items.

After processing, decontaminate the crime scene. If it is to be left for future decontamination, place biohazard warning signs and notify the cleaning team of possible contamination.

Further information on procedures for dealing with evidence with potential of transmitting an infectious disease can be obtained from the Centers for Disease Control and Prevention, Office of Health and Biosafety, 1600 Clifton Road N.E., Atlanta, GA 30333. 1-800-311-3435. http://www.cdc.gov

SUMMARY

Criminal investigations rely heavily upon various types of evidence. To be of value, evidence must be legally and properly seized and processed. Processing physical evidence includes discovering or recognizing it; collecting, recording, and identifying it; packaging, conveying, and storing it; examining it; exhibiting it in court; and disposing of it when the case is closed. The relative importance of physical evidence depends on its ability to establish that a crime was committed, as well as how, when, and by whom.

To determine what is evidence, first consider the apparent crime. Then look for any objects unrelated or foreign to the scene, unusual in their location or number, damaged or broken, or whose relation to other objects suggests a pattern that fits the crime. The more individual the evidence, the greater its value.

Common errors in collecting evidence are (1) not collecting enough of the sample, (2) not obtaining standards of comparison, and (3) not maintaining the integrity of the evidence.

Mark or identify each item of evidence in a way that can be recognized later. Include the date and case number as well as your identifying mark or initials. Record in your notes the date and time of collection, where it was found and by whom, case number, description of the item, and who took custody of it. Package each item separately in durable containers to maintain the integrity of evidence. Personal delivery, registered mail, insured parcel post, air express, Federal Express (FedEx), and United Parcel Service (UPS) are legal ways to transport evidence. Always specify that the person who receives the evidence is to sign for it.

Package evidence properly to keep it in substantially the same condition in which it was found. Document custody of the evidence at every stage. To ensure admissibility of the evidence in court, be able to (1) identify the evidence as that found at the crime scene, (2) describe exactly where it was found, (3) establish its custody from discovery to the present, and (4) voluntarily explain any changes that have occurred in the evidence. After a case is closed, evidence is returned to the owner, auctioned, or destroyed.

Frequently examined physical evidence includes fingerprints; voiceprints; language; DNA; body fluids (including blood); scent; hairs and fibers; shoe and tire impressions; bite marks; tools and tool marks; firearms and ammunition; glass; soils and minerals; safe insulation; rope, strings, and tape; drugs; bioterror agents; documents; laundry and dry-cleaning marks; paint; skeletal remains; wood; and many other types of evidence.

Know how to locate, develop, photograph, lift, and submit fingerprints for classification by experts. Any hard, smooth, nonporous surface can contain latent fingerprints. Do not powder a print unless it is necessary; do not powder a visible print until after photographing it. Prints of persons with reason to be at the scene are taken and used as elimination prints. Fingerprints are positive evidence of a person's identity. They cannot, however, indicate a person's age, sex, or race.

DNA profiling uses material from which chromosomes are made to positively identify individuals. DNA can tell investigators the sample donor's gender, race, eye color, and hair color. Blood can be identified as animal or human and is very useful in eliminating suspects. Age or race cannot be determined from blood samples. DNA analysis, however, can provide positive identification. Microscopic examination determines whether hair is animal or human. Many characteristics can be determined from human hair: the part of the body it came from; whether it was bleached or dyed, freshly cut, pulled out or burned; and whether there is blood or semen on it. Race, sex, and age cannot be determined.

After photographing, cast shoe or tire tread impressions found in dirt, sand, or snow. Identify each suspected tool with a string tag, wrap it separately, and pack it in a strong box to send to a laboratory. Photograph tool marks and then either cast them or send the object on which they appear to a laboratory. A tool mark is compared with a standard-of-comparison impression rather than with the tool itself.

Examine firearms for latent fingerprints. Photograph firearms and then identify them with a string tag. Unload guns and record their serial number on a string tag and in your notes. Label the packing container "Firearms." Identify bullets on the base, cartridges on the outside of the case near the bullet end, and cartridge cases on the inside near the open end. Put ammunition in cotton or soft paper and ship to a laboratory. Never send live ammunition through the mail; use a common carrier instead.

Label glass fragments using adhesive tape on each piece. Wrap each piece separately in cotton to avoid chipping and place in a strong box marked "fragile" to send to a laboratory. Put one pound of comparison soil into a container identified on the outside. Collect evidence soil the same way. Seal both containers to prevent loss, wrap them, and send them to a laboratory.

Put samples of safe insulation in paper containers identified on the outside. Put labeled rope, twine, and string in a container. Put tapes on waxed paper or cellophane and then place them in a container. Put liquid drugs in a bottle and attach a label. Put powdered and solid drugs in a pillbox or powder box and identify the same way.

Do not touch documents with your bare hands. Place them in a cellophane envelope and then in a manila envelope identified on the outside. Use ultraviolet light to detect invisible laundry marks. Submit the entire garment to a laboratory, identified with a string tag or with a marking directly on the garment. In hit-and-run cases, collect paint samples from any area of the vehicle that had contact with the victim. Take paint samples down to the original metal to show the layer composition. If adequate human skeletal remains are available, the sex, race, approximate age at death, approximate height, and approximate time since death can be determined.

CHECKLIST

Physical Evidence

- Was all physical evidence photographed before anything was moved?
- Was the physical evidence located in the crime scene sketch?
- Were relevant facts recorded in your notebook?
- Was the evidence properly identified, including the date, case number, your initials or mark, and a description of the evidence?
- Was the evidence properly packaged to avoid contamination or destruction?
- Were standards of comparison obtained if needed?
- Was the evidence sent in a way that kept it secure and provided a signed receipt, such as by registered mail?
- Was the evidence kept continuously secure until presented in court?

The following types of physical evidence are frequently found at a crime scene and should be searched for, depending on the type of crime committed:

- Blood
- Cigarettes, cigars, smoking materials
- Clothing and fragments
- Containers and boxes
- Documents and papers
- Dirt and dust particles
- Fibers, ropes, and strings
- Fingernail scrapings
- Fingerprints, visible and latent
- Footprints
- Glass objects and fragments
- Greases, oils, salves, emulsions
- Hairs, human and animal
- Inorganic materials
- Insulation from safes, buildings, and homes
- Metal objects and fragments
- Organic materials, plant and animal
- Paint and paint chips
- Palmprints
- Personal possessions
- Photographs
- Plastic impressions
- Soils
- Tires and tire tracks
- Tools and tool marks
- Weapons
- Wood chips or fragments

DISCUSSION QUESTIONS

1. What kind of physical evidence would you expect to find at a burglary scene?
2. What kind of physical evidence would you expect to find at the scene of an armed robbery? Why does this differ from your response to Question 1?
3. What is *material*, *relevant*, and *competent* evidence?
4. What legal rule requires the submission of original evidence, and when is this rule followed? When is it permissible to substitute evidence that is not original?
5. What general procedures would you follow in finding and collecting evidence at a crime scene?
6. How would you mark for identification the following items of evidence? a broken window pane; a damaged bullet; dried blood scraped from a wood floor; a shotgun shell casing; a piece of clothing with semen stains
7. How would you locate, preserve, lift, and identify a latent fingerprint on a wall in a house? How would you have the print examined?
8. What determines whether a government or private laboratory is used to examine evidence? What laboratory facilities are available to your police department?
9. *Continuity of evidence* is a legal term describing the chain of evidence necessary to make evidence legally admissible in court. Describe a chain of evidence from the time of discovery to introduction in court.
10. How does your police department dispose of evidence after it is no longer of value or has been released by the court?

MEDIA EXPLORATIONS

Internet

Select one assignment to complete, and be prepared to share your findings with the class.

* Go to the FBI website at http://www.fbi.gov/programs/lab/handbook/intro.htm to view the *Handbook of Forensic Services.* List the five sections of the handbook. Select one section and outline it.

* Go to the website of the Association for Crime Scene Reconstruction (ACSR) at http://www.acsr.com and take part in their online forum that tests your crime-scene knowledge.

* Go to http://www.ojp.usdoj.gov/nij/pubs-sum/000614.htm to view the document *What Every Law Enforcement Officer Should Know about DNA Evidence.* Outline the most important information.

Crime and Evidence in Action

Select one of three criminal case scenarios and sign in for your shift. Your Mobile Data Terminal (MDT) will get you started and update you throughout the case. During the course of the case you'll become a patrol officer, detective, prosecutor, defense attorney, judge, corrections officer, or parole officer to conduct interactive investigative research. Each case unfolds as you respond to key decision points. Feedback for each possible answer choice is packed full of information, including term definitions, web links, and important documentation. The sergeant is available at certain times to help mentor you, the Online Resources website offers a variety of information, and be sure to take notes in your e-notebook during the suspect video statements and at key points throughout (these notes can be saved, printed, or e-mailed). The Forensics Exercise will test your ability to collect, transport, and analyze evidence from the crime scene. At the end of the case you can track how well you responded to each decision point and join the Discussion Forum for a postmortem. **Go to the CD and use the skills you've learned to solve a case.**

REFERENCES

Akin, Louis L. "Blood Spatter Interpretation at Crime and Accident Scenes: A Basic Approach." *FBI Law Enforcement Bulletin*, February 2005, pp. 21–24.

Barbeau, Janet. "Evidence and Property Control." *Law and Order*, August 2003, pp. 96–99.

Bloodborne Pathogens for Law Enforcement. Virginia Beach, VA: Coastal Training Technologies, Corp., no date.

Bodziak, William. "Electrostatic Lifting of Shoe Impressions." *Law Enforcement Technology*, June 2003a, pp. 94–100.

Bodziak, William. "It's All in the Tire." *Law Enforcement Technology*, September 2003b, pp. 82–90.

Casey, William. "Perspectives on Livescan Imaging and Image Quality." *Law Enforcement Technology*, April 2005, pp. 108–113.

Colwell, Kimberly. "Evidence Collection: Preservation and Presentation for Civil Litigation." *Law and Order*, November 2003, pp. 60–65.

Dees, Tim. "The 'Hound' Drug Sniffer System." *Law and Order*, May 2005, p. 113.

Estersohn, Glenn. "Gardena Police Department Lays Down the Law." *Law Enforcement Technology*, April 2003, pp. 60–64.

Federal Bureau of Investigation. CODIS: Combined DNA Index System. http://www.fbi.gov/hq/lab/codis

Federal Bureau of Investigation. "Glass Fractures." *Forensic Science Communications*, January 2005. http://www.fbi.gov/hq/lab/fsc/backissu/jan2005/standards/2005standards7.htm. Retrieved June 21, 2005.

Federal Bureau of Investigation. *Handbook of Forensic Services.* Quantico, VA: Federal Bureau of Investigation, 2003.

Finley, Joseph A., Jr. "Geologic Material as Physical Evidence." *FBI Law Enforcement Bulletin*, March 2004, pp. 1–6.

Gahn, Laura. "DNA Evidence Collection Procedures." *Law and Order*, March 2005, pp. 72–75.

Glass, Jane. "Solving Space and Security Challenges When It Comes to Evidence." *Law Enforcement Technology*, August 2004, pp. 36–42.

Hanson, Doug. "Bloodstain Pattern Analysis: Recreating the Scene of the Crime." *Law Enforcement Technology*, February 2004a, pp. 84–90.

Hanson, Doug. "Shining Light on Fingerprints to Fibers to Fluids." *Law Enforcement Technology*, October 2004b, pp. 134–140

Hanson, Doug. "The Sound of Crime." *Law Enforcement Technology*, September 2004c, pp. 96–102.

Houck, Max. "The Nature of Physical Evidence." *Law Enforcement Technology*, October 2004, pp. 124–133.

Jones, Phillip. "DNA Profiling." *Law and Order*, August 2004, pp. 92–96.

Kanable, Rebecca. "Collecting Scent Evidence." *Law Enforcement Technology*, June 2003a, pp. 130–134.

Kanable, Rebecca. "Fingerprints Making the Case." *Law Enforcement Technology*, March 2003b, pp. 48–53.

Kanable, Rebecca. "Almost Anything Can Yield Evidence." *Law Enforcement Technology*, March 2005, pp. 36–46.

Kinman, Barney. "The Property Room: Important Considerations." *FBI Law Enforcement Bulletin*, July 2004, pp. 28–32.

Law and Order Staff. "New CVPI Trunk Pack." *Law and Order*, July 2003, pp. 52–54.

LeMay, Jan. "Detection of Blood with Luminol." *Law Enforcement Technology*, June 2003, pp. 140–145.

Lovrich, Nicholas P.; Pratt, Travis C.; Gaffney, Michael J.; Johnson, Charles L.; Asplen, Christopher H.; Hurst, Lisa H.; and Schellberg, Timothy M. *National Forensic DNA Study Report, Final Report*. U.S Department of Justice, unpublished report. Document No. 203970, February 2004.

Lundrigan, Nicole. "Gunshot Residue Technology." *Law and Order*, May 2004, pp. 66–68.

Mertens, Jennifer. "Lessons from the Body Farm." *Law Enforcement Technology*, June 2003, pp. 32–38.

Moore, Carole. "Crime Scene Integrity." *Law Enforcement Technology*, February 2005, p. 130.

National Institute of Justice. "Without a Trace? Advances in Detecting Trace Evidence." *NIJ Journal*, July 2003, pp. 2–9.

Nielsen, Eugene. "Instant Shooter Identification Kit." *Law and Order*, November 2004, pp. 112–114.

Nislow, Jennifer. "Giving Identification the Finger: Questions Surround Accuracy of Digital Fingerprinting Images." *Law Enforcement News*, April 2005, pp. 1, 15.

Nyberg, Ramesh. "Learn to Read Product DNA." *Police*, March 2005, pp. 41–45.

Page, Douglas. "Fingerprinting Bioterror Agents." *Law Enforcement Technology*, January 2004a, pp. 68–73.

Page, Douglas. "Scene of the Grime." *Law Enforcement Technology*, March 2004b, pp. 108–113.

"Psycholinguistics." Britannica Concise Encyclopedia. Retrieved June 23, 2005, from Encyclopedia Britannica Premium Service. http://www.britannica.com/ebc/article?tocId=9376064

Robin, Lisa, and Smith, Tim. "Zebra Technology Evidence Tracking." *Law and Order*, May 2004, pp. 44–48.

Scarborough, Steve. "More Than Meets the Eye." *Law Enforcement Technology*, June 2004, pp. 80–87.

Scarborough, Steve. "A Match Made in Heaven." *Law Enforcement Technology*, April 2005, pp. 42–49.

Spraggs, David. "The Eliminator." *Police*, March 2005, pp. 36–40.

Steck-Flynn, Kathy. "Getting Down and Dirty." *Law Enforcement Technology*, February 2005a, pp. 32–40.

Steck-Flynn, Kathy. "Through the Looking Glass." *Law Enforcement Technology*, March 2005b, pp. 54–60.

Taylor, Royce, and Knapp, Michael. "Indianapolis PD Converts to Full-Hand Scanning." *Law Enforcement Technology*, June 2004, pp. 154–161.

Turner, Shannon. "From Log Books to Barcodes." *Law Enforcement Technology*, August 2004, pp. 138–142.

Van Nostrand, George, and Auletta, Ray. *Forensic Psycholinguistics*. Barraclough Legal Publishing, 2005. http://barracloughltd.com/forensic_psych.html

Wallace, Ronald. "Duke Projectile Recovery System." *Law and Order*, May 2004, pp. 36–39.

Weiss, Jim, and Davis, Mickey. "Managing the Evidence Room." *Law and Order*, August 2003, pp. 92–95.

Wilson, Bob. "Technology Speeds Up DNA Processing." *Law Enforcement Technology*, January 2005, pp. 88–93.

CASES CITED

Daubert v. Merrell Dow Pharmaceuticals, 113 S.Ct. 2728 (1993)

Frye v. United States, 54 App. D.C. 46, 293 F. 1013 (1923)

Obtaining Information

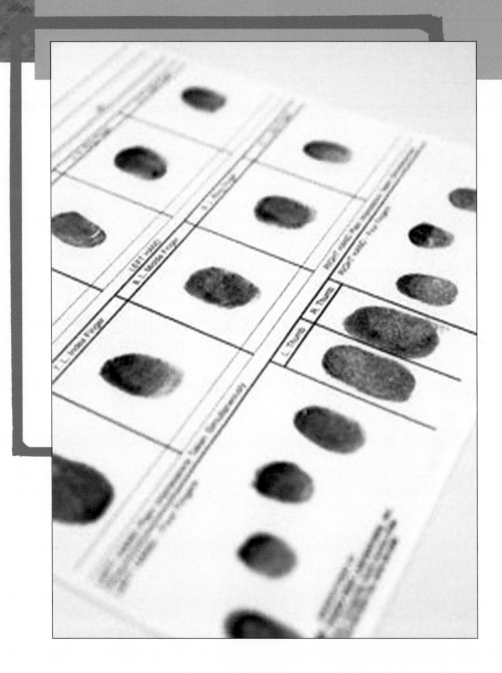

Can You Define?

Do You Know?

- What sources of information are available to investigators?
- What a sources-of-information file is and what it contains?
- What the goal of interviewing and interrogation is?
- What the characteristics of an effective interviewer or interrogator are?
- How to improve communication?
- What the emotional barriers to communication are?
- What two requirements are needed to obtain information?
- What the difference between direct and indirect questions is and when to use each?
- What technique is likely to assist recall as well as uncover lies?
- When and in what order individuals are interviewed?
- What basic approaches to use in questioning reluctant interviewees?
- What the *Miranda* warning is and when to give it?
- What the two requirements of a place for conducting interrogations are?
- What techniques to use in an interrogation?
- What third-degree tactics are and what their place in interrogation is?
- What restrictions are placed on obtaining a confession?
- What significance a confession has in an investigation?
- What to consider when questioning a juvenile?
- What a polygraph is and what its role in investigation and the acceptability of its results in court are?

 nowledge obtained through both questioning and physical evidence is equally important. Most solved cases rely on both physical evidence and information obtained by interviewing and interrogating. Physical evidence can provide a basis for questioning people about a crime, and questioning can provide leads for finding physical evidence. Either or both provide the knowledge required to end an investigation successfully. Although physical evidence is important by itself, supporting oral testimony adds considerable value when presented in court. On the other hand, although a confession may appear conclusive, it cannot stand alone legally. It must be supported by physical evidence or other corroboration.

This chapter begins with a discussion of sources of information, followed by an in-depth look at interviewing and interrogating, including questioning young children and juveniles. Next is a discussion on evaluating and corroborating information received during an interview or interrogation and an explanation of scientific aids available for obtaining information. The chapter concludes with the importance of sharing information to enhance efforts to prevent crime, solve criminal cases, and provide homeland security.

Sources of Information

In addition to physical evidence, three primary sources of information are available.

> Important sources of information include (1) reports, records, and databases, including those found on the Internet; (2) people who are not suspects in a crime but who know something about the crime or those involved; and (3) suspects in the crime.

Often these sources overlap. For example, information in a hotel's records may be supplemented by information supplied by the hotel manager or the doorkeeper.

Because so many informational sources exist in any given community, it is helpful to develop a sources-of-information file. Each time you locate someone who can provide important information on criminal activity in a community, make a card with information on this source or enter the information into a computer file. For example, if a hotel manager provides useful information, make a card with the manager's name, name of the hotel, address, telephone number, type of information provided, and other relevant information. File the card under *hotel.*

> A **sources-of-information file** contains the name and location of people, organizations, and records that may assist in a criminal investigation.

We have progressed from the stone age to the agricultural age to the industrial age to the **information age,** a period driven by words rather than by agriculture or industry as in the past. Knowledge is doubling every two and a half years. In no area have more advances been made than in movement of information. The challenge is in how to keep abreast of it all.

Among the most important advances for law enforcement is the availability of computerized infor-

mation. Such information has been in existence for several years but not in individual squad cars and easily accessible by the average officer on the beat. Officers now receive information on stolen vehicles, individual arrest records, and the like within minutes.

Reports, Records, and Databases

Reports, records, and databases at the local, state, and federal level can be of assistance in criminal investigations.

Local Resources An important information source is the records and reports of your police department, including all preliminary reports, follow-up investigative reports, offense and arrest records, modus operandi files, fingerprint files, missing persons reports, gun registrations, and wanted bulletins. Closely examine a suspect's prior record and modus operandi. Examine all laboratory and coroner's reports associated with a case.

Also check records maintained by banks, loan and credit companies, delivery services, hospitals and clinics, hotels and motels, newspapers, telephone books, city directories, street cross-directories, utility providers, personnel departments, pawnbrokers, storage companies, schools, and taxi companies. Each time you locate a source whose records are helpful, add it to your sources-of-information file.

Caller ID The telephone number from which a call is placed can be recorded by a caller ID service, even if the call is not answered. Caller ID also provides the date and time of the call and can store numbers in its memory when more than one call is received.

In some criminal investigations, evidence has been obtained from telephones served by caller ID. For example, a person who committed a burglary first called the business's office to see if anyone was there. The office telephone recorded the number of the phone the burglar used, enabling the police to locate the suspect. Caller ID could be helpful in cases involving telephoned threats, kidnappings, and the like.

State Resources Investigators also use information from the state police, the Department of Motor Vehicles, the Department of Corrections, and the Parole Commission.

Federal Resources Federal resources include the U.S. Post Office; the Immigration and Naturalization Service; the Social Security Administration; the Federal Bureau of Investigation (FBI), the Bureau of Alcohol, Tobacco, Firearms and Explosives (ATF); and the Drug Enforcement Administration.

The FBI's National Crime Information Center (NCIC) contains online databases on wanted and missing persons; stolen guns, securities, articles, boats, license plates, and vehicles; criminal histories; foreign fugitives and deported felons; gang and terrorist members; and persons subject to protection orders. The newest generation, NCIC 2000, includes mug shots (e.g., of sexual offenders and persons on probation or parole or incarcerated in federal prisons) and other personal identifying images, such as scars and tattoos; images of vehicles; an enhanced name search (of all derivatives of a name, e.g., Jeff, Geoff, Jeffrey); automated single-finger fingerprint matching; and information linking. These provide the ability to associate logically related records across NCIC files for the same criminal or the same crime. For example, an inquiry on a gun also could retrieve a wanted person or a stolen vehicle.

The Internet

The Internet is an extremely valuable source of information. Fast-breaking cases, such as a kidnapping, can be aided by an investigator's ability to distribute photographs and important details efficiently and quickly.

Another resource is the website of the International Association of Chiefs of Police, http://www.theiacp.org. The FBI's website, http://www.fbi.gov, provides information on major investigations, wanted felons, various FBI programs and initiatives, and ways to contact FBI agents regarding various crimes.

Another resource for investigators is Law Enforcement Online (LEO), sponsored by the FBI. Membership is free but tightly restricted. Access is through a dedicated toll-free telephone line. LEO provides electronic mail, newsgroups , real-time chat sessions, links to national crime alerts, bulletins on terrorist activity, and training courses with multimedia features.

Scoville (p.44) suggests using the Internet search engines Google (www.google.com) and Ask Jeeves (www.ask.com) for help in computer forensics. He also suggests that professional investigators can use Black Book Online, at www.crimetime.com/online.htm. This site provides reports from telephone directories, reverse telephone number searches, business and real estate records, news archives, death and criminal records, professional licenses, bank accounts, and more. According to Scoville, investigators who are unfamiliar with starting an investigation on the Web should try the Law Library Resource Xchange (www.llrx.com), a free site providing articles on conducting research on the Internet and links that can "help you draw a bead on companies and individuals of interest in your investigation" (p.48).

In addition to reports and records, databases, and other Internet resources, investigators obtain information from people associated with the investigation.

Complainants, Witnesses, Victims, and Informants

Vast amounts of information come from people with direct or indirect knowledge of a crime. Although no one is legally required to provide information to the police except personal identification and accident information, citizens are responsible for cooperating with the police for their own and the community's best interests. Everyone is a potential crime victim and a potential source of information. Interview anyone other than a suspect who has information about a case. This includes complainants, witnesses, victims, and informants.

A **complainant** is a person who requests that some action be taken. The complainant is especially important in the initial stages of a case. Listen carefully to all details and determine the extent of the investigative problems involved: the type of crime, who committed it, what witnesses were present, the severity of any injuries, and any leads. Thank the complainant for contributing to the investigation.

A **witness** is a person who saw a crime or some part of it being committed. Good eyewitnesses are often the best source of information in a criminal investigation. Record the information a witness gives, including any details that can identify and locate a suspect or place the suspect at the crime scene. Although not always reliable, eyewitnesses' testimony remains a vital asset in investigating and prosecuting cases.

Sometimes a diligent search is needed to find witnesses. They may not want to get involved, or they may withhold information or provide it for ulterior motives. Make every effort to locate all witnesses. Check the entire crime scene area. Conduct a neighborhood canvass to determine whether anyone saw or heard anything when the crime occurred. Check with the victim's friends and associates. Make public appeals for information on radio, television, and the Internet. An informational checkpoint might also be used, as described in Chapter 4.

Be aware that witness statements are not always reliable. A group of police officers attended a session on the reliability of witnesses' memory and were given a memory recall test. Every officer failed the test. Witnesses are often more confident in their knowledge of what happened than they are accurate. Many people see only a part of the commission of a crime but testify as though they witnessed the entire event.

A **victim** is a person injured by a crime. Frequently the victim is also the complainant and a witness. Victims are emotionally involved and may be experiencing anger, rage, and fear. Such personal involvement can cause them to exaggerate or distort what occurred. Victims may also make a dying declaration that can provide valuable information to investigators. A dying declaration usually qualifies as a hearsay exception and is admissible as evidence.

An **informant** is anyone who can provide information about a case but who is not a complainant, witness, victim, or suspect. Informants may be interested citizens or individuals with criminal records.

Criteria for determining the reliability of informants' information were discussed in Chapter 4. The Court ruled in *Alabama v. White* (1990): "An anonymous tip can provide the foundation for reasonable suspicion when the tip predicts future activities that the officer is able to corroborate, which makes it reasonable to think that the informant has inside knowledge about the suspect."

Informants are frequently given code names, and only the investigator knows their identity. In some instances, however, informants may not remain anonymous, and their identity might have to be revealed. Be extremely careful in using such contacts. Never make promises or deals you cannot legally fulfill. Many jurisdictions have policies regarding the use of juveniles as informants, specifying a certain age or that police get permission from a court or parental permission.

Suspects

A **suspect** is a person considered to be directly or indirectly connected with a crime, either by overt act or by planning or directing it.

Do not overlook the suspect as a chief source of information. An individual can become a suspect either through information provided by citizens or by his or her own actions. Any suspicious individuals should be questioned. Complete a field-interview card for any suspicious person you stop. This card places a person or vehicle in a specific place at a specific time and furnishes data for future investigative needs. A sample field-interview card is shown in Figure 6.1.

A person with a known modus operandi fitting a crime may be spotted at or near the crime scene. The person may be wanted for another crime or show an exaggerated concern for the police's presence, or the person may be in an illegal place at an illegal time—often the case with juveniles.

When questioning occurs spontaneously on the street (referred to as a **field interview**), it is especially advantageous to officers to question someone suspected of

involvement in a crime right after the crime has occurred.

Sometimes direct questioning of suspects is not the best way to obtain information. In cases in which direct contact would tip off the person, it is often better to use undercover or surveillance officers or various types of listening devices, as discussed in Chapter 7.

Interviewing and Interrogating

Information is obtained continuously throughout an investigation. Some is volunteered, and some the police officer must really work for; some is useful and some worthless or even misleading. Most of an officer's time is spent meeting people and obtaining information from them, a process commonly referred to as either an *interview* or an *interrogation*.

An **interview** is questioning people who are not suspects in a crime but who know something about it or the people involved. An **interrogation** is questioning those suspected of direct or indirect involvement in a crime.

> The ultimate goal of interviewing and interrogating is to determine the truth, that is, to identify those responsible for a crime and to eliminate the innocent from suspicion.

Investigators must obtain all the facts supporting the truth, whether they indicate a person's guilt or innocence. The best information either proves the elements of the crime (the corpus delicti) or provides leads.

Characteristics of an Effective Interviewer/Interrogator

Many of the emotional and intellectual traits of an investigator (discussed in Chapter 1) are especially valuable in communicating with others. Presenting a favorable appearance and personality and establishing rapport are more important than physical attributes. Sometimes, however, it is an advantage to be of the same race or gender as the person being questioned. Under some circumstances it is better not to wear a uniform. Sometimes a suit or jeans and a sweater are more appropriate. Chandler (p.65) contends that the most important skills in interpersonal communication are empathy, calmness, patience, warmth, sincerity, strength, and conviction.

OP. LIC. NO.	STATE	NAME (Last name first)					
476-18-4681	NV	Pirino, John W.					

RESIDENCE ADDRESS	CITY	STATE	SEX	DESCENT	HAIR	EYES
7801 Dupoint	Las Vegas, Nv.		M	It	Bl	Br

HEIGHT	WEIGHT	BIRTHDATE	CLOTHING
5-11	187	5-14-40	Blue Jeans, Striped Shirt, Brown Jacket

PERSONAL ODDITIES	PHONE NO.
Limp-inj. left leg	421-1170

BUSINESS ADDRESS/SCHOOL/UNION AFFIL.	SOC. SEC. NO.
None	321-14-8645

MONIKER/ALIAS	GANG/CLUB
Jack	None

SUBJ. INFO.	1 LOITERER 3 SOLICITOR 5 GANG ACTIVITY 7 ON PAROLE 2 PROWLER 4 HITCHHIKER 6 HAS RECORD 8 X ON PROBATION	☒ DRIVER ☐ PASSENGER

	YEAR	MAKE	MODEL	TYPE	COLOR	VEH. LIC. NO.	STATE
V	1986	Chev St. Wagon		4 dr	beige	491-AMU	Nv

E	INSIDE COLOR	I N T	1 BUCKET SEATS 2 DAMAGED INSIDE	E X T	1 CUST. WHEELS 3 LEVEL ALTER. 5 CUST. PAINT 2 PAINTED INSC 4 RUST/PRIMER 6 VINYL TOP
	Brown				

H	**BODY**	⊠ DAMAGE 3⊠ STICKER 4 LEFT 6 FRONT 2 MODIFIED 5 RIGHT 7 REAR	**WIN-DOWS**	⊠ DAMAGE 3 CURTAINS 4 LEFT 6 FRONT 2 CUST. TINT 5 RIGHT 7 ⊠REAR

Persons with subject:

LAST NAME	1st init.	SEX	LAST NAME	1st init.	SEX
Bixley, W C		M	Gurley, M S		F
LAST NAME	1st init.	SEX	LAST NAME	1st init.	SEX
Thoms, G A		M	Lecher, R L		F

ADDITIONAL INFO (ADDITIONAL PERSONS WITH SUBJECT, BKG. NOS., I.D. NOS., NARRATIVE, ETC.)

Vehicle going slow in alley, passengers in rear looking out rear
window. No other persons or vehicles in alley, late at night.

DATE	TIME	LOCATION	Rept. Dist.
5-4-20__	0130	Alley behind 602 Pine	

OFFICER'S NAME	SERIAL NO.	OFFICER'S NAME	SERIAL NO.
Wesley Jones	162	Thomas Begley	153

FIELD INTERVIEW BOULDER CITY POLICE DEPARTMENT	DIVISION	DETAIL	SUPERVISOR'S INITS.
	Patrol	Drug	HVM

Figure 6.1
Field interview card, front and back
Courtesy of the Boulder City (Nevada) Police Department.

An effective interviewer/interrogator is adaptable and culturally adroit, self-controlled, patient, confident, optimistic, objective, sensitive to individual rights, and knowledgeable of the elements of crimes.

- *Adaptable and culturally adroit.* Your cultural and educational background and experience affect your ability to understand people from all walks of life, to meet them on their own level on varied subjects, and to adapt to their personalities, backgrounds, and lifestyles (Figure 6.2).

- *Self-controlled and patient.* Use self-control and patience to motivate people to talk. Be understanding yet detached, waiting for responses while patiently leading the conversation and probing for facts. Remain professional, recognizing that some people you interview may feel hostile toward you.

© Paul Conklin/PhotEdit

Figure 6.2
Police officers should be skilled at communicating with people of all ages and from other cultures. Cultural diversity within the department can be of great benefit. Here two officers talk with a Vietnamese refugee mother and her daughter in their home.

- *Confident and optimistic.* Do not assume that because the person you are questioning is a hardened criminal, has an attorney, is belligerent, or is better educated than you that no opportunity exists to obtain information. Show that you are in command, that you already know many answers, and that you want to corroborate what you know. If the conversation shifts away from the subject, steer the discussion back to the topic.

- *Objective.* Maintain your perspective on what is sought, avoiding preconceived ideas about the case. Be aware of any personal prejudices that can interfere with your questioning.

- *Sensitive to individual rights.* Maintain a balance between the rights of others and those of society. Naturally, suspects do not want to give information that conflicts with their self-interests or threatens their freedom. Moreover, many citizens want to stay out of other people's business. Use reason and patience to overcome this resistance to becoming involved.

- *Knowledgeable of the elements of the crime.* Know what information you need to prove the elements of the crime you are investigating. Phrase questions to elicit information related to these elements.

Enhancing Communication

Successful questioning requires two-way communication between the investigator and the person being questioned. There are several ways to improve communication, whether in interviewing or interrogating.

> To improve communication: Prepare in advance, obtain the information as soon after the incident as possible, be considerate and friendly, use a private setting, eliminate physical barriers, sit rather than stand, encourage conversation, ask simple questions one at a time, listen, and observe.

Emotional Barriers to Communication People often have reasons for not wanting to answer questions that police ask. Even though these reasons may have no logical basis, be aware of the common barriers to communication.

> Emotional barriers to communication include ingrained attitudes and prejudices, fear, anger, and self-preservation.

One important barrier to communication between police and the public is the ingrained attitude that telling the truth to the police is wrong. The criminal element, those closely associated with crime, and even the police often use such terms as *fink* and *snitch,* which imply that giving information to the police is wrong, unsavory, or illegal.

Prejudices concerning a person's race, beliefs, religion, appearance, amount of education, economic status, or place of upbringing can be barriers to communication. You may encounter prejudice because you are a police officer or because of your race, physical appearance, or religious beliefs. Equally important, prejudices you hold can interfere with your communicating with some people and therefore with your investigation.

Fear is another barrier to communication. Some witnesses fear that criminals will harm them or their family if they testify, or they fear the imposition on their time and the negative impact on their wages of having to go to court to testify.

People actually involved in a crime can be reluctant to talk for many reasons, the most important of which is self-preservation. Although suspects naturally do not want to implicate themselves, other factors may also cause them to not answer questions. Severe guilt feelings can preclude telling anyone about a crime. Fear of consequences can be so great that nothing will induce them to tell the truth. They may fear that if they are sent to prison they will be sexually assaulted or beaten, or they may fear that any accomplices they implicate will seek revenge.

Other Barriers to Communication As ethnic diversity increases and other languages proliferate, language barriers become an increasing challenge to law enforcement. Language barriers might be minimized or eliminated by seeking a mix of bilingual officers in hiring, training officers in conversational foreign languages, and matching officers to appropriate beats and assignments.

One of the most common techniques used to help officers communicate with non-English-speaking people is the Point Talk Law Enforcement Translator, in which an officer locates the appropriate language either in a handbook or on a computer screen and then points to appropriate phrases to ask specific questions or elicit desired responses.

Mertens (p.18) describes a similar aid, the Kwik-point Law Enforcement Visual Language Translator, which allows officers to assist non-English speakers in understanding and following search procedures, and the "ID" Panel, a visual aid to help victims in describing suspects. Witnesses can point to different heights, weights, eye shapes and colors, hair styles and colors, clothing, and the like.

Additional barriers to communication exist with individuals who are hearing impaired, who have Alzheimer's disease, or who are mentally retarded. It is highly recommended that officers learn sign language to help them communicate with the hearing impaired. This skill also allows officers to communicate silently among themselves when confronting suspects. In addition, it can be a universal means of recognition for undercover officers from different agencies or from large agencies where officers often do not know each other.

Effective Questioning Techniques

Most cases are solved through effective questioning techniques. Investigators use questions and repetition effectively and also know how to question reluctant subjects. No matter which technique or combination of techniques you select, you should follow two key requirements:

 Two basic requirements to obtain information are to listen and to observe.

How people act during questioning can tell as much as or more than their words. Signs of unusual nervousness, odd expressions, rapid breathing, visible perspiration, or a highly agitated state are cause to question the person's truthfulness. Table 6.1 summarizes the guidelines for a successful questioning.

Direct Versus Indirect Questions   A subtle but important difference exists between direct and indirect questions. A **direct question** is to the point, allowing little possibility of misinterpretation—for example, "What time did you and your husband leave the restaurant?" In contrast, an **indirect question** is disguised. For exam-

ple, a question such as, "How do you and your husband get along?" could elicit a variety of answers.

Ask direct questions, that is, questions that come right to the point. Use indirect questions—those that skirt the basic questions—sparingly.

The axiom that the shortest distance between two points is a straight line is generally true in obtaining information. Knowing the elements of the crime you are investigating lets you select pertinent questions.

Repetition   Anyone who watches detective shows has heard victims or suspects complain, "I've already told my story to the police." This is true to life. Individuals *are* asked to tell and retell their version of what happened and for very good reasons. Someone who is lying will usually tell a story exactly the same way several times. A truthful story, however, will contain the same facts but be phrased differently each time it is retold. After a person has told you what happened, guide the discussion to some other aspect of the case. Later, come back to the topic and ask the person to repeat the story.

Repetition is an effective technique to obtain recall and to uncover lies.

Often repeating what someone has told you helps the person provide additional information. Sometimes it also confuses the person being questioned, and if the original version was not true, another repetition will reveal this fact. If inconsistencies appear, go back over the information and attempt to account for them.

Table 6.1 / **Interview/Interrogation Guidelines**

- Ask one question at a time and keep your responses simple and direct.
- Avoid questions that can be answered "yes" or "no"; a narrative account provides more information and may reveal inconsistencies in the person's story.
- Be positive in your approach, but let the person save face if necessary so that you may obtain further information.
- Give the person time to answer. Do not be uncomfortable with pauses in the interview.
- Listen to answers, but at the same time anticipate your next question.
- Watch your body language and tone of voice.
- Start the conversation on neutral territory.
- Tape recorders can be frightening.
- React to what you hear.
- As you move into difficult territory, slow down.
- Don't rush to fill silences.
- Pose the toughest questions simply and directly.
- No meltdowns. You must establish professional distance. Keep your role clear.

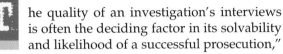

The Interview

"The quality of an investigation's interviews is often the deciding factor in its solvability and likelihood of a successful prosecution," says Reece (p.66), citing the following "rewards" of quality interviews:

- They promote victims' and the public's confidence in law enforcement.
- They increase the likelihood of guilty pleas, reducing time spent testifying and saving tax dollars.
- They reduce the time spent re-interviewing witnesses due to an earlier officer's inexperience.
- They direct investigators to additional suspects, evidence of the crime, additional victims, and the recovery of property.
- They reduce the likelihood of false arrests.
- They improve morale among the investigating officers in the department.

Interviewing involves talking to people, questioning them, obtaining information, and reading between the lines. The main sources of information at the crime scene are the complainant, the victim, and witnesses. (These may be the same person.) Separate the witnesses and then obtain a complete account of the incident from each one. Listen, prompt if necessary, and explore for new leads.

Interview witnesses separately if possible. Interview the victim or complainant first, then eyewitnesses, and then people who did not actually see the crime but who have relevant information.

Finding, detaining, and separating witnesses is a high priority. Witnesses who are not immediately detained can drift off into the crowd or decide not to become involved. Obtain the information as rapidly as possible. Identify all witnesses and check their names and addresses against their identification. Ask witnesses not to speak to one another or to compare stories until they have written down in their own words what happened.

If there are many witnesses, discuss the incident briefly with each. Then establish a priority for obtaining statements based on the witnesses' availability and the importance of their information.

In most cases, interview complainants first, because they can often provide enough information to determine whether a crime has been committed and, if so, what type of crime. If department policy requires it, have complainants read and initial or sign the information you record during the interview.

Anyone who saw what happened, how it happened, or the person(s) who made it happen is inter-

viewed next. Such witnesses may be in a state of panic, frustration, or anger. In the presence of such emotions, remain calm and detached, yet show empathy and understanding—a difficult feat. After interviewing witnesses, interview people who can furnish facts about what happened before or immediately after the crime or who have information about the suspect or the victim.

Not all people with relevant information are at the crime scene. Some people in the general area may have seen or heard something of value. Even people miles away from the scene may have information about the crime or the person committing it. Explain to such individuals why you are questioning them, check their identification, and then proceed with your interview.

The main sources of immediate information away from the crime scene are neighbors, business associates, people in the general area such as motel and hotel personnel, and longtime residents. Longer-term contacts may include informants, missing witnesses, friends, and relatives. Appeals for public cooperation and reports from various agencies and organizations may also produce information.

Record both positive and negative information. The fact that a witness did *not* see anyone enter a building may be as important as having seen someone.

Conduct the interviews like a conversation, but with a purpose. Interviewing skills can be learned and perfected. After each interview, critique it and identify your mistakes and aspects that you want to improve. Then when you are planning your next interview, review what you have decided to do differently. Keep doing this with each new interview, and you will become an expert.

Advance Planning

Many interviews, at least initial ones, are conducted in the field and allow no time for planning. If time permits, plan carefully for interviews. Review reports about the case before questioning people. Learn as much as possible about the person you are going to question before you begin the interview.

Selecting the Time and Place

Sometimes there is no time to decide when and where to conduct an interview. Arriving at a crime scene, you may be confronted with a victim or witness who immediately begins to supply pertinent information. Recall that these *res gestae* statements are extremely valuable. Therefore, record them as close to verbatim as possible.

Determine as soon as possible who the complainant is, where and how many witnesses exist, and whether the suspect has been apprehended. If more than one officer is present, the officer in charge decides who will be questioned and assigns personnel to do it.

Immediate contact with people who have information about a crime improves the chances of obtaining information (Figure 6.3). Although emotions may be running high, witnesses are usually best able to recall details immediately after an incident. They are also less likely to embellish or exaggerate their stories, because others present can be asked to verify the information. Moreover, witnesses can be separated so they will have no opportunity to compare information. Finally, the reluctance to give the police information is usually not so strong immediately after a crime. Given time to reflect, witnesses may fear that they will have to testify in court, that cooperation will take them away from work and cost them financially, or that the criminal will retaliate.

Beginning the Interview

How an interview is started is extremely important. At this point the interviewee and the interviewer size each other up. Mistakes in beginning the interview can establish insurmountable barriers. Make your initial contact friendly but professional. Begin by identifying yourself and showing your credentials. Then ask a general question about the person's knowledge of the crime.

Establishing Rapport

Rapport is probably the most critical factor in any interview. **Rapport** is an understanding between individuals created by genuine interest and concern. It requires empathy. *Empathy* means accurately perceiving and responding to another person's thoughts and feelings. This differs from *sympathy,* which is an involuntary emotion of feeling sorry for another person.

People who are approached civilly may volunteer a surprising amount of useful information. Most people do not condone criminal behavior and will assist you. However, they often do not know what is important to a specific investigation. Provide every opportunity to establish rapport and to assist citizens in providing information.

Not everyone with information can provide it easily. People who are emotionally unstable or mentally deficient, have temporary loss of memory, or fear the police often cannot or will not be forthcoming. With them, establishing rapport is critical. If a person is deaf or speaks a foreign language, arrange for an interpreter. If a person appears unwilling to talk, find out why.

Give reluctant witnesses confidence by demonstrating self-assurance. Give indifferent witnesses a sense of importance by explaining how the information will help a victim. Remind them that someday they may be victims themselves and would then want others to cooperate. Find a way to motivate every witness to talk with you and answer your questions.

Careful listening enhances rapport. Do not indicate verbally or nonverbally that you consider a matter trivial or unimportant; people will sense if you are merely going through the motions. Take a personal interest. Discuss their family, their work, or their hobbies. Be empathetic and assure them that everything possible will be done but that you need their help.

Chandler (p.65) recommends that while establishing rapport interviewers observe the interviewees' baseline behaviors, including their normal eye contact, posture, and speech patterns. The investigators can then detect behavioral changes such as failure to make eye contact or speaking more rapidly during the more intensive stages of the interview, which could indicate deception.

Networking an Interview

Most people are familiar with the concept of a business or professional **network**—a body of personal contacts that can further one's career. In reality, networks can extend much farther than this.

Networks also establish relationships between people and between people and their beliefs. They produce a context in which to understand a person. These networks may be social, ethnic, cultural, business, professional/occupational, religious, or political. As American society becomes more diverse, officers will have to understand the networks in their jurisdictions.

Reluctant Interviewees   Most people who are reluctant to be questioned respond to one of two approaches: logical or emotional.

Appeal to a reluctant interviewee's reason or emotions.

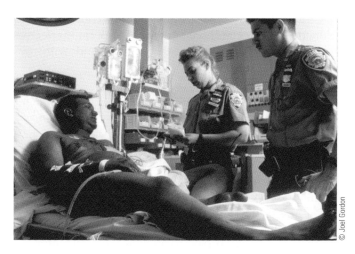

Figure 6.3
Some interviews are conducted under extremely difficult circumstances. Here investigators interview a hospitalized convenience store clerk who was shot during a robbery of the convenience store he worked at. What interview techniques should the investigators use in this situation to conduct a successful interview that is also sensitive to the needs of the interviewee?

The *logical approach* is based on reason. Use logic to determine why the person refuses to cooperate. Explain the problems that result when people who know about a crime do not cooperate with investigators.

The *emotional approach* addresses such negative feelings as hate, anger, greed, revenge, pride, and jealousy. You can increase these emotions or simply acknowledge them (e.g., "Anyone in your situation would respond the same way"). If such tactics do not work, warn the person of the serious consequences of withholding important information.

Whether to select a logical or an emotional approach depends on the person being interviewed, the type of investigation, and your personal preference.

The Cognitive Interview   Interview style has important implications for how much information is received from subjects. The **cognitive interview** tries to get the interviewee to recall the scene mentally by using simple mnemonic techniques aimed at encouraging focused retrieval. These techniques include allowing interviewees to do most of the talking; asking open-ended questions; allowing ample time for answers; avoiding interruptions; and encouraging the person to report all details, no matter how trivial.

The cognitive interview method calls for using a secluded, quiet place free of distractions and encouraging a subject to speak slowly. The interviewer first helps the interviewee *reconstruct the circumstances* by asking, "How did you feel . . . ?" Have the interviewee describe the weather, the surroundings, objects, people, and smells. Interviewees are encouraged to *report everything,* even if they think something is unimportant. They might also be asked to *relate the events in a different order* or to *change perspectives.* What would another person present have seen?

Among the drawbacks of this method are the amount of time it takes and the need for a controlled environment. Nonetheless, the cognitive interview is especially effective for obtaining information from victims and witnesses who have difficulty remembering an event.

Avoiding Contaminating the Interview

Sandoval (p.2) states: "The objective of any interview should be to acquire accurate and complete information without contaminating the interview process." He explains: "Contamination occurs when investigators impede or negatively influence the interview process, thereby causing the subject to provide inaccurate information." This is akin to contamination of a crime scene and can be equally devastating to successful resolution of a case. According to Sandoval (p.2), studies have found that the "single most important determinant" of satisfactory resolution of a criminal case is the information gained from interviews.

Sandoval (p.3) cites three critical dimensions of an interview: (1) the environment, (2) the interviewer's behavior, and (3) the questions asked. He cautions that interviewing subjects on noisy, busy streets with numerous onlookers is "fraught with danger." Most interviews will be much more successful if conducted in a quiet, private location. Interviewers should also project sincerity, patience, and a willingness to listen. They should begin with broad, open-ended questions and end with very direct, closed questions. Table 6.2 provides guidelines for avoiding interview contamination.

The questioning process, according to Sandoval (p.7), is in itself a complex skill that can be thought of as a funnel, as illustrated in Figure 6.4.

A recent development in interviewing individuals with knowledge of a crime has changed the timing of questioning in some situations, i.e., those dealing with testimonial hearsay.

Testimonial Hearsay   Rutledge (2004b, p.63) defines **testimonial hearsay** as "prior testimony (whether at a grand jury hearing, preliminary hearing, prior trial or civil deposition), as well as statements resulting from police interrogation." What this means is that if officers use "structured questioning" to obtain a witness's statement, that statement will be inadmissible in a criminal trial unless the witness is unavailable to testify and was cross-examined by the defendant (*Crawford v. Washington,* 2004).

Rutledge (2004b, p.63) says that the implications of this ruling are that police reports must now try to differentiate between statements that resulted from structured questioning and those that did not. He suggests that interviewers not start asking questions in the middle of a subject's volunteered statements (e.g., "Tell me what happened"). Officers should listen well, take good notes, and make it clear in the notes and report that they did not direct or extract the specific information. If an interview yields substantial information related to a case, a statement should be obtained.

Statements

A **statement** is a legal narrative description of events related to a crime. It is a formal, detailed account. It begins with an introduction that gives the place, time, date, and names of the people conducting and present at an interview. The name, address, and age of the person questioned are stated before the main body of the statement. Figure 6.5 shows a sample statement.

The body of the statement is the person's account of the incident. A clause at the end states that the information was given voluntarily. The person making the statement reads each page, makes any needed corrections, initials each correction, and then signs the statement.

Obtain statements in private, with no one other than police officers present, and allow no interruptions. However, other people will need to be called in to witness the signing of the statement.

Table 6.2 / **Tips for Avoiding Interview Contamination**

Focus on Interview Environment	
Questions to Consider	Strategies to Use
Where should the interview take place?	A location free of distractions
How should the room be configured?	Without barriers (e.g., desk or plants) between interviewer and subject
Who should conduct the interview?	One interviewer builds rapport and engenders trust more easily. Two interviewers should use a team approach; one asks questions and the other takes notes.
Focus on Interviewer's Behavior	
Questions to Consider	Strategies to Use
How can interviewers encourage subjects to talk?	Use an open and relaxed posture, facing the subject; lean forward, make eye contact, nod, and occasionally say "uh huh" and "okay"
How can interviewers encourage subjects to listen?	Speak slowly, softly, and deliberately; avoid stressing or emphasizing one word over another.
Focus on Interviewer's Questions	
Questions to Consider	Strategies to Use
What is a model for posing questions?	A funnel, with open-ended followed by closed questions
What are the benefits of open-ended questions?	Gather complete information, minimize the risk of imposing views on subject, and help assess subject's normal behavior
What are the benefits of closed questions?	Elicit specific details, ensure accuracy, and help detect deviations/changes in subject
How can interviewers ensure thoroughness?	Address the basics of who, what, when, where, how, and why
What are other cautions during questioning?	Never ask questions that disclose investigative information and lead the subject toward a desired response

Source: Vincent Sandoval. "Strategies to Avoid Interview Contamination." *FBI Law Enforcement Bulletin,* October 2003, p.8.

Statements can be taken in several ways: prepared in longhand by the person interviewed, dictated to a typist in question/answer format, or tape-recorded for later typing and signing.

A combination of questions and answers, with the answers in narrative form, is often the most effective format. However, a question/answer format is often challenged in court on grounds that questions guide and control the response. Another alternative is for you to write down the words of the person and have the person read and sign your notes. Also record the ending time.

Beginning and ending times may be of great value in court testimony.

Closing the Interview

End each interview by thanking the person for cooperating. If you have established good rapport with the interviewee, that person will probably cooperate with you later if needed.

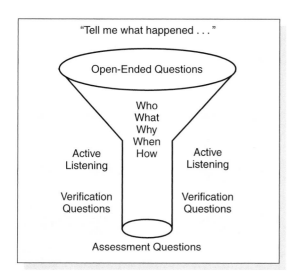

Figure 6.4
The questioning process
Source: Vincent Sandoval. "Strategies to Avoid Interview Contamination." *FBI Law Enforcement Bulletin,* October 2003, p.10.

The Interrogation

s Caplan (p.1) explains: "Interrogation occurs whenever an officer engages in conduct which he should know is likely to elicit an incriminating response from the suspect." Questioning

Figure 6.5
Sample voluntary statement

POLICE DEPARTMENT

VOLUNTARY STATEMENT

DR# ___943210___

DATE OCCURRED ___12 Nov. 20__ ___ LOCATION OF

TIME OCCURRED ___0315___ OCCURRENCE __Rear of bar and grill__

I, ___Walter Wilson___ , am ___28___ years of age,

home phone: ___444-4444___

and my address is ___100 Main St., this city___

bus. phone: ___444-4443___

1. ___I left the bar and grill at about 0300 on the 12th of Nov. 20__. I went out the___

2. _back door, got in my car and drove home. I did not see anyone at the rear of the bar_

3. _and grill.___

4. ___

5. ___

6. ___

7. ___

8. ___

9. ___

10. ___

11. ___

12. ___

13. ___

14. ___

15. ___

16. ___

I have read this statement consisting of ___1___ page (s) and I affirm to the truth and accuracy of the facts contained herein.

This statement was completed at (Location) ___The Police Dept.___

on the __14th__ day of __Nov.___ at __1300___ , 20__.

WITNESS _W^m Barnett_

WITNESS _John H Pratt_

Walter Wilson
Signature of person giving
voluntary statement.

suspects is usually more difficult than questioning witnesses or victims. Once identified and located, a suspect who *is* involved in a crime may make a statement, admission, or confession that, corroborated by independent evidence, can produce a guilty plea or obtain a conviction.

Many procedures used in interviewing are also used in interrogating, but you should note some important differences in how you question suspects. One of the most critical is ensuring that you do not violate suspects' constitutional rights, so that the information you obtain will be admissible in court. It is imperative that officers distinguish between questioning in a *Terry*-type stop/detention situation and a custodial situation requiring giving the *Miranda* warning.

The Miranda Warning

Before interrogating any suspect in custody, you must give the **Miranda warning,** as stipulated in *Miranda v. Arizona* (1966). In this decision, the U.S. Supreme Court ruled that suspects must be informed of their right to remain silent, to have an attorney present, and to have a state-appointed attorney if they cannot afford private counsel. Suspects must also be warned that anything they say may be used against them in court. As Rutledge (2003, p.140) observes: "In *Miranda v Arizona,* the Supreme Court created a judicial presumption that any police interrogation conducted while the subject is in custody inherently urges the person to talk." This jeopardizes the person's privilege against self-incrimination. Many officers read suspects their rights from a card (Figure 6.6).

 The *Miranda* warning informs suspects of their Fifth Amendment rights. Give the *Miranda* warning to every suspect you interrogate while in custody.

The Fifth Amendment states: "No person shall be compelled in any criminal case to be a witness against himself." The *Miranda* decision established that this right must be made known to suspects in custody before any questioning can occur.

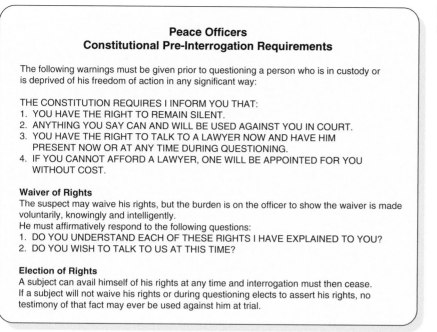

Figure 6.6
Miranda warning

Thousands of words have been written for and against this decision. The general interpretation and application of the *Miranda* decision is that once you have reasonable grounds to believe a person has committed a crime, that person's constitutional rights are in jeopardy unless the *Miranda* warning is given *before* any questioning.

Many court cases illustrate the gray area that exists in determining when to give the warning. The terms most often used to describe when it should be given are **in custody** or **custodial arrest.** *In custody* generally refers to a point at which an officer has decided a suspect is not free to leave, there has been considerable deprivation of liberty or the officer has in fact arrested the suspect.

In *Oregon v. Mathiason* (1977), the U.S. Supreme Court defined **custodial interrogation** as questioning initiated by law enforcement officers after a person has been taken into custody or otherwise significantly deprived of freedom. If a suspect chooses to remain silent, ask no further questions. If the suspect requests counsel, ask no more questions until counsel is present.

Judge (p.10) points out that the *Miranda* custody standard is no different for juveniles. In *Yarborough v. Alvarado* (2004) the Supreme Court held that a trial court need not consider age in determining whether a "reasonable person" is in custody for *Miranda* purposes.

Another *Miranda*-related concern, the fruit-of-the-poisonous-tree doctrine (Chapter 4), is explained by Rutledge (2004a, p.82). Recall that this doctrine makes inadmissible any evidence obtained through an earlier violation of the defendant's constitutional rights (*Wong Sun v. United States*, 1963). That same consequence does *not* follow from a failure to follow the *Miranda* procedures. According to Rutledge, if an officer learns the whereabouts of contraband or evidence from a state-

ment that does not comply with *Miranda*, the contraband or evidence need not be suppressed as "poisonous fruit" of the inadmissible statement (*United States v. Patane*, 2004).

When *Miranda* Does Not Apply   The *Miranda* warning has never applied to voluntary or unsolicited, spontaneous statements, admissions, or confessions. Someone can approach a police officer and say, "I want to confess that I killed Mark Jones. I took a gun from my car and shot him." If this remark was unsolicited and completely voluntary, the police officer is under no obligation to interrupt the person giving the confession. In one instance, a person telephoned the police long-distance to voluntarily confess to a felony.

Miranda warnings are *not* required during identification procedures such as fingerprinting, taking voice or handwriting exemplars, or conducting a lineup or sobriety tests. They are *not* required during routine booking questions, during brief on-the-scene questioning, or during brief, investigatory questioning during a temporary detention such as a *Terry* stop. A *Miranda* warning is also *not* required during roadside questioning following a routine traffic stop or other minor violation for which custody is not ordinarily imposed. Finally, a warning is *not* required during questioning by a private citizen who is not an agent of the government.

Waiving the Rights   A suspect can waive the rights granted by *Miranda* but must do so intelligently and knowingly. A **waiver,** that is a giving up of a right, is accompanied by a written or witnessed oral statement that the waiver was voluntary (Figure 6.7).

Silence, in itself, is *not* a waiver. A waiver of rights must be articulated by the suspect. Therefore, many officers read the *Miranda* warning aloud from a printed

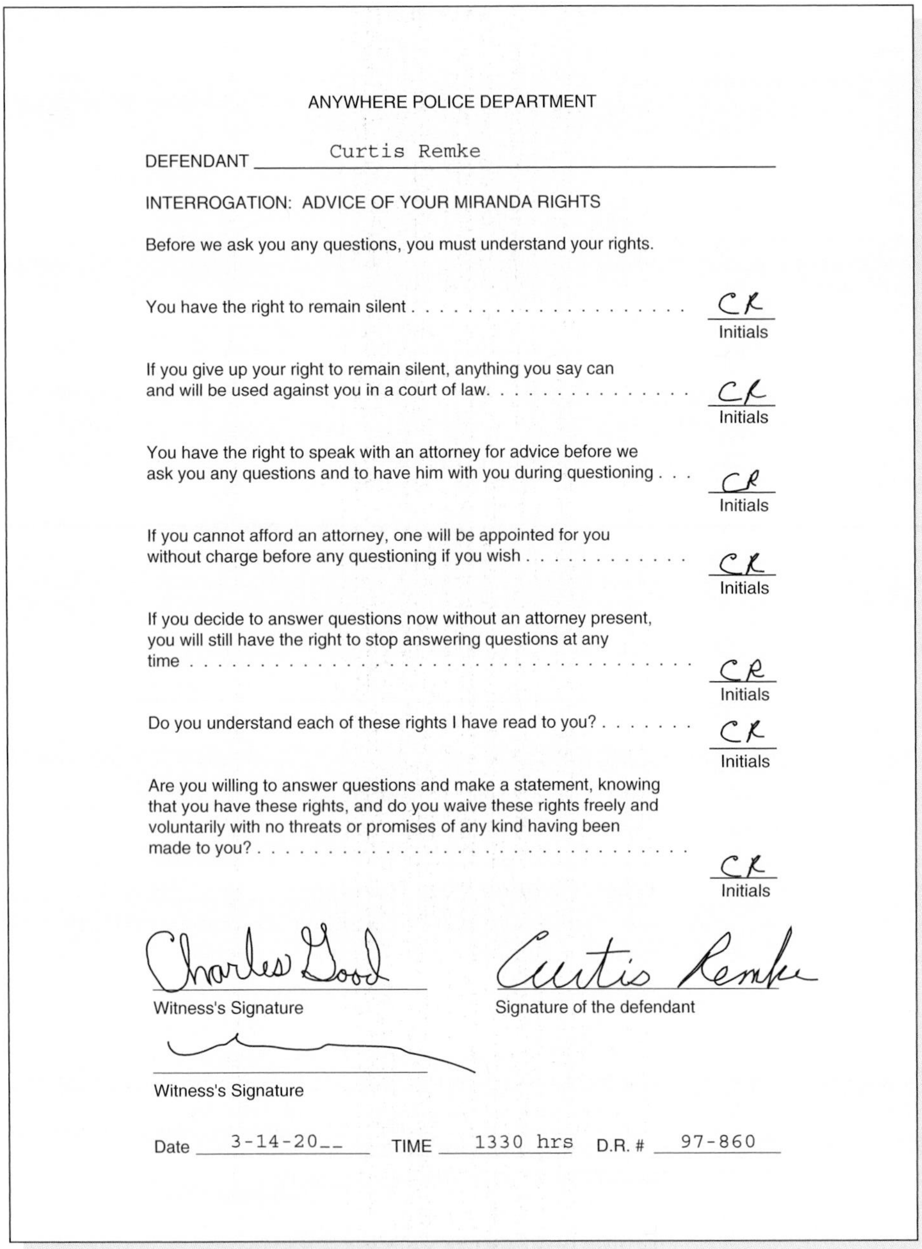

Figure 6.7
Miranda waiver form

ANYWHERE POLICE DEPARTMENT

DEFENDANT _____ Curtis Remke _____

INTERROGATION: ADVICE OF YOUR MIRANDA RIGHTS

Before we ask you any questions, you must understand your rights.

You have the right to remain silent . . . . *CR*
Initials

If you give up your right to remain silent, anything you say can
and will be used against you in a court of law. . . . . *CR*
Initials

You have the right to speak with an attorney for advice before we
ask you any questions and to have him with you during questioning . . . *CR*
Initials

If you cannot afford an attorney, one will be appointed for you
without charge before any questioning if you wish . . . . *CR*
Initials

If you decide to answer questions now without an attorney present,
you will still have the right to stop answering questions at any
time . . . . *CR*
Initials

Do you understand each of these rights I have read to you? . . . . *CR*
Initials

Are you willing to answer questions and make a statement, knowing
that you have these rights, and do you waive these rights freely and
voluntarily with no threats or promises of any kind having been
made to you? . . . . *CR*
Initials

Charles Good
Witness's Signature

Curtis Remke
Signature of the defendant

_____
Witness's Signature

Date __3-14-20__ TIME __1330 hrs__ D.R. # __97-860__

Figure 6.7
Miranda waiver form

card and then have the suspect read and sign the card (see Figure 6.6). The date and time are also recorded. If no card is available, a summary of the *Miranda* warning can be written, read, and signed. Police have the legal burden of proving that the suspect did waive his or her rights. The suspect retains the right to stop answering questions at any point, even when he or she originally waived the right to remain silent.

The Effects of *Miranda* The *Miranda* warning does not prevent suspects from talking. It simply requires that suspects be advised of and fully understand their constitutional rights. The basic intent of the *Miranda* decision is to guarantee the rights of the accused. The practical effect is to ensure that confessions are obtained without duress or coercion, thereby removing any inferences that third-degree tactics were used.

Several Court decisions relate to the *Miranda* warning. *Edwards v. Arizona* (1981) established that once a suspect in custody states that he or she wants an attorney, police must halt all questioning and may not engage in further questioning unless the suspect requests it. The defendant in *Edwards v. Arizona* interrupted a statement and said to FBI agents, "Maybe I should get a lawyer" but then resumed his story without prompting. The Court ruled that neither the Fourth nor the Fifth Amendment prohibits agents from merely listening to a defendant's voluntary statements and using them at a trial. Even if one inferred that the agents' silence amounted to "subtle compulsion," this would not necessarily vitiate the voluntariness of the defendant's statements.

In 1983 in *United States v. Dockery,* the Court ruled that telling a suspect she was "free to leave at any time" and then asking her to wait in a reception area for further questioning was within the *Miranda* rule. In 1984 *Minnesota v. Murphy* established that probation officers do not need to give the *Miranda* warning, and *Berkemer v. McCarty* ruled that the *Miranda* warning is not required for traffic violations.

The Supreme Court ruled in *Illinois v. Perkins* (1990) that jailed suspects need not be told of their right to remain silent when they provide information to undercover agents. Justice Anthony Kennedy wrote that the intent of the *Miranda* decision was to ensure that police questioning of suspects in custody is not sufficiently coercive to make confessions involuntary. Suspects must be told of their rights not to incriminate themselves. *Miranda* was *not* meant to protect suspects who boast about their criminal activities to individuals they believe to be cellmates.

***Miranda* Challenged**   The Supreme Court's ruling in *Dickerson v. United States* (2000) held that *Miranda* is a constitutional decision and therefore could not be overruled by an act of Congress. In declining to strike down *Miranda,* the Court said it found no compelling reason to overrule a 34-year-old decision that "has become embedded in routine police practice to the point where the warnings have become part of our national culture."

The "Question First" or "Beachheading" Technique

An interrogation technique commonly used in some departments is the "question first," or "beachheading," technique: An officer questions a custodial suspect without giving the *Miranda* warnings and obtains incriminating statements; the officer then gives the warning, gets a waiver, and repeats the interrogation to obtain the same statement (Rutledge, 2004c, p.74). Greenhouse (p.A9) contends that suspects typically will waive their *Miranda* rights and repeat what they said earlier in response to officers' leading questions, sensing that it is too late to turn back. The thinking behind this technique is that even though the first statement would be suppressed, the second, waived statement would be admissible. However, in *Missouri v. Seibert* (2004) the Supreme Court found this technique unconstitutional: "It is likely that if the interrogators employ the technique of withholding warnings until after interrogation succeeds in eliciting a confession, the warnings will be ineffective in preparing the suspect for successive interrogation, close in time and similar in content."

Rutledge (2004c, p.77) points out that it is sometimes difficult to tell exactly when a suspect is in custody or whether a particular line of questioning qualifies as interrogation. He maintains that if an unwarned custodial interrogation occurs, no matter what the reason, an admissible statement can still be obtained if officers allow the suspect a one- to two-hour break, change locations and interrogators, then give full warnings, obtain a waiver, and make no references back to any previous statements.

The Interplay of the Fourth and Fifth Amendments

Chapter 4 discussed how the Fourth Amendment restricts searches. This chapter discusses how the Fifth Amendment restricts confessions. Often the two amendments become intertwined, as may be seen in *New York v. Quarles* (1984), a case in which an exigent search resulted in a Fifth Amendment issue because of the statements elicited pursuant to the search.

In *New York v. Quarles* (1984), the U.S. Supreme Court ruled on the **public safety exception** to the *Miranda* warning requirement. In 1980 two police officers were stopped by a young woman who told them she had been raped and gave them a description of her rapist, who, she stated, had just entered a nearby supermarket and was armed with a gun. The suspect, Benjamin Quarles, was located, and one officer ordered him to stop. Quarles ran, and the officer momentarily lost sight of him. When he was apprehended and frisked, he was found to be wearing an empty shoulder holster. The officer asked Quarles where the gun was, and he nodded toward some cartons and said, "The gun is over there." The officer retrieved the gun, put Quarles under formal arrest, and read him his rights. Quarles waived his rights to an attorney and answered questions.

At the trial the court ruled pursuant to *Miranda* that the statement "The gun is over there" and the subsequent discovery of the gun as a result of that statement were inadmissible.

After reviewing the case, the U.S. Supreme Court ruled that the procedural safeguards that both deter a suspect from responding and increase the possibility of fewer convictions were deemed acceptable in *Miranda* to protect the Fifth Amendment privilege against self-incrimination. However, if *Miranda* warnings had deterred the response to the officer's question, the cost would have been more than just the loss of evidence that might lead to a conviction. As long as the gun remained concealed in the store, it posed a danger to the public safety.

The Court ruled that in this case the need to have the suspect talk (an exigent circumstance) took precedence over the requirement that the defendant be read his rights. The Court ruled that the material factor in applying this "public safety" exception is whether a public threat could possibly be removed by the suspect making a statement. In this case, the officer asked the question only to ensure his and the public's safety. He then gave the *Miranda* warning before continuing questioning.

The Fourth and Fifth Amendments also came into play in one case that was argued twice. The trials involved the same defendant (Williams) but different prosecutors. In the first trial, *Brewer v. Williams* (1977), the issue revolved around information solicited from Williams without his being Mirandized. An arrest warrant was issued in Des Moines, Iowa, for Williams, an escapee from a mental institution wanted for murdering a little girl on Christmas Eve. Williams turned himself in to police in Davenport, Iowa. Des Moines police went to Davenport to transport Williams back to Des Moines, with all agreeing that Williams was not to be questioned on the way. However, one detective, knowing Williams was a psychiatric patient who possessed a strong religious faith, told Williams that he wanted him to think about where the little girl was buried. He could perhaps show them where the body was on the way back because it was sleeting and they might not be able to find it in the morning. The officer told Williams that the little girl who was snatched away on Christmas Eve needed a Christian burial (the Christian Burial Speech). Williams complied and showed the officers where he had buried the girl.

As Harr and Hess (p.185) note: "While the lower courts admitted Williams' damaging statements into evidence, the Supreme Court in *Brewer v Williams* affirmed the court of appeals' decision that any statements made by Williams could not be admitted against him because the way they were elicited violated his constitutional rights to counsel." The Court granted Williams a new trial.

At the second trial, in *Nix v. Williams* (1984), the Court allowed the body of the little girl to be admitted into evidence because a search party had been approaching the location of the burial site and would have discovered the body without Williams' help. This case established the *inevitable-discovery doctrine* discussed in Chapter 4.

Right to Counsel under the Fifth and Sixth Amendments

The Supreme Court concluded in *Miranda* that custodial interrogation creates an inherently coercive environment that violates the Fifth Amendment protection against compelled self-incrimination by requiring that suspects be told of their right to an attorney. The Sixth Amendment right to counsel, however, does not hinge on the issue of custody. The right to counsel under the Sixth Amendment does not apply until proceedings against a suspect have begun.

Kruger (pp.11–12) uses the case of *Fellers v. United States* (2004) to clarify the distinction between these two rights. Officers went to Fellers' home to "discuss" his involvement in methamphetamine distribution. They told him that a grand jury had indicted him and four others and that they had a federal warrant for his arrest. The officers did not advise Fellers of his *Miranda* rights and asked him no questions, but Fellers told them he knew the four others and had used methamphetamine with them. The officers transported Fellers to jail and advised him of his rights, which he waived. At trial

Fellers filed a motion to suppress all his statements, claiming they were obtained in violation of his rights. The Supreme Court ruled in favor of Fellers, emphasizing that the Sixth Amendment right to counsel differs from the Fifth Amendment (*Miranda*) custodial-interrogation principle and applies even when the police do not question a defendant. The Court stated: "There is no question that the officers in this case deliberately elicited information from Fellers during the contact at his home." As Kruger (p.12) explains: "Although he may not have been in custody, he had been formally charged. The Fifth Amendment right to counsel may not have attached, but the Sixth Amendment right to counsel certainly had. There may have not been any interrogation, but officers deliberately elicited incriminating information." Officers erred in not obtaining a waiver of Fellers' Sixth Amendment right to counsel.

Foreign Nationals, the Vienna Convention Treaty, and Diplomatic Immunity

In part because of concern that foreign nationals charged with crimes in the United States will not fully understand their rights within the complex U.S. legal system, the Vienna Convention Treaty, signed in 1963, gives foreign nationals the right to contact their consulate in the event of their detention or arrest. Another treaty signed in 1972 provides diplomatic immunity for certain individuals. Rutledge (2005, p.74) explains that the State Department issues identification cards to all diplomatic personnel with a description of their particular immunities printed on the back. If officers wish to interrogate a person who claims diplomatic immunity, they should request the diplomatic identification and check the reverse of the card. Rutledge (2005, p.75) suggests that a general guideline is to treat foreign nationals and diplomats as you would want Americans to be treated under similar circumstances abroad, noting: "Compliance with treaties is not an option—it's the law."

Selecting the Time and Place

Like interviews, interrogations are conducted as soon as possible after a crime. Selecting the right place to question suspects is critical because they are usually reluctant to talk to police. Most interrogations are conducted at police headquarters. However, if a suspect refuses to come to the station and evidence is insufficient for an arrest, the interrogation may take place at the crime scene, in a squad car, or at the suspect's home or place of work. If possible, suspects should be interrogated in an unfamiliar place, away from their friends and family.

Conduct interrogations in a place that is private and free from interruptions.

Ideal conditions exist at the police station, where privacy and interruptions can be controlled. Visible movements or unusual noises distract a suspect undergoing questioning. Only the suspect, the suspect's attorney, and the interrogator should be in the room. Having two officers conduct the interrogation helps deflect false allegations or other untrue claims by the suspect. Allow no telephone calls and no distracting noises; allow no one to enter the room. Under these conditions, communication is more readily established.

Opinions differ on how interrogation rooms should be furnished. An austere, sparsely furnished room is generally less distracting; pictures can reduce the effectiveness of questioning. Many interrogation rooms have only two chairs: one for the investigator and one for the suspect. Some include a small, bare table. Some officers feel it is better *not* to have a desk or table between the officer and the suspect because the desk serves as a psychological protection to the suspect. Without it, the suspect tends to feel much more uncomfortable and vulnerable. Keep all notebooks, pencils, pens, and any objects of evidence to be used in the interrogation out of view, preferably in a drawer, until the appropriate time. An austere setting develops and maintains the suspect's absolute attention and allows total concentration on the conversation.

Other investigators, however, contend that such a setting is not conducive to good rapport. It may remind suspects of jail, and a fear of going to jail may keep them from talking. Instead, some investigators prefer a normally furnished room or office for interrogations. Doctors, lawyers, insurance investigators, and others have shown that a relaxed atmosphere encourages conversation. Even background music can reduce anxiety and dispel fear—major steps in getting subjects to talk.

Starting the Interrogation

Conducting the interrogation at the police station allows many options in timing and approach. A suspect can be brought to the interrogation room and left alone temporarily. Often the suspect has not yet met the investigator and is apprehensive about what the investigator is like, what will be asked, and what will happen. Provide time for the anxiety to increase, just as a football team sometimes takes a time-out before the opposing team attempts a critical field goal.

As you enter the room, show that you are in command, but do not display arrogance. The suspect is in an unfamiliar environment, is alone, does not know you, has been waiting, is apprehensive, and does not know what you will ask. At this point select your interrogation technique, deciding whether to increase or decrease the suspect's anxiety. Some investigators accomplish their goals by friendliness, others by authoritarianism. Show your identification and introduce yourself to the suspect, state the purpose of the interrogation, and then give the *Miranda* warning. Avoid violating the suspect's personal zone. Try to stay 2 to 6 feet away when questioning.

Do not become so wrapped up in yourself and your quest for information that you overlook body language or **nonverbal communication** that may indicate deception, anger, or indifference. Research has shown that 10 percent of a message delivered is verbal and 90 percent is nonverbal. Officers who can correctly interpret what they see arm themselves with a powerful tool.

Deception, for example, may be indicated by looking down, rolling the eyes upward, placing the hands over the eyes or mouth, or rubbing the hands around the mouth. Other possible indicators of deception include continual licking of the lips, twitching of the lips, intermittent coughs, rapid breathing, change in facial color, continuous swallowing, pulsating of the carotid artery in the neck, face flushing, tapping the fingers, and avoiding eye contact. Excessive protestations of innocence should also be suspect, for example, "I swear on my father's grave."

Establishing Rapport

As with interviewing, specific approaches during interrogating may either encourage cooperation or induce silence and noncooperation. The techniques for establishing rapport during an interview also apply in an interrogation. You may decide to instill the fear that there will be serious consequences if the suspect fails to cooperate. You may choose to appeal to the suspect's conscience, emphasizing the importance of getting out of the present situation and starting over with a clean slate. Try any approach that shows the person that cooperation is more desirable than having you find out about the crime another way.

It also helps to know why the crime was committed. Some crimes are committed out of uncontrollable passion, panic, or fear without consideration of the consequences. Other crimes result from the demands of the moment; the presumed necessity of the crime appears to justify it. Some criminals' guilt becomes so overpowering that they turn themselves in to the police. Other criminals turn to drugs or alcohol or leave the area to start over somewhere else.

It takes skill to obtain information from those involved in crime, especially if they know that the consequences can be severe. Suspects who understand that there is no easy way out of a situation may become cooperative. At this point, offering alternatives may be successful. Because most people respond to hard evidence, show suspects the physical evidence against them. Acknowledge to the suspect that there is no totally agreeable solution, but point out that some alternatives may be more agreeable than others.

Make no promises, but remind the suspect that the court decides the sentence and is apt to be easier on those who cooperate. Also point out that family and friends are usually more understanding if people admit they are wrong and try to "go straight."

If the suspect will not provide the names of accomplices because they are friends, explain that such "friends" have put the suspect in the present predicament.

Approaches to Interrogation

As with interviews, interrogations can follow an emotional or a logical approach. An emotional approach is either empathetic or authoritarian. After talking with the suspect, select the approach that seems to offer the best chance for obtaining information.

Server (2003, p.52) observes: "Well-trained detectives know the keys to police interrogation are rapport, rationalization, projection and minimization." Rapport has been stressed previously. Rationalization, projection, and minimization are among techniques commonly used in interrogation.

 Interrogation techniques include inquiring directly or indirectly, forcing responses, deflating or inflating the ego, minimizing or maximizing the crime, projecting the blame, rationalizing, and combining approaches.

Inquiring Indirectly or Directly   Indirect inquiry draws out information without mentioning the main subject. For example, an indirect approach may be phrased, "Have you ever been in the vicinity of Elm Street? Grove Street? the intersection of Elm and Grove?" In contrast, a direct question would be, "Did you break into the house on the corner of Elm and Grove Streets on December 16th?"

Forcing Responses   A forced response is elicited by asking a question that will implicate the suspect, regardless of the answer given. For example, the question "What time did you arrive at the house?" implies that the suspect *did* arrive at the house at some time. Answering the question with a time forces the suspect to admit having been there. Of course, the suspect may simply state, "I never arrived there," or may refuse to answer at all.

Deflating or Inflating the Ego   Belittling a suspect is often effective. For example, you may tell a suspect, "We know you couldn't be directly involved in the burglary because you aren't smart enough to pull off a job like that. We thought you might know who did, though." Question the suspect's skill in committing a crime known to be his specialty. Suggest that the suspect's reputation is suffering because his latest burglaries have

been bungled. The suspect may attempt—out of pride—to prove that it was a professional job.

The same results can be obtained by *inflating* suspects' egos, praising the skill shown in pulling off the job. Suspects may want to take the credit and admit their role in the crime.

Minimizing or Maximizing the Crime   Concentrate your efforts on the crime itself, ignoring for the moment the person committing it. Instead of using the word *crime,* say "the thing that happened." Refer to stolen property as "the stuff that was taken." Do not use terms such as *robbery, homicide,* or *arson.* Use other, less threatening terms. For example, asking the suspect "to tell the truth" is much less threatening than asking someone "to confess." Overstating the severity of an offense can be as effective as understating it. Mentioning that the amount of stolen money was $5,000 rather than the actual $500 puts the suspect on the spot. Is a partner holding out? Is the victim lying about the losses? Will the suspect be found guilty of a felony because of such lies? Making the offense more serious than it actually is can induce suspects to provide facts implicating them in lesser offenses.

Projecting the Blame   Projecting blame onto others is another effective way to get suspects talking. When suspects feel as if others are at fault, they may be more willing to share information that will ultimately incriminate them. This is often seen in rape cases where the officer suggests that the woman "was asking for it" by the way she was dressed.

Rationalizing   Rationalizing is another technique that shifts fault away from a suspect. Even though the suspect committed the act, there was a good reason to justify it. Skilled interrogators understand this psychology and convey empathy by saying they understand where the suspect is "coming from."

Combining Approaches   Having the suspect tell the story using different methods can reveal discrepancies. If an oral statement has been given, have the suspect put this information in writing and compare the two versions. Then give the story to two different investigators and have them compare the versions.

Using Persuasion during Interrogation

Sometimes investigators may obtain much better results using persuasive techniques: making sure the suspect is comfortable and has basic needs taken care of, such as being allowed to go to the restroom and to get a drink of water. Once the suspect has been made comfortable, begin by acknowledging that a problem exists but that before talking about it, the suspect needs to be informed of his rights. Then suggest that the suspect probably already knows all about these rights, and ask the suspect to tell what he does know. Usually the suspect can paraphrase the *Miranda* warning, and you can then compliment him on his knowledge. This helps establish rapport. Next, encourage the suspect to tell his side of the story in detail, intervening only to give encouragement to continue talking. When the suspect has finished, review the account step by step.

Following this, begin a "virtual monologue about robbery" and how some people's desperate financial circumstances lead them into such a crime. The monologue describes how no one starts out planning a life of crime, but some, like an addict, fall into a criminal pattern that leads either to getting shot and killed or to spending a lifetime in prison. End the monologue by "emphasizing that the inevitable result of this pattern of crime is life in prison or death."

Next, suggest that the suspect can avoid this fate only by breaking this pattern and that the first step is to admit that it exists. Add that a person's life should not be judged by one mistake, nor should that person's life be wasted by a refusal to admit that mistake. Following this monologue, begin to talk about the suspect's accomplices and how they are still free, enjoying the fruits of the crime.

Finally, talk about the suspect's previous encounters with the criminal justice system and how fairly it has treated the suspect. In the past the suspect has probably always claimed to be not guilty. Judges are likely to go easier on suspects who indicate remorse for what they have done. This cannot happen unless the suspect first admits the crime. Point out that intelligent people recognize when it is in their best interest to admit a mistake.

Dillingham (2003a, p.71) cautions that the courts have ruled that custodial interrogations are "inherently psychologically coercive." He points out that juveniles, drug abusers, and mentally ill subjects are especially susceptible to persuasion to falsely confess.

Ethics and the Use of Deception

Police officers are supposed to be honest, but what happens when they are lied to? Unfortunately, criminal interrogations do not follow a set of rules that mandates everyone to tell the truth. The fact is, criminals lie as a matter of course. Faced with scant evidence, yet a positive belief that a suspect has committed a particular crime, what might an investigator do?

Several cases support officer use of deception. *United States ex rel. Caminito v. Murphy* (1955) held that it is permissible to tell suspects that they have been identified by witnesses even though that is untrue. *Roe v. State of New York* (1973) held that it is permissible to tell suspects that their fingerprints or other physical evidence was located at the scene of the crime, when this is

in fact untrue. *Moore v. Hopper* (1975) allowed telling suspects that material evidence, such as a firearm used to commit a crime, has been found, when it has not. *Frazier v. Cupp* (1978) held that it is permissible to tell suspects that an accomplice has already confessed, when this is untrue.

Interrogatory deception may include fabricating evidence, making promises, misrepresenting the seriousness of the offense, misrepresenting identity (for example, pretending to be a cellmate or a reporter), or using the "good cop/bad cop" routine. Creating false evidence, however, is not ethical or legal.

Television and movies often depict the good-cop/bad-cop method of interrogation, portraying one officer as very hostile and another one as trying to protect a suspect from the hostile officer. Routines such as this could be considered illegal if carried to an extreme. Some interrogation techniques, even if not illegal, may be unethical. The use of deception in interrogation and the determination of ethical, professional behavior remain important issues.

A letter from an inmate, incarcerated for a murder he pled guilty to but later claimed innocence for, sheds light on the reasons a suspect in jail awaiting trial might confess:

> [Jail] can be hell. I was locked in a cell alone 23 hours a day. The other hour I was still alone, but able to take a shower, etc. The doors are solid steel. When it closes there is no more contact for another day. I used to dread the closing of that door. . . . Try and imagine sitting in a room the size of your bathroom with no window, not knowing when that door will open or what your family is doing outside it. Then picture that for a year.
>
> They told me many times in many different ways how much better things would be if I cooperated with them. I don't know if I did it hoping things would get better or if I just didn't care. I do remember very clearly my feelings of being at the end of my rope. I would of sold my soul to the devil not to hear that door bang again, locking me in for another 23 hours with myself.

To some observers, such treatment might border on third-degree tactics.

Third-Degree Tactics

Considerable literature deals with the use of the third degree in police interrogations. It is not known how widely these methods are used and how much of what is claimed is exaggeration.

Third degree is the use of physical force; the threat of force; or other physical, mental, or psychological abuse to induce a suspect to confess to a crime. Third-degree tactics, which are illegal, include striking or hitting a suspect, denying food or water or sleep for abnormal time periods, not allowing a suspect to go to the restroom, having a number of officers ask questions in shifts for prolonged periods, and refusing normal privileges. Obtaining information by these methods is inexcusable.

Third-degree tactics—physical force; threats of force; or other physical, mental, or psychological abuse—are illegal. Any information so obtained, including confessions, is inadmissible in court.

The image of police brutality is difficult to offset when third-degree tactics are used. Such tactics create a loss of respect not only for the officer involved but also for the entire department and the police profession.

Although physical force is not permitted, this does not rule out physical contact. Placing a hand on a shoulder or touching a suspect's hand can help to establish rapport. Looking directly at a suspect while talking and continuing to do so during the conversation is not using physical force, even though it usually makes the suspect extremely uncomfortable.

If you give a suspect all the privileges you yourself have within the interrogation context, there is no cause for a charge of third-degree tactics. Allow the suspect the same breaks for meals, rest, and going to the restroom that you take. Law enforcement officers are obligated to protect both the public interest and individual rights. No situation excuses a deliberate violation of these rights.

Recording Interrogations

Audio or video recordings of interrogations are becoming increasingly popular and provide documentation of the circumstances surrounding the interrogation. As Judge (p.10) contends, providing the court with complete information about where, when, and how questioning is conducted allows the court greater ability to assess the reasonableness of officers' actions and whether they comply with constitutional requirements.

According to Sullivan (p.46) the "vast majority" of law enforcement agencies do not record custodial interrogations, but pressure is building to require complete electronic recordings in major felony investigations. Sullivan (p.47) reports that all departments in Alaska and Minnesota have recorded full custodial interviews for many years and voice "virtually unanimous support" for the practice. Recording custodial interrogations greatly reduces motions to suppress statements and confessions. In Kankakee County (Missouri), for example, from 1996 to 2003, the agency videotaped 636 interrogations with no statements ever being suppressed ("Lights, Camera, Interrogation," p.7). In addition, officers are spared hostile cross-examination related to coercion and perjury. Further, when detectives review recordings, many discover important information they overlooked during the interrogation. Such recordings also increase public confidence and may be useful in teaching interrogation techniques.

Kanable (2004, p.44) reports on an unscientific study that found that more than 235 law enforcement agencies were in favor of recording custodial interrogations of felony suspects from the reading of their *Miranda* rights until the interrogation ends.

Laws vary from state to state as to whether suspects must consent to being recorded. According to Sullivan (p.47), most states allow police to record without informing suspects (one-party consent), under eavesdropping laws discussed in the next chapter. Of those that object to recording interrogations, most have never attempted to do so. Sullivan (p.48) says that the most common objection is that suspects will "clam up" and refuse to talk, causing the loss of admissions and confessions. Covert recording of the interrogation would alleviate such objections.

Another objection is that detectives believe judges and juries may be offended at accepted interrogation techniques they see or hear (Sullivan, p.49), including "shouting at suspects; using foul language and street talk; suggesting leniency; expressing sympathy for suspect; blaming victims; [and] falsely asserting that incriminating evidence has been obtained." However, given the proper groundwork, judges and juries should accept that such tactics may be needed to obtain information from reluctant suspects.

Admissions and Confessions

When a suspect has become cooperative, you can increase the amount of conversation. Once rapport is established, listen for words indicating that the suspect is in some way connected with the crime, such as "I didn't do it, but I know who did." If the suspect is not implicated in the crime but has relevant information, attempt to obtain a statement. If the suspect is implicated, try to obtain an admission or confession.

The format for obtaining admissions and confessions from suspects in criminal cases is fairly standard. However, state laws, rules, and procedures for taking admissions and confessions vary, so you need to know the rules and requirements of your jurisdiction.

An **admission** contains some information concerning the elements of a crime but falls short of a full confession (Figure 6.8).

A **confession** is information supporting the elements of a crime given by a person involved in committing it. It can be oral or written and must be voluntary and not given in response to threats, promises, or rewards. It can be taken in question/answer form or in a narrative handwritten by the suspect or the interrogator (Figure 6.9).

A confession, oral or handwritten, must be given of the suspect's free will and without fear or in response to threats, promises, or rewards.

The voluntary nature of the confession is essential. For example, Ernesto Miranda had an arrest record and was familiar with his rights; yet his confession was ruled inadmissible because these rights had not been clearly stated to him. Although formal education is not required for making a confession, a suspect must be intelligent enough to understand fully everything stated.

Figure 6.8
Sample admission

```
                        POLICE DEPARTMENT
                           ADMISSION              DR# __933210_____

DATE OCCURRED __12 Nov. 20__ ____  LOCATION OF

TIME OCCURRED ___0315_____  OCCURRENCE __Rear of bar and grill__

I, ___Walter Wilson_____ , am ___28___ years of age,
                                     home phone: __444-4444_____
and my address is ___100 Main St.,this city___
                                     bus. phone: __444-4443_____

1. ____I came out of the bar and grill at approx. 0300 on 12 Nov. 20__ and saw__

2. __Mr. Victim standing there.  He spoke to me and we had an argument.  We_____

3. __argued a little while and I left.  He was alive when I saw him last._____

4. _____

5. _____

6. _____

7. _____

8. _____

9. _____

10. _____

11. _____

12. _____

13. _____

14. _____

15. _____

16. _____

17. _____

18. _____

I have read this statement consisting of ____1____ page (s) and I affirm to the truth and
accuracy of the facts contained herein.

This statement was completed at (Location) ___The Police Dept._____
on the __14th____ day of __Nov._____ at __1300_____ , 20__ .

WITNESS _____

WITNESS _____          _____
                                          Signature of person giving
                                          voluntary statement.
```

In most states, oral confessions are admissible in court, but written confessions usually carry more weight. Put an oral confession into writing as soon as possible, even if the suspect refuses to sign it. Have the suspect repeat the confession in the presence of other witnesses to corroborate its content and voluntariness. In extremely important cases, the prosecutor often obtains the confession to ensure that it meets all legal requirements. Many departments are now videotaping statements and confessions.

After obtaining a confession, you may also go with the suspect to the crime scene and reenact the crime before witnesses. Take pictures or films of this reenactment. Go over the confession and the pictures with the suspect to verify their accuracy. (Such confessions and reenactments can also be used for police training.)

Even though a confession is highly desirable, it may not be true, it may later be denied, or there may be claims that it was involuntary.

 A confession is only one part of an investigation. Corroborate it by independent evidence.

Your investigation will proceed in much the same way with or without a confession. However, a confession often provides additional leads. Although it cannot stand alone, it is an important part of the case.

Questioning Children and Juveniles

Special considerations exist when you question children and juveniles. As in any interview, the first step is to build rapport. You might give the child a tour of the building and show

Figure 6.9
Sample confession

POLICE DEPARTMENT

CONFESSION

DATE __14 Nov. 20__ __ TIME __1300__ PLACE __Police Dept.__

I, __Walter Wilson__ , am __28__ years of age,

and my address is __100 Main St., this city__ ,

I have been duly warned by __police officer name__ , who has identified

himself as __a police officer__
that I do not have to make any statement at all, and that any statement I make may be used in evidence against me on the trial for the offense concerning which this statement is herein made. Without promise of hope or reward, without fear or threat of physical harm, I freely volunteer the following statement to the aforesaid person:

__I left the bar and grill at about 0300 on 12 Nov. 20__. I went out the back__

__door and I met Mr. Victim coming in. He bumped into me and we got in an argument.__

__He picked up a rock to hit me with, so I took out my knife and stabbed him. I__

__think he was dead when I left.__

I have read the __1__ pages of this statement and the facts contained therein are true and correct.

WITNESS: _W^m Bennett_

WITNESS: _John H Scott_

Walter Wilson
Signed by the arrested party.
Page __1__ of __1__ pages.

---

him or her where the parent(s) will be waiting. You must obtain parental permission before questioning a juvenile, unless the situation warrants immediate questioning at the scene. Parents usually permit their juveniles to be questioned separately if the purpose is explained and you have valid reasons for doing so. Overprotective parents can distract and interfere with an interview or interrogation. Often, however, parents can assist if the youth is uncooperative. They can ask questions and bring pressures to bear that you cannot. They know and understand the child and can probably sense when the child is lying. Decide whether to question a juvenile in front of the parents or separately after you determine their attitudes when you explain to them the reasons for the inquiry.

 Obtain parental permission before questioning a youth. Do not use a youth as an informant unless the parents know the situation.

Your attitude toward youths will greatly influence how well you can communicate with them. Ask yourself whether you consider the youth a person who has a problem or a youth who *is* a problem.

Many juveniles put on airs in front of their friends. For example, in one case a juvenile and some other youths were brought into a room for observation by witnesses. The suspect youth knew he was being watched and challenged his school principal by stating that he had a right to know who was looking at him and why. This 10-year-old boy wanted to impress his friends. A few days later the boy's parents brought him to the police station at the officer's request. It took two questions to determine that he had set a fire that resulted in an $80,000 loss. After a third question, the youth admitted his guilt. Although he had acted like a big shot in front of his friends, his action weighed heavily on his conscience. The presence of the police and the knowledge that his parents were waiting in another room motivated him to cooperate.

Many youths also have very active imaginations, tend to exaggerate, and may have periods of fantasy. They may describe suspects as bigger than they really are or may view an event as more serious or important than it is.

Finally, juveniles may have definite opinions about the police. Some dislike adults in general and the police in particular. Like adults, however, most of them do not dislike the police and will cooperate with them. Put yourself in their shoes; learn their attitudes and the reasons for them. Time and patience are your greatest allies when questioning juveniles. Explain why you are questioning them, and you will probably gain their confidence.

Do not underrate the intelligence or cleverness of young people. They are often excellent observers with good memories. Talk to them as you would to an adult. Praise them and impress upon them their importance to the investigation.

If a juvenile confesses to a crime, bring in the parents and have the youth repeat the confession to them. The parents will see that the information is voluntary and not the police's account of what happened. Parents often provide additional information once they know the truth. For example, they may be alerted to stolen items at home and report them.

Evaluating and Corroborating Information

Do not accept information obtained from interviews and interrogations at face value. Verify all information. You cannot know the motives of all those who provide information. Do not assume that all information, even though volunteered, is truthful. Corroborate or disprove statements made during questioning.

To cross-check a story, review the report and the details of the offense. Determine the past record, family status, hobbies, and special interests of the persons questioned. If a person has a criminal record, determine his or her prior modus operandi. With such information, you will be able to ask questions in a way that indicates you know what you are talking about and that deceptive answers will be found out.

A person who resorts to half-truths or lies usually ends up on the defensive and becomes entangled in deceit. Knowing the facts of a case allows you to neutralize deliberate lies. If discrepancies in statements occur, question the suspect again or use polygraph or psychological tests. Compare the replies of people questioned and assess whether they are consistent with the known facts.

Breaking a "Pat" Story

A person who is telling the truth can usually repeat the story the same way many times, although he or she may use different words and a different sequence in retelling it. Times and dates may be approximate, and the person may simply not be able to remember some things. In contrast, a person who is telling a fabricated story can usually repeat it word for word innumerable times. Dates and times are usually precise, and all details are remembered. However, it is difficult to repeat lies consistently; each one sounds better than the other, and the story becomes distorted with mistakes and exaggerations.

To break a pat story, ask questions that require slightly different answers and serve to alter memorized responses.

Detecting Deception

Dillingham (2004b, p.49) reports on research showing that Americans tell an average of three to five lies per day. Some are harmless—the tactful untruths we use to spare others' feelings. Other lies are told to make a person feel important or to cover up for mistakes. A great many lies are told by people who have broken the law in an effort to remain undetected. Dillingham (2004b, p.51) recommends that officers should regard every statement made to them in the line of duty as possibly being deceptive.

Researchers Hartwig et al. (p.429) report that similar to the general public, police officers fail to detect deception at a rate better than chance. Navarro (p.19) asserts that repeated studies have found that traditional methods of detecting deception during questioning succeed only 50 percent of the time, even for experienced detectives. Many techniques to improve this finding and to assist officers in detecting deception in a suspect have been advocated. Earlier the importance of paying attention to nonverbal clues, that is, factors other than the actual words spoken, was discussed.

Nonverbal Clues Dillingham (2003a, p.71) observes: "Studies on deception and body language reveal a wide array of nonverbal behaviors which have been associated with deception." Server (2004–2005, p.21) believes that verbal response latency (i.e., how long it takes a person to respond to a question) can help an officer detect deception: "The average person generally responds to a question within .5 to 1.5 seconds. Answers beyond that time frame may be strongly considered unreliable or misleading." Server also suggests that changes in volume and speed can be indicative of deception: "Truthful responses usually increase in volume and tempo while deceptive answers commonly decrease in rate and trail off in volume"—as can a suspect's posture: "A truthful respondent will generally be relaxed and change positions intermittently throughout the interview/interrogation . . . A deceptive subject may purposely freeze nonverbal communication by maintaining a singular posture."

Dillingham (2003b, p.70) examines using neurolinguistic programming (NLP) to detect deception, particularly the study of subjects' eye movements. He provides the example of the common belief that dishonest people have "shifty eyes" and do not make good eye contact. Children are taught to "look you in the eye" to prove they are being honest. Dillingham notes that NLP techniques are taught to law enforcement officers throughout the nation to help determine whether a person is being honest. However: "There is no evidence that NLP can detect deception. NLP has never been scientifically proven to be a valid method of determining if a person is being deceptive" (Dillingham, 2003b, p.70).

Navarro (p.19) suggests yet another way to detect deception—the Four-Domain model—consisting of the following critical domains: (1) comfort/discomfort, (2) emphasis, (3) synchrony, and (4) perception management. Navarro (p.20) notes that the first domain, a person's comfort/discomfort level, is one of the most important clues to establish veracity: "Tension and distress most often manifest upon guilty people." He explains that people usually show discomfort nonverbally by rearranging themselves, jiggling their feet, fidgeting, or drumming their fingers. They may also continually look at a watch or clock, sit tensely, or not move ("flash frozen").

In the second domain—emphasis—untruthful people do not emphasize using nonverbals. A truthful person would use his or her eyebrows, head, hands, and arms to assert a point. According to Navarro (p.21), as a rule, when people are truthful, they emphasize.

The third domain, synchrony, refers to the match between what is said vocally and presented nonverbally, the match between the present circumstances and what the subject's version is, and the match between events and emotions, including time and space. (Syncrony is at the heart of Ekman's research.)

Navarro's fourth element, perception management, occurs both verbally and nonverbally. He (p.23) points out that liars, like psychopaths, often use perception management to influence the person questioning them. Nonverbally, liars may yawn to show they feel bored. They may slouch or stretch out to try to demonstrate their comfort. They may vocalize the implausibility of their committing a crime—for example, "I would never do such a thing." Or they may try to manage perception by using such phrases as "to be perfectly frank," "to be totally honest," and the like.

Navarro (p.23) concludes that detectives can enhance their ability to detect deception by focusing on these domains: "The research in this area over the last 20 years is unequivocal. Nonverbal behaviors, in and of themselves, do not clearly indicate deception. However, when interviewers notice a display of discomfort and a lack of comfort, emphasis, synchrony and perception management, a greater certitude for assessing deception exists."

Statement Analysis Midcentury German psychologist Udo Undeutsch developed this hypothesis: "Statements that are the product of experience will contain characteristics that are generally absent from statements that are the product of imagination." The *Undeutsch hypothesis* has evolved into statement analysis, the word-by-word examination of language, which has become a valuable investigative tool (Klopf and Tooke, p.6). Klopf and Tooke describe the FBI's Statement Analysis Field Examination Technique (SAFE-T), designed to determine accuracy and completeness of statements using two culpable elements: lack of conviction and extraneous information.

Lack of conviction is embodied in the use of such terms as "I believe," "kind of," "to the best of my recollection," "possible," and "as far as I know" and indicates the person's attempt to avoid personal accountability and employ deception. *Extraneous information* is introduced to avoid answering the question. A truthful person will usually explain what happened chronologically and concisely. The following statement, given by someone involved in a crash, is an example of a statement that is probably not truthful (Klopf and Tooke, p.11). The information in parentheses is extraneous; lack of commitment is indicated by italics:

> . . . continued forward up onto the garden area of a building. (Which leads me to believe that the other vehicle was moving at a rate of speed in excess of the posted 25 mph limit. This is *probably* another reason that I did not see the other vehicle). I . . .

Technology Innovations

Paul Ekman at the University of California at San Francisco is doing research on how to "read faces." Ekman's Facial Action Coding System (FACS) has become an essential tool in the science of facts (Conniff, pp.44–50). The FACS CD-ROM describes the 43 movements facial muscles can perform.

Ekman has concluded that facial expressions are universal as well as biologically determined, with smiling probably our oldest natural expression, as a way to disarm and reassure those around us. Ekman has identified about 30 "savants," people who consistently score 80 percent or better on his one-hour test of their ability to detect lies. Most of them are in law enforcement. He calls the group the Diogenes Project after the Greek philosopher who peered into citizens' faces by lantern light in search of one honest man.

The Diogenes group has developed the habit of listening harder and watching more closely. Careful questioners look for discrepancies—places where words, facial expressions, and body language are not in sync.

Klopf and Tooke (p.14) stress: "Determining the truth represents one of the most important tasks that law enforcement officers must accomplish." The FBI's SAFE-T is a helpful tool, but it is not a "scientific or precise instrument." Additional research is needed here.

Adams and Jarvis (p.7) studied the relationship between truthfulness and certain features of written statements. They found three features that accurately discriminated between truthful and deceptive statements in written incident accounts: (1) the length of the criminal incident section, (2) the presence of unique sensory details, and (3) the inclusion of emotions. To examine the first feature, they note that suspects and victims typically include information before and after the description of the criminal incident itself. The incident section should be the longest, since this is the focus of the statement. They recommend drawing a border around the criminal incident section of the written statement and visually determining whether this is the case. Subjects who write a longer introduction than the incident section may be delaying the discussion of the incident.

The second feature, use of unique sensory details, can be examined by highlighting detailed sensory description, which usually indicates truthfulness. Adams and Jarvis (p.10) suggest that subjects who include sensory details in the introduction but not in the incident section should be questioned further to explore why such details were left out of the most important part of their statement.

The third feature, inclusion of emotions, is also easily examined. By highlighting such information if/when it occurs, investigators can gain insight into veracity, as memory studies have found that recall of actual experienced events include more emotional information than recall of created events.

Adams (2004) uses even more precise analysis of written statements to gain insights into a subject's truthfulness. Nouns, words that name things, can be revealing. For example, a subject writes: "My story has never changed. I did not hurt that child," referring to the death of the 3-year-old daughter of the woman he was living with. The word *story* is worth looking at, as it may imply that the person made up a tale. The word *child,* when the subject knew the child's name, is also revealing. This depersonalization might show a lack of caring. Adams (p.23) also looks at the verbs (action words) in a written statement. The use of the word *hurt* minimizes the severity of the crime being investigated. Adams also examines adjectives, or descriptive words. The use of the word *that* is an example of distancing, placing space between the writer and the person being referred to. Adams (p.23) concludes: "The insight gained from examining the choice of words in suspects' and alleged victims' statements can help investigators prepare effective interviewing strategies to lead them to the truth."

Scientific aids have also been developed to help determine the truthfulness of information provided during an investigation.

Scientific Aids to Obtaining and Evaluating Information

 Many attempts have been made to determine the truth through scientific instruments. Even before instruments were developed, however, trials by ordeal and other tests relied on psychological and physiological principles. For example, it was common knowledge for centuries that when a person was lying or nervous, visible or measurable physiological changes in the body occurred. These include dryness of the mouth, shaking or trembling, perspiration, increased heartbeat, faster pulse, and rapid breathing. The ancient Chinese capitalized on the symptom of mouth dryness when they made a suspect chew rice. If the rice remained dry after being chewed, the suspect was assumed to be lying.

Science and technology have provided aids to help determine the reliability of information. Among them are the polygraph, the computerized voice stress analyzer (CVSA), hypnosis, and truth serums.

The Polygraph and Voice Stress Tests

As implied by the name, a **polygraph** (literally, "many writings") records several measurements on a visible graph.

The polygraph scientifically measures respiration and depth of breathing, changes in the skin's electrical resistance and blood pressure, and pulse.

The same factors measured by the polygraph may be visible to a trained observer through such signs as flushing of the face, licking the lips, slight pulsing of the neck arteries, beads of perspiration, rapid breathing, and other signs of nervousness. A person does not actually have to respond verbally for a polygraph to work because the machine measures the mental and emotional responses regardless of whether the person answers questions.

Measurements taken by the polygraph can be interpreted at the time the test is administered or later. The results can be shown to the subject to demonstrate which responses were shown to be truthful and which were not.

Many law enforcement agencies use polygraphs in their investigations; however, the effectiveness of the polygraph has been questioned. Among supporters of the polygraph, opinions differ as to its accuracy, which depends on the subject, the equipment, and the operator's training and experience. In some cases, the machine may fail to detect lies because the subject has taken drugs, makes deliberate muscular contractions, or has a psychopathic personality.

The subject must be physically, mentally, and emotionally fit for the examination. The examination must be voluntary and completed under conditions conducive to cooperation. A clear, concise summary of the test results is furnished only to authorized personnel.

Despite advances in technology, improved training of polygraph operators, and claims of 95 percent accuracy, polygraph results are not now accepted by the courts. The Supreme Court has said, "There is simply no consensus that polygraph evidence is reliable. To this day, the scientific community remains extremely polarized about the reliability of polygraph techniques. . . . There is simply no way to know in a particular case whether a polygraph examiner's conclusion is accurate, because certain doubts and uncertainties plague even the best polygraph exams" (*United States v. Scheffer,* 1998). Some authorities claim that the results violate hearsay rules because it is impossible to cross-examine a machine.

> The polygraph is an instrument used to verify the truth, not a substitute for investigating and questioning. Although the results are not presently admissible in court, any confession obtained as a result of a polygraph test is admissible.

Many polygraph inaccuracies have been failures to detect lies, not failures to indicate truthful statements. Thus the polygraph is sometimes useful to develop leads, verify statements, and cross-check information. Moreover, it provides the police with a psychological advantage that may lead to a confession. Such confessions are admissible in court even though the test results are not. Even in jurisdictions in which the polygraph is not admissible in court, prosecuting attorneys often give weight to the findings of a polygraph examination in deciding whether to prosecute a case.

Competent questioning is as important as the instrument used. As in an interrogation, the right questions must be asked in the right sequence. Although examiners are trained to give the test and interpret the graphs, they rely heavily on background information that the investigator provides.

The normal procedure for setting up a polygraph test is for the police agency to request in writing that a polygraph test be conducted. The examiner reviews the complete case, including any statements made by the subject before the test is conducted. A pretest interview with the subject covers the information to be included in the test, a review of the questions to be asked, and an advisement of the suspect's constitutional rights.

The polygraph examiner will need the following information before the test:

- The case facts—the precise criminal offense involved, the complete case file, and a summary of the evidence
- Information about the subject—complete name; date of birth; physical, mental, emotional, and psychological data if known; and criminal history.

Technology Innovations

Dillingham (2004a, pp.50–51) describes technologies under development that may prove more reliable than the polygraph. One such technique uses functional magnetic resonance imaging (fMRI) to track brain activity. According to Dillingham, fMRI is a more direct measure of brain activity than the polygraph.

Another "up-and-coming" technique analyzes a specific brain wave, P300. Subjects wear a headband of electrodes and watch photos being flashed on a computer screen. If a person looks at random photos of weapons without activating a P300 brain wave, the objects presumably are unknown to him. If, however, the murder weapon is shown and a P300 wave activates, the person likely has some familiarity with that weapon.

The proper tests are then decided on and the questions prepared and reviewed with the subject. After the test is completed, the subject and the police are advised of the results in person or by letter. If the test indicates deception, an individual interrogation may follow. Any confessions that follow from such tests are almost universally accepted by the courts. The examiner's testimony is not conclusive evidence but rather opinion evidence regarding either guilt or innocence.

Computerized polygraphy eliminates most of the mechanical equipment, replacing it with a virtual graph on a computer monitor. The graph can be printed, if desired. In computerized polygraph systems, the software analyzes physiological changes and reports the probability that the person has answered the question truthfully.

In the 1970s the psychological stress evaluator (PSE) was introduced. The PSE measured stress in the microtremors of the human voice. A more recent version of this technology is the CVSA (Figure 6.10). Voice stress tests have not, however, undergone peer-reviewed, independent research to show that they have accuracy. The only recent independent university research shows that the voice stress devices are less than 35 percent accurate and that what they measure has nothing to do with deception or the detection of deception.

Both the polygraph and the CVSA reduce investigative costs, focus on specific suspects, increase conviction rates (because many tests are followed by confessions), and eliminate suspects. Police agencies should not go on "fishing expeditions," however. Through normal investigative practices, the number of suspects should be narrowed to not more than two people before a polygraph examination or CVSA is used.

Hypnosis and Truth Serums

Like the polygraph, hypnosis and truth serums are supplementary tools to investigation. They are not used as

Figure 6.10
Detectives Steven Geckle (left), Paul Richard (center), and Al Everson (right) pose with a Computer Voice Stress Analyzer (CVSA) at the Upper Merion Township Police Department in King of Prussia, Pennsylvania, Thursday, February 7, 2002. The computer, software, and microphone are supposedly able to tell when an interview subject is lying through frequency modulations in the human voice.

shortcuts but rather in specific cases where the criteria for their use have been determined by thorough review. Cases that meet these criteria are normally crimes of violence or cases where loss of memory or ability to recall is involved and all other standard investigative efforts have been exhausted. Because of the restricted criteria, these techniques are used in a comparatively small number of cases.

Hypnosis Hypnosis psychically induces a trancelike condition in which the person loses consciousness but responds to a hypnotist's suggestions. Hypnosis is used with crime victims and witnesses to crimes, not with suspects. It should be used only after careful consultation with the person to be hypnotized and after a detailed review of the case as well as of the subject's mental, physical, and emotional condition. Written consent from the subject and permission from the prosecutor's office should be obtained, and an attorney should be present.

A professional should carefully analyze the subject and the case before hypnosis is conducted. The actual act of hypnotism and interrogation should be performed only by a psychiatrist, psychologist, or physician specifically trained in the techniques.

Courts have established guidelines for using testimony gained from hypnosis. The guidelines require that a trained professional perform it and that the professional be independent of, rather than responsible to, the prosecution. The number of persons present should be restricted to the hypnotist and the coordinator from the police agency who has knowledge of the case and perhaps an artist who can draw a sketch based on any descriptions of suspects. And although forensic hypnosis has finally been accepted as a valuable crime-fighting tool, many states remain reluctant to allow into court testimony elicited from hypnosis.

The session should be videotaped, if possible. Questions should relate only to what the witness states under hypnosis. The witness should not be prompted or induced in any way.

Truth Serums Truth serums are fast-acting barbiturates of the type used to produce sleep at the approximate level of surgical anesthesia. Alcohol produces somewhat the same effects to a much lesser degree. The theory is that the drug removes a person's inhibitions so that he or she is more likely to tell the truth. In the past, scopolamine and hyascine were the most used drugs, but sodium amatol and sodium pentathol are more commonly used today.

Truth serums are not used extensively by the police because the accuracy of the information obtained with them is questionable. Truth serum is administered by a physician, preferably a psychiatrist, who remains to monitor the person's condition while the questions are asked. The drugs can cause serious side effects, so the subject must be monitored continually. Some patients also become violently excited. Moreover, individuals vary greatly in their response to truth serums. Some can withhold information even under the influence of a large dose of the serum.

The courts do not officially recognize truth serums or their reliability, nor do they admit the results as evidence.

Use of Psychics and Profilers

Television shows have popularized the use of psychics and profilers in criminal investigations, and to many viewers, the incidents depicted are entirely believable. Although use of psychics in criminal investigations is controversial, some agencies are willing to consider any possible lead or source of information, including psychics.

Profilers are more commonly accepted. Profiling combines art and science, resting on the premise that careful analysis of the crime scene and the crime will yield clues as to the type of person who would commit such a crime. Effective profiling relies on the profiler's ability to combine investigative experience, training in forensic and behavioral sciences, and information about the characteristics of known offenders.

Sharing Information

In the beginning of this chapter, the vast amount of information available on the Internet was discussed. The Internet allows information related to criminal investigations to be

Technology Innovations

According to Stanek, CriMNet links Minnesota's 1,100 criminal justice jurisdictions by using common business practices and a standard computer language. It provides statewide case processing, pretrial release data, domestic and restraint conditions, postconviction restrictive probation conditions, weapons prohibition information, juvenile arrests and conviction data, arrest warrant information, electronic warrant information, electronic fingerprinting and photo images, conviction status on all offense levels, detention and incarceration data, alcohol and driving restrictions, and total case records from incident report to outcome and sanctions compliance and completion.

Technology Innovations

Careless (pp.84–85) describes Informant, a software approach allowing police departments to access each other's databases through a password-protected website, whether the databases are compatible or not. He explains that Informant has two major functions. First it allows different systems to speak to each other, providing a bridge between departmental databases. Second, it serves as a Google-style search engine. When a suspect's name is entered, Informant searches all available databases for information on the suspect, checking every computer connected to it.

In short: "Using Informant, police can share access to each other's information, even across incompatible formats; use one search to get multi-jurisdictional records on suspects; get access through desktop PCs, laptops, WAP-enabled cell phones and wireless PDAs; get information fast—in the station or out in the field."

shared across jurisdictional lines as never before. Regional networks have been established in several areas. As Garrett (p.6) stresses: "Information in the hands of law enforcement is power—the power to solve and possibly prevent crime. In homeland security efforts, access to information is critical—the lives of officers, the public and even the country's welfare might be at stake."

Stanek (p.167) reports that law enforcement agencies in Minnesota took a "giant stride" toward information sharing with the creation of CriMNet.

Careless (p.84) contends that sharing information is one of the most effective crime-fighting tools available to law enforcement (Figure 6.11). Although information sharing has become a top priority for U.S. police departments, it is also a major headache, with the reason for the "grief" being database incompatibility between departments (Careless, p.84). Noting that the obvious answer is to

develop a nationwide database platform, Careless also notes that this is not practical given budget constraints, turf fights, and other problems that thwart standardization attempts. An alternative does exist (see the Box above).

Since September 11, 2001, the sharing of information has become even more important as the United States focuses on homeland security. Hess and Wrobleski (p.298) note: "The key to combating terrorism lies with the local police and the intelligence they can provide to federal authorities." The role of police in the "war on terrorism" is discussed in Chapter 20.

Figure 6.11

Members of the Clackamas County multi-agency major crimes team with the assistance of the FBI begin to examine the area where the body of Matel Zachery Sanchez, 4, was found near Estacada, Ore., Saturday July 2, 2005. His stepgrandmother, Christine Coffman, 43, led investigators to the boy's body in a remote area near Estacada in the foothills of the Cascade Range. Specific charges had not been filed against Coffman because police were still questioning her, said Officer Kevin Krebs, spokesman for the Milwaukie Police Department.

© AP/Wide World Photos

SUMMARY

Most solved cases rely on both physical evidence and information obtained from a variety of sources. Important sources of information include (1) reports and records, including those found on the Internet; (2) people who are not suspects in the crime but who know something about the crime or those involved; and (3) suspects in the crime. A sources-of-information file contains the name and location of people, organizations, and records that may assist in a criminal investigation.

The ultimate goal of interviewing and interrogating is to determine the truth, that is, to identify those responsible for a crime and to eliminate the innocent from suspicion. The effective interviewer/interrogator is adaptable and culturally adroit, self-controlled, patient, confident, optimistic, objective, sensitive to individual rights, and knowledgeable about the elements of the crime.

Two basic requirements to obtain information are to listen and to observe. Ask direct questions that come right to the point. Use indirect questions—those that skirt the basic question—sparingly. Repetition is the best way to obtain recall and to uncover lies. Appeal to a reluctant interviewee's reason or emotions.

Regardless of whether you are interviewing or interrogating, there are several ways to improve communication: Prepare in advance and obtain the information as soon after the incident as possible; be considerate and friendly; use a private setting and eliminate physical barriers; sit rather than stand; encourage conversation; ask simple questions one at a time; listen and observe. Emotional barriers to communication include ingrained attitudes and prejudices, fear, anger or hostility, and self-preservation.

Interview anyone other than a suspect who has information about the case. This includes complainants, witnesses, victims, and informants. Interview witnesses separately if possible. Interview the victim or complainant first, then eyewitnesses and then those who did not actually see the crime but who have relevant information.

Although many of the same principles apply to interrogating and interviewing, interrogating involves some special considerations. One important consideration is when to give the *Miranda* warning, which informs suspects of their rights and must be given to any suspect who is interrogated while in custody. It is also important to conduct interrogations in a place that is private and free from interruptions. Interrogation techniques include inquiring directly or indirectly, forcing responses, deflating or inflating the ego, minimizing or maximizing the crime, projecting the blame, rationalizing, and combining approaches. Third-degree tactics—physical force; threats of force; or other physical, mental, or psychological abuse—are illegal. Any information so obtained, including confessions, is inadmissible in court. Any confession, oral or handwritten, must be given of the suspect's free will and not in response to fear, threats, promises, or rewards. A confession is only one part of the investigation. It must be corroborated by independent evidence.

Special considerations are also observed when questioning children and youths. Obtain parental permission before questioning a juvenile. Do not use a juvenile as an informant unless the parents know the situation.

In addition to skills in interviewing and interrogating, you can sometimes use scientific aids to obtain information and determine its truthfulness. The polygraph scientifically measures respiration and depth of breathing, changes in the skin's electrical resistance, and blood pressure and pulse rate. It is an instrument used to verify the truth, not a substitute for investigating and questioning. Although the results are not presently admissible in court, any confession obtained as a result of a polygraph test is admissible. Other scientific aids include hypnosis and truth serums, but such aids must be monitored closely, and the results are seldom admissible in court.

CHECKLIST

Obtaining Information

- Were the complainant, witnesses, victim, and informants questioned?
- Were all witnesses found?
- Was all information recorded accurately?
- Was the questioning conducted in an appropriate place? at an appropriate time?
- Was the *Miranda* warning given to all suspects before questioning?
- Were the type of offense and offender considered in selecting the interviewing or interrogating techniques?
- Were answers obtained to the questions of who, what, where, when, why, and how?
- Were checks made of all available reports and records? the sources-of-information file? field-identification cards? the National Crime Information Center? other police agencies? public and private agencies at the local, county, state, and national levels?
- Were confidential informants sought?
- Was a request for public assistance or an offer of a reward published?

- Is there a private number to call or a private post office box to write to for persons who have information about a crime?
- Was a polygraph used to check the validity of information given?
- Were all statements, admissions, and confessions rechecked against other verbal statements and against existing physical evidence?
- Were those providing information thanked for their help?
- Were all statements, admissions, and confessions properly and legally obtained? recorded? witnessed? filed?

DISCUSSION QUESTIONS

1. What do you consider to be the essential steps in developing information about a crime?

2. What advantages do you see in the concept of *interroview*? What disadvantages?

3. Emphasis is often placed on obtaining a confession, or at least an admission, from a suspect in a criminal inquiry. Under what conditions is a confession of greatest value? of no value?

4. The *Miranda* warning is now accepted by law enforcement agencies as a necessary requirement of interrogation under specific circumstances. What circumstances make it mandatory? What circumstances do not require its use?

5. Do you believe that use of the *Miranda* warning has increased or decreased the number of confessions obtained in criminal cases?

6. How could polygraph results be used in plea bargaining?

7. What categories are included in your police department's sources-of-information file?

8. Should informants be protected by law from having to testify in court about information they have furnished police? What are the effects on investigative procedures and the frequency of cases cleared if informants are not protected?

9. Criminals or others who give the police information about a crime that eventually leads to an arrest or a conviction are sometimes paid for the information. Is this a legitimate use of tax funds, or should private donations be used?

10. How accurate is the typical television portrayal of an informant?

MEDIA EXPLORATIONS

Internet

Using a search engine such as Google, enter the key words *police interrogation*. Select an article of interest and outline it.
OR
Go to the following websites and outline the differences between the polygraph and voice stress machines:

- http://www.polygraphplace.com
- http://www.voicestress.com

Crime and Evidence in Action

Select one of three criminal case scenarios and sign in for your shift. Your Mobile Data Terminal (MDT) will get you started and update you throughout the case. During the course of the case you'll become a patrol officer, detective, prosecutor, defense attorney, judge, corrections officer, or parole officer to conduct interactive investigative research. Each case unfolds as you respond to key decision points. Feedback for each possible answer choice is packed full of information, including term definitions, web links, and important documentation. The sergeant is available at certain times to help mentor you, the Online Resources website offers a variety of information, and be sure to take notes in your e-notebook during the suspect video statements and at key points throughout (these notes can be saved, printed, or e-mailed). The Forensics Exercise will test your ability to collect, transport, and analyze evidence from the crime scene. At the end of the case you can track how well you responded to each decision point and join the Discussion Forum for a postmortem. **Go to the CD and use the skills you've learned to solve a case.**

REFERENCES

Adams, Susan H. "Statement Analysis: Beyond the Words." *FBI Law Enforcement Bulletin*, April 2004, pp. 22–23.

Adams, Susan H., and Jarvis, John P. "Are You Telling Me the Truth? Indicators of Veracity in Written Statements." *FBI Law Enforcement Bulletin*, October 2004, pp. 7–12.

Caplan, Gerald M. *Model Procedures for Police Interrogation.* Washington, DC: Police Executive Research Forum, no date.

Careless, James. "Electronic Informant Solves Crimes." *Law and Order*, December 2003, pp. 84–86.

Chandler, Barb. "Sharpening Your Interviewing Skills." *Police and Security News*, December 2003, pp. 63–64.

Conniff, Richard. "Reading Faces." *Smithsonian*, January 2004, pp. 44–50.

Dillingham, Christopher. "Detecting Pinocchio's Lies: Valid Clues to Deception." *Police and Security News*, November/December 2003a, pp. 71–74.

Dillingham, Christopher. "Using Neuro-Linguistic Programming to Detect Deception." *Police and Security News*, September/October 2003b, pp. 70–73.

Dillingham, Christopher. "Proxy Devices and the State of Lie Detection." *Police and Security News*, July/August 2004a, pp. 47–51.

Dillingham, Christopher. "Why Does Pinocchio Lie?" *Police and Security News*, May/June 2004b, pp. 49–52.

Garrett, Ronnie. "Sharing Info Begins with Interoperability." *Law Enforcement Technology*, January 2003, p. 6.

Greenhouse, Linda. "High Court Further Clarifies Police Use of Miranda Warnings." *New York Times* as reported in the (Minneapolis/St. Paul) *Star Tribune*, June 29, 2004, p. A9.

Harr, J. Scott, and Hess, Kären M. *Constitutional Law and the Criminal Justice System*, 3rd ed. Belmont, CA: Wadsworth Publishing Company, 2005.

Hartwig, Maria; Granhag, Pär Anders; Strömwall, Leif A.; and Vrij, Aldert. "Police Officers' Lie Detection Accuracy: Interrogating Freely Versus Observing Video." *Police Quarterly*, December 2004, pp. 429–456.

Hess, Kären M., and Wrobleski, Henry M. *Police Operations*, 4th ed. Belmont, CA: Wadsworth Publishing Co., 2006.

Judge, Lisa. "Is the Miranda Custody Standard Different for Juveniles?" *The Police Chief*, August 2004, p. 10.

Kanable, Rebecca. "For the Record." *Law Enforcement Technology*, October 2004, pp. 44–56.

Klopf, Gene, and Tooke, Andres. "Statement Analysis Field Examination Technique: A Useful Investigative Tool." *FBI Law Enforcement Bulletin*, April 2003, pp. 6–15.

Kruger, Karen J. "New U.S. Supreme Court Decision Further Illuminates the Two Rights to Counsel." *The Police Chief*, April 2004, pp. 11–12.

"Lights, Camera, Interrogation." *Law Enforcement News*, January 15/31, 2003, p. 7.

Mertens, Jennifer. "Learning to Dance the Language Tango." *Law Enforcement Technology*, March 2004, pp. 16–24.

Navarro, Joe. "A Four-Domain Model for Detecting Deception: An Alternative Paradigm for Interviewing." *FBI Law Enforcement Bulletin*, June 2003, pp. 19–24.

Reece, Hunter. "The Keys to Quality Interview Techniques." *Law and Order*, November 2003, pp. 66–69.

Rutledge, Devallis. "Demystifying Miranda." *Police*, July 2003, pp. 140–141.

Rutledge, Devallis. "Does Miranda Bear Poisonous Fruit?" *Police*, September 2004a, pp. 82–83.

Rutledge, Devallis. "Hearsay and Confrontation." *Police*, May 2004b, pp. 62–63.

Rutledge, Devallis. "Timing is Everything." *Police*, December 2004c, pp. 74–77.

Rutledge, Devallis. "Arresting Foreign Nationals." *Police*, April 2005, pp. 72–75.

Sandoval, Vincent A. "Strategies to Avoid Interview Contamination." *FBI Law Enforcement Bulletin*, October 2003, pp. 1–12.

Scoville, Dean. "Screen Gems." *Police*, October 2003, pp. 40–48.

Server, Michael J. "Revealing Deception." *Minnesota Police Chief*, Summer 2003, pp. 52–53.

Server, Michael J. "Nonverbal Communication in Police Interrogations." *Minnesota Police Chief*, Winter 2004–2005, pp. 21–22.

Stanek, Rich. "CriMNet: Minnesota Catches Up with Criminals." *The Police Chief*, April 2004, pp. 167–168.

Sullivan, Thomas. "Recording Custodial Interrogations." *Law and Order*, March 2005, pp. 46–50.

CASES CITED

Alabama v. White, 496 U.S. 235, 329 (1990)

Berkemer v. McCarty, 468 U.S. 420 (1984)

Brewer v. Williams, 430 U.S. 398 (1977)

Crawford v. Washington, No. 02-9410 (2004)

Dickerson v. United States, 120 S. Ct. 2326 (2000)

Edwards v. Arizona, 451 U.S. 477 (1981)

Fellers v. United States, 124 S.Ct. 1019 (2004)

Frazier v. Cupp, (1978)

Illinois v. Perkins, 496 U.S. 292 (1990)

Minnesota v. Murphy (1984)

Miranda v. Arizona, 384 U.S. 436 (1966)

Missouri v. Seibert, 124 S.Ct. 2601 (2004)

Moore v. Hopper (1975)

New York v. Quarles, 467 U.S. 649 (1984)

Nix v. Williams, 467 U.S. 431 (1984)

Oregon v. Mathiason, 429 U.S. 492 (1977)

Roe v. State of New York (1973)

United States v. Dockery (1983)

United States v. Patane, 124 S. Ct. 2620 (2004)

United States v. Scheffer (1998)

United States ex rel. Caminito v. Murphy (1955)

Wong Sun v. United States, 371 U.S. 471 (1963)

Yarborough v. Alvarado, No. 02-1684 (2004)

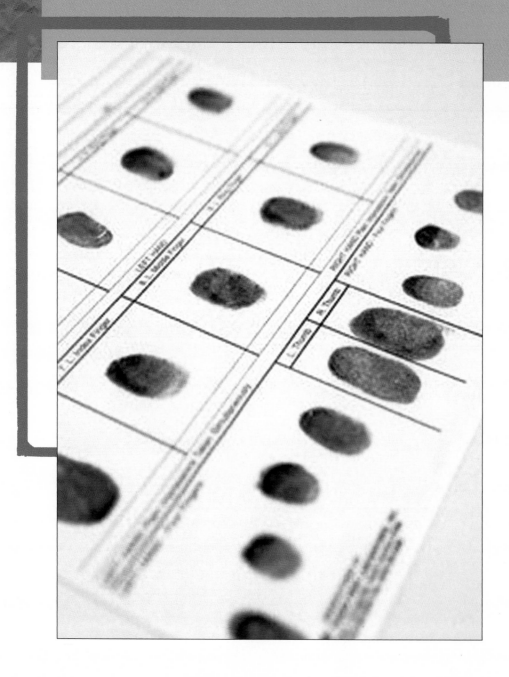

CHAPTER 7

Identifying and Arresting Suspects

Can You Define?

Do You Know?

- What field identification or show-up identification is and when it is used?
- What rights a suspect has during field (show-up) identification and what case established these rights?
- How a suspect is developed?
- How to help witnesses describe a suspect and/or a vehicle?
- When mug shots are used?
- What the four basic means of identifying a suspect are?
- What photographic identification requires and when it is used?
- What a lineup requires and when it is used?
- What rights suspects have regarding participation in a lineup and which cases established these rights?
- When surveillance is used? What its objectives are?
- What the types of surveillance are?
- When wiretapping is legal and what the precedent case is?
- What the objectives of undercover assignments are? What precautions you should take?
- What the objectives of a raid are?
- When raids are legal?
- What precautions should be taken when conducting a raid?
- When a lawful arrest can be made?
- When probable cause must exist for believing that a suspect has committed a crime?
- What constitutes an arrest?
- In what areas officers leave themselves open to civil liability when making an arrest?
- When force is justified in making an arrest? How much force is justified?

Outline

The classic question in detective stories is "Whodunit?" This question is also critical in criminal investigations. In some cases the suspect is obvious. However, in most cases, there is no suspect initially. Although many crimes are witnessed, victims and witnesses may not recognize or be able to describe the suspect. Further, many crimes are not witnessed.

191

Factors crucial to resolving criminal investigations are called **solvability factors.** These are factors you should consider when deciding whether to investigate a crime. Among the most important are the existence of one or more witnesses and whether a suspect can be named or at least described and located.

Even if a suspect is known or has confessed, you must prove the elements of the crime and establish evidence connecting the suspect with the criminal act. Some cases require that suspects be developed, located, identified, and then arrested. Others begin with an arrest and proceed to identification. No set sequence exists. Regardless of whether an arrest begins or ends an investigation, the arrest must be legal.

This chapter explains the most immediate forms of suspect identification, field (show-up) identification, and identification by driver's license. This is followed by a discussion of how to develop, locate, and identify suspects, including photographic identification and lineup identification. Next is a description of three specialized areas of suspect development and identification: surveillances, undercover assignments, and raids. The chapter concludes with a discussion of what constitutes a legal arrest and how much force is allowed when making an arrest.

Identifying Suspects at the Scene

I f a suspect is at the scene, you can use the person's driver's license, mobile identification technology, or field/show-up identification.

Identification by Driver's License

"Despite variations in its appearance among the 50 states, the driver's license is still as close as the United States comes to having a national identity card. . . . As such, the question of who gets to have one and who does not has taken on greater significance in the aftermath of September 11, 2001" ("ID or Not ID," p.5). Asking to see a suspect's driver's license is routine. However, often suspects do not carry identification or, if they do, it may be fake. Investigators need to determine whether licenses are legitimate as well as whether they belong to those using them.

One aid in determining authenticity of driver's licenses is the *Drivers License Guide*, which contains information and graphics of over 200 driver's licenses, as well as other documents commonly used for identification. Keep a current copy of this publication on hand.

Mobile Identification Technology

An important advance in law enforcement is the ability to receive information about suspects through officers' laptops or in-car computers. The amount of time it takes

Technology Innovations

Facial recognition is being used by Department of Motor Vehicles offices in West Virginia to compare a photograph of someone applying for a replacement or renewal license to prior images to be sure the applicant is the same person. Such a system could improve the millions of manual ID verifications performed daily.

to identify a suspect is directly correlated to the length of time it takes to solve a crime.

Field Identification/Show-Up Identification

If a suspect is apprehended while committing a crime, you can have witnesses identify the suspect. The same is generally true if the suspect is apprehended at or near the crime scene.

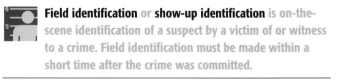

Field identification or **show-up identification** is on-the-scene identification of a suspect by a victim of or witness to a crime. Field identification must be made within a short time after the crime was committed.

The critical element in field identification is *time.* Identification must occur very soon after the crime was committed (usually 15–20 minutes). Some experts, however, suggest that if a suspect has been temporarily detained, the show-up may occur up to two hours after the crime was committed. If the suspect has fled but is apprehended within minutes, you can either return the

Technology Innovations

An integrated biometric identification system (IBIS) shrinks this time factor and solves a problem continually faced by police—the need to obtain positive identification and information on suspects at a crime scene or during a traffic stop.

Gerber (p.18) explains that an IBIS is a comprehensive data system allowing field officers to capture forensic-quality fingerprints and facial images on a handheld device called a remote data terminal (RDT). The captured information is transmitted by a device the size of a clothing iron using cell phone technology to access a central database and matched against criminal and fugitive records. The images can also be transmitted across the law enforcement communications network to two Federal Bureau of Investigation (FBI) databases: the Automated Fingerprint Identification System (AFIS) and the 2000 National Crime Information Center (NCIC). If a match is found, the system returns the individual's name and date of birth directly to the RDT. The system also can query existing criminal history and warrant files and provide information within minutes.

suspect to the scene or take the witness to where the suspect was apprehended. It is usually preferable to take the witness to the suspect than to return the suspect to the crime scene.

Whether the identification is made at or away from the scene, the victim or witness must identify the suspect as soon after the crime as possible so that details are still clear. However, a reasonable basis must exist for believing that immediate identification is required before using field identification. Rutledge (2003b, p.74) stresses that when using field identification it is important to document in the report why a prompt ID was needed and any steps taken to ensure a fair opportunity for an accurate ID. It's best not to tell the witness you think you have the suspect. It might be sufficient to say, "We have someone we want you to look at and tell us if you recognize him."

United States v. Ash, Jr. (1973) established that a suspect does not have the right to have counsel present at a field identification.

Read suspects the *Miranda* warning before questioning them. Suspects may refuse to answer questions and may demand a lawyer before any questioning occurs, but they do not have the right to have a lawyer present before field identification is made. Suspects may not even know such identification is occurring. Victims

or witnesses may be positioned so they can see the suspect while the suspect cannot see them.

Field identifications have been attacked on the basis that the victim or witness is too emotionally upset at the time to make an accurate identification, but such objections are seldom upheld. Mistaken identification is less likely if the person committing the crime is apprehended at the scene and is identified immediately. Have the victim or witnesses put their positive identification in writing and sign and date it, and then have it witnessed.

Developing a Suspect

If a suspect is not at the scene and not apprehended nearby, you must develop a suspect.

Suspects are developed through the following means:
- Information provided by victims, witnesses, and other persons likely to know about the crime or the suspect
- Physical evidence left at the crime scene
- Psychological profiling
- Information in police files
- Information in the files of other agencies
- Informants

The popular television series *CSI*'s theme song "Who Are You" emphasizes the importance of identifying a suspect (or a body). Many sources are sometimes needed to develop a suspect. Most of these sources were introduced in the preceding chapter. At other times the victim or witnesses provide the required information. Then your task is to corroborate the identification through associative evidence such as fingerprints or DNA analysis, shoe prints, personal belongings left at the scene, tools used, weapons, stolen property in the possession of the suspect, injuries sustained, soil in shoes, safe insulation, and other such evidence described in Chapter 5. Police agencies also have automated fingerprint identification systems and computerized imaging systems to assist in identifying suspects.

Victims and Witnesses

Developing a suspect is much easier if the victim or witnesses can describe and identify the person who committed the crime. Witnesses may not have observed the actual crime but may have seen a vehicle leaving the scene and can describe it and its occupants. Obtain a complete description of the suspect(s) and any vehicles involved.

Ask very specific questions and use an identification diagram to assist witnesses in describing suspects and vehicles.

Rather than simply asking a witness to describe a suspect, ask specific questions about each item in Table 7.1. A description sheet with a diagram also helps people to describe suspects (Figure 7.1).

Obtain information about how the suspect left the scene—on foot or in a vehicle. If in a vehicle, obtain a complete description of it. Identifying the car may lead to identifying the suspect.

Victims can provide information about who has a motive for the crime, who has the knowledge required to commit it, and who is not a likely suspect. For example, in an "inside" burglary, the employer may be able to provide important information about which employees may or may not be suspects.

Green (p.195) notes that several studies have found that juries base their verdicts on confident eyewitness identification even if other factors like poor vision, visibility, or bias call the validity of the ID into question. He contends: "Although jurors rely heavily on eyewitness identification, there is overwhelming evidence that eyewitness identification is highly fallible and that eyewitness confidence is a poor guide to accuracy." Green cites several reasons that mistaken identity is common, including poor visibility, brief duration, distance, and faulty memory.

Because of such problems with witness identification, victim or eyewitness identification of a suspect should be corroborated by as much physical and circumstantial evidence as possible.

Table 7.1 / **Key Items in Suspect Identification**

Gender

Height

Weight

Build—stout, average, slim, stooped, square-shouldered

Age

Nationality

Face—long, round, square, fat, thin; pimples, acne, scars

Complexion—flushed, sallow, pale, fair, dark

Hair—color; thick, thin, partly bald, completely bald; straight, curly, wavy; long, short

Forehead—high, low; sloping, straight, bulging

Eyebrows—bushy, thin, average

Eyes—color; close together or wide-set; large, small; glasses or sunglasses

Nose—small, large; broad, narrow; crooked, straight; long, short

Ears—small, large; close to head or protruding; pierced

Mustache—color; short, long; thick, thin; pointed ends

Mouth—large, small; drooping, upturned

Lips—thick, thin

Teeth—missing, broken, prominent, gold, conspicuous dental work

Beard—color; straight, rounded; bushy, thin; long, short

Chin—square, round, broad; long, narrow; double, sagging

Neck—long, short; thick, thin

Distinctive marks—scars, moles, amputations, tattoos

Peculiarities—peculiar walk or talk, twitch, stutter, foreign accent, distinctive voice or dialect

Clothing—shabby or well-dressed, monograms, association with an occupation or hobby, general description

Weapon—(if any) specific type, how carried, how displayed and when

Jewelry—any obvious rings, bracelets, necklaces, earrings, watches

Mug Shots

If the victim or witness does not know the suspect but saw him or her clearly, mug shots may be used.

 Have victims and witnesses view mug shots in an attempt to identify a suspect you believe has a record.

This procedure, frequently depicted in television detective shows, is very time-consuming and is of value only if the suspect has a police record and has been photographed. Using facial recognition to scan the face of a suspect against a database of thousands of mug shots of known criminals helps officers pare down a list of suspects or solve a case.

Technology Innovations

The **Integrated Law Enforcement Face-Identification System (ILEFIS)** deploys a three-dimensional system to match images from surveillance or still photographs to existing mug shots with a high degree of accuracy.

Composite Drawings and Sketches

If witnesses can provide adequate information, a composite image can be made of the person who committed the crime. Composite drawings are most commonly used to draw human faces or full bodies, but they can also be used for any inanimate object described by a witness—for example, vehicles, unusual marks or symbols, tattoos, or clothing. Police officers may also be trained to sketch freehand while interviewing a victim or witness.

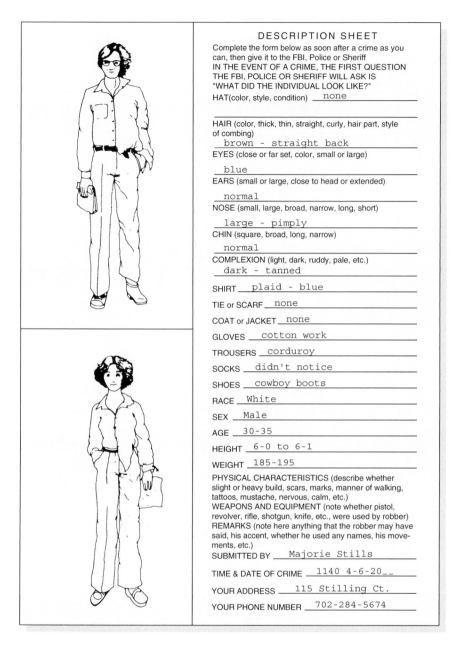

DESCRIPTION SHEET

Complete the form below as soon after a crime as you can, then give it to the FBI, Police or Sheriff
IN THE EVENT OF A CRIME, THE FIRST QUESTION THE FBI, POLICE OR SHERIFF WILL ASK IS "WHAT DID THE INDIVIDUAL LOOK LIKE?"

HAT (color, style, condition) __none__

HAIR (color, thick, thin, straight, curly, hair part, style of combing)
__brown - straight back__
EYES (close or far set, color, small or large)
__blue__
EARS (small or large, close to head or extended)
__normal__
NOSE (small, large, broad, narrow, long, short)
__large - pimply__
CHIN (square, broad, long, narrow)
__normal__
COMPLEXION (light, dark, ruddy, pale, etc.)
__dark - tanned__

SHIRT __plaid - blue__

TIE or SCARF __none__

COAT or JACKET __none__

GLOVES __cotton work__

TROUSERS __corduroy__

SOCKS __didn't notice__

SHOES __cowboy boots__

RACE __White__

SEX __Male__

AGE __30-35__

HEIGHT __6-0 to 6-1__

WEIGHT __185-195__

PHYSICAL CHARACTERISTICS (describe whether slight or heavy build, scars, marks, manner of walking, tattoos, mustache, nervous, calm, etc.)
WEAPONS AND EQUIPMENT (note whether pistol, revolver, rifle, shotgun, knife, etc., were used by robber)
REMARKS (note here anything that the robber may have said, his accent, whether he used any names, his movements, etc.)
SUBMITTED BY __Majorie Stills__

TIME & DATE OF CRIME __1140 4-6-20__ __

YOUR ADDRESS __115 Stilling Ct.__

YOUR PHONE NUMBER __702-284-5674__

Figure 7.1
Witness identification diagram

Sketching courses may be available at local colleges or through the FBI Academy. Composite sketches can also be created using a computerized identification kit such as Identi-Kit®, although some training is required to use them.

Identi-Kit® 2003 is a computerized version of the original Identi-Kit®, developed in the late 1950s. The process starts with a police officer asking a series of initial questions, which creates a general likeness of a suspect based on a victim's or witness's description. After creating a general composite, officers can fine-tune the image of the criminal. Figure 7.2 illustrates how Identi-Kit® helps develop suspects.

Other software such as CompuSketch or Visatex is also becoming more popular for drafting computer-generated composites. Rogers (p.46) notes that computerized composites can be sent electronically to other agencies. She (p.48) also notes that by using a printer in the field, a composite can be immediately distributed in the area of the crime and sent electronically to the police department. However (p.44): "Hand-drawn sketches can include subtleties that can't compare to a composite software program." In addition, hand-drawn sketches have a higher "hit rate" than digital composites.

Developing a Suspect through Modus Operandi Information

A series of crimes often creates a recognizable modus operandi (MO). For instance, a forger may use the same or a very similar name on each forgery, or a burglar may take the same type of property. If a series of burglaries occurs at the same time of day, this may be the suspect's time away from a regular job. Such MOs furnish important investigative leads.

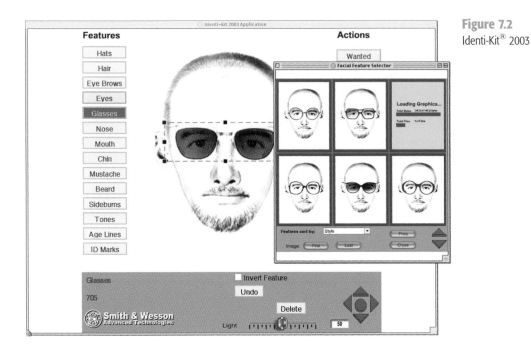

Figure 7.2
Identi-Kit® 2003

Check the details of a specific crime against your department's MO files. If no similar MO is listed, a new criminal may be starting activity in your area, or this may be the only crime the suspect intends to commit. In such cases, the suspect must be developed through sources other than MO information, such as information contained in a psychological or criminal profile.

Psychological or Criminal Profiling and Geographic Profiling

One method of suspect identification is **psychological or criminal profiling,** which attempts to identify an individual's mental, emotional, and psychological characteristics. Profiles are developed primarily for violent acts such as homicides, sadistic crimes, sex crimes, arson without apparent motive, and crimes of serial or ritual sequence. The profile provides investigators with corroborative information about a known suspect or possible leads to an unknown suspect.

The psychological profile is determined by examining all data and evidence from a specific crime scene, including, but not only, crime scene photographs, detailed photos of bodily injuries to victims, photos of any mutilation evidence, information related to the condition of the victim's clothing or absence thereof, information regarding whether the crime scene was altered or unaltered, photos of the area beyond the immediate crime scene, available maps of the area, the medical examiner's report and opinion, and any other relevant information concerning the crime, particularly abnormalities such as multiple slashings, disembowelment, drinking of the victim's blood, beheading, or dismembering of the body.

Specific information is then categorized to produce predictive information regarding the suspect's likely age, sex, race, weight, height; physical, mental, and psychological condition; area of residence; whether known to the victim; whether the suspect has a criminal record; and other details.

The psychological profile produced by experts in criminal behavior analysis can provide excellent leads for investigators. Investigators who desire such assistance may provide a complete crime report to the local office of the FBI, Domestic Cooperative Services. If the report is accepted, it is then forwarded to the FBI Behavioral Science Unit.

In one criminal investigation, the FBI's Behavioral Science Unit advised a police department that the serial rapist they were seeking was probably a 25- to 35-year-old, divorced or separated white male, with a high school education who worked as a laborer, lived in the area of the rapes, and engaged in voyeurism. Based on this information, the agency developed a list of 40 suspects with these characteristics. Using other information in the profile, they narrowed their investigation to one suspect and focused on him. Within a week they had enough information to arrest him.

Another case involved the rape/murder of a 25-year-old white married woman. The criminal profiler told a very surprised detective that he had probably already interviewed the killer. The profiler gave the detective a scenario based on color photographs, physical evidence, and interviews.

Interestingly, William Tafoya of the FBI developed a psychological profile of the Unibomber that many rejected. However, after the arrest of Theodore Kaczynski, Tafoya's assessment was observed to be much more accurate than many in the FBI had believed.

Psychological profiling is most often used in crimes against people in which a motive is unknown. The profile seeks to disclose a possible motive. Continued use of the technique has shown that the more information the police furnish to the FBI, the greater is the possibility of obtaining accurate leads. Reporting the unusual is extremely important. Psychological profiling can help to both eliminate and develop suspects, thereby saving investigative time.

Geographic profiling can also be helpful in identifying suspects who commit multiple crimes (serial criminals). As Weiss and Davis (p.34) point out, geographic profiling is based on the fact that everyone has a pattern to their lives, particularly in relation to the geographical areas they frequent. The serial criminal operates within a comfort zone—near to where he lives but far enough away to remain anonymous and still feel comfortable because he knows the area (Figure 7.3).

Weiss and Davis (p.34) observe: "[Geographic profilers] don't solve crimes, but rather, help to ease information overload, prioritize subjects, focus investigative strategies and conserve limited fiscal resources."

Despite its usefulness, profiling is not infallible. Investigators should not rely solely on a profile without supporting evidence. For example, in the Atlanta Olympic bombing case of 1996, the profile resulted in the arrest of the security guard, who was cleared. In addition, the legitimate use of profiling is sometimes confused with racial profiling.

Racial Profiling

Batton and Kadleck (p.31) define **racial profiling** as "the use of discretionary authority by law enforcement officers in encounters with minority motorists, typically within the context of a traffic stop, that result in the disparate treatment of minorities." Peed and Wexler (p.vii) state: "The term 'racial profiling' emerged only in the late 1990s, but concerns about whether some police are racially biased in their decision making date back decades, arguably even centuries, in U.S. history, and it is not limited to traffic stops." (Peed is director of the U.S. Office of Community Oriented Policing Services [COPS] and Wexler is executive director of the Police Research Executive Forum [PREF].)

Racial profiling occurs when an officer singles out and focuses on an individual as a suspect based solely on that person's race. This is unconstitutional, period.

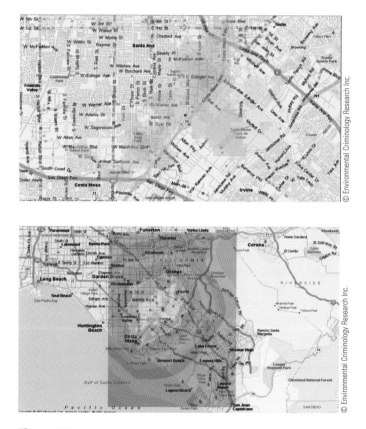

© Environmental Criminology Research Inc.

Figure 7.3

In December 2003, the city of Garden Grove, California, began experiencing a series of armed robberies involving several suspects. The robberies consisted of one to three offenders robbing liquor stores and motel desk clerks at gunpoint. All offenders were wearing masks. The offenders would often commit two or three robberies a night in a spree.

A geographic profile was initially done for this case in late December and was updated in January. At that point the total had reached 32 robberies. The area of the crimes covered 546 square miles. There were now 11 police jurisdictions with crimes in the series.

The offenders were captured in early February 2004 after the suspects had completed a total of 45 robberies. It was found that all offenders were staying at one of the motels they had previously robbed.

The peak profile area shown by the geographic profile was 8 square miles. The location of the motel (the offender's anchor point for the series) was in the top one percent of the updated profile (32 crimes), a highly accurate result.

Technology Innovations

Environmental Criminology Research Inc. (ECRI) has developed the Rigel Profiler, built specifically for geographic profiling (Kanable, p.124). Built on concepts developed by Kim Rossmo and tested on several notorious historical cases, the patented algorithm is a mathematical model of a serial criminal's behavior and how he moves within his "hunt zone" (Miller, p.130).

The street maps produced by Rigel have color overlays giving a visual idea of where the offender probably lives. Bright red shows the greatest probability, with the colors spreading outward in the order of the colors in a rainbow, to denote less and less probability.

In one case, police investigating a sexual assault were prepared to test over 300 suspects' DNA. However, a Rigel geographic-profile prioritized list identified a hit on the first person on the list. Rigel saved $350,000 directly, not counting time that would have been wasted. Says Miller (p.132): "Rigel's purpose is to help focus and direct an investigation, allowing police to deploy their resources more effectively."

Perhaps profiling should be renamed "building a case." Airport security personnel are taught to watch for certain traits—young, African American male paying for a ticket in cash, no luggage, nervousness, etc.—to profile possible drug dealers and are frequently criticized for such profiling. However, change the African American description to one of Middle Eastern descent and it is suddenly appropriate conduct for law enforcement.

A 2004 Amnesty International report (*Threat and Humiliation*) states: "Just as it is inaccurate to talk about racial profiling in the context of the 'War on Drugs' as simply as 'Driving While Black or Brown,' it is wrong to characterize racial profiling committed in the name of the 'War on Terror' as simply 'Flying While Arab.'"

Cooke (p.18) suspects that the perception of racial profiling has been "fueled" by discussions of **pretextual traffic stops,** that is, stopping vehicles when the officer's intent (pretext) was not the real reason for the stop. For example, an officer may stop someone for a traffic violation when he really suspects that the person has drugs in the car, but he does not have reasonable suspicion to make the stop for drug possession. In *Whren v. United States* (1996) the Supreme Court affirmed that officers could stop vehicles to allay any suspicions even though they have no evidence of criminal behavior. The legality of the stop will be gauged by its objective reasonableness.

In some instances racial profiling has not targeted racial *minorities*. For example, in the case of the Washington, D.C., snipers, police relied on racially based profiles of serial killers and were searching for antisocial white males. John Muhammad and John Lee Malvo, two black males, were convicted in 2003.

Gallo (p.19) stresses the importance of distinguishing between *profiling* as a policing technique and the politically charged term *racial profiling*. He suggests: "The purpose of profiling is to provide a scientific method for focusing resources. . . . As a scientific method, profiling can be viewed as pattern recognition through systematically collecting, organizing and analyzing information collected by observation or measurement; drawing conclusions in assessing criminal suspicion; and sharing data with others."

Fridell (2004, p.1), who also stresses the importance of distinguishing profiling (legitimate) from racial profiling (not legitimate), prefers for the latter the term *racially biased policing,* which she defines as "the inappropriate consideration by law enforcement of race or ethnicity in deciding with whom and how to intervene in an enforcement capacity."

The courts *have* ruled that race can be one factor among others to use in developing suspects. In *United States v. Weaver* (1992), a Drug Enforcement Administration (DEA) agent stopped and questioned Arthur Weaver at a Kansas City airport "because he was 'roughly dressed,' young, black, and on a direct flight from Los Angeles, a source city for drugs." Weaver was carrying illicit drugs but challenged the legality of the arrest. The Eighth Circuit Court of Appeals upheld the officer's conduct:

> Facts are not to be ignored simply because they may be unpleasant—and the unpleasant fact in this case is that the [DEA agent] had knowledge, based upon his own experience and upon the intelligence reports he had received from Los Angeles authorities, that young, male members of the African-American Los Angeles gangs were flooding the Kansas City area with cocaine. To that extent then, race, when coupled with the other factors [the agent] relied upon, was a factor in the decision to approach and ultimately detain [the suspect]. We wish it were otherwise, but we take the facts as they are presented to us, not as we would wish them to be.

Shortly after 9/11, on October 1, 2001, the U.S. Supreme Court refused to hear the only remaining case previously docketed concerning an equal protection claim in a case where police officers stopped persons based primarily on racial or ethnic descriptions. In *Brown v. City of Oneonta,* a U.S. Court of Appeals for the Second Circuit held that where law enforcement officials have a description of a suspect that consists only of the suspect's race and gender, and lacking evidence of discriminatory intent, they can act on that description without violating the equal protection clause of the Fourteenth Amendment. Subjecting officers to equal-protection scrutiny when they detain or arrest could hamper police work. Officers who fear personal liability from equal-protection violations might fail to act when they are expected to. If police effectiveness is hobbled by special racial rules, inner-city residents would be harmed the most.

Tracking

Sometimes knowledge of tracking is helpful in developing suspects. Forensic tracking is the science of locating, retaining, and interpreting footprint impressions for the purpose of solving criminal cases.

The length of stride and depth of impression of footprints can help to determine the size or height of the person or whether the person was carrying a heavy load. Tracking skill can be developed for impressions other than footprints and can provide many investigative leads. For example, the direction of vehicle travel from a crime scene can be determined by tire tread marks. People hiding in outside areas may leave foot, knee, hand, heel, or body impressions. Broken tree branches provide evidence of when the branch was broken—the lighter the color of the break, the more recent it is. Recent overturning of a stone may be indicated by the dirt or by the moist side being on top.

Other Identification Aids

Visual aids such as newspaper photos or video and news films disseminated to the public may provide rapid identification of suspects. Yearbooks have also proved to be of value in developing suspects. Fingerprints and footprints are other commonly used means of positive identification, and voiceprints and DNA profiling are becoming more frequently used, as discussed previously (Chapter 5).

If a suspect or victim is deceased and the identity is unknown, dental and orthopedic records may help. Facial reconstruction is also used in many areas to identify unknown victims or suspects if sufficient skull and facial parts are available. Amazing likenesses can be achieved to assist in identifying unknown deceased persons.

Information in Police Files and Files of Other Agencies

Police records on solved crimes and on suspects involved in certain types of crimes often suggest leads. For example, in the "Son of Sam" case in New York City, one lead was provided by a woman who saw an illegally parked car that fit the description of the car reported as being used in the crimes. Police then checked all parking tickets issued on that date for that time and location. This, combined with other information, eventually led to the suspect.

Police files contain considerable information about people who have committed or are suspected of committing crimes. The files contain such information as their physical characteristics, date of birth, age, race, general build, kind of clothing usually worn, height, weight, hair color and style, facial features, unusual marks, scars, tattoos, deformities, abnormalities, alcohol or drug use, MO, and other information.

Field-interview cards that patrol officers file when they stop people under suspicious circumstances can also provide leads. An officer may not know of an actual crime committed at the time of a stop but may later learn that a business or residence in the area of the stop was burglarized at about the same time. Descriptions of vehicles in a high-crime area that do not fit the neighborhood also help to identify suspects.

If the MO is discernible or if you have a good description of the suspect, check with other police departments in the area. Review all reports on the case and any cases that seem similar. Many other official sources of information at all levels of government as well as private agencies can also provide leads in developing and locating a suspect.

Community Level Almost every department of community government can provide some type of information during a criminal investigation. These sources include the city clerk, city attorney's office, municipal court, finance office, public utilities, building inspectors, public works departments, voter registration records, school files, welfare files, and civil service files. Local agencies can often furnish names, birth dates, addresses, changes of address, occupations, places of birth, parents' names, family names, property ownership, legal descriptions of

property, proposed businesses and business ownership, prior employment, past criminal offenses, and many other details. Banks and credit unions are another excellent source of information.

County Level Sources of information at the county level include the treasury department, the health department, engineering departments, license bureaus, the assessor's office, courts, probate courts, the welfare department, the coroner's office, civil service, the building inspector, the register of deeds, the sheriff's office, and the fire marshal. Such sources can furnish information on the payroll of county employees, names, addresses, changes of address, employment, and building inspections.

County agencies are also a source for birth and death certificates showing parents' names, maps, legal descriptions and values of property, deeds, mortgages, court records, marriage license and divorce records, handwriting specimens, criminal records, business listings, diagrams of buildings, and similar information.

State Level State agencies from which information is available include the liquor control board, secretary of state, highway department, highway patrol, bureau of investigation, bureau of narcotics and drug abuse, fish and game agency, insurance department, motor vehicles department, personnel department, state supreme court, state board of probation and parole, state prisons, and juvenile detention facilities. These agencies provide access to criminal records within the restrictions of the Privacy and Security Act, as well as to vehicle registrations, real estate sales records, licensing information, names, present and past addresses, business associates, civil suits, election information, birth and death records, and other personal information.

Federal Level The federal government has many agencies—not only in Washington, D.C., but also in regional offices throughout the United States—that provide information valuable in developing and locating suspects. The investigative agencies of the U.S. Navy, Army, Marines, Coast Guard, Merchant Marine, and Air Force can provide much information. Other federal sources include the Civil Service Commission; Department of Health, Education, and Welfare; Internal Revenue Service; Department of Commerce; Federal Bureau of Investigation; Central Intelligence Agency; Secret Service; State Department; Immigration and Naturalization Service; Federal Communications Commission; Postal Service; Interstate Commerce Commission; Department of Labor; Federal Aviation Administration; Veterans Administration; Department of the Interior; and task forces on organized crime activities. Such agencies provide information on military service, military criminal records, census data, drug abuse and narcotics involvement, aliens, firearms registration, airplane registration and licensing, as well as information on security investigations.

One of the most important federal-level information sources is the FBI's NCIC, discussed in Chapter 6. The 2000 version of this database contains criminal fingerprint records and information on wanted criminals and stolen property, including vehicles and guns. Image transmission to and from officers in the field is one goal of NCIC 2000. The ability to have photographs and fingerprints sent within seconds to and from a patrol car provides officers with information about whether an individual temporarily detained is a wanted person on file at the local, state, or national level.

Another federal information source is the FBI's Uniform Crime Reports (UCR) and its evolving National Incident Based Reporting System (NIBRS). The advantage of the NIBRS is that it reports every crime that occurs instead of just the most serious crime or event. For example, under the UCR summary requirements, if a burglar burglarizes a home and assaults and then kills the owner, only the murder would be reported. NIBRS would report this case as one burglary, one assault, and one murder.

Another advantage of the NIBRS is that it is collected at the incident level, and the data can be recorded on the day they are reported. In addition, it has four times as many inclusive crime categories as the UCR and can be forwarded by electronic transmission (rather than "snail" mail).

Interpol The International Criminal Police Organization (Interpol) is a network of national central bureaus (NCBs) in 177 member countries. Originated in 1914 and headquartered in Lyon, France, Interpol compiles and dispenses information on criminals and cases that cross national boundaries.

The main U.S. office is in Washington, D.C., and Interpol has operations in all the states of the union. Available 24 hours a day to public law enforcement, Interpol's telecommunications network links it with nearly all U.S. investigative agencies, such as the DEA, FBI, Central Intelligence Agency, and the Treasury Department. Interpol can provide criminal history checks, license plate traces, and information on the location of suspects, fugitives, and witnesses; on terrorists; and on stolen artworks, weapons, and motor vehicles.

Private Agencies Many private agencies also assist in developing and locating suspects. These include gas and electric companies, credit bureaus, financial institutions, educational facilities, the National Auto Theft Bureau, telephone companies, moving companies, offices of the Better Business Bureau, taxi companies, real estate sales and rental agencies, laundry and dry-cleaning associations, and insurance underwriters. Check your local city directory for possible additional private sources of information.

Informants

Informants have been a source of police information for centuries, as discussed in Chapter 6. Informants may work in a position that places them in frequent contact with criminals, or they may have committed crimes themselves or be associates of active criminals.

Most informants closely associated with the criminal world insist on remaining anonymous. This is usually to law enforcement's advantage because much information would no longer be available to informants if their cooperation with the police were known. Assign a code name to such informants and keep records of their information in a confidential file to help preserve their anonymity. Be aware of circumstances under which anonymity cannot be preserved and make informants aware of these circumstances.

One disadvantage of using anonymous informants is that information they provide is not accepted as evidence in court. It must be independently corroborated. However, such information can save much investigative time and lead to the recovery of valuable property or the arrest of suspects.

The information that some informants provide is of such value in solving or preventing crimes that the informants are paid. Many police agencies, at all levels of government, have informant-payment funds. Care must be used in paying informants because the payment motivates some of them to give contrived, false information. Cross-checking for truthfulness is required, and informants' reliability should be documented for future reference.

Hendrie (p.14) explains that concerned citizens are sometimes informants and that if a concerned citizen's identity is known to the police, the informant is presumed credible. Departments that use community-oriented policing may develop informants more easily because officers are closer to the people in their patrol area. Because of the negative connotations of the word *informant*, many agencies refer to these individuals as *citizens who assist the police with information.*

Locating Suspects

Many information sources used to develop a suspect can also help to locate the suspect. If the suspect is local and frequents public places, the victim may see the suspect and call the police. In one instance, a rape victim saw the alleged rapist in a shopping center and remembered that she had seen him there just before her rape occurred. The investigator accompanied the victim to the shopping center for several evenings until the victim saw the suspect and identified him.

Telephoning other investigative agencies, inquiring around the neighborhood of the suspect's last known address or checking the address on a prison release form, questioning relatives, and checking with utility companies and numerous other contacts can help locate suspects.

Identifying Suspects

 ield identification and mug shots have been discussed previously.

> Suspects can be identified through field or show-up identification, mug shots, photographic identification, or lineups.

Photographic Identification

Often the victim or witnesses get a good look at the suspect and are able to make a positive identification.

> Use **photographic identification** when you have a good idea of who committed a crime but the suspect is not in custody, or when a fair lineup cannot be conducted. Tell witnesses they need not identify anyone from the photographs.

Photographs can be obtained through surveillance or from files. Select pictures of at least five people of comparable race, height, weight, and general appearance. The photographs can be kept separate or mounted on a composite board. Write a number or code on the back of each photograph to identify the individual, but do not include any other information, especially that the person has a criminal record. Tell witnesses that they need not identify anyone from among the photographs and that it is as important to eliminate innocent people from suspicion as it is to identify the guilty.

> A suspect does not have the right to a lawyer if a photographic lineup is used (*United States v. Ash, Jr.,* 1973).

Rutledge (2003b, p.74) suggests that many officers use a "six pack" photo display of mug shots or other photos of the suspect and five other individuals. If there are several witnesses, have each one view a separate set of pictures independently—preferably in a different room if other witnesses are viewing the photographs at the same time. If witnesses recognize a photograph, have them

indicate this by placing their initials and the date on the *front* of the photograph. Then have them initial and date the *back* of each remaining photograph. This procedure establishes the fairness of the identification.

Holtz (2003a, p.102), however, advocates a sequential approach to showing photographs to witnesses. Patenaude (p.178) also recommends using a sequential rather than a simultaneous identification procedure, showing one photograph at a time rather than an array of photos simultaneously. He explains that a sequential showing allows a witness to decide about each photo before looking at the next, reducing the comparison process or relative judgment that often occurs when a "six pack" is shown.

Green (p.197) states that several studies demonstrate that explicitly telling witnesses that the suspect may not be in the photo array greatly reduces false identifications without having much effect on correct IDs.

It is unwise to show a single photograph to a victim or witness to obtain identification. Such identification is almost always inadmissible as evidence because it allows little chance of mistaken identity. The Supreme Court decision in *Manson v. Brathwaite* (1977), however, did approve the showing of a single picture in specific circumstances.

Rutledge (2005a, p.72) points out that most courts will accept the legality of using an image from the crime scene to jog a witness's memory: "If you show a surveillance photo of the actual criminal taken during the commission of the crime, a subsequent ID will not be considered tainted and can be used in evidence, if otherwise admissible."

After identification is made, review with the witness the conditions under which the suspect was seen, including lighting at the time and distance from the suspect. Patenaude (p.184) advocates also obtaining a confidence statement from the witness—just how certain are they? This and the conditions of the identification should be recorded, and the witness should be asked to sign the document.

A study by Iowa State researchers determined that feedback regarding an identification, whether immediate or delayed, is harmful to correct identification. The researchers showed staged crime videos to 253 participants and asked them to pick out a suspect from a photo lineup. The suspect was never in the lineup. Reluctant witnesses were encouraged to "just try to pick out the person as best you can." All identified someone. Each witness was given immediate or delayed (48-hour) feedback about the choice. By random selection, the feedback either falsely confirmed the choice, disconfirmed it, or was neutral. The witnesses who received confirming feedback experienced significant distortions in their recollection and overestimated how confident they were in their identification ("Feedback, Even When," p.3).

Figure 7.4
This lineup shows five suspects of comparable race, height, weight, age, and general appearance in accordance with lineup standards set by the U.S. Supreme Court. A computer was used to select lineup subjects and generate a useable composite for a witness to look at.

Lineup Identification

Lineup identification is commonly used when the suspect is in custody and there were witnesses to the crime. Police have adopted lineup procedures to ensure accurate, fair identifications and to meet the standards established by Supreme Court decisions. Basically, a lineup has the same requirements as photographic identification (Figure 7.4).

Use lineup identification when the suspect is in custody. Use at least five individuals of comparable race, height, weight, age, and general appearance. Ask all to perform the same actions or speak the same words. Instruct those viewing the lineup that they need not make an identification.

Lineups may have from five to ten people. The suspect must not be of a different race, exceptionally taller or shorter, have longer or shorter hair, or be dressed very differently from the others in the lineup. The suspect must not be handcuffed unless everyone in the lineup is handcuffed. Nor may the suspect be asked to step forward, turn a certain direction, or speak certain words unless everyone in the lineup is asked to do the same.

If the suspect refuses to participate in the lineup or a lineup cannot be conducted for some reason, simply photograph the suspect and each individual in the lineup separately and use photographic identification.

Suspects may refuse to participate in a lineup, but such refusals can be used against them in court (Schmerber v. California, 1966). Suspects have a Sixth Amendment right to have an attorney present during a lineup (United States v. Wade, 1967).

In the case of *United States v. Wade* (1967), on September 21, 1964, a robber forced a cashier and a bank official to place money in a pillowcase. The robber had a piece of tape on each side of his face. After obtaining the money, he left the bank and drove away with an accomplice who had been waiting outside in a car.

In March 1965, an indictment was returned against Wade and an accomplice for the bank robbery. He was arrested April 2, 1965. Approximately two weeks later, an FBI agent put Wade in a lineup to be observed by two bank employees. Wade's counsel was not notified of the lineup. Each person in the lineup had strips of tape similar to those worn by the bank robber, and each was requested to say words allegedly spoken at the robbery. Both bank employees picked Wade out of the lineup as being the robber, and both employees again identified Wade in the courtroom.

The defense objected that the bank employees' courtroom identifications should be stricken because the original lineup had been conducted without the presence of Wade's counsel. The motion was denied, and Wade was found guilty. Counsel held that this violated his Fifth Amendment right against self-incrimination and his Sixth Amendment right to counsel being present at the lineup.

The *Wade* decision ruled: "Prior to having a suspect participate in a lineup, the officer must advise the suspect of his constitutional right to have his lawyer present during the lineup." Recall that this right to a lawyer does not apply to field identification or photographic identification. If suspects waive their right to counsel, get the waiver in writing. A waiver such as the one in Figure 7.5 can be used.

The Court held that a suspect has the right to have counsel present at the lineup because a lineup is held for identification by eyewitnesses and may involve vagaries leading to mistaken identification. The Court cited the many cases of mistaken identification and the improper manner in which the suspect may have been presented. The Court commented that neither the lineup nor anything that Wade was required to

Figure 7.5
Sample waiver

WAIVER OF RIGHT TO LEGAL COUNSEL AT LINEUP

Your Rights Are: The police are requesting you to personally appear in a lineup. There will be a number of other persons similiar in physical characteristics with you. The purpose of the lineup is to permit witnesses to observe all persons in the lineup, to make an identification. You may be asked to perform certain actions such as speaking, walking or moving in a certain manner or to put on articles or clothing. You must appear in the lineup, but you have a right to have legal cousel of your choice present. If you do not have an attorney, one can be appointed for you by the court, and the lineup will not be held until your legal counsel is present. An attorney can help you defend against an identification made by witnesses at the lineup.

You have the right to waive legal counsel being present at the lineup.

WAIVER

I have read, or have had read to me, this statement of my rights and I understand these rights. I am willing to participate in a lineup in the absence of legal counsel. I fully understand and give my consent to what I am being asked to do. No promises or threats have been made to me, and no pressure of coercion has been used against me. I understand that I must appear in the lineup, but this consent is to the waiver of legal counsel being present at the lineup.

Signed _____   Place _____

Witness _____   Date _____

Witness _____   Time _____

---

do in the lineup violated his privilege against self-incrimination.

The Court stated in *Schmerber v. California* (1966) that protection against self-incrimination involved disclosure of knowledge by the suspect. Both state and federal courts have held that compulsion to submit to photographs, fingerprinting, measurements, blood analysis, or samples of writing and speaking is not self-incrimination under the Fifth Amendment.

As with photographic identification, many experts recommend using a sequential lineup rather than a simultaneous lineup, having one person at a time appear before the witness to avoid having the witness identify someone through the process of elimination. According to Holtz (2004, p.19), studies have proved that witnesses tend to compare one member of a lineup with another, making relative judgments about who looks most like the perpetrator.

Adams (2005) reports on a Hennepin County (Minnesota) study in which Minneapolis and three suburban police departments compared lineups using the "six pack" photo procedure and using sequential lineups. Witnesses identified the suspect in about half the cases

using either method, but witnesses picked the wrong person only 8 percent of the time in the sequential lineup, compared with up to 25 percent in the "six pack" lineup. Adams notes that sequential lineups were mandated by New Jersey's attorney general about three years ago.

Avoid having the same person make both photographic and lineup identification. If you do so, do not conduct both within a short time period.

If suspects choose to have a lawyer, they may either select their own or ask you to obtain one. The lawyer may confer with the suspect in private before the lineup and may talk with witnesses observing the lineup, but witnesses are not obligated to talk with the lawyer. Witnesses may wear face covers to avoid recognition by the suspect. Usually the lineup room ensures viewers' anonymity.

Give witnesses clear instructions before the lineup. Tell them that they need not identify anyone in the lineup, that they are not to confer with any other witnesses viewing the lineup, and that they are not to indi-

Figure 7.6
Police report of lineup

POLICE REPORT OF LINEUP

Boulder City Police
Police Department

Name of suspect ___John Vance___ Birth date ___2-14-1964___

Address ___1424 Colten Street, Boulder City___

Case Number ___6432___ Complainant or victim ___Thelma Crump___

Name of legal counsel ___John Simmons___ Present: Yes _X_ No ___

Was waiver signed: Yes _X_ No ___

Place of lineup ___Las Vegas, Nevada, Police Dept.___

Date of lineup ___5-12-20__ ___ Time of lineup ___1640___

Names of persons in lineup (left to right, facing the lineup)

	Name	Height	Weight	Birth date	Other
1.	Charles Upright	5-11	184	4-10-1966	
2.	Gary Starrick	5-10	178	2-14-1965	
3.	Jerry Stilter	5-11	190	10-11-1967	
4.	Ralph Barrett	5-10	185	12-24-1968	
5.	John Vance	5-10	183	2-14-1964	
6.	Christian Dolph	5-11	190	6-12-1964	
7.					
8.					
9.					
10.					

Subject identified by witness: Number ___5___ Name ___John Vance___

Recording taken of lineup: Yes _X_ No ___ Photos taken of lineup: Yes _X_ No ___

Persons present at lineup ___Thelma Crump   Alfred Nener___
___John Simmons   Emmanuel Sorstick___

Person conducting lineup ___Sgt. Lloyd Brenner, LVPD___

---

cate an identification in any way. Tape record or video-tape the proceedings and take a color photograph of the lineup to nullify any allegations by the defense counsel of unfair procedure. The form in Figure 7.6 provides additional evidence of the fairness and reliability of a lineup identification.

Establishing the Reliability of an Identification

Rutledge (2003b, p.75) states that courts examine five factors to establish the reliability of both the pretrial ID and the trial ID:

1. Witness opportunity to observe the suspect during the crime or flight

2. Witness degree of attention

3. Accuracy of the description given by the witness before making the ID

4. Level of certainty in making an ID

5. Time period between the crime and the ID

Information related to all these factors should be contained in the police report.

In addition, Green (p.198) suggests that when conducting photographic or lineup identification, the person conducting the identification session should *not* know who the suspect is. It is possible that this person may signal expectations. In fact, asserts Green: "The tendency to signal expectations is so pervasive that drug and other important scientific studies are rejected without a double blind procedure, one where neither the subject nor the experimenter knows the expected outcome." To assure this double blind procedure, it is important that the witness be told that the examiner has no idea of who the suspect is. As Penrod states: "Blind presentation is the order of the day. Cops should not know who the suspect is, and they should tell the witness they have no idea who the suspect is" ("Altering Lineups," p.11).

Biometric Identification

Just as facial recognition (a biometric technology) can help identify suspicious people and possible terrorists, biometric identification is being used at our borders. According to Mertens (p.8), one initiative of the Department of Homeland Security (DHS) has been the US-VISIT program, designed to strengthen national security through the use of biometric identifiers. In January 2004, 115 U.S. airports and 14 seaports began using a new biometric entry process that uses fingerprints and photographs of foreigners entering the country. The program is to be extended to cover all entry/exit points at all land borders, north and south.

A recent advance in biometrics is the development of gait recognition.

Technology Innovations

Garrett (2003b, p.82) suggests that although people's stride may not be as distinctive as John Wayne's swagger or Marilyn Monroe's sashay, an individual's gait may be unique enough to identify the person from a distance: "Gait recognition may soon be added to the arsenal of biometric methods used to help separate the bad guys from the good." According to Garrett the goal is to detect, classify, and identify people from up to 500 feet away in all weather and lighting conditions, allowing authorities to identify suspects from a safe distance. This technology may help law enforcement detect potential suicide bombers or people smuggling contraband because suicide bombers and smugglers who carry bombs or drugs alter the way they walk—another tool in the "arsenal in the fight against terrorism."

Surveillance, Undercover Assignments, and Raids: The Last Resort

"Follow that car!" "I think we're being tailed!" "I lost him!" "My cover's blown!" "We've been made!" "It's a raid!" Police officers, criminals, and the public are very aware of investigative practices such as observing suspects or their houses or apartments, tailing suspects, staking out locations, and conducting raids. Television shows and movies, however, usually depict the glamorous, dangerous sides of this facet of investigation. They seldom show the long hours of preparation or the days—even weeks—of tedious watchfulness frequently required.

 Surveillance, undercover assignments, and raids are used only when normal methods of continuing the investigation fail to produce results.

These techniques are expensive and potentially dangerous and are not routinely used.

Surveillance

The covert, discreet observation of people or places is called **surveillance** ("to watch over"). Nason (2004, p.1) contends: "Second only to operating confidential sources, surveillance is the most frequently employed investigative technique in obtaining arrests, indictments and convictions for the FBI."

The objective of surveillance is to obtain information about people, their associates, and their activities that may help to solve a criminal case or to protect witnesses.

Surveillance can help do the following:

- Gain information required for building a criminal complaint
- Determine an informant's loyalty
- Verify a witness's statement about a crime
- Gain information required for obtaining a search or arrest warrant
- Gain information necessary for interrogating a suspect
- Identify a suspect's associates
- Observe members of terrorist organizations
- Find a person wanted for a crime
- Observe criminal activities in progress
- Make a legal arrest
- Apprehend a criminal in the act of committing a crime
- Prevent a crime
- Recover stolen property
- Protect witnesses

Because surveillance is a time-consuming, expensive operation that can raise questions of invasion of privacy, first exhaust all alternatives. Balance the rights of the individual against the need for public safety.

The Surveillant

The **surveillant** is the plainclothes investigator who makes the observation. Surveillants must be prepared for tedium. No other assignment requires as much patience and perseverance while simultaneously demanding alertness and readiness to respond instantly. Surveillants must display ingenuity in devising a cover for the operation. Lack of resourcefulness in providing adequate answers at a moment's notice can jeopardize the entire case. The most successful surveillants do not attract attention but blend into the general populace.

Multiple surveillants may also compose a surveillance team (ST). An effective ST requires everyone to be "on the same page," which calls for communication and briefings.

The Subject

The **subject** is whom or what is observed. It can be a person, place, property, vehicle, group of people, organization, or object. People under surveillance are usually suspects in a crime or their associates. Surveillance of places generally involves a location where a crime is expected to be committed: the residence of a known criminal; a place suspected of harboring criminal activities such as illegal drug transactions, gambling, prostitution, or purchase of stolen goods or fencing operations; or the suspected headquarters of a terrorist organization.

Types of Surveillance

The type of surveillance used depends on the subject and the objective of the surveillance. In general, surveillance is either stationary or moving.

 The types of surveillance include stationary (fixed, plant, or stakeout) and moving (tight or close, loose, rough, foot, or vehicle).

Stationary Surveillance Stationary, or **fixed**, **surveillance**, also called a **plant** or **stakeout**, is used when you know or suspect that a person is at or will come to a known location, when you suspect that stolen goods are to be dropped, or when informants have told you that a crime is going to be committed. Such assignments are comparatively short. An outside surveillance simplifies planning. The observation may be from a car, van, or truck or by posting an officer in an inconspicuous place with a view of the location. A "dummy" van or a bor-

rowed business van and a disguise as a painter, carpenter, or service technician are often used. Take photographs and notes throughout the surveillance.

In longer surveillances, it is often necessary to photograph people who frequent a specific location, such as a store suspected of being a cover for a bookmaking operation or a hotel or motel that allows prostitution or gambling. If the subject of surveillance is a place rather than a person, obtain a copy of the building plan and personally visit the building in advance if possible. Know all entrances and exits, especially rear doors and fire escapes. To properly record what is observed, use closed-circuit camera equipment, movie or video cameras, binoculars with a camera attached, telephoto lenses, or infrared equipment for night viewing and photographing.

Lengthy fixed surveillance is often conducted from a room with an unobstructed view of the location, such as an apartment house opposite the location being watched. Naturally, the surveillant must not be noticed entering the observation post.

Whether the stationary surveillance is short or long, have adequate communications such as radio, horn signals, or hand signals. Use simple hand signals such as pulling up the collar, buttoning the shirt, pulling down the brim on a hat, tying a shoelace, running the hand through the hair, or checking a wristwatch. If you use radio communications, find out whether the subject might be monitoring police radio frequencies, and if likely, establish a code.

Select the surveillance team to fit the case and area, and have enough surveillants to cover the assignment. Scout the area in person or by studying maps. Sketch the immediate area to determine possible ways the subject could avoid observation or apprehension. Be aware of alleys, abnormal street conditions, one-way streets, barricades, parking ramps, and all other details. This is especially critical when the objective of the surveillance is to apprehend people committing a crime. In such cases, all members of the stakeout must know the signal for action and their specific assignments.

Moving Surveillance The subjects of **moving surveillance** are almost always people. The surveillant may be referred to as a **tail**. The first step in planning such a surveillance is to obtain as much information about the subject as you can. View photographs and, if possible, personally observe the subjects. Memorize their physical descriptions and form a mental image of them. Concentrate on their appearance from behind, as this is the view you normally have while "tailing" them. Although subjects may alter their physical appearance, this usually presents no problem. The major problem is to keep subjects under constant surveillance for the desired time. Know the subjects' habits, where they are likely to go, and whether they walk or drive. If they drive, find out what kind of vehicle(s) they use. Also find out who their associates are and whether they are likely to suspect that they are being observed.

Other problems of moving surveillance are losing the subject and having the subject recognize you as a surveillant. Sometimes it is not important if the subject knows of the surveillance. This is often true of material witnesses the police are protecting. It is also true of organized crime figures, who know they are under constant surveillance and take this into account. In such instances, a **rough tail** or **open tail** is used. You need not take extraordinary means to remain undetected. The major problem of a rough tail is that it is liable to the charge of police harassment or invasion of privacy.

At other times it is more important to remain undetected than to keep the subject under constant observation. In such cases, a **loose tail** is used. Maintain a safe distance. Nason (p.3) suggests that a rule of thumb is to stay one or two vehicles behind the subject and to "hand off" the subject to another officer after taking one turn. If the subject is lost during surveillance, you can easily relocate the subject and resume the surveillance. A loose tail is often used when you need general information about the subject's activities or associates.

Often, however, it is extremely important not to lose the subject, and a very **close (tight) tail** is maintained. On a crowded street this means staying within a few steps of the subject; on a less crowded street, it means keeping the subject in sight. A close tail is most commonly used when you know the subject is going to commit a crime, when you must know the subject's exact habits, or when knowledge of the subject's activities is important to another critical operation.

When tailing a subject on foot, you can use numerous delaying tactics. You can cross to the other side of the street, talk to a person standing nearby, increase your distance from the subject, read a magazine or newspaper, buy a soda, tinker with the engine in your car, tie your shoe, look in windows or in parked cars, or stall in any other way.

If the subject turns a corner, do not follow closely. When you do turn the corner, if you find the subject waiting in a doorway, pass by without paying attention. Then try to resume the tail by guessing the subject's next move. This is often possible when you have advance information on the subject's habits.

If the subject enters a restaurant, you can either enter and take a seat on the side of the room opposite from the subject, making sure you are near the door so you can see the subject leave, or you can wait outside. If a subject enters a building that has numerous exits, follow at a safe distance, noticing all potential exits. If the subject takes an elevator, wait at the first floor until the subject returns, noticing the floors at which the elevator stops. If there is a stairway near the elevator, stand near the door so you can hear if the subject has gotten off the elevator and taken the stairs. Such stairs are seldom used, and when someone is going up or down, his or her footsteps echo and can easily be heard.

When tailing a subject on the street, do not hesitate to pass the subject and enter a store yourself. The less obvious you are, the more successful you will be. Use the glass in doors and storefront windows to see behind you.

Subjects who suspect they are being followed use many tricks. They may turn corners suddenly and stand in a nearby doorway, go into a store and duck into a restroom, enter a dressing room, hide behind objects, or suddenly jump on a bus or into a taxi. They may do such things to determine *whether* they are being followed or to lose someone they *know* is following them. *It is usually better to lose subjects than to alert them to your presence or to allow them to identify you.*

Surveillants often believe they have been recognized when in fact they have not. However, if you are certain the subject knows you are following you, stop the surveillance, but do not return to the police department right away, because the subject may decide to tail *you.*

If it is critical not to lose the subject, use more than one surveillant, preferably three. Surveillant A keeps a very close tail immediately behind the subject. Surveillant B follows behind Surveillant A and the subject. Surveillant C observes from across the street parallel with the other two. If the subject turns the corner, Surveillant A continues in the previous direction for a while, and Surveillant B or Surveillant C picks up the tail. Surveillant A then takes the position previously held by the surveillant who picked up the close tail.

When tailing by vehicle, have descriptions of all vehicles the subject drives or rides in. The subject's vehicle can be marked in advance by an electronic device or beeper monitored by a receiver in your car, or you can place the beeper in an object the subject will be carrying. A small amount of fluorescent paint can be applied to the rear bumper of the vehicle to make it easily identifiable day or night.

Your own vehicle should be inconspicuous. Obtain unregistered ("dead") plates for it from the motor vehicle authorities and change them frequently, or change your vehicle daily, perhaps using rental cars. Changing the number of occupants tends to confuse a suspicious subject. If surveillance is to be primarily at night, install a multiple contact switch to allow you to turn off one of your headlights at will.

Like subjects being tailed on foot, subjects being tailed by vehicle often use tricks to determine whether they are being tailed or to lose an identified tail. They may turn in the middle of the block, go through a red light, suddenly pull into a parking stall, change traffic lanes rapidly, go down alleys, or go the wrong way down a one-way street. In such cases, if temporarily losing the subject causes no problem, stop the surveillance.

If it is critical not to lose the subject, use more than one vehicle for the surveillance. The ideal system uses four vehicles. Vehicle A drives ahead of the subject and observes through the rearview mirror. (This vehicle is not used if only three vehicles are available). Vehicle B follows right behind the subject. Vehicle C and Vehicle D follow on left and right parallel streets to pick up the tail if the subject turns in either direction.

Avoiding Detection

Criminals are often suspicious of stakeouts or of being followed and may send someone to scout the area to see whether anybody has staked out their residence or their vehicle. This person may stand on the corner near the residence or drive around the block several times to see if everything is clear. Criminals often watch the windows or roofs of buildings across the street for movements. When they leave their residences, they may have an accomplice trail behind to see if anyone is following. Anticipate and plan for such activities. Sometimes a counter-countersurveillance is used if personnel are available.

Not every surveillance is successful. In some instances the subject is lost or the surveillant is recognized, despite the best efforts to avoid either. Like any other investigative technique, failure results from unforeseen circumstances such as vehicle malfunction, illness of the surveillant, unexpected absence of the subject due to illness or emergency, abnormal weather conditions or terrain, and other factors beyond control. Usually, however, information and evidence obtained through surveillance are well worth the time and effort invested. In most instances a form such as the one shown in Figure 7.7 should be completed after a surveillance assignment.

Surveillance Equipment

Surveillance equipment includes binoculars, telescopes, night-vision equipment, body wires, and video systems. Surveillance systems have become extremely sophisticated. One system, for example, conceals a periscope in what looks like a standard air vent in the roof of a van.

Figure 7.7
Surveillance intelligence form

Surveillance Report

Date 4-16-20__ Time started 1130 Time finished 1330 Case No. 6432

Address, location or name of subject ___ 116 7th St-Ralph Burns ___

Purpose of surveillance ___ Sales of controlled substance ___

Weather conditions ___ Fair ___ Equipment used ___ binoculars ___

Conversations with subject ___ None ___

Telephone calls made ___ None ___

Persons contacted by subject ___ None ___

Record of observations during surveillance ___

Time ___ Female adult entered garage 1142 ___

Time ___ Male, adult subject met Burns on step 1154 ___

Time ___ 2 males in 1974 brown car stopped at above address 1232 ___

Time ___ Burns left residence in car 1315 NV; 134-MMN ___

Time ___

Signature of surveillant ___

The periscope rotates 360 degrees and is undetectable. Remote motion detectors activate the system to videotape the area under surveillance.

Global Positioning System (GPS) technology is also being used in surveillance operations. According to Cerullo (p.12), investigators can install a GPS tracking device to monitor a vehicle's movement. Installing and monitoring such a device *probably* does not require a court order because it is used in a public area. Says Cerullo (p.11): "The Big Brother aspect of this technology calls into question its legality." He notes that because the technology is new, little case law addresses it. He also notes that two cases have affirmed warrantless use of a GPS tracking device based on U.S. Supreme Court precedent dealing with bird dog tracking devices. In *United States v. Knotts* (1983) the Court ruled that installing and monitoring a bird dog tracking device in a public location did not violate a suspect's rights.

Aerial Surveillance

Aerial surveillance may provide information about areas inaccessible to foot or vehicle surveillance. Communication between air surveillance and ground vehicles facilitates the operational movement in and around the target area. The aerial pilot should either be a police officer or be carefully selected by the police. The pilot should be familiar with the landmarks of the area, because many such surveillances involve moving-suspect vehicles.

Photographs taken from navigable air space, usually 1,000 feet, do not violate privacy regulations. In one aerial surveillance, officers viewed a partially covered greenhouse within the residential curtilage from a helicopter 400 feet above the greenhouse. The greenhouse, which contained marijuana plants, was located 10 to 20 feet behind the residence, a mobile home. A wire fence surrounded the entire property, and "Do Not Enter" signs were posted. Nonetheless, *Florida v. Riley* (1989) approved the warrantless aerial surveillance, noting that there should be no reasonable expectation of privacy from the skies above.

Visual/Video Surveillance

Fredericks (p.70) notes that video images are often crucial evidence in high-profile criminal investigations, with tens of thousands of lesser crimes caught on video each year. He suggests: "In many cases the videotape is the sole survivor, the silent witness." Fredericks provides the example of the black-and-white video image of Timothy McVeigh's Ryder truck passing in front of an apartment complex a block from the Alfred P. Murrah Federal Building as providing a "critical link," placing the suspected vehicle at the scene.

Covert video systems can be disguised in many ways—in clocks, picture frames, exit signs, and domes. Such systems can record drug buys, money laundering, shoplifting, and bank robberies and are usually admissible in court.

Although a warrant is usually required to use surveillance, the courts have allowed law enforcement to protect certain investigative techniques, to protect information regarding sensitive equipment, or to protect surveillance locations. The courts have allowed warrantless surveillance if revealing the technique may endanger law enforcement officers' lives or the lives of those who allow their property to be used in such activity, or they may no longer allow their property to be used for surveillance. They have also allowed warrantless surveillance if once a technique is revealed it is of no further value to law enforcement or might show criminals how to do the technique. Visual/video surveillance is often used in conjunction with audio/electronic surveillance.

Rotondo (p.71) says that across the country cities have installed video surveillance cameras at traffic signals. An officer in a vehicle can use a laptop to select and view specific cameras to determine the fastest route to an incident or get a real-time view of the situation before arriving on the scene.

Many visual surveillance systems have night-vision and/or telephoto lenses as well as time-and-date generators. Many also have hard-copy printers that produce black-and-white or color photographic copies on site. One of the most valuable pieces of equipment is often high-quality binoculars.

Clifford (p.31) points out that the FBI's Electronic Surveillance Technology Section (ESTS) focuses on evaluating newer technologies for conducting electronic surveillances. According to Davis (p.38): "Surveillance equipment used under the proper circumstances can be a force multiplier. Used inappropriately, however, you'll find yourself and your department bogged down in

Technology Innovations

Douglas (p.36) describes the newest tactical video units as smaller, lightweight, versatile, wireless, and extremely adaptable. The Camlite, for example, is both a flashlight and a portable video system that can transmit images 1,000 feet. The ThermoVision Scout can see suspects in the dark as well as through smoke, foliage, and fog. Davis (p.41) notes: "Soon police surveillance will be just like a James Bond movie. Video cameras have become so small that they can be easily concealed in ball caps, tie clips and fountain pens."

endless litigation as the privacy laws are in a tremendous state of flux."

Audio or Electronic Surveillance

In special instances electronic devices are used in surveillance (Figure 7.8). Such **electronic surveillance** techniques include wiring a person who is going to be talking with a subject or entering a suspicious business establishment, "**bugging**" a subject's room or vehicle, or **wiretapping** a telephone.

The most common forms of lawfully authorized electronic surveillance available to law enforcement are pen registers, trap-and-trace devices, and content interceptions. Pen registers and trap-and-trace devices record dialing and signaling information used in processing and routing telephone communication, such as the signals that identify the dialed numbers of outgoing calls or the originating numbers of incoming calls.

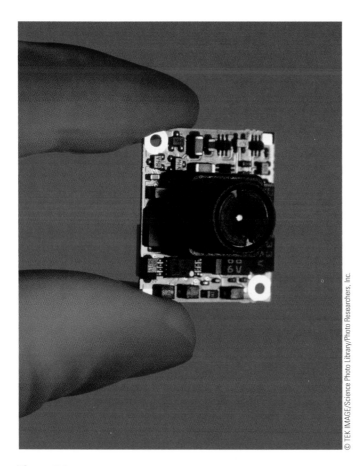

Figure 7.8
Gloved fingers hold a miniature video camera. These cameras, known as board cameras, are used for covert surveillance at home or in the work place. They can be located where they will not be noticed and used to surveil suspects. The cameras can be connected to standard video and television equipment.

© TEK IMAGE/Science Photo Library/Photo Researchers, Inc.

The exclusionary rule requires that all evidence against a suspect be acquired according to the standards set forth in the Fourth Amendment.

> Electronic surveillance and wiretapping are considered forms of search and are therefore permitted only with probable cause and a court order (*Katz v. United States*).

In a landmark case, *Katz v. United States* (1967), the U.S. Supreme Court considered an appeal by Charles Katz, who had been convicted in California of violating gambling laws. Investigators had observed Katz for several days as he made telephone calls from a particular phone booth at the same time each day. Suspecting he was placing horse-racing bets, the investigators attached an electronic listening/recording device to the telephone booth and recorded Katz's illegal activities. The evidence was used in convicting Katz. The Supreme Court reversed the California decision, saying: "The Fourth Amendment protects people not places. . . . Wherever a man may be, he is entitled to know that he will remain free from unreasonable searches and seizures." The investigators did have probable cause, but they erred in not presenting their information to a judge and obtaining prior approval for their actions.

The importance of electronic surveillance is recognized in the Introduction to Title III of the Omnibus Crime Control and Safe Streets Act of 1968, which authorized court-ordered electronic surveillance of organized crime figures. The U.S. Congress stated:

> Organized criminals make extensive use of wire and oral communications in their criminal activities. The interception of such communications to obtain evidence of the commission of crimes or to prevent their commission is an indispensable aid to law enforcement and the administration of justice.

According to Schott (p.27), Title III does not prohibit the surreptitious recording of telephone conversations when one party consents: "Federal case law makes clear that law enforcement may use individuals working for the government to record conversations to which they are a party or overhear without violating the Fourth Amendment."

To avoid wiretaps, suspects often use "drop phones," prepaid cell phones that are disposed of regularly. Prepaid phone cards serve the same purpose and can be easily purchased in many places without a person's having to produce identification.

Federal and state laws allow electronic surveillance (eavesdropping), provided it is authorized by a federal or state judge and specified procedures are followed. Advertisements in police magazines describe state-of-the-art surveillance systems that make undercover work more efficient and effective. Laser technology can direct a beam at the glass in a window with another beam modulated by sonic vibrations inside the room, bouncing the sound back to a receiver so officers can hear what is being said. Eavesdropping with "bugs" is now easier than ever. Criminals are using high-tech electronic countermeasures to detect such devices in a room before they hold a meeting or conversation there.

Schott (p.28) describes three places where a person does not have an expectation of privacy and where conversations can be recorded: squad cars, jail or prison cells, and interrogation rooms.

The courts have thus far upheld the right of officers to tape conversations that occur inside their squad cars. In the case of *United States v. McKinnon* (1993), two suspects were stopped for a traffic violation and asked to sit in the patrol car while the officer conducted a consent search in the vehicle for drugs. While in the patrol car, the suspects made incriminating statements that were recorded without their knowledge. Although one defendant argued that the recording violated his right to privacy, the Court disagreed, stating "no reasonable expectation of privacy exists in the back seat of a patrol car."

The courts have also held that no expectation of privacy exists in prison cells or in interrogation rooms. Schott (p.31) points out that telephone conversations made from jail or police stations usually do not enjoy Title III protection either.

Surveillance and the Constitution

Throughout the discussion on surveillance, of most importance is the balance between acting without violating suspects' constitutional rights and the need for law enforcement to do its job of protecting society. The Court's desire to maintain this balance was seen in *Kyllo v. United States* (2001), introduced in Chapter 4. In this case the Court held that thermal imaging of a house was a search and required a warrant.

Davis (p.43) cautions: "Remember, terrorists or not, we still live in a free society. Just because the PATRIOT Act has loosened the rules for the federal government, your local jurisdiction still needs to be aware of, and obey, local or state regulations when conducting surveillance." He stresses finding the "balancing point" between legal electronic surveillance and an individual's right to privacy.

Undercover Assignments

The nonuniformed or plainclothes investigator is in a good position to observe illegal activities and obtain evidence. For example, a male plainclothes officer may appear to accept the solicitations of a prostitute, or any plainclothes police officer may attempt to buy stolen goods or drugs or to place illegal bets. Many such activities require little

more than simply "not smelling like the law." Unlike other forms of surveillance in which a prime objective is not to be observed, **undercover** surveillants make personal contact with the subject using an assumed identity, or **cover**.

> The objective of an undercover assignment may be to gain a person's confidence or to infiltrate an organization or group by using an assumed identity and to thereby obtain information or evidence connecting the subject with criminal activity.

Undercover assignments can be designed to:
- Obtain evidence for prosecution.
- Obtain leads into criminal activities.
- Check the reliability of witnesses or informants.
- Gain information about premises for use in later conducting a raid or an arrest.
- Check the security of a person in a highly sensitive position.
- Obtain information on or evidence against subversive groups.

Some undercover assignments are relatively simple and are referred to as *ruses*. The two general types of ruses are (1) deception as to identity—for example, posing as a drug dealer or prostitute, and (2) deception as to purpose—for example, pretending to investigate a different person.

Many undercover assignments are more elaborate. Such undercover assignments are frequently made when criminal activity is greatly suspected or even known but no legal evidence of it exists. Such assignments can be extremely dangerous and require careful planning and preparation.

The undercover agent selected must fit the assignment (Figure 7.9). Age, sex, race, general appearance, language facility, health, energy level, emotional stability, and intelligence are all important selection considerations. Undercover agents must be good actors—able to assume their role totally. They must be intelligent and able to deal with any problems that arise, make quick decisions, improvise plans and actions, and work with the person or within the group or organization without arousing suspicion. Wexler (p.89) adds that they need a "gift of gab." Be flexible and have an extremely high moral fiber—have the highest integrity.

A good cover is essential. Rookies are often used because they are not yet known and because they have not been in law enforcement long enough to acquire expressions or mannerisms that hardened criminals recognize as "the law."

In addition to devising a good cover, the undercover agent learns everything possible about the subject, regardless of whether it is a person or an organization. If you are going to be working undercover, make

Figure 7.9
An undercover narcotics investigator makes a drug buy. "Looking the part" is essential to a successful undercover operation.

plans for communicating with headquarters. Make telephone calls from public pay phones, or mail letters to a fictitious friend's post office box. Have a plan for communicating emergency messages, and know what to do if the authorities move in on the subject when you are there. Have a plan for leaving the subject when you have acquired the desired information or evidence.

It is vital that undercover investigators keep accurate notes during their investigation, yet they must not allow the subject to be aware of such documentation.

Precautions for undercover agents:
- Write no notes the subject can read.
- Carry no identification other than the cover ID.
- Ensure that any communication with headquarters is covert.
- Do not suggest, plan, initiate, or participate in criminal activity.

The fourth precaution is important because if you ignore it, the defense can argue that entrapment occurred. The Supreme Court has defined **entrapment** in *Sorrells v. United States* (1932) as "the conception and planning of an offense by an officer, and his procurement of its commission by one who would not have perpetrated it except for the trickery, persuasion or fraud of the officer." *Sorrells* also explained the need for trickery in obtaining evidence: "Society is at war with the criminal classes, and the courts have uniformly held that in waging this warfare the forces of prevention and detection may use traps, decoys and deception to obtain evidence of the commission of a crime." *Sorrells* con-

cludes: "The fact that government agents merely afford opportunities or facilities for the commission of the offense does not constitute entrapment."

These Court rulings still stand. In *Sherman v. United States* (1958) the Court explained:

> Entrapment occurs only when the criminal conduct was "the product of the creative activity" of law enforcement officials. To determine whether entrapment has been established, a line must be drawn between the trap for the unwary innocent and the trap for the unwary criminal.

Because it is possible that you may be arrested if the subject is arrested, learn ahead of time whether you are to "blow your cover" or submit to arrest. In some instances, outside sources may interfere with the lawful arrest, posing great danger for an undercover agent whose identity has become known during the arrest. When the assignment is successfully completed, give the subject a plausible explanation for leaving because it may be necessary to reestablish the undercover contact later.

It is often better to use undercover agents than informants because the testimony of a reliable, trained investigator is less subject to a defense attorney's attack than that of an informant.

The legality of placing an undercover officer in a high school to investigate student drug use was decided in *Gordon v. Warren Consolidated Board of Education* (1983). High school officials had put an undercover officer into classes. The claimants alleged deprivation of their civil rights, but the case was dismissed by the federal district court for failure to state a cause of action. On appeal, the Supreme Court affirmed the prior judgment, stating that the presence of the undercover officer did not constitute any more than a "chilling" effect on the First Amendment right because it did not disrupt classroom activities or education and had no tangible effect on inhibiting expression of particular views in the classroom.

According to Rutledge (2004a, p.78), undercover officers posing as prison inmates can acquire key information from other inmates suspected of other crimes. He (p.80) suggests that often a ploy is needed to motivate an inmate to talk—for example, plotting an escape together.

Another area where officers may operate undercover is online. Malcolm and Girardi (p.12) point out that investigators can conduct investigations using the same anonymity criminals use. They stress: "Creating an undercover identity is crucial to establishing Internet investigative capability for a law enforcement organization."

Raids

police **raid** is a planned, organized operation based on the element of surprise. Consider all other alternatives before executing a raid.

The objectives of a raid are to recover stolen property, seize evidence, or arrest a suspect.

Sometimes all three objectives are accomplished in a single raid. The first consideration is whether there are alternatives to a raid. A second consideration is the legality of the raid.

 A raid must be the result of a hot pursuit or be under the authority of a no-knock arrest or search warrant.

If you are in hot pursuit of a known felon and have no time to plan a raid, make sure enough personnel and weapons are available to reduce danger. Call for backup before starting the raid. If time permits, however, careful planning and preparation will enhance the likely success of the raid.

Planning, organizing, and executing a raid are somewhat similar to undertaking a small military attack on a specific target. Without careful planning the results can be disastrous, as illustrated in the 1993 federal raid on the compound of the Branch Davidian cult in Waco, Texas, in which 80 cult members were killed.

Planning a Raid

Begin planning a raid by gathering information on the premises to be raided, including the exact address and points of entry and exit for both the raiding party and the suspect. Obtain a picture or sketch of the building and study the room arrangement. Additional location information might be obtained from aerial photographs, surveillance photos, walking the neighborhood, and the city planning department.

Next, study the suspect's background. What crimes has the suspect committed? What difficulties were encountered in making past arrests? Is the suspect a narcotics addict? An alcoholic? Likely to be armed? If so, what type of weapon is the suspect likely to wield?

Obtain the appropriate warrants. Most raids are planned and result from an arrest warrant. In such cases the subject is usually living under circumstances that necessitate a raid to make an arrest. In addition, if the raid is conducted to obtain evidence or property, obtain not only an exact description of the property sought and its likely location on the premises but also a legal search warrant. Specify that you require a no-knock warrant to conduct the raid and also perhaps a nighttime warrant to enhance the element of surprise.

Throughout the entire planning process, keep the raid plan as simple as possible. Because the subject may be extremely dangerous, intend to use adequate firepower and personnel. Determine the required weapons and equipment. Plan for enough personnel to minimize violence, overcome opposition through superiority of forces, and prevent the suspect's escape or destruction

of evidence. Make sure all entrances and exits will be covered and that a communication system is established. Decide how to transport the raiding party to the scene and how to take the suspect or evidence and property away. Determine who will be in command during the raid.

Remember that other people may be in the vicinity of the raid. If possible, evacuate everyone from the area of the raid without making the suspect suspicious. It is not always possible to do this without losing the element of surprise vital to the success of the raid.

Executing a Raid

A raid should occur only after a careful briefing of all members of the raiding party. Each participant must know the objective, who the suspect is or what evidence or property is sought, and the exact plan of the raid itself. Give each participant proper equipment such as body armor, weapons, radios, whistles, megaphones, and signal lights. Give each participant a specific assignment, and answer all questions about the raid before leaving the briefing. The raid commander directs the raid, giving the signal to begin and coordinating all assignments.

Decisions about the initial entry and control phase of a raid must be made rapidly, because control is usually established within the first 15 to 30 seconds of a successful raid. No two raids are executed in precisely the same manner. The immediate circumstances and events dictate what decisions and actions are made (Figure 7.10).

Handguns are still the most versatile weapon during a raid, but shotguns and other assault-type weapons are useful in the perimeter operations and to control arrested individuals. If guard animals are known to be inside the raid area, provide for their control. Special equipment such as sledgehammers or rams may help in breaking down fortified entrances. An ambulance should be on standby, or raid personnel should at least know the fastest route to the nearest hospital.

Because raids are highly visible, the public and the news media often take interest. Therefore, raids are likely to be the object of community praise or criticism. They are also often vital to successfully prosecuting a case.

Precautions in conducting raids:

- Ensure that the raid is legal.
- Plan carefully.
- Assign adequate personnel and equipment.
- Thoroughly brief every member of the raiding party.
- Be aware of the possibility of surreptitious surveillance devices at the raid site.

Drug busts and raids on crack houses have become increasingly common. In some instances police have used front-end loaders and other tank-like vehicles to break through the walls of suspected crack houses. Langerman (p.76) notes that in the past, entry teams would use a

Figure 7.10
Police officers raiding a suspected crack house. Surprise, swiftness, and sufficient personnel are required for a successful raid.

shotgun or explosive for forced entry, but such methods can cause major liability problems. He suggests that officers now have alternative tools and technologies such as pry bars, spreaders, rams, lock busters, and cutters.

SWAT Teams

Many police agencies have developed tactical squads, sometimes called special weapons and tactics (SWAT) teams, to execute raids. These units, also called para-military police units (PPUs), are thoroughly trained to search areas for criminals, handle sniper incidents and hostage situations, execute arrest and search warrants, and apprehend militants who have barricaded themselves inside a building or other location. Scoville (2003, p.28) describes the differing views of SWAT teams:

> To the appreciative hostage whose life they have saved, SWAT team members are knights in shining ballistic armor. To their critics, they are gung-ho macho men, prone to wrong house entries and preemptive shootings. Somewhere between the images, the perceptions and accusations lies a truth: If ever an entity embodied the

> **Technology Innovations**
>
> Garrett (2003a, p.102) describes new equipment that uses ultra-wide-band (UWB) technology to allow tactical teams to literally see through walls and view any hidden dangers, including any people present and where they are. UWB technology allows officers to look, undetected, through walls built with common construction materials such as reinforced concrete, concrete block, sheetrock, brick, wood, and wood composites.

philosophy of "hope for the best, but plan for the worst," it is the SWAT unit.

Sanow (2003, p.4) believes that the most important consideration is whether a SWAT team has enough members, noting that the "vast majority" of teams are understaffed. He suggests that seven officers are not enough and that teams of 30 or more make more sense, noting: "The future of SWAT is multi-agency and regional teams, and this goes far beyond a simple mutual aid agreement."

In the 1990s two seemingly contradictory models of policing emerged: community-oriented policing (COP) and SWAT teams. COP is a philosophy that stresses community partnerships and proactive problem solving, in contrast to the militaristic, reactive approach used by SWAT teams to deal with high-risk situations. Such teams generally adhere to the approach used by General Colin Powell of being the "meanest dog in town." According to the Powell Doctrine, force should be used sparingly, but if used, it should be used decisively.

In most jurisdictions both approaches are needed depending on specific circumstances, with community policing being the predominant approach, but with SWAT teams at the ready for emergency situations. Raids, undercover operations, and surveillance often end in officers making arrests.

Legal Arrests

 nce a suspect has been located and identified, the next step is generally an arrest. Police powers to arrest (or search) are restricted by the Fourth Amendment, which forbids unreasonable searches or seizures without probable cause. Just as state laws define and establish the elements of crimes, they also define arrest and establish who may make an arrest, for what offenses, and when. Most state laws define an **arrest** in general terms as "the taking of a person into custody in the manner authorized by law for the purpose of presenting that person before a magistrate to answer for the commission of a crime."

An arrest may be made by a police officer or a private citizen. It may be made with or without a warrant, although a warrant is generally preferred because this places the burden of proving that the arrest was illegal on the defense.

Police officers are authorized to make an arrest:
- **For any crime committed in their presence.**
- **For a felony (or for a misdemeanor in some states) not committed in their presence if they have probable cause to believe the person committed the crime.**
- **Under the authority of an arrest warrant.**

Most arrests are for misdemeanors such as disorderly conduct; drunkenness; traffic violations; minor larceny, drug offenses, assaults, and sex offenses; nuisances; and other offenses of lesser severity. In most states, the police officer must *see* such offenses to make

an arrest without a warrant. In *Atwater v. City of Lago Vista, TX* (2001), the U.S. Supreme Court allowed personally observed probable cause to permit an arrest and custodial detention for a minor misdemeanor. In other words, warrantless arrests for nonjailable offenses such as failing to wear a seatbelt were held to be constitutional. As Walker and McKinnon (p.239) note, common law prevented officers from making warrantless arrests for misdemeanor offenses unless the offenses were personally observed. *Atwater* authorized police to arrest drivers of vehicles for violations punishable by only a monetary fine, widening police authority in traffic-related stops.

In many states an arrest may also be made by a "private person" who witnesses a misdemeanor and then turns the suspect over to law enforcement authorities. Figure 7.11 shows a sample citizen's arrest form.

If you have probable cause to believe a suspect has committed a felony and there is no time to obtain an

Figure 7.11
Certificate of citizen's arrest

CERTIFICATE AND DECLARATION OF ARREST BY PRIVATE PERSON AND DELIVERY OF PERSON SO ARRESTED TO PEACE OFFICER

DATE ___5-3-20__ ___
TIME ___1440___
PLACE ___Boulder City___
___1115 Bolt St.___

I, ___Joyce Mayberry___ , hereby declare and certify that I have arrested
(NAME) ___John Mayberry___
(ADDRESS) ___1115 Bolt St. Boulder City, Nevada___
for the following reasons: _____
John arrived home about fifteen minutes ago and we had
an argument about his drinking and spending all the
money. He struck me twice on the side of my face and
twice in the stomach. He told me that next time he
would kill me.

and I do hereby request and demand that you ___Officer James McGraw___ , a peace officer, take and conduct this person whom I have arrested to the nearest magistrate to be dealt with according to law; and if no magistrate can be contacted before tomorrow morning, then to conduct this person to jail for safekeeping until the required appearance can be arranged before such magistrate, at which time I shall be present, and I will then and there sign, under oath, the appropriate complaint against this person for the offense which this person has committed and for which I made this arrest; and I will then and there, or thereafter as soon as this criminal action or cause can be heard, testify under oath of and concerning the facts and circumstances involved herein. I will save said officer harmless from any and all claim for damage of any kind, nature and description arising out of his acts at my direction.

Signature of private person making this arrest ___Joyce S Mayberry___

Peace Officer Witnesses to this statement
___James McGraw___
___C S Steiner___

arrest warrant, you can make an arrest without the warrant. Facts gathered *after* the arrest to justify probable cause are *not* legally admissible as evidence of probable cause. They can, however, strengthen the case if probable cause was established *before* the arrest.

> Probable cause for believing the suspect committed a crime must be established *before* a lawful arrest can be made.

An arrest for a felony or gross misdemeanor can usually be made any time if there is an arrest warrant or if the arresting officer witnessed the crime. An arrest may be made only in the daytime if it is by warrant, unless a magistrate has endorsed the warrant with a written statement that the arrest may be made at night. This is commonly referred to as a **nightcap provision.**

Officers are allowed to break an inner or outer door to make an arrest after identifying themselves, stating the purpose for entry, and demanding admittance. This is often necessary when officers are in plainclothes and hence not recognized as police. The courts have approved no-knock entries in cases in which the evidence would be immediately destroyed if police announced their intention to enter. Officers may break a window or door to leave a building if they are illegally detained inside. They may break a door or window to arrest a suspect who has escaped from custody. Finally, officers may break an automobile window if a suspect rolls up the windows and locks the doors to prevent an arrest. You should give proper notification of the reason for the arrest and the intent to break the window if the suspect does not voluntarily comply.

You can accomplish the physical act of arrest by taking hold of or controlling the person and stating, "You are under arrest for . . ." In most jurisdictions the arresting officer's authority must be stated, and the suspect must be told for what offense the arrest is being made. In some cases, the apparent reason for the arrest turns out to be incorrect, with a different charge being brought. In *Devenpeck et al. v. Alford* (2004) the Supreme Court ruled that an arrest is not rendered unlawful even if an arresting officer's probable cause for making it is not the precise criminal offense as to which the known facts provided probable cause (Holtz, 2005, p.19). The Court held that while clearly it is a "good police practice" to inform a person of the reason for his arrest at the time he is taken into custody, the Court has "never held that to be constitutionally required."

Rutledge (2005b, p.66) cautions that sometimes it is prudent to wait before executing an arrest warrant: "Arresting a suspect too soon could hinder or even jeopardize your case." He (p.68) points out that arresting a suspect requires that the *Miranda* warning be given before any questioning can occur. He also notes

that an arrest also "starts the clock" on the time limits within which judicial officers must review the case, usually within 48 hours (*County of Riverside v. McLaughlin,* 1991). Officers who postpone an arrest can conduct additional investigation before starting the *McLaughlin* clock and can bolster their probable cause for arrest as well.

In some departments it is common practice to take a suspect who is not under arrest to the department for questioning. Holtz (2003b, p.118) says of this practice: "In the absence of probable cause for arrest, it is unlawful for law enforcement to transport a suspect against his will to the station for questioning."

Rutledge (2003a, p.74) cautions that "bringing suspects in for questioning" may result in civil liability. If bringing someone in for questioning appears to be an arrest without probable cause, even if the suspect is not told he's under arrest, and even if the officers don't personally consider him to be under arrest, the courts are likely to rule that the officers have, in effect, made an illegal *de facto* **arrest,** that is, the functional equivalent of an arrest. As a result the court will suppress any evidence so obtained (*Kaupp v. Texas,* 2003). Rutledge (2003a, p.77) notes that the Court has "unambiguously declared at least four times that if police take someone from one location to another involuntarily to a police facility for investigation, this will be considered a *de facto* arrest." The first case was in 1969 (*Davis v. Mississippi*), followed by *Dunaway v. New York* (1979), then *Hayes v. Florida* (1985), and more recently *Kaupp v. Texas*. If you are going to question the suspect, read the Miranda warning first.

> If your intent is to make an arrest and you inform the suspect of this intent and then restrict the suspect's right to go free, you have made an arrest.

Officers may also pursue a fleeing suspect to make a *Terry*-type stop that could escalate into an arrest. In *Illinois v. Wardlow* (2000), the Supreme Court ruled that a person's sudden flight upon seeing a police officer can be used to establish reasonable suspicion for a *Terry* stop. If, during the *Terry* stop, an officer establishes probable cause to arrest, and if the suspect resists, the officer may use force, but if he does, he may leave himself open to civil liability.

Connor (p.41) has developed a *seizure scale* illustrating the possible progression from a simple suspicious contact to a *Terry* stop and the intermediate steps (always based on articulable facts) that may culminate in an arrest. Garner (p.41) stresses: "Officers are especially vulnerable to attack once they get close enough to handcuff and arrest a suspect." He urges that whenever and wherever possible, an officer should make an arrest under the "protection of an observant cover officer."

Off-Duty Arrests

Every department needs a policy that allows off-duty officers to make arrests. A suggested policy for off-duty arrests requires officers to:

- Be within the legal jurisdiction of their agency.
- Not be personally involved.
- Perceive an immediate need for preventing a crime or arresting a suspect.
- Possess the proper identification.

Unless all these conditions exist, officers should not make an arrest but should report the incident to their department for disposition.

Avoiding Civil Liability When Making Arrests

fficers should be aware of the situations in which they may find themselves names in a lawsuit and should be aware of case law in these areas. According to Hougland et al. (p.25), lawsuits against police fall into five categories: false arrest, excessive force, shootings, wrongful death, and federal civil rights violations. Note that four of the five categories are relevant to this chapter.

 Officers leave themselves open to lawsuits in several areas related to arrests, including false arrests, excessive force, shootings and wrongful death.

False Arrest

Police officers always face the possibility of false arrest. Some officers carry insurance to protect themselves against such lawsuits. Most are idle threats, however.

A false-arrest suit is a civil tort action that attempts to establish that an officer who claimed to have authority to make an arrest did not have probable cause at the time of arrest. The best protection is to be certain that probable cause to arrest does exist, to have an arrest warrant, or to obtain a conviction in court.

Even when the defendant is found not guilty of the particular offense, a basis for a false-arrest suit is not automatically established. A court will consider the totality of the circumstances at the time of the arrest and will decide whether they would lead an ordinarily prudent person to perceive probable cause and take the same action.

Police officers reduce the probability of valid false-arrest actions by understanding the laws they enforce, the elements of each offense, and what probable cause is needed to prove each element. Police officers who honestly believe they have probable cause for an arrest can use the "good-faith" defense, as established in *Pierson v. Ray* (1967):

> A policeman's lot is not so unhappy that he must choose between being charged with dereliction of duty if he does not arrest when he has probable cause, and being mulcted [penalized] in damages if he does. Although the matter is not entirely free from doubt, the same consideration would seem to require excusing him from liability for acting under a statute that he reasonably believed to be valid but that was later held unconstitutional on its face or as applied.

Use of Force

The most difficult lawsuits to deal with are those dealing with use of force. Physical force is not a necessary part of an arrest; in fact, most arrests are made without physical force. The amount of resistance to arrest varies, and this determines how much force you should use.

When making an arrest, use only as much force as is necessary to overcome any resistance. If no resistance occurs, you may not use any force.

Deciding how much force to use in making an arrest requires logic and good judgment. However, in the heat of the moment, police officers may use more force than intended. Courts and juries have usually excused force that is not blatantly unreasonable, recognizing that many factors are involved in such split-second decisions.

Ederheimer and Fridell (p.4) define **force** as "any non-negotiable use of police authority to influence citizen behavior." **Reasonable force** is the amount of force a prudent person would use in similar circumstances. **Excessive force** means more than ordinary force. Ederheimer and Fridell (p.4) characterize excessive force as "the illegal or unreasonable use of force, with reasonableness determined by whether a reasonably prudent officer would have used the same amount of force in the same situation, in light of the information available to the officer at the time." Use of excessive force (such as striking with a nightstick) is justified only when exceptional resistance occurs and there is no other way to make the arrest. As Moore (p.110) stresses: "Excessive force charges undermine the hard work by the other 99.9 percent of law enforcement in one of the toughest and most important jobs one can hold."

Beasey (p.106) stresses that sometimes shooting someone or striking him or her with a baton is "absolutely necessary and absolutely reasonable." He advises that it is important to distinguish a brutal appearance from brutality: "Police work is, at times, bone breaking, bloody, flesh-tearing, bruising, sweaty, lethal and ugly." Fortunately, investigators are not as often faced with such situations as patrol officers, but it can happen.

Luna (p.3) reports that research indicates only a small percentage of police-public interactions involve use of force, with the most frequent being the low-level force needed to safely take suspects into custody.

The landmark case on use of force, *Graham v. Connor* (1989), set parameters on use of force. As Fridell (2005, p.22) explains: "The Court ruled that judgments about force would be in accordance with the reasonableness standard of the Fourth Amendment." It stated: "Our Fourth Amendment jurisprudence has long recognized that the right to make an arrest or investigatory stop necessarily carries with it the right to use some degree of physical coercion or threat thereof to effect it." In *Graham*, the Court explained: "The reasonableness of a particular use of force must be judged from the perspective of a reasonable officer on the scene, rather than with the 20/20 vision of hindsight." In *Graham*, the Court established five factors to evaluate alleged cases of excessive force:

- The severity of the crime
- Whether the suspect posed an immediate threat to the officer or others
- Whether the circumstances were tense, uncertain, and rapidly evolving
- Whether the suspect was attempting to evade arrest by flight
- Whether the suspect was actively resisting arrest

Graham v. Connor further held that plaintiffs alleging excessive use of force need show only that the officer's actions were unreasonable under the standards of the Fourth Amendment. As Gundy (p.63) explains: "The more heinous the person's activities or threat level, the more force that an officer may justifiably use." In effect, as Ederheimer and Fridell (p.138) conclude: "In the end, it all comes down to split-second decisions made by humans in extremely stressful situations."

In *Saucier v. Katz* (2001) the Supreme Court held that "the inquiry as to whether an arresting police officer is entitled to qualified immunity for the use of excessive force is distinct from the inquiry as to whether the use of force was objectively reasonable under Fourth Amendment excessive force analysis."

In the aftermath of the Rodney King case in Los Angeles and the alleged use of excessive force in other cities since then, much national attention has focused on the question of the definition of excessive force. Sometimes the force used is obviously excessive and outrageous. For example, New York City police officer Justin Volpe admitted assaulting and sodomizing Abner Louima with a broomstick in an attempt to humiliate and intimidate the handcuffed Haitian immigrant. Officer Charles Schwartz was charged with holding down Louima during the assault.

The public is very aware of and sensitive to police use of force. The instantaneous decisions and actions by police officers at the scene are subject to long-term review by the public and the courts. Police departments must review their use-of-force policies to ensure that they are clear and in accordance with court decisions as well as effective in ensuring officer safety.

Officers should know their department's policies regarding use of force. Further, uses of force in making arrests should be critiqued, and complaints of excessive force should be thoroughly reviewed.

Officers should also be aware of research findings as to when force is most likely to be used. For example, Terrill and Reisig (p.291) found that officers were significantly more likely to use higher levels of force with suspects encountered in disadvantaged neighborhoods and those neighborhoods with higher homicide rates. Reisig et al. (p.241) report that suspects who are disrespectful to the police are more likely to have their behavior reciprocated. Researchers Alpert et al. (2004) reviewed the use-of-force literature and concluded that force is most likely to be used when suspects show signs of alcohol or drug intoxication or engage in hostile behavior.

Officers should be aware of this finding and not take any disrespect shown to them too personally or be goaded into using more force than necessary. Rutledge (2004b, p.58) suggests: "Documentation and self-control are the keys to protecting yourself against charges of unreasonable force on persons in custody."

Most police departments know of officers who tend to become involved in resistance or violent situations more frequently than others. In some instances these officers' approach seems to trigger resistance. However, in any situation that is *not* out of control when you arrive, give a friendly greeting and state who you are and your authority if you are not in uniform. Speak calmly and convey the impression that you are in control. Show your badge or identification and give your reason for the questioning. Ask for identification and listen to their side of the story. Then decide on the appropriate action: Warn, release, issue a citation, or make an arrest.

Although voluntary compliance is the "best" arrest, there are always situations that are not peaceful. In such cases use only as much force as is necessary to overcome the resistance, progressing from control by empty-hand methods (defensive tactics) to the use of control agents (such as mace or tear gas) to the use of a police baton or—in the case of life-threatening resistance—deadly force.

Use-of-Force Continuums Many different types of force-option continuums exist. Terrill (p.108) explains that most continuum guidelines focus on a suspect's degree of resistance and specify what level of force is appropriate in response. Traditionally, use-of-force continuums have been linear, going from no resistance to aggravated aggression, as shown in Figure 7.12.

Critics of linear use-of-force continuums note that the continuums seem to imply that force events are

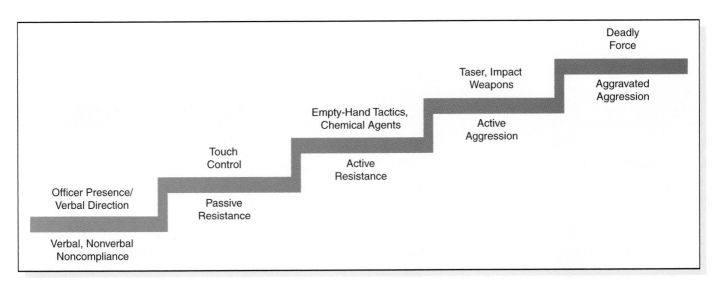

Figure 7.12
Linear use-of-force continuum

Joshua A. Ederheimer and Lorie A. Fridell. *Chief Concerns: Exploring the Challenges of Police Use of Force.* Washington, DC:
Police Executive Research Forum, April 2005, p. 48. Reprinted with permission.

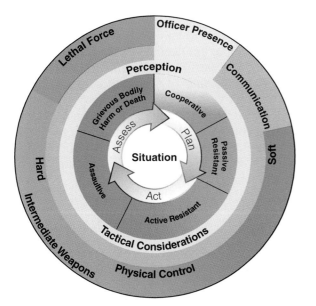

Figure 7.13
Circular use-of-force continuum of the Canadian Association of Chiefs of
Police.

Joshua A. Ederheimer and Lorie A. Fridell. *Chief Concerns: Exploring the Challenges of
Police Use of Force.* Washington, DC: Police Executive Research Forum, April 2005,
p. 50. Reprinted with permission.

One such model is circular, a force wheel, with the spokes in the wheel representing a specific type of force, as shown in Figure 7.13.

Fridell (p.48) observes that the circular configuration avoids the implied stepwise progression of linear models, but such models otherwise provide little guidance to officers' force decisions. One option on most force continuums is use of less-lethal weapons.

Less-Lethal Weapons

Whether they are called less-than-lethal, less-lethal, or nonlethal weapons, their intent is to avoid the use of deadly force. Hougland et al. (p.29) contend: "In this time of community-oriented policing, the use of less-lethal technology clearly is the most socially acceptable and humane means of maintaining peace and order." Scoville (2005, p.46) describes four types of less-lethal weapons available: physical restraints such as handcuffs and Ripp Hobble restraints, chemical weapons such as oleoresin capsicum (OC) spray, electrical shock devices such as Tasers, and impact weapons such as batons. Probably the best known and most controversial less-lethal weapon is the Taser.

Oldman (p.50) contends that the Taser is "arguably the safest and most effective (94 percent) option." He (p.52) reports that Tasers are used by over 7,000 police departments in the United States and abroad. The advanced Taser X26's dataport function stores the time and date the weapon was fired. Sanow (2005, p.6) lists the advantages of the Taser: "Officer injuries . . . down by 80%. Suspect injuries down by 67%. Use of lethal force down by 78%. A 94% effectiveness in immediately stopping aggressive behavior. Immediate recovery of

predictable and escalate in an orderly fashion, when this is not reality. However, even if officers are taught that they can skip steps and go up and down on the continuum, linear continuums are sometimes explained in court as calling for such an orderly progression. Aveni (2003, p.75) suggests that force continuums should evolve just as policing is evolving and that a shift is occurring in continuum design from linear to nonlinear models.

Technology Innovations

Scoville (2005, p.46) also describes some of the "wonder weapons currently being tested by the military and select law enforcement agencies, including super glue, a sticky foam that solidifies on contact with its target and, as the chemical hardens, immobilizes the suspect (not to be confused with forensic superglue, cyanoacrylate). Scoville calls it the "equivalent of Spider-Man's webs."

Another innovation is WebShot, a net that can be launched by a standard weapon or recyclable launcher. WebShot envelops its target in a net that constricts both flight and fight.

Taser International (Scottsdale, AZ) is developing Extended Range Electronic Projectile technology that would overcome the drawback of the current Taser's range of up to 25 feet.

Another innovation is a reloadable handheld OC weapon that can accurately launch 10 milliliters of the chemical out to 21 feet, providing intermediate-range delivery of OC.

the suspect. Millions of dollars saved in liability claims." Yet he notes that "the police use of the Taser has become intensely controversial in the past few months." Reports of 70 to 80 deaths cased by the Taser have made headlines around the country. The debate is beyond the scope of this text, but officers whose departments use Tasers should be aware of the strategy endorsed in an executive brief from the International Association of Chiefs of Police (Estey, 2005).

Use of less-lethal alternatives is not required when use of deadly force is justified.

Use of Deadly Force

Police officers carry guns and are trained in using them. They also have department policy on deadly force as a guide. Unfortunately, the point of last resort may be immediate, because many police situations rapidly deteriorate to the point of "deadly force decision making." When such situations occur, they must be viewed in the light of both department policies and the individual situation. Nowicki (2003) points out that deadly force situations arise rapidly and officers must act quickly and decisively or risk the life of an innocent person or of themselves.

Department policies on deadly force should be reviewed periodically in the light of the most recent Supreme Court decisions. They must be restrictive enough to limit unreasonable use of deadly force but not so restrictive that they fail to protect the lives of officers and members of the community. One important consideration is the observation by Reuland (p.10) that if a supervisor arrives on the scene of a potentially lethal situation, the chances of an officer-involved shooting are reduced 80 to 90 percent.

Use of a deadly weapon is carefully defined by state laws and department policy. Such policies usually permit use of a gun or other weapon only in self-defense or if others are endangered by the suspect. Some policies also permit use of a deadly weapon to arrest a felony suspect, to prevent an escape, or to recapture a felon when all other means have failed. Warning shots are not usually recommended because they can ricochet, harming others.

The landmark case on use of deadly force is the Supreme Court ruling in *Tennessee v. Garner* (1985), where the Court ruled:

> It is not better that all felony suspects die than that they escape. Where the suspect poses no immediate threat to others, the harm resulting from failing to apprehend him does not justify the use of deadly force to do so. It is no doubt unfortunate when a suspect who is in sight escapes, but the fact that the police arrive a little late or are a little slower afoot does not always justify killing the suspect.

In this case, the Court banned law enforcement officers from shooting to kill fleeing felons unless an imminent danger to life exists. This ruling invalidated laws in almost half the states that allowed police officers to use deadly force to prevent the escape of a suspected felon. In this case police shot and killed an unarmed 15-year-old boy who had stolen $10 and some jewelry from an unoccupied house. The Court ruled: "A police officer may not seize an unarmed, nondangerous suspect by shooting him dead."

The *Garner* decision did not take away police officers' right to use deadly force. The Court acknowledged legitimate situations in which deadly force is not only acceptable but also necessary:

> Where the officer has probable cause to believe that the suspect poses a threat of serious physical harm, either to the officer or to others, it is not constitutionally unreasonable to prevent escape by using deadly force. Thus, if the suspect threatened the officer with a weapon or there

Technology Innovations

Gerber (p.20) describes how biometric devices are being developed to help protect officers from having their sidearms used against them. A prototype gun holster has a built-in fingerprint scanner designed to verify that the person who reaches into a holster to grab a pistol is an authorized user. If the fingerprint is not recognized, the gun will not release.

is probable cause to believe that he had committed a crime involving the infliction or threatened infliction of serious physical harm, deadly force may be used if necessary to prevent escape and if—where feasible—some warning has been given.

In some deadly force incidents, officers have had suspects attempt to grab the officers' sidearms to use against them.

In situations that involve a fleeing felon, officers must assess the situation rapidly, considering the law, department policy, and the specific existing conditions. An officer need not wait to see a flash from a suspect's gun muzzle before taking action. On the other hand, the *Garner* decision caused policy changes in many departments that had previously approved shooting fleeing felons under all circumstances, including unarmed fleeing felons.

Whether to use deadly force is a major and difficult decision for police officers. When it should be used is generally defined in state statutes, but in any case of use of deadly force the suspect must be threatening the life of an officer or another person.

Remsberg (2004a, p.9) describes the New Force Science™ Center, founded by Dr. Bill Lewinksi, that researches deadly force. During an interview, Lewinski explained how it might appear that an officer shot a suspect in the back: "We have documented that a young, agile assailant can turn from facing and pointing a gun at an officer to presenting a square back to him in just 14/100 of a second. The officer may make an unretractable decision to shoot when the suspect is facing him and threatening deadly force, but before the officer's gunfire reaches the suspect, he has turned to run and unavoidably is hit in the back" (Remsberg, 2004b, pp.59-60).

Remsberg (2004b, p.60) also reports that Lewinski has explained "extra" shots being fired. He has documented that once a high-stress, life-threatening situation arises, most officers will still squeeze off two to three more rounds before the message to stop goes from the brain to the trigger finger. Says Lewinski: "It's not a case of malicious over-reaction. It's a law of physiology."

Aveni (2005, p.38) points out that "recent hard empirical research" from the New Force Science™ Center has illustrated "more compellingly than ever how a mere fraction of a second might separate the perception that a police shooting is either 'in-policy' or 'out of policy.'"

One consideration not to be overlooked is the psychological effect on an officer who has shot a suspect. Based on his 20-year study of deadly force, Brubaker (p.8) reports: "The majority of officers commented that they were not prepared for the psychological impact upon themselves, their families and their departments." He (p.13) says: "One officer summed it up best when he said, 'All officers should have training and knowledge concerning the postshooting experience. All officers need to know when you pull that trigger, your department and family also are pulling it.'"

Everyone understands that force should be used as a last resort. Use other less-lethal means when you have opportunity and time. Millions of arrests—many with the potential for use of deadly force—have been made without such force. Yet, even when officers try every possible means to avoid using deadly force, the actions of the subject or suspect may demand a response with deadly force.

Use of Force and the Mentally Ill   Dealing with people who are mentally ill or otherwise emotionally disturbed can present a use-of-force challenge. Use of less-lethal weapons may contain the situation or worsen it. When individuals who are mentally ill force police officers into shooting them, the question often arises, Is this a case of suicide by cop?

Suicide by Police   *Suicide by police* is a phenomenon in which someone intentionally acts so threatening toward officers as to force them to fire, accomplishing the subject's ultimate goal of dying, albeit not by their own hand.

Parent (p.15) explains that suicide by cop differs from other officer-involved shootings because the individuals provoke a lethal response from police by, for example, taunting or threatening officers or reaching for a toy or unloaded weapon.

A 10-year study of suicide by cop (Honig, pp.90-93) found that 98 percent of the precipitators were male and the weapon of choice was a firearm (48 percent). Sixty-five percent had a history of alcohol or drug abuse, 63 percent had a psychiatric history, and 58 percent had asked police to kill them. Honig (p.93) reports that in 70 percent of the incidents, shootings occurred within 30 minutes, and 37 percent occurred within 5 minutes of officers arriving on the scene.

Pinizzotto et al. (p.11) stress that like any other serious crime, suspected suicide by cop incidents must be thoroughly investigated. They recommend that responding officers include in their initial offense report specific elements possibly present at the scene, including the following:

- Statements made by the offender, including the names of witnesses to the event
- Type of weapon possessed by the offender
- Offender's specific actions that resulted in the use of deadly force
- Conduct that the officer deemed bizarre or inappropriate on the part of the offender
- Circumstances indicating that the offender's motivation may have been suicide

Sometimes it seems very implausible that a person really wants to die in what appears to be a suicide-by-cop situation. Such instances have been presented as "death by indifference." Williams (p.67) calls "death by indifference an incredibly accurate term." According to Williams, when it seems that suicide by cop is not a probable explanation, investigators should consider the possibility of death by indifference on the part of an offender apathetic to his or her own fate. He notes that almost all such deaths involve alcohol intoxication, being under the influence of drugs, or being mentally ill. All also involve emotionally charged circumstances. In addition, all involve either violence, threatened violence, and/or presence of a weapon that ends up with the police becoming involved.

Ryan (2004, p.25) contends: "Any time a law enforcement officer uses deadly force, the likelihood that a lawsuit will follow is almost a certainty." That underscores the criticality of use-of-force reports.

Use of Force Reports

As has been stressed, thorough, accurate, well-written reports are critical to the investigator. As Rutledge (2004a, p.59) puts it: "The accuracy and completeness of the force report are extremely important, not only for purposes of internal investigations, but also for criminal and civil liability and public relations purposes."

Robinson (2006, p.30) notes that litigation has prompted a push for precision in describing what happened during the incident in a use of force report, and to differentiate between trained techniques and "street fighting." She also points out the hazards of using clinical-sounding terminology before a jury in the following scenario:

Officer, would you read the marked section from your report?

"I attempted to apply an escort hold to the subject, but I noted resistive tension in his arm, so I applied pain compliance instead. The subject actively resisted, so I administered a focused knee strike to the lower abdominal area, and decentralized the subject."

In other words, Officer, you tried to grab my client's arm, and when he pulled away, you twisted his wrist, and then kicked him in the groin and threw him down on the pavement. Is that about it?

"Well, I wouldn't put in quite those words."

No, Officer, I imagine you wouldn't. No further questions.

Language intended to convey precision and professionalism may sound like euphemisms to a jury, as though the officer is being evasive (p.31). Robinson (p.32) suggests that officers need to articulate their use of force in everyday language to show the reasonableness of their actions. For example, rather than writing "I decentralized the subject," the officer might have written: "I used a push in/pull down technique to take Mr. Jones to the ground, while also verbally commanding him to get down." Robinson concludes: "A good report can make an excessive-force lawsuit less likely to be filed in the first place, and, if it does go to court, less likely to be successful. . . . We have a duty to teach officers to use force effectively so they can survive on the street. If we don't also teach them to report it effectively, they may not survive in court."

SUMMARY

Developing, locating, identifying, and arresting suspects are primary responsibilities of investigators.

Field or show-up identification is on-the-scene identification of a suspect by a victim of or witness to a crime. To be admissible, field identification must be made shortly after a crime is committed, usually within 15 to 20 minutes. Suspects do *not* have the right to counsel at a field identification (*United States v. Ash, Jr.,* 1973).

If the suspect is not immediately identified, you must develop a suspect through information provided by victims, witnesses, and other people likely to know about the crime or the suspect; through physical evidence at the crime scene; through psychological profiling; through information in police files; through information in other agencies' files; or through informants. Help witnesses describe suspects and vehicles by asking very specific questions and using an identification diagram.

Suspects can be identified through field identification, mug shots, photographic identification, or lineups. Use field identification when the suspect is arrested at or near the scene. Use mug-shot identification if you believe the suspect has a police record. Use photographic identification when you are reasonably sure who committed the crime but the suspect is not in custody or a fair lineup cannot be conducted. The pictures should portray at least five people of comparable race, height, weight, age, and general appearance. Tell witnesses they need not identify anyone from the photographs. A suspect does *not* have the right to a lawyer if a photographic lineup is used (*United States v. Ash, Jr.,* 1973).

Use lineup identification when the suspect is in custody. Again, use at least five people of comparable race, height, weight, age, and general appearance. Ask them all to perform the same actions or speak the same words. Instruct those viewing the lineup that they need not make an identification. Suspects may refuse to participate in a lineup, but such refusal may be used against them in court (*Schmerber v. California,* 1966). Suspects have a right to have an attorney present during a lineup (*United States v. Wade,* 1976). Avoid having the same person make both photographic and lineup identification. If you do so, do not conduct both within a short time.

Some investigations reach a point after which no further progress can be made without using surveillance, undercover agents, or a raid. Before taking any of these measures, you should exhaust all alternatives.

The objective of surveillance is to obtain information about people or their associates and activities that may help solve a criminal case or protect witnesses. Surveillance can be stationary (fixed, plant, or stakeout) or moving (tail or shadow). Moving surveillance can be rough, loose, or close (tight) and done on foot or by vehicle. Electronic surveillance and wiretapping are considered forms of search and therefore are permitted only with probable cause and by direct court order (*Katz v. United States,* 1967).

The objective of an undercover assignment may be to gain a person's confidence or to infiltrate an organization or group by using an assumed identity and to thereby obtain information or evidence connecting the subject with criminal activity. If you are working undercover, write no notes the subject can read, carry no identification other than the cover ID, make sure any communication with headquarters is covert, and do not suggest, plan, initiate, or participate in any criminal activity.

The objective of a raid is to recover stolen property, seize evidence, or arrest a suspect. To be legal, a raid must be the result of a hot pursuit or under authority of a no-knock arrest warrant or a search warrant. Precautions in conducting raids include ensuring that the raid is legal, planning carefully, assigning adequate personnel and equipment, thoroughly briefing every member of the raiding party, and being aware of the possibility of surreptitious surveillance devices at the raid site.

An arrest may occur at any point during an investigation. Police officers are authorized to make an arrest (1) for any crime committed in their presence, (2) for a felony (and in some states for a misdemeanor) not committed in their presence if they have probable cause to believe the person committed the crime, or (3) under the authority of an arrest warrant. A lawful arrest requires that probable cause for believing the suspect committed a crime be established *before* the arrest.

If your intent is to make an arrest and you inform the suspect of this intent and then restrict the suspect's right to go free, you have made an arrest. Officers leave themselves open to lawsuits in several areas related to arrests, including false arrests, excessive force, shootings, and wrongful death. When making an arrest, use only as much force as is necessary to overcome any resistance. If no resistance occurs, you may not use any force.

CHECKLISTS

Identifying and Arresting Suspects

- Was a suspect observed by police on arrival at the scene?
- Was a suspect arrested at the scene?
- Was anyone observed at the scene by any other person?
- Was a neighborhood check made to determine suspicious people, vehicles, or noises?
- Was the complainant interviewed?

- Were statements taken from witnesses or people with information about the crime?
- Was a description of the suspect obtained?
- Was the description disseminated to other members of the local police force? to neighboring police departments?
- Was any associative evidence found at the scene or in the suspect's possession?
- Were informants checked?
- Were similar crimes committed in the area? the community? neighboring communities?
- Were field-identification cards checked to determine who was in the area?
- Were modus operandi files reviewed to determine who commits the type of crime? Are the suspects in or out of prison?
- Were traffic tickets checked to see whether any person or vehicle was in the area at the time of the crime? How does the vehicle or crime compare with the suspect vehicle or person?
- Have other agencies been checked—municipal? county? state? federal?
- How was the person identified? Field identification? Mug shots? Photographic identification? Lineup identification? Was it legal?
- Was the arrest legal?

Surveillance

- Is there any alternative to surveillance?
- What information is needed from the surveillance?
- What type of surveillance is needed?
- Have equipment and personnel needs for the surveillance area been determined?
- Are the required equipment and personnel available?
- Are proper forms available for recording necessary information during the surveillance?
- Are all signals preestablished?

Undercover Assignments

- Is there any alternative to undercover work?
- What information is needed from the assignment?
- Is adequate information about the subject available?
- Have you established a good cover?
- How will you communicate with headquarters?
- What are you to do if you are arrested?
- Do you have an alternative plan if the initial plan fails?
- Do you have a plausible explanation for leaving once the assignment is completed?

Raids

- Is there any alternative to a raid?
- Have appropriate warrants been obtained?
- Have the objectives of the raid been clearly specified?
- Has a presurveillance of the raid location been conducted?
- Are adequate personnel and equipment available?
- Has a briefing been held?

DISCUSSION QUESTIONS

1. Imagine that a burglary has occurred each of the last four nights in a 10-block residential area in a city of 200,000 people. How might an investigator start to determine who is committing these crimes? What sources of information and techniques can be used in developing a suspect?

2. Suppose you have obtained information concerning a suspect in a rape case. Two witnesses saw someone near the rape scene at about the time of the offense, and the victim was able to describe her assailant. How should identification be made?

3. How do cooperation of the public and of other police agencies each help in identifying and arresting suspects? Which is more important: public cooperation or the cooperation of other police agencies?

4. How are people selected for a lineup? How should a lineup be conducted according to legal requirements? What is done if the suspect refuses to participate?

5. What balance must be maintained between an individual's right to privacy and the public interest when using surveillance?

6. Under what conditions should a police raid be considered?

7. In what types of crimes would the use of an undercover agent be justified?

8. What type of "tail" would you use for each of the following: Checking the loyalty of an informant? A suspected bank robber planning to "case" a bank? A burglar known to meet frequently with another burglar? Someone suspected of being an organized crime leader?

9. How much risk is involved in undercover assignments and raids? How can you minimize this risk?

10. When do outside agencies participate in surveillances, undercover assignments, and raids?

MEDIA EXPLORATIONS

Internet

Select one of the following assignments to complete:

- Go to http://www.driverslicenseguide.com and outline the contents of the *Drivers License Guide.*

- Search for these key words: *criminal profiling, psychological profiling,* and *racial profiling.* Write a brief report defining each and explaining how they are alike and different.

- Search for one of the following key words: *entrapment, undercover officer,* or *wiretapping.* Select one article to outline and share with the class.

- Search for *Miranda v. Arizona.* Select and outline one of the articles to share with the class.

Crime and Evidence in Action

Select one of three criminal case scenarios and sign in for your shift. Your Mobile Data Terminal (MDT) will get you started and update you throughout the case. During the course of the case you'll become a patrol officer, detective, prosecutor, defense attorney, judge, corrections officer, or parole officer to conduct interactive investigative research. Each case unfolds as you respond to key decision points. Feedback for each possible answer choice is packed full of information, including term definitions, web links, and important documentation. The sergeant is available at certain times to help mentor you, the Online Resources website offers a variety of information, and be sure to take notes in your e-notebook during the suspect video statements and at key points throughout (these notes can be saved, printed, or emailed). The Forensics Exercise will test your ability to collect, transport, and analyze evidence from the crime scene. At the end of the case you can track how well you responded to each decision point and join the Discussion Forum for a postmortem. **Go to the CD and use the skills you've learned to solve a case.**

REFERENCES

Adams, Jim. "Police Test New Tactic for Lineups." Minneapolis/St. Paul *Star Tribune*, February 20, 2005.

Alpert, Geoffrey P.; Dunham, Roger G.; and MacDonald, John M. "Interactive Police-Citizen Encounters that Result in Force." *Police Quarterly*, 2004.

"Altering Lineups Could Reduce ID Errors." *Law Enforcement News*, May 2005, pp. 1, 11.

Amnesty International USA. *Threat and Humiliation: Racial Profiling, Domestic Security and Human Rights in the United States.* 2004. www.amnestyusa.org.

Aveni, Thomas J. "The Force Continuum Conundrum." *Law and Order*, December 2003, pp. 74–77.

Aveni, Thomas. "'Must-Shoot vs May-Shoot' Controversy." *Law and Order*, January 2005, pp. 38–44.

Batton, Candice, and Kadleck, Colleen. "Theoretical and Methodological Issues in Racial Profiling Research." *Police Quarterly*, March 2004, pp. 30–64.

Beasey, Dale. "Brutal v. Brutality." *Law and Order*, October 2004, pp. 105–108.

Brubaker, Larry C. "Deadly Force: A 20-Year Study of Fatal Encounters." *FBI Law Enforcement Bulletin*, April 2002, pp. 6–13.

Cerullo, Rob. "GPS Tracking Devices and the Constitution." *The Police Chief*, January 2004, pp. 11–12.

Clifford, Michael P. "Electronic Surveillance Technology." *The Police Chief*, July 2003, pp. 31–35.

Connor, Greg. "The Seizure Scale." *The Law Enforcement Trainer*, January/February 2003, pp. 40–41.

Cooke, Leonard G. "Reducing Bias in Policing: A Model Approach in Virginia." *The Police Chief*, June 2004, pp. 18–22.

Davis, Bob. "Spy Gear." *Police*, 2004, pp. 38–43.

Douglas, Dave. "I See You." *Police*, 2003, pp. 34–43.

Ederheimer, Joshua A., and Fridell, Lorie A., editors. *Chief Concerns: Exploring the Challenges of Police Use of Force.* Washington, DC: Police Executive Research Forum, April 2005.

Estey, Joseph G. "Electro-Muscular Disruption Technology: A Step-by-Step Guide for Law Enforcement." *The Police Chief*, May 2005, p. 6.

"Feedback, Even When Delayed, Found to Distort Lineup Memories." *Criminal Justice Newsletter*, April 15, 2003, pp. 3–4.

Fredericks, Grant. "CCTV: A Law Enforcement Tool." *The Police Chief*, August 2004, pp. 68–74.

Fridell, Lori, editor. *By the Numbers: A Guide for Analyzing Race Data from Vehicle Stops.* Washington, DC: Community Oriented Policing Services and Police Executive Research Forum, 2004.

Fridell, Lori. "Improving Use-of-Force Policy, Policy Enforcement and Training." In *Chief Concerns: Exploring the Challenges of Police Use of Force* edited by Joshua A. Ederheimer and Lorie A. Fridell. Washington, DC: Police Executive Research Forum, April 2005, pp. 21–55.

Gallo, Frank J. "Profiling v. Racial Profiling: Making Sense of It All." *The Law Enforcement Trainer*, July/August 2003, pp. 18–21.

Garner, Gerald W. "Surviving Arrest and Control." *Police*, January 2005, pp. 41–43.

Garrett, Ronnie. "Device Lessens the Risk in Tactical Entries." *Law Enforcement Technology*, April 2003a, pp. 102–105.

Garrett, Ronnie. "Gait Recognition Strides Ahead." *Law Enforcement Technology*, May 2003b, pp. 82–85.

Gerber, Greg. "Let Your Fingers Do the Locking." *Law Enforcement Technology*, May 2003, pp. 14–23.

Green, Marc. "Proper Eyewitness Identification Procedures." *Law and Order*, 2003, pp. 195–198.

Gundy, Jess. "The Complexities of Use of Force." *Law and Order*, December 2003, pp. 60–65.

Hendrie, Edward M. "When an Informant's Tip Gives Officers Probable Cause to Arrest Drug Traffickers." *FBI Law Enforcement Bulletin*, December 2003, pp. 8–21.

Holtz, Larry E. "Conducting Photo and Live Lineups." *Law Enforcement Technology*, November 2003a, p. 102.

Holtz, Larry E. "Transporting Suspects for Questioning." *Law Enforcement Technology*, August 2003b, p. 118.

Holtz, Larry E. "Photo and Live Lineup Procedures: Improving 'Reliability.'" *Police and Security News*, January/February 2004, pp. 19–20.

Holtz, Larry E. "Impersonator Case Leads to Supreme Court Ruling." *Police and Security News*, May/June 2005, pp. 19–20.

Honig, Audrey L. "Police Assisted Suicide: Identification, Intervention, and Investigation" *The Police Chief*, October 2001, pp. 89–93.

Hougland, Steve; Mesloh, Charlie; and Henych, Mark. "Use of Force, Civil Litigation and the Taser." *FBI Law Enforcement Bulletin*, March 2005, pp. 24–30.

"ID or Not ID? That Is the Question." *Law Enforcement News*, April 2005, pp. 8–9.

Kanable, Rebecca. "A Profile of a Geographic Profiler." *Law Enforcement Technology*, July 2003, pp. 124–129.

Langerman, Andrew. "Entry by Force." *Law Enforcement Technology*, March 2003, pp. 76–80.

Luna, Andrea Morrozoff. Introduction. In *Chief Concerns: Exploring the Challenges of Police Use of Force*, edited by Joshua A. Ederheimer and Lorie A. Fridell. Washington, DC: Police Executive Research Forum, April 2005, pp. 1–20.

Malcolm, Mark, and Girardi, Brian. "Protecting Your Anonymity Online." *Law Enforcement Technology*, November 2004, pp. 8–14.

Mertens, Jennifer. "Putting a Finger on Border Security." *Law Enforcement Technology*, May 2004, pp. 8–14.

Miller, Christa. "Geographic Profiling Serial Offenses with ECRI's Rigel." *Law Enforcement Technology*, July 2003, pp. 130–135.

Moore, Carole. "Excessive Force." *Law Enforcement Technology*, November 2004, p. 110.

Nason, John T. "Conducting Surveillance Operations: How to Get the Most Out of Them." *FBI Law Enforcement Bulletin*, May 2004, pp. 1–7.

Nowicki, Ed. "Deadly Force: More than Firearms." *Law and Order*, June 2003, pp. 24–26.

Oldman, Scott. "The Quest for Less Lethal Systems." *Tactical Response*, May-June 2005, pp. 42–52.

Parent, Rick. "Officer's Research Shows that Suicide by Cop Incidents on the Rise in North America." *Police*, February 2004, p. 15.

Patenaude, Ken. "Improving Eyewitness Identification." *Law Enforcement Technology*, October 2003, pp. 178–185.

Peed, Carl, and Wexler, Chuck. Foreword. In *By the Numbers: A Guide for Analyzing Race Data from Vehicle Stops*, edited by Lori Fridell. Washington, DC: Community Oriented Policing Services and Police Executive Research Forum, 2004, pp. vii–xi.

Pinizzotto, Anthony J.; Davis, Edward F.; and Miller, Charles E. "Suicide by Cop: Defining a Devastating Dilemma." *FBI Law Enforcement Bulletin*, February 2005, pp. 8–20.

Reisig, Michael D.; McCluskey, John D.; Mastrofski, Stephen D.; and Terrill, William. "Suspect Disrespect toward the Police." *Justice Quarterly*, 2004, pp. 241–268.

Remsberg, Charles. "A New Force Science™ Center Unravels Vital Mysteries of Extreme Encounters." *The Law Enforcement Trainer*, Third Quarter 2004a, pp. 8–14.

Remsberg, Charles. "Rethinking Reaction Tome." *Police*, December 2004b, pp. 58–61.

Reuland, Melissa. "The Critical 15 Minutes—Perspectives of Chief William Lansdowne." In *Chief Concerns: Exploring the Challenges of Police Use of Force*, edited by Joshua A. Ederheimer and Lorie A. Fridell. Washington, DC: Police Executive Research Forum, April 2005, pp. 10–11.

Robinson, Patricia A. "What You Say Is What They Write: Everybody Teaches Report Writing." *The Law Enforcement Trainer*, January/February 2006, pp. 30–32.

Rogers, Donna. "Drawing the Line." *Law Enforcement Technology*, May 2003, pp. 44–50.

Rotondo, Rick. "Using Wireless Data with Video." *Law Enforcement Technology*, May 2004, pp. 68–72.

Rutledge, Devallis. "Avoiding De Facto Arrests." *Police*, August 2003a, pp. 74–77.

Rutledge, Devallis. "Eyewitness Identification." *Police*, December 2003b, pp. 74–75.

Rutledge, Devallis. "Undercover Interrogation." *Police*, August 2004a, pp. 78–79.

Rutledge, Devallis. "Use of Force on Prisoners." *Police*, January 2004b, pp. 58–59.

Rutledge, Devallis. "ID-ing with Surveillance Photos." *Police*, March 2005a, pp. 72–75.

Rutledge, Devallis. "The Waiting Game." *Police*, January 2005b, pp. 66–69.

Ryan, Jack. "Training Liability in the Use of Deadly Force." *The Law Enforcement Trainer*, May/June 2004, pp. 25–28.

Sanow, Ed. "SWAT Capability Assessment." *Law and Order*, March 2003, p. 4.

Sanow, Ed. "Taser and Force Continuums." *Law and Order*, May 2005, p. 6.

Schott, Richard G. "Warrantless Interception of Communications: When, Where and Why It Can Be

Done." *FBI Law Enforcement Bulletin*, January 2003, pp. 25–32.

Scoville, Dean. "How to . . . Start a SWAT Team." *Police*, March 2003, pp. 28–33.

Scoville, Dean. "In Search of the StarTrek Phaser." *Police*, March 2005, pp. 46–50.

Terrill, William. "Police Use of Force: A Transactional Approach." *Justice Quarterly*, March 2005, pp. 107–138.

Terrill, William, and Reisig, Michael D. "Neighborhood Context and Police Use of Force." *Journal of Research in Crime and Delinquency*, 2003, pp. 291–321.

Walker, Jeffery T., and McKinnon, Kristi M. "*Atwater v. City of Lago Vista*: Police Authority to Make Warrantless Misdemeanor Arrests." *Journal of Contemporary Criminal Justice*, May 2003, pp. 239–252.

Weiss, Jim, and Davis, Mickey. "Geographic Profiling Finds Serial Criminals." *Law and Order*, December 2004, pp. 22–38.

Wexler, Sanford. "Working Undercover." *Law Enforcement Technology*, November 2004, pp. 86–93.

Williams, George T. "Death by Indifference." *Law and Order*, December 2003, pp. 66–69.

CASES CITED

Atwater v. City of Lago Vista, TX, 121 S.Ct. 1536 (2001)

Brown v. City of Oneonta, 122 S.Ct. 44 (2001)

County of Riverside v. McLaughlin, 500 U.S. 44 (1991)

Davis v. Mississippi, 394 US 721 (1969)

Devenpeck et al. v. Alford, decided December 17, 2004

Dunaway v. New York, 442 U.S. 200 (1979)

Florida v. Riley, 488 U.S. 445 (1989)

Gordon v. Warren Consolidated Board of Education (1983)

Graham v. Connor, 490 U.S. 386 (1989)

Hayes v. Florida, 470 US 811 (1985)

Illinois v. Wardlow, 528 U.S. 119 (2000)

Katz v. United States, 389 U.S. 347 (1967)

Kaupp v. Texas, 123 S.Ct. 1843 (2003)

Kyllo v. United States, 121 S.Ct. 2038 (2001)

Manson v. Brathwaite, 432 U.S. 98 (1977)

Pierson v. Ray (1967)

Saucier v. Katz, 121 S.Ct. 2151 (2001)

Schmerber v. California, 384 U.S. 757 (1966)

Sherman v. United States, 356 U.S. 369 (1958)

Sorrells v. United States, 287 U.S. 435 (1932)

Tennessee v. Garner, 471 U.S. 1 (1985)

Terry v. Ohio, 392 U.S. 1 (1968)

United States v. Ash, Jr., 413 U.S. 93 (1973)

United States v. Knotts, 460 U.S. 276 (1983)

United States v. McKinnon, 985 F.2d 525 (11th Cir. 1993)

United States v. Wade, 388 U.S. 218 (1967)

United States v. Weaver, 966 F.2d 391, 396 (8th Cir. 1992)

Whren v. United States, 116 S.Ct. 1769 (1996)

Section 3

INVESTIGATING VIOLENT CRIMES

Part One of the Federal Bureau of Investigation's (FBI) Uniform Crime Reports (UCR) contains statistics on eight types of serious crimes, previously called Index offenses: murder, aggravated assault, forcible rape, robbery, burglary, larceny/theft, motor vehicle theft, and arson. In years past, data were collected for each of these Index offenses and published in an annual UCR to serve as a national barometer of crime in the United States. However, as noted (FBI, Uniform Crime Report):

> In June 2004, the CJIS [Criminal Justice Information System] Advisory Policy Board (APB) approved discontinuing the use of the Crime Index in the UCR Program and its publications. The CJIS APB recommended that the FBI publish a violent crime total and a property crime total until a more viable index is developed. In recent years, the Crime Index has not been a true indicator of the degree of criminality of a locality. The Crime Index was calculated by adding the totals of seven Part I crimes. (The Modified Crime Index included arson.) Currently, larceny-thefts account for almost 60 percent of the total crimes reported. Consequently, the volume of larcenies overshadows more serious but less frequently committed crimes.

Thus, while previous editions of this text discussed crime statistics in the context of the Crime Index, this edition will simply divide such data into two categories—violent crime and property crime—as overall Crime Index data is no longer available or relevant. The Crime Clock (on page 230) illustrates the relative frequency of

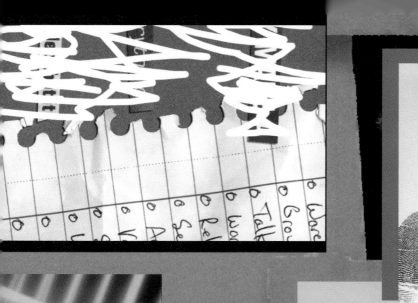

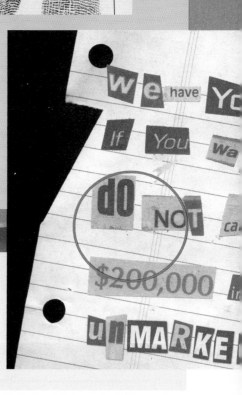

occurrence of these two categories of Part One offenses. This section looks at violent crime; property crime is the focus of Section 4.

According to the Uniform Crime Reports for 2004, a violent crime occurred nationally every 23.1 seconds:

- 1 robbery every 1.3 minutes
- 1 aggravated assault every 36.9 seconds
- 1 forcible rape every 5.6 minutes
- 1 murder every 32.6 minutes

FBI data also indicate that an estimated 1,367,009 violent crimes were committed in the United States in 2004, representing a decrease of 1.2 percent from the 2003 violent crime count. As in previous years, aggravated assaults comprised the largest portion of violent crime in 2004 at 62.5 percent, followed by robbery (29.4 percent), forcible rape (6.9 percent), and murder (1.2 percent). According to *Crime in the United States* (p.11):

The occurrence of violent crime throughout the Nation in 2004 was estimated at a rate of 465.5 violent offenses per 100,000 inhabitants, continuing a 13-year decline. . . .

The only violent crime to show any increase from 2003 to 2004 was forcible rape at 0.8 percent.

The 2004 Crime Clock
Source: The FBI's Uniform Crime Reports, October 2004.

CRIME CLOCK

Every 23.1 seconds	One Violent Crime
Every 32.6 minutes	One Murder
Every 5.6 minutes	One Forcible Rape
Every 1.3 minutes	One Robbery
Every 36.9 seconds	One Aggravated Assault

Every 3.1 seconds	One Property Crime
Every 14.7 seconds	One Burglary
Every 4.5 seconds	One Larceny-theft
Every 25.5 seconds	One Motor Vehicle Theft

The Crime Clock should be viewed with care. The most aggregate representation of UCR data, it conveys the annual reported crime experience by showing a relative frequency of occurrence of Part I offenses. It should not be taken to imply a regularity in the commission of crime. The Crime Clock represents the annual ratio of crime to fixed time intervals.

This decrease continues a decades-long trend, as the overall violent crime rate in 2003 had decreased by nearly 50 percent since 1993. The decline in crime rates has been partially attributed to the strong economy of the 1990s and tougher sentencing laws. Caution must be used when interpreting such figures, however, as they do not include crime data for categories not included in the UCR program and are underrepresentative of the true extent of violent crime.

Another measure of crime is achieved via the National Crime Victimization Survey (NCVS), which tallied 5.2 million crimes of violence in 2004 (Catalano, p.1). This instrument also reveals crime rates to be at a 30-year low, with people who have historically been the most vulnerable to violent crime—males, blacks, and youths—continuing to be victimized at higher rates than others. The NCVS data for 2004 also show that 22 percent of all violent crimes in that year were committed by an armed offender, 6 percent by an offender with a firearm (Catalano, p.1).

Investigating violent crimes is made more difficult by the emotionalism usually encountered not only from

the victim but also from the public. Generally, however, investigating violent crimes results in more and better information and evidence than investigating crimes against property, discussed in Section 4. Indeed, data from the NCVS indicate that crimes of violence are more often brought to the attention of police than are crimes against property, with 50 percent of all violent victimizations in 2004 being reported to law enforcement, compared with only 39 percent of all property crimes (Catalano, p.10).

In violent crimes, the victim is often an eyewitness, an important source of information, and a key to identifying the suspect. The victim and other witnesses are often able to provide important information on the type of crime, the person attacked, how and by what means the attack was made, what the attacker's intent or motive was, and what words may have been spoken.

Weapons may provide physical evidence, as may any injuries the victim suffered. Typically, violent crimes yield much physical evidence, with the type of evidence to anticipate directly related to the type of crime committed. Normally you can expect to find such evidence as a weapon, blood, hair, fibers, fingerprints, footprints, and so on, depending on the specific crime. Consequently the arrest rate is high.

In recent years, violent-crime investigations have been enhanced by the establishment of the Violent Crime Apprehension Program (VICAP) at the FBI National Police Academy in Quantico, Virginia. The goal of this program is to coordinate major violent-crime cases, regardless of their location, in the United States. Information considered viable is published in the *FBI Law Enforcement Bulletin.* If the case merits interagency cooperation, a major case investigation team of investigators from all involved agencies may be formed.

Viability is determined by specialists at VICAP who review the information submitted and compare it with information received from other departments about similar cases and their MOs. This is especially important in serial killings and other major violent crimes in which the suspects have moved to other areas and committed similar crimes.

The chapters in this section of the book discuss specific considerations in investigating deaths/murder (Chapter 8); assault, domestic violence, stalking, and elder abuse (Chapter 9); sex offenses (Chapter 10); crimes against children (Chapter 11); and robbery (Chapter 12). In actuality, more than one offense can occur in a given case. For example, what begins as a robbery can progress to an assault, then a forcible rape, and finally a murder. Each offense must be proven separately.

REFERENCES

Catalano, Shannan M. *Criminal Victimization, 2004.* Washington, DC: Bureau of Justice Statistics, National Crime Victimization Survey, September 2005. (NCJ 210674) *Crime in the United States 2003.* Washington, DC: Federal Bureau of Investigation, 2004. Retrieved from www.fbi.gov August 13, 2005.

FBI. "Uniform Crime Reporting—Summary Reporting: Frequently Asked Questions." http://www.fbi.gov/ucr/ucrquest.htm. Retrieved June 27, 2005.

CHAPTER

Death Investigations

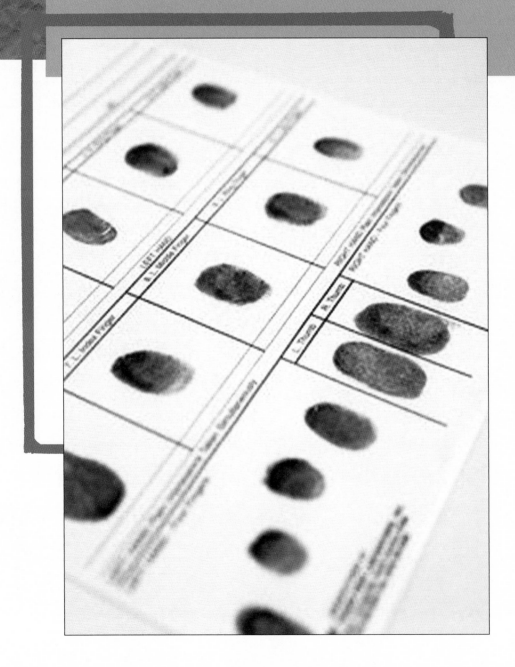

Can You Define?

Do You Know?

- What a basic requirement in a homicide investigation is?
- What the four categories of death are?
- How to define and classify homicide, murder, and manslaughter?
- What degrees of murder are frequently specified?
- How criminal and noncriminal homicide differ?
- How excusable and justifiable homicide differ?
- What the elements of each category of murder and manslaughter are?
- What special challenges a homicide investigation presents?
- What the first priority in a homicide investigation is?
- How to establish that death has occurred?
- What physical evidence is usually found in homicides?
- How to identify an unknown homicide victim?
- What factors help in estimating the time of death?
- What cadaveric spasm is and why it is important?
- What effect water has on a dead body?
- What information is provided by the medical examiner or coroner?
- What the most frequent causes of unnatural death are and what indicates whether a death is a suicide or a homicide?
- What information and evidence are obtained from a victim?
- Why determining a motive is important in homicide investigations?
- What similarities exist between school and workplace mass murders?
- How the conventional wisdom about homicide has changed in some departments?

Outline

You arrive at the scene of a death in response to an emergency call and find the body of a 55-year-old white male crumpled at the bottom of a steep staircase—obviously dead. Did the victim trip and fall (accidental death)? Did he suffer a fatal heart attack at the top of the stairs and then fall (natural death)? Did he throw himself down the stairs to end some intense physical or mental suffering (suicide)? Or was he pushed (homicide)?

Only the fourth explanation involves a criminal action meriting an official police investigation. However, because the police must determine whether it actually was homicide, the other three possible explanations must be investigated.

 A basic requirement in a homicide investigation is to establish whether death was caused by a criminal action.

Statistically, murder is the least significant of the Index crimes, with the FBI reporting 16,503 criminal homicides in the United States during 2003 (*Crime in the United States 2003* [*CIUS*], p.15). However, deaths reported as accidents or suicides may actually have been murder, and vice versa. It may be necessary to determine whether a death was a murder made to appear as a suicide to eliminate further investigation or a murder made to appear as an accident to collect life insurance.

Because homicides have received increasingly extensive media attention, it may appear as if this crime is occurring more frequently. However, it is actually declining—to its lowest level since the late 1960s. According to *CIUS* (p.15), when measured against the 1994 murder rate, the 2003 figures reflect a 29.3 percent decrease. Males are most often the victims and the perpetrators in homicides, being 10 times more likely to commit murder than females (Fox and Zawitz, p.2). In addition, people of African American descent are six times more likely than whites to be homicide victims and seven times more likely to be homicide perpetrators (Fox and Zawitz, p.2).

No other crime is measured as accurately and precisely. Fox and Zawitz (p.1) assert: "Homicide is of interest not only because of its severity but also because it is considered by experts to be a fairly reliable barometer of violent crime." Homicides continue to receive the most attention by police, not only because they are considered the most serious crime but also because they are complex cases to investigate. Furthermore, the national clearance rate for homicides is the highest of all the Part One offenses—62.4 percent of murders were cleared in 2003 (*CIUS*, p.255). However, as Litwin (p.327) points out: "Although clearance rates are highest for homicide, they have steadily decreased from 92 percent in 1960 to 63 percent in 2000, despite advances in investigative technology, such as DNA testing."

This chapter begins with a classification of deaths and descriptions of criminal homicide, noncriminal homicide, and suicide. It then discusses the elements of the crime, challenges in investigating homicides (including equivocal death scenes), suicides, and the preliminary investigation. Next the chapter focuses on discovering and identifying the victim, estimating the time of death, and the medical examination. Then it looks at unnatural causes of death and the methods used. Then follows an examination of victims, witnesses, and suspects; a look at the physical evidence often found in homicide investigations; and reheating a cold case. Next are suggestions on how to handle the unpleasant task of death notification. The chapter concludes with using community policing strategies and problem solving to reduce homicides.

Classification of Deaths

 The four types of death are:
- Natural
- Accidental ⎫ Noncriminal
- Suicide ⎭
- Homicide: Noncriminal or criminal

Natural Causes

Natural causes of death include heart attacks, strokes, fatal diseases, pneumonia, sudden crib deaths, and old age. Frequently, a person who dies of natural causes has been under a physician's care, and a death from natural causes is easily established.

Sometimes, however, a death is made to look as though it resulted from natural causes. For example, drugs that simulate the effects of a heart attack may be used in a suicide or homicide.

Accidental Deaths

Among the causes of accidental death are falling; drowning; unintentionally taking too many pills or ingesting a poisonous substance; entanglement in industrial or farm machinery; or involvement in an automobile, boat, train, bus, or plane crash. Some people advocate that certain accidental deaths be investigated as criminal homicide—for example, fatal crashes. A murder investigation can routinely involve 30 officers. A fatal-crash clearance is usually completed by just 1 or 2 officers.

As with natural deaths, an apparently accidental death can actually be a suicide or a homicide. For example, a person can jump or be pushed from a roof or in front of a vehicle or can voluntarily or involuntarily take an overdose of pills.

Suicide

Suicide—the intentional taking of one's own life—can be committed by shooting, stabbing, poisoning, burning, asphyxiating, or ingesting drugs or poisons. However, homicides are often made to look like suicides, and many suicides are made to look like accidents, usually for insurance purposes or to ease the family's suffering.

Although suicide is not a criminal offense, in most states it is a crime to attempt to commit suicide. This allows the state to take legal custody of such individuals for hospitalization or treatment. It may also be a crime to help someone commit or attempt to commit suicide by either intentionally advising, encouraging, or actually assisting the victim in the act. The topic of assisted suicide is extremely controversial. The U.S. Supreme Court has found that there is no constitutional "right to die" and has left the decision on whether to legally permit or prohibit physician-assisted suicide up to each individual state. One high-profile figure in this controversy is Jack Kevorkian, "Dr. Death," a pathologist-turned-assisted-suicide-crusader who facilitated more than 130 suicides during the 1990s. After being tried multiple times on assisted suicide charges, Kevorkian was eventually tried for murder, found guilty, and sent to prison in 1999. He will be eligible for parole in 2007.

Homicide

If another individual is the direct or indirect cause of the death, the death is classified as homicide.

Homicide is the killing of one person by another.

Homicide includes the taking of life by another human or by an agency, such as a government. It is either criminal or noncriminal, that is, felonious or nonfelonious. **Criminal homicide** is subdivided into murder and manslaughter, both of which are further subdivided. **Noncriminal homicide** is subdivided into excusable and justifiable homicide.

Classification of homicides:
- **Criminal (felonious)**
  Murder (first, second, or third degree)
  Manslaughter (voluntary or involuntary)
- **Noncriminal (nonfelonious)**
  Excusable homicide
  Justifiable homicide

Thus, *murder* and *homicide* are not synonymous. All murders are homicides (and criminal), but not all homicides are murders (or criminal).

Criminal Homicide   The two classes of criminal homicide—murder and manslaughter—have several similarities but also important differences.

Murder is the most severe statutory crime, one of the few for which the penalty can be life imprisonment or death. (In some states treason and ransom kidnapping carry a similarly severe penalty.) Some laws classify murder into first, second, or third degrees. **First-degree murder** requires **premeditation** (advanced planning) and the intent to cause death. Some statutes include in this classification any death that results during the commission of or the attempt to commit a felony such as rape or robbery. **Second-degree murder** includes the intent to cause death, but not premeditation. An example is a violent argument that ends in one person spontaneously killing the other. **Third-degree murder** involves neither premeditation nor intent. It results from an act that is imminently dangerous to others and shows a disregard for human life, such as shooting into a room where people are likely to be present or playing a practical joke that may result in someone's death.

Manslaughter is the unlawful killing of another person with no prior malice. It may be voluntary or involuntary. **Voluntary manslaughter** is the intentional causing of the death of another person in the heat of passion, i.e., because of words or acts that provide adequate provocation. For example, the law generally recognizes such acts as adultery, seduction of a child, or rape of a close relative as outrageous enough to constitute adequate provocation. This provocation must result in intense passion that replaces reason and leads to the immediate act. The provocation, passion, and fatal act must occur in rapid succession and be directly, sequentially related; that is, the provocation must cause the passion that causes the fatal act.

Involuntary manslaughter is accidental homicide that results from extreme (culpable) negligence. Examples of involuntary manslaughter include handling a firearm negligently; leaving poison where children may take it; and operating an automobile, boat, or aircraft in a criminally negligent manner. Some states, such as California, have a third category of manslaughter: manslaughter with a motor vehicle.

Other acts that can be classified as involuntary manslaughter include shooting another person with a firearm or other dangerous weapon while mistakenly believing that person to be an animal; setting a spring gun, pitfall, deadfall, snare, or other dangerous device designed to trap animals but capable of harming humans; and negligently and intentionally allowing a known vicious animal to roam free.

- Murder
  First degree—premeditated and intentional, or while committing or attempting to commit a felony
  Second degree—intentional but not premeditated
  Third degree—neither intentional nor premeditated, but the result of an imminently dangerous act
- Manslaughter
  Voluntary—intentional homicide caused by intense passion resulting from adequate provocation
  Involuntary—unintentional homicide caused by criminal (culpable) negligence

Noncriminal Homicide Although the term *homicide* is usually associated with crime, not all homicides are crimes.

Excusable homicide is the unintentional, truly accidental killing of another person. **Justifiable homicide** is killing another person under authorization of the law.

Excusable homicide results from an act that normally would not cause death or from an act committed with ordinary caution that, because of the *victim's* negligence, results in death, as when a person runs in front of a moving car.

Justifiable homicide includes killing in self-defense or in the defense of another person if the victim's actions and capability present imminent danger of serious injury or death. Killing an enemy during wartime is also classified as justifiable homicide. This classification further includes capital punishment, death caused by a public officer while carrying out a court order, and deaths caused by police officers while attempting to prevent a dangerous felon's escape or to recapture a dangerous felon who has escaped or is resisting arrest.

Officers need not risk their lives when faced with a shoot-or-be-shot situation.

Elements of the Crime

Laws on criminal homicide vary significantly from state to state, but certain common elements are usually found in each, as summarized in Table 8.1.

The degree eventually charged is decided by the prosecuting attorney based on the available evidence. For example, the only difference between first- and second-degree murder is the element of premeditation. If thorough investigation does not yield proof of premeditation, a charge of second-degree murder is made.

Causing the Death of Another Human Usually the death of a human is not difficult to prove; a death certificate completed by a physician, coroner, or medical examiner suffices. If a death certificate is not available, the investigator must locate witnesses to testify that they saw the body of the person allegedly killed by the suspect. When insufficient remains exist to identify the body positively, death is proven by circumstantial evidence such as examination by a qualified pathologist or by other experts and their expert testimony regarding dental work, bone structure, and the like.

A more difficult portion of the element to prove is the cause of death. To show that the suspect's act caused the death, (1) prove the cause of death and (2) prove that the suspect, through direct action, inflicted injury sufficient to cause the death with some weapon or device. For example, if the cause of death was a fatal wound from a .22-caliber weapon, it is necessary to show that the suspect produced the cause of death. Did the suspect

Table 8.1 / **Degrees of Homicide**

	MURDER			MANSLAUGHTER	
Element to be Proven	First Degree	Second Degree	Third Degree	Voluntary	Involuntary
Causing the death of another human	*	*	*	*	*
Premeditation	*				
Malicious intent	*	*			
Adequately provoked intent resulting from the heat of passion				*	
†While committing or attempting to commit a felony	*				
†While committing or attempting to commit a crime not a felony			*	*	
When forced or threatened				*	
Culpable negligence or depravity				*	
Negligence					*

† Indicates that starred elements other than causing the death of another human need not be proven.

own such a weapon? Can witnesses testify that the suspect had such a weapon immediately before the fatal injury? Was the suspect seen actually committing the offense? Did the suspect admit the act by statement or confession?

Premeditation Premeditation is the consideration, planning, or preparation for an act, no matter how briefly, before committing it. Laws use such terms as *premeditated design to kill* or *malice of forethought*. Whatever the law's wording, it is necessary to prove some intention and plan to commit the crime before it was actually committed.

> Premeditation is the element of first-degree murder that sets it apart from all other classifications.

Were oral statements or threats made during a heated argument? Did the suspect buy or have a gun just before the crime was committed or travel a long distance to wait for the victim? Premeditation can be proved in many ways. Sometimes the time interval between thought and action is only a minute; other times it may be hours, days, weeks, months, or even years.

Determine at what time before the killing the suspect considered, planned, threatened, or made some overt act to prepare to commit the murder. This may be established by statements from witnesses or from the victim before death, from evidence at the crime scene, or through a review of the suspect's criminal history and past statements.

Intent to Effect the Death of Another Person Intent is a required element of most categories of criminal homicide. Evidence must show that the crime was intentional, not accidental. **Malicious intent,** an element of first- and second-degree murder, implies ill will, wickedness, or cruelty. How the act was committed shows the degree of intent. The type of weapon used, how and when it was acquired, and how the suspect and victim came together help prove the intent as well as the act that caused the death.

Intent and *premeditation* are not the same. Premeditation is not a requirement of intent. Most crimes of passion involve intent but not premeditation or malicious intent.

This element also applies to a death caused to someone other than the intended victim. For example, in one case a woman intended to kill her husband by placing poison in a bottle of whiskey he kept under the seat of the family car. Unknowingly, the husband offered a drink from the bottle to a friend, who died as a result. The wife was charged with first-degree murder and convicted, even though the person who died was not her intended victim.

It was a reasonable consequence of her act. An explosive that was set for one person may detonate prematurely and kill someone else. A person shooting at an intended victim may miss and kill an innocent bystander. Both of these would constitute first-degree murder.

Adequately Provoked Intent Resulting from Heat of Passion This element is the alternative to premeditation. It assumes that the act was committed when the suspect suddenly became extremely emotional, thus precluding premeditation. **Heat of passion** results from extremely volatile arguments between two people, from seeing a wife or family member raped, from a sudden discovery of adultery, or from seeing a brutal assault being committed against a close friend or family member.

While Committing or Attempting to Commit a Felony In some states a charge of first-degree murder does not require that the murder was committed with premeditation if the victim died as a result of acts committed while the suspect was engaged in a felony such as rape, robbery, or arson. Proof of the elements of the felony must of course be established.

While Committing or Attempting to Commit a Crime Not a Felony If a death results from an act committed by a suspect engaged in a nonfelonious crime such as purse snatching or petty theft, it can be charged as either third-degree murder or voluntary manslaughter, depending on the state in which the offense occurs.

Culpable Negligence or Depravity The act and the way it is committed establish this element. The act must be so dangerous that any prudent person would see death of a person as a possible consequence. A person causing a death while depraved and committing acts evident of such depravity is guilty of third-degree murder.

Negligence A fine line separates this element from the preceding element. Some states make no distinction, classifying both in a separate category of **criminal negligence.** Where separate categories exist, this lesser degree of negligence involves creating a situation that results in an unreasonable risk of death or great bodily harm.

 olice have an obligation to act on behalf of the deceased and their families. They are expected to conduct a professional investigation to identify, arrest, and prosecute suspects. One apparent injustice in the criminal justice system is that to an outsider, it appears that the police are constantly trying to protect the rights of the perpetrator and pay slight attention to the rights of the deceased or the family.

 Challenges in homicide investigations include pressure by the media and the public, the difficulty of establishing that a crime has been committed, identifying the victim, and establishing the cause and time of death.

Homicides create high interest in the community, as evidenced by increased sales of newspapers and higher ratings for the news media. Indeed, the media have a special interest in police investigations of deaths—accidental or otherwise. Police officers who have dealt with the news media understand the important relationship between law enforcement and the media, as discussed in Chapter 1.

Police policies and guidelines should specify what information is to be released: the deceased's name, accused's name, and general identifying information; any details regarding formal charges; and general facts about the investigation that are not harmful to the continuing investigation of the case.

Do not pose the accused for photographs, and do not permit the accused to talk to the press. If investigators have details known only to them and the accused, that information must not be released. Exercising good sense, getting to know the reporters personally, and refraining from giving off-the-record comments will prevent many problems. Reporters have a right to be at the scene, and cooperation is the best policy—within the policies and guidelines of the department.

From time to time, public outrage over particular crimes places increased pressure on the police to solve murders. A more serious problem is the difficulty of establishing that a crime has, in fact, been committed. Search warrants can be issued if proof of a crime exists; however, such proof may not be legally available without a warrant. In addition, many perpetrators attempt to make the crime scene look as if a robbery or burglary has taken place. It can also be difficult to determine whether the death was homicide or suicide.

Equivocal Death

Equivocal death investigations "are those inquiries that are open to interpretation. There may be two or more meanings and the case may present as homicide, suicide or accidental death. The facts may be purposefully vague or misleading as in the case of the staged crime scene" (Geberth, 2005, p.53).

A staged crime scene is one where a killer hopes to cover his or her tracks by making it look like the victim committed suicide, suffered a fatal accident, or died of natural causes. As Geberth (2004, p.117) asserts: "Staging is a conscious-criminal action on the part of an offender to thwart an investigation." Inexperienced investigators who jump to the hasty conclusion that a man found hanging in his garage or the dead woman in the bathtub with slit wrists must have committed suicide may be allowing a perpetrator to get away with murder. A critical piece of the investigation, stresses Geberth, is assessment of the victimology of the deceased: What was the victim's state of mind in the days and weeks leading up to the death? Had the victim made long-term plans, such as having purchased plane tickets for a vacation, prepaid membership dues, or begun a major house renovation project? Answers to these questions may not support an initial assessment of suicide. Therefore, the prudent investigator approaches all equivocal death scenes as if they were homicide cases, bringing each factor to its ultimate conclusion, until forensic evaluation of evidence can point one way or the other—homicide or not.

Another equivocal death situation involves sudden, unexplained infant death (SUID), which is not to be confused with SIDS, or sudden infant death syndrome. SIDS is the sudden death of a child under age 1 that remains unexplained even after a thorough investigation involving a complete autopsy, examination of the death scene, and review of the infant's clinical history. It is a "diagnosis of exclusion," when all other possible causes of death (disease, illness, abuse, etc.) have been explored and ruled out. SUID is a preinvestigative term. A SUID case, after a thorough investigation, may be classified as SIDS (approximately 85 percent of cases) or will identify another cause of death, such as homicide (Weyland, p. 11). Investigating SUID will be covered again in Chapter 11.

In-custody deaths present a tremendous challenge to investigators. These cases typically involve suspects who have been restrained for some time, during which they enter a state of medical crisis and die. Families of the deceased frequently file lawsuits claiming that police brutality caused the death, while the officers involved contend that the restrained person succumbed to some type of preexisting physical defect (weak heart, aneurysm, etc.) brought about by the subject's own state of agitation. As with SUID cases, in-custody deaths must be thoroughly investigated, beginning with a complete autopsy to determine whether a heart attack, stroke, or other physical condition caused the death. Lawrence and Mohr (p.44) suggest:

When professionals can establish no obvious mechanism of death after pursuing all the routine elements of a competent investigation, detectives can scaffold their investigation through a protocol that is informed by several bodies of research. The first, and perhaps most common, is the psychiatric research. Psychiatric illness and substance abuse figure prominently in many instances of sudden in-custody death. Given this knowledge, investigators should examine [the] subject's personal history, the nature of the custody incident, and the environmental factors surrounding the incident.

A checklist for investigating sudden in-custody deaths is provided in Appendix A. Sometimes an equivocal death investigation reveals the cause to be suicide.

Suicide

Suicide ranks eleventh among causes of death in the United States (Pinizzotto et al., p.9). Griffith (p.6) states: "Suicide, even when the victim leaves a note explaining his or her reasons, is the ultimate murder mystery." In fact, suicide often presents as a homicide. Investigators should keep in mind that more Americans die by suicide than by homicide. Often depression or schizophrenia is involved, and usually these people have made their intentions known to someone. Therefore, investigators should try to determine whether a suspected suicide victim was suffering from depression or schizophrenia or whether the victim had talked to anyone about committing suicide.

The reason for an apparent suicide must be determined. An act that appears to be too violent for suicide and is therefore a suspected homicide may actually be a natural death. Never exclude the possibility of death from natural causes in the initial phase of an investigation because of the presence of obvious marks of violence. The abnormal activity of a person suffering from an acutely painful attack can create the appearance of a struggle. The onset of more than 70 diseases can produce sudden death. People who experience such an attack may disarrange their clothing and sustain severe injury by falling. In one case a man shot himself to relieve excruciating pain, and the autopsy showed that a ruptured aorta caused his death, not the gunshot. What appeared to be suicide was declared to be death by natural causes.

Check for weapons on or near the body. Were there any prior suicide attempts, a history of mental illness, or recent traumatic incidents? Were there any recent changes or conflicts in the victim's personal relationships? Was the victim being treated for a medical condition? Were any prescription drugs found at the scene? What was the cause of death?

When investigating suspected suicides, attempt to find a note or letter. However, lack of a note does not eliminate the possibility of suicide—a suicide note is left in only a fourth of the cases investigated. If you do find a note, have it compared with the deceased's handwriting.

Preserve all evidence until the medical examiner or coroner's office rules whether the death is a suicide.

Also look for videos or cassettes describing the actions taken. Examine any pads of paper near the body for the presence of indentation remaining from writing on sheets of paper torn from the pad and destroyed. Look for manuals on how to commit suicide. Check on prior arrangements with an undertaker or other evidence of putting one's affairs in order.

Learn whether the victim was left- or right-handed and see whether this fits with the method of committing suicide. Note lividity conditions and the body's location to determine how long the person has been dead and whether the body has been moved. Note the condition of rigor mortis. Are there "hesitation marks" indicating indecision before the final act? Do not assume that any blood on the victim is the victim's; it may be from a murderer. (These issues are discussed later in the chapter.)

When smaller-caliber weapons are fired, blood may not appear on the hands of the person firing the gun. In fact, in most suicide cases blood does not appear on the hands. A test for gunshot residue (GSR), as explained in Chapter 5, will confirm whether the deceased fired the weapon. In more than 75 percent of suicide cases in which a gun is used, the gun is not found in the victim's hand but is near the body. In a number of suicides the victims have multiple wounds. If evidence surfaces after the initial investigation that proves a suicide was actually a homicide, do not hesitate to reopen the case.

What appears to be a double suicide can also present problems. It may be a murder-suicide. Determine who died first or who inflicted the fatal wounds. Attempt to determine the motive. Search for a note. Look for signs of a violent struggle before death. Sometimes suicide is obvious, as when suspects kill themselves to avoid being captured by the police.

To gain a better understanding of the victim's frame of mind when the suicide occurred or to reveal that the act was perhaps not suicide at all, it is vital for investigators to study the personality traits, character, and lifestyle of the victim, reconstructing as accurately as possible the days and hours preceding the victim's death.

Suicide by Police

Suicide by police was introduced in Chapter 7 and refers to a situation in which a person decides he or she wants to die but does not want to pull the trigger. Such people may not have the courage to do so and take the option of forcing a police officer to do it for them; or they may view suicide as socially or religiously unacceptable but believe that if they are killed by police, the stigma of suicide will be averted and society may see them as victims. Some insurance policies will not pay if a person commits suicide, making suicide by cop an attractive option for those bent on killing themselves.

Often such cases involve a "man-with-a-gun" call. Arriving police are confronted with a person acting bizarrely and threatening to shoot himself/herself, a hostage, or the responding officers. In many instances the gun is not loaded, is a fake, or is inoperative, but if it is pointed at the police, the police are forced to shoot. The actions of armed individuals who go out of their way to provoke a lethal response by police have led those in academia to refer to such suicide-by-cop incidents as "victim-precipitated" ("Officer's Research Shows," p.15).

When investigating a suspected case of suicide by cop, a critical element to determine is the probable motivation of the offender/victim. Pinizzotto et al. (p.12) stress: "[The] investigating officer or unit must sift carefully through the facts and circumstances using stringent criteria to determine if the incident probably was motivated by the offender's *will* to commit suicide." They (p.12) list the following items of evidence for investigators to collect, if possible:

- Notes or recent correspondence from/to the offender
- Detailed and verbatim statements from family members, friends, and associates
- Images captured from in-car or security cameras
- Forensic evidence such as the firearm brandished by the offender and whether it was loaded
- Personal history of the offender

Suicide-by-cop offender profiles indicate that such subjects often have a poor self-image, feel a sense of guilt for great harm they have caused, talk about death and express a desire to be with deceased loved ones, speak often of a higher being, are aggressively confrontational with police, and possess an unloaded or nonfunctioning (toy) gun. Other issues that may potentially indicate suicidal motivations include:

- Substantial loss of funds or outstanding and pressing debts
- Divorce
- Pending or actual loss of a job, including retirement
- Imminent arrest of the individual or a close friend/associate
- Health problems (Pinizzotto et al., p.14)

Keeping these factors in mind may help officers identify potential suicide-by-cop cases. Investigators must evaluate the totality of physical evidence and behavioral indicators to accurately assess whether the incident is one of suicide by cop, as no single piece of evidence, action, or behavior is usually sufficient to establish an offender's motivation (Pinizzotto et al., p.13).

Whatever the circumstances, a police officer who is forced to take a life may suffer emotionally. In some instances officers who have taken a life end up taking their own.

Suicide of Police Officers

There is no question—police work is stressful. And it can take its toll in tragic ways. Although many consider police work to be a dangerous profession primarily because of the risk of encountering violent and armed individuals, more officers lose their lives to suicide than to homicide.

Contributing factors in police suicides, as with other victims of suicide, are alcohol, family issues, and the breakup of relationships. The public's image of the police, and indeed officers' image of themselves, is that of the strong protector of society. Yet police work forces officers to confront daily the dark side of human nature and may eventually cause officers to lose their faith in the goodness of humanity or in their abilities to make a positive impact on the lives of others. This sense of weakness and failure is so contradictory to the image of the police that some officers may simply see no other choice than to "take themselves out of the game."

When an officer commits suicide, the family—and sometimes the first officers on the scene—may attempt to make the death look accidental or like a homicide to avoid the stigma of suicide or to ensure that the family can collect the life insurance. Any officer's death requires a thorough investigation. As with suspected suicide-by-cop incidents, investigation into the officer's prior mental/emotional status (presence of depression, post-traumatic stress disorder), substance use or abuse, family situations (divorce, death of a spouse or child), financial status (large debts), and health (serious or chronic illness) provide critical insight into possible motivations for suicide. Being under an internal affairs investigation and facing the potential loss of one's identity as an officer is the most compelling reason for an officer to make a hasty decision to commit suicide (Nislow, p.1).

Once forensic examination concludes that a death was caused by suicide, the investigation is over and the case closed. For those cases that are homicides, a thorough criminal investigation must be conducted.

Preliminary Investigation of Homicide

The initial investigation of a homicide is basically the same as for any other crime, although it may require more flexibility, logic, and perseverance. The primary goals of the investigation are (1) to establish whether a human death was caused by the criminal act or omission of another and (2) to determine who caused the death.

Death Investigation: A Guide for the Scene Investigator (1999) is a valuable resource for homicide investigators because it details not only the steps to take when arriving at the scene but also important investigative tools and equipment, documenting and evaluating both the scene and the body, establishing and recording decedent profile information, and completing the scene investigation.

The homicide case normally begins with a report of a missing person or the discovery of a body. The officer in the field seldom makes the initial discovery. The first notification is received by the police communications center or a dispatcher who records the date, time, and exact wording used. Because the original call is sometimes made anonymously by a suspect, a voice recording is made for comparison with later suspects.

In *Flippo v. West Virginia* (1999), the Supreme Court held that police may make warrantless entries onto premises where they reasonably believe a person is in need of immediate aid, or may make a prompt warrantless search of a homicide scene for other victims or a killer on the premises. However, the Court specifically rejected the idea that there is any general "murder scene exception" to the search warrant requirement of the Fourth Amendment. The situation qualifies as simply an exigent circumstance.

A study of 800 homicide cases ("Secrets of Success," p.1) found that investigators are more likely to clear a homicide if they arrive within 30 minutes of being notified, as compared with half an hour or longer. It also found that following up on witness information made it more than twice as likely that a case would be solved; and if that information proved valuable, more than 17 times as likely. Furthermore, the study (p.6) found: "The behavior of police at crime scenes plays a significant role, as well. Cases were less likely to be solved if the first officer at the scene failed to notify the homicide unit, medical examiner or crime lab. The chances of solving the case also fell if the first officer did not attempt to round up witnesses." As in any crime scene investigation, the first officer on the scene is extremely important.

As you enter the scene, it is important to introduce yourself, identify key personnel, establish rapport, and assess the safety of the scene. Of course, if you discover upon arrival that the victim is still alive, the first priority is to render emergency aid and make sure an ambulance is en route.

 The first priority is to give emergency aid to the victim if he or she is still alive or to determine that death has occurred.

If the suspect is still at the scene, priorities may differ drastically. Normally, however, the suspect is not at the scene, and the victim is the first priority. If the victim is obviously dying, take a dying declaration. The live victim is taken to a hospital as rapidly as possible.

The first officer on the scene determines the path to the victim that will least disturb evidence. If the victim is obviously dead, the body remains at the scene until the preliminary investigation is complete. It is then taken to the morgue by the medical examiner or coroner for postmortem examination or autopsy.

Following the assessment of the victim, investigators must document everything they can about the scene. This includes detaining and identifying everyone present, obtaining brief statements from each, maintaining control of the scene and everyone present, listing all officers present upon the investigator's arrival and throughout the investigation, and recording the presence of all other personnel at the scene (medical personnel, coroner, family members). A death-scene checklist developed by the Federal Bureau of Investigation (FBI) can help ensure a thorough preliminary investigation. This checklist is reprinted in Appendix B.

Determining That Death Has Occurred

Medically, death is determined by the cessation of three vital functions: heartbeat, respiration, and brain activity. The first two signs are observable.

 Signs of death include lack of breathing, lack of heartbeat, lack of flushing of the fingernail bed when pressure is applied to the nail and then released, and failure of the eyelids to close after being gently lifted.

Cessation of respiration is generally the first visible sign of death. However, in cases such as barbiturate overdoses, breathing can be so shallow that it is undetectable. Therefore, always check for a heartbeat and pulse. Except in some drug overdoses and with certain types of blindness, failure of the pupils to dilate in reaction to light is also a sign of death.

If the victim appears to have died at the moment of the officer's arrival or dies in the presence of the officer, he or she should attempt resuscitation with the standard cardiopulmonary resuscitation methods.

The Focus of the Homicide Investigation

As with any other criminal investigation, the homicide scene must be secured, photographed, and sketched. Videotaping the crime scene can produce excellent results and is becoming more frequently done. All evidence must be obtained, identified, and properly preserved. Physical evidence can be found on the body, at the scene, or on the suspect.

 Physical evidence in a homicide includes a weapon, a body, blood, hairs, and fibers.

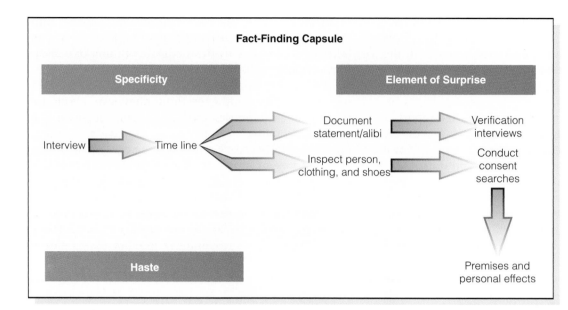

Figure 8.1
Fact-finding capsule

Source: John B. Edwards. "Homicide Investigative Strategies." *FBI Law Enforcement Bulletin,* January 2005, p. 12.

Table 8.2 / **Prompt Investigative Trilogy**

	IMMEDIATE	PENDING
	Specific Focus	General Coverage	Informative
Specific witnesses	Neighborhood canvass	Cell phone records
Specific evidence	Friends, family, and associates (victimology)	Computer hard drives
Specific events	Coworkers	Other records
Specific facts	Victim/suspect time lines	Private papers

Source: John B. Edwards. "Homicide Investigative Strategies." *FBI Law Enforcement Bulletin,* January 2005, p.13.

Any of the various types of evidence discussed in Chapter 5 can be present at a homicide scene. Especially important are the body and the weapon.

After priority matters are completed, the focus of the homicide investigation is to:

- Identify the victim.
- Establish the time of death.
- Establish the cause of and the method used to produce death.
- Develop a suspect.

The preliminary investigation either accomplishes these things or provides leads that investigators can follow up.

Edwards (p.11) suggests using a strategy known as "the fact-finding capsule" to guide homicide investigations (Figure 8.1). Three important rules govern these investigative tactics:

- *Specificity.* Explore all issues to obtain precise facts and enough details to make objective judgments and correlations.
- *Element of surprise.* Keep witnesses from comparing stories and deny suspects time to cover their tracks or create alibis.
- *Haste.* Accomplish all tasks quickly to gather and promptly develop facts.

Edwards (p.12) reminds investigators that the first 48 hours are critical to an ongoing investigation and advocates a prompt investigative trilogy that addresses (1) a specific focus (immediate), (2) general coverage (immediate), and (3) informative records and facts (pending). Table 8.2 lists the investigative avenues to pursue. Edwards (p.12) asserts: "Teams of investigators must address each area simultaneously during the investigation and direct information from all three areas to the central clearinghouse (e.g., the lead investigator, case agent, or detective in the case). At that time, teams should process information, form theories, and take steps regarding the focus, scope, and need for additional resources."

Discovering and Identifying the Victim

 n some cases no body is present. It may have been burned, cut up beyond recognition, or dissolved in a vat of acid. Some states allow the use of circumstantial evidence to prove the corpus delicti when no body can be found. In other cases there is a body, but locating it is a challenge. It may have been weighted and sunk in a body of water or buried underground.

When searching for human remains, investigators can use technologies such as ground-penetrating radar, magnetometers, metal detectors, and infrared thermography, as well as specially trained dogs. Infrared thermography can distinguish between hidden new and old gravesites faster and more accurately than other techniques. In addition, cadaver-search canines have proven effective.

Once a body is found, it must be identified.

> Homicide victims are identified by immediate family, relatives, or acquaintances; personal effects, fingerprints, DNA analysis, and dental and skeletal studies; and clothing and laundry marks; or through missing-persons files.

In many cases identifying the deceased is no problem. The spouse, parents, a close friend, or a relative makes the identification. If possible, have several people identify the body, because people under stress make mistakes. In a number of cases, a homicide victim has been identified only to turn up later alive. Although personal identification by viewing the deceased is ideal, corroborate it by other evidence. Personal effects found on the victim assist in identification. However, such personal effects may not necessarily belong to the deceased. Therefore, check them carefully.

If identification cannot be made by relatives or acquaintances or by personal effects, the most positive identification is by fingerprint or DNA analysis. Comparative fingerprints are not always available, however, and blood type does not provide a positive identification, although it can prove that a body is *not* a specific person.

For an unknown victim, record a complete description and take photographs if possible. Check these against missing-persons files. Circulate the description and photograph in the surrounding area. Check the victim's clothing for possible laundry marks or for labels that might indicate where the clothes were purchased.

If the body is badly decomposed, the bones provide a basis for estimating height, sex, and approximate age as well as proof that the deceased was a human. If there are leads as to who the victim might be, you can attempt identification by comparing dental charts and X-rays of prior fractures and by examining signs of prior surgical procedures, such as scars or other abnormalities (Figure 8.2).

Estimating the Time of Death

In many homicides, there is a delay between the commission of the crime and the discovery of the body, sometimes only minutes, other times years. This time period between death and corpse discovery is called the postmortem interval (PMI). Understanding the processes that occur in a body during the PMI can help investigators estimate a time of death. Research facilities, such as the Body Farm outside of Knoxville, Tennessee, are allowing forensic scientists to study and document these processes under various environmental conditions in an effort to help investigators more accurately determine the time of death.

The time of death relates directly to whether the suspect could have been at the scene and to the sequence of multiple deaths. It is also important to the victim's family in settling insurance claims and Social Security and pension payments.

Both the investigator and the medical examiner or coroner are responsible for estimating the time of death. Knowing how the professional examiner estimates time of death helps investigators to understand better what circumstances are important at the crime scene and alerts them to observe and record specific factors that aid in estimating the time of death, including environmental (or ambient) temperature. Some of these factors are available only to the first officers at the scene.

Without eyewitnesses, the time of death is seldom completely accurate. Normally, however, the time of the death—if it has occurred within the past four days—can be determined to within four hours, depending on the examiner's expertise and the factors available for examination. Figure 8.3 shows the timing of various body changes after death.

© AP/Wide World Photos

Figure 8.2

Bones often assist in identification of victims through comparison with health and dental records. If a victim's identity is unknown, bones can be used to create a facial model of what the victim may have looked like. Here, Trooper Sarah Foster, a Michigan State Police forensic artist, measures a three-dimensional facial reconstruction from an unidentified human skull at Richmond post in Richmond, Mich., Tuesday, Dec. 16, 2003. Foster didn't have formal art training when she joined the Michigan State Police three years ago, but she has since used her artistic talents to help bolster the agency's investigative work.

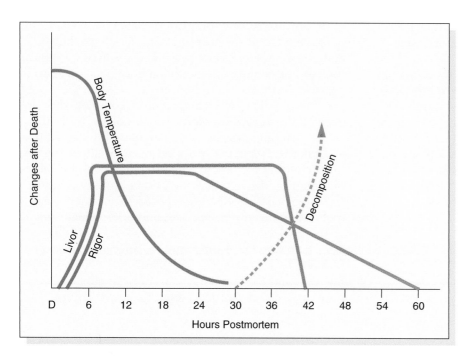

Figure 8.3

Timing of postmortem body cooling, livor, rigor mortis, and putrefactive changes

Source: Irwin M. Sopher. "The Law Enforcement Officer and the Determination of the Time of Death." *FBI Law Enforcement Bulletin,* October 1973.

Factors that help in estimating the time of death are body temperature, rigor mortis, postmortem lividity (livor), eye appearance, stomach contents, stage of decomposition, and evidence suggesting a change in the victim's normal routine.

Recent Death

A time of death that is less than one half hour before examination is normally the easiest determination to make. The body is still warm; mucous membranes are still moist but drying; blood is still moist but drying; the pupils have begun to dilate; and in Caucasians the skin is becoming pale. (For the purpose of convenience, subsequent references to external body color will be to those of light-skinned people.)

Death That Occurred One Half Hour to Four Days Prior

Generally, if the death occurred within the past four days but more than one half hour ago, the mucous membranes and any blood from the wounds are dry, there are skin blisters and skin slippage, the body is slightly pink, body temperature has dropped, rigor mortis and postmortem lividity are present, and the pupils are restricted and cloudy.

Body Temperature   Although not an accurate measure of time of death, body temperature is helpful in conjunction with other factors. **Algor mortis** refers to the postmortem cooling process of the body and can be

extremely helpful in homicide investigations. After death, the body tends to assume the temperature of its environment. Record the temperature of the surroundings and the amount of clothing on the body. Reach under the clothing to determine the warmth or coldness of the body. Compare this with exposed parts of the body to determine whether body heat is being retained by the clothing.

Body temperature drops 2 to 3 degrees in the first hour after death and 1 to 1.5 degrees for each subsequent hour up to 18 hours.

Some investigators use the formula of 1.5 degrees cooling per hour, assuming an internal temperature of 98.6° F and an environmental temperature of 70° to 75° F, with the rate of loss adjusted up and down depending on the actual environmental temperature and with the accuracy decreasing after 10 hours. The formula would be $98.5 - T / 1.5 = N$, where T equals rectal temperature in degrees Fahrenheit and N is the number of hours since death.

These times vary in abnormally hot or cold environments. Also, body temperature drops more slowly in large or obese people, if a high fever was present before death, if humidity prevents evaporation, or if strenuous physical activity occurred immediately before death.

Rigor Mortis   The body is limp after death until rigor mortis sets in. **Rigor mortis,** a Latin term that literally translates to "stiffness of death," is a stiffening of the joints of the body after death due to partial skeletal muscle contraction. Onset may occur anywhere from 10 minutes to several hours postmortem, depending on physical conditions concerning the body and the environment. Excitement, vigorous activity, heavy clothing, and abnormally high temperatures increase the rapidity of rigor; cold slows it. Babies and the aged have little rigor.

Rigor mortis is first noticed in smaller muscles, such as those of the face, and spreads to larger muscle groups throughout the body, reaching maximum rigor between 12 and 24 hours. The body remains rigid for approximately three days, until the muscles themselves begin to decompose.

 Rigor mortis appears as a stiffening of muscles several hours after death, with maximum stiffness occurring 12 to 24 hours after death and lasting for approximately three days.

The degree of rigor mortis as an indicator of time of death is usually accurate to within four hours when used along with other factors, such as ambient temperature.

Closely associated with rigor mortis is **cadaveric spasm,** a condition that occurs in specific muscle groups rather than the entire body. It occurs most often when the victim is holding something in the hand at the time of death. The hand closes tightly around the object because of the stress and tension of death occurring. The condition does not disappear as rigor mortis does, and it cannot be induced by another person. Cadaveric spasm does not always occur, but when it does, it helps to establish whether death was a homicide or a suicide. If a dead person is found with a gun or knife tightly clutched in the hand and this is the only area of the body showing this condition, the victim was holding the weapon at the moment of death.

A weapon tightly clutched in the victim's hand as the result of cadaveric spasm indicates suicide.

Ensure that the weapon clutched *was* the murder weapon. It might be that both the victim and an assailant were armed and that the death was not suicide. Likewise, absence of cadaveric spasm does not preclude suicide, because it does not always occur.

Postmortem Lividity   When the heart stops beating at death, the blood no longer circulates and gravity drains the blood to the body's lowest levels. This causes a dark blue or purple discoloration of the body called **postmortem lividity,** or **livor mortis** (Figure 8.4). Lividity is cherry red or a strong pink if death has been caused by carbon monoxide poisoning (Figure 8.5), and various other poisons give lividity other colors.

If a body is on its back, lividity appears in the lower portion of the back and legs. If facedown, it appears on the face, chest, stomach, and legs. If the body is on its side, lividity appears on the side on which the body is

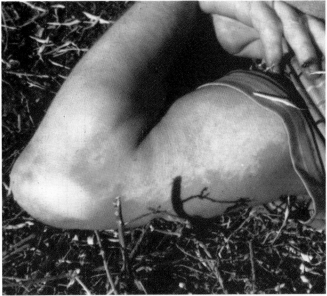

Figure 8.4
Postmortem Lividity. When the heart stops beating at death, the blood no longer circulates, and gravity drains the blood to the body's lowest levels. This results in a dark blue or purple discoloration of the body called postmortem lividity. Lividity patterns can indicate whether a body has been moved after death. This 48-year-old white male fell asleep against a fence and died of heart disease. When he was found the following afternoon, lividity indicated he had been dead approximately 18 hours and had died in that position.

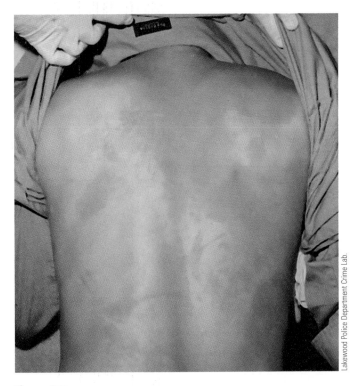

Figure 8.5
Carbon monoxide poisoning. When carbon monoxide is inhaled, it enters the bloodstream and displaces oxygen from the blood. Reddish lividity, as seen on the body in this photo, indicates carbon monoxide poisoning. This 35-year-old white male committed suicide by lying next to a running vehicle in a closed garage.

resting; and if the body is upright, it appears in the buttocks and lower legs.

Postmortem lividity starts one half to 3 hours after death and is congealed in the capillaries in 4 to 5 hours. Maximum lividity occurs within 10 to 12 hours.

Any part of the body pressing directly on a hard surface does not show lividity because the pressure of the body's weight prevents blood from entering the blood vessels in that area. If there are large wounds from which blood has been released, very little if any lividity occurs.

Postmortem lividity and bruises appear similar, but they are easy to distinguish. When bruises are pressed with the thumb or fingers, they remain the same, whereas lividity turns white, or blanches, when pressure is applied. If the blood has already congealed, an incision reveals whether the blood is still in the vessels (lividity) or outside them (bruise). In addition, the color of a bruise varies, whereas the color of lividity is uniform.

The location of lividity can indicate whether a body was moved after death.

Besides helping to establish time of death and sometimes the cause, lividity helps determine whether the body was moved after death occurred. Postmortem lividity in a body moved immediately after death would provide no clues. However, if the body was moved to a different position after lividity had set in, lividity will occur in unlikely areas, indicating that the body was moved.

Examination of the Eyes   The appearance of the eyes also assists in estimating the time of death. After death, eye muscle tone lessens and tends to disappear. The pupils tend to dilate.

A partial restriction of the pupil occurs in about 7 hours. In 12 hours the cornea appears cloudy.

The cornea clouds more rapidly if the eyes are open after death. During the medical examination, fluid can be withdrawn from the eyeball (or the spine) to determine the level of potassium, which tends to rise at a predictable rate after death.

Examination of Stomach Contents   Although the stomach contents must be examined during the medical examination, the investigator can provide important information for the examiner.

Determine when and what the victim last ate. If any vomit is present, preserve it as evidence and submit it for examination.

Attempt to find out when the victim last ate. The medical examiner can often determine how long the victim lived after eating because digestion is a fairly constant process, measurable in hours. Mertens (2003, p.63) notes: "The standard scientists follow involving stomach contents states that the stomach empties 2 to 4 hours after eating," after which time it empties into the small intestine, where it takes another 2 to 4 hours to pass into the large intestine. If the stomach is full, death occurred within less than four hours after eating. If the small intestine is full, death occurred 4 to 8 hours after eating. If the large intestine is empty, 12 or more hours passed after the victim ate and before death occurred. Digestive time is affected by many factors, however. Mental and emotional upsets, poor health, fatigue, and constipation all decrease digestive time; diarrhea increases it.

If the victim has vomited, the stomach is empty and will distort the estimate of time of death; therefore, report the presence of any vomit near the body. Preserve such vomit as evidence, as it may provide information on drugs or poisons related to the cause of death.

Many Days after Death

It is more difficult to estimate the time of death if death occurred several days before discovery of the body. The cadaver is bloated, lividity is darkened, the abdomen is greenish, blisters are filled with gas, and a distinct odor is present.

Decomposition   The medical examiner makes a rough estimate of time of death based on the body's state of decomposition. Decomposition is first observed as an extended stomach and abdomen, the result of internal gases developing. In general, decomposition is increased by higher temperatures and decreased by lower temperatures.

If the body is in a hot, moist location, a soapy appearance called **adipocere** develops. This takes up to three months to develop fully. Attacks by insects, bacteria, animals, and birds also increase the decomposition rate.

Complete dehydration of all body tissues results in **mummification.** A cadaver left in an extremely dry, hot area will mummify in about a year and will remain in this condition for several years if undisturbed by animals or insects.

The presence on the body of insect eggs, their stage of development, and the life cycle of the species, as well as various stages of vegetation on or near the body, also provide information on the time of death. A forensic entomologist (FE) can examine various types of insects to assist in estimating the time of death. Mertens (2004, p.63) stresses: "Forensic entomologists cannot always be present at a scene. Therefore, it is law enforcement's responsibility to properly collect, label and transport entomological evidence. There also are many other factors an entomologist needs to know from the investigating authority regarding a death site." Table 8.3 provides a checklist for investigators working a homicide where entomological evidence is found.

Examination of insects is especially helpful when death occurred more than a week before. Insects can detect newly dead body odors two miles away. Because particular insects work or rest during the day or the night, the types of insects at the scene provide clues as to the timing of the body's deterioration. Furthermore, it is possible to tie a suspect to the area in which a body is found by comparing evidence on the body with insect parts smashed on the suspect's windshield, grille, or other vehicle parts.

Effects of Water

Bodies immersed in water for a period of time undergo changes that help to determine time of death. A body immersed in water may decompose rapidly, depending on the water temperature, salinity, mineral content, and effects of fish and other marine life.

 A dead body usually sinks in water and remains immersed for 8 to 10 days in warm water or 2 to 3 weeks in cold water. It then rises to the surface unless restricted. The outer skin loosens in 5 to 6 days, and the nails separate in 2 to 3 weeks.

The medical examination also determines whether the person was alive or dead at the time the body was immersed in water. This provides evidence to support homicide, suicide, or accidental death.

As with insects found on bodies on land, diatoms and algal material can help forensic biologists determine the time of death for bodies found in water, as well as whether the person was drowned. Diatoms are tiny, single-celled aquatic organisms that live in both saltwater and freshwater environments. The composition of diatoms in one particular body of water or aquatic ecosystem is often unique and can be distinguished from other groups of diatoms from other locations. Thus, forensic biologists who collect diatoms from a suspect's shoes and match them to the population of diatoms existing in a pond where a murder victim was found can help investigators place that suspect at the scene of the crime.

Factors Suggesting a Change in the Victim's Routine

Check telephone calls made to and by the victim. Check dates on mail and newspapers and expiration dates on

Table 8.3 / **Checklist: Entomological Evidence at a Homicide Scene**

Habitat
General—is it woods, a beach, a house, a roadside?
Vegetation—trees, grass, bush, shrubs?
Soil type—rocky, sandy, muddy?
Weather—at time of collection sunny, cloudy?
Temperature and possible humidity at time of collection?
Elevation and map coordinate of the death site?
Is the site in shade or direct sunlight?
Anything unusual, such as the possibility that the body may have been submerged at any time?

Remains
Presence, extent, and type of clothing
Is the body buried or covered? If so, how deep and with what (soil, leaves, cloth)?
What is the cause of death, if known? In particular, is there blood at the scene?
Other body fluids?
Are there any wounds? If so, what kind?
Are drugs likely to be involved? This may affect the decomposition rate.
What position is the body in?
What direction is the body facing?
What is the state of decomposition?
Is a maggot mass present? How many? This will affect the temperature of the body.
What is the temperature of the center of the maggot mass(es)?
Is there any other meat or carrion around that also might attract insects?
Is there a possibility that death did not occur at the present site?

Source: Jennifer Mertens. "It's a Bug Life." *Law Enforcement Technology,* November 2004, p. 63. Reprinted by permission.

food in the refrigerator. Determine who normally provides services to the victim, such as dentists, doctors, barbers, hairdressers, and clerks. Find out whether any appointments were not kept. Were any routines discontinued, such as playing cards or tennis, going to work on schedule, or riding a particular bus? Was there food on the stove or the table? Was the stove on? Were the lights, television, radio, or stereo on or off? Were pets fed? Were dirty dishes on the counters or in the sink? Was this normal for the victim? Was a fire burning in the fireplace? Was the damper left open? The determination of all such facts help to estimate the time of death and can corroborate the estimate based on physical findings.

The Medical Examination

 fter the preliminary investigation, the body is taken to the morgue for an autopsy (Figure 8.6). Most large departments have

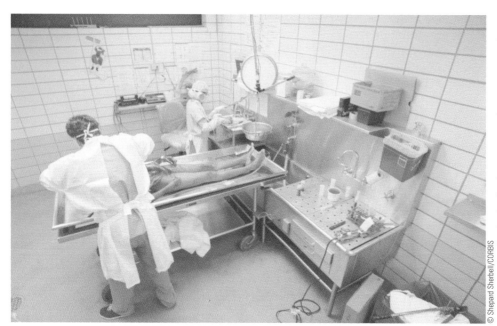

Figure 8.6
A medical examination or an autopsy provides legal evidence related to the cause and time of death and the presence of alcohol or drugs in the system of the deceased. The main job of the coroner's or medical examiner's office is to determine the cause of death. Much of the evidence that leads the examiner to conclude a death was murder also provides corroborating evidence for investigating and prosecuting the case; therefore, pathologists and investigators work together closely. Before an autopsy, the body condition is kept intact and is photographed in this state. In addition to being weighed and measured, the body is periodically photographed as each stage of the examination is completed.

© Shepard Sherbell/CORBIS

medical examiners and forensic pathologists on staff or available as consultants for autopsies. The medical or forensic pathologist assists investigations by relating the evidence to the findings of the autopsy. The study of 800 homicides ("Secrets of Success," p.6) found that the presence of detectives at the postmortem examination nearly doubled the likelihood of a clearance.

The main purpose of the coroner's or medical examiner's office is to determine the cause of death. If no unnatural cause is found, no crime exists. Much of the evidence that leads the examiner to conclude that the death was murder also provides corroborating evidence for investigating and prosecuting the case; therefore, pathologists and investigators work together closely.

Certain types of death must be investigated. These include all violent deaths, whether homicide, suicide, or an accident; sudden deaths not caused by a recognizable disease; deaths under suspicious circumstances, including those of persons whose bodies will be cremated, dissected, buried at sea, or otherwise made unavailable for further examination; deaths (other than from disease) of inmates in prisons or public institutions; deaths due to disease that may constitute a public threat; and deaths due to hazardous employment.

Before an autopsy, the body condition is kept intact. An investigator present at the autopsy records the location, date, time, names of those attending, and the name of the person who performs the autopsy. The body is weighed, measured, and photographed before the autopsy begins and is then periodically photographed as each stage is completed. Facial features and any marks, cuts, wounds, bruises, or unusual conditions are photographed close up. The deceased, including clothing, is completely described. The clothing is tagged,

marked for identification, and sent to the police laboratory for examination. Fingerprints are usually taken, even if the body has been personally identified.

> The medical examination provides evidence related to the cause and time of death and to the presence of drugs or alcohol.

After the autopsy is completed, the cause of death, if determined, is recorded. Deaths not recorded as natural, suicide, or accidental are recorded as either undetermined or homicide. Before making a final determination, the medical examiner reads the police investigation reports to date. These reports indicate prior symptoms such as vomiting, a comatose state, partial paralysis, slow or rapid respiration, convulsions, and various colorations.

During the investigation, report everything relating to the cause of death to the pathologist. Likewise, information discovered by the pathologist is immediately conveyed to the investigative team.

Pennsylvania has passed a law mandating that before any body is cremated, the coroner must approve the cremation. Although an autopsy is not done, the body is examined and X-rays are usually taken. This law is intended to decrease the likelihood of a murder going unnoticed.

Exhuming a Body for Medical Examination

It is not common procedure to exhume a body. Usually this is done to determine whether the cause of death stated on the death certificate is valid. It may also be done if the body is suspected of having been buried to conceal the cause of death or if the identity of the body is in question.

Exhuming a body requires adherence to strict legal procedures to prevent later civil action by relatives. First obtain permission from the principal relatives. If they do not grant it, it is necessary to obtain a court order to proceed. Arrange to have the coroner or medical examiner, a police representative, a gravedigger, a cemetery official, and a family member present at the exhumation. Have the cemetery official or the person who placed the marker identify the grave. Photograph the general area, the specific grave with the marker, and the coffin before exhumation.

Present at the lid opening at the morgue are the coroner, police, family, undertaker, and pathologist. The body is then identified by the persons present if they knew the deceased, and the examination is conducted.

Unnatural Causes of Death and Method Used

As just discussed, in all cases of violent death, industrial/accidental death, or suicide, the medical examiner determines the cause of death. A number of deaths involve circumstances that are investigated by police and the medical examiner, even though many are not criminal homicides.

> Among the most common causes of unnatural death are gunshot wounds; stabbing and cutting wounds; blows from blunt objects; asphyxia induced by choking, drowning, hanging, smothering, strangulation, gases, or poisons; poisoning and drug overdose; burning; explosions, electrocution, and lightning; drug-related deaths; and vehicular deaths.

Table 8.4 indicates the probability of a specific cause of death being the result of an accident, suicide, or homicide.

Gunshot Wounds

Most deaths due to gunshot wounds result from discharges of handguns, rifles, or shotguns. Knowing the type of weapon is important for making comparison tests and locating unknown weapons. The major cause of death from gunshot wounds is internal hemorrhaging and shock. The size, number, and velocity of the ammunition used and the type of weapon determine the effect on the body.

Shots fired from a distance produce little or no powder tattooing or carbons on the skin around where the bullet entered the body, and it is difficult to determine

Table 8.4 / **Cause of Death and the Likelihood It Resulted from Accident, Suicide, or Homicide**

Cause of Death	Accident	Suicide	Homicide
Gunshot wound	*	*	*
Stabbing and cutting wounds	Rare	*	*
Blow from blunt object			
Fall	*	*	*
Hit-and-run vehicle			*
Asphyxia			
Choking	*		
Drowning	*	*	*
Hanging	Autoerotic	*	Rare
Smothering	*		Rare
Strangulation	Autoerotic	Rare	*
Poisoning and overdose	*	*	*
Burning	*		
Explosion	*		
Electric shock	*	Rare	
Lightning	*		

the exact distance—even though the angle of trajectory can be determined from the bullet's path through the body. In the middle-distance range, tattooing appears on the clothing or the body when handguns are fired from up to approximately two feet away (Figure 8.7). Powder tattooing results from both burned and unburned powder. By using test-firing pattern comparisons with the same weapon and ammunition, the actual firing distance can be determined. GSR evidence was discussed in Chapter 5.

If the muzzle of the weapon was in direct contact with the body, contact wounds will be evident. You may notice a muzzle impression on the skin and soot or powder fragments in the entrance area or around the wound. At the entry point, the hole is smaller than the bullet because the skin's elasticity closes the entry point slightly. Entrance wounds are normally round or oval with little bleeding. As the bullet passes through the skin, it leaves a gray to black abrasion collar around the edges of the entrance wound.

The exit wound is usually larger than the entrance wound, but this is not always the case. The exit wound also bleeds more profusely and has no abrasion collar. It is typically larger because gases build up in the body, especially from shots at close range, and tissues bunch up ahead of the bullet until reaching the outer skin. Elasticity then forces the skin outward until it breaks, permitting the bullet and the gases to pass through. The exit wound is generally jagged and torn. The difference between entrance and exit wounds is observable.

Shotgun wounds are distinctly different because numerous pellets penetrate the body. At close range these leave a much larger hole than does a bullet, and at farther range they produce a discernible pellet pattern. Both the entrance and exit wounds are larger than those produced by single bullets.

Shotgun-wound patterns and the appearance of entrance and exit wounds from handguns and rifles help determine the distance from which the gun was fired. Contact wounds (fired at point-blank range) cause a large entrance wound with smudging around the edges. The principal damage is due to the blasting and flame of the powder. Smudging around a wound can be wiped off, but the tattooing pattern cannot be eliminated. If the gun is more than 18 inches from the body when fired, no tattooing or smudging occurs.

In addition, a bullet or pellets from any weapon produce a track through the body that follows the angle between the weapon and the victim at the time of firing. The bullet's path or angle helps to determine the angle at which the weapon was fired and therefore the suspect's possible location at the time of firing. This angle also helps differentiate between suicide and murder.

When investigating gunshot deaths, determine whether the death was due to the wound or to some other injury. Was the wound impossible for the victim to have produced? What is the approximate distance from which the weapon was fired? Were there one or more wounds? Examine the victim's hands to determine whether he or she fired the gun. What was the position of the body when found?

Gunshot wounds

Suicide indicators:

- **Gun held against skin**
- **Wound in mouth or in right temple if victim is right-handed and left temple if left-handed**
- **Not shot through clothing, unless shot in the chest**
- **Weapon present, especially if tightly held in hand**

Murder indicators:

- **Gun fired from more than a few inches away**
- **Angle or location that rules out self-infliction**
- **Shot through clothing**
- **No weapon present**

Stabbing and Cutting Wounds

Stabbing and cutting wounds differ in shape, size, and extent of external and internal bleeding. A knife is the most frequently used weapon. The weapon and wound can be different sizes, depending on the depth and severity of the wound and whether it is into or across the tissues and fibers.

Stab Wounds Stab wounds are caused by thrusting actions. They vary in size in different areas of the body but are usually smaller than cutting wounds. A stab

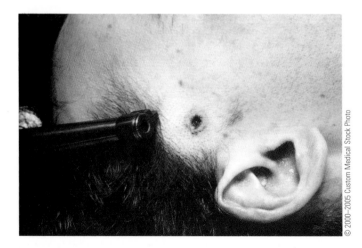

Figure 8.7
The muzzle impression on the skin around the gunshot wound indicates the weapon was held in direct contact with the body. Gun powder residue on the victim's hand may support suicide, as would a wound occurring on the same side of the head as the victim's handedness (i.e., a right-handed victim would usually hold a gun to the right side of his or her own head).

© 2000–2005 Custom Medical Stock Photo

wound in a soft part of the body produces a larger hole than one in the head or a bony area. Ice-pick wounds in a skull covered by a substantial amount of hair can easily be missed on initial examination.

The major damage in stab wounds is to internal tissues, followed by bleeding, primarily internal. The extent and rapidity of internal bleeding depends on the size of the blood vessels affected. In most cases, the cause of death is bleeding rather than damage to a vital organ. A stab wound can be deeper than the length of the weapon used because the force of the thrust on the softer tissues can compress the body's surface inward.

Even if a weapon is found, it can rarely be designated as the murder weapon unless part of it separates and remains in the body or it contains blood, tissue, and fibers from the deceased.

Most stabbing deaths are murders. In murders, stab wounds can be single or multiple and can be in several areas of the body if the victim attempted self-defense. **Defense wounds**—cuts on the hands, arms, and legs—result when the victim attempts to ward off the attacker.

Cutting Wounds   With cutting wounds, external bleeding is generally the cause of death. Cutting wounds are frequently the result of suicide. It is common in such cases to observe **hesitation wounds** in areas where the main wound occurs. These less severe cutting marks are caused by attempts to build up courage to make the fatal wound.

Suicidal cutting wounds are made at an angle related to the hand that held the weapon, generally in a downward direction because of the natural pull of the arm as it is brought across the body.

Stabbing and cutting wounds
Suicide indicators:
- **Hesitation wounds**
- **Wounds under clothing**
- **Weapon present, especially if tightly clutched**
- **Usually wounds at throat, wrists, or ankles**
- **Seldom disfigurement**
- **Body not moved**

Murder indicators:
- **Defense wounds**
- **Wounds through clothing**
- **No weapon present**
- **Usually injuries to vital organs**
- **Disfigurement**
- **Body moved**

Blows from Blunt Objects

Fatal injuries can result from hands and feet and blows with various blunt objects, including hammers, clubs, heavy objects, and rocks. It is often impossible to determine the specific type of weapon involved. The injuries can occur to any part of the body and can result in visible external bruises. The size of the bruise may not correspond to the size of the weapon because blood escapes into a larger area. Severe bruises are not often found in suicides.

In battered-child investigations, it has been found that death rarely results from a single blow or a single series of blows but rather from physical abuse over an extended period. An autopsy reveals prior broken bones or injuries. Death may also have been caused by starvation or other forms of neglect.

Falls can cause death or can be used to conceal the real cause of death. In some cases the victim is taken to a staircase and pushed down after being severely beaten. Intoxication is often given as the reason for the fall, but this can easily be checked through blood tests.

Asphyxia

Asphyxiation results when the body tissues and the brain receive insufficient oxygen to support the red blood cells. An examination of blood cells shows this lack of oxygen. Discoloration occurs in all dead bodies, but in asphyxia deaths, it is usually more pronounced and varied due to the lack of oxygen—especially in the blood vessels closest to the skin surface. It is most noticeable as a blue or purple color around the lips, fingernails, and toenails. Although you need not know the varied coloration produced by different causes and chemicals, be certain to record precise descriptions of coloration that can be interpreted by the medical examiner and related to probable cause of death.

Asphyxia deaths result from many causes, including choking, drowning, smothering, hanging, strangulation, swallowing of certain chemicals, poisoning, and overdosing on sleeping pills. Asphyxiation may also result from certain types of autoerotic behavior.

Choking   Foreign bodies in the throat cause choking, as do burial in grain or sand slides or rapid pneumonia in infants in cribs. Such deaths are almost always accidental.

Drowning   The majority of drownings are accidental. Murder is rarely proven unless witnesses are present. If a dead body is placed in water to make it appear as though death was caused by drowning, a medical examination can determine whether the person was dead when immersed. As Dr. Henry Lee, renowned forensic scientist, explains: "If accidental or suicide, diatoms and algae material would be found in lungs; breathing would suck them into the trachea and lungs. In an instance of homicide, diatoms or algae may be found on the mouth or lips but not in the lungs" (Trent, p.93). However, if the victim was killed by drowning, these organisms would be sucked into the lungs as the person struggled to escape and surface, similar to what happens to someone who accidentally drowns.

Smothering Smothering is an uncommon means of murder, despite many fictional depictions of this method. Intoxicated persons, the elderly, and infants are most likely to be victims of smothering, usually by the hands or a pillow. Often, however, such deaths are accidental. For example, an infant weak from disease may turn over, face downward, or become tangled in bedclothes and accidentally suffocate.

Hanging Hangings are normally suicides, but murders have been made to appear as hanging suicides. Some hangings result from experimentation to achieve sexual satisfaction, as discussed later. In suicides the pressure on the neck is usually generated by standing on a chair or stool and kicking the support away, jumping off, or simply letting the body hang against the noose. (A body need not be completely suspended to result in death by hanging.) Although it is commonly thought that death results from a broken neck, it is usually the result of a broken trachea or a complete constriction of the air supply.

In hangings the ligature marks start from the area of the neck below the chin and travel upward to the point just below the ears. Observe the condition and angle of these marks and save the entire rope, including the knot, as evidence.

Strangulation Strangulation by rope, hands, wire, or scarf produces the same effect as hanging. In both, the cause of death is total constriction of air. In contrast to hangings, however, the ligature marks caused by strangulation are normally evenly grooved and are horizontal around the neck. In cases of manual strangulation, marks often remain from the hand pressure.

In asphyxiation deaths, most cases of choking, drowning, and smothering are accidental; most cases of hanging are suicides; most cases of strangulation are murder.

Poisons, Chemicals, and Overdoses of Sleeping Pills
Asphyxiating chemicals, including ammonia and chloroform, can cause irritation severe enough to totally constrict the breathing passages. Ingestion of certain chemicals and drugs can also cause constriction and blockage of the airways. Examination of the air passages indicates paralysis.

Asphyxiation can occur by breathing carbon monoxide (CO), a method chosen by some to commit suicide. Accidental carbon monoxide poisoning can occur from improperly installed or malfunctioning gas appliances, such as furnaces, water heaters, and clothes dryers. Using charcoal grills indoors or burning wood in an improperly vented fireplace can also lead to CO poisoning.

Autoerotic Asphyxiation In autoerotic asphyxiation, the victim has sought to intensify sexual gratification by placing a rope or other ligature around the neck and causing just enough constriction to create *hypoxia,* or a deficiency of oxygen in the bloodstream that results in semiconsciousness. Such experimentation may be successful a number of times, but then results in total unconsciousness rather than semiconsciousness. In such a case, the body goes limp in the noose, and the weight of the body causes the noose to tighten, causing death. Although not common, autoerotic asphyxiation should be recognized by police officers. In these instances suicides are in fact tragic accidents that occurred during dangerous autoerotic acts. Such deaths are classified into three categories: suffocation, strangulation, and chemical asphyxia—the most common of which is strangulation resulting from suspension of the body. In such cases the body is usually touching the ground and the victim is often bound. Analysis will show, however, that the binding could have been done by the victim.

Indicators of accidental death during autoerotic practices include:

- Nude or sexually exposed victim
- Evidence of solo sexual activity
- Mirrors placed to observe the ritual
- Evidence of masturbation and presence of such items as tissues or towels for cleanup
- Presence of sexual fantasy aids or sexually stimulating paraphernalia (vibrators, dildos, sex aids, and pornographic magazines)
- Presence of bondage

In addition to asphyxiation, there are other types of autoerotic fatalities of which investigators should be aware.

Other Types of Autoerotic Death

There is limited clinical or forensic information about other autoerotic fatalities, but there are several documented cases where an act of risky solitary sexual behavior went further than anticipated, leading to accidental death. Such fatalities have involved electrocution, crushing, sepsis following perforation of the bowel, and accidental self-impalement. Investigators should look for similar types of indicators as described under "Autoerotic Asphyxiation" above.

Noting that such accidental fatalities can easily be misinterpreted as suicide, Cooley (2005), an assistant federal public defender with the capital habeas unit for the District of Nevada in Las Vegas, presents some features of an autoerotic death scene that will help investigators correctly diagnose these cases:

- Presence of a failed self-rescue mechanism
- No evidence of suicidal ideation (no suicide note, no history of depression, etc.)
- Activity performed in a secluded location
- Evidence of repetitive behavior, such as old ligature marks/bruises, use of worn ropes, etc.

According to Cooley: "If it cannot be determined that the death scene location afforded the victim a reasonable expectation of privacy, then investigators should question the true motive behind the death. Meaning, was this a true autoerotic accident or was this a suicide staged as an autoerotic death. Discovering no evidence of previous high-risk behavior should also force investigators to question the motive for death. No evidence of previous behavior may provide more support for either homicide or suicide."

Poisoning

Poisoning, one of the oldest methods of murder, can occur from an overwhelming dose that causes immediate death or from small doses that accumulate over time and cause death. Poisons can be injected into the blood or muscles, inhaled as gases, absorbed through the skin surface, taken in foods or liquids, or inserted into the rectum or vagina. Experts in **toxicology** (the study of poisons) can determine the type of poison, the amount ingested, the approximate time ingested, and the effect on the body.

If a child is poisoned by accidentally ingesting cleaning fluid, detergents, pills, or other such substances, the parents are sometimes charged with manslaughter or negligent homicide. In one case, an 8-month-old baby boy had stopped breathing and was transported to the local hospital, where he died. The case was initially presumed to be one of SIDS, but the autopsy showed that the child had a blood ethanol level of 0.12. Further investigation revealed that the father had given his son a lethal dose of peppermint schnapps. The father was arrested and charged with negligent homicide for the alcohol poisoning of his child (Westveer et al., p.5).

An overdose death is not necessarily a suicide. It might have been accidental—a result of the person's not knowing when medication was last taken or being in a semistupor and taking more pills than intended. If a prescription bottle is found, determine from family members how many pills were in the bottle before the death. Check with the issuing pharmacist to determine whether it was a legal prescription, how many pills were prescribed, and the date the prescription was last filled. Preserve all evidence until the coroner's office rules the death accidental or a suicide. Other important evidence includes the contents of the medicine cabinet, any excretions or vomit at the scene, and any food the victim recently ate.

Westveer et al. (p.3) state: "The effective investigation of homicides generally, and poisoning cases in particular, often depends upon a number of factors, including such basic investigative data as victim demographics, possible offender characteristics, geographic and temporal features of the case, and any particular incident attributes that may assist law enforcement." These researchers (p.7) note that while documented poisoning cases remain relatively rare compared with other types of homicides, the number could actually be somewhat higher due to a lack of understanding on the part of investigators regarding what to look for in these types of cases—"more of these types of homicides remained undetected because of the many holes in the investigative net through which the homicidal poisoner can slip." Westveer et al. (p.7) conclude that more research into homicidal poisoning is needed, particularly as it relates to identifying killers who use this method: "Understanding some of the attributes of homicidal poisoners may enhance the ability of the law enforcement and forensic communities when they are called upon to assist in the prevention and investigation of homicides."

Burning

Most deaths by burning are accidental. However, a death resulting from burns received in a fire caused by arson is classified as murder. Moreover, people sometimes try to disguise murder by burning the victim's body. Even in the most destructive fires, however, considerable information is available from an autopsy, because bones are not easily burned. Even in extreme heat, enough blood usually remains to enable a carbon monoxide analysis to determine whether the victim was alive at the time of the fire. However, in extremely hot fires the heat may cause the skin to break open on the surface, and the resulting wounds may appear to be knife or other wounds inflicted by an assailant prior to the fire.

Explosions, Electrocution, and Lightning

Death due to explosives can result from the direct tearing force of the blast, from a shock wave, or from the victim being blown off the top of a structure or against an object with enough force to cause death. Such deaths are usually accidental.

Electrocution paralyzes the heart muscle, causing rapid death. Nearly all electrocution deaths are accidental (except, of course, in capital punishment cases). High-voltage lines and lightning are the main causes. Lightning leaves linear stripes on the body, turns the skin blue, and burns the skin, especially at the lightning bolt's entry and exit points.

Poisoning deaths can be accidental, suicide, or murder. Most deaths caused by burning, explosions, electrocution, and lightning are accidental, although burning is sometimes used in an attempt to disguise murder.

Drug-Related Deaths

Many studies have documented the relationship between drugs and homicide and the prominent role drugs play in homicide events (Varano et al., p.372). The same techniques used in general death investigations also apply to drug-related death investigations. Look for evidence of alcohol use and/or consumption of drugs (pill bottles or paraphernalia). Alcohol mixed with certain drugs can pose a particularly lethal combination. Keep in mind that prescription drugs are the leading cause of drug-related deaths in the United States.

Different categories of drug-related homicides include deadly disputes involving individuals high on drugs (no organized drug/gang affiliation); deaths caused during the commission of economically motivated crimes, such as robbery, in the offender's effort to get money to buy drugs; and murders associated with the systemic violence surrounding the drug business itself. This third category includes hits on traffickers, dealers, or buyers (may be gang related); assassinations of law enforcement officers or others fighting drug trafficking; and the killing of innocent bystanders in drug-related disputes. Each category presents specific investigative options, summarized in Table 8.5.

According to Varano et al. (p.372): "Drug motivation or the presence of drugs not only are the prevalent characteristics of homicide events but also have implications for understanding certain features of homicide events." One such feature involves the victim-offender relationship (VOR) and requires an understanding of the difference between *expressive* and *instrumental* violence.

Expressive violence is that stemming from hurt feelings, anger, or rage, such as when the jealous lover stabs her ex-boyfriend while he's on a date with his new girlfriend. In these cases, the VOR is close and established. **Instrumental violence** is goal-directed predatory behavior used to exert control—for example, the carjacker who shoots his victim before stealing the vehicle. The VOR in events involving instrumental violence may or may not be close, with such events commonly occurring between strangers who have no preestablished relationship.

A prevalent theory regarding VOR and risk of instrumental vs. expressive violence is that a close relationship (spouse/lover, family member, close personal friend) may protect a person from certain types of instrumental violence (e.g., robbery) because they have someone to watch out for them, but it may also make them more vulnerable to expressive violence. Indeed, as

Table 8.5 / Drug-Related Homicides and Investigative Options

Category	Investigative Options
Drug hits	Intelligence information
	Narcotics buy operation
	Buy and bust operation
	Informant information
Interpersonal drug disputes	Buy and bust operation
	Informant information
	Narcotics buy operation
Murder of innocent bystanders	Reward money
	Crime Stoppers program
	Use of news media
	Community activists
	Buy and bust operation
	Informant information
Drug assassinations	Intelligence operations
	Electronic eavesdropping
	Narcotics buy operations
	Reward money
	Crime Stoppers program
	Use of news media

Source: Vernon J. Geberth. "Investigation of Drug-Related Homicides." *Law and Order,* November 1990, p. 76. Reprinted by permission.

Varano et al. (p.386) acknowledge, results of numerous studies support this theory. However, from their study on the drugs/homicide connection, Varano et al. (pp.386–387) found:

> Homicide events involving friends were nearly 23 times more likely to be drug-motivated events compared to those involving strangers. This finding runs counter to what was hypothesized, namely, that events involving strangers would be more likely to involve drug circumstances. The nature of the VOR is an indicator of regularity and type of interaction between individuals. Relationships characterized by closer social distances (e.g., family and friends) often involve more frequent interactions. . . .
>
> Drugs have diminished the protective features of VOR and exposed individuals to types and degrees of violence not previously thought to be common.

The investigator who is aware of such findings, which seem to run counter to conventional thinking, will have a better chance at solving a drug-connected homicide.

Drug trafficking operations commonly cross jurisdictional boundaries, a factor that severely impedes the progress of an investigator working a drug trafficking murder. To better address this challenge, some areas have developed a Violent Traffickers Task Force (VTTF). Describing the effort in St. Louis, Missouri, Renton and Mokwa (pp.32–33) state: "The new VTTF initiated investigations targeting longstanding, well-entrenched criminal drug organizations that sustained themselves through violence to protect their identification and suppress the willingness of law-abiding citizens to assist law enforcement agencies. . . . Since the task force inception, the murder rate in the city of Saint Louis has declined by 38 percent. Although VTTF is not solely responsible for Saint Louis's drastic decline in violent crime, it has greatly contributed to the public safety." Investigating drug offenses is discussed in greater detail in Chapter 19.

Vehicular Deaths

The National Highway Traffic Safety Administration ("The Facts") proclaims: "The only difference between a vehicular homicide and other homicides is the use of a motor vehicle as a weapon, as opposed to a gun or knife." Vehicular homicide can result from reckless driving, driving under the influence, or other circumstances where a driver's failure to obey the rules of the road, either intentionally or negligently, leads to the death of another person. Aggressive driving and road rage can escalate to a case of vehicular homicide.

When a traffic crash results in a fatality, all vehicles involved must be thoroughly examined. Document the condition of the vehicles through photographs and written observations. Also of extreme importance are weather and road conditions at the time of the incident. An accident reconstruction expert must be brought in to help the investigator make sense of skid marks, impact dynamics, and other factors present at the scene.

If the driver or drivers are still at the scene, obtain evidence for a toxicology examination to determine whether there were any drugs in the person's system at the time of the incident. Toxicology evidence is also necessary for the victim, even if that person wasn't driving a car, as his or her condition prior to the incident may have played a role. For example, Shankar (p.5) reports that of all pedestrians killed in traffic crashes in 2001, "33 percent were intoxicated, with blood alcohol concentration (BAC) of 0.08 grams per deciliter (g/dL) or greater."

If the case is one of hit-and-run, physical evidence left at the scene, such as paint, metal shavings, tire impressions, and glass, can help link a suspect and a vehicle to the crime. Evidence to look for on the suspect's vehicle include hairs, fibers, blood, and other biological fluids from the victim. The vehicle may contain evidence of the impact. Evidence of fresh paint jobs or recent repairs warrant further investigation.

The Homicide Victim

In most crimes the victim provides verbal details of what occurred. In homicides the victim may be able to provide such information if witnesses or the police are present before death occurs. However, the information usually comes from the crime scene, witnesses, physical and circumstantial evidence, and the suspect.

Victims often know the person who killed them, so information about the deceased can furnish leads to the suspect. Obtain the victim's name, address, age, sex, nationality, and type and place of work. Also find out the names of family members, close friends, and known enemies and learn about the victim's habits. Ask about any religious, political, or business actions or remarks that might have enraged someone. Take the victim's fingerprints and determine whether any criminal history may lead to a suspect.

Interview personal contacts such as doctors, pastors, or counselors to learn about the victim's physical and emotional condition, especially if it has not yet been determined whether the death was an accident, suicide, or homicide. The person's medical background may provide information about an extremely painful or terminal disease that could motivate suicide. Inquire about the victim's mental stability. Most suicide victims attempt to avoid inflicting severe pain on themselves when they take their lives, but this is not always true. One woman cut off both her feet before fatally stabbing herself in the chest. Some people set themselves on fire to commit suicide.

> The victim's background provides information about whether the death was an accident, suicide, or homicide. If a homicide, the background often provides leads to a suspect. Evidence on the victim's body can also provide important leads.

In violent murders the victim may grab the suspect's hair, shirt buttons, or other parts of clothing or scratch and claw the suspect. A victim may leave injuries on the suspect, and traces of the suspect's flesh may be found under the victim's fingernails. Identify and preserve all belongings and evidence on or near the deceased. Carefully examine the location where the body was found if it is not where death occurred.

After the entire scene and the evidence have been photographed and sketched, move the body carefully. Lift it a few inches off the surface and slide a sheet under it to catch any evidence that may fall while transporting the body to the vehicle. Itemize other possessions and send them along with the body to the morgue for later release to the family if they are not evidence.

Although you may use a body bag, first wrap the body in a clean, white sheet. Evidence on the body that falls off is much easier to see on a sheet. The sheet also absorbs moisture.

Domestic-Violence Homicide

Many batterers eventually kill their intimate (one out of six murders is a partner homicide), and women who leave their batterers face a 75 percent greater risk of being killed by them than do those who stay. In some cases batterers themselves become victims of homicide.

Many of these murders occurred despite restraining orders on the intimate partner. In addition, four out of five murders by females are reported to be responses to domestic violence.

Law Enforcement Officers Killed

The risk of being killed in the line of duty "comes with the job." Although fewer than half of the officers killed on the job are gunned down or otherwise murdered, being shot and killed in the line of duty is still considered a very real risk of police work.

More than 230 police officers were killed in the line of duty in 2001, including 70 officers who died at the World Trade Center on September 11. FBI statistics (*Law Enforcement Officers*, p.5) indicate that 52 law enforcement officers were feloniously killed during 2003. The average age of these officers was 38, and these victim-officers averaged 10 years of law enforcement experience. Of the 52 slain officers, 50 were male. Fourteen officers were killed during traffic stops or pursuits, 11 were murdered in arrest situations, 10 died while investigating disturbance calls; 9 were slain in ambush situations; 6 were killed while investigating suspicious persons or circumstances; and 2 died while transporting or handling prisoners. The data (p.6) also show that the majority of slain officers were killed with a firearm: 34 with handguns, 10 with rifles, and 1 with a shotgun. Eleven of these officers were shot with their own

weapons. Six other officers were intentionally struck by vehicles and one officer was beaten to death with a police baton. Of the 45 officers killed with a firearm, 31 were wearing body armor—one officer received a fatal wound below the waist; the others died from wounds to the upper torso or head.

Witnesses

In violent criminal deaths, struggles often create noise and attract the attention of neighbors or passersby. Witnesses may know and name a suspect, or they may have seen the suspect or vehicle. Often, however, there are no witnesses, and information must be sought from family members, neighbors, and associates. Conducting a neighborhood canvass is a critical step in a thorough homicide investigation.

St. Louis police have set up a homicide hotline with an untraceable number that murder witnesses can call to offer anonymous tips. The hotline is answered by a message machine and requires no staffing to implement. Figure 8.8 shows the card distributed to bystanders at homicide scenes.

Suspects

If the suspect is arrested at the crime scene, follow the procedures described in Chapter 1. If the suspect is known but is not at the scene, immediately disseminate the description to other investigators, field officers, and police agencies.

If the suspect is not known, identification becomes a priority. Often several suspects are identified and eventually eliminated as information and evidence are

---

"STOP THE KILLING"

If you have information regarding this or any homicide investigation, contact the

HOMICIDE HOTLINE
444-5830

*THE HOTLINE IS CONFIDENTIAL AND NONTRACEABLE
St. Louis Metropolitan Police Department

Figure 8.8
Homicide Hotline card handed out to bystanders at St. Louis murder scenes
Source: Courtesy of the St. Louis Police Department.

obtained and the list is reduced to one or two prime suspects. In major cases any number of suspects may be developed from information at the scene, from informants, and from intelligence files.

Discovering a motive is not a specific requirement in the investigation, but motive is so closely tied to intent and to developing a suspect that it should be determined. Murders are committed for many reasons. Common types of criminal homicide include the anger killing, the love-triangle killing, the revenge or jealousy killing, killing for profit, random killing, murder-suicide, the sex-and-sadism killing, and felony murder. Anger killings often begin as assaults. The possibility of killing for profit almost always exists. Thus it is always critical to determine who would stand to profit from the victim's death.

Determine the motive for a killing, because it provides leads to suspects and strong circumstantial evidence against a suspect.

Some murders are contracted or hired. This is frequently the case in murders of organized crime figures.

Mass Murderers

A **mass murder** occurs when multiple victims are killed in a single incident by one or a few suspects. Recent years have seen several highly publicized cases of mass familicides, particularly parents killing their children—the Fresno, California, man who murdered nine of his children; the Texas mom who methodically drowned her five kids. Without a doubt, the terrorist attacks of September 11, 2001, were the most horrific mass murder events ever witnessed by contemporary Americans in their homeland.

Felony-related mass murder, such as the killing of eyewitnesses during a robbery or a group of participants at a drug buy, has increased over the last part of the 20th century. Duwe (p.754) reports: "The surge in felony-related massacres since the 1960s has had an impact on the overall patterns of mass murder. For example, over the last several decades, mass murderers have become younger and less suicidal." Duwe also notes a modest increase in mass murders involving strangers and multiple offenders during the past 30 years.

The well-publicized episodes of school shootings and attacks at the workplace, in which a lone gunman or pair of gunmen opened fire on students, coworkers, or others within a building or institution, are other examples. Frequently these killers unleash their murderous fury on total strangers. School shootings resulting in multiple deaths have occurred throughout the United States, as shown in Table 8.6.

It is important to realize that school violence almost never occurs without warning, with most school shooters dropping hints about their intentions. Wen (2004) notes:

"Researchers say the discovery that teenage killers tend to scheme over time and spill secrets can be used to the advantage of educators and police if they stay in touch with students."

Workplace violence may also result in multiple murders. As Hess and Wrobleski (p.245) note: "The perpetrators are frequently loners with poor social skills, often obsessed with violence and weapons. The targets include authority figures and peers who are in conflict with them. The perpetrators often bring an arsenal of weapons and kill all who get in their way." As with school shootings, workplace violence may sometimes be anticipated by noting personality changes in the potential shooter as well as the occurrence of certain precipitating events, such as a missed promotion or a termination. Other triggers include divorce and severe financial troubles.

Similarities between school and workplace murders include the perpetrators' profiles, the targets, the means, and the motivation.

In many of these cases the killers take their own lives at the end of the shooting rampage, leaving investigators to wonder about possible motives. Research by Duwe (p.733) found that 21 percent of mass murderers committed suicide, 2 percent attempted suicide, and 3 percent were fatally shot by police. Duwe (p.754) hypothesizes that those who commit felony-related massacres, where the violence is more instrumental in nature than expressive, are much less likely to engage in suicidal behavior, perhaps as a consequence of the relative lack of emotion involved in the killings. In other cases the shooters are easily identified and apprehended, are sometimes quite boastful about what they have just "accomplished," and are eager to provide authorities with their motives.

Another type of murder suspect who also kills multiple victims is the serial killer.

Serial Killers

Serial murder is the killing of three or more separate victims, with a "cooling off" period between the killings. A number of serial killers in the United States have received national attention: Henry Lucas, who confessed to 188 murders in 24 states; Gary Ridgway, the Green River strangler, 48 murders over two decades; Theodore (Ted) Bundy, 40 murders; John Wayne Gacey, 33 murders; Jeffrey Dahmer, 16 murders; David Berkowitz, the "Son of Sam," 6 murders (he blinded one person, paralyzed another, and wounded 7 others); and Aileen Wuornos, 7 murders. In 1997, Andrew Cunanan went on a cross-country murder spree of five men that culminated in the slaying of fashion designer Gianni Versace on the front steps of his Miami mansion and the suicide of Cunanan a week later. The Washington, D.C., "Beltway snipers," John Allen Muhammad and Lee

Table 8.6 / **Summary of School Shootings in the United States, 1996–2005**

Date	Location and Estimated Population	Number Killed	Number Wounded	Shooter(s)
February 2, 1996	Moses Lake, WA (16,300)	2 students, 1 teacher	1	Barry Loukaitis, 14
February 19, 1997	Bethel, AK (6,500)	1 student, principal	2	Evan Ramsey, 16
October 1, 1997	Pearl, MS (23,600)	2 students	7	Luke Woodham, 16
December 1, 1997	West Paducah, KY (25,800)	3 students	5	Michael Carneal, 14
December 15, 1997	Stamps, AR (2,400)	0	2	Colt Todd, 14
March 24, 1998	Jonesboro, AR (52,500)	4 students, 1 teacher	10	Mitchell Johnson, 13; Andrew Golden, 11
April 24, 1998	Edinboro, PA (6,800)	1 teacher	2	Andrew Wurst, 14
May 19, 1998	Fayetteville, TN (7,500)	1 student	0	Jacob Davis, 18
May 21, 1998	Springfield, OR (50,700)	2 students	22	Kip Kinkel, 15
June 15, 1998	Richmond, VA (199,300)	0	2	Male, 14
April 20, 1999	Littleton, CO (41,300)	14 students (including 2 shooters), 1 teacher	23	Eric Harris, 18; Dylan Klebold, 17
May 20, 1999	Conyers, GA (8,500)	0	6	Thomas Solomon, 15
November 19, 1999	Deming, NM (14,900)	1 student	0	Victor Cordova Jr., 12
December 6, 1999	Fort Gibson, OK (3,800)	0	4	Seth Trickey, 13
February 29, 2000	Mt. Morris, MI (3,100)	1 (6-year-old)	0	Male, 6
May 26, 2000	Lake Worth, FL (29,000)	1 teacher	0	Nathaniel Brazil, 13
March 5, 2001	Santee, CA (53,900)	2 students	13	Charles Andrew Williams, 15
March 7, 2001	Williamsport, PA (29,900)	0	1	Elizabeth Catherine Bush, 14
March 22, 2001	El Cajon, CA (90,200)	0	5	Jason Hoffman, 18
March 23, 2005	Red Lake Indian Reservation, MN	10 (including 5 students, 1 teacher, 1 security guard, and the shooter)	7	Jeffrey Weise, 16

*Population data from the U.S. Bureau of the Census.

Source: Updated from Henry M. Wrobleski and Kären M. Hess. *Police Operations: Theory and Practice,* 4th ed. Belmont, CA: Wadsworth Publishing Company, 2006, p. 235.

Boyd Malvo, terrorized the nation, particularly citizens along the Northeast coast, with their 21-day random shooting rampage that left 10 people dead and 3 wounded. And Dennis Rader was sentenced in August 2005 to 10 consecutive life terms for the 10 killings he confessed to as the BTK (Bind, Torture, Kill) serial killer.

Investigating a murder committed by a serial killer may initially seem the same as investigating any other murder. As a case is investigated, however, and if no suspect can be developed, the investigator should consider reporting the crime to the FBI's National Center for the Analysis of Violent Crime (NCAVC) at Quantico, Virginia. NCAVC provides a profiling program as well as research and development, training, and the Violent Criminal Apprehension Program (VICAP). Police departments investigating cases that they believe involve serial murder can submit their cases to VICAP. Other cases with similar modus operandi submitted by other agen-

cies are then compared, and information is furnished to the submitting agencies. As the Henry Lucas cases illustrate—where murders were committed in 24 states—VICAP is an important resource in investigating and prosecuting this type of killer. If VICAP determines that a serial murderer is probably involved, a multijurisdictional Major Crime Investigation Team may be assembled to handle the case.

In some cases, where media coverage leads to an avalanche of citizen tips to authorities, investigators find themselves overwhelmed by the flood of potentially useful, but more often useless, information.

Because of improved information sharing, interjurisdictional communication, and media coverage, some homicide investigations that begin as single-incident investigations may now have the potential to develop into serial killing investigations. For example, Donald Blom, who confessed to abducting and murdering

Technology Innovations

Computer software is available to help investigators effectively handle an onslaught of tips. Wexler (2003, p.22) describes a relatively new tracking software application called Voyager Query that was used by the Beltway snipers task force to quickly check background information on suspicious individuals, at any time, from any location. The handheld device was also used to track down addresses and phone numbers and for recording information gathered during field interviews.

19-year-old Katie Poirier in Minnesota, is now a possible suspect in several other unsolved disappearances and murders around the state and in neighboring states. Carey Staner, a handyman suspected of the murder of a national park tourist, is suspected of three other killings. Authorities speculate that if Staner's last victim had not put up such a struggle, leaving behind a small but invaluable collection of physical evidence, Staner's first three victims—and potentially more in the future—may have forever remained untraceable and unconnected to him.

DNA evidence obtained in any homicide can provide valuable leads for investigators, and the importance of such evidence is magnified greatly in serial killings, even if investigators are at first unaware of any links to other crimes. For example, the head of the task force created to catch the Baton Rouge serial killer recalls how crucial DNA was to solving the case: "If you look at the first two homicides, there were very few similarities. [One victim was strangled, the other stabbed to death.] I've been a cop for 30 years and without DNA, I'd probably still be scratching my head trying to figure out if those two murders were committed by the same guy" (Hustmyre, p.100).

Police officers who understand the psychology underlying serial killings will be more effective in investigating the murders and in interviewing the murderers. Whereas motivational factors for other types of homicide may be simply financial gain, revenge, or jealousy, Brantley and Kosky (p.28) explain: "A serial murderer's motivations are multifaceted and most often reinforced by internal desires for gratification versus external rewards, such as profit or financial gain." In studying a subset of serial killers—health-care-worker serial murderers—Brantley and Kosky (p.30) found motivational factors to include the desire for power, control, excitement, stimulation, attention, recognition, and revenge. Furthermore: "Some serial murderers in health-care facilities and elsewhere have reported that the act of murder relieved tension, stress, and frustration." To lower the risk of detection, many health-care serial killers opt to work the night shift, when there are fewer coworkers present (Brantley and Kosky p.30).

Andreu (p.90), speaking from his experience in working six serial murder cases that collectively involved nearly 50 victims, states: "In nearly all cases, deviant and recurring sexual desires and fantasies are what drive these people to murder multiple victims."

Serial killers generally select strangers as their victims, although by the time the actual murder occurs, they may have become quite familiar with them. According to Andreu (p.92):

> As a serial killer steps away from his base to begin the hunt for human prey, it is almost always true that he knows absolutely nothing about the person who is fated to become his victim. . . .
>
> It may be that having no prior knowledge of a future victim further enables the process of that victim's objectification. The serial killer often views his victims as little more than [objects], depersonalized in advance, existing only for himself and his enjoyment, as to be seized and used as he sees fit.

Dennis Rader, the BTK serial killer, divulged in court how he selected victims as he played out his sexual fantasies. During this self-described "trolling phase," Rader would look for several potential victims, referring to them as "projects," and begin stalking them. Multiple projects were selected so that if one didn't work out, he'd have some backups. Over time, Rader explained, he'd start really honing in on one person he would want to become *the* victim.

The acts of serial killers are typically considered in discussions of homicides, and, indeed, the very term used to describe this group of offenders focuses on the killing part of the crime. However, to the perpetrator, the actual homicide is more of an incidental event. Andreu (p.94) explains:

> The actual commission of the murder itself is usually nothing more than a postscript to a serial killer's overall scheme of violence. The killer's real gratification comes from the subjugation, terrorization and brutalization of his victim, not the murder itself. Once the killer's need to terrorize and abuse is satisfied, his victim is perceived as an object of inconvenience.

Profiles of serial killers show they are extremely selfish and narcissistic. They know right from wrong—they simply do not care, an awareness that distinguishes them from being insane. Brantley and Kosky (pp.29–30) observe: "Serial murderers are mentally abnormal and exhibit traits and characteristics of a variety of mental disorders without reaching the threshold of mental illness necessary for exculpability." They are often quite intelligent and very much in touch with reality, which partially explains their success in eluding capture. According to Andreu (p.90): "A serial killer is among the most alert and cautious of all human beings. Such caution can be explained by the killer's foremost concern—being able to carry out his activities without being caught."

Given these personality traits, bear in mind that when interviewing serial killers, any attempts to evoke sympathy for the victims or surviving relatives will probably be futile. Appeals to their ego, on the other hand, may succeed. It is also important not to display shock at the atrocities that may have been committed, because this is often what serial murderers want.

The acts of serial murderers seem incomprehensible to "normal" people. For example, in 1991 the killing and mutilation of 16 young men and boys by Jeffrey Dahmer made national headlines. When police entered Dahmer's stench-filled apartment, they found body parts of 11 males—painted human skulls, severed heads and body parts in cold storage, and torsos disintegrating in an acid-filled vat. Dahmer's murders can also be classified as lust murders.

Lust Murderers

A **lust murder** is a sex-related homicide involving a sadistic, deviant assault. In lust murder the killer depersonalizes the victim, sexually mutilates the body, and may displace body parts. Two types of lust murderers are often described—organized and disorganized. The *organized offender* is usually of above-average intelligence, methodical, and cunning. He is socially skilled and tricks his victims into situations in which he can torture and then murder them. In contrast, the *disorganized offender* is usually of below-average intelligence, has no car, and is a loner who acts on impulse.

Both the organized and the disorganized offenders usually murder victims from their own geographic area, and the murders involve fantasy, ritual, fetishes, and symbolism. They also both usually leave some sort of physical evidence.

Lethal Predators

A new category has been proposed for a small, identifiable, and extremely dangerous subpopulation of lethal criminals—lethal predators. Brantley and Ochberg (p.18) define **predation** as "an intentional act of selecting, pursuing, and overpowering a person and then inflicting harm on that person for the pleasure of the predator." They (pp.18–19) define a **lethal predator** as possessing *all* four of these elements:

- Lethal violence—has criminally killed in a manner that meets the legal definitions of murder or manslaughter, and at least once in the context of sexual predation

- Multiple acts of sexual predation—has used physical force or the threat of force, on more than one occasion, to coerce another person to submit to sexual behavior or to produce sexual excitement or release in the offender

- Mental abnormality—traits and characteristics consistent with severe personality disorder or para-

philia, based upon traditional mental health assessment techniques

- Legal sanity—able to understand the nature and quality of their acts and to commit them with conscious intent

Brantley and Ochberg (p.18) note that sexual predators escalate their activities over the course of their careers, regardless of whether or not they murder. Likewise: "The lethal predator also will demonstrate increasing skill in selecting, pursuing, capturing, and controlling the victim and carrying out the murder." To emphasize the threat posed by these deranged individuals, Brantley and Ochberg (p.20) recount a case that involved a boy who had been missing for nearly 5 years. The lethal predator, having just been released from a Massachusetts prison after serving only 12 years of his original 18-to-20-year sentence for the attempted murder and kidnapping of two 13-year-old boys, moved across the country to settle in Montana, where he set his sights upon a fifth-grade boy. He eventually kidnapped, raped, and tortured the boy before killing him. Once the boy was dead, the predator dismembered, cooked, and ate the remains. When he was finally discovered and captured (again), police found in his home a stack of photographs and a handwritten list with names and dates, appearing to link him to dozens of other cases of child abduction and molestation in several states.

Cold Cases

Of all violent crimes, homicide has the highest clearance rate. Yet, as the statistics given at the beginning of this chapter attest, nearly 40 percent of all murders go unsolved. At any given time, a large metropolitan jurisdiction may have thousands of cold homicide cases on its shelves. In late 2001, the Los Angeles Police Department had more than 9,000 unsolved killings. As Turner and Kosa (p.1) contend: "Cold cases are among the most difficult and frustrating cases detectives face. These cases are, in effect, cases that other investigators, for whatever reason, could not solve."

Many departments have created cold case squads dedicated to handling these challenging cases. While the mantra for fresh homicide investigations is typically "time is of the essence"—assuming that, if after 72 hours no suspect has been found, the case is unlikely to be solved—cold case squads use the passing of time to their advantage. Different squads use different criteria in deciding which cases to reinvestigate, but in general the presence of well-preserved physical evidence and the ability to identify and locate original witnesses raise the priority level of a case.

Turner and Kosa (p.5) note: "Although forensic analysis and investigative techniques have greatly improved over the years, the resolution of cold cases is primarily rooted in a squad's ability to identify, locate, and secure the testimony and cooperation of witnesses and informants." Over time, witnesses who were once uncooperative, either feeling too threatened or intimidated to get involved or still in shock from what they saw, may no longer be afraid to talk to the police; people who had once had a relationship with the suspect but no longer do may decide to come forward with incriminating information.

In addition to getting information from witnesses, investigators may generate leads by having physical evidence reexamined. Advances in technology over the past decade, particularly DNA analysis techniques, are helping to crack once unsolvable cases. Ellis (2004) reports how a cold case squad in Kansas City, Missouri, was able to use new DNA testing methods to help solve a string of 12 unsolved murders, some having been committed more than 25 years previously. If fingerprint, DNA, or other evidence in a cold homicide case had been previously examined but not entered into a national database, such as the Integrated Automated Fingerprint Identification System (IAFIS), the Combined DNA Index System (CODIS), or VICAP, that information should certainly be entered now; as Wexler (2004, p.19) reminds investigators, new fingerprints and DNA profiles are added to IAFIS and CODIS daily: "An offender who is arrested today for an unrelated offense may very well register a fingerprint or DNA match to evidence that is related to a cold case."

Besides national forensic evidence databases, cold case investigators have several other resources they should tap for help, including the media, the public, and the inmate population. When he was first assigned to Miami-Dade's cold case homicide squad, Nyberg (p.46) expected to have to take a proactive approach, hitting the streets hard to generate viable leads. However, when the squad was publicized, the detectives suddenly found themselves receiving many unanticipated tips, such as letters from prison inmates, leads from prosecutors, and hunches from retired officers. Nyberg (p.46) also notes the necessity of including the original detective when a tip comes in, if he or she is still in the homicide unit: "The sensibility of this requirement is hard to dispute: if a lead comes in on a case that's five years old and Det. Bill Jones was the lead investigator, it goes to him, if he's still in the unit. He's the one with the working knowledge, and he's the one who put the sweat and toil into it in the first place."

Cold case investigators also need to work closely with prosecutors to ensure that their efforts will meet the requirements to get a case to court. Lord (p.5), who interviewed nearly two dozen district and state attorneys with experience prosecuting cold homicides, notes: "Because prosecutors fear that the premature arrests or the presentation of weak cases could undermine the credibility of the cold case unit and needlessly raise the hopes of victims' families, they evaluate the cold cases presented by the unit based on the same cri-

teria that they use for all other homicides." She adds that while prosecutors believe that cold case investigations should be a priority, the enormous publicity such cases generate makes it politically disastrous to lose them: "These prosecutors recognized that it took additional work and skill to convict defendants of murders where the crimes occurred many years before, where witnesses must search their memories for events that have receded to the far corners of their minds, and where physical evidence may have deteriorated." Figure 8.9 is a checklist of the criteria used by the Charlotte-Mecklenburg, North Carolina, Police Department in determining which cold case homicides to reopen.

Cold cases are, without a doubt, one of the most challenging tasks a homicide investigator may face. Another difficult responsibility, perhaps even more so, is that of making a death notification.

Death Notification

Departments may use a police dispatcher, a police chaplain, or an officer to perform death notifications, but such messages should be delivered by a two-person team. Generally, if the police chaplain or a pastor from the deceased's religious faith accompanies the officer, the chaplain or the pastor performs the initial notification, and the officer fills in the details. If the relative is in another community or state or is out of the country, ask police of that jurisdiction to make the notification, using the telephone to make the actual notification only as a last resort. Noting that the survivors always remember the words used to notify them of their loss, verbatim, Moore (p.107) advises: "Officers should be compassionate and careful with their choice of words, but they should tell the truth." She continues:

> Your son has been killed in a car accident. . . . Your daughter was murdered. . . . Your husband is dead. . . . Your son has committed suicide.
>
> Killed, murdered, dead and suicide are harsh, harsh words. These are words no one wants to have to say. But these are the words that should be used when making a death notification. Sugar coating will make it more difficult to get the message across, and can actually cause more pain and distress to the person receiving the bad news.

Regarding word choice and delivery, Dewey-Kollen (2005, p.12) adds:

> Join the survivors in their grief without being overwhelmed by it. *Say*: "I'm so sorry." "Most people who have gone through this react similarly to you." *Do not say*: "I know how you feel," or "Time heals all wounds" as these statements discount the mourner's grief. A statement like "You must be strong for your children and wife, etc." creates an unhealthy expectation, and saying "You don't need to know that detail" is disempowering.

Criteria for Opening Cold Case Homicides

1. Does physical evidence exist?
   DNA   yes_____ no_____
   Latent prints   yes_____ no_____
   Ballistics   yes_____ no_____
   Other   yes_____ no_____

2. Is physical evidence still in property control or available?   yes_____ no_____
   Location_____

3. Have witnesses been identified?   yes_____ no_____
   Number of witnesses_____
   Eye witnesses_____ Other witnesses_____
   Witness availability_____

4. Have suspect(s) been identified?   yes_____ no_____
   In custody   yes_____ no_____   Status_____
   Terminally ill   yes_____ no_____   Deceased   yes_____ no_____

5. Is there opportunity for multiple clearances?   yes_____ no_____

6. Has the case been previously presented to the District Attorney's Office?
   yes_____ no_____   Arrest made   yes_____ no_____

7. Clearance potential   excellent_____ good_____ poor_____

8. Should case be submitted to review team?   yes_____ no_____

Case reviewed by_____ Date_____

Supervisor_____

Figure 8.9
Checklist for reopening cold cases
Source: John B. Edwards. "Homicide Investigative Strategies." *FBI Law Enforcement Bulletin,* January 2005, p. 13

Additional guidelines to follow when making death notifications include (Moore, p.107):

- Make certain you have the right address and right person before beginning the notification.

- Choose a private location—at a home, go inside. Do not deliver the news from the front doorway. At a workplace, contact the survivor's supervisor and ask to speak to the survivor privately.

- If a language barrier exists, arrange for a translator to be present so no mistakes are made in delivering the news.

Officers must be prepared for a wide range of emotional and physical reactions people may have upon hearing such news. They may collapse or suffer another reaction that requires first aid. They may become aggressive or even violent and require physical restraint. Having two officers perform death notifications will afford better control of such reactions. Furthermore, if two or more survivors are to be notified at the same location, it may be advisable to do the notifications separately, particularly if one or more individuals will be asked to provide investigative information (Holtz, 2003, p.218). Because some homicides are in fact committed by the survivor receiving the notification, officers should be sure to observe and later record how the survivor reacted.

Finally, family members should be allowed to see the body, whether it is at the hospital or the morgue. Viewing a body at the scene may compromise the investigation.

Notifying the family of an officer who has been killed is even more difficult. Because a line-of-duty death is always a risk for law enforcement personnel, Moore (p.108) suggests that departments develop a protocol for handling these notifications, including having officers fill out a questionnaire covering the following points:

- Who should be notified after a line-of-duty death? Include address and relationship to officer.

- Are there any special circumstances to be aware of, such as a survivor's heart condition?

- Is there a clergy preference?

- Is there a family friend who can provide support?

Moore (p.108) recommends keeping each form in a sealed envelope on file at the department and having officers update their forms at least annually.

Strategies for Reducing Homicide

Traditionally police have treated homicide as a crime relatively immune from police suppression efforts, a crime over which they had little control. Two trends are changing this reactive view. The first trend is crime analysis showing that homicide is greatest for young people in core, inner-city neighborhoods and is often related to drugs, guns, and gangs. The second trend is the emergence of community-oriented policing and a problem-solving approach to crime. In this approach, homicide is viewed as part of a larger, more general problem—violence. Results of numerous studies of police departments across the country that have implemented community-oriented policing support the theory that greater community involvement and a shift in policing philosophy to one that emphasizes proactive problem solving can reduce overall levels of violence within a community. Reporting on their study of the Richmond (California) Police Department's Comprehensive Homicide Initiative, researchers White et al. (p.217) announce:

> Both the nature and frequency of homicides in Richmond changed in important ways following the RPD's adoption of the new [community] policing philosophy and that many of the decreases were greatest among homicides that have been most directly addressed by the RPD's new efforts (i.e., outdoor homicides, homicides involving guns and drugs). Additional analysis showed that similar reductions were witnessed among other types of nonfatal violence (robbery, aggravated assault, and rape measured as a combined violent crime rate).

> The conventional wisdom about homicide has changed in some departments from viewing it as a series of unconnected, uncontrollable episodes to seeing it as part of the larger, general problem of violence, which can be addressed proactively.

This change in perspective allows departments to be proactive rather than reactive and to develop strategies to reduce homicides in their jurisdictions. One strategy being used by the New York City Police Department is CompStat, which uses computer software to perform statistical analysis of crime data and target geographic areas throughout the city with high levels of violent crime. By focusing law resources and efforts on those areas, law enforcement is able to effect greater change and have a more positive impact (Domash, p.31). Other departments are implementing early intervention programs to keep small issues from growing into bigger, more violent events. In Detroit, for example, the department recognized that the majority of shootings occurred as the result of arguments that boiled over because, in many cases, the people involved lacked conflict-resolution or anger-management skills (Domash, p.34).

SUMMARY

Homicide investigations are challenging and frequently require all investigative techniques and skills. A basic requirement is to establish whether death was caused by a criminal action. The four basic types of death are death by natural causes, accidental death, suicide, and homicide. Although technically you are concerned only with homicide, you frequently do not know at the start of an investigation what type of death has occurred; therefore, any of the four types of death may require investigation.

Homicide—the killing of one person by another—is classified as criminal (felonious) or noncriminal. Criminal homicide includes murder and manslaughter. Noncriminal homicide includes excusable homicide—the unintentional, truly accidental killing of another person—and justifiable homicide—killing another person under authorization of law. Premeditation is the essential element of first-degree murder, distinguishing it from all other murder classifications.

Special challenges in homicide investigations include pressure by the public and the media, difficulty in establishing homicide rather than suicide or an accidental or natural death, identifying the victim, and establishing the cause and time of death.

The first priority in a preliminary homicide investigation is to give emergency aid to the victim if he or she is still alive or to determine that death has occurred—provided the suspect is not at the scene. Signs of death include lack of breathing, lack of heartbeat, lack of flushing of the fingernail bed when pressure is applied and then released, and failure of the eyelids to close after being gently lifted. After priority matters are completed, the focus of the homicide investigation is on identifying the victim, establishing the time of death and cause of death and the method used to produce it, and developing a suspect.

Homicide victims are identified by their relatives, friends, or acquaintances; by personal effects, fingerprints, DNA analysis, skeletal studies including teeth, clothing, and laundry marks; or through missing-persons files.

General factors used to estimate time of death are body temperature, rigor mortis, postmortem lividity, appearance of the eyes, stomach contents, stage of decomposition, and evidence suggesting a change in the victim's normal routine. Body temperature drops 2 to 3 degrees in the first hour after death and 1 to 1.5 degrees for each subsequent hour up to 18 hours. Rigor mortis appears in the head 5 to 6 hours after death; in the upper body after about 12 hours; and in the entire body after about 18 hours. After about 36 hours, rigor mortis usually disappears in the same sequence as it appeared. Any weapon tightly clutched in the victim's hand as the result of cadaveric spasm indicates suicide rather than murder. Postmortem lividity starts one-half to 3 hours after death and is congealed in the capillaries in 4 to 5 hours. Maximum lividity occurs within 10 to 12 hours. The location of lividity can indicate whether a body was moved after death. A partial constriction of the pupil occurs in about 7 hours. In 12 hours the cornea appears cloudy. The investigator should determine when and what the victim last ate. If any vomit is present, it should be preserved as evidence and submitted for examination. A dead body usually sinks in water and remains immersed for 8 to 10 days in warm water or 2 to 3 weeks in cold water. It then rises to the surface unless restricted. The outer skin loosens in 5 to 6 days, and the nails separate in 2 to 3 weeks.

Among the most common causes of unnatural death are gunshot wounds; stabbing and cutting wounds; blows from blunt objects; asphyxia induced by choking, drowning, hanging, smothering, strangulation, gases, or poisons; poisoning and drug overdoses; burning; explosions, electrocution, and lightning; drug-related deaths; and vehicular deaths. In the case of a gunshot wound, suicide may be indicated if the wound shows gun contact against the skin, the wound is in the mouth or temple, the shot did not go through clothing, or the weapon is present. Murder may be indicated if the gun was fired from more than a few inches away or from an angle or location that rules out self-infliction, if the victim was shot through clothing, or if there is no weapon present.

Stabbing and cutting wounds may be the result of suicide if the body shows hesitation wounds; if the wounds appear under clothing or on the throat, wrists, or ankles; if the weapon is present; or if the body has not been moved. Defense wounds, cuts through clothing or to vital organs, disfigurement, the absence of a weapon, and signs that the body has been moved indicate murder. Most cases of choking, drowning, and smothering are accidental; most cases of hanging are suicides; most cases of strangulation are murder. Poisoning deaths can be accidental, suicide, or murder. Most deaths caused by burning, explosions, electrocution, and lightning are accidental, although burning is sometimes used in attempting to disguise murder. The victim's background can also provide information about whether the death was an accident, a suicide, or a homicide. This background and the evidence on the victim's body often lead to a suspect.

Determine a motive for the killing to develop a suspect against whom to provide strong circumstantial evidence. Similarities between school and workplace murders include the perpetrators' profiles, the targets, the means, and the motivation.

Physical evidence in a homicide includes a weapon, a body, blood, hairs, and fibers. A medical examination or an autopsy provides legal evidence related to the cause and time of death and the presence of alcohol or drugs, and corroborates information obtained during the investigation.

The conventional wisdom has changed in some departments from viewing homicides as a series of unconnected, uncontrollable episodes to viewing homicides as part of the larger, general problem of violence, which can be addressed proactively.

CHECKLIST

Homicide

- How were the police notified? By whom? Date? Time?
- Was the victim alive or dead when the police arrived?
- Was medical help provided?
- If the victim was hospitalized, who attended the victim at the hospital? Are reports available?
- Was there a dying declaration?
- What was the condition of the body? Rigor mortis? Postmortem lividity?
- How was the victim identified?
- Has the cause of death been determined?
- Was the medical examiner notified? Are the reports available?
- Was the evidence technician team notified?
- Was the crime scene protected?
- Were arrangements made to handle the news media?
- Are all the elements of the offense present?
- What types of evidence were found at the scene?
- How was the time of death estimated?
- Was the complainant interviewed? witnesses? suspects? victim if alive when police arrived?
- What leads exist?
- Was a description of the suspect obtained? disseminated?
- Was a search or arrest warrant necessary?
- Was all evidence properly collected, identified, and preserved?
- Were photographs taken of the scene? victim? evidence?
- Were sketches or maps of the scene made?

APPLICATION

A. Mary Jones, an 18-year-old high school girl, quarreled with her boyfriend, Thomas Smith. At 3 A.M. following the evening of their quarrel, Mary went to Smith's home to return his picture. Smith stated that after receiving the picture, he went to his room, went to sleep, and awoke about 8 A.M. When he looked out his window, he saw Mary's car parked out front.

Looking into the car, he discovered Mary sitting erect behind the steering wheel, shot through the chest, a .22 revolver lying beside her on the front seat. She was dead—apparently a suicide. The revolver had been a gift to Mary from her father. Smith called the police to report the shooting.

Mary had been shot once. The bullet entered just below the right breast, traveled across the front of her body, and lodged near her heart. The medical examiner theorized that she did not die immediately. When found, she was sitting upright in the car, her head tilted slightly backward, her right hand high on the steering wheel, her left hand hanging limp at her left side.

When questioned, Smith steadfastly denied any knowledge of the shooting. Mary's clothing, the bullet from her body, and the gun were sent to the FBI laboratory for examination. An examination of her blouse where the bullet entered failed to reveal any powder residues. The bullet removed from her body was identified as having been fired from the gun found beside her body.

Questions

1. Is the shooting likely to be a suicide or a homicide? What facts support this?
2. How should the investigation proceed?

B. Ten-year-old Denise was playing in a school parking lot with her nine-year-old stepbrother, Jerry. A car pulled up to the curb next to the lot, and the man driving the car motioned for Denise and Jerry to come over. When the man asked where they lived, Denise described their house. The man then asked Denise to take him to the house, saying he would bring her right back to the lot afterward. Denise got into the car with the man, and they drove away. When they did not return after an hour, Jerry went into the school and told a teacher what had happened. Denise did not return home that evening. The next day the police received a report that a body had been found near a lover's lane. It was Denise, who had been stabbed to death with a pocketknife.

Questions

1. What steps should be taken immediately?
2. Where would you expect to find leads?
3. What evidence would you expect to find?
4. Specifically, how would you investigate this murder?

DISCUSSION QUESTIONS

1. Questions still remain regarding the assassination of President John F. Kennedy. Why is this murder so controversial? What special problems were involved in the investigation?
2. What special problems were encountered in investigating the shooting of Lee Harvey Oswald?
3. How many murders were committed in your community last year? in your state?

4. How do your state laws classify criminal homicide? What are the penalties for each classification? Are they appropriate? Are they more or less severe than in other states?

5. Are you for or against capital punishment for persons convicted of first-degree murder? Is execution of murderers a deterrent to crime? Is media publicity concerning such cases a deterrent to murder? Do television shows and movies showing criminal violence contribute to such crimes? Would gun-control laws deter murder?

6. If patrol officers are dispatched to a murder scene, what are their duties and responsibilities there?

7. An investigator is called to a murder scene by the patrol officer at the scene. What are the duties and responsibilities of the investigator? What activities can be performed jointly by the patrol officer and the investigator? Who is in charge?

8. The investigation of murder is considered the classic crime investigation. Are there factors that make this crime more difficult to investigate, or is it basically the same as any other criminal investigation?

9. What investigative procedures are required in homicides resulting from drowning? gunshot? electrocution? stabbing? hanging? poisoning?

10. Mass deaths in Nazi concentration camps during World War II and in Guyana and Waco, Texas, involving religious cults introduce entirely new problems into homicide investigation. Who should be charged and with what degree of murder? What special problems are associated with such investigations?

MEDIA EXPLORATIONS

Internet

Select one of the following assignments to complete.

- Search for the key phrase *National Institute of Justice*. Click on "NCJRS" (National Criminal Justice Research Service). Click on "law enforcement." Click on "sort by Doc#." Search for one of the NCJ reference numbers from the reference pages. Outline the selection to share with the class.

- Go to the FBI website at www.fbi.gov. Click on "library and reference." Select "Uniform Crime Reports" and outline what the report says about homicides.

- Select one of the following key words: *homicide, homicide prevention, mass murder, serial murders, sui-*

cide. Find one article relevant to homicide investigations to outline and share with the class.

- Find and outline the article "Deadly Ambivalence" by Meredith Maran at www.salon.com/news/feature/2001.

Crime and Evidence in Action

Go to the CD and choose the **domestic violence case.** During the course of the case you'll become patrol officer, detective, prosecutor, corrections officer, and probation officer to conduct interactive investigative research. Each case unfolds as you respond to key decision points. Feedback for each possible answer choice is packed full of information, including term definitions, web links, and important documentation. The sergeant is available at certain times to help mentor you, the Online Resources website offers a variety of information, and be sure to take notes in your e-notebook during the suspect video statements and at key points throughout (these notes can be saved, printed, or e-mailed). The Forensics Exercise will test your ability to collect, transport, and analyze evidence from the crime scene. You'll even have the opportunity to consider a plea bargain offered by the defense. At the end of the case you can track how well you responded to each decision point and join the Discussion Forum for a postmortem. **Go to the CD and use the skills you've learned in this chapter to solve a case.**

REFERENCES

Andreu, Nelson. "Serial Killers: A Homicide Detective's Take." *Law Enforcement Technology*, February 2005, pp. 88–95.

Brantley, Alan C., and Kosky, Robert H., Jr. "Serial Murder in the Netherlands: A Look at Motivation, Behavior, and Characteristics." *FBI Law Enforcement Bulletin*, January 2005, pp. 26–32.

Brantley, Alan C., and Ochberg, Frank M. "Lethal Predators and Future Dangerousness." *FBI Law Enforcement Bulletin*, April 2003, pp. 16–21.

Cooley, Craig M. "Literature Review of Autoerotic Asphyxia and Fatalities." http://www.law-forensic.com/autoerotic_2.htm#_ftnref277 Updated June 12, 2005. Retrieved June 28, 2005.

Crime in the United States 2003: Uniform Crime Reports. U.S. Department of Justice, Federal Bureau of Investigation, October 2004. http://www.fbi.gov/ucr/cius_03/pdf/toc03.pdf

Death Investigation: A Guide for the Scene Investigator. Washington, DC: National Institute of Justice, November 1999.

Dewey-Kollen, Janet. "Death Notification Training." *Law and Order*, May 2005, pp. 12–14.

Domash, Shelly Feuer. "Death Takes a Holiday." *Police*, June 2003, pp. 30–34.

Duwe, Grant. "The Patterns and Prevalence of Mass Murder in Twentieth-Century America." *Justice Quarterly*, December 2004, pp. 729–761.

Edwards, John B. "Homicide Investigative Strategies." *FBI Law Enforcement Bulletin*, January 2005, pp. 11–13.

Ellis, Kate. "Kansas City Cold Case Squad Solves String of Murders." *Subject to Debate*, July 2004, pp. 1, 7.

"The Facts: Vehicular Homicide and the Impaired Driver." National Highway Traffic Safety Administration. No date. http://www.nhtsa.dot .gov/people/outreach/safesobr/13qp/facts/facthom .html. Retrieved June 28, 2005.

Fox, James Alan, and Zawitz, Marianne W. *Homicide Trends in the United States: 2002 Update*. Washington, DC: Bureau of Justice Statistics, Crime Data Brief, November 2004. (NCJ 204855)

Geberth, Vernon J. "An Equivocal Death and Staged Crime Scene." *Law and Order*, November 2004, pp. 117–119.

Geberth, Vernon J. "Equivocal Death Investigation with Staged Crime Scene." *Law and Order*, March 2005, pp. 52–55.

Griffith, David. "Suicide Is Not Painless." *Police*, May 2003, p. 6.

Hess, Kären M., and Wrobleski, Henry M. *Police Operations: Theory and Practice*, 4th ed. Belmont, CA: Thomson Wadsworth, 2006.

Holtz, Larry. "Policy Goes a Long Way in Death Notification." *Law Enforcement Technology*, December 2003, p. 218.

Hustmyre, Chuck. "The Hunt for a Serial Killer." *Law and Order*, November 2003, pp. 97–101.

Law Enforcement Officers Killed and Assaulted 2003. Washington, DC: U.S. Department of Justice, Federal Bureau of Investigation, November 2004.

Lawrence, Chris, and Mohr, Wanda K. "Investigator Protocol: Sudden In-Custody Death." *The Police Chief*, January 2004, pp. 44-52.

Litwin, Kenneth J. "A Multilevel Multivariate Analysis of Factors Affecting Homicide Clearances." *Journal of Research in Crime and Delinquency*, Vol. 41, No. 4, November 2004, pp. 327–351.

Lord, Vivian B. "Implementing a Cold Case Homicide Unit: A Challenging Task." *FBI Law Enforcement Bulletin*, February 2005, pp. 1–6.

Mertens, Jennifer. "Forensics Follows Foliage." *Law Enforcement Technology*, March 2003, pp. 62–68.

Mertens, Jennifer. "It's a Bug's Life." *Law Enforcement Technology*, November 2004, pp. 60–69.

Moore, Carole. "Breaking Bad News." *Law and Order*, May 2003, pp. 106–109.

Nislow, Jennifer. "Before the Going Gets Tough. . . Police Suicide Awareness and Prevention Gets Agencies' Attention." *Law Enforcement News*, November 2004, pp. 1, 15.

Nyberg, Ramesh. "Justice Served Cold." *Police*, October 2004, pp. 44–52.

"Officer's Research Shows That Suicide by Cop Incidents on the Rise in North America." *Police*, February 2004, p. 15.

Pinizzotto, Anthony J.; Davis, Edward F.; and Miller, Charles E., III. "Suicide by Cop: Defining a Devastating Dilemma." *FBI Law Enforcement Bulletin*, February 2005, pp. 8–20.

Renton, William J., Jr., and Mokwa, Joseph. "Drug Trafficking Murderers." *The Police Chief*, March 2005, pp. 32–33.

"Secrets of Success." *Law Enforcement News*, February 29, 2000, pp. 1, 6.

Shankar, Umesh. *Pedestrian Roadway Fatalities*. Washington, DC: U.S. Department of Transportation, National Highway Traffic Safety Administration, April 2003.

Trent, Gayle. "Something in the Water." *Law and Order*, June 2004, pp. 92–93.

Turner, Ryan, and Kosa, Rachel. *Cold Case Squads: Leaving No Stone Unturned*. Washington, DC: U.S. Department of Justice, Bureau of Justice Assistance Bulletin, July 2003. (NCJ 199781)

Varano, Sean P.; McCluskey, John D.; Patchin, Justin W.; and Bynum, Timothy S. "Exploring the Drugs-Homicide Connection." *Journal of Contemporary Criminal Justice*, November 2004, pp. 369–392.

Wen, Patricia. "Accused Teen Fits No Single Profile: School Violence Defies Stereotype." *The Boston Globe*, October 10, 2004.

Westveer, Arthur E.; Jarvis, John P.; and Jensen, Carl J., III. "Homicidal Poisoning: The Silent Offense." *FBI Law Enforcement Bulletin*, August 2004, pp. 1–8.

Wexler, Sanford. "Cracking the Serial Sniper Case." *Law Enforcement Technology*, February 2003, pp. 20–25.

Wexler, Sanford. "Cold Cases Are Getting Hot." *Law Enforcement Technology*, June 2004, pp. 18–23.

Weyland, Ernst H. "Sudden, Unexplained Infant Death Investigations." *FBI Law Enforcement Bulletin*, March 2004, pp. 10–16.

White, Michael D.; Fyfe, James J.; Campbell, Suzanne P.; and Goldkamp, John S. "The Police Role in Preventing Homicide: Considering the Impact of Problem-Oriented Policing on the Prevalence of Murder." *Journal of Research in Crime and Delinquency*, May 2003, pp. 194–225.

CASE CITED

Flippo v. West Virginia, 120 S.Ct. 7 (1999)

CHAPTER 9

Assault, Domestic Violence, Stalking, and Elder Abuse

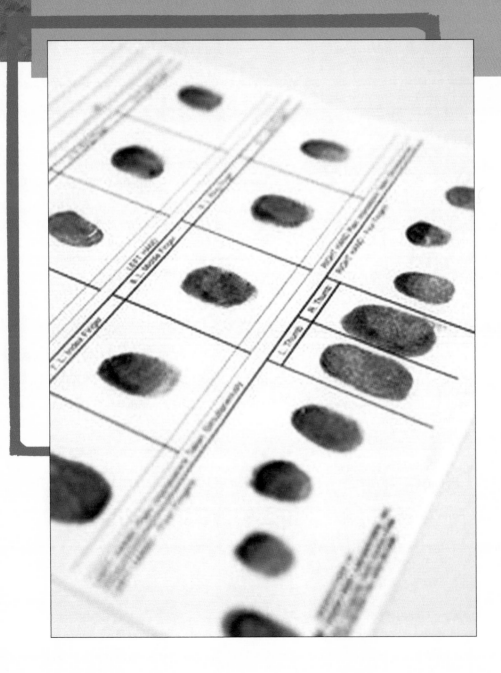

Can You Define?

Do You Know?

- What constitutes assault?
- How simple assault differs from aggravated assault?
- When force is legal?
- What the elements of simple assault, aggravated (felonious) assault, and attempted assault are?
- What special challenges are posed in an assault investigation?
- How to prove the elements of both simple and aggravated assault?
- What evidence is likely to be at the scene of an assault?
- To aid in data collection, what offenses might be categorized as separate crimes?
- What constitutes domestic violence?
- What constitutes stalking?
- What constitutes elder abuse? How prevalent it is?

Outline

Two people have a violent argument and hurl insults at each other. A bouncer physically ejects a belligerent drunk from a bar; a mob enforcer breaks all the fingers of a man who is past due on a gambling debt. An angry wife hurls a frying pan, striking her husband in the back. A teacher slaps a disrespectful student. A group of teenagers mugs an old man. A jealous lover stabs a rival with a knife. Each of these scenarios has one thing in common—each is an assault.

Some assaults take place very publicly, often with victims and witnesses who are willing to press charges and testify in court. Others take place behind closed doors in the privacy of the home. Domestic violence, once viewed as a family matter, has become a priority in many departments, partly because such violence may end in homicide. Psychological assaults or stalking behaviors have become law enforcement concerns since 1990. According to the FBI (*Crime in the United States 2003*, p.37), the volume of aggravated assaults reported throughout the nation declined in 2003 for the tenth consecutive year, with an estimated total of 857,921 offenses. Of all aggravated assaults investigated in 2003, 55.9 percent were cleared.

This chapter begins with an overview and discussion of the classification of assault. This is followed by an explanation of the elements of the crime and special challenges involved in investigating assaults. Next the chapter discusses the preliminary investigation and how to prove the elements of the crime. Then a close-up look at domestic violence is presented, including a brief history, the cycle of violence, the victims, and the police response. This is followed by an exploration of stalking. The chapter concludes with a discussion of elder abuse.

Assault: An Overview

ssault is "an intentional, unlawful act of injury to another by force, or force directed toward another person, under circumstances that create fear of imminent peril, coupled with an apparent ability to execute the attempt, if not prevented. The intention to harm is of the essence. Mere words, although provoking or insulting, are not sufficient" (*Naler v. State*, 1933).

> Assault is unlawfully threatening to harm another person, actually harming another person, or attempting unsuccessfully to do so.

Assaults range from violent threats to brutal gangland beatings, from a shove to a stabbing. Many assaults arise from domestic conflicts, often during periods of heavy drinking by one or both parties. Some result from long-developing ill feelings that suddenly erupt into open violence. Some result from an argument such as a barroom dispute that ends in a brawl. They often are connected with robberies. In fact, 50 percent of all robberies include an assault of some form.

Formerly, in many states the term *assault* referred to threats of or attempts to cause bodily harm, whereas **battery** referred to the actual carrying out of such threats. Actual physical contact is not required for assault. The threat or fear of an assault along with ability to commit the act is sufficient.

In most revised state statutes, the term *assault* is synonymous with *battery,* or the two terms have been joined in a single crime termed *assault.* Some states, however, still have separate statutory offenses of assault and battery. Where one statute remains, battery includes the lesser crime of assault.

Classification

ssaults are classified as either simple or aggravated (felonious).

> **Simple assault** is intentionally causing another person to fear immediate bodily harm or death or intentionally inflicting or attempting to inflict bodily harm on the person. **Aggravated**, or **felonious, assault** is an unlawful attack by one person on another to inflict severe bodily injury.

Simple assault is usually a misdemeanor. It does not involve a deadly weapon, and the injuries sustained, if any, are neither severe nor permanent. Aggravated assault, on the other hand, is a felony. Nationally, it is the most frequent of the violent crimes. Aggravated or felonious assault is sometimes further classified as assault with a deadly weapon or assault with intent to commit murder.

Legal Force

Physical force may be used legally in certain instances.

> In specified instances, teachers, people operating public conveyances, and law enforcement officers can legally use reasonable physical force.

Teachers have the authority of *in loco parentis* ("in the place of the parent") in many states and are allowed to use minimum force to maintain discipline, stop fights on school property, or prevent destruction of school property. Bus drivers, train conductors, airplane pilots, and ship captains have authority to use force to stop misconduct by passengers. Law enforcement officers may use as much force as needed to overcome resistance to a lawful arrest. Force used in self-defense is also justifiable.

Elements of the Crime

 he elements of the crime of assault are not as straightforward as most other crimes and vary significantly from state to state.

Simple Assault

Most state statutes have common elements for simple assault.

 The elements of the crime of simple assault are:
- Intent to do bodily harm to another.
- Present ability to commit the act.
- Commission of an overt act toward carrying out the intention.

Intent to Do Bodily Harm to Another   Evidence of specific *intent* to commit bodily injury must be present. Injury that is caused accidentally is not assault. A suspect's words and actions or any injuries inflicted on a victim imply this intent. The injury must be to another person; injury to property or self-inflicted injury—no matter how serious—is not assault.

The bodily harm or injury in simple assault need not cause severe physical pain or disability. The degree of force necessary in simple assault ranges from a shove or a slap to slightly less than that required for the great bodily harm that distinguishes aggravated assault.

Present Ability to Commit the Act   The suspect must have been physically able to commit the act at the time. A suspect who hurled a knife at a victim who was obviously out of range would not have had the ability to hit the target.

Commission of an Overt Act   An overt act, more than a threat or gesture, must have been completed. If the suspect was in range to strike the victim, even if someone intervened, an assault can be proven. Intentionally pushing, shoving, or physically preventing someone from entering or leaving property is often determined to be simple assault.

Aggravated Assault

Aggravated assault includes the three elements of simple assault plus an element relating to the severity of the attack. Aggravated assault is usually committed with a weapon or by some means likely to produce great bodily harm or death.

An additional element of aggravated assault is that the intentionally inflicted bodily injury must have resulted in one of the following:
- A high probability of death
- Serious, permanent disfigurement
- Permanent or protracted loss or impairment of the function of any body member or organ or other severe bodily harm

---

As with simple assault, the act must be intentional—not accidental.

High Probability of Death   An assault is considered aggravated if it is committed by any means so severe that a reasonable person feels it would result in a high probability of death. Examples include a blow sufficient to cause unconsciousness or coma, a gunshot or knife wound that causes heavy bleeding, or burns inflicted over most of a person's body.

Serious, Permanent Disfigurement   Permanent disfigurement includes such things as losing an ear, eye, or part of the nose, or permanent scarring of the face or other parts of the body that are normally visible. It cannot be a temporary injury that will eventually heal and not be evident.

Loss or Impairment of Body Members or Organs   Regardless of the body part affected, a charge of aggravated assault is supported by the loss or permanent impairment of body members or organs, or maiming. "Maiming signifies to cripple or mutilate in any way which deprives of the use of any limb or member of the body, to seriously wound or disfigure or disable" (*Schackelford v. Commonwealth*, 1945).

Only one of these additional elements is needed to show aggravated assault, although two or all three are sometimes present. Some states do not require permanent or protracted injury or loss if the weapon used in the assault is a dangerous weapon that causes fear of immediate harm or death.

Attempted Assault

Attempted aggravated assault is also a crime in many states. If the suspect intended to assault someone but was prevented from doing so for some reason, it is still a punishable offense categorized as "unlawful attempt to commit assault."

 Attempted assault requires proof of intent along with some overt act toward committing the crime.

Intent or preparation is not enough to prove attempted assault. For example, a suspect must have done more than obtain a weapon or make a plan or even arrange to go to the scene. Rather, the suspect must actually have gone there and have had the weapon in possession when the effort was aborted.

A person who intends to rob a grocery store and whose gun accidentally discharges while the person is in the store has indeed committed an overt act. However, if the gun discharges while the person is driving to the store, there is no overt act to support an attempted assault charge. Likewise, if a potential rapist approaches a woman and has raised his arm to strike her when he is apprehended, an overt act toward an assault has been committed. But if the man is apprehended while still lurking behind a bush, reasonable doubt exists.

Special Challenges in Investigation

Sometimes it is difficult to know who started a fight. Both parties may claim the other person struck the first blow. In such cases, both may be charged with disturbing the peace until officers can obtain more information.

Special challenges in assault investigations include distinguishing the victim from the suspect, determining whether the matter is civil or criminal, and determining whether the act was intentional or accidental. Obtaining a complaint against a simple assault also is sometimes difficult. Moreover, such calls may be dangerous for responding officers.

It is also necessary to determine whether the altercation is a civil or a criminal matter. A person who accidentally injures someone is not guilty of a criminal offense but may be sued in civil court by the victim.

It is sometimes difficult, especially in cases of wife and child beating, to obtain a complaint from the victim. If it is simple assault, which is a misdemeanor, you must see the offense committed or obtain a complaint and arrest warrant or have the victim make a citizen's arrest. Some states, such as Pennsylvania, have given the same right of arrest for domestic assaults that exists for felony arrest—police can arrest without victim complaint and without actually witnessing the assault, as discussed later in the chapter.

Patrol officers usually make the first contact with the complainant or assault victim. Police on regular patrol sometimes observe an assault occurring. Usually, however, they are sent to the assault scene by the dispatcher. Assault calls are potentially dangerous for the police. In fact, according to the Federal Bureau of Investigation (FBI) (*Law Enforcement*, p.5), more police officers were killed in 2003 while investigating disturbance calls, such as family quarrels or bar fights, than in responding to robbery and burglary calls. Of the officers who were assaulted in 2003, 30.6 percent were responding to disturbance calls (*Crime in the United States 2003*, p.64).

Officers may arrive at the point of most heated emotions and in the middle of a situation that stems from a deep-rooted problem entirely unknown to them. Their first act is to stop any assaultive action by disarming, separating, or arresting the people involved. This reduces the possibility of further conflict.

Officers should be on their guard and not take sides in any dispute. If people are injured, first aid must be administered or emergency personnel summoned to the scene. The first officer on the scene should determine whether more help is needed and whether a description of the suspect must be broadcast.

In most assault cases, arriving police officers find that the assault has been completed. However, verbal abuse and considerable confusion may still exist (Figure 9.1). Interview the victim as soon as possible to obtain details about the injury, the degree of pain, medical assistance rendered, and other facts related to the severity of the attack. The extent and nature of the injury determines the degree of assault to be charged. Further facts supporting the severity of the attack are obtained by noting what treatment the victim requires and by talking to medical personnel.

The victim frequently knows who committed the assault, either by name or by an association that can be checked. Determine the reason for the assault. Find out what actions the victim and assailant took before, during, and after the assault. If the victim of an aggravated assault is severely injured and indicates by words, gestures, or appearance that death may be imminent, obtain a dying declaration.

If the suspect is at the scene, an arrest should be made if the situation warrants, or the victim may make a citizen's arrest. If the suspect is known but is not at the scene, the suspect's description should be broadcast and the investigation begun.

The Preliminary Investigation

At a minimum, an officer arriving on the scene of an assault should:

- Control and disarm those involved in the altercation.
- Provide medical aid to injured people.
- Separate suspects.
- Protect the crime scene.

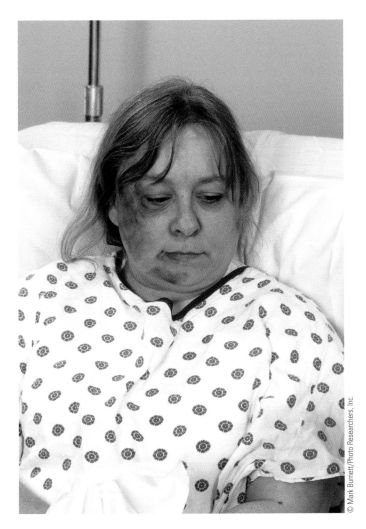

© Mark Burnett/Photo Researchers, Inc.

Figure 9.1
Some domestic assaults are severe enough to require hospitalization of the victim. Despite injuries, the assault victim is normally conscious and can provide critical information about the assailant and details about the severity of the attack. Battered spouses, however, are commonly reluctant to give investigators such details, either out of loyalty to their abuser or fear of reprisal.

- Give the *Miranda* warning if applicable.
- Obtain preliminary statements.
- Photograph evidence.
- Collect and preserve evidence.
- Reconstruct the crime.

Proving the Elements of Assault

An assault that involves no dangerous weapon and results in no serious injury is a relatively minor crime. In contrast, aggravated assault is an extremely serious crime.

 To prove the elements of assault, establish the intent to cause injury, the severity of the injury inflicted, and whether a dangerous weapon was used.

Establish intent by determining the events that led up to the assault. Record the suspect's exact words and actions, and take statements from the victim and any witnesses.

Establish the severity of the assault by taking photographs and describing all injuries in your notes. Describe the size, location, number, color, depth, and amount of bleeding of any injuries. Some bruises do not become visible for several hours or even a day or two. Assault victims should be advised of this and told that additional photographs should be taken. Obtain an oral or written statement from a qualified medical person as to the severity and permanence of the injuries and any impairment of bodily functioning.

Determine the means of attack and the exact weapon used. Was it hands, fists, feet, a gun, or a knife?

Evidence in Assault Investigations

Corroborate the victim's information with physical evidence.

 Physical evidence in an assault includes photographs of injuries, clothing of the victim or suspect, weapons, broken objects, bloodstains, hairs, fibers, and other signs of an altercation.

Two important pieces of evidence are photographs of injuries and the weapon used in the assault. If the hands, fists, or feet were used, examine them for cuts and bruises, and photograph any injuries. Obtain fingernail scrapings from both the victim and the suspect.

Take as evidence any weapons found at the scene. The victim's clothing may contain evidence such as bullet holes or tears made by a knife or other cutting instrument.

If you suspect that alcohol or drug use may have contributed to the assault, arrange for the appropriate urine, blood, and saliva tests. Photograph and make notes regarding evidence that indicates the intensity of the assault—for example, overturned furniture, broken objects, torn-up sod, and bent shrubs.

Reflective ultraviolet photography can allow investigators to document injuries on flesh up to nine months after they have visibly healed. Reflective ultraviolet photography can reveal pattern injuries—that is, injuries that have a recognizable shape—including cigarette burns, whip or belt marks, bruising, contusions, abrasions, injury margins from immersion burns, bite marks, and scratches.

 To aid in data collection, special categories of assault are domestic violence, stalking, and elder abuse.

Investigating Domestic Violence

Officers may not understand that although it appears that the victim can change the circumstances, victims often do not believe they have this capability.

> **Domestic violence** is a pattern of behaviors involving physical, sexual, economic, and emotional abuse, alone or in combination, by an intimate partner, often to establish and maintain power and control over the other partner.

History of Domestic Violence: From Male Privilege to Criminal Act

Domestic violence has deep roots in the patriarchal systems the colonists brought with them when they settled in the New World. At the time, however, such violence was perceived not as a crime but as a man's duty, for he, as head of the family and the authority figure in the home, was expected to keep control over his wife and children and was allowed to use any means necessary to achieve order. In the case of *State v. Rhodes* (1868), the North Carolina Supreme Court ruled that although a husband had the right to whip his wife, if the switch was thicker than the thumb, it was considered abuse. This Rule of Thumb standard, adopted by most state courts across the nation during the colonial period, was derived from English common law and permitted men to use any instrument to physically enforce family obedience as long as the object was no larger than the thickness of the man's thumb.

The use of force was an acceptable male privilege and was considered a family matter to be handled privately. But times have changed. Researchers Lutze and Symons (p.322) acknowledge how slowly the change occurred: "Although activists of the 1800s questioned male violence towards women and children, it was not until the early 1900s that states would begin to consider punishing abusive husbands. For the most part, however, men's legal right to discipline their wives remained intact until the 1970s." Kingsnorth and MacIntosh (p.301) report: "During the last 25 years, social definitions of domestic violence have evolved from private wrongs to acts meriting an aggressive response from the criminal justice system. The change reflects the impact of the women's movement, civil liability lawsuits, changing criminal justice system ideology, and academic research."

Despite the criminalization of such assaults, domestic violence remains a persistent problem for thousands of households across the country, in part because the abusive behavior is part of the family dynamic, tightly woven into the fabric of family relationships and passed from generation to generation through a cycle of violence.

The Cycle of Violence

Domestic violence is commonly thought of as occurring in a three-phase cycle: (1) the tension-building stage, (2) the acute battering episode, and (3) the honeymoon. This cycle, which typically increases in both frequency and severity, is illustrated in Figure 9.2.

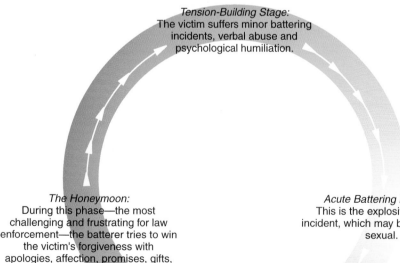

Tension-Building Stage: The victim suffers minor battering incidents, verbal abuse and psychological humiliation.

Acute Battering Episode: This is the explosive, violent incident, which may be physical or sexual.

The Honeymoon: During this phase—the most challenging and frustrating for law enforcement—the batterer tries to win the victim's forgiveness with apologies, affection, promises, gifts, etc. This often works, and the cycle continues.

Figure 9.2
Three-phase cycle of violence.

Source: Kären M. Hess and Henry M. Wrobleski. *Police Operations: Theory and Practice,* 4th ed. Belmont, CA: Wadsworth Publishing Company, 2006, p.208.

This pattern of abuse often becomes a vicious inter-generational cycle, as research has found that children who witness abuse or are abused themselves are more likely to abuse a spouse or child when they become adults. Jennings (2001) asserts: "Reenactment of childhood victimization is the major cause of violence in our society." Citing numerous studies, Jennings contends that if no one notices, listens, or helps, childhood abuse will lead to problem behavior later in the adult years: "Without help, one-third of those abused in childhood may abuse or neglect their own children, perpetuating an intergenerational cycle of abuse." Crimes against children are the focus of Chapter 11.

Table 9.1 shows the type of assault and gender of domestic violence victims.

Prevalence of Domestic Violence and Its Victims

Data from the *National Crime Victimization Survey* (Klaus, p.2) indicate that 3 households in 1,000 were affected by intimate partner violence during 2003. Domestic violence is found at all income levels and in all races, but it occurs more often in households facing economic distress. Benson and Fox (p.ii) report: "When the economically distressed household is located in a disadvantaged neighborhood, the prevalence of intimate violence jumps dramatically: women living in these circumstances are most at risk."

According to Durose et al. (p.8), of the roughly 3.5 million violent crimes committed against family members from 1998 to 2002, 48.9 percent were committed against a spouse, 10.5 percent involved children victimized by parents, and the remaining 40.6 percent involved violence between other family members, such as grandchildren abusing grandparents, children abusing parents, or siblings abusing each other. Furthermore (p.1), the majority (73 percent) of family abuse victims were female.

These figures, however, are an undercount because much of the domestic violence that occurs goes unreported. Research reveals that from 1998 to 2002, approximately 1.4 million family violence victims failed to report the abuse to law enforcement (Durose et al., p.26). Roughly one-third of the victims not reporting gave as their reason their belief that it was a "private/personal matter," with another 12 percent saying they did not report the crime because they wanted to "protect the offender."

Domestic abuse in families from diverse ethnic or cultural backgrounds also commonly goes unreported. For example, female abuse victims of Asian descent are reluctant to notify the police because they do not want to bring shame on their family or community (Kingsnorth and MacIntosh, p.305).

Fear is another reason such crimes go unreported. Many women do not report domestic assaults because of threats such as "I'll take the kids and you'll never see them again" or "I'll kill you if you call the police." In

Table 9.1 / **Percentage of Persons Physically Assaulted by an Intimate Partner**[a] **in Lifetime by Type of Assault and Sex of Victim**

Type of Assault[b]	Women, % (n = 8,000)	Men, % (n = 8,000)
Total physical assault by intimate partner	22.1	7.4
Threw something	8.1	4.4
Pushed, grabbed, shoved	18.1	5.4
Pulled hair	9.1	2.3
Slapped, hit	16.0	5.5
Kicked, bit	5.5	2.6
Choked, tried to drown	6.1	0.5
Hit with object	5.0	3.2
Beat up	8.5	0.6
Threatened with gun	3.5	0.4
Threatened with knife	2.8	1.6
Used gun	0.7	0.1
Used knife	0.9	0.8

[a]*Intimate partner* includes current or former spouses, opposite-sex cohabiting partners, same-sex cohabiting partners, dates, and boyfriends/girlfriends.
[b]With the exception of "Used knife," differences between women and men are statistically significant: *p*-values < 0.001.

Source: Patricia Tjaden and Nancy Thoennes. *Prevalence, Incidence, and Consequences of Violence against Women: Findings from the National Violence against Women Survey.* National Institute of Justice, Centers for Disease Control and Prevention Research in Brief, November 1998, p. 7. (NCJ 172837)

many instances the wife fails to report the abuse (and to leave the relationship) because she has no work skills and no independent income, because of the stigma and embarrassment associated with the offense, or because she has one or more children to support.

Statistics document that many batterers eventually kill their intimate. Some victims choose to stay with their batterers for fear that leaving would further enrage their partner. In some instances the male batterer becomes the victim of homicide. In such cases the defense often attributes the murder to the "battered-woman syndrome," which is based on the concept of duress and results from a cycle of violence.

Women as Abusers Although the majority of abuse victims are women, women may also perpetrate such violence. Durose et al. (p.14) report that of violent crimes against a spouse between 1998 and 2002, 13.9 percent of the offenders were female. Statistics regarding total family violence incidents (including violence against children and the elderly) indicate that females comprised 22.6 percent of offenders (p.14). Data presented in the 2005 *National Crime Victims' Rights Week* (*NCVRW*) *Resource Guide* (p.108) indicate that 15 percent of victimization episodes by intimate partners in 2001 were against men, and according to the most recent large-scale survey of the extent of violence against women, it was revealed that 835,000 men in the United States were raped or physically assaulted by an intimate partner from 1995 to 1996.

While it is common for battered women to feel shame at being victims of domestic abuse, the stigma for battered men is even greater. Many reports of husband abuse go unreported because these men anticipate an unsympathetic or incredulous reaction from responding officers. Indeed, the misperception persists that women who commit violence against men have been driven to it through years of victimization at the hands of these men (the battered-woman syndrome), and thus the men "have it coming." However, officers responding to a domestic violence call must not assume that the male is always the perpetrator and the female always the victim.

Gay and Lesbian Domestic Violence Traditionally the issue of gay and lesbian domestic violence was ignored and its extent undocumented. That law enforcement once considered abuse within a heterosexual couple's relationship a private and personal matter makes understandable the lack of police concern regarding violence between homosexual partners. Today, however, limited research on the topic has shown that domestic violence does exist within gay and lesbian relationships. A study of same-sex domestic violence in 2002 by the National Coalition of Anti-Violence Programs (NCAVP) found 5,092 reported incidents, of which 42 percent involved females and 51 percent involved males, the remainder being of unspecified

gender (*2005 NCVRW Resource Guide*, p.108). The study also revealed that gay and bisexual men experienced intimate partner abuse at a rate comparable to that experienced by heterosexual women (p.108).

When the Abuser Is a Police Officer Knowing the seriousness of the crime and the damage it causes to victims and families does not make officers immune from committing domestic violence themselves. In fact, research suggests that domestic abuse may occur more often in police families than among the general public (Gallo, 2004, p.132). According to Graves (p.109): "Research shows that at least 40% of law enforcement families experience domestic violence each year, in comparison with about 11 to 12% of families in the general U.S. population."

When the abuser is a police officer, special challenges exist. Lonsway and Conis (p.133) contend: "Victims of domestic violence involving an officer are uniquely vulnerable because the officer who is abusing them holds all the cards. Perhaps most obvious, the officer who is perpetrating the violence has a gun and all the authority of a position with law enforcement to use against his victim." Noting that officers are well versed in use-of-force applications and trained to articulate to various investigative entities, if questioned, how they used force in a particular situation, Graves (p.108) asserts: "The very characteristics, techniques and experiences instilled in police officers, when used in intimate relationships, make police officers the most dangerous of domestic abusers."

Few professions are characterized by the fierce loyalty to one's coworkers that prevails in law enforcement. This allegiance is put to the test when responding to a domestic violence call at an officer's home. In the past, responding officers would simply separate the parties and persuade the battered spouse to give the abuser time to cool off, explaining away the violence as the result of a stressful job and convincing the spouse that an arrest would only jeopardize the security of the entire family. Typically, no official report would be filed about the incident, and the abuse would be allowed to go on. Yet, as Gallo (2005, p.40) points out: "All those cops who maintain a code of silence about police domestic abuse think they are helping, but all they are doing is making the situation worse."

Sometimes the abuse continues to escalate until the officer kills his spouse and then, commonly, himself. In many, if not most, of these cases, the officer's service weapon is used in the crime. Spurred by research that showed how domestic abuse can evolve to domestic homicide, particularly when a firearm is available to the abuser, a federal law was passed in 1996 prohibiting anyone, including a police officer, who has been convicted of a qualifying misdemeanor domestic violence offense from owning or using a firearm or possessing ammunition. This law, known as the Lautenberg Act (18. U.S.C. § 925), amended the Gun Control Act of 1968, which barred only those convicted of a felony offense from owning or using a firearm. This law also puts another wrinkle in the issue of police-involved domestic violence, as an officer who is unable to carry a gun is unlikely to find or retain a job. However, as Lonsway and Conis (p.137) state: "Research on the effects of the Lautenberg Amendment consistently shows that the use of the law has been rather limited and officers have often been able to circumvent the ban and retain their weapons."

Predictors and Precipitators of Domestic Violence

Research has attempted to identify factors that predict or precipitate episodes of domestic violence, in terms of both victimization and perpetration. As mentioned, one well-documented predictor of the likelihood of family abuse is a past history of family violence. A report by the National Institute of Justice (*Violence against Women*, p.ii) notes: "Being sexually or physically abused both as a child and as an adolescent is a good predictor of future

victimization. Child sexual abuse on its own, however, did not predict adult victimization" (Figure 9.3).

Acknowledging that the primary risk factor for intimate-partner homicide of women is prior domestic violence, results of a recent study ("Domestic Homicide Tipoffs," p.9) warn of the danger in overlooking potential homicide victims if domestic violence investigators focus exclusively on such a history to predict future episodes of violence, as less overt factors such as controlling behavior, stalking, and social isolation were also recognized as common precursors to near lethal attacks. Other risk factors identified by the study included gun ownership by the abuser, unemployment of the batterer, and estrangement, where the victim has moved out of the previously shared residence.

Analysis of domestic assault reports in the Charlotte-Mecklenburg, North Carolina, Police Department Baker One District ("Domestic Violence Intervention," p.4) revealed that on average, domestic assault victims had filed nine previous police reports, most involving the same suspect named in the domestic assault case.

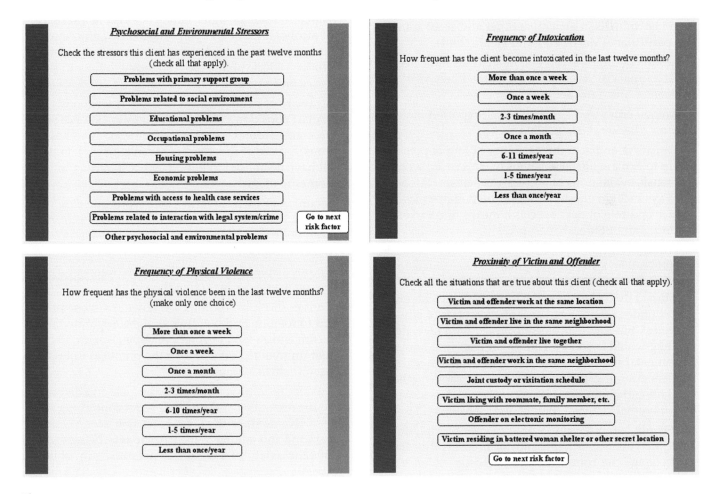

Figure 9.3

Domestic violence risk-assessment software helps investigators take comprehensive histories of both perpetrators and victims. These screen shots show examples of the types of information collected and used by investigators to evaluate the likelihood of domestic violence continuing and, perhaps, escalating to intimate-partner homicide.

Sonkin, Daniel J. (2000. rev. 2003). Domestic Violence: The Court Mandated Perpetrator Assessment and Treatment Handbook. Sausalito, CA: Daniel Sonkin (www.danielsonkin.com).

However, most of these prior reports concerned not domestic assault but other crimes, which were referred to as **indicator crimes.**

Indicator crimes are offenses that, in situations involving the same victim and suspect, can establish a pattern of events indicative of an abusive relationship: "These indicator crimes can range from harassing phone calls to hit-and-run, depending upon the particular victim-suspect pair. In many cases, the pattern of behavior that the suspect displayed against the victim followed the accepted domestic violence continuum of verbal abuse, harassment, stalking-related offenses, escalating violence, and, finally serious assault or death."

Animal cruelty is another predictor of abusive or violent behavior. Results of numerous studies have demonstrated a link between animal abuse and domestic violence, with some research going beyond the surface correlation to explore deeper aspects of the abusive psyche:

- "Violent offenders who committed crimes as adults were significantly more likely than nonviolent offenders to have committed childhood acts of cruelty against animals in general and pet and stray animals in particular" (Merz-Perez and Heide, 2004).
- "Results of multiple regression analyses indicated that animal cruelty is indeed a learned behavior" (Hensley and Tallichet, p.37).
- "Animal cruelty was related to self-reported violent crime" (Becker et al., p.905).
- "Threats of and actually harming/killing of pets can help to explain illegal behavior by an abused woman. Forensic evaluations of abused women should always include questions about the possible existence and role of pet abuse as a means of coercion" (Loring and Bolden-Hines, p.27).
- "Within the framework of the graduation hypothesis, children who are cruel to animals may graduate to aggressive behaviors toward humans. It can be assumed that if killing animals made them feel powerful under a persistent psychological state of powerlessness and low self-esteem coupled with rage, then killing would become a pattern for resolving intolerable mental states. It is interesting that the five serial killers examined in this study used the same method of killing their human victims as they had used with their animal victims" (Wright and Hensley, p.71).

Finally, although not a predictor or precipitator of domestic violence, the presence of firearms can drastically change the complexion of domestic violence and make responding to such calls exponentially more dangerous for officers.

The Police Response

Response to such calls may be initiated by the dispatcher, who can save hours of legwork by exploring with the victim her frame of mind and that of the potential attacker. From that point on, responding officers' actions are critical.

The availability of laptop computers in patrol vehicles and the use of real-time response software enable a premises and individual records check as part of the preliminary investigation. This may include previous calls for service from the complainant's residence, complaints of illegal activities at this address, open warrants for involved parties, and background information on the victim or alleged assailant. This information enhances the safety of the officers and helps them better assess the situation upon arrival at the scene.

Garner (p.44) acknowledges the high risk in responding to a domestic disturbance call, stressing that such an assignment should never be handled solo. He (pp.44–46) suggests the following guidelines when responding to a domestic violence call:

- Wait for backup.
- Do not rush into the scene or rush while you are at the scene.
- Watch for danger signs: hands not visible, presence of alcohol and/or weapons, heightened emotions and agitation, multiple offenders, threats against the officers—these oblige the responding officer to slow down and proceed with caution.
- Be aware of items that can be used as weapons. "Smart cops don't interview domestic violence suspects in residential kitchens or garages." Clothes irons, a piece of firewood, a portable oxygen tank—all have been used to kill officers responding to domestic disturbances.
- Secure your own sidearm—keep your gun side turned away from those you are dealing with, and keep your arm folded down over your weapon whenever possible.
- Do not disregard potential attackers. Keep an alert eye on everyone, including the victim.
- Control the surroundings. Do not allow those present to roam in and out of your sight. Separate the victim and suspect beyond each other's sight. Request that uninvolved others leave the premises unless you need them as witnesses.

Police officers must listen to the facts and determine who the offender is if the assault is not continuing when they arrive. Reduce the level of tension at the scene by separating and talking to the participants, being vigilant about the safety of the participants and any children present.

Gather evidence of the offense. In any assault, one of the most important kinds of evidence are photographs of any injuries. Be aware that some bruises do not become visible until well after the battering episode. Obtain all evidence, including photographs of injuries, victim's statements, prior police reports, doctor or hospital reports, weapons used, damaged clothing or other property, and statements from neighbors or other witnesses. Explain to the victim that an *order of protection* may be obtained from a court to help prevent future assaults, as discussed shortly.

The importance of the incident report should not be overlooked. The better the report, the better the chance of obtaining a conviction. Describe completely any injuries and the victim's physical condition. Some departments have a supplemental report form to document evidence in domestic violence cases (Figures 9.4 A and B).

To Arrest or Not? Basically, any evidence that would lead an officer to make an arrest in any other situation also applies to spousal situations. All states permit an arrest based on probable cause. Many states now mandate police to make an arrest in domestic violence incidents if there is a protective or restraining order against the attacker, and some require an arrest even though no such order exists.

Many departments have a mandatory arrest policy for domestic abuse, requiring the officer to make an arrest if there is probable cause, even without a signed complaint by the victim. In Nevada, for example, if the police have sufficient reason to believe that a person, within the preceding four hours, committed an act of domestic violence or spousal battery, the officer is required to arrest that person if there are no mitigating circumstances. Some states have legislated that police must have and implement such a policy. This philosophy was due in large part to the results of the "Minneapolis Experiment" conducted by Sherman and Berk in the early 1980s, which concluded that arrest was a more effective deterrent to repeat offenses than advising or sending the suspect away. This report, sometimes summarized as "arrest works best," helped create a nationwide pro-arrest sentiment in domestic violence situations. Sherman and Berk (pp.6–7) had advised, however: "It may be premature to conclude that arrest

PAGE ___ OF ___

SAN DIEGO POLICE DEPARTMENT DOMESTIC VIOLENCE SUPPLEMENTAL 137000 P.C.

VICTIM'S NAME (L, M, F) DATE OF BIRTH SDPD CASE NUMBER

I responded to a call of at (SDPD Dispatch Center #)

I found the victim The victim displayed the following emotional and physical conditions:

ORIGIN/CRIME DESCRIPTION

VICTIM

- ☐ ANGRY
- ☐ APOLOGETIC
- ☐ CRYING
- ☐ FEARFUL
- ☐ HYSTERICAL
- ☐ CALM
- ☐ AFRAID
- ☐ IRRATIONAL
- ☐ NERVOUS
- ☐ THREATENING
- ☐ OTHER: EXPLAIN
- ☐ COMP. OF PAIN
- ☐ BRUISE (S)
- ☐ ABRASION (S)
- ☐ MINOR CUT (S)
- ☐ LACERATION (S)
- ☐ FRACTURE (S)
- ☐ CONCUSSION (S)
- ☐ OTHER: EXPLAIN

ALWAYS explain OPPOSITES in narrative.

DESCRIBE ALL CONDITIONS OBSERVED; PHYSICAL, EMOTIONAL AND CRIME SCENE

SUSPECT

- ☐ ANGRY
- ☐ APOLOGETIC
- ☐ CRYING
- ☐ FEARFUL
- ☐ HYSTERICAL
- ☐ CALM
- ☐ AFRAID
- ☐ IRRATIONAL
- ☐ NERVOUS
- ☐ THREATENING
- ☐ OTHER: EXPLAIN
- ☐ COMP. OF PAIN
- ☐ BRUISE (S)
- ☐ ABRASION (S)
- ☐ MINOR CUT (S)
- ☐ LACERATION (S)
- ☐ FRACTURE (S)
- ☐ CONCUSSION (S)
- ☐ OTHER: EXPLAIN

ALWAYS explain OPPOSITES in narrative.

RELATIONSHIP BETWEEN VICTIM AND SUSPECT
MARK ALL THAT APPLY

- ☐ SPOUSE
- ☐ FORMER SPOUSE
- ☐ COHABITANTS
- ☐ FORMER COHABITANTS
- ☐ DATING/ENGAGED
- ☐ FORMER DATING
- ☐ SAME SEX
- ☐ EMANCIPATED MINOR
- ☐ PARENT OF CHILD FROM RELATIONSHIP

LENGTH OF RELATIONSHIP
___ YEAR(s) ___ MONTH(s)

IF APPLICABLE, DATE RELATIONSHIP ENDED: ________

PRIOR HISTORY OF DOMESTIC VIOLENCE? ☐ YES ☐ NO
PRIOR HISTORY OF VIOLENCE DOCUMENTED? ☐ YES ☐ NO
NUMBER OF PRIOR INCIDENTS ☐ ☐ MINOR ☐ SERIOUS
CASE NUMBER(S) ________
INVESTIGATING AGENCY ________

MEDICAL TREATMENT PARAMEDICS AT SCENE ☐ YES ☐ NO HOSPITAL: ________

- ☐ NONE
- ☐ WILL SEEK OWN DOCTOR
- ☐ FIRST AID
- ☐ PARAMEDICS
- ☐ HOSPITAL
- ☐ REFUSED MEDICAL AID

UNIT NUMBER: ________
NAME(S) ID#:

ATTENDING PHYSICIAN(S):

EVIDENCE

EVIDENCE COLLECTED
FROM: ☐ Crime Scene ☐ Hospital ☐ Other; Explain
PHOTOS: ☐ Yes ☐ No Number ________
TYPE: ☐ 35mm ☐ Polaroid

DESCRIBE ALL EVIDENCE AND DISPOSITION

TAKEN BY: ________

DESCRIBE ALL PHOTOGRAPHS
Photos of victim's injuries: ☐ Yes ☐ No
Photos of suspect's injuries: ☐ Yes ☐ No
Weapon used during incident: ☐ Yes ☐ No

Type of weapon used: ________
Weapon impounded: ☐ Yes ☐ No
Firearm(s) impounded for safety: ☐ Yes ☐ No

PROPERTY TAG NUMBER: ________ ☐ CONTINUED

REPORTING OFFICER | ID NUMBER | DIV. WATCH | DATE & TIME | APPROVED BY: NAME & ID

PD-965-FDS (Rev. 10/94) *This information is available in alternate formats upon request.*

Figure 9.4A
Sample report form to document evidence in domestic violence cases, front
Source: Kathryn Bourn. "Battles on the Homefront." *Police,* March 1996, p. 62. Reprinted by permission of Bobit Publishing, Redondo Beach, CA.

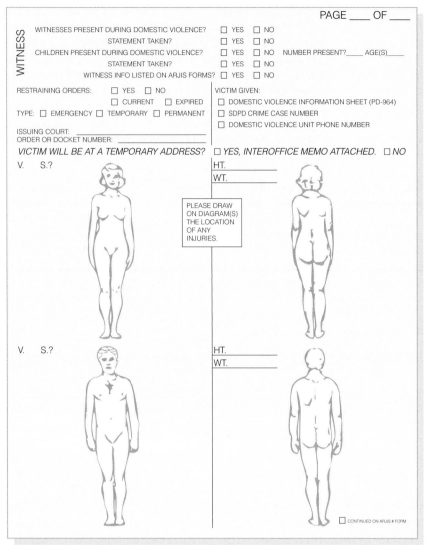

Figure 9.4B

Sample report form to document evidence in domestic violence cases, back

Source: Kathryn Bourn. "Battles on the Homefront." *Police,* March 1996, p. 62. Reprinted by permission of Bobit Publishing, Redondo Beach, CA.

is always the best way for police to handle domestic violence, or that all suspects in such situations should be arrested. A number of factors suggest a cautious interpretation of the finding."

Indeed, since that time, numerous other studies have found that alternatives to arrest may be better in specific circumstances. In fact, Sherman (p.207) himself has asserted that arrest can backfire, and mandatory arrest laws can actually compound the domestic violence problem rather than alleviate it. A more recent study by Dugan (p.303) found that although households in states with mandatory arrest laws are less likely to experience spousal violence, police in these same states are also less likely to discover such abuse: "This suggests that mandatory arrest laws not only reduce the chances of violence, but also keep people from calling the police." According to Dugan, while domestic violence victims are no more likely to report an incident in states with mandatory arrest laws, third parties are significantly less likely to make a report, thus bringing fewer cases to the attention of law enforcement.

Officers should not base their decisions regarding arrest on their perception of the willingness of the victim or witnesses to testify. The victim need not sign a complaint. However, citing how mandatory and pro-arrest policies for domestic violence incidents have strained prosecutorial and court resources, Davis et al. (pp.279–280) urge investigators to take into account the victim's wishes when pursuing prosecution: "Our results speak strongly to the importance of involving victims. Decisions made to prosecute without the victim's acquiesce need to be carefully considered by legislatures and prosecutors. . . . Arresting more batterers does not necessarily result in more prosecutions. Our results show that prosecuting more domestic violence cases can increase court delay, increase pretrial recidivism, and lower conviction rates."

Departments vary in their policies regarding mutual abuse. Some departments require the responding officer to determine who the primary physical aggressor was and then arrest that person, while other agencies have a dual arrest policy. Dual arrest policies, which gained use following passage of pro-arrest laws, allow officers to circumvent the primary aggressor assessment and arrest both parties when injuries to both sides are observed. Critics of dual arrest policies have argued that they result in more arrests than are necessary, as officers find it easier to simply arrest both parties than try to determine who the primary aggressor was, even if only one party shows injury. Furthermore, with a dual arrest option available, officers were using mediation and other nonarrest options less frequently, even when they were more appropriate responses (Finn et al., p.583).

A dual arrest policy does not preclude the single arrest of the primary aggressor only, if the officer is able to make that determination. Factors to consider in making this assessment include:

- Prior domestic violence involving either person.
- The relative seriousness of the injuries inflicted upon each person involved.
- The potential for future injury.
- Whether one of the alleged batteries was committed in self-defense.
- Any other factor that helps the officer decide which person was the primary physical aggressor.

Durose et al. (p.28) found that police were as likely to make an arrest for violence between spouses (35.5 percent) as they were for parental violence against a child (37.9 percent) or for any other type of violence between family members (35.9 percent).

Police Nonresponse One reason officers are criticized for not responding to domestic violence incidents is that they commonly receive calls from uninvolved third parties. For example, an apartment tenant calls to say the couple across the hall is shouting at each other and it sounds like things are being thrown and glass is breaking. When officers arrive, the couple may be embarrassed or angry because this is how they argue. They see no reason to involve the law and are irritated at the interference of neighbors and police. In other cases, a spouse may report a false domestic violence incident just to see the other party punished or the threat of punishment inflicted.

Several studies have examined whether the police response to domestic violence calls does in fact receive a lower priority than other crime calls. The results generally show an increasingly high priority being placed on such calls.

Effectiveness of Various Interventions

Increasing numbers of departments throughout the United States are adopting a "zero-tolerance" approach to domestic violence, which appears to be highly suc-

cessful. While many departments view arrests as a critical part of a zero-tolerance stance, some researchers contend that it is not the arrest itself but what happens *after* the arrest that ultimately determines the effectiveness of the response.

In some jurisdictions, batterers who are arrested are processed through the justice system like many other types of criminal offenders—jail, prosecution, and, hopefully, conviction. However, Wooldredge and Thistlethwaite (p.76) observe: "An emerging theme from studies of court dispositions and subsequent domestic violence is that prosecution and conviction does not appear to reduce recidivism."

In other jurisdictions, arrested abusers are required to participate in a batterer intervention program (BIP), a counseling and treatment alternative to sending these offenders to jail. The most common BIP used throughout the country is based on the Duluth Model, founded on the feminist theory that domestic violence is the result of a patriarchal ideology in which men are encouraged and expected to control their partners. The Duluth Model BIP seeks to enlighten abusive men by exploring their attitudes about control and teaching them strategies to better interact with their partners. Other BIPs are based on cognitive-behavioral modification to correct faulty thinking patterns, group practice models that seek to root out the multiple causes of battering and customize treatment to fit the offender's needs, and group therapy BIPs that take the controversial position that spouses are equal participants in creating disturbances in relationships.

As with arrest research findings, results of studies that have examined the effectiveness of BIPs are mixed. Jackson et al. (p.iii) report:

> Batterer intervention programs were introduced as a way to hold batterers accountable without incarcerating them. Initial studies suggested that the programs reduced battering. Two evaluations of programs in Broward County, Florida, and Brooklyn, New York, based on more rigorous experimental designs, claim that they have little or no effect.

Sanow (p.4), in bold criticism of the Duluth Model, states: "The Duluth Model has two glaring weaknesses: 1) Since the batterers' motivations for violence differs, the same type of program may not work with all batterers. 2) The Duluth Model, based on white feminist theories, doesn't work with minority populations." In defending the Duluth Model, Pence and Paymar (p.376) assert: "The Duluth Model focuses on intervention and on stopping an offender's use of violence, not fixing the relationship. . . . While an objective of our counseling program is to change the attitudes of men who batter, the ultimate goal of the Duluth Model has always been to ensure that victims are safer by having the state intervene to stop the violence."

Results of other studies that have examined the effectiveness of BIPs suggest that perhaps the most significant factor in the rehabilitation of a batterer is the offender's **stake in conformity,** a constellation of variables that, in effect, comprise "what an offender has to lose," such as marital status, residential stability, and/or employment. Post-BIP recidivism among batterers who were married, owned homes, and had steady employment was significantly lower than for offenders who were less stable in terms of property ownership, employment, or marriage (Jackson et al., p.12).

Some jurisdictions have implemented intervention programs that draw on the cultural strengths of the community. In New Mexico, for example, domestic violence in Indian Country had become a significant problem, and the traditional route of incarceration was not having positive results. In fact, according to Leftoff (p.53): "Experience has shown that jail can provide opportunities to learn more subtle approaches to abuse and better ways to hide it." A sergeant with the local sheriff's department, who was himself a Navajo, suggested an intervention program built on a fundamental aspect of Native American communities—the clan, and the wisdom of elders. Leftoff (p.53) explains: "Focusing on clan puts a priority on connections between individuals. [The] program also connects Navajo elders, who serve as mentors, teachers, and resources of traditional knowledge, to offenders and victims who come through the program. This is a collaboration that is working across generations." The elders' knowledge and experience in resolving conflicts through peacemaking is what makes this unique intensive intervention program a success in Indian Country.

As important as intervention programs aimed at batterers are, of equal importance are efforts to help victims. It is fairly common for abuse victims who have filed a report and begun the process of pressing charges to change their minds and express a desire to drop charges, either out of guilt for having "turned on" their partner or because the batterer threatens or tries to intimidate them into dropping the charges. Bune (p.16) contends that such actions are generally not beneficial to abuse victims because, without any intervention, counseling, or assistance, these victims will likely return to a violent domestic situation and be victimized again: "Therefore, it is important for victim services and domestic violence units to become immediately involved with the victims following a report of a violent incident."

One option commonly suggested to victims of violent abuse is to obtain an order of protection, also called a restraining order.

Restraining Orders

Domestic violence victims themselves are taking a more active role in preventing recurring assaults through the attainment of restraining orders. These court-issued documents aim to restrict an alleged abuser's behavior so as to protect his intended victim. A provision of the

Violence Against Women Act (VAWA) of 1994 assigns **full faith and credit** to valid orders of protection, meaning that an order issued anywhere in the country is legally binding and enforceable nationwide.

Restraining orders typically take several weeks to obtain, but if the victim is in immediate life-threatening danger, an emergency restraining order can generally be issued within 24 hours. A court hearing is usually conducted before a restraining order is issued, allowing a judge time to review the facts of the case provided by the victim on the request form and to hear from the abuser, if he appears at the hearing. If an order of protection is granted, it may contain a variety of conditions regarding the abuser's personal conduct, use of alcohol, child custody or visitation, child and/or spousal support, a stay-away order, a move-out order, and a ban on the possession or use of firearms.

This final condition obviously poses a problem for officers who have a restraining order filed against them, as they are prohibited from possessing a weapon even while on duty. Some restraining orders automatically expire after a specified time limit, unless renewed, while others are valid indefinitely unless a request is made for dismissal and a court grants such dismissal.

Although abuse victims are certainly encouraged to protect themselves, they cannot rely solely on a piece of paper for security. In fact, some studies have found that women who seek restraining orders are well aware of their potential ineffectiveness. According to Kane (p.561): "Civil restraining or protective orders issued pursuant to domestic violence offenses carry the force of law and the threat of arrest. But research shows that less than half of restraining order violations actually result in arrest."

As the Office for Victims of Crime (*Enforcement of Protective Orders,* p.5) cautions: "Unless protective orders are enforced, they can prove harmful to victims by creating a false sense of security. Around the United States, legislatures have put laws into place that enable law enforcement personnel to act quickly in cases of violation and permit courts to impose severe sanctions. As use of protective orders increases, victim service providers and advocates can expect further developments in the area of enforcement."

Legislation

In addition to mandatory arrest laws, other laws address issues concerning convicted domestic abusers. One such statute already discussed is the Lautenberg Amendment to the Crime Control Bill of 1968, which enforces an aspect of gun control in supporting domestic violence victims. Section 658 of HR 4278, signed September 30, 1996, prohibits individuals convicted of misdemeanor crimes involving domestic violence from owning or possessing a firearm. The statute is retroactive. This statute obviously presents a problem for law enforcement officers, for if officers are caught and convicted of domestic violence, they will lose their jobs. Interestingly, the Ninth Circuit Court of Appeals has ruled that the portion of the law denying possession of firearms to police officers convicted of spouse abuse is unconstitutional.

Despite the many laws devoted to reducing or eliminating domestic violence, criminal justice should not expect too much from such legislation.

Avoiding Lawsuits

Failure to respond appropriately to domestic violence can result in serious financial liability to local governments. More and more, victims of domestic violence are suing local governments for failure to protect them. Perhaps the most well-known case is that of Tracy Thurman in Torrington, Connecticut. The police department was ordered to pay almost $1 million because they failed to protect Tracy from her husband, who had a history of battering her (*Thurman v. City of Torrington,* 1984).

To reduce lawsuits, departments should have a pro-arrest policy if officers have probable cause to believe a domestic assault has occurred. They should train officers in this pro-arrest policy and require them to document why an arrest has or has not been made.

Closely related to investigating domestic violence cases is the challenge of investigating stalking cases.

Investigating Stalking

 stalker is someone who intentionally and repeatedly follows, tries to contact, harasses, and/or intimidates another person. This repeated harassing or threatening behavior is called *stalking,* the primary motives for which are power, control, and possession (Rugala et al., p.9).

> Although legal definitions vary among jurisdictions, **stalking** is generally defined as the willful or intentional commission of a series of acts that would cause a reasonable person to fear death or serious bodily injury and that, in fact, does place the victim in fear of death or serious bodily injury.

Data from the National Center for Victims of Crime (NCVC) (*Stalking Fact Sheet*) indicate more than 1 million women and over 370,000 men are stalked in the United States every year. Of those, 28 percent of females and 10 percent of males had obtained a restraining order against their stalker.

Stalking is a crime in every state and the District of Columbia and at the federal level. As of June 2004,

13 states classified stalking as a felony upon the first offense; 35 states classified stalking as a felony upon the second offense and/or when the crime involves aggravating factors, including possession of a deadly weapon, violation of a court order, violation of a condition of parole/probation, a victim younger than 16, or the same victim as in prior incidents (*Stalking Fact Sheet*).

Stalking often leads to homicide. Statistics on **femicide,** the murder of a woman, reveal that 76 percent of femicide victims had been stalked by the person who killed them, and 54 percent had reported the stalking to the police before they were murdered by their stalkers (*Stalking Fact Sheet*). Research findings support a strong connection between stalking and domestic violence, with studies showing that more than 80 percent of women stalked by husbands or cohabiting partners had been battered by that individual (Rugala et al., p.12). The seriousness of this problem is further reflected in the fact that almost one-third of the women killed in the United States are murdered by their husbands or boyfriends, and as many as 90 percent are stalked before the murder. One unfortunate event illustrates how stalking can evolve into more overtly violent behavior. On July 5, 2005, a man in a pickup truck, aiming to run over his ex-girlfriend, instead ended up running over and killing a 2-year-old boy who was playing nearby. At the time, the driver was wanted on other charges, including aggravated stalking ("Driver Aiming at Ex-Girlfriend," 2005).

Types of Stalking

Stalkers are typically categorized as a certain typology, usually based on the relationship between the stalker and the victim. One system of stalking typologies involves the three categories of intimate or former intimate, acquaintance, and stranger stalking.

In *intimate or former intimate stalking,* the stalker and victim may be married or divorced, current or former cohabitants, serious or casual sexual partners, or former sexual partners. This is the most common relationship involved in stalking cases. In *acquaintance stalking,* the stalker and victim know each other casually. They may be neighbors or coworkers. They might have even dated once or twice but were not sexual partners. In *stranger stalking,* the stalker and victim do not know each other at all.

The NCVC presents a different set of typologies for stalkers, also including three varieties: the simple obsessional, the love obsessional, and the erotomanic. *Simple obsessional* stalkers are the basic equivalent of the aforementioned intimate stalkers but also include acquaintance stalkers. These cases are the most common type and most often occur in the context of domestic violence. *Love obsessional* stalkers have no prior relationship with their victim but become fixated on that person, often a

© AP/Wide World Photos

Figure 9.5
Dawnette Knight reacts in court as a letter from Catherine Zeta-Jones is read during Knight's sentencing for stalking the actress Friday, July 8, 2005, in Los Angeles. Zeta-Jones, who almost suffered a nervous breakdown because of the vicious death threats, and her husband, Michael Douglas, testified that the 32-year-old Knight wrote more than a dozen letters describing how she was going to "slice [Zeta-Jones] up like meat on a bone and feed her to the dogs," so that when she finished with "this bitch/whore she will not be this pretty face actress." Knight's lawyer, Richard P. Herman (pictured at right), claimed his client simply had a "girlish crush" on Douglas, and was upset when she read in the tabloids that the actress was allegedly having an affair with one of her "Ocean's 12" co-stars. Knight was given three years in state prison, but with credit for time served she could be imprisoned for as little as seven months.

celebrity, believing they belong together (Figure 9.5). *Erotomanic* stalkers, the rarest of the three types, believe that their victim is in love with them.

Cyberstalking The growth of e-mail and use of the Internet has resulted in **cyberstalking,** which, in previous editions of this text, was simply defined as preying on a victim via computer. However, the problem has grown in such scope and severity that more elaborate and specific definitions are now used. The Department of Justice defines cyberstalking as the repeated use of the Internet, e-mail, or other digital electronic communications devices to stalk another person. Stalking generally involves harassing or threatening behavior that an individual engages in repeatedly. Hitchcock (p.18) states: "Cyberstalking is an escalated form of online harassment directed at a specific person that causes substantial emotional distress and serves no legitimate purpose. The action is to annoy, alarm, and emotionally abuse another person." Like other forms of stalking, cyberstalking can turn violent.

Working to Halt Online Abuse ("Online Harassment") received 196 reports of online harassment and cyberstalking for calendar year 2004, with 42 percent of cases originating as e-mail communications, 14 percent as message board conversations, 18 percent from instant messaging, 6 percent from a website, and 6 percent from chat rooms. In the remaining cases, the origin of the

harassment was unknown. In 2004, 69 percent of the cyberstalking victims were female, 18 percent were male, and 13 percent were of unspecified gender ("Online Harassment").

The perception of anonymity afforded by online activity is thought to be one reason cybercrime, including cyberstalking, is on the rise. Consequently, states have turned to legislation to address this problem.

Legislation and Department Policies

The first antistalking laws were passed in 1990 in California. Since that time, all 50 states and the District of Columbia have enacted general stalking laws, many of which are also applicable to cyberstalking offenses. Currently 45 states have passed cyberstalking and related laws; New Mexico has a bill pending; and Idaho, Nebraska, New Jersey, Utah, and the District of Columbia have not yet enacted any specific cyberstalking legislation ("Online Harassment"). Title 18, §875 of the U.S. Code makes it a federal offense to transmit, electronically or otherwise, any threatening communication in interstate or foreign commerce, with such acts punishable by fine and/or imprisonment for up to five years.

Antistalking laws describe specific threatening conduct and hold the suspect responsible for proving that his or her actions were not intended to frighten or intimidate the victim. Hitchcock (p.18) notes that most stalking laws require the showing of a credible threat made by the perpetrator against the victim or the victim's family. This element of the crime of stalking can be problematic in prosecuting cases of cyberstalking because: "Cyberstalkers often do not threaten their victims in person; rather, they engage in conduct that, when taken in context, would cause a reasonable person to fear violence" (pp.18, 20). Hitchcock (p.20) stresses the importance of structuring cyberstalking legislation to include both the location where the communication originated and where it was received as constituting the venue of the offense.

Although legislation makes stalking a specific crime and empowers law enforcement to combat the offense, a great deal of variation and subjectivity exists among the states' legal definitions of stalking. Many officers are unaware of antistalking legislation in their state. And many officers do not know about their own department's policy on stalking.

The Police Response

The traditional law enforcement response to stalkers has been to issue restraining orders. Unfortunately, such orders are often ineffective, as demonstrated when one offender dramatically stabbed his wife to death and "knifed" the court order to her chest. According to the *2005 NCVRW Resource Guide* (p.119), restraining orders against stalkers were violated, on average, 40 percent of the time, and in nearly 21 percent of cases, the victim perceived a worsening of stalking behavior after seeking and receiving a restraining order. Because of this proven ineffectiveness of restraining orders, the perceived inability of criminal justice to effectively handle stalkers, and victims' fear of antagonizing and angering their stalkers, many stalking incidents go unreported.

Law enforcement faces a unique challenge in addressing and investigating stalking incidents because of the lack of clear definitions of stalking or of the elements comprised by the offense. Kinkade et al. (pp.4–5) contend: "In the case of stalking, state law dictates that an above-average level of interpretation is placed on the shoulders of law enforcement to make the subjective decision to arrest and then is placed on juries, judges, and prosecutors to decide whether or not to convict. Put simply, 'Stalking lies in the eye of the beholder.'"

In general, victims should be encouraged to use an answering machine to screen their calls and to document the threatening messages. All threatening electronic communications should be saved and a hardcopy printed. Victims should obtain an unlisted phone number or a new e-mail address or change their user name if the harassment involves cyberstalking. In short, investigators should support victims in gathering evidence and in helping to keep themselves safe until the stalker can be stopped.

One of the initial steps an officer should take is to assess the threat in order to determine the credibility and overall capability of the stalker to actually carry out his expressed intent to cause harm. Regarding cyberstalking, Hitchcock (p.20) states: "A quick assessment of the nature of the contact will determine if the elements of the crime are present and if an investigation is necessary." Elements to consider include the target, the stalker's motivation or intent, the means of transmission for cyberstalking cases, the perpetrator's ability to follow through on threats, the stalker's personal background (criminal, psychological, etc.), and the nature of the victim/offender relationship (Rugala et al., p.11).

Evaluating the potential for violence is an important part of a stalking investigation, since stalking behavior can, and in some cases does, elevate to homicide. The FBI's National Center for the Analysis of Violent Crime (NCAVC) is a valuable resource in helping stalking investigators assess an offender's potential for violence. The NCAVC (Rugala et al., pp.11–12) stresses the need to consider a stalker's behavior in its totality by taking into account specific actions and other factors, including:

- Threats to kill.
- Access to or recent acquisition of weapons.
- Symbolic violence.
- Violations of protective orders.
- Prior physical violence against the victim or others, including pets.
- Substance abuse.
- Location of violence (private vs. public setting).
- Status of the victim/offender relationship.
- Continued harassment by phone, computer, fax, or letters sent to the victim's home or work.
- Surveillance of the victim and "chance" meetings.
- Mental illness.
- Prior intimacy between victim and offender.
- Fantasy—homicidal/suicidal ideation.
- Obsessive jealousy.
- Offender viewing self as the victim.
- Desperation.
- Blaming the victim for personal problems.
- Loss of power/control.
- Mission-oriented mindset with a focus on the victim.

The Family Protection Unit (FPU) of the Westminster, California, Police Department has developed a stalking protocol that has proven successful, not only for their agency but for others who have adopted it (Proctor, pp.96–97). When a possible stalking case comes into the department, it is forwarded to either a detective in charge of stalking investigations or a domestic violence investigator. This investigator conducts an in-depth threat assessment interview with the victim, which is used to develop a profile on the stalker.

Information about the victim is cataloged to help the police if the incident should later escalate into a kidnapping, violent assault, or homicide. Cataloged information includes fingerprints and photographs of the victim and any children that may be at risk, and photos of the vehicles used regularly by the victim.

The victim is given a stalking log in which to enter dates, times, and descriptions of actions or behaviors taken by the stalker. The log is used by the investigator to develop a stalking chronology, which forms the basis of the crime report. According to Proctor, the average stalking crime report for the FPU is 200 to 500 pages long. In addition to logs, some departments advise victims to keep a journal in which they describe how the stalking has affected them and their lifestyle. For example, how many days of work have been missed? Have they felt the need to seek counseling or take medication to counter the effects of the stalking? Research has shown that the prevalence of anxiety, insomnia, social dysfunction, and severe depression is much higher among stalking victims than the general population (Blaauw et al., 2002).

The FPU develops search warrants for every stalking case. Over the course of a dozen years investigating stalking cases, the unit has compiled a standard list of items to be included in such search warrants, with each new case having the potential to add items to the list. Since the unit tries to serve the search warrant at the same time as the stalker's arrest, it attempts to bolster the case beforehand with information gained through a tape-recorded phone call to the stalker. As Proctor (p.97) explains: "Stalkers are usually more comfortable on the phone, give more information, and officers do not have to issue Miranda rights." After the stalker is arrested, all interviews are videotaped.

Hitchcock (pp.22–23) offers the following protocol for investigating cyberstalking (many of these steps are also applicable to investigations of other types of stalking):

- Obtain from the complainant a detailed description of the harassing behavior (phone calls, being followed, etc.).
- Ask the complainant if she knows who is sending the harassing messages.
- Obtain copies of the messages, which will show an e-mail address, chat room nickname, website URL, or other leads to identifying the offender.
- Ask the complainant if she knows why she is being harassed.
- Record when and how the harassment began.
- Ask whether the complainant has been threatened with physical harm or has actually been assaulted.
- Secure any physical evidence available and start a chain of custody to protect the evidence (e-mails, instant messaging (IM) correspondences, webpage images, message board conversations, answering machine messages, letters sent in the mail, etc.).
- Determine the nature and extent of communication the complainant has had with the harasser—did the complainant reply to any messages? how long have the communications been exchanged? This helps the investigator understand whether the incident has escalated or the threats occurred without mitigating factors.
- Ask if there are any witnesses. Did the victim forward the harassing messages to friends or relatives or otherwise alert people of the threats? Can any of these people add information to the case?
- Determine what steps, if any, the complainant has taken to stop the harassment. Has she notified her Internet service provider (ISP), filed any court actions, or made return threats to the harasser?
- Assess the steps the complainant has taken to protect herself. Has she discontinued service with a particular ISP? taken any physical safety precautions?

Hitchcock (p.23) adds: "If the harassment has escalated to cyberstalking or real-life stalking, proceed from there by filing charges, getting protective orders, or helping the victim find a lawyer to file a civil suit."

Complications in investigating cybercrime include the unwillingness of some ISPs to give law enforcement access to subscribers' records and the increased availability of anonymizing Internet tools, such as remailers that strip identifying information from e-mail headers and erase transactional data from servers that would otherwise be used to trace a message's author.

According to D'Ovidio and Doyle (p.16): "Cyberstalkers who use an anonymous remailer as the sole means to send threatening or harassing e-mail messages will remain virtually undetectable to the victim and law enforcement." Online resources for cyberstalking investigators include ForensicsWeb (www.forensicsweb.com), Net Crimes and Misdemeanors (www.netcrimes.net), and Sam Spade (www.samspade.org) (Hitchcock, pp.26–27).

A final area to examine in the investigation of assault and family violence is elder abuse.

Investigating Elder Abuse

The U.S. Census Bureau projects that by 2020 nearly 61 million people will be over the age of 65, and by 2040 that number will climb to 92 million. As the U.S. population ages, a growing concern in law enforcement is elder abuse. Elder abuse is not a specific crime category in many states, which makes its frequency data difficult to obtain. It is typically included in the assault, battery, or murder category.

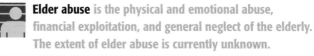

Elder abuse is the physical and emotional abuse, financial exploitation, and general neglect of the elderly. The extent of elder abuse is currently unknown.

While incidents of burglaries, robberies, motor vehicle thefts, assaults, rapes, and homicides of the elderly are relatively well documented in official reports, or at least at rates comparable to those documenting offenses against other age groups, cases of elder abuse typically involve the types of victimization that occur outside the spotlight focused on Part One crimes, in the shadowy fringes of crime collection.

Prevalence and Nature of Elder Abuse

Elder abuse has been called a "hidden" or "silent" crime because a large percentage of cases are not reported. Determining the prevalence of elder abuse is a challenge because of the lack of data, a problem compounded by a reluctance to report the crime—similar to the situation with domestic assault. Some elderly individuals are physically incapable of providing information or may be suffering from conditions such as senility or Alzheimer's disease that might cause others not to believe their statements. In other cases, victims may fear further abuse or loss of the care of the only provider they have, or they may be embarrassed that their child could mistreat them.

Bonnie and Wallace (2003) report that an estimated one to two million Americans age 65 or older are injured, exploited, or otherwise mistreated every year by someone on whom they depend for care or protection. A 50-state survey of adult protective services by the National Center on Elder Abuse (NCEA) (*A Response to Abuse*) found 472,813 reports of elder abuse in domestic and institutional settings during 2000. The survey revealed that 84 percent of the reports received were investigated, with nearly half substantiated, and that adults over 80 were the most frequent victims of abuse, excluding self-neglect. A majority (61.7 percent) of abusers were family members (e.g., spouses, children, grandchildren, siblings, other family members).

Hunt (p.61) observes that the elderly are more vulnerable to a variety of victimizations because they are easier to manipulate and control. The damaging effects of such victimization are often more severe for the elderly. Of the various ways the elderly are victimized, the NCEA survey showed 19 percent of cases involved caregiver neglect/abandonment, 13 percent were cases of financial abuse or exploitation, 11 percent involved physical abuse, 7 percent were emotional/verbal abuse cases, and 1 percent of cases involved sexual abuse. Self-neglect accounted for 39 percent of allegations investigated. Self-neglect may occur because of declining mental or physical health and includes poor hygiene, inability to attend to housekeeping, wearing inappropriate clothes for the weather, dehydration or malnourishment, failing to take necessary medications, refusing to seek medical treatment for serious illness, and careless actions such as leaving a stove burner on or forgetting to turn off a car and then shutting the garage door, thus allowing the buildup of deadly carbon monoxide to seep into the home.

The ultimate act of self-neglect among elderly people is suicide. According to Slatkin (p.30), the highest rate of suicide in the United States occurs in the elderly population: "Rates remain level until ages 65 to 69, when they rise steeply. For this age group, 25 suicides occur per 100,000 individuals; for those 70 to 74 years of age, 30 people per 100,000 took their own lives." He notes that the rates peak for persons 85 and older, where 65 out of 100,000 people take their own lives. Elderly suicide is often the result of a deepening, unnoticed, and untreated depression. Slatkin (p.29) cites research that indicates the occurrence of depressive symptoms in approximately 15 percent of the elderly population living in the community and in 15 to 25 percent of the elderly living in nursing homes.

Financial Abuse and Exploitation of the Elderly

Financial abuse and exploitation of the elderly is an area of growing concern. According to CARE (Curtailing Abuse Related to the Elderly), a program administered by Riverside County, California, older Americans account for 60 percent of all victims contacting the National Fraud Information Center (NFIC). Data from the NFIC (*2003 Telemarketing*) indicate that older consumers are particularly vulnerable to certain types of telemarketing fraud. For example, in 2003 consumers age 60 and over made 66 percent of the reports received for sweepstakes fraud, 59 percent of the reports of lottery club scams, and 52 percent of reports regarding magazine sales scams.

Olinger (2005) reports that nearly one-third of economic crime cases in Denver, Colorado, involve elderly victims. He notes that justice for these victims is often elusive, as prosecutors relate stories of losing victims to mental illness, physical illness, and death before getting the case to trial. According to Olinger: "Many victims are too frail or confused to endure a criminal trial and appear as credible witnesses. Some have sent money to swindlers calling from cellphones in Canada. Others know the perpetrators well—and are reluctant to testify against a nephew, a son or a daughter."

Johnson (pp.2–7) divides elderly financial abuse crimes into two categories: (1) fraud committed by strangers and (2) exploitation by relatives and caregivers. Listed among the types of fraud commonly committed against the elderly by strangers are prize and sweepstakes scams, investment fraud, charitable contribution fraud, home and automobile repair scams, loan and mortgage fraud, bogus or unnecessary duplicates of health and life insurance policies, fraudulent funeral plans, false health remedies and "miracle cures," travel fraud, confidence games, telemarketing fraud, mail fraud, and face-to-face contacts that give an offender a chance to steal from or otherwise scam the elderly victim, such as posing as a utility worker to gain access to the home to commit a robbery.

Even more unsettling than falling victim to a smooth-talking scam artist is the victimization endured at the hands of trusted family members or others with whom the victim has an ongoing relationship. According to Johnson (p.5), this type of financial exploitation can occur when a relative or caregiver borrows money without repaying, withholds medical care or other services to conserve funds, sells the elder's possessions without permission, signs or cashes pension or Social Security checks without permission, misuses the elder's automated teller machine (ATM) or credit cards, forces the elder to sign over property, or simply takes away the elder's money, property, or valuables. Other opportunities for exploitation occur with financial and legal arrangements like joint bank accounts, deed or title transfers, powers of attorney and durable powers of attorney, and living trusts and wills. Johnson (p.7) notes:

"Distinguishing between an unwise, but legitimate, financial transaction and an exploitative transaction resulting from undue influence, duress, fraud, or lack of informed consent can be difficult. Suspicious transactions may be well-intentioned but guided by poor advice. Generally, financial exploitation involves a pattern of behaviors, rather than single incidents."

Indicators of Elder Abuse

It cannot always be assumed that a broken bone on an elderly person or an unwise financial investment are the direct results of elder abuse or exploitation. Older people have weaker muscles and bones. They fall and bruise. They make bad choices on how to invest their money. But when these unfortunate events become a matter of routine, they may warrant further investigation.

Signs of Physical Abuse of the Elderly Signs of physical abuse of the elderly that investigators should be aware of include:

- Injury incompatible with the given explanation.
- Burns (possibly caused by cigarettes, acids, or friction from ropes).
- Cuts, pinch marks, scratches, lacerations, or puncture wounds.
- Bruises, welts, or discolorations.
- Dehydration and/or other malnourishment without illness-related causes; unexplained loss of weight.
- Pallor; sunken eyes or cheeks.
- Eye injury.
- Soiled clothing or bedding.
- Lack of bandages on injuries or stitches where needed, or evidence of unset bone fractures.
- Injuries hidden under the breasts or on other areas of the body normally covered by clothing.
- Frequent use of the emergency room and/or clinic.

The American Medical Association provided doctors with the following questions, which are equally applicable to law enforcement officers:

- Has anyone at home ever hurt you?
- Has anyone ever scolded or threatened you?
- Have you ever signed any documents that you didn't understand?
- Are you often alone?
- Are you afraid of anyone at home?
- Has anyone ever touched you without your consent?
- Has anyone ever made you do things you didn't want to?

Signs of Financial Abuse of the Elderly Johnson (pp.23–24) offers the following indicators for those investigating financial abuse and exploitation of the elderly:

- A recent acquaintance expresses an interest in finances, promises to provide care, or ingratiates himself or herself with the elder.
- A relative or caregiver has no visible means of support and is overtly interested in the elder's financial affairs.
- A relative or caregiver expresses concern over the cost of caring for the elder, or is reluctant to spend money for needed medical treatment.
- The utility and other bills are not being paid.
- The elder's placement, care, or possessions are inconsistent with the size of his or her estate.
- A relative or caregiver isolates the elder, makes excuses when friends or family call or visit, and does not give the elder messages.
- A relative or caregiver gives implausible explanations about finances, and the elder is unaware of or unable to explain the arrangements made.
- Checking account and credit card statements are sent to a relative or caregiver and are not accessible to the elder.
- At the bank, the elder is accompanied by a relative or caregiver who refuses to let the elder speak for himself or herself, and/or the elder appears nervous or afraid of the person accompanying him or her.
- The elder is concerned or confused about "missing money."
- There are suspicious signatures on the elder's checks, or the elder signs checks and another party fills in the payee and amount sections.
- There is an unusual amount of banking activity, particularly just after joint accounts are set up or someone new starts helping with the elder's finances.
- A will, power of attorney, or other legal document is drafted, but the elder does not understand its implications.

The Police Response

Controversy exists about the role of law enforcement in dealing with elder abuse, especially in identifying "hard-to-detect" cases. Some departments believe that this is the responsibility of social services, not law enforcement. Other departments feel that they are in an ideal position to learn from and to assist social services in dealing with cases of elder abuse. Payne and Berg (p.440) observe that the political shift that occurred in the early 1990s to criminalize elder abuse and redefine it not as a social problem but as a criminal one made it incumbent on law enforcement to partner with other social service agencies in responding to actions of elder abuse.

Johnson (pp.36–48) provides a list of possible responses and strategies for agencies involved in investigating fraud and financial exploitation of elderly victims:

- Create a multiagency task force to include representatives from law enforcement, financial management, insurance, investments, real estate, probate law, criminal law, civil law, mental health, and social services for the elderly.
- Develop interjurisdictional cooperation—share information and intelligence with agencies in other jurisdictions.
- Improve reporting mechanisms.
- Train police in how to interview elderly victims of financial crimes.
- Reduce elders' social isolation—get them involved in Adopt-A-Senior programs, neighborhood watches, etc.
- Educate seniors and other concerned parties about scams known to be prevalent in the local area or that commonly target the elderly, including how to report these scams and how to protect themselves from being victimized.
- Identify high-risk seniors.
- Reverse the "boiler room," those mass mailings of postcards offering free and guaranteed prizes to

recipients if they call the number on the card. Those who call your number receive detailed information on sweepstakes fraud and how to protect themselves.

Reducing Elder Abuse

One approach to reducing elderly victimization is Triad, a cooperative effort of the International Association of Chiefs of Police (IACP), AARP (formerly the American Association of Retired Persons), and the National Sheriffs' Association (NSA). These three organizations are working together to design programs to reduce victimization of the elderly, assist those who have been victimized, and generally enhance law enforcement services to older adults and the community at large. According to Hunt (p.61), more than 32 states are currently committed to Triad, and several other state attorney general's offices are promoting the program.

AARP is another resource to tap when trying to reduce the occurrence of elder abuse. Their website (www.aarp.org) posts numerous articles on how to protect against financial exploitation and what to do if nursing-home or other caregiver problems exist, along with various other links to resources able to assist elderly victims.

SUMMARY

Assault is unlawfully threatening to harm another person, actually harming another person, or attempting unsuccessfully to do so. *Simple assault* is intentionally causing another to fear immediate bodily harm or death or intentionally inflicting or attempting to inflict bodily harm on another. It is usually a misdemeanor. *Aggravated assault* is an unlawful attack by one person on another to inflict *severe* bodily injury. It often involves use of a dangerous weapon and is a felony. In specified instances, teachers, persons operating public conveyances, and law enforcement officers use physical force legally.

The elements of the crime of simple assault are (1) intent to do bodily harm to another, (2) present ability to commit the act, and (3) commission of an overt act toward carrying out the intent. An additional element in the crime of aggravated assault is that the intentionally inflicted bodily injury results in (1) a high probability of death; (2) serious, permanent disfigurement; or (3) permanent or protracted loss or impairment of the function of any body member or organ or other severe bodily harm. Attempted assault requires proof of intent and an overt act toward committing the crime.

Special challenges in investigating assaults include distinguishing the victim from the suspect and determining whether the matter is civil or criminal and whether the act was intentional or accidental. Obtaining a complaint against simple assault is also sometimes difficult.

To prove the elements of the offense of assault, establish the intent to cause injury and the severity of the injury inflicted and determine whether a dangerous weapon was used. Physical evidence in an assault includes photographs of injuries, clothing of the victim or suspect, weapons, broken objects, bloodstains, hairs, fibers, and other signs of an altercation.

Domestic assault, stalking, and elder abuse are, for reporting and research purposes, candidates for categorization as separate crimes rather than being lumped into the general category of assault. Domestic violence is defined as a pattern of behaviors involving physical, sexual, economic, and emotional abuse, alone or in combination, by an intimate partner often for the purpose of establishing and maintaining power and control over the other partner.

Stalking generally refers to repeated harassing or threatening behavior. Elder abuse is the physical and emotional abuse, financial exploitation, and general neglect of the elderly. The extent of elder abuse is currently unknown.

CHECKLIST

Assault

- Is the assault legal or justifiable?
- Are the elements of the crime of assault present?

- Who committed the assault?
- Is the suspect still at the scene?
- Who signed the complaint? Who made the arrest?
- Has the victim made a written statement? Have witnesses done so?
- Are injuries visible?
- Have photographs been taken of injuries? In color?
- If injuries are not visible, has the victim received medical attention?
- If medical attention was received, has a report on the nature of the injuries been received? Did the victim grant permission?
- What words did the assailant use to show intent to do bodily harm?
- Was a dangerous weapon involved?
- Has a complete report been made?
- If the assault is severe enough to be aggravated assault, what injuries or weapons support such a charge?
- If the victim died as a result of the attack, was a dying declaration taken?
- Was it necessary and legal to make an arrest at the scene? away from the scene?
- How was the suspect identified?

APPLICATION

Read the following and then answer the questions: Mike S. was drinking beer with friends in a local park at about 9:00 P.M. It was dark. He knew Tom C. was at the other end of the park and that Tom had been seeing Mike's girlfriend, Suzy H. Suzy was with Mike, trying to talk him out of doing anything to Tom. Mike said he was going to find Tom and "pound him into the ground. When I get through with him, they'll have to take him to the hospital."

Mike left the group and Suzy then, telling them to wait for him. Tom C. was found later that night two blocks from the park, lying unconscious on a boulevard next to the curb. His clothes were torn, and his left arm was cut. When he regained consciousness, he told police he was walking home from the park when someone jumped out from some bushes, grabbed him from behind, beat him with fists, and then hit him over the head with something. He did not see his assailant.

Mike S. was arrested because a person at the park overheard his threats.

Questions

1. What is the probability that Mike committed the assault?

2. Did he have the intent? the present ability to commit the act?

3. Did he commit the act? Should he have been arrested?

DISCUSSION QUESTIONS

1. If a police officer wearing a concealed armored vest confronts a man burglarizing a store and the burglar fires a gun at the officer, striking him in the chest, is this assault? If so, what type? Which elements of the offense are and are not present?

2. What if the same situation existed except that as the burglar fired, he slipped and the bullet struck a tree at some distance from the officer?

3. Under what circumstances is a person justified in using force against another person? When is a police officer justified in using force?

4. Imagine that Mrs. Jones has reported to the police department that she and her husband were arguing over his drinking and that Mr. Jones had just beaten her. She wants the police to come to their home and arrest her husband. How would you proceed with this complaint? What precautions would you take?

5. Do your state's laws differentiate between the crimes of assault and battery?

6. Suppose a teacher is having a serious discipline problem with a 5-year-old student and sends the student to the principal's office. The principal spanks the student. Under the *in loco parentis* doctrine, is this action legal? Do you agree with this doctrine? Does your state have such a law?

7. Does a sniper firing on a crowd commit assault?

8. In what crimes is assault often an additional crime?

9. If two people become involved in a violent struggle that seriously injures one or both of them, and if both claim the other started the fight, what do you do?

10. Can police officers be sued for making verbal threats to a suspect?

MEDIA EXPLORATIONS

Internet

Select one of the following assignments to complete.

- Search for the key phrase *National Institute of Justice.* Click on "NCJRS" (National Criminal Justice Research Service). Click on "law enforcement." Click on "sort by Doc#." Search for one of the NCJ reference numbers from the reference pages. Outline the selection to share with the class.

- Go to the FBI website at www.fbi.gov. Click on "library and reference." Select "Uniform Crime Reports" and outline what the report says about assault.

- Select one of the following key words: *assault, assault prevention, cyberstalking, domestic violence, elder abuse, stalking.* Find one article relevant to assault investigations to outline and share with the class.

Crime and Evidence in Action

Go to the CD and choose the **domestic violence case.** During the course of the case you'll become patrol officer, detective, prosecutor, corrections officer, and probation officer to conduct interactive investigative research. Each case unfolds as you respond to key decision points. Feedback for each possible answer choice is packed full of information, including term definitions, web links, and important documentation. The sergeant is available at certain times to help mentor you, the Online Resources website offers a variety of information, and be sure to take notes in your e-notebook during the suspect video statements and at key points throughout (these notes can be saved, printed, or e-mailed). The Forensics Exercise will test your ability to collect, transport, and analyze evidence from the crime scene. You'll even have the opportunity to consider a plea bargain offered by the defense. At the end of the case you can track how well you responded to each decision point and join the Discussion Forum for a postmortem. **Go to the CD and use the skills you've learned in this chapter to solve a case.**

REFERENCES

2003 Telemarketing Fraud Report. National Fraud Information Center. Washington, DC: National Consumer League, 2004.

2005 National Crime Victims' Rights Week Resource Guide. Washington, DC: Department of Justice, Office for Victims of Crime, 2005.

Becker, Kimberly D.; Stuewig, Jeffrey; Herrera, Veronica M.; and McCloskey, Laura A. "Study of Firesetting and Animal Cruelty in Children: Family Influences and Adolescent Outcomes." *Journal of the American Academy of Child and Adolescent Psychiatry*, July 2004, pp. 905–912.

Benson, Michael L., and Fox, Greer Litton. *When Violence Hits Home: How Economics and Neighborhood Play a Role.* Washington, DC: National Institute of Justice, Research in Brief, September 2004. (NCJ 205004)

Blaauw, Eric; Winkel, Frans W.; Arensman, Ella; Sheridan, Lorraine; and Freeve, Adriënne. "The Toll of Stalking: The Relationship Between Features of Stalking and Psychopathology of Victims." *Journal of Interpersonal Violence*, January 2002, pp. 50–63.

Bonnie, R., and Wallace, R. *Elder Mistreatment: Abuse, Neglect and Exploitation in an Aging America.* Washington, DC: National Academy Press, 2003.

Bune, Karen. "NCJA Member Explores Domestic Violence and Calls for More Proactive Solutions to Combating It." *NCJA Justice Bulletin*, February 2005, pp. 16–17.

Crime in the United States 2003: Uniform Crime Reports. Washington, DC: U.S. Department of Justice, Federal Bureau of Investigation, October, 2004. http://www.fbi.gov/ucr/cius_03/pdf/toc03.pdf

Davis, Robert C.; Smith, Barbara E.; and Taylor, Bruce. "Increasing the Proportion of Domestic Violence Arrests That Are Prosecuted: A Natural Experiment in Milwaukee." *Criminology and Public Policy*, Vol. 2, No. 2, 2003, pp. 263–282.

"Domestic Homicide Tipoffs May Be Missed." *Law Enforcement News*, February 2004, p. 9.

"Domestic Violence Intervention in Charlotte-Mecklenberg." *Problem Solving Quarterly*, Spring 2003, pp. 3–6.

D'Ovidio, Robert, and Doyle, James. "A Study on Cyberstalking: Understanding Investigative Hurdles." *FBI Law Enforcement Bulletin*, March 2003, pp. 10–17.

"Driver Aiming at Ex-Girlfriend Kills Toddler." The Associated Press, as reported on MSNBC.com, July 5, 2005. http://www.msnbc.msn.com/id/8474515

Dugan, Laura. "Domestic Violence Legislation: Exploring Its Impact on the Likelihood of Domestic Violence, Police Involvement, and Arrest." *Criminology and Public Policy*, Vol. 2, No. 2, 2003, pp. 283–312.

Durose, Matthew R.; Harlow, Caroline Wolf; Langan, Patrick A.; Motivans, Mark; Rantala, Ramona R.; Smith; Erica L.; and Constantin, Elizabeth. *Family Violence Statistics: Including Statistics on Strangers and Acquaintances.* Washington, DC: Bureau of Justice Statistics, June 2005. (NCJ 207846)

Enforcement of Protective Orders, Legal Series Bulletin #4. Washington, DC: Office for Victims of Crime, January 2002. (NCJ 189190)

Finn, Mary A.; Blackwell, Brenda Sims; Stalans, Loretta J.; Studdard, Sheila; and Dugan, Laura. "Dual Arrest Decisions in Domestic Violence Cases: The Influence of Departmental Policies." *Crime and Delinquency*, October 2004, pp. 565–589.

Gallo, Gina. "Airing Law Enforcement's Dirty Laundry." *Law Enforcement Technology*, June 2004, pp. 132–137.

Gallo, Gina. "A Family Affair." *Police*, February 2005, pp. 36–40.

Garner, Gerald W. "Surviving Domestic Violence Calls." *Police*, January 2005, pp. 44–46.

Graves, Alex. "Law Enforcement Involved Domestic Abuse." *Law and Order*, November 2004, pp. 108–111.

Hensley, Christopher, and Tallichet, Suzanne E. "Learning to Be Cruel? Exploring the Onset and Frequency of Animal Cruelty." *International Journal of Offender Therapy and Comparative Criminology*, February 2005, pp. 37–47.

Hitchcock, J.A. "Cyberstalking and Law Enforcement." *The Police Chief*, December 2003, pp. 16–27.

Hunt, Russ. "The TRIAD Program: A Partnership between Seniors, Law Enforcement and the Community." *The Law Enforcement Trainer*, Fourth Quarter 2004, pp. 58–61.

Jackson, Shelly; Feder, Lynette; Forde, David R.; Davis, Robert C.; Maxwell, Christopher D.; and Taylor, Bruce G. *Batterer Intervention Programs: Where Do We Go from Here?* Washington, DC: National Institute of Justice, Special Report, June 2003. (NCJ 195079)

Jennings, Ann. "What Can Happen to Abused Children When They Grow Up, If No One Notices, Listens, or Helps? Some Statistics from the Research." January 2001. http://www.state.sc.us/dmh/abused_children.htm. Retrieved July 7, 2005.

Johnson, Kelly Dedel. *Financial Crimes Against the Elderly.* Washington, DC: Office of Community Oriented Policing Services, Problem-Oriented Guides for Police, Problem-Specific Guides Series, No. 20, August 4, 2004.

Kane, Robert J. "Violations of Restraining Orders Only Sometimes Lead to Arrest." *Criminal Justice and Behavior*, Vol. 27, No. 2, 2000, p. 561.

Kingsnorth, Rodney F., and MacIntosh, Randall C. "Domestic Violence: Predictors of Victim Support for Official Action." *Justice Quarterly*, June 2004, pp. 301–328.

Kinkade, Patrick; Burns, Ronald; and Fuentes, Angel Ilarraza. "Criminalizing Attractions: Perceptions of Stalking and the Stalker." *Crime and Delinquency*, January 2005, pp. 3–25.

Klaus, Patsy A. *Crime and the Nation's Households, 2003.* Washington, DC: Bureau of Justice Statistics, Bulletin, October 2004. (NCJ 206348)

Law Enforcement Officers Killed and Assaulted 2003. Washington, DC: U.S. Department of Justice, Federal Bureau of Investigation, November 2004.

Leftoff, Sondra. "Stopping Domestic Violence in Indian Country." *The Police Chief*, August 2004, pp. 53–56.

Lonsway, Kim, and Conis, Pete. "Officer Domestic Violence." *Law and Order*, October 2003, pp. 133–140.

Loring, Marti T., and Bolden-Hines, Tamara A. "Pet Abuse by Batterers as a Means of Coercing Battered Women into Committing Illegal Behavior." *Journal of Emotional Abuse*, 2004, pp. 27–37.

Lutze, Faith E., and Symons, Megan L. "The Evolution of Domestic Violence Policy through Masculine Institutions: From Discipline to Protection to Collaborative Empowerment." *Criminology and Public Policy*, Vol. 2, No. 2, 2003, pp. 319–328.

Merz-Perez, Linda, and Heide, Kathleen M. *Animal Cruelty: Pathway to Violence Against People.* Walnut Creek, CA: AltaMira Press, 2004.

Olinger, David. "Abuse of Elderly a Difficult Crime to Prosecute." *Denver Post*, January 23, 2005.

"Online Harassment Statistics." Working to Halt Online Abuse. Accessed July 14, 2005. http://www.haltabuse.org/.

Payne, Brian K., and Berg, Bruce L. "Perceptions About the Criminalization of Elder Abuse Among Police Chiefs and Ombudsmen." *Crime and Delinquency*, July 2003, pp. 439–459.

Pence, Ellen, and Paymar, Michael. "Defense of the Duluth Model." *Law and Order*, February 2004, p. 376.

Proctor, Michael. "The Family Protection Unit." *Law and Order*, April 2005, pp. 94–97.

A Response to Abuse of Vulnerable Adults: The 2000 Survey of State Adult Protective Services. Washington, DC: National Center on Elder Abuse, 2002.

Rugala, Eugene; McNamara, James; and Wattendorf, George. "Expert Testimony and Risk Assessment in Stalking Cases: The FBI's NCAVC as a Resource." *FBI Law Enforcement Bulletin*, November 2004, pp. 8–17.

Sanow, Ed. "Goodbye, Duluth Model." *Law and Order*, November 2003, p. 4.

Sherman, Lawrence W. "Domestic Violence and Defiance Theory: Understanding Why Arrest Can Backfire." In *Australian Violence, Contemporary Perspectives II*, edited by Duncan Chappell and Sandra Egger, 1995, pp. 207–220.

Sherman, Lawrence W., and Berk, Richard A. *The Minneapolis Domestic Violence Experiment*. Washington, DC: Police Foundation Reports, April 1984.

Slatkin, Arthur A. "Suicide Risk and Hostage/Barricade Situations Involving Older Persons." *FBI Law Enforcement Bulletin*, April 2003, pp. 26–32.

Stalking Fact Sheet. Washington, DC: National Center for Victims of Crime. U.S. Department of Justice, 2005. Retrieved July 13, 2005. http://www.ncvc.org/src/AGP.Net/Components/DocumentViewer/Download.aspxnz?DocumentID=38733

Violence against Women: Identifying Risk Factors. Washington, DC: National Institute of Justice, Research in Brief, November 2004. (NCJ 197019)

Wooldredge, John, and Thistlethwaite, Amy. "Court Dispositions and Rearrest for Intimate Assault." *Crime and Delinquency*, January 2005, pp. 75–102.

Wright, Jeremy, and Hensley, Christopher. "From Animal Cruelty to Serial Murder: Applying the Graduation Hypothesis." *International Journal of Offender Therapy and Comparative Criminology*, February 2003, pp. 71–88.

CASES CITED

Naler v. State (1933)

Schackelford v. Commonwealth (1945)

State v. Rhodes (1868)

Thurman v. City of Torrington (1984)

Sex Offenses

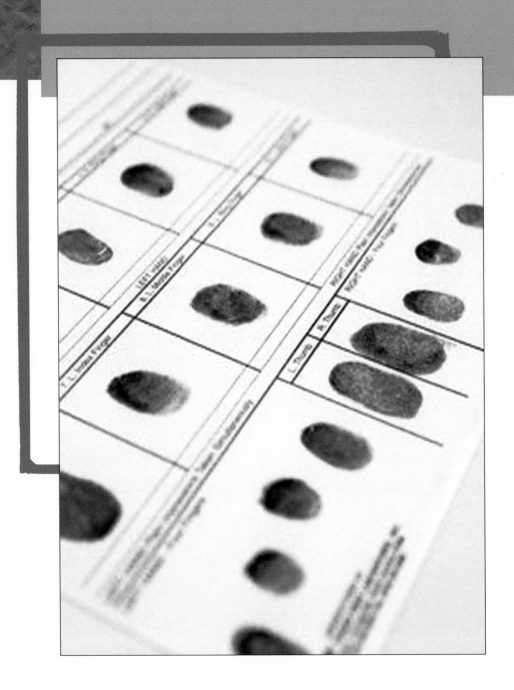

Can You Define?

Do You Know?

- How sex offenses are classified?
- How rape is defined and classified?
- What the elements of sexual assault are?
- What modus operandi factors are important in investigating a sexual assault?
- What special challenges exist in investigating sex offenses?
- What blind reporting is and what its advantages are?
- What evidence is often obtained in sex offense investigations?
- What evidence to seek in date rape cases?
- What agencies can assist in a sexual assault investigation?
- What is generally required to obtain a conviction in sexual assault cases?
- Whether recent laws have reduced or increased the penalties for sexual assault and why?
- Which three federal statutes form the basis for sex offender registries?

Outline

Physically attractive or unattractive people of any age—from very young children to senior citizens—may be victims of sexual assault. Sex offenses range from **voyeurism** (the Peeping Tom) to rape and murder. Sex offenses can be difficult to investigate because the victim is often emotionally distraught. Moreover, investigating officers may be uncomfortable because they lack special training in interviewing sex offense victims or offenders.

Some sex offenders are emotionally disturbed and feel no remorse for their actions. For example, a 38-year-old man with a 20-year history of sex offenses admitted to a prison psychiatrist that even he could not remember how many rapes and sexual assaults he had committed. The suspect also talked freely about his sexual exploits with children and showed no emotion at all. A **pedophile**—a person who is sexually attracted to young children—can be extremely dangerous, as can a **sadist,** a person who derives sexual gratification from causing pain to others, often through mutilation.

Although some sex offenders are emotionally disturbed, the fact remains that most victims know their attacker and that most attacks occur not in dark alleys but in living rooms and bedrooms. According to the Federal Bureau of Investigation (FBI) Uniform Crime Reports (*Crime in the United States 2003,* p.27), an estimated 93,433 forcible rape offenses occurred nationwide in 2003, a 1.9 percent decline from 2002. Of the total number of forcible rape offenses, rapes by force accounted for 91.0 percent. The remainder were attempts. The clearance rate for rape was 44.0 percent.

This chapter begins with a discussion of two offenses closely related to sex offenses: the investigation of obscene phone calls and of human trafficking. Next the chapter provides a classification of sex offenses and definitions of rape/sexual assault. This is followed by an explanation of the elements of the crime, a description of sex offenders, the special challenges in investigating sex crimes, and the benefits of blind reporting. Other topics covered are the police response, an explanation of relevant physical evidence, factors to consider when investigating date rape, and the importance of the victim's medical examination. Next is a discussion of victim interviews, the importance of behavioral profiling in sex offense cases, methods of conducting the follow-up investigation, and interviewing witnesses. This is followed by an explanation of arresting and interrogating sex offenders and prosecuting them, as well as the importance of coordinating efforts with other agencies. The chapter concludes with a look at the prosecution of rape cases and statutory changes affecting sexual assault cases, including the civil commitment of sex offenders following release from prison and the establishment of sex offender registries and notification laws.

Investigating Obscene Telephone Calls

Making obscene telephone calls is a crime. Recall that this is a frequent form of harassing stalking behavior. Police departments receive complaints of many types of harassment calls that are not of a sexual nature and have established procedures for investigating such calls. The same procedures apply to phone calls with sexual implications.

In most obscene phone calls, the callers want to remain anonymous, using the phone as a barrier between themselves and their victims. The callers receive sexual or psychological gratification from making contact with victims, even from a distance. Calls involving sexual connotations are threatening to the victims because they have no way of knowing the caller's true intent. Although such calls may be made randomly, in many cases the caller knows the victim.

If the victim wants to prosecute, the first contact may be the phone company. The information section at the front of most phone directories provides information about what constitutes a violation of phone company regulations and the law, and provides instructions on what to do if a person receives obscene or harassing calls (stay calm, do not respond, and quietly hang up the

phone; if the calls persist, call the phone company). The company will assist the victim in contacting the police for further investigation. Caller ID may discourage obscene calls, although a caller may still be able to block his or her name and/or phone number. The police may also use traps and traces if given a signed affidavit from the victim stating the facts related to the obscene calls.

A more serious challenge to investigators is the problem of human trafficking, which often involves sex offenses as well.

Investigating Human Trafficking

The Thirteenth Amendment to the U.S. Constitution, ratified in 1865, clearly states: "Neither slavery nor involuntary servitude, except as a punishment for crime whereof the party shall have been duly convicted, shall exist within the United States, or any place subject to their jurisdiction." But it has yet to be truly abolished in this country. "Human trafficking," according to Braun (p.68), "is modern-day slavery." She reports that as many as 200,000 people are trafficked into the United States yearly, forced to work in slave-like conditions or be

sexually exploited. A more conservative estimate is given by the Central Intelligence Agency, which has estimated that anywhere from 14,500 to 17,500 people are smuggled into the country each year. Yet only 550 have been identified as victims nationwide (Nislow, p.6). Nislow cites one officer who likened human trafficking to the problem of domestic violence 10 or 15 years ago: "Everyone knew that it was happening, but it was still occurring under the radar."

According to the Department of Justice (*Assessment of U.S. Government*), the largest number of those trafficked into the United States come from East Asia and the Pacific (5,000 to 7,000). The next largest numbers come from Latin America, Europe, and Eurasia (between 3,500 and 5,500 victims from each). The U.S. State Department (*Victims of Trafficking*) reports: "Victims of human trafficking pay a horrible price. Psychological and physical harm, including disease and stunted growth, often have permanent effects. . . . Another brutal reality of the modern-day slave trade is that its victims are frequently bought and sold many times over—often sold initially by family members." The slaves are commonly kept from trying to escape or harm their owners by being continuously drugged.

Venkatraman (p.36), a federal prosecutor and special counsel for trafficking in persons, contends: "Identifying and pursuing human trafficking crimes is an effective control strategy." He cites studies that demonstrate a link between trafficking in people and trafficking in drugs and arms and suggests that organized crime syndicates may be heavily involved in these three illicit activities.

Venkatraman (p.37) points out that a number of federal statutes allow vigorous investigation, prosecution, and punishment of trafficking. He (p.39) also notes that the statute against involuntary servitude is one of the most commonly used federal trafficking laws, which carries a 20-year maximum penalty and up to life imprisonment in cases involving kidnapping, sexual abuse, or death. The Trafficking Victims Protection Act (TVPA) became law in 2000. Its three functions are to prevent human trafficking, to protect victims of human trafficking, and to prosecute those who traffic in humans.

Braun (p.72) suggests: "No police department should try to fight human trafficking alone. Assistance is available from federal agencies and local service providers who can help victims find housing, health care, mental health services and government benefits." However, according to Braun (p.73), the challenge is to get victims to come forward and help in arresting and prosecuting those who traffic in humans. Many victims are undocumented and are afraid of deportation, which their traffickers have threatened will happen if they go to the police.

Venkatraman (p.41) offers the following tips for detecting and investigating trafficking cases: First, know where to look. Although trafficking can occur anywhere, patterns have been observed. Strip clubs, massage parlors, brothels, clothing manufacturing sweatshops, agricultural sites with migrant laborers, restaurants, and homes hiring domestic help are common sites. Second, know what to look for. Victims work long hours for very little (or no) pay, are afraid of their employers, and may be guarded by other employees or family of the suspect. "Be aware of fatigue, bruises or other evidence of injury. Look for withdrawn workers who are afraid of unsanctioned contact with outsiders, or whose statements are censored by overseers."

Third, know what questions to ask—for example, How did you arrive in the United States? What are your work hours and conditions? How much are you paid? Can you come and go as you like? Did anyone take your passport? Fourth, be very careful in selecting interpreters. Make certain that the interpreter is not on the side of the suspect. Fifth, know when to stop asking questions. Never ask the ultimate question: "Were you a slave?"

Very often, human trafficking involves several different types of sex offenses, including prostitution and rape. The U.S. Department of Health and Human Services (*Human Trafficking Fact Sheet*) states: "Many victims of trafficking are exploited for purposes of commercial sex, including prostitution, stripping, pornography and live-sex shows."

On June 30, 2005, 27 people were arrested in connection with an alien-harboring conspiracy. Fifty brothels, residences, and businesses were searched as part of Operation Gilded Cage, a federal investigation into sex trafficking, harboring of illegal aliens, conspiracy to transport female Korean nationals across state lines to engage in prostitution, and money laundering through massage parlors. During Operation Gilded Cage, approximately $2 million was seized at the search locations and approximately one hundred women were transported to an undisclosed, nondetention location where they received health care and other services ("19 Charged"). Operation Gilded Cage resulted from a joint investigation by the U.S. Attorney's Office for the Northern District of California, the U.S. Department of Justice's Civil Rights Division, the FBI, U.S. Immigration and Customs Enforcement (ICE), the San Francisco Police Department, the Internal Revenue Service (IRS), and the State Department's Diplomatic Security Service.

Classification of Sex Offenses

Sex crimes are sometimes classified according to whether they involve physical aggression and a victim—for example, rape—or are victimless acts between consenting adults, such as sodomy. The former are most frequently reported to police and investigated. The latter are often simply offensive to others and are seldom reported or investigated.

Sex offenses include bigamy, child molestation, incest, indecent exposure, prostitution, sodomy, and rape (*sexual assault*).

Bigamy is marrying another person when one or both parties are already married.

Child molestation is usually a felony and includes lewd and lascivious acts, indecent exposure, incest, or statutory rape involving a child, male or female, under age 14. This is a difficult charge to prove because children frequently are not believed. Moreover, parents are often reluctant to bring charges in such cases. (This offense is discussed in depth in the next chapter.)

Incest is sexual intercourse with another person nearer of kin than first cousin when the relationship is known. In some states incest extends beyond bloodlines to include people who are related by adoption.

Indecent exposure is revealing one's genitals to another person to such an extent as to shock the other's sense of decency. It is not necessary to prove intent. The offense is a misdemeanor, although repeated offenses can be charged as a felony in many states. Ordinarily, **exhibitionists**—those who expose themselves—are not dangerous but may become so if they are humiliated or abused.

Not only does **prostitution**—soliciting sexual intercourse for pay—contribute to the spread of venereal disease, but profits from it often go to organized crime. Of special concern to law enforcement officers is the practice of enticing very young girls into prostitution. Legislation—for example, the Mann Act—attempts to prevent such actions. Section 2423 of the act prohibits "coercion or enticement of minor females and the taking of male or female persons across the state line for immoral purposes." Another concern regarding prostitution is the spread of deadly diseases.

Sodomy is any form of anal or oral copulation. Although commonly thought of as being performed by homosexual males, sodomy can occur between a male and female, between two females, or between a human and an animal (bestiality). Oral or anal penetration must be proven. Both parties are guilty if the act is voluntary. Because sodomy is usually a private act between consenting adults, it is difficult to obtain sufficient evidence for prosecution. In some states sodomy between consenting adults is no longer a crime. Such acts between adults and juveniles remain crimes, however.

Rape—or sexual assault—is sexual intercourse with a person against his or her will. Rape is usually considered the most serious crime after murder and carries a heavy penalty in most states. It is now viewed as a violent assault rather than a type of deviance.

Sex offenses may include a wide range of forbidden sexual activity, including the following:

- **Cunnilingus**—sexual activity involving oral contact with the female genitals
- **Fellatio**—sexual activity involving oral contact with the male genitals
- **Oral copulation**—the same as cunnilingus and fellatio; the act of joining the mouth of one person with the sex organ of another person
- **Penetration**—any intrusion, however slight, of any part of a person's body or any object manipulated or inserted by a person into the genital or anal openings of another's body, including sexual intercourse in its ordinary meaning
- **Sadomasochistic abuse**—fettering, binding, or otherwise physically restraining; whipping; or torturing for sexual gratification
- **Sexually explicit conduct**—any type of sexual intercourse between persons of the same or opposite sex, bestiality, sadomasochistic abuse, lewd exhibition, or mutual masturbation

Other Sex Offense Terminology

Intimate parts usually refers to the primary genital areas, groin, inner thighs, buttocks, and breasts.

Sexual contact usually includes any act committed without the complainant's consent for the suspect's sexual or aggressive satisfaction. This includes touching the complainant's intimate parts, forcing another person to touch one's intimate parts, or forcing another person to touch the complainant's intimate parts. In any of these cases, the body area may be clothed or unclothed.

Sexual penetration includes sexual intercourse, cunnilingus, fellatio, anal intercourse, or any other intrusion, no matter how slight, into the victim's genital, oral, or anal openings by the suspect's body or by an object. An emission of semen is not required. Any act of sexual penetration by the suspect without the affirmative, freely given permission of the victim to the specific act of penetration constitutes the crime of sexual assault.

Rape/Sexual Assault

Although males report a significant number of rapes every year, women are by far the predominant victims. In view of that, please note that this discussion assumes that the victim is usually female and the suspect male. Rape is often classified as either forcible or statutory.

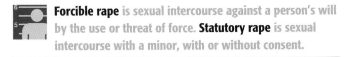 **Forcible rape** is sexual intercourse against a person's will by the use or threat of force. **Statutory rape** is sexual intercourse with a minor, with or without consent.

Forcible rape is the only sex offense that is a Part One crime, and most of the remainder of this chapter addresses this offense. According to the Uniform Crime Reports, forcible rape, like robbery and assault, has doubled in frequency in the past 10 years even though it is the least reported of the Part One crimes.

Researchers Baumer et al. (p.841) found that sex crimes are underreported for a variety of reasons, the most frequently cited being ambiguity about what illicit sexual conduct is, fear of reprisal from the offender, and feelings of embarrassment and stigma (Figure 10.1).

When investigating cases of sexual assault, officers should be aware of several assumptions that are not based on fact (Table 10.1).

Most states have substituted the term *sexual assault* for *rape.* In this chapter the words *rape* and *sexual assault* are used synonymously and interchangeably. In some states statutory rape is classified as "illegal intercourse." In other states it is classified as "assault with intent to commit rape" or as "attempted rape" when the suspect is prevented from completing the act. Some states have broadened their definition to provide that the victim *and*

Figure 10.1
Rape is underreported for a number of reasons. Many victims feel worthless or guilty afterward. Some fear the social stigma associated with rape. Others have a close relationship with their rapist and fear that a charge of rape would damage the relationship. Many victims appear to be intimidated by the criminal justice system in general or by the way the system appears to have dealt with rape cases in the past. Here, a policewoman takes oral evidence from a rape victim who is seated in the officer's squad car.

Table 10.1 / Assumptions versus Facts About Sexual Assault

Assumption	Fact
Most rapes are impulsive acts.	Most rapes are planned.
Victims are attacked suddenly, without conversation	The attack is usually preceded by conversation.
Men rape because they lack sexual outlets.	Many rapists have access to sex; they rape to express power, dominance, and control.
Rape is a sex crime.	Rape is a crime of violence. Sex is often not the goal.

Source: Minnesota Board of Police Officer Standards and Training (POST), *Learning Objectives.*

the perpetrator may be of either sex. In addition, several states provide greater penalties for attacks on the very young and the very old.

Elements of the Crime of Rape

Rape is defined in various ways by state laws, but certain elements of the offense are fairly universal.

> The elements of the crime of rape or sexual assault commonly include:
> - An act of sexual intercourse
>   - with a person other than a spouse,
>   - committed without the victim's consent, and
>   - against the victim's will and by force.

An Act of Sexual Intercourse The element of sexual intercourse does not require establishing that a complete sex act accompanied by ejaculation occurred. Any degree of penetration is sufficient to constitute sexual intercourse. An emission of semen is not required.

With a Person Other Than a Spouse This element now allows the possibility of a man being raped, either by a male or female. Some states, as noted, are revising their laws to include as rape forcible sex acts committed by an adult male against another male. Although most states require that the victim not be the man's wife, a husband can be charged with assault. Moreover, some states include as rape an act of forced sexual intercourse with a wife during a legal separation if the act fulfills the other requirements of rape. Other states are considering laws that would include as rape a husband's forced sexual intercourse accompanied by serious threats against a wife's life. Oregon has such a law and has tried (and acquitted) a husband.

Committed without the Consent of the Victim Consent given because of fear, panic, emotional disturbance, mental illness, or retardation; while on drugs or unconscious; or by a child is *not* considered true consent.

Against the Victim's Will and by Force This element has traditionally been the most difficult to prove and the most subject to attack by the defense. Although laws require the victim to use the utmost resistance possible, such resistance can result in additional violence and even death. A person willing to rape is often willing to injure. Therefore, legislation in many states emphasizes the rapist's words, actions, and intent rather than the victim's degree of resistance.

Police officers are often asked whether it is better for a victim to resist or to submit to a sexual attack. Does resistance increase the attacker's violence? It is a difficult question to answer because researchers have arrived at different conclusions. Some results indicate that resisting reduces the likelihood of continued assault; others, that it makes the attacker more violent. Some people who have been sexually assaulted reported that they fought back only after they had already been harmed, which would appear to preclude that resisting caused increased violence. It has been found that people who have been attacked previously are more apt to resist.

One study pointed out that in no other crime are victims expected to resist or not to resist their assailants. Certainly everyone has a right to defend themselves, but whether it is more harmful to the victim to choose to defend is not possible to state. This must be an individual decision. Some police departments do not give advice on this question because of the possibility of lawsuits.

More emphasis should be placed on the attacker's behavior than on that of the victim. Increasing the penalty where the attacker uses extreme violence may help reduce the severity of the attacks, although this is problematic because of the emotional status and possible mental instability of this type of criminal.

Sex Offenders

W right (pp.97–98) provides the following operational definition of a sexual offender: "(1) A person or persons who [use or attempt] to use physical force on another person, against [his or her] will, . . . to commit an act intended to provide sexual gratification to the aggressor(s). (2) A person or persons who [use] coercion on another person who is incapable or in a diminished capacity to voice [his or her] will, in an attempt to commit an act intended to provide sexual gratification to the aggressor(s)."

Some sexual assault offenders are sadistic and commit physical abuses in hostile, vicious manners that result in injury or even death to the victim. Others seek to control their victims through threats and physical strength but do not cause permanent physical injuries. Still others act out aggression and hatred in short attacks on women

selected as random targets. Rapists may be categorized as motivated by either power or anger. Each category is further divided into two subcategories (Table 10.2).

However, as one reviewer of this text noted: "Many rapists commit their acts not because of anger or power issues, but because they can. They want sex, and they are simply going to take it. Sometimes it's about evil people acting on their own hedonism against weaker individuals." No personality or physical type can be automatically eliminated as a sex offender. Sex offenders include those who are married, have families and good jobs, are college educated, and are active churchgoers.

Suspects fall into two general classifications: those who know the victim and those who are known sex offenders. In the first category are friends of the victim, people who have daily contact with the victim's relatives, those who make deliveries to the victim's residence or business, and neighbors. In the second category are those on file in police records as having committed prior sex offenses. Known offenders with prior arrests are prime suspects because rehabilitation is often unsuccessful.

Information to Obtain

If a suspect is arrested at or near the scene, conduct a field identification. If much time has elapsed between the offense and the report, use other means of identification. If the victim knows the assailant, obtain the suspect's name, address, complete description, and the nature of the relationship with victim. Then obtain arrest and search warrants. If the suspect is unknown to the victim, check modus operandi (MO) files and have the victim look at photo files on sex offenders.

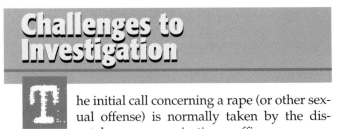

MO factors important in investigating sex offenses include type of offense, words spoken, use of a weapon, actual method of attack, time of day, type of location, and victim's age.

These MO factors are manifested in the offender's behavior and should be asked about when interviewing victims, as discussed shortly.

Challenges to Investigation

T he initial call concerning a rape (or other sexual offense) is normally taken by the dispatcher, communications officer, or complaint clerk. The person taking the call immediately dispatches a patrol unit, not only because rape is a felony but also because it is a crime in which the offender may be

Table 10.2 / **Profiles of Rapists**

	POWER RAPISTS		ANGER RAPISTS	
	Manhood Reassurance	Manhood Assertion	Retaliatory/Punishment	Excitation/Sadism
Purpose	Confirm manhood to self	Express manhood to victim	Punish women for real or imagined wrongs	Obtain
Preassault behavior	Fantasizes about success-ful sexual relationships; plans attack	Seldom pre-planned; crime of opportunity	Spontaneous act in response to a significant stressor	Violent fantasies; careful planning
Victim selection	Observes (prowler, window peeker)	By chance	Spontaneous	Cruises
Victim characteristics	Same race; meek, nonassertive	Same age and race	Resembles female in his life	Same age and race
Location of approach	Inside victim's residence	Singles bars	Near his residence or job	Any location
Type of approach	Stealth; hand over mouth	Smooth talker; con	Blitz; immediate excessive use of force	Brandish a weapon
Weapon	Of opportunity (if used)	Of opportunity (if used)	Of opportunity (if used)	Of choice or planned
Time of day	Nighttime	Nighttime	Anytime	Anytime
Sexual acts	Normal	Self-satisfying; vaginal/penile intercourse; vaginal/anal intercourse; fellatio; spends long time	Violent, painful sex acts; degrading, humiliating acts; spends short time	Experimental sex; inserts objects into body cavities; spends long time
Sexual dysfunction	Erection problems; premature ejaculation	Retarded ejaculation	–	–
Other behaviors	Relatively nonviolent	Tears clothing off	Profanity; injury provoking; assaultive	Excessive, brutal force; bondage; torture; cuts clothing off; protects identity (mask, gloves); most likely to kill
Postassault behavior	Likely to apologize; takes personal items; keeps a diary	Likely to threaten; takes items as trophies; boasts of conquests	Leaves abruptly; may or may not threaten	Straightens scene; shows no remorse

Source: William C. Bradway. "Stages of a Sexual Assault." *Law and Order,* September 1990, pp. 119–124. Reprinted by permission of the publisher.

known or close to the scene. The person taking the call then tells the victim to wait for the police to arrive if at a safe location and not to alter her physical appearance or touch anything at the scene. The victim is asked whether she can identify or describe the suspect, whether she has sustained serious injuries, and whether she needs immediate medical assistance. The victim should also be advised not to wash, shower, or douche before having a medical exam. As with any violent crime, early response is critical not only in apprehending the suspect but also in reducing the victim's anxiety.

 Special challenges to investigating rape include the sensitive nature of the offense, social attitudes, and the victim's horror and/or embarrassment. A rape investigation requires great sensitivity.

To help investigators overcome some of these challenges, many departments are implementing a procedure for victims of sexual assault known as *blind reporting.*

Blind Reporting

Rape victims may feel foolish, hurt, ashamed, vulnerable, and frightened. Furthermore, the prospect of reliving the entire experience by having the police ask detailed and personal questions is more than many victims can bear, particularly immediately after the incident. However, given time, victims may come to trust others enough to recount the attack, even hoping to prevent the same assailant from attacking others. The U.S. Department of Justice (*A National Protocol*, p.45) recommends jurisdictions consider implementing a blind reporting system for sexual assault cases in which victims

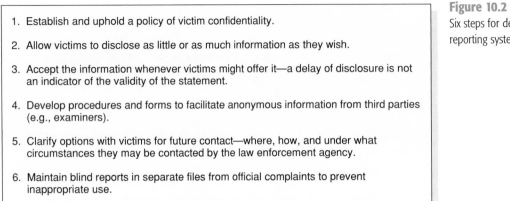

1. Establish and uphold a policy of victim confidentiality.

2. Allow victims to disclose as little or as much information as they wish.

3. Accept the information whenever victims might offer it—a delay of disclosure is not an indicator of the validity of the statement.

4. Develop procedures and forms to facilitate anonymous information from third parties (e.g., examiners).

5. Clarify options with victims for future contact—where, how, and under what circumstances they may be contacted by the law enforcement agency.

6. Maintain blind reports in separate files from official complaints to prevent inappropriate use.

Figure 10.2
Six steps for developing an effective blind reporting system

do not want to report immediately or are undecided about reporting.

Blind reporting allows sexual assault victims to retain their anonymity and confidentiality while sharing critical information with law enforcement. It also permits victims to gather legal information from law enforcement without having to commit immediately to an investigation.

The success of blind reporting hinges on whether trust can be established between the victim and the investigator (Garcia and Henderson, p.14). Figure 10.2 outlines six steps law enforcement agencies can take to develop an effective blind reporting system (*A National Protocol*, p.47).

The legal acceptability of blind reporting varies from state to state, and even from county to county. In jurisdictions where prosecutors do accept blind report records, such records become the "founding document" in the formal sexual assault investigation should the victim decide to file a complaint and proceed with a full investigation.

Blind reporting procedures provide for the collection of crucial medical-legal evidence from sexual assault victims, as discussed shortly. However, for the sexual assault victims who do report the attack immediately, law enforcement personnel must be prepared for a swift yet sensitive response.

The Police Response

Lonsway and Cassidy (2005) report on a study supported by the District of Columbia Metropolitan Police Department in which female interviewers with extensive professional experience in sexual assault and domestic violence cases made approximately 1,100 contacts with victims of sexual assault. From this number, 323 were interviewed. The study concluded: "Evidence from research and experi-

ence from across the country is that law enforcement agencies have considerable room for improvement in their response to victims of sexual assault" (Lonsway and Cassidy, p.115).

The first officers to arrive can make or break a rape case depending on how they approach the victim. All police officers should have special training in handling sexual assault victims. Whenever possible, an officer without such training should not be assigned to this kind of case.

As soon as you arrive at the scene, announce yourself clearly to allay fears the victim may have that the suspect is returning. Explain to the victim what is being done for her safety. If the rape has just occurred, if there are serious injuries, or if it appears the victim is in shock, call for an ambulance.

Protect the crime scene and broadcast a description of the assailant, means and direction of flight, and the time and exact location of the assault. The victim may be unable to describe the suspect because of stress or darkness or because the perpetrator wore a mask or other identity-concealing clothing. A time lapse before reporting the offense can occur because of the victim's embarrassment, confusion, or shock or because the victim was taken to a remote area, giving the suspect time to escape.

Establish a command post away from the scene to divert attention from the address of the victim and also to preserve the scene. Conduct the preliminary investigation as described in Chapter 1. Ascertain the background of both the accuser and, if possible, the accused. At a minimum, officers on the scene should do the following:

- Record their arrival time.
- Determine the victim's location and condition. Request an ambulance if needed. Obtain identification of the suspect if possible.
- Determine whether the suspect is at the scene.
- Protect the crime scene.
- Identify and separate witnesses. Obtain valid identification from them and then obtain preliminary statements.
- Initiate crime broadcast if applicable.

Sometimes it is difficult to determine whether an assault or homicide is a sex-related crime. Evidence of sexual activity observable at the crime scene or on the victim's body includes torn or no clothing, seminal fluid on or near the body, genital bruising or injury, and sexually suggestive positioning of the body.

Physical Evidence

Evidence in a rape case shows the amount of force that occurred, establishes that a sex act was performed, and links the act with the suspect.

> Evidence in a rape case consists of stained or torn clothing; scratches, bruises, or cuts; evidence of a struggle; and semen and bloodstains.

Because such evidence deteriorates rapidly, obtain it as soon as possible. Some police departments have rape kits that contain the equipment needed to collect, label, and preserve evidence (Figure 10.3).

Photograph all injuries to the victim, and take as evidence any torn or stained clothing. Examine the scene for other physical evidence such as fingerprints, footprints, a weapon, stains, or personal objects the suspect may have left behind. Examine washcloths or towels the suspect may have used. Photograph any signs of a struggle such as broken objects, overturned furniture, or, if outdoors, disturbed vegetation.

If the assault occurred outdoors, take soil and vegetation samples for comparison. If the assault occurred in a vehicle, vacuum the car seats and interior to obtain soil, hairs, and other fibers. Examine the seats for blood and semen stains. DNA analysis has become increasingly important in sexual assault cases.

If a suspect is apprehended, photograph any injuries, marks, or scratches on the suspect's body. Obtain blood and hair samples, and give the appropriate tests to determine whether the suspect is intoxicated or on drugs. Obtain any clothing or possessions of the suspect that might connect him with the rape. If necessary, obtain a warrant to search his vehicle, home, or office. Such searches may reveal items associated with perversion or weapons of the type used in the assault.

Lonsway and Cassidy (pp.115–116) contend that a key to improving the response to sexual assault victims is a team approach with victim advocacy organizations such as rape crisis centers: "By coordinating with victim service organizations, police agencies are better able to work with victims and advocates to conduct an investigation that meets the highest standards for professionalism and compassion." They (p.118) recommend that officers give all sexual assault victims a form with resources for victim services, the criminal justice process, their case number, and how to get further information on how their case is progressing.

Investigating Cold Sexual Assault Cases Markey (pp.1–5) describes how new technologies and traditional police methods can combine to solve cold sexual assault cases. An internal audit of the Phoenix Police Department identified over 1,700 sexual assault examination kits waiting for evaluation and screening, with 800 new

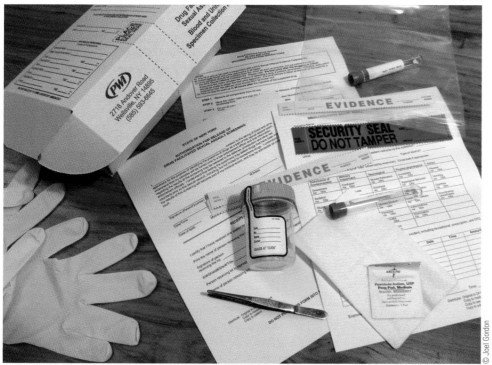

Figure 10.3
Sex crimes evidence collection kits are designed to assist in the uniform collection of evidentiary specimens in sexual assaults. Most kits include instructions for handling trace evidence, clothing and underwear, debris, dried secretions, fingernail scrapings, head and pubic hairs, saliva, blood, vaginal/penile smears, and anal smears.

cases being added each year. This was the impetus for the formation of a multidisciplinary team to address the problem, with investigation and laboratory and victim services forming the nucleus of the team. The team applied for and received an Arizona grant providing 18 months of funding for the Phoenix Cold Case Sex Crime Team.

The first hurdle was the bottleneck in the lab. The team decided to transfer a grant-funded position of detective to the lab to hire a new analyst and deal with the bottleneck. The next hurdle was how to approach the "neglected" victims. The solution was to use victim advocates, generally civilian police employees specialized in victim assistance. Two other hurdles of investigations and prosecutions were deceased and unwilling victims. Here the unit worked closely with prosecutors to develop a review process to address each case individually. Yet another hurdle was the Arizona statute of limitations of seven years for sexual assault. In 2001, to remedy this problem, the Arizona legislature removed the statute of limitations for sexual assault.

According to Markey (p.3), by June 2003, the team had reviewed over 1,000 cases dating back to the 1960s, identified 31 suspects with DNA evidence or another method of forensic or trace evidence, and cleared 58 cases. Markey (p.5) contends: "Technology, old-fashioned police work, victim advocacy and interagency cooperation need to work in harmony to produce positive results."

The Significance of Fantasy in Sexual Assaults   Geberth (p.94) suggests that fantasies are a "normal" consequence of human sexuality. He (p.98) contends that fantasy can indicate the "signature" of an offender, allowing detectives to link an offender to a particular series of crimes that this offender commits. Because fantasy is so strongly associated with sexual assault, Geberth (p.99) recommends that search warrant applications include a list of the materials they would expect to recover from an offender who indulged in sexual fantasies, such as sadistic pornography, drawings, videotapes, women's lingerie and clothing, and fantasy stories featuring sexual sadism.

Geberth also notes that sexual sadists often are obsessed with keeping trophies and recordings of the assaults. Therefore, any search warrant applications in such cases should include photographs, records, scripts, letters, diaries, audiotapes, videotapes, and newspaper reports of the crimes as possible evidence to be seized.

Anchorage's Antirape Unit

When the Anchorage (Alaska) Police Department discovered that it averaged 122 percent more rapes than any other urban police department in the country, with one-third of the cases left uninvestigated because of lack of personnel, it created a Crime Intervention Unit (CIU)

to address the problem (Whitehead, 2005). The Anchorage mayor asked the Alaska congressional delegation for funding for the CIU and received $2 million. The CIU is a test program involving volunteers and undercover police officers who target areas where sexual violence is most likely to take place.

As Whitehead (p.64) explains, approximately 40 volunteers attended a one-day training session conducted by the Sexual Assault Unit. They learned what constituted suspicious behavior, how to contact the police, the needed information for a police report, and how to make a citizen's arrest.

The CIU detectives work in plainclothes at targeted "hot spots" around town, going into bars and blending in with the patrons to watch for suspicious behavior. The officers get to know the bar owners and employees and enlist their aid in preventing sexual assaults. According to the developer of the program, alcohol is the most typical ingredient in sexual assault cases: "Alcohol is almost always present either on the suspect, the victim or both" (Whitehead, p.65). This approach can be especially effective in curbing instances of date rape.

Investigating Date Rape

A particularly difficult type of sexual assault is **date rape,** in which the victim knows the suspect. Frequently drugs, including alcohol, are involved in such cases.

Additional evidence in date rape cases may include the presence of alcohol and/or drugs in the victim's system.

Rohypnol, or the "date rape drug," is the oldest drug used in this crime and is up to 10 times more powerful than Valium and Halcion in producing a slowing of physical and mental responses, muscle reflexes, and amnesia. According to DePresca (p.210), Rohypnol looks like aspirin and, when dropped in a drink, is colorless and odorless, taking full effect between 30 and 60 minutes after ingestion. The effects may include confusion, light-headedness, and disorientation; lowered values; a loss of inhibitions; and eventually being physically unable to resist a sexual attack. Although not legally produced or dispensed in the United States, it is legally used in almost 70 countries across South America, Latin America, and Europe. One tablet can be bought for about 40 cents in Mexico (DePresca, p.210).

DePresca (p.211) also describes gamma hydroxybutyrate, or GHB: "This date rape drug is strong, with potential deadly consequences. Also called Grievous Bodily Harm, Liquid X, Saltwater and Easy Lay, the drug is primarily made in home laboratories. Like Rohypnol, GHB is colorless, odorless and can easily be slipped into a drink. It has a powerful amnesia effect that lasts three to four hours and is much more severe than Rohypnol."

Another date rape drug is Ecstasy, or MDMA (3,4 methylenedioxymethamphetamine). Ecstasy is a stimulant with psychedelic effects that can last from four to six hours. It is usually taken orally in pill form. Its psychological effects include confusion, depression, anxiety, sleeplessness, drug craving, and paranoia. Adverse physical effects include muscle tension, involuntary teeth clenching, nausea, blurred vision, feeling faint, tremors, rapid eye movement, and sweating or chills (*MDMA*, p.1).

Acknowledging the severe and dangerous nature of such drug-assisted sexual assaults, the Drug-Induced Rape Prevention and Punishment Act was signed in 1996, allowing courts to impose prison sentences of up to 20 years on anyone intending to use illicit drugs to aid in the commission of sexual assault.

Officers investigating a sexual assault where the victim cannot give much information about the crime should suspect that a date rape drug is involved. Therefore, in addition to following the usual protocol for investigating sexual assault, officers should inform emergency medical technicians and emergency room (ER) personnel that a date rape drug is suspected. Blood and urine tests may show the presence of a specific drug.

Technology Innovations

Kanable (p.78) describes how osmolality can be used to detect tampered beverages. (*Osmolality* is a science that looks at osmotic pressure, which is based on the number of dissolved particles in a solution.) Automated osmometers are available that can do 30 tests per hour. According to Kanable (p.81): "Osmolality, an effective analytical tool of the hospital laboratory, food and consumer products industries, can be an excellent, low cost, rapid and non-destructive screening tool for the forensic drug testing laboratory."

A disadvantage of osmometers is that they do not tell you what you have, only that somebody has tampered with a liquid by adding something that has a small molecular weight. It is just a screen.

The Victim's Medical Examination

he rape victim should have a medical examination as soon as possible to establish injuries, to determine whether intercourse occurred, and to protect against venereal disease and pregnancy. Some hospitals provide drugs at the initial

examination to lessen the possibility of pregnancy. Further examination for venereal disease is also conducted.

Although each hospital has its own procedures, ER doctors and nurses are trained to observe and treat trauma; therefore, they can provide counseling and support services to the victim during this initial critical phase. Good examination-stage care promotes later cooperation from the victim.

The hospital obtains medical-legal evidence that includes a detailed report of an examination of the victim for trauma, injuries, and intercourse. The report contains precise descriptions of all bruises, scratches, cuts, and other injuries. The physician's report contains descriptions of the physician's findings and treatment, the victim's statements, documentation of the presence or absence of semen, documentation of the presence of drugs in the victim's system, the specific diagnosis of trauma, and any other specific medical facts concerning the victim's condition. The report should contain no conclusions as to whether the woman was raped because this is a legal matter for the court to decide. However, in some states, hospitals are required by law to report suspected rape cases to the police.

Most hospitals have a sexual assault and vaginal kit in the examination room with the proper forms and tests for semen. Tests can be made of the vagina, anus, or mouth, depending on the type of assault. After the examination, these kits are given to the police at the victim's request and sent to a crime laboratory for analysis.

The victim should be asked to sign a release form that authorizes the medical facility to provide police a copy of the examination record. Hospital reports may be introduced as evidence even if a police officer was not present during the examination. Also ask the hospital and the victim for the clothing the victim was wearing at the time of the assault if it was not obtained earlier.

The victim is reimbursed for medical examination costs in jurisdictions that have victim compensation laws. In other states, local or state health agencies may cover the costs. Personnel at rape crisis centers can assist in these arrangements. Such information is important to many victims.

As mentioned, many rape victims choose not to go to the police immediately following their attack. Such victims, however, must be encouraged to seek prompt medical attention and to allow for the collection of evidence at a medical examination in case they later decide to proceed with an investigation. Given these victims' overwhelming need for privacy and confidentiality at this critical time, the availability of blind reporting is extremely beneficial in motivating sexual assault victims to proceed with collecting and processing medical evidence.

A suspect apprehended at or near the scene also usually undergoes a similar medical examination.

Interviewing the Victim

ape is typically a horrifying, violent experience of violation to the victim. Reporting it to the police is frequently a courageous act because the victim knows that she will be forced to relive the experience through numerous retellings and that her word may be doubted. In addition, rape is humiliating and can involve numerous undesirable repercussions such as ostracism by friends and family, hospitalization, pregnancy, venereal disease, and even AIDS. At the time of the interview, the rape victim may be hysterical or unusually calm. Remember: Rape is a crime of aggression and hostility and is usually conducted violently. Attempt to establish rapport by using sympathetic body language and explaining the necessity for asking sensitive questions.

Attempt to reinforce the victim's emotional well-being, but also obtain the facts. The pressure and stress caused by rape can make victims uncooperative. Insensitive actions by a male investigator may reinforce the female victim's image of male aggressiveness and result in refusal to answer questions.

Rape victims sometimes complain that investigative personnel question the complaint's validity even before hearing the facts, are rude and overly aggressive, fail to explain the procedures used in the investigation, ask highly personal questions too early in the interview, or have or express unsympathetic or negative attitudes about the victim's personal appearance, clothing, or actions, implying that the victim may be partly responsible for the crime.

Both uniformed and investigative personnel, male and female, can help the victim cooperate if they are understanding and supportive. Such an approach not only contributes to the victim's psychological well-being but also helps obtain information and evidence required to apprehend and prosecute the offender. Some departments require that two investigators or a victim's advocate be present when a rape victim is interviewed.

Although some police feel that professional medical personnel should obtain the personal details of a sexual attack, this is shirking responsibility. Deal with the victim's emotional and psychological needs completely while investigating the case and preserving evidence.

Whether the investigator's gender affects the victim's cooperation is debatable. Some believe that a female investigator should interview female victims. Others feel that a male can better show victims that men can be understanding and nonaggressive. How much victims cooperate usually depends less on the interviewer's gender than on his or her attitude, patience, understanding, competence, and ability to establish rapport. Treat the victim with care, concern, and understanding. Assume that the sexual assault is real unless facts ultimately prove otherwise.

The interview location is also important. The police station may be unsatisfactory. The victim's home may be ideal—if the rape did not occur there. Tell the victim that you must ask questions about the incident and ask where she would be most comfortable talking about it. If the victim is hospitalized, consult with the medical staff as to when you can question her.

No matter where the interview is conducted, do it privately. Although the victim should be allowed to have a relative or friend nearby to talk to, it is better to be alone with the victim when specific questions are asked. If the victim insists on having someone with her, discuss with this person the procedure to be followed. Explain that the person's presence is important to the victim for reassurance and security but that the person must allow the victim to talk freely and not interrupt.

The victim's family and friends can considerably influence whether the victim relates the entire story. A wide range of emotions can occur from mothers, fathers, husbands, or other family members. They may be silent, hysterical, or angry to the point that they have every intention of killing the perpetrator if they find him. Sometimes such anger is turned against the victim.

Make a complete report of the victim's appearance and behavior: presence of liquor or drugs; bruises, scratches, or marks; manner of speech; emotional condition; appearance of clothes or hair; color of face; smeared makeup; torn clothes; and stains. Take photographs to supplement your notes.

The needed initial information includes the victim's name, age, home address, work address, telephone number(s) and any prior relationship with the offender, if the offender is known. At a *later* interview, investigators should obtain additional information about the victim, including the following:

- Children and their ages
- Victim's educational level
- Family, parents, and the nature of the victim's relationship with them
- Fears
- Financial status, past and present
- Friends and enemies
- Hobbies
- Marital status
- Medical history, physical and mental
- Occupation, past and present
- Personal habits
- Physical description, including attire at the time of the incident
- Recent court actions
- Recent changes in lifestyle
- Reputation on the job and in the neighborhood
- Residence, past and present

- Social habits
- Use of alcohol and drugs

Obtain a detailed account of the crime, including the suspect's actions and statements, special characteristics or oddities, and any unusual sexual behaviors. Determine exactly where and how the attack occurred, what happened before and after the attack, and whether the victim can give any motive for the attack. Explain what you need to know and why, the procedures you will follow, and how important the victim's cooperation is. Use open-ended questions such as, "Take your time and tell me exactly what happened."

Determine the exact details of resistance, even if not required by law. Was there any unconsciousness, paralysis, or fainting? Was there penetration? Who did the victim first talk to after the assault? How soon was the report made, and if there was a delay, what was the reason?

Establish lack of consent. Obtain the names of any witnesses. Determine where the victim was before the attack and whether someone might have seen her and followed her. The suspect's description can then be used at that location to see whether anyone there can identify him. Obtain as much information as possible about the suspect: voice, mannerisms, clothing, actions, and general appearance.

It is important to obtain as many details as possible even though they may appear insignificant at the time. How the initial contact was made; attempts at concealment; the suspect's voice, appearance, and exact words; unusual behavior, including unusual sexual acts performed—all these can be helpful.

Establishing the Behavioral Profile in Sex Offense Cases

Because rapists are generally recidivists (about 70 percent of them commit more than one rape), it is possible that the details and MOs of offenses in another area of the same city or another community may be identical to the present case. For this reason, the usefulness of behavioral profiling becomes apparent, and interviews with victims should focus on the *offender's* behavior.

Several specific areas should be covered in the behavior-oriented interview of rape victims, embodied in three essential basic steps: (1) Carefully interview the victim about the rapist's *behavior,* (2) analyze that behavior to ascertain the *motivation* underlying the assault, and (3) compile a *profile* of the individual likely to have committed the crime.

The three types of rapist behavior of concern to investigators are physical (use of force), verbal, and sexual. First, ascertain the method of approach. Three common approaches are the "con" approach, in which the offender is initially friendly, even charming, and dupes the victim; the "blitz" approach, in which the offender directly physically assaults the victim, frequently gagging, binding, or blindfolding the victim; and the "surprise" approach, in which the offender hides in the back seat of a car, in shrubbery, or behind a wall or waits until the victim is sleeping.

After determining the approach, you should determine how the perpetrator maintained control. Four common methods of control are (1) mere presence, (2) verbal threats, (3) display of a weapon, and (4) use of physical force.

If the rapist used physical force, it is important to determine the amount of force, as this gives insight into the offender's motivations. Four levels of physical force may be used: (1) *minimal,* perhaps slapping; (2) *moderate,* repeated hitting; (3) *excessive,* beating resulting in bruises and cuts; and (4) *brutal,* sadistic torture. This last type of offender is typically extremely profane, abusive, and aggressive, and the victim may require hospitalization or die.

Sexual sadists become more sexually excited the more the victim suffers. The pleasure of complete domination over another person is the essence of the sadistic drive. Most sadists are cunning and deceitful and feel no remorse or compassion. They feel superior to society, especially the law. They often use pliers, electric cattle prods, whips, fire, bondage, amputation, and objects inserted into the vagina. They may keep diaries, audiotapes, sexual devices and devices to torture victims, photographs of victims, and other incriminating evidence—all items to be included in a search warrant.

In addition to the offender's sexual behavior, investigators should inquire about the offender's verbal behavior. Themes in rapists' conversations include threats, orders, personal inquiries of the victim, personal revelations, obscene names, racial epithets, and inquiries about the victim's sexual enjoyment. Also ask about the *victim's* verbal behavior. Did the offender demand that the victim say certain words or demand that she beg, plead, scream? Such demands also shed insight into the offender's motivation.

Specifically ask victims about any change in the offender's behavior, either verbal, physical, or sexual. Such changes can indicate weakness or fear if the offender lessens his efforts, or anger and hostility if he suddenly increases his efforts.

A further area of inquiry relates to the offender's experience level. Did he take actions to protect his identity, to destroy or remove evidence, or to make certain he had an escape route? The novice rapist may take minimal or obvious actions to protect his identity—for example, wearing a ski mask and gloves, changing his voice tone, affecting an accent, ordering the victim not to look at him, or blindfolding and binding the victim. These are common precautions a person not knowledgeable of phosphotate tests of hair and fiber evidence would be expected to take. In contrast, the experienced rapist may walk through the residence or prepare an escape route, disable the phone, order the victim to shower or douche, bring bindings or gags, wear surgical gloves, or take or force the victim to wash items the rapist touched or ejaculated on, such as bedding and the victim's clothing.

Also determine whether any items other than those of evidentiary value were taken by the offender. Of interest are not only items of value but also items of a personal nature. It is important to determine not only whether items were taken but also why. Again, such information may provide insight into the offender's motivation.

Ending the Victim Interview

End the interview with an explanation of available victim assistance programs, such as Sexual Offense Services (SOS). Arrange for relatives, friends, or personnel from a rape crisis center to help the victim. If the victim refuses to be questioned, is incapable of answering questions because of shock or injuries, or begins the interview but then breaks down emotionally, terminate the interview for the time being, but return later.

Explain to the victim what will happen next in the criminal justice system. Give the victim the case number and a phone number to call at the police department if any other details are remembered or if questions arise.

Follow-Up Investigation

After the preliminary investigation, medical examination, and initial interview are completed, conduct a follow-up investigation. Interview the victim again in two to five days to obtain further information and to compare the statements made after time has elapsed. Following that interview, determine whether the crime scene or evidence has been altered or contaminated and also interview all possible witnesses to the offense.

It is worth noting that many prosecutors discourage the practice of conducting follow-up interviews with sexual assault victims, contending that the only thing these interviews accomplish is to provide the defense with inconsistent statements. Instead, these prosecutors argue, the victim should be interviewed by the on-the-scene officer and then formally interviewed by the investigator. It is advised that sexual assault investigators be cognizant of this hazard of inconsistent statements and be familiar with the practices and preferences of prosecutors in their jurisdiction.

Interviewing Witnesses

Locate witnesses as soon as possible, and obtain their names, addresses, and phone numbers. Canvass the neighborhood for possible witnesses. Even though witnesses may not have seen the incident, they may be able to describe the suspect or his vehicle. They may have heard screams or statements made by the victim or the offender.

Determine whether a relationship exists between the witness and the victim or offender. Determine exactly what the witness saw and heard. Did the witness see the victim before, during, or after the assault? Did the witness see the victim with the suspect? How did the witness happen to be in the vicinity where the offense occurred? Interview acquaintances and individuals known to the victim, because many victims know their rapists. In fact, the incidence of date rape has been increasing. In such cases it is a matter of proving lack of consent.

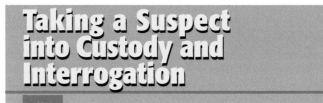 Taking a Suspect into Custody and Interrogation

If a suspect is apprehended at the scene, record any spontaneous statements made by the suspect and photograph him. If more than one suspect is present, separate them. Do not allow communication among suspect, victim, and witness. Remove the suspect from the scene as soon as possible.

When interrogating sex offenders, obtain as much information as possible, yet remain nonjudgmental. The suspect should be the last person interviewed. This allows the interviewer to have all information possible by the time of the suspect interview: facts about the victim, the type of offense, and the location of the crime; statements from witnesses, neighbors, and informants; and information about the suspect's background.

As in most interrogation situations, building rapport is the first step. Suggest to the suspect that you understand what he is going through. Ask about his family, his job, and his interests. Assess the suspect's character. After rapport is established, ask the suspect to tell his side of the story from beginning to end and do not interrupt him. Show interest in what he is saying and keep him talking. The interrogator's approach should be one of "you tell me what happened and I will understand," even though that may not be the investigator's actual feelings.

The objective is to obtain the truth and the information necessary for proving guilt or innocence. To help accomplish this goal, attempt to gain the suspect's confidence. Many suspects feel they can justify their actions by putting some blame on the victim—for example, "She came on to me."

During the interrogation, remember that the seriousness of the charge to be brought will be based on the information you obtain. All elements of the charged offense must be proven, so keep the possible charges in mind and prepare questions to elicit supporting information.

Coordination with Other Agencies

 number of other agencies and individuals assist in handling rape cases.

The public and the news media can greatly influence the prosecution of a rape case. Medical and hospital personnel influence the victim's attitude and cooperation in obtaining facts for medical reports and the necessary evidence for use in court. Rape crisis centers can provide various kinds of support to victims and encourage them to sign a complaint.

Gomez (pp.45–51) describes the Miami-Dade (Florida) Police Department's Sexual Crimes Clearinghouse (SCCH), a multijurisdictional link established in 1999 to promote communication and coordination among all law enforcement agencies sharing a common geographical boundary: "The SCCH provides real-time intelligence information relating to sexual crime offenses for the purpose of identifying trends and patterns in criminal behavior." SCCH analysts prepare victim surveys, create computerized lineups and photo stacks, provide visual maps in serial cases, and coordinate information between agencies.

According to Gomez (p.49) the SCCH receives case information from Miami-Dade, Broward, Monroe, and Collier Counties and enters it into its database. It then forwards any information related to the case back to the department. It also responds to requests for information on similar cases and subject background. Says Gomez (p.50): "The successes of the SCCH can be seen in the numerous arrests since its inception—the direct result of the clearinghouse's contact with other law enforcement agencies."

Prosecution of Rape and Statutory Charges

 ew criminal cases are as difficult to prosecute as rape, at least under older laws. Despite changes in the law, it is virtually impossible to obtain a conviction on the victim's testimony alone.

Defendants usually want a jury trial because of present laws and attitudes regarding rape, and because the defendant is not required to testify. However, the victim not only must relate a very difficult ordeal but also be subjected to cross-examination that can make *her* appear to be the one on trial.

Juries tend to be unsympathetic with a victim who was drinking heavily, hitchhiking, or using drugs or who left a bar with a stranger or engaged in other socially "unacceptable" actions. Many newer laws make it very explicit that such conditions are not to be considered during the trial. Newer laws also state that the victim's testimony need not be corroborated and that testimony about the degree of resistance—although it may be admitted—is not required.

Moreover, testimony about the victim's previous sexual conduct is not admissible unless (1) the victim has had prior sexual relations with the defendant, (2) there is evidence of venereal disease or pregnancy resulting from the assault, (3) circumstances suggest that consent occurred within the calendar year, or (4) the victim has not told the truth or has filed a false report.

Juries must not be instructed that a victim who consented to sexual intercourse with other persons would be likely to have consented with the defendant, that the victim's prior sexual conduct may be used to determine credibility, or that the victim's testimony should be subjected to any greater test of credibility than in any other crime. Some have argued, however, that victims' characters are being judged even before a case has a chance to go to trial. These critics contend that victim characteristics and credibility issues frequently prevent sexual assault cases from ever reaching court by negatively affecting prosecutors' charging decisions in sexual assault cases.

Some states have made it illegal to publish the names or addresses of sex crime victims and have required that the county where the crime occurred pay the medical examination expenses.

Former penalties were so severe that many juries hesitated to convict. More recent laws usually include both oral and anal sexual conduct, and many classify sexual offenses by degrees.

Some victims decide not to prosecute because of pressure from family or friends, fear of reprisal, shame, fear of going to court, or emotional or mental disturbance.

Sometimes the prosecuting attorney refuses to take the case to court because the case is weak and thus has little chance of conviction. For example, there may not be enough physical evidence to corroborate the victim's complaint, or the victim may be a known prostitute or a girlfriend of the rapist, or she may be pregnant because of prior sexual relations with the assailant. At other times the report is unfounded and unsubstantiated by the evidence.

False Reports

Women make false reports of sexual assault for a number of reasons, including getting revenge on lovers who have jilted them, covering up a pregnancy, or getting attention. Such circumstances need to be ruled out when investigating a reported sexual assault. The credibility of rape reports is probably questioned more frequently than that of any other felony report. A polygraph can help determine the truth of the complainant's statements. If the evidence of a false report is overwhelming, include all the facts in your closeout report.

If the victim admits orally or in writing that her story was false, close the case. When the victim's credibility is in serious doubt because of contradictory evidence, the investigating officer's superior or the prosecutor can close the case.

Civil Commitment of Sex Offenders after Sentences Served

Because of the high recidivism rate of sex offenders following their release from jail or prison, many advocate legislation that allows the civil commitment of sex offenders upon completion of their sentence. Such legislation acknowledges that although sex offenders may have paid a debt to society by spending time behind bars, often little if anything is accomplished during this period of incarceration to address and treat the disorders that lead offenders to commit sexual assault.

"More than a decade after the passage of Megan's Laws and related civil commitment statutes, states and localities are still struggling to balance the rights of the community with those of convicted sex offenders who must have someplace to live when they are released back into society" ("Problems Still Linger," p.12). Although many contend that these acts violate offenders' civil rights, the Supreme Court has upheld the constitutionality of at least one state's civil commitment law. In *Kansas v. Hendricks* (1997), the Court upheld

Kansas' Sexually Violent Predator Act, which establishes procedures by which that state may civilly commit to a mental hospital people likely to commit predatory acts of sexual violence due to a mental abnormality or personality disorder.

However, in *Kansas v. Crane* (2001), the Supreme Court began refining its 1997 ruling in *Hendricks,* adding a new limitation on such civil commitments, saying that there must be "proof of [an offender's] serious difficulty in controlling [his] behavior."

Sex Offender Registry and Notification

With the realization that many convicted sex offenders have committed one or more such crimes prior to the current act for which they are serving time has come a flurry of legislation designed to notify the public of such predators living in their communities and to assist law enforcement in keeping track of these recidivism-prone individuals.

However, because of the highly mobile nature of today's society, it is increasingly difficult to keep tabs on these offenders as they move from jurisdiction to jurisdiction, changing their names and appearances along the way. Nonetheless, state and national sex offender registries have proliferated in recent years, as mandated by law (Figure 10.4).

> The evolution of sex offender registries can be traced to a trilogy of federal statutes: the Jacob Wetterling Act, Megan's Law, and the Pam Lychner Act.

The first act was named for 11-year-old Jacob Wetterling, who was abducted in October 1989 near his home in rural Minnesota and has never been found. The Jacob Wetterling Crimes against Children and Sexually Violent Offender Registration Act was enacted as part of President Clinton's 1994 Crime Act. It required states to establish registration systems for convicted child molesters and other sexually violent offenders. States could release the information to the public, but they were not required to do so.

The second act was named for 7-year-old Megan Kanka, raped and murdered by a convicted sex offender who lived across the street from Megan's family with two other released sex offenders. Megan's Law, signed by President Clinton in 1996, amends the Jacob Wetterling Act in two ways: (1) It requires states to release any relevant information about registered sex offenders necessary to maintain and protect public

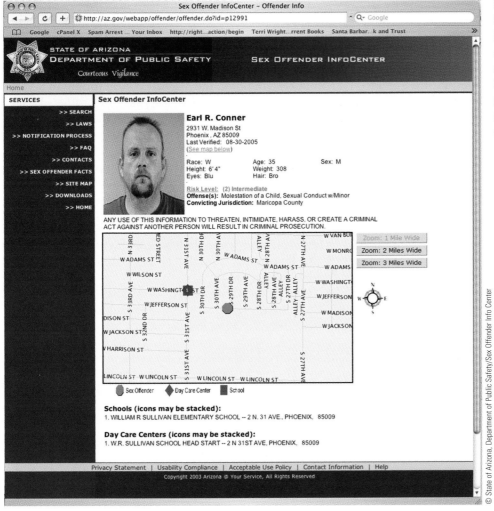

Figure 10.4
Sex offender registries vary from state to state, but most contain similar information. Many can be found on a state's website, such as this one taken from the Arizona Department of Public Safety. A disclaimer, shown above the map, is important to protect the offender's rights. Without such a disclaimer, the registry could be declared unconstitutional.

safety, and (2) it allows disclosure of information collected under a state registration program for any purpose permitted under the laws of the state.

The third law in the federal trilogy was named for a victims' rights advocate killed in a plane crash in July 1996. Officially called the Pam Lychner Sexual Offender Tracking and Identification Act, it directed the FBI to establish a national sex offender database. The permanent National Sex Offender Registry File is part of the FBI's National Crime Information Center (NCIC) 2000 project and includes fingerprint and photo images of registered offenders.

The first sex offender registry was created in California in 1947, before it was legally required. By 1996 all states had enacted laws requiring sex offenders to register within their states to help law enforcement agencies manage offenders released from secure confinement (*Sex Offender Registries*, p.1). In California, failure to register as a sex offender is a felony, making punishment more severe. If the previous sex crime itself was a felony, failure to register carries a mandated prison term. In 2005 Attorney General Alberto R. Gonzales instituted a nationwide sex offender list, the National

Sex Offender Public Registry (NSOPR) ("Justice Department to Create," p.4). The registry is intended to provide "one-stop access" to available information on the 48 states that have sex offender registries (Oregon and Rhode Island will be assisted in developing registries). As of September 2005, sex offender registries of 32 states, the District of Columbia, and Guam were accessible online via the NSOPR.

Many arguments exist both for and against sex offender registries and notification laws. People who advocate sex offender registration and notification cite the significant number of sex offenders under community supervision, the fear of recidivism, and the protection of children and their families.

The three basic objections to notification laws center around punishment, privacy, and due process issues. Some offenders claim that registering subjects them to additional punishment. However, in April 1998, the Supreme Court rejected constitutional challenges that claimed that the laws' notification requirements represented an unconstitutional added punishment. Another concern of opponents is that notification will lead to harassment of offenders and increased acts of vigilantism.

Sometimes the stigma placed on sex offenders is too great a burden to handle. A convicted child molester in Maine shot himself to death, saying in a tape-recorded message that he feared living in a world "with no forgiveness."

Pallone (pp.83–84) contends: "Despite the (generally well-founded) concerns of civil libertarians who decry the 'double jeopardy' provisions of such laws [requiring sex offenders to register], especially when applied *ex post facto* to offenders who had completed their legislatively-prescribed, court-imposed sentences before these laws were enacted, they have consistently been supported by appellate courts and even, in *Kansas v Hendricks* (1997), by the U.S. Supreme Court."

It appears that sex offender registration and notification have more supporters than opponents. Internet access is quickly revolutionizing the way the public keeps informed of the whereabouts of convicted sex offenders. In many jurisdictions residents are now able to access a registry online, enter their zip codes, and obtain information on sex offenders living in their area.

Perhaps the more relevant question is, do such registries work? One recent study found that "[a]t any given time, nearly one-quarter of the nation's convicted sex offenders cannot be located because they failed to register with local law enforcement as required under Megan's Law" ("Hiding in Plain Sight," p. 1). Laura A. Ahearn, executive director of Parents for Megan's Law, gives one explanation: "We are actually asking the most cunning of our criminals to take part in an honor system." According to Ahearn, to expect that sex offenders are going to provide accurate, current information to law enforcement agencies is "just unreasonable" ("Hiding in Plain Sight," p.1).

A case in point: the May 2005 kidnapping of 8-year-old Shasta Groene and her 9-year-old brother, Dylan, from their Idaho home by registered sex offender Joseph Edward Duncan III. The children's mother, older brother, and the mother's boyfriend had been slain in their home just prior to the kidnappings, and Dylan's remains were later discovered after Shasta had been rescued and Duncan apprehended. At the time of the murders and kidnappings, Duncan was being sought for jumping bail on child molestation charges he faced in Minnesota and was listed as delinquent (missing) with both the North Dakota and Washington state sex offender registries.

One solution described by Moore (p.4A) is use of GPS (global position system) technology to track convicted and released sex offenders. Florida and Oklahoma have passed laws requiring lifetime GPS satellite tracking for those whose victims were under 12 and for repeat offenders, respectively. Pennsylvania, New Jersey, and New York are considering such legislation. GPS works everywhere. An ankle bracelet and transmitter send a continuous signal to the parole officer's computer. The offender knows he is being watched around the clock.

SUMMARY

Sex offenses include bigamy, child molestation, incest, indecent exposure, prostitution, rape (sexual assault), and sodomy. The most serious of these is rape—sexual intercourse with a person against the person's will. Rape is classified as forcible (by use or threats of force) or statutory (with a minor, with or without consent).

Most states include the following elements in defining the crime of rape or sexual assault: (1) an act of sexual intercourse, (2) with a person other than a spouse, (3) committed without the victim's consent, (4) against the victim's will and by force.

MO factors important in investigating sex offenses include type of offense, words spoken, use of a weapon, method of attack, time of day, type of location, and age of the victim. Special challenges in investigating rape include the sensitive nature of the offense, social attitudes, and the victim's embarrassment. A rape investigation requires great tact. To help overcome some of these challenges, many departments are implementing a procedure known as blind reporting, which allows sexual assault victims to retain their anonymity and confidentiality while sharing critical information with law enforcement. It also permits victims to gather legal information from law enforcement without having to commit immediately to an investigation.

Physical evidence commonly found in rape cases includes stained or torn clothing; scratches, bruises, and cuts; evidence of a struggle; and semen and bloodstains. Additional evidence in date rape cases may include the presence of drugs in the victim's system.

A rape case often involves cooperation with medical personnel, social workers, personnel of rape crisis centers, and news media. Conviction in sexual assault cases requires medical evidence, physical evidence such as torn clothing, evidence of injuries, and a complaint that is reported reasonably close to the time of the assault. Many recent laws have reduced the penalties for sexual assault, which should lead to more convictions.

The evolution of sex offender registries can be traced to a trilogy of federal statutes: the Jacob Wetterling Act, Megan's Law, and the Pam Lychner Act.

CHECKLIST

Sexual Assault

- What specific sex offense was committed?
- Are all the elements of the crime present?
- Who is the victim? Were there any injuries? Were they described and photographed?
- Were there any witnesses?
- Was the surrounding area canvassed to locate possible leads?
- Is there a suspect? a description of a suspect?
- Has there been a relationship between the suspect and the victim?
- What evidence was obtained at the scene?
- Was evidence submitted to the crime laboratory? Were reports received?
- Was the victim taken to the hospital for a medical examination?
- What evidence was obtained at the hospital? Is a medical report available?
- Was the victim interviewed? Will he or she sign a complaint?
- Was the victim reinterviewed four to five days after the assault?
- Was a background check made of the victim?
- Were other police agencies in the area notified and queried?
- Were field interrogation cards, MO files, and other intelligence files checked?
- Have patrol divisions been checked for leads on cars or people in the area?
- Has a sexual assault or rape crisis center been contacted for help?

APPLICATION

Several young people in a car wave down a police car and tell the officers that screams are coming from the south end of a nearby park. At about the same time, the police dispatcher receives a call from a resident who says she hears screams and cries for help but cannot tell exactly what part of the park they are coming from. The officers talk to the juveniles, get their names and a description of the area, and then head for the park without red lights and siren to avoid warning the attacker. Arriving at the south end of the park, the officers see a man running from some bushes. He is wearing a dark jacket and is bareheaded. One officer goes to find the victim; the other attempts to follow the fleeing man. At the scene the officer observes a woman with torn clothing and a cut on the side of her head. She is unable to speak coherently, but she has obviously been assaulted. The juveniles have followed the squad car to the scene and crowd around the victim to offer help. The officer chasing the suspect has lost him and has returned to the scene. Both officers help the victim into the squad car and leave the scene with red lights and sirens, heading for the hospital. After leaving the victim at the hospital, they return to the scene. They find that branches are broken from some of the bushes. They also find an article of clothing from the victim and a switchblade knife on the ground. They secure the scene by posting several of the juveniles around the area until further help arrives.

Questions

1. Should red lights and siren have been used in going to the scene?
2. Was it correct for the officers to split up as they did?
3. Evaluate the effectiveness of the officers' actions after arriving at the scene.

DISCUSSION QUESTIONS

1. What myths and prejudices have you heard about prosecuting rape cases? Are rape cases more difficult to prosecute than other crimes?
2. What are the penalties for rape in your state? Are these penalties adequate, or should they be more or less severe?
3. Past rape laws have required the utmost resistance on the part of the victim. Present laws have reduced this requirement. Do you support this change?
4. What persons or agencies can assist the police in rape investigations? What functions or services can they provide? What resources are available in your community? your state?
5. Should the rape victim be interviewed by male or female investigators?
6. Rape victims often complain about the attitudes of police and medical personnel during a rape investigation. Do you believe this is justified, or is it due to the victim's emotional stress?
7. A case in Oregon received wide publicity because a husband was charged with raping his wife during a temporary separation and was acquitted. Do you agree with this verdict? Are there circumstances under which such a charge should be supported?
8. What environment is best for interviewing the victim of a rape or sexual assault? How would you start the interview? How supportive of the victim would you be? What questions would you ask? Who would you allow to be present? How would you close the interview?
9. How vigorously should sex offenses such as sodomy, indecent exposure, and prostitution be investigated? Should unnatural sexual acts between consenting adults be considered criminal acts?
10. Why is semen, rather than sperm, the evidence sought in a rape case?

MEDIA EXPLORATIONS

Internet

Select one of the following assignments to complete.

- Search for the key phrase *National Institute of Justice*. Click on "NCJRS" (National Criminal Justice Research Service). Click on "law enforcement." Click on "sort by Doc#." Search for one of the NCJ reference numbers from the reference pages. Outline the selection to share with the class.
- Go to the FBI website at www.fbi.gov. Click on "library and reference." Select "Uniform Crime Reports" and outline what the report says about sexual assault.
- Select one of the following key words: *blind reporting, date rape, prostitution, rape, sex crimes prevention, sexual assault, statutory rape*. Find one article relevant to sexual assault investigations to outline and share with the class.

 ### Crime and Evidence in Action

Go to the CD and choose the **domestic violence case.** During the course of the case you'll become a patrol officer, detective, prosecutor, corrections officer, and probation officer to conduct interactive investigative research. Each case unfolds as you respond to key decision points. Feedback for each possible answer choice is packed full of information, including term definitions, web links, and important documentation. The sergeant is available at certain times to help mentor you, the Online Resources website offers a variety of information, and be sure to take notes in your e-notebook during the suspect video statements and at key points throughout (these notes can be saved, printed, or e-mailed). The Forensics Exercise will test your ability to collect, transport, and analyze evidence from the crime scene. You'll even have the opportunity to consider a plea bargain offered by the defense. At the end of the case you can track how well you responded to each decision point and join the Discussion Forum for a postmortem. **Go to the CD and use the skills you've learned in this chapter to solve a case.**

REFERENCES

"19 Charged in Connection with Alien Harboring Conspiracy." Press Release, Department of Justice, U.S. Attorney's Office, Northern District of California, July 1, 2005.

Assessment of U.S. Government Activities to Combat Trafficking in Persons. Washington, DC: U.S. Department of Justice, June 2004.

Baumer, Eric P.; Felson, Richard B.; and Messner, Steven F. "Changes in Police Notification for Rape: 1973–2000." *Criminology*, August 2003, pp. 841–870.

Braun, Joy M. "Collaborations: The Key to Combating Human Trafficking." *The Police Chief*, December 2003, pp. 68–74.

Crime in the United States 2003. Washington, DC: Federal Bureau of Investigation, Uniform Crime Reports, 2003.

DePresca, John. "Date Rape Drugs." *Law and Order*, October 2003, pp. 210–213.

Garcia, Sabrina, and Henderson, Margaret. "Blind Reporting of Sexual Violence." *FBI Law Enforcement Bulletin*, June 1999, pp.12–17.

Geberth, Vernon. "Investigative Significance of Fantasy in Sex Crimes." *Law and Order*, September 2004, pp. 94–99.

Gomez, Halli. "The Sexual Crimes Clearinghouse: Linking Intelligence Information." *The Police Chief*, March 2003, pp. 45–51.

"Hiding in Plain Sight." *Law Enforcement News*, February 24, 2003, pp. 1, 8.

Human Trafficking Fact Sheet. Washington, DC: U.S. Department of Health and Human Services, 2004.

"Justice Department to Create Nationwide Sex Offender List." *Criminal Justice Newsletter*, June 1, 2005, p. 4.

Kanable, Rebecca. "Osmolality Helps Detect Tampered Beverages." *Law Enforcement Technology*, May 2003, pp. 78–81.

Lonsway, Kimberly, and Cassidy, Michael. "Investigating Sexual Assault." *Law and Order*, May 2005, pp. 114–121.

Markey, James. "New Technology and Old Police Work Solve Cold Sex Crimes." *FBI Law Enforcement Bulletin*, September 2003, pp. 1–5.

MDMA (Ecstasy). Washington, DC: Office of National Drug Control Policy, April 2002.

Moore, Martha T. "States Look to High-Tech Tools to Track, Map Sex Offenders." *USA Today*, June 20, 2005, p. 4A.

A National Protocol for Sexual Assault Medical Forensic Examinations: Adults/Adolescents. Washington, DC: U.S. Department of Justice, Office on Violence Against Women, September 2004. (NCJ 206554)

Nislow, Jennifer. "How to Spot Trafficking in Human Beings." *Law Enforcement News*, Fall 2004, p. 6.

Pallone, Nathaniel J. "Without Plea-Bargaining, Megan Kanka Would Be Alive Today." *Criminology and Public Policy*, Vol. 3, No. 1, 2003, pp. 83–96.

"Problems Still Linger with Megan's Law." *Law Enforcement News*, May 2004, p. 12.

Sex Offender Registries and Community Notification: States' Use of Technology for Public Safety. Washington, DC: National Criminal Justice Association, no date.

Venkatraman, Bharathi A. "A Guide to Detecting, Investigating and Punishing Modern-Day Slavery." *The Police Chief*, December 2003, pp. 34–43.

Victims of Trafficking and Violence Protection Act of 2000: Trafficking in Persons Report. Washington, DC: U.S. Department of State, 2005.

Whitehead, Christy. "Anchorage Anti-Rape Unit." *Law and Order*, March 2005, pp. 62–65.

Wright, Richard G. "Sex Offender Registration and Notification: Public Attention, Political Emphasis and Fear." *Criminology and Public Policy*, Vol. 3, No. 1, 2003, pp. 97–104.

CASES CITED

Kansas v. Crane (2001)

Kansas v. Hendricks, 521 U.S. 346 (1997)

Crimes against Children and Youths

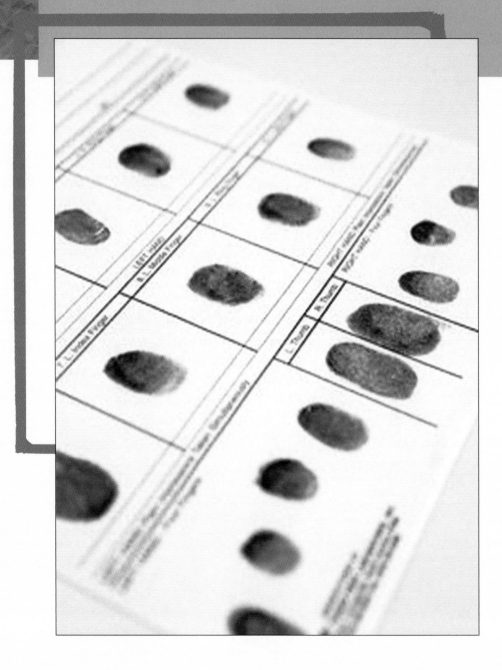

Can You Define?

Do You Know?

- What crimes against children are frequently committed?
- What effects child abuse can have?
- What challenges are involved in investigating crimes against children?
- When a child should be taken into protective custody?
- What factors to consider in interviewing child victims?
- Whether children are generally truthful about abuse?
- Who usually reports crimes against children?
- What evidence is important in these cases?
- What things can indicate child neglect or abuse?
- What types of sex rings exist in the United States?
- How pedophiles typically react when discovered?
- What the Child Protection Act involves?
- What three law enforcement approaches are models to combat child sexual exploitation?
- What challenges a missing child report presents?
- What the most common type of child abduction is?
- What the AMBER Alert program is?
- What the NCAVC's four-pronged approach to assessing the potential for a school shooting incident consists of?
- How crimes against children can be prevented?

Outline

 man admitted to a law enforcement investigator that he had molested 5,000 boys in his lifetime; a 42-year-old man admitted more than 1,000; and a 62-year-old oil executive stated he had molested a boy a day for 30 years. Recently the Catholic Church has endured several cases of adults reporting having been molested as children by priests.

Marshall (2005) reports on a nationwide search being conducted by the FBI and California law enforcement officials for Dean A. Schwartzmiller, a convicted child molester who kept meticulous journals of his exploits. Law enforcement records in Alaska, Idaho, Oregon, New York, and Washington show that Schwartzmiller has been arrested or served time on multiple child molesting charges. Most recently, police learned about Schwartzmiller from a 12-year-old boy. The boy and his parents told the police that he had been forced to commit sex acts. When authorities raided Schwartzmiller's house, they seized seven spiral notebooks that logged more than 36,000 sexual acts, many in code. They also found more than 100 pornographic videos, DVDs, and CD-ROMs, as well as boys' clothing, including underwear, in the master bedroom. Hundreds of people from around the United States have called offering help. The police believe there may be hundreds of his victims across the country.

In Boston the Catholic archdiocese and 86 alleged victims of child-molesting priest John Geoghan reached a final settlement of $10 million, four months after the church backed out of a much costlier offer. Geoghan was killed in his prison cell August 23, 2003. Hotakainen et al. (p.A1) report that, overall, 4,392 priests—about 4 percent of all priests in the country between 1950 and 2002—were responsible for sexually abusing more than 10,000 children over the 52-year period.

Child molestation is but one type of crime against children. Other crimes against children may occur repeatedly with the same victim, as in most instances of child abuse, whether physical, emotional, or sexual. Hess and Drowns (p.111) state:

Throughout history children have been subjected to physical violence. Infants have been killed as a form of birth control, to avoid the dishonor of illegitimacy, as a means of power, as a method of disposing of retarded or deformed children and as a way of protecting financial security.

In ancient Greece a child was the absolute property of the father, and property was divided among the male children. The father would raise the first son and expose subsequent children to the elements. Under Roman law the father had the power of life and death (*patria potestas*) over his children and could kill, mutilate, sell or offer them as a sacrifice.

Just as domestic violence used to be considered a family matter, so was mistreating children considered a family matter. Now both are considered crimes, and they must be thoroughly investigated. Youths are also victims of the various other crimes that occur, but those crimes are usually investigated in the same ways as for adult victims, other than some changes in interviewing techniques, discussed later in this chapter.

This chapter begins with a discussion of the classification of crimes against children, followed by some clinical definitions, important terminology, and a look at the extent of the problem and the effects on children. It then discusses challenges in investigating crimes against children. Next the chapter describes the initial report, the police response, guidelines for interviewing children, a sample protocol, examples of the evidence to collect, and possible suspects, including pedophiles and members of child sexual abuse rings. Next is a discussion of child pornography and juvenile prostitution. This is followed by an explanation of investigating missing children, including parental abduction. The chapter concludes with an examination of children as witnesses in court and a discussion of preventing crimes against children.

Classification

Law enforcement agencies are charged with investigating all crimes, but their responsibility is especially great where crimes against children are involved. Children need the protection of the law to a greater degree than do other members of society because they are so vulnerable, especially if the offense is committed by one or both parents. Even after the offense is committed, the child may still be in danger of further victimization.

 Crimes against children include kidnapping, abandonment, and maltreatment, which may take the form of neglect, exploitation, physical abuse, emotional abuse, incest, and sexual assault.

Kidnapping is taking someone away by force, often for ransom. Child kidnapping is especially traumatic for the parents and for those called upon to investigate. A highly publicized child kidnapping case in 1989 involved the abduction of 11-year-old Jacob Wetterling, who was taken at gunpoint from near his home in Minnesota by a masked man. No ransom was demanded, and despite

© Jacques M. Chenet/CORBIS

Figure 11.1
Two children play near their home and an open sewer. This poverty-stricken area in Tunica, Mississippi, is sometimes referred to as "Sugarditch."

national publicity and a nationwide search, Jacob remains missing.

Some child kidnappings are committed by a parent who has lost custody of the child in divorce proceedings. In such cases, ransom is not demanded. Rather, the parent committing the kidnapping may take on a new identity and move to another part of the country. Parental abduction is discussed later in this chapter. Childless couples have also been known to kidnap babies or young children to raise as their own.

Abandonment refers to a parent's desertion of a child. This may occur not because the parents no longer love the child but because they feel the child would have a better life without them. It sometimes occurs when a young girl has a child and does not want anyone to know about it.

Maltreatment categories typically include neglect, medical neglect, physical abuse, sexual abuse, and psychological maltreatment. **Neglect** refers to failure to care for a child properly and can include not providing humane living quarters, adequate food, or adequate love and attention (Figure 11.1). An example of physical abuse or neglect is the case of a couple who raped and drugged their four children over a period of at least four years. These children were fed a regular diet of skinned and boiled rats rolled in flour and deep-fried and boiled cockroaches served with hot sauce.

Exploitation refers to taking unfair advantage of children or using them illegally. This includes using children in pornography and prostitution. It can also involve forcing children to perform physical labor beyond what could be reasonably expected of a child.

Physical abuse refers to beating, whipping, burning, or otherwise inflicting physical harm upon a child. Child abuse has been identified as the biggest single cause of

death of young children. One study found that between 3 and 4 million children have at some time been kicked, beaten, or hit with a fist by their parents; and between 900,000 and 1.8 million have been assaulted with a knife or gun. In several tragic instances, the abuse resulted in death.

Emotional abuse refers to causing fear or feelings of unworthiness in children by such means as locking them in closets, ignoring them, or constantly belittling them.

Child sexual abuse includes sexually molesting a child, performing sexual acts with a child, and statutory rape and seduction. Sexual assault victims may number in the millions, and perhaps some 90 percent of child molestations are not reported. Finkelhor and Jones (p.1) report that the number of sexual abuse cases substantiated by child protective service (CPS) agencies dropped a "remarkable" 40 percent between 1992 and 2000, from an estimated 150,000 cases to 89,500 cases. The reason is unclear. Some cultures sanction sexual relationships between adults and children, but such acts are illegal in this country.

Other Terminology

State statutes differ in their definitions of **minor,** with the most common specifying under the age of 16 or 18. When classifying crimes against children, several state statutes are applicable, including offenses of physical assault, sexual assault, incest, sexual seduction, indecent exposure, lewdness, and molestation. Physical and sexual assault and incest have been previously defined.

Sexual seduction means ordinary sexual intercourse, anal intercourse, cunnilingus, or fellatio committed by a nonminor with a consenting minor. **Lewdness** means touching a minor to arouse, appeal to, or gratify the perpetrator's sexual desires. The touching may be done by the perpetrator or by the minor under the perpetrator's direction. **Molestation** is a broader term, referring to any act motivated by unnatural or abnormal sexual interest in minors that would reasonably be expected to disturb, irritate, or offend the victim. Molestation may or may not involve touching of the victim.

Legislatures in a number of states are attempting to broaden penalties to make them match the severity of the offense, especially if the victim is very young. There is also a concerted effort to expand the offenses to make genders equal, recognizing that victims and offenders may be male or female. The age of the offender as well as the type of crime are both taken into account. Illinois, for example, has consolidated 9 sex offenses into 4 but provides for 24 combinations of charges.

At the federal level, child abuse statutes pertain mainly to exploitation, but they also set forth important definitions that apply to any type of child abuse. Public Law 95–225 (1978) defines **sexual exploitation** as follows:

> Any person who employs, uses, persuades, induces, entices, or coerces any minor to engage or assist in engaging in any sexually explicit conduct for the purpose of producing any visual or print medium, knowing that such visual or print medium will be transported interstate or in foreign commerce or mailed, is guilty of sexual exploitation. Further, any parent or legal guardian who knowingly permits such conduct, having control and custody of the child, is also subject to prosecution.

Visual print or **medium** means any film, photograph, negative, slide, book, magazine, or other visual print or medium. **Commercial exploitation** means having as a direct or indirect goal monetary or other material gain.

The Extent of the Problem

According to the National Child Abuse and Neglect Data System (NCANDS) (maintained by the National Clearinghouse on Child Abuse and Neglect Information) (*Child Maltreatment 2003*), an estimated 906,000 children were determined to be victims of child abuse or neglect in 2003. The rate of victimization per 1,000 children in the nation dropped from 13.4 children in 1990 to 12.4 children in 2003:

> More than 60 percent of child victims experienced neglect. Almost 19 percent were physically abused; 10 percent were sexually abused; and 5 percent were emotionally

maltreated. In addition, 17 percent were associated with "other" types of maltreatment.

Children ages birth to 3 years had the highest rates of victimization at 16.4 per 1,000 children. Girls were slightly more likely to be victims than boys.

In 2003 an estimated total of 2.9 million referrals concerning the welfare of approximately 5.5 million children were made to child protection agencies (CPAs) throughout the United States. Of these, approximately two-thirds (an estimated 1.9 million) were accepted for investigation or assessment.

Pacific Islander, American Indian or Alaska Native, and African-American children had the highest rates of victimization when compared to their national population. While the rate of White victims of child abuse or neglect was 11.0 per 1,000 children of the same race, the rate for Pacific Islanders was 21.4 per 1,000 children, the rate for American Indian or Alaska Natives was 21.3 per 1,000 children, and for African-Americans 20.4 per 2,000 children.

Child fatalities are the most tragic consequence of maltreatment. For 2003, an estimated 1,500 children died due to abuse or neglect. More than three-quarters (79 percent) of children who were killed were younger than 4 years old. Unfortunately, studies have estimated as many as 50 to 60 percent of deaths resulting from abuse or neglect are not recorded and that neglect is the most unrecorded form of child maltreatment (*Child Abuse and Neglect Fatalities*).

In 2004 President Bush signed the Unborn Victims of Violence Act, or Laci and Conner's Law. This law amended the U.S. Code and the Uniform Code of Military Justice to punish separately the harming of a child in utero. The punishment is the same as provided under federal law for conduct causing the injury to, or death of, the unborn child's mother, but the imposition of the death penalty is prohibited. This separate offense does not require proof that the person who committed the offense knew or should have known that the victim was pregnant or that the accused intended to harm the unborn child.

A complicating factor in investigating child abuse is the perceived ambiguity of what it is. Is spanking a child abuse? Belittling a child? Sending a child to bed without dinner?

The underreporting of child abuse is another concern. It is estimated that for every report of abuse the police and child protective services receive, there are 10 unreported cases.

A major concern involves the frequency with which children are abused by people they know. Although many parents stress to their children the importance of staying away from strangers, the sad truth is that the overwhelming majority of sexual abuse is committed by persons known to the child. The report by the National Clearinghouse on Child Abuse and Neglect Information (*Child Maltreatment 2003*) states that more than 80 percent of perpetrators were parents. Other relatives accounted for 7 percent, and unmarried partners of parents accounted for 3 percent.

In addition, as noted by Harris (p.8), methamphetamine abuse and production have become major factors in the severity of child abuse and neglect cases handled by the child welfare system. Harris notes that children are found in about one-third of all seized meth labs and that of those children, about 35 percent test positive for toxic levels of chemicals in their bodies. Worse, as Harris notes, it is likely that 90 percent of all meth labs go undetected. Children who live in such homes not only risk exposure to dangerous chemicals and their by-products, but also endure filthy homes often lacking water, heat and electricity with little to eat. Such conditions can lead to "serious short- and long-term health problems, including damage to the brain, liver, kidneys, lungs, eyes and skin." That child abuse and neglect in any of its many forms can have serious consequences is well known.

The Effects of Child Abuse

The effects of child abuse can be devastating.

Child abuse can result in serious and permanent physical, mental, and emotional damage, as well as future criminal behavior.

Physical damage may involve the brain, vital organs, eyes, ears, arms, or legs. Severe abuse may also cause mental retardation, restricted language ability, restricted perceptual and motor-skill development, arrested physical development, blindness, deafness, loss of limbs, or even death.

Emotional damage may include impaired self-concept as well as increased levels of aggression, anxiety, and tendency toward self-destructiveness. These self-destructive tendencies can cause children to act out antisocial behavior in the family, the school, and the community at large. Such self-destructiveness can also manifest itself in risky behavior that endangers youths' health and safety.

Researchers Kilpatrick et al. (p.281) report: "The emotional consequences that youths experience because of victimization, such as psychological disorders, substance abuse and dependence, and delinquency problems, are often overlooked." They conclude: "Clearly, victimization in early childhood and adolescent years is the root of many problems later in life."

English et al. (*Childhood Victimization*) followed 877 youths for 15 to 24 years following dependency and found "strong support" for the relationship between child abuse and neglect and delinquency, adult criminality, and violent criminal behavior: "Abused and neglected children are 4.8 times more likely to be arrested as juveniles; 2 times more likely to be arrested as [adults], and 3.1 times more likely to be arrested for a violent crime than matched controls."

Research by Siegel and Williams (p.71) found that child sexual abuse was a statistically significant predictor of certain types of offenses, but other indicators of familial neglect and abuse were significant factors as well. "Child sexual abuse may indeed play a central role in some girls' pathway to delinquency and subsequent crime." They (p.84) conclude: "Sexual abuse victims were significantly more likely to have been arrested as adults than their matched counterparts even after controlling for a childhood history characterized by family problems serious enough to have resulted in a dependency hearing." Cohen et al. (*Effects of Childhood*) report similar results, finding that victims of officially identified abuse were more likely to be arrested as adults.

Another likely effect of child abuse is that as an adult, the former victim frequently becomes a perpetrator of child abuse, thereby creating a vicious circle sometimes called the *intergenerational transmission of violence*. Research shows that a child's history of physical abuse predisposes that child to violence in later years. Victims of neglect are also likely to engage in later violent criminal behavior.

The Cycle of Abuse

A study of the effects of exposure to violence on problem behavior among 306 African American middle school and high school students by McGee and Baker (p.74) found "a strong association between victimization experience and adjustment outcomes including internalizing (i.e., self-rejection, depression) and externalizing (i.e., offenses) problem behavior."

"General delinquency research shows that childhood abuse (physical and sexual) is often associated with delinquency and that the early onset of maltreatment may increase the variety, seriousness and duration of problems. It is also widely suggested that violence begets violence—that today's abused children become tomorrow's violent offenders" (Widom and Maxfield, p.1).

Challenges to Investigation

Many prosecutors at all levels of the judiciary system perceive crimes against children as among the most difficult to prosecute and for which to obtain convictions. Therefore, officers interviewing child witnesses and victims should have specialized training not only to convict the guilty but also to protect the innocent. Regardless of whether crimes against children are handled by generalists or specialists within the department, certain challenges are unique to these investigations.

 Challenges in investigating crimes against children include the need to protect the child from further harm, the possibility of parental involvement, the difficulty of interviewing children, credibility concerns, and the need to collaborate with other agencies.

Protecting the Child

When child abuse is reported, investigators may initiate an investigation on their own, or they may investigate jointly with the welfare department. Regardless of the source of the report and regardless of whether the investigation is a single or joint effort, the primary responsibility of the investigator assigned to the case is the immediate protection of the child.

 If the possibility of present or continued danger to the child exists, the child must be removed into protective custody.

Under welfare regulations and codes, an officer may take a child into temporary custody without a warrant if there is an emergency or if the officer has reason to believe that leaving the child in the present situation would subject the child to further abuse or harm. **Temporary custody without hearing** usually means for 48 hours. Conditions that would justify placing a child in protective custody include the following:

- The child's age or physical or mental condition makes the child incapable of self-protection.
- The home's physical environment poses an immediate threat to the child.
- The child needs immediate medical or psychiatric care, and the parents refuse to get it.
- The parents cannot or will not provide for the child's basic needs.
- Maltreatment in the home could permanently damage the child physically or emotionally.
- The parents may abandon the child.

Consultation with local welfare authorities is sometimes needed before police officials ask the court for a hearing to remove a child from the parents' custody or for protective custody in an authorized facility. Because police rarely have such facilities, the child should be taken to the nearest welfare facility or to a foster home as soon as possible, as stipulated by the juvenile court.

The parents or legal guardians of the child must be notified as soon as possible.

Difficulty in Interviewing Children

When children are very young, a limited vocabulary can pose a severe challenge to investigators. Unfortunately, by the time children are old enough to possess the words or other skills needed to communicate and describe their abusive experiences, they have also developed the ability to feel such shame, embarrassment, and fear over these events as to resist talking about them.

Interviewing a child abuse victim takes special understanding, skill, and practice. Children often have difficulty talking about abuse, and often they have been instructed not to tell anyone about it. They may have been threatened by the abuser, or they may have a close relationship with the abuser and not want anything bad to happen to that person.

When interviewing children, officers should consider the child's age, ability to describe what happened, and the potential for retaliation by the suspect against a child who "tells."

Another difficulty in interviewing children is their short attention spans. Questions should be brief and understandable, a skill that often proves difficult and requires training and practice. Interviewers who are excellent with adults may not be so successful with children.

Investigators may consider inviting a social service professional to help conduct the interview because they often have more formal training and experience in interviewing children at their level and may therefore be better able to establish rapport. More specific guidelines for interviewing abused children are discussed in detail shortly.

Credibility Concerns

Assessing the credibility of people reporting child abuse is a constant challenge for investigators. As repulsive as society finds child abuse, particularly sexual abuse, investigators must exercise great care to protect the innocent and falsely accused. No other crime is so fraught with stigma. Consequently, accusations of this type can be difficult to dispel even if false.

Because of the "loaded" nature of child sexual abuse allegations, parents who are divorcing may be tempted to use such claims as ammunition against their soon-to-be ex-spouse. For investigators, sorting through details of such allegations to determine their credibility can be extremely challenging. Occasionally the credibility of the child victim is called into question. However, investigators must approach each case and each victim with an open mind.

 In the vast majority of child abuse cases, children tell the truth to the best of their ability.

People who work with child abuse cases point out that children will frequently lie to get out of trouble, but they seldom lie to get into trouble. Although most child abuse reports are valid, investigators must use caution to weed out those cases reported by a habitual liar or by a child who is telling a story to offset other misdeeds he or she has committed. A child's motivation for lying may be revenge, efforts to avoid school or parental disapproval, efforts to cover up for other disapproved behavior, or, in the case of sexual abuse, an attempt to explain a pregnancy or to obtain an abortion at state expense.

The Need to Involve Other Agencies: The Multidisciplinary Team Approach

Another challenge facing law enforcement is the need to collaborate with various social service, child welfare, and health agencies to more effectively handle child abuse cases. Traditionally, law enforcement and social service agencies have worked fairly independently on child abuse cases, with each conducting its own separate interviews and investigations. In fact, many police departments have seen no need to collaborate with social services unless their investigation determines a need to remove the child from parental custody. However, it is increasingly evident that this lack of communication and coordination among these agencies has led to numerous cases "falling through the cracks" of the disjointed system, sometimes with devastating results.

A multidisciplinary team (MDT) consists of professionals who work together to ensure an effective response to reports of child abuse and neglect. Co-ordinated responses can also minimize the likelihood of conflicts among agencies with different philosophies and mandates. Joint investigations often result in more victim corroborations and perpetrator confessions than do independent investigations. In addition, referral agencies provide support and assistance to families and victims experiencing child abuse or neglect. A collaborative, community-based approach to problems associated with children and youths should result in identifying, developing, and implementing more effective, multiagency solutions.

A community-involvement program that can assist in the investigation of abused, abandoned, or abducted children is the National Fingerprint for Children Identification project, which provides information to law enforcement agencies about the identification of children who have been fingerprinted and are listed in their files. These confidential files contain the prints of some 40,000 children. The prints are submitted by parents, police, and sometimes civic organizations as a community project.

Other technological developments allow police to communicate more effectively with organizations such as the media in cases involving child abductions—cases where speed of information dissemination is critical.

On November 2, 2002, President Bush signed into law legislation making changes to the Juvenile Justice and Delinquency Prevention Act (JJDPA). While maintaining the core protections for youths in the justice system, the new law includes important linkages between juvenile justice and child welfare (*Summary of Juvenile*).

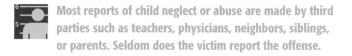
The Initial Report

According to the NCANDS, of the 2.6 million referrals to CPS agencies, more than one-half (56.5 percent) were made by such professionals as educators, law enforcement and legal personnel, social services personnel, medical personnel, mental health personnel, child day-care providers, and foster care providers. Friends, neighbors, and relatives submitted approximately 43.8 percent of reports.

Most reports of child neglect or abuse are made by third parties such as teachers, physicians, neighbors, siblings, or parents. Seldom does the victim report the offense.

In most states certain individuals who work with or treat children are required by law to report cases of suspected neglect or abuse. This includes teachers, school authorities, child-care personnel, camp personnel, clergy, physicians, dentists, chiropractors, nurses, psychologists, medical assistants, attorneys, and social workers. Such a report may be made to the welfare department, the juvenile court, or the local police or sheriff's department. It may be made verbally, but it should also be put in writing as soon as possible after the initial verbal report is made. Some states have special forms for child abuse cases. These forms are sent to a central location in the state, thereby helping to prevent child abusers from taking the child to different doctors or hospitals for treatment and thus avoiding the suspicion that would accompany multiple incidents involving the same child.

Child neglect/abuse reports should contain the name, age, and address of the child victim; the name and address of the child's parents or others responsible for the child's care; the name and address of the person suspected of the abuse; the nature and extent of the neglect or abuse; and any evidence of this or previous neglect or abuse. These reports are confidential.

In most states, action must be taken on a report within a specified time, frequently three days. If in the judgment of the person receiving the report it is necessary to remove the child from present custody, this is discussed with the responsible agency, such as the welfare department or the juvenile court. If the situation is deemed life-threatening, the police may temporarily remove the child. No matter who receives the report or whether the child must be removed from the situation, it is the responsibility of the law enforcement agency to investigate the charge.

The Police Response

As noted, traditionally, as with domestic violence, child abuse/neglect was viewed as a family matter—a social issue regulated by child protection agencies. It was not a crime. Currently, child abuse is viewed as a crime and within the jurisdiction of the criminal justice system. Therefore it needs to be investigated by trained criminal investigators.

The investigator must talk with people who know the child and obtain background information on the child. For example, does the child have behavior problems? Is the child generally truthful?

If interviews are conducted with the parents, every attempt should be made to conduct the interviews in private. Explain why the interview is necessary. Be direct, honest, understanding, and professional in your approach. Do not accuse, demand, give personal opinions about the situation, request information from the parents unrelated to the matter under discussion, make judgments, place blame, or reveal the source of your information. If the parents are suspects, provide them the due process rights granted by the Fourth and Fifth Amendments, including the *Miranda* warning.

Harris (p.9) suggests special measures that need to be taken with drug-endangered children (DEC), including the formation of a multidisciplinary child abuse and neglect (CAN) team, including law enforcement officers, child protection service workers, mental health employees, medical personnel, prosecutors, and other professionals. He advises that law enforcement officers should take such children into protective custody, move them to a safe place, and see to it that their immediate needs are tended to. He (p.10) recommends that officers have a standing court order from the jurisdictional judge when children are found in meth labs to expedite assuming temporary custody for the child protection workers. He also suggests a standing court order regarding toxicology testing for ingested or assimilated chemicals and drugs.

Interviewing Abused Children

Interviewing children requires special skills. Before the interview, obtain relevant background information from the parents or guardian and anyone else involved in the case, including caseworkers, counselors, and physicians. Also review the assault report.

Often several interviews are necessary to get a complete statement without overwhelming the child. The initial interview should be brief, merely to establish the facts supporting probable cause, with a second interview later.

Generally it is best to conduct the interview in private in the child's or a friend's home or in a small room at a hospital or the police station. An interview room in a police station can be converted into a friendly environment for youngsters with the addition of some simple toys or coloring books (Figure 11.2). If the interview is to take place at the child's home, it might be best not to wear a uniform, especially if the child thinks he or she is to blame. The uniform could be too intimidating and frighten the child into thinking that he or she is going to be arrested. Casual, comfortable clothes are usually best.

Regardless of whether the interview is conducted at the child's home or at the police station, it is usually not advisable to have a family member present—but if the child so desires, the wish should be respected. The family member should be seated out of the child's view so as not to influence the interview. However, if a parent is suspected of being the offender, neither parent should be present. The investigator should record the time the interview begins and ends. Because taking written statements from children is difficult, it is sometimes better to videotape the interview. Videotapes may be used by other officers, prosecutors, and the courts, which eliminates having to requestion the victim.

When conducting an interview with a child, investigators must maintain rapport. The gender of the interviewer generally does not matter—the ability to elicit accurate information is the key quality. The interviewer should sit next to the child and speak in a friendly voice, without talking down to the child. It may help to play a game with the child or to get down on the floor at the child's level to get attention and to encourage the child to talk naturally. Allow the child freedom to do other things during the interview, such as moving around the room or playing with toys, but do not allow distractions from the outside. Learn about the child's abilities and interests by asking questions about everyday activities, such as school and household chores. Ask about the child's siblings, pets, friends, and favorite games or television shows. It may help to share personal informa-

Figure 11.2
This girl is being interviewed by a plain-clothes investigator in a child-friendly room. Achieving a comfortable rapport with the child is essential to getting that victim to open up and discuss the abuse. Doll play often helps the child relax and recount important details of the abuse event(s).

tion when appropriate, such as about your own children or pets. Evaluate the child's cognitive level by asking if he or she can read, write, count, or tell time. Does the child know his/her birthdate? Can the child recount past events (yesterday, holidays)? Does the child know about various body parts and their functions? Assess the child's maturity level by asking about his/her responsibilities—making his/her own breakfast, walking the dog, and so on. Does the child enjoy any privileges (staying home alone, going places on his/her own)?

Make the child feel comfortable, and keep in mind that questioning children is apt to be more of a sharing experience than a formal interview. Because young children have a short attention span, fact-finding interviews should last no more than 15 or 20 minutes. Questions should pertain to what happened, who did it, when it happened, where it happened, and whether force, threats, or enticements were involved. Ask simple, direct, open-ended questions. Avoid asking "why" questions, because they tend to sound accusatory. To alleviate the anxiety, fear, or reluctance found in children who have been instructed or threatened not to tell by the offender (*especially* if a parent), try statements such as, "It's not bad to tell what happened," "You won't get in trouble," "You can help your dad/mom/friend by telling what happened," and "It wasn't your fault." Never threaten or try to force a reluctant child to talk, because such pressure will likely lead a child to "clam up" and may cause further trauma.

To obtain the most thorough and accurate account of the abuse possible, investigators should be proficient in cognitive interview techniques, discussed in Chapter 6.

It is extremely important not to put words into a child's mouth. When the child answers your questions, be certain you understand the meaning of his or her words. A child may think "sex" is kissing or hugging or touching. If the child uses a word, learn what the word really means to the child to get to the truth and avoid later embarrassment in court.

In the case of sexual abuse of young children, it may be helpful to use drawings or anatomical dolls to assist the children in describing exactly what happened and the positions of the child and the abuser when the offense took place (Figure 11.3). Controversy exists, however, in whether such anatomically detailed dolls help or hinder interview progress.

To assess the credibility and competence of children in sexual abuse cases, consider the following criteria, courtesy of the Sexual Assault Center, Seattle, Washington:

● Does the child describe acts or experiences to which a child of his or her age would not normally have

Figure 11.3
Anatomical dolls are sometimes used to diagnose and treat sexual abuse victims. The dolls enable victims (generally children) to better express thoughts and actions by "acting out" their trauma. These adolescent dolls feature a male or female sex organ, breasts, ears, mouth, navel, jointed legs, and individual fingers.

been exposed? The average child is not familiar with erection or ejaculation until adolescence.

- Does the child describe circumstances and characteristics typical of a sexual assault situation? "He told me that it was our secret"; "He said I couldn't go out if I didn't do it"; "She told me it was sex education."
- How and under what circumstances did the child tell? What were the child's exact words?
- How many times has the child given the history, and how consistent is it regarding the basic facts of the assault (times, dates, circumstances, sequence of events, etc.)?
- How much spontaneous information does the child provide? How much prompting is required?
- Can the child define the difference between the truth and a lie? (This question is not actually very useful with young children because they learn these terms by rote and may not truly understand the concepts.)

During the interview, do not try to extract promises from the child regarding testifying in court, because an undue emphasis on a trial will have little meaning and may frighten the child, causing nightmares and apprehension. Investigators should avoid asking leading questions, repeated interviews, and confusing questions.

After the interview is completed, give the parents simple, straightforward information about what will happen next in the criminal justice system and approximately when, the likelihood of trial, and so on. Enlist their cooperation. Let them know who to contact for status reports or in an emergency; express appreciation and understanding for the efforts they are making by reporting and following through on the process. Answer any questions the child or parents have.

One final note: Exact notes are critical in interviews of child sexual abuse victims because such cases are an exception to the hearsay rule, meaning an officer *may* testify in court about the victim's statements. Therefore, officers should be meticulous in recording all statements verbatim. The child may not be able to repeat the statements due to fear or anxiety. For this reason, as well as others mentioned earlier, interviews should be videotaped whenever possible.

Sample Protocol

The following excerpt from the Boulder City (Nevada) Police Department's protocol for investigating reports of sexual and physical abuse of children is typical.

It is the policy to *team* investigate all abuse allegations.

When a report comes in, a juvenile officer is immediately assigned all abuse cases. This officer is responsi-

ble for maintaining a 72-hour time frame. Contact is made as soon as possible.

The investigative process includes the following:

- The investigator contacts Nevada Welfare, and together they contact the victim at a location where the victim can be interviewed briefly, and not in the presence of the alleged perpetrator of the crime.
- During the initial interview the juvenile officer tries to determine if the report is a substantiated abuse, unsubstantiated or unfounded.
- If the report is substantiated, the juvenile officer or Nevada State Welfare removes the child from the home and books the child into protective custody. If the juvenile officer and Nevada State Welfare investigator determine the child is not in danger of *any* abuse, the child can be allowed to remain in his/her home environment.
- If the report is unsubstantiated, the child is left in the home.
- If the report is unfounded, the reason for the false report is also investigated to identify other problems.
- If the case is substantiated abuse, the victim is housed at Child Haven, and there is a detention hearing at 9:00 A.M. the following working day.

An in-depth interview is conducted with the victim by the juvenile officer and the Nevada State Welfare investigator. Several aids are used, depending on the child's age and mental abilities: structured and unstructured play therapy, picture drawings and use of anatomical dolls.

The juvenile officer also contacts the accused person and interviews him/her about the specific allegations, makes a report or statement relevant to the interview and makes these reports available to Nevada State Welfare and/or Clark County Juvenile Court. Nevada State Welfare is encouraged to attend these interviews, and a team approach is used during this phase of the investigation also.

The juvenile officer also interviews other people, including witnesses or victims—anyone who might have information about the case. The officer prepares an affidavit and presents the case to the district attorney's office to determine whether the case is suitable for prosecution. If so, a complaint is issued, and a warrant or summons is issued for the accused. Once a warrant is obtained, the investigating officer locates and arrests or causes the accused person to be arrested.

Klain et al. (p.39) stress that investigators must not only know their own state laws, but also be familiar with federal statutes and the possibility of dual prosecution. They (p.40) also note that to apply federal or state child pornography statutes, the investigation must collect evidence to support the charges. This evidence can also corroborate the victim's account, identify other victims or offenders, uncover other crimes, or provide additional information about the offender.

Evidence

ll the investigator's observations pertaining to the victim's physical and emotional condition must be recorded in detail.

 Evidence in child neglect or abuse cases includes the surroundings, the home conditions, clothing, bruises or other body injuries, the medical examination report, and other observations.

Photographs may be the best way to document child abuse and neglect where it is necessary to show injury to the child or the home environment conditions. Pictures should be taken immediately, because children's injuries heal quickly and home conditions can be changed rapidly. Pictures in both color and black-and-white should be taken, showing bruises, burns, cuts, or any injury requiring medical treatment (Figure 11.4). These photographs should be witnessed by people who can later testify about the location and extent of the injuries, including medical personnel who examined the child. Explain the need for the pictures to the child to avoid further fear or excitement. All procedures for photography at a crime scene (discussed in Chapter 2) should be followed.

Additional types of evidence that may be obtained in sexual assault cases include photographs, torn clothing, ropes or tapes, and trace evidence such as the hair of the offender and the victim and, in some instances, semen.

Indicators of Child Neglect and Abuse

 Indicators of neglect or abuse may be physical or behavioral or both.

Caution: The lists of indicators in this section are not exhaustive; many other indicators exist. In addition, the presence of one or more of these indicators does not prove that neglect or abuse exists. All factors and conditions of each specific case must be considered before you make a decision.

Neglect Indicators The *physical* indicators of child neglect may include frequent hunger, poor hygiene, inappropriate dress, consistent lack of supervision (especially in dangerous activities or for long time periods), unattended physical problems or medical needs, and abandonment. Such indicators often appear in families where the parents are drug addicts. The *behavioral* indicators may include begging, stealing (e.g., food), extend-

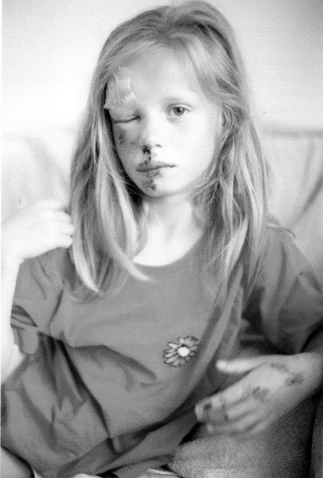

© Hill Creek Pictures/Index Stock Imagery

Figure 11.4
Injuries caused by abuse are best documented through photographs. Some of this girl's injuries will heal quite rapidly; thus, the severity of the battering will become less evident over time and must be captured as soon after the assault as possible. Note the scrapes and bruises on the girl's hand. Be sure to photograph all injuries.

ing school days by arriving early and/or leaving late, constant fatigue, listlessness or falling asleep in school, poor performance in school, truancy, alcohol or drug abuse, aggressive behavior, delinquency, and stating that no one is at home to care for them.

Emotional Abuse Indicators *Physical* indicators of emotional abuse may include speech disorders, lags in physical development, and general failure to thrive.

Behavioral indicators may include habit disorders such as sucking, biting, and rocking back and forth and conduct disorders such as antisocial, destructive behavior. Other possible symptoms are sleep disorders, inhibitions in play, obsessions, compulsions, phobias, hypochondria, behavioral extremes, and attempted suicide.

Physical Abuse Indicators *Physical* indicators of physical abuse include unexplained bruises or welts, burns, fractures, lacerations, and abrasions. These may be in various stages of healing. One obvious and important indicator of physical abuse is bruising.

Behavioral indicators include being wary of adults, being apprehensive when other children cry, extreme aggressiveness or extreme withdrawal, being frightened of parents, and being afraid to go home.

Parental indicators may include contradictory explanations for a child's injury; attempts to conceal a child's injury or to protect the identity of the person responsible; routine use of harsh, unreasonable discipline inappropriate to the child's age or transgressions, and poor impulse control.

Sexual Abuse Indicators *Physical* indicators of sexual abuse include difficulty urinating and irritation/bruising/tearing around the genital and/or rectal areas. Venereal disease and pregnancy, especially in preteens, are also indicators.

Behavioral indicators of sexual abuse may include unwillingness to change clothes for or to participate in physical education classes; withdrawal, fantasy, or infantile behavior; bizarre sexual behavior, sexual sophistication beyond the child's age, or unusual behavior or knowledge of sex; poor peer relationships; delinquency or running away; and reports of being sexually assaulted.

Parental indicators may include jealousy and overprotectiveness of a child. Incest incidents are insidious, commonly beginning with the parent fondling and caressing the child between the ages of 3 and 6 months and then progressing over a long time period, increasing in intensity of contact until the child is capable of full participation, usually between the ages of 8 and 10. A parent may hesitate to report a spouse who is sexually abusing their child for fear of destroying the marriage or for fear of retaliation. Intrafamily sex may be viewed as preferable to extramarital sex.

The Suspect

As noted, in many instances of child neglect and physical or emotional abuse, the suspect is one of the parents. According to the Uniform Crime Reports, in abuse or neglect of children under 5 years of age, the perpetrator was the father in 32 percent of the cases, the mother in 30 percent, a male acquaintance in 23 percent, other relatives in 6 percent, and a stranger in 3 percent.

People who have normal behavior patterns in all other areas of life may have very abnormal sexual behavior patterns. Child sexual abusers may commit only one offense in their lifetime, or they may commit hundreds. Surveys indicate that 35 to 50 percent of offenders know their victims. Some studies indicate an even higher percentage. Therefore, the investigator of a child sexual crime may not be looking for an unknown suspect or stranger.

The Parent as Suspect

Sexual abuse of one or more children in a family is one of the most common child sexual abuse problems, but it is not often reported. Because of the difficulties in detecting it, it is the least known to the public. The harm to the child from continued, close sexual relationships with a family member may be accompanied by shame, fear, or even guilt. Additional conflict may be created by admonitions of secrecy.

Although girls are more frequently victims, keep in mind that if a girl is sexually abused by a family member, a boy in the same family may also be a victim. Incest usually involves children under age 11 and becomes a repeated activity, escalating both in severity and frequency.

Courts have ruled that the spousal immunity rules do not apply to child sexual abuse cases. One spouse may be forced to testify against the other in court.

Munchausen Syndrome and Munchausen Syndrome by Proxy **Munchausen syndrome** involves self-induced or self-inflicted injuries. If a child's injuries appear to be self-induced or self-inflicted, the child may be seeking attention or sympathy or may be avoiding something. Parents—usually the mother—may inflict injuries on their children for basically the same reasons. **Munchausen syndrome by proxy (MSBP)** is a form of child abuse in which a parent or adult caregiver deliberately provides false medical histories, manufactures evidence, and causes medical distress in a child (Figure 11.5). MSBP is usually done so that the child will be treated by a physician and the abuser may gain the attention or sympathy of family, friends, and others.

MSBP allegations frequently come from an anonymous source or a health-care professional. An unknown percentage of the anonymous calls come from health-care professionals concerned with liability issues. One of the most logical first steps is to contact the primary-care physician. Early contact should be made with a child-care agency to coordinate issues regarding the child's safety when the investigation becomes known to the parent. MSBP should be considered as a possible motive in any questionable or unexplained death of a child.

Investigators assigned to work child abuse cases should investigate cases of MSBP as they do similar cases of abuse. In general, however, when confronted with possible cases of MSBP, investigators should:

- Review the victim's medical records.
- Determine from contact with medical personnel the reporting parent's concerns and reactions to the child's medical treatment.
- Compile a complete family history.

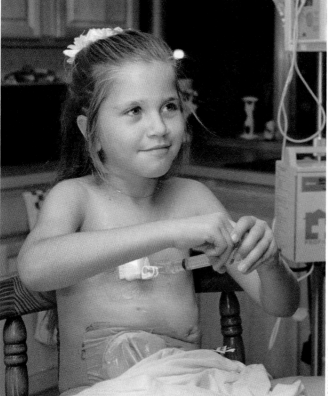

Figure 11.5
At her Coral Springs, Florida, home, Jennifer Bush applies medicine from a syringe as treatment for a rare disease. She has been hospitalized more than 200 times, undergone 40 operations, and accumulated $3 million in medical expenses. Jennifer has been placed under state care and her mother jailed for allegedly causing her illnesses as a result of Munchausen syndrome by proxy, a rare form of child abuse in which an adult intentionally makes a child ill to get attention.

- Interview family members, neighbors, and babysitters.
- Consider using video surveillance in the hospital.
- Use a search warrant for the family's residence when collecting evidence.

Chiczewski and Kelly (p.22) note: "Distinguishing between MSBP and other forms of child abuse remains extremely difficult." They (p.21) suggest that investigators be suspicious of a person who exhibits knowledge of diseases and medical procedures beyond what most parents may know. Offenders often have a medical background or have been around the medical profession in some way.

Whereas MSBP is a disorder that clearly results in a form of child abuse, another disorder whose symptoms closely resemble child abuse, and for which parents are often mistakenly accused of abuse, is osteogenesis imperfecta.

Osteogenesis Imperfecta Osteogenesis **imperfecta (OI)**, or brittle bone disease, is a genetic disorder characterized by bones that break easily, often from little or

no apparent cause. However, child abuse may also result in broken bones. Consequently, improper diagnosis of OI can lead to the parents of children with the disease being wrongly accused of child abuse. The U.S. Osteogenesis Imperfecta Foundation (OIF) states: "A minor accident may result in a fracture; some fractures may occur while a child is being diapered, lifted, or dressed." The most routine child-care activities, performed by the most careful and loving parents, can easily and spontaneously break the bones of a child with OI, and, in some severe cases, the condition may be lethal. The OIF reports:

> False accusations of child abuse may occur in families with children who have milder forms of OI and/or in whom OI has not previously been diagnosed. Types of fractures that are typically observed in both child abuse and OI include fractures in multiple stages of healing, rib fractures, spiral fractures and fractures for which there is no adequate explanation of trauma.

The similarities between OI and child abuse symptoms can easily confuse investigators and anger parents wrongly accused of abuse. For example, in addition to displaying different types of fractures in various stages of healing, a child with OI often bruises easily. Furthermore, many children with OI are of shorter stature than average, a condition often mistaken as indicative of neglect (OIF).When these symptoms are detected, how do investigators determine whether the suspected abuse case is actually OI? First, a medical professional experienced in diagnosing OI should evaluate the child. Genetic counseling may also reveal a previously unrecognized family history of mild OI. Investigators should also look for inconsistencies between the explanation for the injury given by the child or parent and the diagnosis provided by the treating physicians and other medical personnel. Parents may also try to conceal child abuse by frequently changing doctors or hospitals, thus avoiding a buildup of incriminating records at any one office or facility. Keep in mind also that the presence of OI does not automatically preclude the existence of child abuse.

Sudden Infant Death Syndrome Another tragic condition that takes the lives of young victims and for which parents may become suspected of child abuse is **sudden infant death syndrome (SIDS)**, briefly introduced in Chapter 8.

Weyland (p.10) differentiates between investigating sudden unexplained infant death (SUID) and SIDS. He explains that SIDS is a "diagnosis by exclusion" after a thorough case investigation and that it is the most frequently determined cause of SUID. He (p.11) reports that about 15 percent of SUID investigations will identify a cause of death other than SIDS.

Because examination of the death scene is a critical factor in determining SIDS, officers responding to a call of an "infant not breathing" must be observant of several elements, including the infant's position when found, the condition of the crib and surrounding area, the presence of objects in the crib, any unusual or dangerous items in the room, any medications being given to the baby, room temperature, and air quality.

Officers may also observe certain bodily appearances in the victim that typically occur in SIDS cases resulting from the death process, including discoloration of the skin, frothy drainage from the mouth or nose, and cooling rigor mortis that takes place quickly, usually in about three hours in infants.

Weyland (p.13) suggests the following considerations during a SUID investigation:

● Remain sensitive to the family, but stay focused.

● Time is critical.

● Trust your investigative instincts.

● Use a SUID investigative protocol.

(See also "Guidelines for Death Scene Investigations of Sudden, Unexplained Infant Deaths," available [Sept. 20, 2005] at http://www.cdc.gov/mmwr/preview/mmwrhtml/00042657.htm)

Table 11.1 compares the characteristic features of SIDS with child abuse, and Table 11.2 summarizes the characteristics of MSBP, OI, and SIDS.

Investigating Child Fatalities   Investigating the death of a child can be one of the most difficult tasks an investigator ever encounters. Tough questions must be asked to grieving parents or caregivers so that the investigator may determine whether the fatality resulted from an unknown medical condition, an accident, or a criminal act. Walsh (p.25) notes that many child fatalities are first reported as natural deaths or accidents. He offers the following checklists of potential witnesses and other information sources for investigators working a child fatality case (pp.14, 18).

Potential witnesses include:

● Parents—including current and former step-parents and parents' significant others

● Siblings and other children

● Family members

Table 11.1 / Comparison of Sudden Infant Death Syndrome (SIDS) and Child Abuse Characteristics

Characteristic/Feature	SIDS	Child Abuse/Neglect
Age typically affected	May occur from birth to 24 months, but most common from 2 to 4 months of age	May occur at any time, but most abused children are 1 to 3 years of age
External signs of injury?	Not usually	Yes—distinguishable and visible signs
Signs of malnourishment?	Not usually; appears well developed	Common
Do siblings show any symptoms	Not usually; siblings appear normal and healthy	May show patterns of injuries
Parents' account of investigated event	Placed healthy baby to sleep in the crib and later found infant lifeless	May sound suspicious or may not account for all injuries to the child
Annual number of deaths in the United States	3,000–4,000 infants	1,000–4,000 children; 300 are infants

Source: Adapted from Linda Esposito, Larry Minda, and Claire Forman. "Sudden Infant Death Syndrome." *FBI Law Enforcement Bulletin,* September 1998, pp. 1–5.

Table 11.2 / Comparison of the Characteristics of Munchausen Syndrome by Proxy (MSBP), Osteogenesis Imperfecta (OI), and Sudden Infant Death Syndrome (SIDS)

Characteristic/Feature	MSBP[a]	OI[b]	SIDS[a]
Age of child affected	Any age	Any age	Occurs in typically afflicted newborn to 24 months but is most frequent from 2 to 4 months
Number of children who die every year in the United States due to it	Unknown	Unknown	3,000–4,000
External signs of injury (parent-inflicted)	Occasionally	Not usually	Not usually
Is it child abuse?	Yes	No	No

Source: [a] Adapted from Linda Esposito, Larry Minda, and Claire Forman. "Sudden Infant Death Syndrome." *FBI Law Enforcement Bulletin,* September 1998, pp. 1–5.

[b] U.S. Osteogenesis Imperfecta Foundation: http://www.oif.org/tier2/childabuse.htm

- Caretakers—babysitters, childcare employees
- Teachers—daycare, preschool, school, church
- Neighbors—current and previous
- First responders—police and emergency medical technicians
- Emergency room personnel—physicians and nurses
- Medical providers who have seen the child previously, including school nurses
- Agency personnel—Child Protection Services (CPS), daycare licensing, law enforcement personnel who have had prior contact with the family and/or child

    Other potential information sources include:

- CPS records—for the deceased child, siblings, other children that the child's caretakers have had contact with
- Law enforcement records—criminal history, victim or suspect history, calls for service
- Medical records for the deceased child and siblings—birth, prenatal care, pediatrician, medical, emergency room
- 911 calls
- Emergency medical services (EMS) reports
- Telephone calls or other communications made or received by the suspect around the time of the child's death—including cell phones, pagers, e-mails, messages on answering machines
- Autopsy results

    If the child's family or suspect has previously lived in another community, check there for potential witnesses and other agency records that may document a history of abuse or neglect.

    Walsh (p.25) provides the following tips and reminders for investigators working possible child fatality cases:

- An unreasonable delay in seeking medical attention is often a "red flag" that the child's injuries may have been caused by abuse.
- 911 call records often contain important information about how a child's injuries were initially reported.
- Treat cases involving severe injury as potential child fatalities, as it is not uncommon for severely injured children to die days or weeks after the original injury.
- Delayed deaths often involve more than one crime scene. Examine the place where the injury occurred, the hospital where the child died, and any private vehicle used to transport the child to the hospital.
- There is no substitute for a timely, professional crime-scene search, including evidence collection, documentation, and photodocumentation.
- Coordinate and communicate with CPS investigators in child fatality cases. They have a legitimate role in

the investigation and can often provide important information on the child and family involved.

Successful child fatality investigations hinge on three factors: effectively conducted, well-documented interviews of witnesses; through background checks on every witness and suspect involved in the case; and competent interrogation of the suspect(s) (Walsh, p.25). A final word of caution: Do not automatically exclude children as potential suspects. Children have been known to inflict severe injuries on other children.

Sex Crimes by Other Children

Although seldom discussed, an increasing number of child sex crimes are being committed by other children. Many people think that such crimes cannot occur because they often view children as not being sexually capable. However, arrests of 12 to 14 year olds for sexual offenses increased 70 percent during the 1980s. Some child sexual abusers were molested themselves. When investigators receive reports of children committing sex crimes against other children, they must not automatically dismiss them as fantasy and must thoroughly investigate all such reports.

The Nonparent Suspect

Perpetrators other than parents have included babysitters, camp counselors, school personnel, clergy, and others. Habitual child sex abusers, whether they operate as loners or as part of a sex ring, have been classified into three types. First is the **misoped**, the person who hates children, has sex with them, and then brutally destroys them. The second type is the **hebephile**, a person who selects high school–age youths as his or her sex victims. The pedophile is the third and most common habitual child sex abuser.

The Pedophile

 he **pedophile**, sometimes referred to as a **chicken hawk,** is an adult who has either heterosexual or homosexual preferences for young boys or girls of a specific, limited age range. Although pedophiles are typically male, this is not always the case. Women are also involved in the sexual abuse of children. Pedophilia is a sex offense in all states.

Rarely deviating from the preferred age range, the pedophile is an expert in selecting and enticing young people. The pedophile frequently selects children who stand apart from other children, who are runaways, or who crave attention and love. Although some pedophiles are child rapists, the majority rarely use force, relying instead on befriending the victims and gaining their confidence and friendship. They may become involved in activities or programs that interest the type of victims they want to attract and that provide them with easy access to these children. They may also use drugs or alcohol as a means of seduction, reducing the child's inhibitions.

Pedophiles may obtain, collect, and maintain photographs of the children with whom they are or have been involved. Many pedophiles maintain diaries of their sexual encounters with children. They may collect books, magazines, newspapers, and other writings on the subject of sexual activities with children. They may also collect addresses, phone numbers, or lists of people who have similar sexual interests. Pedophiles also locate and attract victims through the computer, as discussed shortly. In addition, many pedophiles are members of sex rings.

Child Sexual Abuse Rings

Adults (at least 10 to 15 years older than the victims) are usually the dominant leaders, organizers, and operators of sex rings. The adult leader selectively gathers young people together for sexual purposes. The involvement varies, with the longest periods occurring when prepubescent children are involved. Most cases involve male ringleaders, but some involve a female as well, usually a husband/wife pair.

Many ringleaders use their *occupation* as the major access route to the child victims. The adult has a legitimate role as an authority figure in the lives of the children selected for the ring or is able to survey vulnerable children through access to family records or history.

Sometimes rings are formed by an adult targeting a specific child, who then uses his or her associations and peer pressure to bring other children into the group. The initial child may be a relative or previously unknown. One common technique is to post a notice on a store bulletin board requesting girls to help with housework.

The adult's status in the neighborhood sometimes helps to legitimize his or her presence with the children and their parents and to permit unquestioned movement of young people into the offender's home. Such an offender often is well liked by his neighbors.

 Investigators should be aware of three types of sex rings: solo, transition, and syndicated. Certain cults are also involved in the sexual abuse of children.

Solo Sex Rings The organization of *solo sex rings* is primarily by the age of the child—for example, toddlers (ages 2 to 5), prepubescent (6 to 12), or pubescent (13 to 17). This type of offender prefers to have multiple children as sex objects, in contrast to the offender who seeks out one child at a time.

Transition Sex Rings Pedophiles have a strong need to communicate with others about their interest in children. In *transition sex rings*, experiences are exchanged, whereas in solo rings, the pedophile keeps his or her activities and photographs totally secret. In transition rings, photographs of children as well as sexual services may be traded and sold.

The trading of pornography appears to be the first move of the victim into the "possession" of other pedophiles. The photographs are traded, and victims may be tested by other offenders and eventually traded for their sexual services.

Syndicated Sex Rings The third type of ring is the *syndicated sex ring*, a well-structured organization that recruits children, produces pornography, delivers direct sexual services, and establishes an extensive network of customers. Syndicated rings have involved a Boy Scout troop, a boys' farm operated by a minister, and a national boy prostitution ring.

Cults

Cults are groups that use rituals or ceremonial acts to draw their members together into a certain belief system. According to Wrobleski and Hess (p.89): "When the rituals of a group involve crimes, . . . [including] child sexual abuse . . . , they become a problem for law enforcement." Crimes associated with cults are discussed in Chapter 18.

Victimology

People involved in intervening, investigating, or prosecuting child pornography and sex ring cases must recognize that a bond often develops between the offender and the victims. Many victims find themselves willing to trade sex for attention, affection, and other benefits. Pedophile ring operators are, by definition, skilled at gaining the continued cooperation and control of their victims through well-planned seduction. They are skilled at recognizing and then *temporarily* filling the emotional and physical needs of children. They know how to listen to children—an ability many parents lack. They are willing to spend all the time it takes to seduce a child.

This positive offender/victim bond must not be misinterpreted as consent, complicity, or guilt. In one case a prosecutor announced to television reporters that the victims were as guilty as—if not more guilty than—the offenders. Police investigators, in particular, must be sensitive to this problem.

Offender Reactions

When a child pornography and sex ring is discovered, certain reactions by the pedophile offenders are fairly predictable. The intensity of these reactions may depend on how much the offenders have to lose by their identification and conviction.

Usually a pedophile's first reaction to discovery is complete denial. The offenders may act shocked, surprised, or even indignant about an allegation of sexual activity with children. This denial frequently is aided by their friends, neighbors, relatives, and coworkers, who insist that such upstanding people could not have done what is alleged.

If the evidence rules out total denial, offenders may switch to a slightly different tactic, attempting to minimize what they have done in both quantity and quality. Pedophiles are often knowledgeable about the law and might admit to acts that are lesser offenses or misdemeanors.

Either as part of the effort to minimize or as a separate reaction, pedophiles typically attempt to justify their behavior. They might claim that they care for these children more than their parents do and that what they do is beneficial to the children. They may claim to have been under tremendous stress, to have a drinking problem, or not to have known how young a certain victim was. The efforts to justify their behavior often center on blaming the victim. Offenders may claim that they were seduced by the victims, that the victims initiated the sexual activity, or that the victims were promiscuous or even prostitutes. When various reactions do not result in termination of the investigation or prosecution, pedophiles may claim to be sick and unable to control themselves.

> Pedophiles' reactions to being discovered usually begin with complete denial and then progress to minimizing the acts, justifying the acts, and blaming the victims. If all else fails, they may claim to be sick.

Pedophiles are usually very involved in child pornography, but they are not the only individuals who participate in child pornography.

Child Pornography and Sexual Exploitation

Finkelhor and Ormrod (*Child Pornography*) note that the FBI's emerging National Incident-Based Reporting System (NIBRS) is becoming an effective tool in understanding the pornography problem. They (p.1) report that NIBRS data suggest that approximately 2,000 crime incidents of pornography with juvenile involvement were known to state and local police in 2000. These offenses most often were committed by a lone adult male offender,

occurred in a residence, and did not involve a computer. According to Finkelhor and Ormrod (p.6), juvenile-related pornography has been rising, which is notable because it is occurring in the context of an overall decline in reported cases of sexual abuse of children.

> The Child Protection Act (1984) prohibits child pornography and greatly increases the penalties for adults who engage in it.

According to the Child Protection Act of 1984, child pornography is highly developed into an organized, multimillion-dollar industry producing and distributing pornographic materials nationally, exploiting thousands of children, including runaways and homeless youths. It states that such exploitation is harmful to the physiological, emotional, and mental health of the individual and to society.

Many states have passed similarly worded statutes and have also increased penalties for sexual abuse and the production and distribution of child-pornographic materials. Although adult pornography has always been objectionable to many people, it has not resulted in the aggressive public and legislative action that child pornography has received. In 1977 Congress passed the Protection of Children Against Sexual Exploitation Act. This and other federal and state laws have prohibited commercial and noncommercial distribution of pornographic materials and more recently have made it a violation of law to *possess* such materials. The basis for these laws has been the acceptance of a relationship between child-pornographic materials and child sexual abuse offenders and offenses.

Indeed, in many cases, arrested pedophiles have had in their possession child-pornographic literature used to lower their selected victims' inhibitions. It is often necessary to obtain search warrants for the suspect's premises to obtain these materials. It is necessary in the investigation to gain as much evidence as possible, because the problems of child testimony in court are well established. Klain et al. (p.41) recommend that the following specific items be listed in a child pornography search warrant:

- Any correspondence concerning either adult or child pornography, including e-mails, Internet chats, and similar communication
- Telephone listings, address books, mailing lists, or other records of communications concerning adult or child pornography
- Books, magazines, photographs, slides, negatives, films, videotapes, and similar items of adult or child pornography
- Photographs, albums, or drawings of children, whether clothed or unclothed
- Computer data, including floppy diskettes, fixed hard drives, tapes, modems, laser disks, CDs, zip

drives, and other media that can store magnetic coding or data

- Computer hardware, including computer components, peripherals, word-processing equipment, and other electronic devices
- Computer software, including operating systems, application software, utility programs, and other programs used to communicate via telephone lines, radio, or other means of transmission

Models to Combat Child Sexual Exploitation

Three law enforcement approaches have emerged as models to combat child sexual exploitation: special task forces, strike forces, and law enforcement networks.

Special Task Forces According to Klain et al. (p.47), this model is most useful in jurisdictions with a steady load of child sexual exploitation cases. In addition to steady caseload, other characteristics of the model include a centralized location, a standing team of experts, specialized staffing, victim services, and a multijurisdictional (federal, state, local) approach. Klain et al. (p.49) cite the following advantages of special task forces:

- The explicit dedication of personnel and resources
- A formalized structure for sharing expertise and equipment
- An extensive communications network to prevent duplicative efforts and maximize impact
- An increased esprit de corps among task force members and the community

The Child Exploitation Unit (CEU) of the Dallas (Texas) Police Department is a nationally recognized law enforcement special task force responding to child pornography (Klain et al., pp.48–49). The unit, part of the Youth and Family Crimes Bureau, uses six detectives to investigate out-of-family pornography and other offenses and two detectives to manage covert and sting operations. The unit works closely with the Dallas County District Attorney's Office and Dallas Children's Advocacy Center. Much of the unit's work is self-generated through its sting operations and extensive monitoring. When a lead is produced, the unit investigates it thoroughly, gathering evidence for a sexual abuse case, identifying children depicted in the pornography, and aggressively investigating sexual predators.

Strike Forces Under this model, no core is dedicated exclusively to the problem. Rather, team members come together from individual agencies in response to a particular case. According to Klain et al. (p. 49), strike forces are characterized by having no central location

and only a few dedicated resources and being mobilized as needed with limited caseloads, but providing victim services.

A nationally recognized Child Sexual Exploitation Strike Force of the U.S. Postal Inspection Service, Northern Illinois, was established in the late 1980s when law enforcement agencies discovered that they often investigated the same cases, resulting in duplication of efforts and wasted resources (Klain et al., p.50). The strike force includes a U.S. postal inspector, four investigators from the Cook County Sheriff's Police Department, three investigators from the Chicago Police Department, and a Cook County state's attorney's investigator. The strike force maintains strong ties with many federal, state, and local law enforcement units, including the FBI and Illinois State Police, allowing the strike force to call on individual agents with specialized expertise as needed case by case. Strike force investigators, who have been deputized as U.S. marshals, use covert mail and electronic correspondence to apprehend those seeking to send or receive child pornography. The investigators also meet with adults seeking children to include in pornography productions. When child victims are identified, the strike force works with local advocacy centers to obtain interviews and provide services.

Law Enforcement Network Klain et al. (p.51) describe this model as the "most loosely configured. In this model, law enforcement officers, prosecutors, victims' services providers, social service agents, and others come together as needed on a case-by-case basis. The model is characterized by having no dedicated resources and focusing on education and recruitment. They (p.52) suggest that a strength of this model is "the immediate and comprehensive effort to increase awareness about the issue of child sexual exploitation."

The Massachusetts Child Exploitation Network is one nationally recognized law enforcement network of investigators and victim-assistance professionals who share an interest in crimes against children, particularly child sexual exploitation (Klain et al.). The group, which has more than 200 members, seeks to raise awareness and enhance expertise among law enforcement and victim-serving professions regarding child sexual exploitation. In addition to being a coalition builder and educator, the network collaborates with the Massachusetts State Police to develop regional task forces coordinated by each district attorney's office to investigate child sexual exploitation cases.

Federal Agencies Working against Child Pornography

Several federal agencies are involved in combating child pornography. The FBI's Crimes Against Children (CAC) unit provides quick and effective responses to all incidents of sexual exploitation of children. The CAC program focuses on multidisciplinary and multiagency resource teams to investigate and prosecute crimes against children, enhanced interagency sharing of intelligence, and specialized skills (Klain et al., p.46).

The U.S. Customs Service targets the illegal importation and trafficking of child pornography and fights child sex tourism. The Customs CyberSmuggling Center (C3) is a front line of defense against smuggling over continental borders as well as through the Internet.

The U.S. Postal Inspection Service is responsible for investigating crimes involving the U.S. mails, including child pornography and child sexual abuse offenses. It is the lead agency in the federal government's efforts to eliminate the production and distribution of such material.

International Initiatives

Klain et al. (p.38) describe the First World Congress against Commercial Exploitation of Children, convened in Stockholm, Sweden, in 1996. This world congress adopted a Declaration and Agenda for Action calling upon states to, among other things:

- Accord high priority to action against the commercial exploitation of children and allocate adequate resources to the effort.
- Promote stronger cooperation between states and all sectors of society and strengthen the role of families
- Criminalize the commercial sexual exploitation of children
- Condemn and penalize the offenders while ensuring that child victims are not penalized
- Review and revise laws, policies, programs, and practices
- Enforce laws, policies, and programs

Interpol has established a Standing Working Party (SWP) on Offenses against Minors that seeks to improve international cooperation in preventing and combating child pornography and other forms of child sexual exploitation (Klain et al., p.52). The group meets twice a year and is working on producing best-practices manuals and recommendations for investigations of child exploitation.

Advances in computer technology and the expansion of the Internet have created an entirely new global forum in which sex offenders can access potential victims and distribute or trade child pornography (Figure 11.6).

Internet Sex Crimes against Children

Collins (p.3) contends that more than 45 million children were online in 2002. In addition, pedophiles run more than 20,000 websites, and hundreds more are created monthly. According to Bowker and Gray (p.12): "From the safety of their homes, pedophiles can use the Internet to anonymously and simultaneously prepare numerous children for future molestation." They cite the following statistics from a recent study of 1,501 Internet users ranging in age from 10 to 17:

- Approximately 1 in 5 received a sexual solicitation over the Internet in the past year.
- One in 33 experienced an aggressive approach—an individual who requested a meeting, telephoned, or sent regular mail, money, or gifts.

Figure 11.6
Pedophiles lurk in cyberspace, waiting to lure unsuspecting children into ongoing online "friendships" and hoping to persuade the child to eventually meet them in person.

© L. Clarke/CORBIS

- One in 4 had unwanted exposure to explicit pictures in the past year.

- One in 17 faced threats or harassment.

- Youths reported less than 10 percent of sexual solicitations and only 3 percent of unwanted exposure episodes to authorities.

Wolak et al. (p.vii) describe a national study of juvenile online victimization, the National Juvenile Online Victimization (N-JOV) Study, to serve as a baseline for monitoring the growth of Internet sex crimes against minors. The study found that law enforcement at all levels made an estimated 2,577 arrests during the 12 months starting July 1, 2000, for Internet sex crimes against minors. These crimes were categorized in three mutually exclusive groups: (1) Internet crimes against identified victims involving Internet-related sexual assaults and other sex crimes, such as the production of child pornography committed against identified victims (39 percent of arrests); (2) Internet solicitations unknowingly to undercover law enforcement officers posing as minors that involved no identified victims (25 percent of arrests); and (3) the possession, distribution, or trading of Internet child pornography by offenders who did not use the Internet to sexually exploit identified victims or unknowingly solicit undercover investigators (36 percent of arrests). Figure 11.7 illustrates the categories.

The study also found that the vast majority of offenders were non-Hispanic white males older than 25 acting alone. Most investigations (79 percent) involved more than one law enforcement agency.

Investigating Cybersex Offenders

Wolak et al. (p.5) provide the following description of how typical investigations of solicitations to undercover law enforcement are conducted:

- A law enforcement investigator posts a profile on the Internet or goes into a chat room posing as a girl or boy, usually in the age range of 13 to 15, and waits to

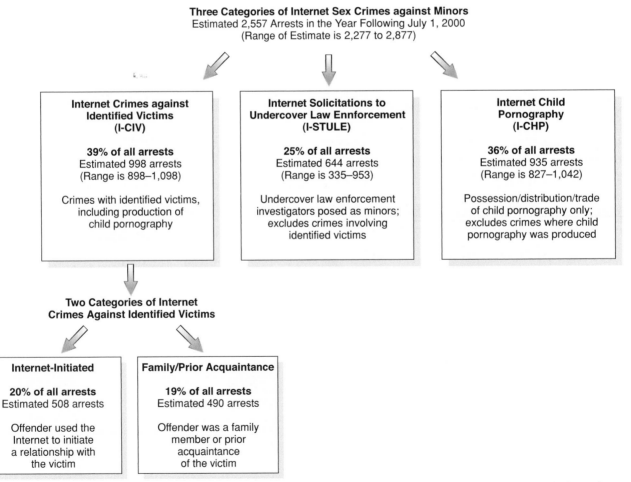

Three Categories of Internet Sex Crimes against Minors
Estimated 2,557 Arrests in the Year Following July 1, 2000
(Range of Estimate is 2,277 to 2,877)

Internet Crimes against Identified Victims (I-CIV)

39% of all arrests
Estimated 998 arrests
(Range is 898–1,098)

Crimes with identified victims, including production of child pornography

Internet Solicitations to Undercover Law Ennforcement (I-STULE)

25% of all arrests
Estimated 644 arrests
(Range is 335–953)

Undercover law enforcement investigators posed as minors; excludes crimes involving identified victims

Internet Child Pornography (I-CHP)

36% of all arrests
Estimated 935 arrests
(Range is 827–1,042)

Possession/distribution/trade of child pornography only; excludes crimes where child pornography was produced

Two Categories of Internet Crimes Against Identified Victims

Internet-Initiated

20% of all arrests
Estimated 508 arrests

Offender used the Internet to initiate a relationship with the victim

Family/Prior Acquaintance

19% of all arrests
Estimated 490 arrests

Offender was a family member or prior acquaintance of the victim

Note: The ranges for each estimate constitute margins of error, calculated separately, for each estimate using a statistical formula based on the weighted number of cases in each category.

Figure 11.7

Categories of Internet sex crimes against minors

Source: Janis Wolak, Kimberly Mitchell, and David Finkelhor. *Internet Sex Crimes against Minors: The Response of Law Enforcement.* Washington, DC: National Center for Missing & Exploited Children, November 2003. Reprinted by permission.

be contacted by an adult seeking a young adolescent for a sexual encounter. The investigator responds to a conversation initiated by an offender and allows the offender to develop a relationship that culminates in a face-to-face meeting, where the offender is arrested. The investigator is careful not to initiate conversations about sexual topics or propose sexual activity—this could be considered entrapment.

- The agent uses investigative resources to track down the identity of the offender and keeps logs of all online interactions, which constitute evidence of the crime.

- The offender is charged with attempted sexual assault and, in some jurisdictions, illegal use of a computer to solicit a minor. In some cases, other crimes, like distribution of child pornography, are committed.

- The legal decisions pertaining to entrapment apply to Internet undercover operations. Investigators may not improperly induce a person to commit a criminal act.

- These cases are often referred to as "proactive" because they allow law enforcement to act without waiting for an offender to commit a crime against a juvenile victim.

Bowker and Gray (p.15) suggest that investigators examine any files found in an offender's possession to determine the subject's level of interest and deviancy and foreclose several defenses. They should consider file quantity, themes, types, organization, locations, and uses. They should also examine an offender's online activites. For example, how many screen names does the offender use? Does the offender have a screen profile with the offender's photo? Is the profile accurate or does it give false information? Also of importance is the subject's real life. Does current or prior employment involve juveniles? Does the person volunteer in activities involving children? A challenge to monitoring child pornography sites is that they are constantly moving, because many Internet service providers (ISPs) expel them once they become aware of the nature of the site.

Welch (p.51) contends that one of the greatest challenges for Internet-related investigations is determining the identity behind an Internet Protocol (IP) address and where it is located. IP tracing technologies can provide valuable tools to identify the source of Internet communications. Helpful clues to the location of a suspect can be found by analyzing e-mail header information, which reveals the IP address of the system the e-mail came from. Once the IP address is obtained, investigators can easily identify the location with an IP tracing tool.

Bowling and Resch (p.3) suggest an interview strategy to obtain a confession from cybersex offenders. Initially investigators should show appropriate identification, state the purpose of the interview, and state their accusation. The suspect typically will deny involvement. If this occurs, investigators should immediately interrupt and use whatever the protestation consisted of, for example, "I'm glad to hear you say that you couldn't do such

a thing." Then the investigators should detail the evidence against the person. Follow the accusation, denials, and protests with a series of theme-development strategies. They (pp.2–3) suggest: "Interrogation themes consist of rationalizing the crime, projecting the blame onto others, and minimizing the offense (RPMs)." These techniques were explained in Chapter 6. Bowker and Gray (p.16) provide some common defenses investigators should be prepared for: "I downloaded them by accident." "I did not know it was child pornography." "It was just a fantasy. I never intended to have sex with a minor." "I just had dirty pictures. I did not hurt anyone." "A hacker put these files on my computer." "I have them so I will not abuse children."

After the subject has been given reasonable time to confess, investigators can present a bad–good option, with the bad choice presented first—for example, "Either you're a monster who preys on little children [bad] or you just possess a few photographs of kids [good]. Which is it?" Such an approach is usually successful in eliciting a confession.

The Innocent Images National Initiative   The *Innocent Images National Initiative* (IINI), part of the FBI's Cyber Crimes Program, is an "intelligence driven, proactive, multi-agency investigative initiative to combat the proliferation of child pornography/child sexual exploitation (CP/CSE) facilitated by an online computer" (Federal Bureau of Investigation, *Innocent Images*). The program provides a coordinated FBI response to this nationwide problem by collating and analyzing information and images obtained from numerous sources, avoiding duplication of effort by all FBI field offices. To date, 32 IINI subjects placed on the FBI's ten most wanted list have been apprehended.

Between fiscal years 1996 and 2003 (second quarter), this initiative has accomplished the following:

- 9,366 cases opened
- 2,520 informations/indictments
- 2,608 arrests/locates/summons
- 2,569 convictions/pretrial diversions

IINI undercover operations are being conducted in several FBI field offices by task forces that combine the resources of the FBI with other federal and state and local law enforcement agencies. International investigations are coordinated through the FBI's Legal Attache program as well as with the Internet Crimes Against Children (ICAC) task forces (discussed next).

FBI agents and task force officers go online undercover into predicated locations using fictitious screen names and engage in real-time chat or e-mail conversations to obtain evidence of criminal activity. Investigating specific online locations is initiated through a citizen complaint, a complaint by an ISP, or a referral from a law enforcement agency.

Another approach to combating online sex crimes against children is to establish an ICAC task force.

Internet Crimes against Children Task Forces In September 1998 the Office of Juvenile Justice and Delinquency Prevention (OJJDP) of the U.S. Department of Justice began a national program to counter the growing threat of offenders using the Internet to sexually exploit children by making 10 awards to state and local law enforcement agencies across the country. Miller (pp.64–65) reports that currently 45 regional ICAC task forces exist in the United States, half of which are run by state agencies, the other half being situated in city or county agencies. According to Miller (p.68), weekly ICAC meetings occur between agents from the FBI, Immigration and Customs Enforcement (ICE), the U.S. Postal Service (USPS), the U.S. Army's Criminal Investigative Division (CID), and the U.S. Attorney General's office. Getting federal agents involved allows an ICAC to bring both state and federal charges if warranted. Miller (p.62) notes that 95 percent of state and 93 percent of federal investigations of Internet-based sex offenses against children resulted in convictions, owed in large part to electronic evidence.

CyberTipline The National Center for Missing and Exploited Children's (NCMEC) CyberTipline (www .cybertipline.com) maintains a 24-hour-a-day number (1-800-843-5678) that receives leads in five basic areas: (1) possession, manufacture, and distribution of child pornography, (2) online enticement of children for sexual acts, (3) child prostitution, (4) child sex tourism, and (5) child sexual molestation outside the family.

Yet another challenge for investigators involved in crimes against children is that of prostitution.

Prostitution of Juveniles

Finkelhor and Ormrod (*Prostitution*) report that the prostitution of juveniles occurs in a variety of contexts. Both international rings and interstate crime operations traffic young girls to far-away places, promising them employment and money. Runaway and homeless youths are recruited by pimps or engage in "survival sex." Drug dealers get youths addicted and then force them to prostitute themselves to receive drugs or have a place to stay. Some parents have advertised and prostituted their children over the Internet. The big question becomes, are these young prostitutes offenders or victims?

Finkelhor and Ormrod (p.1) note that the NIBRS provides a better way to analyze the problem of prostitution of juveniles, treating juvenile prostitutes as both offenders and victims. They (pp.1–2) provide the following highlights of the NIBRS analysis of juvenile prostitution:

- Juvenile prostitution as encountered by police is more likely than adult prostitution to involve multiple offenders and more likely to occur indoors and in large urban areas.
- Police report more contacts with male juvenile prostitutes than with female juvenile prostitutes.
- Male juvenile prostitutes tend to be older than female juvenile prostitutes and more likely to operate outdoors.
- Police are less likely to arrest juvenile prostitutes than adult prostitutes, more likely to arrest male juveniles than female juveniles, and more likely to refer female juveniles to other authorities, such as social services agencies.
- Police are more likely to categorize juveniles involved in prostitution as offenders than as crime victims, but those categorized as victims are more likely to be female and young.

Finkelhor and Ormrod (p.7) note that male juvenile offenders were arrested more often than females (59 percent versus 82 percent). Law enforcement's differential treatment of male and female prostitutes goes beyond arrest disparities in that most female juveniles (74 percent) arrested for prostitution were referred to other authorities, while a majority (57 percent) of male juveniles arrested for prostitution were handled within the department—released to parents, released with warnings, and the like.

In December 2002, the Office of Justice Programs of the U.S. Department of Justice hosted a national summit to address the problem of prostituted children and youth, called *Protecting Our Children: Working Together to End Child Prostitution.* The goals of the summit were:

- To create a forum for networking and information sharing
- To raise national awareness about prostituted children
- To build a base of knowledge about good practices
- To assess the needs and strengths of the field
- To develop consensus for action (*Protecting Our Children,* p.1)

Among the "critical and central themes" at this summit were two of importance to law enforcement. First (p.3): "Prostituted children should be treated as victims, not offenders, using the same victim-sensitive interview techniques as those used in child abuse cases." Second: "Consistent language needs to be adopted nationwide." The term *sexual exploitation of children* should be used rather than *child prostitution* or *prostituted children.* Against offenders and traffickers, the summit (p.7) recommended specialized training for law enforcement in corroboration of cases, interviewing skills, warrants, cell phone records, date books, surveillance, and the like.

Another major challenge facing law enforcement involves cases of missing children.

Missing Children: Runaway or Abducted?

"**T**he words 'missing child' call to mind tragic and frightening kidnappings reported in the national news. But a child can be missing for many reasons, and the problem of missing children is far more complex than the headlines suggest" (Sedlak et al., p.1).

 A special challenge in cases where a child is reported missing is to determine whether the child has run away or been abducted.

Garrett ("AMBER Bill Just," p.8) reports that in any given year between 1.3 and 1.8 million children are reported missing. Spratley (p.60) points out that law enforcement agencies nationwide receive more than 2,000 missing child calls per day: "Too many of these cases end tragically, with homicides or accidental death." According to Welch (p.50), although parents and their teenage children may have day-to-day arguments, when a disagreement causes a teenager to run away from home, a parent's mood "ricochets from anger to worry to sheer terror."

Steidel (p.134) reports that data from the NCMEC indicate that 68 percent of the total registered missing child cases involved endangered runaways. Twenty-six percent were family abductions; 3 percent were lost/injured/otherwise missing; and 2 percent were nonfamily abductions.

National Estimates of Missing Children: Selected Trends, 1988–1999 describes the findings of the second National Incident Studies of Missing, Abducted, Runaway and Thrownaway Children (NISMART-2) (OJJDP, *National Estimates*). This study considers three categories: runaways; family abductions; and lost, injured, or otherwise missing children. Each of the categories is subdivided into *broad scope*—all cases in the category—and *policy focal*—cases considered to be more serious.

Cases of children running away from home (defined broadly as those who left without permission and were away at least one night) declined, but again, not at a statistically significant level. The policy-focal cases of running away, in which the child was without a familiar and secure place to stay for at least one night, also declined, but not significantly.

Declining significantly were family abductions, defined broadly as any case in which a family member took a child or failed to return a child at the appointed time and the child was kept at least overnight. Policy-focal family abductions—in which the abductor attempted to conceal the child's whereabouts, took the child out of state, or intended to keep the child indefi-

Technology Innovations

Spratley (pp.58–62) describes a new program to help find lost children called A Child Is Missing (ACIM), based in Ft. Lauderdale, Florida. This telephone notification system is simple, taking only an hour or so of training.

Once an officer at the scene verifies that a child is missing, the officer immediately contacts ACIM using the toll-free number on a wallet card supplied by the program. The officer gives basic descriptive information to a technician at ACIM's offices, who enters the information into a database and discusses with the officer the radius surrounding the child's last known location to determine the size of the geographical area to alert. ACIM's unique telephone system can deliver a recorded message to a thousand homes in 60 seconds.

Spratley (p.60) notes that the recorded message begins with something like, "This is an urgent message from the Fulton County Sheriff's Office" to distinguish the call from telemarketers' robotic sales pitches. Most people pay attention when they hear that their law enforcement agency has an important message.

The message not only describes the missing child, but also asks the receiver to look out their windows or step outside and check the area. This 98 percent "listen rate" adds up to a lot of eyes. The message instructs anyone who sees the missing child or has any information about him or her to call the police, and gives the phone number to call. In less than half an hour, ACIM can mobilize an entire community to help search for a missing child. The initial round of phone calls usually develops a lead within 15 minutes.

nitely—increased slightly, but the increase was not statistically significant.

The "lost, injured, or otherwise missing" category was defined by the child's age: children age 11 to 13 had to be missing at least eight hours, but children under age 3 are included if missing for any period of time. This category showed a significant decrease. Policy-focal cases, in which police were contacted to help locate the child, declined at a close to statistically significant level. Figure 11.8 summarizes the findings from the two NISMART studies.

This report (p.6) states: "The most important finding is the absence of increases in any of these problems. This finding is consistent with growing evidence of improvements in child and youths' well-being during the 1990s."

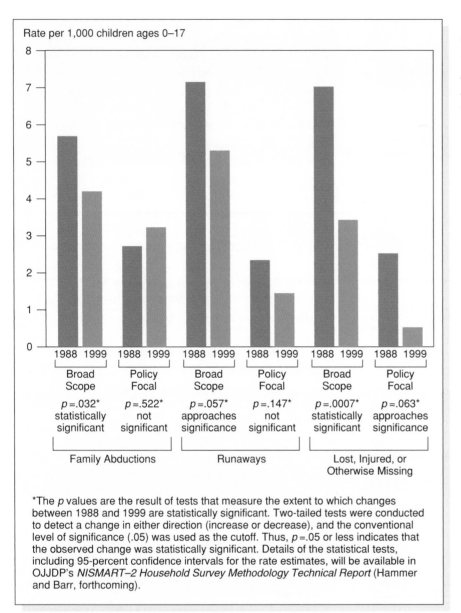

Figure 11.8

Comparison of incidence rates for missing children, 1988 (NISMART-1) and 1999 (NISMART-2)

Source: National Estimates of Missing Children: Selected Trends, 1988–1999, Washington, DC: Office of Juvenile Justice and Delinquency Prevention, December 2004. (NCJ 206179)

Runaway Children

Steidel (p.87) stresses: "Today, we know that when many children run, it is often to escape from a protracted and painful family conflict or from physical, sexual or psychological abuse. We also know what may lie in wait for the long-term runaway [including] homelessness, drugs, crime, sexual exploitation and suicide."

Considerations as to whether youths are missing voluntarily include resources available to them to satisfy basic needs, such as food and shelter, access to money or credit cards, skills to get a job, and access to a vehicle or public transportation. Another indicator that the absence is voluntary is that items such as clothing and treasured personal possessions are missing. Sometimes information can be obtained by examining the teenager's computer e-mails.

Sometimes a note is left confirming that the youth has indeed run away, but often there is no note. In other cases there is evidence that the child has not run away but rather has been abducted.

Abducted Children

The most frequent type of child abduction is parental abduction.

In some cases, parents are simply poorly educated about the law, not knowing it to be a crime to abscond with their children. Other risk factors or warning signs of a possible parental abduction include the following: prior threats of abduction or a history of hiding the child or withholding visitation; a parent's lack of emotional or financial ties to the area where the child is living; signs that a parent has liquidated assets, borrowed money, or made maximum withdrawals of funds against credit cards; and various forms of mental illness in a parent.

Regardless of whether the investigator knows whether the child is a runaway or has been abducted, specific investigative steps should be taken.

Investigating a Missing Child Report

The first responder conducts the preliminary investigation. Interview the parent(s) or person who made the initial report, verify that the child is in fact missing, and verify the child's custody status. Conduct a search to include all surrounding areas, including vehicles and other places of concealment, treating the area as a crime scene. Steidel (p.36) suggests that, based on the circumstances of the child's disappearance, the officer should consider using canine units, using forced entry into abandoned cars, sealing off any apartment complex where the child was last seen, and considering use of search-and-rescue organizations, fire departments, military units, and scout groups and other volunteers for a large-scale search.

Officers should evaluate the contents and appearance of the child's room and determine whether any of the child's personal items are missing. Obtain photographs/videotapes of the missing child. Prepare reports. Enter the missing child into the National Crime Information Center (NCIC) Missing Persons File and report it to NCMEC. Interview other family members and friends/associates of the child and of the family to determine when each last saw the child and what he or she thinks happened to the child. Ensure that everyone at the scene is identified and interviewed separately.

As time permits, prepare and update bulletins for local law enforcement agencies, state missing children's clearinghouses, the FBI, and other appropriate agencies. Also prepare a flyer/bulletin with the child's photograph and descriptive information and distribute it in appropriate geographic regions. Secure the child's latest medical and dental records. Establish a telephone hotline for tips and leads. As Steidel (p.32) notes, although the initial steps in the response are extensive, time-consuming, and labor intensive, the preliminary investigation should be commenced as soon as possible after the original missing child report is received.

If the preliminary investigation does not resolve the situation, a follow-up investigation must be conducted. Responsibilities of the investigative officer are many:

- Obtain a briefing from the first responding officer and other on-scene personnel.
- Verify all information developed during the preliminary investigation.
- Obtain a brief, recent history of family dynamics.
- Correct and investigate the reasons for any conflicting information offered by witnesses and others submitting information.
- Develop an investigation plan for follow up.

Runaways If it is determined—either through a note or other evidence—that the child has run away, investigators (in addition to doing the investigative steps already described) should initially check agency records for recent contact with the child (arrests, other activities)

(Steidel, p.85). Review school records and interview teachers, other school personnel, and classmates and check the contents of the school locker.

Steidel (p.90) recommends that investigators also determine whether the runaway child is endangered, providing the following criteria:

- Is the missing child younger than 13 years of age?
- Is the missing child believed to be out of the physical or geographic zone of safety for his or her age and developmental stage?
- Is the missing child mentally incapacitated?
- Is the missing child drug dependent—on a prescribed medication and/or an illegal substance— and is the dependency life-threatening?
- Was the missing child absent from home for more than 24 hours before being reported to police?
- Is the missing child believed to be in a life-threatening situation?
- Is the missing child believed to be in the company of adults who could endanger his or her welfare?
- Is the child's absence inconsistent with his or her established patterns of behavior and the deviation not readily explained?
- Are there other circumstances involved in the disappearance that would cause a reasonable person to conclude that the child should be considered at risk?

If the child fits any of these criteria, he or she should be categorized as an endangered runaway, and "strenuous efforts" to locate the child should be immediately put into effect.

Abductions Steidel (p.76) suggests that for officers considering criminal charges against a parent who has abducted his or her child, the following questions are pertinent:

- Is there sufficient documentation to demonstrate parentage and the individual's right to physical custody or access?
- Can the suspect-parent actually be identified as the abductor?
- A vacation or change of address is not necessarily illegal. Can it be clearly established that the intent of the move was to unlawfully deny access to the complainant?
- If removal from the state is an element of the offense, can it be proven that the child has been physically taken across the state line?
- Can it be demonstrated that the suspect-parent is responsible for the removal?
- Have mitigating factors (such as domestic violence and abuse) been evaluated that, by statute, could undermine the filing of a charge?
- If an accomplice was involved, can it be proven that he or she had sufficient personal knowledge of the legal custody issues to form criminal intent?

- If the accomplice was the abductor, can the suspect-parent's complicity be demonstrated? How can he or she be directly implicated?

Steidel (p.75) recommends that, if the situation warrants, officers use the federal Unlawful Flight to Avoid Prosecution (UFAP) statute. Although UFAP warrants are not required for out-of-state arrests, they can be very helpful.

The investigation becomes exponentially more complicated when the suspect-parent leaves the country with the child. Steidel (p.78) stresses: "As soon as it has been determined that a child may have been taken to a foreign country, the left-behind parent should immediately contact the U.S. Department of State to discuss filing an application invoking the Hague Convention." The Hague Convention is an international treaty calling for the prompt return of an abducted child, usually to the country of his or her residence. Rapid action is necessary, because after a child has been in another country for one year, the treaty is no longer binding.

Because of the seriousness of missing child cases and the critical need for a prompt response, investigators are strongly advised to seek the assistance of national resources and specialized services. Steidel (p.33) contends: "Major cases will arise . . . when the investigative resources available from other agencies and organizations will be needed to supplement those of the initial agency."

Additional Resources Available

One valuable resource in missing children cases is the Missing and Exploited Children's Program. This program provides direct services through NCMEC, the Association of Missing and Exploited Children's Organizations (AMECO), and Project HOPE (Health Opportunities for People Everywhere). It also provides training and technical assistance to law enforcement, and it conducts research.

The Team HOPE (Help Offering Parents Empowerment) project, established in 1998, helps families of missing children handle the day-to-day issues of coping. Team HOPE links victim-parents with experienced and trained parent volunteers who have gone through the experience of having a missing child. Because they speak from firsthand experience, these volunteers provide compassion, counsel, and support in ways no other community agency can.

Another resource used in all 50 states is the AMBER Alert plan.

The AMBER Alert Plan AMBER (America's Missing: Broadcast Emergency Response) Alert was created in the Dallas–Fort Worth region after the murder of Amber Hagerman, a 9-year-old girl who was abducted from her home. AMBER Alert is an early-warning network that law enforcement can use to quickly convey key information to the general public via television and radio soon after a child has been abducted.

> The National AMBER Alert Network Act of 2002 encouraged development of a nationwide alert system for abducted children. The PROTECT (Prosecutorial Remedies and Other Tools to end the Exploitation of Children Today) Act of 2003 provided $25 million to support state AMBER Alert plans.

The AMBER Alert is a voluntary partnership between law enforcement and broadcasters to activate an urgent bulletin in the most serious child abduction cases. The president and chief executive officer of NCMEC calls the bill "the most far-reaching legislation to date to protect American children" ("AMBER Becomes Law," p.10). As AMBER Alert (*Bringing Abducted*) describes itself:

> The goal of AMBER Alert is to recover abducted children before they meet physical harm. Statistics show that time itself is the enemy of an abducted child, because most children who are kidnapped and later found murdered die within the first three hours after being taken.
>
> AMBER Alert aims to turn that statistic around. Studies show that when ordinary citizens become the eyes and ears of law enforcement, precious lives can be saved.

A law enforcement agency can activate an AMBER Alert only if the circumstances surrounding a child's disappearance meet local or state criteria. The AMBER Alert criteria recommended by the U.S. Department of Justice are as follows (AMBER Alert, *Bringing Abducted*):

1. Law enforcement officials must have a reasonable belief that an abduction of a child age 17 or younger has occurred.

2. Law enforcement officials must believe that the child is in imminent danger of serious bodily injury or death.

3. Enough descriptive information must exist about the victim and the abductor for law enforcement to issue an AMBER Alert.

4. The child's name and other critical data elements—including the child abduction (CA) and AMBER Alert (AA) flags—must have been entered into the NCIC system.

AMBER Alerts can be posted on electronic road signs and broadcast on radio and television (Figure 11.9). Attorney General Alberto R. Gonzales contends: "A missing child is every parent's worst nightmare. AMBER Alerts have already made a significant difference, and the establishment of AMBER Alert plans in all 50 states marks an important milestone in our efforts to prevent child abductions" ("AMBER Alert Plans," p.17). Johnson (p.3A) reports that from early 2002 through October 1, 2004, 143 children were recovered through

© AP/Wide World Photos

Figure 11.9
An AMBER Alert highway advisory sign over Interstate 80 in Nebraska engages the driving public as vital partners to law enforcement in the search for abducted children. Such advisories have met with considerable success in retrieving children alive.

the AMBER Alert system. He also reports that NCMEC estimates that 90 percent of AMBER Alerts issued across the nation have resulted in authorities finding a child alive.

Beyond AMBER Alerts   Garrett (p.68) suggests that law enforcement agencies look beyond AMBER Alert for technologies to supplement the program, such as e-mails to law enforcement agencies, a call to a cell phone, a fax blast, an Internet pop-up window, or the A Child Is Missing system.

Technology Innovations

Garrett (p.72) notes: "An AMBER Alert is just one part of a series of things that should happen when a child goes missing." She describes one tool to supplement an AMBER Alert, BeyondMissing, a missing person's flyer creation and distribution system. This program sits on a separate platform and does not interfere with other technologies that states are using. BeyondMissing lets an agency distribute English- and Spanish-language flyers over a 200-mile radius from the point of an abduction. Flyers go to every law enforcement agency, media outlet, highway motel, service station, convenience store, and bus station in that area.

The worst possible outcome of a missing child case is that it becomes a child abduction homicide investigation.

Child Abduction Homicides

Geberth (p.32) contends that the abduction and murder of a child under 18 years of age by a stranger is a rare event, occurring in 100 to 200 cases annually: "Although the data indicates that these incidents are statistically rare, they are horrendous crimes." He (p.33) underscores the criticality of reporting missing children: "A little under half of the children are murdered within one hour of being abducted, three quarters are dead within three hours, and nine out of 10 are often killed within 24 hours." Geberth (p.36) advises that a neighborhood canvass is an important step in child abductions. Officers should interview all potential witnesses in the victim's last known location, the victim/killer contact site, the body recovery site, and any other site related to the investigation.

According to Geberth (pp.36–37), the initial contact site is usually within a quarter of a mile, or three city blocks, of the victim's last known location. A third of the time it is within a quarter mile of the suspect's residence. He recommends canvassing and searching a minimum half-mile radius out from the contact site. Geberth (p.38) notes that the majority of abducted child victims are killed within 200 feet of the body recovery site and that over half of the victims' bodies are concealed: "Unfortunately due to their small size [the body] can be placed in small areas."

While there is no question that child abduction homicides are horrendously tragic crimes, the media coverage of such events may make them appear more commonplace than they actually are. This phenomenon is also observed in the instances of school shootings that have occurred over the past several years. However, in these cases the offender is one of the youths themselves.

Mass Murders in Our Schools

According to Alvarez and Bachman (p.123): "April 20, 1999, marks the date of one of the most notorious mass murders in modern American history." That was the date of the Columbine school shootings. As noted by Lawrence and Mueller (p.330): "Extensive media coverage [of school shootings] has given rise to widespread fears that similar acts of violence can erupt anywhere, at anytime" (Figure 11.10). However, just as the murders of abducted children are relatively rare, so are school shootings. Table 8.6 (Chapter 8) provides a summary of the most well-known school shootings.

Wen (2004) reports on a Marshfield (Massachusetts) High School junior, Tobin Kerns, who was accused of plotting a Columbine-style massacre. The interesting aspect of this case is that the youth had contradictory traits exhibited by teenagers accused of planning or actually carrying out violence against their schools. In common with known school shooters, Kerns had exploded a homemade bomb and had had brushes with the law for vandalism and stealing, and his computer had detailed plans of the school. However, he was not a loner, had loyal friends and a girlfriend, and was willing to seek therapy for his emotional swings. Wen notes that U.S. Secret Service researchers looked at cases of 41 children who committed an act of violence within their schools and found only one characteristic in common: They were all adolescent males.

© AP/Wide World Photos

Figure 11.10
In this image made from a video released by the Jefferson County (Colorado) Sheriff's department, Eric Harris, left, and Dylan Klebold, are shown walking the halls of Columbine High School in Littleton, Colorado, the day of their deadly rampage. The two student gunmen killed 13 and wounded 21 before turning their guns on themselves.

Their plans for attacking the school, recovered by investigators after the tragedy had occurred, evolved over one year's time. Klebold and Harris intended to kill as many students and faculty as possible by placing two 20-lb. propane bombs inside the cafeteria, set to detonate during the peak lunch time, and then shoot any survivors trying to run out of the building.

Witnesses to the shooting spree heard one of the gunmen shout, "This is what we always wanted to do. This is awesome!" Another witness hiding in the cafeteria reports hearing one of the shooters say, "Today the world's going to come to an end. Today's the day we die."

O'Toole (p.4) suggests that news coverage "magnifies" many widespread but wrong or unverified impressions of school shooters, including the following:

- School violence is an epidemic.
- All school shooters are alike.
- The school shooter is always a loner.
- School shootings are exclusively revenge motivated.
- Easy access to weapons is *the* most significant risk factor.

O'Toole (pp.5–9) describes the threat assessment model of the FBI's National Center for the Analysis of Violent Crime (NCAVC), outlining a methodical procedure for evaluating a threat and the person making the threat. A *threat* is "an expression of intent to do harm or act out violently against someone or something. A threat can be spoken, written, or symbolic; for example, motioning with one's hand as though shooting at another person (p.6). The threat assessment model rests on two critical principles: (1) All threats are not equal and (2) most threateners are unlikely to carry out their threats, but all threats must be taken seriously and evaluated.

The threat assessment model classifies threats into four categories: direct, indirect, veiled, and conditional (O'Toole, p.7). A *direct threat* identifies a specific act against a specific target and is delivered in a straightforward, clear, explicit manner: "I am going to place a bomb in the school gym." An *indirect threat* is vague, unclear, and ambiguous. The plan, the intended victim, the motivation, and other aspects of the threat are masked or equivocal: "If I wanted to, I could kill everyone at this school!" The threat implies violence, but is tentatively phrased. A *veiled threat* strongly implies but does not explicitly threaten violence: "We would be better off without you around anymore." This hints at possible violence, but leaves interpretation of the message to the potential victim. A *conditional threat* often is used in extortion cases: "If you don't pay me one million dollars, I will bomb the school."

O'Toole (pp.8–9) explains how to assess levels of risk. A *low level of threat* poses a minimal risk to the victim and public safety. The threat is vague and indirect, and information contained in the threat is inconsistent or implausible or lacks detail. The threat lacks realism and suggests that the person is unlikely to carry it out.

A *medium level of threat* is one that could be carried out, although it may not appear to be entirely realistic. It is more direct and concrete and suggests that the threatener has given thought as to how it would be carried out. There may be specific statements to convey that the threat is not empty: "I am serious" or "I really mean this."

A *high level of threat* appears to pose an imminent, serious danger to the safety of others. The threat is direct, specific, and plausible, suggesting concrete steps that have been taken to carry it out. Says O'Toole (p.9):

"NCAVC's experience in analyzing a wide range of threatening communications suggests that in general, the more direct and detailed a threat is, the more serious the risk of its being acted on. A threat that is assessed as high level will almost always require immediate law enforcement intervention."

The NCAVC assessment model consists of four prongs: (1) the student's personality, (2) family dynamics, (3) school dynamics and the student's role in those dynamics, and (4) social dynamics.

O'Toole (p.12) suggests that clues to a student's *personality* can be obtained by observing the student's behavior when:

- Coping with conflicts, disappointments, failures, insults, or other stressors encountered in everyday life.
- Expressing anger or rage, frustration, disappointment, humiliation, sadness, or similar feelings.
- Demonstrating or failing to demonstrate resiliency after a setback, a failure, real or perceived criticism, disappointment, or other negative experience.
- Demonstrating how the student feels about himself, what kind of person the student imagines himself to be, and how the student believes he appears to others.
- Responding to rules, instruction, or authority figures.
- Demonstrating and expressing a desire or need for control, attention, respect, admiration, confrontation, or other needs.
- Demonstrating or failing to demonstrate empathy with the feelings and experiences of others.
- Demonstrating his or her attitude toward others—for example, does the student view others as inferior or with disrespect?

As the name suggests, *family dynamics* refers to patterns of behavior, thinking, beliefs, traditions, roles, customs, and values that exist in a family. Knowing how these dynamics are perceived by both the student and the parents is a key factor in understanding circumstances and stresses in the student's life that could affect a decision to carry out a threat.

Likewise, as the name suggests, *school dynamics* and *social dynamics* are patterns of behavior, thinking, beliefs, customs, traditions, roles, and values existing in a school's or a community's culture. Some of these dynamics are obvious, others very subtle.

O'Toole (p.26) stresses: "It is especially important that a school not deal with threats by simply kicking the problem out the door. Expelling or suspending a student for making a threat must not be a substitute for careful threat assessment and a considered, consistent policy of intervention. Disciplinary action alone, unaccompanied by any effort to evaluate the threat or the student's intent, may actually exacerbate the danger."

After a school shooting, a thorough investigation is required, even though in almost all instances the perpetrators are known. Investigators should learn as much about the incident as possible to prevent future shootings. In addition, if a police officer is assigned to a school as a resource officer, or SRO, that officer should be as proactive as possible, watching for warning signs that a student might go on a shooting rampage. Busse (p.33) recommends that officers and teachers watch for the four primary characteristics identified by the FBI as common among juvenile school shooters: (1) access to a weapon, (2) grievances, (3) pre-incident indicators such as persistent themes of violence in their schoolwork, and (4) an obsession with violent media.

Busse says that if officers believe they have reliable information, they can institute a home search of a potential perpetrator's residence. Dorn (p.16) notes: "Under the right circumstances, SROs can search students based upon reasonable suspicion and, with appropriate signage, they can search student and non-student vehicles with only articulable suspicion. Courts have regularly upheld these and other actions that would not be within an officer's scope of authority on the street."

Having looked at the various incidents involving children as victims of crime, consider next their role in presenting a case in court. This discussion will be expanded on in Chapter 21.

another room during the trial and/or using a videotape of the child's testimony as evidence.

- Some courts remove the accused from the courtroom during the child's testimony.

Many of these changes in rules and procedures are being challenged. Sixth Amendment issues arise concerning the right to confront witnesses. In *Coy v. Iowa* (1988) the Supreme Court ruled that a protective screen violated the Sixth Amendment, but Justice O'Connor opined that the *Coy* decision did not rule out using videotapes or closed-circuit television (CCTV). In *Maryland v. Craig* (1990) the Supreme Court carved out an exception to the Sixth Amendment by stating that alleged child abuse victims could testify by CCTV if the court was satisfied through testimony that face-to-face confrontation would traumatize the victim.

Despite some courts' stance that children should be made to testify in court as any other victim or witness, some studies have provided evidence that courtroom testimony is not always the best way to elicit accurate information from children. If children will be testifying in court, several courtroom preparation techniques might improve their testimony and place them more at ease, such as giving them a tour of the courtroom, making coloring or activity books depicting courtrooms and trials available, or showing them videotapes about the court process.

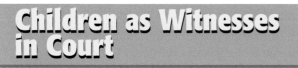

Children as Witnesses in Court

With the increase in criminal cases involving physical and sexual abuse of children, the problems associated with children providing testimony in court have increased proportionately. Court procedures and legal practices that benefit the child witness may not be balanced with the rights of the accused, and vice versa. To resolve some of these problems, the courts have changed a number of rules and procedures, such as the following:

- Some courts give preference to these cases by placing them ahead of other cases on the docket.

- Some courts permit videotaping child interviews and then providing access to the tapes to numerous individuals to spare the child the added trauma of multiple interviews.

- Courts are limiting privileges for repeated medical and psychological examinations of children.

- To reduce the number of times the child must face the accused, the courts are allowing testimony concerning observations of the child by another person who is not a witness, allowing the child to remain in

Preventing Crimes against Children

Child abusers can be of any race, age, or occupation; they can be someone close or a complete stranger. When given adequate information, children can avoid dangerous situations and better protect themselves against such predators.

> Crimes against children may be prevented by educating them about potential danger and by keeping the channels of communication open.

The following specific suggestions should assist in preventing crimes against children. Although the suggestions refer to parents, they apply equally to guardians or other individuals who care for children:

- Parents should teach their children about sexual abuse, what forms it may take, and what to do about it. Children should learn to discuss sex questions with their parents. They should know what sexual abuse is, including anyone touching their anus, penis, vagina, or breasts. They should learn to tell their parents if they encounter any abnormal sexual behavior from adults.

- Parents should listen to their children. Children may drop subtle hints such as "Uncle Charlie was not very nice to me today." An appropriate response may be "Oh? How was he not nice?" Such a response may elicit a statement such as, "He asked me to take down my pants when I was in the car."

- Children should be instructed to tell their parents when someone tells them, "Don't tell anyone." Usually if someone says not to tell, it is about something that is wrong.

- Parents should understand that children do not usually tell tales about sexual abuse. Experience has taught parents and police that the vast majority of sexual abuse incidents that children tell of are true. Therefore, if a child tells a parent about being sexually abused, the parents should report it to the police immediately.

- Older children should be taught to tell their parents where they are going, with whom, and approximately when they expect to return. They should learn to call home if plans change.

- Children should be taught to stay with the group when they are at events away from home and that if they become lost, they are to go to an area where people are present and seek help.

- Children should be taught that when they are home alone they should lock the doors and windows and never let strangers in. Parents should see that doors and windows are locked before they leave the child alone. They should also give proper instructions for leaving the home in case of fire.

- Children should be taught that sometimes it is all right to tell a lie. For example, if a child is home alone and receives a phone call for one of the parents, it is all right to say the parents are home but cannot come to the phone because they are resting or in the shower or some other excuse.

- Parents should help children plan safe routes to and from school and their friends' homes. Children should then travel these routes. "Block parent" programs can provide places where children can stop if

in danger, or the parents should tell their children what houses they can stop at where family friends live. Children should be taught to play in groups; to avoid vacant buildings, alleys, and restrooms; and to walk with friends when possible.

- Babysitters should be selected carefully. Parents should always request and check references.

A guidebook, *Personal Safety for Children: A Guide for Parents,* is designed to help parents take specific steps to improve their children's safety. It is available at http://www.missingkids.com. Collins (p.3) describes one way to protect children from online predators.

Technology Innovations

Mousetrap: Protecting America's Children from Online Predators is an interactive CD-ROM guide for parents, educators, and children about the dangers online. Its three goals are to: (1) educate adults on the basics of online activities, such as chat rooms and instant messaging, (2) raise awareness of adults on the tactics used by Internet predators, and (3) provide adults with tools to prevent and detect possible exploitation. The program was developed by the Virginia Community Policing Institute and Blue Ridge Thunder, a group of cybercops who patrol the Internet for molesters and child pornographers.

Digital technology is allowing police to become more effective in preventing and handling crimes against children. For example, some law enforcement departments are teaming up with schools and the community to create digital files of local children in a step toward discouraging child abduction. Such files contain digitized photographs, fingerprints, and other personal information of area students and, because of their digital nature, can be dispatched within minutes to any law enforcement agency, business, or other organization involved in the search for a missing child.

SUMMARY

Crimes against children include kidnapping, abandonment, neglect, exploitation, physical abuse, emotional abuse, incest, and sexual assault. Such crimes can result in serious and permanent damage physically, mentally, and emotionally, and in future criminality. The Child Protection Act prohibits child pornography and greatly increases the penalties for adults who engage in it.

Challenges in investigating crimes against children include the need to protect children from further harm, the possibility of parental involvement, the difficulty in interviewing children, credibility concerns, and the need to collaborate with other agencies.

The primary responsibility of the responding officer is the child's safety; and if the possibility of present or continued danger to the child exists, the child must be placed in protective custody. When interviewing children, officers should consider the child's age, ability to describe what happened, and the potential for retaliation by the suspect against a child who "tells." In the vast majority of child abuse cases, children tell the truth to the best of their ability.

Most reports of child neglect or abuse are made by third parties such as teachers, physicians, neighbors, siblings, and parents. Seldom does the victim report the offense. When such reports are received, investigators must look for evidence of the crime, including the surroundings, the home conditions, clothing, bruises or other body injuries, the medical examination report, and other observations.

Investigators should also listen carefully to children and should look for indicators of neglect or abuse. These indicators may be physical or behavioral or both.

Investigators should also be aware of pedophiles—adults who have either heterosexual or homosexual preferences for young boys or girls of a specific, limited age range. Many pedophiles are members of sex rings, three types of which have been identified: solo, transition, and syndicated. Certain cults also practice sexual abuse of children. Pedophiles' reactions to being discovered usually begin with complete denial and progress through minimizing the acts, justifying the acts, and blaming the victims. If all else fails, they may claim to be sick.

A special challenge when a child is reported missing is to determine whether the child ran away or was abducted. The most frequent type of abduction is parental abduction. The National AMBER Alert Network Act of 2002 encouraged development of a nationwide alert system for abducted children. The PROTECT Act of 2003 provided $25 million to support state AMBER Alert plans. Crimes against children can be prevented by educating them about potential dangers and by keeping the channels of communication with them open.

CHECKLIST

Crimes against Children

- What statute has been violated, if any?
- What are the elements of the offense charged?
- Who initiated the crime?
- Are there witnesses to the offense?
- What evidence is needed to prove the elements of the offense charged?
- Is there physical evidence?
- Has physical evidence been submitted for laboratory examination?
- Who has been interviewed?
- Are written statements available?
- Would a polygraph be of any assistance in examining the victim? the suspect?
- Is there probable cause to obtain a search warrant?
- What items should you include in the search?
- Is the victim able to provide specific dates and times?
- Is the victim able to provide details of what happened?
- What physical and behavioral indicators are present in this case?
- Were photographs taken of the victim's injuries?
- Is the victim in danger of continued abuse?
- Is it necessary to remove the victim into protective custody?
- Has the local welfare agency been notified? Was there a joint investigation to avoid duplication of effort?
- Is there a file on known sexual offenders in the community?
- Is a child sexual abuse ring involved in the offense?
- Could the offense have been prevented? How?

APPLICATION

A. A police officer receives an anonymous call reporting sexual abuse of a 10-year-old white female. The caller states that the abusers are the father and brother of the girl and provides all three names and their address. When the officer requests more details, the caller hangs up. You are assigned the case and initiate the investigation by contacting the alleged victim at school. She is reluctant to talk to you at first but eventually admits that both her father and brother have been having sex with her for almost a year. You then question the suspects and obtain written statements in which they admit the sexual abuse.

Questions

1. Should the investigation have been initiated on the basis of the anonymous caller?
2. What type of crime has been committed?
3. Was it appropriate to make the initial contact with the victim at her school?
4. Who should be present at the victim's initial interview?
5. What should be done with the victim after obtaining the facts?
6. What would be the basis for an affidavit for an arrest warrant?

B. A police officer receives an anonymous phone call stating that a child is being sexually assaulted at a specific address. The officer goes to the address—an apartment—and through an open door sees a child lying on the floor, apparently unconscious. The officer enters the apartment and, while checking the child for injuries, notices blood on the child's face and clothing. The child regains consciousness, and the officer asks, "Did your dad do this?" The child answers, "Yes." The officer then goes into another room and finds the father in bed, intoxicated. He rouses him and places him under arrest.

Questions

1. Was the officer authorized to enter the apartment on the basis of the initial information?
2. Was the officer authorized to enter without a warrant?
3. Should the officer have asked whether the father had injured the child? If not, how should the question have been phrased?
4. Was an arrest of the father justified without a warrant?
5. What should be done with the victim?

C. A woman living in another state telephones the police department and identifies herself as the ex-wife of a man she believes is performing illegal sexual acts with the daughter of his present lover. The man resides in the police department's jurisdiction. The woman says the acts have been witnessed by her sons, who have been in the area visiting their father. The sons told her that the father goes into the bathroom and bedroom with his lover's 8-year-old daughter and closes the door. They also have seen the father making suggestive advances to the girl and taking her into the shower with him. The girl has told the woman's sons that the father does "naughty" things to her. The woman's sons are currently at home with her, but she is worried about the little girl.

Questions

1. Should an investigation be initiated based on this thirdhand information?
2. If the report is founded, what type of crime is being committed?
3. Who has jurisdiction to investigate?
4. What actions would be necessary in the noninitiating state?
5. Where should the initial contact with the alleged victim be made?

D. A reliable informant has told police that a man has been molesting children in his garage. Police establish a surveillance of the suspect and see him invite a juvenile into his car. They follow the car and see it pull into the driveway of the man's residence. The man and the boy then go into the house. The officers follow and knock on the front door but receive no answer. They knock again and loudly state their purpose. Continuing to receive no answer, they enter the house through the unlocked front door, talk to the boy, and based on what he says, arrest the suspect.

Questions

1. Did the officers violate the suspect's right to privacy and domestic security?
2. Does the emergency doctrine apply?
3. What should be done with the victim?
4. Was the arrest legal?

Note: In each of the preceding cases, the information is initially received not from the victim but from third parties. This is usually the case in child abuse offenses.

DISCUSSION QUESTIONS

1. At what age does a child cease to be a minor in your state?
2. What is the child sexual abuse problem in your community? How many offenses were charged during the past year? Is there any method of estimating how many unreported offenses occurred?
3. What are some common physical and behavioral abuse indicators?
4. What evidence is commonly found in child sexual abuse cases?
5. What types of evidence are needed for establishing probable cause for a search warrant?

6. Who are suspects in child sexual abuse cases?

7. What statutes in your state or community are applicable to prosecuting child sexual abuse cases?

8. What are some special difficulties in interviewing children? In having children testify in court?

9. What is being done in your community to prevent crimes against children?

10. Have any sex rings been exposed in your community? your state?

MEDIA EXPLORATIONS

 ## Internet

Select one of the following assignments to complete.

- Search for the key phrase *National Institute of Justice*. Click on "NCJRS" (National Criminal Justice Research Service). Click on "law enforcement." Click on "sort by Doc#." Search for one of the NCJ reference numbers from the reference pages. Outline the selection to share with the class.

- Search for the acronym *OJJDP*. Select Office of Juvenile Justice Delinquency Prevention. Then click on "publications." Explore the publications available related to child abuse and neglect. Find one article to outline and share with the class.

- Select one of the following keywords: *child abuse, child sexual abuse, hebephile, misoped, missing children, Munchausen Syndrome by Proxy, pedophile, sexual exploitation of children, sudden infant death syndrome*. Find one article relevant to crimes-against-children investigations to outline and share with the class.

Crime and Evidence in Action

Go to the CD and choose the **domestic violence case.** During the course of the case you'll become a patrol officer, detective, prosecutor, corrections officer, and probation officer to conduct interactive investigative research. Each case unfolds as you respond to key decision points. Feedback for each possible answer choice is packed full of information, including term definitions, web links, and important documentation. The sergeant is available at certain times to help mentor you, the Online Resources website offers a variety of information, and be sure to take notes in your e-notebook during the suspect video statements and at key points throughout (these notes can be saved, printed, or e-mailed). The Forensics Exercise will test your ability to collect, transport, and analyze evidence

from the crime scene. You'll even have the opportunity to consider a plea bargain offered by the defense. At the end of the case you can track how well you responded to each decision point and join the Discussion Forum for a postmortem. **Go to the CD and use the skills you've learned in this chapter to solve a case.**

REFERENCES

Alvarez, Alex, and Bachman, Ronet. *Murder American Style*. Belmont, CA: Wadsworth Publishing, 2003.

AMBER Alert. *Bringing Abducted Children Home*. April 2005. http://www.ncjrs.gov/html/ojjdp/amberalert/000712. Retrieved September 21, 2005.

"AMBER Alert Plans in Place in All 50 States." *NCJA Justice Bulletin*, March 2005, p. 17.

"AMBER Becomes Law." *Law Enforcement Technology*, June 2003, p. 10.

Bowker, Arthur, and Gray, Michael. "The Cybersex Offender and Children." *FBI Law Enforcement Bulletin*, March 2005, pp. 12–17.

Bowling, Randy, and Resch, Dave. "Child Pornography Cases: Obtaining a Confession with an Effective Interview Strategy." *FBI Law Enforcement Bulletin*, March 2005, pp. 1–7.

Busse, Nick. "Speaker Coaches Officers, Educators on Preventing School Violence." *Minnesota Police Chief*, Spring 2005, pp. 31–33.

Chiczewski, Deborah, and Kelly, Michael. "Munchausen Syndrome by Proxy: The Importance of Behavioral Artifacts." *FBI Law Enforcement Bulletin*, August 2003, pp. 20–24.

Child Abuse and Neglect Fatalities: Statistics and Interventions. Washington, DC: National Clearinghouse on Child Abuse and Neglect Information, 2004.

Child Maltreatment 2003: Summary of Key Findings. Washington, DC: National Clearinghouse on Child Abuse and Neglect Information, 2004.

Cohen, Patricia; Smailes, Elizabeth; and Brown, Jocelyn. *Effects of Childhood Maltreatment on Adult Arrests in a General Population*. Washington, DC: National Institute of Justice, 2004. (NCJ 199707)

Collins, Geneva. "Protecting Children from Online Predators." *Community Links*, August 2004, pp. 3–4.

Dorn, Michael. "How to . . . Start an SRO Program." *Police*, October 2004, pp. 16–24.

English, Diana J.; Spatz, Cathy Widom; and Brandford, Carol. *Childhood Victimization and Delinquency, Adult Criminality, and Violent Criminal Behavior: A Replication and Extension, Final Report*. Washington, DC: U.S. Department of Justice, February 1, 2002.

Federal Bureau of Investigation. *Innocent Images National Initiative: Online Child Pornography/Child Sexual Exploitation Investigations*. Washington, DC: Author, September 24, 2003.

Finkelhor, David, and Jones, Lisa M. *Explanations for the Decline in Child Sexual Abuse Cases.* Washington, DC: Juvenile Justice Bulletin, January 2004. (NCJ 199298)

Finkelhor, David, and Ormrod, Richard. *Child Pornography: Patterns from NIBRS.* Washington, DC: Juvenile Justice Bulletin, December 2004a. (NCJ 204911)

Finkelhor, David, and Ormrod, Richard. *Prostitution of Juveniles: Patterns from NIBRS.* Washington, DC: Juvenile Justice Bulletin, June 2004b. (NCJ 203946)

Garrett, Ronnie. "AMBER Bill Just the First Step." *Law Enforcement Technology*, June 2003, p. 8.

Garrett, Ronnie. "Looking Beyond AMBER Alerts." *Law Enforcement Technology*, February 2004, pp. 68–74.

Geberth, Vernon. "Child Abduction Homicides." *Law and Order*, March 2004, pp. 32–38.

Harris, Jerry. "Drug-Endangered Children." *FBI Law Enforcement Bulletin*, February 2004, pp. 8–11.

Hess, Kären M., and Drowns, Robert W. *Juvenile Justice*, 4th ed. Belmont, CA: Wadsworth Publishing, 2004.

Hotakainen, Rob; Johns, Emily; and Allen, Martha Sawyer. "Bishops Failed to Protect Children, Report Says." Minneapolis/St. Paul *Star Tribune*, February 28, 2004, pp. A1, A15.

Johnson, Kevin. "AMBER Alert Successes Jump Sharply." *USA Today*, December 16, 2004, p. 3A.

Kilpatrick, Dean G.; Saunders, Benjamin E.; and Smith, Daniel W. *Youth Victimization: Prevalence and Implications.* Washington, DC: National Institute of Justice, April 2003. (NCJ 194972)

Klain, Eva J.; Davies, Heather J.; and Hicks, Molly A. *Child Pornography: The Criminal Justice System Response.* Washington, DC: The American Bar Association Center on Children and the Law for the National Center for Missing and Exploited Children, March 2001.

Lawrence, Richard, and Mueller, David. "School Shootings and the Man-Bites-Dog Criterion of Newsworthiness." *Youth Violence and Juvenile Justice*, January 2003, p. 330.

Marshall, Carolyn. "Child Molesting Case Leads to a National Investigation." *The New York Times*, June 25, 2005.

McGee, Zina T., and Baker, Spencer R. "Impact of Violence on Problem Behavior among Adolescents." *Journal of Contemporary Criminal Justice*, February 2002, pp. 74–93.

Miller, Christa. "Does Your Agency Need an ICAC Unit?" *Law Enforcement Technology*, March 2005, pp. 62–70.

OJJDP [Office of Juvenile Justice and Delinquency Prevention]. *National Estimates of Missing Children: Selected Trends, 1988-1999.* Washington, DC: Author, December 2004.

O'Toole, Mary Ellen. *The School Shooter: A Threat Assessment Perspective.* Quantico, VA: Federal Bureau of Investigation, no date.

Protecting Our Children: Working Together to End Child Prostitution. Washington, DC: Office of Juvenile Justice and Delinquency Prevention, December 13–14, 2002.

Sedlak, Andrea J.; Finkelhor, David; and Hammer, Heather. *National Estimates of Children Missing Involuntarily or for Benign Reasons.* Washington, DC: Office of Juvenile Justice and Delinquency Prevention, July 2005.

Siegel, Jane, and Williams, Linda M. "The Relationship between Child Sexual Abuse and Female Delinquency and Crime: A Prospective Study." *Journal of Research in Crime and Delinquency*, February 2003, pp. 71–94.

Spratley, Lynnette. "Telephone Notification Finds Missing Children." *Law and Order*, August 2004, pp. 58–62.

Steidel, Stephen E., editor. *Missing and Abducted Children: A Law Enforcement Guide to Case Investigation and Program Management*, 2nd edition. Alexandria, VA: National Center for Missing and Exploited Children, May 2000.

Summary of Juvenile Justice Provisions in 21st Century Department of Justice Appropriations Act. Washington, DC: Child Welfare League of America, 2003.

Walsh, Bill. *Investigating Child Fatalities.* Washington, DC: Office of Juvenile Justice and Delinquency Prevention, August 2005.

Welch, George. "E-Mail Tracing Tools." *Law and Order*, May 2004, pp. 50–51.

Wen, Patricia. "Accused Teen Fits No Single Profile: School Violence Defies Stereotype." *Boston Globe*, October 10, 2004.

Weyland, Ernst H. "Sudden, Unexplained Infant Death Investigations." *FBI Law Enforcement Bulletin*, March 2004, pp. 10–16.

Widom, Cathy S., and Maxfield, Michael G. *An Update on the "Cycle of Violence."* Washington, DC: National Institute of Justice, Research in Brief, February 2001. (NCJ 184894)

Wolak, Janis; Mitchell, Kimberly; and Finkelhor, David. *Internet Sex Crimes against Minors: The Response of Law Enforcement.* Washington, DC: National Center for Missing and Exploited Children, November 2003.

Wrobleski, Henry M., and Hess, Kären M. *Introduction to Law Enforcement and Criminal Justice*, 8th ed. Belmont, CA: Wadsworth Publishing, 2006.

CASES CITED

Coy v. Iowa, 487 U.S. 1012 (1988)
Maryland v. Craig, 497 U.S. 836 (1990)

Robbery

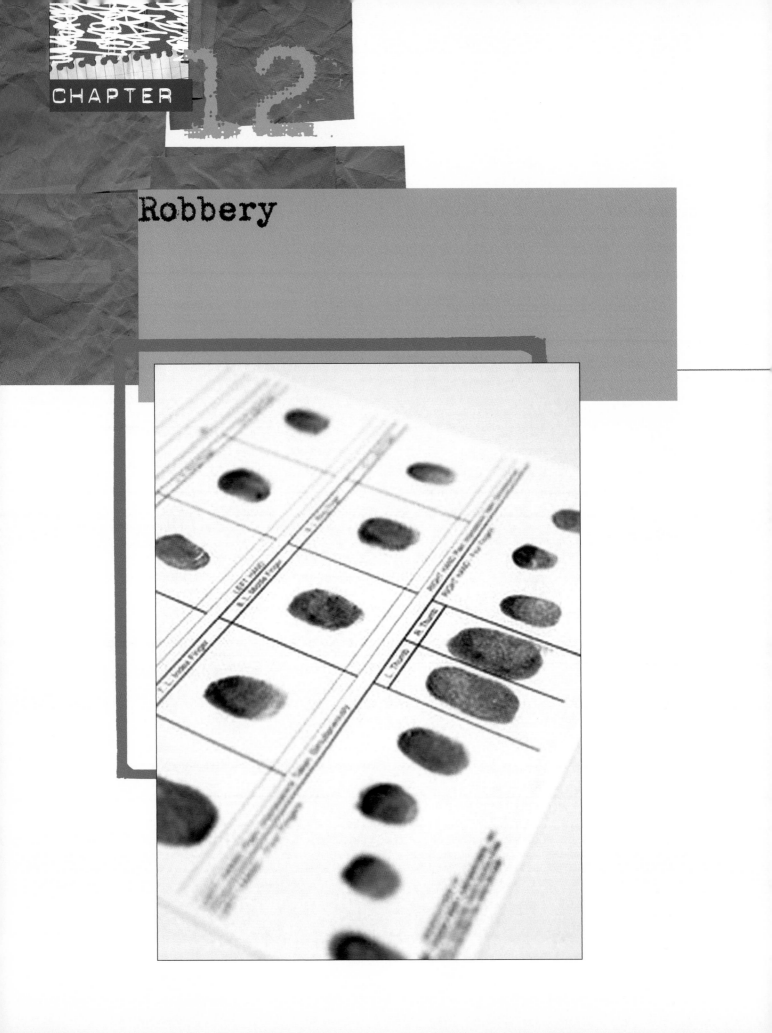

Can You Define?

Do You Know?

- How robbery is defined?
- How robberies are classified?
- What home invaders are?
- In what types of robbery the FBI and state officials become involved?
- What relatively new category of robbery has become a national concern?
- What the elements of the crime of robbery are?
- What special challenges are posed by a robbery investigation?
- What factors to consider in responding to a robbery-in-progress call?
- How to prove each element of robbery?
- What descriptive information is needed to identify suspects and vehicles?
- What modus operandi information to obtain in a robbery case?
- What physical evidence can link a suspect with a robbery?

Outline

Robbery has plagued the human race throughout history. During the 1930s John Dillinger, America's number-one desperado, captured the attention of citizens and law enforcement officers alike. This notorious bank robber's tools of the trade were a Thompson submachine gun and a revolver. Although admired by many for his daring and cast as a folk hero, Dillinger gunned down 10 men. "Pretty Boy" Floyd began his criminal career by robbing a local post office of $350 in pennies.

Like Dillinger, he also killed 10 people. Who has never heard of Bonnie Parker and Clyde Barrow's murder and robbery spree through Missouri, Texas, and Oklahoma?

More recently, two Los Angeles police officers on patrol drove by the Bank of America and saw what turned out to be two armed robbers dressed like Ninja Turtles enter the bank. The officers called for backup and within five minutes the bank was surrounded. The bank robbers emerged with five fully automatic reflex rifles, a semiautomatic pistol, and a Molotov cocktail. The ensuing gun battle ended in injuries to 11 officers and 7 civilians and the deaths of both suspects.

The preceding are vivid examples of the violent nature of many robberies. Robbery is one of the three most violent crimes against the person. Only homicide and rape are considered more traumatic to a victim. According to the FBI Uniform Crime Reports, there were an estimated 413,402 robberies in the nation in 2003, a 1.8 percent decrease from the 2002 estimate. Robbery accounted for 29.9 percent of all violent crimes. In 2003 robbery offenses occurred at a rate of 142.2 offenses per 100,000 population, a 5.3 percent decline from 1999 and a 40.2 percent decline from 1994. The clearance rate for robbery was 26.3 percent in 2003 (*Crime in the United States 2003*, p.31).

This chapter begins with an overview of robbery and a description of how robberies might be classified. This is followed by an explanation of the elements of the crime of robbery. Next is a discussion of special challenges in investigating robberies, the preliminary investigation, proving the elements of the offense, and conducting the complete investigation. The chapter concludes with a look at the problem of false robbery reports as well as ways to prevent robbery.

Robbery: An Overview

Robbery takes many forms, from the daring exploits of criminals such as Dillinger to purse snatching and muggings. Whatever the form, the potential for violence exists.

> **Robbery** is the felonious taking of another's property, either directly from the person or in that person's presence, through force or intimidation.

Most robbers carry a weapon or other threatening item or indicate to the victim that they are armed (Figure 12.1). Therefore, little direct personal contact occurs between the robber and the victim, which reduces the probability of physical evidence remaining at the crime scene. Despite the inherent danger to the victim during a robbery, most robberies do not result in personal injury. Sometimes, however, a violent physical act is performed against the victim early in the robbery, either by original intent or because of unexpected circumstances or resistance. Such cases involve additional charges of aggravated assault or, in the case of death, murder.

According to the FBI's Uniform Crime Reports, the use of violence during robberies has increased during the past 10 years, but such violence is not nearly as frequent as the public might expect. One theory about the low rates of injury and death during robberies is that the threat of force, the use of force, or the presence of a weapon reduces the likelihood of the victim resisting.

Confronted with threatening statements, a threatening note, or a visible weapon, most robbery victims obey the robber's demands.

However, the behavior of an armed robber is unpredictable. In some cases when the victim resists, the robber may flee without completing the robbery. In one case, a man armed with a shotgun demanded and obtained $10,000 from a bank teller. Instead of leaving, he talked to the teller for 15 minutes, telling her that he was drunk and considering suicide. Then he handed the money back to the teller and walked out of the bank. In another case, a robber handed a bank teller a note that said, "Please put the money in this bag and no one will get hurt. Thank you very much." The teller called a bank guard and handed him the note. The guard read the note and told the robber, "Get out, you bum, or I'll blow your brains out." The robber quickly left the bank. In other instances, however, resisting victims have been injured or killed.

Violence against the victim also occurs in muggings and purse snatchings in which the victim is struck with a weapon, club, or the fists or is knocked down. Older people are often injured by the fall resulting from such violent acts. Any such violent contact increases the probability of hair, fibers, scratches, or other evidence being found on the victim or the suspect.

Most robbers are visibly armed with a weapon or dangerous device and make an *oral demand* for the desired money or property. For example, a robber uses a gun to obtain money from an attendant inside a service station. Either the gun is visible or the robber's hands are in a coat or jacket pocket in such a way as to indicate possession of a weapon.

Figure 12.1

Sometimes a robber will stage an auto accident or other incident to gain access to a victim. Here, a man rear-ended a car stopped at a red light and used the incident as an excuse to approach the car and engage its occupants. Her guard down, the passenger allows the attacker to get close enough to carry out a brutal assault before taking her purse and other valuables. Occasionally, this tactic is used by carjackers to gain possession of their targeted vehicle.

Some robbers present a *note* rather than speaking. The robber may or may not ask for the note to be returned. It is important evidence if left behind.

Hostages are held in some robberies. In one case a bank's head cashier, his wife, and their child were held captive by a robber for five hours one Saturday. The cashier was ordered to go to the bank and get money. The wife and child were tied up but left unharmed. In another case a woman was taken from her home and forced to drive two men to a bank in her car. They forced her to accompany them into the bank, robbed it, left her there, and used her car for their getaway. Bank robberies and hostage situations are discussed later in this chapter.

Robbers use various ruses to get themselves into position for the crime. They may loiter, pose as salespeople, or feign business, watching for an opportune moment to make their demands. Once the opportunity presents itself, robbers act quickly and decisively. Sometimes, however, their actions before the robbery give them away. One such case involved a robber who was captured by two FBI agents just as the teller was handing over the money. The robber was unaware that the FBI agents had been watching him since he'd entered the bank. His nervous actions had attracted their attention, even though they were in the bank on other business at the time.

Stolen jewelry or cash usually cannot be recovered unless an arrest is made immediately after the crime. Stolen purses and wallets are usually discarded within minutes of the robbery.

The vast majority of robberies are committed by males. Robbers are usually serial criminals and may commit 15 to 25 robberies before being apprehended. People who commit robberies are often egotistical braggarts, prone to boasting of their crimes. Because of this, informants can provide excellent leads in robbery cases.

The most frequent victims of robberies are drug houses, liquor stores, fast-food places, jewelry stores, convenience stores, motels, gambling houses, and private residences. The elderly are frequently robbery victims of purse snatchings and snatches of packages committed by amateurs or juveniles.

Characteristics of robberies typically include the following:

- They are committed by strangers rather than acquaintances.

- They are committed with the use of stolen cars, stolen motor-vehicle license plates, or both.

- They are committed by two or more people working together.

- The offender lives within 100 miles of the robbery.

- Robberies committed by a lone perpetrator tend to involve lone victims and are apt to be crimes of opportunity (spur of the moment).
- Youths committing robberies tend to operate in groups and to use strong-arm tactics more frequently than do adults.
- Less physical evidence is normally found after robberies than in other violent crimes.
- They take much less time than other crimes.
- Middle-aged and older people tend to be the victims.

In confrontational robberies, regardless of the offender's weapon, victims who defend themselves in some way are less likely to lose property than victims who take no actions. However, victims who defend themselves against armed offenders are more likely to be injured than those who take no actions during the crime.

Classification

obberies are classified into four categories, each committed by different types of people using different techniques.

Robberies are classified as residential, commercial, street, and vehicle driver.

Residential Robberies

Residential robberies include those that occur in hotel and motel rooms, garages, elevators, and private homes. These robberies are less frequent than the other types but are dangerous and traumatic because they tend to involve entire families.

Entrance is frequently gained by knocking on the door and then forcing entrance when the occupant appears. Most residential robberies occur in the early evening when people are apt to be home. Victims are frequently bound and gagged or even tortured as the robber attempts to learn the location of valuables. In some cases, people are robbed because they arrive home to discover a burglary in progress. The burglar is thus "forced" to become a robber.

Hotel, motel, garage, or elevator robberies are carried out rapidly and frequently involve injury. Information from employees that a person has a large amount of jewelry or money determines the victim for some robberies.

A relatively new type of residential robber that is challenging police departments across the country has been dubbed the *home invader*. Home invaders usually target a resident, not a residence—often women, senior citizens, or drug dealers.

Home invaders are typically young Asian gang members who travel across the country robbing Asian families, especially Asian business owners.

Home invaders know that many Asian families distrust banks and keep large amounts of cash and jewelry in their homes. Home-invading robberies are increasing in rural areas.

Commercial Robberies

Convenience stores, loan companies, jewelry stores, liquor stores, gasoline or service stations, and bars are especially susceptible to robbery. Drugstores are apt to be targets of robberies to obtain narcotics as well as cash.

Commercial robberies occur most frequently toward the end of the week between 6 P.M. and 4 A.M. Stores with poor visibility from the street and few employees on duty are the most likely targets. Many stores now keep only a limited amount of cash on hand during high-risk times. Stores also attempt to deter robbers by using surveillance cameras, alarm systems, guards, and guard dogs.

Many commercial robberies are committed by individuals with criminal records; therefore, their modus operandis (MOs) should be compared with those of past robberies. Because of the offenders' experience, commercial robberies are usually better planned than street or vehicle-driver robberies.

Many robbers of convenience stores are on drugs or rob to pay for drugs. Convenience stores that are robbed once are likely to be robbed again. In fact, about 8 percent of convenience stores account for more than 50 percent of these robberies. The National Association of Convenience Stores' *Robbery and Violence Deterrence Manual* lists these deterrents:

- Keep the cash-register cash balance low.
- Provide good lighting outside and inside the store.
- Elevate the cash-register area so the clerk has better viewing ability and is in sight of passersby.
- Remove outdoor pay phones from the premises. (NACS, *Robbery and Violence*)

Bank Robbery "Bank robbery!" The call could mean a possible shootout or a hostage situation. Bank robbery is both a federal and a state offense. U.S. Code Title 18, Section 2113, defines the elements of the federal crime of bank robbery. This statute applies to robbery, burglary, or larceny from any member bank of the Federal Reserve system, any bank insured by the Federal Deposit Insurance Corporation (FDIC), any bank organized and operated under the laws of the United States, any federal savings and loan association, or any federal credit union.

 Bank robberies are within the jurisdictions of the FBI, the state, and the community in which the crime occurred and are jointly investigated.

Most banks have surveillance cameras that might catch a robbery on tape. Byers (2004) describes a bank that has installed three cameras inside that are connected to the police department. The cameras allow dispatchers to observe what is going on inside the bank as it happens and give instructions to the officers. The bank is also considering posting signs to say that the bank is connected via secure video link to the police department.

Because of the large sums of money involved, bank robberies are committed by rank amateurs as well as by habitual criminals. Amateurs are usually more dangerous because they are not as familiar with weapons and often are nervous and fearful.

Bank robbers often act alone inside the bank, but most have a getaway car with lookouts posted nearby. These individuals pose additional problems for the approaching police. The robbery car often has stolen plates or is itself stolen. Robbers use this "hot" car to leave the robbery scene and to transport them and their loot to a "cold" car left a distance from the robbery. Even if only one robber has been reported at the scene, an armed accomplice may be nearby.

The number of bank robberies has increased with the number of branch banks, many of which are housed in storefront offices and outlying shopping centers, thus providing quick entrance to and exit from the robbery scene.

Adding clerks is not necessarily a deterrent, because a person with a gun has the advantage regardless of the number of clerks. Adding bulletproof glass around the cashier may increase the incidence of hostage taking. This problem has been reduced in some banks by enclosing and securing the bank's administrative areas.

Other deterrents to bank robberies involve the use of bait money and dye packs, required by federal banking regulations for federally insured financial institutions. **Bait money** is U.S. currency with recorded serial numbers placed at each teller position. A **dye pack** is a bundle of currency containing a colored dye and tear gas. Taken during a robbery, it is activated when the robber crosses an electromagnetic field at the facility's exit, releasing the brightly colored dye that stains the money and emits a cloud of colored smoke.

Bank robberies at automatic teller machines (ATMs) are also of concern. Brazen robbers wait nearby for people either on foot or in their vehicles to approach the ATM for a withdrawal. These types of robberies tend to occur after dark in poorly lit areas but can occur any time of the day. Scott (p.2) reports: "The best one can conclude is that the overall rate of ATM-related crime is somewhere between one per 1 million and one per 2.5 million transactions, suggesting that such crime is relatively rare." Scott (p.4) describes the most common ATM robbery patterns: "Most robberies are committed by a lone offender—using some type of weapon—against a lone victim. Most occur at night, with the highest risk between midnight and 4 A.M. Most involve robbing people of cash after they have made a withdrawal. Robberies are somewhat more likely to occur at walk-up ATMs than at drive-through ATMs. About 15 percent of victims are injured. The average loss is between $100 and $200." Scott (pp.15–19) suggests the following responses to reduce ATM robberies:

- Ensuring adequate lighting at and around ATMs
- Ensuring that the landscaping around ATMs allows for good visibility
- Installing rearview mirrors on ATMs
- Installing ATMs where there is a lot of natural surveillance
- Installing ATMs in police stations
- Relocating, closing, or limiting the hours of operation of ATMs at high-risk sites
- Providing ATM users with safety tips
- Installing and monitoring surveillance cameras at and around ATMs
- Installing devices to allow victims to summon police during a robbery

Street Robberies

Street robberies are most frequently committed on public streets and sidewalks and in alleys and parking lots. Most are committed with a weapon, but some are strong-arm robberies, in which physical force is the weapon. Both the victim and the robber are usually on foot.

Speed and surprise typify street robberies, which are often crimes of opportunity with little or no advance planning. Because such robberies happen so fast, the victim is often unable to identify the robber. Sometimes the victim is approached from behind and never sees the attacker. Because most street robberies yield little money, the robber often commits several robberies in one night.

Alvarez and Bachman (p.89) note that about 55 percent of robberies take place on streets and highways and tend to be fairly violent, with one in every three robberies resulting in injury to the victim.

In areas with large influxes of diverse groups of immigrants, especially undocumented ones, special problems occur. In Yonkers, New York, for example, great numbers of illegal immigrants from Mexico, Central America, and South America are preyed upon by robbers.

Because of their illegal status, few of these immigrants have Social Security numbers. Without these, they are unable to open a bank account or get paid by check. Therefore, they tend to carry large amounts of cash, sometimes their entire savings. Compounding the problem are the language barrier, fear and mistrust of police, fear of deportation, and lack of understanding of the justice system.

Vehicle-Driver Robberies

Drivers of taxis, buses, trucks, delivery and messenger vehicles, armored trucks, and personal cars are frequent targets of robbers. Taxi drivers are vulnerable because they are often alone while cruising for fares or are dispatched to addresses in vulnerable locations. Some taxi companies have taken preventive steps such as placing protective shields between the passenger and driver and reducing the amount of cash that drivers carry. To reduce the amount of cash in the driver's possession, buses in many cities require passengers to have the exact change. Delivery vehicle drivers may be robbed of their merchandise as they arrive for a delivery, or the robbers may wait until after the delivery and take the cash.

Armored-car robberies (Figure 12.2) are of special concern because they are usually well planned by professional, well-armed robbers and involve large amounts of money. One approach to this problem is to develop an intelligence network between the police department and the armored-car industry.

Drivers of personal cars are often approached in parking lots or while stopped at red lights in less-traveled areas. These robberies are generally committed by teenagers. Drivers who pick up hitchhikers leave themselves open not only to robbery but also to assault and auto theft. Some robbers force people off roads or set up fake accidents or injuries to lure motorists into stopping. A combination of street and vehicle-driver robbery that has increased drastically over the past few years is carjacking.

Carjacking

A new category of robbery appeared late in 1990 and has increased substantially. An average of 34,000 carjackings or attempted carjackings were committed annually over a 10-year period, and the rate is headed downward according to a study by the Bureau of Justice Statistics (*Carjacking, 1993–2002*).

> **Carjacking,** a category of robbery, is the taking of a motor vehicle by force or threat of force. It may be investigated by the FBI.

The force may consist of use of a handgun, simulated handgun, club, machete, axe, knife, or fists. A weapon was used in 74 percent of carjacking victimization; firearms were used in 45 percent, knives in 11 percent, and other weapons in 1 percent. About 12 percent of the victims of completed carjackings, and 16 percent of the victims of attempted carjackings, were injured. Almost all the perpetrators (93 percent) were male. Victims identified 56 percent of the offenders as black, 21 percent as white, and 16 percent as members of other

Figure 12.2
Crime scene investigators confer in the Bank of Texas parking lot where two gunmen attempted to rob an armored car in the south Oak Cliff section of Dallas. A gun battle ensued between the guards and the alleged robbers, wounding a guard, a suspect, and a bank customer.

races. Carjacking rates were highest in urban areas, with two-thirds of the incidents occurring at night (6 P.M. to 6 A.M.) (*Carjacking, 1993–2002*).

The federal carjacking statute provides that a person possessing a firearm who takes a motor vehicle from the person or presence of another by force and violence or by intimidation shall (1) be imprisoned not more than 15 years; (2) if serious bodily injury results, be imprisoned not more than 25 years; and (3) if death results, be imprisoned for any number of years up to life.

Nearly every major city has experienced armed carjacking offenses in sufficiently substantial numbers that Uniform Crime Reports may soon be required to use carjacking as a designation rather than report these crimes without uniformity as armed robbery, auto theft, or some other offense.

Carjackings have resulted in car thefts, injuries, and deaths. Initially, the more expensive vehicles were involved, but this trend now covers all types of motor vehicles. The stolen vehicle is then used as in the conventional crime of vehicle theft: for resale, resale of parts, joyriding, or use in committing another crime.

Parking lots are the favorite location for carjacking, followed by city streets, private residence driveways, sporting events, car dealerships, gas stations, and ATMs. Handguns are the most frequently used weapon.

The motivation for carjacking is not clear because the vehicles are taken under so many different circumstances and for so many different reasons. One theory for the sudden increase is that the increased use of alarms and protective devices on vehicles, especially on more expensive ones, makes it more difficult to steal a vehicle by traditional means. Car operators are easy prey compared with convenience stores or other commercial establishments that may have surveillance cameras and other security measures in effect. Another theory suggests that status is involved: A criminal who carjacks a vehicle achieves higher status in the criminal subculture than one who steals it in the conventional manner. And some police officers believe that the crime is becoming a fad among certain groups of young people as a way to enhance their image with their cohorts.

Carjackers employ many ruses to engage a victim. Some stage accidents. Others wait for their victims at workplace parking lots or residential driveways. Other likely locations include commercial parking lots, stoplights, service stations, ATMs, drive-up bank windows, and pay telephones.

Carjackings have become a serious problem for police, who investigate them in the same way as other armed robberies. Publication of prevention techniques has become standard policy for police agencies in an effort to prevent property losses, injuries, and deaths. Some agencies use decoys in an effort to apprehend carjackers.

In October 1992, Congress passed, and President Bush signed, the Anti-Car Theft Act, making armed carjacking a federal offense. Under this law, automakers must engrave a 17-digit vehicle identification number on 24 parts of every new car.

In addition to knowing how robberies are generally classified, investigators must be familiar with the elements of the crime of robbery in their particular jurisdictions.

tate statutes define *robbery* precisely. Although the gen-

Elements of the Crime: Robbery

Seral public tends to use the term *robbery* interchangeably with *burglary, larceny,* and *theft,* the specific elements of robbery clearly distinguish it from these offenses. A businessman might say that his store was robbed when, in fact, it was burglarized. A woman may have money taken from her purse at work while she is busy waiting on customers and say that she was robbed when, legally, the crime was larceny. Such thefts are not robbery because the necessary elements are not present.

Some states have only one degree of robbery. Others have both simple and aggravated robbery. Still others have robbery in the first, second, and third degree. However, in most state statutes common elements exist.

The elements of the crime of robbery are:
- the wrongful taking of personal property,
- from the person or in the person's presence,
- against the person's will by force or threat of force.

Wrongful Taking of Personal Property

Various statutes use phrases such as *unlawful taking, felonious taking,* and *knowing he is not entitled thereto.* Intent is an element of the crime in some, but not all, states. To take "wrongfully," the robber must have no legal right to the property. Moreover, property must be *personal property,* as distinguished from real property.

From the Person or in the Presence of the Person

In most cases, *in the presence of a person* means that the victim sees the robber take the property. This is not always the case, however, because the victim may be locked in a separate room. For example, robbers often take victims to a separate room such as a restroom or a bank vault while they search for the desired items or cash. Such actions do not remove the crime "from the presence of the person" as long as the separation from the property is the direct result of force or threats of force used by the robber.

Against the Person's Will by Use of Force or Threat of Force

This essential element clearly separates robbery from burglary and larceny. As noted, most robberies are committed with a weapon or other dangerous device or by indicating that one is present. The force or threat is generally sufficient to deter resistance. It can be immediate or threatened in the future. It can be directed at the victim, the victim's family, or a person who is with the victim.

Alvarez and Bachman (p.89) point out: "When one considers the characteristics of robberies, it is not surprising they often end in murder." They quote one offender who said: "We try not to kill our victims. If we can avoid killing them, then we try not to. But if they force your hand, then you have to kill them. It's just that simple."

Special Challenges in Investigation

As a violent crime, robbery introduces challenges that require special attention from the dispatcher, patrol officers, investigators, and police administrators. Three major problems occur in dealing with robberies: (1) They are usually not reported until the offenders have left the scene, (2) it is difficult to obtain good descriptions or positive identification from victims, and (3) the items taken, usually currency, are difficult to identify.

> The speed of a robbery, its potential for violence and the taking of hostages, and the usual lack of evidence at the scene pose special challenges for investigators.

Police response time can be reduced if the robbed business or residence has an alarm system connected to the police department or a private alarm agency. Silent alarms can provide an early response, and audible alarms sometimes prevent a robbery. The "late-time"—that is, the elapsed time between the commission of a robbery and the time the police are notified—is usually much longer than the actual police response time.

A robbery-in-progress call involves an all-units response, with units close to the scene going there directly while other units cover the area near the scene, looking for a possible getaway vehicle. Other cars go to checkpoints such as bridges, converging highways, freeway entry and exit ramps, dead-end streets, and alleys.

Roskind (p.144) explains that in most robbery calls, it is advisable to establish a containment circle, an area within which the robbers would logically be found based on information received from dispatch regarding what time the suspects left the scene. He suggests that with a speed limit of 44 mph, a vehicle could travel at about one mile for every minute "time-late" (time passed since suspects departed the crime scene) that police arrive on the scene.

Officers should observe all vehicles as they approach a robbery scene. Whether to use red lights and sirens depends on the information received from the dispatcher. It is often best to arrive quietly to prevent the taking of hostages. If shooting is occurring, using lights and siren may cause the robber to leave before police arrive.

Roskind (p.142) says: "It is scary to think of how many times I must have driven my marked patrol car directly past a violent, armed robber, not realizing it as I ran to a hold-up alarm. The robber could see us a mile away, but we could not see him. As long as the robber was driving calmly in the flow of traffic, he became the 'invisible man.'" Roskind suggests that if police could check every license plate within the containment circle to see whether it was on a stolen car, and then accumulate that information, they might identify serial robbers. He (p.146) contends that license plate records are basic information that should be collected for any violent event and that even capturing large percentages of the plates within the containment circle could eventually identify suspect vehicles. This is now possible.

Technology Innovations

Roskind (p.147) describes HotSheet, a program that uses off-the-shelf voice recognition programs to make such license plate searches possible and inexpensive. The program limits the vocabulary to state names and alphanumeric input, and the system has a directional microphone in the high-noise environment of the patrol car. Officers simply read off the license plate, and HotSheet completes a license plate search in less than one second, returning a simple, audible answer of "wanted" or "clear." Roskind (p.148) suggests: "With HotSheet and a well-designed containment circle, the 'invisible man' won't be invisible much longer."

When responding to a robbery-in-progress call:
- Proceed as rapidly as possible, but use extreme caution.
- Assume that the robber is at the scene, unless otherwise advised.
- Be prepared for gunfire.
- Look for and immobilize any getaway vehicle you discover.
- Avoid a hostage situation if possible.
- Make an immediate arrest if the suspect is at the scene.

Officers should guard against the dangers inherent in stereotyping when responding to robberies in progress. For example, an officer responding to a robbery alarm at a convenience store, expecting to see a young male running from the scene, sees a young female walking calmly from the store; and after she passes the officer (who is ignoring her) she shoots him in the back, because she was the robber. (This scenario could apply to an elderly person, a disabled person, or other assumed nonsuspect.)

Upon arrival at a robbery scene, attempt to locate any vehicle that the suspects might use, even if you have no description of it. It will probably be within a block of the crime scene, and its engine may be running. It generally has a person in it (the "wheelman," or lookout) waiting for the robber to return. If the vehicle is identified through prior information and is empty, immobilize it by removing the distributor cap or letting the air out of a tire. If a cohort is waiting in the car, arrest the person and then immobilize the vehicle.

Decide whether to enter the robbery location immediately or to wait until sufficient personnel are in position. Department policy determines whether it is an immediate or a timed response. Too early an entry increases the chances of a hostage situation or of having to use weapons. The general rule is to avoid a confrontation if it will create a worse situation than the robbery itself.

If you arrive at the robbery scene and find a suspect there with the victim, surround the building and order the suspect to come out. Get other people in the area to leave because of possible gunfire. Know the operational limitations imposed by the number of officers and the amount of equipment available at the scene. Take advantage of vehicles and buildings in the area for cover.

Because the robber is committing a violent crime and is usually armed, expect that the robber may use a weapon against the police and that a hostage may be taken.

Hostage Situations

Regini (p.1) explains: "Hostage incidents involve a subject who has taken hostages and has a substantive demand, something that the individual cannot attain without extorting authorities through the act of hostage-taking."

The priorities in a hostage situation are to (1) preserve life, (2) apprehend the hostage taker, and (3) recover or protect property. Accomplishing these priorities requires specialized training in hostage situations. It also requires that the media be dealt with effectively.

In general, direct assault should be considered only if there has already been a killing or if further negotiations would be useless. Hostage situations may last for less than an hour or for more than 40 hours; the average length is approximately 12 hours.

However, this approach may result in conflict within the department between special weapons and tactics (SWAT) teams and crisis negotiation teams (CNTs). SWAT is action oriented, whereas CNTs are communication-oriented. Both types of team have a common goal but use a different approach. In reality, to successfully resolve a hostage situation, both teams must often work together. A successful hostage-incident outcome is not possible without a well-coordinated strategy.

The Tactical Response Staff (p.55) contends that the success of hostage negotiations in most cases relies on subjects' desire to live. They do not fear jail time as much as the belief that they are going to be killed by the police. Negotiators' biggest task is to convince subjects that no harm will come to them if they cooperate with the negotiation: "Are SWAT guys with big guns out there?" the subject may be very anxious to know. Assure the subject: "Sure, but they do what I tell them."

The need for negotiation is based on the principle that the main priority is to preserve life—that of the hostages or the hostage takers, as well as of police or innocent bystanders. SWAT teams or expert sharpshooters are often at or near the scene but do not participate in negotiations and in some cases are not visible except as a last resort. Figure 12.3 illustrates the typical emotions hostage takers experience during negotiations.

Usually you do not need to rush into the scene immediately and proceed with direct contact. In a few cases it may be better not to do anything, but to let the hostage taker resolve the situation. To its advantage, passage of time can:

- Provide the opportunity for face-to-face contact with the hostage taker.
- Allow the negotiator to attempt to establish a trustful rapport.
- Permit mental, emotional, and physical fatigue to operate against the hostage taker.
- Increase the hostage taker's needs for food, water, sleep, and elimination.
- Increase the possibility of the hostage taker's reducing demands to reasonable compliance levels.
- Allow hostage-escape possibilities to occur.

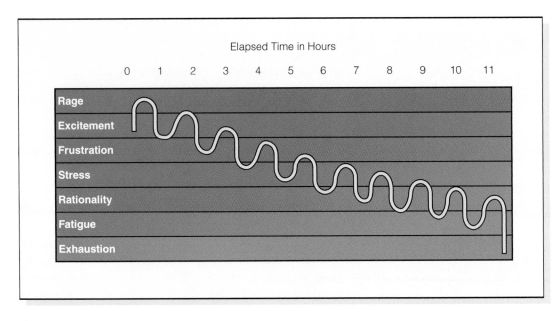

Figure 12.3

Time-line pattern for emotions of hostage takers during negotiations

Source: Thomas Strentz. "The Cyclic Crisis Negotiations Time Line." *Law and Order,* March 1995, p. 73. Reprinted by permission of the publisher.

- Provide for more rational thinking, in contrast to the emotionalism usually present during the initial stage of the crime.

- Lessen the hostage taker's anxiety and reduce his or her adrenalin flow, allowing more rational negotiations.

- Allow for important intelligence gathering concerning the hostage taker, hostages, layout, protection barriers, and needed police reinforcement.

A disadvantage of the passage of time is that it could possibly foster the *Stockholm syndrome,* by which hostages begin to identify with their captors and sympathize with them.

The **Stockholm syndrome** occurs when hostages report that they have no ill feelings toward the hostage takers and, further, that they feared the police more than they feared their captors. However, according to Tactical Response Staff (p.56), police administrators, the public, and the media all have "serious misconceptions" of the Stockholm syndrome. The Staff states that a true Stockholm syndrome almost never occurs. In fact, it suggests that negotiators encourage a *reverse* Stockholm syndrome, with the hostage taker beginning to see the hostages less like pawns and more like people.

The negotiator should have street knowledge and experience with hostage incidents. Sometimes the first officers at the scene have established rapport with the hostage taker, and the negotiator only advises. In some cases a trained clinical psychologist may be called to the scene, not as a negotiator but as a consultant regarding possible behavioral deviations of the hostage taker.

Face-to-face negotiations are ideal because they provide the best opportunity for gathering knowledge about and personally observing the reactions of the hostage taker. Such contact should be undertaken only if circumstances indicate that the negotiator will not be in danger. An alternative is telephone contact, allowing for personal conversation and establishing rapport without the dangers of face-to-face contact. Use of a bullhorn is not the personal type of communication desired—nonetheless, it may be the only available method of communication.

Negotiable items may include food and drink (but not liquor, unless it is known that liquor would lessen the hostage taker's anxieties rather than increase them), money, media access, and reduced penalties. Transportation is generally not negotiable because of the difficulty in monitoring and controlling the situation. Police departments should establish policies regarding hostage negotiations in advance. In general, nothing should be granted to a hostage taker unless something is received in return. Complicating the situation may be that the hostage taker is alcohol or drug impaired.

When criminals caught in the act of robbery take hostages, it is usually a spontaneous reaction to being cornered, and they know what to expect from the police. They generally desire media attention or want to escape safely from the crime scene. They may ask for more money to prove they are serious. Law enforcement response will invariably ensure safe apprehension of the criminal in return for release of the hostages. There are other types of hostage situations—for instance, involving terrorists, mentally disturbed persons, prisoners, and the like—but the motives of the hostage taker and guidelines for action require handling consistent with the characteristics of those situations.

In the several instances in which author Bennett was a negotiator, each incident both lent itself to the general guidelines and also was unique. Decisions had to be made based on the immediate factors involved. In the vast majority of cases, effectively handled negotiations can resolve the situation without injury or death.

If a robber emerges on request or is already outside the building, he or she should be immediately arrested. The victim and any witnesses should make a field identification, and then the suspect should be removed from the scene.

A wounded suspect presents an especially dangerous situation. Officers should be alert to the possibility that a suspect is feigning more serious injury than exists to draw them off guard and get them close enough to be shot. Suspects should be covered at all times and immobilized with handcuffs as soon as possible. If a suspect is seriously injured, an armed escort should accompany the robber in the ambulance and take a dying declaration if necessary. If the suspect is killed, the coroner or medical examiner is notified.

In a successfully resolved hostage situation, the robber is apprehended and the case is closed. In most robberies, however, an investigation is required.

The Preliminary Investigation

 requently, officers arriving at the scene of a robbery find that the robber has just fled. After taking care of emergencies, broadcast initial information about the suspect, the getaway vehicle, and the direction of travel. Follow-up vehicles dispatched to the general area of the robbery can then attempt to apprehend the escaping robbers. Early information helps determine how far the suspect may have traveled and the most likely escape routes.

Robbery usually leaves victims and witnesses feeling vulnerable and fearful, making it difficult for them to give accurate descriptions and details of what occurred. Be patient.

Witnesses to a robbery suffer varying degrees of trauma even though they have not lost any property. They may have had to lie on the floor or been placed in a locked room or a bank vault, possibly fearing that the robber would return and kill them. Their ability to recall precise details is further impaired by the suddenness of the crime. Victims and witnesses may be asked to complete a form such as the one in Figures 12.4A and 12.4B.

Proving the Elements of the Offense

 now the *elements of robbery* in your jurisdiction so you can determine whether a robbery has in fact been committed. Each element must be proven separately. Proving only some of the elements is not sufficient.

The Elements of Robbery

Most state statutes have at least three elements for the crime of robbery.

Was Personal Property Wrongfully Taken? *Taking of property* necessitates proving that it was carried away from the lawful owner or possessor to permanently deprive the owner of the property. Prove that the robber had no legal right to the property taken.

Determine the legal owner of the property taken.
Describe completely the property and its value.

Who is the legal owner? Take statements from the victim to show legal possession and control of the property before and during the robbery.

Was property taken or intended to be taken? Obtain a complete description of the property and its value, including marks, serial numbers, operation identification number (if available), color, size, and any other identifying characteristics.

Obtain proof of what was lost and its value. In a bank robbery, the bank manager or auditor can give an accurate accounting of the money taken. In a store robbery, any responsible employee can help determine the loss. Cash-register receipts, sales receipts, quotations of retail and wholesale prices, reasonable estimates by people in the same business, or the estimate of an independent appraiser can help determine the amount of the loss. In robberies of the person, the victim determines the loss. Some robbery victims claim to have lost more or less than was actually taken, thus complicating the case.

Was Property Taken from the Person or in the Person's Presence? *From the person or in the presence of the person* necessitates proving that the property was under the victim's control before the robbery and was removed from the victim's control by the robber's direct actions.

Record the exact words, gestures, motions, or actions the robber used to gain control of the property.

Figure 12.4A
Robber identification form, front

ROBBER IDENTIFICATION FORM

DO NOT DISCUSS DETAILS OF THE CRIME OR ROBBER DESCRIPTIONS WITH ANYONE EXCEPT OFFICER IN CHARGE OR LAW ENFORCEMENT OFFICIALS.

RECORD YOUR OWN OBSERVATIONS, NOT WHAT SOMEONE TELLS YOU.

Use separate form for each robber.

Time of Robbery _____ A.M. _____ P.M.   No. of robbers involved _____   This form describes Robber No. _____

Race   White ☐   Black ☐   Am. Indian ☐
Mexican Am. ☐   Puerto Rican ☐   Cuban ☐
Asian ☐   Other _____

Sex: Male ☐   Female ☐

Age _____   **Height** _____   **Weight** _____

Build: Small ☐   Medium ☐   Large ☐

Stature: Thin ☐   Medium ☐   Heavy ☐

Complexion: Light ☐   Medium ☐   Dark ☐
Ruddy ☐   Fair ☐   Wrinkled ☐

Hair: Bald ☐   Partially Bald ☐
Color _____ Very Short (close cropped) ☐
Short ☐   Medium ☐
Long ☐   Very Long ☐

Beard: No ☐   Yes ☐   **Mustache:**   No ☐   Yes ☐

Sideburns: No ☐   Yes ☐
If Yes — Short ☐   Medium ☐   Long ☐

Glasses: No ☐   Yes ☐
If Yes — Regular ☐   Sunglasses ☐

Size of Frame: Small ☐   Medium ☐   Large ☐

Type of Frame: Wire ☐   Plastic ☐   Color _____

Shape of Frame: Regular ☐   Round ☐
Square ☐   Rectangular ☐

Hat: No ☐   Yes ☐   If Yes — Color _____

Type _____

Tie: No ☐   Yes ☐   If Yes — Color _____

Shirt or Blouse: Color _____
Type: Work ☐   Sport ☐   Dress ☐   T-Shirt ☐
Sweatshirt ☐   Other Data _____

Sweater: No ☐   Yes ☐   If Yes — Color _____
Type: Button ☐   Pullover ☐
Other Data _____

Pants: Color _____
Type: Work ☐   Jeans ☐   Dress ☐

Shoes: Color _____
Style: Work ☐   Sport ☐   Dress ☐
Type of Heel _____

Coat: No ☐   Yes ☐   If Yes — Color _____
Type: Business Suit ☐   Sport Suit ☐
Jacket ☐   Overcoat ☐   Raincoat ☐
Style: Button ☐   Zipper ☐   Other _____
Length: Hip Level ☐   Knee Level ☐
Thigh Level ☐   Other _____

Gloves: No ☐   Yes ☐   If Yes — Color _____
Type _____

Mask or Disguise: No ☐   Yes ☐
If Yes — Describe _____
_____
_____
_____

Continued other side

Answer such questions as: Where was the property before it was taken? Where was the victim?

Against the Person's Will by Force or the Threat of Force?   *By force or the threat of force* may be the most difficult element to establish. If the victim perceived a threat, it is real.

 Obtain a complete description of the robber's words, actions, and any weapon used or threatened to be used.

If nothing was said, find out what gestures, motions, or other actions compelled the victim to give up the property.

The force need not be directly against the robbery victim. For example, a woman may receive a call at work, telling her that her husband is a hostage and will be killed unless she brings money to a certain location, or the robber may grab a friend of the victim or a customer in a store and direct the victim to hand over money to protect the person being held from harm.

Describe any injuries to the victim or witnesses. Photograph them, if possible, and have them examined by a doctor, emergency room personnel, or ambulance paramedics.

The Complete Investigation

Most robberies are solved through prompt actions by the victim, witnesses, and the police patrolling the immediate area or by police at checkpoints. In many cases, however, a robbery investigation takes weeks or even months. Begin

Figure 12.4B
Robber identification form, back

Weapon: None Seen ☐ Gun ☐ Knife ☐   **Motor Vehicle:**   Colors:

Other (describe)_____   Top _____

If gun, Rifle ☐ Shotgun ☐   Bottom _____

Pistol ☐ Revolver ☐ Automatic ☐   Make: _____

Color of Gun: Black ☐ Chrome ☐ Blue ☐   Model: _____

Speech: Coarse ☐ Refined ☐ High ☐ Low ☐   2 Dr. ☐ 4 Dr. ☐ Sedan ☐ Wagon ☐

Accent ☐ Drawl ☐ Stutter ☐   Van ☐ Other_____

Lisp ☐ Normal ☐   License Plate No.: _____

Manner: Polite ☐ Gruff ☐ Nervous ☐   State_____

Calm ☐ Alcoholic ☐   Color of Plate:_____

Direction of Escape: _____   Color of numbers _____

_____   Number of people in vehicle _____

Scars, marks, or moles _____

Does subject resemble any acquaintance?_____

Subject first observed: Remarks_____

_____

Actions of subject: Remarks _____

_____

Words spoken by subject: _____

_____

Was the money placed in a container?   No ☐   Yes ☐   If Yes — Describe _____

_____

Other remarks; peculiarities; jewelry, etc. _____

_____

Other Details _____

_____

_____

_____

Location of Employee/Customer in relation to subject(s)_____

_____

Name of Witness (Print) _____ Tele. Home _____ Business _____

Address _____ City _____ State_____ Zip_____

Signature_____ Date_____

your investigation with an immediate canvass of the neighborhood because the suspect may be hiding in a parked car, in a gas station restroom, or on the roof of a building. Check motels and hotels in the area. If another city is nearby, check the motels there. Look for discarded property such as the weapon, a wallet, money bag, or other items taken from victims. Check car rental agencies if no vehicle was reported stolen. Check airports, bus and train stations, and taxi companies for possible links.

Recheck all information and physical descriptions. Have a sketch of the suspect prepared and circulate it. Alert your informants to listen for word of the robbery. Check known "fences." Check MO files. Where applicable, check police field-interview/contact forms and communications records relating to recent citizen calls complaining about suspicious people or vehicles in the area of the robbery.

Prepare your report carefully and thoroughly and circulate it to any officers who may assist. Even if you do not apprehend your suspect, the suspect may be apprehended during a future robbery, and his or her MO and other evidence may implicate him or her in the robbery you investigated.

Identifying the Suspect

The various techniques used in suspect identification (discussed in Chapter 7) are relevant at this point.

Obtain information about the suspect's general appearance, clothing, disguises, weapon, and vehicle.

If the suspect is apprehended within a short time (20 minutes or so), he or she may be taken back to the scene for identification by the victim. Alternatively, the victim may be taken to where the suspect is being held.

Technology Innovations

Brooks (pp.8–9) describes MassMostWanted, an online tool developed in Massachusetts by the Bank Robbery Working Group to identify suspects. This group consists of executives of the Massachusetts Bankers Association and bank security officers, as well as representatives from the FBI, Massachusetts State Police, Massachusetts Chiefs of Police Association, and the Boston and Wellesley Police Departments. The centerpiece of the working group is its easy-to-use website, www.MassMostWanted.org, which provides a central source of information about bank robbers. Each page features 15 thumbnail photographs of criminals caught in the act by surveillance cameras. Viewers can click on one of the images and then view the "case page," which has a larger picture, any additional images, a description of the offense (date, time, location), and the name and phone number of the investigator. A toolbox on the screen allows viewers to e-mail a tip to the investigator or send the page to a friend. Viewers can navigate the site according to desired criteria such as gender, complexion, and type of crime, as well as search the site for occurrences in their own cities.

Law enforcement officers investigating bank robberies rely on MassMostWanted as a "standard investigative tool." In addition to using it to help identify subjects, officers can link robberies throughout the region. Because many bank robbers are serial offenders, catching them is a primary goal of law enforcement agencies. Investigators update cases when they obtain a subject's identity. In one case, officers did not have to identify the subject. After the robber saw his picture on MassMostWanted, he became frightened and turned himself and the money in.

Soon after it went online, agencies from bordering states began sending investigations to include on the website. However, the working group soon determined that it would be better for bordering states to develop their own websites. They could simply replicate what they had done in Massachusetts. To date, Maine, New Hampshire, and Rhode Island have developed such sites. They are linked to each other with access provided by a drop-down box. Brooks (p.9) says: "This central, easy-to-use source of information pertaining to these crimes serves investigators and citizens alike and continues to prove its value in the fight against bank robberies."

Several people should be in the area of the suspect to witness that the victim makes any identification without assistance from the police. Photo lineups may be used if no suspect is arrested at or near the scene of the crime. Photo lineups should include five other people in addition to the suspect. A person who has been arrested does not have the right to refuse to have a photo taken.

Eyewitness identification is affected by many factors: the distance between the witness and the suspect at the time of the robbery, the time of day and lighting conditions, the amount of violence involved, whether the witness had ever seen or knew the suspect, and the time it took for the crime to be committed.

Disguises To conceal their identities, many robbers use ski masks, nylon stockings pulled over their heads, or paper sacks with eyeholes. Other disguises include wigs, dyed hair, sideburns, scarves, various types of false noses or ears, and makeup to alter appearance. Gauze is sometimes used to distort the shape of the cheeks or mouth, and tape is used to simulate cuts or to cover scars.

Clothing also can serve as a disguise. Collars can be pulled up and hats pulled down. False heels and soles can increase height. Various types of uniforms that fit in with the area of the robbery scene, such as delivery uniforms or work clothes, have been used.

Clothing and disguises may be discarded by the robber upon leaving the scene and are valuable evidence if discovered because they may provide DNA evidence.

Weapons Pistols, revolvers, and automatic weapons are frequently used in robberies. Sawed-off shotguns, rifles, air guns, various types of imitation guns, knives, razors, and other cutting and stabbing instruments, explosives, tear gas, and various acids have also been used. Such weapons and devices are often found on or near the suspect when arrested, but many are hidden in the vehicle used or are thrown away during the escape. Robbery victims are the most likely of all victims of violent crime to face an armed offender.

Vehicles Most vehicles used in robberies are inconspicuous, popular makes that attract no attention and are stolen just before the robbery. Some robbers leave the scene on foot and then take buses or taxis or commandeer vehicles, sometimes at gunpoint.

Establishing the Modus Operandi

Even if the suspect is apprehended at the scene, the MO can help link the suspect with other robberies.

Important MO information includes:
* Type of robbery
* Time (day and hour)
* Method of attack (real or threatened)
* Weapon

- Number of robbers
- Voice and words
- Vehicle used
- Peculiarities
- Object sought

Finding that an MO matches a previous robbery does not necessarily mean that the same robber committed the crime. For example, in one instance three masked gunmen robbed a Midwestern bank of more than $45,000 and escaped in a stolen car. The MO matched a similar robbery in the same town a few weeks earlier in which $30,000 was obtained. The three gunmen were identified and arrested the next day, and more than $41,000 of the loot was recovered. One gunman told the FBI agent that he planned the robbery after reading about the successful bank robbery that three other masked gunmen had pulled off. The FBI agent smiled and informed the robber that the perpetrators had been arrested shortly after the robbery. Aghast, the copycat robber bemoaned the fact that he had seen no publicity on the arrest.

Physical Evidence

Physical evidence at a robbery scene is usually minimal. Sometimes, however, the robbery occurs where a surveillance camera is operating. The film can be processed immediately and used as evidence.

 Physical evidence that can connect a suspect with a robbery includes fingerprints, shoe prints, tire prints, restraining devices, discarded garments, fibers and hairs, a note, or the stolen property.

Fingerprints may be found at the scene if the suspect handled any objects, on the holdup note if one was left behind, on the getaway car, or on recovered property. They might also be found on pieces of tape used as restraints, which in themselves are valuable as evidence.

In one residential robbery, the criminal forced entrance into a home, bound and gagged the residents, stole several items of value, and then left. As he backed up to turn his car around, he inadvertently left the impression of the vehicle's license plate clearly imprinted on a snow bank. He was apprehended within hours of the robbery.

Mapping Robbery

Because robbery is inherently serial, mapping it has proven successful. The Charlotte-Mecklenburg (North Carolina) Police Department used mapping to address an increase in robbery victimization among Charlotte's growing Hispanic population ("Hispanic Robbery Initiative," pp.27–35).

Officers used the Global Information Software (GIS) mapping capabilities in the department's Crime Analysis Unit to map all robbery incidents with Hispanic victims citywide. Overlaying the maps revealed a close correlation between Hispanic robbery incidents and areas of high concentrations of Hispanic residents. Mapping narrowed the problem to robberies of Hispanic victims in the apartment complexes where they lived. It then identified a particular complex, the Park Apartments, that was a hot spot for the robberies. This complex consisted of 51 buildings with approximately 2,000 residents. Hispanics constituted 49 percent of the complex population but 64 percent of its robbery victims. The analysis then identified a number of factors that increased the risk of robbery, including the fact that victims often carried large sums of money instead of using banks, that poor lighting and poor security made robberies easy to commit, and that partly because of language barriers the police had done little community outreach.

In cooperation with complex managers, police officers addressed the identified physical factors. In addition to improving lighting, they restricted access to the apartment grounds and to the high-risk laundry area. An enforcement component with the department's robbery unit worked to arrest several suspects. Officers also built relationships with the residents to increase their willingness to report crime.

From December 1, 2000, to November 2002, overall robberies in the Park Apartments declined by 72.7 percent, in contrast to a jurisdiction-wide 13.1 percent increase. In that same period, robberies with Hispanic victims at the Park Apartments decreased by 66.7 percent, as opposed to a city-wide increase of 29.7 percent. GIS mapping revealed that the Park Apartments were no longer a chronic robbery hot spot. Based on the project's success, five replication locations were selected throughout the city. Its future replication is anticipated throughout Charlotte-Mecklenburg and, ultimately, across the state.

The maps and predictions were also helpful in supporting the postarrest case.

False Robbery Reports

Investigators need to rule out the probability that a robbery report is false. Among the indicators of a false robbery report are the following:

- Unusual delay in reporting the offense
- Amount of the loss not fitting the victim's apparent financial status
- Lack of correspondence with the physical evidence
- Improbable events
- Exceptionally detailed or exceptionally vague description of offender
- Lack of cooperation

SUMMARY

Robbery is the felonious taking of another's property from his or her person or in his or her presence through force or intimidation. Robberies are classified as either residential, commercial, street, or vehicle driver. One relatively new category is carjacking—the taking of a motor vehicle by force or threat of force. The FBI may investigate carjacking.

A relatively new type of residential robber is the home invader. Home invaders are typically young Asian gang members who travel across the country robbing Asian families, especially Asian business owners. The FBI and state and local law enforcement personnel jointly investigate bank robberies.

The elements of robbery are (1) the wrongful taking of personal property, (2) from the person or in the person's presence, (3) against the person's will by force or threat of force.

The rapidity of a robbery, its potential for violence and the taking of hostages, and the usual lack of evidence at the scene pose special challenges. When responding to a robbery-in-progress call, proceed as rapidly as possible but use extreme caution. Assume that the robber is at the scene unless otherwise advised, and be prepared for gunfire. Look for and immobilize any getaway vehicle you discover. Avoid a hostage situation if possible, and make an immediate arrest if the situation warrants.

Prove each element of robbery separately. To prove that personal property was wrongfully taken, determine the legal owner of the property and describe the property and its value completely. To prove that it was taken from the person or in the person's presence, record the exact words, gestures, motions, or actions the robber used to gain control of the property. To prove that the removal was against the victim's will by force or threat of force, obtain a complete description of the robber's words, actions, and any weapon the robber used or threatened to use.

Obtain information about the suspect's general appearance, clothing, disguises, and vehicle.

Important MO information includes type of robbery, time (day and hour), method of attack (threatened or real), weapon, object sought, number of robbers, voice and words, vehicle, and any peculiarities. Physical evidence that can connect the suspect with the robbery includes fingerprints, shoe prints, tire prints, restraining devices, discarded garments, fibers and hairs, a note, and the stolen property.

CHECKLIST

Robbery

- Are maps and pictures on file of banks and other places that handle large amounts of cash? Are there plans for police response in the event that these facilities are robbed?
- Was the place that was robbed protected by an alarm? Was the alarm working?
- Was the place that was robbed protected by a surveillance camera? Was the camera working? Was the film immediately removed and processed?
- What procedure did police use in responding to the call? Did they enter directly? To avoid a hostage situation, did they wait until the robber had left?
- Did police interview separately everyone in the robbed place? Did they obtain written statements from each?
- Are all elements of the crime of robbery present?
- How was the robber dressed? Was a disguise used?
- What were the robber's exact words and actions?
- What type of weapon or threat did the robber use?
- Was anybody injured or killed?
- Was there a getaway car? Description? Direction of travel? A second person in the car?
- Was a general description of people and vehicles involved quickly broadcast to other police agencies?
- Did police secure and photograph the scene?
- What property was taken in the robbery? What was its value?
- Who is the legal owner?
- If a bank was robbed, were the FBI and state officials notified?
- If the suspect was arrested, how was identification made?
- If money or property was recovered, was it properly processed?

APPLICATION

Read the following account of an actual robbery investigation. As you read, list the steps the investigators took. Review the list and determine whether they took all necessary steps. (Adapted from a report by Captain Raymond J. Eagan, New Haven, Connecticut.)

> On December 16, close to midnight, a woman looked in the window of the grocery store owned by Efimy Romanow at 187 Ashmun Street, New Haven, Connecticut, and saw Romanow lying behind the

counter with the telephone receiver clutched in his right hand. Thinking Romanow was sick, the woman notified a neighbor, Thomas Kelly, who went to the store and then called an ambulance. Romanow was pronounced dead on arrival at the hospital.

Autopsy revealed he had been shot near the heart. The bullet was removed and turned over to detectives, who immediately began an investigation. Officers protected the crime scene and made a thorough search for possible prints and other evidence. They found a small amount of money in the cash register. At the hospital, $15.50 was found in Romanow's pockets, and $313 in bills was found in his right shoe. A thorough check of neighborhood homes was made without result. One report received was that two white men were seen leaving the store before Romanow's body was discovered.

About 7 A.M., December 17, Mrs. Marion Lang, who lived directly opposite the store but was not home when the officers first went there, was contacted. She stated that at about 11:10 p.m. she had heard loud talking in the street, including the remark, "Damn it, he is shot, let's get out of here." She had not looked out the window, so she was unable to describe the people she had heard talking.

The investigation continued without any tangible clues until 9:25 P.M., December 17, when a phone call was received from George M. Proctor, owner of a drugstore on a street parallel to Ashmun Street and one block away. He had just overheard a woman talking in the phone booth in his store say, "I will not stand for her taking my fellow away. I know who shot the storekeeper on Ashmun. It was Scotty and Almeda at 17 Dixwell." Mr. Proctor did not know the woman he had overheard.

Two detectives were assigned to this lead, and they began a search. A few hours later they learned that Scotty and Almeda were in a room at 55 Dixwell Avenue. Arriving with several uniformed officers, they entered and found Francis Scott and Henry Almeda in bed with their clothes on. Both had previous records and were well known to the local police. The detectives took the two men to headquarters for questioning and then returned to the room. Their search revealed five .32 caliber bullets at the top of a window casing where plaster had been broken up.

They also received information that Scott and Almeda had earlier visited Julia Redmond, who had a room in the same house. They asked Ms. Redmond if Scott and Almeda had left anything there. She responded, "They put something under the mattress." Turning over the mattress, the detectives found a .32 caliber Harrington and Richardson revolver, serial number 430-087. Ms. Redmond said, "That belongs to Scott and Almeda."

The detectives returned to headquarters and searched the stolen gun files. They discovered that this gun had been reported stolen in a burglary at the home of Geoffrey Harrell, 46 Webster Street, in November. Both suspects were questioned during the night and denied any part in the shooting.

The questioning resumed on the morning of December 18 at 9:00 A.M. At 3:45 P.M. that day, Almeda broke and made a confession in which he involved Scott. Almeda's statement was read to Scott with Almeda present. When Almeda identified the confession and stated it was true, Scott also admitted his part in the shooting.

When Almeda was shown the .32 caliber H&R revolver, he identified it as the gun used in shooting Romanow. He explained that they had to shoot Romanow because he refused to give up his money and placed himself between them and the door. In order to get out, he shot Romanow. Both stated that they had no car and that no one else was involved.

A preliminary examination of the bullet taken from Romanow's body did not satisfy the detectives that the bullet had been fired from the gun in their possession, even though it had been identified by both Almeda and Scott as the one used.

A detective took the gun and bullet to the FBI Technical Laboratory in Washington, D.C., where a ballistics comparison established that the gun furnished for examination was not the gun that fired the fatal bullet. A search of the Technical Laboratory files revealed that the gun matched a bullet furnished by the same department as evidence in a holdup of Levine's Liquor Store on December 1 of that year. One shot had been fired, striking a chair and deflecting into a pile of rubbish in the rear of the store. The bullet had been recovered by detectives after sifting through the rubbish.

When confronted with this information, Scott and Almeda admitted that they had committed this holdup and shooting while masked. They also admitted that they had stolen an automobile to use that night and that they had burglarized Harrell's home in November, when they took the gun.

The detectives conducted an extensive search for the gun used in killing Romanow. They cut a hole in the bottom of the flue leading from the room occupied by Scott and Almeda and even had the sewer department clean out 15 sewer catch basins in the area of the crime, but no weapon was discovered.

Both Almeda and Scott were indicted by the grand jury for first-degree murder. They were scheduled for trial February 13. The night before the trial was to begin, they told their lawyers that a third man had furnished the gun and driven the getaway car. In a conference with the state attorney and detectives, the lawyers identified the third man as William Sutton. Within half an hour, Sutton was apprehended and brought to the state attorney's office where, in the presence of Scott and Almeda, their statements were read to Sutton. He admitted participating in the crime.

This new turn in the case also revealed that the gun used in the killing was loaned to Sutton by John Foy. The morning after the shooting, Sutton brought the gun back to Foy and left it with him. A short time later Sutton returned and asked for the gun. He had decided he should get rid of it because it was hot. Sutton then took the cylinder from the gun while Foy broke the rest of it into small parts, which he threw in various places. Foy, who admitted he knew the gun was to be used in a holdup, was charged with conspiracy.

Sutton, Almeda, and Scott pled guilty to second-degree murder and received life sentences in the Connecticut State Prison. Foy received a one-year jail sentence.

Questions

1. List the steps the investigators followed.
2. Did they omit any necessary steps?
3. What comparison evidence was helpful in the case?
4. How did law enforcement agencies cooperate?
5. What interrogation techniques did they use?
6. How important was citizen information?

7. What other crimes often occur along with a robbery?
8. What types of establishments are most susceptible to robbery? What types of establishments are most often robbed in your community?
9. What measures can a police department take to prevent robbery? What preventive measures does your department take?
10. What measures can citizens take to help prevent robberies? How can the police assist citizens in these measures?

DISCUSSION QUESTIONS

1. In a robbery of a neighborhood grocery store, how important is citizen information? Should a neighborhood check be made if the incident occurred at 3 A.M.? How would you attempt to locate two witnesses who saw the robber enter the store if the owner does not know their names? How else could you develop information on the robber's description, vehicle, and the like?

2. Imagine that you are a police officer responding to the scene of a bank robbery. Should you enter the bank immediately? Should you close the bank to business during the investigation? Can the drive-up window be used for business if it was not involved in the robbery? What should be done with the bank employees after the robbery? with customers in the bank at the time of the robbery? What agencies should work jointly on this type of crime?

3. How important is an immediate response to a robbery call? What vehicles should respond to the scene? to the area surrounding the scene? What types of locations near the scene are most advantageous to apprehending the suspect?

4. If a robber takes a hostage inside a building, what are immediate considerations? If the hostage situation is not resolved in the first 15 minutes, what must be considered? Should a police officer offer to take the hostage's place? What might you say to the robber to induce him or her to release the hostage? to surrender after releasing the hostage?

5. Why is a robbery in progress dangerous for the police? for the victim? What can the police do to reduce the potential danger while responding? to reduce the danger to the hostage?

6. Which takes priority: taking the robber at all risks (to remove him or her from the street and prevent future robberies) or ensuring the safety of the victim and witnesses?

MEDIA EXPLORATIONS

 ### Internet

Select one of the following assignments to complete.

- Go to the FBI website at www.fbi.gov. Click on "library and reference." Select "Uniform Crime Reports" and outline what the report says about robbery.
- Select one of the following key words: *bait money, dye pack, carjacking, robbery, robbery prevention, Stockholm syndrome.* Find one article relevant to robbery investigations to outline and share with the class.

 ### Crime and Evidence in Action

Go to the CD and choose the **robbery case**. During the course of the case you'll become a patrol officer, detective, prosecutor, corrections officer, and probation officer to conduct interactive investigative research. Each case unfolds as you respond to key decision points. Feedback for each possible answer choice is packed full of information, including term definitions, web links, and important documentation. The sergeant is available at certain times to help mentor you, the Online Resources website offers a variety of information, and be sure to take notes in your e-notebook during the suspect video statements and at key points throughout (these notes can be saved, printed, or e-mailed). The Forensics Exercise will test your ability to collect, transport, and analyze evidence from the crime scene. You'll even have the opportunity to consider a plea bargain offered by the defense. At the end of the case you can track how well you responded to each decision point and join the Discussion Forum for a postmortem. **Go to the CD and use the skills you've learned in this chapter to solve a case.**

REFERENCES

Alvarez, Alex, and Bachman, Ronet. *Murder American Style.* Belmont, CA: Wadsworth Publishing, 2003.

Brooks, William G., III. "MassMostWanted: An Online Tool for Law Enforcement." *FBI Law Enforcement Bulletin,* 2005, pp. 8–9.

Byers, Christine. "Camera System Links Bank with Police." Chicago *Daily Herald,* October 19, 2004.

Carjacking, 1993–2002. Washington, DC: Bureau of Justice Statistics, July 2005. (NCJ 205123)

Crime in the United States 2003. Washington, DC: Federal Bureau of Investigation, 2003.

"Hispanic Robbery Initiative." *Excellence in Problem-Oriented Policing: The 2002 Herman Goldstein Award Winners.* Washington, DC: Police Executive Research Forum, November 2002.

NACS [National Association of Convenience Stores]. *Robbery and Violence Deterrence Manual.* Alexandria, VA: Author, 2000. http://www.nacsonline.com

Regini, Chuck. "Crisis Intervention for Law Enforcement Negotiators." *FBI Law Enforcement Bulletin,* 2004, pp. 1–6.

Roskind, Michael. "Technology Traps for the Invisible Man." *Law Enforcement Technology,* July 2004, pp. 142–148.

Scott, Michael S. *Robbery at Automated Teller Machines* (Problem-Oriented Guides for Police Series No. 8). Washington, DC: Office of Community Oriented Policing Services, 2001.

Tactical Response Staff. "Special Report: NYPD Hostage Negotiation Course." *Tactical Response,* May-June 2005, pp. 54–60.

Section 4

INVESTIGATING CRIMES AGAINST PROPERTY

Most of the crimes discussed in this section do not involve the use of force or violence against people and therefore are often not considered to be as serious as assault, robbery, rape, or murder. However, according to various official reports, crimes against property occur much more frequently than crimes against persons. For example, 77 percent of all crimes reported to the Bureau of Justice Statistics (BJS) National Crime Victimization Survey (NCVS) in 2003 were property crimes (Catalano, p.1), and more than 88 percent of the Part One crimes reported to law enforcement agencies in 2003 were property crimes (*Crime in the United States 2003*). According to Klaus (p.1), 13 percent of households participating in the NCVS experienced one or more property crimes during 2003, with theft the most frequent type. Furthermore, over 5.8 million households were vandalized in 2003 (Klaus, p.1).

In 2003 a crime against property occurred every 3.0 seconds in the United States:

- One larceny/theft every 4.5 seconds
- One burglary every 14.6 seconds
- One motor vehicle theft every 25.0 seconds

As high as these numbers sound, the rate of property crime in 2003 was actually 1.2 percent lower than that in 2002 (*Crime in the United States 2003*, p.41).

Many property crimes are difficult to investigate because there is little evidence and there are usually no eyewitnesses. Physical evidence in property crimes is often similar to that found in violent crimes: fingerprints, footprints, tire impressions, hair, fibers, broken glass, and personal objects left at the crime scene. Other important evidence in crimes against property includes tools, tool fragments, tool marks, safe insulation, disturbance of paint, and evidence of forcible entry.

The modus operandi of a property crime often takes on added importance because there are no other significant leads. In addition, crimes against property tend to occur in series, so solving one crime may lead to solving an entire series of similar crimes.

The chapters in this section discuss specific considerations in investigating burglary (Chapter 13); larceny/theft, fraud, and white-collar crime (Chapter 14); motor vehicle theft (Chapter 15); and arson, bombs, and explosives (Chapter 16).

REFERENCES

Catalano, Shannan M. *Criminal Victimization, 2003.* Washington, DC: Bureau of Justice Statistics, National Crime Victimization Survey, September 2004 (NCJ 205455).

Crime in the United States 2003. Washington, DC: Federal Bureau of Investigation, Uniform Crime Reports, October 27, 2004.

Klaus, Patsy A. *Crime and the Nation's Households, 2003.* Washington, DC: Bureau of Justice Statistics, Bulletin, October 2004 (NCJ 206348).

CHAPTER 13

Burglary

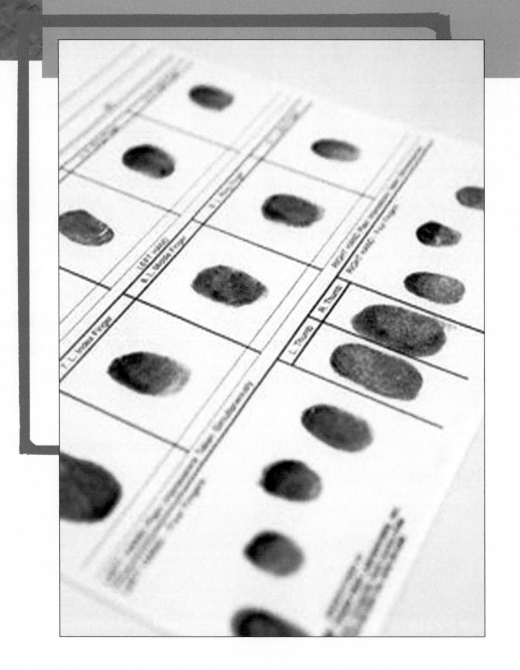

Can You Define?

Do You Know?

- What the basic difference between burglary and robbery is?
- What the two basic classifications of burglary are?
- What three elements are present in laws defining burglary?
- What additional elements can be included in burglary?
- What determines the severity of a burglary?
- What the elements of the crime of possession of burglary tools are?
- How to proceed to a burglary scene and what to do on arrival?
- What the most frequent means of entry to commit burglary is?
- How safes are broken into?
- What physical evidence is often found at a burglary scene?
- What modus operandi factors are important in burglary?
- Where to search for stolen property?
- What the elements of the offense of receiving stolen goods are?
- What measures may be taken to prevent burglary?

Outline

In a western city, police officers noticed what they believed was safe insulation on the steps of a cabin occupied by a known burglar. They obtained a warrant and searched the premises for evidence of a burglary. The substance found on the steps and some burglary tools found inside the home were mailed to a laboratory, where the substance was confirmed as safe insulation. The suspect was arrested and convicted of burglary. On appeal, the courts held that such knowledge on the officers'

375

part was in effect an extension of the laboratory and was therefore probable cause even without the laboratory examination. The verification by the laboratory only strengthened the probable cause, and the charge of burglary was sustained.

The FBI's Uniform Crime Reports (UCR) define **burglary** as "the unlawful entry of a structure to commit a felony or theft, even though no force was used to gain entry." All such attempts also count as burglaries. The common-law definition of *burglary* (originating in sixteenth-century England) required that the breaking and entering be committed during the nighttime or "between sunset and sunrise." Many changes have been made in burglary statutes since that time, including eliminating the requirement that it occur at night.

 Burglary is the unlawful entry of a structure to commit a crime.

The word *burglar* comes from the German words *burg,* meaning "house," and *laron,* meaning "thief"; thus the meaning "house thief."

Burglary is reported by frequency and by the value of the property stolen and recovered. This is because many burglaries yield low losses, although a single burglary can yield a high loss. According to the FBI (*Crime in the United States 2003,* p.45), an estimated 2,153,464 burglary offenses occurred throughout the nation during 2003, virtually the same number as were reported for 2002. Burglary offenses made up 20.6 percent of all property crimes reported, with an estimated burglary rate of 740.5 offenses per 100,000

inhabitants. Fass and Francis (p.173) estimate the net market value of merchandise stolen in the United States at $40 billion to $45 billion annually, based on data from the UCR, the National Crime Victimization Survey (NCVS), and the National Retail Security Survey (NRSS). Of all burglaries reported in 2003, law enforcement cleared 13.1 percent by arrest or exceptional means (*Crime in the United States 2003,* p.47).

The public regards burglary as a major crime problem. Many people fear arriving home or at work and confronting a burglar, a situation that can develop into an assault and robbery. Moreover, it is traumatic for people to realize that they have been doubly victimized when someone has invaded the privacy of their home or business and stolen their possessions. Although the items taken may be covered by insurance, some may be irreplaceable because of their sentimental value.

This chapter first explains the basic differences between burglary and robbery and presents a classification of various types of burglary. It then discusses the elements of the crime of burglary, how to determine its severity, and the elements of the crime of possession of burglary tools. Next the chapter describes the "typical" burglar, how to respond to a burglary call, and how to conduct the preliminary investigation, including determining entry methods into structures, safes, and vaults. Then it explores physical evidence to obtain at the scene of a burglary and modus operandi (MO) factors to consider, followed by a discussion of effective case management. The chapter concludes with a look at recovering stolen property, the elements of receiving stolen goods, and burglary prevention.

Burglary versus Robbery

 burglar seeks to avoid contact with people near the scene or on the premises.

best chances of apprehending a burglar in the act are when a silent alarm is tripped, a surveillance camera records the crime, a witness hears or sees suspicious activities and reports them immediately to the police, or alert patrol officers observe a burglary in progress. However, most burglaries are not solved at the crime scene but through subsequent investigation.

Burglary differs from robbery in that burglars are covert, seeking to remain unseen, whereas robbers confront their victims directly. Burglary is a crime against property; robbery is a crime against person.

Most burglaries occur in unoccupied homes and businesses; therefore, few witnesses exist, and few alarms are given to provide advance notice to the police. The

Classification

Burglaries are classified as residential or commercial.

Residential Burglaries

A **residential burglary** occurs in buildings, structures, or attachments that are used as or are suitable for dwellings, even though they may be unoccupied at the time of the burglary. Residential units include private homes, tenements, mobile homes, cabins, apartments, rooms within a house leased by a renter, houseboats used as dwellings, and any other structure suitable for and used as a dwelling. About two-thirds of all burglaries are residential burglaries.

Residential burglaries are often committed by one or more juveniles or young adults who live in the same community. The targets are cash, items to convert to personal use, or items to "fence" or sell, such as televisions, radios, computers, guns, jewelry, and tools and other small household goods. Residential burglaries typically occur during weekdays when most people are away from their homes, either at work or at school (Figure 13.1).

Whereas the study of burglary and related crime rates has historically focused on the offender, new theories shift the focus toward the victims and particular times and places. For example, the **routine-activity theory** proposes that crime results from the simultaneous existence of three elements: (1) the presence of likely or motivated offenders, (2) the presence of suitable targets, and (3) an absence of guardians to prevent the crime. This theory acknowledges the role, however indirect, of victims in their own victimization and suggests that certain locations may be more susceptible to burglary at certain times because of the routine absence of residents.

A study by Bernasco and Luykx (p.981) of residential burglaries found that an area's attractiveness, potential for opportunity, and accessibility all act to pull burglars toward it as a target. *Attractiveness* is measured as the value of goods that can be stolen from a particular neighborhood, with higher percentages of home ownership and higher average real estate values increasing residential burglary rates. *Opportunity* refers to areas with increased likelihood of successfully completing the crime; higher levels of ethnic/racial diversity and higher residential mobility rates increase residential burglary rates.

© Digital Vision, Ltd./Super Stock

Figure 13.1
Burglars often ransack rooms looking for valuables, making it difficult for the victim to know what is missing. Often there are no leads and, therefore, little hope of apprehending the burglar or recovering the stolen property.

Accessibility is defined by how far offenders must travel to reach the area and how familiar they are with its social and physical infrastructure once they get there; closer proximity to homes of burglars and the area's central business district (CBD) increases residential burglary rates.

Commercial Burglaries

A **commercial burglary** is one that involves churches, schools, barns, public buildings, shops, offices, stores, factories, warehouses, stables, ships, or railroad cars. Most commercial burglaries are committed in service stations, stores, schools, manufacturing plants, warehouses, and office buildings. Burglars often specialize in one type of facility. Businesses located in out-of-the-way places are very susceptible to burglary because of a lack of police coverage and street lighting and because there are usually few witnesses to observe wrongdoing and notify the police. Businesses in high-poverty, rundown neighborhoods are also at high risk of burglary. In contrast to residential burglaries, most commercial burglaries take place after-hours, either at night or on weekends, whenever the establishment is closed.

Commercial burglaries are often committed by two or more people, depending on the type of premises, size and location of the building, and the planned burglary attack. Sometimes a lookout is used who acts like a drunk, works on a stalled car, or walks an animal near the location. The building is "cased" in advance to learn about security devices, opening and closing times, employee habits, people in the neighborhood, and the presence of a private security officer. Casing is also done by obtaining information from an employee or by posing as a worker, repairperson, or salesperson to gain ostensibly legitimate entrance.

Elements of the Crime: Burglary

lthough burglary laws vary from state to state, statutes of all states include three key elements.

Elements of the crime of burglary include:
- Entering a structure,
- without the consent of the person in possession,
- with the intent to commit a crime therein.

Entering a Structure

Paths of entry may be through an open door, window, or transom; a ventilation shaft; a hole in a wall; or a tunnel. Means of entry can be by jimmying a door or window (Figure 13.2), reaching through an open door or window with a long stick or pole, using a celluloid strip to open a door lock, climbing a ladder or stairs outside a building, descending through a skylight, hiding in an entryway, or breaking a window and taking items from the window display (called **smash and grab**). Entry also includes remaining in a store until after closing time and then committing a burglary.

Some state laws include vehicles, trailers, and railroad cars as structures.

Without the Consent of the Person in Possession

To constitute burglary, the entry must be illegal and must be effected without permission of a person with lawful authority, that is, the owner of the property, the legal agent of such person, or the person in physical control of the property, such as a renter or part-owner.

Entering a *public* place is done with consent unless consent has been expressly withdrawn. The hours for

© 911 Pictures

Figure 13.2
Shoeprints indicate the burglar may have tried kicking the door to gain entry. In the end, the doorknob was broken off.

legal entry usually are posted on public buildings; for example, "Open Weekdays 9 A.M. to 5 P.M." Entrance at any other time is without consent. If a specific individual is restricted from entering a public place during its open hours, that individual must be notified orally or in writing that consent has been withdrawn.

With Intent to Commit a Crime

Regardless of whether the burglary is planned well in advance or committed on the spur of the moment, intent must be shown. When the first two elements are present, the third is often presumed present; that is, if a person enters a structure without the owner's consent, the presumption is that it is to commit a crime, usually larceny or a sex offense.

Additional Elements

Three additional elements are found in the laws of some states.

 Elements of burglary can also include breaking into the dwelling of another during the nighttime.

Breaking Into   Actual "breaking" is a matter of interpretation. Any force used during the burglary to enter or leave the structure, even if a door or window is partly opened or closed, constitutes breaking. Entrance through trick or ruse or through threats to or collusion with any person residing in the building is also considered breaking.

Breaking and entering is strong **presumptive evidence** that a crime is intended; that is, it provides a reasonable basis for belief. Some laws include such wording as:

> Every person who shall unlawfully break and enter a building or dwelling or other structure shall be deemed to have broken and entered or entered the same with intent to commit grand or petit larceny or a felony therein, unless such unlawful breaking and entering shall be explained by testimony satisfactory to the jury to have been made without criminal intent.

This, in effect, places the burden of proof on the defendant.

The Dwelling of Another   Some states still require that the structure broken into be a dwelling, that is, a structure suitable for sheltering humans. This remnant from common law restricts burglary to residential burglaries.

During the Nighttime   Common law also specified that burglary occur under the cover of darkness, an element still retained in some state statutes. *Nighttime* is defined as the period from sunset to sunrise as specified by official weather charts.

Establishing the Severity of the Burglary

Most burglary laws increase the crime's severity if the burglar possesses a weapon or an explosive. Obtain the weapon and connect it with the burglar if possible. Check with the National Crime Information Center (NCIC). If the weapon is stolen, a separate felony charge of theft or illegal possession of a weapon can be made.

A burglary's severity is determined by (a) the presence of dangerous devices in the burglar's possession or (b) the value of the property stolen.

If other crimes are committed along with the burglary or if the burglary is for the purpose of committing another crime such as rape, the additional crime is separate and must be proven separately.

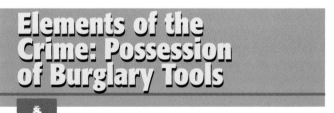
Elements of the Crime: Possession of Burglary Tools

A companion crime to burglary is possession of burglary tools, an offense separate from burglary. The charge of possession of burglary tools can be made even if a burglary has not been committed if circumstances indicate that the tools were intended for use in a burglary.

Elements of the crime of possessing burglary tools include:
- Possessing any device, explosive, or other instrumentality,
- with intent to use or permit their use to commit burglary.

Burglary tools include nitroglycerin or other explosives and any engine, machine, tool, implement, chemical, or substance designed for the cutting or burning open of buildings or protective containers.

A person with a large number of automobile keys probably intends to use them to open varied makes and models of vehicle doors. Portable key cutters, codes, and key blanks such as those used in hardware stores and key-making shops are also classified as burglary tools, as are *slam pullers,* devices that look like oversized screwdrivers and are inserted in car locks to force them open.

Many other tools used in burglaries are commonly obtained in hardware stores. These include pry bars, screwdrivers, bolt cutters, extension cords, pipe wrenches, channel locks, and tire irons. Lock picks and tension wrenches, lever-type wrenches, warded pass keys, pick guns, cylinder drill jigs, and various types of metal blades to open car doors can also be used as burglary tools.

Because many people, especially mechanics and carpenters, have tools that might be used in a burglary in their car or on their person, circumstances must clearly show an intent to use or allow their use in committing a crime.

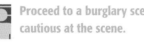

The Burglar

The burglar is often portrayed as a masked person with a bag over his shoulder loaded with silverware and candlesticks. In reality, burglars fit no set image; they are of all sizes, ages, races, and occupations. They are either amateurs or longtime professionals whose sole income is derived from burglaries. Citing results from various criminological studies, Mullins and Wright (pp.813–814) observe: "Residential burglary is a prototypically social offense, shaped by ongoing relationships and interactions set in the broader world of streetlife." Noting that one key characteristic of a "good burglar" is "the ability to get along well with others," Mullins and Wright (p.814) also state that residential burglars tend to offend in groups, use inside information collected during their daily routines to choose their targets, and commonly convert their stolen goods to cash through an established network of buyers.

Most amateur burglars are between the ages of 15 and 25; most professionals are 25 to 55. The amateur is usually an unskilled, "infancy-level" burglar who steals radios, televisions, cash, and other portable property and who learns through trial and error. In contrast, the professional burglar usually steals furs, jewelry, and more valuable items and has been carefully trained by other professional burglars.

Even though amateurs gain experience in burglaries, they are apt to make a mistake sooner or later and be observed by the police while committing a burglary. If caught and sentenced to prison, amateur burglars gain the opportunity to learn more about the "trade" from the professionals.

Professional burglars may have lookouts who are in communication through two-way radios. A getaway vehicle is usually close to the burglary site, and the lookout monitors police radio frequencies.

Although most burglars' motives are monetary or drug related, sometimes the excitement of committing burglary and evading detection is equally or more important. One burglar said it was a "thrill" not to know what was waiting for him and whether he would get away with the crime.

Responding to a Burglary Call

On the way to the burglary scene, watch for anyone fleeing the area, suspicious-looking people still at the scene, and suspicious automobiles. Do not use a siren on the way to the scene. Cut your flashing lights some distance from the scene, and do not use a spotlight or flashlight to determine the address. Park several doors away from the address of the call, turn the radio down, and close car doors quietly. Approach the immediate area with low-tone conversation and avoid jangling keys or coins or flashing lights.

Proceed to a burglary scene quietly. Be observant and cautious at the scene.

The first two officers arriving place themselves at diagonally opposed corners of the building. This places them out of the other's line of fire but in position to protect each other.

Search the premises inside and outside for the burglar.

Use maximum cover and caution in going around corners. In a dark room, use a flashlight rather than room lights to prevent silhouettes. Hold the flashlight in front of you at a 45-degree angle. Have your gun drawn but not cocked.

Be alert for the possible presence of explosives at a burglary scene. If a bomb threat is connected with a burglary, notify the FBI. If explosives are actually detonated, notify the Alcohol, Tobacco, and Firearms Division of the U.S. Treasury Department. To dispose of explosives at the scene or in the suspect's possession, call the bomb squad of the nearest large metropolitan area or the explosives ordnance unit of the closest military installation. If an explosion has already occurred at the burglary scene, intentionally or accidentally, it may leave behind potentially valuable evidence. The collection and handling of such evidence is discussed shortly.

False Burglar Alarms

False burglar alarms from personal residential and commercial security systems are a huge problem for law enforcement agencies, accounting for up to 98 percent of all alarm calls received in some jurisdictions. Nislow (p.1) contends: "The unreliability of alarm systems is turning overloaded police forces into false alarm managers." False alarms are typically caused by user error, although occasionally they occur because of faulty equipment.

The growing problem of false alarms has led many departments to implement policies on how to handle such nuisance calls. Some law enforcement agencies have implemented a **verified response policy,** meaning that they will not respond to a burglary alarm unless criminal activity is first confirmed through either an onsite security officer or some method of electronic surveillance, such as closed-circuit television. An aggressive form of verified response is Enhanced Call Verification (ECV), which requires that a minimum of two phone calls be made from the alarm monitoring center, to assess whether user error activated the alarm. Only then will a law enforcement response be requested (Martin, p.160). Mowrey and Rice (p.15) assert: "Enhanced Call Verification is becoming an industry standard." They note how Lee County, Florida—believed to be the country's first jurisdiction to include ECV in its city's alarm ordinance—has successfully reduced the number of alarm calls coming into dispatch and anticipate reaching their targeted goal of a 70 percent reduction in 2005. The officer in charge of the system is quoted as saying: "The success of Lee County's effort is the direct result of its initial public education program, public acceptance and partnership with the alarm industry in finding a solution for a community-wide problem" (Mowrey and Rice, p. 15).

Another approach that departments are taking is to use an escalating series of fines and fees for police dispatch when the alarm turns out to be false. For chronic abusers, alarm response by police is suspended entirely. As Martin (p.160) reports: "On average, 10 percent of alarm system users will generate 50 percent of the alarm dispatches."

Not only are false alarms a waste of time for responding officers, but, more important, they may cause officers to be caught off guard when a genuine alarm occurs. Betten and Mervosh (p.166) assert: "Without verified-response policies, police become complacent about replying to alarms that they expect to be false."

The Preliminary Investigation

While burglary is a very basic crime to investigate, many investigators cut corners or simply skip the necessary steps of a preliminary investigation because, with a national clearance rate of only about 13 percent, such cases are perceived as being high time investments for low-result rewards.

Yet, for this very reason, the preliminary investigation is of utmost importance.

If no suspect is found at the scene of a burglary, conduct the preliminary investigation as described in Chapter 1. Obtain detailed information about the type of structure burglarized, the means of entry, the time and date, the whereabouts of the owner, other persons recently on the premises, the property taken, and the MO.

Determine who the occupants are and where they were at the time of the burglary. Were they on the premises? If not, when did they leave? Were the doors and windows locked? Who had keys? What visitors had recently been there? Obtain descriptions of salespeople, agents, service installers, or maintenance workers on the premises recently. Was the burglar familiar with the premises? Could the location of the stolen items be known only to a person who worked on the premises; that is, was it an inside job?

Obtain a complete list of the property taken and an estimate of the value from the victim. Find out where the property was obtained and where it was stored. Where and when did the owner last see it? What type of property was *not* stolen?

Interview witnesses. In many burglaries there is a connection between the victim and the suspect. The suspect may have recently performed work, made a delivery, or attended a party in the home. Conduct a neighborhood canvass to see whether anyone saw anything and to alert neighbors. An important point to keep in mind is that concern should be shown for the victim. Surveys indicate that victims' impressions of the police are related to how professionally investigators conduct the crime scene investigation. If officers are thorough, courteous, considerate, concerned, and conscientious about keeping the victims informed of the progress of the investigation, victims generally express favorable opinions of the investigators. Solving the crime is the first priority for the police, but the victims' feelings must be considered as well. They may feel devastated, violated, angry, or completely dejected. Investigators must keep these feelings in mind as they conduct interviews with victims.

Search for physical evidence, including latent fingerprints, items left on the premises by the burglar, or tool marks on doors or windows. Without physical evidence, there is little chance of charging anyone. It is especially important to search for prints at the scene and to obtain elimination prints of those with normal access to it.

Check pawnshops where stolen items may have been left. Log articles with serial numbers into NCIC.

Preliminary Investigation of Residential Burglaries

The preliminary investigation of a residential burglary should include the following steps as a minimum:

- Contact the resident(s).
- Establish points and methods of entry and exit.

- Collect and preserve evidence.
- Determine the type and amount of loss, with complete descriptions.
- Describe the MO.
- Check for recent callers such as friends of children, salespeople, and maintenance people.
- Canvass the neighborhood for witnesses, evidence, discarded stolen articles, and so on.

Interviews of burglars have revealed that they prefer middle- to upper-class homes and corner homes that allow them to see people approaching from a maximum of directions. They may knock on doors before entering to determine whether a dog is inside, and they may call in advance to see if anyone is home. The advent of caller ID may bring about some change in this technique.

When processing the crime scene in a residential burglary, process the exit as well as the entry area. When looking for fingerprints, check the inside of drawers that have been ransacked, smooth glass objects, papers strewn on the floor, countertops, and clocks. The same procedures are followed if the burglary has occurred in a multiple-dwelling or a commercial-lodging establishment such as an apartment building or a hotel.

Preliminary Investigation of Commercial Burglaries

Preliminary investigation of a commercial burglary (of, for example, a market, shop, office, liquor store) should minimally include the following steps:

- Contact the owner.
- Protect the scene from intrusion by the owner, the public, and others.
- Establish the point and method of entry and exit.
- Locate, collect, and preserve possible evidence.
- Narrow the time frame of the crime.
- Determine the type and amount of loss.
- Determine who closed the establishment, who was present at the time of the crime, and who had keys to the establishment.
- Describe the MO.
- Identify employees' friends, maintenance people, and any possible disgruntled employees or customers.
- Rule out a faked or staged burglary for insurance purposes.

Fake Burglaries

Do not overlook the possibility of faked burglaries, especially in commercial burglaries where the owner appears to be in financial difficulty. Check the owner's financial status.

So-called combination safe jobs, in which the safe is opened by the combination without the use of external force, are usually due to the combination being found on the premises, the safe being carelessly left open or improperly locked, a dishonest present or former employee using the combination or selling it to the burglar, or the employer faking a burglary to cover a shortage of funds.

Determining Entry into Structures

Burglary is a crime of opportunity and concealment. Entry is made in areas of a structure not normally observed, under the cover of darkness, in covered entryways, through windows screened by shrubbery or trees, or through ruse and trickery. Sometimes, however, the burglar breaks a shop window, removes some items on display, and rapidly escapes by jumping into a nearby vehicle driven by an accomplice.

> Jimmying is the most common method of entry to commit burglary.

Almost every means imaginable has been used by burglars to gain entry, including tunneling; chopping holes in walls, floors, and ceilings; and using fire escapes. Tool marks, disturbed paint, footprints and fingerprints, broken glass, or forced locks help determine how the burglar gained entry.

Some burglars have keys made. For example, some people leave their car at a repair shop along with their full set of keys—an open invitation to make a duplicate house or office key. At other times burglars hide inside a building until after closing. In such cases they often leave behind evidence such as matches, cigarette butts, or candy wrappers because their wait is often lengthy.

The **hit-and-run burglary,** also called "smash and grab," (Figure 13.3) in which the burglar smashes a window to steal merchandise, is most frequently committed by younger, inexperienced burglars. Jewelry and furs are the most common targets.

In recent years enterprising burglars have taken advantage of the prevalence of electric garage door openers. Using "code grabbers," burglars can record and replicate the electronic signal emitted from an automatic garage door opener. When a person leaves the house and activates the garage door opener, the burglar is able to capture the signal from up to several hundred yards away and reopen the door once the resident is safely out of sight. Some burglars are bold enough to back their own car into the garage, load it up with stolen

Figure 13.3
Some burglars use a rock or brick to smash a display window and then steal valuable merchandise. Such smash-and-grab burglaries often set off an alarm.

items, and drive away, leaving no sign of forced entry. To combat the code-grabbing technique to gain entrance into homes, a device called a "code rotator" is available. Each time an automatic door opener is used, the internal code rotates to a new one, rendering a code grabber useless.

Determining Entry into Safes and Vaults

afes are usually considered a good way to protect valuables, but most older safes provide little more than fire protection. Unless they are carried away or demolished by a burglar or lost in a fire, safes last many years; therefore, many old safes are still in use.

A **safe** is a semiportable strongbox with a combination lock. The size of the safe or lock does not necessarily correlate with its security. A **vault** is a stationary room of reinforced concrete, often steel lined, with a combination lock. Both safes and vaults are common targets of burglars (Figure 13.4).

Safes and vaults are entered illegally by punching, peeling, chopping, pulling, blowing, and burning. Sometimes burglars simply haul the safes away.

In **punching,** the dial is sheared from the safe door by a downward blow with a sledge or by holding a chisel to the dial and using a sledge to knock it off, exposing the safe mechanism spindle. Sometimes tire inner tube, or similar material, will be placed over the safe's dial to deaden the noise. Punching is most successful in attacking older-model fire-resistant safes and is less successful on newer models that have tapered spindles that will jam when someone attempts to punch them.

In **peeling,** the burglar drills a hole in a corner of the safe and then makes this hole successively larger by using other drills until the narrow end of a jimmy can be inserted in the hole to pry the door partially open. The burglar then uses the larger end of the jimmy to complete the job. Although slow, this method is less noisy than others.

In **chopping,** the burglar uses a sledge and chisels or a heavy chopping instrument, such as an axe, to chop a hole in the bottom of the safe large enough to remove the contents. Also called a *rip* or *peel,* all three terms are used to describe the opening by physical force of a hole, which is expanded until it is big enough to fit a hand inside the safe. A chop/rip/peel is commonly used on fire-resistant safes (sometimes after an unsuccessful punch).

In **pulling,** also called **dragging,** the burglar inserts a *V* plate over the dial, with the *V* in place behind the dial. The burglar then tightens the screw bolts one at a time until the dial and the spindle are pulled out. This method, the opposite of punching, works on many older safes but not on newer ones.

In **blowing,** the burglar drills a hole in the safe near the locking bar area or pushes cotton into an area of the safe door crack and puts nitroglycerin on the cotton. The burglar then places a primer cap against the cotton, tapes it in place, and runs a wire to a protected area. Mattresses and blankets are often used to soften the blast. The burglar ignites the nitroglycerin, which blows the safe open. This dangerous, noisy method requires experience and is rarely used.

The process of **burning** often uses a "burning bar," a portable safecracking tool that burns a hole into the safe to gain entry. This hole may be burned near the safe's locking mechanism, or the safe may be tipped over and the hole burned through the bottom. An arc-air burning tool can punch a hole completely through a one-inch steel plate in about 10 seconds.

Figure 13.4
Safes are a frequent target of burglars.

Some burglars prefer a site of their own choosing at which to employ one or more of these methods. So, they steal the entire safe, haul it away in a truck, and open it when they get there.

The preceding methods are used on older safes still found in many smaller stores. Often the safe can be entered in less than 15 minutes. Modern safes, however, do not have spindles and cannot be punched, peeled, or pulled. Safes of newer steel alloys are highly resistant to burning and drilling.

Obtaining Physical Evidence

ost burglars are convicted on circumstantial evidence. Any physical evidence at the burglary scene is of the utmost importance.

 Physical evidence at a burglary scene includes fingerprints, footprints, tire prints, tools, tool marks, broken glass, paint chips, safe insulation, explosives residue, and personal possessions.

The competent, professional burglar will wear gloves to avoid leaving behind fingerprints and palm prints. However, an offender's inexperience and haste could result in such prints being scattered throughout the crime scene. Therefore, process the scene for prints, particularly at the entry point (Figure 13.5).

Shoe impressions and footprints may be visible inside and/or outside the structure and should be cast per the guidelines given in Chapter 5. Similarly, any tire impressions located around the burglary scene should be cast as possible evidence.

Tools and tool marks are especially important items of evidence. Pry bars, augers, picks, and screwdrivers are common tools used to commit burglary. Locksmith tools can also be used and are illegal to possess unless one is a licensed locksmith. Burglars often have a "tool

Figure 13.5
Glass doors pose a security risk in that they can be easily broken by burglars. While an investigator may find fingerprints or tool marks on a door used to gain entry to a burglary scene, experienced burglars typically wear gloves to avoid leaving prints. In this case, evidence to link a suspect with the scene would include glass fragments on the suspect's clothes or fibers found at the scene that match the suspect's glove or other clothing.

of choice" they use to gain entry, and this same tool, used over and over at different crime scenes, will leave behind characteristic striation marks (Figure 13.6) that can connect one burglary to another. Tools used to pry open a door or window always leave a mark behind (recall Locard's principle of exchange [Chapter 1]). If the frame is made of wood, striation marks may be visible and can be cast. Before casting an impression in wood, however, spray the surface with a silicone oil-based release agent to ensure that the silicone casting material, once cured, does not stick to the wood and pull out wood fibers when the cast is removed. (A helpful website is that of BVDA America, Inc., at http://usa.bvda.com.)

Be alert to the variety of containers used to carry burglary tools—handbags, suitcases, musical-instrument cases, and packages that appear to contain merchandise. Tools can also be concealed under coats, inside pant legs, or under car seats. Tools found on the premises are also sometimes left there by the burglar to avoid being caught with burglary tools in possession and to thwart efforts to link multiple burglaries to one offender.

Broken glass and paint chips are common items of evidence at burglary scenes. An offender who smashes a window to gain entry to a building may unwittingly carry away tiny fragments of glass on his clothing or the soles of his shoes. Samples of glass or chipped paint collected at the scene can be matched to glass and paint fragments detected on the suspect, helping to establish his presence at that location of the crime.

Evidence at the scene of a safe burglary may also include safe insulation. As with glass and paint fragments, the burglar often has some of this insulation on his or her clothing, either in pants, coat, or jacket pockets or in the nail holes of shoes. Take comparison standards of safe insulation to be matched with particles found on the suspect, on tools the suspect used, or

in the vehicle used during the crime. In some cases safe insulation can also be matched with a series of burglaries.

Sometimes explosives are encountered at a burglary scene. Use extreme caution in handling and preserving such evidence. If an explosion has already occurred at the burglary scene, intentionally or accidentally, identify and preserve fragments from the explosive device and send them to a crime laboratory.

Figure 13.6
A 25x magnification of a toolmark comparison. Note the detail of how the impression can be matched to the marks on the tool that made it.
Source: United States Department of Justice/Bureau of Alcohol, Tobacco, Fire Arms, and Explosives.

DNA is also becoming important in burglary investigations. If a burglar gets cut breaking into a structure, he or she may leave blood behind that can be analyzed for DNA, perhaps linking the burglary to others. Noting the high recidivism rates of property crime offenders, that their crimes and violence often escalate, and that many property crime cases go unsolved, the National Institute of Justice (NIJ) (p.1) has advocated the collection of DNA evidence in "minor" crime investigations as a way to yield major public safety benefits:

> It has been estimated that each burglar in the top 10 percent of burglars commits more than 232 burglaries per year. Several police departments in the United States are finding that . . . when they analyze DNA from a burglary, they get evidence that often solves several other cases as well.

For investigators who consider the collection of DNA evidence at burglary scenes to be "overkill" for such relatively minor crimes, the NIJ (p.2) provides the following counterpoint:

> Mark Dale, crime lab director at the NYPD, said that in his experience, when DNA from a no-suspect murder scene is checked against records in the Combined DNA Index System (CODIS), it often matches DNA from a no-suspect burglary. Review of the State's first 1,000 hits showed that the vast majority were linked to crimes like homicide and rape, but of these, 82 percent of the offenders were already in the databank as a result of a prior conviction for a "lesser" crime such as burglary or drugs. According to a Florida State study, 52 percent of database hits against murder and sexual assault cases matched individuals who had prior convictions for burglary.

Modus Operandi Factors

Effective MO files are essential in investigating burglaries because most burglars commit a series of burglaries. Look for patterns in the location, day of week, time of day, type of property stolen, and method of entry or exit. The burglar may commit vandalism, ransack, write with lipstick on mirrors, take only cash or jewelry, drink liquor from the scene, or eat from the refrigerator. Such peculiarities can tie several burglaries to one suspect.

 Important MO factors include the time, type of victim, type of premises, point and means of entry, type of property taken, and any peculiarities of the offense.

Suspects often commit burglaries on only a certain day of the week, perhaps related to their day off from a regular job. The time of the burglary should be as accu-

rate as possible, but when victims are gone on vacation, this is not easy to determine. Knowing the time also helps in checking alibis, interviewing witnesses, and, in some states, determining the degree of the burglary.

Determine any peculiarities of the offense, including oddities of the suspect. What method of search was used? Was anything else done besides committing the burglary? Did the burglar telephone first to ensure that no one was home or pose as a delivery person? Did neighbors see such activities? Determine any trademarks of the burglar. Some burglars take such pride in their professionalism that they leave a calling card of some type to let the police know whose work it is.

Check the MO with local files. Talk to other officers, inquire at other agencies within a 100-mile radius, and discuss the case at area investigation meetings. Other officers may have encountered a similar MO.

Effective Case Management

Because burglary is predominantly a serial crime, the serial burglar should be the primary target of the burglary unit. This requires effective case management, including an effective system for prioritizing cases. Profiling and mapping may be of considerable help.

Using the computer's search capabilities, information retrieval is fast and simple, and investigations can proceed on information that in the past would have taken hundreds of hours to retrieve if indeed it could have been retrieved at all.

Effective case management also recognizes the mobility of burglars and makes assignments on the MO rather than on the geographic area—for example, burglaries involving forcible entry, daytime burglaries involving no force, and nighttime residential burglaries. All information should be shared with the drug enforcement unit because many burglaries are drug related.

In fact, the rise in narcotics and other prescription drug thefts from pharmacies has led to the creation of a new national database called RxPATROL (Rx Pattern Analysis Tracking Robberies and Other Losses). Gibbs (p.18) explains: "RxPATROL is designed to be a quick and easy way for law enforcement officers and pharmacists to enter information regarding a theft or loss into a clearinghouse, via a secure Internet site. The information [includes] data on the store, suspect description, method of operation, store security systems, items stolen, and weapons displayed or inferred. Any photos captured by security cameras . . . can be sent to RxPATROL for analysis."

Recovering Stolen Property

Stolen property is disposed of in many ways. Because many people are looking for a bargain, thieves can often sell the property on the streets, thus avoiding a record of the sale but also risking being reported to the police by someone who sees the transaction.

In the case of property being sold to pawnshops or secondhand stores or left at a store on consignment for sale, most states and communities have statutes or ordinances requiring a permanent record of the transaction. The seller must be given a receipt describing the property purchased and the amount paid, with the seller's name and address. A copy of the transaction is often sent to the police department of the community listed as the seller's home address. If the property is identified as stolen, the police contact the shop owner and, upon proof that the property is stolen, can recover it. Shop records are open to police inspection at all times. Information in these records can lead to the arrest of the seller as the person who committed the burglary.

Informants can often locate stolen property because they usually know who is active in the area. Surveillance of pawnshops also is often productive. Circulate a list of the stolen property to all establishments that might deal in such merchandise in your own community and surrounding communities. If the property is extremely valuable, enter it into the FBI's NCIC files.

> The elements of the offense of receiving stolen goods are:

Check with pawnshops, secondhand stores, flea markets, and informants for leads in recovering stolen property.

As with so many other types of crimes and evidence, national database and tracking tools are being implemented to help law enforcement find and recover stolen goods. One technology, l.e.a.d.s.online (Law Enforcement Automated Database Search), allows investigators to search a single Internet database for pawned property items, eliminating the tedious job of searching through stacks of paper records and visiting numerous pawnshops and secondhand stores (Payne, p.154).

When you recover stolen property, record the date on which the property was recovered, where it was recovered, who turned it in, and the circumstances surrounding the recovery. List the names and addresses of anyone present at the time of recovery. Mark the property as evidence and take it into custody. In some states, it is legal to return the property as long as its identification is recorded and a photograph is taken. There is no reason the original property must be produced in court unless it was an instrument that caused death or serious injury.

Recovering stolen property and returning it to the rightful owner is aided by Operation Identification programs. In such programs homeowners mark all easily stolen property with a personal identification number (PIN). The numbers are recorded and placed in a secure location.

The Offense of Receiving Stolen Goods

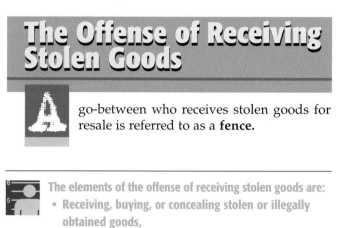

A go-between who receives stolen goods for resale is referred to as a **fence**.

> The elements of the offense of receiving stolen goods are:
> • Receiving, buying, or concealing stolen or illegally obtained goods,
> • knowing them to be stolen or otherwise illegally obtained.

Receiving stolen property for resale is a crime, as is concealing stolen property, even though not purchased. A burglar does not have to personally sell goods to a fence. An "innocent" third party can sell the property for the burglar, but it is still an offense if the buyer knows the property was stolen.

It is difficult to prove that a buyer knew the purchased goods were stolen. The property must be found in the receiver's possession and identified as the stolen property by the owner's testimony, marks, serial numbers, or other positive identification. Knowing can then be proved by the very low price paid for the goods in comparison with the true value.

Usually evidence of the sale is provided through an informant who either made the sale or knows who did. The property may have been resold, and the person buying the item may be the informant who identifies the receiver of stolen goods. This person assists the police in making another sale or identifying property in the receiver's possession.

The receiver of stolen goods is often discovered when the person who stole the property is arrested and identifies the receiver. It is necessary to show that the receiver could not legitimately own the item unless he or she had bought it from a thief. Show that it was not purchased through a normal business transaction. The character of the person selling the property or any indication that the property was being concealed is evidence. Evidence that markings or serial numbers have been altered or removed indicates concealment and intent to deprive the rightful owner of the property. The seller can testify to conversations with the receiver about the property and the fact that it was stolen. The receiver's records may not show the transaction, which would be evidence of intent to conceal. The charge of receiving stolen goods can be used when possession of stolen items can be shown but there is not sufficient evidence to prove theft.

One indicator of fencing activity is an operation that makes merchandise available to retailers at extremely low wholesale prices provided they pay cash. Another possible indicator is a small local outlet that offers significant savings to customers, conducts a large volume of business over a short period, and then closes suddenly. Sales from fenced goods amount to tens of billions of dollars annually.

Sting Operations

Many cities have established sting operations, in which the police legally establish a fencing operation. A suitable shop is set up as a front for the operation. Normally, secondhand stores, repair shops, salvage dealers, appliance dealers, or pawnshops make good front operations. The store is stocked with items to support the type of business selected.

Word is spread through informants and the underworld that the business will "buy anything." Attractive prices are paid to get the business started. All transactions between the fence and the seller of stolen goods are recorded by closed-circuit television. The camera is usually focused on an area in which a calendar and clock are clearly visible to establish the date and time of each transaction. A parking lot surveillance camera shows the vehicle used to transport the property and its license number.

When an item is presented at the counter, the seller, the amount paid for the property, and the buyer are recorded. The property is then dusted for fingerprints to further prove the seller's possession. The stolen goods are checked through normal police channels to determine where they were stolen.

The shop is run for two to three months and then discontinued. Arrest warrants are then issued for those implicated during the store's operation.

Preventing Burglary

R esearch shows that premises that are burglarized are likely to be burglarized again. The National Burglar and Fire Alarm Association (NBTAA) states on its website (http://www.alarm.org):

Homes without security systems are about 3 times more likely to be broken into than homes with security systems. (Actual statistic ranges from 2.2 times to 3.1 times, depending on the value of the home.) Businesses without alarm systems are 4.5 times more likely to be burglarized than commercial locations with electronic security in place. Losses due to burglary average $400 less in residences with security systems than for a residence without security systems.

Officers who work with burglary victims can help them avoid future burglaries by conducting a security check of the premises and "hardening" the target. **Target hardening**, also called **crime prevention through environmental design (CPTED)**, involves altering physical characteristics of the property so as to make it less attractive to criminals. CPTED measures include removing dense shrubbery next to windows and doors, as this provides concealment to burglars and increases the attractiveness of the target. High privacy fences around homes also give cover to people attempting to break in. Inadequate lighting increases the attractiveness of a property to burglars. Open garages and unlocked service doors from the home to the garage are other ways burglars gain entry.

Weisel (*Burglary of Single-Family*) lists factors burglars use to select their targets. Knowledge of these selection criteria can help burglary victims and potential victims turn the tables on burglars and make their property a less attractive target. For example, burglars select houses that appear vacant for an extended period, and accumulated mail or newspapers by the front door can indicate that the homeowners are out of town. To prevent burglaries, advise homeowners to have their mail and newspaper stopped while they are away, or to ask a neighbor to collect it until they return.

Officers can also assist their jurisdiction in reducing burglaries by having input into building codes that would require adequate locks, lighting, and other security measures to deter burglaries.

Measures that deter burglaries include:
- Installing adequate locks, striker plates, and doorframes.
- Installing adequate indoor and outdoor lighting.
- Providing clearly visible addresses.
- Eliminating bushes or other obstructions to windows.
- Securing any skylights or air vents over 96 inches.
- Installing burglarproof sidelight window glass beside doors.
- Installing a burglar alarm.

SUMMARY

Burglary is the unlawful entry of a structure to commit a crime. It differs from robbery in that burglars are covert, seeking to remain unseen, whereas robbers confront their victims directly. Burglary is a crime against property; robbery is a crime against person.

Burglaries are classified as residential or commercial. The primary elements of the crime of burglary are (1) entering a structure (2) without the consent of the person in possession (3) with the intent to commit a crime therein. Additional elements of burglary that may be required include (1) breaking into (2) the dwelling of another (3) during the nighttime. A burglary's severity is determined by the presence of dangerous devices in the burglar's possession or by the value of the stolen property. Attempted burglary and possession of burglary tools are also felonies. The elements of the crime of possessing burglary tools include (1) possessing any device, explosive, or other instrumentality (2) with intent to use or permit its use to commit burglary.

When responding to a burglary call, proceed to the scene quietly. Be observant and cautious. Search the premises inside and outside for the burglar. Determine the entry point, keeping in mind that jimmying is the most common method to enter a structure to commit burglary. Attacks on safes and vaults include punching, peeling, chopping, pulling or dragging, blowing, burning, and, for safes, hauling them away.

Physical evidence at a burglary scene often includes fingerprints, footprints, tire prints, tools, tool marks, broken glass, safe insulation, paint chips, and personal possessions. Important MO factors include the time, the types of premises, the type of victim, point and means of entry, type of property taken, and any peculiarities of the offense.

Check with pawnshops, secondhand stores, flea markets, and informants for leads in recovering stolen property.

The elements of the offense of receiving stolen goods are (1) receiving, buying, or concealing stolen or illegally obtained goods (2) knowing them to be stolen or otherwise illegally obtained.

Measures to deter burglaries include installing adequate locks, striker plates, and door frames; installing adequate indoor and outdoor lighting; providing clearly visible addresses; eliminating bushes or other obstructions to windows; securing any skylights or air vents over 96 inches; installing burglar-proof sidelight window glass beside doors; and installing a burglar alarm.

CHECKLIST

Burglary

- Was a thorough preliminary investigation conducted?
- What is the address and description of the structure burglarized?
- What time and date did the burglary occur?
- What means was used to enter? Was it forcible?
- Who is the rightful owner? Was consent given for the entry?
- What visitors had recently been on the premises?
- Was the burglar familiar with the premises?
- What was taken (complete description and value of each item)?
- Where was the property located, and when was it last seen by the owner?
- What was *not* taken?
- What pattern of search did the burglar use?
- What was the burglar's MO?
- What physical evidence was found at the scene?
- Did any witnesses see or hear anything suspicious at the time of the burglary?
- Does the owner have any idea who might have committed the burglary?
- Have the MO files been checked?
- Have neighboring communities been informed of the burglary?
- Have you checked with fences, pawnshop owners, and secondhand stores for the stolen property? Have you circulated a list to the owners of such businesses?
- Might this be a fake burglary?

APPLICATION

Read this account of a criminal investigation and evaluate its effectiveness:

> In a California city two janitors showing up for work were met at the door of the restaurant they were to clean by two armed men. One janitor was taken inside; the other escaped and notified the police. When the police arrived, both suspects were outside the building in different areas and claimed they knew nothing of a crime being committed. Inside, the one janitor was tied up in the kitchen, unharmed. The safe had been punched open. A substance believed to be safe insulation, along with paint chips, was found in the trouser cuffs and shoes of both suspects. Both janitors made a positive field identification of the two suspects. Laboratory analysis of the substance found in the suspects' clothing and shoes matched a comparison sample of the safe insulation, and the paint chips matched the top two layers of paint on the safe. The men were charged with burglary.

Questions

1. Was it legal to take the men into custody?
2. Was field identification appropriate?
3. Was it legal to submit the safe insulation and paint chips for laboratory analysis?
4. Was the charge correct?
5. What additional evidence should have been located and seized?

DISCUSSION QUESTIONS

1. Many people think of *burglary* and *robbery* as interchangeable terms. What is the principal difference between these two offenses from an investigative viewpoint?
2. Describe the following methods of entering a safe: a pull job; a peel job; a chopping; blowing a safe; burning.
3. What types of evidence would you expect to find at the scene of a safe burglary? How would you collect and preserve it?
4. What are the elements of burglary in your state? What is the penalty?
5. How frequent is burglary in your community? your state? Has burglary been increasing or decreasing in the past five years?
6. If you are investigating a burglary, which persons would you be most interested in talking to at the scene? away from the scene?
7. What other crimes are often committed along with burglary?
8. Is it legal to "steal back" your own property if someone has stolen it from you?
9. If the object stolen in a burglary is valued below $100, is the crime a misdemeanor?
10. What can the police do to increase the reporting of burglaries? What can they do to help the public prevent burglaries?

MEDIA EXPLORATIONS

Internet

Select one of the following assignments to complete.

- Go to the FBI website at www.fbi.gov. Click on "library and reference." Select "Uniform Crime Reports" and outline what the report says about burglary.
- Select one of the following keywords: *burglary, routine activity theory, smash and grab*. Find one article relevant to burglary investigations to outline and share with the class.

Crime and Evidence in Action

Go to the CD and choose the **burglary/arson case.** During the course of the case you'll become patrol officer, detective, judge, corrections officer, and parole officer to conduct interactive investigative research. Each case unfolds as you respond to key decision points. Feedback for each possible answer choice is packed full of information, including term definitions, web links, and important documentation. The sergeant is available at certain times to help mentor you, the Online Resources website offers a variety of information, and be sure to take notes in your e-notebook during the suspect video statements and at key points throughout (these notes can be saved, printed, or e-mailed). The Forensics Exercise will test your ability to collect, transport, and analyze evidence from the crime scene. At the end of the case you can track how well you responded to each decision point and join the Discussion Forum for a postmortem. **Go to the CD and use the skills you've learned in this chapter to solve a case.**

REFERENCES

Bernasco, Wim, and Luykx, Floor. "Effects of Attractiveness, Opportunity and Accessibility to Burglars on Residential Burglary Rates of Urban Neighborhoods." *Criminology*, August 2003, pp. 981–1002.

Betten, Michael, and Mervosh, Mitchell. "Should Police Respond to Alarms?" *Security Management*, June 2005, pp. 166–168.

Crime in the United States 2003. Washington, DC: Federal Bureau of Investigation, Uniform Crime Reports, October 27, 2004.

Fass, Simon M., and Francis, Janice. "Where Have All the Hot Goods Gone? The Role of Pawnshops." *Journal of Research in Crime and Delinquency*, May 2004, pp. 156–179.

Gibbs, Landon S. "A New Tool to Combat Pharmacy Theft." *The Police Chief*, September 2004, pp. 17–19.

Martin, Stan. "What's Best for Alarm Response Policies?" *Security Management*, March 2005, pp. 160–162.

Mowrey, Glen M., and Rice, Derek. "Alarm Industry Steps Up to Reduce False Alarm Calls through Enhanced Call Verification." *The Police Chief*, September 2004, pp. 14–15.

Mullins, Christopher W., and Wright, Richard. "Gender, Social Networks, and Residential Burglary." *Criminology*, August 2003, pp. 813–840.

National Institute of Justice. *DNA in "Minor" Crimes Yields Major Benefit in Public Safety.* Washington, DC: Author. November 2004. (NCJ 207203)

Nislow, Jennifer. "Cause for Alarm: Industry and User Resistance Thwart Solution to False-Alarm Problem." *Law Enforcement News*, April 15, 2003, pp. 1, 6.

Payne, Chris. "Property Crime Investigation Enters New Technology Era." *Law Enforcement Technology*, July 2003, pp. 152–156.

Weisel, Deborah Lamm. *Burglary of Single-Family Houses.* Washington, DC: Office of Community Oriented Policing Services, Problem-Oriented Guides for Police Series, No. 18, July 25, 2002.

Larceny/Theft, Fraud, and White-Collar Crime

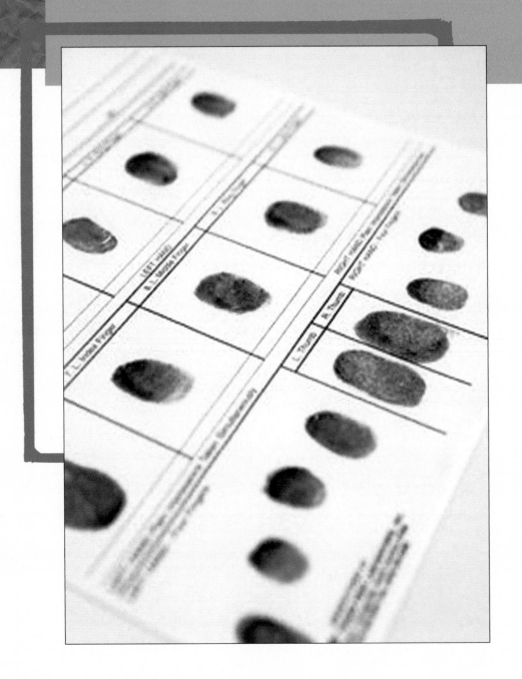

Can You Define?

Do You Know?

- How larceny differs from burglary and robbery?
- What the elements of larceny/theft are?
- What the two major categories of larceny are and how to determine them?
- What legally must be done with found property?
- What the common types of larceny are?
- Whether a shoplifter must leave the premises before being apprehended?
- When the FBI becomes involved in a larceny/theft investigation?
- What fraud is and how it differs from larceny/theft?
- What the common means of committing fraud are?
- What the common types of check fraud are?
- What the elements of the crime of larceny by debit or credit card are?
- What form of larceny/theft headed the FTC's top 10 consumer fraud complaints in 2004?
- What white-collar crime is and what offenses are often included in this crime category?
- What the nature of the FBI's two-pronged approach to investigating money laundering is?
- What the main problems in prosecuting environmental crime are?

Outline

Larceny/theft is one of the eight Part One crimes. Although fraud, white-collar crime, and environmental crime are not Part One crimes, they are so closely related to larceny/theft that they are included in this chapter. Furthermore, they all have elements in common and are investigated in similar ways.

Some states eliminate the distinctions between larceny, fraud, and white-collar crimes, combining them into the single crime of *theft*. However, because many states have separate offenses, this chapter discusses them separately. The distinction may be unimportant in your jurisdiction.

Reported larceny/thefts exceed the combined total of all other Part One crimes. Data from the FBI (*Crime in the United States 2003,* p.49) show that there were more than 7 million estimated larceny/thefts in the United States during 2003, costing victims an estimated $4.9 billion in losses. Larceny/thefts accounted for 67.3 percent of the estimated total property crimes. Nationwide, law enforcement cleared 18.0 percent of all reported larceny/thefts in 2003 (*Crime in the United States 2003,* p.53).

Investigators may find themselves working a case with the FBI if the matter involves fraud, theft, or embezzlement within or against the national or international financial community. The FBI notes: "These crimes are characterized by deceit, concealment, or violation of trust, and are not dependent upon the application or threat of physical force or violence" (*Financial Crimes,* p.A1). The priority problem areas of this category of crime identified by the FBI's Financial Crimes Section (FCS) include corporate fraud, health care fraud, mort-

gage fraud, identity theft, insurance fraud, and money laundering. One unit of the FCS, the Economic Crimes Unit, investigates significant frauds targeted against individuals, businesses, and industries such as corporate fraud, securities and commodities fraud, telemarketing fraud, insurance fraud not related to health care, Ponzi schemes, advance fee schemes, and pyramid schemes. While these crimes may be investigated and prosecuted at the federal level, the victims typically call the local police first.

This chapter begins with an overview of larceny/theft, a discussion of the elements of the crime, classification of such crimes, and how "found property" fits. Then follows a description of the preliminary investigation, the various types of larceny/theft that might be investigated, and proving the elements of the crime. The chapter then focuses on the various types of fraud that investigators might encounter, including the devastating crime of identity theft. The chapter concludes with a presentation of white-collar crime as a constellation of numerous economic or corporate crimes, including corporate fraud, money laundering, embezzlement, and environmental crime.

Larceny/Theft: An Overview

 arceny/theft is the unlawful taking, carrying, leading, or driving away of property from the possession of another. Larceny is committed through the cunning, skill, and criminal design of the professional thief or as a crime of opportunity committed by the rank amateur. The adage that "there is a little larceny in everyone" has considerable truth. Although some thefts result from revenge or spite, the motive for most larcenies is the same for the professional and the amateur thief—monetary gain: either actual cash or articles that can be converted to cash or personal use.

> Both larceny and burglary are crimes against property, but larceny, unlike burglary, does not involve illegally entering a structure. Larceny differs from robbery in that no force or threat of force is involved.

Elements of the Crime

 he crime of larceny/theft takes many forms, but the basic elements of the offense are similar in the statutes of every state.

> The elements of the crime of larceny/theft are:
> - The felonious stealing, taking, carrying, leading, or driving away,
> - of another's personal goods or property,
> - valued above (grand) or below (petty) a specified amount,
> - with the intent to permanently deprive the owner of the property or goods.

Felonious Stealing, Taking, Carrying, Leading, or Driving Away This element requires an unlawful, wrongful, or felonious removal of the property; that is, the property is removed by any manner of stealing. Taking items such as fuel and electricity is also included in this element. Withholding property is a form of larceny by a failure to ever return, or properly account for, the property or to deliver the property to the rightful owner when it is due. Failure to pay a debt is *not* larceny, even though there is a failure to pay. Civil remedies are sought for this type of theft.

The Personal Goods or Property of Another Goods or **property** refers to all forms of tangible property, real or personal. It includes valuable documents; electricity, gas, water, and heat supplied by municipalities or public utility companies; and domestic animals such as cats, dogs, and livestock. It also includes property in which the accused has a co-ownership, lien, pledge, bailment, lease, or other subordinate interest. Larceny laws also cover cases in which the property of a partnership is converted to one partner's personal use adverse to the other partner's rights, except when the accused and the victim are husband and wife.

In the definition of larceny/theft, *another* refers to an individual, a government, a corporation, or an organization. This element refers to the true owner or the one authorized to control the property. Care assignment, personal custody, or some degree of legal control is evidence of possession. In numerous cases ownership has been questioned. Ownership usually designates the true owner or the person who has superior rights at the time of the theft. The owner must support the charge of larceny; otherwise, there is no prosecution.

Of a Value above or below a Specified Amount
Value determines whether the offense is grand or petty larceny. Value refers to the market value at the time of the theft. Value is determined by replacement cost, legitimate market value, value listed in government property catalogs, fair market value, or reasonable estimates.

If the property is restored to the owner, value means the cost-equivalent of the property's use or the damage it sustained, whichever is greater, during the time the owner was deprived of its possession. However, this cannot exceed the original value declared.

If several items are stolen in a single crime, the value of *all* items combined determines the value of the loss, even if the property belonged to more than one owner. Identical items stolen from different larceny locations are not combined but are treated as separate offenses.

With the Intent to Permanently Deprive the Owner of the Property or Goods
Intent either exists at the time the property was taken or is formed afterward. The person may have intended only to borrow the property but then decided to keep it permanently. Intent is usually the most difficult element to prove. Establish ownership through documents of purchase, statements describing how the property was possessed, the length of time of possession, and details of the delegation of care and control to another by the true owner.

Because of its frequency, much police time is devoted to larceny, and individual merchants and private security forces are also involved (Figure 14.1). Millions of dollars in losses go unreported each month. Those that are reported are usually for the purpose of collecting insurance rather than in the hope of recovering the property or clearing the case.

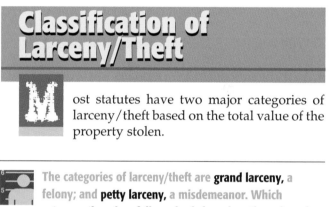

Classification of Larceny/Theft

Most statutes have two major categories of larceny/theft based on the total value of the property stolen.

The categories of larceny/theft are **grand larceny,** a felony; and **petty larceny,** a misdemeanor. Which category the crime falls under is based on the value of the property stolen.

In many states the amount of theft that predicates grand larceny is $100 or more; any lesser amount is petty (petit) larceny. Check the laws in your jurisdiction

Figure 14.1
To help prevent theft, a security guard monitors the facilities of a California computer company using multi-image closed-circuit television sets.

© Bill Varie/CORBIS

for the dollar value that distinguishes petty and grand larceny. It is important to know whether the crime is a misdemeanor or a felony before proceeding with the investigation.

Found Property

 Keeping or selling property lost by the owner is a form of theft.

 In most states taking found property with the intent to keep or sell it is a crime.

Although the finder has possession of the property, it is not legal possession. Thieves apprehended with stolen property often claim to have found it—an invalid excuse. A reasonable effort must be made to find the owner of the property—for example, by making inquiries or advertising in a newspaper. The owner, if located, must pay the cost of such inquiries before the property is returned.

If the owner is not located after reasonable attempts are made to do so and after a time specified by law, the finder of the property can legally retain possession of it.

The Preliminary Investigation

Investigating larceny/theft is similar to investigating a burglary, except that in a larceny/theft, even less physical evidence is available because no illegal or forcible entry occurred. Physical evidence might include empty cartons or containers, empty hangers, objects left at the scene, footprints, and fingerprints.

Do not give the complainant or victim the impression that the investigation of the reported theft is unimportant. If there is little hope of recovering the property or finding the thief, inform the complainant of this, but only after you obtain all the facts.

Types of Larceny/Theft

The Uniform Crime Reports for 2003 indicate the relative frequency of each type of larceny (Figure 14.2). The growing problem of identity theft is discussed later in the chapter.

 Common types of larceny are purse snatching, pocket picking, theft from coin machines, shoplifting, bicycle theft, theft from motor vehicles, theft from buildings, theft of motor vehicle accessories, and jewelry theft.

Pickpockets and Purse Snatchers

Pickpockets are difficult to apprehend because the victim must identify the thief. This proves challenging, if not impossible, unless the thief is observed by someone else or is caught in the act. The purse opener and purse snatcher are modern versions of the pickpocket. These thieves use force if necessary but generally rely instead on their skills of deviousness and stealth to avoid the use of force and evade identification. These types of thefts are sometimes called *distraction thefts* because of how the offender gains access to the victim's property. The two necessary elements of this crime are a distraction followed by an extraction, the actual theft. According to Vincent (p.117): "Distract theft reports may fall into either larceny or robbery statistics, but the vast majority of incidents aren't reported at all." Lost wallets and purses, often the work of the pickpocket, are often not reported as thefts because the victims do not realize that theft has occurred. Vincent (p.117) surmises: "Lost property reports, therefore, may be an indicator of a distraction theft problem."

Vincent (p.116) states: "Pickpocketing may be an inconspicuous problem, yet major public events attract hoards of thieves along with the tourists and their fat wallets." Sporting events, New Year's Eve parties, Mardi Gras and other parades, rock concerts, fairs and festivals, public transportation, and commuter trains present ideal situations for the pickpocket, full of potential victims in tight, distracted crowds. Vincent (p.118) suggests some behaviors to watch for when investigating possible pickpocket operations:

> Watch for suspicious behaviors, such as constantly looking around, meeting and separating, frequent changing of seats at an event, and positioning around a target. Look for unnatural elbow and shoulder movement. Work in two-person teams, and get close enough to see an extraction, even at the risk of being noticed.
>
> Say you spot an extraction, who do you arrest? Follow the money, while your partner secures the victim. If the incident occurs before or during a concert, game, or show, get the victim's driver's license and follow up with him when it's over.

Other behavior that may indicate a pickpocket at work is "looping," in which a suspect exits at one train or bus door and reboards at another (p.119). Another common tactic is for pickpockets to immerse themselves in a crowd getting onto a bus or train and take advantage of the jostling body contact that almost always occurs during a boarding rush. Watch for "passengers"

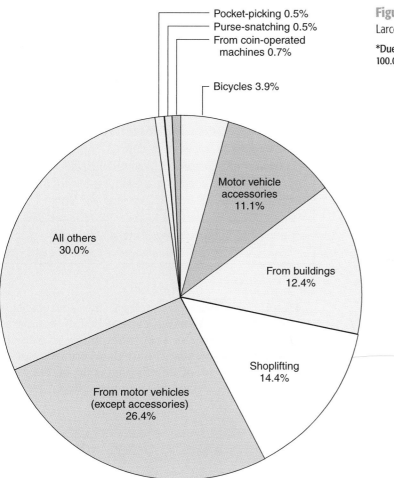

Figure 14.2

Larceny/theft, percent distribution,* 2003

*Due to rounding, the percentages may not add to 100.0.

who join the crowd rushing toward the vehicle doorway but then, at the last minute, fail to board.

Purse snatching may be a larceny/theft or a robbery depending on whether force is used. There are two distinct types of purse snatches. One type occurs when a victim is seated at a bus stop, outdoor restaurant, gambling casino, or similar public place and sets a purse, bag, or like item on the seat or floor next to her, and a thief grabs the property and runs off with it. Because this act lacks the element of use of force, it qualifies as a larceny/theft. The other type occurs when a victim is clutching a bag or purse tightly, has a purse strap over her shoulder or has used some similar means of securing the property, and force is used by the thief to seize it, qualifying the act as a robbery. As a general rule, investigators should determine whether the victim experienced any sensation of force being used, since any force, no matter how slight, would satisfy the element of robbery. The statement of the victim on this point will be a critical factor for the prosecutor to determine whether to charge robbery or larceny/theft.

Obtain from the victim a description of what was stolen and its value. Ask if the victim recalls being jostled or distracted momentarily, and, if so, obtain complete details. Keep careful records of pickpockets and purse snatchers, as often they are caught.

Retail Shrinkage: Employee Theft, Shoplifting, and Vendor Theft/Fraud

Shrinkage refers to the unexplained or unauthorized loss of inventory, merchandise, cash, or any other asset from a retail establishment. Shrinkage results from employee theft, shoplifting, vendor theft/fraud, and human error. The 2004 National Retail Security Survey (Hollinger and Langton, p.6) compiled data regarding these sources of inventory shrinkage and reports the following percentages attributed to each category:

- 47.0 percent employee theft
- 34.0 percent shoplifting
- 14 percent administrative/paper error
- 5 percent vendor fraud

According to Lamb (p.46), the retail industry in the United States suffers an annual estimated loss of $46 billion because of shrinkage.

Employee Theft Although many assume that the majority of a retail company's shrinkage is the result of shoplifting, more thefts and losses from stores are internal, committed by employees. Lamb (p.46) notes that

30 percent of all business failures are due to employee theft and concludes: "By any measure, employee crime is a large and growing problem." Although retail shrinkage as a whole has declined for four consecutive years, the dollar loss per employee theft incident has increased over that time (Beaulieu, p.17). Hollinger and Langton (p.6) state: "Assuming a total shrinkage dollar total of approximately $31 billion, this [47% loss due to employee theft] translates into an annual employee theft price tag of $14.6 billion. This is a staggering monetary loss to come from a single crime type."

One recommendation for reducing employee theft is to keep the more expensive items under security lock and to have frank discussions with employees regarding the problem. Employees who are aware of management's policy regarding employee theft are less likely to steal. Some companies attempt to eliminate potential employee thieves by informing job applicants that a drug test is required, even if it is not. This announcement alone may weed out applicants who have a drug habit and therefore are more prone to steal to support it. According to Lamb (p.48), over 90 percent of Fortune 100 companies currently conduct preemployment substance abuse testing.

Shoplifting **Shoplifting,** also known as *boosting,* involves taking items from retail stores without paying for them. It is usually committed by potential customers in the store during normal business hours. It does *not* include thefts from warehouses, factories, or other retail outlets or thefts by employees.

Shoplifting has increased with modern merchandising techniques that display goods for sale, remove barriers between customers and merchandise, and permit potential buyers to pick up and handle goods. Most shoplifted items are on the main floor, from where it is easy to leave the store. Clarke (p.6) suggests the acronym CRAVED to highlight the characteristics of "hot products," those most likely to be shoplifted: "They are concealable, removable, available, valuable, enjoyable, and disposable. The last of these attributes, disposability, may be the most important in determining the volume of goods shoplifted."

Security technology is being employed to limit losses caused by shoplifting. For example, electronic article surveillance (EAS) uses small security tags applied to high-theft merchandise that alert retailers when shoplifters try to take stolen items through electronic sensors at exit doors. Systems using radio frequency identification (RFID) are also becoming more popular among retailers.

Closed-circuit television (CCTV) has become a standard security tool to curb shoplifting and help in the apprehension and prosecution processes (Figure 14.3). Martinez ("CCTV," p.58) asserts that shoplifters who seek to remain invisible to store employees cannot usually hide from well-placed CCTV cameras. Furthermore: "Stores with visible CCTV systems are less likely to be targeted by burglars."

> ## Technology Innovations
>
> RFID is an emerging technology housed in tiny tags or devices—some smaller than a grain of rice—that emit unique identifying codes when read by special scanners. . . .
>
> RFID applications range from inventory control to cattle tracking to law enforcement. . . . The Department of Defense and giant retailers like Wal-Mart, Target, and Albertsons are moving toward universal use of the technology. The Food and Drug Administration has decided to use RFID to thwart prescription drug counterfeiting (Page, p.128).

Despite advancing technology, the apprehension rate for shoplifters remains extremely low compared with the total number of shoplifting offenses committed. Clarke (p.1) contends: "Police data seriously underrepresent the extent of shoplifting—one of the most common but least detected and reported crimes." He (p.2)

Figure 14.3

Inventor F. Jerry Gutierrez demonstrates one of his surveillance mannequins designed to watch for shoplifters. They are being photographed by the photographer shown on the television monitor.

cites a study that found that only about 1 in 150 shoplifting incidents resulted in the offender's apprehension and subsequent police action. Of all shoplifters apprehended, less than one-quarter are prosecuted (Dabney et al., p.695).

Most apprehensions are by private security forces working for department stores and shopping centers or by floorwalkers or supervisory personnel. Stores that detect and apprehend shoplifters often do not prosecute because it is a relatively expensive course of action to take when compared with the value of the item(s) shoplifted. Other reasons for not prosecuting are fear of facing a false arrest suit, the hope that a reprimand will cure the problem, or the belief that notifying a juvenile shoplifter's parents will control the situation. Managers sometimes call the police for the chastening effect it will have on the shoplifter, but if the property is recovered, they often decline to sign a formal complaint.

If a charge is made by a merchant or merchant's employee, officers may arrest a suspected shoplifter without a warrant if reasonable cause exists for believing that the person has attempted or actually committed shoplifting. In some states store personnel themselves are encouraged to interview the suspect because they are not police officers and thus do not have to warn suspects of their rights.

Elements of Larceny by Shoplifting
The elements of shoplifting are very similar to those required for general larceny. They include:

- Intentionally taking or carrying away, transferring, stealing, concealing, or retaining possession of merchandise or altering the price of the merchandise,
- without the consent of the merchant,
- with intent to permanently deprive the merchant of possession or of the full purchase price.

 Altering the price of an item is considered larceny. It is usually not required that the person leave the premises with the stolen item before apprehension.

Early laws required that a shoplifter leave a store before an apprehension could be made. However, many laws have been changed to permit apprehension after the suspect has passed the last cashier's counter in the store for the particular level or department. The farther the suspect is from the normal place of payment, the greater the degree of intent shown to permanently deprive the merchant of the item. After being told why, the suspect may be detained for a reasonable time and then delivered to a police officer, parent, or guardian.

Because intent is absent, it is not a crime for a person to walk out of a store after simply forgetting to pay for an item. This is a common problem for individuals who suffer from Alzheimer's disease and some other types of mental impairment. Such people may forget that they have picked up an item, may forget to pay for it, or may honestly believe that they have paid for it when they have not. Such incidents require officers to exhibit patience and excellent communication skills in resolving the situation.

Because shoplifting can be either petty or grand larceny, a misdemeanor or a felony, the value of the property must be established. If the shoplifter is placed under arrest, the stolen item should be recovered and retained as evidence. Whether the individual is prosecuted depends on the individual's attitude, the policy of the store and the police department, the value of the property taken, and how many of the legal requirements for prosecution are fulfilled. Evidence to support shoplifting or altering a price requires an eyewitness or proof that the item could not have been removed except by the person charged. The property must be carried away or removed but not necessarily to outside the store. The manager or clerk should identify the property and show proof of the store's ownership.

Proving the intent to permanently deprive is the most difficult problem in investigating shoplifting. This intent is shown by the shoplifter's actions from the time the item was stolen until the arrest was made. Stores are legally within their rights to recover items taken from a store if there is no proof of purchase. This does not mean the person is guilty of shoplifting. It may be impossible to prove intent to steal.

If a store manager wants to prosecute, review the store's reports to determine whether a crime has been committed. If it has, take the shoplifter to the police station and book and search him or her for additional property. The store personnel making the arrest must sign a complaint. Most shoplifters never reach the stage of arrest and release to the police. When it does occur, encourage store cooperation, because good arrests by store personnel aid convictions and can deter shoplifting in the particular store.

Overcrowded courts have become a problem to retailers who want to prosecute for shoplifting. Prosecutors have difficulty obtaining convictions. Many states have passed statutes providing for civil fines instead of or in combination with criminal penalties. Retailers are dissatisfied with criminal prosecution because of the delays, low conviction rate, and lack of restitution for the lost property. The civil approach permits the retailer to sue in small claims court, even in cases in which the offender is not convicted of a crime. Penalties under civil action range from $50 to $500, or in some cases actual damages plus five times the value.

Faced with the many challenges encountered in prosecuting shoplifters, Clarke (p.3) observes: "It is tempting for police to wash their hands of shoplifting and let the shops bear the consequences." However, this attitude may be shortsighted on the part of law enforcement because, according to Clarke:

- Shoplifting is often considered an entry crime from which juveniles or others graduate to more serious offenses.

- Shoplifting seriously erodes profits and leads to store closures, which, particularly in economically deprived neighborhoods, depresses employment prospects and further erodes the amenities and overall quality of life in such neighborhoods.
- Shoplifting is often thought to fuel the drug trade by providing an "income" with which addicts can buy more drugs.

In addition to contributing to the trade in and abuse of drugs, shoplifting has been recognized as a way for terrorist and organized crime groups to generate revenue.

Terrorist and Organized Crime Theft According to Hayes and Rogers (p.82): "Organized Retail Crime (ORC) is extensive, multilayered, and complex," generating between $12 billion and $35 billion in losses to U.S. retailers every year. They (p.83) also stress that ORC is more than simple property crime; it can involve sophisticated credit card and check fraud schemes as well as cargo hijacking. Martinez ("Selling Retail," p.46) notes: "One trend that is just beginning to be taken seriously is that of terrorist groups using organized retail theft as a significant funding source." Terrorist and other ORC groups "subcontract" with professional shoplifters, called *boosters,* to carry out the actual shoplifting of specific small, high-priced items that have a high resale value on the black market, such as baby formula, coffee, steaks, cigarettes, smoking cessation products, eyeglass frames, over-the-counter health products, razor blades, fragrances, batteries, Polaroid film, electronic goods, printer ink cartridges, power tools, and athletic apparel.

As Martinez ("Selling Retail", p.46) explains, the appeal of shoplifting as a fundraising avenue for terrorists and other ORC groups, as opposed to drug sales or other crimes, is that it is not treated as a serious crime and carries less severe consequences. A further benefit to offenders of this type of crime is the lack of specific legislation directed toward it. Smith (p.9) states:

> The FBI's Interstate Theft Task Force has been tracking the spread of these organized retail theft rings, and a number of major arrests have been made as a result of its investigations. To an extent, however, the FBI's efforts to combat organized interstate shoplifting has been limited by the fact that there is no federal law that specifically addresses organized retail theft. Because of the seriousness of this growing problem, organized retail theft is now the second highest domestic priority for the FBI due to the link that organized retail theft may have in helping to fund terrorism.

In addition to shoplifting, the retail industry also suffers shrinkage as a result of vendor fraud.

Vendor Fraud The Georgia Retail Association proclaims simply: "Vendor fraud is one of the easiest ways someone can steal from your business without being detected" (*Vendor Fraud*). Corporate Security Services has available on its website a list of possible indicators of retail vendor theft, the details of which exceed the scope of this discussion ("Possible Indicators"). What the list does provide in overview, however, is that vendors have successfully used a variety of techniques to defraud or steal from retailers. As with other sources of shrinkage, surveillance cameras and well-trained, vigilant employees can help greatly reduce a company's loss due to vendor fraud.

Bicycle Theft

As bicycles have increased in popularity, so has bicycle theft. According to the website of the National Bike Registry (www.nationalbikeregistry.com), more than 1.5 million bicycles, worth an estimated $200 million, are stolen each year in the United States. Experienced thieves can steal a locked bike in less than 20 seconds. And while nearly 50 percent of all stolen bicycles are recovered every year by law enforcement, only 5 percent are returned to their owners, because most bikes are unregistered.

Bicycles are most frequently stolen from schoolyards, college campuses, sidewalk parking racks, driveways, and residential yards. Juveniles are responsible for the majority of thefts, although some professional bike theft rings operate interstate, even exporting stolen bicycles out of the country. Stolen bikes are used for transportation; are sold on the street, at flea markets, or to bike stores; and are disposed of through fences. The National Bike Registry notes: "Within the drug trade, stolen bicycles are so common they can almost be used as currency. On the street, the value of a stolen bicycle is approximately 5–10% of the bicycle's original retail value, with an inverse relationship between value and percentage worth on the street" ("Crime and No Punishment"). In other words, less expensive bikes are resold for a higher percentage of their original price than are top-of-the-line bikes. In some bicycle thefts, the crime is grand larceny due to the high value of the stolen bike.

The professional thief, often using a van or covered truck, steals several expensive bikes at one time, takes them to a garage, and repaints them or dismantles them for parts. Bicycles are easy to disguise by painting over or removing ID tags. Many are immediately disassembled and sold for parts and are easily taken from one location to another by simply riding them or placing them in a vehicle trunk, van, or truck.

A single bike theft is best investigated by the patrol force. Determine the bicycle's value and have the owner sign a complaint. A juvenile apprehended for a single theft can be prosecuted, especially with a prior record of similar or other offenses. Restitution for damage and an informal probation are usually initiated. If multiple thefts have occurred, the offender usually goes to juvenile court. Adults are prosecuted by the same procedures used for other larcenies.

The investigative division compiles a list of bike complaints organized by make of bike, serial number, and color. Bike thefts are also entered into the police computer system. Patrol officers are given a bike "hot sheet" similar to that for stolen vehicles and periodically check bike racks at parks, schools, and business areas against this sheet.

Bikes are sometimes reported stolen to defraud insurance companies. Even if the bike is recovered, the owner has already collected its value, and there will seldom be a prosecution. Large numbers of thefts in a short time may indicate an interstate ring has moved into the community. These use covered trucks to transport bicycles from the area, making recovery almost impossible. However, when interstate or international bicycle theft rings attempt to dispose of their stolen inventory, their activity may become identifiable. For example, customs officials at a port in New Jersey have, at various times, noticed spikes in the number of shipments of both bicycles and bicycle parts ("Crime and No Punishment").

Identification of bicycles is difficult due to failure to have a registration system or to use one that exists, the complex method of providing serial numbers, and the fact that stolen bikes are often altered, dismantled, repainted, and resold.

Mail Theft

In the quest for new and easier ways to steal money, thieves are now targeting sites used daily as repositories for hundreds of thousands of dollars, sites often left unsupervised for hours—mailboxes. On certain days of the month, with tremendous predictability, many households receive government assistance checks. Other mailboxes hold numerous applications for credit cards or the actual cards themselves.

Mailboxes are used not only to receive money but to submit payments as well. Millions of people leave their bills, accompanied by checks, for pickup in their mailboxes. Thieves known as **flaggers** go around neighborhoods targeting mailboxes with their flags up, searching for envelopes containing checks and other forms of payment. Thieves may also raid the large blue mailboxes used by people who may not trust leaving their own flag up.

Once thieves have a check, they may call the bank posing as a legitimate business to confirm that the funds are available, or they may simply go ahead and alter the check, assuming it will clear. The thieves protect the check signer's signature using a "liquid skin" coating and then use another solution to strip off the remaining ink, thus enabling them to rewrite the check payable to another source and for another amount.

Jewelry Theft

According to the FBI ("Jewelry and Gem"), the jewelry industry loses more than $100 million each year to jewelry and gem theft. Most often stolen by sophisticated professional thieves, jewelry is also the target of armed robbers and burglars. Jewel thieves know the value of jewels, that they are extremely difficult to identify once removed from their settings, and that the rewards are higher for the amount of risk involved than in other types of larceny. They also have ready outlets for disposition.

Most jewelry thefts are from vehicles owned by jewelry salespeople, who typically carry thousands of dollars in jewels, and from private individuals known to be careless about the security of their jewelry. Jewel thieves also operate in stores, distracting the salesperson and then substituting a cheap facsimile for expensive jewelry. Jewel thieves tend to operate interstate and to use locally known fences. They have many ingenious methods to steal and hide jewelry.

The Jeweler's Security Alliance (JSA) published an alert in July 2005 to inform retail jewelry shop owners of a new trend in jewel theft—burglars entering a store overnight via the roof with the intention of carrying out an armed robbery when employees arrive at work the next morning (Goldman, "JSA Alert"). Four such robberies occurred between March 23, 2005, and June 12, 2005, and were spread around the country, with thefts occurring in Florida, New York, Nevada, and California.

Because jewel thieves operate interstate, the FBI becomes involved. The local FBI office maintains files of known jewel thieves and their last known operations; their pictures, descriptions, and modus operandis (MOs); and information about whether they are in or out of prison.

> Always inform the FBI of jewel thefts, even without immediate evidence of interstate operation.

Since 1992, the FBI's Jewelry and Gem (JAG) Program has helped local law enforcement investigators by providing a sophisticated and multijurisdictional response to these types of thefts ("Jewelry and Gem"). FBI jurisdiction is attained under Title 18, Sections 2314 and 2315. Section 2314 gives the FBI jurisdiction when the value exceeds $5,000 and the items are transported interstate or in foreign commerce and when the criminal knows the goods to be stolen, converted to personal use, or obtained fraudulently. Section 2315 gives the FBI jurisdiction when buyers of the goods know they are stolen, that they have been transported interstate or by foreign commerce, and that they are worth more than $5,000. Mailing packages that contain illegally obtained jewels to another state also constitutes interstate operation.

Investigating jewelry theft is the same as for any other larceny. To obtain physical evidence, search the crime scene as you would in a burglary. Obtain the names of people in neighboring rooms at motels and hotels. Interview employees and other possible witnesses.

Review the victim's account of the theft. Obtain a complete description of the jewelry, the value of each item, and the amount of insurance carried. Contact informants and have them be on the alert for information about the thieves and also the location of the stolen items.

Art Theft

The FBI ("Art Theft") reports losses due to art theft of $8 billion a year. This offense usually comes to the attention of law enforcement through an art gallery's report of a burglary or theft. In other instances art objects are recovered during the investigation of another crime, or the theft is reported by another police agency. The stolen objects are frequently held for a long time and are then sold or moved coast to coast or internationally for disposition.

Art theft is an international problem that is increasing. To cope with the problems resulting from the interstate and international nature of these thefts, the FBI created the National Stolen Art File (NSAF) in 1979. Administered through the FBI's Criminal Investigative Division, Violent Crimes and Major Offenders Section, Major Theft/Transportation Crimes Unit, the NSAF provides a computerized index of stolen art and cultural property as reported to the FBI by law enforcement agencies throughout the United States and internationally (FBI, "Art Theft"). For an object to be eligible for entry into the NSAF, it must meet the following criteria:

- The object must be of artistic or historical significance; this includes fine arts, decorative arts, antiquities, Asian art, Islamic art, ethnographic objects (Native American, African, Aboriginal), archaeological material, textiles, books and manuscripts, clocks and watches, coins, stamps, musical instruments, and scientific instruments.
- The object must be valued at $2,000 or more, or less if associated with a major crime.
- The request must come through a law enforcement agency accompanied by a physical description of the object, a photograph of the object, if available, and a copy of any police reports or other information relevant to the investigation.

Thefts of valuable art should be reported to the FBI and to Interpol, which also has an international stolen art file.

Few police officers have any training in identifying art, so they should conduct only the normal burglary, theft, or fraud investigation. Then an authenticity check of the art object should be conducted by the FBI and national art dealers. People who own art objects rarely have adequate descriptions or photos of each piece, and the pieces rarely have identification numbers. Investigators should submit to the FBI all known information concerning the theft and a photograph of the art if available.

The FBI's specialized art crime team consists of eight agents working in major art markets around the country, including New York, Los Angeles, and Philadelphia; two assistant U.S. attorneys; and several FBI analysts. The field agents are art savvy and can tell a Monet from a Manet; know the dealers, appraisers, collectors, curators, and auction houses; are well versed in the art markets; and are knowledgeable about the unique laws that apply. Art theft cases the FBI has handled in recent years include:

- January 2004: the return of a Civil War sword stolen from the U.S. Naval Academy museum in 1931.
- March 2004: the arrest of a Manhattan art dealer and gallery owner, later convicted on federal mail fraud charges for an international art forgery operation that spanned nearly two decades.
- February 2005: the return of eight ancient stone seals looted from Iraq during the aftermath of Saddam Hussein's fall.

The FBI is currently working a March 14, 2004, theft from the Las Vegas Elvis-A-Rama museum, in which thieves got away with several of the legendary performer's rings, other pieces of jewelry, and some other effects.

Numismatic Theft: Coins, Metals, and Paper Money

Thefts of coins, metals of various types, and paper money have also been increasing. Coin collections are typically stolen during commercial and residential burglaries. Obtain the exact description of the coins, the condition, any defects, scratches, dye breaks, how they were jacketed, and any other identifying information. The condition of coins determines their value; a coin in mint condition may be worth twice the value of a coin in poor condition. Stolen coins may be taken from one coast to the other for disposition. Large coin shows are held throughout the year in larger cities, usually at convention centers or hotels. If interstate transportation is suspected, notify the FBI.

Metals such as gold, copper, silver, and aluminum are valuable. Copper is obtained from electrical and telephone lines or from storage yards of these companies. Thieves have been known to cut down telephone lines and to strip electrical lines in remote areas. A weekly check of scrap yards may be advisable in some jurisdictions.

Agricultural Theft

In certain areas of the country, agricultural theft is an increasing problem that requires investigation. Such crimes may include theft of timber, cactus, livestock, farm equipment, and chemicals.

Timber Theft The U.S. Forestry Service estimates $100 million in lumber is stolen annually through illegal logging. Tree "rustlers" harvest **burls,** the large gnarly root at the base of walnut trees. Burls can weigh as much as 2,000 pounds and are used to make fine woodwork. Tree "tippers" harvest the tips of pine trees to make into wreaths. In one such theft case in northern Minnesota, thieves took more than 10,000 black spruce treetops valued at up to $80,000 ("A Possible Lead"). Investigators note that the thieves spared a 50-foot-wide buffer of trees around the crime scene so the missing treetops would be less visible from the nearby highway. If caught, the suspects would face felony theft and trespass charges.

A timber theft crime scene will usually contain traceable evidence, such as tire tracks, stumps, and other items the thief may have discarded or accidentally left behind. As part of a stolen timber investigation, investigators should know how the timber might be used. For example, Douglas fir is harvested for firewood, cedar for shake shingles and fence posts. Investigators can then contact area mills and timber buyers to obtain information that might help them apprehend the thief.

Cactus As communities have cropped up in the desert Southwest, the demand for landscape cactus has soared, and poachers have found a lucrative business in stealing these prickly plants. The theft of cactus has become such a problem in some areas of Arizona, Texas, and other western states that special police units have been formed to crack down on the crime. As noted in *Law Enforcement News*: "The black market for ocotillo, saguaro, hedgehog and barrel cactuses, fueled primarily by desert landscaping, exceeds $20 million a year in Arizona, where theft of a plant worth more than $500 is considered a felony" ("Crimes against Nature," p.6). A saguaro cactus, which can reach a height of 20 feet, can go for as much as $5,000 ("Crimes against Nature," p.6). Some jurisdictions, such as Lake Mead, Nevada, have gone so far as to implant computer ID chips in certain species of cactus to be able to track them if they go missing.

As with a timber theft, a cactus theft crime scene will likely contain tire tracks, shoe imprints, and perhaps residue from tools and equipment used to harvest the plants. Soil and sand samples from the crime scene may be linked to a particular vehicle used by the thieves or with transplanted cactuses at residences or commercial businesses.

Livestock Just as in the days of the Wild West, cattle rustlers are still around, stealing millions of dollars worth of cattle annually and showing no signs of stopping. For example, the South Dakota State Brand Board reported a 300 percent increase in cattle thefts between

2001 and 2002 and estimated that South Dakota ranchers lost in excess of $12 million to cattle theft in 2003 ("Forgoing Lassos," p.11). According to Barbassa (2004), cattle theft began soaring in 2003 as beef prices rose and high-protein diets gained popularity.

Most livestock is stolen from the open range and consequently may go undetected for weeks or even months. Cattle are usually stolen at night and are fairly easy to lure away because they are herd animals—once rustlers get one animal to come, the rest soon follow. Cattle rustlers are almost always armed because they often slaughter the animals on the spot, butcher them, and load them into refrigerated trucks. Investigators may need the help of stock auctioneers, slaughterhouses, feedlot operators and livestock associations when looking into these crimes.

Evidence in such cases again includes shoe and tire impressions, soil samples, broken fences and perhaps forged bills of sale. Livestock branding, a practice dating back to 2700 B.C., can also provide valuable evidence in cattle thefts. Brands, both hot irons and freeze brands, are unique identifying symbols placed on each animal of a specific ranch's herd. Brands are registered through a state's brand inspection office, which is generally under the jurisdiction of the state's department of agriculture. Blanton ("Reading") notes that even as early as 1885, Colorado had 12,000 registered brands and that Texas, in 2005, has approximately 230,000 brands registered.

Laughlin ("Brands") asserts: "Branding can be very important in proving ownership of lost or stolen animals. An unbranded animal is called a 'slick,' and is almost impossible to legally identify." Investigators working a livestock theft should be familiar with the branding process, where brands are typically placed on certain animals, and how to read brands. Laughlin notes: "Most states require a brand to be in a certain place on the animal's body and of sufficient size to be readily seen." In addition: "Brands, to the inexperienced, resemble hieroglyphics; to the experienced livestock person, however, they become a readable language. With practice and an understanding of some important brand terms, the average person can easily acquire basic skills in reading brands." Brands are read from left to right, top to bottom, and outside to inside (Figure 14.4).

Cattle are also ear marked and wattle marked, commonly with a knife, according to branding protocol. These cuts are further means of identification.

Horse rustling is another problem, with over 50,000 horses stolen annually. Like cattle, horses are herd animals and are fairly easy to steal once rustlers have lured one animal away. Sometimes after the desired horses are loaded onto a truck, the rustlers break down the fence and scatter the remaining horses. Owners may then think the horses broke out themselves, and those not recovered are simply lost. Most stolen horses are slaughtered, and the meat is sold in Europe and Japan. The United States is the world's leading exporter of

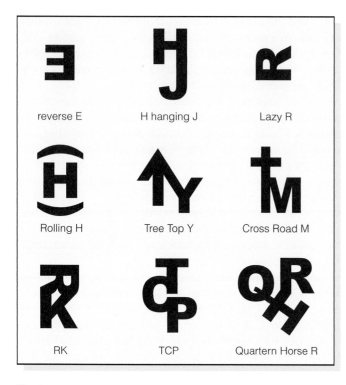

Figure 14.4
Cattle branding irons. Brands are composed of capital letters of the alphabet, numerals, pictures, and characters such as slashes, circles, crosses, and bars, with many combinations and adaptations. Letters can be used singly, joined, or in combinations. They can be upright, lying down ("lazy"), or reversed.

www.bbqblanton.com/puread.htm

horsemeat, which in many countries is considered better than our best steaks.

As with cattle, horses are branded, with various breeds being marked in specific locations: BLM (Bureau of Land Management) Mustangs are branded on the left side of their necks, registered Arabians on the right side of the neck, and Thoroughbreds have registration numbers tattooed under the upper lip (Laughlin, "Brands").

Brand altering is a common method used by livestock thieves to disguise the stolen animals, although with well-chosen and -designed brands, such alterations are very difficult to make appear original. To foil brand-altering rustlers, DNA analysis is now being used to identify stolen cattle (Barbassa, 2004). According to Babitsky (2004), director of the North American Rural Futures Institute, digital livestock identification software is now available to help identify and track ownership of branded cattle within minutes instead of days, as was previously the case.

Farm Equipment and Chemicals Farm equipment and chemicals are also targets for thieves. Because of their expense, pesticides and herbicides are especially attractive. Farmers themselves may be the thieves, or they may buy their chemicals and equipment at ridiculously low prices from such thieves. Evidence of this crime may be uncovered by examining purchasing records.

Fish and Wildlife Theft

Poaching is illegally taking or possessing fish, game, or other wildlife, including deer, elk, bear, pheasant, ducks, wild turkeys, and grouse. This crime may be committed by the amateur—the usually law-abiding hunter who is faced with an unexpected opportunity to poach, such as coming across an animal not in season to hunt while hunting another animal that is in season—or the professional poacher, who, in contrast, sets out to hunt prey illegally, often as a "trophy hunter." Hunting-license verifications and vehicle stops to check limits are two means of detecting poachers.

Game wardens may be of help in investigating fish and wildlife theft. Wardens know the hunting and wildlife laws, and they may be familiar with many of the local hunters and poachers and of certain poachers' MOs. Wardens can also help gather evidence.

A powerful computerized database, Green Parrot, has about 3,300 images and textual data for some 7,000 animal and 15,000 plant species. This database should enable police and customs authorities worldwide to more effectively investigate wildlife theft.

Cargo Theft

Nearly everything we wear, eat, and use at home or work has, at some point, been on the back of a truck. The amount of cargo crisscrossing our country is mind-boggling and critical to daily life. The increasing popularity of cargo theft is due to two primary features: It is low risk (few thieves are apprehended, prosecuted, or incarcerated), and it is extremely profitable. The direct cost of cargo theft in the United States is $12–15 billion annually ("Cargo Theft"). According to Hayes and Rogers (p.84): "Because trucks often travel in remote areas with large concentrations of desirable products and usually have just one person onboard, cargo theft can offer more reward with less risk than boosting."

The illegal or unauthorized removal of cargo from the supply chain is called **leakage**, a concept similar to that of shrinkage. Cargo theft can occur from an 18-wheel trailer, a shipping container left on a dock or placed on a railway, or a warehouse. While some cargo thieves will take whatever commodity crosses their path, many groups steal to order. Common commodities targeted include consumer electronics, designer clothing and fragrances, alcohol, and tobacco (author's e-mail correspondence with Tim Kennedy, former security expert for New York Harbor and Target Corp., August 3–4, 2005).

Methods used to steal cargo vary, and such crimes are generally extremely difficult to detect after they occur. In some cases, thieves break the locking mechanism off the back door of a trailer or container, or drill out a rivet holding the door in place, empty the cargo, and then shut the door again, sometimes taking the time to replace the rivet or otherwise visually disguise the

/Users/Chapter 14 / Larceny/Theft, Fraud, and White-Collar Crime / **405**

theft so that nothing looks amiss to a passing security guard. Other times the driver is highjacked en route. These "driver give-ups" typically happen close to major interstate corridors (author's interview with Thomas Bibb, Marion County [Florida] Sheriff's Office, August 11, 2005).

A large portion of cargo theft occurs from commercial truck stops. Thieves know that truck drivers usually cannot offload their cargo over a weekend; thus, drivers who stop on a Friday evening are likely to drop their trailer and take only the tractor for transportation until Monday morning. During that time, the unsupervised trailer is extremely vulnerable to theft (author's interview, Bibb). Other times, thieves wait at truck stops and, knowing that many drivers simply leave their truck running for the few minutes it takes them to grab some food or use a restroom, get in and drive the entire rig away.

Not uncommon are drivers who are part of the theft crew itself. For example, South American crews operating along the east coast, primarily in New York and New Jersey, commit "leakage theft," where one member works as a truck driver, picks up a legitimate load from a marine terminal or distribution center, and then diverts the cargo prior to delivery. The thieves enter the container or trailer, leaving the manifested seal intact, take out a portion of the load, and then close the container. When the load is delivered, it appears to be short-shipped (author's correspondence, Kennedy), i.e., that the mistake was made by the shipper.

Although arresting thieves is still a goal, many agencies, including the FBI, are now focusing on finding the source—the organized crime (OC) groups and their front businesses. Approximately half of all domestic cargo thefts are the result of OC, and law enforcement is now using criminal statutes that target money laundering to shut down cargo theft. Kennedy notes the existence of certain nontraditional OC groups who engage in cargo theft. Cuban and South American (Ecuadorian, Peruvian, etc.) groups operate nationwide and are fairly sophisticated. These groups typically work in cells or crews of three or four, occasionally more, and lack the typical hierarchy found in more traditional OC groups, such as La Cosa Nostra. The MOs do not vary much by group, except for the Asian and street gangs in Southern California who tend to be quite violent and will use guns to conduct armed hijackings.

Numerous challenges face cargo theft investigators. One problem is that cargo theft is not an Index crime. Such offenses may be reported as robbery, fraud, or theft. Efforts, however, are being made to overcome this inconsistency. Another problem centers on the mobile nature of the crime. Numerous jurisdictions around the country, particularly those close to major seaports and cargo distribution hubs, have developed cargo theft task forces to increase their effectiveness in conducting investigations. The success of these units has demonstrated that the surveillance and investigative abilities

of a multijurisdictional team surpass those of any single agency. Examples of these teams include the California Highway Patrol's Cargo Theft Interdiction Program (CTIP), which from 1994 through 2004 recovered more than $148 million in stolen property and 1,245 cargo loads ("Cargo Theft"), and the Tactical Operations Multi-agency Cargo Anti Theft Squad (TOMCATS) based in Miami-Dade County, Florida, comprising local, state, and federal law enforcement agencies engaged in complex investigations of commercial vehicle and cargo theft by OC groups. TOMCATS recovers approximately $30 million in stolen property each year ("Commercial Motor").

In the absence of a task force, experts recommend that an investigator work a cargo theft case backward, from the point of recovery to the initial loading of the product (author's correspondence, Kennedy). Contact the container or trailer carrier for information on where the load should be. If the theft was from a refrigerated container, known as a *reefer*, collect the temperature chart as evidence. This chart will reveal a spike in temperature whenever the container was opened and will, presumably, indicate when the theft occurred (author's correspondence, Kennedy)

Often discussed with cargo theft, particularly post-9/11, is the broader topic of supply chain integrity, which is concerned not only with those items taken out of the supply chain but also with those inserted into the chain. Rogers et al. (p.26) stress that while cargo theft remains a concern, "of equal or even greater importance is the illicit introduction of things like weapons of mass destruction or bioterrorism into the supply chain." Furthermore, a proven nexus exists between organized retail crime, cargo theft, and terrorism (author's correspondence, Kennedy).

Proving the Elements of the Crime

T o prove the felonious stealing, taking, carrying, leading, or driving away of property, you must gather enough evidence to prove that the property is missing—not simply misplaced. Obtain proof of ownership through bills of sale or receipts or through evidence that the owner had custody or possession of or responsibility for the item. Determine the item's value by ascertaining its replacement cost or legitimate market value or by obtaining reasonable estimates. The owner can testify to the actual value if he or she is familiar with the specific item and its quality and condition at the time of the theft. Persons with business knowledge of similar items can help determine value. If certain items obviously exceed the petty larceny limitation, it is not necessary to know their exact value. Take statements from the owner regarding where the property was located and what security was provided. Also obtain evidence that the owner no longer possesses the property.

Intent to permanently deprive the owner of the property is shown by the suspect's selling, concealing, hiding, or pawning the property or converting it to personal use. Intent is proven by a motive of revenge, possession under circumstances of concealment, denial of possession where possession is proven, or flight from normal residence.

Fraud

 raud is a general term used for deceit, trickery, and cheating as well as to describe the activity of individuals who pretend to be what they are not. Legally, however, fraud has a narrower meaning.

 Fraud is an intentional deception to cause a person to give up property or some lawful right. It differs from theft in that fraud uses deceit rather than stealth to obtain goods illegally.

Advances in technology and, in particular, the proliferation of electronic commerce have given innovative criminals yet another way to commit fraud. Use of computers to commit fraud is discussed in Chapter 17.

Fraud victims are in a good position to provide information regarding suspects because they have had firsthand dealings with the suspects.

 Fraud includes confidence games, real estate fraud, insurance fraud, health care fraud, telephone fraud, mail fraud, and fraud committed through counterfeiting or the use of checks or debit/credit cards. An increasingly serious and pervasive type of fraud is identity theft.

Because fraud often involves use of interstate communications devices (e.g., phones, computers), the mail system, and/or financial and banking institutions, many, if not most, types of fraud fall under the jurisdiction of the FBI.

Confidence Games

Confidence games have separated people from their money for centuries; in fact, con games were known as early as 100 B.C. Changing times require changing techniques, but four basic elements are always present: (1) locating a mark from whom to obtain money,

(2) selecting the game, (3) conducting it, and then (4) leaving the area as rapidly as possible.

A **confidence game** obtains money or property by a trick, device, or swindle that takes advantage of a victim's trust in the swindler. The confidence game purports to offer a get-rich-quick scheme. The victim is sworn to secrecy and told that telling anyone could cause the deal to fall through or the profits to be divided among more people. The game may require the victim to do something dishonest or unethical, thus making the victim less apt to report the swindle to the police. It is often conducted away from the victim's hometown so that the victim cannot obtain advice from friends.

A particular type of person is needed to make the con game work. Con artists develop cunning, guile, and skills through their own systems of learning and education. They are taught by older persons in the "trade," usually starting as the "number two" or "straight man." As they gain experience, they work their way up until they are the "number one" in a swindle of their own. Con artists understand human nature, are extremely convincing, lack conscience, have an uncanny ability to select the right victim, and have no mercy for their victims, often extracting the life savings of elderly people.

Two basic approaches are used in con games: the short con and the long con. **Short-con games** take the victims for whatever money they have with them at the time of the action. For example, three-card monte, similar to the old shell game, entices victims to bet on whether they can select one card from among three. "Huge Duke" involves betting on a stacked poker hand, with the victim dealing the final hand. "The Wipe" involves tying money into a handkerchief for safekeeping and then switching it with one containing newspaper bits. **Long-con games** are usually for higher stakes. For example, in "The Wire," the original long-con game, the victim is enticed to bet on horse races, convinced through an elaborate telegraph office setup that the manager can beat the bookmaker by delaying the results of the race long enough to let the victim and other cohorts in the scheme make bets. After allowing the victim to win a few games at low stakes, the "big bet" is made in which the victim may lose thousands of dollars.

When investigating con-game fraud, obtain a complete description of the confidence artists and the type of fraud, trick, or false pretense they used, as well as the exact amount of money involved.

Because the victim usually sees and talks with the con artists, it is often easy to identify them, but unless the police are notified quickly, the suspects will be gone from the area. Obtain descriptions of the perpetrators and their MO. Keep this information on file for future reference.

The FBI maintains a confidence artist file to assist in locating such suspects, as well as a general appearance file of con artists (even though photographs are not available). The FBI assists in investigating violations that occur on interstate conveyances such as planes, boats, and trains. It also assists if there is evidence that radio, television, or telegraph was used in committing the crime or if a money order was sent to a person in another state. If the swindle exceeds $5,000, the FBI has jurisdiction under the Interstate Transportation of Stolen Property Act. (Many con games exceed this amount.) Postal authorities may assist investigators in cases in which confidence artists use the mails to execute their crimes.

Most states include con games in statutes relating to larceny by trick and to obtaining money under false pretenses. Check the statutes in your jurisdiction for the specific elements that must be proven.

Other Scams   Other scams that investigators may be summoned to examine include:

- *Easy-credit scams.* Con artists target people who seek to repair damaged credit ratings by offering credit cards in exchange for advanced payments or deposits.

- *Bogus prize offers.* Mail or phone announcements proclaim, "You're a big winner!" The winner is instructed to wire money to cover taxes or fees to receive the "grand prize."

- *Phony home repairs.* Workmen knock on a door and explain that they are finishing several jobs (roofing, siding, driveways) in the neighborhood. They have leftover material and can offer to fix anything at a great discount. They may take a deposit or the entire payment and never return to complete the job, or they may begin the work and then claim the job is more involved than they had thought and state they will need additional payment to finish the job.

- *Travel scams.* Victims are promised an exciting, free vacation in an exotic location but must first provide a credit card number for "verification."

- *Cyber-scams.* The Internet offers numerous sites to sell or trade merchandise, and con artists are taking advantage of this lucrative virtual swap shop to sell defective or nonexistent products.

Although it may be hard to believe that people would fall for some of these scams, con artists are extremely well versed and tend to target more typically vulnerable and trusting victims, such as the elderly.

Real Estate and Mortgage Fraud

In many areas of the country, populations are booming, and the corresponding real estate markets and mortgage industries are also thriving. In some communities, however, real estate scams, such as phantom down payments and "flipping," are costing lenders and homebuyers tremendous amounts of money. The FBI states: "People want to believe their homes are worth more than they are, and with housing booms going on throughout the U.S., there are people who try to capi-talize on the situation and make an easy profit" (*Financial Crimes*, p.D11).

According to the FBI: "Each mortgage fraud scheme contains some type of 'material misstatement, misrepresentation, or omission relied upon by an underwriter or lender to fund, purchase or insure a loan'" (*Financial Crimes*, p.D1). Common mortgage fraud schemes include equity skimming, air loans, foreclosure schemes, inflated appraisals, nominee loans/straw buyers, and silent seconds (pp.D10–D11). In **property flipping,** the offender buys a property near its estimated market value, artificially inflates the property value through a false appraisal, and then resells (flips) the property, often within days of the original purchase, for a greatly increased price. This process can be repeated several times with a single property through the help of the flipper's associates, ultimately leading to foreclosure by the victim lenders. Many deals rely on fraudulent appraisals inflating the property's value. Although flipping *per se* is not illegal, it often involves mortgage fraud, which is illegal.

Insurance Fraud

The insurance industry is one of the largest in the United States, comprising more than 7,000 companies collecting over $1 trillion in annual premiums (*Financial Crimes*, p.F1). Insurance fraud affects every policyholder in the form of higher premiums. According to the FBI, insurance fraud (not including health care insurance) costs the average American family $400–700 every year, for a total cost in excess of $40 billion.

The most prevalent type of insurance fraud involves premium diversion by insurance agents and brokers, where customers' payments are pocketed for personal gain instead of being sent to the policy underwriter (*Financial Crimes,* p.F1). Scams run by unauthorized, unregistered, and unlicensed agents are also common and involve the collection of premiums for nonexistent policies. The scam lasts as long as customers have no claims. Once claims start to be filed, the fraudster closes up shop and relocates. These kinds of fraudulent operations take advantage of individuals who seek high-risk lines of insurance for which few legitimate providers exist.

Another type of insurance fraud involves worker's compensation, in which, like other insurance fraud schemes, the con operator collects a premium without providing any legitimate protection against claims. This type of fraud can leave injured victims and families of deceased victims with little or no coverage to pay their medical bills.

Insurance companies are duty-bound to hold customer premiums secure until such time as a claim is made. However, when the economy takes a downturn and finances become strained, some insurance executives fraudulently dip into this premium pool to cover their own company's operating expenses. This illegal act leads to further illegal acts as accounting documents and financial statements must be doctored to cover up the misuse of customer premiums (*Financial Crimes*, p.F1).

The FBI has recently investigated and shut down several highly profitable insurance fraud schemes. For example, Operation Short Tail involved a network of 70 bogus insurance companies that, once closed and liquidated, yielded more than $50 million in recovered premiums. Operation Soft Assets focused on a married couple who, with the help of more than 90 accomplices, ran a Ponzi-type nationwide property and casualty insurance scam, collecting customer premiums on high-risk insurance products, backed by nonexistent offshore assets (FBI, "Insurance Fraud"). A **Ponzi scheme,** named after Charles Ponzi, whose pyramid-type fraud scheme during the 1920s led to a major federal investigation, involves using capital from new investors to pay off earlier investors. This scheme requires an ever-expanding base of new investors to support the financial obligations to the existing "higher ups," hence the pyramidal shape used to depict such structures.

Insurance businesses are regulated primarily by the states in which they operate. The National Association of Insurance Commissioners (NAIC) is a nonprofit association of state officials who help state insurance regulators achieve fundamental industry goals and serve the public interest. The NAIC assists the FBI in insurance fraud investigations, helping to identify not only those perpetrating fraud but also the most commonly used schemes to commit insurance fraud. The FBI is also a member of the International Association of Insurance Fraud Agencies (IAIFA), a nonprofit group that addresses insurance-related financial crimes on a global basis (*Financial Crimes*, p.F1).

Insurance fraud investigations often require the collaborative efforts of the FBI, NAIC, IAIFA, state fraud bureaus, and state insurance regulators. In addition to traditional investigation methods, the FBI uses covert undercover investigations to apprehend fraudsters.

Health Care Fraud

As with insurance fraud, health care fraud adds billions of dollars each year to U.S. health care costs. Noting that Medicare and Medicaid are the most visible programs affected by such fraud, the FBI reports: "Estimates of fraudulent billings to health care programs, both public and private, are . . . between 3 and 10 percent of total health care expenditures. The fraud schemes are not specific to any general area, but are found throughout the entire country" (*Financial Crimes*, p.C1). The FBI expects health care fraud to continue rising as people live longer. One of the most serious trends observed involves the increased number of medical professionals willing to risk patient harm in their fraud schemes, which can include unnecessary surgeries, dilution of cancer and other lifesaving drugs, and fraudulent lab tests (p.C3).

Telephone Fraud

Telemarketing fraud and other types of fraud using the telephone have proliferated, and the victims are predominantly the elderly. In one such scam, a "representative" informs potential victims that they have won a sweepstakes prize and that the company needs their name, address, and Social Security number to process the award. The company then uses the Social Security number for fraudulent purposes. Other scams simply involve informing the "winner," aka victim, that he or she must first pay a service fee or tax for their prize and that once the payment has been received, the prize will be shipped. Of course, it never is. According to the FBI: "Telemarketing fraud, predominantly emanating from Canada, is a flourishing crime problem with estimated losses to U.S. elderly citizens exceeding $500 million per year. In the past it has been difficult to prosecute Canadian telemarketers due to a variety of factors. However, substantial strides have been made to address these issues through the cross-border initiative, Canadian Eagle" (*Financial Crimes*, p.G1).

Frauds involving cellular phones and personal communication services (PCS) are growing problems. One prevalent form of high-tech fraud is cloning, or "grabbing." Individuals obtain legitimate account information by theft from an owner carrier or by on-the-air interception. The thief then programs the account number into a cellular or PCS telephone, creating a clone of the legitimate phone (Figure 14.5). Dodge (p.358) notes: "The 1984 divestiture of AT&T created a proliferation of telecommunication services and wide-spread opportunities for corporate and consumer fraud." She (pp.359–363) describes some of the most popular telephone scams:

- **Slamming** is the unauthorized switch of a long-distance carrier, representing the number-one and fastest-growing category of complaints to the FCC.
- **Cramming** involves billing consumers for unauthorized, misleading, or deceptive charges, such as a personal 800 number, paging, and voice mail. The vendor levies the charge against a phone number, and the phone company is required by law to pass the charges on to the customer. Because the amounts are typically quite small, many customers never even notice they have been scammed.
- **Gouging** refers to companies charging undisclosed fees when calls are made from pay phones or hotel rooms.
- **Sliding** occurs when an unauthorized carrier switches a specific call from the long-distance carrier.
- **Jamming** refers to setting up roadblocks to make it difficult to switch in-state long distance.
- **Fluffing** occurs when rates are increased without notification.

Caller ID can both enhance *and hinder* fraud investigations. It can identify perpetrators of fraud, but it can

© Ingram Publishing/Alamy

Figure 14.5
While talking on a cell phone, a person is vulnerable to having the phone number "grabbed" and used by someone illegally.

also pose a danger to officers who work undercover. They may be exposed by having their telephone numbers revealed to the criminals they telephone.

Mail Fraud

Mail fraud involves the perpetuation of scams through use of the mail—for example, bogus sweepstakes entries and notices. If mail fraud is suspected, police officers should contact the postal inspector through their local post office. Postal authorities can assist in investigating if the fraud scheme uses the mails to obtain victims or to transport profits from crime.

Counterfeiting

Counterfeiting of money generally comes to the attention of the police through a retailer or a bank. The U.S. Secret Service publishes pamphlets on identifying counterfeit money (Figure 14.6). The most common denominations of counterfeit money are $10, $20, and $50. The paper of authentic bills has red and blue fibers embedded in it, and the bills have intaglio printing. The portrait is detailed and lifelike; the Treasury seal is clear and distinct on sawtooth points; the borders are clear and unbroken; and serial numbers are distinct, evenly spaced, and the same color as the Treasury seal.

If a bill is suspect, give a receipt to the retailer or bank, and turn the bill over to the nearest Secret Service office to determine its authenticity. Obtain details of how the bill came into the complainant's possession as well as an accurate description of the bill passer.

A felt-tip marker can instantly detect even the finest-quality counterfeit money with a single stroke.

With the felt-tip marker, a dot or short line is made on the suspected bill. If the "ink" remains gold, the bill is authentic. If the "ink" turns black, the bill needs scrutiny.

Commercial Counterfeiting Currency is not the only item targeted for counterfeiting. Commercial counter-

© AP/Wide World Photos

Figure 14.6
Lorelei W. Pagano, a counterfeit specialist with the U.S. Secret Service, talks about the different styles of counterfeiting at their anti-counterfeiting lab, Monday, June 14, 2004, in Washington.

feiting includes trademark counterfeiting and copyright pirating. *Trademark counterfeiting* is the illegal production of cheap "knock-offs" of well-known pricier products, such as Rolex watches, Gucci handbags, or Mont Blanc fountain pens. *Copyright pirating* is making—for trade or sale—unauthorized copies of copyrighted material, including print and sound media. In contrast to trademark counterfeiting, however, where products are sold far below the retail value of their legitimate counterparts, pirated music or movies impose much steeper prices on the consumer. The FBI ("Pirates of Hollywood") reports that movie pirating is a multibillion-dollar industry largely dominated by global criminal networks. However, individual movie pirates can also cause harm and make a significant amount of money through the illegal recording and distribution of motion pictures.

A case in point: Johnny Ray Gasca, 35, also known to law enforcement as "the prince of pirates." Gasca would go to Hollywood theaters showing advanced movie screenings, talk his way in as a movie industry insider, and proceed to covertly record the film with high-end equipment he had smuggled in. Afterward, he'd rush home to mass-produce copies and sell them online before the films began showing nationwide, claiming in his diary to clear as much as $4,500 a week. Fortunately, as the FBI stated in an account of the case (made as the result of an investigation by the cyber crimes division of the FBI in Los Angeles), Gasca had a habit of getting caught, betrayed repeatedly by the green glow coming from his camera bag:

> Burbank police arrested him when he was caught at a screening of *The Core*. Then at *Anger Management*. Then *8 Mile*. Our law enforcement partners called us in to search Gasca's apartment and there it all was: things like two video camcorders, a micro-camera built onto a trouser belt, two DVD recorders, the 11 linked VCRs, a stolen Social Security card, and his two diaries, which happily chronicled all the bad things he'd been doing.
>
> Gasca later threatened to sell up to 20 more unreleased movies online and "laugh all the way to jail" unless the Motion Picture Association of America (MPAA) helped him get his equipment back. He was charged in April 2003 (the first person ever indicted on federal charges of movie piracy) . . . and was placed in his lawyer's custody to discuss legal strategy . . . at which point he disappeared without a trace. Two years passed before U.S. Marshals got a tip and chased him down at a motel in Kissimmee, Florida. What was he doing? Illegally copying movies. Of course.
>
> Gasca was tried in Los Angeles and found guilty on eight criminal counts. He faces a maximum of 33 years in prison, with his sentencing scheduled for this September [2005]. ("Pirates")

It is also a felony in most states to pirate sound recordings, and nearly every state has some type of law related to pirated recordings. Despite the illegalities of this business, the practice continues, particularly on the Internet, as discussed in Chapter 17.

Check Fraud

Losses from bad-check operations cannot be determined exactly because no single clearinghouse gathers statistics on this offense. Estimates range from $815 million to $5–10 billion annually.

Checks used to defraud include personal, business, counter, draft, and universal checks, as well as money orders. Fraudulent checks are made to appear genuine in many ways. The check blank can be similar to the one normally used and difficult to detect. In fact, many fraudulent and forged checks are written on stolen check blanks. Handwriting is practiced to look authentic. Various stamps, check writers, date stamps, and cancellation stamps are placed on the front and back of the check to give it a genuine appearance.

In some cases, the checks are not stolen but handed over willingly to thieves—for a price. The checking account owner benefits by being paid more money than is actually in the account, while the thief is allowed to cash checks or purchase merchandise for a few days before the bank is notified of the check "theft."

Common types of check fraud are issuing insufficient-fund or worthless checks and committing forgery.

The *insufficient-* or *nonsufficient-fund check* falls into one of two categories: (1) accidental, in which people carelessly overdraw their checking account and are generally not prosecuted unless they do so habitually or (2) intentional, in which professionals open a checking account with a small deposit, planning to write checks well in excess of the amount deposited. This is intent to defraud—a prosecutable offense.

Most bad checks are not written with intent to defraud. They may have been mistakenly drawn against the wrong bank, the account balance may have been less than the writer thought, two or more people may have used the same account without knowing the actual balance, or the bank may have made an error.

Issuing a worthless check occurs when the issuer does not intend the check to be paid. Proof of intent is shown if the issuer has no account or has insufficient funds or credit or both. A worthless check is normally prosecuted the same as one for insufficient funds. Obtain the check as well as statements from the person who accepted it, any other witnesses, and bank representatives. Also obtain a signed complaint.

Forgery is signing someone else's name to a document with the intent to defraud. This includes actually signing the name and using a rubber stamp or a check-writing machine. To prosecute, obtain the forged check or document, statements from the person whose name is forged, any witnesses to the transaction, and the testimony of a handwriting expert if necessary. Blank checks are often obtained through burglaries or office thefts committed by professionals. The check is authentic and therefore easier to cash once the endorsement is forged.

It is also forgery to alter the amount on a check or to change the name of the payee. The person who initially draws the check must testify as to the authorized amount and payee. It is also forgery to change a name on a charge account slip.

Investigating bad or fraudulent checks requires precise details about the check and the entire transaction. The check itself is the main evidence. Carefully examine the front and back of the check and note peculiarities. Describe the check: type, firm name, and whether it is personal, payroll, federal, or state. Was it written in pencil or ink or typed? Were any special stamps used? Was anything altered: the payee, the date, the amount? Was the signature forged? Were there erasures or misspellings? Were local names and addresses used? Put the check in a protective polyethylene envelope or plastic container so that it can also be processed for fingerprints at the laboratory.

Where was the check passed? Who took it? Were there other witnesses? If so, obtain their names and addresses. If currency was given, what were the denominations? Obtain an exact description of the check passer. Was the suspect known to the person taking the check? Had he or she ever done business with the store before? What identification was used: driver's license, Social Security card, bank identification card, credit card? Was the suspect left- or right-handed? Was the suspect alone? If with others, what did they look like? What approach was used? What words were spoken? If the check passer used a car, did anyone notice what it looked like or the license number?

The National Fraudulent Check File Professional check passers who write several checks in a city in a short time and then move to another city or state often use the same technique. The FBI's National Fraudulent Check File helps identify such people and often shows a pattern of travel. The FBI maintains other files that assist in tracing bad-check writers. These include files on check-writer standards, watermarks, confidence operators, safety paper standards, rubber stamps, anonymous letters, and typewriter standards.

Debit and Credit Card Fraud

A **debit card,** sometimes called a check card, refers to a card presented to a merchant exactly as a credit card would be, with the amount instantly credited before verification of the existence of funds is established. A **credit card** refers to any credit plate, charge plate, courtesy card, or other identification card or device used to obtain a cash advance, a loan, or credit or to purchase or lease property or services on the issuer's credit or that of the holder. The **holder** is the person to whom such a card is issued and who agrees to pay obligations arising from its use.

Use of debit and credit cards has become a way of life in the United States. The cards have opened a new avenue for criminals to obtain goods and services by theft and fraud. Losses from debit and credit card fraud are in the billions annually. Despite these losses these cards, like checks, reduce cash thefts from individuals and reduce the amount of cash-on-hand in places such as filling stations, as well as the amount of cash transferred to banks from businesses. Use of these cards also aids in identifying criminals who have the cards in their possession, more so than does cash, which is not as easily identifiable.

Because credit card fraud is often spread throughout many jurisdictions, many police departments place low priority on this type of offense. Further complicating this crime, many businesses accept credit card telephone purchases. Fraudulent orders are placed, and if the victims do not review their bills, the fraud can go completely undetected.

Most people involved in credit card fraud are also involved in other types of crimes. The credit cards are obtained principally by muggers, robbers, burglars, pickpockets, purse snatchers, thieves, and prostitutes. They can also be obtained through fraudulent application or by manufacturing counterfeit cards.

Credit cards can be stolen by mailbox thieves who may have been tipped off by a postal employee, by someone at apartment boxes, or by dishonest employees of the card manufacturer. Cards from the manufacturer are desirable because they are unsigned. The criminal can sign the holder's name in his or her own handwriting. These cards also provide more time for use before the theft is discovered. For the same reasons, these cards are more valuable for resale to other fraudulent users. To take maximum advantage without being detected, the criminal obtains the card by fraud, theft, or reproduction, uses it for a short time, and then disposes of it.

Ballezza (p.8) describes a relatively new trend in credit card theft: stealing cards from health club lockers to use in obtaining cash at casinos. He (pp.9–10) offers the following scenario of a health-club credit card theft:

> A group of between four to six thieves goes to a health club. At least one of them will be a member, sometimes under an alias, of the club the group targeted for locker thefts. Other coconspirators may sign in as guests of the member or may sign in on a day-use basis. These thieves also target health clubs offering 1-week free, trial memberships. . . .
>
> Once the thieves enter the locker room, they separate into prearranged roles. At least one person will act as a "blocker" and lookout at the main entrance to the locker room. Other thieves will target certain lockers and will carry various "shims"—extremely thin pieces of metal cut to a small size—to "shim" open the combination padlocks on the lockers. A skilled "shimmer" can open these padlocks faster than a person who uses the combination. . . .
>
> After opening the lock, the thieves carefully avoid disturbing the contents in the locker, looking only into

the member's wallet to find any credit cards. They remove one or two of the credit cards . . . but never take any cash.

After leaving the club or clubs, and before hitting the casinos, the thieves use laptop computers, color scanners, and color printers to produce counterfeit identification matching the names on the credit cards. Just before using the stolen card at a casino, the thieves will try making a small purchase with the card at a convenience store. If the transaction is approved, the thieves know the card has not yet been reported stolen. They then proceed to max out each card through the various cash-advance services available at casinos (Ballezza, p.10).

 The elements of the crime of larceny by debit or credit card include:
- Possessing a credit card obtained by theft or fraud,
- by which services or goods are obtained,
- through unauthorized signing of the cardholder's name.

To use another person's debit or credit card illegally, the criminal must either forge the cardholder's signature on sales slips or alter the signature on the card. The latter is made difficult by colored or symbol undertones that indicate when erasures and alterations are attempted.

The criminal must also operate under the floor-release limit to avoid having a clerk check the card's validity. The **floor-release limit** is the maximum dollar amount that may be paid with a charge card without getting authorization from the central office unless the business assumes liability for any loss. The limit is set by each company and is subject to change. It can be $50 or $100; in some gas stations, it is only $10. **Zero floor release** means that all credit card transactions must be checked. A suspicious merchant usually runs a check regardless of the amount of credit requested. Often the criminal is asked for additional identification, which is difficult to produce unless other identification was also obtained in the theft.

Credit cards are attractive to criminals who operate interstate. Such criminals know that few companies will pay the witness fees for out-of-state prosecutions and that extradition is difficult to obtain unless the losses are great.

Many laws cover larceny or fraudulent use of credit cards. Possessing a forged credit card or one signed by a person other than the cardholder is the basis for a charge of possession of a forged instrument. Possessing two such cards is the basis for presuming intent to defraud. Illegally making or embossing a credit card or changing the expiration date or account number also subjects the person to a charge of intent to defraud. In most jurisdictions it is not necessary to prove that the person possessing the card signed it. Persons who have machinery or devices to counterfeit or forge credit cards can be charged with possession of forgery devices.

It is larceny to fail to return a found credit card or to keep one that is sent by mistake if the finder or recipient uses the card. Airline tickets bought with a stolen or forged credit card are also stolen property. The degree of larceny, petty or grand, is determined by the ticket's value. It is also larceny to misrepresent credit information or identity to obtain a credit card. If a person sells his or her credit card to someone who uses it and the original cardholder then refuses to pay, the cardholder can be charged with larceny.

Some merchants and businesspeople commit credit card fraud themselves. For example, a merchant may direct an employee to make more than one authorized record of charge per sale and then forward the charges for payment or raise the amount on the credit card charge slip. This is larceny, with the degree determined by the difference between the actual charge and that forwarded for payment. It is also forgery because a document was altered. It is an attempt to commit larceny if such actions are not completed because of intervening circumstances such as the cardholder becoming suspicious.

Most large credit card issuers assign personnel to work with local police in cases of credit card larceny. These people can be contacted for help or for information on the system used to manufacture and issue the cards.

When investigating credit card fraud, obtain samples of handwriting from sales slips signed by the suspect. If a card is obtained by false credit application, handwriting is available on the credit application form. If the card is used for a car rental, other information about the rented vehicle is available. Gas stations often record the state and license number of vehicles they service. Driver's licenses are used for identification. If a suspect is arrested, obtain a warrant to search the suspect's vehicle and residence for copies of sales slips or tickets obtained with the card, even though it has been discarded or sold.

Examine credit cards for alteration of the signature panel; the numbers or name can be shortened by using a razor blade to shave them off. New numbers can be entered to defeat the "hot card" list. Merchandise on sales slips found in the criminal's possession can provide further proof of illegal use. If the service obtained is a motel room, telephone calls can be traced to pinpoint accomplices. Clerks who handle the transactions often initial the sales slip, which enables the company or store to furnish the name of a witness.

As serious as credit card fraud is, it can have an even graver consequence—identity theft.

Identity Fraud/Theft

A type of theft that can wreak enormous havoc on a person's credit and financial security is identity fraud, alternately called **identity theft.** Whitlock (p.62) contends: "Identity theft continues to be the fastest growing crime problem in the U.S." In fact, the last edition of this text cited 2002 data indicating that identity theft hit an estimated 900,000 Americans every year. In 2004, however, the number of victims of identity theft had grown to more than 9 million a year, as Lim (p.46) observes: "What used to be considered a nuisance is now a full-blown epidemic." He notes that from 1999 to 2004, 28 million Americans—13 percent of the U.S. adult population—had their identities stolen.

To the question: "Why is ID theft such a threat?" Sivy et al. (p.97) answer: "Two words: organized crime." Dadisho (2005c, p.25) notes: "Identity theft is an emotionally abusive crime, and its psychological effects on the victim may last for years. It is a repetitive crime, as victims receive continual notices by phone or mail from creditors." Identity theft is *not* the crime when someone takes your credit card number and goes on a shopping spree—that is simple credit card fraud. Identity crime is a more encompassing offense, when someone acquires enough personal information to assume another person's identity, opening credit card and bank accounts, applying for loans and mortgages, even getting jobs—all by using someone else's name. Newman (p.1) states:

> Identity theft is a new crime, facilitated through established, underlying crimes such as forgery, counterfeiting, check and credit card fraud, computer fraud, impersonation, pickpocketing, and even terrorism. It became a federal crime in the United States in 1998, with the passage of the Identity Theft and Assumption Deterrence Act. This act identifies offenders as anyone who ". . . knowingly transfers or uses, without lawful authority, any name or number that may be used, alone or in conjunction with any other information, to identify a specific individual with the intent to commit, or to aid or abet, any unlawful activity that constitutes a violation of Federal law, or that constitutes a felony under any applicable State or local law."

The Identity Theft and Assumption Deterrence Act allows for prison sentences up to 25 years for those convicted of the offense and also enables victims to seek restitution for identifiable losses and for expenses related to restoring their credit rating.

Majoras (p.14), chairman of the Federal Trade Commission (FTC), reports that identity theft causes nearly $48 billion in losses each year to businesses and nearly $5 billion in annual losses to individual victims. Furthermore, an estimated 300 million victim hours are spent trying to fix the resulting problems.

 For the fifth consecutive year, identity theft topped the list of fraud-related complaints filed with the FTC in 2004 (*National and State*).

Identity theft is especially prevalent on college campuses. Identity thieves know this and hang around campus post office boxes to gain access to applications and fill them in themselves. Complicating the problem is the fact that there are over 200 valid forms of ID or driver's licenses issued in the United States.

Identity theft has proliferated as use of the Internet has grown. One type of identity theft, called *phishing*, involves tricking consumers into replying to an e-mail or accessing a website that appears to be associated with a legitimate business but is actually a carefully concocted hoax intended to strip consumers of personal identifying information that can be used for criminal purposes, such as identity theft and fraud (Figure 14.7). (Crimes involving use of computers are discussed in Chapter 17.) Figure 14.8 shows the four types of identity theft, based on the combinations of commitment and motive.

Newman (p.30) states: "Identity theft is a complex crime, composed of many sub-crimes and related to many other problems. Thus, identity theft crimes fall under the authority of many different agencies, including the local police, Secret Service, Postal Inspection Service, FBI, Homeland Security, local government offices, and motor vehicle departments, to name just a few." Consequently, an effective police response to and investigation of identity theft will very likely require a multi-jurisdictional approach.

Dadisho (2005c, p.28) remarks on the exceptionalness of identity theft investigations in that there are no witnesses or physical evidence at the crime scene, and

```
-----Original Message-----
From: XXXXX@argolink.net [mailto:XXXXX@argolink.net]
Sent: Thursday, January 10, 2002 4:53 AM
To: XXXXX@argolink.net
Subject: The $10,000 Big Money Club! New International Membership$$$
Time: 4:52:47 AM


IT'S TIME TO LIVE YOUR DREAMS!
THE MOST HONEST ONE TIME PAY PROGRAM AVAILABLE!
WE SHOW YOU THE MONEY!

   FINALLY, a MLM Gifting Program that CAN'T FAIL, because we do all the
work and Guarantee Your Success! We print all the Flyers, we stuff all the
Envelopes, and we do all the mailing using our own Exclusive mailing list.

   We guarantee each participant 10 people in their Downline, because we
mail until each participant has 10 people no matter how man flyers we have
to mail. YOU CAN'T FAIL!!!

INTERESTED, GO TO OUR WEBSITE LISTED BELOW!
```

Figure 14.7

An excerpt from a spam e-mail targeted by law enforcement. This example is posted on the Federal Trade Commission's website, along with additional information on identifying and addressing spam and other fraudulent e-mail.

Courtesy of the U.S. Federal Trade Commission.

	Financial Gain	Concealment
High commitment (lots of planning)	*Organized:* A fraud ring systematically steals personal information and uses it to generate bank accounts, obtain credit cards, etc. *Individual:* The offender sets up a look-alike Internet website for a major company; spams consumers, luring them to the site by saying their account information is needed to clear up a serious problem; steals the personal/financial information the consumer provides; and uses it to commit identity theft.	*Organized:* Terrorists obtain false visas and passports to avoid being traced after committing terrorist acts.* *Individual:* The offender assumes another's name to cover up past crimes and avoid capture over many years.
Opportunistic (low commitment)	An apartment manager uses personal information from rental applications to open credit card accounts.	The offender uses another's name and ID when stopped or arrested by police.

* An Algerian national facing U.S. charges of identity theft allegedly stole the identities of 21 members of a Cambridge, Massachusetts, health club and transferred the identities to one of the people convicted in the failed 1999 plot to bomb the Los Angeles International Airport (Wilcox 2002).

Figure 14.8
There are four types of identity theft, based on the combinations of commitment and motive. Of course, any single case could reflect aspects of more than one type.

From Newman, *Identity Theft,* p. 15.

the crime scene may be thousands of miles from where the victim lives. He (2005a, p.46) advises that every identity theft investigation require a determination of the point of compromise—that place where the offender obtained the victim's identification information: "This will help lead to possible suspects and will often lead to additional victims." Dadisho (2005a, p.46) stresses the need for a properly structured preliminary investigation, which will save further investigative time and lay the foundation for prosecution.

The investigation begins with the victim reporting the theft to police per the provisions of the 2004 Fair and Accurate Credit Transactions Act (FACT Act). This federal law provides new rights and remedies to victims of identity theft, but with a catch—the victim must first file a police report. While this would appear to be common sense on the part of the victim, the act was intended primarily to serve as an impetus to law enforcement in developing identity theft prevention and investigation policies and protocols. To comply with the FACT Act, agencies must now have personnel trained in completing identity theft crime reports; investigating identity

theft crimes, including the collection of evidence; and preparing identity theft cases for possible prosecution (Dadisho, 2005c, p.28). Once a victim is armed with a police report proving that he has, indeed, suffered a theft of his identity, the lengthy and difficult process of repairing the victim's damaged credit becomes somewhat easier through the use of certain privileges not available to other consumers, such as blocking fraudulent trade lines on credit reports and obtaining the suspect's credit application (White and Einhorn, p.38).

Dadisho (2005a, p.48) suggests that one of the first things an investigator should do is conduct a detailed interview with the victim to determine the motive for the identity theft. Knowing whether the crime was motivated by greed, drugs, revenge, or some other cause will help direct the investigation. Victim interviews may also provide suspect leads. According to Dadisho (2005b, p.20), nearly 70 percent of identity theft complaints received by the FTC contain some information regarding the suspect. He notes that victims often learn, by way of the creditors, collection agencies, or other entities involved in trying to collect the fraudulent charges, the names, addresses, or phone numbers used by the suspect, information that can help investigators link seemingly unrelated complaints to common suspects. The U.S. Secret Service, in collaboration with the International Association of Chiefs of Police (IACP), has created an 11-page questionnaire for investigators to give to victims of identity theft to elicit information useful to the investigation.

White and Einhorn (p.38) offer these suggestions for interviewing identity theft victims:

- Provide the police report as quickly as possible.
- Refer the victim to the FTC's ID Theft website (www.consumer.gov/idtheft) to file their complaint, learn their rights, and find out what else to do.
- Encourage victims to complete the ID theft affidavit to use in disputing fraudulent accounts with creditors.

If the identity theft case begins with a report of fraudulent checks, the investigator should:

- Verify that the routing numbers on the checks are real.
- Contact the bank to verify that the name on the check matches that of a legitimate bank customer.
- Ask the bank to determine if "the account number is legitimate."
- Ask the merchant where the check was passed if they use a check cashing company that can help detect patterns.
- Seek FBI assistance in having handwriting samples analyzed.
- Search databases for similar complaints in other jurisdictions.
- Refer the victim to the FTC's website (White and Einhorn, p.38).

Databases that investigators should search include the Financial Crimes Database, which includes information on stolen U.S. mail as well as stolen and fraudulently used checks and credit, ATM, and debit cards (Heath, 2005). The FTC's Identity Theft Data Clearinghouse is a national identity theft database containing more than 815,000 victim complaints, allowing investigators to search for information on identity theft victims and/or suspects across the country. FinCEN (Financial Crimes Enforcement Network) is another valuable resource for investigators, as it links approximately three dozen independent databases in three main areas: law enforcement, finance, and commerce. Also, with authorization from the victim, an investigator can get the victim's identity theft–related transaction records from creditors without first obtaining a subpoena, under the 2003 amendments to the Fair Credit Reporting Act, section 609(e).

In addition to victim interviews, investigators should also seek information from informants. Dadisho (2005a, p.48) suggests identifying possible informants by using intelligence from other law enforcement agencies or the private sector. Other possible sources of informants include peripheral players in the identity theft, such as store employees who sold to suspects they knew were using stolen identities.

Identity theft is unique in that not only is it a crime in itself but it is also an MO to commit other crimes. A challenge for investigators, therefore, may be deciding in what offense to accuse a suspect of involvement. John E. Reid and Associates (2003) offer the following advice for interrogating an identity theft suspect:

> The general guideline here is to base the accusation on the strongest evidence. For example, if there is strong evidence indicating that a suspect (using someone else's identity) made fraudulent credit card purchases, the confrontation statement should only address the illegal purchases. At a later stage, the investigator can develop the details of how the suspect obtained the fraudulent credit card. This approach is similar to one investigators would take in an arson-homicide case, in which it is best to confront the suspect with the killing and later develop the details of starting the fire to cover up the homicide.

Reid and Associates suggests that when multiple crimes are suspected, the investigator work on only one crime at a time; once a suspect confesses to one crime, information about others is usually forthcoming. Investigators may get a suspect to open up by:

- Blaming banks and credit card companies for making identity theft so easy to commit: "George, I realize this thing isn't entirely your fault. Banks are so eager to get customers, they rush applications, promise quick approval, never even meet their customers . . ."
- Blaming the victim for being so careless with sensitive, personal information as to allow the suspect access to it: "Those people should have shredded their bank and credit card statements before tossing them in the trash."
- Blaming curiosity and the media: "Joe, I think what happened here is that you read an article about how easy it is to get credit using another person's information, so you decided to test the system and fill out an application. And to your amazement, a card arrived in the mail, maybe the same day as a bunch of bills . . ."

Reid and Associates lists the following questions for investigators to consider asking suspects in identity theft cases:

- "How many false identities (false credit cards, fraudulent loans) have you established? Dozens or just a few?"
- "How much have you charged to this card? Did you charge the maximum limit, $10,000, or was it less than that?"
- "Are you a member of an organized network, perhaps with a terrorist affiliation, or did you just do this to hide from your ex-wife?"
- "Did you pay money to bribe people to get this credit card, or did they simply accept your application at face value?"

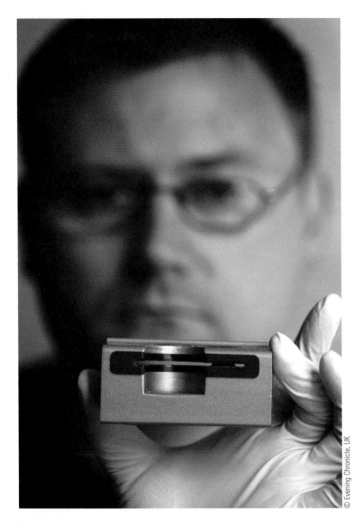

© Evening Chronicle, UK

Figure 14.9
Credit cards have replaced cash and checks in many people's wallets. Thieves have adapted to changing consumer habits by using devices such as credit card skimmers to steal individuals' financial data. Here, DC Gary Dickson from Whickham Police holds a credit card skimmer device.

Investigators should recognize the tools of the identity thief's trade, including blank checks, laminating machines, laptop computers, typewriters, color scanners and copiers, and skimming devices, through which a user can swipe a credit card and retrieve information from the card's magnetic strip (Dadisho, 2005b, p.25) (Figure 14.9).

Noting that the average American possesses 20 IDs in various forms—credit cards, bank accounts, personal identification numbers (PINs), Social Security numbers, driver's licenses, username/password combinations—all of which can be easily compromised, LaCous (2005) suggests that the key to stopping identity theft may lie in biometrics, which relies on unique biological properties to positively identify an individual. Biometric identifiers include fingerprints, voiceprints, retinal scans, and facial recognition—IDs that are extremely difficult to steal or forge.

Just as identity theft can overlap with and include other crimes such as credit card fraud and counterfeit-

ing, identity theft can also be classified as white-collar crime.

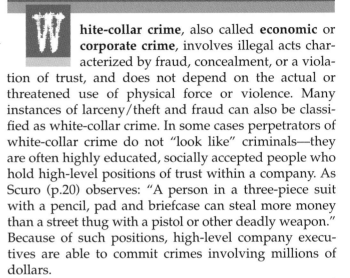

White-Collar Crime

White-collar crime, also called **economic** or **corporate crime**, involves illegal acts characterized by fraud, concealment, or a violation of trust, and does not depend on the actual or threatened use of physical force or violence. Many instances of larceny/theft and fraud can also be classified as white-collar crime. In some cases perpetrators of white-collar crime do not "look like" criminals—they are often highly educated, socially accepted people who hold high-level positions of trust within a company. As Scuro (p.20) observes: "A person in a three-piece suit with a pencil, pad and briefcase can steal more money than a street thug with a pistol or other deadly weapon." Because of such positions, high-level company executives are able to commit crimes involving millions of dollars.

White-collar crime makes headlines: the frauds and crooked accounting involved in the Enron and WorldCom bankruptcies, the scandals involving Tyco International and Adelphia Communications, and the ImClone stock debacle that sent the all-things-domestic guru Martha Stewart to prison for five months. With CEOs pocketing millions, even billions, of dollars, investors and pensioners lost everything (Figure 14.10). This is probably the ultimate white-collar crime, perhaps better termed *corporate terrorism*. It is of interest to note that the American Society of Industrial Security (ASIS) Standing Committee on White-Collar Crime has changed its name to the Economic Crime Committee.

Much white-collar crime is never reported because it involves top-level executives of organizations that do not want their reputations damaged. White-collar crimes may be committed by individuals against other individuals such as family members, lawyers, real estate agents, insurance agents, and physicians. They may be committed against organizations by insiders such as business partners, office managers, computer programmers, and senior executives. White-collar crimes may also be committed by individuals with no relationship to the victim, such as corporate spies, forgers, counterfeiters, computer hackers, and information pirates.

The FBI's categories of white-collar criminal activity are money laundering, securities and commodities fraud, bank fraud and embezzlement, environmental crimes, fraud against the government, health care fraud, election law violations, copyright violations, and telemarketing fraud. Scuro (p.20) lists as some of the most common white-collar crimes securities fraud; computer crime; crimes against consumers; crimes involving the banking, insurance, and pension fund industries; med-

Figure 14.10

Former WorldCom CEO Bernard Ebbers is escorted from court. Ebbers and five other ex-officials of the telecommunications giant were charged with violating Oklahoma's securities laws in connection with the demise of WorldCom, which collapsed in 2002 and filed the largest bankruptcy action in U.S. history. Ebbers was convicted of nine felonies that carried a maximum prison term of 85 years but, in July 2005, received a sentence of only 25 years in prison for leading the largest corporate fraud in the history of our nation. He plans to appeal.

ical fraud; corruption of public officials; environmental crimes; unsafe products; and media-induced crimes against consumers. Clearly, differences exist in how to define white-collar crime and what types of other crimes should fall within this classification. Many of the aforementioned crimes have already been discussed.

White-collar or economic crime includes (1) securities and commodities fraud; (2) insurance fraud; (3) health care and medical fraud; (4) telemarketing fraud; (5) credit card and check fraud; (6) consumer fraud, illegal competition, and deceptive practices; (7) bankruptcy fraud; (8) computer-related fraud; (9) bank fraud, embezzlement, and pilferage; (10) bribes, kickbacks, and payoffs; (11) money laundering; (12) election law violations; (13) corruption of public officials; (14) copyright violations; (15) computer crimes; (16) environmental crimes; and (17) receiving stolen property.

Investigate these crimes as you would any larceny or fraud case. Whether they are felonies or misdemeanors depends on the value involved.

White-collar crimes can be committed by any employee within a business or organization. However, low-level employees usually do not have the opportunity to steal a large amount from their employer. Most often their crimes consist of pilferage. Many employees do not see taking office supplies or placing personal long-distance phone calls from a work phone as dishonest. However, they would not think of doing the same thing in a place where they did not work. Over time, the losses from pilferage are often much more than what a high-level employee might embezzle.

Few law enforcement agencies are equipped to investigate white-collar crime, encouraging such investigations to be conducted internally by in-house or contracted private investigators. The National White Collar Crime Center (NW3C) links criminal justice agencies across international borders and also bridges the gap between local and state criminal justice agencies. This center provides assistance in preventing, investigating, and prosecuting economic crime.

Corporate Fraud

Corporate fraud has gained national attention in recent years. Despite all the media coverage and heightened scrutiny of business practices in corporations nationwide, the FBI anticipates no reduction in the number of such cases in the foreseeable future. As noted in the *Financial Crimes Report to the Public* (p.B1), corporate fraud remains the top priority of the FBI's Financial Crimes Section. FBI field offices throughout the United States are currently juggling 405 corporate fraud cases, a number that represents a 100 percent increase over the number of such cases pending at the end of fiscal year 2003 (p.B1).

FBI investigations show that corporate fraud involves such activities as falsification of financial information ("cooking the books"); self-dealing by corporate insiders, including insider trading and kickbacks; fraud in connection with an otherwise legitimately operated mutual or hedge fund; and obstruction of justice designed to conceal criminal conduct (pp.B1–B2). Many cases of corporate fraud involve securities and commodities. The FBI's Economic Crimes Unit website helps put into perspective the serious consequences of such illegal activities:

> The economic stability of the United States and the soundness of the nation's financial markets are directly related to the integrity of the securities and commodities markets. The trading volume in the United States' securities and commodities markets has grown dramatically over the last decade. This growth has led to an increase in fraud and misconduct by investors, executives, shareholders, and other market participants. Securities regulators and other prominent groups have estimated that securities and commodities fraud totals approximately

$40 billion per year. The fraudulent schemes perpetrated in the securities and commodities markets can ultimately have a devastating impact on the viability and operation of those very markets.

The highly publicized Enron scandal involved numerous illegal practices committed over the course of several years by high-ranking company executives who sought to hide Enron's growing debt and keep perceived stock market value high. The deception and fraud began to receive notice when, in October 2001, the company made public the fact that it was actually worth $1.2 billion less than previously reported. This announcement set off an investigation by the Securities and Exchange Commission (SEC), which remains ongoing as this text goes to print. Thus far, the SEC's investigation has uncovered a tangled conspiracy between Enron executives, investment banking partners, and members of Enron's accounting firm, Arthur Anderson, to commit securities fraud, wire fraud, mail fraud, money laundering, and insider trading.

Other notable recent corporate fraud cases have included WorldCom and ImClone, companies both charged with securities fraud and other illegal accounting practices. These types of corporate fraud are generally discovered during routine auditing procedures and are often jointly investigated by the SEC and the FBI. In the WorldCom case, the company and its executives have also been investigated by two congressional committees.

Money Laundering

Money laundering is converting illegally earned (dirty) cash to one or more alternative (clean) forms to conceal its illegal origin and true ownership. Drug traffickers and other racketeers who accumulate large cash inventories face serious risks of confiscation and punishment if considerable, unexplained cash hoards are discovered. For these criminals to fully benefit from their illicit activities, they must first convert those cash proceeds to an alternative medium—one that is both easier than cash to use in everyday commerce and avoids pointing, even indirectly, to the illegal activity that generated it.

Federal laws that drive the need for money laundering include the Bank Secrecy Act (BSA) of 1970, the first major piece of legislation to address the problem and require the reporting of certain cash transactions. Specific sections of this act include:

- 31 U.S.C. § 5313: requires U.S. banks and other financial institutions to report cash transactions exceeding $10,000.

- 31 U.S.C. § 5324: prohibits intentionally dividing cash sums exceeding $10,000 into smaller amounts so as to evade detection by ducking in under the required reporting threshold.

Other federal laws pertaining to money laundering include:

- 18 U.S.C. § 982: allows the seizure of all property or money associated with a money laundering scheme and the forfeiture of such assets to the federal government.

- 18 U.S.C. § 1951: the Hobbs Act; addresses government corruption and makes illegal the act of extortion, through the actual or threatened use of violence or fear, exercised by someone in a position of authority or official capacity, for the purpose of personal gain.

- 26 U.S.C. § 7201 and § 7206(1): prohibits the filing of a false federal income tax return or the commission of tax evasion through failure to report income.

- 26 U.S.C. § 60501: requires all entities (individuals or organizations) engaged in commerce to report all cash transactions exceeding $10,000.

- The Money Laundering Control Act of 1986.

- The Anti-Drug Abuse Act of 1988.

- The 2001 USA PATRIOT (Providing Appropriate Tools Required to Intercept and Obstruct Terrorism) Act, which created a new money laundering statute, 18 U.S.C. § 5316, to deal with bulk cash smuggling.

The basic process of laundering money begins with **placement** of the funds into the legitimate U.S. market (Sheetz, p.106). Common methods of placement include creating shell corporations or fake cash-intensive businesses, and **smurfing,** more technically known as **structuring,** whereby large amounts of cash are broken into increments less than $10,000, to avoid federal reporting requirements, and deposited into various bank accounts.

The second step in the laundering process is **layering,** where the money is cleaned by moving it around through a series of elaborate transactions, often involving offshore bank accounts and international business companies (IBCs). These multiple, complex transactions aim to obscure the connection between the money and the criminal group and to continue until the organization feels confident the money is adequately clean.

The third and final step in the money laundering cycle is **integration,** where criminals repatriate their money through seemingly legitimate business transactions. For example, the launderer creates a bogus export company in a free trade zone and a bogus import company owned through an IBC in a different country. A trading relationship is established where the exporter sends nonexistent goods or goods invoiced at greatly inflated prices to the importer, who pays the exporter in cleaned money, thus completing the laundry cycle.

A variety of types of businesses are used in the laundering of money. In 2001, 22 commercial defendants were charged with money laundering, including auto dealerships, banks, beauty shops, construction firms, grocery stores, and furniture stores (Motivans, p.1). The amount of money laundered through these types of businesses and financial institutions across the country has been estimated at hundreds of billions of dollars and, despite efforts to curb such criminal practices, many expect money laundering to continue to increase with both domestic and international enforcement challenges in light of the ever-expanding potential of the Internet.

As part of the Money Laundering Strategy Act of 1998, High Intensity Financial Crimes Areas (HIFCA) were designated to help focus law enforcement efforts in those parts of the country where money laundering and related financial crimes were most prevalent (Motivans, p.3). As of July 2003, six HIFCAs had been identified by the secretary of the treasury and the U.S. attorney general: New York/New Jersey; San Juan, Puerto Rico; Los Angeles; the southwestern U.S. border including Arizona and Texas; the northern district of Illinois (Chicago); and the northern district of California (San Francisco) (Motivans, p.3).

Investigating money laundering usually uses white-collar-crime investigative techniques such as financial auditing and accounting, undercover operations (perhaps through sting operations), and electronic surveillance. The FBI has developed a proactive, two-pronged approach to investigating money laundering.

- Prong 1: The investigation of the underlying criminal activity. In simple terms, if there is no criminal activity, or Specified Unlawful Activity that generates illicit proceeds, then there can be no money laundering.
- Prong 2: A parallel financial investigation to uncover the financial infrastructure of the criminal organization. This involves following the money and discerning how it flows through an organization and what steps are taken to conceal, disguise, or hide the proceeds (*Financial Crimes*, p.H2).

Sheetz (pp.110–111) offers several suggestions to help investigators follow the money trail and effectively work a money laundering case, beginning with maintaining a strong working relationship with local financial professionals, as these are the first line of defense against money laundering. Investigators should also routinely monitor the anti–money laundering initiatives of other countries. The Financial Action Task Force (FATF) is an international assembly of member countries deemed to have strong anti–money laundering controls. While FATF has no enforcement authority, its value lies in information sharing and promoting cooperation among nations (Sheetz, p.110). FATF's various member-country websites are good resources for information on current methods and trends in money laundering and the investigative techniques used to uncover them (p.110).

Third, investigators should carefully scrutinize the business activity of the suspected launderer, paying par-

ticular attention to cash-intensive businesses like restaurants and bars, import/export companies, and diamond and fine jewelry businesses (p.110). Furthermore, know your community and the surrounding area, and avoid tunnel vision when developing the case (p.111).

Embezzlement

Embezzlement is the fraudulent appropriation of property by a person to whom it has been entrusted. The property is then used by the embezzler or another person contrary to the terms of the trust. The owner retains title to the property during the trust period. The property so entrusted may be real or personal property. Even though the title remains with the owner, the embezzler usually has control through appointment as agent, servant, bailee, or trustee. Because of the relationship between owner and embezzler, the embezzler has custody of the property. Most embezzlements involve employees. Most bank losses are from embezzlement, often involving large sums of money.

Businesses, industries, and other financial institutions besides banks are also victims of embezzlement. Embezzlement includes committing petty theft over a period of time, "kiting" accounts receivable, overextending credit and cash returns, falsifying accounts payable records, and falsifying information put into computers—a highly sophisticated crime. (Computer-related crimes are discussed in Chapter 17.)

Bank embezzlements often start small and gradually increase. Surprisingly, many embezzlements are not committed for the benefit of the embezzler. Many start by providing unauthorized credit extensions to customers. As the amount increases, the employee is afraid to make the error known to the employer and attempts to cover the losses. In other cases, the employee uses funds to start other businesses, fully intending to replace the borrowed funds, but the businesses often fail. Other motives for embezzlement are to cover gambling debts, to support a drug habit, to make home improvements, to meet heavy medical expenses, or to get even with the employer for real or imagined grievances.

Embezzlement losses may be discovered by accident, by careful audit, by inspection of records or property, by the embezzler's abnormal behavior, by a sudden increase in the embezzler's standard of living, or by the embezzler's disappearance from employment. Bank embezzlement is jointly investigated by the local police and the FBI. However, the prosecution rate is low because of adverse publicity for both the individual and the company. Often the employee has been trusted for many years, and sympathy overrules justice.

Because police training rarely includes accounting courses, investigating embezzlement cases often requires help from professional accountants. In embezzlement cases, prove fraudulent intent to convert property contrary to the terms of a trust by establishing how and when the property was converted, what the exact amount was, and who did the converting. Establish that a financial loss did in fact occur. Determine the amount of the loss. Describe the property accurately if it is not money. Describe and prove the method of obtaining the property. Establish the nature of the trust. Seize all relevant books and financial records as evidence. It is necessary to determine the motive to prove fraudulent intent.

Environmental Crime

Our environment—air, land, and water—has become a casualty in the battle among companies, worldwide, for higher profits and lower costs. Investigation of environmental crime is a new area of specialization that mixes elements of law, public health, and science. It is considered within the larger realm of white-collar crime because the motive behind these offenses is almost always an economic one. And contrary to what many believe, environmental crime is not victimless—the victims are our children and our children's children. Environmental crime is far-reaching and pervasive, and its consequences are often hidden for years or even decades.

Interpol entered the fight against environmental crime in 1992 when its general assembly adopted a resolution authorizing the creation of the Environmental Crimes Committee, with an initial participation of approximately 40 countries from all regions of the world. Interpol states on its website:

> Environmental crime is a serious and growing international problem, with criminals violating national and international laws put in place to protect the environment. These criminals are polluting the air, water and land. They are pushing commercially valuable wildlife species closer to extinction and they are significantly impacting the biological integrity of the planet.
>
> Across the world, environmental crime takes on a number of forms which include: poaching, trafficking in ozone-depleting substances (ODSs), trafficking and use of illegal pesticides, illegal diversion of rivers, trafficking in endangered species, and illegal dumping of hazardous waste onto land or in water. Environmental criminals, including those associated with organized crime, regularly cause permanent and extensive damage to ecosystems, which may result in serious human health problems. The incentives to carry out environmental crimes are financial, coupled with a perception, on the part of criminals, that they are unlikely to be caught and face severe penalties. Examples of environmental crimes which have become more common and lucrative are the trade of collectible species and illegal disposal of waste in an effort to avoid legitimate disposal costs, which results in an unfair competitive advantage for the criminals over legitimate, law-abiding businesses. ("Environmental Crime")

The most common environmental crimes prosecuted in the United States involve illegal waste disposal.

The most common substances involved in such offenses are hazardous wastes. Also included are used tires and oil. Collecting and processing evidence in these cases often require special training and equipment. Many law enforcement officers lack the scientific background needed to put together an environmental pollution case or to deal safely with the illegal disposal of hazardous waste. Indeed, walking into a hazardous waste site without proper protective gear or skills for handling the material may be just as deadly as facing an armed robber in a dark alley.

Furthermore, most officers have little or no idea of the existence of the complex array of environmental control laws with all their exceptions, changes, and omissions. For example, Congress and administrative agencies are continuously amending environmental laws and regulations to increase punishments for environmental criminal offenses, in many cases making them felonies rather than misdemeanors. Among such acts are the following:

- Comprehensive Environmental Response, Compensation and Liability Act (CERCLA)
- Resource Conservation and Recovery Act (RCRA)
- Federal Water Pollution Control Act (FWPCA)
- Clean Air Act (CAA)

In each of these acts, amendments were made converting misdemeanors to felonies.

In 1990 the Pollution Prosecution Act was enacted, making enforcement of environmental crimes a new concern for law enforcement. Violations of various environmental crime acts call for penalties of up to $25,000 per day for noncompliance or imprisonment up to 10 years.

The main problems in investigating environmental crimes are understanding the numerous laws regarding what constitutes environmental crime, the fact that it is often considered a civil matter, and collaborating with civil regulatory agencies.

Civil regulatory agencies are knowledgeable in these laws and have the resources to document evidence of a violation. For these reasons, in addition to the safety issues, many investigators find it beneficial to seek assistance from an environmental regulatory agency. Collaboration with specially equipped environmental labs, as opposed to crime labs, may also be necessary.

Some jurisdictions have designated specially trained law enforcement officers to investigate environmental crimes. Although many such officers are derisively being called "the garbage police," some agencies' sanitation police are gaining respect and recognition for their efforts in keeping the city clean and free of environmental wrongdoings. Massachusetts is one of several states that have created an environmental crimes strike force, an interagency law enforcement initiative that combines the technical, investigative, and legal resources necessary to detect, investigate, and prosecute environmental crimes.

Environmental hazards once common in industry, in America and abroad, include lead, asbestos, and chlorofluorocarbons (CFCs)—all of which have become regulated under various environmental laws. For example, when Freon, a brand name the public generally equates with the broader class of CFCs, was shown to contribute to the global problem of ozone depletion, countries from around the world gathered to find a solution. Through an international agreement signed by more than 160 countries at the 1987 Montreal Convention, the United States agreed to completely phase out CFC production by the year 2000. However, as the FBI found, continued demand for CFCs and dwindling supplies created an enormous black market, second only to the black market for narcotics. The FBI ("Criminal Fraud") notes: "To date, cooperative law enforcement efforts have resulted in the seizure of 1.5 million pounds of illegally imported CFCs with a 'street' value of $18 million."

Many of the problems associated with investigating environmental crime are similar to investigating other crimes that have become more prevalent in the twenty-first century. Definitions of environmental crimes vary from state to state. Statistics are not uniformly compiled. The suspects are often otherwise upstanding businesspeople who often do not feel they are committing crimes.

Gibbons (2005) cites one legal definition of environmental crime as any *"willful* criminal violation that results in actual and substantial harm to the water, ambient air, soil, or land." Premeditation or malice is not required to prove an environmental crime. All that must be proved is that an act that violated the law was done knowingly rather than by mistake (Figure 14.11). For example, the owner of a company makes a conscious decision to dump hazardous materials into a waterway or unload a truck full of construction and demolition (C & D) debris in a remote location off a desolate road under cover of darkness. Evidence of "knowing" may include tire tracks in remote locations and documented "after hours" activities, for it may be concluded that such "detours" are made to illegally dump and are not in fact accidental.

As in any other crime, there must be a victim. Officers should determine who owns the property. Most judges do not like to see *State of X v. X* unless the state actually owns the property. In addition, officers should conduct a standard administrative interview, obtaining

Figure 14.11
Premeditation or malice is not required to prove an environmental crime. All that must be proved is that an act violated the law and was done knowingly rather than by mistake.

such information as name, date of birth, address, and whatever information is routinely asked *before* giving the *Miranda* warning if an interrogation is to take place.

Of special concern in environmental crime investigations is the search warrant. Investigators must know what substances they may seek and how they should collect such samples to avoid becoming contaminated. Again, regulatory personnel may provide assistance.

Through criminal prosecution of environmental crimes, local prosecutors have a crucial function and can assume the role of protector of the public health. Often such prosecution is most successful using **parallel proceedings,** that is, pursuing civil and criminal sanctions at the same time.

SUMMARY

Larceny/theft is the unlawful taking, carrying, leading, or driving away of property from another's possession. It is synonymous with theft. Both larceny and burglary are crimes against property, but larceny, unlike burglary, does not involve illegally entering a structure. Larceny also differs from robbery in that no force or threat of force is involved.

The elements of the crime of larceny/theft are (1) the felonious stealing, taking, carrying, leading, or driving away of (2) another's personal goods or property (3) valued above or below a specified amount (4) with the intent to permanently deprive the owner of the property or goods. The two major categories of larceny/theft are grand larceny, a felony based on a value of stolen property usually more than $100; and petty larceny, a misdemeanor based on a value of stolen property usually less than $100. In most states, taking found property with the intent to keep or sell it is also a crime.

Among the common types of larceny are purse snatching, picking pockets, theft from coin machines, shoplifting, bicycle theft, theft from motor vehicles, theft from buildings, theft of motor vehicle accessories, and jewelry theft.

When dealing with shoplifters, remember that altering the price of an item is considered larceny. Also remember that it is not usually required that a shoplifter leave the premises with the stolen item before apprehension. When investigating jewelry theft, inform the FBI of the theft even if there is no immediate evidence of interstate operations. The elements of the offense of receiving stolen goods are (1) receiving, buying or concealing stolen or illegally obtained goods and (2) knowing them to be stolen or illegally obtained.

Fraud is intentional deception to cause a person to give up property or some lawful right. It differs from theft in that fraud uses deceit rather than stealth to obtain goods illegally. Fraud is committed in many ways, including through the use of checks, debit and credit cards, confidence games, and embezzlement. Common types of check fraud are issuance of insufficient-fund or worthless checks and forgery.

Elements of the crime of larceny by debit and credit card include (1) possessing such cards obtained by theft or fraud (2) by which services or goods are obtained (3) through unauthorized signing of the cardholder's name. For the fifth consecutive year, identity theft topped the list of fraud-related complaints filed with the FTC in 2004.

White-collar, or economic, crime includes (1) securities and commodities fraud; (2) insurance fraud; (3) health care and medical fraud; (4) telemarketing fraud; (5) credit card and check fraud; (6) consumer fraud, illegal competition, and deceptive practices; (7) bankruptcy fraud; (8) computer-related fraud; (9) bank fraud, embezzlement, and pilferage; (10) bribes, kickbacks, and payoffs; (11) money laundering; (12) election law violations; (13) corruption of public officials; (14) copyright violations; (15) computer crimes; (16) environmental crimes; and (17) receiving stolen property. The FBI's two-pronged approach to investigating money laundering involves (1) the investigation of the underlying criminal activity (in simple terms, if there is no criminal activity, or "specified unlawful activity" that generates illicit proceeds, then there can be no money laundering) and (2) a parallel financial investigation to uncover the financial infrastructure of the criminal organization. This involves following the money and discerning how it flows through an organization and what steps are taken to conceal, disguise, or hide the proceeds.

The main problems in investigating environmental crimes are understanding the numerous laws regarding what constitutes the crime, the fact that it is often considered a civil matter, and collaborating with civil regulatory agencies.

CHECKLIST

Larceny

- What are the name, address, and phone number of the complainant or the person reporting the crime?
- What are the name, address, and phone number of the victim if different from the complainant?
- Has the victim made previous theft complaints? If so, obtain all details.
- What were the date and time the crime was reported and the date and time the crime was committed if known?
- Who owns the property or has title to it or right of possession?
- Will the owner or person in control or possession sign the complaint?
- Who discovered the loss? Was this the logical person to discover it?
- Where was the item at the time of the theft? Was this the usual place for the item, or had it been recently transferred there?
- When was the item last seen?
- Has the area been searched to determine whether the property might have been misplaced?
- What security precautions had been taken? Were these normal?
- Exactly what property was taken? Obtain a complete description of each item, including number, color, size, serial numbers, and other identifying marks.
- What was the value of the items? How was the value determined: estimated original price, replacement price, or estimated market value?

- How easily could the items be sold? Are there likely markets or buyers?
- Were there any witnesses to the theft or people who might provide leads?
- Who had access to the property before and during the time of the theft?
- Who were absentee employees?
- Who are possible suspects and why? What might be the motive?

APPLICATION

A cash box was left on top of a desk at a university office. Some students had registered early that day, so there was about $600 in the box. The box was closed but not locked. The office manager went to lunch, leaving a college student in charge. The student took a phone call in the dean's office, and the box was out of her sight for about five minutes. Later she heard a noise in the hallway outside the office. She went out to see what had happened and discovered that a student had been accidentally pushed through a glass door across the hallway from the main office. She observed the scene in the hallway for about five minutes and then went back to the registration office, where she did not notice anything out of order.

After a half hour the office manager returned from lunch and helped register two students at the front counter. When she went to the cash box to make change, she found that the $600 was missing. She immediately notified the administrator's office, and a controller was sent over to the registration office. The controller conducted a brief investigation and then notified the police. You are the investigator arriving at the registration office.

Questions

1. What procedure would you use upon arrival?
2. What steps would you take immediately?
3. What evidence is likely to be located?
4. What questions would you ask?
5. What is the probability of solving the case?

DISCUSSION QUESTIONS

1. Larceny has been called the most underreported crime in the United States. What factors might account for failure to report larceny? Is there a way to determine how many larcenies actually occur when you consider shoplifting, bicycle thefts, and minor thefts of property that victims may regard as having been simply lost or misplaced?

2. What are possible motives for committing a larceny such as bicycle theft? shoplifting? embezzlement? thefts from autos? gasoline thefts? theft by check or credit card?

3. How can you protect yourself against identity theft? If it should occur, what would you expect the police to do?

4. How do petty and grand larceny differ in your state? Do the elements that must be proved for each of these crimes differ in your state?

5. A con artist has bilked a senior citizen in your community out of $2,000. The senior citizen has filed a complaint in hopes of having the money returned and the perpetrator arrested. What crime has been committed under your state laws, and what is the procedure for following up the complaint?

6. A man has been arrested for shoplifting and taken to the police station for booking. During the search for this offense, the police discover several credit cards that are not issued in the name of the person arrested. What offense is involved? Is there a separate offense from the original offense of shoplifting? Can the person be tried on both offenses? What procedure is necessary to prove the second charge?

7. Embezzlement is most frequently associated with white-collar crime. Has it been a problem in your community?

8. How do the following differ: stealing a suitcase (a) from the baggage claim area at an airport, (b) from an automobile, and (c) from a retail store?

9. If a customer knows an article is priced much higher in the store where she is shopping than in another store and can prove it, is it legal for her to change the price on the article?

10. What can the police do to reduce the number of larcenies in a community? Does your community have an antishoplifting program? an anti–bike theft program? Do banks send literature to senior citizens concerning con games? What other measures have been initiated in your community? What additional measures may be taken?

MEDIA EXPLORATIONS

 Internet

Select one of the following assignments to complete.

- To learn more about identity theft, go to www.identitytheft.org, www.privacyrights.org, or www.futurecrime.com. Write a brief report on what new information you learned about this crime.
- Go to the FBI website at www.fbi.gov. Click on "library and reference." Select "Uniform Crime Reports" and outline what the report says about larceny/theft.
- Select one of the following key words: *confidence games, cramming (phone), embezzlement, environmental crime, fraud, fraud prevention, identity theft, identity theft prevention, larceny/theft, larceny/theft prevention, poaching, shoplifting, white-collar crime, white-collar crime prevention.* Find one article relevant to larceny/theft, fraud, white-collar crime, and environmental crime investigations to outline and share with the class.

Crime and Evidence in Action

Go to the CD and choose the **burglary/arson case.** During the course of the case you'll become patrol officer, detective, judge, corrections officer, and parole officer to conduct interactive investigative research. Each case unfolds as you respond to key decision points. Feedback for each possible answer choice is packed full of information, including term definitions, weblinks, and important documentation. The sergeant is available at certain times to help mentor you, the Online Resources website offers a variety of information, and be sure to take notes in your e-notebook during the suspect video statements and at key points throughout (these notes can be saved, printed, or e-mailed). The Forensics Exercise will test your ability to collect, transport, and analyze evidence from the crime scene. At the end of the case you can track how well you responded to each decision point and join the Discussion Forum for a postmortem. **Go to the CD and use the skills you've learned in this chapter to solve a case.**

REFERENCES

Babitsky, Timlynn. "Cattle Rustlers Beware . . . ." North American Rural Futures Institute website, http://narfi.org/node/45. Posted August 6, 2004. Accessed July 29, 2005.

Ballezza, Richard A. "Health Club Credit Card Theft: A National Crime Problem." *FBI Law Enforcement Bulletin*, November 2003, pp. 8–13.

Barbassa, Juliana. "Cattle Rustlers Defeated by DNA." *CBS News*, January 29, 2004. http://www.cbsnews.com/stories/2004/01/29/tech/main596571.shtml. Accessed July 29, 2005.

Beaulieu, Elizabeth. "Retail Survey Reports Slight Drop in Shrink." *Security Director News*, November 2004, pp. 1, 16–17.

Blanton, Bobby. "Reading Branding Irons." http://www.bbqblanton.com/puread.htm. Accessed July 29, 2005.

"Cargo Theft Interdiction Program." California Highway Patrol website, http://www.chp.ca.gov/html/vtask.html. Accessed July 29, 2005.

Clarke, Ronald V. *Shoplifting.* Washington, DC: Office of Community Oriented Policing Services, Problem-Oriented Guides for Police Series No. 11, January 24, 2002.

"Commercial Motor Vehicle and Cargo Theft," Florida Department of Transportation website, http://www.dot.state.fl.us/mcco/cmv_cargo_theft.htm. Accessed July 29, 2005.

"Crime and No Punishment." http://www.nationalbikeregistry.com/crime.html. Accessed October 3, 2005.

Crime in the United States 2003. Washington, DC: Federal Bureau of Investigation, Uniform Crime Reports, October 27, 2004.

"Crimes Against Nature: Special Units Tackle Spike in Cactus Theft." *Law Enforcement News*, April 30, 2003, p.6.

Dabney, Dean A.; Hollinger, Richard C.; and Dugan, Laura. "Who Actually Steals? A Study of Covertly Observed Shoplifters." *Justice Quarterly*, December 2004, pp. 693–728.

Dadisho, Ed. "Identity Theft and the Police Response: The Investigation." *The Police Chief*, March 2005a, pp. 46–52.

Dadisho, Ed. "Identity Theft and the Police Response: Prevention." *The Police Chief*, February 2005b, pp. 17–26.

Dadisho, Ed. "Identity Theft and the Police Response: The Problem." *The Police Chief*, January 2005c, pp. 25–29.

Dodge, Mary. "Slams, Crams, Jams, and Other Phone Scams." *Journal of Contemporary Criminal Justice*, November 2001, pp. 358–368.

"Environmental Crime." Interpol website. http://www.interpol.int/Public/EnvironmentalCrime/default.asp. Accessed August 2, 2005.

FBI. "Art Theft Program." http://www.fbi.gov/hq/cid/arttheft/arttheft.htm. Accessed July 28, 2005.

FBI. "Criminal Fraud Cases: Environmental Crimes." http://www.fbi.gov/hq/cid/fc/gfu/cases/criminalfatg.htm. Accessed August 2, 2005.

FBI. "Insurance Fraud Video Text." http://www.fbi.gov/hq/cid/fc/video_text/if_txt.htm. Accessed September 10, 2005.

FBI. "Jewelry and Gem Program." http://www.fbi.gov/hq/cid/jag/jagpage.htm. Accessed July 28, 2005.

FBI. "Pirates of Hollywood or, the Curse of the Green-Glow Camcorder." http://www.fbi.gov/page2/july05/pirate072005.htm. Accessed August 1, 2005.

Financial Crimes Report to the Public. Washington, DC: Federal Bureau of Investigation, Financial Crimes Section, May 2005.

"Forgoing Lassos, Rustlers Have S. Dakota Ranchers Reeling." *Law Enforcement News*, November 15/30, 2003, p.11.

Gibbons, Whit. "How Do We Curtail White-Collar Environmental Crime?" University of Georgia, Savannah River Ecology Laboratory, *Ecoviews* Environmental Commentaries, March 13, 2005. http://www.uga.edu/srel/ecoview3-15-05.htm. Accessed August 1, 2005.

Goldman, Jeanette. "JSA Alert: Increasing Jewelry Theft Via Roof." *Rapaport News* on Diamonds.net, http://www.diamonds.net/news/newsitem.asp?num=12675. Accessed July 14, 2005.

Hayes, Read, and Rogers, King. "Catch Them If You Can." *Security Management*, October 2003, pp. 80–88.

Heath, Lee R. "U.S. Postal Inspectors: Partners in the Investigation of Identity Theft and Crimes Involving the U.S. Mail." *The Police Chief*, March 2005.

Hollinger, Richard C., and Langton, Lynn. *2004 National Retail Security Survey: Final Report*. Gainesville: University of Florida Press, 2005.

John E. Reid and Associates, Inc. "Interrogating a Suspect on the Issue of Identity Theft." December 2003. http://www.reid.com/educational_info/r_tips.html?serial=107046662252680&print=[print]. Accessed August 1, 2005.

LaCous, Mira. "Computer Technology." *Law Enforcement Technology*, June 2005, pp.144–148.

Lamb, John. "An Ounce of Prevention." *Security Products*, November 2004, pp. 46–49.

Laughlin, Mike. "Brands: Page One." http://www.cowboyshowcase.com/brands.htm. Accessed July 29, 2005.

Lim, Paul J. "Gimme Your Name and SSN." *U.S. News and World Report*, March 7, 2005, pp. 46–48

Majoras, Deborah Platt. "Combating Identity Theft: Partnerships Are Powerful." *The Police Chief*, February 2005, pp. 14–15.

Martinez, Liz. "CCTV in the Retail Environment." *Security Technology and Design*, March 2004a, pp. 58–62.

Martinez, Liz. "Selling Retail Security Successfully." *Security Technology and Design*, July 2004b, pp. 46–48.

Motivans, Mark. *Money Laundering Offenders, 1994–2001*. Washington, DC: Bureau of Justice Statistics, Special Report, July 2003. (NCJ 199574)

National and State Trends in Fraud and Identity Theft, January–December 2004. Washington, DC: Federal Trade Commission, February 1, 2005.

Newman, Graeme R. *Identity Theft*. Washington, DC: Office of Community Oriented Policing Services, Problem-Oriented Guides for Police, Problem-Specific Guides Series No.25, July 26, 2004.

Page, Douglas. "RFID Tags: Big Brother in a Small Device." *Law Enforcement Technology*, August 2004, pp. 128–133.

"Possible Indicators of Vendor Theft." Corporate Security Services website. http://www.corpsecure.com/css/members/Retail_security/VENDOR_%20THEFT.htm Accessed July 29, 2005.

"A Possible Lead on a Treetop Thief." Associated Press, as reported in the Minneapolis/St. Paul *StarTribune*, November 28, 2003, p.B3.

Rogers, King; Guffey, Ben; and Markle, Anne. "The Retail Loss Prevention Tool Bag." *Security Technology and Design*, February 2005, pp. 22–26.

Scuro, Joseph, Jr. "White Collar Crime." *Law and Order*, May 2003, pp. 20–22.

Sheetz, Michael. "Investigating Global Money Laundering," *Law and Order*, August 2004, pp. 106–111.

Sivy, Michael; Regnier, Pat; and Bigda, Carolyn. "What No One Is Telling You about Identity Theft." *Money*, July 2005, pp. 95–99.

Smith, Kevin. "Organized Retail Theft: A Low-Risk, High-Profit Threat." *Security Director News*, October 2004, p. 9.

Vendor Fraud. Georgia Retail Association. http://www.georgiaretail.org/VendorFraud.htm Accessed July 28, 2005.

Vincent, Bambi. "Workshop Teaches Pickpocket Recognition." *Law and Order*, June 2005, pp. 116–119.

White, Stephen, and Einhorn, Monique. "Identity Theft: Resources for Police." *The Police Chief*, April 2005, pp. 36–42.

Whitlock, Chuck. "Identity Theft Recognition." *The Law Enforcement Trainer*, Fourth Quarter 2004, pp. 62–64.

Motor Vehicle Theft

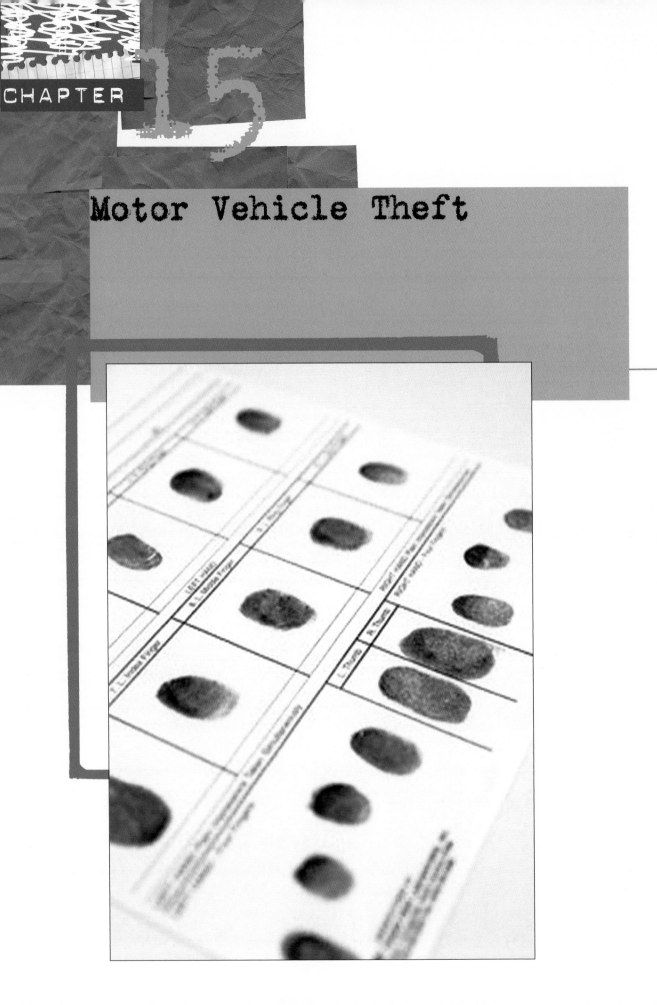

Can You Define?

Do You Know?

- What a VIN is and why it is important?
- What the five major categories of motor vehicle theft are?
- What the elements of the crime of unauthorized use of a motor vehicle are?
- What types of vehicles are considered "motor vehicles"?
- What embezzlement of a motor vehicle is?
- How the Dyer Act assists in motor vehicle theft investigation?
- Why false reports of auto theft are sometimes made?
- What two agencies can help investigate motor vehicle theft?
- How to improve effectiveness in recognizing stolen vehicles?
- How to help prevent motor vehicle theft?

Outline

I t is not unusual for an American family to finance or own more than $30,000 in motor vehicles. Yet the motor vehicle, even though highly vulnerable, is the least protected of all property subject to theft. The vehicle, its accessories, and the property inside are all targets for thieves.

Most people use motor vehicles to travel to work and for pleasure. Thousands of recreational vehicles are also targets for theft and burglary.

Aircraft and watercraft thefts add to the problems facing police investigators.

A car is stolen every 26 seconds in the United States ("Is Your Car," p.23). According to the FBI Uniform Crime Reports (*Crime in the United States 2003*), motor vehicle thefts increased by 1.1 percent in 2003. An estimated 1,260,471 motor vehicles were stolen in 2003 with a value of $8.6 billion. The average value of a stolen vehicle was $6,797. Automobiles represented 73.3 percent of all motor vehicles stolen. The clearance rate was 13.1 percent, with 30 percent of the vehicles never recovered. Tables 15.1 and 15.2 list the most commonly stolen vehicles in the United States for 2003 and 2004, respectively.

Table 15.1 / **Top Stolen Cars in the United States, 2003**

1. 2000 Honda Civic
2. 1989 Toyota Camry
3. 1991 Honda Accord
4. 1994 Chevrolet Full Size C/K 1500 Pickup
5. 1994 Dodge Caravan
6. 1997 Ford F150 Series
7. 1986 Toyota Pickup
8. 1995 Acura Integra
9. 1987 Nissan Sentra
10. 1986 Oldsmobile Cutlass

Source: "Hot Wheels: Now You See Them, Now You Don't! No Surprise, Auto Thieves Continue to Favor Popular Models." National Insurance Crime Bureau press release, February 28, 2005. http://www.nicb.org/public/newsroom/ hotwheels/pressrelease.cfm

Table 15.2 / **Top Stolen Cars in the United States, 2004**

1. 1999 Acura Integra
2. 2002 BMW M Roadster
3. 1998 Acura Integra
4. 1991 GMC V2500
5. 2002 Audi S4
6. 1996 Acura Integra
7. 1995 Acura Integra
8. 2004 Mercury Marauder
9. 1997 Acura Integra
10. 1992 Mercedes-Benz 600

Source: "Acura Integra Is Most-Stolen Car in America." *Consumer Affairs News*, July 19, 2005. http://www.consumeraffairs.com/news04/2005/acura _moststolen.html

This chapter begins with an explanation of motor vehicle identification and motor vehicle theft classification. This is followed by descriptions of the elements of the crimes of unauthorized use of a motor vehicle, embezzlement, and interstate transportation of motor vehicles. Next the chapter describes the preliminary investigation as well as the problem of insurance fraud and names various agencies that might cooperate in investigating and/or preventing motor vehicle theft. Following this is a discussion of how to recognize a stolen motor vehicle or an unauthorized driver, how to recover an abandoned or stolen motor vehicle, and efforts to prevent motor vehicle theft. The chapter concludes with a discussion of thefts of other types of motor vehicles.

Motor Vehicle Identification

iven the millions of motor vehicles operating on our roads, an identification system is imperative. The most important means of vehicle identification is the **vehicle identification number (VIN).**

> The VIN is the primary nonduplicated, serialized number assigned by a manufacturer to each vehicle made. This number–critical in motor vehicle theft investigation– identifies the specific vehicle in question.

The Motor Vehicle Theft Law Enforcement Act of 1984 requires manufacturers to place the 17-digit VIN on 14 specified component parts including the engine, the transmission, both front fenders, the hood, both front doors, both bumpers, both rear quarter panels, both rear doors, and the deck, lid, tailgate, *or* hatchback. In most late-model cars the VIN is located on the left instrumentation or dash plate by the window, on the driver's door or post, or on the firewall.

A fictional example of a VIN would be "1F1CY62X1YK555888," where:

1 = nation of origin (U.S. 1 or 4, Canada 2, Mexico 3)

F = manufacturer symbol (Audi A, BMW B, Honda H)

1 = make

C = restraint

Y = car line

62 = body type

X = engine symbol

1 = check digit

Y = model year

K = assembly plant

555888 = sequential production number

The VIN of a vehicle is comparable to human DNA. No two VINs are identical. The VIN allows investigators to trace a vehicle from the factory to the scrap yard. Some manufacturers position the label in plain view; others hide it. Car thieves often attempt to change or replace VINs to conceal vehicles' true identities (Figure 15.1). As one investigator put it: "I often refer to the labels as our guardian angels—you can't see them, but you know they're constantly working in your favor."

Manufacturers also use numbers to identify engines and various vehicle components.

Figure 15.1

A section of the front subframe of the truck that was used in the bombing of the U.S. embassy in Dar Es Salaam, Tanzania. This critical piece of evidence was used in the trial against the suspected terrorists—the number stamped in the metal is the vehicle identification number which was instrumental in tracking down the suspects. This embassy and another in Nairobi, Kenya, were bombed almost simultaneously on August 7, 1998.

Classification of Motor Vehicle Theft

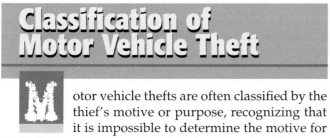

 otor vehicle thefts are often classified by the thief's motive or purpose, recognizing that it is impossible to determine the motive for thefts that end in the vehicle's being abandoned.

Classifications of motor vehicle theft based on the motive of the offender include:
- Joyriding.
- Transportation.
- Commission of another crime.
- Stripping for parts and accessories.
- Reselling for profit.

Joyriding

The joyrider and the person stealing for transportation are sometimes grouped together, but there is an important distinction between them. The joyrider is generally a younger person who steals for thrills and excitement.

Joyriders look for cars with keys in the ignition that can be started and driven away rapidly. The vehicle is taken for a comparatively short time and then abandoned near the location of the theft or near the joyrider's destination. A vehicle taken to another community is generally left there, and another vehicle is then stolen for the return trip.

Stolen vehicles are often found where young people congregate: fast-food places, malls, and athletic events. Several vehicle thefts within a short time may follow a pattern, providing clues for investigators. For example, most cars stolen by the same individual or group in a short period are the same make, entered in the same manner, and stolen and dropped off in the same general area. Juvenile informants can be extremely helpful in investigating such auto thefts.

Motor vehicle thefts by juveniles are often not regarded seriously by the courts, even though they account for most vehicle thefts and can cause injury or death to others. It is not unusual for juveniles to be involved in up to a hundred car thefts before apprehension.

Vehicle theft by juveniles is a serious problem. In fact, in some states joyriding is a separate offense.

Transportation

Theft of a motor vehicle for transportation can involve a joyrider but is more apt to involve a transient, a hitchhiker, or a runaway. The objective is to travel from one point to another at no cost. These offenders are generally older than joyriders. Late fall and winter are peak periods for this type of theft.

A vehicle stolen for transportation is kept longer than one stolen for joyriding. Frequently it is operated until it runs out of gas or stops running. It is then abandoned (often to avoid suspicion) and another vehicle is stolen. The license plates may be changed, or a plate may be stolen and put on the rear of the vehicle.

Commission of Another Crime

Automobiles are used in most serious crimes. Robberies of banks, bank messengers, payroll offices, businesses, and service stations, as well as criminal escapes, almost always involve a getaway in a stolen vehicle. Vehicles provide both rapid transportation and a means to transport the loot. Other crimes frequently committed while using stolen vehicles include rapes, kidnappings, burglaries, larcenies to obtain gas, and assaults of police officers attempting to apprehend a suspect. Records indicate that many habitual criminals have stolen at least one car in their criminal career. Some began as car thieves.

Stolen cars are used in committing other crimes to escape detection at the crime scene and to avoid being identified by witnesses. Therefore, the criminal normally uses the stolen vehicle only briefly. In fact, a stolen vehicle report may not yet have been made when the crime is committed. Stolen plates are often used to cause confusion in identification. The vehicle used in committing the crime—the "hot" car—is usually soon abandoned for a "cold" car—a vehicle used to escape from the crime scene vicinity.

Stolen vehicles played a major role in the search for serial killer Andrew Cunanan. Authorities were able to re-create the route taken by Cunanan in his cross-country killing spree by locating one victim's vehicle in the vicinity of the next victim's body. Cunanan's homicidal rampage began in late April 1997 in Minnesota with the killing of two men. Cunanan then stole the Jeep Grand Cherokee of one of the victims, and police later discovered this vehicle near the home of a third victim in Chicago. The Chicago victim's Lexus was reported missing and was later found in New Jersey at the murder scene of Cunanan's fourth victim. In continuing the pattern, the fourth victim's pickup truck was stolen and later turned up in a Miami Beach parking ramp, several blocks from where fashion designer Gianni Versace was murdered in front of his home by Cunanan, who then killed himself.

A stolen motor vehicle driven by a criminal is 150 to 200 times more likely to be in an accident than a vehicle driven by a noncriminal; therefore, regard as suspicious any damaged abandoned vehicles you observe. Conditions contributing to this high accident rate include operating the vehicle on unfamiliar streets and roads, driving at high speeds in an attempt to escape police pursuit, testing the vehicle's speed, unfamiliarity with the vehicle, and use of drugs.

A criminal apprehended with a stolen vehicle after committing another crime is usually prosecuted for only the major crime, not the auto theft.

Stripping for Parts and Accessories

Many vehicles are stolen by juveniles and young adults who strip them for parts and accessories to sell: transmissions, rear ends, motors, and wheels. Batteries, radiators, and heaters are sold to wrecking yards, used car lots, and auto repair shops. Expensive accessories such as car phones, stereo tape decks, radios, CB radios, and CD players also are removed for resale. The stripped vehicle is often crushed for scrap metal. The profit is extremely high.

Sometimes thieves steal specific items for friends, other vehicle owners, or themselves (Figure 15.2). These

Figure 15.2
This vehicle was taken by car thieves, who stripped it for parts and then dumped it in a remote rural area.

© Malcom Fife/zefa/CORBIS

are often parts that are impossible to buy or are very expensive.

Airbag Theft The National Insurance Crime Bureau (NICB) reports that airbags are a primary accessory on the black market for stolen vehicle parts. A new airbag retails for approximately $1,000. Unscrupulous collision repair shops may replace a deployed airbag with a stolen one and charge the customer or the customer's insurer the full price (which constitutes insurance fraud). Insurance statistics show that approximately 50,000 airbags are stolen each year, resulting in an annual loss of more than $50 million to vehicle owners and their insurers ("Airbag Theft").

Stealing for Chop Shops A **chop shop** is a business, usually a body shop, that disassembles stolen autos and sells the parts. The chop shop deals with car thieves who steal the cars specifically for them, often on demand, stealing the exact make, model, and color. The vehicle may triple in value when sold for parts. There is no waiting period and no tax to the customer. The cars are dismantled, and the parts are cataloged. In some cities this business is so big that organized crime has been heavily involved and network organizations dispose of the stolen parts. Auto parts are also sought outside the United States.

The chop shop may also deal directly with the owner of a vehicle who wants to dispose of it for insurance purposes due to dissatisfaction with its performance. The owner leaves the vehicle registration with the chop shop. The shop returns the registration to the owner after the vehicle is dismantled and crushed. The insurance company has no chance of recovery.

Reselling

Auto thefts are also committed by professional thieves who take an unattended vehicle, with or without the keys, and simply drive it away. Or they may go to a used car lot, posing as a buyer, and drive the vehicle away on a no-return test drive. Another method is to answer an ad in the paper for a particular car, try it out, and then never return it. This gives the thief time to escape because the owner gave permission to take the vehicle—which makes the case one of embezzlement. Cars are also stolen by using bad checks. Recovering a vehicle stolen by professionals requires a specialized knowledge of investigative techniques and often depends on a reliable informant to get started. Moreover, such thieves are difficult to detect and prosecute. As specialists in automobiles, the thieves know how to steal cars and how to alter them or the documents needed to make them eligible for resale. The professional is rarely the actual thief; rather, the professional hires others to steal cars and bring them to a specified location, usually a garage, for making the necessary alterations.

Alterations include repainting, changing seat covers, repairing existing damage, and altering the engine number. The car is also completely searched to eliminate any items that connect it with the former owner. The VIN is almost always altered or replaced. The most common method of changing the VIN is to buy a similar vehicle from a salvage lot and then remove and replace the entire dash, making the change undetectable. If the VIN is not located on the dash, the car thief has a much more difficult time. In some cases the VIN plate itself is removed and carefully altered, or the car thief can make embossed tape with a handheld tape-numbering device and place it over the regular VIN plate. Unless the inside of the car is investigated, a false VIN plate is not usually detected.

After all number changes on the motor and the VIN plate are completed, the vehicle is prepared for resale with stolen or forged titles, fictitious bills of sale, or titles received with salvage vehicles bought by the thieves. When the mechanical alterations and paperwork are completed, the vehicle is registered through the Department of Motor Vehicles (DMV) and resold, usually at a public car auction, to a used car dealer or a private individual.

Many stolen cars are exported for resale in other countries, the most common destinations being Central and South America. According to the NICB, 200,000 vehicles are illegally exported each year. One international car theft ring was indicted by a federal grand jury for illegally obtaining vehicles from Reno, Nevada, car dealers and transporting them to the Port of Long Beach in California, where the cars were loaded onto freighters and shipped to China to be sold at three to four times their original price. The ring members then reported the cars stolen to police and insurance companies for reimbursement of their losses. Charges against ring members included making false statements on loan and credit applications, mail fraud, interstate and foreign transportation of stolen property, aiding and abetting, and attempting to evade financial reporting requirements. The FBI estimated that the scheme involved total losses of up to $6 million.

Elements of the Crime

Unauthorized Use of a Motor Vehicle

Most car thieves are prosecuted not for auto theft but for unauthorized use of a motor vehicle. Prosecution for auto theft requires proof that the thief intended to permanently deprive the owner of the vehicle, which is often difficult or impossible to establish.

Intentionally Taking or Driving *Intent* is often described in state laws as "with intent to permanently or temporarily deprive the owner of title or possession" or "with intent to steal." Intent can be inferred from the act of taking or driving, being observed taking or driving, or being apprehended while taking or driving. Laws often include as culpable any person who voluntarily rides in a vehicle knowing it is stolen.

A Motor Vehicle **Motor vehicle** is not restricted to automobiles. It includes any self-propelled device for moving people or property or pulling implements, whether operated on land, on water, or in the air.

Homemade motor vehicles are also included.

Without the Consent of the Owner or the Owner's Authorized Agent Legitimate ownership of motor vehicles exists when the vehicle is in the factory being manufactured, when it is being sold by an authorized dealership, or when it is owned by a private person, company, or corporation. *Owner* and *true owner* are not necessarily the same. For example, the true owner can be a lending agency that retains title until the loan is paid.

Usually the owner or the owner's authorized agent reports the theft. Thus, it can be determined immediately whether consent was given. Previous consent is not a defense, although it may be considered.

If you stop a suspicious vehicle and the driver does not have proof of ownership, check the registration with the state DMV to determine who the legal owner is. If that person is not the driver, check with the legal owner to determine whether the driver has permission to use the vehicle.

Motor Vehicle Embezzlement

his most frequently occurs when a new or used-car agency permits a prospective buyer to try out a vehicle for a specific time. The person decides to convert the vehicle to personal use and does not return it. This is fraudulent appropriation of property. Motor vehicle embezzlement can also occur under rental or lease agreements or when private persons let someone test-drive a vehicle that is for sale.

Interstate Transportation

In 1919 the need for federal control of motor vehicle theft was recognized, and Congress approved the National Motor Vehicle Theft Act, commonly known as the *Dyer Act*.

The act was amended in 1945 to include aircraft and is now called the *Interstate Transportation of Stolen Motor Vehicles Act.* Since the Dyer Act was passed, more than 300,000 vehicles have been recovered and more than 100,000 criminals have been convicted in interstate car theft cases.

The elements of the crime of interstate transportation of a motor vehicle are:

- The motor vehicle was stolen.
- It was transported in interstate or foreign commerce.
- The person transporting or causing it to be transported knew it was stolen.
- The person receiving, concealing, selling, or bartering it knew it was stolen.

The vehicle thief may be prosecuted in any state through which the stolen vehicle passed. Prosecution is normally in the state in which the vehicle was stolen, but sometimes it is in the state in which the person was arrested.

Intent is not required. The stolen vehicle could accidentally be driven over the state line or forced to detour into another state. If the vehicle is transported by train or truck through another state, prosecution is also possible.

The Anti-Car Theft Act of 1992 provides tougher legislation against auto theft, previously a low-profile crime. The penalty for importing or exporting stolen vehicles was increased from 5 to 10 years, as was the penalty for interstate transportation of stolen vehicles. The act empowers U.S. Customs with new authority in checking for stolen vehicles and provides funds to states that participate in the National Motor Vehicle Title Information System. It also made armed carjacking a federal offense.

The Preliminary Investigation

hen a motor vehicle theft is reported, initial information obtained by police includes the time, date, and location of the theft; the make, model, and color of the vehicle; the state of issue of the license plate; license plate number; direction of travel; description of any suspect; and the complainant's present location.

The complainant is asked to remain at his or her present location, and a police officer is dispatched to obtain further information and to complete the proper complaint form (Figure 15.3).

False motor vehicle theft reports are often filed when a car has been taken by a family member or misplaced in a parking lot, when the driver wants to cover up for an accident or crime committed with the vehicle, or when the driver wants to provide an alibi for being late for some commitment.

It is also possible that the vehicle has been reclaimed by a loan company—a civil matter.

A preliminary description is provided to patrol officers, who are told that the theft has not been verified; therefore, no all-points bulletin is issued. During this time patrol officers are alerted, but they make no move if they see the stolen vehicle because the report has not been validated. The officer in the field obtains informa-

Figure 15.3
Sample Motor Vehicle Report

| ST. LOUIS PARK POLICE DEPT. MN0272100 | SUPERVISOR APPROVED S/A | | MOTOR VEHICLE REPORT | | | |
| DATE & TIME REPORT MADE 4-5-20__ 1330 | | FOR ALL ATTEMPTS AND THEFTS OF MOTOR VEHICLES | | PAGE | |

DATE/TIME COMPLAINT RECEIVED 4-5-20__ 1245

UDC / GRID NO. / COMPLAINT NO.

HOW COMPLAINT RECEIVED FOUND BY POLICE ☐ RADIO ☐ CITIZEN ☐ STATION ☐ LETTER ☐ PHONE ☒

Date of Theft (DOT) 4-5-20__ 1115 Time of Theft, Between 4-4-20__ and 4-5-20__

Owner: Jerald Combs Person Reporting same

Address: 646 13th Street Address:

Telephone: Res.: 293-2415 Bus.: Telephone: Res.: Bus.:

License No. (LIC) AMU 345 State of Issue (LIS) Minnesota License Plate Yr.: (LIY) 1994 License Plate Type: (LIT) P

Vehicle Serial No. (VIN) 643210 Vehicle Year (VYR) 1992 Vehicle Make: (VMA) Chev Vehicle Model: (VMO) 4 cyl

Vehicle Style (VST) 4 dr Vehicle Color (VCO) Beige Other Ident. Characteristics (MIS)

Special Equipment: Spotlight-left side Odometer Reading 18,000

Damage to Vehicle prior to theft none Where?

Personal Property in Vehicle Little value Value of Vehicle 7,500

Car was Parked at 646 13th St. Vehicle Locked Yes X No Location of Keys in house

Is anyone Permitted to use vehicle? wife Under What Conditions? all times

Do you have Absolute Ownership? Yes Name of Finance Co. none Name of Insurance Co. Farmers Life

Will Owner Prosecute? Yes Does Owner Suspect Anyone? No

I Hereby Certify That The Foregoing Statement is True and Correct X

Date (DOR) Recovered 4-6-20__ Time Recovered 2330 Where Recovered accident-St. Louis Park

Vehicle Impounded At St. Louis Park PD Owner Notified By St. Louis Park Date of Notice 4-6-20__

Vehicle Recovered By St. Louis Park PD

Vehicle NCIC Entered into MINCIS Yes Date of Entry 4-5-20__ NCIC MINCIS No.: 162345

Recovery NCIC Cancelled-MINCIS Yes Date of Cancel 4-5-20__ NCIC MINCIS No.: 162345

Officer Taking Report: Milo Prins Date of Report: 4-6-20__ Time of Report: 0015

Case Investigated By: Det. Thomas Strong, St. Louis Park PD

DETAILS OF OFFENSE: Vehicle was parked on street at about 8:30 PM, 4-4-20__ and was missing at early morning 4-5-20__. Didn't report until several hours after checking with friends.

DEFENSE CLEARED BY ARREST ☒ EXCEPTIONALLY ☐ CASE UNFOUNDED ☐ INACTIVE (Not Cleared) ☐ OTHER ☐

PERSONS ARRESTED, SUSPECTS, WITNESSES & ADDITIONAL DETAILED REPORT ON SUPPLEMENTARY

Douglas Amherst, 1614 College Street, St. Louis Park, Minnesota

tion to determine the validity of the theft charge: the circumstances surrounding the alleged theft, identification of characteristics of the stolen vehicle, any details of items in the car, and any possible suspects. Interviews with witnesses are another crucial aspect of the preliminary investigation. Frequent false reports impair cooperation from other agencies, especially when the errors should have been detected by the investigating officers.

Recovered vehicles must be examined for usable latent prints and other physical evidence. If a vehicle is found with accident damage, it is necessary to determine whether the damage occurred before or after the report. Vehicles involved in a hit-and-run incident are sometimes abandoned by the driver and then reported as stolen. Younger persons sometimes report a car stolen if they crash and are afraid to tell their parents.

Computerized police files can assist in searching for suspects. Investigators can enter data concerning past suspects and other individuals in vehicles, types of vehicles stolen, the manner in which vehicles were entered or stolen, the types of locations from which they were stolen (apartment complexes, private residences, or commercial parking lots, for example), where vehicles were abandoned, and where vehicles were if the suspects were arrested in them.

Common Tools and Methods

Investigators must be familiar with the tools and methods commonly used to commit vehicle theft, including car openers, rake and pick guns, tryout keys, impact tools, keyway decoders, modified vise grips, tubular pick locks, modified screwdrivers, and hot wiring. Be familiar with these items and techniques and know what evidence to collect to prove their use.

Insurance Fraud

Vehicle insurance fraud is a major economic crime that affects every premium payer through increased insurance rates. According to the NICB, insurance criminals cost $30 billion annually.

Many police departments facilitate insurance fraud by allowing car theft reports to be phoned in or by taking them "over the counter" at the police station and then never investigating the reports. The primary reason the auto theft is reported is often for insurance purposes. To avoid this situation law enforcement agencies should investigate all auto theft reports and should not discount the possibility that the "victim" is actually committing insurance fraud.

For example, a luxury car stolen from a suburban mall parking lot was found four days later on fire on a rural road. The case seemed routine until a detective

began an investigation to eliminate the car's reported owner. The detective found that there were three pending lawsuits against the "victim," who had filed for bankruptcy shortly after the lawsuits and months before the car was stolen. He had filed an affidavit claiming he no longer owned the car because he had sold it six months before. Investigation revealed that the buyer was a friend who let the car be transferred into his name so it would not be involved in the bankruptcy proceedings.

This was a clear case of filing false information with the police. Further, after a fire investigator and a mechanic inspected the car, they reported that the lab tests showed ongoing engine failure. The victim wanted the insurance company to pay for a replacement—an obvious case of fraud. A growing type of insurance fraud is vehicle cloning.

Vehicle Cloning

The NICB describes vehicle cloning as a crime in which stolen vehicles assume the identity of legally owned, or "nonstolen," vehicles of a similar make and model. Criminals apply counterfeit labels, plates, stickers, and titles to these stolen cars, making them appear legitimate. The nonstolen vehicles can be actively registered or titled in another state or country, resulting in multiple vehicles having the same VIN being simultaneously registered and/or titled—but, of course, only the nonstolen vehicles are legitimate. The rest are fakes, or clones. According to the NICB president: "Conservative U.S. vehicle cloning profits are estimated to exceed more than $12 million annually, with an average net of $30,000 per cloned vehicle" ("Vehicle Cloning," p.1).

The first step in the cloning process is to copy a VIN from a legally owned car. Then the criminal steals a vehicle similar to the one from which the VIN had been lifted. The stolen vehicle's legitimate VIN is replaced with a counterfeit one, making the stolen vehicle a clone of the legally owned original vehicle. The criminal then creates counterfeit ownership documents and sells the stolen vehicle to an innocent buyer ("It's Not a Feat"). Table 15.3 lists the most popular cloned vehicles uncovered during recent NICB investigations.

Cooperating Agencies in Motor Vehicle Theft

Police most frequently use state DMVs to check owners' registrations. They also use them to compare the driver of a vehicle with the registered owner. When vehicle registration and driver's registration checks are completed, further

Table 15.3 / **Most Popular Cloned Vehicles (in alphabetical order)**

1. BMW X5
2. Cadillac Escalade
3. Chevrolet Avalanche and Tahoe
4. GM Hummer
5. GMC Yukon
6. Jeep Grand Cherokee
7. Lexus GX, LX, and RX
8. Mercedes-Benz
9. Mitsubishi Montero
10. Toyota Camry and 4Runner

Source: "Vehicle Cloning." *UpClose* (Special Edition), National Insurance Crime Bureau, November 2004, Issue 2, p.1. http://www.nicb.org/uploaded_documents/upclose/upclose11.04.pdf.

checks can be made in the FBI's National Crime Information Center (NCIC) files to determine whether the vehicle is stolen and whether the driver has a criminal record.

 The FBI and the NICB provide valuable help in investigating motor vehicle thefts.

The FBI

The FBI assists local and state authorities who notify the Bureau that a stolen motor vehicle or aircraft has been transported interstate—which places it within the provisions of the Interstate Transportation of Stolen Motor Vehicles Act. The FBI works with local authorities to find the vehicle and the person who stole it. The FBI can also examine suspicious documents relating to false sales or registrations. The Bureau's NCIC contains information on stolen vehicles and stolen auto accessories. Its National Automobile Altered Numbers File is an additional resource.

The National Insurance Crime Bureau

In 1992 the National Auto Theft Bureau was incorporated into the National Insurance Crime Bureau (NICB), a nonprofit organization supported and maintained by hundreds of automobile insurance companies. The organization helps law enforcement agencies reduce and prevent auto thefts and investigate questionable or fraudulent vehicle fires and thefts.

The NICB also disseminates reports on stolen cars to law enforcement agencies and serves as a clearinghouse for information on stolen cars. Computer files are

maintained for several million wanted or stolen cars, listed by make, engine number, VIN, and component part number. This information is available free upon request to law enforcement agencies. The bureau can also trace cars from the factory to the owner. Its staff of specialists and technicians are experts in identifying stolen cars and restoring mutilated, changed, or defaced numbers. They also restore altered or obliterated VINs.

The NICB publishes and distributes to police agencies its *Manual for the Identification of Automobiles*. This publication describes the location of identifying numbers, gives license plate reproductions, and provides a short legal digest of each state's motor vehicle laws. In an emergency, call the bureau collect. Otherwise, send a letter requesting specific assistance.

Also of assistance is the National Vehicle Identification Program (NVIP). This program promotes use of vehicle identification technology and provides a $1,000 reward for information leading to recovery of an NVIP-registered vehicle and the arrest and conviction of the auto thief.

Recognizing a Stolen Motor Vehicle or an Unauthorized Driver

 asquale (p.34) contends that in the fight against car thieves, sometimes the most effective tools are the eyes of a police officer: "Patrol officers have always been the backbone of the police department, and they play a crucial role in the fight against auto theft. A well-trained, experienced officer can spot a stolen car driving down the highway or one 'dumped' on the side of a country road." As with other crimes, a suspicious nature and an alert mind help an officer detect motor vehicle thefts. Detection is sometimes improved by an instinct developed through training, observation, and experience. Police officers develop individual techniques for recognizing stolen cars. No absolute, single peculiarity identifies a stolen car or its driver, but either one can draw the attention of an observant officer.

 To improve your ability to recognize stolen vehicles:
- Keep a list of stolen vehicles, or a "hot sheet," in your car.
- Develop a checking system to rapidly determine whether a suspicious vehicle is stolen.
- Learn the common characteristics of stolen vehicles and car thieves.
- Take time to check suspicious persons and vehicles.
- Learn how to question suspicious drivers and occupants.

A *potential car thief on foot* usually appears nervous. He or she may be looking into cars on the street or in parking lots, trying door handles and carrying some sort of entry tool. Observe such an individual from a distance until an overt act is committed.

Characteristics of a driver of a stolen vehicle include making sudden jerks or stops, driving without lights or excessively fast or slow, wearing gloves in hot weather, and attempting to avoid or outrun a squad car. Any unusual or inappropriate driving behavior may be suspicious.

Characteristics of a stolen vehicle include having one license plate when two are required, or two when one is required. Double or triple plates with one on top of the other can indicate lack of time to take off the original plates. A set of old plates with new screws, wired-on plates, altered numbers, dirty plates on a clean car or clean plates on a dirty car, differing front and rear plate numbers, plates bent to conceal a number, upside-down or hanging plates, and homemade cardboard plates are all suspicious. Observe whether the trunk lid has been pried or whether side windows or door locks are broken. Look for evidence of a broken steering column or of tampering with the ignition switch. Abandoned vehicles are also suspicious.

When *questioning drivers and any occupants of cars* you have stopped on suspicion of motor vehicle theft, observe their behavior. Watch for signs of nervousness, hesitancy in answers, overpoliteness, and indications that the driver does not know the vehicle. Request the driver's license and the vehicle registration papers for identification. Examine the driver's license and ask for the driver's birth date. The driver will probably not know the correct date unless it is his or her license. Compare the description on the license with the person. Compare the state of issuance of the license with the car's license plates. Ask the driver to sign his or her name and compare the signature with that on the driver's license.

Ask the driver the year, make, and model of the car and compare the answers with the registration papers. Ask the mileage. The driver of a stolen car rarely knows the mileage, whereas the owner or regular driver knows within a reasonable number of miles. Ask the driver to describe the contents of the car's trunk and glove compartment.

Check inside the vehicle for an extra set of license plates, bullet holes or other damage, bloodstains, and service stickers showing where and when the car was last serviced. Inspect the VIN plate for alterations. A roll of adhesive tape can indicate it was used to tape windows before breaking them. Wire or coat hangers bent straight to open doors, rubber gloves, jumper cables, or tools for breaking into a car are also alerting signals.

Parked cars may have been stolen if debris under the car indicates it has been in the same place for a long time. Check with neighbors to determine how long the vehicle has been parked there. The neighborhood canvass is one of the most effective techniques in investigating abandoned cars. Check for illegal entrance, for open car windows in inclement weather, and for dirty vehicles indicating lack of care. A citation under the wiper can indicate when the car was abandoned. Keys left in the ignition and lack of license plates are also grounds for checking.

A warm or running motor and firearms or valuables left in the car may indicate that the thief has temporarily parked the car and intends to return. Stake out stolen vehicles (identified by license number or description) because the thief may return. Consider partially immobilizing the vehicle to prevent an attempted escape.

Recovering an Abandoned or Stolen Motor Vehicle

Most motor vehicle thefts are local problems involving a locally stolen and recovered vehicle. The majority of stolen vehicles are recovered, most of them within 48 hours, especially those stolen by juveniles. Stolen vehicles are recovered when patrol officers observe a vehicle on a hot sheet, a suspicious vehicle or driver, or an apparently abandoned vehicle or when private citizens report an abandoned vehicle.

Although patrol units are responsible for most of the stolen vehicles recovered, investigative personnel play a major role in furnishing information to the uniformed patrol in all areas of motor vehicle theft.

The initial patrol officer at the scene examines recovered and abandoned vehicles unless there is reason to believe the vehicle was involved in a serious crime. Investigators assigned to such a crime may want to look for specific items in the vehicle that might not be known to the patrol officers. In these cases the vehicle is protected until the specialists arrive.

Once recovery and impound reports have been completed, the car is removed from the hot sheet, and the owner is notified of the recovery. A vehicle recovery report, such as the one in Figure 15.4, should be completed and filed.

If a crime has recently been committed in the area or if the vehicle's position and location suggest that the suspect may return, drive by and arrange for a stakeout. If the car is locked and the keys are gone, if heavy rain or fog exists and the windshield-wiper marks indicate they were recently used, or if no dry spot appears under the car, the vehicle was probably used recently and the driver may return. Round rain spots on the vehicle mean that it has been parked for a longer period than if there are elongated raindrops, which indicate recent movement. A quick check of heat remaining on the hood, radiator, or exhaust pipe also indicates whether

DISTRICT NUMBER	St. Louis Park Police Department **VEHICLE RECOVERY REPORT**	COMPLAINT NUMBER

LICENSE _____ STATE _____ YR. _____ SERIAL _____

MAKE _____ YR. _____ TYPE _____ RECOVERED BY _____ DATE _____ TIME _____

WHERE RECOVERED _____ ON STREET - ALLEY - PARKING LOT - GARAGE

RECOVERED ON INFORMATION FROM: RADIO - CITIZEN - FOUND BY POLICE - OTHER _____

REASON FOR IMPOUNDING: INVOLVED IN ACCIDENT -ARREST - ABANDONED - OTHER _____

EXTENT OF DAMAGE TO VEHICLE _____

VEHICLE LOCKED? _____ TRUNK LOCKED? _____ WERE KEYS IN CAR? _____

PERSON ARRESTED _____ CHARGE _____

TOW TRUCK ORDERED AT _____ ARRIVED _____ TOW COMPANY _____ DRIVER (SIGNATURE) _____

VEHICLE OWNER _____ ADDRESS _____

VEHICLE DRIVER _____ ADDRESS _____

O.K. TO RELEASE   YES ☐   NO ☐   TO OWNER ☐   DRIVER ☐   OTHER ☐

LIST VEHICLE EQUIPMENT		INVENTORY OF PERSONAL PROPERTY IN VEHICLE
	LICENSE PLATES	BATTERY	
	WHEELS	HEAD LIGHTS	
	TIRES	TAIL LIGHTS	
	RADIO	BUMPERS	
	EXPOSED AERIAL	TAPE PLAYER	

OTHER EQUIPMENT _____ | DISPOSITION OF PROPERTY: _____
| IF RELEASED PRIOR TO VEHICLE, HAVE RECEIVER SIGN HERE: _____
| RELEASED BY _____ RECEIVER _____
| DATE _____ TIME _____

REPORT MADE BY _____ DATE _____ TIME _____ REMARKS _____

HOLD ☐   AUTHORITY _____ REASON _____

RELEASED BY _____ | I HEREBY ACKNOWLEDGE RECEIPT OF ABOVE DESCRIBED VEH. & PROP.

DATE _____ TIME _____ | NAME _____

AUTHORIZED BY _____ | ADDRESS _____

CERT. OF REGISTRATION ☐   BILL OF SALE ☐   INS. POLICY ☐ | TELEPHONE _____ DATE _____ TIME _____

Figure 15.4

Vehicle Recovery Report Form

Source: Courtesy of the St. Louis Park (Minnesota) Police Department.

the car was recently parked. Consider attempting to apprehend the criminal on return to the vehicle.

On the other hand, if a car has a flat tire or is up on blocks, it is probably abandoned and can be immediately processed at either the scene, the police station, or a storage location. Consider the possibility that the vehicle was used in committing another crime such as robbery, burglary, murder, hijacking, or abduction/kidnapping. Search the vehicle's exterior first and then the interior as described in Chapter 4. Many car thieves have been located through items left in a vehicle.

If you suspect that the vehicle was used in another crime, take it to a garage or lock and seal it with evidence tape; then notify the proper authorities. After processing, notify the rightful owner.

Technology is facilitating the recovery of stolen vehicles. LoJack, a Massachusetts company, has developed a system that places a homing device in an obscure place on a vehicle. If the vehicle is reported stolen, the device is activated and a tracker picks up a signal that is displayed on a lighted compass. An illuminated strength meter tells operators when they are nearing the stolen vehicle. The display also shows the model and color of the car. The LoJack website reports that the radiofrequency-based system is used in 20 countries by 2.4 million customers. It has helped recover 50,000 vehicles worth nearly $1 billion and has a consistently high 90 percent recovery rate.

The system is not without its drawbacks, however. First, unless police departments across the country install tracking devices in their squad cars, the devices are ineffective. Second, the lag time between a car theft and its report may be hours or even days. Third, there

are some dead spots—locations where transmitted radio signals will not be detected. Fourth, some departments hesitate to become a partner with a private company. Finally, some departments worry that the public will perceive them to be focused on preventing car theft from the more affluent members of the community, those who can afford the $600 auto recovery system.

Other systems also are available, some of which activate automatically. If someone drives off in the car without deactivating the system, an alarm is sent to the tracking center. Such systems might, however, result in false alarms and pose as great a problem as false burglar alarms. Other systems provide a personal alert service that allows motorists to signal authorities in case of emergencies. One system allows controllers to shut off a stolen car's engine by remote control if police tracking the car believe it would be safe to do so.

Combating Motor Vehicle Theft

Police departments are using several strategies to combat rising auto theft levels:

- Setting up sting operations—for example, a body shop that buys stolen vehicles
- Providing officers with auto theft training
- Coordinating efforts across jurisdictional lines

- Instituting anti–car theft campaigns
- Increasing penalties for stealing vehicles

Clarke (pp.17–22) suggests several measures to combat thefts of and from cars in parking lots: hire parking attendants, improve surveillance at deck and lot entrances/exits, hire dedicated security patrols, install and monitor closed-circuit television (CCTV), improve lighting, secure the perimeter, install entrance barriers and electronic access, and arrest and prosecute persistent offenders.

To combat auto theft in Atlanta, the Auto Theft Task Force (ATTF) was initiated to target high-risk areas at high-risk times. The approach involved high-visibility uniformed patrol, members' making frequent traffic stops, and heavy reliance upon field investigative interviews. The efforts of the task force paid off, with the seven ATTF officers making 2,500 arrests in the first year and recovering more than 400 vehicles.

To combat the rising auto theft rate at Newark International Airport in New Jersey, airport police took several steps, including the following:

- Increasing the candlepower of parking lot lights
- Conducting weekly inspections of the lot perimeter to locate access points for thieves (e.g., broken or cut fences)
- Offering monetary rewards to the public for information leading to the arrest of car thieves
- Securing unused remote entrances
- Touring the lots with marked and unmarked patrol cars

Technology Innovations

Dees (p.34) describes a new product, the License Plate Reading (LPR) system, which can watch 22,000 cars in both directions at the same time in an hour. The system has micro digital cameras mounted into the existing light bar system of a patrol car and a trunk-mounted processing unit. The unit's software locates the license plate of each vehicle, translates it into machine-readable form, and compares each license plate number against a list of stolen vehicles. The LPR can recognize 95 percent of the license plates moving past the cameras at up to 75 miles per hour. It will work in stationary or moving mode, in all types of weather, and at night using infrared flash technology.

In 2004 the Ohio State Highway Patrol ran a four-month test on the Ohio Turnpike, which led to the recovery of 24 stolen vehicles worth $221,000 and the arrests of 23 suspects—a 50 percent increase in recovery and arrest rates. The system also removes the issue of racial bias from vehicle stops.

In areas where police have made special efforts to educate the public and to assign extra squads to patrol high-auto-theft areas, auto theft has significantly decreased.

New York City has instituted the Combat Auto Theft (CAT) program, which has been highly successful. Participating car owners sign a form indicating that they do not normally operate their automobiles between 1 A.M. and 5 A.M., the peak auto-theft hours. They also sign a consent form that authorizes the police to stop their vehicle during these hours without probable cause. Owners are given a CAT program decal to affix prominently on the inside of the car's rear window. Officers may stop any car having the decal, without probable cause, if they see it traveling on city streets between 1 A.M. and 5 A.M.

Minnesota's Help Eliminate Auto Theft (HEAT) program offers up to $5,000 for information leading to the arrest and trial of suspected auto-theft-ring members or chop shop operators. The program's toll-free number is answered by the Minnesota Highway Patrol.

Curtin et al. (p.3) report on the Bureau of Justice Assistance Watch Your Car (WYC) program. This national program involves motor vehicle owners who place stickers in their windshields that alert police that they can stop the vehicle for a theft check during certain hours of the night and in certain locations. They (p.ii) report that WYC states reported that the program was easily incorporated into existing programs. The member states also indicated that a major shortcoming was the inability to easily check a vehicle's status across state lines or in other jurisdictions and that a national database would be preferable to the current state-by-state system.

Curtin et al. (p.ii) also reported on a myriad of other auto theft programs being used, including license plate readers at border crossings, marking of vehicle parts with VIN numbers, inspection of salvaged cars to ensure that salvaged VIN numbers were not being used on stolen cars, cargo inspections, and a bilingual information center that law enforcement officers used to combat auto theft between the United States and Mexico. Parts-marking programs and public awareness were perceived to be the most effective of those program approaches.

The increased use of alarms and protective devices may in part account for the rise in armed carjackings, as explained in Chapter 12. Unwilling to give up their lucrative "trade," car thieves may use force against a vehicle operator to gain control of the vehicle rather than risk being thwarted by antitheft devices. Whereas carjacking is treated as quite a severe crime, regular unarmed auto theft remains a relatively minor offense and, from a criminal perspective, a safe crime to commit.

Routine Activities and Motor Vehicle Theft

The routine-activity approach to crime suggests that the daily routine activities of populations influence the availability of targets of crime. The existence of potential offenders, suitable targets, and lack of guardianship explains variation in the rate of motor vehicle theft. Research indicates that city blocks with bars have almost twice as many auto thefts as city blocks without bars and that blocks adjacent to high schools have higher levels of auto theft than blocks that are not near high schools. In addition, parking lots with attendants have lower rates of auto theft than similar lots with no attendants on duty. Such findings might be used in designing auto theft prevention programs such as using bait cars.

Bait Cars The basic idea of a bait car is simple. A model of vehicle with a high theft rate is selected and placed in a high crime area. Officers then simply sit back and wait for the vehicle to be stolen. The Los Angeles Sheriff's Department's Taskforce for Regional Autotheft Prevention (TRAP) uses a traditional, watch-and-wait method of bait vehicles. According to Mertens (p.36), the bait car usually gets stolen within two to five minutes. If it is not stolen in five minutes, it is picked up and moved. The longest time a bait car sits in one location is half an hour. Six TRAP teams run bait operations once or twice a week, averaging 5 to 15 arrests in a four-hour period.

Chu (p.109) explains how bait cars can be enhanced using **telematic technology,** which is the transfer of data between a remote vehicle and a host computer. The data are transferred using the Internet and wireless technology as well as a global positioning system (GPS). A small radio transceiver called a vehicle locator unit (VLU) is hidden in the bait vehicle. The VLU transmits a silent homing signal, revealing the vehicle's location to an officer's remote control unit (RCU), a handheld two-way radio equipped with a keypad from which commands are entered, activating the tracking transmitter and controlling the bait vehicle's engine, door locks, flashers, and horn. The car is tracked by satellite and located. Mapping software can display the location, direction, and speed of the vehicle. When an officer catches up with the thief, he or she can remotely kill the stolen car's engine and lock the car's door ("Police Catch Car Thieves," p.12).

Whitely (p.7A) reports that the Everett (Washington) Police Department has added video to its bait car program. In one video a female car thief is shown pulling down her sleeves to cover her hands, in an effort to avoid leaving fingerprints, before spinning a bait car's steering wheel and driving off. Auto thefts in Everett have dropped 14.8 percent in the first five months of the program.

Border-Area Auto Theft

According to the NICB, many of the top metropolitan areas for vehicle theft are in or near ports and/or the Mexican or Canadian borders. Bailer (p.27) stresses that the first step in putting a dent in border-area auto theft

is to "acknowledge that there is no international border when it comes to this highly mobile crime." Particularly hard hit by auto theft are California and Arizona, which the NICB ranks as the leading car theft states in the nation ("California Leads"). In 2003, Modesto, California, topped the list for most auto thefts within a city and surrounding metropolitan area. The Phoenix/Mesa (Arizona) area, which ranked number one in 2002, dropped to second place in 2003.

In Arizona between 1985 and 2001, vehicle theft rates jumped more than 356 percent. In 2002, 57,600 vehicles were reported stolen in Arizona (Bailer, p.30). Arizona law enforcement agencies use many of the same anti–auto theft initiatives found in other states. What makes their approach different is that the law enforcement community has created programs to encourage binational cooperation. At the center of this effort is Policia Internacional Sonora y Arizona (PISA), a cross-border networking group that began modestly 20 years ago when a few Arizona and Sonora (Mexico) officers gathered informally over breakfast. The group now has hundreds of members throughout the border region. Each year it hosts a well-attended, binational conference on combating crime along "the line." Relationships established at these conferences create personal connections that could not be made any other way.

In 2003 Arizona established a Border Auto Theft Information Center (BATIC), a toll-free, long-distance telephone line that Sonoran police can use to seek and share information about vehicles recovered in or stolen from Mexico. The program averages about 50 calls a day from Mexican law enforcement officers. Just as border-area auto theft presents unique challenges, so does the theft of police vehicles.

Theft of Patrol Cars

"Police vehicles are more vulnerable to thieves than you might think," warns Kariya (p.32). He reports that in the first four months of 2003, more than 30 police departments nationwide experienced a theft of one of their vehicles. About the only police vehicle that appears to be immune from theft is a K-9 vehicle. A stolen unit driven by a fleeing felon might run down civilians, practically guaranteeing that the department will be sued. In addition, police cars grant the drivers access to high-security areas, so terrorists would jump at the chance to obtain one.

Kariya (p.33) notes that most reports of stolen police vehicles involve suspects who get into a unit an officer has left unattended, usually to take a report or chase a suspect: "Walking away from a car with the keys in the ignition is standard operating procedure for some law enforcement agencies." In fact, many officers need to keep their vehicles running almost nonstop through a shift. Turning the engine off drains the car's battery quickly due to the power demands of emergency lights, communications systems, laptops, and other computers.

Not only does the battery drain, but turning off the engine powers down those instruments, requiring inconvenient rebooting.

Technology offers some answers here. One solution is a brake-light kill switch. With the brake lights cut off, the car will not come out of park even when running. This solution works only with later-model vehicles that require the driver to step on the brake before the transmission can shift out of park.

Another solution is a secure-idle system in which an officer presses a button, places the transmission in park, turns the key to the normal off position, and removes the key. The engine keeps running and all accessories remain on. However, any unauthorized attempt to step on the brake or move the shift lever out of park cuts all electrical power. It can also trigger an optional alarm. The system is deactivated by putting the key back into the ignition and turning it to the on position.

Preventing Auto Theft

Effective preventive measures could eliminate many motor vehicle thefts. Vehicle theft requires both desire and opportunity, and it is often difficult to know which comes first. An unlocked automobile with keys in the ignition is a temptation. A parked vehicle with the motor running is also extremely inviting. Many juveniles take cars under such conditions and then boast of their ability to steal.

> Numerous motor vehicle thefts can be prevented by effective educational campaigns and by installing antitheft devices in vehicles during manufacture.

Educate motor vehicle owners about the importance of removing their keys from the ignition and locking their vehicles when parked. Public education campaigns might include distributing dashboard stickers with the reminder "Have you removed your keys from the ignition?" or "Don't forget to take your keys and lock your car."

To deter theft some automakers have developed ignition systems and keys that use microchips with electronic codes embedded in them. However, car thieves have been able to duplicate these antitheft keys by using code grabbers similar to the devices used to duplicate codes that open garage doors. In response, as with garage door makers, some auto manufacturers are now using rolling codes and encrypted systems that use randomly generated codes to defeat thieves. They have also developed a buzzer system that warns the driver that the keys are still in the vehicle. **Keyless doors**—requiring the owner to enter a combination by pushing numbered pads in a programmed sequence to gain access to the

car—may make it harder for thieves to break into vehicles to steal them.

The NICB website suggests a four-layered approach to combat auto theft:

1. *Common sense.* Remove keys, close windows, and lock doors. Park in well-lit areas.

2. *Visible and audible warning devices.* Use steering wheel locks (Figure 15.5), wheel locks, theft deterrent decals, identification markers such as the VIN etched in the window, and audible alarms.

3. *Immobilizing devices.* Use cut-off switches, kill switches, smart keys, and fuel disablers.

4. *Tracing devices.* Give police the location of the vehicle.

Thefts of Trucks, Construction Vehicles, Aircraft, and Other Motorized Vehicles

Investigating thefts of trucks and trailers, construction vehicles and equipment, recreational vehicles, motorized boats, snowmobiles, motorcycles, motor scooters, mopeds, and aircraft is similar to investigating auto thefts.

Trucks and Trailers

Usually trucks and trailers are stolen by professional thieves, although they are also stolen for parts. A "fingerman" often provides information to the thief. In most cases the fingerman is an employee of the company that owns the truck. A "spotter" locates the truck

Figure 15.5
Antitheft devices such as the Club are one effective way to deter car thieves.

after getting information from the fingerman and then follows the truck to the point where it is to be stolen. A driver experienced in operating the targeted vehicle then commits the actual theft.

Truck trailers are usually stolen by simply backing up a tractor to the trailer and hauling it away. The trailer's cargo is generally the target.

Stolen trucks and trailers are identified much as passenger vehicles are—by the manufacturer or through the *Commercial Vehicle Identification Manual* published by the NICB.

Construction Vehicles and Equipment

The NICB website notes that heavy equipment theft is a growing problem, with approximately 5,500 heavy equipment thefts reported to the NCIC in 2001, including backhoes, bulldozers, and dump trucks. The recovery rate was only 9 to 18 percent. Most of the thefts were committed by organized crime rings, which often had targeted equipment shopping lists. Many of the rings are international, filling equipment needs in underdeveloped countries ("Heavy Equipment").

Sider (p.42) reports on national surveys suggesting that the total cost of heavy equipment theft could be as much as $1 billion each year in the United States alone. More worrisome is that as little as 10 to 15 percent of stolen heavy equipment is ever recovered. Adding to the problem is the fact that product identification numbers (PIN) are nonstandard, vary dramatically in format among manufacturers, and may be located in numerous, often hard-to-find locations (Sider, p.43).

The NICB website notes that rubber-tired equipment is most likely to be stolen because it can be driven away under its own power. The most popular targets are skid steers, backhoes, and dump trucks. Most vulnerable are less-secure construction sites on weekends. The stolen vehicles usually stay intact.

In 2002 the National Equipment Register (NER) was launched, a significant step toward reducing this ongoing problem. According to the NER, heavy equipment is stolen because the reward for the thief far outweighs the risk. Heavy equipment has little physical machine or site security, is valuable, and is easy to sell. In addition, the theft often is not discovered for hours, even days, after it is committed. Furthermore, a lack of due diligence in the used-equipment market contributes to the problem ("The Problem of Heavy").

The NER has registered more than 70,000 theft reports and provides access to more than 12 million equipment ownership records. The NER provides law enforcement officers with expert, free assistance in investigating and prosecuting equipment theft, including:

- 24/7 access to specialist NER operators who will offer expert advice on equipment identification, PIN locations, and other identification techniques.
- 24/7 searches of the NER database online via a toll-free number (866-FIND-PIN).
- 24/7 access to millions of ownership records through NER operators.
- Additional online investigation tools such as PIN location information.
- Local and national training programs.

Many construction companies have formed protection programs, have identified their equipment with special markings, and have offered rewards for information about thefts. Local construction firms can also provide information about possible outlets for stolen parts.

The NER recommends that site security be enhanced by posting "no trespassing" signs and using fencing, gates, locks, and good lighting (*Loss Prevention*). Vehicle security can be enhanced by marking, anchoring, and immobilizing equipment. Equipment not being used should be arranged in a way so that a missing unit would be obvious. Equipment should not be left on a trailer unattended.

The NER has a pocket-sized reference, *Law Enforcement Identification Guide for Construction and Agricultural Equipment,* which includes among other things theft indicators, commonly stolen equipment, location of PIN numbers, and other useful items for investigators. The NER (pp.3-4) offers the following "red flags" as theft indicators, cautioning that legitimate explanations might exist for any of the indicators.

Transport

- Equipment being transported late at night or on weekends or holidays. Equipment theft most often happens at those times.
- Hauled equipment that is being moved in a hurry and therefore lacks the proper tie-downs, over-width/over-weight signs, or lights.
- Equipment being hauled on trucks not designed to haul such equipment.
- Equipment being hauled with buckets in the up position or booms not lowered.
- New equipment on old transport.
- The labels/markings on a piece of equipment do not match those of the unit carrying or hauling it.

Use and Location

- Equipment in an unsecured location that has not been moved for some time—either by repeat observation or the age of the tracks leading to the equipment.
- The type of equipment does not suit the location or use—such as construction equipment on a farm or in a residential area with no building activity.

Equipment and Markings

- Equipment with missing PIN plates. Manufacturers generally use mounting techniques that make it unlikely for a PIN plate to fall off during normal use.

- Equipment that has been entirely repainted or that has decals removed or painted over.
- Manufacturer decals or model number stickers do not match the piece of equipment to which they are affixed.
- A commercially manufactured trailer with registration plates reflecting a homemade trailer (certain states only).

Price

- Equipment that is being offered, or has been purchased, at a price well below market value.

When looking for "red flags," focus on the 10 most commonly stolen pieces of equipment, which account for 90 percent of all stolen equipment reported to the NER. Figure 15.6 shows the location of PIN numbers on these commonly stolen types of equipment.

Recreational Vehicles

More than 450 makes and models of recreational vehicles (RVs) are marketed in the United States. Because there are so many makes and models, contact the manufacturer for any special numbers not readily visible. Recreational vehicles are also targets for vehicle burglaries because many contain CB radios, televisions, and appliances. Many false theft claims are made because of the high cost of operating these vehicles.

Motorized Boats and Jet Skis

Since 1972 many states have required licensing of boats, including an identification number on the boat's hull. Most such identification numbers are 10 to 13 digits. The first several digits are the manufacturer's number. This is followed by 4 or 5 identification digits and several certification digits.

Boat Watch USA offers these suggestions to prevent boat theft: Mark the vessel by etching your driver's license number in several inconspicuous places and affixing a Boat Watch USA decal in a prominent location. Record the specifics and effects of the boat by inventorying not only the boat and trailer but also all electronics and other gear. Photograph the boat. Secure it using the best locks you can buy ("Boaters Watching Out").

Skid Steer Loader

Also referred to as: Bobcat, Uniloader, Skid Steer

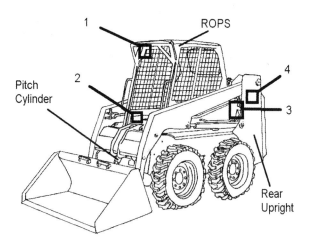

1. On upper portion of front post of ROPS, may be either left or right side.

2. In operator's area, on either side or in the middle (usually near the operator's knees while seated).

3. On rear upright below loader arm mounting point, may be in the interior of the channel shape of the rear upright.

4. On outside face of the loader arm upright, may be on either side.

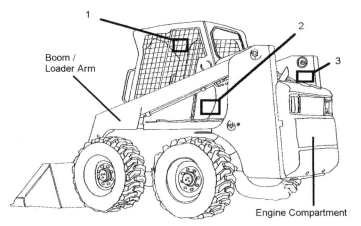

1. On upper portion of front post of ROPS, may be either left or right side.

2. On body of machine, visible below the loader arm and above the fender. May be somewhat obscured by the loader hydraulic lines (usually left side of machine).

3. On interior facing vertical surface of rear upright, may be on either left or right side.

Common Manufacturers: Bobcat, Case, John Deere, New Holland, Caterpillar, ASV, Gehl, Daewoo, JCB, Scat Trac, Thomas, Hyundai, Hydra-Mac, Takeuchi

Figure 15.6
The 10 most commonly stolen pieces of equipment reported to the NER and PIN number locations

Front End Loader

Also referred to as: Loader, Skip Loader, Rubber Tired Loader, Wheel or Articulated Loader, Tool Carrier (with different front end)

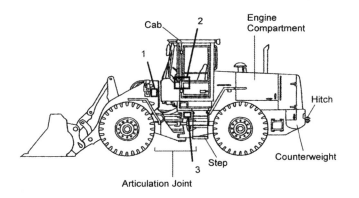

1. On loader arm mounting structure or frame, forward of articulation joint, left or right side.

2. Inside operator's area on instrument panel, console, or seat pedestal.

3. On frame to the rear of articulation joint, left or right side.

Backhoe Loader

Also referred to as: Backhoe, Tractor Loader Backhoe

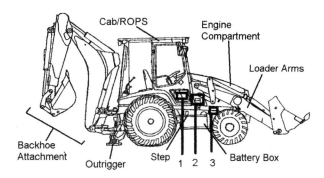

1. In operator's area, affixed to instrument panel, control console, or seat pedestal.

2. Below loader arm mounting point, forward of operator's area, left or right side.

3. On left or right frame near front axle.

Common Manufacturers: Case, Caterpillar, John Deere, JCB, Ford New Holland, Volvo, Kubota, Fermec, Terex, Terramite, MF Industrial

Agricultural Tractor

Also referred to as: Ag, Farm, Vineyard or Utility Tractor (Tractor names may be interchangeable between types.)

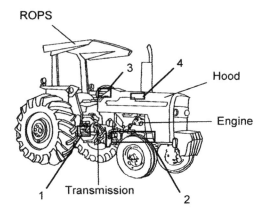

1. On transmission near steps, left or right side.

2. On frame near front axle, left or right side.

3. On instrument panel or steering column.

4. On underside of hood.

Warehouse Forklift

Also referred to as: Forklift, High-Low

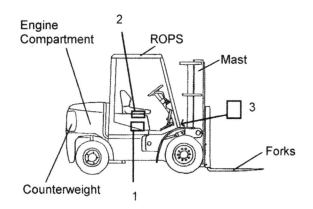

1. On frame near entry step, left or right side.

2. On flat surface next to operator's seat, near mast and fork control levers.

3. On instrument panel or forward facing portion of machine frame.

Figure 15.6 *(continued)*

Tracked Dozer

Also referred to as: Crawler Dozer, Bulldozer, Crawler Tractor (without attachments), Crawler Loader (with loader attachment)

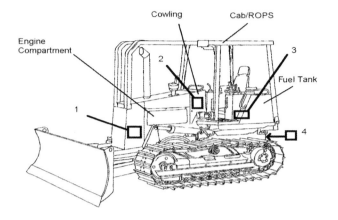

1. On either the left or right side of radiator housing.

2. On either left or right side of cowling, just in front of operator's area.

3. On either left or right side of bodywork surrounding operator (fuel tank, control console, seat pedestal).

4. On either side of rear facing portion of transmission or frame.

Trencher

Also referred to as: Rock Saw, Wheel, Chain or Belt Trencher

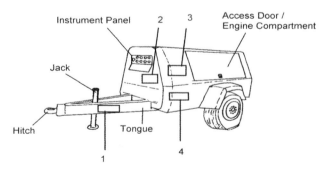

1. On front facing panel in operator's area, or seat pedestal.

2. In operator's area, on instrument panel or control console.

Utility Cart

Also referred to as: Gator, Mule, Utility ATV

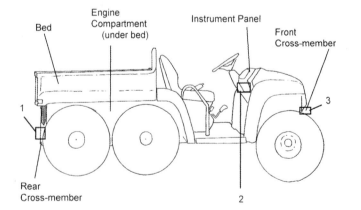

1. On rear frame or rear cross-member.

2. On instrument panel or steering column.

3. On front frame or front cross-member.

Generator / Compressor

1. On tongue frame, generally near hitch, left or right side.

2. On front face of body.

3. Inside engine compartment, on interior bulkhead near operator instructions, left or right side.

4. On frame inside engine compartment.

Figure 15.6 *(continued)*

Other options include arming the vessel with an alarm system and insuring it. The same precautions are applicable to jet skis.

Because boats also are the objects of many fraudulent insurance claims, investigators should determine whether the theft claim is legitimate.

Snowmobiles

Snowmobiles are easy to steal because they can be transported inside vans and trucks. Most major snowmobile manufacturers use chassis and engine numbers that aid in identification.

A popular snowmobile resort in Lanaudiere, Quebec, reduced snowmobile theft in 2004 by more than 50 percent through the joint efforts of tourism operators and law enforcement. Tourism operators invested heavily in video surveillance and alarm equipment at restaurants, lodges, hotels, motels, and other tourist-oriented businesses. Police involvement was stepped up as well, with local law enforcement waging a "deliberate war on snowmobile thieves," making the region known as a bad place to steal snowmobiles, trucks, and trailers ("Solution to Sled").

Wells ("Stopping") offers the following suggestions to thwart snowmobile thieves: Never leave the ignition key in an unattended snowmobile; always park the machine where you can keep an eye on it; keep it in a locked garage or shed when possible; use a universal fit track lock; and take out theft insurance. Wells suggests that probably the best solution is to secure the snowmobile to an immovable object or at least to another snowmobile.

Motorcycles, Motor Scooters, and Mopeds

"Just because motorcycles have half the wheels as most vehicles does not mean they are not tempting targets for thieves and insurance fraud scams. Like cars, sport utility vehicles and trucks, stolen motorcycles offer criminals a full-throttle avenue to huge profits" ("Motorcycle Theft").

The NICB states that many motorcycles cost $20,000 or more. It also notes that in 2001, 44,000 motorcycle thefts were reported to the NCIC, with a low recovery rate of 25 to 30 percent ("Motorcycles Offer"). Motorcycles, motor scooters, and mopeds are easy to steal because they lack security devices and are often left unprotected. The lock number is easily identified, and substitute keys can be made. These cycles can be driven away or loaded onto trailers or into vans and transported, perhaps several at a time. A professional thief takes only 20 seconds to steal a motorcycle.

In January 2005 a multistate motorcycle theft ring was busted in a coast-to-coast undercover sting operation. Sixteen individuals were charged with stealing 81 imported and domestic motorcycles valued at over $1 million and selling them on the Internet ("Multi-State Motorcycle").

Identifying motorcycles is difficult because of the many types and the fact that parts are not readily identifiable. However, identification numbers can often be obtained through the NICB, local dealers, and manufacturers.

The NICB offers the following prevention suggestions: Lock your motorcycle, even when it is stored in a garage; be wary of used cycles titled or registered as an "assembled vehicle"; be wary of cloned motorcycles; and obtain an expert appraisal and/or insurance policy preinspection before purchasing and insuring a used cycle.

Yet another area of motor vehicle theft that may be investigated, although relatively rare, is theft of aircraft.

Aircraft

Aircraft theft, although infrequent, is a high-value theft. Such thefts are jointly investigated by the FBI and the Federal Aviation Administration. Many stolen aircraft are used in narcotics smuggling, so that the plane can be sacrificed at no cost if there is danger of apprehension.

Aircraft identification consists of a highly visible N identification number painted on the fuselage. Many aircraft parts, including the engine, radio equipment, landing gear, and tires, also have individual serial numbers. Aircraft identification can be verified through the manufacturer.

After the 9/11 attack on the World Trade Center and the Pentagon, security of aircraft has become more of a priority. However, a security brief by the Aircraft Owners and Pilots Association (AOPA) stressed: "General aviation (GA) aircraft do not pose a significant terrorist threat to the United States. In fact, there has been no terrorist attack anywhere in the world using a general aviation aircraft ("General Aviation"). According to the brief, GA

Technology Innovations

Brecken ("New Anti-Terrorist") describes Secure Start 1000, an antiterrorist security device certified on most King Air, Diamond, Beechjet, and Cessna Caravan models. The system was developed to provide proven theft deterrence that disables the engine's start circuits to unauthorized users. It is operated by a double access code keyboard. The keyboard also indicates prior tampering by unauthorized users, signifying to the authorized flight crew that there has been a security breach. The system can be installed during routine maintenance or during an inspection.

aircraft are incapable of causing significant damage. The typical GA aircraft—for example, a Cessna 172—weighs less than a Honda Civic and carries even less cargo. The number of GA aircraft stolen is down sharply since 9/11 and the additional precautions that have been taken. In 2002, 13 GA aircraft, mostly single-engine piston aircraft, were stolen. In 2003 only 6 GA aircraft were stolen.

The AOPA sponsors an Airport Watch, similar to a community's Neighborhood Watch, with America's pilots and aircraft owners banding together to protect our small airports. Everyone is encouraged to get to know one another and to report anything that appears to be suspicious. Greet strangers. Have a cell phone, a camera, or pen and paper handy to record any suspicious activity, including:

- Pilots who appear under the control of someone else.
- Anyone trying to access an aircraft through force.
- Anyone who seems unfamiliar with aviation procedures.
- Anyone who misuses aviation lingo—or seems too eager to use the lingo.
- People or groups who seem determined to keep to themselves.
- Anyone who appears to be just loitering.
- Any out-of-the-ordinary videotaping of aircraft or hangars.
- Dangerous cargo or loads.
- Anything that strikes you as wrong.

The AOPA urges its members to use common sense. Any of the preceding could have a logical explanation. However, when in doubt it should be checked out ("What Is AOPA's"). Chapter 20 discusses in depth the investigation of terrorist activity.

SUMMARY

Motor vehicle thefts take much investigative time, but they can provide important information on other crimes under investigation. The VIN, critical in motor vehicle theft investigations, identifies the specific vehicle in question. This number is the primary nonduplicated, serialized number assigned by the manufacturer to each vehicle.

Categories of motor vehicle theft based on the offender's motive include (1) joyriding, (2) transportation, (3) stripping for parts and accessories, (4) commission of another crime, and (5) reselling for profit.

Although referred to as "motor vehicle theft," most of these crimes are prosecuted as "unauthorized use of a motor vehicle" because a charge of theft requires proof that the thief intended to deprive the owner of the vehicle permanently, which is often difficult or impossible to establish.

The elements of the crime of unauthorized use of a motor vehicle are (1) intentionally taking or driving (2) a motor vehicle (3) without the consent of the owner or the owner's authorized agent. Motor vehicles include automobiles, trucks, buses, motorcycles, motor scooters, mopeds, snowmobiles, vans, self-propelled watercraft, and aircraft. Embezzlement of a motor vehicle occurs if the person who took the vehicle had consent initially and then exceeded the terms of that consent.

The Dyer Act made interstate transportation of a stolen motor vehicle a federal crime and allowed for federal help in prosecuting such cases. False reports of motor vehicle theft are often filed because a car has been taken by a family member or misplaced in a parking lot, to cover up for a crash or a crime committed with the vehicle, or to provide an alibi for being late to some commitment deemed important enough to file a false police report over. The FBI and the NICB provide valuable help in investigating motor vehicle theft.

To improve your ability to recognize stolen vehicles, keep a hot sheet in your car, develop a checking system for rapidly determining whether a suspicious vehicle is stolen, learn the common characteristics of stolen vehicles and car thieves, take time to check suspicious persons and vehicles, and learn how to question suspicious drivers and occupants.

Numerous motor vehicle thefts can be prevented by effective educational campaigns and by manufacturer-installed security devices.

CHECKLIST

Motor Vehicle Theft

- Description of vehicle: year, make, color, body type?
- Anything unusual about the vehicle, such as color combination or damage?
- Identification of vehicle: VIN, engine number, license number by state and year, registered owner and legal owner, address, telephone number?
- What were the circumstances of the theft: date and time reported stolen, location of theft? Were doors locked? Was the key in the ignition?
- Was the vehicle insured and by whom?
- Was the vehicle mortgaged and by whom? Are payments current?
- Did anyone have permission to use the vehicle? Have they been contacted?
- Was the owner arrested for another crime or suspected in a crime?
- Does the owner have any motive to falsely report the vehicle stolen?
- Was the owner involved in a hit-and-run incident or driving while intoxicated?
- Did the spouse report the vehicle missing?
- What method was used to take the vehicle?
- Has the vehicle been recovered? Where?
- Were crimes committed in the area where the vehicle was stolen or recovered?
- Was anybody seen near where the vehicle was stolen or found? When? How were they dressed? Approximate age?
- Was the vehicle seen on the street with suspects in it? Description of the suspects? Does the owner have any suspects?
- Were police field interrogation cards checked for the day of the theft and the days after to determine whether the vehicle had been stopped by police for other reasons?
- Were pawnshops checked for items that were in the vehicle?
- If the vehicle was a motorcycle, were motorcycle shops checked?
- If the vehicle was a truck, have there been other truck thefts in the area or labor problems?
- Is the vehicle suspected of going interstate? Was the FBI notified?
- Has a check been made with the National Insurance Crime Bureau?
- Have junkyards been checked?
- Have known auto thieves been checked to determine whether they were in the area at the time of the theft?
- Was a check made with the DMV to determine the registered owner?

APPLICATION

A. On July 2 an internist finished his shift at a Veterans Administration hospital and went to the hospital parking lot to find that his Triumph TR4A was missing. He called the local police, but they refused to come, saying that because the theft occurred on federal property, it was the FBI's problem. The doctor called the FBI, which first said it would not investigate a car theft unless the car was transported out of the state. The doctor's insurance company finally convinced the FBI to investigate the theft, which it did. Two days later, local police in a town 529 miles away discovered the TR4A abandoned in the parking lot at a racetrack. Because the car had been hot-wired, they assumed it was stolen and made inquiries to the state DMV about its ownership. The car was towed to a local storage garage. When it was learned who owned the TR4A, local police contacted the police in the doctor's city.

Because that police department had no record of a stolen TR4A, officers there assumed that the message was in error. It was a holiday weekend, they were busy, and the matter was dropped. Eight months later the storage garage called the doctor to ask him when he was coming to get his car.

Questions

1. What mistakes were made in this incident?
2. Who is primarily to blame for the eight-month delay in returning the car to the owner?

B. Samuel Paris parked his 1999 Corvette in front of his home shortly after midnight when he and his wife returned from a party. He locked the car and took the keys with him. He discovered the vehicle missing the following morning at about 7:45 when he was leaving for work. He immediately called the police to report an auto theft.

Questions

1. Were his actions correct?
2. What should the police department do upon receiving the call?
3. What should the officer who is assigned to the case do?

DISCUSSION QUESTIONS

1. How do you identify a stolen vehicle so that you can prove in court that it was in fact stolen?
2. What evidence do you need to charge a suspect with unauthorized use of a motor vehicle? embezzlement of a vehicle?

3. Where would you start looking for a stolen vehicle used in a crime? for joyriding? for transportation? for stripping and sale of parts?
4. How large a problem is auto theft in your community? Are such thefts thoroughly investigated?
5. What agencies besides local police are involved in investigating auto thefts, and under what circumstances can their services be requested? Who would be contacted in your area? What services can they perform?
6. How do juvenile and professional auto thieves differ with regard to motive and type of vehicle stolen? Are there different methods for locating each?
7. A CD player has been taken from a stolen motor vehicle abandoned on a city street. Is this burglary or larceny in your state? Does it make any difference if the car door was closed but unlocked?
8. Does the value of the stolen vehicle affect the charge made? The punishment?
9. What other crimes are frequently committed along with motor vehicle theft?
10. What measures does your community take to prevent motor vehicle theft? What else might it do?

MEDIA EXPLORATIONS

 Internet

Select one of the following assignments to complete.

- Go to the FBI website at www.fbi.gov. Click on "library and reference." Select "Uniform Crime Reports" and outline what the report says about motor vehicle theft.
- Select one of the following key words: *auto theft, motor vehicle theft, motor vehicle theft prevention, vehicle identification number.* Find one article relevant to motor vehicle theft investigations to outline and share with the class.

Crime and Evidence in Action

Go to the CD and choose the **motor vehicle theft case.** During the course of the case you'll become patrol officer, detective, judge, corrections officer, and parole officer to conduct interactive investigative research. Each case unfolds as you respond to key decision points. Feedback for each possible answer choice is packed full of information, including term definitions, Web links, and important documentation.

The sergeant is available at certain times to help mentor you, the Online Resources website offers a variety of information, and be sure to take notes in your e-notebook during the suspect video statements and at key points throughout (these notes can be saved, printed, or e-mailed). The Forensics Exercise will test your ability to collect, transport, and analyze evidence from the crime scene. At the end of the case you can track how well you responded to each decision point and join the Discussion Forum for a postmortem. **Go to the CD and use the skills you've learned in this chapter to solve a case.**

REFERENCES

"Airbag Theft and Fraud: Deflating a Growing Crime Trend." National Insurance Crime Bureau fact sheet. http://www.nicb.org/uploaded_documents/publicfactsheets/airbag.pdf. Accessed July 22, 2005.

Bailer, Bryn. "Grand Theft Arizona." *Police*, October 2004, pp. 26–32.

"Boaters Watching Out for Boaters." Boat Watch USA website: http://www.boatwatchusa.com/crime_prevent.htm. Accessed July 22, 2005.

Brecken, Steve. "New Anti-Terrorist Security Device Prevents Aircraft Theft and Tampering." News release from the Raytheon Aircraft Company, January 19, 2005. http://www.raytheonaircraft.com/press/news_releases .shtml. Accessed July 22, 2005.

"California Leads the Nation in Auto Theft Rates for 2003: Car Thieves Strike Gold in the Golden State." National Insurance Crime Bureau press release, November 15, 2004. http://www.nicb.org/public/newsroom/hotspots/index.cfm. Accessed July 22, 2005.

Chu, Jim. "Bait Cars: Reducing Auto Thefts with Telematics." *Law and Order*, March 2003, pp. 109–111.

Clarke, Ronald V. *Thefts of and from Cars in Parking Facilities.* Washington, DC: Office of Community Oriented Policing Services, Problem-Oriented Guides for Police Series No. 10, January 24, 2002.

Crime in the United States 2003. Washington, DC: Federal Bureau of Investigation, 2004.

Curtin, Patrick; Thomas, David; Felker, Daniel; and Weingart, Eric. *Assessing Trends and Best Practices of Motor Vehicle Theft Prevention Programs.* Washington, DC: National Institute of Justice, February 2005.

Dees, Tim. "Finding Stolen Vehicles." *Law and Order*, March 2005, pp. 34–35.

"General Aviation and Homeland Security." Aircraft Owners and Pilots Association website: http://www.aopa.org. Accessed July 22, 2005.

"Heavy Equipment Is a Tempting Target for Thieves." National Insurance Crime Bureau fact sheet. http://www.nicb.org/uploaded_documents/publicfactsheets/heavyequipment.pdf. Accessed July 22, 2005.

"Is Your Car a Magnet for Thieves?" *USAA* [United Services Automobile Association] *Magazine*, 2005, No.1, pp. 23–25.

"It's Not a Feat of Science: Cloned Vehicles Are a Crime." National Insurance Crime Bureau fact sheet. http://www.nicb.org/uploaded_documents/publicfactsheets/clonedvehicles.pdf. Accessed July 22, 2005.

Kariya, Mark. "Grand Theft Cop Car." *Police*, October 2003, pp. 32–38.

Loss Prevention and Security Techniques for Equipment Owners. National Equipment Register, 2002.

Mertens, Jennifer. "Thieves Tempted by Bait." *Law Enforcement Technology*, April 2003, pp. 36–43.

"Motorcycle Theft and Fraud: Half the Wheels but All the Criminal Opportunity." *UpClose*, Summer 2004, Issue 1, National Insurance Crime Bureau. http://www.nicb .org/uploaded_documents/upclose/upclose08.04.pdf. Accessed July 22, 2005.

"Motorcycles Offer a Tempting Target for Criminals." National Insurance Crime Bureau fact sheet. http://www.nicb.org/uploaded_documents/publicfactsheets/motorcycle.pdf. Accessed July 22, 2005.

"Multi-State Motorcycle Theft Ring Smashed in Undercover Sting Operation." New York State Insurance Department press release, January 6, 2005.

Pasquale, Dan. "Be On the Lookout." *Police*, October 2004, pp. 34–36.

"Police Catch Car Thieves with High-Tech Bait Cars." *Police*, March 2003, p. 12.

"The Problem of Heavy Equipment Theft." National Equipment Register website: http://www.nerusa.com/theft_problem.asp. Accessed July 22, 2005.

Sider, Glen. "Identifying Heavy Equipment." *The Law Enforcement Trainer*, March/April 2004, pp. 41–45.

"Solution to Sled Theft in Lanaudiere, Quebec." *Supertrax*, January 7, 2005.

"Vehicle Cloning." *UpClose* (Special Edition), November 2004, Issue 2, National Insurance Crime Bureau. http://www.nicb.org/uploaded_documents/upclose/upclose11.04.pdf. Accessed July 22, 2005.

Wells, David. "Stopping Snowmobile Theft." *Snowbound*, January 2004.

"What Is AOPA's Airport Watch?" Aircraft Owners and Pilots Association website: http://www.aopa.org/asn/watch.html. Accessed July 22, 2005.

Whitely, Peyton. "'Bait Cars' in Everett Snagging Car-Theft Suspects." *Seattle Times*, July 26, 2005.

Arson, Bombs, and Explosives

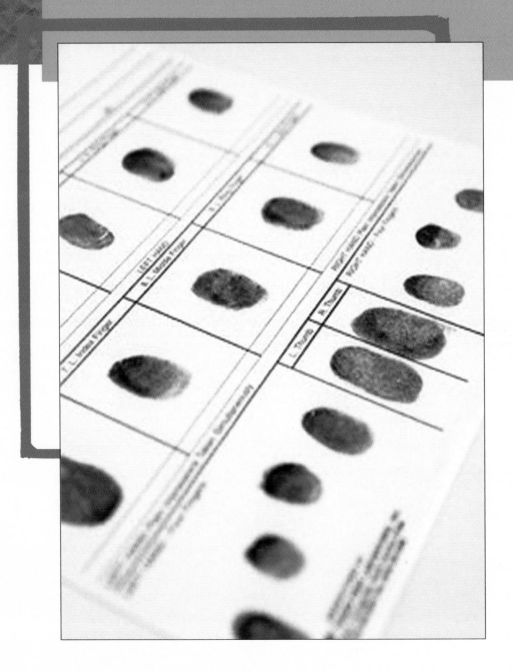

Can You Define?

Do You Know?

- How fires are classified?
- What presumption is made when investigating fires?
- What the elements of arson are?
- What constitutes aggravated arson? simple arson?
- What degrees of arson the Model Arson Law establishes?
- Who is responsible for detecting arson? investigating arson?
- What special challenges exist in investigating arson?
- What the fire triangle is and why it is important in arson investigations?
- What accelerants are and which are most commonly used in arson?
- What common igniters are used in arson?
- What common burn indicators are?
- How to determine a fire's point of origin?
- How fires normally burn?
- What factors indicate the likelihood of arson?
- When an administrative warrant is issued? a criminal warrant?
- When a warrant is needed for investigating a fire scene and what the precedent case is?
- What to check when investigating suspected arson of a vehicle?
- What to pay special attention to when investigating explosions and bombings?

Outline

 rson, the malicious, willful burning of a building or property, is one of the oldest crimes known. It has probably been practiced since soon after fire was discovered. Arson is a combination crime against persons and property, threatening life and causing immense property losses. In October 1978 Congress mandated that the FBI reclassify arson as a Part One Index crime in its Uniform Crime Reporting Program, effective March 1979.

Arson is difficult to prove because in many fires the evidence is consumed and there are few witnesses. Few police officers or investigators have extensive training in investigating arson, and they are often confused by the complications involved in securing evidence and cooperating with other agencies.

Many sources gather statistics on fires, including the FBI, the National Fire Protection Association (NFPA), insurance companies, state fire marshal's offices, state crime bureaus, sheriff's offices, and local police and fire departments. The FBI's Uniform Crime Reports (UCR) show 64,043 arson offenses in 2003, with an average damage of $11,942 and a clearance rate of 16.7 percent (*Crime in the United States 2003*). Of these arson offenses, 42.1 percent were structure fires with an average damage valued at $21,276.

A press release headline (July 11, 2005) from the NFPA reads: "Nearly 4,000 Die in U.S. Fires in 2004." Of these, nearly 82 percent died in their homes. According to the NFPA annual report (Karter, p.i), every 20 seconds a fire department responds to a fire somewhere in the nation. The report (p.ii) says that 3,900 civilian fire deaths occurred in 2004, along with 17,785 civilian fire injuries. Fire caused an estimated $9,794,000,000 in prop-

erty damage (p.iii). An estimated 36,500 intentionally set structure fires occurred in 2004, resulting in 320 civilian deaths and $714,000,000 in property damage. An additional 36,000 set vehicle fires occurred, resulting in $165,000,000 in property damage.

In addition to these losses, Martin (p.125) points out that arson can affect neighborhoods by causing public fear and that on a broader scale, arson to commercial property can cause loss of jobs, diminishing tax revenue, and, in turn, the raising of fire insurance premiums for people across the country.

This chapter begins with a classification of arson crimes, the elements of the crime of arson, and the Model Arson Law. This is followed by a profile of the typical arsonist and a description of the need for police and fire department cooperation as well as the availability of other sources of assistance. Next is a discussion of the special challenges in investigating arson, responding to the scene, the preliminary investigation, and the types of search warrants that might be required. The challenges of investigating vehicle arson, prosecuting arsonists, and preventing arson are covered next. The chapter concludes with an in-depth look at investigating explosions caused by bombs.

Classification of Fires

 Fires are classified as natural, accidental, criminal (arson), suspicious, or of unknown origin.

A *natural fire* is one set intentionally to destroy refuse, weeds, or waste products in industrial processes or to provide warmth. It is easy to determine that such fires are natural.

An *accidental fire,* as the name implies, is not intentional. Fires can be accidentally ignited by the heat of the sun's rays, lightning, faulty wiring, leaking gas, a carelessly tossed cigarette, overheated Christmas tree lights, children playing with matches, and many other causes. Arsonists usually try to make their fires appear accidental.

A *criminal fire* (arson) is ignited intentionally and maliciously to destroy property or buildings. Proof must be obtained that the fire was not natural or accidental.

A *suspicious fire* is one suspected as arson even though proof is lacking.

A fire of *unknown origin* is one in which there is no evidence to indicate whether the fire was natural, accidental, or criminal. The cause is simply not known.

Fires are presumed natural or accidental unless proven otherwise.

The prosecution has the burden of proving that a fire is not accidental or natural. Because arson cases are hard to prove and require a great deal of work, they are unattractive to prosecutors. Moreover, a prosecutor may feel uneasy with the large amount of expert scientific testimony required.

Exercise caution in investigating fires. The vast majority are not the result of arson. Do not unduly suspect property owners who have already been subjected to fire losses.

Elements of the Crime

Under common law, the *crime of arson* was defined as the malicious, willful burning of another's house or outbuilding. It was considered such a serious offense that the penalty was death. Laws have now extended arson to cover other buildings, personal property, crops, and the burning of one's own property. As in other crimes, arson laws vary from state to state but share some common elements.

The elements of the crime of arson include:
• Willful, malicious burning of a building or property,
• of another or of one's own to defraud,
• or causing to be burned, or aiding, counseling, or procuring such burning.

Attempted arson is also a crime in most states.

Willful, Malicious Burning of a Building or Property

Willful means "intentional." If a motive is determined, intent can be proven; therefore, when possible, show motive even if it is not required by law. Merchandise or household goods moved in or out immediately before the fire help to establish motive and intent.

Malicious denotes a "spiteful, vindictive desire to harm others." Malice is shown by circumstantial evidence such as statements of ill will, threats against persons or property, a recent increase in insurance coverage, or past property burned.

Burning is the prime element in the corpus delicti. There must be more than an exposure to heat, although flames need not have been visible nor the property destroyed. Heating to the ignition point is sufficient even if the fire extinguishes itself.

Of Another or of One's Own to Defraud

The motive for burning another's property can range from revenge to economic gain. The burning of one's own property, however, is almost always to defraud. Prove that the property was insured and show a motive for desiring the insurance money. Copies of the insurance policies obtained from the victim after serving proper notice show whether an excessive amount of insurance was taken out, whether recent additions or changes were made in the policy, or whether the insurance was soon to expire. Businesses are sometimes burned because they are failing financially, which can be established by business records or employee statements.

Causing to be Burned, or Aiding, Counseling, or Procuring the Burning

A person who hires a professional (a "torch") to commit arson is also guilty of the crime. Seek evidence connecting this person with the actual arsonist.

Classification of Arson

States vary in how they classify arson and related crimes.

Aggravated and Simple Arson

Some laws categorize arson as either aggravated or simple.

Aggravated arson is intentionally destroying or damaging a dwelling or other property by means of fire or explosives or other infernal device—creating an imminent danger to life or great bodily harm, which risk was known or reasonably foreseeable to the suspect.
Simple arson is an intentional destruction by fire or explosives that does not create imminent danger to life or risk of great bodily harm.

Fire does not require visible burning or an actual flame, but it must involve some extent of burning. *Explosives* include any device, apparatus, or equipment that causes damage by combustion or explosion, such as time bombs, Molotov cocktails, missiles, plastic explosives, grenades, and dynamite. *Destruction or damage* does not require total destruction or consummation. Damage that affects the value or usefulness of the property is sufficient.

Creating an imminent danger to life or risk of great bodily harm is assumed whenever the burned structure is a dwelling or is likely to have people within it. People need not be there at the time. *If the danger or risk was known or reasonably foreseeable* means that even if the suspect did not intend to harm anyone, the risk should have been known or reasonably anticipated. If a person dies in a fire set by an arsonist, the death is first-degree murder, an additional offense to be prosecuted.

Attempted Arson

The elements of attempted arson are the intent to set a fire and some preparation to commit the crime. The intent is normally specific, and the act must be overt. It must be shown that the fire would have occurred except for some intervention. Attempted arson also includes placing any combustible or explosive material or device in or near any property with the intent to set fire, to destroy, or to otherwise damage property. Putting materials together at a location where they could not cause a fire does not constitute attempted arson.

Setting Negligent Fires

Setting a negligent fire is defined as causing a fire to burn or to get out of control through culpable negligence, creating an unreasonable risk and the likelihood of damage or injury to persons or property. This charge is often brought against people who leave smoldering campfires that cause forest fires.

The Model Arson Law

The Model Arson Law was written and promoted in the 1920s by the NFPA. The latest revision is included in *The Fire Almanac*, published annually by the same organization. Many states do not classify fires as aggravated or simple but instead have adopted the Model Arson Law, which specifies four degrees of arson.

The Model Arson Law divides arson into the following degrees:

- *First-degree:* burning of dwellings
- *Second-degree:* burning of buildings other than dwellings
- *Third-degree:* burning of other property
- *Fourth-degree:* attempting to burn buildings or property

The Model Arson Law includes within each degree not only the actual act but also anyone who aids, counsels, or procures the act.

The Arsonist

According to the FBI's UCR, the majority of those arrested for arson are white males and over half are under age 18, a higher rate of juvenile involvement than any other Index crime. The typical adult male arsonist has been reared in a broken or unstable home, has an extensive criminal history, is below average intelligence, lacks marital ties, is socially maladjusted or a loner, is unemployed or working in an unskilled position, and is intoxicated at the time he sets the fire.

Female arsonists usually burn their own property, rarely that of an employer, neighbor, or associate. They are often self-destructive, mentally defective, older, lonely, and unhappy, and often have some psychotic problems, primarily schizophrenia.

Juvenile Firesetting

Putnam and Kirkpatrick (p.1) point out the tragic, costly consequences of juvenile firesetting: "In a typical year, fires set by children and youths claim the lives of approximately 300 people and destroy more than $300 million worth of property. Children are the predominant victims of these fires, accounting for 85 of every 100 lives lost." Their review of the literature reveals a distinction between fireplay and firesetting behavior. Fireplay conveys a low level of intent to inflict harm and an absence of malice. Rather it involves curiosity and fascination. Firesetting is "decidedly different" and involves malice and an intent to inflict harm.

The website juvenilejustice.com (*Juvenile Firesetters*) specifies the following three categories: curious experimenters, intentional firesetters, and crisis firesetters. The curiosity firesetters are mainly children under age 7 who experiment with or cause accidental fires. The intentional firesetters are usually between 8 and 12, whose firesetting represents "underlying psychosocial conflicts." Crisis firesetters are adolescents between ages 13 and 18 with a long history of undetected fireplay and fire-starting behavior resulting from psychosocial conflict or intentional criminal behavior. Each of these classifications is viewed as distinct from arson.

Malcolm Shabazz, grandson of slain black nationalist leader Malcolm X, is an example of a boy who went from the curiosity stage to the crisis stage in nine years (*Juvenile Firesetting*). At age 3 he set his sneakers on fire. At age 9 he fantasized about starting fires with gasoline. Court documents state that he developed an alter-ego called "Sinister Torch" and acted on his desire to set fires. After manifesting seemingly unmanageable problems, he was separated from his mother and sent to live with his grandmother, Dr. Betty Shabazz. Angered by the unwanted move, he allegedly laid a trail of gasoline in Dr. Shabazz's home and lit it. She was burned over 80 percent of her body and died.

Hundreds of jurisdictions have established programs to address the growing concern about juvenile firesetting. According to the director of one such program: "Firesetting is the first major outward sign, usually of more deeply rooted problems" and is a risk factor associated with delinquency, although usually not identified as one (*Juvenile Firesetting*).

In arson, unlike other crimes, the victim is often the prime suspect. Motivation, although it need not be proved, has great significance in arson investigations.

Motivation

Common motives for arson include revenge, spite, or jealousy; vandalism and malicious mischief; crime concealment and diversionary tactics; profit and insurance fraud; intimidation, extortion, and sabotage; and psychiatric afflictions, pyromania, alcoholism, and mental retardation.

Revenge, spite, and jealousy motivate jilted lovers, feuding neighbors, disgruntled employees, quarreling spouses, people who feel cheated or abused, and those who feel racial or religious hostility. In rural areas, disagreements often result in the burning of homes or barns.

Vandalism and malicious mischief are frequent motives for juveniles who burn property merely to relieve boredom or as a general protest against authority. Many fires in schools, abandoned autos, vacant buildings, and trash containers are caused by this type of arsonist.

Crime concealment and diversionary tactics motivate criminals to set fires to destroy evidence of a crime or evidence connecting them to the crime. In murder cases arson can be used to attempt to make it impossible to identify a victim. In other cases people set fires to destroy records containing evidence of embezzlement, forgery, or fraud. Arson is also used to divert attention while criminals commit another crime or cover their escape.

Profit and insurance fraud are frequent motives for arson. A businessperson may wind up in financial straits and decide that the easiest way out is to burn the business and collect the insurance. Some people overinsure property and then burn it, collecting far more than the property was worth. For example, a St. Louis property owner received more than $415,000 in insurance payments for 54 fires occurring within a two-year period. In large cities professional arson rings defraud insurance companies of millions of dollars.

Other methods of obtaining profit have used arson to stimulate business, to eliminate business rivals, or to secure employment—for example, a security guard, firefighter, or police officer might set fires to obtain a job. In South Carolina five firefighters were charged with arson believed to be motivated not by profit but by a desire to practice fighting fires. In other cases firefighters have set fires and then responded to the alarm, receiving attention and praise at having "played the hero." These "vanity" arsonists are called **strikers.**

It is not always firefighters who seek to become heroes. In December 1999 a male nurse set a fire that killed billionaire banker Edmond Safra, stating he hoped to emerge as the hero who saved his employer's life. Safra was terrified that assailants were after him and locked himself in his Monaco penthouse bathroom, refusing to leave even when police and firefighters arrived. He died of asphyxiation.

Intimidation, extortion, and sabotage are motives of striking workers and employers to apply pressure during a strike. Criminals, especially mobsters, use arson to intimidate witnesses and to extort money. Protesters have also used arson as a way of sending a message. For example, an environmental group claimed responsibility for a series of fires that caused $12 million in damage in protest of Vail Associates moving forward with its controversial 885-acre ski resort expansion.

Psychiatric afflictions, pyromania, alcoholism, and mental retardation account for many other fires. Pyromaniacs start fires because of an irresistible urge or passion for fire. Some derive sexual satisfaction from watching fires. Others become arsonists to show power over their environment or because they believe they are acting with divine guidance.

Several studies reveal revenge as the most common motive. Nonetheless, many arson investigators believe that insurance fraud is the most prevalent motive for arson. It may be that arson intended to defraud is often hired out to a professional who is less likely to get caught and, if apprehended, is more likely to have better legal counsel.

The professional torch—the arsonist for hire—is extremely difficult to identify because such individuals have no apparent link to the fire. However, the victim is also under suspicion in many instances. A guilty victim typically has an ironclad alibi. Also to be considered is the unintentional firesetter, that is, the individual who accidentally sets a fire and then is too embarrassed to admit it or who fears that insurance may not cover the loss if the accident is made known.

Computer software can play a pivotal role in identifying serial arsonists by allowing investigators to efficiently organize and manage tips, evidence, and other information about related fires. Such case management can shorten investigations by months.

Police and Fire Department Cooperation

Arson is investigated by many agencies with joint jurisdiction: state fire marshals, state police, county sheriffs, and local police and fire departments (Figure 16.1). In addition, insurance investigators often become involved.

Lack of trained personnel to investigate arson is a major problem in both police and fire departments, except in large cities that have their own arson investigation squads. Although arson is a crime, police tend to give it low priority, believing that the fire department should investigate. However, many firefighters are volunteers who are not trained in arson investigation. Many full-time departments do not train their personnel to investigate arson. Rural areas and cities of up to 75,000 in population rely heavily on the state fire marshal's office, which usually does not have enough staff to conduct full investigations throughout the state. State fire marshal's offices can help local police and fire

© 911 Pictures

Figure 16.1
Law enforcement and fire department personnel must collaborate to solve cases of arson.

agencies by providing advice, coordinating activities, and supplying information on suspect profiles. They cannot, however, assume full responsibility for the investigation. Even fire departments that provide training in arson detection seldom include training on the criminal procedures followed in prosecuting arson.

Attitudes about the responsibility for investigating arson vary. Some fire departments feel that arson investigation and prosecution are their responsibility; others feel just as strongly that arson is a police matter.

> Logic suggests that the fire department should work to detect arson and determine the fire's point of origin and probable cause, whereas the police department should investigate arson and prepare the case for prosecution.

Fire Department Expertise

Recognizing factors concerning smoke and fire conditions, detecting arson evidence, and determining the cause of a fire are specific areas of expertise for the fire department, which investigates many accidental and natural fires. To delegate this responsibility to the police department would be an unnecessary duplication of skill, especially because only a small number of fires are due to arson.

Trained fire personnel know about buildings, how fires are started, and the various components necessary for ignition. Fire marshals also have extralegal powers to summon witnesses, subpoena records, and take statements under oath that police officers do not have.

Moreover, fire personnel may enter buildings after a fire without a warrant, a benefit to criminal investigations.

They also work closely with insurance companies and are apt to recognize people frequently present at fires.

The fire department's basic role is fire investigation and arson detection, not arson investigation. Once the cause of the fire is determined to be arson, the police are notified and the process becomes a joint investigation.

Police Department Expertise

Police on patrol duty and investigators, through intelligence files, are likely to know possible arson suspects. Field-interview cards can include names of people present in an area where arson fires are being set. Specialized techniques such as interviewing witnesses and interrogating suspects are normal police operations. Moreover, police have contacts with informants and arrest power.

Coordinating Efforts

Regardless of the actual agency assigned to an arson investigation, someone must coordinate the efforts of everyone involved. A full-time arson squad has the potential for conducting the best arson investigation. The next best arrangement is to have a well-trained arson investigator from local jurisdictions or the state fire marshal's office. However, police personnel trained in criminal investigation working with fire personnel trained in arson detection can do an effective job if they mutually agree about who is in charge. Cross-training is one way to help police and firefighters understand each other's roles.

However, as Miller (p.86) observes: "Mention the term 'cross-training' to police officers and firefighters and you'll likely get eye rolls, groans and vocal explanations as to why it hasn't worked before, why it can't work now and why it never will." Miller suggests that because the federal government has made agency interoperability a cornerstone of homeland security, and because such interoperability may take years for many agencies to deploy, cross-training deserves consideration.

Other Sources of Assistance in Investigating Arson

Other sources of assistance in investigating arson are the Bureau of Alcohol, Tobacco, Firearms and Explosives (ATF), the news media, insurance companies, and arson task forces.

The Bureau of Alcohol, Tobacco, Firearms, and Explosives

On January 24, 2003, the Bureau of Alcohol, Tobacco and Firearms became part of the Department of Justice under the Homeland Security bill and had its name expanded to the Bureau of Alcohol, Tobacco, Firearms and Explosives to reflect the new focus on explosives-related crime and terrorism. The ATF has extensive resources for investigating arsons, including the ATF National Response Team, ready to investigate within 24 hours of receiving a call. Other ATF resources include arson profilers; national laboratories in Georgia, Maryland, and California; the Explosives Incidents Systems (EXIS) database, an intelligence division; financial auditors; accelerant-detecting canines; photograph examiners; and Certified Fire Investigators.

News Media

One source of assistance frequently overlooked is the news media, which can publish profiles of arsonists and seek the public's help in identifying them. They may also have photographs or videotapes of in-progress fires that can be extremely useful in investigations.

Insurance Companies

Insurance companies can be very helpful in an arson investigation. Insurance companies usually request the insured to sign a release authorizing the company to obtain private records such as income tax returns, financial audits, bank accounts, credit reports, telephone records, and utility company records. Without this release, obtaining such records is a long, complex process.

Private insurance company investigators can assist fire and police efforts in investigating fire losses. Many insurance companies have full-time fire loss investigators, whereas many smaller fire and police agencies do not. The objective is the same for both—obtaining the truth. For fire and police authorities, the goal is to locate the suspect. If the suspect in a fire-for-profit act is arrested, fire loss problems for the insurance company are resolved.

The property owner must work with the fire and police departments and insurance company to collect the insurance money. Consequently, interviewing and interrogating efforts are much enhanced. Background checks, bank and credit inquiries, and financial status are also easier to verify.

Insurance investigators have the additional advantage of being able to enter the fire scene without a warrant in their efforts to examine the damage and to determine the cause of the fire.

Further, several index bureaus gather insurance-claim information in attempting to determine whether the same claim is being made to more than one company or whether a pattern of claims exists. Law enforcement investigators can benefit from information gathered by these bureaus as well. Most states provide limited civil immunity to insurance companies that provide information to law enforcement agencies in their investigations.

Arson Task Forces

A powerful impact can be made on coordinating existing forces and creating new sources. To coordinate existing forces and create new sources for combating arson and related problems in any community, county, or state, arson task forces should be developed comprised of fire and police department personnel; community leaders; insurance representatives; city, county, and district attorneys; federal agency personnel; and others. Arson has the lowest clearance by arrest of the major crimes, due primarily to inadequate training of fire and police department personnel, the difficulty of locating and preserving evidence, and a lack of coordination of personnel of the various organizations involved.

The website of the Office of the Illinois State Fire Marshal describes its Juvenile Firesetters Task Force (www.state.il.us/osfm/jfs/jfs.htm), whose goal is "to develop and coordinate a comprehensive statewide program to identify, intervene with and counsel juveniles to reduce fire deaths, injuries and property damage from criminal and non-criminal fires." This task force approach is described by Martin (p.123) in developing the Utica (New York) Arson Strike Force. Assisted by the Federal Emergency Management Agency (FEMA), a team was assembled that became the model for interagency cooperation across the country. Contributing members and resources were the ATF, the U.S. Marshals Service, the district attorney's office, the Utica Police Department and Fire Department, the Oneida County Sheriff's Office, the New York State Office of Fire Protection and Control, the New York State Police, and the New York State Insurance Fraud Bureau. The task force had three main goals:

1. Detecting arson, including seeking ways to improve on the detection of, as well as methods to properly investigate, arson to successfully prosecute the crime

2. Reducing the number of arsons and deliberately set fires, in turn reducing property damage, physical injuries, and deaths

3. Developing a preventive program aimed at educating and developing a working relationship with the people the task force serves (Martin, p.124)

Their combined efforts resulted in arson dropping 50 percent in one year.

Special Challenges in Investigation

Special challenges in investigating arson include:
- Coordinating efforts with the fire department and others.
- Determining whether a crime has in fact been committed.
- Finding physical evidence, most of which is destroyed by the fire.
- Finding witnesses.
- Determining whether the victim is a suspect.

Investigating arson often requires even more persistence, thoroughness, and attention to minute details than do other crimes. Arson is a difficult crime to investigate because there are seldom witnesses and the evidence needed to prove that a crime has been committed is usually consumed in the fire. Moreover, arson is an easy crime to write off without being publicly criticized because the victim and the suspect are often the same person. However, the innocent victim of arson is frequently frustrated by the lack of evidence and witnesses and by the police's inability to prove that a crime was committed.

Responding to the Scene

hile approaching a fire scene, first responders should observe, mentally note, and, when time permits, record in notes (*Fire and Arson*, pp.13-14):

- The presence, location, and conditions of victims and witnesses
- Vehicles leaving the scene, bystanders, or unusual activities near the scene
- Flame and smoke conditions (e.g., the volume of flames and smoke; the color, height, and location of flames; the direction in which the flames and smoke are moving)

- The type of occupancy, use, and condition of the structure
- Conditions surrounding the scene
- Weather conditions
- Fire-suppression techniques used, including ventilation, forcible entry, and utility shutoff measures
- Status of fire alarms, security alarms, and sprinklers

The Preliminary Investigation

T he fire department usually receives the initial fire call unless the departments have a joint dispatcher or are merged into a public safety department. Fire personnel make out the reports and forward them to the state fire marshal. Insurance companies are also represented, and their efforts are coordinated with those of fire and police personnel.

The scene of a fire is dirty, messy, and complicated, making it difficult to obtain evidence of possible arson. An arson scene may be the most contaminated crime scene you will ever encounter. The Law Enforcement Assistance Administration describes it:

> No other type of crime scene except bombing is characterized by as much destruction and disorder as arson. Investigators must search through piles of debris and rubble, often on their hands and knees. Ashes, soot, and char make fire scenes filthy and malodorous. . . .
>
> The fire-scene search is further aggravated by water and foam remaining from the extinguishment. The scene may be a quagmire, making the rubble wet and heavy to move out of the way. Plaster fallen from walls and ceilings mixes with the water, forming a gray slush retarding the investigator's movements. In cold weather, there is the additional pressure of completing the work before everything freezes and the investigation is severely impeded.
>
> The fire scene may be dangerous to work in because of the imminent collapse of upper parts of the structure. It may be exposed to the elements, making work in foul weather difficult and unpleasant.
>
> In addition to the destruction of the fire, there are further problems caused by firefighter mop-up and salvage operations immediately following the fire. The mop-up process involves finding and eliminating any smoldering spots that might rekindle the fire. This involves tearing open walls, ceilings, roofs, and other partitions, and throwing objects like mattresses and sofas out of the building. The salvage process involves removing any salvageable items, such as furnishings or machinery, to a safe place and covering them from the elements. This process hampers efforts to reconstruct the fire scene and the sequence of events that led to the arson.

Although the fire department is responsible for establishing that arson has occurred, investigators must verify those findings by understanding what distinguishes an accidental fire from arson and by knowing what evidence and information are available for proving the elements of the crime.

The Fire Triangle

The fire triangle is a basic concept critical to an arson investigation.

 The **fire triangle** consists of three elements necessary for a substance to burn: air, fuel, and heat. In arson one or more of these elements is usually present in abnormal amounts for the structure.

Extra amounts of *air* or oxygen can result from opened windows or doors, pried-open vents, or holes knocked in walls. Because firefighters often chop holes in structures, determine whether any such openings were made by the firefighters or by someone else. *Fuel* can be added by piling up newspapers, excelsior, or other combustible materials found at or brought to the scene. Gasoline, kerosene, and other accelerants add sufficient *heat* to the fire to cause the desired destruction after it has been ignited. As Steck-Flynn (p.60) points out: "To say the cause of a fire was arson, and therefore deliberate, the investigator must have sufficient evidence one of the factors in the fire triangle was tampered with."

Arson Indicators

Several factors can alert investigators that the fire was probably the result of arson.

Accelerants

Evidence of **accelerants,** substances that promote combustion, especially gasoline, is a primary form of physical evidence at an arson scene.

Most arson cases involve a flammable liquid, and in 80 percent of these cases, it is gasoline. Perhaps this is because gasoline is easily obtained and widely known to arsonists or because gasoline's familiar odor makes it easier for investigators to detect. Other common accelerants are kerosene, charcoal lighter, paint thinner, and lacquer solvent.

Look for residues of liquid fire accelerants on floors, carpets, and soil because the liquid accelerants run to the lowest level. In addition, these areas often have the lowest temperatures during the fire and may not have enough oxygen to support complete combustion of the accelerant. Accelerants may seep through porous or cracked floors to underlying soil that has excellent retention properties for flammable liquids. Accelerants can also be found on the clothes and shoes of the suspect if apprehended. You can also identify fire accelerants at the scene either by your own sense of smell or by using portable equipment that detects residues of flammable liquids.

Olfactory detection, the sensitivity of the human nose to gasoline vapor, is ineffective if the odor is masked by another strong odor, such as that of burned debris. Moreover, it is often inconvenient or impossible to sniff for accelerant odors along floors or in recessed areas.

Catalytic combustion detectors are the most common type of flammable vapor detector used by arson investigators. Commonly known as a *sniffer,* a *combustible gas indicator,* an *explosimeter* or a *vapor detector,* this detector is portable, moderately priced, and fairly simple to operate. Basically, vapor samples are pumped over a heated, platinum-plated wire coil that causes any combustible gas present to oxidize. The heat from the oxidation raises the coil's electrical resistance, and this change is measured electrically.

Although fire accelerants are the most frequent type of evidence submitted to laboratories for analysis (80 percent), explosives (13 percent) and incendiary devices (4 percent) are also frequently submitted.

Igniters Igniters are substances or devices used to start fires. The most common igniters are matches. To be carrying matches is not damaging evidence unless some have been removed from the book or box and those found at an arson scene match those found in the suspect's possession.

Common igniters include matches; candles; cigars; cigarettes; cigarette lighters; electrical, mechanical, and chemical devices; and explosives.

Electrical devices left on, kerosene-soaked papers in waste baskets, time fuses, shorted light switches, magnifying glasses, matches tied around a lighted cigarette, and numerous other igniters have been used to commit arson.

Candles are often used in arsons because they give the suspect time to leave the scene. The average candle burns about 30 to 45 minutes per inch, depending on its size, shape, composition, and the amount of air in the room. Tapered candles burn faster at the top and slower toward the base. The arsonist may control the length of time by cutting off part of the candle before lighting it. The candle can be set in a material that will ignite once the candle burns down, or the hot wax may be allowed to drip onto a surface to start a fire. The candle's flame can also be used to ignite other materials in the room.

Regardless of whether arsonists use direct or delayed ignition, they usually plan for the fire to consume the igniter; however, this often does not happen. Moreover, in their haste to leave the scene, arsonists may drop parts of the igniter in an area unaffected by the fire. Any igniter not normally present at the location is evidence.

Burn Indicators   **Burn indicators** are visible evidence of the effects of heating or partial burning. They indicate various aspects of a fire such as rate of development, temperature, duration, time of occurrence, presence of flammable liquids, and points of origin. Interpreting burn indicators is a primary means of determining the causes of fires (Figure 16.2).

Figure 16.2
The alligatoring and other burn indicators at this fire scene will provide important information to the investigator regarding the rate of fire development, temperature, duration, time of occurrence, presence of flammable liquids, and points of origin. Interpreting burn indicators is a primary means of determining the causes of fires.

 Common burn indicators include alligatoring, crazing, the depth of char, lines of demarcation, sagged furniture springs, and spalling.

Alligatoring is the checking of charred wood that gives it the appearance of alligator skin. Large, rolling blisters indicate rapid, intense heat. Small, flat alligatoring indicates slow, less intense heat.

Crazing is the formation of irregular cracks in glass due to rapid, intense heat, possibly caused by a fire accelerant.

The **depth of char,** or how deeply wood is burned, indicates the length of burn and the fire's point of origin. Use a ruler to measure depth of char.

A **line of demarcation** is a boundary between charred and uncharred material. A puddle-shaped line of demarcation on floors or rugs can indicate the use of a liquid fire accelerant (Figure 16.3). In a cross section of wood, a sharp, distinct line of demarcation indicates a rapid, intense fire.

Sagged furniture springs usually occur when a fire originates inside the cushions of upholstered furniture (as from a lighted cigarette rolling behind a cushion) or when a fire is intensified by an accelerant.

Spalling is the breaking off of surface pieces of concrete or brick due to intense heat. Brown stains around the spall indicate use of an accelerant.

Point of Origin   Knowing the fire's point of origin helps to establish how the fire spread and whether it followed a normal burning pattern. The more extensive the destruction, the more difficult it is to determine the fire's point of origin.

 The point of origin is established by finding the area with the deepest char, alligatoring, and usually the greatest destruction. More than one point of origin indicates arson.

Incendiary (igniter) evidence might be discovered at the point of origin. In addition, information from witnesses who saw the fire can establish where the flames began.

Burning Pattern

Fires normally burn upward, not outward. They are drawn toward ventilation and follow fuel paths.

Given adequate ventilation, a fire will burn upward. If a door or window is open, it will be drawn toward that opening.

If the arsonist places a path of flammable liquid, the fire will follow that path, known as a **trailer**. Trailers can

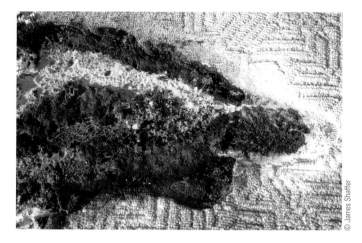

Figure 16.3

A photograph of a line of demarcation, seen in this carpet, is important evidence in an arson investigation. A puddle-shaped line of demarcation on floors or rugs can indicate the use of a liquid fire accelerant.

be made of paper, hay, flammable compounds, or any substance that burns readily, and they result in an abnormal pattern. The char marks will follow the trailer's path.

Areas of uneven burning can also indicate the presence of an incendiary or that a great amount of flammable material was already at the scene.

Appearance of Collapsed Walls   Notice how walls seem to have collapsed, especially if you smell gas. Lighter gases tend to explode walls out from the top of the room; heavier gases explode walls out from the bottom of the room. Fast-exploding gases such as hydrogen,

acetylene, or butane give the appearance of the walls caving in. If odors or the walls' appearance suggests gas as the igniter or accelerator, determine whether the gas is normally on the premises.

Smoke Color   Generally, blue smoke results from burning alcohol; white smoke from burning vegetable compounds, hay, or phosphorous; yellow or brownish yellow smoke from film, nitric acid, sulfur, hydrochloric acid, or smokeless gunpowder; and black smoke from petroleum or petroleum products (Figure 16.4).

Notice the smoke's color if the fire is still in progress. If it has been put out when you arrive, ask the firefighters or witnesses what color the smoke was. Determine whether substances likely to produce smoke of that color were on the premises before the fire.

Summary of Arson Indicators

Arson is likely in fires that:
- Have more than one point of origin.
- Deviate from normal burning patterns.
- Show evidence of trailers.
- Show evidence of having been accelerated.
- Produce odors or smoke of a color associated with substances not normally present at the scene.
- Indicate that an abnormal amount of air, fuel, or heat was present.
- Reveal evidence of incendiary igniters at the point of origin.

Figure 16.4

The black smoke in this fire indicates the involvement of petroleum or petroleum products. If these are not normally on the premises, arson is probable.

Figure 16.5
A firefighter makes his way through the rubble inside of the Cathedral of St. John the Divine December 18, 2001, after a fire broke out in the rear of the cathedral in New York City. After a fire the investigator should take enough pictures to show the entire scene in detail. Pictures taken inside the building should show the extent of burning as well as close-ups of alligatoring and deep charring.

Professional arsonists use a variety of methods to ignite fires, including the following:

- Connecting magnesium rods to timed detonators and placing them in a building's electrical system. The rods burn with extreme intensity and cause a fire that looks as though it was caused by faulty wiring.

- Connecting a timed explosive charge on one or more barrels of gasoline or other highly flammable liquid. This method is often used when large areas such as warehouses are to be burned.

- Pouring acid on key support points in steel-structured buildings to make certain the building will collapse during the fire.

Photographing and Videotaping an Arson Fire

Pictures of a fire in progress show the smoke's color and its origination as well as the size of the fire at different points and times. Pictures are especially useful if there appears to be acceleration of the fire at a specific time that would indicate arson or the presence of highly combustible substances. Many fire departments take such in-progress photographs. Smaller departments may seek help from television or newspaper photographers who may take pictures that can be of immense help. Photographs or videotapes of the fire scene are also ideal to show the judge and jury.

Pictures taken of people at the fire scene might reveal the presence of a known arsonist or show a person who repeatedly appears in photos taken at fires and is therefore an arson suspect.

After the fire, take enough pictures to show the entire scene in detail. Start with the outside of the structure, showing all entries and exits. Also show any obstructions that were placed in front of windows to prevent seeing inside the building. Persons familiar with the structure can review the pictures for anything out of the ordinary.

Take inside pictures to show the extent of burning (Figure 16.5). These will prove the corpus delicti. Take close-up pictures of extra papers, rags, gas cans, or other suspicious substances, as well as examples of alligatoring and deep charring. Take pictures at each stage of the search to show the point of origin, the nature of the burning and the direction and speed of the fire's spread.

Physical Evidence

Preserving evidence is a major problem because much of the evidence is very fragile. Follow carefully the procedures described in Chapter 5. Use disposable cellulose sponges to sop up accelerants for transfer to a container. Use hypodermic or cooking syringes to suck up accelerants between boards or crevices. Sift ashes to detect small objects such as the timing device from an igniter.

Incendiary evidence at the point of origin can be part of a candle, an empty flammable liquid container, excessive amounts of unburned newspaper folded together, or a number of unburned matches.

Paper exposed to high temperatures and sufficient air burns with little ash to examine. However, with a limited supply of air, only partial combustion occurs, leaving charred paper evidence that can be collected for laboratory examination. Paper in a fireplace or stove may be only partially burned, even if the building was totally consumed. These papers may provide a motive for the arson. If the paper is not destroyed, a laboratory may be able to recover any messages on it.

Do not overlook computer data, even if the computer has been involved in an intense fire. The hard drive may survive extreme heat and sometimes even direct flames. It may also survive the water and steam encountered during suppression efforts.

An important step in an arson investigation is identifying potential accelerants at a fire scene. The accepted method is to use gas chromatography with a flame ionization detector (GC-FID), which can make identification in 95 percent of the cases.

Using K-9s in Arson Investigations

Dogs can be of great assistance in arson investigation. Connecticut's K-9 accelerant-detection program, for example, is the result of collaboration among the ATF, the New Haven County state's attorney's office, the State Police Science Laboratory, the Emergency Services Division Canine Unit, and the Bureau of the State Fire Marshal. Their first dog, Mattie, was trained to detect extremely small quantities of highly diluted flammable and combustible liquids, including paint remover and thinner, lacquer thinner, charcoal lighter fluid, kerosene, naphtha, acetone, dry gas, heptone, gasoline, number 2 fuel, diesel fuel, gum turpentine, Heritage lamp oil, transmission fluid, octane, and Jet-A-Fuel.

A lab-certified accelerant-detection canine can detect accelerants at fire scenes and can also search a crowd for possible suspects, search a suspect's clothing and vehicle for the presence of accelerants, and search areas for accelerant containers.

Evidence on a Suspect, at a Residence, or in a Vehicle

If you have a suspect, look for any burns he or she may have received while setting the fire. The suspect may have scorched hair, torn clothing, stains, cuts, and other injuries, or his or her clothing or shoes may have traces of accelerants. The suspect's residence or vehicle may contain clothes noticed at the fire by a witness, objects removed from the scene of the fire, or incendiary devices. You may also find insurance documents or business or financial records that provide a motive.

Observing Unusual Circumstances

Suspicious circumstances implying arson include suddenly emptied premises, the presence of materials not normally part of the business, holes in wall plaster or drywall that expose the wood, disconnected sprinkler systems, blocked-open interior doors, nailed-open fire doors, and other alterations that would provide more air, heat, or fuel to the area.

Interviewing the Victim, Witnesses, and Firefighters

Ask questions such as: How was the fire discovered? Who discovered it? Who were witnesses? What did they see? What color was the smoke, and where was it coming from? What direction was the wind? Did the fire appear to suddenly accelerate? Did anything out of the ordinary occur before the fire? Were there unusual odors? Were the shades up or down? Did obstructions prevent seeing into the building? Were suspicious persons or vehicles observed at the scene before, during, or after the fire?

Also try to learn who had an opportunity to set the fire and who might benefit from it. Determine who had keys and how the property was normally guarded or protected. Check the victim's financial status and find out how much insurance was carried on the property. Interview the firefighters assigned to the fire and obtain copies of their reports.

Search Warrants and Fire Investigations

The U.S. Supreme Court requires a two-step warrant process for investigating fires involving crimes. The initial search may require an **administrative warrant** for searching the premises for cause of fire and origin determination *and* a criminal warrant when evidence of a crime is discovered. Both require probable cause for issuance.

An administrative warrant is issued when it is necessary for a government agent to search the premises to determine the fire's cause and origin. A criminal warrant is issued on probable cause when the premises yield evidence of a crime.

Both require an affidavit in support of the warrant that states the location and legal description of the property, the purpose (to determine the fire's cause and origin), the area and time of the search, the use of the building, and the measures taken to secure the structure or area of the fire. Searches are limited to the items specified in the warrant. Found evidence may be seized, but once the officers leave after finding the evidence, they must have a criminal warrant to return to the premises for a further search.

Administrative warrants allow civil inspections of private property to determine compliance with city ordinances such as fire codes. The Court has established guidelines for arson investigators. In *Michigan v. Clifford* (1984), the Court held:

> If a warrant is necessary, the object of the search determines the type of warrant required. If the primary object is to determine the cause and origin of a fire, an administrative warrant will suffice. . . and if the primary object is to gather evidence of criminal activity, a criminal search warrant may be obtained only on a showing of probable cause to believe that relevant evidence will be found in the place to be searched.

In *Coolidge v. New Hampshire* (1971), the Court held that evidence of criminal activity discovered during a search with a valid administrative warrant may be seized under the plain-view doctrine. Any evidence so seized may be used to establish the probable cause needed to obtain a criminal search warrant.

> Entry to fight a fire requires no warrant. Once in the building, fire officials may remain a reasonable time to investigate the cause of the blaze. After this time an administrative warrant is needed, as established in *Michigan v. Tyler* (1978).

Guidelines on the current legal status of searches conducted during fire investigations include the following:

- Warrants are not required when an authorized individual consents to the search. The consent must be written and must specify the areas to be searched and the purpose of the search. This consent can be revoked at any time.

- Warrants are not required when investigators enter under "exigent circumstances," that is, if investigators enter the premises while firefighters are extinguishing the blaze or conducting overhaul. The scope of the search must be limited to determining the cause and origin. If evidence of a crime is discovered, a criminal warrant is required to continue the search.

- Without consent or an exigency, warrants are required if the premises are subject to a "reasonable expectation of privacy." This includes commercial businesses as well as private residences. Exceptions would be premises that are so utterly devastated by the fire

that no expectation of privacy is reasonable and property that has been abandoned.

- Evidence of a crime discovered during an administrative search may be seized if in plain view.

- Once evidence of arson is discovered, the fire's cause and origin are assumed to be known. The scope of the administrative warrant has been exhausted. A criminal warrant is required to continue the search.

When in doubt, obtain a warrant.

Investigating Vehicle Arson

lthough vehicle fires can be caused by accident, vehicles usually do not burn readily. Accelerants are used on many vehicles to accomplish arson. A quart to a half gallon of flammable liquid is required to cause a major vehicle fire.

> When investigating vehicle fires, look for evidence of accelerants and determine whether the vehicle was insured.

Motives for vehicle arson include the desire to collect insurance, inability to make needed repairs after an unreported accident, desire to eliminate a loan on the vehicle, desire to cover up another crime committed in or with the vehicle, general dissatisfaction with the vehicle's performance, and desire to resolve arguments over the vehicle's use.

A close correlation exists between insurance coverage and vehicle arson; few arsons are committed when there is no insurance coverage. Obtain proof that the vehicle was insured against fire, that the fire was willfully set, that damage resulted, and that there was intent to defraud.

Prosecuting Arsonists

ome studies indicate that well over 90 percent of arsonists go unpunished, probably because arson is most often committed without the benefit of witnesses. According to the International Association of Arson Investigators, approximately 25 percent of all fires in the United States—about 500,000 per year—result from arson, but only about

2 percent of all arsonists are ever arrested and convicted for their crimes.

The difficulty of investigating arson has been discussed, as has the need for cooperation between law enforcement investigators and firefighters. Equally difficult is prosecution. There is a big difference between proving a fire as arson and proving arson in court. Cooperative investigation and prosecution are required if the losses from arson are to be stemmed.

Many prosecutors fail to bring charges because all they have is circumstantial evidence. However, circumstantial evidence can be used to successfully prosecute a case. Look for evidence of planning, such as increasing insurance coverage, removing items, or making offhand remarks or unusual changes. Also look for evidence of disabled or turned-off alarms or sprinkler systems and doors left open. Finally, look for evidence of motive.

Preventing Arson

To prevent arson, various properties at risk of being set on fire might be identified by computer mapping. In some instances crime analysis has determined that the majority of the properties that had experienced an arson fire were either abandoned or vacant properties located near or adjacent to notably high crime locations. In one instance, six key factors were merged into one master map: (1) abandoned properties, (2) negative-equity properties, (3) properties whose gas and/or electric were shut off, (4) sites of prior-year fires, (5) gang locales, and (6) known drug hot spot locations. With accurate predictions, officers can be stationed close to and be more observant of targeted zones.

Investigating Bombings and Explosions

Following the highly publicized bombings of military barracks in Saudi Arabia and numerous sites around the United States, it should come as no surprise that bombs have become a high-profile, almost routine, weapon of mass destruction. Bombs generate substantial media attention and provide an impersonal means of causing considerable damage while allowing a bomber to be a safe distance away when detonation occurs.

Motives for bombings include vandalism, revenge, and protest. Bombs are relatively easy to build from directions that can be found on the Internet. The following are common types of bombs:

- *Dry ice.* Combines dry ice and some water in a 2-liter plastic soda bottle. Depending on the condition of the bottle, the amount of ice, and the weather, the device will explode in 3 to 7 minutes, causing a dangerous, loud explosion.
- *Mailbox bomb.* Combines a bit of sugar and some water in a 2-liter bottle of chlorine. The explosion can launch an average mailbox 20 feet into the air.
- *Car bomb.* A fuse is wrapped around a car's exhaust manifold. The fuse is ignited by the heat of the manifold, detonating the explosion.
- *Nail bomb.* An explosive device packed with nails to increase destructive power when detonated in crowded places. The July 7, 2005, explosion in London atop a double-decker bus near Shoreditch was thought to be this type of bomb.
- *Pipe bomb.* Consists of pipe, end caps, and smokeless powder, detonated by a spark or some heat source. Common containers are pipes, bottles, cans, boxes, pressurized cartridges, and grenade hulls. A pipe bomb laced with nails and other hardware to increase fragmentation caused two deaths in Atlanta's Centennial Park bombing.

Haber (p.14) observes: "Pipe bombs and other improvised explosive devices (IEDs) pose a serious threat to federal, state and local government facilities, considering how easily and inexpensively they can be put together." He suggests that high-traffic public places such as schools, shopping malls, and stadiums are also potential targets.

Numerous websites give detailed instructions on how to make bombs, especially pipe bombs. For example, the Linkbase website offers the following links: homemade explosives, high explosives, how to make a detonator, how to make a pipe bomb, how to make a smoke bomb, how to make a grenade, how to make a time bomb, and the like. It gives detailed instructions "written with the backing of special forces improvised munitions knowledge" ("How to Make"). The instructions are only two pages long, and all the materials needed are readily available.

Bombs, more than any other weapon, make people feel vulnerable. Unlike a gun, a bomb does not have to be aimed. Unlike poison, it does not have to be administered. Bombs are weapons of chance. Victims are simply in the wrong place at the wrong time. For example, the 1993 World Trade Center bombing in New York resulted in six dead, more than a thousand injured, and millions of dollars in property damage. The 1995 bombing at the Murrah Federal Building in Oklahoma City claimed 169 lives, caused nearly 500 injuries, and resulted in losses of $651 million. Bomber Timothy McVeigh was found guilty of the crime and executed. And, of course, there were the explosions in 2001 at the World Trade Center and the Pentagon, resulting in thousands of deaths. Terrorist acts are discussed in Chapter 20.

National attention also focused on the Unabomber case. After 18 years of investigation, 29 injuries, and 3 deaths, Theodore Kaczynski, a Montana hermit who hated our technological society, was arrested, found guilty, and sentenced to life in prison without possibility of release. Evidence found in Kaczynski's cabin included scrap metal and wood, batteries and electric wire, 10 three-ring binders filled with writings and diagrams about constructing and concealing explosive devices, and two manual typewriters that investigators believe Kaczynski used to type his "Unabomber Manifesto."

In the late 1990s Eric Rudolph used nail-laden bombs during the Atlanta summer Olympics as well as at abortion clinics and at nightclubs catering to a mostly gay and lesbian clientele. His 11-page statement was devoid of remorse but rife with anti-abortion and anti-gay rhetoric. The attack at the Olympics was meant to embarrass the government for legalizing abortion (Dewan, p.A37).

In 2002 Luke Helder, age 21 at the time, left a trail of 18 pipe bombs in rural mailboxes in Illinois, Iowa, Nebraska, Texas, and Colorado. The bombs were accompanied by typewritten notes in clear plastic bags indicating the bomber wanted to get people's attention "in the only way I can." Six of the bombs exploded, injuring four letter carriers and two residents, but no one was killed. Law enforcement pulled Helder over three times during the course of his 1,500-mile journey in which he attempted to create a "smiley face" pattern of mailbox bombings. He was stopped in Nebraska and given a speeding ticket. He was stopped in Oklahoma for driving without a seatbelt. And he was stopped in Colorado for speeding. Within 48 hours of these three encounters, Helder was arrested on bombing charges after his cellphone calls were traced ("Wiping a Smile," p.6). The FBI was the lead agency in investigating these bombings and in apprehending Helder.

Responding to a Bomb Threat

Mariani (p.66) contends: "Most bomb threats are the work of pranks, mischief makers and sometimes copycats, who seem to enjoy causing fear and inconvenience to large numbers of people with one simple note or one simple phone call. Terrorists, on the other hand, are not likely to be thoughtful enough to warn their victims of a bomb about to explode." Nonetheless, special safety precautions must be taken when responding to a bomb threat.

The International Association of Chiefs of Police (IACP) has developed detailed bomb threat instructions to be kept near telephones where such a threat might be received (Figure 16.6).

BOMB THREAT INSTRUCTIONS

Place this card under your telephone.

Questions to ask:

1. *When is bomb going to explode?*
2. *Where is it right now?*
3. *What does it look like?*
4. *What kind of bomb is it?*
5. *What will cause it to explode?*
6. *Did you place the bomb?*
7. *Why?*
8. *What is your address?*
9. *What is your name?*

Exact wording of the threat:

_____
_____
_____
_____
_____
_____

Sex of caller: _____ *Race:* _____
Age: _____ *Length of call:* _____

Additional information on reverse.

Number at which call is received:
_____

Time: _____ Date: __/__/__

Caller's Voice:
☐ Loud   ☐ Soft   ☐ High   ☐ Deep
☐ Intoxicated ☐ Disguised ☐ Calm ☐ Angry
☐ Fast   ☐ Slow   ☐ Stutter ☐ Nasal
☐ Distinct ☐ Slurred   ☐ Accent (*Type:* ___)
Other Characteristics: _____
_____

If voice is familiar, who did it sound like? _____

Background Sounds:
☐ Voices   ☐ Quiet   ☐ Animals
☐ Street Traffic ☐ Office Machinery ☐ Airplanes
☐ Trains   ☐ Factory Machinery ☐ Music
Other: _____

Threat Language:
☐ Foul   ☐ Well-spoken (*educated*)
☐ Taped   ☐ Message read by threat-maker
☐ Irrational ☐ Incoherent
Remarks: _____
_____
_____

Report call immediately to: _____
Phone Number: _____

Date: __/__/__
Name: _____
Position: _____
Phone Number: _____

Figure 16.6
Bomb threat instructions

Source: Project Response: The Oklahoma City Tragedy. Alexandria, VA: International Association of Chiefs of Police, p. 10.

Management should assist first responders in devising a thorough search of the building using employees to help in the search, as employees will know if anything is out of place and "doesn't fit." Management will also decide if the building is to be evacuated after the search.

Smith (p.43) advises that searchers pay attention to unattended bags, boxes, or briefcases. Also suspect are areas with suspended ceilings fitted with panels that are easily pushed up to hide an IED. Other items to pay attention to are trash cans, ashtrays, and flowerpots. In addition, any incoming mail or packages should be carefully screened. Smith presents as a caveat: "The search itself may trigger a device." Therefore, when searchers enter a room, they should go to the center and remain there quietly for several seconds, eyes closed, to listen. Any unusual noises may provide clues as to where a bomb might be hidden.

If a bomb is found, the most important rule in handling suspect packages is to NOT TOUCH the package. The area should be cleared to a 300-foot radius. Emergency personnel (fire and emergency medical personnel) should be alerted. All radios should be turned off. If there has been an explosion, investigators should:

- Ensure that a search for secondary explosive devices has been conducted.
- Ensure that the scene has been secured, that a perimeter and staging areas for the investigation have been established, and that all personnel have been advised of the need to prevent contamination of the scene.
- Ensure that the chain of custody is initiated for evidence that may have been previously collected.
- Establish procedures to document personnel entering and exiting the scene.
- Establish and document procedures for evidence collection, control, and chain of custody. Throughout the investigation, safety should be of prime concern (*A Guide for Explosion,* pp.19–21).

Using Technology in Detecting Explosives

Hanson (p.68) notes that airports and cargo terminals use X-ray and computed axial tomography (CAT) equipment to scan large numbers of items and people. Such methods require highly trained operators, are stationary, and cannot readily be used on vehicles or individuals or to investigate where bomb-making activities are ongoing or have taken place. Because of this, law enforcement must rely on what is referred to as "sniffer" technology: "A sniffer detection device is an instrument that takes in a sample of air, processes it through a detector and then identifies and calculates the approximate quantities of explosive material in the air sample."

Technology Innovations

Hanson (p.78) describes how ion mobility spectrometry (IMS) is used in walk-through scanning devices to allow whole body scanning of individuals rapidly, similar to conventional metal detectors used at airports and in building lobbies. Some of the devices can provide head-to-toe screening in the parts per billion range: "As an individual steps into the unit, a gentle puff of air dislodges any particles of explosive residue trapped in hair, clothes, shoes or skin. The unit allows analysis of up to seven people per minute so delay time is minimal."

Another touchless, large vehicle-bomb detection system allows a high vehicle throughput rate. As vehicles enter the unit, they are swept with a blast of air that dislodges any explosives residue and the air sample is fed into the detection devices. Analysis usually takes less than a minute.

Using K-9s in Detecting Explosives

As with arson investigations, dogs have become increasingly useful in bomb detection and in searches for evidence following explosions. Following the precaution of not handling the explosive, bomb dogs are trained to alert the handler by sitting near a suspect package without touching it. Hanson (p.78) contends: "Despite all the advances in technology, the canine 'sniffer' should not be overlooked as a valuable detection device." He points out that a trained dog searching a room full of cargo or luggage will often go almost directly to the explosive, while an officer with a chemical detector may have to test many items before locating the suspect material: "As law enforcement professionals continue their vigilance in finding and destroying explosives and thwarting bomb attacks, both the chemical sniffer and the canine sniffer will play an important role."

Using Robots

Bomb squads in larger departments are using robots to approach and detonate suspected packages. Page (2002a, p.35) suggests: "Robots are ideal for the grim work of searching hostile terrain or close, unstable structures. They don't get tired, they're immune to smoke, toxic fumes, emotional stress and, unlike police and firefighters, they're expendable" (Figure 16.7). According to Laska (p.55): "Although it's an expensive piece of equipment, a robot is a versatile machine that greatly enhances the safety of personnel on incidents."

Robots can be equipped with **disrupters,** devices that use gunpowder to fire a jet of water or a projectile at a particular component of an explosive to make it safe (Cox, p.106). Other features of bomb robots include portable X-ray machines and devices to remotely cut open a car door. Page (2002b, p.136) describes one such robot:

> Government researchers at Sandia National Laboratories, in Albuquerque, New Mexico, have taken a remote-controlled wheeled police robot and given it an embryonic brain. This allows the bomb 'bot to make many "how to" decisions on its own, without human control. It also frees up operators' time so they can make more critical "what to do next" decisions during potentially dangerous bomb-disablement or other law enforcement missions. The purpose of the upgrade is to substantially improve police explosive ordnance disposal (EOD) operations, mainly through enhanced controllability of the manipulator arms. . . . Giving them a better memory is the next step.

Douglas (p.30) notes: "Robots mated with real-time X-ray systems offer remote real-time viewing of explosive devices without endangering bomb techs." He also describes new body cooling systems "that look a little like long underwear with a pump and temperature regulating system. They are worn under bomb suits and greatly extend the time that a tech can spend in the suit."

Figure 16.7
Using a remote-controlled robot to approach and analyze suspected bombs has the advantage of not risking lives.

may thwart an attack or act as a deterrent. The signs should be placed at entrances, exits, and throughout facilities.

Awareness training programs should teach employees to notice individuals wearing clothes unsuitable for the time of year, people trying to blend into a group that he or she clearly doesn't belong to, or an object protruding from a person's clothing. Other behaviors to watch for are people acting very nervous or perspiring profusely, someone obviously staying clear of security personnel, a person walking slowly while constantly glancing back, or a person running suspiciously (Haber, p.13).

Investigating Bomb Explosions

 When investigating explosions and bombings, pay special attention to fragments of the explosive device as well as to powder present at the scene. Determine motive.

Bomb-scene investigations must progress logically. The first step is to determine the scene's parameters. In general, once the farthest piece of recognizable evidence is located, a radius 50 percent wider is established. For example, in the Oklahoma City bombing, the rear axle of the truck carrying the explosives was located three blocks from the blast site, so the scene parameters were approximately four and a half blocks in all directions.

Raising Awareness

Haber (p.13) recommends posting clearly visible signs disclosing where and how to report suspicious activity to allow security personnel to gather intelligence that

Importance of the Team Approach

The teamwork of field investigators and laboratory specialists in investigating bombings is critical. Such teamwork followed a California pipe-bombing incident that killed the driver of a vehicle to which a bomb had been attached. The Rialto Police Department, the San Bernardino Sheriff's Office, and the ATF combined their efforts. They investigated and forwarded evidence from the scene to the ATF laboratory for examination. Chemists identified the type and brand of powder used in the bomb by examining intact powder particles found in the bomb's end caps. A subsequent search at the suspect's home uncovered a can of smokeless powder identical to the identified powder. Additional evidence obtained during the search provided further links between the suspect and the bombing. The suspect was arrested and charged with murder.

Investigators with technical questions about commercial explosives can receive assistance from the Institute of Makers of Explosives (IME) in Washington, D.C. This nonprofit safety organization has 31 member companies and more than 80 subsidiaries and affiliates, which together produce more than 85 percent of the commercial explosives used in the United States. Also of help is the ATF National Response Team (NRT), which can be deployed in the most urgent, difficult bomb cases.

Another source of assistance is the Interpol Explosives Incident System (IEXIS), an explosives index containing descriptions of all explosives materials manu-factured throughout the world. A primary objective of IEXIS is to immediately determine whether a bombing or an attempted bombing in one country is significantly similar to bombings in the same or another country. This combination of explosives-theft information and IED componentry and manner of construction, along with knowledge of the modus operandis of criminal or terrorist groups, should greatly assist in investigating all forms of explosives-related crimes.

SUMMARY

Fires are classified as natural, accidental, criminal (arson), suspicious, or of unknown origin. They are presumed to be natural or accidental unless proven otherwise.

The elements of the crime of arson include (1) the willful, malicious burning of a building or property (2) of another or of one's own to defraud (3) or causing to be burned, or aiding, counseling, or procuring such burning. Attempted arson is also a crime. Some states categorize arson as either aggravated or simple. Aggravated arson is intentionally destroying or damaging a dwelling or other property by means of fire or explosives, creating an imminent danger to life or great bodily harm, which risk was known or reasonably foreseeable to the suspect.

Simple arson is intentional destruction by fire or explosives that does not create imminent danger to life or risk of great bodily harm. Other states use the Model Arson Law, which divides arson into four degrees: First-degree involves the burning of dwellings; second-degree involves the burning of buildings other than dwellings; third-degree involves the burning of other property; and fourth-degree involves attempts to burn buildings or property.

Logic suggests that fire departments should *detect* arson and determine the point of origin and probable cause, whereas police departments should *investigate* arson and prepare cases for prosecution.

Special challenges in investigating arson include coordinating efforts with the fire department and others, determining whether a crime has been committed, finding physical evidence and witnesses, and determining whether the victim is a suspect.

Although the fire department is responsible for establishing whether arson has occurred, law enforcement investigators must be able to verify such findings. To do so requires understanding the distinction between an accidental fire and arson. Basic to this understanding is the concept of the fire triangle, which consists of three elements necessary for a substance to burn: air, fuel, and heat. In arson, at least one of these elements is usually present in abnormal amounts for the structure. Evidence of accelerants at an arson scene is a primary form of evidence. The most common accelerant is gasoline. Also important as evidence are igniters, which include matches; candles; cigars and cigarettes; cigarette lighters; electrical, mechanical, and chemical devices; and explosives.

Burn indicators that provide important information include alligatoring, crazing, depth of char, lines of demarcation, sagged furniture springs, and spalling. The point of origin is established by finding the area with the deepest char, alligatoring, and (usually) the greatest destruction. Fires normally burn upward and are drawn toward ventilation and follow fuel. Arson is likely in fires that:

- Have more than one point of origin.
- Deviate from normal burning patterns.
- Show evidence of trailers.
- Show evidence of having been accelerated.
- Produce odors or smoke of a color associated with substances not normally present at the scene.
- Indicate that an abnormal amount of air, fuel, or heat was present.
- Reveal evidence of incendiary igniters at the point of origin.

An administrative warrant is issued when it is necessary for a government agent to search the premises to determine the fire's cause and origin. A criminal warrant is issued on probable cause when the premises yield evidence of a crime. Entry to fight a fire requires no warrant. Once in the building, fire officials may remain a reasonable time to investigate the cause of the blaze. After this time, an administrative warrant is needed, as established in *Michigan v. Tyler*.

When investigating vehicle fires, look for evidence of accelerants and determine whether the vehicle was insured. It is seldom arson if there is no insurance. When investigating explosions and bombings, pay special attention to fragments of the explosive device as well as to powder present at the scene. Determine motive.

CHECKLIST

Arson

- Who first noticed the fire?
- Who notified authorities?
- Who responded from the fire department?
- Did the fire department record the color of the smoke? the color of the flame?
- What was the fire's point of origin? Was there more than one point of origin?
- What material was used to ignite the fire?
- Was there an explosion before the fire? during the fire? after the fire?
- How did the building explode: inward or outward?
- Was the fire's burn time normal? Did it appear to be accelerated?
- Were any accelerants (newspapers, rags, or gasoline) found at the scene?
- What was the weather: dry, windy, snowy?
- What property was destroyed that was unusual for the premises?
- Were there any unusual circumstances?
- Was anyone injured or killed? Was an autopsy done to determine whether there were other causes for death than fire? Were carbon monoxide tests made of the victim to determine when death occurred— whether before or during the fire?

- Were regular informants checked to determine possible suspects?
- Who had access to the building?
- What appeared to be the motive for the fire? Who would benefit?
- Who owns the property destroyed? For how long?
- Was there insurance and, if so, how much?
- Who was the insurance payable to?
- What is the name of the insurance company? Obtain a copy of the company's report.
- Does the owner have any record of other property destroyed by fire?
- Does the owner have a criminal record for this or other types of crimes?
- Were any suspicious people or vehicles observed at the scene before, during, or after the fire?
- Was the state fire marshal's office notified? Did it send an investigator? If so, obtain a copy of the investigator's report.
- Were photographs or videos taken? Are they available?

APPLICATION

A. It is midafternoon on a Sunday. The fire department has just received a call to proceed to the Methodist Church on St. Anthony Boulevard. Smoke has been reported coming out of the church's windows by a nearby resident. When the fire department arrives, the church is engulfed in flames. By the time the fire is brought under control, the church is gutted, with damage estimated at $320,000. Suspecting arson, the fire department asks for help from the local police department.

Questions

1. Was the request for assistance justified at this point?
2. What are the responsibilities of the investigator assigned to respond to the call?

B. Investigators Ron McNeil and Brett Joyce worked together as part of Boston's special arson task force. Just before midnight they received a call from the dispatcher and were told to proceed to a certain address. They arrived minutes later at a small, one-story frame house and pulled in behind the first fire rig. Orange flames were shooting from every window of the house.

While the firefighters fought the blaze, McNeil and Joyce walked among the bystanders, asking if anyone had seen anything suspicious before the fire, but no one had. When the fire was out and the smoke cleared, floodlights illuminated the house and McNeil and Joyce started their investigation. Beginning in the small front room, they noticed extensive burning and win-

dows totally blackened from the fire. They proceeded through a small alcove, where the top portion had been destroyed, and then entered the kitchen. The glass in a window over the kitchen sink had broken and melted, with a series of intricate cracks running through each fragment. After shoveling out layers of debris and dragging in a fire hose to wash the floor, McNeil and Joyce noticed that the floor was deeply charred and spongy with water. Inspection of the wooden cabinets around the sink revealed large, rolling blisters. The investigators also discovered that the electricity to the structure had been disconnected. Then they began to photograph the fire scene.

Shortly afterward the owner and his wife arrived. The owner calmly answered questions, informing the investigators that he had been letting a carpenter live in the house in exchange for fixing up the place. But when the tenant failed to make the repairs and instead stole the construction materials, much of the furniture, and many appliances, the owner kicked him out. The carpenter threatened to "make him sorry." The owner had no fire insurance because he had intended not to live in the house but to use it as an investment property.

After filing their report, McNeil and Joyce returned to the property at 4 A.M. A heavy rain the day before had soaked the ground, and the mud in the backyard was crisscrossed with footprints. Joyce noticed some boot prints leading from the back door and took a plaster cast of them. Just then a neighbor stopped over to say he had seen a green pickup parked behind the house with the motor running just before the fire. McNeil photographed all the tire tracks in the dirt alley where the pickup was reportedly parked. The next morning the investigators learned that the carpenter, now their prime suspect, had been in jail when the fire broke out. The green pickup was registered to a friend of his, a man who had been previously arrested for arson.

They obtained a search warrant and executed it later that morning. The tires of the carpenter's friend's truck and his boot soles resembled the impressions found at the fire scene, but the impressions were so spongy that it was difficult to match them exactly. The investigators found no further evidence linking the man to the fire. (Adapted from Kevin Krajick's "Seattle: Sifting through the Ashes.")

Questions

1. Where did the fire probably originate? What factors indicate this?
2. What indicated that the fire was probably arson?
3. Did the investigators have probable cause to arrest the carpenter's friend? Would the owner also be a possible suspect? Why or why not?
4. What aspects of this case illustrate an effective arson investigation?

DISCUSSION QUESTIONS

1. Do you agree that investigation of arson cases is the joint responsibility of police and fire departments? Which department should be in charge?

2. What are the respective roles of the police and fire departments in your community during an arson investigation?

3. Arson has a low conviction rate. What factors make an arson investigation difficult? What factors make prosecution difficult?

4. Imagine that you are called to the scene of a fire to determine whether it was accidental or of criminal origin. What initial steps would you take in making this determination?

5. What types of evidence are material to the crime of arson? Where do you find such evidence at a fire scene? How do you collect it? Where do you send it for examination in your area?

6. What are common motives for arson? How do these motives help an investigator locate suspects?

7. Arson was added to the Part One Index crimes in the Uniform Crime Reporting Program. Is arson serious enough to be in this category along with murder and rape? Are there other reasons it should or should not be a Part One Index crime?

8. What agencies outside the police and fire departments can assist in an arson investigation? Who would you contact? What services could they provide?

9. What other types of crimes might be involved along with arson?

10. Organized crime has used arson to bring pressure on uncooperative persons and businesses. Why is arson effective for this purpose? Why is it difficult to prosecute such cases?

MEDIA EXPLORATIONS

Internet

Select one of the following assignments to complete.

- Search for the key phrase *National Institute of Justice* [NIJ]. Click on "NCJRS" (National Criminal Justice Research Service). Click on "law enforcement." Click on "sort by Doc#." Search for one of the NCJ reference numbers from the reference pages. Outline the selection to share with the class.

- Go to the FBI website at www.fbi.gov. Click on "library and reference." Select "Uniform Crime Reports" and outline what the report says about arson.

- NIJ Report 604-00, March 2001, *Flammable and Combustible Liquid Spill/Burn Patterns*, provides an extensive discussion of burn patterns, including numerous illustrations. (Go to NIJ, select "law enforcement" and then the year "2001" to access this report.)

- Select one of the following key words: *administrative warrant, arson, arsonists, bombs, burn indicators, explosives, fire triangle, pyromaniac.* Find one article relevant to arson or bombing investigations to outline and share with the class.

Crime and Evidence in Action

Go to the CD and choose the **burglary/arson case.** During the course of the case you'll become patrol officer, detective, judge, corrections officer, and parole officer to conduct interactive investigative research. Each case unfolds as you respond to key decision points. Feedback for each possible answer choice is packed full of information, including term definitions, web links, and important documentation. The sergeant is available at certain times to help mentor you, the Online Resources website offers a variety of information, and be sure to take notes in your e-notebook during the suspect video statements and at key points throughout (these notes can be saved, printed, or e-mailed). The Forensics Exercise will test your ability to collect, transport, and analyze evidence from the crime scene. At the end of the case you can track how well you responded to each decision point and join the Discussion Forum for a postmortem. **Go to the CD and use the skills you've learned in this chapter to solve a case.**

REFERENCES

Crime in the United States 2003. Washington, DC: Federal Bureau of Investigation, 2004.

Cox, Jennifer. "Recoilless Disrupter Enhances EOD Technology." *Law Enforcement Technology,* February 2004, pp. 106–109.

Dewan, Shalla. "Defiant and Brazen, Rudolph Pleads Guilty to Four Bombings." *New York Times* as reported in the Minneapolis/St. Paul *Star Tribune,* April 14, 2005, p. A3.

Douglas, Dave. "Special Handling." *Police,* June 2002, pp. 24–32.

Fire and Arson Scene Evidence: A Guide for Public Safety Personnel. Washington, DC: National Institute of Justice, June 2000. (NCJ 181584) http://www.ojp.usdoj.gov/nij/pubs-sum/181584.htm. Accessed September 27, 2005.

A Guide for Explosion and Bombing Scene Investigation. Washington, DC: National Institute of Justice, June 2000. (NCJ 181869) http://www.ojp.usdoj.gov/nij/pubs-sum/181869.htm

Haber, Grant. "Facing the Threat of Improvised Explosives." *Law Enforcement News*, May 2004, p. 13.

Hanson, Doug. "Sniffing Out Explosives." *Law Enforcement Technology*, February 2005, pp. 68–79.

"How to Make a Pipe Bomb." http://www.linkbase.org/make-pipe-bomb. Accessed July 15, 2005.

juvenile.justice.com. *Juvenile Firesetters.* http://www.juvenilejustice.com/firesetter.html. Accessed July 25, 2005.

Karter, Michael J., Jr. *Fire Loss in the United States 2004: Abridged Report.* Quincy, MA: National Fire Protection Association, June 2005.

Laska, Paul R. "Bomb Disposal Equipment in the Era of the War on Terrorism." *Law Enforcement Technology*, January 2002, pp. 52–56.

Mariani, Cliff. *Terrorism Prevention and Response.* Flushing, NY: Looseleaf Law Publications, Inc., 2004.

Martin, Richard. "Combating Arson." *Law and Order*, July 2004, pp. 122–126.

Miller, Christa. "The Value of Police/Fire Cross-Training." *Law Enforcement Technology*, August 2004, pp. 86–92.

Page, Douglas. "Small Fry Robots Becoming Big Law Enforcement Deal." *Law Enforcement Technology*, May 2002a, pp. 34–37.

Page, Douglas. "Get Smart: A Bomb 'Bot with Know-How." *Law Enforcement Technology*, July 2002b, pp. 136–142.

Putnam, Charles T., and Kirkpatrick, John T. *Juvenile Firesetting: A Research Overview.* Washington, DC: OJJDP Juvenile Justice Bulletin, May 2005.

Smith, Jim. "How to Conduct a Bomb Search." *Police and Security News*, September/October 2003, pp. 43–46.

Steck-Flynn, Kathy. "Finding Clues in a Fire." *Law Enforcement Technology*, May 2005, pp. 62–67.

"Wiping a Smile from Mailbox Bomber's Face." *Law Enforcement News*, December 15/31, 2002, p. 6.

CASES CITED

Coolidge v. New Hampshire, 403 U.S. 443 (1971)

Michigan v. Clifford, 464 U.S. 287 (1984)

Michigan v. Tyler, 436 U.S. 499 (1978)

Section 5

OTHER CHALLENGES TO THE CRIMINAL INVESTIGATOR

The two preceding sections discussed investigating violent crimes and crimes against property. Many crimes do not fall neatly into one of the eight Part One crimes but involve a combination of illegal acts related to both people and property. Unique investigative challenges are presented by investigating computers and cybercrime (Chapter 17), drug-related and organized crime (Chapter 18), the criminal activities of gangs and other dangerous groups (Chapter 19), and the war against terrorism and fight for homeland security (Chapter 20). Investigating the illegal activities related to these groups is more difficult because the elements of the crimes are not neatly spelled out and statistics are not available as they are for the Part One Uniform Crime Reports crimes. A final and critical challenge is preparing for and presenting cases in court (Chapter 21).

Cybercrime is relatively new, but organized crime, drug- and gang-related crime, bias/hate crime, and ritualistic crime have existed in one form or another for centuries. Not until recently, however, have they had such an impact on law enforcement, straining already limited resources. A further complication is that the areas commonly overlap; people involved in organized crime, drugs, and gangs are often the same people—

but not necessarily. Terrorists fund their activities through drug sales and various types of fraud, including cybertheft. Although each type of crime is discussed separately, you should always keep this overlap in mind. Furthermore, moral and ethical issues are raised by the activities of these organizations that are not raised by the activities of, say, bicycle thieves, rapists, and murderers. Stealing, raping, and murdering are clearly wrong in our society. This is not necessarily true for gambling, worshiping Satan, or smoking pot.

Among the greatest challenges are the "wars" America finds itself in, not only against drugs but now also against terrorism. Homeland defense has become a priority for law enforcement agencies at all levels. Other great challenges for investigators are the preparation of final reports the prosecutor can use to bring criminal cases to trial and the presentation of effective testimony to bring these cases to successful resolution. Without these skills, the best investigations are futile.

CHAPTER 17

Computer Crime and Its Evolution into Cybercrime

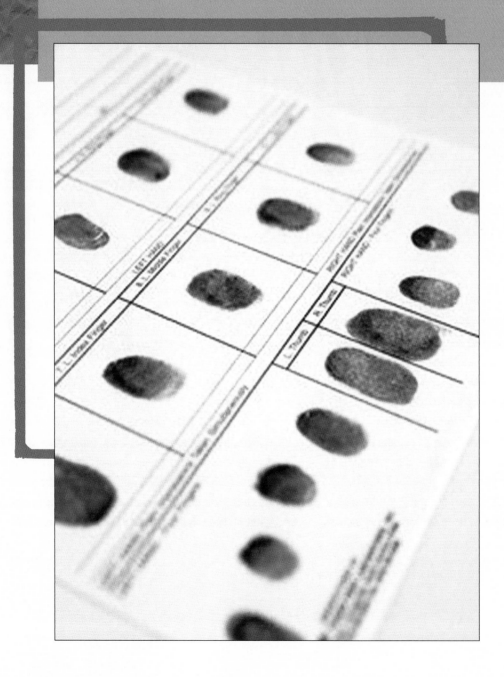

Can You Define?

adware
biometrics
computer crime
computer virus
cracker
cybercrime
cyberspace
cybertechnology
cyberterrorism
data remanence
denial of service
domain name
e-crime
encryption
firewall
hacker
hacktivism
hardware disabler
imaging
Internet Protocol (IP)
    address
ISP
keystroke logging
logic bomb
malware
pharming
phishing
phreaking
piracy
port scanning
sniffing
spam
spoofing
spyware
steganography
trashing
Trojan horse
URL
virtual reality
worm
zombie

Do You Know?

- What two key characteristics of computer crime are?
- How computer crime can be categorized?
- What special challenges are presented by computer-related crimes?
- How an investigator with a search warrant should execute it in a computer crime investigation?
- What a common protocol for processing a crime scene involving electronic evidence is?
- What a basic tenet is for first responders at a computer crime scene?
- What form electronic evidence and other computer crime evidence may take?
- What precautions you should take when handling computer disks?
- How electronic evidence should be stored?
- Whether "deleted" data are really deleted?
- Whether most cybercrimes against businesses are committed by insiders or outsiders?
- How cybercriminals may be categorized?
- What motivates the different types of cybercriminals?
- What approach is often required in investigating computer crime?
- How computer crimes can be prevented?

Outline

The Scope and Cost of the Problem
Terminology and Definitions
Classification and Types of Computer Crimes
Special Challenges in Investigation
Search Warrants
Investigative Tools and Equipment
The Preliminary Investigation
Forensic Examination of Computer Evidence
Legal Considerations in Collecting and Analyzing Computer Evidence
Follow-Up Investigation
Legislation
Security of the Police Department's Computers
The Investigative Team
Resources Available
Preventing Computer Crime

wo computer programmers at an oil company plant who were responsible for the company's purchasing files created a fictitious supply company. They altered the company's computer database so that the oil company bought its supplies twice: once from the real supplier and once from the fictitious supply company, resulting in an embezzlement of several million dollars over a two-year period. The crime was discovered during a surprise audit, but the company declined to prosecute, not wanting to publicize how vulnerable its database was or how long it took to discover the embezzlement. Ironically, rather than being dismissed, the two embezzlers were promoted and placed in charge of computer security.

In another instance, a New York bank hired an outside consultant to work with its computer technicians on transferring funds electronically. In the course of his work, the consultant observed the access code being used to transfer the funds. He later used this access code to transfer a large sum of money to his own bank account. When the loss was finally discovered, management insisted that everyone in the section take a polygraph test, including the consultant. All except the consultant complied, and all passed. Although management was convinced the consultant had stolen the money, they did not prosecute. They simply changed their access code.

These cases illustrate two key characteristics of computer crimes.

- Computer crimes are relatively easy to commit and difficult to detect.
- Most computer crimes are not prosecuted.

Computers are becoming increasingly common in the home, workplace, and school. The most recent U.S. census data show that since 1984, the first year in which the Census Bureau collected information on computer ownership and use, the proportion of U.S. households with computers has grown more than fivefold (Newburger, p.2). In August 2000, 51 percent of American households, or 54 million, had one or more computers, compared with 42 percent in December 1998 (Newburger, p.1).

Prior to the mid-1990s, cybercrime was almost nonexistent. Computer crime typically involved actions performed on a single machine or on a small self-contained network of machines, such as stealing data off a hard drive or planting a malicious code within the software of a company's internal computer network. Whatever the specifics of the crime, the criminal had to come in close physical contact with the computer(s) and the crime scene.

In the last decade, however, crimes involving computers have become much more sophisticated, and the investigations of such crimes considerably more complicated. What makes cybercrime the tremendous problem it is today is the fact that most computers on the planet are connected via the Internet, allowing a criminal thousands of miles away from a crime scene—whether at a computer in a private residence or at an extensive database within a major corporation's mainframe—to carry out theft, fraud, vandalism, or any other number of crimes without ever setting foot in the same city, state,

country, or even continent as the victim. The Internet also provides a medium through which pedophiles access and exchange child pornography, stalkers harass and threaten their targets, and terrorists around the globe communicate with each other. Keeping up with these techno-savvy criminals has pushed law enforcement to develop a new breed of detective—the cybercrime investigator (Figure 17.1).

This chapter begins with a discussion of the scope and cost of the computer crime problem and some basic terminology and definitions. This is followed by an explanation of the various ways computer-related crimes are classified and descriptions of some of the most common types of computer crimes encountered by investigators. Next is a discussion of the special challenges involved in computer-related crimes, followed by a discussion of search warrants and the types of investigative tools and equipment needed to effectively handle cybercrime cases. The chapter then turns to the preliminary investigation and presents a fairly detailed explanation of how a first responder or investigator should approach a computer crime scene, including how to conduct preliminary interviews and how to recognize, document, collect, package, and transport electronic evidence. Forensic examination of computer evidence is covered next, followed by a look at the legal considerations involved in collecting and analyzing computer evidence and conducting the follow-up investigation and the current status of legislation addressing computer-related crimes. Next the security of the police department's computers is briefly explored, followed by a discussion of how a team approach is being used to tackle the rising tide of computer-related crimes. The chapter concludes with a look at the resources available to cybercrime investigators and measures being used to prevent computer crime.

© AP/Wide World Photos

Figure 17.1

Dan Clements, CEO of Cardcops.com, a company that monitors Internet chat rooms and other hacker communications for stolen credit card numbers, then notifies merchants and consumers to block bad purchases.

The Scope and Cost of the Problem

The current hot crime tool is a personal computer linked to the Internet. This *online element* has led to a fundamental change in how many law enforcement agencies refer to such offenses—from computer crime to cybercrime. Census figures show that 42 percent of U.S. households, or 44 million homes, have Internet access, up from 26 percent in 1998 (Newburger, p.2). It should come as no surprise that criminals are capitalizing on this technology. Citing the numerous online communication options available, such as e-mail, chat rooms, and webpages, Girardi and Peterson (p.58) assert: "Criminals have turned to the Internet as their preferred means of interaction. As a medium for evil deeds, the Internet knows no boundaries. . . . and open networks have become the Wild West for crime."

According to Thomas (p.14), chief of the cyber technology section of the Federal Bureau of Investigation (FBI): "The introduction of digital information technologies, the widespread use of computers and computer networks (including the Internet), and the increased production, availability, and use of encryption have dramatically changed the way we communicate, transact business, and maintain records. Terrorists, hackers, and spies are increasingly using computers, computer networks, and encryption products to carry out their heinous acts."

The Internet's capacity for global interconnectivity has made the scope of the cybercrime problem a transnational one, the extent of which, confess most experts, is not yet fully understood. Adding to the uncertainty of the extent of the problem is the fact that a large percentage of police departments do not yet know how to address this new threat and do not keep accurate records involving such incidents. According to Aeilts (p.15): "Many law enforcement agencies do not clearly identify occurrences of high-tech crime. For example, a high-tech related theft of money or resources statistically is identified as a theft based upon historical definitions; the high-tech component of the crime may not be identified at all." What is known, however, is that cybercrime has touched countless individuals and businesses throughout the United States and has the potential to cause a national disaster.

Individuals can be victimized by a variety of different cybercrimes. For example, data from the Federal Trade Commission (FTC) show that nearly 10 million people were victims of identity theft in 2002, many of whom had information stolen from cyberspace (Whitlock, p.13). Internet scams continue to strip unsuspecting consumers of millions of dollars every year,

along with their faith in the security of doing business online. Of all fraud complaints reported to the FTC during 2004, 53 percent were Internet related, accounting for monetary losses of more than $265 million and a median loss of $214 (*National and State*, p.3). The Internet Crime Complaint Center (IC3), formerly called the Internet Fraud Complaint Center, is a partnership between the FBI and the National White Collar Crime Center (NW3C) designed to serve as a clearinghouse for cybercrime data for law enforcement and regulatory agencies at the federal, state, and local levels. The IC3 receives a broad spectrum of complaints including online fraud, computer intrusions (hacking), breaches of intellectual property rights (IPR), online extortion, international money laundering, economic espionage (theft of trade secrets), and, of course, identity theft. For the single month of January 2004, the IC3 received approximately 17,000 online complaints, a 50 percent increase over January 2003 (Lusher, p.17). The proliferation of child pornography on the Internet has also become a serious concern, as thousands of young individuals are victimized every year by this type of exploitation.

Cybercrime also impacts U.S. businesses, institutions, and other organizations, inflicting an estimated financial loss of $10 billion on corporate America every year, although the exact extent of the damage remains unknown, as many attacks go undetected (Whitlock, p.13). Rantala (p.1) reports that of the nearly 200 businesses responding to a 2001 pilot survey, 74 percent reported being victimized by cybercrime. The most frequently reported incidents involved computer viruses (p.3), which were also considered to be the most damaging and significant type of incident by businesses (p.5).

Since 1995, the Computer Security Institute (CSI), with the help of the FBI, has conducted annual surveys of computer security practitioners in corporations, financial and medical institutions, universities, and government agencies throughout the nation to analyze and assess the current state of computer network security. Gordon et al. (2005) present some of the findings from the latest survey:

- Virus attacks ranked as most common, followed by unauthorized access, theft of proprietary information, and **denial of service** (DoS) attacks at a distant fourth.
- Defacement of Internet websites [has] increased dramatically, with 95 percent of organizations reporting more than 10 such incidents in 2004.
- "Inside jobs" occur about as often as external attacks.

Table 17.1 presents a breakdown of the types of electronic crimes reported in the *2005 E-Crime Watch Survey* (p.16).

Besides individuals and companies, the entire United States population faces risk of victimization by cybercriminals because of our increasing reliance on information technology and the role computers play in many aspects of our daily lives:

> The nation's critical infrastructures are composed of public and private institutions in the sectors of agriculture, food, water, public health, emergency services, government, defense industrial base, information and telecommunications, energy, transportation, banking and finance, chemicals and hazardous materials, and postal and shipping. Controlling it all is cyberspace, a composition of hundreds of thousands of interconnected computers, servers, routers, switches, and fiber optic cables that allow the critical infrastructures to work.

Thus the healthy functioning of cyberspace is essential to the United States economy and national security. ("The National Strategy," p.32)

Cyberattacks on any part of this infrastructure could lead not only to tremendous loss of revenue and intellectual property but also to loss of life. For these reasons, the scope of cybercrime, even if undetermined, has the potential to cause extreme damage.

To fully understand and effectively investigate computer crime, officers need a working knowledge of relevant terminology, how documents are stored and retrieved, and how access to the Internet (and others' files) is obtained.

Table 17.1 / Types of Electronic Crimes Committed: 2005 and 2004 Compared

Among respondents whose organizations experienced electronic crimes in 2004, 82% cite virus or other malicious code as the most prevalent type of electronic crime or action, followed by spyware (61%), phishing (57%), and illegal generation of spam e-mail (48%). Phishing, not technically a crime but a precursor to fraud and/or identity theft, shows the largest single percentage increase year over year, jumping to 57% from 31% reported in last year's survey.

Which of the following electronic crimes were committed against your organization in 2004? (base: among those experiencing electronic crimes)	2005 (base: 554)	2004* (base: 342)
Virus or other malicious code	82%	77%
Spyware	61%	N/A
Phishing	57%	31%
Illegal generation of spam e-mail	48%	38%
Unauthorized access to information, systems, or networks	43%	47%
Denial-of-service attacks	32%	44%
Rogue wireless access point	21%	N/A
Exposure of private or sensitive information	19%	N/A
Fraud	19%	22%
(2004: Employee) Identity theft	17%	12%
Password sniffing	16%	N/A
Theft of intellectual property	14%	20%
Zombie machines on organization's network	13%	N/A
Theft of other (proprietary) information	12%	16%
Sabotage	11%	18%
Web site defacement	9%	N/A
Extortion	2%	5%
Other	4%	11%
Don't know/not sure	3%	8%

* Timeframe: 2003

Source: 2005 E-Crime Watch Survey: Summary of Findings. Conducted and printed by *CSO Magazine* in cooperation with the U.S. Secret Service and CERT® Coordination Center. May 3, 2005. http://www.cert.org/archive/pdf/ecrimesummary05.pdf, p.16. Accessed August 10, 2005.

Terminology and Definitions

he FBI previously defined **computer crime** as "that which involves the addition, deletion, change or theft of information." However, as the Internet has become an increasingly common element among crimes committed via the computer, the FBI has refocused its efforts and created the Cyber Investigations unit. Cybercrime, as part of the larger category of computer crime, has been a challenge to define. Early efforts to define cybercrime tended to overgeneralize; for example, "a criminal act in which the computer is used as the principal tool" (Forester and Morrison, 1994). However, as Stephen Brinton, of the Computer Science Department at Gordon College,[1] notes, many crimes that *involve* computers could just as easily be committed using other methods.

Over the past decade, refinements have occurred in how **cybercrime** is defined. Although a single definition has yet to be agreed on, an acceptable definition is that cybercrime is "a criminal act that can only be carried out using cybertechnology, and can only take place in the cyberrealm" (Tavani). **Cybertechnology** is the spectrum of computing and information/communication technologies, from individual computers to computer networks to the Internet. The cyberrealm is more commonly called **cyberspace,** an intangible, virtual world existing in the network connections between two or more computers. Cybercrime has also been referred to as *electronic crime,* or **e-crime,** in describing any criminal violation in which a computer or electronic form of media is used in the commission of that crime.

Regardless of whether an agency calls such offenses computer crimes, cybercrimes, or e-crimes, the effective investigator must be familiar with basic computer terminology as well as terms specifically related to computer crime (additional terms are defined throughout this chapter):

- **Adware.** A type of spyware used by advertisers to gather consumer and marketing information.
- Boot. To start up a computer.
- Browser. A computer program that accesses and displays data from the World Wide Web; for example, Internet Explorer.
- Byte. The amount of space needed to store one character of information.
- Disk drive. Physical location of disks on a computer (internal hard drives are usually labeled as C drive; floppy drives are generally identified as A or B drives).
- DOS. Disk Operating System.
- Download. To receive data, files, or pictures from another computer. Opposite of *upload.*
- E-mail. Electronic mail.
- **Firewall.** A software or hardware protective measure that blocks ports of access to a computer or network to prevent unauthorized access and stop malicious programs from entering.
- Floppy disk. Magnetic media capable of storing large amounts of information (a 3 ½" disk can hold as much information as 470 sheets of paper).
- Gigabyte (GB). One billion bytes.
- **Hacktivism.** Using cyberspace to harass or sabotage sites that conduct activities or advocate philosophies that "hacktivists" find unacceptable.
- Hard disk. A nonremovable means of data storage located inside a computer. Also called *hard drive.*
- Hardware. The computer equipment, such as hard drives, memory, CPUs (central processing units), the monitor, and so on.
- **Imaging.** Making a byte-by-byte copy of everything on the hard drive.
- **Keystroke logging.** A diagnostic technique that captures a user's keystrokes. Used in espionage to bypass security measures and obtain passwords or encryption keys. Also called *keylogging.*
- Kilobyte (KB). One thousand bytes.
- **Logic bomb.** Secretly attaches another program to a company's computer system. The attached program monitors the input data and waits for an error to occur. When this happens, the new program exploits the weakness to steal money or company secrets or to sabotage the system. For example, if a specific name fails to appear in the payroll system, the logic bomb would delete the entire payroll database.
- **Malware.** A contraction of "malicious software." Software developed to cause harm.
- Megabyte (MB). One million bytes (a typical 240MB hard drive could hold up to 27 four-drawer filing cabinets of information).
- Modem. A device linking a computer to telephone or cable lines so information can be exchanged with computers at different locations.
- Network. Two or more computers connected for the purpose of sharing data and resources.
- Operating system (OS). The software installed in a computer responsible for the control and management of the hardware and that allows the computer to run various application software, such as word processing programs, graphics programs, spreadsheets, etc.
- PC. Personal computer.

---

[1] http://www.math-cs.gordon.edu/courses/cs111brinton/index.php. Accessed August 8, 2005.

- **Phreaking.** Exploiting the telephone system's vulnerabilities to acquire free access and usage in a dial-up Internet provider system. Considered a type of electronic hacking.

- **Piracy.** The copying and use of computer programs in violation of copyrights and trade secret laws.

- **Port scanning.** Looking for access (open "doors") into a computer.

- Program. A series of commands instructing a computer to perform a desired task.

- Scanner. A device that can look at a typed page or photograph, convert it to digital format, and copy it onto a disk.

- Script. A text file containing a sequence of computer commands.

- **Sniffing.** Monitoring data traveling along a network.

- Software. Computer programs.

- **Spyware.** Malicious, covert (difficult to detect) software that infects a computer in a manner similar to viruses, collecting information or executing other programs without the user's knowledge. Some programs can track which websites a user visits; some can track and capture personal user information.

- **Trashing.** To scavenge through a business's garbage looking for useful information. Also called *dumpster diving*.

- **Trojan horse.** A malicious program hidden inside an apparently harmless, legitimate program, intended to carry out unauthorized or illegal functions. For example, a program controlling a computer log-on process could log on a user (legitimate) but also record the user's password (unauthorized, illegal).

- Upload. To transfer data, files, or pictures to another computer. Opposite of *download*.

- **Virtual reality.** An artificial, interactive world created by computer technology (usually involving some kind of immersion system, such as a headset).

- **Zombie.** A computer that has been taken over by another computer, typically through infection with hidden software (virus) that allows the zombie machine to be accessed and controlled remotely, often with the intention of perpetrating attacks on other computers.

The Net versus the Web

Confusion exists among many computer users regarding the differences between the Internet (aka "the Net") and the World Wide Web (aka "the Web") (Figure 17.2). Berners-Lee (2005), creator of the Web, explains:

> The Internet ('Net) is a network of networks. Basically it is made from computers and cables. . . . [It] sends around little "packets" of information. . . . A packet is a bit like a postcard with a simple address on it. If you put the right address on a packet, and gave it to any computer

which is connected as part of the Net, each computer would figure out which cable to send it down next so that it would get to its destination. That's what the Internet does. It delivers packets—anywhere in the world, normally well under a second. . . .

> The Web is an abstract (imaginary) space of information. On the Net, you find computers—on the Web, you find document, sounds, videos . . . information. On the Net, the connections are cables between computers; on the Web, connections are hypertext links. The Web exists because of programs which communicate between computers on the Net. The Web could not be without the Net. The Web made the Net useful because people are really interested in information (not to mention knowledge and wisdom!) and don't really want to . . . know about computers and cables.

A basic understanding of the Internet helps investigators trace suspected criminal activity and its perpetrators. To access the Internet, a user must have an **Internet Protocol (IP) address,** which is a unique number, analogous to a phone number. Typically, there is only one IP address per network connection. The IP address is commonly issued by a user's Internet Service Provider (ISP), a company that offers access to the Internet for a fee, such as America Online (AOL), EarthLink, NetZero. The details of IP address distribution and registration are complex and not necessary to go into for a general understanding of cybercrime investigation. The importance lies in recognizing that an IP address and ISP, if known, can lead to a specific computer and, by extension, a specific user.

Deciphering E-mail and Web Addresses It is useful for investigators to understand the parts of an e-mail or web address and to be able to accurately refer to the individual elements of each. E-mail addresses typically have two

Figure 17.2

The Internet and World Wide Web have spread across the globe over the past two decades, pervading every developed country. Here passengers surf the free Internet services at the transit hall of Singapore's Changi International Airport.

parts: the e-mail name or ID and the e-mail domain, separated by @. For example: janedoe@abc123.com

A **domain name** is the unique name of a computer system on the Internet that distinguishes it from all other online systems. It is associated with a specific IP address and is easier to remember than a string of numbers. A domain name is *not* the same as a web address, although many people incorrectly refer to it as such. A web address, or Uniform Resource Locator (**URL**), comprises several more elements. For example:

URL: http://www.abc123.com

Domain name: abc123.com

Subdomain: www

Domain: abc123

Top level domain: com

Common top-level domains include the following:

.com	commercial
.edu	educational
.gov	U.S. government
.mil	U.S. Department of Defense
.net	networks
.int	international organizations

Live Chat and Instant Messaging

Many ISPs provide chat rooms and offer Instant Messaging (IM) to their subscribers, features that allow two or more people to "talk" online in real time. Such conversations can involve criminal activity, including child pornography. Because of its popularity, AOL is fairly well policed, with the names of chat rooms being carefully monitored. The Internet Relay Chat (IRC) environment is similar to AOL but offers worldwide communication. Unlike AOL, IRC chat rooms are not monitored; therefore, it is common to see names such as #teensex or #newidentities (all IRC channel names begin with #). Both AOL and IRC services allow "chatters" to leave a group room and have a private conversation over a more secure connection using DCC (Direct Channel Chat).

Investigators should also be familiar with the types of crimes that may involve computers.

Classification and Types of Computer Crimes

he crimes committed with computers range from students changing school records and grades to thieves embezzling millions of dollars from large corporations to pedophiles luring unsuspecting children into child pornography. The International Association of Chiefs of Police (IACP) points out: "The computer may be contraband, fruits of the crime, a tool of the offense, or a storage container holding evidence of the offense" (*Best Practices*).

The U.S. Secret Service's Electronic Crimes Branch[2] (ECB) of its Financial Crimes Division has investigated matters involving credit card fraud, unauthorized computer access, cellular and land line telephone service tampering, the production of false identification, counterfeit currency, threats made against the president, narcotics, illegal firearms trafficking, and even homicides. In fact, the only limit there appears to be on the range of crimes committed with a computer is the limit of criminals' imaginations. Some even contend there will come a point when cybercrime laws become unnecessary because most crimes will involve computers in some way and, thus, all crime will be cybercrime (Brenner, 2001).

As computer crime evolves and specific offenses emerge, different categories are being identified. The U.S. Department of Justice has delineated three basic ways computers are being used criminally:

1. *Computer as target.* A computer or network's confidentiality, integrity, or availability is attacked, resulting in the theft of services or information or the damaging of victim computers. DoS attacks and the release of malware (viruses and worms) are examples of this type of computer crime.

2. *Computer as tool.* Includes crimes that have migrated from the physical world into cyberspace, such as child pornography, fraud, intellectual property violations, and the online sale of illegal substances and goods.

3. *Computer as incidental to an offense.* Significant for law enforcement because of the role the computer played in facilitating or executing a crime. For example, computers may be used by pedophiles to store child pornography, by drug traffickers to store business contact information, and by prostitution rings to manage payroll and customer accounts.

> Computer-related crimes may be categorized as computer as target, computer as tool, or computer as incidental to the offense.

However one chooses to categorize the various types of computer-related crimes, investigators should be aware of the ever-expanding ways in which computers are used for criminal endeavors.

---

[2] U.S. Secret Service website at http://www.secretservice.gov/fcd_ecb.shtml. Accessed July 29, 2005.

The Computer as Target

Some cybercrimes involve the infection or infiltration of a computer system's software by a malware that, when executed, removes a degree of control over the machine from the authorized user and places it in the hands of an outsider. These crimes can involve viruses, worms, and DoS attacks and almost invariably involve hacking.

Hacking The terms *hacking* and *cracking* are alternately used by law enforcement agencies to refer to the act of gaining unauthorized access to a computer system. However, amongst the people who perform these actions, a clear distinction is made between those who intrude for the challenge and status (hackers) and those who intrude to commit a crime (crackers). A **hacker** is not necessarily a negative term. A **cracker,** on the other hand, is a hacker in the negative sense, someone who cracks software protection and removes it. They deliberately, maliciously intrude into a computer or network to cause damage.

Viruses A computer virus is a program that attacks, attaches itself to, and becomes part of another executable program. The purpose may be to replace or destroy data on the computer's hard drive or to simply leave a back door open to later effect a DoS.

Viruses can be transmitted through communication lines or by an infected disk and can infect any PC. Just as human viruses are spread from one person to another, so computer viruses are spread from program to program. Viruses can be accidentally introduced into a system by infected disks carried between home and work, or passed among students or colleagues.

The prevalence of computer viruses reached epidemic proportions several years ago, with the number of identified viruses surpassing 70,000 in January 2002 (Moore, p.23) (Figure 17.3). The hype surrounding these security threats did much to raise the public's and corporate America's awareness of their computer systems' vulnerabilities and led many to install protective devices, such as antivirus or virus detection programs, downloadable software patches, and firewalls. Nonetheless, vast numbers of machines remain unprotected, and many consumers neglect to keep their virus detection subscriptions current.

Worms While the general computing public fears exposure to computer viruses, many are unaware that worms are actually more powerful and destructive. A **worm** is a self-contained program that travels from machine to machine across network connections, often clogging networks and information systems as it spreads. Whereas viruses require some action on the part of the computer user (clicking or downloading), worms do not. They simply come in through an "open door" or unprotected port on a machine connected to the Internet. And, unlike a virus, a worm need not become part of another program to propagate itself.

Figure 17.3

Established in 2003 to protect the nation's Internet infrastructure, US-CERT coordinates defense against and responses to cyber attacks across the nation.

In August 2003, the Blaster worm spread among computers running specific Microsoft programs and attempted to generate a massive DoS attack on one of Microsoft's websites. In January 2004, the MyDoom mass mailer worm spread rapidly; cyberinvestigators with the U.S. Secret Service have theorized that the worm was created and released by an organized hacker group. And in May 2004 the Sasser worm emerged, causing widespread problems in networks and interrupting business. Cybercrime investigators are becoming increasingly adept at tracking down the authors of these worms.

Denial-of-Service Attacks A DoS attack disrupts or degrades a computer or network's Internet connection or e-mail service, thus interrupting the regular flow of data. Using multiple agents to create a widespread interruption is a *distributed DoS,* or DDoS. When a target company's website is flooded with requests for information or by some other onslaught of incoming data, the system is eventually overloaded and the site shuts down. At this time the company's cost clock starts ticking: Either it submits to extortion by their attackers or it is forced to incur millions of dollars in lost revenue as a result of its website being down. Citing a study by the Aberdeen Group, Srinivasan (2005) reports: "Companies that suffer business disruptions from Internet-based attacks are losing an average of $2 million in revenue per incident." DoS attacks can be perpetrated by individuals, but are increasingly being used by terrorists.

Extortion Cybercriminals may attempt to extort thousands, even millions, of dollars from companies by threatening to or actually damaging the company's computers, network, or web presence. Extortion can be achieved via DoS attacks or threats to expose a company's web vulnerabilities, making the offense fit both categories of computer as *target* and as *tool*. An estimated 7,000 organizations are currently paying online extortion demands (Srinivasan).

The Computer as Tool

A computer connected to the Internet has become the tool of choice for many criminals, as they have taken the traditional methods of committing their illegalities and elevated them to high-tech levels. Keep in mind that many of the theft offenses described below overlap or are commonly committed together and thus may be investigated from a variety of angles and prosecuted under numerous laws.

Fraud Internet fraud can involve several other offenses singled out in this section, such as phishing, spamming, and identity theft. The types of fraud committed online span a wide range of businesses and topics. The Computer Crime Research Center (2005) culled figures from the FTC's database to determine the top 10 types of Internet fraud, which are, in descending order: Internet auction fraud, ISP scams, Internet website design/promotion (web cramming), Internet information and adult services (credit card cramming), multi-level marketing and pyramid scams, business opportunities and work-at-home scams, investment schemes and get-rich-quick scams, travel/vacation fraud, telephone/pay-per-call solicitation fraud, and health care fraud.

Reshipper Schemes In this age of telecommuting and rising gas prices, the appeal of working from home has never been greater. Preying off this interest are scam artists who lure unsuspecting job seekers into reshipping schemes, transforming these citizens into "mules" who unwittingly help their "employers" commit international crime. To top it off, prospective employees must usually complete an application, on which they disclose such information as their birth date and Social Security number—harmless enough in the hands of a legitimate employer, money in the pocket for identity thieves and others with a criminal bent.

Victims are attracted to the scheme through ads posted on popular employment websites, such as Job-Finder.com, Monster.com, and CareerBuilder.com, seeking "correspondence managers," "freight-forwarding coordinators," or other respectable-sounding titles, and are guaranteed to earn money by working from home without even quitting their current job. After applicants are informed that they have been hired—and nearly everyone who applies is hired—they begin receiving parcels at home with instructions on how to forward this merchandise to the company's home office abroad. The reshippers are compensated well, with one correspondence manager earning $24 for every package he reshipped (Acohido and Swartz, p.A1). Thus, employee complaints, at this stage, are few. What the employee does not know, however, is that the products they are reshipping are actually goods ordered online, purchased with fraudulent credit cards, and sent overseas to be sold on the black market, or that they (the mules) have become part of a high-end fencing operation that converts stolen personal and financial data into tangible goods and cash.

Offenders also lure victims into their scheme by establishing relationships with them in online chat rooms. Over a period of time, offenders weave a tale of how, because of various legal restrictions, they are unable to direct business shipments from the United States into their home country. They play up the injustice of these laws and how their government uses such restrictions to keep its citizens in poverty. Eventually the scam artist gains the victim's trust, through either befriending or seduction. Offenders may even send small gifts to their victims as tokens of their affection. Whatever ploy is used, victims ultimately agree to have packages sent to their home, which they will then reship to their "friend" in another country.

The FBI, through IC3, has investigated numerous reshipper schemes throughout the United States and abroad. IC3 has also formed a public/private alliance with the Merchants Risk Council (MRC) in an effort to shut down such Internet fraud through use of real-time data sharing between law enforcement and private industry. The FBI's Operation Cyber Sweep webpage reports that from July 1, 2003, to November 1, 2003, 5,053 addresses within the United States were identified as having been used in the furtherance of reshipper schemes and that according to the MRC, e-commerce in the United States has lost more than $500 million because of activity related to reshipper schemes.

Spam Spam is unsolicited bulk e-mail messages, similar in concept to junk mail and commonly commercial in nature. Lesser known by its formal designation as unsolicited commercial e-mail (UCE), spam is most often perceived by recipients as an annoyance and nothing more. Granted, it is a widespread and persistent annoyance, with some ISPs estimating that nearly 75 percent of the 20.7 billion e-mail messages received weekly in the United States qualify as spam (Donofrio, p.86). Chain letter spam is an example of the type of unsolicited e-mail that clogs the Internet and fills people's inboxes but falls well short of criminal conduct. Sometimes, however, spam is distributed on such a massive scale, with such malicious or contentious content, or with intent to defraud, that the spamming becomes criminal in nature. For example, chain letters calling for a payment to participate may be construed as pyramid schemes, which are illegal in most states. Investment/business opportunity spam, which entices people with the promise of effortless income and financial freedom for the small price of an upfront "investment," commonly results in only the spammer getting rich, while victims file complaints alleging theft or online fraud.

Spam that leaves no question as to its illegality is that intended to phish, commit identity theft, or otherwise extract sensitive information from a computer user with the ultimate goal of using such information to engage in criminal activity.

Identity Theft   Identity theft was already discussed in detail in Chapter 14. However, a brief revisit here is warranted considering how several recent computer security breaches of companies across the country have raised consumers' fears of having their identities stolen. For example, in February 2005, a criminal posing as legitimate businesses accessed databases at Choice-Point, a company that collects and sells personal data and has electronic records containing background information on nearly every U.S. citizen. The "unauthorized third parties" had access to approximately 35,000 individuals' names, addresses, Social Security numbers, credit reports, and other personal information. A month later, on March 9, 2005, Lexis-Nexis, one of the nation's largest information brokers, suffered a security breach in which intruders, using stolen passwords from legitimate customers, accessed a database containing the names, addresses, Social Security numbers, and driver's license numbers of nearly 310,000 people.

Phishing/Spoofing   Phishing is becoming more popular as a way for criminals to obtain sensitive information online from unsuspecting victims to use in identity theft and fraud activities. Phishing is the use of unsolicited e-mails to deceive Internet users into providing sensitive information, such as Social Security or credit card numbers, by pretending to be from legitimate and trustworthy businesses or individuals. **Spoofing,** often considered synonymous with phishing, is acquiring unauthorized access to a computer or network through a message using an IP address that appears to be from a trusted host.

Sabadash (2004) asserts: "Phishing expeditions can be a financial windfall for attackers, since some analysts' estimates put the success rate of such bogus e-mail at about 1 in every 20 recipients." Phishing negatively impacts e-commerce by making consumers hesitant to conduct business or buy products online. Americans have become wary of the legitimacy of any and all e-mails and websites, as phishers are getting better and better at disguising bogus e-mails and websites to look like those of well-known, legitimate businesses, financial institutions, and government agencies ("Special Report"). According to one survey ("Bush Signs," p.A9): "'Phishing' victims lost $1.2 billion to identity-theft related fraud between April 2003 and April 2004 and were three times more likely than the average American to have their identities stolen."

Pharming   Pharming is an emerging cybercrime that is catching even the most cautious, experienced Internet users off guard. Pharming involves the hijacking of a domain name for the purpose of redirecting online traffic away from a legitimate website toward a fake site, such as a bogus bank website. Even if a computer user types in the correct domain name of a legitimate site, if that site has been pharmed, the user will be unknowingly taken to the fraudulent site. Congress has introduced an anti-phishing bill that, if passed, would also apply to pharming and allows prison time and fines for those convicted of these cybercrimes.

Theft of Intellectual Property   This offense involves the pirating of proprietary information and copyrighted material. Illegal online piracy is rampant, with criminals around the globe cashing in on the lucrative black market of illegally copied and distributed software, movies, music, and video/computer games. The U.S. Department of Justice (DOJ) states: "Intellectual property permeates everything we do, and its diversity is reflected in the four distinct areas of law that protect it: copyrights, trademarks, trade secrets, and patents" (*Report of the Department,* p.1) As with a growing number of crimes, special teams are being assembled to increase the effectiveness of attacks on the global threat of intellectual property crime: "Because certain areas of the country have high concentrations of computer crime and intellectual property cases, the Justice Department created "Computer Hacking and Intellectual Property" ("CHIP") Units in those regions" (p.14). The first CHIP unit was launched in February 2000 in San Jose, California, to handle the rising number of cases in the high-tech region of Silicon Valley.

Because successful criminal prosecution of intellectual property theft requires reliable investigative resources, the FBI's Cyber Division and Intellectual Property Rights Division were created to investigate intellectual property theft and fraud. According to the DOJ, FBI computer labs and field offices throughout the country staff forensics experts specially qualified to analyze digital evidence (*Report of the Department,* p.14).

Online Child Pornography and Child Sexual Abuse   An increasingly persistent and pervasive cyber problem for law enforcement is the flow of child pornography. Pedophiles and other sex offenders around the world have discovered how quickly and surreptitiously they can exchange illegal images online. The Internet also provides a forum in which pedophiles can "meet" potential victims, in the hopes of arranging a face-to-face meeting at some point. In one case involving a missing child, detectives asked the family about the child's hobbies and were told he spent a great deal of time on the computer. By examining the computer files, detectives learned that the child had been contacted by a pedophile and had unwittingly arranged a meeting. Detectives went to the meeting site and found the child with the pedophile.

The development of software now enables more computer-savvy pornographers to create virtual child pornography in which an image of an actual child is

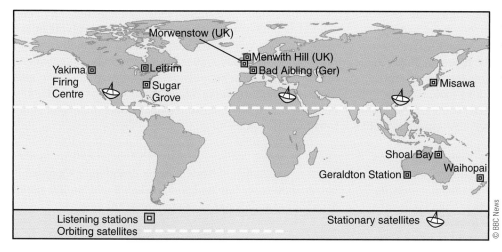

Figure 17.4
World map of satellites of the ECHELON system, a network of computers that automatically scans intercepted messages for keywords indicating potential terrorist activity.

© BBC News

manipulated, or "morphed," into an image no longer identifiable as that particular child. Some programs allow entirely computer-generated children to be depicted in a variety of sexual situations. As these programs become more refined, it is getting more difficult to distinguish between real children and virtual children. Such software presents considerable legal implications and challenges involving how a jurisdiction defines child pornography and how investigators proceed with child pornography cases. Klain et al. (p.3) advise: "Historically child pornographers use new technology as it develops to evade detection, and investigators should be mindful of such new capabilities."

The investigation of crimes against children were discussed in Chapter 11.

Cyberterrorism *Terrorism*—traditionally defined as the actual or threatened use of force or violence, motivated by political or religious ideals or grievances and exacted for the purposes of intimidation, coercion, or ransom—has evolved into cyberterrorism courtesy of the Inter-net. **Cyberterrorism** is the premeditated, politically motivated attack against information, computer systems, computer programs, and data that results in violence against noncombatant targets by subnational groups or clandestine agents. It also refers to the use of a computer system as a conduit for causing terror. Terrorists use this global interconnectivity not only to communicate with each other, but also to commit crimes to fund their other nefarious activities (Figure 17.4).

Cyberterrorism, however, does not merely equate to terrorists communicating through cyberspace. It is the actual use of computers and Internet technology to cause intimidation and destruction. Cyberterrorists can target a specific business or industry, or they can wreak electronic havoc indiscriminately across giant segments of the Internet. In recent years, intense concern has developed over the threat of a possible terrorist attack on the computer networks that link to critical parts of the U.S. infrastructure, such as those dedicated to pub-

lic health and the distribution of emergency services, government and defense operations, energy and utility services, and elements that keep our economy in motion, such as shipping and cargo distribution. According to Srinivasan (2005), the cyberterrorist's weapon of choice is the DoS attack, commonly originating in places like Libya, China, and countries of the former Eastern Bloc, motivated by economic or political reasons.

Special Challenges in Investigation

For the police to deter such crimes, they must be reported, thoroughly investigated, and, when the evidence is sufficient, prosecuted. Too often, however, victims of computer-related crimes either are unaware that a crime has been committed or have a reason for not reporting the crime to authorities. Results from the *2005 E-Crime Watch Survey* (p.24) show numerous reasons why organizations choose not to report electronic crimes or computer intrusions:

- 59 percent chose not to report an incident because they deemed the damage level insufficient to warrant prosecution.
- 50 percent believed they lacked enough evidence to successfully prosecute.
- 15 percent were concerned about the negative publicity that would follow such a report.
- 7 percent chose not to report due to concerns that competitors would use the security breach to their advantage.
- 6 percent were unaware they could report the crime.
- 6 percent opted not to report because of a prior negative response from law enforcement.

Another challenge facing investigators assigned to computer-related crimes is that often they have not been adequately trained or equipped to investigate these felonies. Cybercriminals are usually more technologically sophisticated and have more resources, more access to the newest technology, and more time to devote than the investigators assigned to the cases. The technological disadvantage of many law enforcement agencies is painfully obvious.

Law enforcement at all levels needs additional training in the following areas: the unique requirements of computer-related crimes; digital evidence; identifying, marking, and storing this evidence; the capabilities of present private and state agencies to analyze this evidence; and the procedures for developing teams to conduct investigations of computer-related crimes.

> Special challenges in investigating computer crime include victims' reluctance or failure to report such crimes, the investigator's lack of training and the lack of understanding of computer crimes by others within the justice system, the proliferation of such crimes, the fragility of the evidence, jurisdictional questions, and the need for specialists and teamwork.

Difficulties exist in determining jurisdiction when the equipment being employed criminally is located in one community and the computer that is illegally entered electronically is in another state or even another country. For example, a 28-year-old in St. Petersburg, Russia, hacked into Citibank's cash-management system in New York City and stole millions of dollars. Where did the crime take place—St. Petersburg or New York City? Who has jurisdiction?

Other major challenges in investigating computer-related crimes include the need to determine the exact nature of the crime and to gather evidence in ways that do not disrupt an organization's operation. It is also sometimes difficult to know when a search warrant for computers and their software might be required in an investigation that does not originally implicate computer-related criminal activity.

Search Warrants

Investigators may need to obtain a search warrant to locate the evidence necessary for successful prosecution. Searches may also be conducted by consent; in other words, the owner of the materials may give voluntary consent for a search. However, if the suspect is unknown, this is not desirable because it could alert the person who committed the crime. In such cases, a search warrant must be obtained. Privacy issues surrounding some or all of the informa-

tion contained in the digital evidence desired may pose a legal technicality. If the organization involved is the victim of the crime, its management normally grants permission. If it is not the victim, it may be necessary to obtain permission from individuals named in the evidentiary file, which could be an enormous task. It may be better to take the evidence to a court and obtain court permission if possible.

Investigators may have in their possession both a consent search form and a search warrant, thus avoiding the possibility of destruction of evidence. Consent is better than a search warrant in that it avoids the usual attack by the defense in search-warrant cases.

> Request the consent initially, and if that fails, use the search warrant—in that order.

If the order is reversed, the consent is bastardized because the search warrant was used as a threat in obtaining voluntary consent. The areas of search and the sought items must be specified in the warrant. Determine the computer system used and the types of physical evidence available from this system. Include this information in the application for a search warrant. A person connected with the computer operation in question should assist with the search warrant to provide information to the investigators, and this person should accompany the investigators with the affidavit for warrant in case the judge requires technical explanations that the investigators cannot provide regarding the equipment and the evidence desired.

Investigative Tools and Equipment

Investigators assigned to cybercrimes or other computer-related crimes must have ready certain tools and equipment commonly required in cases involving electronic evidence. Table 17.2 lists the items the National Institute of Justice (NIJ) recommends be included in a cybercrime tool kit, in addition to the general crime scene processing tools such as notepads, sketchpads, cameras, tape measures, markers, and so on (*Electronic Crime*, pp.23–24).

The Preliminary Investigation

The principles of investigating cybercrimes are basically the same as in other felonies. However, because of the highly technical

Table 17.2 / **Cybercrime Investigative Tool Kit**

Documentation Tools

- Cable tags
- Indelible felt tip markers
- Stick-on labels

Disassembly and Removal Tools

- to include a variety of nonmagnetic sizes and types of:
  - Screwdrivers: flat-blade, Philips, and specialized (manufacturer specific, e.g., Compaq, Macintosh, etc.)
  - Hex-nut, star-type nut, and secure-bit drivers
  - Pliers: standard and needle-nose
  - Small tweezers
  - Wire cutters

Package and Transport Supplies

- Antistatic evidence bags
- Antistatic bubble wrap and other packing material (avoid Styrofoam products as they produce static electricity, which can damage electronic/digital evidence)
- Cable ties
- Evidence tape
- Packing tape
- Sturdy boxes of various sizes

Other items

- Gloves
- Hand truck
- Large rubber bands
- Magnifying glass
- Small flashlight
- Printer paper
- Seizure disk
- Unused floppy diskettes (3½ and 5¼ inch) and CDs
- List of contact numbers for assistance*

Source: NIJ, *Electronic Crime Scene Investigation*, pp. 23–24

*As part of a standard computer-crimes toolkit, the NIJ recommends every law enforcement agency identify and contact local computer experts before they are needed and request these experts be "on call" for situations requiring technical expertise beyond that of the first responder or department (*Electronic Crime*, p.7).

nature of computer crimes and the fragile nature of the evidence, officers must receive "first responder" training, and the cybercrime investigator must have extensive knowledge of computers or seek the assistance of a computer expert.

Griffith (p.19) states: "The typical cybercrime investigation begins like most other investigations with a citizen complaint." When a report of a possible computer-related crime is received by a police department, the departmental report procedure is followed for the initial information. The officer assigned to the case interviews the reporting person to obtain the information necessary for determining whether a crime has been committed.

This first responder has a critical role in preserving the crime scene to protect the integrity of the evidence, as this is the point where such digital evidence is most vulnerable: "It only takes one innocent move of the mouse or pressing a key on the keyboard to completely remove key evidence that may have been available on the computer" (Jacobia, p.30).

 A common protocol for processing a crime scene involving electronic evidence is as follows:

- Secure and evaluate the crime scene.
- Recognize and identify the evidence.
- Document the crime scene.
- Collect and preserve evidence.
- Package, transport, and store evidence.

Much of the following discussion is adapted from the following documents: *Best Practices for Seizing Electronic Evidence*, jointly produced by the IACP and the U.S. Secret Service; *Electronic Crime Scene Investigation: A Guide for First Responders*, the first in a six-guide series by the NIJ; and *Forensic Examination of Digital Evidence: A Guide for Law Enforcement*, the second guide in the aforementioned six-part NIJ series. It should be noted, however, that the recommendations presented in these guides, and our discussion based on them, are not to be taken as legal mandates, policy directives, or a representation of the one and only proper course of action to follow with electronic crimes investigations, but rather as a compilation of the diverse views, experiences, and suggestions offered by the technical working group (TWG) members involved in putting these guides together.

Securing and Evaluating the Scene

As with any other crime scene, the first responder's initial priority is to ensure the safety of everyone at the scene and to protect the integrity of evidence, both conventional (physical) and electronic. Next the responding officer should restrict access to any computers, *visually* identify potential evidence (do not touch anything yet), determine whether such evidence is perishable, and formulate a search plan. The recommended steps for securing and evaluating the crime scene are:

- Remove all persons from the immediate area from which evidence is to be collected.
- At this point in the investigation, do not alter the condition of any electronic device: If it is on, leave it on. If it is off, leave it off.
- Protect perishable data on pagers, caller ID boxes, cell phones, etc., physically and electronically, always keeping in mind that devices containing

perishable data should be immediately secured and documented (photographed).

- Identify any communications lines (telephone, LAN/Ethernet connections) attached to devices such as modems and caller ID boxes. Document, label, and disconnect each line from the wall rather than the device, if possible. Communication via such lines must be severed so as to prevent remote access to data on the computers.

- *Do not touch* the keyboard, mouse, diskettes, CDs, or any other computer equipment or electronic devices (evidence) at this stage. (*Electronic Crime*, pp.25–26)

A basic tenet for first responders at computer crime scenes is to observe the ON/OFF rule: If it's on, leave it on. If it's off, leave it off.

Before any evidence is touched, it must be properly documented (a later stage, discussed shortly). However, prior to identifying and documenting evidence, preliminary interviews must be conducted.

Preliminary Interviews If a crime is suspected or determined, further interviewing of the complainant and witnesses should continue. It is essential that information be obtained as soon as possible because evidence is easily destroyed. Preliminary interviews are conducted before collecting evidence, as these interviews help determine the nature of the crime and develop suspects. If the crime involves a computer user in a private residence or other type of singular victim, ask how the user became aware of the crime and who his/her ISP is. The victim will need to provide his/her username(s) and password(s), as such information is typically required to access the system. Ask about security devices or programs installed on the machine, and obtain as much documentation as possible regarding the victim computer's hardware and software configurations.

If the victim is a business or other organization, interview employees and staff, as they are a good source of information unless they are suspected of collusion. Internal reporting of this type of crime is the same as for any other crime within an organization, normally beginning at the lowest level and reporting upward to the supervisor and then to management. However, supervisory or management personnel are conceivably part of the collusion, so care must be used in the initial stages to eliminate those capable of being involved. Persons with security clearance to access sensitive data or areas within a company's network must also be interviewed and evaluated as possible suspects. If a computer has been stolen, determine if it is protected by CompuTrace, computer security and tracking software that helps deter theft and recover stolen machines.

The NIJ (*Electronic Crime*, p.26) recommends the following course of action in conducting preliminary interviews:

- Separate and identify all persons at the scene and record their location at the time of entry.
- Consistent with departmental police and applicable law, obtain from these individuals such information as:
  - Owners and/or users of the electronic devices found at the scene.
  - Usernames and passwords required to access the system, software, or data (*Note:* An individual user may have multiple passwords, e.g., BIOS, system login, network or ISP, e-mail, application files, etc.).
  - Purpose of the system.
  - Unique security schemes or destructive devices.
  - Any off-site data storage.
  - Documentation pertaining to the system's hardware or software.

While on-site, the first responder/investigator should:

- Identify the number and types of computers.
- Determine if a computer network exists.
- Interview the system administrator and users.
- Identify and document the types and volume of media, including removable media, noting the location from which the media were taken.
- Identify proprietary software (*Forensic Examination*, pp.8–9)

Also during this time, the first responder or investigator should attempt to assess the skill levels of the computer users involved, since proficient users may conceal or destroy evidence by employing sophisticated techniques such as **encryption**, which puts information in code and thus obscures a normally comprehensible message, or **steganography**, which is Greek for "hidden writing" and aims to keep everyone except the intended recipient of a message oblivious to its very existence (*Forensic Examination*, p.8). A steganographic message often appears as some type of "cover" message—a shopping list, a picture, etc. Steganography should not be confused with *stenography* (shorthand).

Before evidence can be collected, it must be recognized and documented.

Recognizing Evidence—Traditional and Digital

Computer crimes commonly involve both conventional evidence (fingerprints, documents, computer hard drive, etc.) and digital evidence (electronic computer files, e-mails, etc.). Regarding physical evidence, search techniques and patterns described in Chapter 4 are applicable to computer-related crime searches. Seal the area and search it according to the type and location of the evidence necessary for prosecution. Avoid pressures to speed up the search because of a desire for continued use of the system, but at the same time, return the equipment as soon as possible and be sensitive to the desire of a company to get back to "business as usual" as quickly as possible.

The NIJ's TWG has defined electronic evidence as "[i]nformation and data of investigative value that is stored on or transmitted by an electronic device" (*Electronic Crime*, p.6). It also explains that electronic evidence:

- Is often latent in the same sense as fingerprints or DNA evidence, meaning that the evidence is not discernible in its natural state but must be processed with equipment or software to make it visible.
- Is fragile and can be easily altered, damaged, or destroyed.
- Is sometimes time sensitive.
- Can transcend borders with ease and speed.

It is usually not difficult for an investigator to recognize obvious evidence such as a computer, keyboard, or mouse, but digital evidence may also exist among a host of other electronic devices too often overlooked (Table 17.3). Some of these devices contain perishable data and thus must be immediately secured and documented. Remember: Do not alter a device's condition at this point. If it is off, leave it off.

Technology Innovations

When a cybercrime crime scene presents a plethora of disks among which may exist evidence of illegal activity, the InfinaDyne CD/DVD Inspector 2.1 software application can help an investigator quickly sift through the media to uncover the bad guy's secrets:

One of Inspector's best features is its ability to make a ZIP image of an entire CD. This "true copy" captures everything that ever was burned onto the subject disk, including files that are not listed in the directory, damaged files, and deleted files. . . . Inspector also offers you some great shortcut features. A warrant to search a cyber criminal's office might yield hundreds of CDs and you may be seeking one specific piece of information, for example, an e-mail address. Inspector can search all files on the disk and all sectors on the disk for that e-mail.

Also, with Inspector, you can search "inaccessible" disks for scan specification syntax. This is a great feature for any officer investigating a child pornography case because it lets you identify files containing graphic content regardless of their file extension. In other words, your local pervert can't hide his porn collection merely by removing the BMP, GIF, JPG, or TIF extensions. (Davis, "InfinaDyne," pp.62–64)

Table 17.3 / **Electronic Devices Containing Potential Digital Evidence**

Answering machines—voice messages and other recordings
Audio recorders
Cables
Caller ID boxes
Cell phones
Chips—when found in quantity, may indicate chip theft
Copiers—usage logs, time and date stamps
Databank/digital organizer
Digital cameras—images and video, storage media
Dongle or other hardware protection devices (keys) for software
Drive duplicators
External drives
Fax machines
Flash memory cards
Floppies, diskettes, CD-ROMs
Global positioning systems (GPS)—coordinates, previous destinations, travel logs
Pagers—conventional and e-mail addresses, phone numbers, messages
PCMCIA (Personal Computer Memory Card International Association) cards
Personal digital assistants (PDAs) and electronic organizers
Printers—usage logs, time and date information. If active, allow to complete printing.
Removable media—including the associated device that creates the media (tape drive, cartridge drives such as Zip®, Jaz®, ORB, Clik!™, Syquest, LS-120)
Scanners (film, flatbed, watches, etc.)
Smart cards/secure ID tokens
Telephones
VCRs
Wireless access point

Source: Electronic Crime Scene Investigation: A Guide for First Responders. Washington, DC: National Institute of Justice, July 2001. (NCJ 187736) http://www.ncjrs.gov/txfiles1/nij/187736.txt, p.33.

Figure 17.5 summarizes the nature of information and types of evidence commonly encountered during a computer crime scene search as they relate to specific crimes.

For certain crimes, such as child pornography, identity theft, and computer attacks, CDs, DVDs, diskettes, and tapes are likely to hold an abundance of evidence. Noting how criminals often keep "trophies" or collections to document their activities, Davis (2004, p.62) advises investigators to search the work area around

Figure 17.5

Information and evidence encountered during a computer crime scene search as related to specific crimes

	Sex Crimes		Crimes Against Persons			Fraud/Other Financial Crime								
	Child Exploitation/Abuse	Prostitution	Death Investigation	Domestic Violence	E-Mail Threats/Harassment/Stalking	Auction Fraud	Computer Intrusion	Economic Fraud	Extortion	Gambling	Identity Theft	Narcotics	Software Piracy	Telecommunications Fraud
General Information:														
Databases		✓			✓		✓		✓	✓				
E-mail/notes/letters	✓	✓	✓	✓	✓	✓	✓	✓	✓	✓	✓	✓	✓	✓
Financial/asset records		✓	✓	✓	✓	✓		✓		✓		✓		✓
Medical records		✓	✓	✓										
Telephone records			✓	✓	✓	✓								✓
Specific Information:														
Account data						✓								
Accounting/bookkeeping software						✓								
Address books		✓	✓	✓	✓	✓	✓	✓		✓		✓		
Backdrops										✓				
Biographies			✓											
Birth certificates										✓				
Calendar		✓				✓		✓		✓	✓			
Chat logs	✓					✓							✓	
Check, currency, and money order images							✓			✓				
Check cashing cards											✓			
Cloning software														✓
Configuration files							✓							
Counterfeit money											✓			
Credit card generators											✓			
Credit card numbers											✓			
Credit card reader/writer											✓			
Credit card skimmers							✓							
Customer database/records		✓							✓					✓
Customer information/credit card data						✓		✓	✓					
Date and time stamps	✓								✓					
Diaries			✓	✓	✓									
Digital cameras/software/images	✓					✓					✓			
Driver's license											✓			
Drug recipes												✓		
Electronic money										✓				
Electronic signatures											✓			

continued

computers as well as CD and DVD storage units throughout the premises. Some wily offenders try to hide incriminating CDs and DVDs among legitimate ones or insert illicit data into a disk that contains otherwise aboveboard content.

Documenting Digital Evidence

As with other crime scenes, thorough notes, sketches, and photographs are necessary to create a permanent historical record of the scene. The NIJ TWG suggests the following steps for the first responder or investigator:

- Observe and document the physical scene, such as the position of the mouse and location of components relative to each other (e.g., a mouse to the left of the keyboard may indicate a left-handed user).
- Document the condition and location of the computer system, noting the computer's power status (on, off, sleep mode). Check the power status light if no other obvious indication exists. An "off" machine that still feels warm was most likely just recently turned off.
- Identify and document related electronic components that will not be collected.
- Photograph the entire scene with 360-degree coverage, if possible.
- Photograph the front and back of the computer, the monitor screen, and other peripheral components connected to the computer. An active program may require videotaping or more extensive documentation of screen activity.

Regarding any computers at the scene:

- If the monitor is on with a work product or desktop visible, photograph it and make written notes of the information displayed.

Figure 17.5
Continued

Specific Information (Cont):	Sex Crimes		Crimes Against Persons			Fraud/Other Financial Crime								
	Child Exploitation/Abuse	Prostitution	Death Investigation	Domestic Violence	E-mail Threats/Harassment/Stalking	Auction Fraud	Computer Intrusion	Economic Fraud	Extortion	Gambling	Identity Theft	Narcotics	Software Piracy	Telecommunications Fraud
Erased Internet documents									✓					
ESN/MIN pair records														✓
Executable programs						✓								
False financial transaction forms							✓							
False identification		✓					✓				✓			
Fictitious court documents									✓					
Fictitious gift certificates									✓					
Fictitious loan documents									✓					
Fictitious sales receipts									✓					
Fictitious vehicle registrations									✓					
Games		✓												
Graphic editing and viewing software	✓													
History log								✓						
"How to phreak" manuals														✓
Images	✓		✓	✓	✓									
Images of signatures							✓							
Image files of software certificates											✓			
Image players								✓						
Internet activity logs	✓	✓	✓		✓	✓	✓	✓	✓		✓	✓	✓	✓
Internet browser history/cache files					✓									
IP address and user name				✓										
IRC chat logs				✓										
Legal documents and wills			✓	✓										
Movie files	✓													
Online financial institution access software						✓		✓	✓					
Online orders and trading information									✓					
Prescription form images												✓		
Records/documents or "testimonials"					✓									

continued

- If the monitor is on but shows a blank screen or a screensaver, move the mouse very slightly with a pen, pencil, or other object (do not touch it with your hand or click any buttons) to bring up the active screen. The monitor will display either a work product or a request for a user password. Again, photograph the screen and record the information shown. Do not perform any keystrokes or mouse operations.

- If the monitor is off, note the status and then turn it on (do not turn on or otherwise touch the computer). If an image becomes visible, photograph the screen and make written notes of the information displayed. If no image comes up right away, move the mouse slightly as described above and then photograph the screen and record the information shown.

- After you have noted the status of the computer, remove the power cable from the *computer,* NOT from the wall outlet or power strip. If it is a laptop, remove the battery as well. **IMPORTANT:** If the computer was running when it was seized, it should be powered down in a way least likely to damage any data existing in memory or on the hard disk. The method to use—either normal shutdown procedures or pulling the plug from the back of the computer without first shutting down the operating system—depends on which operating system the computer is running. Table 17.4 lists common operating systems and the recommended method of powering down devices running on them. If the operating system is undetermined, pulling the plug will suffice.

- Check for a modem/cable/DSL (digital subscriber line) connection and, if present, attempt to identify the associated telephone number.

Figure 17.5 Continued

Specific Information (Cont):	Child Exploitation/Abuse	Prostitution	Death Investigation	Domestic Violence	E-mail Threats/Harassment/Stalking	Auction Fraud	Computer Intrusion	Economic Fraud	Extortion	Gambling	Identity Theft	Narcotics	Software Piracy	Telecommunications Fraud
	Sex Crimes		Crimes Against Persons			Fraud/Other Financial Crime								
Scanners/scanned signatures											✓			
Serial numbers													✓	
Social security cards											✓			
Software cracking information and utilities													✓	
Source code							✓							
Sports betting statistics										✓				
Stock transfer documents											✓			
System files and file slack											✓			
Temporary Internet files									✓					
User names							✓		✓					
User-created directory and file names that classify copyrighted software													✓	
User-created directory and file names that classify images	✓													
Vehicle insurance and transfer documentation											✓			
Victim background research					✓									
Web activity at forgery sites											✓			
Web page advertising		✓												

- Remove any floppy disks, package each disk separately, and insert a blank floppy disk back into the drive.
- Do NOT remove CDs or touch the CD drive.
- Place tape over all drive slots and the power connector.
- Record the make, model, and serial numbers.
- Photograph and diagram the connections of the computer and corresponding cables.
- Label all connectors and cable ends to allow exact reassembly later.
- Label unused connection ports as "unused."
- Identify laptop docking stations to identify other storage media.

The preceding guidelines are generally sufficient for most stand-alone computers. However, in a business environment, multiple computers may be connected to each other and/or to a central server. The NIJ (*Electronic Crime*, p.32) cautions: "Securing and processing a crime scene where the computer systems are networked poses special problems, as improper shutdown may destroy data. This can result in loss of evidence and potential severe civil liability." Indicators of a computer network include:

- The presence of multiple computer systems.
- The presence of cables and connectors running between computers or central devices such as hubs.
- Information provided by those on the scene or by informants.

Collecting Physical and Digital Evidence

The biggest difference between traditional evidence and computer evidence is the fragility of the latter. Digital evidence can be altered, damaged, or destroyed simply by turning the computer on or off at the wrong time. The NIJ (*Electronic Crime*, p.6) strongly cautions: "Without having the necessary skills and training, no responder should attempt to explore the contents or recover data from a computer (e.g., do not touch the keyboard or click the mouse) or other electronic device other than to record what is visible on its display." First responders and investigators must be aware that destruction of the program or of information files may be programmed in so that any attempt to access the information or to print it will cause it to self-destruct. Check for a **hardware disabler,** a device designed to ensure a self-destruct sequence of any potential evidence. It may be present on or around a computer, with a remote power switch being the most prevalent of the disabler hardware devices. If found, a disabler switch should be taped in the position in which it was found.

Table 17.4 / **Recommended Powering-Down Methods for Different Operating Systems**

Shutdown Protocol	Pull-the-Plug Protocol
Windows NT Server	DOS
Windows 2000 Server	Windows 3.1
Windows 2003	Windows 95
Linux	Windows 98
Unix	Windows NT
Macintosh OS X	Windows 2000
	Windows XP
	Macintosh OS 9 and older
Shutdown Protocol: Critical for these operating systems so as to commit back to disk data that is normally stored only in memory. Shutting down computers running on operating systems that do not normally store data in memory (DOS, Windows NT, Windows XP, etc.) by the usual method could result in possible changes to data on the hard drive and loss of evidence and, thus, should be powered down by pulling the plug.	*Pull-the-Plug Protocol:* Be sure to pull the lead out from the computer itself because if the machine has an uninterrupted power supply (UPS) connected and the power to this is turned off, the computer itself will remain powered.

Source: Wikipedia, "Computer Forensics," http://en.wikipedia.org/wiki/Computer_forensics. Accessed August 18, 2005.

Evidence in computer cases is also unique in that it is not as readily discernible as evidence in most other criminal cases. Computer disks, for example, although visible in the physical sense, contain "invisible" information.

Digital evidence is often contained on disks, CDs, hard drives, or on any number of peripheral electronic devices; is not readily discernible; and is highly susceptible to destruction. Other computer crime evidence may exist in the form of data reports, logs, programming, or other printed information run from information in the computer. Latent prints may be found on the keyboard, mouse, power button, or any other peripheral equipment near the computer.

Because chemicals used in the processing of fingerprints can damage electronic equipment and data, latent prints should be collected after electronic evidence recovery is complete.

A backup of the hard disk contents should be made as quickly as possible. A portable hard drive duplication tool is available that permits investigators to quickly create a mirror image of one or more hard drives in the field without removing the original to a remote site.

Investigators must reproduce the material within the rules of evidence. Identification should include the case number, date, time, and initials of the person taking the evidence into custody. To mark a metal container, use a carbide metal scribe such as that used in marking items in the Operation Identification program. Use a permanent black-ink marker or felt-tip pen to identify disks. If the evidence is in a container, both the container and the inside disks should be identified in the same way. Marking both identically avoids interchangeability and retains the credibility of the item as evidence. Use normal evidence tape to mark containers and to seal them.

Avoid contact with the recording surfaces of computer tapes and disks. Never write on disk labels with a ballpoint pen or pencil or use paper clips or rubber bands with disks. To do so may destroy the data they contain.

Usually printouts must be made of data contained on computer disks or CDs. These printouts should be clearly identified and matched with the software they represent.

Technology Innovations

A primary responsibility of a cybercrime investigator is to locate and document evidence on computers or other electronic devices used by the suspect. Sometimes, however, it is unreasonable or impractical to seize an individual's or organization's computer assets. In these cases, Davis ("Logicube," p.70) asserts: "The tool for this job is Logicube's portable Forensic MD5. This 16-ounce handheld unit makes exact images or copies of a suspect storage drive or device." This tool, which was used by the FBI to gather evidence against the accused "twentieth 9/11 hijacker" Zacarias Moussaoui, can capture true data from a hard drive at a rate of more than 3 GB per minute and is tamper-proof, "guaranteeing zero chance of alteration of the suspect and evidence drives." Davis ("Logicube," p.70) also notes that the Forensic MD5's operation software includes sample "keyword" lists for terrorism, controlled substances, computer crimes, and hate groups, which can be used during a preliminary screening of a suspect drive. If the program gets a "hit" and detects one or more of these keywords on a suspect drive, it could provide the probable cause necessary to secure a search warrant.

In more complex cases, the volume of evidence is significant because large amounts of information can be stored on a single disk or CD. In the majority of felony investigations, the amount of evidence is not a major problem; but in the case of computer crimes, the evidence may involve hundreds of disks or CDs. Copying this amount of evidence can be costly and time-consuming. In addition, taking equipment into evidence can be a major problem because some equipment is heavy and bulky.

In a very few cases the evidence is the computer equipment. Also, it may be necessary to keep the equipment operating to continue business. Investigators must work with management to determine how to best accomplish this. If the evidence cannot be moved from the premises, management may have to provide on-premises security with their own guards or with temporarily hired security until the evidence can be copied or otherwise secured by court order or by police security.

Other nonelectronic evidence that may prove valuable to the investigation includes material found in the vicinity of the suspect computer system, such as handwritten notes, Sticky notes with passwords written on them, blank pads of paper with the indentations from previous pages torn off, hardware and software manuals, calendars, and photographs.

Any evidence collected and removed from the premises must be entered onto an evidence log, thus creating a chain of custody that must be maintained from this point forward throughout the investigation.

Collecting Evidence from Cyberspace Most, if not all, cybercrimes leave some type of cyber trail or "e-print" as evidence, because ISPs maintain records of everything a subscriber does online, at least for awhile. If an investigator knows a suspect user's screen name, it can be linked to an identifiable IP address. The IP address(es) associated with suspect pieces of data transmitted via the Internet will help an investigator track down the user's ISP. However, no law yet exists requiring the maintenance of online activity data, and the storage policies of ISPs can vary tremendously. For example, large ISPs commonly maintain data for as long as 30 days, whereas others dump these records every 30 minutes. Data storage is a major expense for ISPs, and many look to save money by purging their files fairly quickly (Griffith, pp.19–20). Therefore, if a crime has involved Internet use, investigators should proceed quickly to subpoena the ISP for stored records. If the subpoena will take several days or longer to obtain, send a letter to the ISP requesting that they preserve the data until a subpoena, warrant, or court order can be obtained: "The preservation letter does not legally require the ISP to turn over its records. But many ISPs will cooperate with a request to preserve data" (Griffith, p.20).

These records, once obtained, will provide the investigator with such information as the suspect's billing address and log-in records, which can in turn lead to the location of the computer used, such as in a private residence, a public library, or an Internet cafe. While the

billing information and credit card numbers associated with a user's account can be falsified, this information may still be of value to the investigation. Once the suspect's location is known, the investigation typically expands to involve another jurisdiction, as the perpetrators of cybercrimes can be thousands of miles away from their victims and the investigation's point of origin.

After the desired target information is culled from the general ISP data records, the investigator needs a search warrant to delve further into a particular user's account information. These files are likely to include e-mails, website data, images, spreadsheets, and other digital log files that can help the investigator assess what activity the account is being used for.

Other tools available to cybersleuths are the Internet pen register and Internet Title III Intercept, the use of which also requires court approval. Internet pen registers track transactions originating at the target's computer and can reveal web surfing habits and sites commonly visited, the types of applications being used, and the e-mail addresses of those being communicated with (Girardi and Peterson, p.60). Title III Intercepts are similar in function to the Internet pen but trap more comprehensive data, allowing the investigator to see not only where the target is surfing and whom he communicates with but also what the target sees and to read the content of his e-mail and chat messages. Because the Title III Intercept allows a greater intrusion into the private activities and conversations of the target than any of the preceding surveillance methods, it is typically the most difficult one to obtain court authorization for (Girardi and Peterson, p.60).

Understanding how to decipher e-mail headers is a necessary skill for cyberinvestigators. The following guidelines (*Best Practices*) are provided for tracing an Internet e-mail:

- When an Internet e-mail message is sent, the user typically controls only the recipient line(s) (*To* and *Bcc*) and the *Subject* line.

- Mail software adds the rest of the header information during processing.

Reading an E-mail Header
—— Message header follows ——

(1) Return-path: <ambottom@o167832.cc.nps.navy.mil>

(2) Received: from o167832.cc.army.mil by nps.navy.mil (4.1/SMI-4.1) id AAO868O;

Thur, 7 Nov 96 17:51:49 PST

(3) Received: from localhost byo167832.navy.mil (4.1/SMI-4.1) id AA16514; Thur 7 Nov 96

17:50:53 PST

(4) Message-ID: <9611080150.AA16514@o167832.cc.army.mil>

(5) Date: Thur, 7 Nov 1996 17:50:53 -0800 (PST)

(6) From: "M. Bottoms" <ambottomo167832.cc.nps.navy.mil>

(7) To: Tom Whitt <tom_whitt@tomwhitt.com>

(8) Cc: Real 3D <real3dQmmc.com>, Denis Adams <zzxxms@ldsa.com>, Joe Arion <oerion@aol.com>

- Line (1) tells other computers who really sent the message and where to send error messages (bounces and warning).

- Lines (2) and (3) show the route the message took from sending to delivery. Each computer that receives this message adds a *Received* field with its complete address and time stamp, which helps in tracking delivery problems.

- Line (4) is the *Message-ID*, a unique identifier for this specific message. This ID is logged and can be traced through computers on the message route if there is a need to track the mail.

- Line (5) shows the date, time, and time zone when the message was sent.

- Line (6) shows the name and e-mail address of the message originator (the "*sender*").

- Line (7) shows the name and e-mail address of the primary recipient; the address may be for a:
  - mailing list,
  - systemwide alias,
  - a personal username.

- Line (8) lists the names and e-mail addresses of the "courtesy copy" recipients of the message. There may be "*Bcc:*" recipients as well; these "blind carbon copy" recipients get copies of the message, but their names and addresses are not visible in the headers.

Mobile Evidence   Cell phones, or more specifically the electronic memory devices within them that store digital data, have become an important source of evidence for criminal investigators. Cell phone use may factor into an investigation involving any of the crimes discussed in this text.

Evidence on a mobile or cell phone system may be found on the communication equipment (the phone itself), the subscriber identity module (SIM), a fixed base station, switching network, the operation/maintenance system for the network, and the customer management system. It may also be possible to retrieve deleted items. Call data records (CDRs) obtained from the network service provider are also very valuable as evidence, for they can reveal the location of the mobile phone user every time a call is sent or received.

Because of its digital nature, mobile evidence must be handled carefully, yet few standards have been widely implemented regarding how best to collect such evidence. The following guidelines (*Best Practices*) are offered for investigators collecting wireless phones and electronic paging devices as evidence:

- Wireless Telephones
  - Observe the On/Off Rule

- If it is ON, leave it ON—turning off a device that is on could activate a lockout feature.
- Write down the information on the display and photograph if possible.
- Power down the device prior to transport and take any power supply cords present.
- If it is OFF, leave it OFF—turning it on could alter evidence on the device.

- Upon seizure, get the device to an expert as soon as possible or contact the local service provider.

- If an expert is not available, *use a different telephone* and call 1-800-LAWBUST, a 24/7 service provided by the cellular phone industry.

- Attempt to locate any instruction manuals or other documents pertaining to the device.

- Electronic Paging Devices
  - Once the pager is no longer in proximity to the suspect, turn it off.
  - Continued access to electronic communication over a pager without proper authorization can be construed as unlawful interception of electronic communication.

- A search of the stored contents of the pager is allowed:
  - Incidental to an arrest.
  - With probable cause + exception.
  - With consent.

Packaging, Transporting, and Storing Digital and Other Computer Crime Evidence

To reiterate, computer evidence—electronic devices and the data contained within them—is fragile and sensitive to temperature, humidity, physical shock, static electricity, and magnetic sources. Thus, first responders and investigators must use due diligence when packaging, transporting, and storing the evidence. Furthermore, documenting these procedures is necessary for maintaining the chain of custody.

When packaging electronic evidence:

- Ensure everything is properly documented, labeled, and inventoried.

- Pay special attention to latent or trace evidence and make sure to preserve it.

- Pack magnetic media in antistatic bags.

- Avoid folding, bending, or scratching computer media such as diskettes, CD-ROMs, and tapes.

- Ensure that all containers used to hold evidence are properly labeled.

If multiple computer systems are collected, label each system so it can be reassembled as found. For example, System A—mouse, keyboard, monitor, main base unit; System B—mouse, keyboard, monitor, main base unit.

When transporting computer evidence:

- Keep electronic evidence away from magnetic sources, such as radio transmitters, speaker magnets, and heated seats.
- Avoid leaving electronic evidence in vehicles for prolonged periods of time. Excessive heat, cold, or humidity can damage electronic evidence.
- Secure computers and other components not packaged in containers to avoid exposure to shock and excessive vibration during transport.
- Maintain the chain of custody on all evidence transported.

Storage problems can arise because of the nature of the evidence in computer-related crimes. Store disks in the manufacturers' containers, and store all computer evidence in areas away from strong sources of light. Computers and other electronic devices, and the digital information stored in and on them, are sensitive to temperature extremes and dust. Exposing electronic media to any magnetic field such as radio waves, motors, degaussers, or speakers can alter or destroy data. In addition, plastic bags can cause static electricity and condensation, both of which can damage electronically stored data, and should not be used to store computer equipment or disks. If possible, obtain from management the procedures normally used for storing their disks and other materials. If this is not possible, contact the manufacturer for this information.

> Store electronic evidence in a secure area away from temperature and humidity extremes and protected from magnetic sources, moisture, dust, and other harmful particles or contaminants. Do not use plastic bags.

Also be aware of the time-sensitive nature of perishable data evidence. Potential evidence such as dates, times, and system configurations may be lost due to prolonged storage or the depletion of a device's battery. Therefore, when submitting such evidence for examination, notify the appropriate personnel that a device powered by batteries needs immediate attention.

Forensic Examination of Computer Evidence

Crime laboratories, either public or private, have much of the equipment necessary to examine computer evidence. Computer hardware has individual characteristics, much the same as other items of evidence such as tools. The hardware might also contain fingerprints, but frequently the perpetrator's fingerprints are not unusual because he or she has legal access to the hardware. Printers have individual characteristics, much the same as typewriters. Document examinations of printouts can be made, and these printouts can also be analyzed for fingerprints. Fragments of software may be compared. And, as discussed, the entire file content of a computer's hard drive may be analyzed for incriminating text or images.

Because the skills required for some of today's complex digital and electronic forensic evidence examination are very technical and usually fall outside the realm of what is expected of the typical criminal investigator, this discussion will not delve too deeply into specific techniques required during such examinations but rather will present a fairly superficial overview of what happens to the evidence once it is submitted to the lab.

Data Analysis and Recovery

In an ideal case, digital data on a seized computer's hard drive or contained on other media such as diskettes, CDs, or tapes is intact, unencrypted, and has not been "deleted." In these scenarios, the digital forensic examiner can simply retrieve the data and print it. Another rather obvious place to look for evidence is in the computer's recycle bin, as some less computer-savvy criminals might equate putting a file in "the trash" with deleting it. In many cases, however, the suspect has taken steps to hide evidence of criminal activity, such as through data encryption or steganography, installing booby traps or other destructive programs to keep outsiders from gaining access, or by deleting files. Sometimes computer evidence is damaged through exposure to fire, water, or physical impact. While it may seem as if no useful data could possibly be retrieved in such situations, a skilled computer forensic examiner is often able to achieve the impossible.

Data recovery is a computer forensic technique that requires not only an extensive knowledge of computer technology and storage devices but also an understanding of the laws of search and seizure and the rules of evidence, to be discussed shortly. Software programs can help investigators restore data on damaged hard drives or other computer media or recover information that has been deleted, or so the suspect thought.

Lange and Perrin (p.167) note: "The 'delete' key on the keyboard is not the equivalent of a paper shredder." Modern operating systems often leave copies of "deleted" files scattered about, in temporary directories, unallocated sectors, and swap files. Tsai (2002) explains: "When interacting with the graphic user interface (GUI) in applications and operating system software, users can physically erase, hide, and change data with little or no trace (audit trail). These physical actions are transparent to the users, but the computer performs differently based on its logical design." She lists several technical reasons to explicate why such data persists:

- When deletions of files occur, many computer systems have log mechanisms to record these activities and, typically, only information technology (IT) persons have the skills to defeat the log mechanism, such as in Windows.

- Furthermore, only IT persons have system access and skills to use special programs ("wipers") to clean all the files and used and unused disk space from multiple systems, such as the networks, backup servers, and e-mail servers.

- Deleting files may remove only the file names from the disk's index, and the deleted files may still be intact or in fragments scattered in unused sections of the hard drive.

- Old data do not disappear permanently unless new data are saved or overwritten to cover all the files and fragments.

- Many companies lack policies for purging electronic files, particularly for e-mail via the Internet.

- Even if a company purges its e-mail backlog, e-mail copies may remain on multiple servers at several source and destination points.

> Although deleted files remain on the hard drive in a nonviewable format, their existence hidden from most computer users, the computer forensic expert knows where to look and how to make such files viewable again.

Data remanence refers to the residual physical representation of data that have been erased. In addition to recovering deleted material, a qualified computer forensic analyst may be able to recover evidence of the copying of documents, whether to another computer on the network or to some removable storage device such as a diskette; the printing of documents; the dates and times specific documents were created, accessed, or modified; the type and amount of use a particular computer has had; Internet searches run from a computer; and more (Berryhill, p.127).

Legal Considerations in Collecting and Analyzing Computer Evidence

Throughout the entire evidence collection and analysis processes, investigators and forensic technicians must adhere to strict standards if the evidence is to be of value in the courtroom: "Failure to adhere to strict industry standards regarding

data preservation cannot only result in the loss of critical data, but can also impinge upon the credibility of any data that is recovered" (Lange and Perrin, p.167). As in all cases, the evidence must follow the best-evidence rule. According to the DOJ: "Federal rules state that if data are stored in a computer or similar device, any printout or other output readable by sight, shown to reflect the data accurately, is an 'original'" and, as such, meets the criteria of the best-evidence rule (*Searching and Seizing*). Individuals must testify in court to the authenticity of the disks, CDs, or printouts. The materials must be proven to be either the originals or substitutes in accordance with the best-evidence rule. This evidence must be tied to its source by a person qualified to testify about it.

Because computers often use magnetically produced signals, printouts must be made of these signals, and computer experts must verify that the printouts are copies of the original data. To counter any claims or concerns that the duplication process introduced unintended alterations to the original data, complex algorithms have been developed to test and authenticate digital evidence and are considered to exceed the probability standards accepted by the courts when evaluating DNA evidence (Mercer, p.31).

Besides adhering to authenticity standards, investigators must be alert to situations where the Privacy Protection Act may be implicated. Under this act, with certain exceptions, it is considered unlawful for a government agent to search for or seize materials possessed by a person reasonably believed to have a legitimate purpose for disseminating information to the public. For example, seizure of First Amendment materials such as drafts of newsletters or webpages may implicate the Privacy Protection Act (*Electronic Crime*, p.7). The NIJ also cautions first responders seizing electronic devices that improper access of data stored within may violate provisions of certain federal laws, including the Electronic Communications Privacy Act. The recommended course of action, should this be a concern, is to consult the local prosecutor before accessing stored data on an electronic device (*Electronic Crime*, p.7).

An evolving area of legal wrangling concerns copyright laws and investigative agencies that seize computers that have an operating system installed on them, as most do. Operating systems, which are copyright protected, may not be copied without the author's, or in this case the software company's, expressed permission. When a law enforcement agent images a suspect's hard drive, boots up the mirror image, and loads the Internet browser to see the history file, that agent has, technically, violated the copyright protections of that software. While few cases concerning this issue have passed through the courts thus far, the NW3C has called attention to the topic and advises any agency involved in the forensic examination of electronic data to purchase copies of any publicly available, nonunique, and nonuniquely configurable software that may be needed to access a suspect's files ("Copyright and Law Enforcement").

Follow-Up Investigation

Once the initial report has been completed and the general information has been obtained, a plan is made for the remaining investigation. The plan will assist in a directed investigation even though deviations from the plan may occur because exigencies may not be known at the beginning. The plan should identify the problem and the crime or crimes that have been committed. A suspect must be developed, as well as other peripheral parties to the crime. Determine the areas involved in the crime, equipment used, internal and external staffing needs, approximate length of time required for the investigation, a method of handling and storing evidence, and the assignment of personnel. When developing a suspect, ascertain motive, opportunity, means of commission, the type of security system bypassed, and known bypass techniques. It may be necessary to conduct covert operations as part of the investigation. In such cases, an officer with expert-level knowledge in cybercrime is a critical factor in achieving a successful resolution. It is also necessary to determine which federal, state, or local laws are applicable to the specific type of computer crime committed.

© Getty Images

Figure 17.6

Hacking has evolved significantly over the past three decades and is often, although not necessarily, a negative term used to refer to cybercriminals. Credited as the original hacker, John Draper (aka "Captain Crunch") is the creator of the infamous Blue Box, a device that hacked telephone systems in the early 1970s by mimicking the tones that control phone switches, allowing hackers to make free long distance calls, bill calls to someone else's phone number, etc.

With this first form of hacking, coined "phone phreaking" by Draper, began the custom of "ph" spellings used in many hacker pseudonyms and organizations.

"Phishing," first referenced in hacker literature in 1996, was a term given to the act of "fishing" in the sea of Internet users for sensitive information (passwords, financial data, etc.) hackers could use for personal benefit. First applied to stealing AOL user information, phishing has grown increasingly widespread and malicious, targeting major financial institutions and e-commerce sites.

Developing Suspects

A few decades ago, computer crime was the exclusive domain of a relatively small group of electronic geniuses whose incredibly specialized knowledge and programming skills afforded them unique opportunities to pry into individuals' and corporations' computers and steal money, trade secrets, or other information of value (Figure 17.6). Today, however, cybercrooks are not such an elite bunch. Today's global population of twenty-somethings and younger are often as proficient on the computer as they are with using a TV or cell phone. Rogers (p.22) contends: "International terrorists aside, the reality is that most successful cybercrime being committed, at present, centers around a typical thief stealing money." Griffith (p.18) simply states: "Computer criminals are no longer masterminds, just crooks and creeps doing what crooks and creeps do."

A significant change from previous editions of this text is in the number of crimes committed by insiders versus outsiders. It used to be that most computer-related crimes against businesses and other organizations were committed by insiders, because these people had the best access to the machines. With the expansion of the Internet, however, outsiders have gained increasing levels of access, to the extent that today most (80 percent) of electronic crimes are perpetrated by outsiders (Figure 17.7).

> Most cybercrimes against businesses are committed by "outsiders."

While anyone with the requisite know-how can take up a life of cybercrime, the FBI and other organizations who have been compiling records on the perpetrators of cybercrime have developed a sort of cybercriminal profile of characteristics these individuals are likely to exhibit (Brinton):

- A cybercriminal will likely fall into one of three categories:
  - Crackers (hackers): motivated by achieving prohibited access; inspired by boredom and the desire for intellectual challenge; no real damage done

Who Are The Criminals?

Average Percent of Electronic Crimes by Outsiders vs. Insiders

Organizations appear to be doing a better job identifying criminals. Only 19% of respondents experiencing electronic crimes or intrusions in 2004 do not know whether insiders or outsiders were the cause, down from 30% in last year's survey. Respondents who identify the culprit indicate that an average of 80% of the attacks come from outsiders and 20% from insiders (a drop from 29% in the 2004 survey).

Figure 17.7

Average percentage of electronic crimes by outsiders vs. insiders

Source: 2005 E-Crime Watch Survey: Summary of Findings. Conducted and printed by *CSO Magazine* in cooperation with the U.S. Secret Service and CERT® Coordination Center. May 3, 2005. http://www.cert.org/archive/pdf/ecrimesummary05.pdf, p.18. Accessed August 10, 2005.

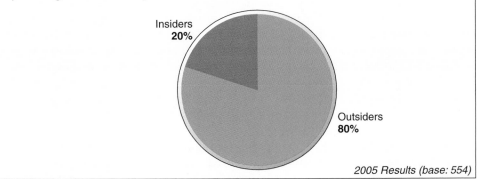

Mean Percent of Electronic Crimes Caused by Outsiders vs. Insiders (base: among those experiencing electronic crimes)

Insiders **20%**

Outsiders **80%**

2005 Results (base: 554)

Number of Electronic Crimes by Outsiders vs. Insiders

The following tables break out the source of electronic crimes or intrusions and support that a greater percentage of electronic crimes (or network, system, or data intrusions) were carried out by outsiders in 2004 compared to the previous year.

How many electronic crimes or network, system, or data intrusions are known or suspected to have been caused by... OUTSIDERS (base: among those experiencing electronic crimes)	*2005 (base: 554)*
None	4%
1 or more (NET)	77%
1–9	42%
10–49	19%
50–99	5%
100–249	4%
250 or more	7%
Mean	102
Median	5
Don't know	19%

How many electronic crimes or network, system or data intrusions are known or suspected to have been caused by... INSIDERS (base: among those experiencing electronic crimes)	*2005 (base: 554)*
None	43%
1 or more (NET)	39%
1–9	24%
10–49	10%
50–99	2%
100–249	2%
250 or more	1%
Mean	10
Median	0
Don't know	19%

NOTE: percents may not sum to 100 due to rounding.

- Vandals: motivated to cause damage and as much harm as possible; are often disgruntled, either at their employer or at life/society in general
- Criminals: motivated by economic gain; use espionage and fraud, among other tactics, to accomplish their goals
- Organization level
  - Most computer criminals, although commonly active in a social underground, commit their criminal act alone.
  - A smaller percentage of cybercriminals will exist in organized groups, such as corporate spies and organized crime groups.

 Three general categories of cybercriminals are crackers, vandals, and criminals. Motivations vary, from the cracker's need for an intellectual challenge, to the vandal's urge to cause damage, to the criminal's desire for financial or other personal gain.

Revenge is a motive when a suspect feels that management has committed injustices or when militants destroy computer centers that deal with controversial issues or products. Brinton suggests that certain types of targets attract specific types of cybercriminals:

- Military/intelligence computers are commonly targeted by spies.

- Banks and other financial organizations are commonly targeted by professional cybercriminals.
- Government entities and utility companies are common targets for terrorists.
- Institutions of higher learning are frequent targets of students and former students.
- Private companies are often targeted by employees and ex-employees.
- Anything can be a target for a cracker, whether for the challenge or because he or she was hired.

Of course, these are generalizations, and exceptions always exist.

Normal or special audit procedures may have brought a computer crime to the attention of the proper persons, as in embezzlement cases. Because computer operations require contact with other employees in collecting computer-input information, suspicion develops when employees appear to withdraw from other normal relationships.

Overloading of the computer system or a lack of accessibility to records that the system was designed for may indicate illegal use of the computer, a crime that occurs more frequently in small computer operations, where greater opportunity exists. However, this makes an investigator's task easier because the number of suspects is reduced.

The suspect may act alone or in collusion in committing the crime. In cases of internal abuse, commission normally occurs during authorized use or during periods of overtime when the employee is working alone. Developing a suspect's work history assists in locating past opportunities for committing the offense. The suspect's training will provide information about his or her knowledge of computers and computer languages. Comparisons of these factors with the equipment at the crime scene will help determine whether the suspect was capable of the crime.

A complete review of everyone within the organization who has access, their type of access, and their technical capability or opportunity greatly assists the investigation if the crime is internal. Check for employees who have a history of computer crimes.

Investigators will often find that computer-related thefts originate from agencies that already have highly trained computer personnel on their staffs. If the theft is internal, the investigator may confidentially involve personnel of that agency who are not suspect. In internal crimes of this nature, the number of suspects will necessarily be limited, as opposed to a crime such as a residential burglary, in which the suspect could be a local or an outsider. In computer crimes for theft, supervisory and management personnel may use computers to hide their offenses and then misdirect the investigative team toward subordinate staff who have committed relatively minor transgressions.

Internal auditing procedures are normally started with the security director involved. If an employee is suspected at this point, management must decide whether to handle the matter internally or proceed with prosecution. If the decision is to handle the matter internally, then the case is closed. If not, the investigation continues, often involving state or private investigators. Such individuals may have the expertise and anonymity not available to local police departments.

Organized Cybercrime Groups Most cybercriminals work alone. However, on occasion these individuals may come together for a common criminal endeavor. They generally are not Mafia-style organizations and usually lack any real loyalty to one another. The transitional nature of these cybercrime rings makes prosecution an effective tool against such groups and sends a message of deterrence to other online criminals, who, because of the anonymity involved with Internet communications, often do not know who they are really dealing with.

While cybercriminal rings have not historically been formally structured like traditional organized crime, a few hacker groups have been observed to have a Mafia-like hierarchy, with virtual godfathers mapping strategy, capos issuing orders, and soldiers carrying out the dirty work: "Their *omertà*, or vow of silence, is made easier by the anonymity of the Web" (Grow, 2005). Some cybergangs have evolved into highly organized criminal enterprises whose membership and illegal activities span the globe. For example ShadowCrew, whose members are proficient in identity theft, bank account pilferage, and the fencing of stolen goods, allegedly has 4,000 members worldwide, including Americans, Russians, Britons, Brazilians, and Spaniards (Grow).

A major hurdle facing cyber investigators are the cybergangs operating in countries with weak hacking laws and lax enforcement, such as Russia, eastern European countries, and China. For example, the HangUp Team is a Russian gang that has been attacking e-commerce websites and taunting authorities for two years. The gang's modus operandi is to plant software bugs in computers that allow it to steal passwords and other sensitive user information. In 2004 the HangUp Team released the Scob worm to infect online stores and wait for web surfers to connect, at which time the worm would lodge in the user's hard drive and spy on the user's keystrokes. This attack sent thousands of consumer passwords and credit card numbers to a server in Russia before being brought under control (Grow, 2005).

An effective tactic being used to apprehend organized cybercrime networks is undercover investigation and surveillance. In fact, many law enforcement agencies have found success in applying to cybercrime the same tactics used in the 1980s to crush organized crime—informants and the cyberspace equivalent of wiretaps (Grow, 2005).

Undercover Investigation and Surveillance

Sometimes it is necessary to develop an undercover operation to further the investigation. This operation must be headed by a computer expert and coordinated with the nonsuspects. Lists must be prepared of all persons to be used in the case and the evidence to be obtained. Undercover work can be undertaken in nearly every aspect of cybercrime. As with undercover work in the real world, investigators must be sensitive to entrapment issues and to undercover involvement with criminal activity.

Covert investigation including ongoing surveillance operations is a method being used to gather evidence against cybercrime gangs. Operation Firewall, an information-age undercover investigation led by the U.S. Secret Service and involving numerous other domestic and foreign law enforcement agencies as well as investigators in the financial services industry, was a year-long operation that began in July 2003 as a case involving access device fraud and evolved into a highly technical, international investigation involving global credit card fraud, identity theft, and other criminal cyber activity targeting the financial infrastructure of the United States. During the course of the investigation, several underground cybergangs were identified—ShadowCrew, Carderplanet, and Darkprofits—as highly organized international criminal enterprises, which had collectively trafficked in at least 1.7 million stolen credit card numbers and had caused more than $4.3 million in losses to various financial institutions ("U.S. Secret Service's"). The operation involved an in-tense collection of electronic evidence through court-authorized intercepts, with the amount of information gathered amounting to approximately two terabytes, or the equivalent of a university's entire academic library.

Undercover tactics are also commonly used in cases of online child pornography and sexual exploitation. An officer will go online, undercover, into predicated locations and, using a fictitious screen name and profile, pose as a child or teenager and engage in real-time chat or e-mail conversations with subjects to obtain evidence of criminal activity. Investigations of specific Internet locations can be initiated through a citizen complaint, a complaint by an ISP, or a referral from another law enforcement agency (FBI, "Innocent Images").

Legislation

ith the proliferation of online child pornography, phishing, and other crimes involving the computer, legislation has necessarily been developed to address the problem. For example, in 1986 President Reagan signed a bill to modernize the federal wiretap law to protect the privacy of high-tech communications. This bill makes it illegal to eavesdrop on electronic mail, video conference calls, conversations on cellular car phones, and computer-to-computer transmissions.

However, following the 9/11 tragedy and the realization that the terrorists had used the Internet and other electronic means to communicate and coordinate their plans, the government took measures to allow law enforcement greater latitude in its surveilling of electronic communication if there is a reasonable suspicion that such activity involves terrorism. On October 26, 2001, President George W. Bush signed the USA PATRIOT Act (Uniting and Strengthening America by Providing Appropriate Tools Required to Intercept and Obstruct Terrorism), a major piece of legislation consisting of more than 150 sections, many of which pertain to electronic communications and other areas of cybercrime investigation.

For instance, the act made several amendments to the Foreign Intelligence Surveillance Act (FISA) of 1978, such as granting "roving" authority to FBI and other law enforcement agents to more efficiently serve orders on communications carriers and thus meet the challenges posed by individuals who rapidly switch telephone carriers, cell phones, or Internet accounts as a way of evading detection and thwarting surveillance.

The PATRIOT Act also changed key features of existing National Security Letter (NSL) protocol. NSLs are a type of subpoena issued in foreign counterintelligence and international terrorism investigations to obtain records under the statutory authority of the Electronic Communications Privacy Act (telephone and ISP records), the Right to Financial Privacy Act (financial institution records), and the Fair Credit Reporting Act (records from credit bureaus). The act expanded signature authority for NSLs to increase the efficiency and effectiveness of processing such subpoenas. Recently the "Emergency Disclosure of E-Mail and Records by ISPs" provision of the act helped law enforcement to quickly track down and restore an abducted 14-year-old girl to her family. The PATRIOT Act was reauthorized in 2006 for five more years.

Other federal statutes relevant to computer-related crimes include patent laws, espionage and sabotage laws, trade secret laws, the Copyright Act of 1976, and the Financial Privacy Act of 1978. In 1998 the Child Protection and Sexual Predator Punishment Act was passed after members of Congress cited horror stories involving sexual predators making initial contact with young children through the Internet.

In the past decade all 50 states have enacted tough computer crime control laws. States address computer crime either by modifying existing statutes such as those pertaining to theft or by adding computer crime chapters to their criminal codes. For example, to address the growing problem of cyberstalking, some states have amended their traditional stalking laws to include threats transmitted via the Internet. Phishing schemes, which are relative newcomers to the crime arena, are likely to violate not only various existing state statutes on fraud and identity theft but also several federal criminal laws. Those who phish may be committing identity theft (18 U.S.C. §1028(a)(7)), wire fraud (18 U.S.C. §1343), credit card or "access-device" fraud (18 U.S.C. §1029), bank fraud (18 U.S.C. §1344), computer fraud (18 U.S.C. §1030(a)(4)), and the newly enacted criminal offenses delineated in the CAN-SPAM (Controlling the Assault of Non-Solicited Pornography and Marketing) Act (18 U.S.C. §1037). Transmission of computer viruses and worms may be prosecuted under the federal provisions of the computer fraud and abuse statute relating to damage to computer systems and files (18 U.S.C. § 1028(a)(5)). These federal criminal offenses can carry substantial penalties and fines, with convictions for wire fraud and bank fraud earning the offender up to 30 years in prison and the possibility of fines as high as $250,000, plus forfeiture of the defendant's property ("Special Report").

Well-defined statutes are critical to investigating and prosecuting computer crimes successfully, and the area of cyber law is rapidly evolving. Lawmakers are challenged, however, by the complex nature of the technology and nontraditional jurisdictional concerns, elements that complicate the effort to define cybercrime and cybercrooks (Figure 17.8). Through it all, cybercrime investigators must stay on top of the ever-changing body of state and federal law regarding electronic crimes.

Figure 17.8

Gary McKinnon, 39, of North London enters the Bow Street Magistrates Court on July 27, 2005, for an extradition hearing. He is wanted by the U.S. government for illegally accessing and making unauthorized modifications to 53 computers belonging to NASA, the Pentagon, the U.S. Army, Navy, Air Force, and the Department of Defense, causing $1 million worth of damage. McKinnon is believed to be the world's biggest military computer hacker.

and other valuable data hijacked in a system takeover following a virus attack.

The Investigative Team

There is no doubt: Criminals around the world have their sticky fingers poised at the keyboard, prepared to click their way into places they don't belong and steal. The rising tide of Internet activity has washed ashore an increasing variety of old crimes in new bottles and shows no signs of ebbing.

For many, if not most, law enforcement agencies throughout the country, keeping up with the high-tech bad guys is a formidable challenge, not only because of the technical skills required to detect, catch, and prosecute cybercriminals but also because limited funds and other resources prevent departments from having the same access to the latest and greatest gizmos and gadgets used by those who commit computer crimes. Furthermore, the Internet allows criminals on one side of the planet to wreak e-havoc on computer users and businesses on the other side of the planet, throwing immense jurisdictional complications on top of an already complex area of criminal investigation.

For these reasons, many departments have found the need to form cybercrime investigative teams comprising various specialists, similar to the approach taken in cases involving complex art thefts, bank embezzlements, narcotics trafficking, or other types of crime in which a generalist investigator has little expert-

Security of the Police Department's Computers

When considering computer crime, law enforcement officers should not overlook the possibility that their own computers may be accessed by criminals. Any computer attached to a telephone line is accessible by unauthorized persons outside the department, even thousands of miles away on a different continent. Considering the critical nature of law enforcement data and communications, such as systems that control computer-aided dispatch, records management applications, and offender databases, ensuring the security of an agency's network should be a top priority (Miller, pp.76–85). Law enforcement departments cannot afford to have their evidence logs hacked or have reports

ise. Computer-related crimes may be relatively low tech, but for cybercrimes of a highly technical nature in which fragile digital evidence must be extracted from extensive database systems with equipment that is unfamiliar to police officers, the proactive law enforcement department has already devised a response protocol and assembled an investigative team of qualified specialists.

 Investigating computer crime often requires a team approach.

For departments intimidated by the prospect of forming a cybercrime unit, Pettinari (p.34) reassures: "There is nothing magical, mystical, or mysterious about starting a high-tech crimes unit. You don't have to be a computer science major or a rocket scientist." Sheetz (p.14) echoes: "In many ways, the process of creating a high-tech investigative response team is similar to creating any other specialized investigative unit." The areas to focus on are selecting the right personnel, establishing a specific protocol to guide investigators, providing the proper training for team members, and acquiring the necessary tools and equipment to do the job.

The investigative team is responsible for assigning all team personnel according to their specialties, including securing outside specialists if necessary; securing the crime scene area; obtaining search warrant applications; determining the specific hardware and software involved; searching for, obtaining, marking, preserving, and storing evidence; obtaining necessary disks, printouts, and other records; and preparing information for investigative reports. In the majority of computer-related crimes, investigators seek assistance from the victim who owns the equipment, database processing technicians, auditors, highly trained computer experts or programmers, and others. If necessary, the team should contact the manufacturer of the equipment, the consulting services of a private computer crime investigative agency, or the technology resources found at local universities and other institutions of higher learning.

To assist in combating increasing computer-related crimes, government and private businesses are developing computer crime teams similar to the FBI's kidnapping crime teams and the arson investigation specialist teams of the Bureau of Alcohol, Tobacco, Firearms and Explosives. The FBI's Computer Analysis Response Team (CART) helps not only federal agents but also state and local law enforcement. CART helps write and execute search warrants, seize and catalog evidence, and perform routine examinations of digital evidence.

In addition to CART, investigators working cybercrime cases may seek assistance from a growing pool of resources, both domestic and international.

Resources Available

Police agencies in many states are forming cooperative groups and providing training seminars on investigating computer crimes. Such groups are especially helpful for small departments, which are less likely to have the needed expertise in-house. For example, Florida's law enforcement agencies can submit computer evidence to the Computer Evidence Recovery (CER) program, which also trains the state's law enforcement agencies to prepare warrants to search computers and to follow specific procedures when seizing computer crime evidence.

Training in computer crimes investigation is also available from other sources. Working in partnership with state, local, federal, and international law enforcement agencies, the DOJ has developed the National Cybercrime Training Partnership (NCTP) to develop and promote a long-range strategy for high-tech police work, including interagency and interjurisdictional cooperation, information networking, and technical training; to garner public and political understanding of the problem and generate support for solutions; and to serve as a proactive force to focus the momentum of the entire law enforcement community to ensure that proposed solutions are fully implemented. The NCTP is open to any law enforcement agency involved in electronic crime investigation, prosecution, or training.

Another resource to help law enforcement handle computer crimes is the IC3 (see above under "The Scope and Cost of the Problem"). The IC3 provides to cybercrime victims a convenient, user-friendly reporting mechanism that notifies authorities of suspected violations. In its first year of operation, the IC3 received over 30,000 complaints, and its website was viewed over a million times.

The ECB of the U.S. Secret Service offers numerous services to its field agents, including technical assistance in the development of a cybercrime case, help in preparing search warrants involving electronic storage devices, laboratory analysis of and courtroom testimony regarding the evidentiary contents of electronic storage devices, and educational seminars for law enforcement officers nationwide.

The Computer Crime and Intellectual Property Section (CCIPS) (U.S. DOJ, "Computer Crime") of the DOJ maintains a web resource for law enforcement (www.cybercrime.gov) and is the closest thing you are likely to find to a one-stop resource for all things related to computer crime. The site offers a collection of documents and links to other sites and agencies that may help prevent, detect, investigate, and prosecute cybercrime.

The list of additional resources available to help law enforcement combat cybercrime is quite extensive and expanding all the time:

- National Fraud Database (NFD): the only cross-industry national repository of verified fraudulent credit activity

- Electronic Evidence Information Center (www .e-evidence.info): a compilation of other digital forensics links, some foreign

- National Infrastructure Protection Center (U.S. DOJ, "Computer Crime"): acts as a clearinghouse for information on cybercrime

- National Cybercrime Training Partnership (http://www.nctp.org)

- *Prosecuting Cases that Involve Computers: A Resource for State and Local Prosecutors* (CD-ROM), National White Collar Crime Center, 2001. (See http://www .training.nw3c.org for information.)

- Infobin (http://www.infobin.org/isplist/isplist.pdf)

- FTC's ID theft website (http://www.consumer.gov/ idtheft)

- Federal Law Enforcement Training Center (FLETC), Glynco, GA: 800-74-FLETC

- Florida Department of Law Enforcement (FDLE), Computer Crime Center: 850-488-8771

- FBI Computer Analysis Response Team, Washington, DC: 202-324-9307

- NIJ/National Law Enforcement and Corrections Technology Centers, El Segundo, CA: 888-548-1618; Rome, NY: 888-338-0584

- National White Collar Crime Center (NW3C), Computer Crime Center, Fairmont, WV: 800-221-4424

- National Cybercrime Training Partnership, Washington, DC: 202-514-0823

Preventing Computer Crime

 lthough computers and related technologies have added immeasurable benefits and value to our quality of life, this technology has opened up new avenues of crime and exploitation. One reason computer crime has proliferated among businesses in the private sector is that many managers are unprepared to deal with it. They may be ignorant, indifferent, or both. They also frequently lack control over their information. Without standards to violate, there is no violation.

 Computer crimes can be prevented by educating top management and employees and by instituting internal security precautions. Top management must make a commitment to defend against computer crime.

Management must institute organization-wide policies to safeguard its databases and must educate employees in these policies and any security measures implemented. Management should also take internal security precautions: Firewalls and virus protection are two safeguards for computers. Data disks and CDs should have backup copies and be kept in locked files. The FBI's National Computer Crime Squad suggests the following procedures for computer users to institute, both prior to becoming a computer crime victim and after a violation has occurred:

- Place a log-in banner to ensure that unauthorized users are warned that they may be subject to monitoring.

- Turn audit trails on.

- Consider keystroke-level monitoring if the adequate banner is displayed.

- Request trap and tracing from your local telephone company.

- Consider installing caller identification.

- Make backups of damaged or altered files.

- Maintain old backups to show the status of the original.

- Designate one person to secure potential evidence.

- Evidence can consist of tape backups and printouts. These should be initialed by the person obtaining the evidence. Evidence should be retained in a locked cabinet with access limited to one person.

- Keep a record of resources used to reestablish the system and locate the perpetrator.

One of the most important, yet most frequently overlooked, security measures is to use a paper shredder for all sensitive documents once they are no longer needed. Another technique gaining momentum in the effort to increase computer security is **biometrics,** using physical characteristics the user cannot lose or give away, including facial, voice, and fingerprint recognition.

Computer crimes also plague and persist among private American citizens because, like corporate managers, they remain uninformed as to how to protect themselves. One of the most common ways home users become victims of cybercrime is through phishing or other scams devised to get computer users to relinquish sensitive information.

Finally, the U.S. Secret Service contends that law enforcement must take a proactive approach to cyberthreats and that prevention coupled with aggressive proactive investigations deliver the best outcome in the fight against cybercrime. The Cyber Incident Detection and Data Analysis Center (CIDDAC) is one initiative helping law enforcement protect the private-sector networks that control 85 percent of the country's technological infrastructure. CIDDAC uses real-time cyber attack detection sensors, or RCADS, to prevent outside attackers from penetrating a system's perimeter defenses and reaching a target's internal database. If a hack is detected, CIDDAC is notified immediately and begins analyzing the incident. They can track the origin of the attack and notify the target, in real time, that an intrusion is being attempted (Moore, C., 2005). Businesses voluntarily subscribed to CIDDAC's services, which in turn guarantee to preserve their client's anonymity should an attack incident occur: "Businesses don't want the public or their competitors to know their databases have been compromised, or even attacked unsuccessfully" (Moore, p.88).

SUMMARY

Computer crimes are relatively easy to commit and difficult to detect, and most are not prosecuted. Computer-related crimes may be categorized as computer as target, computer as tool, or computer as incidental to the offense.

Special challenges in investigating computer crime include victims' reluctance or failure to report such crimes, the investigator's lack of training and the lack of understanding of computer crimes by others within the justice system, the proliferation of such crimes, the fragility of the evidence, jurisdictional questions, and the need for specialists and teamwork.

If investigators possess a search warrant and wish to conduct a search, they should first request permission for the search. If consent is given, the search can proceed right away. If it is not given, then the warrant can be served and the search conducted. A common protocol for processing a crime scene involving electronic evidence is as follows:

1. Secure and evaluate the crime scene.
2. Recognize and identify the evidence.
3. Document the crime scene.
4. Collect and preserve evidence.
5. Package, transport, and store evidence.

A basic tenet for first responders at computer crime scenes is to observe the ON/OFF rule: If it's on, leave it on. If it's off, leave it off. Digital evidence is often contained on disks, CDs, or hard drives, or on any number of peripheral electronic devices, is not readily discernible and also is highly susceptible to destruction. Other computer crime evidence may exist in the form of data reports, logs, programming, or other printed information run from information in the computer. Latent prints may be found on the keyboard, mouse, power button, or any other peripheral equipment near the computer.

Investigators who handle computer disks should avoid contact with the recording surfaces. Never write on computer disk labels with a ballpoint pen or pencil, and never use paper clips on or rubber bands around computer disks, for to do so may destroy the data they contain. Store electronic evidence in a secure area away from temperature and humidity extremes and protected from magnetic sources, moisture, dust, and other harmful particles or contaminants. Do not use plastic bags.

Although deleted files remain on the hard drive in a nonviewable format, their existence hidden from most computer users, the computer forensic expert knows where to look and how to make such files viewable again.

Most cybercrimes against businesses are committed by "outsiders." Three general categories of cybercriminals are crackers, vandals, and criminals. Motivations vary, from the cracker's need for an intellectual challenge, to the vandal's urge to cause damage, to the criminal's desire for financial or other personal gain.

Investigating such crimes often requires a team approach. Computer crimes can be prevented by educating top management and employees and by instituting internal security precautions.

CHECKLIST

Cybercrime

- Who is the complainant?
- Has a crime been committed?
- What is the specific nature of the crime reported to the police?
- What statutes are applicable? Can the required elements of the crime be proven?
- Has the crime been terminated, or is it continuing?
- Is the origin of the crime internal or external?
- Does the reported crime appear to be a cover-up for a larger crime?
- What barriers exist to investigating the crime?
- What are the make, model, and identification numbers of the equipment involved? the hardware? the software?
- Is the equipment individually or company owned?
- Is an operations manual available for the hardware?
- Is a flowchart of computer operations available? Is a computer configuration chart available?
- Is documentation for the software available?
- What computer language is involved? What computer programs are involved?
- What is the degree of technicality involved? Simple or complex?
- What are the input and output codes?
- What accounting procedures were used?
- What is the database system? What are the system's main vulnerabilities?
- Is there a built-in security system? What is it? How was it bypassed?
- What are the present security procedures? How were they bypassed?
- Can the equipment be shut down during the search and investigation or for a sufficient time to investigate the portion essential to obtaining evidence?
- Can the computer records be "dumped" without interfering with the ongoing operations, or must the system be closed down and secured?
- Does the equipment need to be operational to conduct the investigation?

- Does the reporting person desire prosecution or only disciplinary action?
- Are there any suspects? Internal or external?
- If internal, are they presently employed by the reporting organization or person?
- Is a list of current employees and their work histories available? Are all current computer-related job descriptions available?
- What level of employees is involved? Is an organizational table available?
- How can the investigation be carried out without the knowledge of the suspect?
- What is the motive for the crime?
- What competitors might be suspect?
- What types of evidence are needed or likely to be present?
- What external experts are needed as part of the search team?
- Does the available evidence meet the best-evidence requirement?
- What are the main barriers to the continued investigation? How can they be overcome?

APPLICATION

A. (From "Marijuana Buyers Club Sets Up Site on Internet," *Las Vegas Review Journal*, November 14, 1996, p.14E.)

After voters in one state approved a proposition legalizing marijuana use "for medicinal purposes," an Internet site began offering marijuana to severely ill or disabled people who need it, requiring proof of a doctor's recommendation to use marijuana. The site's director states, "I don't want people trying to order marijuana without the proper authorization. I'm really trying to do this in keeping with the proper spirit of [the proposition]."

A police sergeant from the jurisdiction from which the marijuana is being shipped contends the operation is clearly illegal. "Along with supplying and selling marijuana, which are felonies, I imagine you could cook up something extra for using the Internet," he said. The site is receiving orders from all over the state, as well as from people outside the state who are using in-state mailing addresses.

Questions

1. What crime is being committed, if any?
2. Who has jurisdiction?
3. What steps would you take to conduct this investigation?
4. How would you prepare a search warrant?
5. What types of evidence would you look for?

B. A local firm contacts your police department concerning theft of customer credit card and Social Security numbers from their computer records. This operation and theft are suspected to be internal, so present and past employees are the prime suspects.

Questions

1. How would you plan to initiate the investigation?
2. What statements would you obtain?
3. Would you use internal or external assistance?
4. What types of evidence would you need?

DISCUSSION QUESTIONS

1. What do you perceive to be the differences between investigating computer crime and investigating other felonies?
2. What are the differences in interviewing and interrogating individuals involved in computer crime?
3. What are the legal differences between a computer crime investigation and other felony investigations?
4. If you were in charge of a computer crime investigation team, what would you include in your plan?
5. Do you have a computer crime law in your municipality? your state?
6. Is anyone in your police department trained specifically in computer crime investigation? If so, where was this training obtained?
7. Do you have a computer? If so, how do you store your information?
8. What type of computer security is used in your local police department?
9. Of all the various types of computer crime, which do you think is the most serious?
10. What do you consider the greatest challenge in investigating computer crimes?

MEDIA EXPLORATIONS

 Internet

Select one of the following assignments to complete.

- Go to the International Association of Chiefs of Police website at www.theiacp.org to find and outline *Best Practices for Seizing Electronic Evidence*.
- Go to www.cybercrime.gov/s&smanual2002 .htm

and outline *Searching and Seizing Computers and Obtaining Electronic Evidence in Criminal Investigations.*

- Search for the key phrase *National Institute of Justice.* Click on "NCJRS" (National Criminial Justice Research Service). Click on "law enforcement." Click on "sort by Doc#." Search for one of the NCJ reference numbers from the reference pages. Outline the selection to share with the class.

- Go to the FBI website at www.fbi.gov. Click on "library and reference." Select "Uniform Crime Reports" and outline what the report says about computer crime.

- Select one of the following keywords: *computer crime, computer crime prevention, hacker, logic bomb.* Find one article relevant to computer crime investigations to outline and share with the class.

 Crime and Evidence in Action

Go to the CD and choose the **drug bust/gang homicide/sexual assault case.** During the course of the case you'll become patrol officer, detective, defense attorney, corrections officer, and patrol officer to conduct interactive investigative research. Each case unfolds as you respond to key decision points. Feedback for each possible answer choice is packed full of information, including term definitions, web links, and important documentation. The sergeant is available at certain times to help mentor you, the Online Resources website offers a variety of information, and be sure to take notes in your e-notebook during the suspect video statements and at key points throughout (these notes can be saved, printed, or e-mailed). The Forensics Exercise will test your ability to collect, transport, and analyze evidence from the crime scene. At the end of the case you can track how well you responded to each decision point and join the Discussion Forum for a postmortem. **Go to the CD and use the skills you've learned in this chapter to solve a case!**

REFERENCES

2005 E-Crime Watch Survey: Summary of Findings. Conducted and printed by *CSO Magazine* in cooperation with the U.S. Secret Service and CERT® Coordination Center, May 3, 2005. http://www .cert.org/archive/pdf/ecrimesummary05.pdf. Accessed August 10, 2005.

Acohido, Byron, and Swartz, Jon. "Cybercrooks Lure Citizens into International Crime," *USA Today*, July 11, 2005, p. 1A.

Aeilts, Tony. "Defending against Cybercrime and Terrorism," *FBI Law Enforcement Bulletin*, January 2005, pp. 14–20.

Berners-Lee, Tim. "Frequently Asked Questions." www .w3.org/People/Berners-Lee/FAQ.html#InternetWeb. Accessed August 2, 2005.

Berryhill, Jon. "Finding a Qualified Computer Forensic Analyst." *Law Enforcement Technology*, May 2005, pp. 122–127.

Best Practices for Seizing Electronic Evidence. Arlington, VA: International Association of Chiefs of Police, 2001.

Brenner, Susan W. "Is There Such a Thing as 'Virtual Crime'"? *California Criminal Law Review*, vol. 4, no.1, 2001.

Brinton, Stephen, "Defining Cybercrime," www.math-cs .gordon.edu/courses/cs111brinton/impact_websites/ cybercrime/define.html. Accessed April 13, 2006.

"Bush Signs Identity Theft Bill." Associated Press, as reported in the Minneapolis/St. Paul *StarTribune*, July 16, 2004, p.A9.

Computer Crime Research Center. "Fraud in the Internet." April 11, 2005. http://www.crime-research .org/articles/Internet_fraud_0405. Accessed October 15, 2005.

"Copyright and Law Enforcement Use of Seized Computers," *The Law Enforcement Trainer*, March/April 2004, pp. 24–28.

Davis, Bob. "InfinaDyne CD/DVD Inspector 2.1," *Police*, April 2004, pp. 62–64.

Davis, Bob. "Logicube Forensic MD5," *Police*, March 2005, pp. 70–71.

Donofrio, Andrew. "What Can Be Done about Spam?" *Law Enforcement Technology*, May 2004, pp. 86–91.

Electronic Crime Scene Investigation: A Guide for First Responders. Washington, DC: National Institute of Justice, July 2001. (NCJ 187736) http://www.ncjrs .gov/txtfiles1/nij/187736.txt

FBI. "Innocent Images National Initiative: Online Child Pornography/Child Sexual Exploitation Investigations." Washington, DC, September 24, 2003. http://www.fbi.gov/publications/innocent.htm. Accessed August 18, 2005.

Forensic Examination of Digital Evidence: A Guide for Law Enforcement. Washington, DC: National Institute of Justice, April 2004. (NCJ 199408) http://www.ncjrs .org/pdffiles1/nij/199408.pdf

Forester, Tom, and Perry Morrison. *Computer Ethics: Cautionary Tales and Ethical Dilemmas in Computing*, 2nd ed. Cambridge, MA: MIT Press, 1994.

Girardi, Brian, and Peterson, David. "Internet Intercepts Part I: They've Got Mail!" *Law Enforcement Technology*, May 2004, pp. 58–62.

Gordon, Lawrence A.; Loeb, Martin P.; Lucyshyn, William; and Richardson, Robert. *2005 CSI/FBI Computer Crime and Security Survey*. San Francisco: CSI Publications, 2005.

Griffith, David. "How to Investigate Cybercrime," *Police*, November 2003, pp. 18–22.

Grow, Brian. "Hacker Hunters: An Elite Force Takes on the Dark Side of Computing," *BusinessWeek*, May 30, 2005.

Jacobia, Jack. "Computer Forensics: Duties of the First Responder," *Law Enforcement Technology*, April 2004, pp. 28–34.

Klain, Eva J.; Davies, Heather J.; and Hicks, Molly A. *Child Pornography: The Criminal-Justice-System Response.* American Bar Association Center on Children and the Law for the National Center on Missing and Exploited Children, March 2001.

Lange, Michele C. S., and Perrin, Trevor W. A. "Common Computing Landmines to Avoid," *Law Enforcement Technology*, June 2004, pp. 162–167.

Lusher, Gary R. "National White Collar Crime Center: Helping State and Local Police Combat Electronic Crime," *The Law Enforcement Trainer*, March/April 2004, pp. 17–21.

Mercer, Loren D. "Computer Forensics: Characteristics and Preservation of Digital Evidence." *FBI Law Enforcement Bulletin*, March 2004, pp. 28–32.

Miller, Christa. "Part II: Securing Your Data," *Law Enforcement Technology*, May 2004, pp. 76–85.

Moore, Carole. "Protecting Your Backdoor," *Law Enforcement Technology*, June 2005, pp. 80–89.

Moore, Eric. "Network Security: Safeguarding Systems against the Latest Threats," *The Police Chief*, February 2003, pp. 23–31.

National and State Trends in Fraud and Identity Theft: January–December 2004. Washington, DC: Federal Trade Commission, February 1, 2005.

"The National Strategy to Secure Cyberspace," *The Police Chief*, December 2003, pp. 32–33.

Newburger, Eric. C. *Home Computers and Internet Use in the United States: August 2000.* Washington, DC: U.S. Department of Commerce, U.S. Census Bureau, Special Studies, September 2001. (P23-207) http://www.census.gov/prod/2001pubs/p23-207.pdf. Accessed August 17, 2005.

Pettinari, Dave. "How to Start a High-Tech Crimes Unit," *Police and Security News*, September/October 2004, pp. 34–40.

Rantala, Ramona R. *Cybercrime against Businesses: Pilot Test Results, 2001 Computer Security Survey.* Washington, DC: Bureau of Justice Statistics, Technical Report, March 2004. (NCJ 200639)

Report of the Department of Justice's Task Force on Intellectual Property. Washington, DC: U.S. Department of Justice, October 2004.

Rogers, Donna. "Intercepting the Cybersleuth," *Law Enforcement Technology*, November 2003, pp. 22–27.

Sabadash, Victor. "Criminal Legal Descriptions of Computer Crimes: Methods and Practice of Investigation," Computer Crime Research Center, June 9, 2004. http://www.crime-research.org/articles/Sabadash0504. Accessed July 29, 2005.

Searching and Seizing Computers and Obtaining Electronic Evidence in Criminal Investigations. Washington, DC: Department of Justice, July 2002. http://www.cybercrime.gov/s&smanual2002.htm. Accessed August 8, 2005.

Sheetz, Michael. "Cyber Sleuths: Creating the High-Tech Investigative Unit," *Law and Order*, December 2004, pp. 14–20.

"Special Report on 'Phishing.'" U.S. Department of Justice, Criminal Division. http://www.usdoj.gov/criminal/fraud/Phishing.pdf. Accessed August 11, 2005.

Srinivasan, Arun. "Combating Cyberterrorism," *Line56* as reported on the Computer Crime Research Center website, February 27, 2005. http://www.crime-research.org/analytics/Cyberterrorism01. Accessed July 29, 2005.

Tavani, Herman. *Ethics and Technology.* Hoboken, NJ: John Wiley and Sons, 2005.

Thomas, Marcus C. "Study Group Workshops Bring IT Industry and Law Enforcement Together," *The Police Chief*, April 2003, p. 14.

Tsai, Alice. "Computer Forensics: Electronic Trail of Evidence," *New Hampshire Society of CPAs E-News*, May 2002. http://www.nhscpa.org/May2002News/forensics.htm2. Accessed August 18, 2005.

U.S. DOJ. "Computer Crime and Intellectual Property Section (CCIPS)." http://www.usdoj.gov/criminal/cybercrime/ccpolicy.html. Accessed October 16, 2005. This webpage contains links to the NIPC Act and Advisory.

"U.S. Secret Service's Operation Firewall Nets 28 Arrests." Washington, DC: U.S. Department of Homeland Security, Secret Service press release, October 28, 2004.

Whitlock, Chuck. "The Con Artist of the Future," *The Law Enforcement Trainer*, March/April 2004, pp. 11–15.

CHAPTER 18

A Dual Threat: Drug-Related Crime and Organized Crime

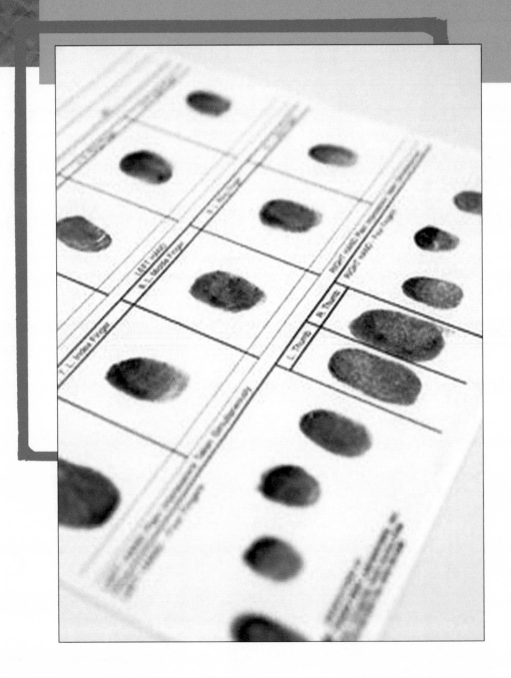

Can You Define?

Do You Know?

- When it is illegal to use or sell narcotics or dangerous drugs and what physical evidence can prove these offenses?
- How drugs are commonly classified?
- What drugs are most commonly observed on the street, in the possession of users, and seized in drug raids, and what the most frequent drug arrest is?
- What the major legal evidence in prosecuting drug use and possession is?
- What the major legal evidence in prosecuting drug sale and distribution is?
- When an on-sight arrest can be made for a drug buy?
- What precautions to take in undercover drug buys and how to avoid a charge of entrapment?
- What hazards exist in raiding a clandestine drug laboratory?
- What agency provides unified leadership in combating illegal drug activities and what its primary emphasis is?
- What the distinctive characteristics of organized crime are? its major activities?
- What organized crime activities are specifically made crimes by law?
- What the investigator's primary role in dealing with the organized crime problem is?
- What agencies cooperate in investigating organized crime?

Outline

he violence inspired by drug-related and organized crime activities translates into murders, arsons, drive-by shootings, car bombs, and other acts that threaten and terrorize communities across the country. Drug gangs have turned many communities into virtual war zones. Sometimes these acts are gang reprisals or witness intimidation; others are designed simply to frighten innocent citizens enough to ensure that they refrain from calling the police. Similarly, organized crime groups

513

have infiltrated some communities to the point where the people looked upon as leaders and role models, or as guardians of the law, have become corrupt themselves.

Organized crime is heavily involved in the drug trade. In fact, many drug cartels, particularly Latino ones, are structured and operated much like other crime syndicates. Thus, these two investigative challenges are discussed in this chapter. Keep in mind, however, that the two topics, while overlapping, are also separate. Organized crime is involved in many more activities than just drug trafficking; and drug-related crimes, while sometimes linked to organized crime, are usually committed by other groups and individuals with no mob associations. Another facet of these two crime problems to be aware of is the response and involvement of different jurisdictional levels. Federal law enforcement has devoted substantial investigative resources to both the illegal drug trade and organized crime. However, in most cases, it is local law enforcement that first detects these problems and opens the cases (Abadinsky, p.313).

This chapter begins with a discussion of the seriousness and extent of the drug problem, an explanation of the legal definitions and problems, identification and classification of controlled drugs, and a discussion of investigating illegal *possession or use* of controlled substances, as well as the illegal *sale and distribution* of controlled substances. Then it presents the hazards involved in investigating clandestine drug laboratories and investigative aids. This is followed by a look at agency cooperation and the role of drug asset forfeitures in combating the drug problem. The discussion of drugs concludes with an exploration of efforts to prevent problems with illegal drugs and the inextricable link between drugs and organized crime.

The second section of the chapter focuses on organized crime in the United States, including an overview, the characteristics of organized crime, applicable laws, major activities, and the threat of specific organized crime groups. Next is a discussion of organized crime and corruption and the police response. This is followed by a look at agencies cooperating in investigating organized crime and methods being used. The chapter concludes with a consideration of whether organized crime is on the decline.

Seriousness and Extent of the Drug Problem

Drug addiction and the crime it engenders place a significant burden on American society and pose a formidable challenge for law enforcement. The *National Drug Control Strategy 2004 Strategy Overview* reports that more than 19 million Americans use drugs on a monthly basis, and roughly 7 million of these users meet the clinical criteria for needing drug treatment. The most recently available data show that approximately 3.8 million users were dependent on or addicted to illicit drugs in 2003 (*National Drug Threat*, 2005a, p.v). Furthermore, in 2002, the total economic cost to society of illegal drug use was an estimated $180.9 billion (*The Economic Costs*, p.vi).

A national survey of police chiefs reveals a commonly held belief that drugs, today, are a far more serious problem than property crime, violent crime, domestic violence, or even the threat of terrorism (*Drugs and Crime,* p.1). Sixty-three percent of police chiefs label **drug abuse** as "extremely serious" or "quite serious," and 60 percent believe the current drug abuse problem in their community is more serious than it was five years ago (*Drugs and Crime,* p.2).

Legal Definitions and Problems

Most narcotics laws prohibit possessing, transporting, selling, furnishing, or giving away narcotics. Possession of controlled substances is probably the most frequent charge in narcotics arrests. Actual or constructive possession and knowledge by a suspect that a drug was illegal must be shown. If the evidence is not on the person, it must be shown to be under the suspect's control.

The legal definitions of *narcotics* and *controlled substances* as stated in local, state, and federal laws are lengthy and technical. The laws define the terms that describe the drugs, the various categories, and the agencies responsible for enforcement.

Laws generally categorize drugs into five Schedules of Controlled Substances, arranged by the degree of danger associated with the drug. The five schedules contain the official, common, usual, trade, and chemical names of the drugs. The laws also establish prohibited acts concerning the controlled substances. Basically, these laws state that no person, firm, or corporation may manufacture, sell, give away, barter or deliver, exchange, distribute, or possess these substances with intent to do any of the prohibited acts. The schedules establish penalties in ratio to the drug's danger, with Schedule I drugs being the most dangerous. Possessing a small amount of marijuana is a felony in some states, a misdemeanor in others, and not a crime at all in a few states.

 It is illegal to possess or use narcotics or dangerous drugs without a prescription and to sell or distribute them without a license.

Laws also define the type of activity drug traffickers are involved in and can be used to impose criminal sanctions even when the intended act is unsuccessful.

Identification and Classification of Controlled Drugs

The sale of prescription drugs, the fastest-growing category of drugs being abused, has skyrocketed nearly 400 percent since 1990 (Mills-Senn, p.48). Consequently, a major challenge for law enforcement officers is to recognize and identify drugs found in a suspect's possession. Because of the countless different types, colors, sizes, trade names, and strengths of commercial drugs, many officers rely on a pharmaceutical reference book, the *Physicians' Desk Reference* (PDR), used widely by health care providers. It is the basis for mobile PDR™ software installed on handheld devices. These portable tools provide instant access to concise monographs about thousands of commonly prescribed drugs.

A reference considered by many in law enforcement to be easier and faster to use than the PDR is the *Drug Identification Bible* (Amera-Chem, Inc., Grand Junction, CO). The revised, expanded 2004/2005 edition contains more than 1,100 full-color actual-size photos of prescription drugs scheduled by the Drug Enforcement Administration (DEA); tablet and capsule imprints for more than 14,000 prescription and over-the-counter (OTC) drugs; hundreds of photos of drug packaging and paraphernalia; sources, methods of use, purity levels, and street prices for all major illicit drugs; and updated street slang to help officers understand the language of the drug culture. For example: "A" is a street name for LSD. "Abe" means $5 worth of a drug.

In the absence of a printed field guide or reference book, street drugs can be identified with a narcotic field-test kit. Officers must understand, however, that field testing cannot be used to *establish* probable cause, only *confirm* it. Probable cause, through observation and evaluation of other factors, must already exist before a substance can be field-tested (Johnson, p.131). For example, an officer working undercover who buys a small bag of white powder from a suspected cocaine dealer has, in essence, established probable cause and may run a substance-specific field test for cocaine (Johnson, p.131). Officers must be properly trained in how to use these field-testing kits, not only to ensure accurate results but also to avoid sample contamination or waste and reduce liability concerns associated with false arrests based on faulty testing procedures.

Knowing the street terms for various drugs, drug paraphernalia, and drug-related activity is also beneficial to the drug investigator. The Office of National Drug Control Policy (ONDCP) maintains a street-term database with more than 2,300 entries referencing current street slang for drug types, the drug trade, drug cost and quantities, and drug use (ONDCP, "Street Terms").

Drugs are commonly classified as belonging in one of the following groups:

- Central nervous system depressants (alcohol, barbiturates, tranquilizers)
- Central nervous system stimulants (cocaine, amphetamines, methamphetamine)
- Narcotic analgesics (heroin, codeine, methadone, meperidine [Demerol], OxyContin)
- Hallucinogens (LSD, PCP [angel dust], peyote, psilocybin, mescaline, DMT, AMT, DXM, and Foxy)
- Cannabis (marijuana, hashish, hash oil)
- Inhalants (hobby model glue, cleaning solvents, lighter fluid, aerosols)

Drugs can be classified as depressants, stimulants, narcotics, hallucinogens, cannabis, or inhalants.

Stimulants and depressants are controlled under the Drug Abuse Control Amendments to the Federal Food, Drug and Cosmetic Act (U.S. Code Title 21).

The most commonly observed drugs on the street, in possession of users, and seized in drug raids are cocaine, codeine, crack, heroin, marijuana, morphine, and opium. Arrest for possession or use of marijuana is the most frequent drug arrest.

Figure 18.1 provides a threat matrix for five commonly encountered drugs including the source and transit countries, primary entry points into the United States, and domestic wholesale and retail price ranges.

Powder Cocaine and Crack

Cocaine and its derivative, crack, are major problems for law enforcement officers, with crack consistently being ranked as the drug with the most serious consequences (*Pulse Check*, p.9). **Crack,** also called *rock* or *crack rock,* is

National Drug Threat Assessment 2005: Threat Matrix

Overall Key Findings

• Mexican criminal groups exert more influence over drug trafficking in the United States than any other group. Mexican criminal groups smuggle most of the cocaine available in domestic drug markets into the country. Moreover, Mexican criminal groups produce and subsequently smuggle into the country much of the heroin, marijuana, and methamphetamine available in the U.S. drug markets.

• Mexican drug trafficking organizations (DTOs) appear to be gaining control of a larger percentage of the cocaine smuggled into the United States. The estimated percentage of cocaine smuggled into the United States via the Mexico–Central America corridor increased sharply from 72 percent in 2002 to 77 percent in 2003, and preliminary data indicate that the percentage may be higher than 90 percent for 2004.

• Domestic drug markets appear to be increasingly supplied with methamphetamine produced in methamphetamine superlabs in Mexico.

• Production and distribution of ice methamphetamine—a higher purity, more addictive form of methamphetamine—by Mexican criminal groups has increased sharply over the past 2 years in many drug markets.

• Colombian DTOs are increasingly relying on Mexican DTOs and criminal groups to transport South American heroin to the United States much as they rely on Mexican DTOs to transport cocaine.

• The threat posed to the United States by the illegal diversion and abuse of prescription drugs has increased sharply since the mid-1990s and is now among the leading drug threats to the country.

• Law enforcement reporting indicates that transportation of bulk currency out of the United States—primarily overland across the U.S.–Mexico border—is the principal form of money laundering by DTOs.

February 2005

Illicit Drug	Key Findings	Source Locations	Seized En Route/Within U.S. in 2003	Transit Countries	Primary Entry Points Into U.S.
Cocaine	• Powder cocaine use by adolescents decreased since 1999 while cocaine use among adults increased slightly. • Cocaine production declined from 700 metric tons in 2001 to 460 metric tons in 2003. • Increased seizures in Texas indicate it is the state through which most cocaine enters the U.S.	**Foreign:** Colombia, Bolivia, Peru **Domestic:** None	116,898 kg (233,000 kg reportedly available to U.S. markets)	Mexico, Central American countries, Caribbean island nations	Southwest Border (SWB) states (Texas, California, Arizona, New Mexico); Miami/S Florida; New York City (NYC)
Methamphetamine	• Increasing methamphetamine availability in the Northeast region. • Ice availability has increased sharply since 2002. • Production of methamphetamine in Mexico is increasing. • Sharp increase in methamphetamine seizures at and between Arizona ports of entry (POEs).	**Foreign:** Mexico and, to a much lesser extent, Southeast Asia **Domestic:** California	3,845 kg	**Mexican:** Direct from source **SE Asian:** Direct from source	**Mexican:** SWB states (California, Texas, Arizona, and New Mexico) **SE Asian:** California, Hawaii
Marijuana	• Since 1994, marijuana emergency department (ED) mentions and treatment admissions increased. • U.S. marijuana production increasing partly because of increased involvement by U.S.-based Mexican DTOs. • Size of marijuana shipments from Canada increased.	**Foreign:** Mexico, Colombia, Canada, Jamaica **Domestic:** California, Appalachia (Tennessee, Kentucky), Hawaii, Pacific Northwest (Washington, Oregon)	1,225,000 kg (seizures in Texas, Arizona, California, and New Mexico account for 1,139,000 kg)	**Mexican:** Direct from source **Colombian:** Mexico, Caribbean island nations **Canadian:** Direct from source **Jamaican:** Caribbean island nations	**Mexican:** SWB states (primarily Texas and Arizona followed by California and New Mexico) **Colombian:** Miami/S Florida, SWB states, New York City **Canadian:** Northern Border states **Jamaican:** Miami/S Florida, New York City
Heroin	• Heroin treatment admissions increased each year since 1992. • Potential worldwide heroin production increased in 2002, 2003, and 2004 primarily because of increased production in Afghanistan. • Sharp increase in South American heroin seizures along Southwest Border.	Mexico, Colombia, Southeast Asia (Burma, Laos, Thailand); Southwest Asia (Afghanistan, Pakistan)	2,361.8 kg	**Mexican (MX):** Direct from source **South American (SA):** Direct from source, Central/South American countries, Caribbean island nations, Mexico **Southeast Asian (SEA):** China, SE Asian countries, Taiwan, Hong Kong, Canada **Southwest Asian (SWA):** European and Central Asian countries, Canada	**MX:** SWB states (primarily California and Texas followed by Arizona and New Mexico) **SA:** Miami/S Florida, NYC, Newark, SWB states (primarily Texas) **SEA:** NYC, Los Angeles, Northern Border states (Washington, Michigan, New York) **SWA:** NYC, Chicago, Detroit, Atlanta, Washington, D.C.
MDMA	• MDMA availability has decreased since 2001. • More adolescents perceive risk in using MDMA. • Decrease in MDMA smuggled directly to the U.S. from source areas. Asian DTOs increasingly are involved in MDMA trafficking and may become the primary domestic suppliers.	**Foreign:** Netherlands, Belgium (also Poland, Germany, Canada, Latin America) **Domestic:** Limited	1,319,492 du	Western European countries, Canada, Mexico, Dominican Republic	New York City, Newark, Miami, Los Angeles (via international airports); Northern Border states (New York, Washington), Texas

continued

Figure 18.1

Threat matrix for cocaine, methamphetamine, marijuana, heroin, and MDMA

Source: National Drug Threat Assessment 2005: Threat Matrix. Washington, DC: National Drug Intelligence Center, February 2005b. (Product No. 2005-Q0317-006)

produced by mixing cocaine with baking soda and water, heating the solution in a pan, and then drying and splitting the substance into pellet-size bits or chunks (Figure 18.2). Crack is generally less expensive than powder cocaine.

Crack is most often smoked in a glass pipe and has ten times the impact of cocaine. It is described as "cocaine intensified or amplified" in terms of its effects on the human body. The intense high produced by crack is usually followed by a severe depression, or "crash," and a deep craving for more of the drug. It is more addictive than cocaine, at a much earlier stage of use, sometimes after the first use. Some users "space-base" the drug; that is, they lace it with PCP or other drugs.

PCP causes out-of-control behavior, an added hazard to the already dangerous effects of crack itself.

For the past two decades the cocaine supply in the United States has been controlled by the Colombian Medellin and Cali mafias. The U.S./Mexico border is the primary point of entry for cocaine into the United States, with an estimated 77 percent of the national supply arriving via the Mexico–Central America corridor.

Heroin

Heroin, a commonly abused narcotic, is synthesized from morphine and is up to ten times more powerful in

Primary Markets and Principal Suppliers	Wholesale Price Range in the U.S.	Principal Retailers	Retail Price Range in the U.S.	Projections
Atlanta: Mexican, Colombian, Dominican **Chicago:** Mexican, Colombian **Houston:** Mexican, Colombian, Dominican, Jamaican **Los Angeles:** Mexican **Miami:** Colombian, Haitian **New York:** Colombian, Dominican, Mexican	$13,000-$30,000 per kg (powder)	African American, Hispanic street gangs; African American, Caucasian, Cuban, Dominican, Haitian, and Puerto Rican independent dealers and criminal groups	$25-$110 per gram (powder) $10-$100 per rock (crack)	• Rates of cocaine use among adolescents likely will continue to decline. • Continued reduction of cocaine production in Colombia and interdiction of cocaine shipments in the transit zone may result in worldwide reductions of retail cocaine availability.
Los Angeles: Mexican, outlaw motorcycle gangs (OMGs) **Phoenix:** Mexican **San Diego:** Mexican **San Francisco:** Mexican (Hawaiian, Filipino, and Asian DTOs distribute ice)	$3,500-$99,000 per kg* (powder); $13,200-$154,000 per kg* (ice) *normally sold in pound quantities: $1,600-$45,000 per pound (powder); $6,000-$70,000 per lb (ice)	Mexican, Caucasian, and Asian criminal groups; Caucasian independent dealers; Asian and Hispanic street gangs; OMGs	$20-$300 per gram (powder) $60-$700 per gram (ice)	• Increases in foreign and domestic production should raise domestic methamphetamine availability. • Production and distribution of ice by Mexican criminal groups is likely to increase.
Chicago: Mexican **Dallas/Houston:** Mexican **Los Angeles/San Diego:** Mexican, Jamaican; street gangs **Miami:** Hispanic, Haitian, African American **New York:** Jamaican, Mexican **Phoenix/Tucson:** Mexican, Jamaican **Seattle:** Caucasian, Hispanic, Vietnamese, OMGs	$770-$4,400 per kg* (commercial-grade); $1,980-$13,200 per kg* (sinsemilla) *normally sold in pound quantities: $350-$2,000 per lb (commercial-grade); $900-$6,000 per lb (sinsemilla)	Caucasian, Jamaican, African American, Hispanic, Asian, and Native American local independent dealers; African American and Hispanic street gangs; Jamaican, Mexican, and Asian criminal groups; OMGs; prison gangs	$5-$50 per gram $2-$10 per joint	• As DTOs continue to expand large-scale domestic cultivation operations, overall marijuana production in the U.S. will increase. • Expansion of cannabis cultivation on public lands may increase the threat of violence against unsuspecting passersby.
Chicago: Colombian (SA), Mexican (MX), Nigerian (SEA, SWA) **Los Angeles:** Mexican **New York:** Colombian, Dominican, Mexican, Chinese, Nigerian, Pakistani	**MX:** $18,000-$50,000 per kg **SA:** $52,000-$90,000 per kg **SEA:** $40,000-$80,000 per kg **SWA:** $60,000-$70,000 per kg	African American (MX, SA), Asian (SEA, SWA), Caucasian (SA), Colombian (SA), Dominican (SA), Guatemalan (MX), Honduran (MX), Mexican (MX), Puerto Rican (SA) criminal groups; African American (MX, SA, SEA, SWA), Hispanic (MX, SA, SEA, SWA) street gangs	$10 per dose (approximately 50-100 mg)	• Demand for heroin will remain lower than for other major drugs. • The increase in worldwide heroin production is unlikely to cause an increase in heroin availability in the U.S. because the increase is mostly attributed to Southwest Asian heroin, which is typically destined for Asian and European drug markets.
Los Angeles: Israeli, Russian, Asian **Miami:** Russian, Israeli, Eastern European, Dominican (also Colombian, Caucasian) **New York:** Israeli, Russian, (also Asian, Eastern European, Dominican, Colombian, OMGs, Traditional Organized Crime [TOC] groups)	$4-$20 per du (1,000 du lots)	Caucasian independent dealers; African American, Asian, and Hispanic street gangs; OMGs; prison gangs	$6-$50 per du	• MDMA abuse likely to continue declining among all age groups. • MDMA smuggling across the Northern Border may increase as MDMA trafficking organizations avoid transporting the MDMA directly to the U.S. by first transporting the drug to Canada.

Figure 18.1
Continued

© Mark Richards/PhotoEdit

Figure 18.2
A shoebox found during a drug raid contains 3 large chunks of crack wrapped in plastic. Rock cocaine, more commonly known as *crack*, is much less expensive than powder cocaine and has ten times the impact.

its effects. It is physically addictive and relatively expensive. Heroin can be injected, smoked, or snorted, with intravenous injection producing the greatest intensity and most rapid onset of euphoria, usually within 7 or 8 seconds (Figure 18.3). Heroin that is sniffed or smoked takes longer to enter the bloodstream (10 to 15 minutes), but these methods have increased in popularity due to the availability of high-purity heroin and the growing fear of sharing needles (Lloyd).

Marijuana

Marijuana is the most widely available and most commonly used illicit drug in the United States, with 14.6 million current users (6.2 percent of the population) (*Nation's Youth*, 2004). It is variously classified a **narcotic,**[1] a **depressant,**[2] and a **halluconogen,**[3] and street

names include grass, pot, dope, joint, herb, Mary Jane, mj, reefer, and weed. Its use was outlawed by the Federal Marijuana Tax Act of 1927.

Marijuana is the most controversial of the illicit drugs, and a wide spectrum of opinion exists regarding its harmfulness. Some feel it should be legalized; others think it is a very dangerous drug. Many opponents of legalizing marijuana contend that it is a "gateway" drug, exposing new and curious experimenters to a fairly benign drug that will eventually lead them to explore other, "harder" chemical substances. Whether marijuana users progress to hard narcotics or other controlled substances has not been thoroughly researched. The vast majority of hard-narcotics users once used marijuana, but how many marijuana users proceed to hard drugs is unknown.

In the never-ending quest to enhance their high, some users lace marijuana with other substances, including PCP, cocaine, and even embalming fluid, or formaldehyde, stolen from funeral homes or university labs. Marijuana laced with PCP or embalming fluid, called "wet" marijuana, will likely cause hallucinations, euphoria, and, sometimes, panic or violence.

Mexican commercial-grade marijuana is the most common variety, but "BC Bud," marijuana from British Columbia, generally has a higher concentration of the active substance tetrahydrocannabinol (THC), and thus greater potency, and has become more sought after (*Pulse Check*, p.9). According to the *National Drug Threat Assessment* (2005a, p.vii), domestic production of marijuana has increased, in part because more U.S.-based Mexican criminal groups are setting up large-scale cultivation operations, principally in the Pacific and Appalachian states.

Large quantities of marijuana are being grown hydroponically indoors, often in abandoned barns or other buildings in rural areas. Such controlled cultivation increases marijuana potency by three to ten times, which increases its value and thus the growers' profits. Known as **sinsemilla,** homegrown marijuana has become extremely popular, and indoor marijuana-growing operations have proliferated, domestically and abroad. For example, the number of indoor marijuana-growing operations in Ontario increased by an estimated 250 percent from 2000 to 2002, with as many as 15,000 operations active throughout the province in 2002 (La Barge and Noakes, p.28).

Methamphetamine

Methamphetamine, identified as an *emerging* drug threat in past revisions of this book, is now firmly entrenched as a major U.S. drug problem that is only getting bigger, with some sources contending that it is on a trajectory to overtake crack cocaine as the nation's most dangerous drug (Thompson, p.2). Methamphetamine is a highly addictive synthetic stimulant that looks like cocaine but is made from toxic chemicals,

---

[1] Narcotic: a drug that is physically and psychologically addicting; examples include heroin, morphine, codeine, and cocaine.
[2] Depressant: a drug that reduces restlessness and emotional tension and induces sleep; most common are the barbiturates.
[3] Hallucinogen: a mind-expanding drug.

Figure 18.3
A heroin addict shooting up. Once a person is addicted, it is extremely difficult for him or her to quit using drugs without special assistance. A high percentage of addicts eventually return to their drug habit, their familiar settings, and their old associates in drug abuse.

© Scott Houston/CORBIS

such as drain cleaner, paint thinner, and other easily obtained OTC products, including cold medications containing pseudoephedrine.

Concocting **crank,** a street name for methamphetamine, is relatively simple and inexpensive. Typical meth users are high school and college students and working-class white men and women, although it is gaining popularity among New York City's and Miami's gay populations and club hoppers (Simon). A **tweaker** is a methamphetamine addict; a **cook** is someone who produces the drug.

The most common form is powder meth, which is usually injected or snorted but can also be ingested orally or smoked. Other forms include ice meth, which resembles shards of ice, is usually smoked, and is highly pure and very addictive; and methamphetamine tablets, commonly the size of a pencil eraser, which is typically ingested orally or smoked, but it can also be crushed and snorted or mixed with water and injected (*National Drug Threat,* 2005a, p.27).

Many sources report the particularly devastating effect meth is having on America's rural communities, where much of the production and abuse occurs and where law enforcement and public health officials lack adequate resources to effectively address the growing problems. For example, the average tweaker in Nebraska commits approximately 60 crimes a year to support his/her habit, a rate that translates into hundreds of crimes by only a handful of meth addicts, which, for a small community, can severely stretch police resources ("Bill Would Increase," p.1).

Technology Innovations

A chemical additive called GloTell is being used to identify those who handle anhydrous ammonia fertilizer, a common ingredient in the production of methamphetamine. GloTell leaves bright pink stains on the skin and clothes of anyone who comes in contact with the fertilizer and is detectable with a black-light for up to 72 hours after exposure. The additive also impedes the production process of meth by making the drug very difficult to dry. Furthermore, GloTell leaves a pink tinge on the finished product, will leave a pink discoloration on the nose of anyone who snorts the drug and will leave a pink mark on the skin of drug users who inject it ("Additive Might," p.37).

In central Missouri, social workers have noticed that nearly every case of child abuse involves meth (Simon). Zernicke (2005) reports that children in homes where meth is produced and/or consumed face repeated neglect by parents who binge on the drug and then spend several days sleeping off the high. Furthermore, children living in meth lab homes commonly test positive for the drug because of their exposure to and inadvertent inhalation of the fumes (Wuestewald and Adcock, "Methamphetamine," p.3).

Club Drugs

Club drugs are those drugs commonly found at **raves,** "dance parties that feature fast-paced, repetitive electronic music and accompanying light shows. . . . Rave culture also entails the use of a range of licit and illicit drugs" (Scott, p.1). According to Valdez (p.74): "Gangs control much of the flow of dangerous recreational drugs at raves." Although tobacco and alcohol are the most common substances found at the club scene, other substances such as Ecstasy, Rohypnol, GHB, and LSD have gained popularity with young people. Methamphetamine has also been increasingly used at raves.

Ecstasy 3,4-Methylenedioxymethylamphetamine (**MDMA**), known more commonly as **Ecstasy** or XTC, is a powerful stimulant derivative of amphetamine, or speed. MDMA is considered a moderate threat in the United States, with reported levels of availability and abuse trending downward (*National Drug Threat*, 2005a, p.83). Increased interdiction efforts and the dismantling of large MDMA trafficking organizations are credited as the major reasons for decreased use and availability.

Rohypnol A second club drug that has made news in the past is the "date-rape" drug, Rohypnol, also known as "roofies." Available by prescription outside of the United States, Rohypnol is a central nervous system depressant ten times more potent than Valium. The drug by itself can produce extreme lethargy and significant reduction in the brain's recall ability. Combined with alcohol, it causes memory loss, blackouts, and disinhibition. Because Rohypnol was originally colorless, odorless, and tasteless, it became used as a way to facilitate sexual assault, hence the tag "date-rape drug." Once it was learned that Rohypnol was being slipped into unwary victims' drinks as an aid for committing sexual assault, the manufacturer of the drug reformulated it to increase its detectability in clear fluid and to retard its dissolution rate. However, it is still used by teenagers and young adults as an "alcohol extender" and disinhibitory agent (*Countering the Spread*, 2005).

GHB Another drug used to commit sexual assault is gamma-hydroxybutyric acid, or GHB, a colorless, odorless, slightly salty liquid or white powder. It is taken orally and costs $5 to $20 per dose (capful or ounce). Investigating cases involving GHB may be very challenging, and investigators have started referring to it as a "stealth drug" because of the difficulty in detecting its use. Because GHB causes unconsciousness, victims may be unable to provide much useful information to investigators regarding any attack that may have occurred following ingestion of the drug.

Ketamine A prescription general anesthetic primarily marketed for veterinary use, ketamine, or "special K," is sold as both a liquid and a powder. In humans it causes some physical effects similar to PCP and visual effects like LSD (*Countering the Spread*, 2005). At low dosage,

ketamine impairs attention, learning ability, and memory. At higher doses, it can produce delirium, impaired motor function, high blood pressure, depression, and potentially fatal respiratory problems (*Community Drug Alert*, 2004). Its amnesiac effects have reportedly led to its use as a date-rape drug.

LSD LSD (lysergic acid diethylamide), a Schedule I Controlled Substance with severe penalties for possession and use, is a potent hallucinogen derived from lysergic acid, a fungus that grows on rye and other grains. Often referred to as *acid* on the club scene, it is clandestinely manufactured in relatively professional laboratory settings, as some chemistry background and a working knowledge of laboratory control are generally necessary to safely and successfully synthesize the drug. The initial synthesis produces a crystalline powder, which is then reduced to a liquid and placed onto blotting paper. LSD can also be sold in tablet or capsule form (*Community Drug Alert*, 2004).

2C-B or Nexus An emerging drug threat is 2C-B, also known as Nexus, an illicit, synthetic, Schedule I hallucinogen. The effects of the drug vary based on dosage, with a small increase in dose capable of producing a radically different and unpredictable, potentially violent, reaction. In low doses (4 mg), the effects resemble those of MDMA; higher doses (20–30+ mg) produce extremely frightening, LSD-type hallucinations and morbid delusions (*2C-B Reappears*, p.4). Some users combine 2C-B with other club drugs, with a 2C-B + MDMA combination referred to as a "party pack," and 2C-B mixed with LSD called a "banana split."

Prescription Drugs

Prescription drug abuse has become a nationwide epidemic, representing 25 to 30 percent of the overall drug problem in the United States (Burke, p.17). Pain relievers, such as Vicodin, Percodan, Percocet, and OxyContin, top the list of abused prescription drugs. Other commonly abused prescription drugs include tranquilizers such as Xanax and Valium, stimulants, and Viagra.

Prescription drug diversion occurs by faking, forging, or altering a prescription; obtaining bogus prescriptions from criminal medical practitioners; or buying drugs diverted from health care facilities by personnel. Pharmacy thefts are increasing nationwide to feed the growing demand for prescription drugs. The rising cost of prescription drugs has also enticed senior citizens to join in the diversion and sell their prescriptions, with "pill ladies" now a common street term for elderly women who engage in this type of illegal conduct (Schanlaub, "A Prescription," p.96). Prescription drugs are also obtained through a practice called *doctor shopping*. A doctor shopper will visit multiple health care providers as a "new patient" or "visiting from out of town," exaggerate or feign medical problems, particularly difficult-to-diagnose ones such as lower back pain or migraines, and seek a prescription (Gibbs and Haddox, p.24).

Frequently involved in prescription fraud are narcotics, stimulants, barbiturates, benzodiazepines, tranquilizers, and other psychoactive substances manufactured for use in legitimate medical treatment. Law enforcement officers spend a significant amount of time investigating cases involving prescription fraud, many of which also involve insurance, Medicare, or Medicaid fraud.

OxyContin OxyContin, a pain medication derived from opium with heroin-like effects, is the number-one prescribed Schedule II narcotic in the United States (Schanlaub, "A Prescription," p.93). Used in the treatment of pain related to cancer and other debilitating diseases, OxyContin is not popular for abusers in its intended long-acting, time-release, swallowed-whole form. Instead, abusers chew it up and swallow the pieces, melt it down to inject intravenously, or crush the tablet and snort it (Burke, p.17). Taking an 80-mg OxyContin tablet in any of these three ways produces an effect similar to ingesting 16 Percocet at one time.

Inhalants

While many drugs have shown steady or declining numbers of users over the past few years, inhalants are one class of drug that has demonstrated clear evidence of increased use during 2004, particularly among eighth graders (Johnston et al., p.4). Inhalants are second only to marijuana in terms of the number of youths who use illicit drugs. The age at which youths first try inhalants is also younger than for any other substances, with reports of six year olds using the drug (Creighton, p.34).

More than 1,000 household and commercial products can be inhaled to produce a high: adhesives, aerosols, anesthetics, cleaning agents, gases, and solvents. Methods used to inhale include sniffing or snorting the inhalant directly from the container, *huffing* the chemical from a saturated piece of cloth held firm to the nose and mouth, and *bagging* the inhalant by spraying or pouring it into a plastic or paper bag and holding the opening over the nose and mouth.

Khat

Khat (pronounced "cot"), a natural narcotic whose primary psychoactive ingredients are chemically similar to amphetamines, is a relative newcomer to the United States drug scene but is well known in eastern African and southern Middle Eastern countries, some of which consider it a legitimate and quite profitable export (Crenshaw and Burke, p.10). The drug is harvested from the leaves of the khat tree. Users either chew the leaves or smoke the powder obtained from dried leaves. Cathinone, one of the main chemicals in khat, is a Schedule I narcotic in the United States and, as such, is regulated by law. Observers note that the rising use of khat in the United States appears to coincide with the increased numbers of

immigrants coming from eastern African and Middle Eastern countries. It is legal in some of those nations, and many immigrants are unaware of khat's illegal status in this country (Crenshaw and Burke, p.12).

Over-the-Counter (OTC) Drugs

Some teens are turning to legal **OTC drugs** for their highs, mistakenly assuming that if something is legal and readily available, it can't be dangerous, or at least not deadly. Youths have their own language to describe the methods used to get these "legal highs." Drinking bottles of cough syrup, such as Robitussin DM, to get high is called **robotripping. Skittling,** so named because the pills resemble small, red pieces of Skittles candy, is ingesting high doses of Coricidin Cough and Cold ("Triple C") tablets. Perhaps the riskiest and most hazardous practice of all is **pharming**—simply rifling through the family medicine cabinet for pills, both OTC and prescription, combining everything in a bowl, scooping out and ingesting a handful, and waiting to see what happens.

OTC drugs are taken in excessive quantities for their psychoactive effects and fall into three general categories: uppers, downers, and all-arounders (Garrett, p.35). The most popular upper is pseudoephedrine, a main ingredient in nasal decongestants such as Sudafed (Garrett, p.36). In the downer category, Benadryl Allergy formula is a top choice (Garrett, p.37). The biggest all-arounder is dextromethorphan, also called DXM or Dex, a primary ingredient in cough and cold medicines. DXM, often purchased over the Internet, has been linked to numerous overdose deaths during the past few years. Investigations following these deaths often reveal that the drug is being used quite commonly among other young people in the community.

The fact that these drugs are legal places law enforcement in a quandary and requires a more proactive approach to the problem, such as educating youths and their parents and networking with professional organizations such as the American Pharmacists Association, public health departments, and school administrations (Garrett, p.43).

Other Narcotics and Drugs

Designer drugs are so named because they can be created by adding to or omitting something from an existing drug. In many instances the primary drug is not illegal. The illicit drugs are called **analogs** of the drug from which they are created—for example, meperidine analog or mescaline analog. These drugs may cause the muscles to stiffen and give the appearance of someone suffering from Parkinson's disease. Because designer drugs are difficult for amateurs to manufacture, they are high-profit drugs for dealers. Due to their complex natures, these drugs must be submitted to a laboratory for analysis.

Table 18.1 summarizes the various narcotics and dangerous drugs. Pay special attention to each drug's

Table 18.1 / **Summary of Controlled Substances**

Drug	Trade or Other Names	Usual Methods of Administration
Narcotics		
Opium	Dover's powder, paregoric, Parepectolin	Oral, smoked
Morphine	Morphine, pectoral syrup	Oral, smoked, injected
Codeine	Tylenol with Codeine, Empirin Compound with Codeine, Robitussin A-C	Oral, injected
Heroin	Diacetylmorphine, horse, smack	Injected, sniffed, smoked
Hydromorphone	Dilaudid	Oral, injected
Meperidine (pethidine)	Demerol, Merpergan	Oral, injected
Methadone	Dolophine, methadone, Methadose	Oral, injected
Other narcotics	LAAM, Leritine, Numorphan, Percodan, Tussionex, Fentanyl, Darvon, Talwin, Lomotil*	Oral, injected
Depressants		
Chloral hydrate	Noctec, Somnos	Oral
Barbiturates	Phenobarbital, Tuinal, Amytal, Nembutal, Seconal, Lotusate	Oral
Benzodiazepines	Ativan, Azene, Clonopin, Dalmane, diazepam, Librium, Xanax, Serax, Tranxene, Valium, Verstran, Halcion, Paxipam, Restoril	Oral
Methaqualone	Quaalude	Oral
Gluethimide	Doriden	Oral
Other depressants	Equanil, Miltown, Noludar, Placidyl, Valmid	Oral
Stimulants		
Cocaine*	Coke, flake, snow	Sniffed, smoked, injected
Amphetamines	Biphetamine, Delcobese, Desoxyn, Dexedrine, Mediatric	Oral, injected
Phenmetrazine	Preludin	Oral, injected
Methylphenidate	Ritalin	Oral, injected
Other stimulants	Adipex, Bacarate, Cylert, Didrex, Ionamin, Plegine, Pre-Sate, Sanorex, Tenuate, Tepanil, Voranil	Oral, injected
Hallucinogens		
LSD	Acid, microdot	Oral
Mescaline and peyote	Mesc, buttons, cactus	Oral
Amphetamine variants	2,5-DMA, PMA, STP, MDA, MDMA, TMA, DOM, DOB	Oral, injected
Phencyclidine	PCP, angel dust, hog	Smoked, oral, injected
Phencyclidine analogs	PCE, PCP, TCP	Smoked, oral, injected
Other hallucinogens	Bufotenine, Ibogaine, DMT, DET, psilocybin, Psilocyn	Oral, injected, smoked, sniffed
Cannabis		
Marijuana	Pot, Acapulco gold, grass, reefer, sinsemilla, Thai sticks	Smoked, oral
Tetrahydrocannabinol	THC	Smoked, oral
Hashish	Hash	Smoked, oral
Hashish oil	Hash oil	Smoked, oral

*Designated a narcotic under the CSA (Controlled Substance Act).

continued

Table 18.1 / **Continued**

Possible Effects	Effects of Overdose	Withdrawal Syndrome
Euphoria, drowsiness, respiratory depression, constricted pupils, nausea	Slow and shallow breathing, clammy skin, convulsions, coma, possible death	Watery eyes, runny nose, yawning, loss of appetite, irritability, tremors, panic, chills and sweating, cramps, nausea
Slurred speech, disorientation, drunken behavior without odor of alcohol	Shallow respiration, clammy skin, dilated pupils, weak and rapid pulse, coma, possible death	Anxiety, insomnia, tremors, delirium, convulsions, possible death
Increased alertness, excitation, euphoria, increased pulse rate and blood pressure, insomnia, loss of appetite	Agitation, increase in body temperature, hallucinations, convulsions, possible death	Apathy, long periods of sleep, irritability, depression, disorientation
Illusions and hallucinations, poor perception of time and distance	Longer, more-intense "trip" episodes, psychosis, possible death	Withdrawal syndrome not reported
Euphoria, relaxed inhibitions, increased appetite, disoriented behavior	Fatigue, paranoia, possible psychosis	Insomnia, hyperactivity and decreased appetite occasionally reported

effects. This information is important in investigating the sale and use of drugs.

Investigating Illegal Possession or Use of Controlled Substances

If you observe someone using a narcotic or other dangerous drug, you may arrest the person and seize the drugs as evidence. The arrested person may be searched incidental to the arrest. If a vehicle is involved but the suspect was not in the vehicle, post a guard at the vehicle or impound it. Drugs found on a person during a legally conducted search for other crimes may also be seized, and additional charges may be made.

Take the suspect into custody quickly. Then make sure the suspect does not dispose of the drugs by swallowing them, putting them between car seat cushions, or placing them in other convenient hiding places. While in custody, the suspect may experience withdrawal pains and other bodily ills that can create special problems for the arresting officers.

Recognizing the Drug Addict: Drug-Recognition Experts

In drug crimes the victims are implicated; thus, they usually avoid contact with the police, conspiring with the sellers to remain undetected. If apprehended and faced with charges, however, the drug addict may be willing to work with the police. Therefore, many drug investigations involve identifying those who buy drugs illegally and who can thus provide information about sources of supply.

Congress has defined a **drug addict** as "any person who habitually uses any habit-forming narcotic drug so as to endanger the public morals, health, safety or welfare, or who is or has been so far addicted to the use of habit-forming narcotic drugs as to have lost the power of self-control with reference to the addiction." Drug addiction is a progressive disease. The victim uses increased amounts of the same drug or harder drugs. Each increase in habit has a corresponding cost increase—thus the frequent necessity for committing crime. In addition, as the addiction increases, the ability to control the habit decreases. Drug addicts become unfit for employment as their mental, emotional, and physical condition deteriorates. Because addicts often help each other obtain drugs, exercise extreme caution when addicts are in jail, to prevent visitors from getting drugs to them.

Police officers are adept at recognizing and legally charging individuals who are under the influence of alcohol, especially if they are driving. They are not always so able to recognize drug-impaired individuals. However, Drug Evaluation Classification (DEC) programs, more commonly known as Drug Recognition Expert (DRE) programs, have demonstrated international success in detecting and deterring drug-impaired driving. The International Association of Chiefs of Police (IACP) sets DRE program guidelines, and the National Highway Traffic Safety Administration (NHTSA) supports the program's operation (Hayes, p.103).

If an officer suspects a driver is impaired, he begins his assessment by using the standard field sobriety tests. If impairment is noticeable, the subject is given a breath test. If the blood alcohol reading is inconsistent with the perceived impairment, a DRE evaluates the individual's appearance, performance on psychological tests, eyes, and vital signs.

The initial interview includes questions about the subject's behavior; response to being stopped; attitude and demeanor; speech patterns; and possible injury, sickness, or physical problems. Physical evidence such as smoking paraphernalia, injection-related material, and needle marks on the subject is sought.

The physical examination includes an eye examination, an improved walk-and-turn test, the Rhomberg Standing Balance test, and the one-leg stand test, as well as the finger-to-nose test. Also tested are vital signs (blood pressure, pulse rate, and temperature) and muscle rigidity. If warranted, a toxicological examination is also conducted.

A pupilometer allows officers to inexpensively conduct sobriety checks in the field. This lightweight, hand-held binocular-type instrument measures absolute pupil dynamics to presumptively detect alcohol, drugs, inhalants, or fatigue in a suspect. If the pass/fail indicators show green, the person is not under the influence of any substances. Yellow suggests the person may be under the influence and that further testing is warranted. Red indicates the person is definitely under the influence. The name of the potential substance appears next to the pass/fail indicator along with the percentage probability level.

Physical Evidence of Possession or Use of Controlled Substances

The suspect's clothing may conceal drugs, which have been found in neckties, shirt collars, coat and pants linings and seams, shoe tongues, soles of shoes or slippers, hat or cap bands, and, naturally, pockets. Suspects are usually strip-searched because drugs can be concealed in any body opening including the rectum or vagina, in the hair, behind the ears, and between the toes. Drugs can also be attached to the body with tape.

Objects in the suspect's possession can also contain drugs, depending on the suspect's ingenuity. Cigarette cases, lighters, holders, and packages, as well as chewing-gum wrappers, fountain pens, jewelry, eyeglass cases, lockets, pencil erasers, and many other objects can conceal illegal drugs.

Vehicles have innumerable hiding places, including under seat covers; behind cushions or seats; in heater pipes, hubcaps, or glove compartments; under floor mats; in false auto batteries and oil filters; and in secret compartments devised for great amounts of smuggled drugs. Put the vehicle on a hoist and examine the undercarriage.

In a residence or building, do not give the suspect a chance to flush the toilet or turn on the water in a sink to destroy evidence. Look for drugs in drawer bottoms, in fuse boxes, in bedposts, behind pictures, in tissue boxes, in overhead light fixtures, under rugs and carpets, in and under furniture, and in holes in walls. If you find evidence, attempt to locate the property owner and inform him or her of the arrest. Gather all correspondence addressed to the person arrested if it is not in a mailbox. Obtain rent receipts, utility bills, and other evidence that establishes that the suspect resides at that location.

One initial problem is identifying the suspected substance. As noted earlier, pharmaceutical manuals and physicians' desk manuals provide information needed to identify various drugs. Field tests can be conducted to serve as the basis for a search warrant, but such tests must always be verified by laboratory examination. A residue-detection swab can be used to test surfaces for traces of cocaine. Investigators simply wipe the swab across the area to be tested. If cocaine residue is present, the swab instantly turns color. Individually wrapped in foil packaging, these swabs are easy to carry and to use and have a relatively long shelf life.

If evidence of narcotics or other dangerous drugs is found on an arrested suspect, as a result of a search of the premises or even by accident, immediately place it in a container, label it, and send it to a laboratory. If it is already in a container, leave it there and process the container for fingerprints. Package uncontained drug evidence carefully to avoid a challenge to its integrity as evidence. Use special precautions to avoid contaminating or altering the drugs by exposure to humidity, light, or chemicals.

> Physical evidence of possession or use of controlled substances includes the actual drugs, apparatus associated with their use, the suspect's appearance and behavior, and urine and blood tests.

Often found along with drugs are various types of pipes, syringes, cotton, spoons, medicine droppers, safety pins, razor blades, hypodermic needles, and the like—common components of a drug addict's "outfit" (Figure 18.4). A suspect's general appearance and signs such as dilated pupils, needle marks or razor cuts in the veins, confusion, aggressiveness, watery eyes, runny nose, and profuse perspiration provide additional evidence of drug use. Table 18.2 lists indicators.

To establish that an arrested person is under the influence of drugs, a urine and blood test, a medical examination, and a report of personal observations are used along with an alcoholic or drug-influence test form.

In-Custody Deaths

Hundreds of people die each year in the United States while in police custody, often without any obvious reason or explanation (Ho, p.47). Sometimes the cause is a

Figure 18.4

A collection of drug paraphernalia

© James Shaffer

Table 18.2 / **Indicators of Drug Abuse**

Drug	Physical Evidence	Observable Conditions
Morphine	Burning spoon, candle, hypodermic needle, actual substance	Needle marks, euphoria
Heroin	Burning spoon, candle, hypodermic needle, razor blade, eyedropper, actual substance	Needle marks or razor cuts, euphoria, starry look, constricted pupils, profuse perspiration
Cocaine	White or colorless crystalline powder, hypodermic needle, pipe	Needle marks, dilated pupils, increased heart rate, convulsing
Crack	Pellets, glass pipes, plastic bottle	Depression, euphoria, convulsions
Stimulants	Pills of various shapes and sizes	Restlessness, nervousness, hand tremor, dilated pupils, dry mouth, excessive perspiration
Depressants	Pills of various shapes and sizes	Symptoms resemble those of drunkenness: slurred, indistinct speech and loss of physical coordination
Hallucinogens	Hypodermic needle, eyedropper, spoon, bottle caps, tourniquets, cotton balls, actual substances	Needle marks on inner elbow, extreme emotionalism, noticeable dilation of pupils, often causing persons to wear dark glasses even at night
Marijuana	Roach holder, pipe with a fine screen placed halfway down the bowl, actual substance	Sweet smoke odor; symptoms resemble those of mild intoxication: staring off into space, glassy eyes, semiconsciousness, drowsiness
Methamphetamine	Makeshift laboratory with ingredients present	Violent behavior, paranoia, other psychotic episodes

medical condition; other times it is a consequence of drug use. Most of the time it is a combination of factors.

One serious problem that may be encountered in dealing with drug users is **excited delirium,** which Ho (p.50) describes as "a behavioral condition whereby a person exhibits extremely agitated and noncoherent behavior, elevated temperature, and excessive endurance without fatigue. Excited delirium is often seen in the context of people under the influence of an illicit stimulant substance such as cocaine or in people with a history of mental illness who are not taking their medication properly." He further explains that people in this mental state do not perceive or respond to the brain's signals to calm down before the body collapses. They continue to push past the point of exhaustion, by running, fighting with officers, or resisting against restraints, until their body reaches a potentially fatal medical condition called metabolic acidosis. Only a few minutes in this lethal condition can lead to cardiac arrest and sudden in-custody death (Ho, p.50).

Occasionally, a suspect in a drug case will attempt to hide or destroy evidence by ingesting it, which could lead to an in-custody overdose death. In an effort to avoid arrest, subjects have also been known to swallow entire packages or bags containing drugs, which results in their suffocating or choking to death. The use of restrictive restraint devices and procedures, such as handcuffing subjects behind their back and placing them face-down, can lead to positional asphyxia where

the person suffocates, and the likelihood of this happening increases when the subject is under the influence of an illicit substance (Ho, p.50). According to one study, 53 percent of the people who die suddenly while in police custody have used illicit substances proximal to their collapse (Ho, p.55).

Investigating Illegal Sale and Distribution of Controlled Substances

 ecause addiction depends on drug availability, drug control must be directed toward the supplier. This is often a joint effort among law enforcement agencies at all levels. Drug users and sellers know the local police, so it is difficult to mount undercover or surveillance operations locally. Outsiders are frequently brought in by the police to make buys and arrests. However, local patrol officers are still responsible for investigating drug offenses, because they see the users and sometimes observe drug sales. Actions they take against users can put pressure on sellers because their market is hurt when users are arrested and jailed.

Drug users often become sellers to support their habit. Many such individuals, called **mules,** sell or transport drugs for a regular dealer in return for being assured of a personal drug supply. Whereas some remain in small operations sufficient to support their needs, others see the profit they can make in large operations and go into business on a larger scale. Further, many drug pushers become users—an occupational hazard. This sometimes occurs accidentally as the result of testing the quality of the merchandise over an extended period.

Investigating the illegal sale and distribution of drugs requires all the basic techniques used for other crimes, plus special investigative skills related to the behavior of drug users and sellers, both of whom can be dangerous and unpredictable. An increasing challenge to narcotics investigators is the evolving use of technology by drug traffickers and street dealers. Law enforcement agencies have encountered all types of devices used by drug sellers, ranging from two-way radios and cellular phones to robot planes. One seller of two-way radios stated that drug dealers were his biggest customers. If a radio was confiscated in an arrest, another was immediately purchased. Drug dealers use personal computers, sophisticated encryption systems that even federal agencies have difficulty deciphering, night-vision equipment, police frequency jamming equipment, scanners, and networking systems. The main advantages drug dealers have over government in using technology are the availability of almost unlimited funds and a lack of bureaucratic approval systems.

Other challenges concern the wide variety of drugs, the difficulty faced when trying to identify them under street conditions, and the special types of searches often required to locate minute amounts of drugs that may be hidden ingeniously. Investigators also encounter special problems in finding drugs smuggled across national borders in a variety of ways and in identifying those who transport and distribute them. It takes much time and expense to develop informants and to make a purchase or otherwise discover and confiscate drugs while ensuring that the evidence will stand up in court. In the past few years, international drug lords have benefited from lowered political and economic barriers as well as easy access to sophisticated communications technology that can be frequently changed to evade law enforcement.

 The actual transfer of drugs from the seller to the buyer is the major legal evidence in prosecuting drug-sale cases.

A patrol officer may see a drug transfer by chance or observe it after long surveillance or when an undercover officer makes a planned buy. Some transfers are quite intricate. In one case, a drug seller put drugs on a dog's back, and the dog brought them to the buyer and then returned to the seller with the payment. Even though the seller did not personally hand the drugs to the seller, there was a sale. In other cases, the seller leaves drugs at a predetermined location and picks up payment at another location. Such subterfuge is countered by personal testimony.

If either the buyer or seller throws the drugs away to avoid being caught with them in possession, the drugs can be recovered as abandoned property and taken into custody. If the suspect was seen discarding the drugs, they can be used as evidence.

Narcotics cases begin with a report of suspicious drug activity, a search warrant obtained on information from a reliable informant, or an on-sight observation of a drug buy. Undercover officers and informants then become central figures in obtaining evidence.

On-Sight Arrests

Patrol officers witnessing a suspected drug buy should obtain as complete a description as possible of the persons and vehicles involved (Figure 18.5). There is usually no urgency in making a drug arrest because the seller and buyer continue to meet over time.

If you observe what appears to be a drug buy, you can make a warrantless arrest if you have probable cause. Often, however, it is better to simply observe and gather information.

Probable cause is established through knowledge of the suspect's criminal record, by observing other people making contact with the suspect and finding drugs on them, by knowing of the suspect's past relationships with other drug users or sellers, and through observing

Figure 18.5
Drugs are commonly bought and sold at raves and other events where young people congregate.

actions of the suspect that indicate a drug buy. The courts usually give weight to officers' experience and to their information about the suspect and the circumstances of the arrest, including actions by the suspect before the arrest commonly associated with drug selling.

If probable cause is based on information supplied by an informant, check the information for accuracy against intelligence files. If no prior intelligence information exists, add the facts provided to the file. Check the informant's reliability by asking about other suspects in drug cases. Are these suspects already in the files? Has the informant helped before? How many arrests or convictions were based on the information? You might ask the informant to obtain a small amount of the drug if possible.

Surveillance

Neighborhood residents often know where the drug dealers live or which houses are the crack houses. They are, however, usually reluctant to provide such information to police for fear of retributive consequences. Therefore, it may be necessary to surveil a property to develop evidence of drug dealing activity. Some common indicators of residential drug trafficking are:

- A high volume of foot and/or vehicle traffic to and from a residence at late or unusual hours.
- Periodic visitors who stay at the residence for very brief periods of time.
- Altering the property to maximize privacy with minimal expense, such as covering windows and glass doors with newspaper, tin foil, etc. (*Drugs: A "Municipal,"* p.26).

It is frequently best simply to watch and obtain information if you witness a drug buy. The suspected seller or the location of the buy can then be put under surveillance, an especially important technique in narcotics investigations. Surveillance can provide protection for planned buys, protect the money used to make the buy, provide credibility for the buyer, provide information regarding the seller's contacts, and provide information to establish probable cause for an arrest or search warrant. It is not necessary to make an arrest on the first surveillance. In fact, it is generally advisable to make several surveillances to gather evidence.

Surveillance officers must have patience because many planned drug buys necessitate a long period of surveillance before the actual sale, or bust, is made. The drug dealer is concentrating on making the sale. No sale, no profit. At the same time, the dealer is trying to avoid being "busted." It is essentially a cat-and-mouse game. Drug dealers often feel they are being observed when they are not, and surveillance officers often feel they have been "burned" when they have not. Prearranged signals and communications between surveillance officers and undercover officers are essential

to prevent untimely drug busts. A detailed plan of action is mandatory. The surveillance team must be prepared with adequate equipment, food, and drink for the estimated surveillance period. Surveillance officers should have specialized training and detailed briefing before actual assignment.

Undercover Assignments

Undercover investigations are used more routinely in drug cases than perhaps any other type of criminal investigation. The downside to this common tactic is that drug dealers also know it is routinely used, and they have become fairly adept at sniffing out a "narc." Street dealers are also aware of the restrictions imposed on undercover agents, such as the fact that law enforcement cannot smoke marijuana legally. As a result, undercover narcotics officers have had to develop more convincing ways to fit into the drug culture.

Technology Innovations

An undercover agent might dress a certain way, use certain slang and talk with an accent, or even gargle with beer or hard liquor just before meeting with a dealer. But several new products by Narc-Scent Incorporated are helping undercover officers gain street credibility by giving them the right smell:

The first is a type of incense stick that, when burned, produces a similar odor to that of smoked marijuana. These sticks can be burned inside the narcotics officer's vehicle before or during street buy operations. . . . The smoke can also fill the undercover operative's clothing . . . deceiv[ing] the dealer into believing the buyer is an actual doper. . . .

The second product is a loose weed version of the stick. This product can be rolled into an imitation marijuana cigarette and used in any application as if it were real marijuana. Both products are composed of totally organic ingredients that contain no THC, the chemical that creates the intoxicating effect of marijuana. The proprietary blend produces a smell that will fool even the most experienced cop and criminal. (Haffner, pp.325–326)

Planned Buys Planned buys usually involve working an undercover agent into a group selling or buying drugs or having an informant make the buy. Before using an informant to buy drugs, determine why the person is involved and keep a strict log of his or her activities. Use care in working with drug users as buyers because they are known by the courts to be chronic liars.

The enormous number of drug buys by undercover agents and informants have made drug sellers wary of new customers. Informants typically introduce the undercover officer. Informants are often involved in criminal narcotics as users or sellers and are "turned" by the police for providing information in exchange for lesser charges. The prosecutor's office usually makes the decision to use an informant in this manner. Most people arrested for dealing drugs who are given the option of either going to jail or becoming an informant choose the latter. Police departments should have written policies on the use of informants.

Undercover agents are usually police officers of the investigating agency (in large cities) or of cooperative agencies on the same level of government in an exchange operation or a mutual-aid agreement that provides an exchange of narcotics officers.

If working undercover, be thoroughly conversant with the language of the user and the seller, know the street prices of drugs, and have a tight cover. Talk little and listen much. Observe without being noticed. Also devise an excuse to avoid using the drugs. Work within the seller's system. Drug pushers, like other criminals, tend to develop certain methods for making their sales.

Asking them to change their method can cause suspicion, whereas going along with the system establishes your credibility for subsequent buys. Avoid dangerous situations by insisting you do not want to get into a situation where you could be ripped off, injured, or killed.

Undercover drug buys are carefully planned, witnessed, and conducted so that no charge of entrapment can be made.

Make careful plans before a drug buy. Select a surveillance group and fully brief group members on the signals to use and their specific assignments. Small transmitters are important communications devices for members of the surveillance team. Have alternative plans in case the original plan fails.

Careful preparation includes searching the buyer immediately before the transaction to avoid the defense that drugs were planted on the suspect. Any items on the buyer other than the money are retained at the police station or with other police officers until after the buy.

Prepare the buy money in advance. It must be marked, identified, counted, and recorded by serial number, date, time, and denomination. Have this procedure witnessed by one or more people. The money is not given to the buyer until immediately before the buy. Fluorescent powders can be used, but some drug sellers check money for these powders before making a transaction. All buys should be observed from a location where the movements of both the seller and the buyer can be seen by the surveillance team.

At the meeting, record the seller's description, the vehicles used, telephone numbers called to set up the buy, and observations about the seller's personal statements and habits. If the informant and the undercover officer are both present, the officer makes the buy to protect the informant's identity if an arrest is planned. If no arrest is planned, both the undercover officer and the informant make buys, providing additional evidence.

If several buys are made from the same seller over a period of time, the seller may relax security and include others higher in the organization. Even if this is not the case, the seller usually visits his or her drug source frequently. The route to or the actual location of the supplier can then be put under surveillance. Such an opportunity seldom arises on the first contact because sellers usually devise very clever ruses to cover their tracks.

The three things valued by dealers are the drugs, the money the drugs can bring, and their freedom to do business. In the middle of the triangle is the officer. When both the money—that is, the **flashroll**—and the drugs are present at the same time, the undercover officer faces the greatest danger.

The ability to negotiate is essential for an undercover officer. Almost everything is negotiable in a drug deal. Remaining cool and collected during the actual buy is absolutely necessary. If the situation does not look right or appears to be too dangerous, walk away from the deal; there is always another time and place. Because of the prevalence of weapons in drug trafficking, undercover officers can be in extreme danger, usually alone.

If the buy is successful, an arrest can be made immediately, or a search warrant can be obtained on the basis of the buyer's observation of other drugs on the premises. After the buy, the buyer is searched again and the exact amount of money and drugs on the buyer recorded.

Make two or more buys to avoid the charge of entrapment.

Although police are responsible for investigating narcotics offenses and arresting violators, they are equally responsible for making every reasonable effort to avoid arresting an innocent person. The illegal act involved in the sale should be voluntary, without special urging or persuasion. An agent who knows that a seller is in business and merely asks for, pays for, and receives drugs is not using entrapment. But continued requests for drugs from a person who does not ordinarily sell them *is* entrapment. If there has been more than one voluntary drug transaction, no basis for a defense of entrapment exists.

Stings A **sting,** or **reverse buy,** is a complex operation organized and implemented by undercover agents to apprehend drug dealers and buyers and to deter other users from making drug purchases at a certain location. As with other planned buys, reverse buys are labor intensive and logistically complex and require participating officers to be very well trained (Karchmer, p.257). In a typical reverse buy, a team of officers conducts a street sweep to clear an area of drug dealers, and a second undercover team moves in posing as dealers. A third group of officers is stationed nearby conducting surveillance on the operation, videotaping transactions, and providing ready backup should a deal go awry. A fourth group of uniformed officers waits just outside the perimeter of the reverse buy, ready to arrest those who have just purchased drugs (Karchmer, pp.256–257).

In a sting called Operation Impunity, federal and local drug enforcement officers arrested 93 suspects in an effort to dismantle the operations of drug trafficker Amado Carillo Fuentes. Fuentes was considered Mexico's number-one drug lord until he died in July 1997 while recovering from plastic surgery meant to help him evade law enforcement. The two-year investigation, which ended in the fall of 1999, had the cooperation of the Mexican government and targeted alleged "cell heads" running the drug operations after Fuentes' death.

Narcotics Raids

Raids are another method used to apprehend narcotics dealers. Surveillance frequently provides enough information for obtaining a no-knock search or arrest warrant. Successful narcotics raids are rarely spontaneous; they are planned on the basis of information obtained over an extended period. They can be designed to occur in two, three, or more places simultaneously, not only in the same community but also in other communities and even in other states. The raid itself must be carried out forcefully and swiftly because drugs can easily be destroyed in seconds.

Narcotics raids are often dangerous; therefore, before the raid, gather information about the people involved and the premises where the drugs are located. Also determine how many police officers are needed, the types of weapons needed, and the location of evidence, as discussed in Chapter 7. A November 2004 raid in and around the Boston area, which also included arrests in New Jersey and Arizona, netted nearly 20 suspects who were part of a multistate OxyContin drug ring that involved organized crime figures, violent street gang members, several pharmacists, and a couple of college students (Ellement, 2004). At its peak, the ring generated $160,000 each week from the illegal sale of the drug. Thousands of pills were allegedly diverted from pharmacies with the help of the pharmacists and forged prescription slips.

The effectiveness of raids as a police intervention strategy has been questioned. While raids, if properly planned and executed, may have a desirable effect in the short term, studies have found that such effects typically do not last (Cohen et al., p.257).

Drug Paraphernalia Stores

Another avenue available to investigators concerns paraphernalia shops and their clientele. Such stores fall into two broad categories. "Head shops" sell products that help the end user ingest drugs, such as pipes, syringes, etc. "Cut or vial stores," in contrast, sell adulterants, diluents, and other "office supplies" used by drug organizations in measuring, separating, chemically altering, and packaging mass quantities of drugs that are then distributed to the street dealers (Sheehy and Rosario, p.1). The trail of drug paraphernalia may help investigators track down drug gangs and other major drug distributors.

Online Drug Dealers

One challenge for 21st-century narcotics investigators involves a move from the street corner into cyberspace, as today's pushers are as likely to conduct business online as they are in the park or a back alley (Domash, p.44). Club drugs, prescription narcotics, and ultra-pure forms of DXM, an ingredient found in OTC cough medication, can all be purchased online and shipped directly to the user's home—transactions that are extremely difficult for law enforcement to detect. Online drug dealers commonly try to disguise their activities by posting their available products as some type of legitimate substance.

Clandestine Drug Laboratories

An increase in clandestine drug laboratories has occurred as more emphasis has been placed on reducing illegal foreign drug imports into the United States. For example, the number of clandestine methamphetamine labs seized nationwide by the DEA increased by more than 500 percent from 1994 to 2000, and the figures continued to rise in 2005 (Schanlaub, "Meth Hazards," p.98). An estimated 80 percent of meth is produced in organized "super laboratories," with the remaining 20 percent manufactured in smaller "mom and pop" labs (McEwen and Uchida, p.12).

These laboratories pose serious hazards to law enforcement agencies conducting raids on the premises, including booby traps and assaults from attack dogs or violent drug "cooks" under the influence of their products. In addition, many of the substances, often unidentified or misidentified, are explosive and extremely flammable. Irritants and corrosives, asphyxiants, and nerve toxins also may be encountered. Figure 18.6 lists the toxic, explosive, and hazardous chemicals commonly found in clandestine drug labs.

Typical Chemicals Found in Lab Sites	Common Legitimate Uses	Poison	Flammable	Toxic Vapors	Explosive	Corrosive	Skin Absorption	Common Health Hazards
Acetone	Fingernail polish remover, solvents	X	X	X				Reproductive disorders
Methonol	Brake cleaner fluid, fuel	X	X	X				Blindness, eye damage
Ammonia	Disinfectants	X		X		X	X	Blistering, lung damage
Benzene	Dye, varnishes, lacquers	X	X		X	X	X	Carcinogen, leukemia
Ether	Starter fluid, anesthetic	X	X		X			Respiratory disorders
Freon	Refrigerant, propellants	X		X		X	X	Frostbite, lung damage
Hydriodic acid	Driveway cleaner	X		X		X	X	Burns, thyroid damage
Hydrochloric acid (HCl gas)	Iron ore processing, mining	X		X		X	X	Respiratory, liver damage
Iodine crystals	Antiseptic, catalyst	X	X		X	X		Birth defects, kidney failure
Lithium metal	Lithium batteries	X				X	X	Burns, pulmonary edema
Muriatic acid	Swimming pool cleaners	X		X		X		Burns, toxic vapors
Phosphine gas	Pesticides	X		X			X	Respiratory failure
Pseudoephedrine	Cold medicines	X						Abuse: health damage
Red phosphorus	Matches, fireworks	X	X	X	X			Unstable, flammable
Sodium hydroxide	Drain cleaners, lye	X		X		X	X	Burns, skin ulcers
Sulfuric acid	Battery acid	X		X		X	X	Burns, thyroid damage
Toulene	Paint thinners, solvents	X	X	X	X		X	Fetal damage, pneumonia
Liquid lab waste	None	X	X	X	X	X	X	Unknown long-term effects

Figure 18.6

Toxic, explosive, and hazardous chemicals found in clandestine drug labs

Law Enforcement Technology, May 2005, p.10. Courtesy of the Clandestine Drug Lab Program of the Division of Environmental Health in the Washington State Department of Health.

 Clandestine drug laboratories present physical, chemical, and toxic hazards to law enforcement officers engaged in raids on the premises.

Most clandestine labs produce one or more types of amphetamine, but a few produce club drugs such as Ecstasy, LSD, and GHB (Hanson, 2005b, p.69). The most serious challenge is posed by covert drug labs involved in the manufacture of methamphetamine, the most widely used and clandestinely produced synthetic drug in the United States (Walters, p.32). Meth labs have cropped up across the country, in cities and rural areas, and have been found in private residences, motel rooms, storage units, garages, barns, and even vehicles (Hanson, 2005a, p.8).

Because of their volatility, these labs present a significant threat to public safety. In fact, it is estimated that of all the clandestine drug labs discovered in the United States, 20 percent come to the attention of law enforcement because of fire or explosion (Hanson, 2005a, p.8). Meth labs run out of homes can have a particularly devastating impact on the health of children living there, as 80 percent of children rescued from such environments test positive for toxic levels of meth (Peed, p.1). These children also face increased risk of adverse neurological, respiratory, and dermatological effects caused by exposure to chemicals and stimulants (Wuestewald and Adcock, "Enlisting," p.34).

Table 18.3 outlines the methamphetamine production process and identifies the various hazards generated at each stage.

Identifying a Clandestine Lab

Drug labs can be set up almost anywhere. Smaller operations are more portable and easily moved, making detection more difficult. Clandestine labs tend to share some common characteristics, however, and knowing which signs to watch for can help investigators uncover these dangerous and unlawful operations ("Additive Might," p.37; Hanson, 2005a, pp.10–14):

From the Outside

- Strong chemical odors—may be similar to fingernail polish or cat urine, ammonia, brake cleaner, ether
- Windows blacked out or boarded up from the inside
- Hoses and pipes sticking out under windows or doors, or through holes cut through the side of the structure—for ventilation of fumes
- Exhaust fans running constantly
- Disturbed ground or dead vegetation—may indicate where chemical wastes have been buried or disposed of
- Excessive traffic, with people coming and going at all times of the day and night, usually staying only a short while

On the Inside

- Coffee grinders and blenders with white residue
- Coffee filters with red stains
- Small propane tanks

Table 18.3 / **Methamphetamine Production Process**

Steps in Process	Chemicals Added	Process	Hazards Generated
Cooking Stage			
Initial mixing and heating	Ephedrine, hydriodic acid, red phosphorous	Chemicals are mixed and heated for about 12 hours to form D-meth in an acidic mixture.	Fires, explosions, toxic gas
Straining	None	Mixture is strained through a bed sheet or pillowcase to remove the red phosphorous.	Discarded bed sheets/pillowcases contaminated with red phosphorous and hydriodic acid
Extraction Stage			
Converting to a base	Sodium hydroxide (lye/caustic soda), ice	Sodium hydroxide is added to convert the acidic mixture to a basic one. Ice is then added to cool the resulting exothermic reaction to prevent evaporation or loss of product. After this step, the mixture is transferred to a separatory vessel, most often a 55-gallon drum with a spigot at its base.	Spills
Extracting D-meth	Freon (cooks have been known to use Coleman fuel or other solvents)	Freon is added to aid in the extraction of the D-meth from the sodium hydroxide solution. The Freon will drag the D-meth to the bottom of the vessel, and the clandestine lab cook will drain it off. If another solvent is used, the D-meth base floats to the top because this solvent is lighter than water.	Large amounts of sodium hydroxide waste
Salting Stage			
Salting and drying	Hydrogen chloride gas	When treated with hydrogen chloride gas, the D-meth oil will convert into a white crystalline powder. Presses or mop buckets are used to remove excess Freon.	Discarded solvents, flammable hazards

Information obtained from U.S. Department of Justice, National Drug Intelligence Center. *Hazards of D-Methamphetamine Production,* June 1995.

Source: Tom Manning. "Drug Labs and Endangered Children." *FBI Law Enforcement Bulletin,* July 1999, p. 13.

- Large quantities of acetone, antifreeze, camping fuel, drain cleaner, lithium batteries, matches, plastic baggies, and glass jars
- Large quantities of cold tablets or cough syrup with the ingredient pseudoephedrine
- Thermos bottles and plastic liter soda bottles
- Mixing containers—Pyrex glassware, Corning Ware, crock pots, large metal pots
- Strips of bed linens for filtering liquid drug mixtures
- Excessive clutter and generally filthy living conditions

Because hotel rooms are a commonly used site for those planning to set up "clan" (clandestine) labs, some law enforcement agencies are training hotel managers and employees on the dangers such labs pose and ways to identify suspected "meth cooks." DEA agents profile a typical meth cook as white, trashy looking, with rotting teeth (the meth cook look) and poor-quality tattoos, and with a local address on his identification. Because the chemicals, such as Drano, used in the production are corrosive and the cooks usually do not get all of them out before using the drug, they suffer corrosion on their teeth and skin.

Entering a Clandestine Drug Lab

When encountering a drug lab or its components, do not use matches, lighters, or items that could ignite fumes. Do not turn switches on or off, because the electric connection could produce sparks and cause an explosion. Do not taste, smell, or touch any substance, and check for booby traps before moving or touching containers.

The various health and safety hazards encountered at a clandestine drug lab necessitate that only properly trained and equipped personnel proceed onto the site. According to Schanlaub ("Meth Hazards," p.100): "The expert recommendation is that any personnel that are to be entering a suspect building should enter only with self-contained breathing apparatus and complete skin protection unless it is known that the lab has not been in recent operation and that all of the chemicals are under control." A safety program developed by the DEA and the California Bureau of Narcotics Enforcement following recommendations by the Occupational Safety and Health Administration and the National Institute for Occupational Safety and Health has four basic elements: policies and procedures, equipment and protective clothing, training, and medical monitoring.

Policies and procedures are aimed at ensuring officer safety through a certification process. Only certified individuals are allowed to seize, process, and dispose of clandestine laboratories. Their procedure for conducting a raid has five stages: planning, entry, assessment,

processing, and exit. During the planning stage, certified agents and chemists identify the chemicals that may be present and arrange for the proper safety equipment and protective clothing.

Entry has the most potential for danger. The entry team faces the possibility of armed resistance by owners and operators, booby traps, and exposure to hazardous chemicals. Still, the entry team wears the least protection because the gear limits mobility, dexterity, vision, and voice communications. Once entry has been successful, the assessment team—an agent and a chemist—enter the site to deal with immediate hazards, to ventilate the site, and to segregate incompatible chemicals to halt reactions. Assessment team members wear fire-protective, chemical-resistant suits, gloves, and boots (Figure 18.7). They also use self-contained breathing devices for respiratory protection. This team determines what safety equipment and clothing the processing team will need. The processing team then enters and identifies and collects evidence. They photograph and videotape the site and collect samples of the various chemicals. The final

Figure 18.7

Assessment team members investigating clandestine drug laboratories wear fire- and chemical-resistant suits, gloves, and boots and use self-contained breathing devices for protection. The team determines what safety equipment and clothing the processing team (who will identify and collect evidence) will need. Here a member of the Southwest Virginia Clandestine Lab Team piles up methamphetamine-making ingredients and cooking devices on the lawn of a Damascus, Virginia, home. Seizures of methamphetamine labs such as this have been on the rise throughout the country, reflecting a growing drug problem and an increased effort to combat it.

step involves removing and disposing of hazardous materials and decontaminating and posting the site.

Training involves 40 hours of classroom instruction followed by a 24-hour in-service training course at the field level. Medical monitoring has two stages: medical screening of potential team members and annual monitoring to learn whether any team members have developed adverse health effects as a result of working with hazardous chemicals. Guidelines and training for clandestine drug laboratory investigations are available through the National Sheriffs Association.

Not only do clan labs pose a danger to officers and the public, they generate an enormous amount of waste and can be very expensive to clean up.

Cleanup of Clandestine Drug Labs

Most estimates calculate that for every pound of meth produced, as much as five pounds of waste are created (Hanson, 2005b, p.73). Much of this waste consists of empty chemical containers, contaminated cooking equipment, and other items that have become hazardous through exposure to the vapors produced during the drug manufacturing process. Such trash requires special handling and disposal, often at great expense. The Comprehensive Methamphetamine Control Act (MCA) of 1996 allows the courts to order a defendant convicted of manufacturing methamphetamine to pay the cost of cleanup of the lab site. Despite efforts to detect and shut them down, clan labs continue to proliferate.

Indoor Marijuana Growing Operations

Another type of clandestinely produced drug is sinsemilla, a potent form of marijuana cultivated indoors. One good indication of indoor marijuana growing operations is the excessive use of electricity needed to run the lighting system. Many grow operations steal electricity by diverting power from a main supply line, with an average bypass stealing between $1,100 and $1,600 worth of electricity each month (La Barge and Noakes, p.29). In one case, police were alerted to a residence that had been using ten times the normal amount of electricity. Based on this information and observations of the type and amount of traffic to and from the house, police were able to obtain a search warrant and break up a large marijuana-growing operation.

In addition to tampered-with electric meters and supply lines, other signs of an indoor grow operation include:

- Water lines or electrical cords running to a basement or outbuilding.
- An outbuilding with air conditioners.
- An unusual number of roof vents in a house or outbuilding.
- Excessive condensation around windows.
- A housetop with no snow on it when roofs of other surrounding properties are snow covered.
- Excessive security measures such as guard dogs, high fences, razor wire, locks on gates, and Keep Out signs (La Barge and Noakes, p.30).

Inherent dangers associated with the high-energy needs of these indoor grow operations include the risk of electrocution from exposing and tampering with high-wattage wires; explosion and fire risks due to the presence and prevalence of chemicals stored inside; and upper respiratory infections caused by mold that thrives in these high-humidity environments.

Investigative Aids

One tool to help federal, state, and local law enforcement agencies investigate drug trafficking is the DEA's National Drug Pointer Index (NDPIX), a nationwide database that became operational across the United States in 1997. The NDPIX is intended to enhance agent/officer safety, eliminate duplication, increase information sharing and coordination, and minimize costs by using existing technology and 24/7 access to information through an effective, secure law enforcement telecommunications system.

Some investigative aids are not so high-tech. For example, using dogs to detect drugs has been common for decades because their keen sense of smell enables them to detect minute traces of illicit drugs. The Supreme Court has ruled that a canine sniff in a public area or during a lawful traffic stop is not a Fourth Amendment "search" and thus requires no suspicion (Rutledge, p.91). However, use of a narcotics-detection dog to sniff at the door of an apartment or a home has been ruled a search within the meaning of the Fourth Amendment and therefore requires a warrant.

Another assist for investigators is a special high-accuracy laser rangefinder developed for the U.S. Customs Service that can find secret compartments that might contain drugs. Investigators use the unit to measure the interior dimensions of cargo containers in their search for hidden compartments in which drugs may be smuggled. The small laser beam allows measurements of loaded containers in which physical access to the rear wall is limited. The handheld, battery-operated laser rangefinder measures distances from 6 to 85 feet with an accuracy of 1 inch.

The Law Enforcement Liaison and Education (LELE) unit of Purdue Pharma L.P., a Connecticut-based pharmaceutical company, comprises retired law enforcement officers from around the country and offers free training and other assistance to law enforcement to help in the efforts to combat prescription drug abuse and diversion. For example, the LELE unit provides placebos of OxyContin tablets for undercover investigators working reverse-buy drug stings. The placebos, which visually appear to be identical to the real drug, contain no active ingredients and are expressly available to only those agencies actively involved in criminal investigations (Gibbs and Haddox, p.20). Purdue Pharma has also developed a project called RxPATROL (Pattern Analysis Tracking Robberies and Other Losses) to help investigators solve pharmacy robberies and other drug thefts involving health care establishments (Burke, p.21).

Agency Cooperation

Investigating illegal drug activities requires the cooperation of all law enforcement agencies, including the exchange of suspect car lists and descriptions of sellers and buyers. Local police assist state and federal narcotics investigators by sharing their knowledge of drug users and sellers in their community. In addition, many narcotics officers exchange vehicles and personnel with other agencies to have less identifiable operators and equipment.

The federal government has mobilized an all-out attack on illegal drug activities. Before 1973 several federal agencies were involved in investigating illegal drug activities. These included the Bureau of Narcotics and Dangerous Drugs (BNDD), the Office for Drug Abuse Law Enforcement, the Office of National Narcotics Intelligence, the drug investigative and intelligence units of the Bureau of Customs, and the drug enforcement sections of the Office of Science and Technology. In 1973 all these agencies were merged into the Federal Drug Enforcement Administration (FDEA), often called simply the DEA.

The Federal Drug Enforcement Administration (FDEA) provides unified leadership in attacking narcotics trafficking and drug abuse. Its emphasis is on the source and distribution of illicit drugs rather than on arresting abusers.

The DEA's emphasis is on stopping the flow of drugs at their foreign sources, disrupting illicit domestic commerce at the highest levels of distribution, and helping state and local police to prevent the entry of illegal drugs into their communities. The DEA's Mobile Enforcement Team (MET), established in 1995, consists of more than 200 agents deployed across the nation to help fight the drug war. The National Drug Intelligence Center (NDIC) also plays a vital role in providing police administrators and officers with the latest information on drug distribution patterns.

U.S. agencies must cooperate with law enforcement in other countries because much of the U.S. domestic drug problem originates across national borders. To overcome interjurisdictional competition and minimize duplication of effort, multijurisdictional drug task forces have been implemented across the country. Sometimes task forces and programs are created not out of a desire to cooperate but out of a need to eliminate dissention. One benefit of working with a task force is shared forfeiture revenues.

Drug Asset Forfeitures

Asset forfeiture is a tool that allows agencies investigating various types of crimes, including drug trafficking, to seize items used in or acquired through the commission of that crime. The Federal Comprehensive Crime Control Act of 1983 initiated procedures for asset forfeitures as a result of drug arrests. The U.S. Congress gave final approval to the Civil Asset Forfeiture Reform Act of 2000. This act lowered the burden of proof from "clear and convincing" to "a preponderance of the evidence." It also reduced the statute of limitations from 11 years to 5 years for a property owner to make a claim on the property.

Confiscating drug dealers' cash and property has been effective in reducing drug trafficking and is providing local, state, and federal law enforcement agencies with assets they need for their fight against drugs. Asset forfeiture laws provide for the confiscation of cash and other property in possession of a drug dealer at the time of the arrest. Seized vehicles, boats, or airplanes may be used directly by the agency or sold at auction to generate funds. Monetary assets may be used to purchase police equipment, to hire additional law enforcement personnel, or to provide training in drug investigation.

Currency seizures pose special challenges to law enforcement because there is no law against possessing a large quantity of cash and, as Steffen and Candelaria (p.42) observe, most currency seizure scenarios arise in the absence of narcotics, sometimes making it difficult to establish a link between the money and criminal activity. The investigator must establish the ownership of the currency (Was it inherited? won at the track? What does the person do for a living?), the origin of the currency, and the packaging and transportation methods used with the currency. An attempt to disguise or otherwise hide the currency is suggestive of criminal involvement.

Precise recording of all proceedings is necessary to avoid allegations of abuse or misuse of these funds. Because of the required legal and judicial proceedings regarding these confiscations, it is often six months or longer after an arrest before the assets are available for police agency use.

A common defense to asset seizure is the Innocent Owner Defense. If an owner can prove that he or she had no knowledge of the prohibited activity, the property is not subject to forfeiture.

The forfeiture program has not been without problems and misunderstandings. The confiscated funds may be used only for police department efforts to increase their fight against drugs. Police budgets cannot be reduced because of the availability of the asset-forfeiture funds.

Preventing Problems with Illegal Drugs: Community Partnerships

Tremendous national, state, and local efforts are being directed to meeting the challenges of drug use and abuse in the United States. A national drug czar serves at the direction of the president, and many states appoint people to similar positions to direct state and local efforts. Federal funding is available through state agencies. Federal, state, and local agencies with roles in the drug war coordinate their efforts. Any successful effort to address drug-related crime and drug addiction must also necessarily involve partnerships with the community. Businesses, schools, public health departments, and individual citizens are invaluable components of an effective response.

Thousands of volunteers, groups, and agencies have joined the fight against illegal drugs. For example, Operation Weed and Seed is a national initiative for marshaling the resources of a number of federal agencies to strengthen law enforcement and revitalize communities. It is a comprehensive, coordinated approach to controlling drugs and crime in targeted high-crime neighborhoods. The Weed and Seed program links community policing and concentrated law enforcement efforts to identify, arrest, and prosecute violent offenders, drug traffickers, and other criminals (weeding) with human services such as after-school, weekend, and summer youth activities; adult literacy classes; parental counseling; and neighborhood revitalization efforts to prevent and deter further crime (seeding).

But crime control is only one of several drug-control strategies that individual communities and the nation as a whole have available. Figure 18.8 depicts the multi-faceted drug-control strategies competing for funds and support now and into the future.

Some communities are developing specific programs to address the drug problem and are recognizing the need for innovative approaches. For example, in jurisdictions facing high incidence of youths abusing OTC drugs, law enforcement can take steps to educate business owners and operators who sell these products about the risks involved. Clerks can be trained to recognize common signs of drug abuse and to understand why they should not sell a dozen packages of Coricidin Cough and Cold medicine to a group of teenagers. Some businesses may voluntarily move the drugs behind the counter, limit the number of packages a customer may purchase at one time or require customers to be over age 18; others will do nothing for fear of hurting sales. Law enforcement cannot force retailers to restrict OTC drugs (Garrett, p.44).

States, however, can and have passed legislation banning OTC sales of certain products deemed threats to public safety. As of April 2005, 27 states had passed or were considering legislation to restrict OTC sales of pseudoephedrine-containing medications in an effort to stop the proliferation of meth labs ("States Crack Down," p.8).

The illegal drug trade has become an essential source of revenue for organized crime.

Organized Crime: An Overview

Organized crime is a global scourge, entangling communities around the world in its web of corruption and violence. Organized crime undermines legitimate commerce, manipulates stock markets, steals merchandise, distributes drugs, controls labor unions, and enslaves innocent women and children. These criminal enterprises have even developed an online presence, with organized crime groups actively and increasingly engaged in Internet fraud and identity theft.

The FBI defines **organized crime** as any group having some manner of a formalized structure and whose primary objective is to obtain money through illegal activities. Organized crime groups achieve and retain their status through the use of actual or threatened violence, corruption of public officials, and other coercive tactics. A **criminal enterprise**, by FBI definition, is a group of individuals with an identified hierarchy, or comparable structure, engaged in significant criminal activity. While *organized crime* and *criminal enterprise* are often equated and used interchangeably, several federal statutes specifically delineate the elements of an *enterprise* that must be proven to convict individuals or groups under those statutes. For example, the Racketeering Influenced and Corrupt Organizations (RICO) Act, or Title 18 U.S.C. 1961(4), passed in 1970, defines an enterprise as "any individual, partnership, corporation,

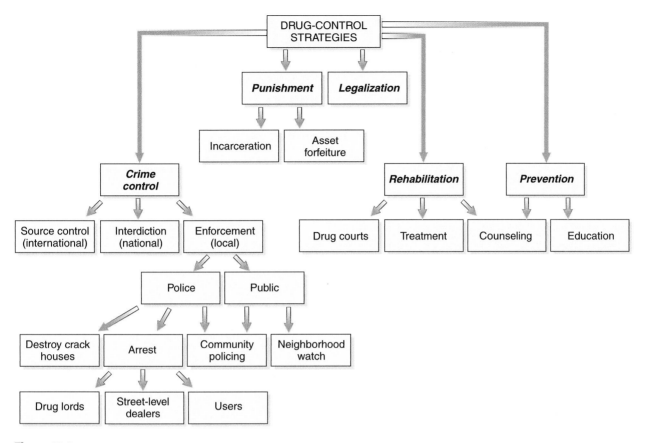

Figure 18.8

Overview of drug-control strategies

Source: Henry M. Wrobleski and Kären M. Hess, *Introduction to Law Enforcement and Criminal Justice,* 8th ed. Belmont, CA: Wadsworth/Thomson Leaning, 2003, p. 323.

association, or other legal entity, and any union or group of individuals associated in fact although not a legal entity."

Several characteristics distinguish organized crime from crimes committed by individuals or unorganized groups.

Characteristics of Organized Crime

 Distinctive characteristics of organized crime include:

- Definite organization and control.
- High-profit and continued-profit crimes.
- Singular control through force and threats.
- Protection through corruption.

The *organization* provides direct *control,* leadership, and discipline. The leaders are isolated from the general operations through field or area leaders, who in turn control the everyday activities that bring in the profits. Organized crime deals primarily in *high-profit* crimes that are susceptible to organizational control and that can be developed into larger operations that will provide the continued profit necessary for future existence.

Organized crime functions through many forms of corruption and intimidation to create a *singular control* over specific goods and services that ultimately results in a monopoly. Monopoly provides the opportunity to set higher prices and profits for that product or service.

Organized crime flourishes most where *protection* from interference and prosecution exist. The first line of immunity is the indifference of the general public and their knowing or unknowing use of the services or purchase of the goods offered by organized crime. Through such activities, citizens provide the financial power that gives organized crime immunity from legal authorities. Moreover, organized crime uses enforcement tactics to ensure compliance with its decrees. Members or paid enforcers intimidate, brutalize, and even murder those who fail to obey the dictates of organized crime bosses.

In the early 1960s Joseph Valachi made public for the first time the awesome power of organized crime and dispelled many misconceptions about it. First, organized crime is not a single entity controlled by one superpower. Although a large share of organized crime is controlled by the Italian Mafia, other organizations throughout the United States have sprung up. As America has become more diverse, so too have the organized crime groups operating within it. Asian and Russian/Eurasian criminal groups, for example, have been spreading across the country in recent years.

Second, organized crime does not exist only in metropolitan areas. Although organized crime operates primarily in larger metropolitan areas, it has associate operations in many smaller cities, towns, and rural areas.

Third, organized crime does not involve only activities such as narcotics, prostitution, racketeering, and gambling. In fact, organized crime is involved in virtually every area where profits are to be made, including legitimate businesses.

Fourth, citizens are not isolated from organized crime. They are directly affected by it through increased prices of consumer goods controlled by behind-the-scenes activities of organized crime. In addition, citizens who buy items on the black market, solicit prostitutes, purchase pornography, bet through a bookie, take chances on punch boards, or participate in other innocent betting operations directly contribute to the financial success of organized crime. Millions of citizens support organized crime by knowingly or unknowingly taking advantage of the goods and services it provides.

Applicable Laws against Organized Crime

In addition to various state laws, two other distinct groups of laws seek to control organized crime: criminal laws that attack the criminal act itself and laws that make violations a criminal conspiracy. Charges have also been brought against some types of organized crime through prosecution under the Internal Revenue laws and initiation of civil lawsuits.

The major federal acts specifically directed against organized crime are the 1946 Hobbs Anti-Racketeering Act, the 1968 Omnibus Crime Control and Safe Streets Act, the RICO Act of 1970, and the Organized Crime Control Act of 1970. These acts make it permissible to use circumstantial rather than direct evidence to enforce conspiracy violations. They also prohibit the use of funds derived from illegal sources to enter into legitimate enterprises (commonly known as *laundering* money). Title 18 U.S. Code, Section 1962, defines three areas that can be prosecuted.

 It is a prosecutable conspiracy to:
- **Acquire any enterprise with money obtained from illegal activity**
- **Acquire, maintain, or control any enterprise by illegal means**
- **Use any enterprise to conduct illegal activity**

Major Activities of Organized Crime

 rganized crime is involved in almost every legal and illegal activity that makes large sums of money with little risk.

Organized crime is heavily involved in the so-called victimless crimes of gambling, drugs, pornography, and prostitution, as well as fraud, loan-sharking, money laundering, and infiltration of legitimate businesses.

Federal crimes prosecutable under the RICO statute include bribery, sports bribery, counterfeiting, embezzlement of union funds, mail fraud, wire fraud, money laundering, obstruction of justice, murder for hire, drug trafficking, prostitution, sexual exploitation of children, alien smuggling, trafficking in counterfeit goods, theft from interstate shipment, and interstate transportation of stolen property. State crimes chargeable under RICO include murder, kidnapping, gambling, arson, robbery, bribery, extortion, and drug offenses. Thus, investigating organized crime effectively means investigating any of these other types of criminal activity in which the organization is involved.

Victimless Crimes

A **victimless crime** is an illegal activity in which all involved are willing participants. Among the crimes categorized as "victimless" are gambling, drug use, pornography, and prostitution. Because there is no complainant, these crimes are difficult to investigate and to prosecute. According to Parker (2005): "Prostitution, pornography and other forms of commercial sex are a multibillion dollar industry. They enrich a small minority of predators, while the larger community is left to pay for the damage. People used in the sex industry often need medical care as a result of the ever-present violence. They may need treatment for infectious diseases, including AIDS."

Arguments for legalizing so-called victimless crimes have been made periodically over the years but without success. Proponents argue that it is not the government's function to regulate morality, that the laws are not only ineffective but also hypocritical and unenforceable. Further, the laws have created a whole class of "criminals" who would not otherwise be considered such. Perhaps most important, the laws create the conditions under which organized crime can thrive.

Opponents of legalizing these activities argue that it *is* the government's proper function to regulate morality and to protect individuals from themselves. As long as the activities are illegal, law enforcement is obligated to enforce the laws. Among the most difficult laws to enforce are those making gambling illegal *in some instances.*

Gambling is regarded by some as a vice, a sinful activity that corrupts society; others see gambling as simply a harmless form of entertainment. In fact, within the gambling industry the term *gambling* is being replaced with the term *gaming,* giving it the appearance of respectability. Legal "gaming" has greatly expanded throughout the country in the form of state lotteries, pari-mutuel betting on horses and greyhounds, bingo, slot machines, and casinos. The Internet has hundreds of gambling-related sites, many of which have set up operations offshore.

Some contend that when casino gambling comes to a city, robberies, check and credit card fraud, property crimes, domestic abuse, and alcohol-related violations increase.

In addition to the problems associated with legal gambling, most reports on organized crime indicate that illegal gambling is the backbone of its activities and its largest source of income. **Bookmaking**—soliciting and accepting bets on any type of sporting event—is the most prevalent gambling operation. In addition, various forms of numbers/policy and other lottery games net substantial portions of the financial gain to organized crime from gambling.

Loan-Sharking

Loan-sharking—lending money at exorbitant interest rates—is supported initially by the profits from gambling operations. The upper hierarchy lends money to lower-echelon members of the organization, charging them 1 to 2 percent interest on large sums. These members in turn lend the money to customers at rates of 20 to 30 percent or more. The most likely customers are people who cannot obtain loans through legitimate sources, often to pay off illegal gambling debts.

Money Laundering and the Infiltration of Legitimate Business

In recent years organized crime has become increasingly involved in legitimate business. The vast profits from illegal activities are given legitimacy by being invested in legal business. This is another way of turning dirty money into clean money, or "laundering" it. (Money laundering was discussed in depth in Chapter 14.) For example, a medium-sized company experiences a lack of business and is unable to get credit. Convinced that an infusion of capital will turn the business around, the president turns to a loan shark and borrows at an interest rate of 50 percent per week. Within months organized crime has taken over the company. The crime boss keeps the president as a figurehead and uses his reputation to order goods worth thousands of dollars, never intending to pay for them. After a few months the company files for bankruptcy.

Although the history of organized crime is filled with bloodshed, violence, and corruption, organized crime bosses no longer wield power through a Thompson submachine gun. They manipulate the business economy to their benefit. Such crimes as labor racketeering, unwelcome infiltration of unions, fencing stolen property, gambling, loan-sharking, drug trafficking, employment of illegal aliens, and white-collar crimes of all types can signal syndicate involvement.

Investigators must be aware that some criminal groups are more involved than others in particular activities. Familiarity with a crime group's "specialties" or crimes of preference will greatly assist in investigations and will help identify the presence of new organized crime factions.

The Threat of Specific Organized Crime Groups

Whereas Italian crime syndicates such as La Cosa Nostra (LCN) may have predominated in the early days of organized crime in the United States, groups from other parts of the world are now cashing in on America's reputation as the "land of opportunity." The rise of Asian, Latino, African, and Russian gangs requires the government to redesign the fight against organized crime. Nonetheless, Italian criminal groups persist as the stereotypical organized crime threat to American society and are indeed the most *organized* criminal presence in America.

Italian Organized Crime

While most Americans lump all organized crime figures of Italian descent into one general group called *the Mafia,* Italian organized crime (IOC) in the United States actually comprises four separate groups: the Sicilian Mafia; the Neapolitan Camorra; the 'Ndrangheta, or Calabrian Mafia; and Sacra Corona Unita, or "United Sacred Crown." These four IOCs have more than 3,000 members and affiliates throughout the United States, but the largest percentage of them operate out of New York, New Jersey, and Philadelphia. IOC groups are heavily involved in drug trafficking and money laundering, as well as illegal gambling, political corruption, extortion, fraud, counterfeiting, weapons trafficking, infiltration of legitimate businesses, bombings, kidnappings, and murders.

LCN is a nationwide alliance of criminals with both familial and conspiratorial connections. Although rooted in Italian organized crime, LCN is an Americanized version of the "old school" mafias from Italy, separate and distinct from the other IOC groups. LCN is, in fact, what most people are referring to when they speak of the Mafia or Italian organized crime. LCN is involved in many of the same activities as other IOC groups, as well as labor racketeering, prostitution, pornography, tax fraud schemes, and stock manipulation schemes. One of the distinguishing features of LCN, compared with all other criminal organizations in the United States, is how it has operated as a bridge between the upperworld and the underworld through its control of labor unions, organization of employer cartels, and impact on major industries throughout the nation (Finckenauer, 2001).

Finckenauer explains: "Made members, sometimes called good fellows or wise guys, are all male and all of Italian descent. The estimated made membership of the LCN is 1,100 nationwide, with roughly eighty percent of the members operating in the New York metropolitan area." Five crime families make up New York City's LCN: the Bonanno, Colombo, Genovese, Gambino, and Lucchese families. Beside the made members, roughly 10,000 associate members work for the families.

Each family has roughly the same organizational structure. The boss controls the family and makes executive decisions. The underboss is second in command, and the consigliere serves as a senior adviser or counselor. Surrounding the boss are captains ("capos") who supervise crews of "soldiers," all of whom are "made guys" (Finckenauer; Abadinsky, p.20). The soldiers and their associates carry out the actual crimes, the proceeds from which go to the capos and those of higher rank (Finckenauer). In LCN, the bosses are connected to each other through some personal relationship, whether actual kinship, friendship, or a mutual respect (Abadinsky, p.20).

LCN was originally grounded on standards of conduct borrowed from southern Italian tradition, particularly loyalty to the family. In the Mafia, however, this meant that loyalty to the crime family took precedence over loyalty to one's own blood family (Abadinsky, p.30). This loyalty began to unravel with the 1992 testimony of an underboss, Salvatore "Sammy the Bull" Gravano, of the Gambino family, against his boss, John Gotti, which sent Gotti to prison for life and set the precedent for other turncoat mobsters to rat out their crime bosses in exchange for reduced prison sentences. The federal racketeering and kidnapping trial of John A. Gotti, who took over as street boss for the Gambino family after his father went to prison, and who allegedly continued ordering crimes after his own imprisonment for a racketeering conviction in 1997, has thus far included testimony from five Gambino crime family defectors (Preston). In 2005, Joseph Massino, the once highly respected "last don" of the Bonanno family, became the first LCN boss to flip.

Asian Organized Crime

Asian organized crime (AOC) groups, referred to as Asian Criminal Enterprises by the FBI, are involved in murder, kidnapping, extortion, prostitution, pornography, loan-sharking, gambling, money laundering, alien smuggling, trafficking in heroin and methamphetamine, counterfeiting of computer and clothing products, and various protection schemes. AOC is often well run and hard to crack, using global networks of criminal associates that are very fluid and extremely mobile. Asian criminal enterprises are classified as either traditional, such as the Yakuza and Triads, or nontraditional, such as ethnic Asian street gangs.

Japanese organized crime is sometimes known as *Boryokudan* but is more commonly known as the *Yakuza*. A *gyangu* (Japanese gangster) is a member of the Yakuza (organized crime family) and is affiliated with the Yamaguchi-gumi (Japan's largest organized crime family) as a *boryokudan* (used primarily for muscle). Triads are the oldest of the *Chinese organized crime* (COC) groups (Figure 18.9). The Triads engage in a wide range of criminal activities, including money laundering, drug trafficking, gambling, extortion, prostitution, loan-sharking, pornography, alien smuggling, and numerous protection schemes.

Vietnamese organized crime is generally one of two kinds: roving or local. As the name suggests, roving bands travel from community to community, have a propensity for violence, and have no permanent leaders or group loyalty. They lack language and job skills and have no family in the United States. Local groups, in contrast, tend to band together in a certain area of a specific community and have a charismatic leader. They also have a propensity for violence and tend to engage in extortion, illegal gambling, and robbery.

Asian organized crime investigations present some unique challenges, due primarily to cultural and social differences. Many Asians are suspicious of the police and the U.S. criminal justice system. Asian criminals exploit this distrust by preying on other Asians, secure in the knowledge that their crimes will most likely go unreported. Another challenge is the fact that many Asian groups are very mobile and have associates or family scattered throughout the United States.

Latino Organized Crime

Latino organized crime groups within the United States include Cubans, Colombians, Mexicans, and Dominicans. These criminal enterprises are heavily involved in drug trafficking, typically bringing their criminal organization into this country along with the drugs they sell (Abadinsky, p.166). For example, most of the world's cocaine market is controlled by Colombian cartels. In the United States, cartel representatives serve as brokers to coordinate cocaine deliveries to various drug networks (Abadinsky, p.170) (Figure 18.10).

Figure 18.9

Indra Lim, 20, an alleged member of the Oriental Lazyboys, a Chinatown street gang, appears in a Los Angeles courtroom during opening statements for the murder of Oscar-winning actor Haing Ngor, Monday, Feb. 23, 1998. Lim, along with alleged gang members Tak Sun Tan and Jason Chan, is charged with killing Ngor outside his Los Angeles home and will share one trial with three different juries.

Because of Mexico's proximity to the United States, its organized crime groups are becoming an increasing threat to the United States and are among the fastest growing gangs in the country. Mexican drug trafficking has had an enormous impact on the United States, as organizations smuggle heroin, cocaine, marijuana, and, most recently, meth. In fact, Mexican trafficking organizations have set up large-scale meth labs in some western and southwestern U.S. states (Abadinsky, p.179). The Mexican Mafia, a prison-based gang, has been growing within the U.S. correctional system for nearly 50 years and is found in at least nine state prison systems (Abadinsky, p.188). The Mexican Mafia also has links to Hispanic street gangs and controls, to varying degrees, their drug trafficking activities (Abadinsky, p.189).

African Organized Crime

The African criminal enterprise problem in the United States has proliferated since the 1980s. While some groups comprise members originating in Ghana and Liberia, by far the predominant nationality in African organized crime is Nigerian. African criminal enterprises are an emerging criminal threat facing law enforcement agencies worldwide and are known to be operating in at least 80 other countries. According to the FBI, Nigerian criminal enterprises in the United States are most prevalent in Atlanta; Baltimore; Washington, DC; Chicago; Milwaukee; Dallas; Houston; New York; and Newark. Financial frauds and advance fee schemes, often perpetrated over the Internet, are common methods used by Nigerian organized crime groups. Known as "4-1-9" scams," after Section 4-1-9 of the Nigerian Penal Code relating to fraudulent schemes, these scams prey on victims' sympathy, naivete, and, often, greed, promising a handsome monetary reward in exchange for help making a financial transaction. Usually received via e-mail or

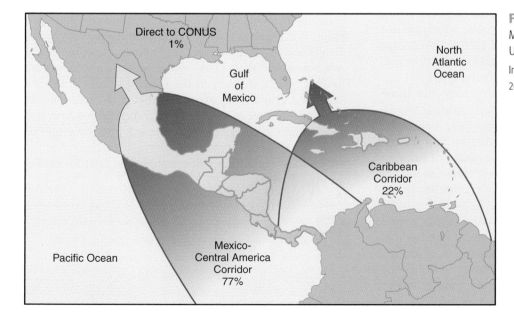

Figure 18.10

Major cocaine trafficking corridors to the United States

Interagency Assessment of Cocaine Movement, 2003.

fax, these frauds are often riddled with misspellings, improper grammar, and other potential "tip-offs" that the correspondence is less than legitimate.

Russian Organized Crime

Russia has a 400-year history of dealing with organized crime groups, which for the most part kept their illegal activities inside the border. However, in the wake of the collapse of the Soviet Union, Russian organized crime has gone international and poses a great threat to and challenge for U.S. justice. The FBI refers to these groups as Eurasian Organized Crime (EOC). Former FBI director Louis Freeh has called the Russian Mafia the fastest-growing criminal organization in the United States.

Unlike members of organized crime groups originating from economically and educationally disadvantaged areas, EOC members tend to be well educated, oftentimes holding Ph.D.s in science-based fields or mathematics (Abadinsky, p.200). EOC has had little to no involvement in some of the more traditional organized crime activities, such as drug trafficking, loan-sharking, and gambling, choosing instead to focus on a wide range of frauds and scams, including insurance scams, securities and investment fraud, and fuel oil scams. In the United States, EOC has become the primary purveyor of credit card scams. Contract murders, kidnappings, and business arson are also common for Russian criminal enterprises (Finckenauer and Voronin, p.26). In addition to transnational money laundering, Russian organized crime is known to traffic in women and children.

They also traffic in such hazardous commodities as weapons and nuclear material smuggled out of their homeland. This removal of otherwise legal raw materials is a major concern to the Russian government, as it deprives the country of export income and diminishes the global market value of these goods (Finckenauer and Voronin, p.25). The large-scale removal of funds or capital from a country is called **capital flight.** Do not confuse *money laundering* and *capital flight*, which are not interchangeable terms. While money laundering is capital flight, not all capital flight is money laundering. Money laundering is illegal; capital flight is not.

U.S. money laundering laws recognize only three offenses committed outside the United States as predicate for a charge of money laundering: drug violations, terrorism, and bank fraud. Any funds resulting from a theft from the Russian government, evasion of Russian taxes, or bribes received by Russian officials can legally be processed through U.S. banks. Such activities do not qualify as money laundering.

Investigating Russian organized crime is challenged by several factors. First, the EOC consists of hundreds of groups, all acting independently. Russian crime groups in the United States are loosely structured, lacking any formal hierarchy. They tend to be fluid groups whose membership fluctuates between 5 and 20 people, depend-ing on the operation involved (Abadinsky, p.200). Most members are already hardened criminals, have military experience, and are highly educated. As with other immigrant organized crime groups, language presents a challenge to investigators. Another problem lies in the cooperation among and pooling of resources between Russian and other organized crime groups.

Organized Crime and Corruption

One of the greatest threats posed by organized crime is the corruption it engenders throughout the entire legal system. Although the police are interested in any corruption by public officials, they are especially concerned about corruption in their own department. Bribes of police officers can take many forms: outright offers of money, taking care of medical bills, or providing free merchandise or free vacations. Any police officer who is offered a bribe must report it immediately to a superior and then attempt to make an arrest that will involve the person making the offer as well as those responsible higher in the organization.

Some officials repay organized crime figures by providing inside information that can be used to manipulate securities or to purchase real estate in areas of future development that can be sold for a much higher price.

The Police Response

It is frequently difficult for local law enforcement officers to understand their role in investigating or controlling organized crime. But there is a direct relationship between what officers do on assignment and investigation of organized crime activities. Local law enforcement officers are the first line of defense in the control of all crime, and organized crime is no exception. Because of the highly structured nature of many organized crime groups, law enforcement officers can seldom break into these hierarchies, but they can remain the "eyes" and "ears" of the information and intelligence system essential to combat organized crime.

The daily observations of local law enforcement officers provide vital information for investigating organized crime. Report all suspicious activities and persons possibly associated with organized crime to the appropriate person or agency.

Because organized crime is involved in a great number of activities, information can arise from many sources. Thus, your street-level observations can be critical. Every day you observe many conditions related to crime and deal with individuals who are part of the community's activities. Seemingly unimportant details can fit into an overall picture that an intelligence unit is putting together (Figure 18.11).

Ways to become aware of people and conditions that suggest organized crime activity are provided by the International Association of Chiefs of Police:

> A retail establishment seems to be doing a brisk business—many customers coming and going. But the customers do not remain in the store very long and do not leave with packages or other evidence that purchases were made. The store may have a meager selection of merchandise, which raises the question of how it can attract so many customers day after day. This could indicate the presence of a policy operation at the writer level or the place of business of a bookmaker's commission man.
>
> At about the same time each day, a package is delivered to a newsstand, bar, or other location. Later the package is picked up by another individual. The location could be a policy drop—the place to which a policy writer sends his slips and/or day's receipts.
>
> You are called to investigate a beating in a bar or at a location near a factory or other place of employment. The incident may occur on a payday or within a couple of days thereafter. The beating may have resulted from the impatience of a loan shark who has not been paid on schedule.
>
> Merchants complain about another price rise by the cartage company that removes their garbage or trash. They also mention that there is either no competitor to deal with or if there is one, it will not accept their business. Frequently, this indicates that an organized crime group is trying to monopolize the cartage business or limit competition through territorial agreements.

> A rash of vandalism strikes a number of establishments engaged in the same type of business—such as dry cleaning. Racketeers may be trying to coerce reluctant owners into joining an association or into doing business with mob-controlled vendors. (Reprinted from *Criminal Intelligence*, Training Key #223, with permission of the International Association of Chiefs of Police.)

Make a habit of checking out new businesses that set up shop in the area. If the enterprise requires a license, such as a bar, ask to see it if for no other reason than to observe who the owners are, ascertain the identity of the company that distributes or services the jukeboxes, etc. If, for example, the jukebox or vending machine distributor is a company controlled by the organized underworld, so also might be the bar in which they are located.

Report in writing all information pertaining to such activities when time permits or immediately if the activity involves an imminent meeting. Report as nearly as possible exact conversations with assault victims suspected of associating with organized crime members. These conversations can include names of people or organizations responsible for violence and crime in the community.

Agencies Cooperating in Investigating Organized Crime

Under the authority of the 1968 Omnibus Crime Control Act, the Safe Streets Act and the Organized Crime Control Act of 1970, the U.S. Justice Department established the Organized

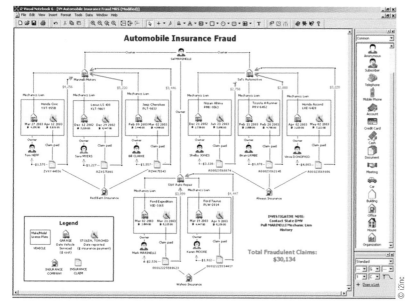

Figure 18.11

The progress and details of an organized crime investigation may make perfect sense to those who have spent months putting it together, but bringing others up to date can be challenging and time consuming. Charts like this, made with Visual Notebook, can graphically organize information as your case progresses to show relationships between suspects, witnesses, vehicles, and events, thus helping investigators identify the most significant areas of an investigation and aid decision makers in targeting their resources.

Crime and Racketeering Unit. Organized crime strike forces were formed throughout the country, mostly in major cities.

 Organized-crime strike forces coordinate all federal organized crime investigation activities and work closely with state, county, and municipal law enforcement agencies.

Other agencies that play important roles in investigating organized crime are the FBI, which often has a member on the strike forces; the Postal Inspection Service, which is in charge of mail fraud, embezzlements, and other crimes involving material distributed through the mails; the U.S. Secret Service, which investigates government checks and bonds as well as foreign securities; the Department of Labor, which investigates organized crime activities related to labor practices and pension funds; the Securities and Exchange Commission, which investigates organized crime activities in the purchase of securities; and the Internal Revenue Service, which investigates violations of income tax laws.

In addition to these agencies, the state attorney general's office and the district attorney's office can assist the police in building a case against organized crime figures who violate local and state laws.

Methods to Combat Organized Crime

Because organized crime groups often have extremely abundant resources and international connections to help protect their interests, law enforcement must deploy a wide variety of tactics to conquer the threat. Proactive community policing and problem-solving approaches hold much promise in combating organized crime. Intra-agency cooperation is also needed, as most organized crime activities cross jurisdictions. Surveillance and undercover operations are also sometimes indicated.

Another resource for combating organized crime is the local citizenry. However, victims, witnesses, and others with knowledge about organized crime activities are usually, and understandably, quite reluctant to come forth with their information. Consequently the government is often prepared to provide federal protection to those whose testimony is deemed crucial in building a case against organized crime (Figure 18.12).

The enterprise theory of investigation (ETI) is a combined organized crime/drug strategy used by the FBI that focuses investigations and prosecutions on entire criminal enterprises rather than on individuals.

Figure 18.12
Salvatore "Sammy the Bull" Gravano, right, appears in Bergen Superior Court Thursday, June 2, 2005, in Hackensack, N.J., with his attorney, Anthony Ricco. Gravano will be allowed to get a new lawyer to defend him on a murder charge stemming from the 1980 killing of a New York City police detective, according to a judge's ruling. Ricco requested to be relieved as counsel because he would have to testify during the trial that the prosecution's star witness, Richard "The Iceman" Kuklinski, solicited a $200,000 bribe from him "to make the case go away."

ETI is a proactive approach to attack a criminal organization's structure, and when combined with appropriate federal and state laws, can enable law enforcement to effectively target and terminate a criminal enterprise with a single criminal indictment. ETI, as with other FBI initiatives, focuses on major regional, national, and international crime groups that control large segments of the illegal activities of organized crime.

Investigative Aids

Electronic surveillance of suspects is essential in investigating organized crime. Organized crime leaders often avoid direct involvement in criminal acts by planning and coordinating criminal activity over the telephone or the Internet. Consequently, electronic surveillance can be used to build an effective case based on a criminal's own words while avoiding the risks associated with using informants or undercover agents.

Pen registers also are important in investigating sophisticated criminal networks. Pen registers record the numbers dialed from a telephone by monitoring the electrical impulses of the numbers dialed. In *Smith v. Maryland* (1979), the Supreme Court held that using a pen register does not constitute a search within the meaning of the Fourth Amendment, so neither probable cause nor a warrant is required to use the device. Several state courts, however, have held that using a pen register *is* a search under the respective state statutes and that a warrant supported by probable cause *is* needed. Investigators must be familiar with their state's statutes in this area. The same situation exists for trap-and-trace devices, which reveal the telephone number of the source of all *incoming* calls to a particular number. Their use may or may not require a warrant, depending on the specific state. Caller ID and phone numbers stored in speed dialers, fax machines, and computer files can also be of assistance, as discussed in Chapter 17.

The Regional Information Sharing System (RISS), a multijurisdictional intelligence sharing system comprising nearly 5,000 local, state, and federal agencies, is another tool available to help investigators identify, target, and remove criminal conspiracies and activities that reach across jurisdictional boundaries.

Asset Forfeiture

An effective weapon against organized crime, as with drug crimes, is the asset-forfeiture program, which allows law enforcement agencies to seize funds and property associated with criminal activity and effectively subjects criminals to 100 percent tax on their earn-ings. Asset forfeiture was presented in detail earlier in the section on drug-related criminal investigations.

The Decline of Organized Crime?

Certainly one hopes that tougher legislation, improved investigative techniques, and increased use of tools such as asset forfeiture have brought about a decline in organized crime. While perhaps these measures have forced a decline in the threat of *traditional* organized crime, the vacancies left by recent LCN associates and Gambino crime family members will easily be filled by any number of new criminal enterprises finding their way onto American soil.

It is sometimes difficult to determine whether criminal events are the work of organized crime or of gangs. In fact, many of the defining characteristics of organized crime groups are strikingly similar to those of better-organized gangs, and prison gangs often have direct ties to organized crime groups. Gangs are the focus of Chapter 19.

SUMMARY

It is illegal to possess or use narcotics or other dangerous drugs without a prescription; it is illegal to sell or distribute them without a license. Drugs can be classified as depressants, stimulants, narcotics, hallucinogens, phencyclidine, cannabis, or inhalants. The most common drugs on the street, in possession of users, and seized in drug raids are heroin, opium, morphine, codeine, cocaine, crack, and marijuana. Arrest for possession or use of marijuana is the most frequent drug arrest.

Physical evidence of possession or use of controlled substances includes the actual drugs, apparatus associated with their use, the suspect's appearance and behavior, and urine and blood tests. Evidence of the actual transfer of drugs from the seller to the buyer is the major legal evidence required for prosecuting drug sale cases. If you observe what appears to be a drug buy, you can make a warrantless arrest if you have probable cause. Often, however, it is better simply to observe and gather information. Undercover drug buys are carefully planned, witnessed, and conducted so that no charge of entrapment can be made. Two or more buys are made to avoid the charge of entrapment. Clandestine drug laboratories present physical, chemical, and toxic hazards to law enforcement officers who raid them.

The Drug Enforcement Administration (DEA) provides unified leadership in attacking narcotics trafficking and drug abuse. The DEA's emphasis is on the source and distribution of illicit drugs rather than on arresting abusers. The illegal drug trade has become an essential source of revenue for organized crime.

Distinctive characteristics of organized crime include definite organization and control, high-profit and continued-profit crimes, singular control, and protection. It is a prosecutable conspiracy to acquire any enterprise with money obtained from illegal activity; to acquire, maintain, or control any enterprise by illegal means; or to use any enterprise to conduct illegal activity.

Organized crime is continuously attempting to do all of the preceding with money obtained through its heavy involvement in gambling, drugs, pornography, prostitution, fraud, loan-sharking, money laundering, and infiltration of legitimate businesses. The daily observations of local law enforcement officers provide vital information for investigating organized crime. All suspicious activities and persons possibly associated with organized crime must be reported to the appropriate person or agency. Organized crime strike forces coordinate all federal organized crime activities and work closely with state, county, and municipal law enforcement agencies.

CHECKLISTS

Drugs and Controlled Substances

- How did the complaint originate? From police? victim? informant? neighbor?
- What is the specific nature of the complaint? Selling? Using? Possessing? Overdose? Are all required elements present?
- What type of narcotics are suspect?
- Is there enough evidence of sale to justify planning a buy?
- Were obtained drugs tested with a department drug-detection kit?
- Has the evidence been properly collected, identified, and preserved?
- Has the evidence been sent to a laboratory for examination?
- Has the drug been determined to be a controlled substance?
- Has everyone involved been interviewed or interrogated?
- Do those involved have prior arrests for similar offenses?
- Is surveillance necessary to obtain evidence for an arrest and/or a search warrant?
- Is a raid called for? (If so, review the checklist for raids in Chapter 6.)
- Have cooperating agencies been alerted?

Organized Crime

- Have people recently moved into the city and purchased businesses that obviously could not support their standard of living?
- Do any public officials appear to live beyond their means?
- Does a public official continuously vote in favor of a business that is suspected of being connected with organized crime?
- Have business owners complained of pressure to use a specific service or of threats to close the business if they do not hire certain people?
- Does a business have high-level executives with police records?
- Have there been complaints of someone on the premises operating as a bookie?
- Have families complained about loss of wages paid to a loan shark?
- Have union officials suddenly been replaced by new, nonlocal persons?
- Has there been damage or injury to property during union problems?
- Are goods being received at a store that do not fit with merchandise sold there?
- Has a discount store suddenly appeared without a clear indication of true ownership?
- Has arson suddenly increased?
- Do nonemployees hang around manufacturing plants or nonstudents hang around a school? (This could indicate a bookie operation or drug sales.)

- Is the same person using a pay telephone at the same time each day?
- Is evidence of betting operations being left in public wastebaskets or trash containers on the streets?
- When assaults occur, what are the motives? Could they be a result of gambling debts owed to a loan shark?
- Are people seen going into and out of certain businesses with which they are not ordinarily associated?
- Are known gamblers or persons with other criminal records repeatedly seen in a specific location?

APPLICATION

The Stakeout (Adapted from an account of an actual narcotics investigation written by David Peterson): It is dark as the five men emerge from the plane. They haul out their luggage and walk to the parking lot of the tiny, one-strip airport. The pilot enters a white shack that is trimmed in red. When the pilot leaves, the others gather around a young man who has driven out to meet them. His name is Bruce Preece, and he looks like an outdoorsman. Bearded, he wears a suede hat and red plaid jacket.

Moments later, a camper occupied by two more men pulls into the parking lot, and most of the group pile into the back. Seated along foam-rubber benches, they are dim in the shadows as the camper moves through the empty town.

"That guy sure was an inquisitive one," the pilot remarks, referring to the man in the shack. "He knew we were here last week, and he wanted to know what we were up to."

"Tourists," someone else replies, his head silhouetted against a window. Everyone looks like a visitor—a hunter, perhaps, or a fisherman. They carry small bags and wear down jackets and jeans. The clothing is deceptive.

Four narcotics agents, or *narcs,* and four agents from the Federal Drug Enforcement Administration are staked out in a camper outside the home of a man who works for a chemical firm. They suspect that at home he is manufacturing illegal drugs in a clandestine laboratory. The agents call him "No. 1."

They suspect that another man is getting illegal drugs and distributing them in nearby towns. They call him "No. 2."

No. 1 came under suspicion when a chemical supply company in Connecticut notified the feds that someone in this little town was ordering chemicals often used to make illegal substances. No. 2 came under suspicion when he told a local deputy sheriff he would be paid $2,000 if he notified him of any narcotics investigations.

The two men have been under surveillance for several weeks. One agent has even been inside the house by taking a shipment of chemicals from the Connecticut firm and making a "controlled delivery"— that is, he pretended to be the mailman and hauled the heavy boxes inside the house.

The agents have noticed a pattern. On Wednesdays, No. 1's wife goes into town and No. 2 stops by. It is Wednesday night. The plan is to watch No. 2 enter and leave the house and arrest him before he reaches his car. Assuming he is carrying illegal drugs, the agents will arrest No. 1 as well, search his home, and seize the contents of the lab. Both men are known to be armed.

By 7 P.M. surveillance has begun in earnest. The eight are waiting for something to happen. Two agents sit in an unmarked car along the highway leading to the house. Two others are in the woods, within view of the house. The other four are in the camper, parked just off the highway. Even from inside, the camper looks normal. But its cabinets contain an array of radios, cameras, lenses, firearms, and other gear. From the camper's bathroom, one agent takes out a tele-photo lens the size of a small wastebasket and attaches it to a "night scope."

At about 7:15, the woman leaves.

Each of the three groups of agents has a radio. However, No. 1 is believed to have a police scanner, which would allow him to monitor their conversation. So they speak in a rough sort of code, as though they were squad cars checking for speeders. "401," for example, will mean that No. 2 has arrived.

Hours pass. None of the agents has eaten since noon. They pass around a bag of Halloween-sized Snickers bars and start telling narc stories.

At 10, a sober, low voice over the radio says, "You may have three visitors shortly." A few minutes later, three agents climb into the camper, shivering. One agent, who has been watching No. 1 through his kitchen window with binoculars, says, "He's busy in there. He's pouring stuff, and he's running something, like a tableting machine."

The agents know that if they could just bust into that house, they'd find a guilty man surrounded by evidence. No. 2 doesn't show. Another night wasted?

Questions

1. Do the agents have probable cause to conduct a raid at this time?
2. Could they seize the materials No. 1 is working with as plain-view evidence? Why or why not?
3. What aspects of the surveillance illustrate effective investigation?
4. Have the agents made any mistakes?
5. What should their next step be?
6. Is there likely to be a link between the suspects and organized crime? Why or why not?

DISCUSSION QUESTIONS

- How serious do you feel the drug problem is nationally? Statewide? Locally?

- Would legalizing drugs be a feasible solution to the problem?

- Why should alcohol abuse be considered an illness and drug abuse a crime?

- How are drug raids treated by the media in your community?

- Do you know anyone with a drug abuse problem? How has it affected that person's life?

- Should the penalty for use of marijuana be reduced to a misdemeanor as it has been in some states? Should it be legalized, or should it remain a felony? In what amounts should the determination be made?

- Most experts believe that organized crime can flourish only in areas where it has corrupted local officials. Do you agree?

- What is your perception of the prevalence of organized crime in your community? your state? the country?

- Has organized crime become more or less of a problem for police in the past decade?

- Have you participated in any victimless crimes—for example, gambling? Do you feel that victimless crimes should be legalized?

MEDIA EXPLORATIONS

 Internet

Select one of the following assignments to complete.

- Go to www.whitehousedrugpolicy.gov and outline the *President's Drug Policy* to share with the class.

- Search for the key phrase *National Institute of Justice.* Click on "NCJRS" (National Criminal Justice Research Service). Click on "law enforcement." Click on "sort by Doc#." Search for one of the NCJ reference numbers from the reference pages. Outline the selection to share with the class.

- Select one of the following keywords: *capital flight, gambling, loan sharking, money laundering, organized crime, organized crime prevention, victimless crimes.* Find one article relevant to organized crime to outline and share with the class.

Crime and Evidence in Action

Go to the CD and choose the **drug bust/gang homicide/sexual assault case.** During the course of the case you'll become patrol officer, detective, defense attorney, corrections officer, and patrol officer to conduct interactive investigative research. Each case unfolds as you respond to key decision points. Feedback for each possible answer choice is packed full of information, including term definitions, web links, and important documentation. The sergeant is available at certain times to help mentor you, the Online Resources website offers a variety of information, and be sure to take notes in your e-notebook during the suspect video statements and at key points throughout (these notes can be saved, printed, or e-mailed). The Forensics Exercise will test your ability to collect, transport, and analyze evidence from the crime scene. At the end of the case you can track how well you responded to each decision point and join the Discussion Forum for a postmortem. **Go to the CD and use the skills you've learned in this chapter to solve a case.**

REFERENCES

2C-B Reappears on the Club Drug Scene. Washington, DC: U. S. Department of Justice, National Drug Intelligence Center, Information Bulletin, May 2001. (Product No. 2001-L0424-002)

Abadinsky, Howard. *Organized Crime* (7th ed.). Belmont, CA: Wadsworth/Thomson Learning, 2003.

"Additive Might Help Police Catch Meth Cooks," *Minnesota Police Chief,* Autumn 2004, p. 37.

"Bill Would Increase Funding for Treatment of 'Meth' Abuse," *Criminal Justice Drug Letter,* June 2005, pp. 1–3.

Burke, John. "Prescription Drug Diversion," *Law Enforcement Technology,* May 2004, pp. 16–21.

Cohen, Jacqueline; Gorr, Wilpen; and Singh, Piyusha. "Estimating Intervention Effects in Varying Risk Settings: Do Police Raids Reduce Illegal Drug Dealing at Nuisance Bars?" *Criminology,* May 2003, pp. 257–292.

Community Drug Alert Bulletin: Club Drugs. Bethesda, MD: National Institutes of Health, National Institute on Drug Abuse, May 2004.

Countering the Spread of Synthetic Drugs. Washington, DC: Office of National Drug Control Policy, Fact Sheet, March 2005.

Creighton, Colleen M. "Inhalant Abuse," *The Police Chief,* June 2003, pp. 34–35.

Crenshaw, M. Justin and Burke, Tod. "Khat: A Potential Concern for Law Enforcement." *FBI Law Enforcement Bulletin,* August 2004, pp. 10–13.

Domash, Shelly Feuer. "Market Report." *Police,* May 2005, pp. 36–45.

Drugs: A "Municipal" Approach. Des Moines (Iowa) Police Department, April 1990.

Drugs and Crime across America: Police Chiefs Speak Out. Conducted for Drug Strategies and the Police Foundation by Peter D. Hart Research Associates, Inc., December 2004.

The Economic Costs of Drug Abuse in the United States: 1992–2002. Washington, DC: Office of National Drug Control Policy, December 2004.

Ellement, John. "Police Thwart OxyContin Drug Ring," *The Boston Globe*, November 12, 2004.

Finckenauer, James O. *La Cosa Nostra in the United States.* Washington, DC: National Institute of Justice, International Center, no date.

Finckenauer, James O., and Voronin, Yuri A. *The Threat of Russian Organized Crime.* Washington, DC: National Institute of Justice, June 2001. (NCJ 187085)

Garrett, Ronnie. "Legal Highs." *Law Enforcement Technology*, May 2005, pp. 34–46.

Gibbs, Landon S., and Haddox, J. David. "Diversion of Prescribed Drugs," *The Police Chief*, June 2003, pp. 18–32.

Haffner, Timothy. "Narc-Scent for Undercover Cops," *Law and Order*, February 2005, pp. 325–326.

Hanson, Doug. "Clandestine Drug Labs Right in Your Backyard," *Law Enforcement Technology*, May 2005a, pp. 8–16.

Hanson, Doug. "Illegal Drug Labs: Hazmat Minefields," *Police and Security News*, May/June 2005b, pp. 69–73.

Hayes, Chuck. "Drug Recognition Experts: A Public Safety Resource," *The Police Chief*, October 2003, pp. 103–106.

Ho, Jeffrey D. "Sudden In-Custody Death," *Police*, August 2005, pp. 47–56.

Johnson, Matt. "Narcotic Field-Testing," *Law and Order*, June 2003, pp. 131–132.

Johnston, Lloyd D.; O'Malley, Patrick M.; Bachman, Jerald G.; and Schulenberg, John E. *Monitoring the Future—National Results on Adolescent Drug Use: Overview of Key Findings, 2004.* Bethesda, MD: National Institute on Drug Abuse, 2004.

Karchmer, Clifford L. "Local Drug Control." In William A. Geller and Darrel W. Stephens, eds., *Local Government Police Management*, 4th ed. Washington, DC: International City/County Management Association, 2003.

La Barge, Armand P., and Noakes, Karen. "Indoor Marijuana Growing Operations," *The Police Chief*, March 2005, pp. 28–31.

Lloyd, Jennifer. *Heroin.* Washington, DC: Office of National Drug Control Policy, Fact Sheet, June 2003. (NCJ 197335)

McEwen, Tom, and Uchida, Craig D. *An Evaluation of the COPS Office Methamphetamine Initiative.* Washington, DC: Office of Community Oriented Policing Services, Institute for Law and Justice and 21st Century Solutions, April 22, 2003.

Mills-Senn, Pamela. "Got an ID," *Law Enforcement Technology*, May 2005, pp. 48–55.

National Drug Control Strategy—2004 Strategy Overview. Washington, DC: The White House, March 2004.

National Drug Threat Assessment 2005. Washington, DC: National Drug Intelligence Center, February 2005a. (Product No. 2005-Q0317-003)

National Drug Threat Assessment 2005: Threat Matrix. Washington, DC: National Drug Intelligence Center, February 2005b. (Product No. 2005-Q0317-006)

Nation's Youth Turning Away from Marijuana, as Perceptions of Risk Rise; Most Adults with Substance Abuse Problems Are Employed. Substance Abuse and Mental Health Services Administration (SAMHSA), Media Advisory, September 9, 2004.

ONDCP [Office of National Drug Control Policy]. "Street Terms: Drugs and the Drug Trade," *Drug Facts.* http://www.whitehousedrugpolicy.gov/streetterms/default.asp. Accessed October 16, 2005

Parker, Joe. "How Prostitution Works." Prostitution Research and Education webpage. http://www.prostitutionresearch.com/parker-how.html. Accessed October 16, 2005.

Peed, Carl R. "COPS Office Attacks the Scourge of Meth," *Community Links*, November 2004, pp. 1–4.

Preston, Julia. "Causing Talk: Turncoat Mobsters on the Stand in the Racketeering Trial of John A. Gotti," *New York Times*, August 29, 2005.

Pulse Check: Trends in Drug Abuse. Washington, DC: Office of National Drug Control Policy, January 2004. (NCJ 201398)

Rutledge, Devallis. "K-9 Sniffs and the Fourth Amendment," *Police*, June 2005, pp. 88–91.

Schanlaub, Russell. "A Prescription for Abuse," *Law and Order*, November 2003, pp. 93–96.

Schanlaub, Russell. "Meth Hazards." *Law and Order*, March 2005, pp. 98–102.

Scott, Michael S. *Rave Parties.* Washington, DC: Office of Community Oriented Policing Services, Problem-Oriented Guides for Police Series No. 14, August 2004.

Sheehy, Robert D., and Rosario, Efrain A. "Connecting Drug Paraphernalia to Drug Gangs," *FBI Law Enforcement Bulletin*, February 2003, pp. 1–6.

Simon, Stephanie. "Meth Strains Police in Midwest: Authorities See a Drug Epidemic in Rural Counties," *Boston Globe*, July 17, 2005.

"States Crack Down on Cold Pills to Curb Meth," *NCJA Justice Bulletin*, April 2005, pp. 8, 13–14.

Steffen, George, and Candelaria, Samuel. "Currency Seizures during Interdiction Investigations," *Law and Order*, March 2004, pp. 40–47.

Thompson, Mark. "'Meth' Close Second to Cocaine as Top Drug Threat in Survey," *Drug Enforcement Report*, April 23, 2004, pp. 1–2.

Valdez, Al. "White Supremacist Gangs," *Police*, October 2002, pp. 90–93.

Walters, John P. "Methamphetamine: A National Response," *The Police Chief*, April 2005, pp. 32–35.

Wuestewald, Todd, and Adcock, Gayla. "Methamphetamine: A Particularly Insidious Drug," *Community Links*, May 2004, p. 3.

Wuestewald, Todd, and Adcock, Gayla. "Enlisting Community Help in the Investigation of Methamphetamine Laboratories." *The Police Chief*, March 2005, pp. 34–37.

Zernicke, Kate. "Officials across U.S. Describe Drug Woes," *New York Times*, July 6, 2005.

CASE CITED

Smith v. Maryland (1979)

Criminal Activities of Gangs and Other Dangerous Groups

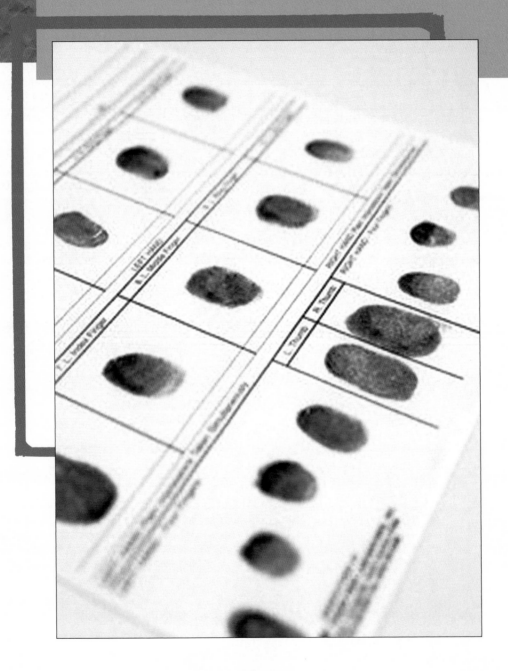

Do You Know?

- Whether the gang problem is increasing or decreasing?
- How criminologists have categorized street gangs?
- What types of crimes gangs typically engage in?
- What the first step in dealing with a gang problem is?
- How to identify gang members?
- What kinds of records to keep on gangs?
- What special challenges are involved in investigating illegal activities of gangs?
- What strategies have been used to combat a gang problem?
- What two defense strategies are commonly used by gang members' lawyers in court?
- What the primary motivation for bias/hate crimes is and who is most frequently targeted?
- What a cult is? How better to refer to cults?
- What a ritualistic crime is?
- What may be involved in ritualistic crime?
- What are indicators of ritualistic crimes?
- What special challenges are involved in investigating ritualistic crimes?

n Minneapolis, a 12-year-old boy and an 18-year-old man, both with ties to a local gang, are shot to death while sitting in a car parked behind an apartment building, allegedly by a reputed member of a rival gang. In Denver, a 16-year-old girl tries to break free from gang life and is stabbed to death a month later by a rival gang member.

In Jasper, Texas, a black man is chained by his ankles to a pickup truck and dragged to his death, his head and arm ripped from his body during the incident. In Laramie, Wyoming, a gay college student is beaten, tied to a fence, and left to die alone.

On a lonely rural road in Wisconsin, a pharmacist who was a member of a voodoo cult arranges to have himself shot and killed by two friends, also cult members. In Rancho Santa Fe, California, 39 members of a high-tech cult pack their bags and commit mass suicide, believing that in death they will rendezvous with a UFO that was trailing the Hale-Bopp comet. In Tavares, Florida, members of a teenage "vampire clan" use cigarettes to burn a "V" onto the body of a man they had just bludgeoned to death.

Scenes from the movie of the week? Unfortunately, no—they are actual events that have occurred across the country and reflect the everyday reality of gangs, hate crime, and ritualistic crime in the United States.

The chapter begins with an overview of gang-related crime. Next are some definitions of gangs and a look at their extent within society. This is followed by a discussion of why people join gangs; a look at the types of gangs in existence; and the connection between gangs, organized crime, and terrorism. Then gang culture, membership, and organization are presented,

followed by a discussion of gang activities, including their relationship to drugs. Next the discussion focuses on ways to recognize the existence of gangs and how to identify gang members, the records to keep, and ways to investigate illegal gang activity. The discussion next looks at approaches to the gang problem, collaborative efforts to combat gangs, and the prosecution of gang-related offenses. The section on gangs concludes with a discussion of federal efforts to tackle the gang problem.

The second topic discussed in this chapter is bias/hate crime, an issue that has been making headlines and presenting major problems for law enforcement. The discussion begins with an overview, a look at the motivation underlying such crimes, and the most common hate groups. This is followed by a discussion of the police response and efforts to combat bias/hate crimes.

The third topic considered is ritualistic crime. First is an overview of ritualistic crime, followed by the terminology and symbolism associated with rituals. Next is a discussion of the nature of ritualistic crimes and who commits them. The chapter concludes with an exploration of investigating ritualistic crimes and the special challenges they present.

The Threat of Gangs: An Overview

The pervasiveness of gangs throughout society is undeniable. They incite fear and violence within our communities. Gangs threaten our schools, our children and our homes. Gangs today are more sophisticated and flagrant in their use of violence and intimidation tactics. As they migrate across the country, they bring with them drugs, weapons and criminal activity (*2005 National Gang*, p.v).

Gangs have been of interest and concern for centuries. Street gangs have existed in the United States for most of the country's history and have been studied since the 1920s. Savelli (p.3) points out: "Gangs are not a new concept. Throughout the 1800s Americans were fascinated with gangs and gangsters. The James Gang, Billy the Kid and other outlaws, legend has it, ruled the Wild West. As the late 1800s roared in, the new generation of gangs and gangsters was created out of the new immigrants." The 1900s saw street gangs flourishing, influenced by such mobsters as Al Capone. And gangs continue to pose a problem for law enforcement in the twenty-first century.

Belonging to a gang is *not* illegal in this country; however, many activities that gangs engage in are illegal. Gangs traffic in drugs; commit shootings, assaults, robbery, extortion, and other felonies; and terrorize neighborhoods. Previously loose-knit groups of juveniles and young adults who engaged in petty crimes have, over time, become powerful, organized gangs, representing a form of domestic terrorism. Gang wars, drive-by shootings, and disregard for innocent bystanders have a chilling effect. Gangs now exist in almost every community.

To investigate gang-related crimes effectively, law enforcement personnel must understand the makeup of these organizations, what types of crimes to expect, how to identify their members, and how to deal with the special challenges of investigating such crimes.

Gangs Defined

gang is a group of individuals with a recognized name and symbols who form an allegiance for a common purpose and engage in continuous unlawful activity. A definition commonly accepted by law enforcement is that a gang is any group gathering continuously to commit antisocial behavior. Klein (p.135) provides the minimalist "consensus Eurogang definition" developed over five years and agreed on by more than 100 gang researchers in the United States and Europe: "A **street gang** is any durable, streetoriented youth group whose own identity includes involvement in criminal activity."

Extent of Gangs

The last quarter of the twentieth century saw significant growth in gang problems across the country. In the 1970s, less than half the states reported youth gang problems, but by the late 1990s, every state and the District of Columbia reported gang activity. During that same period, the number of cities reporting youth gang problems mushroomed nearly tenfold—from fewer than 300 to more than 2,500 in 1998.

Gangs range in size from small groups of 3 to 5 up to several thousand. Nationally known gangs such as the Crips number around 50,000 and the Bloods number about 20,000 to 30,000. Large gangs are normally broken down into smaller groups but are known collectively under one name. More than 90 percent of gangs have between 3 and 100 members, and only 4 percent have more than 100 members. The number of gangs in large cities ranges from 1,200 to 1,500.

According to the *2002 National Youth Gang Survey*, published by the Office of Juvenile Justice and Delinquency Prevention (OJJDP), there were an estimated 21,500 gangs and 731,500 gang members in the United States active in more than 2,300 cities with a population of 2,500 or more and in 550 jurisdictions served by county law enforcement agencies. This was a *decrease* from the previous year, 2001. However, Swecker (*Gangs*), the FBI's top criminal investigative executive, testified before Congress that there are approximately 30,000 gangs with 800,000 members and that today they are "more violent, more organized and more widespread than ever before." The FBI's Uniform Crime Reports state that 115 gangland murders and 819 juvenile gang killings occurred in 2003.

 The number of gangs and gang members has decreased over the last few years, but gang-related crime is still a major concern to law enforcement.

Johnson (2005b, p.3A) contends that statistics on the threat posed by gangs may be too low by at least 20,000

because of the 20,000 state and local police agencies contacted for information, only 455 provided information. Many agencies withhold such information so as not to alarm the public.

Gang Migration

As society in general has become more mobile, gangs and gang members have also increased their mobility, contributing to gang migration. Whereas early gangs tended to exist primarily in large cities near the country's borders (Los Angeles, New York, Miami, Chicago), gangs are now sending members across the country and into the nation's heartland to take advantage of new territory, diminished competition from other gangs, and law enforcement agencies with less experience in dealing with gang activity. The gang problem is not restricted to metropolitan areas. Researchers Weisheit and Wells (p.2) report that gangs are increasingly becoming a problem in rural areas.

In addition, as Hagerdorn (p.153) points out: "Gangs are a significant worldwide phenomenon with millions of members and a voice of those marginalized by processes of globalization." Deep-seated inequalities are too often reinforced by present economic and social conditions and can perpetuate gangs across the globe. Says Hagerdorn (p.163): "Gangs are being reproduced throughout this largely urban world by a combination of economic and political marginalization and cultural resistance. We ignore organizations of the socially excluded at great risk."

Why People Join Gangs

The many factors contributing to the development of delinquent gangs include dropping out of school, unemployment, family disorganization, neighborhood traditions of gang delinquency, and ethnic status. Gangs provide acceptance and protection to inner-city youth.

Kersten (p.B2) suggests: "Kids in gangs often start life differently. Many have young, unmarried mothers, some of whom are high school dropouts or drug abusers. Few have fathers who insist they get home on time or do their homework. As a result, they develop neither a strong moral code nor the ability to control their aggressive impulses."

Shelden et al. (pp.77–78) cite six reasons for joining a gang: (1) material reasons, (2) recreation, (3) a place of refuge and camouflage, (4) physical protection, (5) resistance against parents and/or society, and (6) commitment to community. Shelden et al. focus on the first factor, devoting an entire chapter in their book to "Inequality in American Society."

Types of Gangs

Shelden et al. (pp.42–43) describe the major types of gangs identified by various studies and different researchers nationwide:

- **Hedonistic/social gangs**—only moderate drug use and offending, involved mainly in using drugs and having a good time; little involvement in crime, especially violent crime

- **Party gangs**—commonly called "party crews"; relatively high use and sale of drugs, but only one major form of delinquency—vandalism; may contain both genders or may be one gender; many have no specific dress style, but some dress in stylized clothing worn by street gang members, such as baseball caps and oversize clothing; some have tattoos and use hand signs; their flexible turf is called the "party scene"; crews compete over who throws the biggest party, with alcohol, marijuana, nitrous oxide, sex, and music critical party elements.

- **Predatory gangs**—heavily involved in serious crimes (robberies, muggings) and the abuse of addictive drugs such as crack cocaine; may engage in selling drugs but not in organized fashion.

- **Scavenger gangs**—loosely organized groups described as "urban survivors"; prey on the weak in inner cities; engage in rather petty crimes but sometimes violence, often just for fun; members have no greater bond than their impulsiveness and need to belong; lack goals and are low achievers; often illiterate with poor school performance.

- **Serious delinquent gangs**—heavy involvement in both serious and minor crimes, but much lower involvement in drug use and drug sales than party gangs.

- **Territorial gangs**—associated with a specific area or turf and, as a result, get involved in conflicts with other gangs over their respective turfs.

- **Organized/corporate gangs**—heavy involvement in all kinds of crime, heavy use and sale of drugs; may resemble major corporations, with separate divisions handling sales, marketing, discipline, and so on; discipline is strict, and promotion is based on merit.

- **Drug gangs**—smaller than other gangs; much more cohesive; focused on the drug business; strong, centralized leadership with market-defined roles. (The link between gangs and drugs is discussed later in the chapter.)

Criminologists have classified gangs as cultural or instrumental.

Cultural gangs are neighborhood centered and exist independently of criminal activity. **Instrumental gangs** are formed for the express purpose of criminal activity, primarily drug trafficking.

Girl Gangs

A review of research on girl gangs shows that some young women find themselves trapped in horrible social conditions "characterized by widespread poverty and racism" (Shelden et al., p.174). A general consensus exists in the research literature that girls join gang life for the same reasons as their male counterparts—to meet basic human needs such as belonging/being a member of a family, self-esteem, and protection (p.175).

Shelden et al. (p.142) report three types of female gang involvement: (1) membership in an independent gang, (2) membership in a male gang as a coed, and (3) membership in a female auxiliary of a male gang. Most girls are found within the third type. Although the number of all-female gangs remains low, girls are taking more active roles, assisting in the movement of drugs and weapons, and gathering intelligence from other gangs (*2005 National Gang*, p.v) (Figure 19.1). Gangs are also often classified around race or nationality.

Ethnic Gangs

Much has been written about the various ethnic gangs in the United States. Among the most well known are African American gangs (Bloods, Crips, Vice Lords), Hispanic gangs (Latin Kings and Mara Salvatrucha 13), Asian gangs (Chinese, Filipino, Vietnamese, Hmong), and Indian Country gangs. An in-depth discussion of ethnic gangs is beyond the scope of this text. However,

Figure 19.1
A girl flashes the Playboy Gang's hand sign, the profile of a rabbit head.

the following trends are noted in the *2005 National Gang Threat Assessment* (p.v):

- Hispanic gang membership is on the rise. These gangs are migrating and expanding their jurisdictions throughout the country. Identification and differentiation of these gangs pose new obstacles for law enforcement, especially in rural communities.

- Migration of California-style gang culture remains a particular threat. The migration spreads the reach of gangs into new neighborhoods and promotes a flourishing gang subculture.

- Indian Country is increasingly reporting escalating levels of gang activity and gang-related crime and drug trafficking. The remote nature of many reservations and a thriving gang subculture make youths in these environments particularly vulnerable to gangs.

The literature on ethnic gangs is abundant. However, two of the preceding trends deserve expansion.

Mara Salvatrucha 13 (MS-13) Domash (p.30) contends that the Mara Salvatrucha is America's most dangerous gang: "Spreading from El Salvador to L.A. and across the United States, Mara Salvatrucha 13 is increasingly well organized and deadly." Gang members often wear blue and white, colors from the El Salvador flag. MS-13 has migrated to the East Coast, partially because of the strict antigang laws on the West Coast.

MS-13 is the most pervasive Salvadoran gang to settle in the Washington, D.C., area in the past few years and has approximately 5,000 members in North Virginia, Maryland, and the District ("The Reality," p.A16). MS-13 is active in smuggling people, drugs, and guns across the border (Domash, p.34). Stratman ("Gangs") reports that in 2005 U.S. officials expressed increasing concern about the spillover of gang violence from Latin America, specifically the violent MS-13.

Native American Gangs Martinez (p.20) suggests that the fastest-growing category of gangs is made up of Native Americans. Indian gangs are a significant problem in Minneapolis, throughout Arizona, and in the Pine Ridge area of South Dakota. According to Martinez (p.23), Native Americans suffer all the ills that new immigrants suffer and more, including living on reservations. In addition: "The overall lack of funding, coupled with challenges to the acknowledgment of gangs in Indian Country, mean that tribal police forces are spread mighty thin" (p.25).

Outlaw Motorcycle Gangs

The major outlaw motorcycle gangs (OMGs) are the Hell's Angels, Bandidos, Outlaws, and Pagans. These gangs' primary source of income is drug trafficking, but they are also involved in murder, assault, kidnapping, prostitution, money laundering, weapons trafficking,

intimidation, extortion, arson, and smuggling. The *2005 National Gang Threat Assessment* (p.v.) reports that OMGs are expanding their territory and forming new clubs, as reflected in increased violence among them as they battle over territories.

Prison Gangs

Although prison gangs would seem to be more of a problem for corrections, the *2005 National Gang Threat Assessment* (p.v) notes: "Prison gangs pose a unique threat to law enforcement and communities. Incarceration of gang members often does little to disrupt their activities. High-ranking gang members are often able to exert their influence on the street from within prison." In fact, prison provides a prime recruiting opportunity for some gangs.

Gangs, Organized Crime, and Terrorism

he *2005 National Gang Threat Assessment* (p.v) reports that gangs are associating with organized crime entities, such as Mexican drug organizations, Asian criminal groups, and Russian organized crime groups. Approximately 26 percent of law enforcement agencies surveyed indicated that gangs were associated with organized crime entities in their jurisdiction. These groups often turn to gangs to conduct low-level criminal activity, protect territories, and facilitate drug-trafficking activities. The primary goal of any association between these groups is financial gain.

A more hopeful finding is that few gangs have been found to associate with domestic terrorist organizations. Only 5.7 percent of law enforcement agencies surveyed indicated that gangs were associated with any domestic or international terrorist organizations or extremist groups in their jurisdiction. Of the domestic terrorist groups identified, most were white supremacist groups (2005 National Gang Threat Assessment, p.v). The susceptibility of gang members to any type of terrorist organization appears to be highest in prison.

Gang Culture, Membership, and Organization

ome gang experts talk about the three R's of the gang culture: reputation, respect, and revenge. Reputation is of prime concern to gang members, both individually and collectively. They expect, indeed demand, respect. And they are required to show disrespect for rival gang members, called a "diss" in gang slang. Disrespect inevitably leads to the third R—revenge. Every challenge must be answered, often in the form of a drive-by shooting.

Most gangs are of limited numbers sufficient for the entire group to meet and discuss things in person. Incidents that happen to them or that are expressly initiated by them cause them to identify as a group. This bonding normally takes place over time. Sometimes gang members are multigenerational—that is, father and son may have been members of the same gang. Most gang members are unemployed or work at part-time jobs. Many are most active at night and sleep during the day. Some stay with their gangs into adulthood, and others may go back to school or gain full-time employment, usually in jobs with very low pay.

Most gang members are weak academically because they lack good study habits, although they are mentally capable. This is an important factor because gangs are essentially self-operated and self-governed. Some operate by consensus, but the majority have leaders and a subgoverning structure. Leadership may be single or dual. Status is generally obtained by joining the gang, but equal status within the gang once joined is not automatically guaranteed.

Gang members have differing levels of commitment and involvement in gang activities. Most gang members are either hard-core, associate, or peripheral members. The hard-core members are those most dedicated to the gang. Knowing how a gang is organized and what level of involvement a member has can be of great assistance to investigators. The hard-core member is least likely to cooperate with the police; the peripheral members are most likely to be cooperative.

Turf and Graffiti

Many gangs establish a **turf,** the *geographic* area of domination that gang members will defend to the death. The turf includes the schools, businesses, residential areas, streets, and alleys in the area, all controlled through fear, intimidation, and violence. In the past, turf wars took the form of gang fights. Today, however, they often take the form of drive-by shootings from a moving vehicle, many of which have killed innocent citizens as well as rival gang members.

Gangs identify their turf through **graffiti,** called "throwing a placa." Other gangs may challenge the turf claim by writing over or crossing out the graffiti and replacing it with their own. Such cross-outs are usually found at the edge of a gang's territory. Gang members caught in the act of crossing out graffiti in a rival's territory may be killed, or a turf war can result. Gang graffiti is a source of frustration and expense to property owners and local governments.

Police officers who deal with gangs can learn much by understanding wall graffiti. The center of a gang's turf will have the most graffiti. It may name members of the gang, often in order of authority, listed in neat rows under the gang's logo. Reading graffiti is discussed later in the chapter. Unchallenged graffiti affirms the gang's control. With the increasing mobility of society, graffiti no longer has to necessarily remain within a gang's turf.

Hispanic graffiti is highly artistic and very detailed. It frequently refers to group or gang power. In contrast, graffiti of black gangs shows less flair and attention to detail and often is filled with profanity as well as expressions of individual power. The symbolism is more obvious and often includes weapons.

Symbols

Savelli (p.23) stresses the importance of understanding gangs/groups and creating a keen awareness of their presence. One way to do this is by paying attention to a gang's symbols. These symbols are often personalized and may appear in various combinations.

Gang Activities

Many gang activities are similar to those of other segments of society and are *not* illegal. Gangs gather informally on streets and street corners, in parks, homes, abandoned buildings, vehicles, vacant lots, or recreational areas and buildings. Indeed, many of the defining characteristics of a gang could be applicable to any other organization in society, with the exception of the purpose, which is to engage in antisocial or criminal behavior. Not all gangs engage in criminal behavior, however. Some "gangs" form out of normal relationships in a neighborhood or a school.

If they do not engage in antisocial behavior, nothing ever happens that causes them to feel a need to "band together" to protect their group from outside activity or threats. The gang remains a social group or club.

However, when a gang forms for social reasons and then outside activities occur that endanger one or more of the members, the group may "close ranks" and act as a group in their defense. For example, the group may be having a meeting in the park and an outside group beats up a few of the members. The group may report this to the police or may decide to take matters into their own hands and seek revenge. Other gangs form for the express purpose of committing antisocial behavior or criminal activities, starting with the manner of initiation into the group, which may require shoplifting or a more serious illegal activity.

Gangs offer a sense of belonging and importance to their members that society and family do not provide. Gang members gradually dissociate from social conformity and become responsible only to themselves and their group activities.

Regardless of how or why gangs form, society views them as undesirable. The public often associates drinking and sexual promiscuity with gangs, and this is often the reality. Table 19.1 compares gang and nongang criminal behavior.

Although gang crime often involves only a few members at a time, occasionally the entire gang, or a large portion of it, participates in the illegal activity. For example, a surveillance video from a Las Vegas minimarket showed more than 40 teenagers flooding into the tiny store. Three youths jumped the counter and robbed the cashier at gunpoint while the others flocked to coolers. Teens clogged the doorways as they rushed out, carrying cases of beer and handfuls of food. The whole incident took less than 90 seconds. Police call this technique **swarming.**

Harrell (p.1) cites data from the National Crime Victimization Survey (NCVS) indicating that about 6 percent of violent victimizations between 1993 and 2003 were committed by gang members. Gang members committed about 373,000 of the 6.6 million violent victimizations annually. Harrell (p.2) reports that victims believed offenders were gang members in about 12 percent of all aggravated assaults occurring between 1993 and 2003. Offenders were identified as gang members in about 4 percent of rapes, 6 percent of simple assaults, and 10 percent of robberies.

 In addition to drug dealing, gang members often engage in vandalism, arson, shootings, stabbings, intimidation, and other forms of violence.

Figure 19.2 describes the type of gang-related crime by percentage.

Gangs and Drugs

The *2005 National Gang Threat Assessment* (p.v) reports that gangs remain the primary distributors of drugs throughout the United States. Shelden et al. (p.123) state: "There is little question that drug usage and violent crime are closely related. What is still in doubt, however, is the relationship between drugs (both usage and sales) and gangs. Research on this issue has produced conflicting findings. . . . Gang members are about twice as likely as nongang members to use drugs and to use them more often."

Katz et al. (p.81) found that soft- and hard-drug use among gang members was very common. More than three-quarters of current and past gang members in their sample had used marijuana in the past year and

Table 19.1 / Comparison of Gang and Nongang Criminal Behavior (Cleveland)

Crime (p^1)	Gang (N = 47)	Nongang (N = 49)
Auto theft (***)	44.7%	4.1%
Assault rivals (***)	72.3	16.3
Assault own members (*)	30.4	10.2
Assault police (n.s.)	10.6	14.3
Assault teachers (n.s.)	14.9	18.4
Assault students (n.s.)	51.1	34.7
Mug people (n.s.)	10.6	4.1
Assault in streets (*)	29.8	10.2
Theft-other (***)	51.1	14.3
Intim/assault-vict/wit (***)	34.0	0.0
Intim/assault shoppers (*)	23.4	6.1
Drive-by shooting (***)	40.4	2.0
Homicide (**)	15.2	0.0
Sell stolen goods (*)	29.8	10.2
Guns in school (***)	40.4	10.2
Knives in school (***)	38.3	4.2
Concealed weapons (***)	78.7	22.4
Drug use (**)	27.7	4.1
Drug sales (school) (n.s.)	19.1	8.2
Drug sales (other) (***)	61.7	16.7
Drug theft (***)	21.3	0.0
Bribe police (n.s.)	10.6	2.0
Burglary (unoccupied) (*)	8.5	0.0
Burglary (occupied) (n.s.)	2.1	2.0
Shoplifting (n.s.[.058])	30.4	14.3
Check forgery (n.s.)	2.1	0.0
Credit card theft (n.s.)	6.4	0.0
Arson (*)	8.5	0.0
Kidnapping (n.s.)	4.3	0.0
Sexual assault/molest (n.s.)	2.1	0.0
Rape (n.s.)	2.1	0.0
Robbery (*)	17.0	2.0

(p^1) Level of statistical significance: *$p<.05$; **$p<.01$; ***$p<.001$; n.s. = no significant difference.

Source: C. Ronald Huff. *Comparing the Criminal Behavior of Youth Gangs and At-Risk Youths.* Washington, DC: National Institute of Justice Research in Brief, October 1998, p. 4.

about 70 percent of current gang members tested positive at the time of arrest. They conclude that current gang members are significantly more likely to use marijuana and cocaine compared with former gang members.

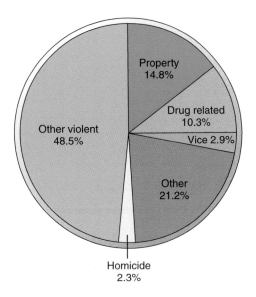

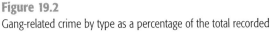

Figure 19.2

Gang-related crime by type as a percentage of the total recorded

Table 19.2 / **Common Differences between Street Gangs and Drug Gangs**

Street Gangs	Drug Gangs
Versatile ("cafeteria-style") crime	Crime focused on drug business
Larger structures	Smaller structures
Less cohesive	More cohesive
Looser leadership	More centralized leadership
Ill-defined roles	Market-defined roles
Code of loyalty	Requirement of loyalty
Residential territories	Sales market territories
Members may sell drugs	Members do sell drugs
Intergang rivalries	Competition controlled
Younger on average, but wider age range	Older on average, but narrower age range

Source: James C. Howell. *Youth Gangs: An Overview.* OJJDP Juvenile Justice Bulletin, August 1998, p. 13.

The gang problem is exceedingly complex. Not all gangs deal with drugs, and not all who use drugs commit other crimes. Law enforcement officers must maintain objectivity and refrain from stereotyping gang members and drug users and pushers. They must know how to deal with gangs effectively and how to do their part in the war on drugs. Keep in mind, however, that many gangs are not involved in drugs, either using or selling.

Until the early 1980s, when crack, or rock cocaine, hit the market, gangs engaged primarily in burglary, robbery, extortion, and car theft. Although drug trafficking existed, it was nowhere near current levels. The reason: enormous profit. Economic gain is often the reason youths join gangs. It is hard to convince a youth that $5.50 an hour for busing tables is preferable to making $400 for two hours' work as a drug courier.

Valdez and Sifaneck (p.82) studied the role of Mexican American gang members in drug marketing and found (1) many gang members are user/sellers and are not profit-oriented dealers, (2) gangs commonly extend protection to drug-selling members, and (3) proximity to Mexican drug markets, adult prison gangs, and criminal family members may play important roles in whether these gang members have access and the profit potential to actually deal drugs.

Some, however, caution that drug trafficking by gangs is not as rampant as others might claim. Aside from expert opinions that most gangs lack the discipline, leadership, and crime skills necessary to sustain a successful drug operation, those gangs that are successful are serious forces to be reckoned with. Table 19.2 compares characteristics of street gangs and drug gangs.

Gangs often purposely exploit the difference between juvenile and adult law in their drug dealing,

using younger gang members whenever possible to avoid adult sanctions. Most states will not allow youths under age 15 to be certified as adults and have statutory restrictions on placing youths under age 18 into adult correctional facilities.

Recognizing a Gang Problem

Failure to recognize or acknowledge the existence of gang activity, whether willingly or through the lack of gang identification training, dramatically increases a gang's ability to thrive and develop a power base. The *2005 National Gang Threat Assessment* (p.v) reports that about 31 percent of survey respondents indicated that their communities refused to acknowledge the gang problem. Several communities began to address gang issues only when high-profile gang-related incidents occurred.

The first step in dealing with a gang problem is to recognize it.

Walker (2005) stresses that gangs' presence can be seen everywhere. They are not an invisible empire, but rather thrive on recognition and constantly seek ways to make their presence known or felt. Walker asserts: "They only go unseen when law enforcement personnel, as well as educators and parents, fail to recognize

Table 19.3 / **Criteria for Defining Gangs**

Criteria Used*	Large Cities	Smaller Cities
Use of symbols	93%	100%
Violent behavior	81	84
Group organization	81	88
Territory	74	88
Leadership	59	48
Recurrent interaction	56	60

*Of the cities surveyed, 70 (89%) of the large cities and 25 (58%) of the smaller cities indicated the criteria used to define gangs.

Source: 1994 National Institute of Justice Gang Survey. Washington, DC.

the signs of gang activity and an individual's involvement."

Warning Signs of a Gang Problem

Identifying gangs is difficult, but law enforcement, a school, or a community can be aware of warning signs of a gang problem: graffiti, obvious colors of clothing, tattoos, initiations, hand signals or handshakes, uncommon terms or phrases, and a sudden change in behavior. Valdez (p.66) suggests that gangs have discovered that wearing sports teams' clothing is a low-profile way to represent their own gang colors. Table 19.3 summarizes some criteria used by some jurisdictions to identify gangs. Additional criteria include the use of graffiti and hand signals.

fter the first step, recognizing a gang problem, the second step is to identify the gang members.

Gang members may be identified by their names, symbols (clothing and tattoos), and communication styles, including graffiti and sign language.

The **Crips,** for example, are associated with blue or purple bandannas, scarves, or rags. The **Bloods** are identified by red or green colors. Mexican gangs often wear brown bandanas as a symbol of ethnic pride. Some gangs wear jackets and caps identified with profes-

sional sports teams, posing a problem for those youths who wear them because of actual loyalty to the particular team. Gang members may also be identified by the hand signals they use. Tattoos (sometimes called body art) are another means of identifying gang members. The most respected tattoos are those earned by serving a prison sentence.

Often, the stylized dress and haircuts, tattoos, graffiti, slang, hand signs, and jewelry used by other street gangs are also used by Southeast Asian gangs. Another characteristic of Southeast Asian street gangs is that they do not claim turf but rather are very mobile, with informal networks throughout the United States.

With rural gangs, according to Weisheit and Wells (p.3), the most frequent indicator is self-identification by youths. They note: "Respondents also frequently used the presence of graffiti and tattoos, the wearing of gang colors and the judgment of criminal justice officials that some youths were gang members." Table 19.4 lists warning signs that a youth may be involved with a gang.

Police also need to identify the gang leaders and the "tough guys." Reducing the effectiveness of the leaders is important but is often difficult and can be accomplished

Table 19.4 / **Warning Signs that a Youth May Be Involved with a Gang**

Admits to "hanging out" with kids in gangs
Shows an unusual interest in one or two particular colors of clothing or a particular logo
Has an unusual interest in gangster-influenced music, videos, movies, or websites
Uses unusual hand signals to communicate with friends
Has specific drawings of gang symbols on schoolbooks, clothes, walls, or tattoos
Has unexplained physical injuries (fighting-related bruises, injuries to hands/knuckles)
Has unexplained cash or goods, such as clothing or jewelry
Carries a weapon
Has been in trouble with the police
Exhibits negative change in behavior such as:
• Withdrawing from family
• Declining school attendance, performance, behavior
• Staying out late without reason
• Displaying an unusual desire for secrecy
• Exhibiting signs of drug use
• Breaking rules consistently
• Speaking in gang-style slang

Source: Washington, DC Office of Community Oriented Policing Services.

only by having sufficient evidence to convict the leader of a crime that results in a prison sentence.

Browne (2004) describes how the Los Angeles Police Department has targeted the top 10 percent of the gang leadership, the "sociopaths" who are committing most of the crimes, as a first step in combating their gang problem.

Records to Keep

The most common way to gather information about gangs is internal contacts with patrol officers and detectives, followed by internal departmental records and computerized files and then by review of offense reports.

Information is an essential tool for law enforcement, and an effective records system is critical in dealing with any gang problem. A gang file should be maintained with the following information: type of gang (street, motorcycle, etc.), ethnic composition, number of active and associate members, territory, hideouts, types of crimes usually committed, method of operation, choice of targets or victims, leadership, and members known to be violent (Figure 19.3). Included within the record system should be a *gang member pointer file* that cross-references the names of suspected gang members with the gang file. This may be a cardex or computerized file.

A *moniker file* connects suspected gang members' street names with their legal names. A **moniker,** or nickname, is the name gang members use among their peers and often during the commission of crimes. Although no two members of the same gang will have the same moniker, several gangs may have members with the same moniker. Therefore, one card should have on it the moniker and all gang members who use it.

A *photograph file* is of great help in conducting photographic identification sessions. A *gang vehicle file* can be maintained, arranged alphabetically by vehicle *make.* Include color, year, body type, license number, distinguishing features, known drivers, and usual parking spots. An *illegal activities file* can also be maintained, arranged alphabetically, listing the gangs known to engage in the activities.

Maintain records on gangs, gang members, monikers, photographs, vehicles, and illegal activities. Cross-reference the records.

A gang information system can provide current crime incident data that can be linked to gang members and used to enhance police and other agency interventions. Table 19.5 shows the methods used for gathering information on gangs.

Investigating Illegal Gang Activity

Gang investigations should proceed like most other criminal investigations. Uniformed officers should establish personal contacts with the gangs in the community and become familiar with their size, the names of as many members as possible, and each gang's identifying symbols, colors, and graffiti.

A mutual understanding between the police and gang members can reduce violence. The police know what gangs do, and gangs know what police do. Gang members try to avoid the police but at times engage in open confrontation because of police interference with their territory and the criminal activities they perpetrate.

Some disenchanted gang members may become police informants. Children know what is going on among their peers even though they may not be gang members themselves. Teachers and school counselors are other sources of information on acceptable and unacceptable youth activities. In addition, recreation department personnel know what is going on in the youth community and are therefore good sources of information.

Obtaining information from gang members is difficult because of the gang's unity. The same techniques police use to obtain information about organized crime and other serious criminal activity can produce information about gang activity. Obtaining witness information from nongang members is difficult because they feel threatened by the gang and have obvious concerns about their personal safety.

Figure 19.3
Canyon County Prosecuter Dave Young points to a map of Caldwell, Idaho, with pins marking public reporting of shots fired during the month of August, during a public meeting on how to fight gang violence.

Table 19.5 / **Methods Used for Gathering Information on Gangs Ranked by "Often Used" Category**

	Never Used	Sometimes Used	Often Used
Internal contacts with patrol officers and detectives	1	22	64
Internal departmental records and computerized files	4	22	62
Review of offense reports	2	25	60
Interviews with gang members	5	26	56
Information obtained from other local police agencies	1	35	51
Surveillance activities	6	37	44
Use of unpaid informants	2	44	42
Information obtained from other criminal justice agencies	3	43	42
Information obtained from other governmental agencies	3	47	37
Provision of information by schools	2	50	35
Reports from state agencies	11	63	14
Use of paid informants	28	46	13
Reports from federal agencies	16	62	9
Information obtained from private organizations	27	51	9
Infiltration of police officers into gangs or related groups	75	11	2

James W. Stevens. "Youth Gangs' Dimensions." *The Encyclopedia of Police Science,* 2nd ed., edited by William G. Bailey. New York: Garland, 1995, p. 832. Reprinted by permission.

The immediate area in which a crime occurs may yield much information. Any graffiti present indicates which gang controls the territory. Keep in mind that gang members do not like to be on foot in a strange area, especially one dominated by their enemies; therefore, commando-type raids on foot are very rare.

If a neighborhood canvass is conducted and information is received, it is important that the canvass not stop at that point. This would implicate the house or business at which the canvass was terminated as the source of information. In addition, more information might be available from a source not yet contacted during the canvass.

Crime scenes that involve gangs are unique. Often the crime scene is part of a chain of events. When a gang assault occurs, for example, often a chase precedes and follows the assault, considerably widening the crime scene. If vehicles are involved, the assault is probably by a rival gang. If no vehicles appear to have been involved, the suspects are probably local, perhaps even members of the same gang as the victim. This frequently occurs when narcotics, girlfriends, or family disputes are involved.

Evidence obtained in gang-related criminal investigations is processed in the same way as evidence related to any other crime. Photograph graffiti for later identification. File field-interview cards on members, vehicles, territory, locations, crimes committed, drug activities, and any other information. Gang members may usually be located within their territory even after they commit a crime—because this is their "home."

Burns (*Gang- and Drug-Related*) describes a novel investigative approach used in Baltimore, Maryland, to combat gangs based on the concept that the gang is an instrument of the leader's will. An investigative goal is to develop conspiracy cases from evidence obtained by turning the gang's violence inward on vulnerable gang members. The approach uses two phases, a *covert phase*, which involves identifying the gang's members, detecting its victims and violent acts, learning its reputation, and developing an informant to observe and record the gang's characteristics and activities over time. When this phase is complete, the investigation moves to the overt phase.

The *overt phase* targets members outside the leadership nucleus. During this phase, targeted gang members are placed in legal jeopardy in a highly structured interview situation designed to change the allegiance from the gang to the investigative team. The overt phase uses one of three methods to place gang members in jeopardy: (1) controlled arrests, (2) interviews of randomly arrested gang members, and (3) grand juries as investigative tools.

The interview uses two major themes. The first theme is a "litany" of the gang's violence, with responsibility placed squarely on the leader. The second theme is self-interest. The subject is promised leniency in exchange for cooperation against the violence-prone nucleus of the gang. In addition to the major themes, interviews introduce other themes, including the investigator's knowledge of the gang, the inevitability of prosecution, and the scope of the investigation.

Technology Innovations

The Analyst's Notebook, a software program that military special forces used to capture Saddam Hussein, can be used by law enforcement officers to track gang activity. The program's visual spreadsheet offers detectives an uncluttered picture of what formerly was a jumble of loose relationships. Investigators can scan photos or download documents into the spreadsheet and draw lines between various elements before typing descriptions under each line. They can include audiotapes and videos. Analyst's Notebook lets the investigator see all the connections, whether it's financial transactions or a name that has three aliases attached to it. The software has also been used in several significant criminal investigations in the United States, including the DC sniper case ("Greensboro Police," 2004).

Another source of information on gangs is the Internet. Thousands of gang-related sites have been posted. In addition, investigators can learn much about gangs in their jurisdiction by paying attention to graffiti.

Reading and Responding to Graffiti

Savelli (p.9) suggests: "The key to understanding gang graffiti is being able to analyze the symbols, indicators and terminology used by gangs. Simply, gangs use graffiti to send messages. The purpose of these messages is:

- To mark the gang's turf (territory).
- To disrespect a rival gang or gang member.
- To memorialize a deceased gang member.
- To make a statement.
- To send a message.
- To conduct business.

    Savelli (p.15) notes: "While it is important to read the writing on the walls, it is equally important to cover it over as soon as possible. Don't give the gang a chance to claim your community as their turf by allowing their graffiti to stay intact." To document graffiti evidence:

- Photograph it whole and in sections.
- Analyze it while it is intact.
- Remove it (paint over it, sandblast it, etc.).
- Archive the photo.
- Record the colors used.
- Record the gang "Tag" names.
- Record indicators of "beef" or violence.
- Create an anti-graffiti program to cover over all graffiti.

An area of Los Angeles prone to graffiti has used video surveillance to reduce graffiti by 60 percent (Lee, 2005). The anti-graffiti effort is called UNTAG, which stands for Uniting Neighborhoods to Abolish Graffiti. The program also gives investigators useful information about who is responsible for the graffiti, invaluable for their investigations of local gangs.

Challenges in Investigating Illegal Gang Activities

Illegal activities of gangs usually involve multiple suspects, which makes investigation much more difficult. Evidence may link only a few of the suspects with the crime, and, as with organized crime figures, gang members maintain fierce loyalty to each other.

A further difficulty is that many "witnesses" may actually be gang members or people who at least sympathize with the gang, so their information is highly suspect. In addition, others within the neighborhood may have information but may be afraid to become involved. Because they live in the neighborhood with the gang and may fear for their lives, they may provide information and then later deny it. For this reason, tape-record or videotape all such interviews.

> Special challenges in investigating the illegal activities of gangs include the multitude of suspects and the unreliability or fear of witnesses.

Approaches to the Gang Problem

> Four general strategies are being used to deal with gang problems: (1) suppression or law-enforcement efforts, (2) social intervention, (3) opportunities provision, and (4) community organization.

The most effective approach is probably a combination of prevention, intervention, and suppression strategies. More specific strategies might include not tolerating graffiti, targeting hard-core gang leaders, and consolidating major gang-control functions. Table 19.6 shows the law enforcement strategies being used, with what frequency, and with what perceived effectiveness if used.

Although in-state information exchange was the most used strategy, it was also among those judged least effective. Street sweeps and other suppression tactics were used by less than half the departments, but their effectiveness was judged high.

Table 19.6 / **Law Enforcement Strategies and Perceived Effectiveness***

Strategy	Used (Percent)	Judged Effective (If Used) (Percent)
Some or a lot of use		
Targeting entry points	14	17
Gang laws	40	19
Selected violations	76	42
Out-of-state information exchange	53	16
In-state information exchange	90	17
In-city information exchange	55	18
Federal agency operational coordination	40	16
State agency operational coordination	50	13
Local agency operational coordination	78	16
Community collaboration	64	54
Any Use		
Street sweeps	40	62
Other suppression tactics	44	63
Crime prevention activities	15	56

*Percentage of cities n = 211. The number of cities responding to each question varied slightly.

SOURCE: James C. Howell. *Youth Gang Programs and Strategies.* Washington, DC: OJJDP, August 2000, p.46. (NCJ 171154)

Suppression

As might be expected, law enforcement agencies view the following, in this order, as most effective in preventing and controlling gang crime: suppression tactics, such as street sweeps, intensified surveillance, and hot-spot targeting; crime prevention activities; and community collaboration. Fritsch et al. (p.267) point out: "Suppression tactics include tactical patrols by law enforcement, vertical prosecution by district attorneys and intensive supervision by probation departments. Generally, suppression involves the arrest, prosecution and incarceration of gang members." Weisheit and Wells (p.6) report that the most frequent agency response in rural areas to gang activity was suppression through strict enforcement—"zero tolerance." Although suppression is the primary strategy used in many jurisdictions, Fritsch et al. suggest it is also frequently viewed as the least effective.

A Youth Violence Strike Force (YVSF) reviewed what had been done in the past and found one program mentioned over and over: the Wendover Street operation. In that operation police disrupted gang violence by cracking down on any type of criminal activity and by telling gang members that the crackdown would continue until the violence stopped. The YVSF decided to take this approach, called **pulling levers,** telling gang members: " 'We're here because of the shooting. We're not going to leave until it stops. And until it does, nobody is going to so much as jaywalk, nor make any money, nor have any fun.' The plan involved pulling every legal lever the police could, which was not diffi-

cult as many gang members were on probation, selling drugs or otherwise chronically offending" (Kennedy et al., p.28). Tita et al. (2005, p.115) list several other levers police can use, including property (vehicle, housing) ownership, vehicle licensure, child support payments, children's truancy, asset forfeiture, and warrants.

Tita et al. (*Reducing Gun,* p.1) describe Operation Ceasefire in Los Angeles, an intervention intended to send gang members the message that there would be consequences for *all* members of a gang if any one member committed a crime involving guns. This program was modeled after Boston's well-known Operation Ceasefire. The message that something would happen if gun violence continued was retailed in advance. **Retailing** is forewarning gang members that violent crime will bring consequences and offering incentives, such as services, to reject crime (Tita et al., 2005, p.4).

Gang Units

Many departments have established gang units, which use a combination of prevention, suppression, and intervention. The suppression component involves collaboration among police, probation, and prosecution, targeting the most active gang members and leaders. According to Johnson (2005a, p.1A), watching and restricting one gang leader is equivalent to watching 200 gang members. The intervention component includes giving gang members the chance to finish high school or obtain a GED (general equivalency diploma), to have tattoos removed, and to obtain gainful employment and legal assistance. The prevention component includes conflict resolution skills and peer counseling.

Loudoun County, Virginia, formed a gang unit of five full-time investigators after an alert from a neighboring county that MS-13 was becoming active in the area (Collins, pp.11–12). According to the county sheriff, "We got very aggressive at going out and identifying gang members, finding the hotspots where they were hanging out and doing business. This was important to us because we started gathering statistics and could see where we stood, what was going on throughout the county."

Gang Impact Teams

Collins (p.12) describes the gang problem facing Los Angeles: "More than 400 gangs, comprising 52,000 members are known to operate in Los Angeles, population 4 million. . . . Of the 516 homicides in the city last year 263, or 41 percent, were gang-related, costing the city nearly $875 million per homicide. Intangible costs cover quality-of-life issues, such as revenue loss due to fear of crime or declining property values, and are estimated at more than $2.16 million per homicide. And that's just for homicide. Add to that the dollar costs for rape, robbery and aggravated assault and you're looking at a $946 million price tab." One approach to this problem was the formation of gang impact teams and strategic targeting:

> In L.A., where gangs are so pervasive, the police department has formed gang impact teams to manage investigations. Previously, LAPD's narcotics work was handled in a separate, centralized division. However, when it was recognized that gang activity and drug activity went hand in hand, narcotics officers and gang officers were assembled into teams that operate out of each of the city's 18 precincts. This arrangement gives the teams autonomy to address neighborhood gang problems as they see fit, but the teams also meet once or twice monthly to coordinate a centralized strategy. . . .
>
> [According to the overseer of the teams] Given the totality of our resources against the magnitude of the problem, we like to concentrate on the 10 percent factor—that is, the concept that 10 percent of suspects are responsible for 50 percent of crime and that 10 percent of locations account for 60 percent of all crime scenes. (Collins, p.13)

Civil Gang Injunctions and Ordinances

Civil gang injunctions (CGIs) are legal tools used with urban gangs that focus on individuals and the locations of their routine activities. These neighborhood-level intervention strategies target specific individuals who intimidate residents and cause other public nuisance issues and restricts these gang members' activities within a specific geographic area (Maxon et al., p.239).

Another approach to the gang problem in some cities is to pass a gang ordinance. Santa Clara, California, recently passed such an ordinance, and as O'Rourke (2004) states: "Gang members bent on intimidating others by loitering in public places have been put on notice by the city that they are breaking the law. An ordinance adopted Tuesday empowers the Sheriff's Department to arrest gang members who loiter in public areas with the intent to mark their domain or to conceal illegal acts."

Collaborative Efforts

Collaboration among law enforcement agencies can greatly enhance efforts to cope with the gang problem. In addition, as noted by the *2005 National Gang Threat Assessment* (p.v): "Forming multiagency task forces and joint community groups is an effective way to combat the gang problem."

Even though law enforcement unquestionably plays a major role in effectively combating the gang problem, partnerships with the community, parents, and schools significantly increase the likelihood of a successful response.

Gangs and Community Policing

Greene (p.11) contends: "The police have begun to learn that for their actions to become effective and perhaps lasting, they must mobilize external others." This is as true for investigators as it is for patrol officers. Weisel and Shelley (*2004*) studied the extent to which community policing and specialized gang units are complementary or conflicting approaches to gangs. They conclude: "There is little evidence that specialized gang units conflict with community policing in principle or practice, indeed, gang units can complement community policing by providing resources to focus on specific problems related to gangs." They also note, however, that the fit of gang units with community policing will continue to reflect the organizational tension in balancing proactive and reactive approaches to investigations.

One valuable resource available to all communities is the National Gang Crime Research Center website (http://www.ngcrc.com).

Prosecuting Gang-Related Crimes

Throughout the investigation of illegal gang activities, be aware of the most common defenses gang members use in court.

Table 19.7 / **Prosecution Problems by Size of Jurisdiction**

Problem	LARGE JURISDICTIONS (N = 118)			
	Not a Problem	Minor Problem	Moderate Problem	Major Problem
Obtaining cooperation of victims and witnesses	2.6%	8.8%	27.2%	61.4%
Intimidation of victims and witnesses	1.8	17.0	30.4	50.8
Lack of appropriate sanctions for juvenile gang members who commit crimes	9.7	22.2	21.2	46.9
Lack of early intervention for youth at risk of gang involvement	9.7	11.5	32.8	46.0
Lack of resources for witness protection	6.1	20.2	31.6	42.1
Victim and witness credibility	6.2	16.8	46.9	30.1
Inadequate police preparation of crime reports	33.3	41.2	20.2	5.3
	SMALL JURISDICTIONS (N = 74)			
Obtaining cooperation of victims and witnesses	10.1	15.9	30.4	43.5
Intimidation of victims and witnesses	13.2	19.2	25.0	42.6
Lack of appropriate sanctions for juvenile gang members who commit crimes	2.9	27.5	37.7	31.9
Lack of early intervention for youth at risk of gang involvement	15.7	18.6	34.3	31.4
Lack of resources for witness protection	7.1	27.1	37.2	28.6
Victim and witness credibility	1.4	30.0	41.4	27.2
Inadequate police preparation of crime reports	34.8	39.2	13.0	13.0

Source: Claire Johnson, Barbara Webster and Edward Connors. *Prosecuting Gangs: A National Assessment.*
Washington, DC: National Institute of Justice Research in Brief, February 1995, pp. 6–7.

 The two most often used defense strategies are pleas of diminished capacity and self-defense.

Although some states have eliminated "diminished capacity" as a defense, many have not. Therefore, *document* whether the suspect was under the influence of alcohol or other drugs at the time of the crime. Likewise, *document* whether the suspect was threatened by the victim and could possibly have been acting in self-defense. Table 19.7 summarizes difficulties in prosecuting gang-related crimes. In both large and small jurisdictions, obtaining cooperation of victims and witnesses and intimidation of victims and witnesses present the most problems.

Federal Efforts to Combat the Gang Problem

 n January 2004, an LAPD-FBI collaboration, including federal indictments of 15 gang members, was at the "leading edge of a quiet

sea change inside the FBI." According to FBI Director Robert Mueller, the FBI is obligated to respond to the growing "barbarity and the willingness to utilize homicide, torture and assaults in furtherance of violent gang activities" (Ragavan and Guttman, p.22). Swecker notes the following efforts of the FBI in combating the gang problem:

- More Safe Streets Violent Gang Task Forces (SSVGTFs), from 78 to 108, and 20 more planned. Since 1996, the SSVGTFs have led to nearly 20,000 convictions and the dismantling of more than 250 gangs.

- A National Gang Intelligence Center to coordinate the national collection of gang intelligence and share it with law enforcement agencies throughout the country and around the globe.

- A new MS-13 National Gang Task Force (NGTF) to help speed the flow of information and intelligence on MS-13 nationally and internationally and to coordinate investigations.

Swecker, who oversees criminal investigations for the FBI, has said the MS-13 has surpassed traditional organized crime as the top priority of his division.

The effort is paying off. Gately (2005) reports that on August 25, 2005, a federal grand jury indicted 19 men accused of being members of MS-13 on racketeering charges connected with six murders, three attempted murders, and two kidnappings in suburban Washington, D.C. The indictment charges all the men as being members of a "racketeering enterprise," allowing prosecutors to hold each defendant accountable for crimes committed by the gang. That same day more than 300 federal law enforcement officials, armed with search warrants and arrest warrants, conducted raids and arrested 8 of the men. The 11 others were already being held without bail by law enforcement agencies or immigration authorities. If convicted, each could face a maximum penalty of life in prison.

The Department of Homeland Security's Immigration and Customs Enforcement (ICE) bureau has established a federal program that trains officers to enforce immigration laws and allows them to tap into an immigration database. Those who are trained can use their new knowledge and skills in any special criminal investigation they are conducting, including gang investigations. The training teaches officers how to use federal immigration laws to go after criminals in the same way they used tax laws to go after organized crime figures ("Locals Look," p.8).

Eggen (p.A2) reports that federal immigration and customs officers, through Operation Community Shield, have arrested more than 1,000 suspected gang members and their associates during the first half of 2005. Eggen notes that the crackdown is part of the federal government's renewed focus on violent street gangs after several years of focusing on terrorism. He also notes that under the ICE antigang program, local and state police departments have supplied federal immigration and customs agents with names of thousands of suspected gang members, many of whom may be in the federal database and eligible for deportation.

The National Youth Gang Center (NYGC) in Tallahassee, Florida, is a "one-stop shop for information about gangs and effective responses to them." The center is funded by the Office of Juvenile Justice and Delinquency Prevention (OJJDP). Established in 1995, the NYGC analyzes state and local gang legislation and local antigang ordinances, reviews the literature on gangs, compiles and analyzes data about gangs, and identifies effective gang program strategies. (Its website is www.iir.com/nygc.)

In addition to youth and street gangs, law enforcement is often confronted with the criminal activities of hate groups.

Bias/Hate Crime: An Overview

Hate is a complex subject that can be divided into two general categories: rational and irrational. Unjust acts inspire rational hate.

Hatred of a person based on race, religion, sexual orientation, ethnicity, or national origin constitutes irrational hate (Schafer and Navarro, p.1). Generically, a **bias crime** or a **hate crime** is a criminal act committed because of someone's actual or perceived membership in a particular group. The International Association of Chiefs of Police (IACP) says: "A hate crime is a criminal offense committed against persons, property or society that is motivated, in whole or in part, by an offender's bias against an individual's or a group's race, religion, ethnic/national origin, gender, age, disability or sexual orientation" (Turner, p.3). According to Steen and Cohen (p.91): "Hate crime has emerged over the past 15 years as a distinct category within criminal law." Crimes range from verbal intimidation and harassment to destruction of property, physical violence, and murder.

Hate crime is not a new development in our country. It has probably existed in America for more than 300 years; however, only recently has it become recognized as a violation of the law. According to FBI figures ("Hate Crime," 2004), there were 7,400 incidents of hate crime in 2003. However, as Fantino (p.37) states: "Hate crimes are among the most underreported forms of criminality."

Motivation for Hate Crime

Bias or hate crimes are motivated by bigotry and hatred against a specific group of people. Race is usually the primary motivation for hate crimes, and African Americans are most often the victims.

Data collected by the National Incident-Based Reporting System (NIBRS) from the period 1995–2000 reflects this distribution, as shown in Figure 19.4.

According to the FBI, racial prejudice motivated more than half of the 7,400 hate crimes in 2003 that were reported to the FBI. Intimidation, vandalism, and property destruction accounted for nearly two-thirds of the nation's hate crimes, but there were also hundreds of violent crimes, including 14 murders; more than 2,700 assaults; 444 robberies, burglaries, and thefts related to prejudice; and 34 arsons.

The groups most likely to be victims of hate crime are (in alphabetical order) African Americans, Arabs, Asians, gay males, Jews, Latinos, lesbians, Native Americans, and white women in interracial relationships. Buchanan ("The Rift") reports on a growing rift between blacks and Hispanics, intensified by blacks' 2002 displacement by Hispanics as the largest minority in America for the first time in history.

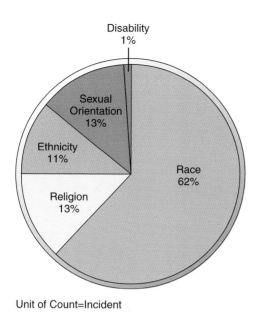

Unit of Count=Incident

Figure 19.4
Distribution of incidents by bias type
Source: National Incident-Based Reporting System

Given the events of September 11, 2001, concern has arisen over an increase of hate crimes against young men of Middle Eastern descent. Arab and Muslim groups reported more than 2,000 September 11–related backlash incidents ("We Are Not," p.3). The FBI reported a seventeen-fold increase in anti-Muslim crimes nationwide during 2001.

A group often overlooked in discussions of hate crime is the homeless. A report by the National Coalition for the Homeless cites incidents of homeless people being run over; hit with stun guns, pellet guns, paint guns, and pepper balls; set on fire; beaten; robbed; raped; and firebombed (*Hate, Violence*). Some characteristics typical of hate-motivated violence are relatively rare in other crimes of violence, as shown in Table 19.8.

Hate Groups

Savelli (p.96) suggests that the main hate groups in the United States are "skin-heads," Christian Identity groups, the Ku Klux Klan (KKK), black separatists, white supremacists, and neo-Nazis (Figure 19.5). The Southern Poverty Law Center ("Active U.S.") counted 762 active hate groups in the United States: 162 KKK, 158 neo-Nazi, 108 black separatists, 97 neo-Confederates, 48 skinheads, 28 Christian Identity, and 161 "other."

Several watchdog organizations like the Southern Poverty Law Center and the Anti-Defamation League track the size and activities of racist groups and are good resources for law enforcement.

Table 19.8 / **Non–Hate-Based Crime Versus Hate-Based Crime**

Characteristics	Non–Hate-Based Incidents	Hate-Based Incidents
Relationship of victim to perpetrator	Most assaults involve two people who know each other	Assaults tend to be "stranger" crimes
Number of perpetrators	Most assaults have one perpetrator and one victim	Involve an average of four assailants for each victim
Nature of the conflict	Tend to be even	Tend to be uneven—hate crime perpetrators often attack younger or weaker victims, or arm themselves and attack unarmed victims
Amount of physical damage inflicted	Not typically "excessive"	Extremely violent, with victims being three times more likely to require hospitalization than "normal" assault victims
Treatment of property	In most property crimes, something of value is taken	More likely that valuable property will be damaged or destroyed
Perpetrator's personal gain	Attacker settles a score or profits from the crime	In most, no personal score is settled and no profit is made
Location of crime	No place with any symbolic significance	Frequently occur in churches, synagogues, mosques, cemeteries, monuments, schools, camps, and in or around the victim's home

Source: Kären M. Hess and Henry M. Wrobleski. *Police Operations,* 4th ed. Belmont, CA: Wadsworth Publishing, 2006, p. 346.

Figure 19.5
Graves scribbled with swastikas and other anti-semitic graffiti in a Jewish cemetery. One of the results of increased awareness of hate crimes is the creation of laws that exact higher penalties from convicted hate-crime offenders.

© Vincent Kessler/Reuters/CORBIS

The Police Response

Research by Wilson and Rubeck (p.373) found that police involvement was significantly related to the seriousness of the offense. Bouman (p.22) stresses: "When working with the victims of a hate/bias crime, the role of the first responder is critical." Respond promptly to reports of hate crime, attempt to reduce the victims' fears, and determine the exact type of prejudice involved. Bouman suggests that investigators ask the following questions to determine whether an incident was hate or bias motivated:

- Was the victim a member of a targeted class?
- Was the victim outnumbered by the perpetrators?
- Did the victim and offender belong to different groups?
- Would the incident have taken place if the victim and offender were of the same group?
- Have other incidents occurred in the same locality or in a similar place?
- Is the timing significant to a hate-motivated group's calendar of special dates?
- Did the offender use biased oral comments, written statements, or gestures?
- Were bias-related objects, items, or symbols used or left at the crime scene?

Then provide follow-up information to the victims. Include in the report the exact words or language used reflecting racial, religious, ethnic, or sexual orientation bias; the perpetrators' actions; symbols; colors; dress; or any other identifying characteristics or actions.

According to *Investigating Hate Crimes on the Internet* (p.15), identifying bias crime indicators and confirming bias motivation are the "essential building blocks for responding to the needs of victims and the community and successfully prosecuting hate crimes." The document defines bias crime indicators as "objective facts, circumstances or patterns attending a criminal act that, standing alone or in conjunction with other facts or circumstances, suggest that the offender's actions were motivated, in whole or in part, by bias."

The IACP (Turner, p.7) has outlined key indicators that a hate crime may have been committed:

- Perception of the victim(s) and witnesses about the crime
- The perpetrators' comments, gestures, or written statements that reflect bias, including graffiti or other symbols
- Any differences between perpetrator and victim, whether actual or perceived by the perpetrator
- Similar incidents in the same location or neighborhood to determine whether a pattern exists
- Whether the victim was engaged in activities promoting his/her group or community—for example, by clothing or conduct
- Whether the incident coincided with a holiday or date of particular significance
- Involvement of organized hate groups or their members
- Absence of any other motive such as economic gain

In addition to finding key indicators, Bune (p.44) suggests: "Photographs of graffiti, epithets and symbols should be taken immediately to preserve the evidence. Police should then see to it that the offending graffiti, epithets or symbols are removed quickly to avoid continued victimization." Symbols commonly associated with extremist or hate groups are shown in Figure 19.6.

American Front

American Nazi Party

Aryan Nation

KuKlux Klan

New Black Panther Party

National Socialist Movement

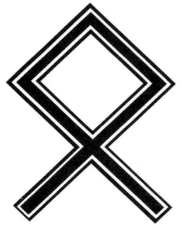

Odin Rune

Posse Comitatus

Storm Front

Nationalist Movement

Triskele

Volksfront

Figure 19.6

A sampling of extremist group symbols. Their origins and meanings may be found online at the Anti-Defamation
League's website: www.adl.org/hate_symbols/default_graphics.asp.

Symbols reprinted with the permission of the Anti-Defamation League.

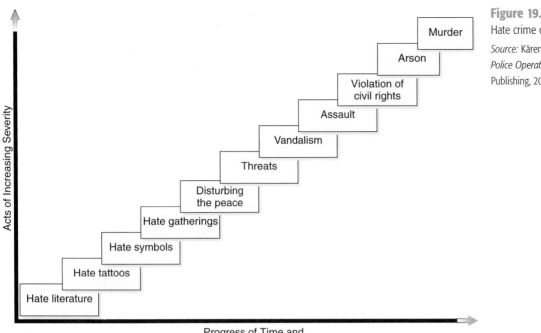

Figure 19.7

Hate crime continuum

Source: Kären M. Hess and Henry M. Wrobleski. *Police Operations,* 4th ed. Belmont, CA: Wadsworth Publishing, 2006, p. 346.

Turner (p.4) notes that officers must differentiate between hate crimes and hate incidents: "**Hate incidents** involve behaviors that, though motivated by bias against a victim's race, religion, ethnic/national origin, gender, age, disability or sexual orientation, are *not* criminal acts. Hostile or hateful speech or other disrespectful/discriminatory behavior may be motivated by bias but is not illegal." Figure 19.7 shows the continuum on which bias-motivated behavior can fall, going from hate incidents to crimes. State statutes will determine where upon this continuum an act becomes illegal.

Investigating Hate Crimes on the Internet

A 2003 report states: "The Internet is vast and perpetrators of online hate crimes hide behind anonymous screen names, electronically garbled addresses and Web sites that can be relocated and abandoned overnight" (*Investigating Hate,* p.3). The report (p.10) stresses that determining whether a message was motivated by bias is at the heart of investigating potential hate crimes. It (p.11) notes that frequently the most difficult investigative issue is identifying the sender of the message. However, many of the same investigative tools investigators use to determine who sent an anonymous letter or placed an anonymous phone call apply equally to anonymous messages over the Internet.

Reporting Bias/Hate Crimes

The passage of the Hate Crime Statistics Act of 1990 encouraged departments to report data on hate crimes to the FBI. Twenty-three states and the District of Columbia require the collection of such data. Appendix C contains a form for collecting data for a bias offense report. Such forms can help assure quality field reports properly identifying the crime, the elements of the offense, and the evidence clearly demonstrating that a hate crime was committed (Bune, p.44).

The FBI has also published manuals concerning the types of statistics needed and has established training programs in major cities. Nonetheless, it is difficult to establish hate crime records because some hate crimes involve groups rather than individuals. Table 19.9 summarizes the variables that may encourage or discourage an agency from reporting hate crimes.

Efforts to Combat Bias/Hate Crimes

egardless of how an agency or individual officer views hate crime, it remains a criminal offense that requires a law enforcement response. Two responses have been taken: legislation to expand the scope of the law and increase the severity of punishment for hate crimes, and more police focus on and fully investigating such crimes. Other efforts include community-based programs to increase awareness of and offer solutions to the problem of hate crime.

Legislation

Shively (p.2) contends that no national consensus exists as to whether hate crimes should be a separate crime,

Table 19.9 / **Variables that Affect Whether Agencies Report Hate Crimes**

Agency Encouragers	Agency Discouragers
Ability to assess intergroup tensions in community	Not deemed important by department
Desire to give support to communities	Perception on part of police that no problem exists
Belief that hate crime reporting will improve police/community relations	Insufficient support staff to process, record, and submit hate crime data
Belief that police help set level of acceptable behavior	Perceived as not being real police work in the community
Understanding that community wants police to report	A belief that reporting hate crimes will make things worse for hate violence victim
Need to know extent of problem as first step to developing solutions	A belief that reporting hate crimes will make things worse for communities
Lets community know that department takes hate crimes seriously	Perception that some minority groups complain unnecessarily
A belief that victims will get help	Not a priority of local government
Will help diffuse racial tensions within the police department	A belief that identifying a crime as a hate crime will have no effect on the outcome
The right thing to do politically	A belief that it is wrong to make these types of crimes special
The right thing to do morally	A belief that hate crime reporting will result in negative publicity for the community
Will help maintain department's good relationship with diverse groups	A belief that hate crime reporting supports the political agendas of gay and minority groups (which is seen as a negative thing)
Consistent with values of department	It creates too much additional work
A belief that identifying problem will keep others safe	Hate crimes are not as serious as other crimes (i.e., a lower priority)
Citizens appreciate the hate crime reporting efforts of police	Agency does not have the adequate technological resources

Source: James J. Nolan and Yoshio Akiyama. "An Analysis of Factors that Affect Law Enforcement Participation in Hate Crime Reporting," *Journal of Contemporary Criminal Justice,* February 1999, p. 118. Reprinted by permission of Sage Publications.

and those supporting hate crime statutes disagree about what should be included. States vary greatly in legislation related to hate crimes. The most common elements of hate crime legislation include:

- Enhanced penalties.
- Criminal penalties for vandalism of religious institutions.
- Collection of data.

Legislation must also keep up with the technology used to spread messages of hate.

Despite such legislation, those who propagate messages of bigotry, intolerance, and hatred claim they have a constitutionally protected right to do so, citing free speech, due process, and equal protection challenges. Nonetheless, state courts have upheld the constitutionality of legislation that enhances penalties for hate-motivated violence. However, in 2003 the U.S. Supreme Court, in *Virginia v. Black et al.,* struck down a Virginia law banning cross burning, saying the statute violated the First Amendment.

Furthermore, research has found minimal public support for harsher penalties for offenders who commit hate crimes than for offenders who commit identical crimes with no biased motivation (Steen and Cohen, p.118).

Sometimes, the hideous nature of hate crimes leaves investigators wondering whether the offense is truly based on bias or whether some type of ritualistic torture was involved.

Ritualistic Crime: An Overview

Ritualistic crimes are most often associated with cults or occult groups. According to Savelli (p.97), occultism is widespread through the United States. For this discussion it is necessary to distinguish between "cults" in two senses. In the general sense, a *cult* is a system of religious beliefs, rituals, and believers. In the sense used in this text and by law enforcement, a *cult* is a group of people whose beliefs and rituals appear to the majority of society to be socially deviant or even violent and destructive. Such cults are commonly connected with the occult, paganism, witchcraft, demonism, and Satanism or devil worship.

 A **cult** is a system of religious beliefs and rituals. It also refers to those who practice such beliefs.

One informal definition of a *cult* is "any religion other than your own." The term is often applied to religious or mystical groups that society does not understand. Most cults involve some form of worship and followers who are dedicated to the concepts promoted by the leader.

Cults range in size from a few followers to worldwide organizations directed by a complex chain of command. According to some estimates, 3,000 cults exist throughout the world, claiming a total estimated membership of more than 3 million people, mostly young adults.

One cult in the late 1970s was the People's Temple, led by Jim Jones, a Protestant clergyman. Hundreds of his followers moved into Jonestown, a rural commune in Guyana, South America, and lived under his absolute rule. In 1978, cult leaders killed a U.S. congressman and three journalists investigating activities in Jonestown. Jones then ordered his followers to commit suicide, resulting in the deaths of over 900 people.

Another well-known group regarded as a cult is the International Society for Krishna Consciousness, better known as the Hare Krishna movement. This cult came from India in 1954. Most members wear orange robes, and the men shave their heads.

Some scholars refer to cults as "new religious movements," or NRMs, because the majority of cults are young religious movements still in their first generation. As such, these authors stress, most NRMs are law abiding. For example, the neo-pagan Wicca movement, although it may have aspects of a cult, continually disclaims association with witchcraft and insists upon its status as a religion.

Moreover, the pervasive effect of mass media has elevated some superficial characteristics of cults—such as goth/vampire makeup and clothing—to an almost pop-culture status; consequently the display of such trappings may not be indicative of serious involvement.

A less negative term than *cult* is *new religious movement* (NRM).

Normally NRMs have a charismatic leader who develops an idea that attracts people looking for fulfillment. The leader is usually self-appointed and claims the right of rule because of a supernatural power of appointment. NRM membership may include males and females, and there is normally no room for democratic participation. Leadership is most often exerted through fear and mysticism. Charles Manson and Jim Jones are examples of such leaders.

An NRM in Waco, Texas, the "Branch Davidians" headed by David Koresh, clashed with federal agents attempting a raid in February 1993. The raid turned into a gun battle in which four federal agents and at least two Branch Davidian members were killed. Sixteen agents were wounded. Weapons inside the compound included at least one tripod-mounted .50-caliber machine gun and many semiautomatic weapons. A child released from the compound who had lived there for four years said she had been taught to put a gun into

her mouth and told how to commit suicide by taking cyanide.

A 51-day standoff between the federal government and Koresh's armed followers ended in April 1993, when fire engulfed the compound. The FBI had sent an armored combat vehicle to ram holes into the buildings and pump tear gas into them. The FBI asserted that Davidians started the blaze, an apparent mass suicide that killed at least 80, including women and children.

Survivors of the fire, however, insisted that it was caused by the tank's hitting a barrel of propane and tipping over lit camping lanterns. The FBI has been cleared of wrongdoing in this incident.

Terminology and Symbols of Cults

O ver the years a number of terms have been associated with cults. Among the terms law enforcement officers should be familiar with are the following:

- **Antichrist**—the son of Satan
- **Beelzebub**—a powerful demon, right under Satan
- **Coven**—a group of witches or Satanists
- **Hand of Glory**—the left hand of a person who has died
- **Incantation**—verbal spell
- **Magick**—the "glue" that binds occult groups, a supernatural act or force that causes a change in the environment
- **Occult**—secret knowledge of supernormal powers
- **Ritual**—prescribed form of religious or mystical ceremony
- **Sabbat**—a gathering of witches

Symbols

Among the satanic and occult symbols are the *circle,* which symbolizes totality and wholeness and within which ceremonies are often performed; the *inverted cross,* which mocks the Christian cross; the *goat's head,* symbolizing the devil; the *heart,* symbolizing the center of life; the *hexagram* (six-pointed star), purported to protect and control demons; the *pentagram* (five-pointed star), representing the four elements of the earth surmounted by "the Spirit"; and the *horned hand,* a hand signal of recognition used between those members. This is similar to the hand signals used by street gangs. Figure 19.8 illustrates symbols commonly associated with satanic and occult groups.

Colors also have significance to many cults:

- Black—darkness, night, sorrow, evil, the devil
- Blue—water, tears, sadness

Figure 19.8
Common satanic and occult symbols

AC/DC	ANTICHRIST/ DEVIL CHILD	
ZOSO	THREE-HEADED DOG THAT GUARDS GATE TO HELL	PENTAGRAM WHITE MAGIC
S	SATAN/STONER	
MARKOS	ABRACADABRA	PENTAGRAM UPSIDE-DOWN STAR SIGN OF OCCULT
FFF	ANTICHRIST	
666	ANTICHRIST	HEXAGRAM CIRCLE
	ANTICHRIST	
NATAS	SATAN REVERSED	INFINITY- CONTAINMENT CONTROL OF EVIL POWER
6, 9, 13, XIII	OCCULT NUMBERS	
	HORN AND TAIL ADDED TO ANY LETTER	ANK
	LIGHTNING BOLT HEAVEN TO HELL STRENGTH	
	SWASTIKA	LUCIFER MORNING STAR
	ANTICHRIST CROSS OF CONFUSION	

- Green—vegetation, nature, restfulness
- Red—blood, physical life, energy, sexuality
- White—cleanliness, purity, innocence, virginity
- Yellow—perfection, wealth, glory, power

The Nature of Ritualistic Crimes

C ults and the occult have created great interest because of recurring stories from children and adults in different areas of the United States concerning bizarre satanic rituals and behaviors. Although some may be fantasies, there appears to be some truth, especially regarding the danger to children of the members of satanic groups.

 A **ritualistic crime** is an unlawful act committed with or during a ceremony. Investigate the crime, not the belief system.

Like gangs, occult groups have three levels of activity: dabbling, serious involvement, and criminal involvement.

 Ritualistic crimes include vandalism, destruction or theft of religious artifacts; desecration of cemeteries; the maiming, torturing, or killing of animals and humans; and the sexual abuse of children.

The "Black Masses" of Satanism often incorporate religious articles stolen from churches. A **Black Mass** mocks the Christian ritual of communion by substituting blood and urine for the wine and feces for the bread. The cross is usually inverted, and candles and cups may be used in sexual acts. "Hymns" that are either obscene or that praise Satan may be sung, and heavy-metal music may be played.

The Black Mass frequently involves animal mutilation and sacrifice and sometimes torture and sacrifice of humans, preferably babies or virgins. The sacrifice often incorporates ritualistic incantations. Victims, animal or human, are tortured and mutilated because it is believed that while the victim struggles, the life forces given off can be captured and stored for later use. Such sacrifices may be followed by a dance and an orgy.

"Stoner" gangs consist of middle-class youths involved in drugs, alcohol, and often Satanism. Although stoners are not as apt to engage in the violent crimes associated with other street gangs, they may mutilate animals, rob graves, and desecrate churches and human remains. Their graffiti frequently depicts satanic symbolism such as inverted crosses and the number 666.

Who Commits Ritualistic Crime?

A psychological profile of males and females involved in the occult reveals that they tend to be creative, imaginative, curious, daring, and thus intelligent and well educated, yet are frequently underachievers. Although they are egocentric, they also have low self-esteem and have suffered peer rejection or persecution. They come from various social and economic backgrounds, can be any age (although the age range of 13 to 24 is the most common), and are of a variety of races, nationalities, and religions. Interestingly, few Jews are involved in Satanism, because Judaism does not believe in the devil.

A number of factors may lead an individual to occult involvement, including family alienation, insecurity and a quest for personal power, unfulfilled ambitions, a spiritual search for answers, idealism, nonconformity, adolescent rebellion, a desire for adventure and excitement, a need for attention and recognition, and a need to escape reality or the circumstances of his/her own birth.

Although the personal appearance of those involved in occult activity is often quite normal, some adopt a less mainstream look. For example, they may dress entirely in black or other dark clothing; pierce various parts of their bodies; grow their hair long and dye it; wear chains as implements of confinement; wear heavy eye shadow and white makeup to appear more ashen or deathlike; wear heavy boots; display tattoos depicting serpents, skulls, or other occult symbols; and have scars indicating cuttings, burnings, or whippings.

Investigating Ritualistic Crimes

Occult reports and activities are investigated in much the same way as any other crime. Interview the people who report these incidents, and prepare reports concerning witnesses or alleged victims of criminal activity. Take photos, sketch symbols, describe colors found, and measure objects. Preserve all objects at the scene as evidence. Work from the outside perimeter to the center or the focus point of the site.

Numerous books on the beliefs and rituals of various cults are available. The background contained in such books is beyond the scope of this book, but investigators should be alert to signs that criminal activity may be cult related.

Signs of Cult-Related Activity

The following items may be important indicators of satanic or cult activity. If you suspect ritualistic crime, list these items in any search warrant sought:

- Altars (stone or metal) or a wooden stand for an altar
- Animal parts (anus, heart, tongue, ears, front teeth, front legs, genitals), cages
- Ashes or bowls with powder, colored salt, drugs, or herbs
- Bells, gongs, drums
- Blood, bottles containing blood (may be in refrigerator), hypodermic needles (for removing blood)
- Body paint, painted rocks
- Body parts (may be in a freezer), skulls, and bones, perhaps taken from graves (femur, fibula, index finger, skull, and other large bones; the upper right leg and joints of the right-hand fingers are valued) (Figure 19.9)
- Booby traps
- Books on Satanism (especially *Book of Shadows*)
- Bullwhips, cat-o'-nine-tails
- Candles, candle holders, candle drippings, incense
- Cauldron for a fire
- Chalices

- Circle with a 9-foot diameter (may contain a pentagram)
- Coffins
- Cords (colored and knotted) and ligatures
- Crystals
- Daggers, knives, swords (particularly double-edged short swords), martial arts weaponry and clothing
- Effigy-like clay figures or voodoo dolls stuck with pins or otherwise mutilated
- Flash powder, smoke bombs
- Hoods, robes (especially red, white, or black), hats, helmets, gloves (black satin or velvet) for the right hand, masks
- Inverted crosses, vandalized Christian artifacts
- Jewelry such as amulets or medallions with satanic symbols
- Nondiscernible alphabet, satanic symbols painted on rocks or trees, unusual drawings or symbols on walls or floors (hexagrams, pentagrams, horns of death, etc.)
- Occult games, Ouija boards, tarot cards
- Parchment (for making contracts)
- Pillows
- Rooms draped in black or red (or nail holes in walls and ceiling indicating that such drapes may have been used)

Ritualistic Crimes

Garrett (p.63) notes that ritualistic crimes may involve everything from church desecration, grave robbing, arson, trespassing, and vandalism, to animal abuse, serial rape, and ritual homicide. Anthony Pinizzotto, senior scientist and clinical forensic psychologist with the FBI, urges law enforcement to remember that a ritualistic crime is still a crime and should be investigated as such: "The rituals are not important, but the crimes that are committed while doing them are" (Garrett).

 Indicators that criminal activity may be cult related include symbols, candles, makeshift altars, bones, cult-related books, swords, daggers, and chalices.

If evidence is found to support the commission of a crime, submit the case to the prosecuting attorney's office, as with other crimes. Also as with other crimes, if illegal acts are being committed in the presence of an officer who arrives at the scene, an immediate arrest may be executed. However, many authorities on cult activity warn that no one, including a police officer, should ever approach or try to stop an occult ritual alone, because in all probability, the officer would be dealing with mentally deranged people high on drugs.

Figure 19.9

Scott Dyleski, 16, appears behind a protective glass barrier in Judge David Flinn's courtroom in Martinez, California, Thursday, Oct. 27, 2005. Dyleski is charged with first-degree murder as an adult in the death of Pamela Vitale, the wife of prominent defense attorney and television commentator Daniel Horowitz. The 16-year old suspect is reported to have been involved in some kind of self-styled Satanism including the reading of Anton LeVay's Satanic Bible and use of occult symbols at the crime scene. Pamela Vitale was killed October 15, having been hit 39 times with a piece of crown molding and stabbed in the abdomen. A Lorraine Cross (a cross with two horizontal lines, the lower one larger than the upper one, which is associated with Satanism and suggests fire and brimstone) was carved into her back.

Dyleski pleaded not guilty Wednesday, Nov. 9, 2005, in Martinez, California.

Investigating Animal Deaths

Unusual circumstances surrounding animal deaths may be important indicators of satanic or cult activity. The following circumstances connected with dead animals should be noted:

- No blood (the blood has been drained from the animal.)
- An inverted cross carved on the animal's chest
- Surgically removed head
- Intestines or other body organs removed

If a rash of missing-animal reports occurs, gather information on the kind of animals they are, when they disappeared, and from what area. Look for patterns, and coordinate efforts with the local humane society/ASPCA and veterinarians.

Investigating Homicides

At the scene of a homicide investigation, the following may suggest a ritualistic death:

- Missing body parts—heart, genitals, left hand, tongue, index finger
- Scarring between index finger and thumb or inside the wrist from past rituals involving members' blood
- Blood drained from body
- Ritualistic symbols such as a pentagram associated with satanic worshipers carved on the body or surrounding area
- Tattoos on armpits or the bottom of feet
- Wax drippings, oils, incense, or powders of ritual on the body
- Urine or human/animal feces smeared on body or found in body cavities
- Semen inside, on, or near body cavities or smeared on the body
- Victim undressed
- Body painted or tied up
- Neck wounds, branding-iron marks, or burn marks on body
- Colored strings near the body

Occult murders are usually stabbings or cuttings—seldom are they gunshot wounds—and many of the victims are cult members or former members. The person who commits the murder is typically a white male from a middle- to upper-class family with above-average intelligence. Some form of drug use is characteristic.

Guard against reacting emotionally when confronted with ritualistic crime, for they tend to be emotionally and spiritually repulsive. Also bear in mind that unusual crimes are also committed by individuals with mental problems who are not connected with cults.

During postmortem examination, the stomach contents can be of great importance in determining what occurred just before death. In many ritualistic homicides the body is not available because it has been burned, leaving no evidence. Further, most juries disbelieve seemingly outlandish charges of Satanism and human sacrifice, and most judges do not regard Satanism as a real problem. Hence, most cases are dismissed.

Investigating Satanic Serial Killings

Serial killings may be linked to satanic-like rituals in the murder act itself as well as in the killer's behavior following the murder. Serial killings frequently linked to Satanism include the following:

- Charles Manson had links with the Process, a satanic group. Many of the murders committed by Manson and his followers had ritualistic overtones.
- The "Son of Sam" murders involving David Berkowitz are claimed by author Maury Terry in *The Ultimate Evil* to have been a conspiracy among satanic cult members of the Process group.
- Some brutal, vicious serial killers find Satanism a justification for their bizarre antisocial behavior.
- "Night Stalker" Richard Ramirez had a pentagram on the palm of his hand, wrote satanic graffiti on the walls of some of his victims' homes, and was obsessed with AC/DC's *Highway to Hell* album featuring the song "Night Stalker." Ramirez shouted "Hail, Satan" as he left the courtroom.

Investigating Youth Suicides

Increasingly, law enforcement has been faced with satanic "overtones" to suicides committed by young people. Lyle Rapacki of Flagstaff, Arizona, has compiled a list of indicators that a youth is involved in cult or occult activities:

- Withdrawal from family and friends
- Changing of friends and associates
- Sudden hostility toward the Christian church and the Bible
- New friends who are loners, academic nonachievers, and problem cases for school officials
- Change of dress to darker, more subdued colors; more jewelry
- Increased rebellion, depression, or aggressive behavior
- Negative change in moral behavior; also a change in priorities to a more narrowly self-centered pattern
- Drop in grades, lack of interest in school, or lack of concentration
- Interest in occult literature; may start his/her own *Book of Shadows*—a notebook containing personal symbols and rituals, often written in code
- Magazines focusing on death, violence, secrecy, and sexual acting out
- Increasing involvement in fantasy role-playing games such as Dungeons and Dragons
- Increased viewing of occultic movies and television programs
- Collection of occultic paraphernalia such as bones, skulls, ritual knives, and candles
- Almost exclusively listening to heavy-metal or punk/goth music
- Nightmares; shades drawn during the day

- Preoccupation with death, destruction, or harming things
- Sudden missing pets or animals in neighborhood

Investigators dealing with youth suicides that they suspect may be occult related should inquire into the kind of music the youths listened to, the kinds of games they played, whether they had Ouija boards or tarot cards, and whether they dabbled in astrology or séances.

Special Challenges in Ritualistic Crime Investigations

 ust as law enforcement officers may have a difficult time relating to gang members and not reacting with scorn toward them because of their gang associations, they will almost certainly have difficulty relating to those who engage in ritualistic activity. This is also true of the general public and the media, which frequently sensationalize cases involving ritualistic or cult-related crimes, particularly sexual abuse of children and homicides.

Special challenges involved in investigating ritualistic or cult-related crimes include separating the belief system from the illegal acts, the sensationalism that frequently accompanies such crimes, and the "abnormal" personalities of some victims and suspects.

Frequently the "victims" of cult-related crimes are former participants in the cult. Many have been or are currently undergoing psychological counseling, which makes their testimony less than credible to some people. Likewise, many of the suspects, the leaders in particular, are beyond the pale of what most people would consider to be normal and consequently may be treated differently because of how they look and what they believe rather than because of their actions.

SUMMARY

Belonging to a gang is not illegal in this country; however, the activities of gang members frequently *are* illegal. The number of gangs and gang members has decreased over the last few years, but gang-related crime is still of concern to law enforcement. Cultural gangs are neighborhood centered and exist independently of criminal activity. Instrumental gangs are formed for the express purpose of criminal activity, primarily drug trafficking.

In addition to drug dealing, gang members often engage in vandalism, arson, shootings, stabbings, intimidation, and other forms of violence. The first step in dealing with a gang problem is to recognize it. Gang members may be identified by their names, symbols (clothing and tattoos), and communication styles, including graffiti and sign language. Maintain records on gangs, gang members, monikers, photographs, vehicles, and illegal activities. Cross-reference the records.

Special challenges in investigating the illegal activities of gangs include the multitude of suspects and the unreliability or fear of witnesses. The two most often used defense strategies in gang-related crime prosecutions are pleas of diminished capacity and of self-defense. Four general strategies are being used to deal with gang problems: (1) suppression or law enforcement efforts, (2) social intervention, (3) provision of opportunities, and (4) community organization.

Other challenges are investigating bias/hate crimes and ritualistic crimes. Bias/hate crimes are acts motivated by bigotry and hatred against a specific group of people. Race is the most frequent motivation for bias/hate crime, and African Americans are the most frequent victims.

Ritualistic crimes are often associated with the occult. A cult is a system of religious beliefs and rituals and those who practice them. A more positive way to refer to cults is as "new religious movements" (NRMs). A ritualistic crime is an unlawful act committed within the context of a ceremony. Investigate the crime—not the belief system.

Ritualistic crimes have included vandalism; destruction and theft of religious artifacts; desecration of cemeteries; the maiming, torturing, and killing of animals and humans; and the sexual abuse of children. Indicators that criminal activity may be cult related include symbols, candles, makeshift altars, bones, cult-related books, swords, daggers, and chalices. Special challenges in investigating ritualistic or cult-related crimes include separating the belief system from the illegal acts, the sensationalism that frequently accompanies such crimes, and the "abnormal" personalities sometimes found in both victims and suspects.

CHECKLIST

Gangs

- What illegal activities have been committed?
- Who reported the activities?
- What evidence is there?
- Who are the suspects?
- What signs tend to implicate a specific gang?
- Who are the leaders of this gang?
- What records exist on this gang?
- Who might provide additional information?

Bias/Hate Crimes

- What specific crime was involved?
- What were the victim(s)' and witnesses' perceptions of motivation for the crime?
- Was there more than one perpetrator?
- What was the relationship between the victim and the perpetrator(s)?
- Was the perpetrator associated with an organized hate group?
- How much physical damage was inflicted?
- Did the perpetrator make any comment, gesture, or written statement reflecting bias, including graffiti?
- Were there any differences between the perpetrator and the victim, whether actual or perceived?
- Have similar incidents occurred in the same location or neighborhood, indicating a pattern?
- Was the victim engaged in activities promoting a group, either by appearance or conduct?
- Did the incident coincide with a holiday or date of particular significance?
- In destruction of property crimes, was there an absence of any other motive such as economic gain?

Cults

- What type of activity brought the cult to the attention of the police?
- Is the activity illegal?
- What statutes or ordinances are applicable?
- Who reported the activity? What is their connection to the cult?
- What evidence is there that the illegal activity is part of a ritual?
- Who are suspected cult members?
- What records exist on the cult?
- Who might provide additional information?

APPLICATION

A. Graffiti has suddenly appeared in increasing amounts in specific areas on walls, public buildings, telephone poles and streetlights in your community. Some are in blue paint and some are in red. Groups in the local park have been seen wearing blue bandannas, whereas in another park they are wearing red kerchiefs. Some of them have been seen flashing particular hand signals to each other. Some of the graffiti symbols represent animals and insects. A blue word *Crips* has the letter *C* crossed out with a red *X*.

Question

If graffiti is truly the "newspaper of the street gangs," what information should the preceding description give to a police officer?

B. While looking for a stolen safe in a wooded area, the police discover a circular clearing about 200 feet in diameter with candles placed around the circumference. A rough altar has been constructed with a cross. A fire has been burned beneath the cross. A five-pointed star is scratched in the dirt, and the word *NATAS* is scrawled on several trees and on the cross. The number 6 also appears on several trees. What appears to be bones are found in the ashes of the fire below the altar.

Question

What do these findings suggest? Is this something the police should investigate further? Why or why not?

DISCUSSION QUESTIONS

1. Are there gangs in your community? If so, in what activities do they engage?
2. What are the signs that a community might have a gang problem?
3. What does gang membership provide for its members that society does not?
4. What do you feel is the most important part of an investigation of gang-related crime?
5. Do you think ordinances against loitering are effective deterrents to gang-related crime?
6. What "levers" might police officers pull to deter gang-related crime in your community?
7. Why do you think the gang problem greatly increased in the 1990s and why is it now declining?
8. What are the signs of occult influence among teenagers?

9. What is the police responsibility with regard to investigating gang activity? hate crimes? ritualistic crimes?
10. Which poses the greatest challenge to law enforcement: gang-related crime, hate crime, or ritualistic crime? Explain your reason(s).

MEDIA EXPLORATIONS

 **Internet**

Select one of the following assignments to complete.

- Go to the website "Gangs Or Us" at www.gangsorus.com. Find your state and list the information provided. Then compare it with that of another state you find interesting. Be prepared to share your findings with the class.
- Search for the key phrase *National Institute for Justice*. Click on "NCJRS" (National Criminal Justice Research Service). Click on "law enforcement." Click on "sort by Doc#." Search for one of the NCJ reference numbers from the reference pages. Outline the selection to share with the class.
- Go to the FBI website at www.fbi.gov. Click on "library and reference." Select "Uniform Crime Reports" and outline what the report says about gangs.
- Select one of the following keywords: *gangs, gang prevention, graffiti, pulling levers, street gang, youth gangs*. Find one article relevant to gang investigations to outline and share with the class.
- Go to the International Association of Chiefs of Police website at www.theiacp.org and find their pamphlet *Responding to Hate Crimes: A Police Officer's Guide to Investigation and Prevention*. Outline the main areas covered by this guide to share with the class.
- Go to the Anti-Defamation League's website at www.adl.org/learn and see if any hate group meetings or rallies are planned for your state within the next 12 months.
- Go to the FBI website at www.fbi.gov. Click on "library and reference." Select "Uniform Crime Reports" and outline what the report says about hate crimes.
- Select one of the following keywords: *coven, cult, hate crimes, hate crime prevention, ritualistic crime, ritualistic crime prevention*. Find one article relevant to gangs, bias/hate crime, or ritualistic-crime investigations to outline and share with the class.

Crime and Evidence in Action

Go to the CD and choose the **drug bust/gang homicide/sexual assault case.** During the course of the case you'll become patrol officer, detective, defense attorney, corrections officer, and patrol officer to conduct interactive investigative research. Each case unfolds as you respond to key decision points. Feedback for each possible answer choice is packed full of information, including term definitions, web links, and important documentation. The sergeant is available at certain times to help mentor you, the Online Resources website offers a variety of information, and be sure to take notes in your e-notebook during the suspect video statements and at key points throughout (these notes can be saved, printed, or e-mailed). The Forensics Exercise will test your ability to collect, transport, and analyze evidence from the crime scene. At the end of the case you can track how well you responded to each decision point and join the Discussion Forum for a postmortem. **Go to the CD and use the skills you've learned in this chapter to solve a case.**

REFERENCES

2005 National Gang Threat Assessment. Washington, DC: Bureau of Justice Statistics, 2005.

"Active U.S. Hate Groups in 2004." Southern Poverty Law Center. http://www.splcenter.org/intel/map/hate.jsp. Accessed August 1, 2005.

Bouman, Walter. "Best Practices of a Hate/Bias Crime Investigation." *FBI Law Enforcement Bulletin*, March 2003, pp. 21–25.

Browne, Phillip. "Gang Problem Needs to Be Tackled in the Schools, Home," *L.A. Daily News*, October 3, 2004.

Buchanan, Susy. "The Rift: Evidence of a Divide Between Blacks and Hispanics Mounting." Southern Poverty Law Center, http://www.splcenter.org/intel/intelreport/article.jsp?aid=548. Accessed August 1, 2005.

Bune, Karen L. "Law Enforcement Must Take Lead on Hate Crimes," *The Police Chief*, April 2004, pp. 43–44.

Burns, Edward. *Gang- and Drug-Related Homicide: Baltimore's Successful Enforcement Strategy.* http://www.ncjrs.org/html/bja/gang. Accessed August 5, 2005.

Collins, Geneve. "Fighting Gangs: Strategic Targeting vs. Kitchen Sink Model," *Community Links*, August 2004, pp. 11–13.

Domash, Shelly Feuer. "America's Most Dangerous Gang," *Police*, February 2005, pp. 30–34.

Eggen, Dan. "Customs Jails 1,000 Suspected Gang Members," *Washington Post*, August 2, 2005, p. A2.

Fantino, Julian. "Hate Crime," *The Police Chief*, August 2003, pp. 36–38, 93.

Fritsch, Eric J.; Caeti, Tory J.; and Taylor, Robert W. "Gang Suppression through Saturation Patrol and Aggressive Curfew and Truancy Effectiveness." In Scott M.

Decker, ed., *Policing Gangs and Youth Violence.* Belmont. CA: Wadsworth Publishing, 2003, pp. 267–284.

Garrett, Ronnie. "Policing the Shadows: The How's and Why's of Investigating Ritualistic Crime," *Law Enforcement Technology*, March 2004, pp. 62–67.

Gately, Gary. "Indictments in Maryland Single Out MS-13 Gang," *New York Times*, August 26, 2005.

Greene, Jack R. "Gangs, Community Policing and Problem Solving." In Scott M. Decker, ed., *Policing Gangs and Youth Violence.* Belmont, CA: Wadsworth Publishing, 2003, pp. 3–16.

"Greensboro Police Use Military Program to Track Gang Activity." Associated Press as reported in the Minneapolis/St. Paul *Star Tribune*, December 7, 2004.

Hagerdorn, John M. "The Global Impact of Gangs," *Journal of Contemporary Criminal Justice*, May 2005, pp. 153–169.

Harrell, Ericka. *Violence by Gang Members, 1993–2003.* Washington, DC: Bureau of Justice Statistics Crime Data Brief, June 2005. (NCJ 208875)

"Hate Crime Statistics, 2003." Washington, DC: Federal Bureau of Investigation, November 2004.

Hate, Violence, and Death on Main Street USA: A Report on Hate Crimes and Violence Against People Experiencing Homelessness 2004. National Coalition for the Homeless. June 2005. http://www.nationalhomeless.org/hatecrimes. Accessed October 19, 2005.

Investigating Hate Crimes on the Internet. University of Southern Maine, Center for the Prevention of Hate Violence, September 2003.

Johnson, Kevin. "Paroled Gangsters Find They Can't Go Home Again," *USA Today*, August 9, 2005a, p.1A

Johnson, Kevin. "U.S. Gang Membership May Be Higher than Reported," *USA Today*, August 4, 2005b, p. 3A.

Katz, Charles M.; Webb, Vincent J.; and Decker, Scott H. "Using the Arrestee Drug Abuse Monitoring (ADAM) Program to Further Understand the Relationship between Drug Use and Gang Membership," *Academy of Criminal Justice Sciences*, 2005, pp. 58–87.

Kennedy, David M.; Braga, Anthony A.; Piehl, Anne M.; and Waring, Elin J. *Reducing Gun Violence: The Boston Gun Project's Operation Ceasefire.* Washington, DC: National Institute of Justice, September 2001. (NCJ 188741)

Kersten, Katherine. "Roots of Gang Violence Feed off '60s," Minneapolis/St. Paul *Star Tribune*, July 18, 2005, p. B2.

Klein, Malcolm W. "The Value of Comparisons in Street Gang Research," *Journal of Contemporary Criminal Justice*, May 2005, pp. 135–152.

Lee, Natasha. "Video Surveillance Cuts Graffiti by 60%," *Los Angeles Times*, August 16, 2005.

"Locals Look to ICE to Chill Street Gangs," *Law Enforcement News*, May 2005, pp. 8–9.

Martinez, Liz. "Gangs in Indian Country," *Law Enforcement Technology*, February 2005, pp. 20–27.

Maxon, Cheryl L.; Hennigan, Karen; and Sloane, David C. "For the Sake of the Neighborhood: Civil Gang Injunctions as a Gang Intervention Tool in Southern California." In *Policing Gangs and Youth Violence*, edited by Scott M. Decker. Belmont, CA: Wadsworth Publishing Co., 2003, pp. 239–266.

O'Rourke, Judy. "City Passes Gang Ordinance," *The Signal*, October 14, 2004.

Ragavan, Chitra, and Guttman, Monika. "Terror on the Streets," *U.S. News & World Report*, December 13, 2004, pp. 21–24.

"The Reality of Gangs," *Washington Post*, August 10, 2005, p. A16.

Savelli, Lou. *Gangs Across America and their Symbols.* Flushing, NY: Looseleaf Law, 2004.

Schafer, John R., and Navarro, Joe. "The Seven-Stage Hate Model: The Psychopathology of Hate Groups," *FBI Law Enforcement Bulletin*, March 2003, pp. 1–8.

Shelden, Randall G.; Tracy, Sharon K.; and Brown, William B. *Youth Gangs in American Society*, 3rd ed. Belmont, CA: Wadsworth Publishing, 2004.

Shively, Michael. *Study of Literature and Legislation on Hate Crime in America.* Washington, DC: National Institute of Justice, March 31, 2005.

Steen, Sara, and Cohen, Mark A. "Assessing the Public's Demand for Hate Crime Penalties," *Justice Quarterly*, March 2004, pp. 91–124.

Stratman, Sam. "Gangs and Crime in Latin America," press release from the U.S. House of Representatives, Committee on International Relations, March 15, 2005.

Swecker, Chris. *Gangs in America. . . and Beyond: FBI Exec Outlines Anti-Gang Strategy to Congress.* Washington, DC: Federal Bureau of Investigation, April 20, 2005.

Tita, George; Riley, K. Jack; and Greenwood, Peter. "From Boston to Boyle Heights: The Process and Prospects of a 'Pulling Levers' Strategy in a Los Angeles Barrio." In Scott M. Decker, ed., *Policing Gangs and Youth Violence.* Belmont, CA: Wadsworth Publishing, 2003, pp. 102–130.

Tita, George; Riley, K. Jack; and Greenwood, Peter. *Reducing Gun Violence: Operation Ceasefire in Los Angeles.* Washington, DC: National Institute of Justice, February 2005. (NCJ 192378)

Turner, Nancy. *Responding to Hate Crimes: A Police Officer's Guide to Investigation and Prevention.* Alexandria, VA: International Association of Chiefs of Police, 1999. Available through the IACP website, http://www.theiacp.org. Accessed October 19, 2005.

Valdez, Al. "Athletic Supporters," *Police*, April 2003, pp. 66–67.

Valdez, Avelardo, and Sifaneck, Stephen J. "'Getting High and Getting By': Dimensions of Drug Selling Behaviors among American Mexican Gang Members in South Texas," *Journal of Research in Crime and Delinquency*, February 2004, pp. 82–105.

Walker, Robert. "Gangs Or Us" website. http://www.gangsorus.com/law.html. Accessed August 22, 2005.

"We Are Not the Enemy." *Human Rights Watch*, November 2002, pp. 2–16.

Weisel, Deborah Lamm, and Shelley, Tara O'Connor. *Specialized Gang Units: Form and Function in Community Policing.* Washington, DC: U.S. Department of Justice, October 2004.

Weisheit, Ralph A., and Wells, L. Edward. "Youth Gangs in Rural America," *NIJ Journal*, July 2004, pp. 2–5. (NCJ 204516)

Wilson, Mindy S., and Rubeck, R. Barry. "Hate Crimes in Pennsylvania, 1983–99: Case Characteristics and Police Responses," *Justice Quarterly*, vol. 20, no. 2, 2003, p. 373.

CASE CITED

Virginia v. Black et al., No. 01-1107, 2003.

CHAPTER 20

Terrorism and
Homeland Security

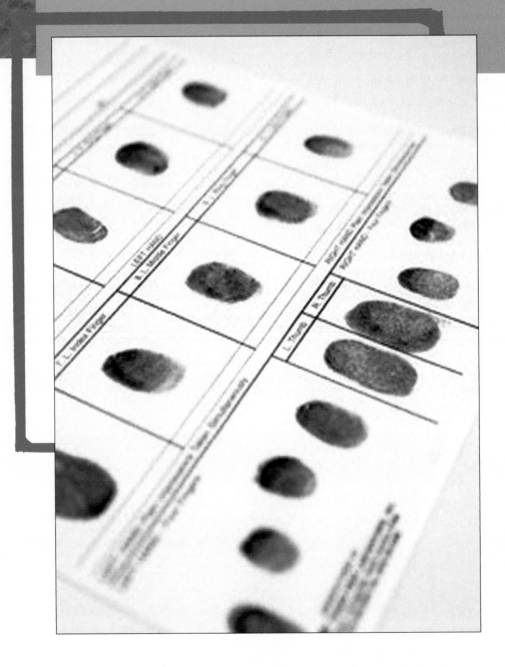

asymmetric warfare
bioterrorism
contagion effect
cyberterrorism
deconfliction
ecoterrorism
hawala
intifada
jihad
sleeper cell
technological terrorism
terrorism

Do You Know?

- What most definitions of terrorism have in common?
- What motivates most terrorist attacks?
- How the FBI classifies terrorist acts?
- What groups are commonly identified as Islamic terrorist organizations?
- What domestic terrorist groups exist in the United States?
- What methods terrorists may use?
- What federal office was established as a result of 9/11?
- What the two lead agencies in combating terrorism are?
- How the USA PATRIOT Act enhances counterterrorism efforts by the United States?
- What the first line of defense against terrorism in the United States is?
- What the three-tiered model of al-Qaeda terrorist attacks consists of?
- What a key to successfully combating terrorism is?
- What the Community Protection Act authorizes?
- What two concerns related to the war on terrorism are?
- What balance must be maintained in investigating terrorism?

"The terrorist attacks of September 11, 2001, sounded a clarion call to Americans: our nation must prepare more vigorously to prevent and, if necessary, to manage the consequences of man-made disasters" (McDonald and McLaughlin, p.14) (Figure 20.1).

"The 9/11 attacks were a shock, but they should not have come as a surprise. Islamist extremists had given plenty of warning that they meant to kill Americans indiscriminately and in large numbers. . . . The most

Figure 20.1

The terrorist attacks of September 11, 2001, rocked the entire nation. First responders to the World Trade Center crime scene, including law enforcement officers and firefighters, were invaluable in saving countless lives but were also among the many casualties of the horrific event. A positive consequence of this tragedy was the galvanization of American patriotism and a resolve of citizens to join law enforcement in the daily efforts to protect our freedoms and valued way of life.

Left: A police officer lowers his face mask and signals to someone near the site of the World Trade Center, Wednesday, Sept. 12, 2001, in New York.

Right: Firemen, police officers, and workers lock arms while observing a moment of prayer during a short interfaith memorial service held at the World Trade Center disaster site, Thursday morning, Oct. 11, 2001, in New York.

important failure was one of imagination. We do not believe leaders understood the gravity of the threat. The terrorist danger from bin Laden and al-Qaeda was not a major topic for policy debate among the public, the media or in the Congress" ("9/11 Report," p.A14).

The Terrorism Research Center (www.terrorism.com) outlined the effects of this attack: "The President of the United States made it very clear in his September 20th speech to the Congress, the nation and the world, that this threat has not achieved its objectives of fear. Rather, it has galvanized the United States into action: 'Tonight we are a country awakened to danger and called to defend freedom. Our grief has turned to anger, and anger to resolution.'" The horrific events of September 11 pulled together and unified the American people. Patriotism was immediately popular. Thousands of volunteers helped search for victims and donated blood and money. The American flag flew everywhere.

In addition to galvanizing the nation, the events of that tragic day had other ramifications. Reuland and Davies (p.5) suggest: "The events of September 11, 2001, forever changed the nation's view of our security if faced with a large-scale terrorist attack." Peed and Wexler (p.vii) point out: "Local, state and federal law enforcement agencies are still feeling the effects of September 11, 2001. In the years that have passed since those tragic events, law enforcement professionals have been working to redefine their roles as they

continue traditional crime-fighting efforts while also taking on tremendous new counterterrorism activities." But the threat remains. The Justice Department's top priority is to support law enforcement and intelligence agencies in the fight against terrorism ("AG Gonzales").

This chapter begins with an overview of terrorism and a discussion of how it is classified. Next is a discussion of international terrorism, a description of the domestic terrorist groups existing in the United States, terrorists as criminals, and the methods terrorists may use. This is followed by how terrorism is funded and a look at the federal response to terrorism, including the formation of the Department of Homeland Security and passage of the USA PATRIOT Act. Next is a discussion of hometown security and homeland security and the critical role of local law enforcement in responding to terrorism. Next, investigating terrorist activities and information gathering and intelligence sharing are discussed. This is followed by a discussion of crucial collaborations and partnerships, as well as initiatives, to assist in the fight against terrorism and the role of the media in this fight. Then the discussion turns to two major concerns related to that fight: erosion of civil liberties and retaliation against people of Middle Eastern descent. The chapter concludes with a discussion of terrorism and community policing.

Terrorism: An Overview

 he United States has not been immune from terrorist attacks from within and without. Consider, for example, the raids of the Ku Klux Klan, the mail bombings of the Unabomber, the 1993 attack on the World Trade Center, and the 1995 bombing of the Alfred P. Murrah Building in Oklahoma City. Most terrorist acts result from dissatisfaction with a religious, political, or social system or policy and an inability to change it through acceptable, nonviolent means.

The United States paid lip service to fighting terrorism in 1995 when the Federal Bureau of Investigation (FBI) established a Counterterrorism Center. In 1996 the Antiterrorism and Effective Death Penalty Act was passed, enhancing the powers of the federal government to deny visas to individuals belonging to terrorist groups and simplifying the process for deporting aliens convicted of crimes. On February 23, 1998, Osama bin Laden called for **jihad**, a holy war, on the United States. He called on "every Muslim who believes in God and wishes to be rewarded to comply with God's order to kill Americans and plunder their money wherever and whenever they find it" (Savelli, p.3).

In 1999 FBI Director Louis Freeh announced, "Our number-one priority is the prevention of terrorism." But it took the horrendous attacks of September 11, 2001, to truly get our attention. Those attacks were criminal and are still being investigated. It is up to law enforcement throughout the country to investigate possible terrorist activities. To do so, it is important to "know the enemy" and to understand terrorism and those who engage in it.

Terrorism Defined

Terrorism is extremely difficult to define because, as the Terrorism Research Center notes: "One man's terrorist is another's freedom fighter." The Center defines **terrorism** as "the use of force or violence against persons or property in violation of the criminal laws of the United States for purposes of intimidation, coercion or ransom." This is similar to the FBI's definition: "Terrorism is the unlawful use of force or violence against persons or property to intimidate or coerce a government, the civilian population, or any segment thereof, in furtherance of political or social objectives" (28 *Code of Federal Regulations* Section 0.85). The U.S. Code Title 22 defines terrorism as the "premeditated, politically motivated violence perpetrated against noncombatant targets by subnational groups or clandestine agents, usually intended to influence an audience."

 Most definitions of terrorism have commonalities, including the systematic use of physical violence, either actual or threatened, against noncombatants to create a climate of fear to cause some religious, political, or social change.

Carter and Holden (p.300) suggest: "Terrorism may be seen as a tactic, strategy, philosophy or pejorative label to describe the activities of one's enemies." They contend: "The most useful definition of terrorism is a form of political or religious militancy that uses violence or the threat of violence in an attempt to change behavior through fear."

Motivations for Terrorism

Most terrorist acts result from dissatisfaction with a religious, political, or social system or policy and frustration resulting from an inability to change it through acceptable, nonviolent means.

Religious motives are seen in Islamic extremism. Political motives are seen in such elements as the Red Army Faction. Social motives are seen in single-issue groups such as those against abortion or active in animal-rights or environmentalist movements. Before looking at specific terrorist groups, consider how they might be classified.

Classification of Terrorist Acts

The FBI categorizes terrorism in the United States as either domestic or international.

Domestic Terrorism

The FBI defines domestic terrorism as "the unlawful use, or threatened use, of force or violence by a group or individual based and operating entirely within the United States or its territories without foreign direction committed against persons or property to intimidate or coerce a government, the civilian population or any segment thereof, in furtherance of political or social objectives" (Murphy and Plotkin, p.84).

The bombing of the Alfred P. Murrah Federal Building and the pipe bomb explosions in Centennial Olympic Park during the 1996 Summer Olympic Games in Atlanta highlight the threat of domestic terrorists. These terrorists represent extreme right- or left-wing and special-interest beliefs. Many are antigovernment, antitaxation, and antiabortion, and some engage in survivalist training to perpetuate a white, Christian nation. Domestic terrorist groups are discussed later in the chapter.

In October 2002 the Washington, D.C., area was terrorized by a sniping spree. The sniper mastermind, John Allen Muhammad, was sentenced to death by a judge who called the shootings that left 10 people dead "so vile that they were almost beyond comprehension" (Barakat). His teenage accomplice, Lee Boyd Malvo, was sentenced to life without parole (Jackman, p.A3).

Brinkley ("Present Threats: Part II," p.43) presents what he describes as "undeniable facts" about terrorism:

1. We as a country will be attacked again.
2. Residents and/or citizens of this country will carry out these attacks.
3. Car bombings will become a tool of choice to be used against us.
4. Threat groups will practice a greater level of organization and sophistication in technologies and weapons.
5. Only by practicing due diligence and using sound and consistent enforcement practices can meaningful safety and security be achieved.

International Terrorism

According to the FBI:

> International terrorism involves violent acts or acts dangerous to human life that are a violation of the criminal laws of the United States or any state, or that would be a criminal violation if committed within the jurisdiction of the United States or any state. These acts appear to be intended to intimidate or coerce a civilian population, influence the policy of a government by intimidation or coercion, or affect the conduct of a government by assassination or kidnapping. International terrorist acts occur outside the United States or transcend national boundaries in terms of the means by which they are accomplished, the persons they appear intended to coerce or intimidate, or the locale in which the perpetrators operate or seek asylum. (Murphy and Plotkin, p.84)

International terrorism is foreign based or directed by countries or groups outside of the United States against the United States. The FBI divides international terrorism into three categories: (1) foreign state sponsors using terrorism as a tool of foreign policy, such as Iraq, Libya, Afghanistan; (2) formalized terrorist groups such as the Lebanese Hezbollah, the Egyptian al-Gamm'a al-Islamiyya, the Palestinian HAMAS (Harakat al-Muqawamah al-Islamiyyah), and bin Laden's al-Qaeda; and (3) loosely affiliated international radical extremists who have a variety of identities and travel freely in the United States, unknown to law enforcement or the government.

These international terrorist groups are likely to engage in what is often referred to as asymmetric warfare. **Asymmetric warfare** refers to combat in which a weaker group attacks a superior group not head-on but by targeting areas where the adversary least expects to be hit, causing great psychological shock, along with loss of life among random victims. Asymmetric warfare aims to empower the powerless and nullify the stronger adversary's ability to use its conventional weapons. A prime example was the use by the 9/11 al-Qaeda terrorists of ordinary box cutters to overpower flight personnel and convert airplanes into weapons of mass destruction, costing billions of dollars of losses to the U.S. economy and tremendous loss of life (at a total estimated cost to the terrorists of $500,000).

The FBI's National Counterterrorism Center (NCTC) states that of the 64 significant terrorist attacks in 2004 involving a U.S. citizen or facility, 53 (83 percent) were committed in the Near East (*A Chronology,* p.84). Only 3 (5 percent) were committed in the Western Hemisphere (Figure 20.2). Of the 651 total terrorist attacks in 2004, 90 percent had no U.S. target (p.86). In addition, U.S. citizens constituted only 1 percent of all victims of international terrorism in 2004 (p.87).

The July 7 bombings in London were evidence of the spread of terrorism to Western societies, particularly the staunch allies of the U.S.-led invasion of Iraq and overthrow of Saddam Hussein's regime. According to Zuckerman (2005a, p.68), London has become the headquarters of "Islamifascism in Europe with hundreds of al-Qaeda–trained terrorists in Britain." He notes that after the London bombings, Islamic websites exclaimed: "Rejoice, Islamic nation! Rejoice, Arab world!" Zuckerman cautions: "With 20 million Muslims in Europe, a population likely to double over the next 20 years, national borders are no defense against the insidious ideology of radical Islam." Zuckerman (2005b, p.60) contends: "Like terrorists in London, Islamic jihadists will try to find ways to exploit the freedoms and openness that are the core of a democratic society."

Confusion often exists when the term *Islamic jihad* is used because, according to White (p.353), several Middle Eastern groups go by that name. These terrorist groups are all parts of the Palestine Liberation Organization's (PLO) military branch but have different ideas on how to go about their militant actions. They share a similar beginning, however, born of the first **intifada**, or uprising, which was a spontaneous Palestinian revolt in Gaza and the West Bank against Israeli crackdowns on rioting.

Who are these groups and where did they come from?

Islamic terrorist groups include Hezbollah, HAMAS, Palestinian Islamic Jihad (PIJ), and the al-Aqsa Martyrs' Brigades.

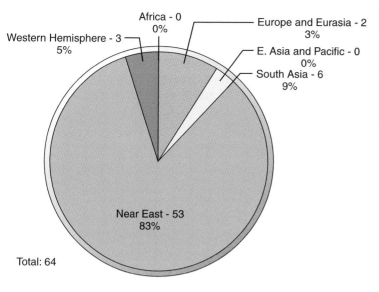

Figure 20.2

Total significant international terrorist attacks involving a U.S. citizen and/or facility, by region, 2004

Source: A Chronology of Significant International Terrorism for 2004. Washington, DC: National Counterterrorism Center, April 27, 2005, p.84.

Hezbollah   Hezbollah, literally the Party of God, "is a militia group and political party that first emerged as a faction in Lebanon following the Israeli invasion of that country in 1982" ("Hezbollah"). Hezbollah began with a group of Lebanese Shi'ite clerics determined to drive Israel from their homeland. They found assistance from Iran, which provided logistical support and an ample supply of recruits, primarily disaffected, younger, more radical Muslims. Hezbollah's tactics include kidnappings and car bombings directed predominantly against Westerners. They also offer a comprehensive social services network for its supporters.

White (p.168) notes that Hezbollah participated in the al-Aqsa intifada and that its international branch "is believed to be the most effective terrorist network in the world." While Hezbollah is part of the jihadist network, its origins are found in the struggle over Palestine and it has "reluctantly formed alliances with non-jihadist groups" (p.140).

HAMAS   HAMAS is a militant Palestinian Islamic movement in the West Bank and Gaza Strip dedicated to destruction of Israel and the creation of an Islamic state in Palestine. Founded in 1987, HAMAS opposed the 1993 Peace Accords between Israel and the PLO. In 1998, HAMAS claimed that Palestine was an Islamic homeland that could never be surrendered to non-Muslims and that waging holy war to wrest control of Palestine from Israel was a religious duty for Palestinian Muslims. This was in direct conflict with the agenda of the PLO ("Hamas"). White (p.169) notes that HAMAS is a large organization, but its terrorist wing is relatively small. Frequently allied with Islamic Jihad, HAMAS competes with other organizations of the Palestinian Liberation Movement, or al-Fatah.

Palestinian Islamic Jihad   White (p.160), in the chapter of his book on the metamorphosis of Middle Eastern

terrorism, describes Palestinian Islamic Jihad (PIJ) as having emerged from Egypt. PIJ founders were influenced by militant factions and were disillusioned with Egypt's traditional Muslim Brotherhood. While the Brotherhood spoke of education and peaceful change, the PIJ founders wanted to create an Islamic state through military action. In the late 1970s they moved into the Gaza Strip and eventually went to southern Lebanon. When they returned to the occupied territories, they believed they could become the vanguard of a local Islamic revolution and began to create a new terrorist organization. White (p.169) notes that the group has strong links in the United States, allegedly in Florida, and is one of the groups that has mastered suicide bombing.

Al-Aqsa Martyrs' Brigades   This terrorist group formed in refugee camps in the West Bank (White, p.168). That some members are motivated by Hezbollah suggests that they have Shi'ite elements. Others believe the brigades represent al-Fatah's attempt to take the intifada's leadership away from HAMAS and the PIJ. The brigades are organized militarily and became one of the first secular groups in the Middle East to use suicide bombers. Their terrorist operations are divided into six geographical areas, controlled by division commanders. They do not always follow the wishes of the command council, formerly led by the late Yasser Arafat.

A totally different terrorist group, and perhaps the greatest threat to the United States, is al-Qaeda.

Al-Qaeda   Al-Qaeda, meaning "the base," is a broad-based Islamic militant organization founded by Osama bin Laden in the late 1980s. It began as a logistical network to support Muslims fighting against the Soviet Union during the Afghan War. When the Soviets withdrew from Afghanistan in 1989, the organization dispersed but continued to oppose what its leaders considered corrupt Islamic regimes and foreign presence in

Islamic lands. The group eventually reestablished its headquarters in Afghanistan under the patronage of the Taliban militia.

Al-Qaeda merged with other Islamic extremist organizations, and its leaders declared jihad on the United States. Tens of thousands of Muslim militants throughout the world were trained in military skills, and its agents have engaged in numerous terrorist attacks, including the bombing of the U.S. embassy in Nairobi, Kenya, the suicide bomb attack against the U.S.S. Cole, and the 9/11 attacks on the United States ("Al Qaeda").

The Dual Threat

Pitcavage (p.35) stresses: "As America goes forward in its war on terrorism, those who wage that war must always remember that there are fronts. Even as the United States seeks to eradicate international terrorist groups such as al-Qaeda, it must never forget to protect its citizens from those among them who would like nothing better but to tear it apart and recast it in their own, warped image. America's police officers are on the front lines of that battle." Such terrorist groups are numerous in the United States.

Terrorist Groups in the United States

ccording to Brinkley ("Present Threats: Part II," p.43): "A wide range of groups on the left and right, including environmentalist groups, pose specific challenges and threats to law enforcement operations and the officers who run them."

Domestic terrorist groups within the United States include white supremacists, black supremacists, militia groups, other right-wing extremists, left-wing extremists, pro-life extremists, animal rights extremists, and environmental extremists.

Garrett (2004a, p.88) cautions: "While not every activist is an extremist, law enforcement should pay attention to those who are." Many of these groups were also discussed in Chapter 19 as hate groups or cults.

White Supremacists

Scoville (p.48) notes: "One of the oldest American terrorist organizations is the Ku Klux Klan. Formed by Confederate veterans following the Civil War, the goal of the original Klan was to terrorize freed blacks and exert

political influence over the Reconstruction south. . . . The Klan is still out there. Members of local and regional Klan groups have been blamed for church burnings, intimidation and harassment of minorities and minority advocates, and other crimes." Neo-Nazi groups also espouse white supremacy, as do "skinheads."

Black Supremacists

The Black Panther Party for Self-Defense was established in 1966 during a time of racial turmoil. According to Scoville (p.46): "Today, a newly reconstituted Black Panther Party for Self-Defense has been organized, and it qualifies as a hate group. These contemporary Panthers are heavily armed, advocate violence against whites, and like their 1960s predecessors, see cops as the enemy."

The Militia Movement

According to White (p.254), most militia groups are heavily armed and practice their sharpshooting skills. Militia members are commonly frustrated, overwhelmed, and socially unable to cope with the rapid pace of change in the modern world. Many militia groups provide the rhetoric for violence.

Other Right-Wing Extremists

The preceding groups might also be described as right-wing extremists. According to White (p.249): "The appearance of modern right-wing extremism came to fruition around 1984 and has remained active since that time." White (pp.250–251) cites three issues that rejuvenated the extreme right: the Brady Bill and the Ruby Ridge and Waco incidents. The Brady Bill caused militia groups to fear federal gun control legislation. The Ruby Ridge incident involved an attempt to arrest Randy Weaver, a white supremacist charged with selling illegal firearms to undercover agents of the Bureau of Alcohol, Tobacco and Firearms (ATF). A shootout ensued, resulting in the death of a U.S. marshal and Weaver's young son. The FBI laid siege to Weaver's Ruby Ridge cabin and killed his pregnant wife before Weaver surrendered.

White (p.251) describes the third galvanizing incident, the federal siege of the Branch Davidian compound near Waco, Texas:

> In 1993, ATF agents attempted to serve a search warrant on the compound, but they were met with a hail of gunfire. Four agents were killed, and several were wounded. After a three-month siege, FBI agents moved in with tear gas. Unknown to the agents, the compound was laced with gasoline. When the FBI moved in, the Branch Davidians burned their fortress, killing over 70 people, including several young children held inside the compound.

1979   1985   1990   1996

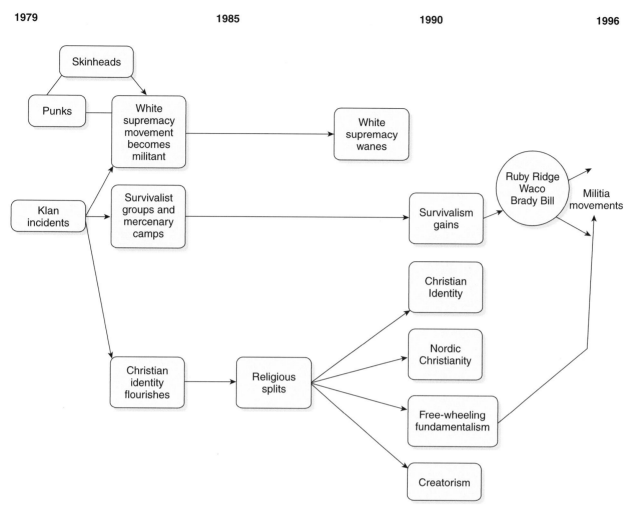

Figure 20.3

American right-wing terrorism from 1979 to 1996

Source: Jonathon R. White. *Terrorism: An Introduction,* 3rd ed. Belmont, CA: Wadsworth, 2002, p. 227.

Figure 20.3 illustrates American right-wing terrorism from 1979 to 1996.

Left-Wing Extremists

Brinkley ("Present Threats," pp.33–34) explains: "The left wing believes in a Pro-Marxist stance where the rich must be brought down and the poor elevated. Presently the largest groups of supporters for this cause are Anarchists. . . . This group believes that one receives according to one's needs."

Pro-Life Extremists

Although many pro-life, antiabortion advocates stay within the law in promoting their beliefs, some groups do not. One such group is an active terrorist organization called the Army of God: "Abortion clinics and their staffs are common Army of God targets, with zealots committing crimes ranging from arson to assault to assassination" (Scoville, p.48).

Animal Rights Extremists

The Animal Liberation Front (ALF), a clandestine, decentralized group, is one of the most active domestic terrorist assemblages, whose targets have included research labs, meat packing plants, and furriers (Scoville, p.46). ALF has claimed credit for numerous acts of vandalism, arson, and the "liberation" of laboratory animals, attacks that have cost millions of dollars in damages and setbacks in medical research.

Environmental Extremists

Environmental extremists are often referred to as "ecoterrorists," with *eco* being derived from *ecology*—the study of the interrelationships of organisms and their environment. **Ecoterrorism** seeks to inflict economic damage on those who profit from the destruction of the natural environment. The term *ecoterrorism* in conjunction with saving the environment is controversial because few people want to harm animals, and even fewer want to harm the planet. However, some cross the line from rhetoric to terror. When they cross this line, their violent actions are criminal.

One such group is the Earth Liberation Front (ELF), often working with the ALF. Arson is a favorite weapon, responsible for tens of millions of dollars of property damage, including a U.S. Department of Agriculture building, a U.S. Forest Service ranger station, and a Colorado ski resort. The group has claimed responsibility for releasing 5,000 mink from a Michigan fur farm, releasing 600 wild horses from an Oregon corral, and burning the Michigan State University's genetic engineering research offices.

Terrorists as Criminals

P olisar (p.8) observes: "Suddenly agencies and officers who have been trained and equipped to deal with more traditional crimes are now focused on apprehending individuals operating with different motivations, who have different objectives and who use much deadlier weapons than traditional criminals." According to McVey (p.174): "Terrorist acts can be identified as being criminal in nature, symbolically targeted and always aggressive. They seek to achieve political goals and communicate a message." The differences between the street criminal and the terrorist are summarized in Table 20.1.

Linett (p.59) notes another striking difference between dealing with a terrorist and a street criminal: "The difference is not just one of semantics; it is a matter of life and death. When fighting terrorists, it's kill or be killed, not capture and convict."

As Page ("Law Enforcement," p.86) suggests: "Terrorism has caused a blurring of war and crime." This has drawn law enforcement directly into the war. He (p.87) notes: "Local law enforcement will be expected to handle complex tactical situations such as chemical, biological and nuclear events." These are among the arsenal of methods terrorists use.

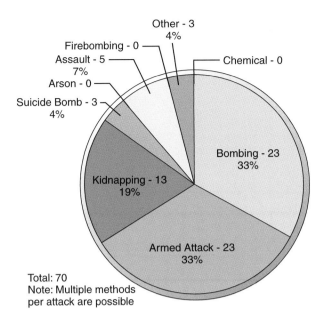

Figure 20.4
Methods used by international terrorists, 2004

Source: A Chronology of Significant International Terrorism for 2004. Washington, DC: National Counterterrorism Center, April 27, 2005, p.85.

Methods Used by Terrorists

T errorists have employed a variety of techniques in furtherance of their cause. (The use of arson has already been discussed.) Figure 20.4 illustrates the methods used in the significant international terrorist attacks involving a U.S. citizen and/or facility during 2004.

Terrorists may use arson, explosives and bombs, weapons of mass destruction (biological, chemical, or nuclear agents), or technology.

Reuland and Davies (p.5) state: "The term 'CBR' is used by law enforcement agencies as shorthand to include all potential terrorist threats that can have consequences for the health of large numbers of people. These threats include chemical agents (C), biological agents (B) and radiation exposure (R)." They present the most likely to least likely terrorist threats (Figure 20.5) and the level of impact by weapon used (Figure 20.6).

Explosives and Bombs

From 1978 to 1996, Theodore Kaczynski, the notorious Unabomber, terrorized the country through a string of 16 mail bombings that killed three people, apparently in a protest against technology. Ramzi Ahmed Yousef,

Table 20.1 / **Differences between the Street Criminal and the Terrorist**

Typical Criminal	Terrorist
Crimes of opportunity	Fight for political objective
Uncommitted	Motivated by ideology or religion
Self-centered	Group focused—even berserkers or lone wolves
No cause	Consumed with purpose
Untrained	Trained and motivated for the mission
Escape/elude oriented	On the attack

Source: Adapted from D. Douglas Bodrero. "Law Enforcement's New Challenge to Investigate, Interdict and Prevent Terrorism," *The Police Chief,* February 2002, p. 44.

Most Likely

Explosives
Toxic Industrial Chemicals
Radiological Dispersal Devices
Biological Agents/Weapons
Nuclear Weapons

Least Likely

Figure 20.5

Terrorist threats from most likely to least likely

Source: Melissa Reuland and Heather J. Davis. *Protecting Your Community from Terrorism: Strategies for Local Law Enforcement,* vol. 3: *Preparing for and Responding to Bioterrorism.* Washington, DC: Community Oriented Policing Services Office and the Police Executive Research Forum, September 2004, p. 7. Reprinted by permission of the Police Executive Research Forum.

Greatest Impact

Biological Agents/Weapons
Nuclear Weapons
Toxic Industrial Chemicals
Radiological Dispersal Devices
Explosives

Least Impact

Figure 20.6

Level of impact by weapon used

Source: Melissa Reuland and Heather J. Davis. *Protecting Your Community from Terrorism: Strategies for Local Law Enforcement,* vol. 3: *Preparing for and Responding to Bioterrorism.* Washington, DC: Community Oriented Policing Services Office and the Police Executive Research Forum, September 2004, p. 8. Reprinted by permission of the Police Executive Research Forum.

found guilty of masterminding the first World Trade Center bombing in 1993, declared that he was proud to be a terrorist and that terrorism was the only viable response to what he saw as a Jewish lobby in Washington. The car bomb used to shatter the Murrah Federal Building in 1995 was Timothy McVeigh's way of protesting the government and its raid on the Branch Davidians at Waco. In 2002 Lucas Helder terrorized the Midwest by placing 18 pipe bombs accompanied by antigovernment letters in mailboxes throughout five states. Six exploded, injuring four letter carriers and two residents. And the most horrific act of terrorism against the United States occurred on September 11, 2001, when two airplanes were used as missiles to explode into the World Trade Center and another plane was used as a missile to attack the Pentagon. A fourth plane crashed in a rural Pennsylvania field before it could reach its intended target.

Incendiary devices and explosives are most likely to be used because they are easy to make. Gips (p.16) describes one terrorist tactic, using a secondary explosive device after a first one is set off. This tactic was used in Bali, Indonesia, in October 2003, when a hand grenade was tossed into a nightclub, causing patrons to

flee into the streets, where a Jeep bomb was detonated. The attack, which killed almost 200 people, was attributed to Muslim extremists in Indonesia with links to al-Qaeda. According to Moore (p.24): "Regardless of the group responsible, the destruction highlights the effectiveness of the car bomb—one of terrorism's more deadly tools."

According to another report: "Car and truck bombings will continue to be the principal modus operandi for terrorists, with the main targets being U.S., British and Israeli military and diplomatic facilities. But also at risk are businesses popular with expatriates, including shopping malls, restaurants, bars and supermarkets" ("The Shape," p.20).

Morgenstern (p.9) points out that bombing requires a certain level of organization, equipment, materials, and a place to put the bomb together, all aspects that an investigator's knowledge can help detect, leading hopefully to the prevention of these crimes.

Suicide Bombers As noted in Table 20.1, whereas a typical criminal will by no means look to lay down his life for the sake of crime, suicide bombers go to their targets knowing that they are going to die there ("Suicide Terrorism," pp.20–21). Most believe that the act makes them martyrs and ensures them a place in their version of heaven. Their families are usually held in reverence and taken care of. Suicide bombers try to kill as many people as possible. "Although the United States has yet to be plagued by the type of routine belt-bomb suicide attacks that Israel experiences, many experts believe that it is only a matter of time before this tactic makes its way across the Atlantic" ("Confronting," p.16).

According to Glasser and Coll (2005), suicide bombers are immortalized online by al-Qaeda websites, with video clips showing the destruction they cause and web biographies attesting to their religious zeal.

Prevention Strategies Levine (p.30) describes the challenge of trying to stop the terrorists' low-tech, lethal weapon of choice, the car bomb: "The simplicity and stealth of these weapons make them a complex foe. It's virtually impossible to screen all the cars and trucks that rumble past critical buildings. So authorities now use simple tools, such as restricting parking and traffic and putting up concrete median barriers and security checkpoints." Moore (p.24) stresses: "A successful line of defense against car bombs would rely heavily on police-civilian coordination." He explains: "Terrorists may unwittingly give away their bombing plans by their actions or behavior" (p.28). According to Moore (p.29): "Beyond standard security that entails intelligence, static physical security [closed circuit television] and active detection methods, there are unique measures to apply that can lessen the car bomb threat: (1) use vehicle registration to conduct background checks for terrorist connections, (2) engage in rigorous registration enforcement and (3) restrict the type and size of vehicles imported." Moore (p.31) contends: "Vehicle registration may discourage terrorists from relying on car bombs because the car may be traced to the owner after the fact."

Among the warning signs revealing a suicide bomber are unseasonable garb; profuse sweating; obvious disguises (such as a police uniform with a security badge); and a well-dressed, perfumed appearance and demeanor commensurate with one who is prepared to meet his maker ("Confronting," p.16).

Weapons of Mass Destruction

Symonds (p.19) notes: "Weapons of mass destruction (WMD) are not the result of any recent technological developments. Biological WMDs have actually been in use since the 1300s. The advent of the 20th century brought with it the first use of artificially produced WMDs—or chemical agents—during World War I. Today the world faces the major problem of how to get the genie back into the bottle. The means and recipes for the development of nuclear, radiological, biological and chemical weapons are well known and documented."

Much concern centers around potential use of nuclear, biological, and chemical (NBC) agents. Some experts suggest that, of these three means, bioterrorism is the least likely to occur whereas chemical attacks are the most likely because the raw materials are easy to get and the devices are simple to assemble and use..

Biological Agents Bioterrorism involves dissemination of anthrax, botulism, and smallpox as WMDs, and is a potential reality following the anthrax scare of 2001 on the heels of the 9/11 attacks (Hanson, "The Nation's," p.18). Raffel (p.1) notes: "Many countries and terrorist groups have the capability to mass produce lethal viruses and distribute them throughout the human population."

A survey of 2,000 hospitals conducted by the U.S. General Accounting Office found that although 80 percent had written emergency response plans for large-scale infectious disease outbreaks, fewer than half had conducted training related to bioterrorism ("Bioterrorism," pp.24–25). Especially susceptible to bioterrorism are the nation's food and water supply, which might also be attacked using chemical agents.

Chemical Agents The attention of security experts was first riveted on the potential for chemical terrorism in 1995 when members of Aum Shinrikyu, a new-age cult, released sarin, a poisonous gaseous substance, into the Tokyo subway system (Nason, p.44; White p.209), killing 12 and sending 5,000 to the hospital. It was what many considered one of their worst nightmares: "A non-state entity could manufacture a viable chemical agent and deliver it in a public location" (Nason, p.44). Unfortunately, anyone with Internet access and a web browser can, in less than 40 minutes,

obtain the chemical formula for the invisible, odorless, and highly toxic sarin gas.

The four common types of chemical weapons are nerve agents, blood agents, choking agents, and blistering agents. One agent, ricin toxin, is both a biological and a chemical weapon. According to Hanson ("Ricin," p.16), ricin is more than 1,000 times more poisonous than cyanide. He (p.18) notes: "In its purest form, an amount of ricin toxin no bigger than a grain of table salt can kill an adult." Hanson also states: "According to a recent Monterey Institute of International Studies report, detailed procedures for ricin extraction and use were found in al Qaeda's military manuals seized in safe houses and caves in Afghanistan."

Nuclear Terrorism The U.S. Nuclear Regulatory Commission (NRC) contends that an average of approximately 375 devices of all kinds containing radioactive material are reported lost or stolen each year. Such devices are also called "dirty bombs." While this may seem another horrific addition to a terrorist arsenal as a weapon of choice (Page, "Dirty Bomb," p.124), Hughes ("Anxiety," p.32) suggests: "The primary destruction and disruption from a dirty bomb detonation will be caused by public panic, not radiation."

A WMD Team Hughes ("How to Start") advocates that local law enforcement agencies select and train officers to form a WMD team. The officers' time is not devoted solely to the unit, but is ready if a need for their skills arises. According to Hughes ("How to Start" p.21): "A WMD unit trains together and is tasked with responding to, assessing and resolving the crisis portion of any Weapons of Mass Destruction event. . . . Responders to a WMD incident must be capable of assessing any agents or products disseminated as well as how rapidly they are spreading and be equipped to contain and neutralize them. These tasks require an above-average knowledge of chemistry, meteorology, physics and tactics, not to mention immediate access to some fairly specialized equipment. HazMat is not enough."

Reuland and Davies (p.36) stress the importance of adequate personal protective equipment (PPE) for investigators involved in bioterrorism incidents. Batista (p.94) points out that implementing a PPE program protects the protectors and results in no "blue canaries." Police officers who walk into hazardous situations and die are sometimes described as blue canaries—from the practice of coal miners releasing a canary into a mine shaft to see whether the shaft was safe for breathing (if the canary died, more ventilation was needed). Table 20.2 illustrates the level of protection, description, type of protection afforded, and circumstance for use of each level of equipment.

Senn (p.102) cautions that storing PPE in a squad car trunk can subject it to extreme temperature changes and damage due to friction caused by rubbing against other items. Officers should store equipment in a gear

Table 20.2 / **Personal Protective Equipment.**

Level	Description	Protection	Circumstance
D	Work uniform	Provides no respiratory protection and minimal skin protection	Should not be worn on any site where respiratory or skin hazards exist
C	Full facepiece, air-purifying, canister-equipped respirator and chemical-resistant clothing	Same skin protection as level B, but a lower level respirator	Worn when airborne substance is known, concentration is measured, criteria for using air-purifying respirators are met, and skin and eye exposures are unlikely
B	Chemical-resistant clothing (overalls and long sleeves) and self-contained breathing apparatus (SCBA)	Provides splash protection	When the highest level of respiratory protection is needed but a lesser level of skin and eye protection is sufficient
A	Fully encapsulating chemical-resistant suit and SCBA Can be worn for only 15 to 30 minutes due to overheating; special training is required	Provides full protection	When the highest level of respiratory, skin, eye, and mucous membrane protection is needed

Source: Melissa Reuland and Heather J. Davies. *Protecting Your Community from Terrorism: Strategies for Local Law Enforcement,* vol. 3: *Preparing for and Responding to Bioterrorism. Washington,* DC: Community Oriented Policing Services and the Police Executive Research Forum, September 2004.

bag and carry it in the car only when on shift. When off shift, the gear should be kept in a dry storeroom or locker (Senn, p.104).

Detecting Radiation and Other Bioterrorism Agents
Dosimeters are described as "small, lightweight devices that use silicon diode technology to instantaneously detect and display the accumulated exposure dose and dose rate" ("Dosimeters Protect," p.105). Dosimeters can identify the specific radionuclide(s) involved and let investigators calculate how long they can safely remain on the scene. Two common dosimeters are a credit card size that can be worn on a lanyard and a pager-sized device that can clip onto a duty belt (Garrett, "Detecting," p.86).

Another advance in detecting hazardous agents is the *electronic nose.* Already used to select fragrant wines and diagnose diseases, electronic noses are now "sniffing" their way into the market for detecting hazardous agents (Kanable, p.74). Electronic nose technology is designed to detect all chemicals within an aroma or fragrance and miss nothing. According to Garrett ("Detecting," p.87), the technology of electronic noses in the future will be smaller, cost less, and merge with wireless technology. Some electronic noses already use wireless technology, allowing an investigator more than a mile away from the device to use a computer to monitor the vapors, smells, odors, and chemistry of the air remotely.

Technological Terrorism

Technological terrorism includes attacks *on* our technology as well as *by* technology. We rely on energy to drive our technology. An attack on the U.S. energy supply could be devastating. Likewise, an attack on the computer systems and networks critical to the functioning of businesses, health care facilities, educational institutions, the military, and all governmental agencies would be catastrophic. **Cyberterrorism** is defined by the FBI as "terrorism that initiates, or threatens to initiate, the exploitation of or attack on information systems." Uner (p.26) cautions: "The threat of cyberterrorism is real; it's only a matter of when."

Damage to our critical computer systems can put our safety and our national security in jeopardy. Each of the preceding types of terrorism poses a threat to our national security.

Technology Innovations

Researchers at the University of California, San Diego, have developed dust-sized chips of silicon capable of rapidly, remotely detecting biological and chemical agents, including substances terrorists might dissolve in drinking water, spray into the atmosphere, or fold into a letter. The head of the research effort notes: "The idea that you can have something that's as small as a piece of dust with some intelligence built into it so that it could be inconspicuously stuck to paint on a wall or to the side of a truck or dispersed into a cloud of gas to detect toxic chemicals or biological materials has obvious law enforcement potential" (Page, "Dust," p.96).

Funding Terrorism

It takes money to carry out terrorism, not only for weapons but for general operating expenses. Terrorist groups commonly collaborate with organized criminal groups to deal drugs, arms, and, in some instances, humans. The concept of *narcoterrorism* refers to the use of terrorist tactics to support drug operations or the use of drug trade profits to finance terrorism (White, p.76). To finance their operations, terrorist groups smuggle stolen goods and contraband, forge documents, profit from the diamond trade, and engage in extortion and protection rackets (White, pp.68–79). In countries across the globe, terrorists are known to generate revenue by offering their security services to narcotics traffickers ("The Growing," p.87).

Many terrorist operations are financed by charitable groups and wealthy Arabs sympathetic to the group's cause. To investigate local charities, any interested individual can access the information by contacting the Better Business Bureau or the Wise Giving Alliance. Billingslea (p.49) elaborates on the illicit sale of goods: "The illicit sale of cigarettes and other commodities by terrorist groups and their supporters has become a crucial part of their funding activities. . . . The trafficking schemes provide the terrorist groups with millions of dollars annually, which fund the purchasing of firearms and explosives to use against the United States, its allies and other targets." He notes that Hezbollah and HAMAS members have established front companies and legitimate businesses in the cigarette trade in Central and South America. In other fundraising efforts, terrorists conspire with cargo theft rings to obtain commodities to sell on the black market.

Fraud has become increasingly common among terrorists, not only as a way to generate revenue but also as a way to gain access to their targets. Fraudulently obtained driver's licenses, passports, and other identification documents are often found among terrorists' belongings (Savelli, p.9). No matter how terrorist groups are financed, they usually need to hide where the money came from.

Money Laundering

Money laundering was discussed in Chapter 14. However, one tactic is especially important in hiding the money trail of terrorist financing—*hawala*. **Hawala** is an informal banking system based on trust and often bartering, common throughout the Middle East and used to transfer billions of dollars every year. No tax records or paper trails exist. This practice has been used for many years to move terrorist money without a trace of banking records or currency transaction reports (CTR). Hawala allows money launderers to secretly hide and send money out of the country without detection (Savelli, p.47).

Operation Green Quest, described by Savelli (p.47), is a multiagency terrorist financing task force to "identify, disrupt and dismantle terrorist financial networks by bringing together the financial expertise from the Treasury and other branches of the U.S. government." Proof exists that millions of dollars were sent directly to al-Qaeda to fund operations leading up to the September 11 attacks.

The Federal Response to Terrorism

On October 19, 1984, President Reagan signed into law the Act to Combat International Terrorism (ACIT), which established a monetary reward program for information involving terrorism. In 1996 the FBI established the National Counterterrorism Center. Also in 1996 the Antiterrorism and Effective Death Penalty Act was passed, including several specific measures aimed at terrorism. It enhanced the federal government's power to deny visas to individuals belonging to terrorist groups and simplified the process for deporting aliens convicted of crimes.

Having announced in 1999 that prevention of terrorism was its top priority, the FBI added a new Counterterrorism Division with four subunits: the International Terrorism Section, the Domestic Terrorism Section, the National Infrastructure Protection Center, and the National Domestic Preparedness Office. But this was not enough to avert the tragic events of September 11, 2001. It took a disaster of that magnitude to make the war on terrorism truly the number-one priority of the United States. One of the first initiatives was establishing a new federal agency at the cabinet level.

The Department of Homeland Security

On October 8, 2001, President Bush signed Executive Order 13228 establishing the Department of Homeland Security (DHS) to be headed by then Pennsylvania Governor Tom Ridge (who resigned to take the post).

 As a result of 9/11, the Department of Homeland Security was established, reorganizing the departments of the federal government.

According to Van Etten (p.31), the national strategy for Homeland Security defines *homeland security* as "a concerted effort to prevent terrorist attacks within the United States, reduce America's vulnerability to terrorism and minimize the damage and recover from attacks that do occur." The mission of the DHS is "to develop and coordinate the implementation of a comprehensive national strategy to secure the United States from terrorist threats or attacks." Figure 20.7 shows the organization of the DHS.

Also in September, Attorney General Ashcroft announced that all U.S. attorneys were establishing

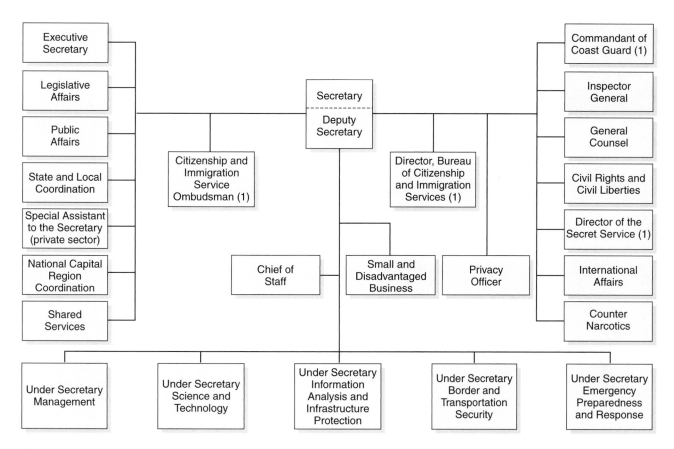

Figure 20.7

Organization of the Department of Homeland Security

[1] Effective March 1, 2003.

antiterrorism task forces to serve as conduits for information about suspected terrorists between federal and local agencies.

 At the federal level, the FBI is the lead agency for responding to acts of domestic terrorism. The Federal Emergency Management Agency (FEMA) is the lead agency for consequence management (after an attack).

The DHS serves in a broad capacity, facilitating collaboration between local and federal law enforcement to develop a national strategy to detect, prepare for, prevent, protect against, respond to, and recover from terrorist attacks within the United States. The DHS has established a five-level color-coded threat system used to communicate with public safety officials and the public at large: green represents a low level of threat, blue a guarded level, yellow an elevated level, orange a high level, and red a severe level (Figure 20.8). (Other information on DHS preparedness and prevention measures can be found at www.ready.gov.)

The USA PATRIOT Act

On October 26, 2001, President Bush signed into law the Uniting and Strengthening America by Providing Appropriate Tools Required to Intercept and Obstruct Terrorism (USA PATRIOT) Act, giving police unprecedented ability to search, seize, detain, and eavesdrop in their pursuit of possible terrorists. The law expands the FBI's wiretapping and electronic surveillance authority and allows nationwide jurisdiction for search warrants and electronic surveillance devices, including legal expansion of those devices to e-mail and the Internet. It includes money laundering provisions, sets strong penalties for anyone who harbors or finances terrorists, and establishes new punishments for possessing biological weapons. Further, it makes it a federal crime to commit an act of terrorism against a mass transit system.

 The USA PATRIOT Act significantly improves the nation's counterterrorism efforts by:
- Allowing investigators to use the tools already available to investigate organized crime and drug trafficking.
- Facilitating information sharing and cooperation among government agencies so they can better "connect the dots."
- Updating the law to reflect new technologies and new threats.
- Increasing the penalties for those who commit or support terrorist crimes.

HOMELAND SECURITY ADVISORY SYSTEM

SEVERE
SEVERE RISK OF
TERRORIST ATTACKS

HIGH
HIGH RISK OF
TERRORIST ATTACKS

ELEVATED
SIGNIFICANT RISK OF
TERRORIST ATTACKS

GUARDED
GENERAL RISK OF
TERRORIST ATTACKS

LOW
LOW RISK OF
TERRORIST ATTACKS

© AP/Wide World Photos

Figure 20.8
This five-level color-coded security alert system is in use throughout the country to communicate a threat level.

Using Tools Already in Use in the War on Drugs   Baveja
(p.36) suggests that the war the United States has waged on illicit drugs may provide lessons in the current fight against terrorism:

> Despite their differences, terrorism and illicit drug activity have several commonalties in their delivery and control, making a compelling case for exploring further to decipher any shared lessons. For example, drugs and terrorism involve covert illegal activities that call for sophisticated undercover enforcement operations. Both terrorism and drug activity do have a domestic component, but the threat from the organized and international component of these activities is far more devastating. In addition, there is evidence to suggest that terrorist cells and networks have structures similar to those of drug cartels.
>
> Further, both counterterror and counterdrug strategies require coordination among various law enforcement agencies, and strategic cooperation and information sharing with other partner countries. Finally, an overall policy for both these problems involves careful

weighing of different strategies that reach beyond U.S. borders and span the globe.

Facilitating Information Sharing   The importance of the
information-sharing provision of the act can be seen in the case of an al-Qaeda cell in Lackawanna, New York, and its implications on updating the law to reflect new technologies and new threats:

> This case involved several residents of Lackawanna, who traveled to Afghanistan in 2001 to receive training at an al Qaeda–affiliated camp near Kandahar. The investigation of the "Lackawanna Six" began during the summer of 2001, when the FBI received an anonymous letter indicating that these six individuals and others might be involved in criminal activity and associating with foreign terrorists. The FBI concluded that existing law required the creation of two separate investigations in order to retain the option of using FISA [the Foreign Intelligence Surveillance Act]: a criminal investigation of possible drug crimes and an intelligence investigation related to terrorist threats. Over the ensuing months, two squads carried on these two separate investigations simultaneously, and there were times when the intelligence officers and the law enforcement agents concluded that they could not be in the same room during briefings to discuss their respective investigations with each other.
>
> The USA PATRIOT Act, however, took down the "wall" separating these two investigations by making clear that the sharing of case-sensitive information between these two groups was allowed. As a result of key information shared by intelligence investigators, law enforcement agents were able to learn that an individual mentioned in the anonymous letter was an agent of al Qaeda. Further information shared between intelligence and law enforcement personnel then dramatically expedited the investigation of the Lackawanna Six and allowed charges to be filed against these individuals. Five of the Lackawanna Six pleaded guilty to providing material support to al Qaeda, and the sixth pleaded guilty to conducting transactions unlawfully with al Qaeda. These individuals were then sentenced to prison terms ranging from seven to ten years.
>
> Before the passage of the USA PATRIOT Act, applications for orders authorizing electronic surveillance or physical searches under FISA had to include a certification from a high-ranking executive branch official that the purpose of the surveillance or search was to gather foreign intelligence information. As interpreted by the courts and later the Justice Department, this requirement meant that the "primary purpose" of the collection had to be to obtain foreign intelligence information rather than evidence of a crime. Over the years, the prevailing interpretation and implementation of the "primary purpose" standard had the effect of limiting coordination and information sharing between intelligence and law enforcement personnel. Because the courts evaluated the government's purpose for using FISA at least in part by examining the nature and extent of such coordination, the more coordination that occurred, the more likely courts would find that law enforcement, rather than foreign intelligence, had become the primary purpose of the surveillance or search. (*Report from the Field*, p.3)

Controversy over the USA PATRIOT Act

According to Boyter (p.17):

> The law [the PATRIOT Act] has come under increasing attack from groups across the political spectrum. Some members of Congress and civil liberties groups say the act has given federal agents too much power to pursue suspected terrorists, threatening the civil rights and privacy of Americans.
>
> Attorney General Ashcroft has defended the law, arguing that repealing it would endanger lives and aid terrorists. He said that any attempt to strip law enforcement agents of their expanded legal powers could open the way to further terrorist attacks.
>
> He said that the law had been essential in preventing another terrorist attack in the United States. Expanding the powers of federal agents to use wiretaps, surveillance and other investigative methods and to share intelligence information "gives us the technological tools to anticipate, adapt and out-think our terrorist enemy," he said.

Report from the Field (p.1) states: "Since the USA PATRIOT Act was enacted, the Department of Justice—ever cognizant of civil liberties—has moved swiftly and vigorously to put its new tools into practice. As of May 5, 2004, the Department has charged 310 defendants with criminal offenses as a result of terrorism investigations since the attacks of September 11, 2001, and 179 of those defendants have already been convicted." The act was reauthorized in 2006 for an additional five years.

The Justice Department has launched a website, www.lifeandliberty.gov, devoted to the PATRIOT Act to dispel some of the myths about it. As Devanney and Devanney (p.10) explain: "The intent of the PATRIOT Act, when it was passed in 2001 as an immediate response to the 9/11 attacks, was to provide *federal* law enforcement with better means to defend against terrorism" (emphasis added). They note: "Even in the first days after 9/11, federal officials recognized the importance of local officers in defense against terror. In October 2001, President Bush signed executive Order 12321, which called for federal agencies to reach out to state and local agencies." The concern about local involvement was later incorporated into the Homeland Security Act (HSA) in November 2002. This acknowledgment notwithstanding, the act focused on reorganizing 22 *federal* agencies to defend against terrorism.

However, in an address at the 56th Biennial FOP Conference on August 4, 2003, FBI Director Robert Mueller told the 2,000 police delegates: "You are the first lines of defense against danger. . . . No one agency can handle these complex, sophisticated threats alone. . . . We in the FBI are proud to be your partners" ("A New Era", 2003).

Devanney and Devanney suggest: "At present, the exact relationship between these local entities and the federal government is still evolving, particularly as it concerns funding issues." Unquestionably, the efforts of local law enforcement agencies are critical in the fight against terrorism.

Hometown Security and Homeland Security

The International Association of Chiefs of Police (IACP) report *From Hometown Security to Homeland Security* (p.2), from its "Taking Command" project, suggests that our nation's current homeland security strategy "is handicapped by a fundamental flaw. It does not sufficiently incorporate the advice, expertise or consent of public safety organizations at state, tribal or local levels." The IACP has identified five key principles that should form the basis for a national homeland security strategy:

1. All terrorism is local.
2. Prevention is paramount.
3. Hometown security is homeland security.
4. Homeland security strategies must be coordinated nationally, not federally.
5. Bottom-up engineering is important, involving the diversity of the state, tribal, and local public safety communities in noncompetitive collaboration.

The criticality of local law enforcement has been recognized ever since homeland security became a focus.

- It is vital that patrol officers correctly see themselves as the country's first line of defense against terrorist attacks (Gardner, p.6).
- When it comes to homeland security, every law enforcement officer can play a vital role. . . . A single law enforcement officer can indeed foil a devastating terrorist attack (Wexler, S., p.30).

The 16,000 state and local law enforcement agencies in the United States employ 700,000 officers who patrol the city streets daily and know their communities intimately.

> The first line of defense against terrorism is the patrol officer in the field.

Berkow (p.25) suggests: "American policing is well into the new post–September 11 era of new duties. Before the attacks, the world[s] of counterterrorism, site security and intelligence gathering were generally restricted to either the largest of police agencies or those departments that were responsible for specific identified threats. Most police agencies in the United States were neither trained to carry out these tasks nor focused on them. Since the attacks, every agency in the United States regardless of size or location has accepted these new homeland security missions to some degree. Every agency has now added a counterterrorism mindset to [its] regular mission and is focused on building and enhancing that capability."

Savelli (pp.65–66) points out: "Keep in mind, any law enforcement officer can potentially come in contact with a terrorist at any time, whether investigating an unrelated crime, conducting normal duties or responding as a back-up for another law enforcement officer. Also, keep in mind how many of the 9-11-01 hijackers had contact with law enforcement officers in various parts of the country and how many unsuspecting law enforcement officers, in any capacity, may have such contact with terrorists today or in the future." He provides the following examples:

- September 9, 2001: Ziad Jarrah, hijacker of the plane that crashed in Shanksville, Pennsylvania, was stopped by police in Maryland for speeding. He was driving 90 mph in a 65 mph zone. He was issued a ticket and released.

- August 2001: Hani Hanjour, who hijacked and piloted the plane that crashed into the Pentagon, killing 289 persons, was stopped by police in Arlington, Virginia. He was issued a ticket for speeding and released. He paid the ticket so he would not have to show up in court.

- Mohammed Atta, who hijacked and piloted the plane that crashed into the north tower of the World Trade Center, was stopped in Tamarac, Florida, for driving without a valid license and issued a ticket. He didn't pay the ticket, so an arrest warrant was issued. A few weeks later he was stopped for speeding but was let go because police did not know about the warrant.

According to Garrett ("The Wolf," p.6), 71 percent of the 4,500 agencies that responded to a survey conducted by the IACP reported being "not at all prepared" or "somewhat unprepared" to prevent terrorism. A mere 1 percent claimed that they were "adequately prepared." An important step in preparedness is learning about the enemy. DeMuro (p.32) emphasizes the need for "focused terrorism awareness training for law enforcement." Wexler ("Homeland," p.35) echoes:

> The only way to successfully fight terrorism in the United States is for law enforcement to gain a clear understanding of the adversary and to establish meaningful inroads with the Arab community. Local law enforcement has to be brought up to speed as to who the adversary is, their thinking processes, their tactics and their mindset. . . . Local law enforcement must try to establish a good foothold in the Arab and Muslim communities so that they can obtain assistance in developing assets that can root out these individuals. It's not going to be done by the INS, the FBI or NSA satellites. It's going to be done by local law enforcement.

Investigating Possible Terrorist Activities

 nvestigating possible terrorist activities is facilitated by the fact that terrorists also often engage in other criminal activities. Savelli (pp.21–36) identifies the following crimes as commonly associated with terrorists: mail theft, coupon fraud, sale of illegal cigarettes, identity theft, credit card scams, automated teller machine fraud, counterfeiting of food products and postage stamps, money laundering, and video/audio piracy. Loyka et al. (p.7) also note the "nexus" existing between traditional crime and terrorism, citing fraudulent identification, trafficking in illegal merchandise, and drug sales as means to terrorists' ends.

Savelli (p.16) recommends: "Law enforcement officers should be aware of terrorist *indicators*. Awareness of these indicators will give the law enforcement officer a strong basis to recognize terrorist related information upon being exposed to it. Such indicators are: negative rhetoric, excessive physical training, anti-American literature or a disregard for U.S. laws. Terrorists and their supporters tend to act similar since many of them have trained in the same terrorist training camps and share the same negative ideology." The U.S. Postal Service has provided indicators of suspicious mail, shown in Table 20.3.

Investigators should also be knowledgeable of vulnerable, valuable targets for a terrorist attack.

Table 20.3 / **Indicators of Suspicious Mail**

What Should Make Me Suspect a Piece of Mail?
It's unexpected or from someone you don't know.
It's addressed to someone no longer at your address.
It's handwritten and has no return address or bears one that you can't confirm is legitimate.
It's lopsided or lumpy in appearance.
It's sealed with excessive amounts of tape.
It's mailed with restrictive endorsements such as "Personal" or "Confidential."
It has excessive postage.
What Should I Do with a Suspicious Piece of Mail?
Don't handle a letter or package that you suspect is contaminated.
Don't shake it, bump it, or sniff it.
Wash your hands thoroughly with soap and water.
Notify local law enforcement authorities.

Source: U.S. Postal Service

Mariani (pp.106–107) suggests the following as valuable targets for terrorists: a high-occupancy structure or any site where a significant number of human lives are affected; a structure containing dangerous substances or articles; any vital, high-use structure comprising an infrastructure; a site of significant historical, symbolic, strategic, defensive, or functional value to the nation; a structure or item with high replacement cost; or a structure holding highly sensitive, rare, historical, or irreplaceable artifacts, documents, or other such content.

A White House report lists the following as critical infrastructures: agriculture and food, water, public health, emergency services, defense industrial base, telecommunications, energy, transportation, banking and finance, chemical industry and hazardous materials, and postal and shipping facilities (*The National Strategy*). It lists the following as key assets: national monuments and icons, nuclear power plants, dams, government facilities, and commercial key assets.

Although focusing on logical targets for terrorist attacks, "soft" targets should not be overlooked. Soft targets include shopping malls, subways, trains, sporting stadiums, theaters, schools, hospitals, restaurants, entertainment parks, compressed gas and oil storage areas, chemical plants, pharmaceutical companies, and many others. Hanson ("What's Next," p.20) explains that soft targets are relatively unguarded or difficult to guard.

In addition to being aware of potential targets in a community, investigators should also make use of the link between terrorism and white-collar crime that often exists.

The Link between Terrorism and White-Collar Crime

Kane and Wall (p.1) suggest that one way to address terrorism is to modify laws and rules that deal with crimes traditionally referred to as white-collar crimes. Such crimes are nonviolent and usually involve some form of deception or fraud to achieve financial gain. These crimes include, but are not limited to, credit card fraud, insurance fraud, identity theft, money laundering, immigration fraud, and tax evasion.

The reasoning behind this approach to counterterrorism includes the belief that terrorist activities require funding for weaponry, training, and travel and living expenses. In addition, terrorists create and use false identifications to enter the country, gain employment, acquire equipment, and accumulate money. Cases involving money laundering should be looked at as not only a white-collar crime but also as potentially linked to terrorism. The investigative techniques described in Chapter 18 would be applicable in this counterterrorism strategy.

The Typical Stages in a Terrorist Attack

Mariani (p. 97) provides additional insight into terrorist attacks by explaining the typical stages. The first stage is research, including surveillance, stakeouts, and local inquiries. The second stage is planning, usually conducted behind closed doors. The third stage is execution, the actual attack, and possible escape. Mariani suggests: "Of these three main stages, local law enforcement in general and the patrol officer in particular can best serve the counter-terrorism effort with stage one. It is at this stage that the terrorists are out in the open . . . mingling amongst us, driving, traveling, shopping, dining out . . . watching us, studying us, noting our habits, discovering our vulnerabilities and reporting back to their handlers with prospective targeting data to begin the planning stage." Most often these attacks are carried out by sleeper cells. A **sleeper cell** is a group of terrorists who blend into a community.

The three-tiered model of al-Qaeda terrorist attacks consists of sleeper cells attacking in conjunction with the group's leaders in Afghanistan, sleeper cells attacking on their own apart from centralized command, and individuals attacking with support from small cells.

It is crucial that investigators identify members of sleeper cells within their community. Mariani (pp.22–23) notes that racial profiling has been used in law enforcement for decades and suggests the following typical appearance of an al-Qaeda terrorist: a young (20 to 30) Middle Eastern–appearing male of average height and weight with prominent facial hair and a foreign accent. But a terrorist operative could just as readily affect atypical features, such as shoulder-length hair or a ponytail, flashy clothing and jewelry, business suits, dress shirts and ties, sport jackets or blazers, designer clothes, wingtip shoes, head gear, and use of alcohol or cigarettes. Mariani (p.24) cautions: "Unfortunately, terrorist operatives are believed to have been instructed by a . . . bin Laden aide to do whatever is necessary to avoid detection (e.g., shave their beards, use cologne, wear Western-style clothing, etc.)."

Heinecke (p.80) describes what she calls "another layer to the security blanket"—behavior pattern recognition (BPR): "BPR is a security methodology based on two components: observation of irregular behaviors for the environment and targeted conversations with suspects. . . . BPR is an extension of trained observation. Officers, whether they are in an airport, sports arena or convention center, need to look for behaviors that are irregular for that location."

Rashbaum (2004) describes a tactic against terrorism being used by the New York City Police Department: "Detectives visit scuba shops and hardware stores. They talk to parking garage attendants and plastic surgeons, hotel managers and tool rental companies, bulk fuel dealers and trade schools." Police officials acknowledge that this is something of a "needle-in-a-haystack approach," but the program, called Operation Nexus, has the potential to identify terrorists. Information from an al-Qaeda manual for terrorist operatives and debriefings of some of the group's leaders and foot soldiers suggest that al-Qaeda has considered using scuba divers to blow up bridges, riding in tourist helicopters for surveillance, turning trucks and limousines into rolling bombs, and using special torches to cut the cables of the Brooklyn Bridge.

Terrorists might be hunted down using confidential informant reward programs established by the 1984 ACIT. The PATRIOT Act amended the reward program by increasing the amount offered to be paid an informant to $250,000.

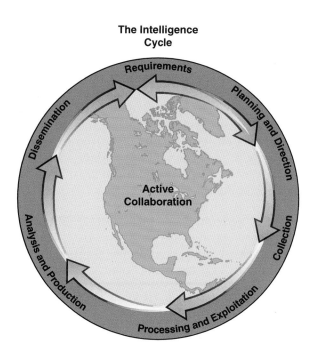

The Intelligence Cycle

Figure 20.9

The intelligence cycle

Source: Loyka, Stephan A.; Faggiani, Donald A., and Karchmer, Clifford. *Protecting Your Community from Terrorism: Strategies for Local Law Enforcement*, vol. 4: *The Production and Sharing of Intelligence*. Washington DC: Community Oriented Policing Services and the Police Executive Research Forum, February 2005.

Information Gathering and Intelligence Sharing

Loyka et al. (p.7) differentiate information and intelligence, with intelligence broadening to become organized information: "Intelligence has come to mean information that has not only been selected and collected, but also analyzed, evaluated and distributed to meet the unique policymaking needs of one particular enterprise."

Loyka et al. (pp.35–36) describe the intelligence cycle (Figure 20.9). The cycle begins with knowing the *intelligence requirements* needed for the investigation. What do investigators need to know to effectively participate in homeland security? These requirements are established by the director of Central Intelligence under the guidance of the president and the National and Homeland Security Advisors. The second step is *planning and direction*, a function of the FBI. The third step is the *collection of raw information* from local, state, and federal investigations. Fourth is *processing and exploitation* of the raw information, that is, converting the collected information into a form usable for analysis. Fifth is *analysis and production*, converting the raw information into intelligence. The final step is *dissemination*, which leads back to refinement of intelligence requirements.

Loyka et al. (p.36) explain: "The Intelligence Cycle is just that, a continuing cycle, which overlaps and drives each of its functions and in turn, drives the investigative mission. This cycle or process is used across all programs—Counterterrorism, Counterintelligence, Cyber and Criminal—to counter all threats."

Local and state law enforcement agencies are critical to the third step in the intelligence cycle and benefit from the sixth step as well. Many of the day-to-day duties of local law enforcement officers bring them into proximity with sources of information about terrorism. Patrol operations, especially traffic officers, properly trained in what to look for and what questions to ask when interacting with citizens, can be a tremendous source of intelligence, not only for local investigators, but also for their state and federal homeland security counterparts.

The difficult tasks of counterterrorism and antiterrorism are made even harder by the operational style that pervades law enforcement—that of withholding, rather than sharing, intelligence (Pilant, p.34). A report by the Senate Governmental Affairs Committee (Lieberman, pp.38–41) states:

> The frontline "first preventers" in the war against terrorism lack simple, streamlined access to the federal databases that are most valuable in the effort to identify and apprehend terrorists. . . .
>
> States and localities still operate far too much as information islands, in relative isolation from their neighbors. Cities, counties and states also have few resources to learn what their counterparts around the country are doing to effectively protect their localities. . . .
>
> Many state and local officials who need high-level information access lack the necessary federal security

clearances to do what their job—and our safety—demands. . . .

States lack a single point of contact for both receiving "downstream" information needs and pushing intelligence and other information "upstream."

Polisar (p.8) also asserts: "For far too long efforts to combat crime and terrorism have been handicapped by jurisdictional squabbles and archaic rules that prevented us from forging cooperative working relationships with our counterparts in local, regional, tribal and federal law enforcement. This must end." Local networking modules developed among local, state, and federal law enforcement agencies are the most effective way to discuss and share investigative and enforcement endeavors to combat terrorism. This networking module approach avoids compromising existing investigations or conducting conflicting cases and should have a built-in **deconfliction** protocol, which essentially means guidelines to avoid conflict. Deconfliction can be applied to declassified and confidential investigations (Savelli, p.43).

The National Criminal Intelligence Sharing Plan

A subtitle of the Homeland Security Act of 2002, called the Homeland Security Information Sharing Act, required the president to develop new procedures for sharing classified information, as well as unclassified but otherwise sensitive information, with state and local police. This charge was fulfilled in May 2002 when the IACP, the Department of Justice, the FBI, the DHS, and other representatives of the federal, state, tribal, and local law enforcement communities endorsed the National Criminal Intelligence Sharing Plan (NCISP). In releasing the plan, Attorney General John Ashcroft said: "The NCISP is the first of its kind in the nation, uniting law enforcement agencies of all sizes and geographic locations in a truly national effort to prevent terrorism and criminal activity. By raising cooperation and communication among local, state and federal partners to an unprecedented level, this groundbreaking effort will strengthen the abilities of the justice community to detect threats and protect American lives and liberties" ("Justice Dept.," p.5).

he importance of partnerships between law enforcement agencies at all levels cannot be overstated as it applies to the war on terrorism. The issue of effective partnerships among local, state, and federal law enforcement agencies has *deserved* attention for at least half a century, and it *demands* attention now (Murphy and Plotkin, p.87).

 A key to combating terrorism lies with the local police and the intelligence they can provide to federal authorities.

Communication should be the number-one priority in any terrorist-preparedness plan, and it is also number one in collaboration among local, state, and federal law enforcement agencies. An extremely valuable resource for investigators is the Regional Information Sharing Systems (RISS) program, which assists state and local agencies by sharing information and intelligence regarding terrorism.

Limitations on information sharing have caused tensions in the past, as often information received by the FBI is classified. Rules of federal procedure and grand jury classified material are two other limitations to how much information can be shared. However, as Johnson (2005) notes, since 9/11 more than 6,000 state and local police officers have been granted access to classified material involving terrorist threats, "the broadest dissemination of secret information in U.S. history." Also to date, some 6,011 clearances have been authorized.

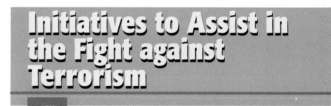

everal initiatives have been undertaken to help in the fight against terrorism. One such initiative is production of the *FBI Intelligence Bulletin*, a weekly online publication containing information related to terrorism in the United States. Recipients include duly authorized members of all law enforcement agencies who have registered with a law enforcement network.

Another initiative that indirectly supports the fight against terrorism is passage of the Community Protection Act.

 The Community Protection Act gives off-duty as well as qualified retired police officers the right to carry their firearms concealed in all 50 states.

According to Garrett ("'V' Is for Victory," p.6): "The men and women of law enforcement who can now carry the tools of their trade will help make America more secure." Other initiatives include increased security at our borders; the Community Vulnerability Assessment Methodology (C-VAM), the National Memorial Institute for the Prevention of Terrorism, the Center for Food Protection and Defense, and the National Incident Management System.

Increased Border Security

Moreno (2004) describes a program of the DHS called US-VISIT (U.S. Visitor and Immigrant Status Indicator Technology), a goal of which is "to enhance the security of our citizens and visitors; facilitate legitimate travel and trade; and ensure the integrity of our immigration system." The program requires visitors to submit to ink-less finger scans and digital photographs, allowing Customs and Border Protection (CBP) officers to determine whether the person applying for entry is the same one who was issued a visa by the State Department (Figure 20.10). Biometric and biographic data will also be checked against watch lists of suspected foreign terrorists and databases of sexual predators, criminals wanted by the FBI, and people deported previously from the United States. The program was implemented in January 2005 at 115 airports and 14 seaports, to be expanded to all 165 land ports of entry by year's end.

Lipton (2005b) reports that the government has created enormous new repositories of digitally recorded biometric data that can be used to identify more than 45 million foreigners. In addition, federal agencies have assembled data on more than 70 million Americans to speed law-abiding travelers through checkpoints.

Lipton (2005a) reports on the strengthening of the country's borders as outlined by Homeland Security Secretary Michael Chertoff following border-related emergency declarations by the governors of New Mexico and Arizona. Chertoff said the strategy went far beyond hiring more Border Patrol agents and installing more surveillance cameras, infrared and motion detectors and fences, initiatives already planned or underway. In addition, Chertoff intends to bolster the deportation process so an overwhelmed detention system does not cause illegal immigrants to be set free instead of being sent home. He plans to add beds for detainees, expedite deportations by making more judges and lawyers available, and try to track down more illegal immigrants who fail to appear for deportation hearings.

Community Vulnerability Assessment Methodology

Another tool available to law enforcement agencies across the country is C-VAM, a back-to-basics approach that identifies a community's weaknesses by using a detailed and systematic analysis of the facilities and their relationship to each other. This initiative examines a community as a whole to help departments focus resources and funds on the areas needing them most. It uses a performance-based system to calculate how effective a community's current physical protection systems are against likely threats (Goldsmith et al., p.100).

The National Memorial Institute for the Prevention of Terrorism

McDonald and McLaughlin (p.15) describe this initiative: "The Memorial Institute grew out of the desire of the survivors and family of the Murrah Federal Building bombing to have a living memorial. The result is an online, national network of best practices and lessons learned."

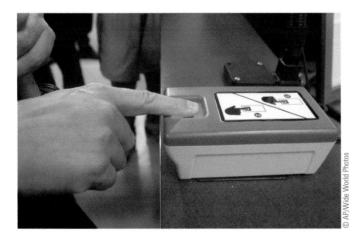

© AP/Wide World Photos

Figure 20.10
An arriving passenger at John F. Kennedy International Airport in New York submits an inkless fingerprint, which will be checked instantly against the national digital database for criminal backgrounds and any terrorist lists. Authorities began scanning fingerprints and taking photographs of arriving foreigners in 2003 as part of an initiative the Department of Homeland Security hopes will keep U.S. borders open to travelers but closed to terrorists and other criminals.

The Center for Food Protection and Defense

In July 2004 the University of Minnesota was awarded a $15 million grant for a national Center for Food Protection and Defense. It won the grant because it is one of only a few universities in the country with experts in agriculture, public health, veterinary medicine, and medicine on the same campus. The university will partner with General Mills, Cargill, 3M, and Hormel. Frank Busta, professor emeritus of food science and nutrition, will direct the grant. According to Busta: "Our charge is to protect and defend safe food from intentional contamination. The vulnerability of food is immense. . . . We hope we can make it sufficiently difficult [so] if and when terrorists decide to look at [attacking the food supply], they will say, 'We'll try something else'" (Smetanka, 2004a, p.A4). In announcing the new Center for Food Protection and Defense, DHS Secretary Ridge noted: "Government can't do it alone. . . . Partnerships between government and our great research universities, businesses and scientists will produce together what would be impossible individually" (Smetanka, 2004b, p.B1).

The National Incident Management System

The DHS in October 2003 created the Initial Response Plan (INRP), described as "an interim plan designed to help develop a unified approach to domestic incident management across the nation" ("Initial National," p.19). As Hamilton (p.11) explains: "The events of September 11, 2001, and subsequent development of the DHS has necessitated a change in the response and management of major domestic incidents."

On March 1, 2004, Secretary Ridge announced the approval of the National Incident Management System (NIMS), the country's first standardized management approach unifying federal, state, and local governments for incident response. NIMS establishes standardized incident management processes, protocols, and procedures that all responders—federal, state, tribal, and local—will use to coordinate and conduct response action ("DHS Secretary," p.14).

Joint Terrorism Task Forces

"Successful management of a joint terrorism task force (JTTF) may represent one of the most important aspects of law enforcement's unified war on terrorism" (Casey, p.1). According to Casey, the FBI has a JTTF in each of its 56 field offices, as well as 10 stand-alone, formalized JTTFs in its largest resident agencies. In an effective JTTF, all investigators, whether FBI agents, other federal officers, or state or local officers, are equal partners. Every investigator is assigned substantive cases and works from established FBI protocols for investigating terrorism, completing paperwork requirements, and using data systems (p.3).

The Role of the Media in the War on Terrorism

he Terrorism Research Center suggests: "Terrorism and the media have a symbiotic relationship. Without the media, terrorists would receive no exposure, their cause would go ignored, and no climate of fear would be generated. Terrorism is futile without publicity, and the media generates much of this publicity." White (p.342) raises the question of the **contagion effect;** that is, the coverage of terrorism inspires more terrorism. It is, in effect, contagious. This controversial issue leads to discussions about censorship in the war on terrorism. Two other pressing concerns relate to efforts to combat terrorism.

Concerns Related to the War on Terrorism

 Two concerns related to the so-called war on terrorism are that civil liberties may be jeopardized and that people of Middle Eastern descent may be discriminated against or become victims of hate crimes.

These two concerns were explored by Getlin (2005), who found that some of those he interviewed saw the searches at New York City's Penn Station as an intrusion on personal freedom, while others wanted police to be able to openly focus on Muslim commuters. One city council member noted: "There is a particular group who engages in these [terrorist] activities. They're not skinny balding Italian Americans from Staten Island."

The first guiding principle of the DHS is to protect civil rights and civil liberties:

> We will defend America while protecting the freedoms that define America. Our strategies and actions will be consistent with the individual rights and liberties enshrined by our Constitution and the Rule of Law. While we seek to improve the way we collect and share information about terrorists, we will nevertheless be vigilant in respecting the confidentiality and protecting the privacy of our citizens. We are committed to securing our nation while protecting civil rights and civil liberties. (*Securing*, p.6)

Concern for Civil Rights

Civil libertarians are concerned that valued American freedoms will be sacrificed in the interest of national safety. For example, the Justice Department has issued a new regulation giving itself the authority to monitor inmate–attorney communications if "reasonable suspicion" exists that inmates are using such communications to further or facilitate acts of terrorism. However, criminal defense lawyers and members of the American Civil Liberties Union (ACLU) have protested the regulation, saying that it effectively eliminates the Sixth Amendment right to counsel because, under codes of professional responsibility, attorneys cannot communicate with clients if confidentiality is not ensured. The ACLU has vowed to monitor police actions closely to see that freedoms protected under the Constitution are not jeopardized.

Bulzomi (p.26) stresses: "The government must use its new tools in a way that preserves the rights and freedoms guaranteed by America's democracy, but, at the same time, ensure that the fight against terrorism is vigorous and effective" (Figure 20.11).

> A difficult challenge facing law enforcement is balancing the need to enhance security with the need to maintain freedom.

Retaliation or Discrimination against People of Middle Eastern Descent

Another concern is that some Americans may retaliate against innocent people of Middle Eastern descent, many of whom were either born in the United States or are naturalized citizens. According to Peed and Wexler (p.vii): "America's multicultural neighborhoods, particularly Arab and Muslim communities, were initially affected by backlash violence and hate crimes following the terrorist attacks." Davies and Murphy (p.1) likewise note: "Within hours of the Twin Towers' collapse and the attack on the Pentagon, U.S. residents and visitors, particularly Arabs, Muslims and Sikhs, were harassed or attacked because they shared—or were perceived to share—the terrorists' national background or religion. . . . Law enforcement's challenge since then has been to maintain an appropriate balance between the security interests of our country and the constitutional rights of every American." We must remember the Japanese American internment camps during World War II and make sure we do not repeat that mistake.

Closely related concerns are the rights of citizens detained as enemy combatants and the rights of detained foreign nationals. In *Hamdi v. Rumsfeld* (2004) the Supreme Court ruled that a citizen detained in the

Figure 20.11
New Jersey Transit Police Officer Elizabeth Farrell (left) conducts a random passenger bag search.

United States as an enemy combatant must be afforded the opportunity to rebut such a designation. Petitioner Hamdi was captured in an active combat zone in Afghanistan following the September 11, 2001, attacks on the United States and surrendered an assault rifle. The U.S. District Court found that the declaration from the Defense Department did not support Hamdi's detention and ordered the government to turn over numerous materials for review. The U.S. Court of Appeals for the Fourth Circuit reversed the decision, stressing that because it was undisputed that Hamdi was captured in an active combat zone, no factual inquiry or evidentiary hearing allowing Hamdi to rebut the government's assertions was necessary. The U.S. Supreme Court voted 6 to 3 to vacate and remand, concluding that Hamdi should have a meaningful opportunity to offer evidence that he was not an enemy combatant.

In *Rasul v. Bush* (2004) the Supreme Court ruled that U.S. courts have jurisdiction to consider challenges to the legality of the detention of foreign nationals captured in Afghanistan in a military campaign against al-Qaeda and the Taliban regime that supported it. The petitioners, 2 Australians and 12 Kuwaitis, were being held at Guantanamo Bay, Cuba,

Figure 20.12

An inmate of Camp X-Ray is escorted by two guards while other prisoners are seen in their cells in Guantanamo Bay U.S. Navy Base, Cuba, in this March 15, 2002 photo. Debate has centered on whether foreigners detained at Guantanamo, a territory legally outside of the U.S., should enjoy the Constitutional rights that they would have if they were held on U.S. soil. In 2004, the Supreme Court ruled that prisoners in Guantanamo do have access to American courts, citing the fact that the U.S. has exclusive control over Guantanamo Bay (*Rasal v. Bush*, No. 03-334, U.S. June 28, 2004)

without charges (Figure 20.12). These and other legal issues regarding civil rights will be debated as the country seeks to balance the need for security with civil rights.

Community Policing and Homeland Security

"The community policing philosophy is an important resource for preparing for and responding to acts of terrorism" (Scheider et al., p.158). Officers in departments that fully embrace community policing will have an advantage in recognizing potential terrorist threats and targets in their jurisdictions because their daily work requires and imparts an intimate familiarity with their regularly assigned patrol area (p.160). Such officers interact with citizens and can educate them to be alert to suspicious activity. As Griffith (p.6) points out, "real" homeland security depends on alert, aware, and vigilant citizens. Information they provide officers on their beat can be invaluable to investigators.

"In order to truly protect our communities from terrorism we must enlist [citizens] as partners in our fight to prevent the next attack. If we are to be successful, it is imperative that we have the full cooperation of the communities we are trying to serve. The onus is on law enforcement to expand our community policing capabilities and continue to build relationships with our citizens, so that we can work together to reduce crime, violence and fear" (Wexler, C., p.2). Scheider et al. (p.162) conclude: "In the 21st Century, the community policing philosophy is well positioned to take a central role in preventing and responding to terrorism and in efforts to reduce citizen fear."

Being Proactive

A 2004 *New York Times* poll shows that while Americans are divided on their views of how prepared the United States is for another terrorist attack, the overwhelming majority of citizens have done nothing personally to prepare for such an attack (Sims, 2004). In addition, Savage (2004) reports: "Large numbers of Americans say they would probably ignore official instructions for how to respond to a terrorist attack involving a radiological dirty bomb or a smallpox attack according to a new study." Clearly, officers engaged in community policing can do much to educate citizens in their jurisdictions on preparedness plans, including a meeting place in case of a terrorist attack.

Citizen Corps is a component of the USA Freedom Corps focusing on opportunities for people across the country to participate in a range of measures to make their families, homes, and communities safer from the threats of terrorism, crime, and disasters of all kinds ("Homeland Security," p.27). In addition, Citizen Corps brings together a community's first responders, firefighters, emergency health care providers, law enforcement, and emergency managers with its volunteer resources.

The New York City police are providing antiterrorism training to building supers and doormen to be the eyes and ears of the department. Plans call for training 28,000 building employees through 2005 (Butler, p.A7). Giannone and Wilson (p.37) describe the Community Antiterrorism Training initiative, or CAT Eyes, designed to enlist community members in the fight against terrorism: "The CAT Eyes program was designed to help local communities combat terrorism by enhancing neighborhood security, heightening the community's powers of observation, and encouraging mutual assistance and concern among neighbors."

SUMMARY

The threat of terrorism has become a reality in America. Most definitions of terrorism have common elements, including the systematic use of physical violence, either actual or threatened, against noncombatants to create a climate of fear to cause some religious, political, or social change. Most terrorist acts result from dissatisfaction with a religious, political, or social system or policy and frustration resulting from an inability to change it through acceptable, nonviolent means.

The FBI classifies terrorist acts as either domestic or international. Domestic terrorist groups include white supremacists, black supremacists, militia groups, other right-wing extremists, left-wing extremists, pro-life extremists, animal rights extremists, and environmental extremists. Terrorists may use arson, explosives and bombs, weapons of mass destruction (biological, chemical, or nuclear agents), and technology.

As a result of 9/11 the DHS was established, reorganizing the departments of the federal government. The FBI is the lead agency for responding to terrorism. The Federal Emergency Management Agency (FEMA) is the lead agency for consequence management (after an attack).

The USA PATRIOT Act significantly improves the nation's counterterrorism efforts by:

- Allowing investigators to use the tools already available to investigate organized crime and drug trafficking.
- Facilitating information sharing and cooperation among government agencies so they can better "connect the dots."
- Updating the law to reflect new technologies and new threats.
- Increasing the penalties for those who commit or support terrorist crimes.

The first line of defense against terrorism is the patrol officer in the field.

The three-tiered model of al-Qaeda terrorist attacks consists of sleeper cells attacking in conjunction with the group's leaders in Afghanistan, sleeper cells attacking on their own apart from centralized command, and individuals attacking with support from small cells. A key to combating terrorism lies with the local police and the intelligence they can provide to federal authorities. The Community Protection Act gives off-duty as well as qualified retired police officers the right to carry their firearms concealed in all 50 states.

Two concerns related to the "war on terrorism" are that civil liberties may be jeopardized and that people of Middle Eastern descent may be discriminated against or become victims of hate crimes. A difficult challenge facing law enforcement is balancing the need to enhance security with the need to maintain freedom.

CHECKLIST

Terrorism

- What method of attack was used?
- What was the target of the attack?
- Who had access to the location?
- What was the likely motivation?
- Has any group claimed responsibility?
- What was the damage?
- Were there injuries? fatalities?
- Who notified authorities?
- Who responded first?
- Were there any witnesses?
- Were any suspicious individuals or vehicles observed at the location before the attack? during the attack? after the attack?
- Was the scene photographed and/or videotaped?
- What evidence was found at the scene?
- Were there any unusual circumstances?
- Was a canvass of the area conducted?

APPLICATION

Detective Smith has had a young Middle-Eastern appearing male under surveillance as a suspected terrorist. She has followed him for several days and has observed him buy a newspaper from a machine every morning, walk to the state capitol building several times each day and take pictures from various angles, enter the building, and come out shortly. He then returns to an inexpensive motel on the edge of town. He has visits from other Middle-Eastern appearing young males who bring him packages. He does not appear to be employed but wears expensive clothing and eats at expensive restaurants.

On this particular day she sees that the suspect is carrying a briefcase, something he has not done before. He goes directly to the state capitol building and enters. Approximately one hour later he comes out, but without the briefcase.

Questions

1. Does Detective Jones have reasonable suspicion to stop the suspect and question him?
2. If so, based on what?
3. What should be the next step?

DISCUSSION QUESTIONS

1. Which is the greater threat—domestic or international terrorism? Why?

2. Does your police department have a counterterrorism strategy in place? If so, what?

3. What type of terrorist attack would you fear most? Why?

4. Do you feel Americans have become complacent about terrorism?

5. What provisions of the PATRIOT Act do you think are most important?

6. What barriers to sharing information among the various local, state, and federal agencies do you think are most problematic?

7. Does media coverage of terrorist acts lead to more terrorism, that is, do you think the contagion effect is in operation?

8. Should Americans expect to give up some civil liberties to allow law enforcement officers to pursue terrorists?

9. Do you think a terrorist sleeper cell could operate in your community? What signs might indicate that such a cell exists?

10. What means might terrorists use to attack the United States in the future? Are we more vulnerable at home or at our interests abroad?

MEDIA EXPLORATIONS

Internet

Select one of the following assignments to complete.

- Go to the websites of the Drug Enforcement Administration (www.dea.gov), the FBI (www.fbi.gov), the Department of Justice (www.usdoj.gov), and the Department of the Treasury (www.ustreas.gov) and note how the different agencies are addressing the issue of terrorism. How do their focuses differ? Be prepared to share your findings with the class.

- Search for *USA PATRIOT Act* (2001). List specific applications of the act to law enforcement practices and explain how they might differ from conventional practices. Do you believe the phrase "extraordinary times demand extraordinary measures" and that it justifies bending the rules, so to speak, in the war on terrorism? In other words, do the ends justify the means? Should law enforcement be permitted to

use roving wiretaps and breach privileged inmate-attorney communications in the name of national security, or is this the beginning of the end of our civil liberties? Be prepared to discuss your answers with the class.

- Go to the Department of Justice website devoted to the PATRIOT Act and list the myths the site dispels.

- Go to www.policeforum.org and find "Local Law Enforcement's Role in Preventing and Responding to Terrorism." Read and outline the article. Be prepared to share your outline with the class.

- To learn what the U.S. Department of Homeland Security is doing to keep America safe, go to http://www.ready.gov.

- Go to the Counterterrorism Training and Resources website at http://www.counterterrorismtraining.gov and outline what resources are available for local police departments.

- Search for the key phrase *National Institute of Justice*. Click on "NCJRS" (National Criminal Justice Research Service). Click on "law enforcement." Click on "sort by Doc#." Search for one of the NCJ reference numbers from the reference pages. Outline the selection to share with the class.

 ## Crime and Evidence in Action

Go to the CD and choose the **drug bust/gang homicide/sexual assault case.** During the course of the case you'll become patrol officer, detective, defense attorney, corrections officer, and patrol officer to conduct interactive investigative research. Each case unfolds as you respond to key decision points. Feedback for each possible answer choice is packed full of information, including term definitions, web links, and important documentation. The sergeant is available at certain times to help mentor you, the Online Resources website offers a variety of information, and be sure to take notes in your e-notebook during the suspect video statements and at key points throughout (these notes can be saved, printed, or e-mailed). The Forensics Exercise will test your ability to collect, transport, and analyze evidence from the crime scene. At the end of the case you can track how well you responded to each decision point and join the Discussion Forum for a postmortem. **Go to the CD and use the skills you've learned in this chapter to solve a case.**

REFERENCES

"9/11 Report: Excerpts." Reported in the Minneapolis/St. Paul *Star Tribune*, July 21, 2004, p. A14.

"AG Gonzales Outlines Key Priorities for the Justice Department," *NCJA Justice Bulletin*, March 2005, pp. 1–2.

"Al Qaeda," *Encyclopedia Britannica Online,* http://www .britannica.com. Accessed September 11, 2005.

Barakat, Matthew. "Muhammad Sentenced to Death in Sniper Killings," Associated Press as reported in the Minneapolis/St. Paul *Star Tribune,* March 20, 2004, p. A3.

Batista, Ernie. "No Blue Canaries," *Law Enforcement Technology,* August 2005, pp. 94–101.

Baveja, Alok. "War on Illicit Drugs May Offer Lessons in Fight Against Terrorism," *The Police Chief,* March 2002, pp. 30–36.

Berkow, Michael. "The Internal Terrorists," *The Police Chief,* June 2004, pp. 25–30.

Billingslea, William. "Illicit Cigarette Trafficking and the Funding of Terrorism," *The Police Chief,* February 2004, pp. 49–54.

"Bioterrorism," *Security Management,* July 2003, pp. 24–25.

Boyter, Jennifer. "Attorney General Ashcroft Defends Patriot Act," *The Police Chief,* September 2003, p. 17.

Brinkley, Larry. "Present Threats." *The Law Enforcement Trainer,* November/December 2003, pp. 30–35.

Brinkley, Larry. "Present Threats: Part II," *The Law Enforcement Trainer,* January/February 2004, pp. 43–48.

Bulzomi, Michael J. "Foreign Intelligence Surveillance Act: Before and after the USA PATRIOT Act," *FBI Law Enforcement Bulletin,* June 2003, pp. 25–32.

Butler, Desmond. "Building Supers Standing Watch," Associated Press as reported in the Minneapolis/St. Paul *Star Tribune,* June 23, 2004, p. A7.

Carter, David L., and Holden, Richard N. "Terrorism and Community Security." In *Local Government Police Management.* Washington, DC: International City/County Management Association, 2003, pp. 291–311.

Casey, James. "Managing Joint Terrorism Task Force Resources." *FBI Law Enforcement Bulletin,* November 2004, pp. 1–6.

A Chronology of Significant International Terrorism for 2004. Washington, DC: National Counterterrorism Center, April 27, 2005.

"Confronting the Suicide-Bomber Threat," *Security Management,* November 2003, p.16.

Davies, Heather J., and Murphy, Gerard R. *Protecting Your Community from Terrorism: The Strategies for Local Law Enforcement Series,* vol. 2: *Working with Diverse Communities.* Washington, DC: Office of Community Oriented Policing Services and the Police Executive Research Forum, 2004.

DeMuro, Joseph G. "Terrorism and Extremist Training: The Rationale for Focused Terrorism Awareness Training for Law Enforcement," *The Law Enforcement Trainer,* January/February 2003, pp. 32–33.

"DHS Secretary Ridge Approves National Incident Management System (NIMS)," *NCJA Justice Bulletin,* March 2004, pp. 14–16.

Devanney, Joe, and Devanney, Diane. "Homeland Security and Patriot Acts," *Law and Order,* August 2003, pp. 10–12.

"Dosimeters Protect Officers from Radiological Terror," *Law Enforcement Technology,* August 2003, pp. 102–107.

From Hometown Security to Homeland Security: IACP's Principles for a Locally Designed and Nationally Coordinated Homeland Security Strategy. Alexandria, VA: International Association of Chiefs of Police, May 17, 2005.

Gardner, Gerald W. "Getting Ready for the Big One: Terrorism Can Happen Anywhere, at Any Time," *Police,* October 2003, p. 6.

Garrett, Ronnie. "Detecting Radiation," *Law Enforcement Technology,* August 2003, pp. 84–89.

Garrett, Ronnie. "Tree Huggers with Hand Grenades?" *Law Enforcement Technology,* September 2004a, pp. 88–95.

Garrett, Ronnie. "'V' Is for Victory," *Law Enforcement Technology,* September 2004b, p. 6.

Garrett, Ronnie. "The Wolf Is at the Door: What Are We Waiting For?" *Law Enforcement Technology,* March 2004c, p. 6.

Getlin, Josh. "Profiling Fears Surface in Subway," *Los Angeles Times,* August 8, 2005.

Giannone, Donald, and Wilson, Robert A. "The CAT Eyes Program: Enlisting Community Members in the Fight Against Terrorism," *The Police Chief,* March 2003, pp. 37–38.

Gips, Michael A. "Secondary Devices a Primary Concern," *Security Management,* July 2003, pp. 16–20.

Glasser, Susan B., and Coll, Steve. "Al Qaeda Uses Web as a Weapon," *Washington Post,* August 8, 2005.

Goldsmith, Michael; Weiss, Jim; and Davis, Mickey. "Community Vulnerability Assessment Methodology," *Law and Order,* May 2004, pp. 100–103.

Griffith, David. "Watching the Neighborhood," *Police,* April 2004, p. 6.

"The Growing Threat from Terrorist Operations," Los Angeles: Los Angeles Early Warning Group/Analysis/Synthesis Section. *Police and Security News,* May/June 2005, pp. 87–91.

"Hamas," *Encyclopedia Britannica Online,* http://www .britannica.com. Accessed September 11, 2005.

Hamilton, Randy C. "The Implementation of a National Incident Management System (NIMS)," *The Law Enforcement Trainer,* May/June 2003, pp. 11–12.

Hanson, Doug. "Ricin Toxin: What Law Enforcement Needs to Know," *Law Enforcement Technology,* August 2003, pp. 16–22.

Hanson, Doug. "The Nation's Food and Water Supply: A New Target for Terrorists?" *Law Enforcement Technology,* January 2004, pp. 18–24.

Hanson, Doug. "What's Next—Soft Target Attacks," *Law Enforcement Technology,* August 2005, pp. 18–27.

Heinecke, Jeannine. "Adding Another Layer to the Security Blanket," *Law Enforcement Technology,* March 2004, pp. 78–85.

"Hezbollah," *Encyclopaedia Britannica Online,* http://www .britannica.com. Accessed September 11, 2005.

"Homeland Security Funding Sources," *The Police Chief,* February 2004, pp. 23–27.

Hughes, Shawn. "How to Start a WMD Unit," *Police,* September 2003, pp. 20–24.

Hughes, Shawn. "Anxiety Attack," *Police*, September 2004, pp. 32–36.

"Initial National Response Plan," *The Police Chief*, February 2004, pp. 19–21.

Jackman, Tom. "Teen Sniper Gets Life without Parole for Virginia Shooting," *Washington Post*, as reprinted in the Minneapolis/St. Paul *Star Tribune*, March 11, 2004, p. A3.

Johnson, Kevin. "FBI Gets Local Police in the Loop," *USA Today*, August 2, 2005.

"Justice Dept. Announces Plan for Local Police Intelligence Sharing," *Criminal Justice Newsletter*, June 1, 2004, p.5.

Kane, John, and Wall, April. *Identifying the Links Between White-Collar Crime and Terrorism*. National White-Collar Crime Center, September 2004.

Kanable, Rebecca. "What's That Smell?" *Law Enforcement Technology*, August 2003, pp. 74–77.

Levine, Samantha. "The Car Bomb Conundrum: Trying to Stop the Terrorists' Low-Tech, Lethal Weapons of Choice," *U.S. News & World Report*, August 16/August 23, 2004, p. 30.

Lieberman, Senator Joseph I. *State and Local Officials: Still Kept in the Dark about Homeland Security*. Washington, DC: Senate Governmental Affairs Committee, August 13, 2003.

Linett, Howard. "Counter-Terrorism," *Police*, August 2005, pp. 58–64.

Lipton, Eric. "Homeland Security Chief Tells of Plan to Stabilize Border," *New York Times*, August 24, 2005a.

Lipton, Eric. "Hurdles for High-Tech Efforts to Track Who Crosses Borders," *New York Times*, August 10, 2005b.

Loyka, Stephan A.; Faggiani, Donald A.; and Karchmer, Clifford. *Protecting Your Community from Terrorism: Strategies for Local Law Enforcement*, vol. 4: *The Production and Sharing of Intelligence*. Washington, DC: Community Oriented Policing Services and the Police Executive Research Forum, February 2005.

Mariani, Cliff. *Terrorism Prevention and Response: The Definitive Law Enforcement Guide to Prepare for Terrorist Activity*. Flushing, NY: Looseleaf Law Publications, Inc., 2003.

McDonald, Kathleen, and McLaughlin, W. Sean. "First Responders: Ready or Not?" *The Law Enforcement Trainer*, May/June 2003, pp. 13–19.

McVey, Philip M. "Homeland Defense: An Effective Partnership," *The Police Chief*, April 2002, pp. 174–180.

Moore, Jeffrey. "Car Bomb Security," *Law Enforcement Technology*, August 2003, pp. 24–33.

Moreno, Sylvia. "Border Security Measures to Tighten Next Month," *Washington Post*, October 15, 2004.

Morgenstern, Henry. "Bomb Basics: What Law Enforcement Needs to Know and Why." *Law Enforcement Technology*, August 2005, pp. 8–17.

Murphy, Gerard R., and Plotkin, Martha R. *Protecting Your Community from Terrorism: Strategies for Local Law Enforcement*, vol. 1: *Local-Federal Partnerships*. Washington, DC: Community Oriented Policing

Services and the Police Executive Research Forum, March 2003.

Nason, Randall R. "Chemical Agent Terrorism: A Refresher in Strategic Approach," *Security Technology and Design*, February 2003, pp. 44–46.

The National Strategy for the Physical Protection of Critical Infrastructures and Key Assets. Washington, DC, February 2003. http://www.whitehouse.gov/pcipb/physical.html. Accessed October 19, 2005.

"A New Era of Law Enforcement Partnerships: FBI Director Addresses 56th Biennial F.O.P. Conference." Washington, DC: Federal Bureau of Investigation, August 5, 2003. http://www.fbi.gov/page2/aug03/fop080503.htm. Accessed August 1, 2005.

Page, Douglas. "Dust in Time: Detecting Bioterror with Tiny Particles," *Law Enforcement Technology*, August 2003, pp. 98–101.

Page, Douglas. "Law Enforcement Renaissance: The Sequel," *Law Enforcement Technology*, March 2004, pp. 86–90.

Page, Douglas. "Dirty Bomb Detection: What's Hot," *Law Enforcement Technology*, August 2005, pp. 124–129.

Peed, Carl R., and Wexler, Chuck. Foreword. In Heather J. Davies and Gerard R. Murphy, eds., *Working with Diverse Communities*, volume 2 of the *Protecting Your Community from Terrorism: The Strategies for Local Law Enforcement* series. Washington, DC: The Office of Community Oriented Policing Services and the Police Executive Research Forum, 2004, pp. vii–viii.

Pilant, Lois. "Strategic Modeling: Los Angeles County's Counterterrorism Program Is Being Duplicated Nationwide," *Police*, May 2004, pp. 34–38.

Pitcavage, Mark. "Domestic Extremism: Still a Potent Threat," *The Police Chief*, August 2003, pp. 32–35.

Polisar, Joseph M. "The National Criminal Intelligence Sharing Plan," *The Police Chief*, June 2004, p. 8.

Raffel, Robert. "Weapons of Mass Destruction and Civil Aviation Preparedness," *FBI Law Enforcement Bulletin*, May 2003, pp. 1–5.

Rashbaum, William K. "Police Tactic against Terror: Let's Talk," *New York Times*, August 14, 2004.

Report from the Field: The USA PATRIOT Act at Work, Washington, DC: Department of Justice, July 2004.

Reuland, Melissa, and Davies, Heather J., et al. *Protecting Your Community from Terrorism: Strategies for Law Enforcement*, vol. 3: *Preparing for and Responding to Bioterrorism*. Washington, DC: Community Oriented Policing Services and the Police Executive Research Forum, 2004.

Savage, Charlie. "Terror Response Study Spurs Concern: Many Americans Would Disobey," *Boston Globe*, September 15, 2004.

Savelli, Lou. *A Proactive Law Enforcement Guide for the War on Terrorism*, Flushing, NY: Looseleaf Law Publications, Inc., 2004.

Scheider, Matthew C.; Chapman, Robert E.; and Seelman, Michael E. "Connecting the Dots for a Proactive

Approach," *BTS (Border and Transportation Security) America,* no date, pp. 158–162.

Scoville, Dean. "The Enemies Within," *Police,* September 2003, pp. 44–50.

Securing Our Homeland. Washington, DC: U.S. Department of Homeland Security, no date.

Senn, Pamela. "Protecting Your PPE," *Law Enforcement Technology,* August 2005, pp. 102–112.

"The Shape of Things to Come," *Security Management,* March 2003, p. 20.

Sims, Calvin. "Poll Finds Most Americans Have Not Prepared for a Terror Attack," *New York Times,* October 28, 2004.

Smetanka, Mary Jane. "'U' Studies Terrorism at Your Table," Minneapolis/St. Paul *Star Tribune,* July 6, 2004a, pp. A1, A4.

Smetanka, Mary Jane. "'U' Center Safeguards Food Supply," Minneapolis/St. Paul *Star Tribune,* July 7, 2004b, pp. B1, B4.

"Suicide Terrorism," *Security Management,* August 2003, pp. 20–22.

Symonds, Daniel R. "A Guide to Selected Weapons of Mass Destruction," *The Police Chief,* March 2003, pp. 19–29.

Uner, Eric. "Cyber Terrorism: Count on It," *Security Products,* February 2003, pp. 26–28.

Van Etten, John. "Impacts of Domestic Security on Law Enforcement Agencies," *The Police Chief,* February 2004, pp. 31–35.

Wexler, Chuck. "Policing a Multicultural Community." *Subject to Debate,* July 2003, p. 2.

Wexler, Sanford. "Homeland Security: Think Locally." *Law Enforcement Technology,* January 2003, pp. 30–35.

White, Jonathan R. *Terrorism and Homeland Security,* 5th ed. Belmont, CA: Wadsworth Publishing, 2006.

Zuckerman, Mortimer B. "Confronting the Threat." *U.S. News & World Report,* August 1, 2005a, p. 68.

Zuckerman, Mortimer, B. "The Poison Among Us," *U.S. News & World Report,* August 8, 2005b, p. 60.

CASES CITED

Hamdi v. Rumsfeld, No.03-6696, U.S. June 28, 2004

Rasul v. Bush, No. 03-334, U.S. June 28, 2004

USEFUL RESOURCES

- The Counterterrorism Training and Resources website: http://www.counterterrorismtraining.gov
- U.S. Department of Homeland Security: www.ready.gov
- Federal Emergency Management Agency: http://www.fema.gov/areyouready
- Federal Bureau of Investigation: http://www.fbi.gov
- Centers for Disease Control and Prevention: www.cdc.gov

CHAPTER 21

Preparing for and Presenting Cases in Court

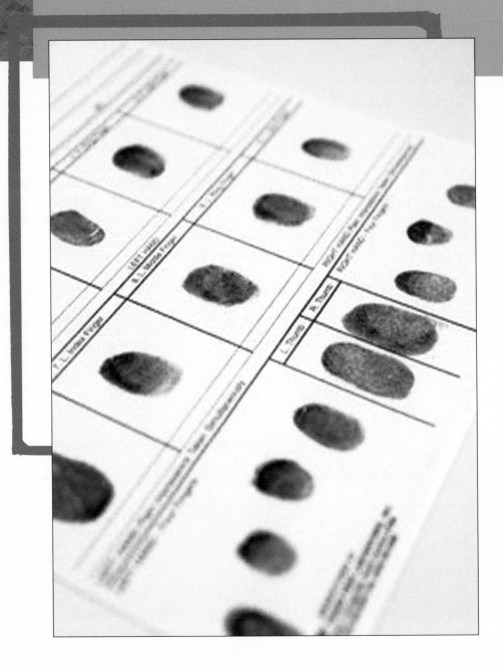

Do You Know?

- What the most important rule to eradicate fear of testifying in court is?
- What to include in the final report?
- The relative importance of the prosecutor in the court system?
- Why some cases are not prosecuted?
- How to prepare a case for court?
- How to review a case?
- What occurs during the pretrial conference?
- What the usual sequence in a criminal trial is?
- What the "win" is for an investigator who testifies in court?
- What kinds of statements are inadmissible in court?
- How to testify most effectively?
- When to use notes while testifying?
- What nonverbal elements can influence courtroom testimony positively and negatively?
- What strategies can make testifying in court more effective?
- What defense attorney tactics to anticipate?
- What a key to testifying during cross-examination is?
- How to avoid objections to your testimony?

fter all the leads in a case have been exhausted, all the witnesses interviewed, all the suspects interrogated and all the evidence properly collected and stored, if the investigation has been successful, the case will be ready for prosecution. Before this can occur, however, a *final* report on the case must be written, establishing the elements of the crime and proving the corpus delicti. Officers and prosecutors must ensure that the evidence has not been contaminated, that the witnesses have not been corrupted, and that the suspect's constitutional rights have not been infringed upon. With these assurances in place, the case can proceed to court, where the investigator's testimony is almost always critical to a successful outcome. Even the most experienced investigator may worry about having to testify, perhaps fearing the responsibility.

 The most important rule to eradicate fear of testifying in court is to always tell the truth.

Garland and Stuckey (p.502) stress: "The officer who tells the truth will not have to be concerned about being tripped up on cross-examination, being contradicted, or not having his or her testimony corroborated by other witnesses."

This final chapter begins with a discussion of the importance of the final report and what is to be included. Next the role of the prosecutor is presented, as is an explanation of how to prepare a case for prosecution. This is followed by an overview of the trial, an explanation of the American adversary system, and a description of the typical sequence of events in a criminal trial. Then suggestions are provided for behavior while waiting to testify as well as for testifying under direct examination, strategies for excelling as a witness, providing expert testimony, and testifying under cross-examination. The chapter ends with a discussion on concluding your testimony and advice and examples of testimony from Detective Gautsch.

The Final Report

 he effectiveness of the final report is often the determining factor in whether a case is prosecuted. The recommendations and guidelines presented in Chapter 3 apply to the final report as well. Therefore, you might wish to review that chapter.

The final report presents the facts of the case, a criminal history of the person charged, the types of evidence available, and the names of those who can support such evidence by testimony in court, names of people the prosecutor can talk to for further information, and a chronological account of the crime and subsequent investigation.

The final report contains (1) the complaint; (2) the preliminary investigation report; (3) all follow-up reports; (4) statements, admissions, and confessions; (5) laboratory reports; (6) photographs, sketches, and drawings; and (7) a summary of all negative evidence.

Prepare the report after a careful review of all information. Organize the facts logically.

The Complaint

Include a copy of the original complaint received by the police dispatcher and complaint desk. This should include the date and time of the complaint, location of the incident, brief details, times when officers were

dispatched, and the names of the officers assigned to the initial call.

The Preliminary Investigation Report

The report of the officer's initial investigation at the crime scene provides essential information on the time of arrival, lighting and weather conditions, observations at the scene, and immediate and subsequent actions taken by officers responding to the call.

Follow-Up Reports

Assemble each contact and follow-up report in chronological order, presenting the sequence of the investigation and the pattern used to follow leads. These reports contain the essential information gathered in proving the elements of the crime and in linking the crime to the suspect. The reports can be in the form of progress notes.

Statements, Admissions, and Confessions

Include the statements of all witnesses interviewed during the investigation, as discussed in Chapter 6. If written statements were not obtained, report the results of oral interviews with witnesses. Assemble all statements, admissions, or confessions by suspects in a separate part of the report. Include the reports of all polygraphs or other examinations used to determine the truth of statements, admissions, or confessions.

Laboratory Reports

Assemble laboratory results in one segment of the final report. Make recommendations on how these results relate to other areas of the report.

Photographs, Sketches, and Drawings Include photographs, sketches, and drawings of the crime scene to show conditions when officers arrived and the available evidence, as discussed in Chapter 2.

Summary of Negative Evidence Include a summary of all negative or exculpatory evidence developed during the investigation. Statements of witnesses who claim the suspect was elsewhere at the time of the crime are sometimes proved false, but the prosecution must consider such statements and develop a defense. If information exists that the suspect committed the crime but did so in self-defense or accidentally, state this in the report. Include all recognizable weaknesses in proving the corpus delicti or the offender's identity.

Write the report clearly and accurately, following the guidelines presented in Chapter 3. The quality of the final report influences its credibility. Arrange the material in a logical sequence and a convenient format. A binder or loose-leaf notebook works well for this because it allows the various units of information to be separated, with a labeled, tabbed divider for each unit. Although the prosecutor may have been consulted at various stages of the investigation, it is at this point that the prosecutor might offer a plea bargain to the defendant based on the strength of the case and of the final report. In fact, it has been said that some cases are, in effect, trial by report.

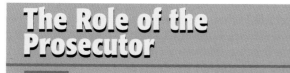

The Role of the Prosecutor

The prosecutor is the gatekeeper of the court system, determining which cases are prosecuted and which are not. As Neubauer (p.126) comments:

> The prosecutor is of critical importance because of the office's central position in the criminal justice system. Whereas police, defense attorneys, judges and probation officers specialize in specific phases of the criminal justice process, the duties of the prosecutor bridge all of these areas. This means that on a daily basis the prosecutor is the only official who works with all actors of the criminal justice system. As Justice Robert Jackson once remarked, "The prosecutor has more control over life, liberty and reputation than any other person in America."

According to Neubauer and Meinhold (p.259), at the county level the prosecutor, or district attorney (DA), is the chief law enforcement official for the community. DAs are typically elected and are responsible for prosecuting felonies and serious misdemeanors in the trial courts of general jurisdiction. Neubauer and Meinhold point out that their activities are not monitored by the state's attorney general, making the prosecutor "the most powerful official in the criminal courts."

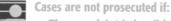

> The prosecutor is the most powerful official in the court system.

According to Neubauer (p.126): "A key characteristic of the American prosecutor is broad discretion." He notes that the various actors in a trial have conflicting views about how this discretion should be used: "The police push for harsher penalties, defense attorneys for giving their clients a break and judges to clear the docket." In addition, Neubauer notes that although the prosecutor tries cases in the court, the office is part of the executive branch of government, independent from the judiciary. This independence is crucial for the adversary system to function because prosecutors often challenge judicial decisions. The adversary system is reviewed later in the chapter.

Tensions and conflicts sometimes exist between investigators and prosecutors. An investigator may feel a case is strong and the suspect should be brought to trial, but the prosecutor may disagree. However, the prosecutor is an investigator's legal adviser throughout the process—during the investigation, the pretrial conference, and the court presentation. It is ultimately the prosecutor's decision. Investigators should follow prosecutors' advice even if they disagree, for it is best to work out the issues of cases together. Investigators should listen to and learn from prosecutors. There may be valid reasons for not prosecuting a case.

Nonprosecution

For many possible reasons, most criminal cases are resolved without a trial. An excellent investigation and report may cause the defendant to plead guilty, the defendant may desire to plead guilty without going through a trial, or the plea-bargaining process may bring about a satisfactory resolution.

> Cases are not prosecuted if:
> - The complaint is invalid.
> - The prosecutor declines after reviewing the case.
> - The complainant refuses to prosecute.
> - The offender dies.
> - The offender is in prison or out of the country and cannot be returned.
> - No evidence or leads exist.

Administrative policy sometimes closes cases to further investigation. Specific criteria are established for these decisions. The caseload of investigative personnel has grown so large that cases with little probability of successful prosecution must be closed as a matter of maintaining priorities.

Many police departments have incorporated such criteria into their crime report forms. If enough criteria are met, the department closes the case to further investigation and notifies the complainant. This often happens when the complainant files a report "only because my insurance company requires me to report the loss to the police." The loss may have occurred many days before the report, or there may be no leads. In some cases there are insufficient facts to support the complaint, but the victim insists on filing a complaint and has the right to do so.

In other cases, there is a valid report, but investigation reveals that witnesses have left the area or that no physical evidence remains at the crime scene. Without physical evidence, witnesses, identifiable leads, or information to follow up, it is unwise to pursue the case when more pressing cases abound. Such a case is placed in an inactive file and is reopened only if time is available or new information is received. Occasionally such cases are cleared by the admission or confession of a suspect arrested for another crime. Cases are **exceptionally cleared** when circumstances outside the investigation result in no charges being filed—for example, the suspect dies. If the prosecutor decides to bring the case to trial, the investigator must thoroughly prepare for testifying in court.

Preparing a Case for Prosecution

nce the decision is made to prosecute a case, more than "probable cause" is required. The prosecution must prove the case *beyond a reasonable doubt*—the degree of proof necessary to obtain a conviction. To do so, the prosecution must know what evidence it can introduce, what witnesses will testify, the strengths and weaknesses of the case, and the type of testimony police investigators can supply.

To prepare a case for court:
- Review and evaluate all evidence, positive and negative, and the chain of custody.
- Review all reports on the case.
- Prepare witnesses.
- Hold a pretrial conference with the prosecutor.

Review and Evaluate Evidence

Each crime consists of one or more elements that must be proven. The statutes and ordinances of the particular jurisdiction define these elements.

Concentrate on proving the elements of the crime and establishing the offender's identity.

Review physical evidence to ensure that it has been properly gathered, identified, transported, and safeguarded between the time it was obtained and the time of the trial. Make sure the evidence is available for the trial and that it is taken to the courtroom and turned over to the prosecuting attorney. Arrange for trained laboratory technicians' testimony if necessary. As discussed in detail in Chapter 4, select evidence that is material, relevant, and competent and that helps to establish the corpus delicti: what happened and who is responsible. How evidence is moved along in the system is shown in Figure 21.1.

The pretrial **discovery process** requires the prosecution and defense to disclose to each other certain evidence they intend to use at trial, thus avoiding "trial by surprise" (Schott, p.26). There is no general constitutional right to discovery in criminal trials (*Weatherford v. Bursey*, 1977). According to Neubauer (p.263), courts have expressed concern that requiring too much prosecutorial disclosure might put the prosecution at a disadvantage or that witnesses for the defense might be intimidated. He points out that the type of information that is discoverable varies greatly from state to state, with some states allowing only limited discovery, others taking a middle ground, and yet others adopting liberal discovery rules. Moore (p.78) cautions: "Any evidence not properly documented and available during discovery can run a risk of being excluded when the case goes to trial."

The landmark Supreme Court case in the discovery process is *Brady v. Maryland* (1963), in which the Court held: "The suppression by the prosecution of evidence favorable to the accused upon request violates due process where the evidence is material either to guilt or to punishment, irrespective of the good faith or bad faith of the prosecution." As noted by Gardner and Anderson (p.28): "Although an accused does not have a right to all information available to the prosecutor, he does have the right to information as provided by the statutes of the state and to information required under the **Brady rule.**" As discussed in Chapter 4, exculpatory evidence, that is, evidence that tends to show innocence of the accused, must be disclosed. Investigators who are aware of such evidence are obligated to bring it to the prosecutor's attention. Schott (p.30) cautions: "When officers intentionally withhold *Brady* material from the prosecutors with whom they work, they are clearly subjecting themselves to personal liability for violating a defendant's constitutional rights to due process."

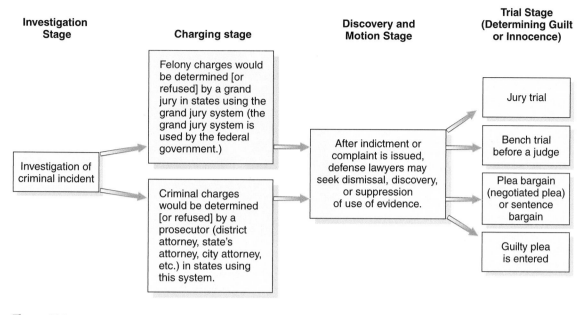

Figure 21.1

The use of evidence in the stages of the criminal justice process

Source: Thomas J. Gardner and Terry M. Anderson. *Criminal Evidence: Principles and Cases*, 5th ed. Belmont, CA: Wadsworth Publishing, 2004, p. 47. Reprinted by permission.

Gardner and Anderson (p.30) note that in most states "missing" evidence or failing to turn over evidence violates the Brady rule only if it can be shown that it was done in bad faith; that is, it was known the evidence was exculpatory and was intentionally withheld. The defense must prove a "conscious effort" to suppress exculpatory evidence.

Schott (p.27) also points out that the Supreme Court took a "short step" in deciding that due process requires the government to disclose to a defendant information regarding witness credibility before trial, extending *Brady* to impeachment material in *Giglio v. United States* (1972). Defense attorneys will try to **impeach** the testimony of prosecution witnesses; that is, they will try to discredit the testimony, to call into question the truth or accuracy of what a prosecution witness testified to under direct examination. This obviously applies to police officers and investigators who testify.

In 1996 the U.S. Department of Justice (DOJ) issued a policy for all DOJ investigative agencies obligating each of their *employees* to inform prosecutors of potential impeachment material as early as possible before providing a sworn statement or testimony in any criminal investigation or case. The DOJ guidelines suggest that the following must be disclosed: substantiated allegations; pending investigations or allegations; and criminal charges, past or pending.

Schott (p.29) points out that there are limits on what the defense is entitled to learn about law enforcement witnesses, notwithstanding that the information relates to the witness's veracity. In *Pennsylvania v. Ritchie* (1987) the Supreme Court held: "Evidence is material only if

there is a reasonable probability that had the evidence been disclosed to the defense, the result of the proceeding would have been different. . . . The government has the obligation to turn over evidence in its possession that is both favorable to the accused and *material* to guilt or punishment." Schott (p.31) stresses: "Officers who intentionally withhold information that affects their credibility deprive defendants of their constitutional right to due process. No matter how destructive to the prosecution or personally embarrassing the information may be, it must be disclosed at least to the government prosecutor." The issue of credibility also applies to witnesses other than those of law enforcement who may testify for the prosecution.

Review and evaluate witnesses' statements for credibility. If a witness claims to have seen a specific act, determine whether the light was sufficient and whether the witness has good eyesight and was in a position to see the act clearly. Also assess the witness's relationship to the suspect and the victim.

Establish the identity of the suspect by eyewitness testimony, transfer evidence, and supporting evidence such as motive, prior knowledge, opportunity, and known modus operandi.

Videotapes are being used increasingly in court, especially in child abuse and sex crime cases. Expert witnesses with heavy time commitments may be allowed to testify by videotape, saving the time and expense of a trip to the city where the trial is taking place. Videotapes have also been made of witnesses who are severely injured and cannot appear in court. In addition, videotapes of suspects' confessions and of crime scenes are invaluable.

Reviewing every aspect of the case before entering the courtroom is excellent preparation for testifying. Do not memorize answers to imagined questions, but be prepared.

Review Reports

Review written reports of everything done during the investigation. This includes the preliminary report, memorandums, summary reports, progress reports, evidence records and receipts, photographs and sketches, medical examiner's reports, emergency squad records, laboratory test reports on evidence, statements of witnesses (positive and negative), and any other reports on actions taken during the investigation.

Prepare Witnesses

Re-interview witnesses to refresh their memories. Read their previous statements to them and ask if this is the evidence they will present in court. Such a review also helps allay any fears witnesses have about testifying in court. Describe trial procedures to the witnesses so they understand what will occur. Explain that they can testify only to facts from their own personal knowledge or from common knowledge. Emphasize that they must tell the truth and present the facts as they know them. Explain the importance of remaining calm; having a neat, clean appearance; and remaining impartial (Figure 21.2).

By experience, police officers know of the many delays in court proceedings and of the waits in the courtroom or in the hall outside before they can testify. This should also be explained to witnesses who may be testifying for the first time so they can make flexible arrangements for the day. In addition, the complainants should be prepared for the possible delays and continuances that may be part of the defense's strategy to wear them down so they will drop the charges.

Pretrial Conference

Before testifying in court and after you have made the final case preparation, arrange for a pretrial conference with the prosecuting attorney. Organize the facts and evidence and prepare a summary of the investigation. Include in this summary the focal points and main issues of the case, an envelope containing copies of all reports, and all other relevant documents.

 At the pretrial conference with the prosecutor:
- Review all the evidence.
- Discuss the strengths and weaknesses of the case.
- Discuss the probable line of questioning by the prosecutor and the defense.

Figure 21.2

An important step in preparing a case for prosecution is to reinterview witnesses to refresh their memories. Officers should read the witnesses' previous statements to them and ask if this is the evidence they will present in court. This review helps alleviate any fears witnesses have about testifying in court.

Victims and witnesses may also have the opportunity to speak to the court during the sentencing phase of a trial, should a conviction occur. Statements made during this stage are often emotionally charged and intended to provide the court with insight as to the impact of the crime on the victim(s) and/or witness(es). Preparation is also important in making the most of these "statement of opinion" opportunities.

Brendan Costin, shown here speaking at the sentencing trial of Thomas Junta, the man found guilty of beating Brendan's father to death at the boy's hockey practice, is noticeably choked up as he states: "I can still remember being hysterical, trying to wake him up as the blood streamed down his face. Rushed to the hospital in the ambulance, my father had stopped breathing and had no pulse and his heart stopped beating. After two days in the hospital I realized I had just witnessed my dad literally getting beaten to death."

The 6-foot-1, 270-pound Junta was convicted of involuntary manslaughter for beating 160-pound Michael Costin to death at a Reading ice rink in 2000, after Junta got angry over rough play on the ice. Junta testified that he struck Costin only in self-defense. Others said Junta was red-faced with rage.

After hearing both sides, the judge determined there were aggravating circumstances surrounding Costin's death, including the fact that the beating took place in front of children.

Discuss complicated or detailed information fully to avoid misunderstanding. Discuss any legal questions concerning admissibility of evidence or testimony. The prosecutor may be able to offer insights into the style of the defense attorney as well as the judge hearing the case.

Sometimes witnesses are included in the pretrial conference. If so, listen carefully to what each witness says to the prosecuting attorney and to what the prosecuting attorney says in response. During the trial, the judge may exclude all witnesses from the courtroom except the person testifying. Therefore, you may have no opportunity to hear the testimony of other witnesses or the approach used by the prosecuting attorney.

It is also a good idea to review the case with other officers who are going to testify. You may not hear their actual testimony, and it will help you if you know in advance what they are going to say.

Final Preparations

Shortly before the trial, again review your notes and your final report. Take with you only those notes you want to use in testifying. Be certain that the physical evidence is being taken to the courtroom and will be available for the prosecuting attorney when needed. Also make sure that laboratory technicians are available to appear when necessary. Find out which courtroom you will be testifying in and look it over before the trial.

Rutledge ("Courthouse," p.71) recommends that if you are asked to bring physical evidence with you to the trial, use an appropriate container to prevent passersby from seeing it: "If you have a bloody shirt or a sawed-off shotgun across your lap in the waiting area or the courthouse snack shop, potential jurors might be exposed to it before it's introduced in evidence. (And if the judge excludes the evidence, the prejudice has already been created.)"

Know What Is Expected and the Rules of the Court

Gunderson (p.112) contends: "The rules change depending on the nature of the trial and the judge assigned to hear the case." When an officer receives a **subpoena,** an order to appear before the court, it may not indicate what kind of hearing it is. It might be a grand jury or a preliminary hearing or a criminal trial. The rules of evidence are different, as is the burden of proof required. If the subpoena does not specify the type of hearing, call the prosecutor or the attorney who sent the subpoena to determine the nature of the hearing.

The subpoena will also usually indicate whether the officer is to make a personal appearance or be on-call, meaning that the officer need not appear personally unless called by the prosecution. On-call officers should provide the prosecutor or county clerk with a phone or pager number where he or she can be reached and should be available to receive the call and respond within a relatively short time.

Garland and Stuckey (p.506) explain that usually witnesses are excluded from the courtroom during a trial to prevent one witness from hearing another witness's testimony. This is known as the **rule on witnesses** or **witness sequestration rule.** They recommend that investigators find out before going into the courtroom whether witnesses have been excluded. If they have and an investigator goes into the courtroom and sits, the investigator may be severely reprimanded or, worse, be the cause for a mistrial.

Be familiar with any pretrial rulings a judge has issued. In some instances, a judge may have issued a **motion in limine,** a motion requesting the judge to issue a protective order against prejudicial questions or statements. For example, a defense attorney may ask a judge to restrict any reference to his client's criminal record during the trial. An investigator who is unaware of this motion and violates it may cause the judge to order a mistrial.

Dress Appropriately   Most police departments have regulations regarding attire when officers appear in court. Some departments specify that officers should appear in uniform. A weapon may not be worn into the courtroom without special permission. If one is worn, it should not be visible. Do not wear dark or deeply tinted glasses. If you wear street clothes, dress conservatively. Avoid bright colors and large plaids. Do not overdo on accessories, and avoid bizarre haircuts. Your personal appearance reflects your attitude and your professionalism and will have a definite effect on the jury.

According to Navarro (p.27): "Ample evidence suggests that for males, the traditional dark blue suit, white shirt and conservative tie projects success, competency and even veracity. . . . Female officers should choose comfortable business suits with a conservative length and style." He recommends that officers not testify in their uniforms because jurors may associate the uniform with a traffic citation they received or some other negative encounter with a uniformed officer.

Be on Time   If you are delayed for any reason, phone the prosecutor or the court clerk, explain the reason, and give an approximate time when you can be expected to appear.

The Trial

The main participants in a trial are the judge, jury, attorneys, defendant, and witnesses. The *judge,* or *magistrate,* presides over the trial; determines whether a witness is qualified and competent; addresses questions of law, including motions, objections, and procedures; rules on the admissibility of the evidence; keeps order; interprets the law for the jurors; and passes sentence if the defendant is found guilty.

The *jurors* hear and evaluate the testimony of all witnesses. Called *fact finders,* jurors consider many factors other than the words spoken. The attitude and behavior of witnesses, suspects, and attorneys are constantly under the jury's scrutiny. Jurors notice how witnesses respond to questions and their attitudes toward the prosecution and the defense. They reach their verdict based on what they see, hear, and feel during the trial. Typical jurors will have had limited or no experience with the criminal justice system outside of what they have read in the newspaper and seen on television.

Legal counsel presents the prosecution and defense evidence before the court and jury. Lawyers act as checks against each other and present the case as required by court procedure and the rulings of the presiding judge.

Defendants may or may not take the witness stand. The Fifth Amendment protects defendants against self-incrimination. If a defendant chooses not to testify, this fact cannot be used against him or her. However, if a defendant does choose to testify, waiving the privilege against self-incrimination, that defendant cannot tell only a part of the story. As Neubauer (p.329) explains, if a defendant testifies, the state can ask questions about all the facts surrounding the event testified to. In addition, once the defendant takes the stand, the state can impeach the defendant's credibility by introducing any prior felony convictions. Says Neubauer: "The defense attorney must make the difficult decision whether to arouse the jury's suspicion by not letting the accused testify or [let] the defendant testify and be subjected to possibly damaging cross-examination."

Witnesses present the facts as they know them. Gardner and Anderson (p.93) contend: "To qualify as a witness a person must have relevant information, must be competent and must declare that he or she will testify truthfully. To be competent, a witness must be able to remember and tell what happened, must be able to distinguish fact from fantasy and must know that he or she must tell the truth. . . . Anglo-Saxon law seeks to keep witnesses honest by having them testify under oath or affirmation in the presence of the fact finder and the accused, subject to cross-examination and subject to possible perjury charges for failure to tell the truth."

Police officers are witnesses for the prosecution. Law enforcement witnesses present a challenge to the prosecution's case because the prosecuting attorney must establish the burden of proof beyond a reasonable doubt.

The American Adversary System

ardner and Anderson (p.21) explain that the **adversary system** establishes clearly defined roles for both the prosecution and the defense and sets the judge as the neutral party. Figure 21.3 illustrates the key players in this system.

This has important implications for the investigator, who is on the "side" of the prosecutor in the proceeding, as will be discussed shortly.

Sequence of a Criminal Trial

trial begins with a case being called from the court docket. If both the prosecution and the defense are ready, the case is presented before the court.

The sequence in a criminal trial is as follows:
- Jury selection
- Opening statements by the prosecution and the defense
- Presentation of the prosecution's case; cross-examination by the defense
- Presentation of the defense's case; cross-examination by the prosecution
- Rebuttal and surrebuttal testimony
- Closing statements by the prosecution and the defense
- Instructions to the jury
- Jury deliberation to reach a verdict
- Reading of the verdict
- Acquittal or passing of sentence

If the trial is before a judge *without a jury,* called a **bench trial,** the prosecution and the defense make their opening statements directly to the judge. The opening statements are brief summaries of both the prosecution and defense attorneys' plans. In a *jury trial,* the jury is selected and then both counsels make their opening statements before the judge and jury.

The prosecution presents its case first. Witnesses for the prosecution are sworn in, and the prosecuting attorney asks them questions. Then the defense attorney may cross-examine the witnesses. After this cross-examination the prosecuting attorney may redirect-examine, and then the defense attorney may re-cross-examine.

Direct examination is the initial questioning of a witness or defendant by the lawyer who is using the person's testimony to further his or her case. **Cross-examination** is questioning by the opposing side for the purpose of assessing the validity of the testimony.

After the prosecutor has completed direct examination of all prosecution witnesses, the defense presents its case. After the direct examination of each defense witness, the prosecutor may cross-examine, the defense counsel may redirect-examine, and the prosecutor may re-cross-examine.

After each side has presented its regular witnesses, both sides may present *rebuttal* and *surrebuttal* witnesses. The prosecution can call **rebuttal** witnesses to contradict the testimony (or evidence) presented by the defense. The defense, in turn, can call **surrebuttal** witnesses to contradict the testimony (or evidence) presented by the

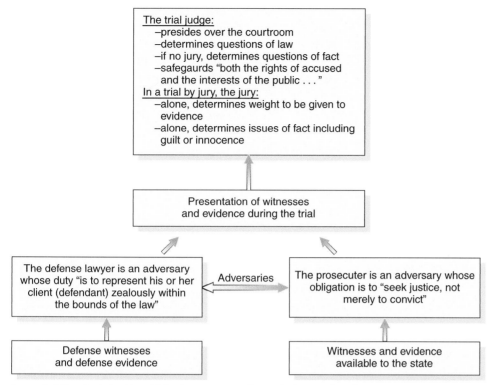

The trial judge:
  –presides over the courtroom
  –determines questions of law
  –if no jury, determines questions of fact
  –safegaurds "both the rights of accused
    and the interests of the public . . . "
In a trial by jury, the jury:
  –alone, determines weight to be given to
    evidence
  –alone, determines issues of fact including
    guilt or innocence

Presentation of witnesses
and evidence during the trial

The defense lawyer is an adversary
whose duty "is to represent his or her
client (defendant) zealously within
the bounds of the law"

Adversaries

The prosecuter is an adversary whose
obligation is to "seek justice, not
merely to convict"

Defense witnesses
and defense evidence

Witnesses and evidence
available to the state

Figure 21.3
The American adversary system

Source: Thomas J. Gardner and Terry M. Anderson.
Criminal Evidence: Principles and Cases, 5th ed.
Belmont, CA: Wadsworth Publishing, 2004, p. 22.
Reprinted by permission.

In most civil and criminal jury trials, the names and addresses of jurors are available from public records for people with the interest and knowledge of how to go about obtaining them. It does not occur to most people sitting on juror panels that this could be a problem. However, jurors sitting on criminal cases where defendants are potentially dangerous or retaliatory should have some concerns for their families and themselves.

Trial courts can restrict the disclosure of juror information if the court determines that jurors are in need of protection. Courts have held that factors that could justify restricting jury information could include ". . . but are not limited to: (1) the defendant's involvement in organized crime; (2) the defendant's participation in a group with the capacity to harm jurors; (3) the defendant's past attempts to interfere with the judicial process; and (4) extensive publicity that could enhance the possibility that jurors' names would become public and expose them to intimidation or harassment." *United States v. Darden*, 70 F.3d 1507, 1532 (8th Cir. 1995); *United States v. Ross*, 33 F3d at 1520.

prosection. When the entire case has been presented, prosecution and defense counsel present their closing arguments. In these arguments the lawyers review the trial evidence of both sides and tell the jury why the defendant should be convicted or acquitted. Sometimes the lawyers also make recommendations for penalty.

The judge instructs the jury on the laws applicable to the case and on how they are to arrive at a decision. The jury then retires to the jury room to deliberate and arrive at a verdict. When the jury reaches a verdict, court is reconvened and the verdict is read. If the verdict is for acquittal, the defendant is released. If the verdict is guilty, the judge passes sentence or sets a time and date for sentencing.

While Waiting to Testify

Do not discuss the case while waiting in the hallway to testify. If a juror or another witness hears your statements, you may have

created grounds for a mistrial. According to Rutledge ("Courthouse," p.72): "Perhaps the thing that's most likely to torpedo your case in the middle of trial is unauthorized communication with members of the jury." He acknowledges that it is not possible to avoid all contact with jurors and that chance contacts—passing in the hall or crowded in an elevator—may not be avoidable. In such instances, **deminimus communication,** that is, a simple hello or giving of directions, is allowable. It is important not to appear aloof or unfriendly.

Testifying under Direct Examination

Rutledge (*Courtroom*, p.15) asserts: "No matter how brilliant the investigation, how careful the arrest, and how thorough the report, if an officer isn't just as competent on the stand as he is in the field, he is just processing bodies." He (p.12) stresses: "You are on trial, too—your credibility, your professionalism, your knowledge, your competence, your judgment, your conduct in the field, your use of force, your adherence to official policies, your observance of the defendant's rights—they're all on trial."

As you enter the courtroom, keep in mind your goal. It is probably in line with the thinking of Van Brocklin (p.48): "The goal for officers in their courtroom confrontations is the same as in their street confrontations—win." But, surprisingly, Van Brocklin (p.44) does not mean win the case:

> The "win" for every honest officer in every courtroom confrontation is as simple as it is difficult: at the end of their testimony, when the last question has been answered, the jury must find them *credible.* Credibility is the degree to which the jury believes a witness. That's it. That's the only goal, the only win, the only job for the testifying officer—to be believed by the jury.

 The "win" for an investigator who testifies is to have established credibility.

First impressions are critical. Know what you are doing when you enter the courtroom. When your name is called, answer "Here" or "Present" and move directly to the front of the courtroom. Do not walk between the prosecutor and the judge; go behind the attorneys. Garland and Stuckey (p.509) caution that officers should never walk in front of the judge or between the judge and the attorneys' tables. This area, called **the well,** is off-limits and is to be entered only if the judge so directs or permission is granted. Traditionally, the area is a sword's length and was intended for the judge's protection.

Walk confidently; the jurors are there to hear the facts from you. If your investigation has been thorough and properly conducted, the jury will give a great deal of weight to your testimony.

If you have notes or a report, carry them in a clean manila file folder in your left hand so your right hand is free for taking the oath. Taking the oath in court is basically the same as taking your oath of office. Stand straight and face the clerk of the court, holding the palm of your hand toward the clerk. Use a clear, firm voice to answer "I do" to the question "Do you promise to tell the truth, the whole truth, and nothing but the truth, so help you God?" Do not look at the judge, either legal counsel, or the jury.

Sit with your back straight but in a comfortable position, usually with your hands folded in your lap or held on the arms of the chair. Do not move the chair around or fidget, because this is distracting. Hold notes and other reports in your lap. If the reports are bulky, many experts on testifying recommend placing them under the chair until needed.

The witness chair in all courtrooms is positioned so you can face the judge, legal counsel, jury, or the audience, depending on to whom your answers are directed.

In most instances, if the judge asks you a question, look directly at the judge to answer. If either the prosecutor or defense counsel asks you a question, look directly at the jury to give your answer. The prosecutor will ask you to state your name, department, and position. As you respond, keep in mind the types of statements that are not admissible.

Inadmissible statements include:
- Opinions and conclusions (unless the witness is qualified as an expert)
- Hearsay
- Privileged communication
- Statements about character and reputation, including the defendant's criminal record

---

Testify only to what you actually saw, heard, or did, not what you believe, heard from others, or were told about. You can testify to what a defendant told you directly, but any other statements must be testified to by the person making them.

Preparation is the key to being a good witness. After a review of your personal notes and all relevant reports, you will be familiar with the case and can "tell it like it is." This will come across well to the jury and establish your credibility.

Guidelines for effective testimony are:
- Speak clearly, firmly, and with expression.
- Answer questions directly. Do *not* volunteer information.
- Pause briefly before answering.
- Refer to your notes if you do not recall exact details.
- Admit calmly when you do not know an answer.
- Admit any mistakes you make in testifying.
- Avoid police jargon, sarcasm, and humor.
- Tell the complete truth as you know it.

How you speak is often as important as what you say. Talk slowly, deliberately, and loudly enough to be heard by everyone. Never use obscenity or vulgarity unless the court requests a suspect's or victim's exact words. In such cases, inform the court before you answer that the answer requested includes obscenity or vulgarity.

Ignore the courtroom's atmosphere. Devote your entire attention to giving truthful answers to questions. Answer all questions directly and politely with "yes" or "no" unless asked to relate an action taken, an observation made, or information told to you directly by the defendant. Refer to the judge as "your honor" and to the defendant as "the defendant." Do not volunteer information. Instead, let the prosecution decide whether to pursue a particular line of questioning.

Take a few seconds after hearing the question to form your answer. If the counsel or the court objects to a question, wait until instructed to proceed. If it takes some time for the judge to rule on an objection, ask to have the question repeated.

 Refer to your notes if you are uncertain of specific facts, but do not rely on them excessively.

Reviewing the case thoroughly before your courtroom appearance does not mean that you should memorize specific dates, addresses, or spellings of names and places. Memorization can lead to confusion. Instead use notes to help avoid contradictions and inconsistencies. An extemporaneous answer is better received by the judge and jury than one that sounds rehearsed.

Using notes too much detracts from your testimony, weakens your presentation, and gives the impression you have not adequately prepared for the case. It can also lead to having your notes introduced into the record. If, as you refer to your notes, you discover you have given erroneous testimony such as an incorrect date or time, notify the court immediately. Do not try to cover up the discrepancy. Everyone makes mistakes. If you admit them in a professional manner, little harm results. Do not hesitate to admit that you do not know the answer to a question or that you do not understand a question. Never bluff or attempt to fake your way through an answer.

In addition, be aware of certain phrases that may leave a negative impression on the jury. Phrases such as "I believe" or "to the best of my recollection" will not impress a jury. Do not argue or use sarcasm, witticisms, or "smart" answers. Be direct, firm, and positive. Be courteous, whether in response to a question from the prosecutor or an objection from the defense or the judge. Do not hesitate to give information favorable to the defendant. Your primary responsibility is to state what you know about the case.

If asked to identify evidence with your personal mark, take time to examine the item thoroughly. Make sure that all marks are accounted for and that your mark has not been altered. A rapid identification may make a bad impression on the jury and may lead you into an erroneous identification.

Nonverbal Factors

Do not underestimate the power of nonverbal factors as you testify. Over 25 years ago, Dr. Albert Mehrabian conducted his famous, often-cited study at UCLA and concluded that communication is made up of several components consisting of:

- *What* is said—the actual words spoken (7 percent of the total message communicated)
- *How* it is said—tone of voice, pitch, modulation, and the like (38 percent of the message)
- *Nonverbal factors*—body language, gestures, demeanor (55 percent)

Thus, the bulk of a message is conveyed not through which words are used but in how they are delivered. Never overlook the importance of how you present information and nonverbal factors when testifying (Figure 21.4).

 Important nonverbal elements include dress, eye contact, posture, gestures, mannerisms, and facial expressions.

Navarro (p.28) suggests: "Officers should make eye contact often, but respectfully, with the jury while testifying." He also suggests: "Facial expressions can prove revealing and problematic. Displays of indifference, disgust, antipathy, displeasure, or arrogance interfere with a jury's perception either on the stand or at the prosecutor's table."

Figure 21.4
Testifying in court is part of working in law enforcement. Officers must never underestimate the power of nonverbal communication when they testify. While what is being said (the "facts" to which the officer is testifying) is certainly important, the way these facts are presented can speak just as loudly, if not louder, to the judge and jury. Important nonverbal elements include dress, eye contact, posture, gestures, mannerisms, rate of speech, and tone of voice. These factors can provide far more insight and depth into an officer's statement of fact and experience, particularly as pertains to a brutal or otherwise horrific crime scene, than can mere words recorded onto the court transcript.

Consider the expression of Montgomery County police officer Cynthia Martin, the first officer on the scene of the shooting of sniper shooting victim Sarah Ramos, as she testifies during the trial of Washington area sniper suspect John Allen Muhammad.

Avoid actions associated with deception such as putting a hand over your mouth, rubbing your nose, preening, straightening your hair, buttoning your coat, picking lint off your clothing, or tugging at your shirt or a pant leg.

Strategies for Excelling as a Witness

 To excel as a witness: (1) set yourself up, (2) provoke the defense into giving you a chance to explain, (3) be unconditional, and (4) do not stall.

Rutledge (*Courtroom*) suggests several basic points to enhance the chance of success, some of which you have heard before:

- Get into the habit of thinking ahead to the trial while you are still out in the field. Ask yourself, "What if they ask me this in court?" (p.20).

- The rules of court severely restrict your answers to questions. No competent defense attorney is ever going to give you a chance to explain anything. So, you need to know how to provoke the defense attorney into giving you a chance to explain. Some of these provokers are: *definitely; of course, certainly; certainly not; naturally; naturally not;* and one that always works: *Yes . . . and no* (pp.24–27).

- Be unconditional. Some police officers seem to like the sound of the conditional word *would*. When I am prosecuting a case, I cringe at the sound of it because it is too indefinite.
  Example:
  Q: Who was your partner?
  A: That would be Officer Hill. (p.72)

- Do not stall. Do not repeat the attorney's question.
  Example:
  Q: Were you holding a flashlight?
  A: Was I holding a flashlight? Yes, I was. (p.75)

In some instances officers may qualify to testify as *expert witnesses*. In such cases, the restrictions on testimony are somewhat more relaxed.

Expert Testimony

Rule 702 of the Federal Rules of Evidence states:

If scientific, technical or other specialized knowledge will assist the trier of fact to understand the evidence or to determine a fact in issue, a witness qualified as an expert by knowledge, skill, experience, training or education, may testify thereto in the form of an opinion or otherwise, if (1) the testimony is based upon sufficient facts of data, (2) the testimony is the product of reliable principles and methods, and (3) the witness has applied the principles and methods reliably to the facts of the case.

An **expert witness** is a person who has had special training, education, or experience (Gardner and Anderson, p.91). Kruger ("The Police Officer," p.11) explains: "Expert testimony is testimony that seeks to explain matters beyond the usual comprehension or knowledge of a typical jury. It is based on specialized knowledge, training, experience or skills, the application of which will help the jury understand the evidence."

Daubert v. Merrell-Dow Pharmaceuticals, Inc. (1993) established standards for the admission of expert testimony in federal courts. Under *Daubert*, an expert's testimony must be specialized and relate directly to some fact at issue in the case: "Expert testimony which does not relate to any issue in the case is not relevant and, ergo, non-helpful." The U.S. Supreme Court noted that expert testimony must fit the case. Fitness is determined by examining how helpful the testimony is. This "helpfulness" standard requires a "valid connection" between the expert testimony and "the pertinent inquiry" in a case (Kruger, "The Role," p.48).

Officers who qualify as experts in an area are allowed to give opinions and conclusions, but the prosecution must qualify the officer as an expert on the stand. The prosecution must establish that the person has special knowledge that others of moderate education or experience in the same field do not possess. To qualify as an expert witness, one must have as many of the following as possible:

- Present or prior employment in the specific field
- Active membership in a professional group in the field
- Research work in the field
- An educational degree directly related to the field
- Direct experience with the subject if not employed in the field
- Papers, treatises, or books published on the subject or teaching experience in it

Police officers can become experts on sounds, firearms, distances, lengths of time, visibility problems, and so on simply by years of experience in police work. Other areas, such as firearms identification, fingerprint classification, and handwriting analysis, require specialized training. Just who qualifies as an expert is not always clear, and different qualifications may exist for scientific and nonscientific evidence.

Rutledge (*Courtroom*, pp.182–184) strongly recommends that officers document their training, studies, and experience in a format such as that shown in Figure 21.5.

IN-SERVICE TRAINING

	Date	Place	Subject	Number Hours
Basic Academy				
Advanced Academy				
Special Schools				
Roll-Call Training				

Figure 21.5

Record of training, studies, and experience

Source: Devallis Rutledge. *Courtroom Survival: The Officer's Guide to Better Testimony.* Belmont, CA: Wadsworth Publishing, 2000, pp. 182–184. Reprinted by permission.

SPECIAL STUDIES/EXPERIMENTS

Dates	Place	Subject	Description

COLLEGE, UNIVERSITY, TECH SCHOOL

Dates	Place	Subject	Description

READINGS

Dates	Title	Subject	Description

PROFESSIONAL ASSOCIATIONS

OJT
Supervised Training

Dates	Supervisor	Subject	No. Hrs. or Cases

INVESTIGATIONS, ARRESTS, EVALUATIONS, ETC.
Approximate Number

Narc	Prints	T/A	Bkmkg	Ballis.	DWI	Handwriting	Poly

continued

PRIOR EXPERT TESTIMONY (Number)								
Court	Narc	Prints	T/A	Bkmkg	Ballis.	DWI	Handwriting	Poly
Justice								
Municipal								
Superior								
Supreme								
Federal								
Other States								
OTHER QUALIFICATION								

Figure 21.5
(continued)

Take this record to court to establish yourself as an expert witness. Knight and Callanan (p.15) stress: "Competent police procedure experts are not advocates, legal scholars or truth finders. They are simply 'subject matter experts.'"

Testifying under Cross-Examination

ecall the earlier description of the adversary system. It is understandable that an investigator would consider the defense attorney's cross-examination as an attack on the prosecution's case. However, also recall that according to Van Brocklin (p.46) investigators' *attitudes* determine their testimony style and their body language. During cross-examination, while the defense attorney attempts to impeach your testimony or at least undermine your credibility, Van Brocklin (p.48) enumerates behaviors that juror comments from posttrial interviews indicate weaken a witness's credibility:

- Uses a defensive or evasive tone of voice
- Appears ill at ease or nervous
- Avoids eye contact
- Crosses arms defensively across chest
- Quibbles over common terms
- Sits stiffly
- Looks to attorney for assistance during cross-examination
- Cracks jokes inappropriately
- Uses lots of "ah's" or "uh's"

In contrast, jurors have noted that the following behaviors enhance credibility:

- Displays an even temperament on direct and cross
- Doesn't become angry or defensive when pressed
- Appears relaxed and at ease
- Is likeable and polite
- Maintains eye contact with attorney and jury
- Is not affected by interruptions or objections

Rutledge (*Courtroom*, p.60) notes: "You're not an advocate—you're a witness. Don't try to help the prosecutor. Don't try to thwart the defense lawyer." Cross-examination is usually the most difficult part of testifying. "The defense lawyer's most important task is to destroy your credibility—to make you look like you're either a . . . bungler, a liar, or both. How does he do that? He attacks you. He tricks you. He outsmarts you. He confuses you. He frustrates you. He annoys you. He probes for your most vulnerable characteristics" (Rutledge, p.118). How does this make officers feel?

Van Brocklin (pp.46–47) suggests that when officers are given a word-association test and the words *defense attorney* are given, "Exclamations fly—*snake, shark, weasel, slime, dishonest, deceptive, liar*, and several that need not be printed." According to Van Brocklin this negative attitude explains why an officer can do a competent job in the investigation, be truthful, and still not be believed by the jury. If jurors perceive that an investigator is acting defensively, they may think that the investigator is not testifying truthfully: "Jurors think that only a guilty person—a person with something to hide—acts defensively." The key is to recognize this tendency and remain professional and objective.

The defense attorney will attempt to cast doubt on your direct testimony in an effort to win an acquittal for the defendant. Know the methods of attack for cross-examination to avoid being trapped.

During cross-examination the defense attorney may:
- Be disarmingly friendly or intimidatingly rude.
- Attack your credibility and impartiality.
- Attack your investigative skill.
- Attempt to force contradictions or inconsistencies.
- Ask leading questions or deliberately misquote you.
- Ask for a simple answer to a complex question.
- Use rapid-fire questioning.
- Use the silent treatment.

The defense attorney can be extremely friendly, hoping to put you off guard by making the questioning appear to be just a friendly chat. The attorney may praise your skill in investigation and lead you into boasting or a show of self-glorification that will leave a very bad impression on the jury. The "friendly" defense attorney may also try to lead you into testifying about evidence of which you have no personal knowledge. This error will be immediately exposed and your testimony tainted, if not completely discredited.

At the opposite extreme is the defense attorney who appears outraged by statements you make and goes on the attack immediately. This kind of attorney appears very excited and outraged, as though the trial is a travesty of justice. A natural reaction to such an approach is to exaggerate your testimony or lose your temper, which is exactly what the defense attorney wants. If you show anger, the jury may believe you are more interested in obtaining a conviction than determining the truth. It is often hard for a jury to believe that the well-dressed, meek-appearing defendant in court is the person who was armed with a gun and robbed a store. Maintain your dignity and impartiality, and show concern for only the facts.

The credibility of your testimony can be undermined in many ways. The defense may attempt to show that you are prejudiced, have poor character, or are interested only in seeing your arrest "stick." If asked, "Do you want to see the defendant convicted?" reply that you are there to present the facts you know and that you will abide by the court's decision. No contemporary case demonstrated these cross-examination attacks on police credibility more effectively than the O. J. Simpson murder trial. The defense was successful in shifting the focus away from the issue of the defendant's guilt and putting it directly on the incompetence of the police investigators.

The defense may also try to show that your testimony itself is erroneous because you are incompetent, lack information, are confused, have forgotten facts, or could not have had personal knowledge of the facts you have testified to. Do not respond to such criticism. Let your testimony speak for itself. If the defense criticizes your reference to notes, state that you simply want to be completely accurate. Be patient. If the defense counsel becomes excessively offensive, the prosecutor will intervene. Alternatively, the prosecutor may see that the

defense is hurting its own case by such behavior and will allow the defense attorney to continue.

The defense attorney may further try to force contradictions or inconsistencies by incessantly repeating questions using slightly different wording. Repeat your previous answer. If the defense claims that your testimony does not agree with that of other officers, do not change your testimony. Whether your testimony is like theirs or different is irrelevant. The defense will attack it either way. If it is exactly alike, the defense will allege collusion. If it is slightly different, the defense will exaggerate this to convince the jury that the differences are so great that the officers are not even testifying about the same circumstances.

Rutledge (*Courtroom*, p.77) explains that a favorite tactic of defense lawyers to destroy credibility is to try to get you to commit yourself to something and then later have to admit you could be wrong about it. He suggests that if either attorney asks for any kind of *measurement* you did not personally make, including distance, time, height, weight, speed, age, and the like, allow yourself some leeway. Either give an *approximation*—for example, "he was approximately 45 feet away"—or put your answer in brackets. **Brackets** provide a range—for example, "he was 40 to 50 feet away."

Another defense tactic is to use an accusatory tone in asking whether you talked with others about the case and what they told you about how to testify. Such accusations may make inexperienced officers feel guilty because they know they have talked about the case with many people. Because the accusing tone implies that this was legally incorrect, the officers may reply that they talked to no one. Such a response is a mistake because you may certainly discuss the case before testifying. Simply state that you have discussed the case with several people in an official capacity, but that none of them told you how to testify.

If defense counsel asks whether you have refreshed your memory before testifying, do not hesitate to say "yes." You would be a poor witness if you had not done so. Discussions with the prosecution, officers, and witnesses and a review of notes and reports are entirely proper. They assist you in telling the truth, the main purpose of testimony.

Leading questions are another defense tactic. For example, defense counsel may ask, "When did you first strike the defendant?" This implies that you did in fact strike the defendant. Defense attorneys also like to ask questions that presume that you have already testified to something when in fact you may not have done so. If you are misquoted, call it to the counsel's attention and then repeat the facts you testified to. If you do not remember your exact testimony, have it read from the court record.

In addition, defense counsel may ask complicated questions and then say, "Please answer 'yes' or 'no.'" Obviously, some questions cannot be answered that simply. Ask to have the question broken down. No rule requires a specific answer. If the court does not grant your request, answer the question as directed and let the prosecutor bring out the information through redirect examination.

Rapid-fire questioning is yet another tactic that defense attorneys use to provoke unconsidered answers. Do not let the attorney's pace rush you. Take time to consider your responses.

Do not be taken in by the "silent treatment." The defense attorney may remain silent for what seems like many seconds after you answer a question. If you have given a complete answer, wait patiently. Do *not* attempt to fill the silence by saying things such as, "At least that's how I remember it," or "It was something very close to that."

Another tactic frequently used by defense attorneys is to mispronounce officers' names intentionally or address them by the wrong rank. This is an attempt to distract the officer.

Regardless of how your testimony is attacked, treat the defense counsel as respectfully as you do the prosecutor. Do not regard the defense counsel as your enemy. You are in court to state the facts and tell the truth. Your testimony should exhibit no personal prejudice or animosity, and you should not become excited or provoked at defense counsel. Be professional.

Few officers are prepared for the rigor of testifying in court, even if they have received training in this area. Until officers have actually testified in court, they cannot understand how difficult it is. Because police officers are usually the primary and most damaging witnesses in a criminal case, defense attorneys know they must attempt to confuse, discredit, or destroy the officers' testimony.

The best testimony is accurate, truthful, and in accordance with the facts. Every word an officer says is recorded and may be played back or used by the defense.

> A key to testifying during cross-examination is to NEVER volunteer any information.

Garland and Stuckey (p.515) explain that during cross-examination the defense attorney can ask questions about only subjects raised by the prosecution during direct examination. If an investigator volunteers additional information, he or she may open up areas the prosecution did not intend to present and may not be prepared for.

Handling Objections

Gardner and Anderson (p.97) describe three categories of objections. The first category is objections to the *form of the question*: leading, speculative, argumentative, misstates facts in evidence, assumes facts not in evidence, vague and ambiguous, repetitive or cumulative, or misleading. The second category is objections to the *substance of the question*: irrelevant, immaterial, incompetent, calls for hearsay, insufficient foundation, calls for inadmissible opinion, or beyond the scope of the direct examination. The third category is objections to the *answer*: unresponsive, inadmissible opinion, inadmissible hearsay statement.

Rutledge (*Courtroom*, pp.97–115) gives the following suggestions for handling objections (reprinted by permission of the publisher):

> There are at least 44 standard trial objections in most states. We're only going to talk about the two that account for upwards of 90 percent of the problems a testifying officer will have: that your answer is a conclusion, or that it is nonresponsive.
>
> - How to avoid conclusions. One way is to listen to the form of the question. You know the attorney is asking you to speculate when he starts his questions with these loaded phrases:
>
>   Would you assume . . . ?
>   Do you suppose . . . ?
>   Don't you think that . . . ?
>   Couldn't it be that . . . ?
>   Do you imagine . . . ?
>   Wouldn't it be fair to presume . . . ?
>   Isn't it strange that . . . ?
>   And the one you're likely to hear most often:
>   Isn't it possible that . . . ?
>
> - Another major area of conclusionary testimony is what I call mindreading. You can't get inside someone else's brain. That means you don't know for a fact—so you can't testify—as to what someone else sees, hears, feels, thinks or wants; and you don't know for a fact what somebody is trying to do, or is able to do, or whether he is nervous, excited, angry, scared, happy, upset, disturbed, or in any of the other emotional states that can only be labeled with a conclusion.
>
> - How to give "responsive" answers. You have to answer just the question you're asked—no more, no less. That means you have to pay attention to how the question is framed. You answer a yes-or-no question with a "yes" or "no."
>
>   Q: Did he perform the alphabet test?
>   A: Yes, twice—but he only went to "G."
>
> Everything after the "yes" is nonresponsive. The officer anticipated the next three questions and volunteered the answers. He should have limited each answer to one question:
>
>   Q: Did he perform the alphabet test?
>   A: Yes.
>   Q: How many times?
>   A: Twice.
>   Q: How far did he go correctly the first time?
>   A: To the letter "G."

> To avoid objections to your testimony, avoid conclusions and nonresponsive answers. Answer yes-or-no questions with "yes" or "no."

Concluding Your Testimony

o not leave the stand until instructed to do so by counsel or the court. As you leave the stand, do not pay special attention to the prosecution, defense counsel, defendant, or jury. Return immediately to your seat in the courtroom or leave the room if you have been sequestered. If you are told you may be needed for further testimony, remain available. If told you are no longer needed, leave the courtroom and resume your normal activities. To remain gives the impression that you have a special interest in the case.

If you are in the courtroom at the time of the verdict, show neither approval nor disapproval at the outcome. If you have been a credible witness and told the truth, win or lose in court, you have done your job and should not take the outcome personally.

The complainant should be notified of the disposition of the case. A form such as the one shown in Figure 21.6 is frequently used.

Advice on Testifying from a Seasoned, "Officer of the Year" Investigator

Y ou were introduced to Detective Richard Gautsch at the beginning of the text. He returns to furnish the book's conclusion, emphasizing the areas to focus on when giving courtroom testimony and providing examples of some of his experiences testifying.

Although everything in this chapter is important, Gautsch emphasizes three major areas:

1. *Preparation.* While testifying, an investigator should not use his or her report as a crutch or a script. It should be a safety net—seldom used. Constantly referring to a report gives the jury the impression that you do not know the case. Officers should *study* their reports and the reports of fellow officers before testifying.

2. *Communication.* Understand that words are a small part of communicating. Expressions, demeanor, personality, appearance, and more are what jurors use to form an opinion. If you remind them of the obstinate cop who wrote them a ticket for going two miles over the speed limit, they're going to sympathize with the defendant.

3. *Credibility.* If jurors question your credibility, the case is in big trouble. If you get caught in a lie, an embellishment, or an obvious omission, why should a juror believe anything you say? In the O. J. Simpson murder trial, a detective lied about whether he had ever used racial slurs. While it had nothing to do with the evidence he was presenting, once he lost his credibility, his testimony lost its value and, indeed, severely damaged the prosecution's case.

Detective Gautsch was nervous the night before his first major trial, his mind filled with stories of defense attorneys ripping cops to shreds during cross-examination—stories artfully embellished by fellow cops—and the knowledge that a bad day testifying can lose a case. He had good reason to be nervous, as the defense attorney assigned to the case was infamous for picking apart police reports. He studied his reports as if he were taking a final exam and rehearsed responses to every dirty trick a defense attorney could throw at him. He wasn't going to be some ill-prepared cop referring to his report for the suspect's name or the location of an arrest.

He took the stand, scanned the packed courtroom, and hoped his voice would not crack. The direct testimony went smoothly, but he knew what was coming. The defense attorney smiled and greeted him. His voice was calm and reassuring. He knew all about the detective's background and that he had reached the rank of detective at a very young age. The attorney's tone was complimentary, and Gautsch's fear of being ripped to shreds was replaced with a sense of importance. He began to enjoy the cross-examination.

Most of the initial questions were general and easy to answer. The defense attorney asked several questions about the defendant's level of cooperation. He cited things that his client had done at their request, including having his hands swabbed for gunpowder residue. Gautsch acknowledged that the defendant had been cooperative. The defense attorney asked if his client had refused any of their requests. Gautsch paused to think, and the defense attorney quickly added, "Did you ask him to do anything else?"

It seemed to Gautsch that the defense attorney was helping him remember something in his report without making him look stupid. Then Gautsch remembered, "Oh, yes. He agreed to take a polygraph test." The defense attorney thanked Gautsch and sat down. The prosecutor slowly slumped in his chair. Gautsch had been tricked into telling the jury that the defendant was willing to take a lie-detector test—something that wasn't admissible and that the defense could not have presented without the detective's help. In fact, the defendant offered to take the test, but later refused—something the jury would never hear. His mistake left the jury with the impression that the defendant had passed a polygraph test. The jury returned a guilty verdict for a lesser charge and left Gautsch wondering what role his mistake on the stand had played in its decision.

Figure 21.6
Case disposition notice

CASE DISPOSITION REPORT

Date Disposition Made: __4-25-20__ __   D.R. #: __97-1002__
Date of Incident: __2-10-20__ __   Type of Incident: __Burglary__

DISPOSITION:
(X) Case Clearance
(X) Property Recovered
( ) Disposition of Property: (X) Owner ( ) Police Evidence
( ) Other
If Other, specify type: _____

VICTIM: (If Runaway Juvenile or Missing Adult, disregard this section)
Name___Jerome Slater___ Address _3041 Harding, Edina, Minnesota_

SUSPECT(S):
NO. 1: __John Toben__   Arrested? __Yes__   BCPD I.D. # __20146__
NO. 2: __William Moss__   Arrested? __Yes__   BCPD I.D. # __20147__
NO. 3: _____   Arrested? _____ BCPD I.D. # _____

PROPERTY RECOVERED:
Item No. 1: _One Car Radio, Sears_____   Value __$87.00__
Item No. 2: _One car battery, Sears____   Value __60.00__
Item No. 3: _Micro Wave Oven-GE_____   Value __250.00__
Item No. 4: _One 17" TV-Sears Solid State_   Value __350.00__
Recovering Agency: _Edina Police Department_   Total Value Recovered Property: _$747.00_

CANCELLATIONS: (Specify date, time, agency and officer receiving cancellation and officer making cancellation)

NCIC: _____
Other Agencies: _Hennepin County Sheriffs Office_____
Other Agencies: _____

OFFICER MAKING DISPOSITION: _____
SUPERVISOR APPROVING: _____
DETAILS: _Full recovery of property_____

Another defense attorney taught Detective Gautsch a more positive lesson during his first murder trial—a case described at the beginning of the text. Two men robbed and murdered a teenage boy working as an attendant at a gas station. They netted less than $50, but decided the boy had to be killed because he had seen their faces. They forced him into their car, bound his hands, and drove him to secluded woods. They shot him nine times and left him to bleed to death. The boy was missing for a week before his body was found. During that week Detective Gautsch got to know the boy's family as wonderful people. He fought back tears when he brought them the news of their son's death.

Experienced detectives do not allow their emotions to influence their professionalism. At age 24, Gautsch was inexperienced and emotional. The scene was chaotic as the team of detectives raided a house where one of the suspects was living. Cops rushed in to secure the scene and control a group of suspects. Gautsch grabbed the first person he could get his hands on and forced him against a wall. He recognized him as one of the murderers. As Gautsch held him against the wall, he felt the suspect tremble. Gautsch asked why he was shaking, and he said they had scared him. Gautsch asked how scared the boy had been when they had marched him into the woods. The suspect smirked and laughed nervously. At that instant Gautsch made a stupid, unprofessional mistake—he punched the smirk off the suspect's face, satisfying his need for retribution, but jeopardizing the entire case.

Seasoned detectives interviewed the suspect for several hours. He denied any involvement in the murder. During a break in the questioning, the suspect and Detective Gautsch were left alone in the interview room.

They were the same age, and the suspect felt more comfortable talking to Gautsch. Eventually he confessed to the murder.

Gautsch did not include the striking incident in his report, but it was ever present in his mind. He was the key witness at the trial, and the confession was the most important evidence. The defense attorney was one of the very best. He methodically questioned the detective about various aspects of the investigation, then paused and switched legal pads. "Detective, did you punch my client before he confessed to you?"

Gautsch's heart pounded so loudly he was sure everyone could hear it. The confession, the case, and his job were all about to be lost. The murdering little creep was going to get off because of Gautsch's stupidity. The courtroom was silent. The jury, the prosecutor, the judge, the press, and the victim's family all stared at him, waiting for his answer. For the sake of justice, Gautsch wondered if one lie would really hurt. He looked squarely into the defense attorney's eyes and responded, "Yes sir, I did."

For a moment the defense attorney looked perplexed. He asked a few more questions and sat down. The prosecutor was furious that Gautsch had neglected to share that damaging information with him. Fortunately, the defendants were found guilty and sentenced to life in prison. After the trial the defense attorney asked to meet with Gautsch in the prosecutor's office. Gautsch arrived expecting some type of sanctions. Instead, the defense attorney extended his hand and commended Gautsch for telling the truth on the stand. The attorney said he had hoped Gautsch would deny hitting his client. If he had, the attorney was prepared to show that the detective was lying and ruin his credibility with the jury. When Gautsch told the truth, the attorney's strategy failed, and the detective's credibility with the jury was actually enhanced.

The lesson to be learned is never lie, exaggerate, or embellish your testimony. It is more obvious to a jury than you may realize. Once you lose your credibility, it is nearly impossible to recover it. The truth can only strengthen a good case.

SUMMARY

The most important rule to eradicate fear of testifying in court is to always tell the truth.

Before testifying, the final report must be written and presented to the prosecutor. The final report contains (1) the complaint; (2) the preliminary investigation report; (3) all follow-up and progress reports; (4) statements, admissions, and confessions; (5) laboratory reports; (6) photographs, sketches, and drawings; and (7) a summary of all negative evidence. The quality of the content and writing of the report influences its credibility.

The prosecutor is the most powerful official in the court system. To prosecute or not to prosecute is often a question. Some cases are never prosecuted because the complaint is invalid, it is exceptionally cleared, or no evidence or leads exist. If the decision is made to prosecute, thorough preparation is required. To prepare a case for court: (1) review and evaluate all evidence, positive and negative; (2) review all reports on the case; (3) prepare witnesses; (4) write the final report; and (5) hold a pretrial conference with the prosecutor. Concentrate on proving the elements of the crime and establishing the offender's identity.

Before the trial, hold a conference with the prosecutor to review all the evidence and to discuss the strengths and weaknesses of the case and the probable line of the prosecutor's and defense attorney's questioning.

A criminal trial begins with the jury selection. When court convenes, prosecution and defense make their opening statements. The prosecution then presents its case, followed by presentation of the defense's case. After closing statements by the prosecution and the defense, the judge instructs the jury, which then retires to deliberate its verdict. When a verdict is reached, court is reconvened and the verdict read. If the defendant is found guilty, the judge passes sentence or sets a sentencing date.

The "win" for an investigator who testifies is to have established credibility. This includes avoiding inadmissible statements, including opinions, conclusions, hearsay, privileged communications, and statements about the defendant's character and reputation. To present testimony effectively, speak clearly, firmly, and with expression; answer questions directly, and *do not* volunteer information; pause briefly before answering; refer to your notes if you do not recall exact details; admit calmly when you do not know an answer; admit any mistakes you make in testifying; avoid police jargon, sarcasm, and humor; and above all, tell the complete truth as you know it. Refer to your notes if you are uncertain of specific facts, but do not rely on them excessively; this would give the impression that you are not prepared for the case and thus weaken your testimony. Important nonverbal elements include dress, eye contact, posture, gestures, mannerisms, rate of speech, and tone of voice.

Strategies for testifying in court include (1) setting yourself up, (2) provoking the defense into giving you a chance to explain, (3) being unconditional, and (4) not stalling. Anticipate the tactics commonly used by defense attorneys during cross-examination. They may be disarmingly friendly or intimidatingly rude; attack your credibility and impartiality; attack your investigative skill; attempt to force contradictions or inconsistencies; ask leading questions or deliberately misquote you; request a "yes" or "no" answer to complex questions; use rapid-fire questioning; or use the "silent treatment." To avoid objections to your testimony, avoid conclusions and nonresponsive answers. Answer yes-or-no questions with "yes" or "no."

If you are well prepared, know the facts, and present them truthfully and professionally, you have done your part in furthering the cause of justice. The disposition of a case should be made known to the complainant.

CHECKLIST

Final Report

- Have I met all the criteria for an effective report? (See Chapter 3)
- Have I included all relevant information?
- Have I included headings?
- Have I proofread the paper to spot content and composition errors?

Preparing to Testify

- Have all reports been reviewed?
- Have all reports been organized for presentation to the prosecutor?
- Has all evidence been located and made available for court presentation?
- Has all evidence been examined by competent laboratories and the results obtained? Are copies of the reports available?
- Have all known leads been developed?
- Have both negative and positive information been submitted to the prosecuting attorney?
- Has all arrest information been submitted?
- Has a list of witnesses been prepared? Addresses? Telephone numbers?
- Has the final report been assembled? Does it contain copies of investigators' reports? photographs? sketches? evidence? lab reports? medical examiner's reports? statements? confessions? maps? all other pertinent information?
- Has a pretrial conference been held with the prosecutor's office?
- Have all witnesses been reinterviewed? notified of the date and time of the trial?

- Have all expert witnesses been notified of the date and time of the trial?
- Has someone been designated to take the evidence to court?
- Have notes needed for testimony been removed from your notebook?
- Is your personal appearance professional?

DISCUSSION QUESTIONS

1. Plea bargaining has become very controversial in many states, and some states have eliminated it as a part of the prosecution process. Is plea bargaining good or bad?

2. The news media can affect jury and court decisions by publicizing information about a criminal case before it goes to trial. May police refuse to give information to the press if doing so might jeopardize the case in court? How significantly does such publicity affect the trial?

3. Should criminal trials be televised? What are the advantages and disadvantages?

4. What is the investigator's role in preparing a case for court? How does the investigator cooperate with the prosecutor to enhance the courtroom presentation?

5. Imagine that you are preparing a final report for the prosecutor. What materials should you include? How should you organize them to show the continuity of your investigation and the way you gathered evidence related to the elements of the offense charged?

6. If you were accused of a crime, would you prefer a trial with or without a jury?

7. Is there a better system than the jury system?

8. Does an acquittal mean that the investigator failed?

9. How prevalent do you believe "testilying" (not telling the truth) is by law enforcement officers?

10. If you were to testify in a major case, what would you wear?

MEDIA EXPLORATIONS

Internet

Select one of the following keywords: *expert witness, report writing in law enforcement, testifying.* Find one article relevant to writing offense reports and testifying in court to outline and share with the class.

 Crime and Evidence in Action

Go to the CD and choose the **drug bust/gang homicide/sexual assault case.** During the course of the case you'll become patrol officer, detective, defense attorney, corrections officer, and patrol officer to conduct interactive investigative research. Each case unfolds as you respond to key decision points. Feedback for each possible answer choice is packed full of information, including term definitions, web links, and important documentation. The sergeant is available at certain times to help mentor you, the Online Resources website offers a variety of information, and be sure to take notes in your e-notebook during the suspect video statements and at key points throughout (these notes can be saved, printed, or e-mailed). The Forensics Exercise will test your ability to collect, transport, and analyze evidence from the crime scene. At the end of the case you can track how well you responded to each decision point and join the Discussion Forum for a postmortem. **Go to the CD and use the skills you've learned in this chapter to solve a case.**

REFERENCES

Gardner, Thomas J., and Anderson, Terry M. *Criminal Evidence: Principles and Cases,* 5th ed. Belmont, CA: Wadsworth Publishing Company, 2004.

Garland, Norman M., and Stuckey, Gilbert B. *Criminal Evidence for the Law Enforcement Officer.* New York: McGraw Hill, 2000.

Gunderson, M. P. "Five Tips for Testifying in Court," *Law and Order,* July 2003, pp. 110–113.

Knight, Susan, and Callanan, Joe. "Police Expert Malpractice," *The Law Enforcement Trainer,* July/August 2003, pp. 10–15.

Kruger, Karen J. "The Role and Impact of Police Practice Experts on Litigation," *The Police Chief,* June 2004, pp. 48–57.

Kruger, Karen J. "The Police Officer as Expert Witness," *The Police Chief,* June 2005, pp. 10–11.

Moore, Carole. "Taking the Stand," *Law Enforcement Technology,* July 2005, pp. 76–84.

Navarro, Joe. "Testifying in the Theater of the Courtroom," *FBI Law Enforcement Bulletin,* September 2004, pp. 26–30.

Neubauer, David W. *America's Courts and the Criminal Justice System,* 8th ed. Belmont, CA: Wadsworth Publishing, 2005.

Neubauer, David W., and Meinhold, Stephen S. *Judicial Process: Law, Courts and Politics in the United States,* 3rd ed. Belmont, CA: Wadsworth Publishing, 2004.

Rutledge, Devallis. *Courtroom Survival: The Officer's Guide to Better Testimony.* Belmont, CA: Wadsworth Publishing, 2000.

Rutledge, Devallis. "Courthouse Conduct," *Police*, June 2004, pp. 70–72.

Schott, Richard G. "The Discovery Process and Personnel File Information," *FBI Law Enforcement Bulletin*, November 2003, pp. 25–32.

Van Brocklin, Valerie. "Winning Courtroom Confrontations: A New Approach to Training," *The Law Enforcement Trainer*, April/May/June 2005, pp. 44–49.

CASES CITED

Brady v. Maryland, 373 U.S. 83 (1963)

Daubert v. Merrell-Dow Pharmaceuticals, Inc., 509 U.S. 579 (1993)

Giglio v. United States, 405 U.S. 150 (1972)

Pennsylvania v. Ritchie, 480 U.S. 39 (1987)

Weatherford v. Bursey, 429 U.S. 545 (1977)

Sudden In-custody Death: An Investigator's Checklist

The following checklists are designed to help investigators organize the collection of evidence suggested by this protocol, especially transient evidence, which can become altered within a few minutes, during the first few minutes after a subject dies in custody.

Subject's History

❑ Residential ❑ Educational ❑ Family ❑ Medical ❑ Behavioral
❑ Employment ❑ Financial History ❑ Police Contact ❑ Nutritional ❑ Substance Abuse
❑ The Common Link

The Incident

❑ Duration of unusual behavior prior to police contact?_____
_____
_____
_____
_____

❑ Detailed history of behavior immediately prior to police intervention?_____
_____
_____
_____
_____
_____

❑ Subject utterances _____
_____
_____
_____

❑ Subject actions, activities _____
_____
_____
_____
_____

❑ Hyperventilation ❑ Shouting ❑ Other_____
❑ Running ❑ Pacing furiously _____

❑ Type of resistance_____
❑ Duration of resistance_____
❑ Length of time taken to subdue subject_____
❑ Number of officers involved _____
❑ Method of subject transport _____
❑ Time transport begins _____ ❑ Time transport ends _____
❑ Struggle against restraints during transport?_____

❑ Describe struggle _____
_____
_____
_____
_____
_____

❏ Describe breathing pattern _____

_____

_____

_____

_____

❏ Shouting? _____

_____

_____

_____

_____

❏ Presence or absence of sweating by the subject? _____

❏ Pulse rate during incident _____

❏ Strength during incident _____

❏ Determined by _____

❏ Time _____

❏ Name _____

❏ Presence or absence of sweating by persons involved with subject? _____

_____

_____

_____

_____

The Scene

❏ Air temperature _____

❏ Relative humidity _____

❏ Determined by _____

❏ Time _____

❏ Name _____

❏ Transport vehicle interior temperature _____

❏ Climate control settings _____

❏ Functional? _____

❏ Used _____

❏ Determined by _____

❏ Time _____

❏ Name _____

❏ Treatment facility temperature _____

❏ Relative humidity _____

❏ Climate control settings _____

❏ Functional? _____

❏ Used _____

❏ Determined by _____

❏ Time _____

❏ Name _____

❏ Additional location temperature _____

❏ Relative humidity _____

❏ Climate control settings _____

❏ Functional? _____

❏ Used _____

❏ Determined by _____

❏ Time _____

❏ Name _____

❑ Describe surface where subject was restrained _____
_____
_____
_____
_____
_____

❑ Surface temperature _____
❑ Determined by _____
❑ Time _____
❑ Name _____

Resuscitation Efforts

❑ Describe _____
_____
_____
_____
_____
_____

❑ Subject's core temperatures	Before	Upon death	PM
Times			
Determined by			
Name	Name _____	Name _____	Name _____

Thyroid/cricoid pressure (pressure over the front of the windpipe used _____
Number of times the attempt was made _____
ID of person making efforts _____
_____
_____

Environmental Factors

❑ External air temperature _____   ❑ Humidity _____
❑ Humidex _____   ❑ Wind chill _____
❑ Wind speed _____   ❑ Direction _____
❑ Determined by _____
❑ Time _____
❑ Name _____

❑ Weather trend _____
❑ Surface temperature of the ground _____
❑ Determined by _____
❑ Time _____
❑ Name _____

❑ Duration of contact with ground _____
❑ Position _____

❑ Other _____
_____
_____
_____
_____
_____
_____
_____
_____
_____
_____
_____
_____

Death Scene Checklist

This form is to be used as a supplementary source sheet for readily available information and is not intended to replace conventional reports. Copies should be distributed to investigating officers and medical examiners.

Name of deceased:

First   Middle   Last

Address:

Age: **Race:** White Black Hispanic Asian Native American Unknown

Sex: Male   Female

Telephone number:

Marital status: S   M   W   D   Separated   Unknown

Next-of-kin:

Name:

Address:

Telephone number:

Police notified by:

Date: Time:

Name:

Address:

Telephone number:

Relationship to deceased:

Deceased found:

Date: Time:

Address: (if different from above)

Location: Apartment   House   Townhouse   Other (describe)

Entrance by: Key   Cutting chain   Forcing door   Other (describe)

Type of lock on door:

Condition of other doors and windows: Open   Closed   Locked   Unlocked

Body found:

Living Room   Dining Room   Bedroom   Kitchen   Attic   Basement   Other (describe)

Location in room:

Position of body: On back   Face down   Other:

Condition of body:

Fully clothed   Partially clothed   Unclothed

Preservation: Well preserved   Decomposed

Estimated Rigor: Complete   Head   Arms   Legs

Livor: Front   Back   Localized

Color:

Blood: Absent   Present   Location

Ligatures: Yes   No

Apparent wounds: None   Gunshot   Stab   Blunt force

Number:

Location: Head   Neck   Chest   Abdomen   Extremities

Hanging: Yes   No   Means:

Weapon(s) present: Gun (estimate caliber)

Type:

Knife:

Other (describe)

Condition of surroundings: Orderly   Untidy   Disarray

Odors: Decomposition   Other

Evidence of last food preparation:

Where:

Type:

Dated material:

Mail:

Newspapers:

TV guide:

Liquor bottles:

Last contact with deceased:

Date:

Type of contact:

Name of contact:

Evidence of robbery: Yes   No   Not determined

Identification of deceased: Yes   No

If yes, how accomplished:

If no, how is it to be accomplished:

Evidence of drug use: (prescription and nonprescription)   Yes   No

If drugs present, collect them and send with body.

Evidence of drug paraphernalia: Yes   No

Type:

Evidence of sexually deviant practices: Yes   No

Type: (collect and send with body)

Name and telephone number of investigating officer:

Source: James C. Beger, M.D., and William F. Enos, M.D. *FBI Law Enforcement Bulletin.* August 1981, pp. 16–18. Reprinted by permission of the FBI.

Sample Form for Reporting Bias Crime

BIAS OFFENSE REPORT

AGENCY IDENTIFIER (ORI)_____

MONTH AND YEAR_____   AGENCY NAME_____

This form is to be used to report any bias motivated crimes in violation of Minnesota State Statute 626.5531. The chief law enforcement officer for an agency must complete form and return to the Department of Public Safety, Office of Information Systems Management, 314 Transportation Building, 395 John Ireland Blvd., St. Paul, Minnesota 55155 within 30 days (Laws of Minnesota, 1996, Chapter 643).

A. GENERAL OFFENSE INFORMATION

1) Agency Case Number: _____ 2) Date of Offense: _____

3) Bias offense base on: ❑ Officer's belief ❑ Victim's belief

4) *Description of Offense: _____ 5) *Disposition: _____

6) *Type of Bias and Description: _____ / _____

                         Type Code   Description Code or Literal

7) *Target: _____ 8) Place of Occurrence: _____

B. VICTIM/OFFENDER INFORMATION

9) VICTIMS				10) OFFENDERS			11) *RELATIONSHIP TO VICTIM	12) AFFILIATION (if any)
#	Age	Sex	Race	Age	Sex	Race		
1								
2								
3								
4								
5								
6								
7								
8								
9								
10								
11								
12								
13								
14								
15								

COMMENTS: _____

_____

_____

_____

*Use code tables on reverse.

Return to: DPS/OISM
314 DOT Building
395 John Ireland Blvd.
St. Paul, MN 55155

CODE TABLES

4) *DESCRIPTION of OFFENSE:*

To be used in further identifying offense
01-Cross Burning
02-Swastika
03-Bombing
04-Hanging in Effigy
05-Disturbing Public Meeting
06-Graffiti
07-Spitting
08-Letter
09-Verbal Abuse (Person to Person)
10-Telephone
11-Homicide
12-Criminal Sexual Conduct
13-Robbery
14-Burglary
15-Aggravated Assault
16-Arson
17-Larceny Theft
18-Disturbing the Peace
19-Property Damage
20-Simple Assault
00-Other (Describe)

5) *DISPOSITION:* Based on CJRS Reporting
System—Major Offenses
A-Arrest of Adult and/or Adult & Juvenile
J-Arrest of Juvenile
E-Exceptionally Cleared
U-Unfounded
P-Pending

6) *TYPE of BIAS and DESCRIPTION:*

Type	Description
01-Racial	W-White
	H-White/Hispanic Origin
	N-Negro/Black
	B-Black/Hispanic Origin
	I-Indian or Alaskan Native
	M-Indian w/Hispanic Origin
	O-Asian or Pacific Islander
	A-Asian or Pacific Islander w/Hispanic Origin
02-Religious	01-Catholic
	02-Hindu/Buddhist
	03-Islamic/Moslem
	04-Jewish
	05-Protestant
	06-Fundamentalist
	07-Other (Describe)
03-National Origin	Specify

04-Sex	M-Male
	F-Female
05-Age	Specify age(s)
06-Disability	Specify disability
07-Sexual Orientation	01-Homosexual Male
	02-Homosexual Female
	03-Heterosexual Male
	04-Heterosexual Female

7) *TARGET CODES:*

01-Person
02-Private Property
03-Public Property

8) *PLACE of OCCURRENCE:*

01-Residence
02-Hotel, Motel or Other Commercial Short-Term Residence
03-Parking Lot Areas
04-Business
05-Vehicle
06-Street/Sidewalk
07-Highway/Freeway
08-Park/School Ground
09-Vacant Lot
10-Jail
11-Rural Area/Country Road
12-Cemetery
13-Religious Building
14-Government Building
15-School Building
16-Private Club
17-Other (Describe)

11) *RELATIONSHIP of OFFENDER to VICTIM:*

01-Family Member
02-Neighbor
03-Acquaintance
04-Boyfriend/Ex-Boyfriend
05-Girlfriend/Ex-Girlfriend
06-Ex-Husband
07-Ex-Wife
08-Employee
09-Employer
10-Friend
11-Homosexual Relation
12-Other-Known to Victim
13-Stranger
14-Gang Member
15-Peace Officer Related
16-Unknown
17-Other (Describe)

Source: Reprinted by permission of the Minnesota Bureau of Criminal Apprehension.

Glossary

Number in parentheses is the chapter in which the term is discussed.

A

ABANDONMENT desertion of children by their parents. (11)

ACCELERANTS substances that cause fires to burn faster and hotter. (16)

ACTIVE VOICE the subject performs the action of the sentence. In contrast to passive voice. (3)

ADIPOCERE soapy appearance of a dead body left for weeks in a hot, moist location. (8)

ADMINISTRATIVE WARRANT official permission to inspect a given property to determine compliance with city regulations; for example, compliance with fire codes. (16)

ADMISSION statement containing some information concerning the elements of a crime, but falling short of a full confession. (6)

ADVERSARY SYSTEM the justice system used in the United States; establishes clearly defined roles for both the prosecution and the defense and sets the judge as the neutral party. (21)

ADWARE a type of spyware used by advertisers to gather consumer and marketing information. (17)

AGGRAVATED ARSON intentionally destroying or damaging a dwelling or other property, real or personal, by means of fire or explosives, creating an imminent danger to life or great bodily harm, which risk was known or reasonably foreseeable to the suspect. (16)

AGGRAVATED ASSAULT (FELONIOUS ASSAULT) an unlawful attack by one person on another to inflict severe bodily injury. (9)

ALGOR MORTIS the postmortem cooling process of the body. (8)

ALLIGATORING checking of charred wood giving the appearance of alligator skin. Large, rolling blisters indicate rapid, intense heat; small, flat blisters indicate long, low heat. (16)

ANALOGS drugs created by adding to or omitting something from an existing drug. (18)

ANTICHRIST the son of Satan. (19)

ARREST taking a person into custody in the manner authorized by law. (7)

ARSON the malicious, willful burning of a building or property. *See also* **aggravated arson.** (16)

ASPHYXIATION death or unconsciousness resulting from insufficient oxygen to support the red blood cells reaching the body tissues and the brain. (8)

ASSAULT unlawfully threatening to harm another person, actually harming another person or attempting to do so. Formerly referred to threats of or attempts to cause bodily harm, but now usually includes *battery*. (9)

ASSOCIATIVE EVIDENCE evidence that links a suspect with a crime. (5)

ASYMMETRIC WARFARE combat used by a weaker state or nonstate entity challenges even a superpower by refusing to confront the stronger adversary head-to-head, striking where they least expect it. (20)

AUTOEROTIC ASPHYXIATION accidental death from suffocation, strangulation or chemical asphyxia resulting from a combination of ritualistic behavior, oxygen deprivation, danger, and fantasy for sexual gratification. (8)

AUTOMATED FINGERPRINT IDENTIFICATION SYSTEM (AFIS) a computerized system of reviewing and mapping fingerprints. (5)

B

BACKING marking photographs on their back with a felt-tip pen or label to indicate the photographer's initials, date photo was taken, brief description of what it depicts and the direction of north. Evidence can be circled on the back of the photo in the same way. (2)

BAIT MONEY currency whose serial numbers are recorded and which is placed so it can be added to any robbery loot. (12)

BALLISTICS broadly defined as the study of the dynamics of projectiles, from propulsion through flight to impact; a narrower definition is the study of the functioning of firearms. (5)

BASELINE (PLOTTING) METHOD establishes a straight line from one fixed point to another from which measurements are taken at right angles. (2)

BATTERY actually hitting or striking someone. (9)

BEELZEBUB a powerful demon, subordinate only to Satan, according to Satanists. (19)

BENCH TRIAL a trial is before a judge without a jury. (21)

BEST EVIDENCE the original object, or the highest available degree of proof that can be produced. (5)

BIAS CRIME a crime motivated by bigotry and hatred against a specific group of people. (19)

BIGAMY marrying another person when one or both of the parties are already married. (10)

BIOMETRICS the statistical study of biological data such as fingerprints. (5,17)

BIOTERRORISM involves such biological weapons of mass destruction (WMD) as anthrax, botulism and smallpox. (20)

BLACK MASS diabolical communion ritual performed by Satanists that mocks and desecrates the Christian mass. (19)

BLIND REPORTING allows sexual assault victims to retain their anonymity and confidentiality while sharing critical information with law enforcement. It also permits victims to gather legal information from law enforcement without having to commit immediately to an investigation. (10)

BLOODS an African American gang; associated with the colors red and green. (19

BLOWING A SAFE opening a safe using cotton, primer cap, copper wire and nitroglycerine. (13)

BOOKMAKING soliciting and accepting bets on any type of sporting event. (18)

BOOT to start up a computer. (17)

BORE the inside portion of a weapon's barrel, which is surrounded by lands and grooves. (5)

BRACKETS a testimony tactic that allows the witness some leeway and helps him or her retain credibility; provides a range, for example, he was 40 to 50 feet away. (21)

BRADY RULE entitles the accused to information as provided by the statutes of the state and disclosure of exculpatory evidence. (21)

BROWSER a computer program that accesses and displays data from the World Wide Web, for example, Internet Explorer. (17)

"BUGGING" using a machine to record conversations within a room without the consent of those involved. (7)

***BUIE* SWEEP** synonymous with *protective sweep*; the authorized search by police of areas immediately adjoining the place of arrest. Held constitutional in *Maryland v Buie* (1990). (4)

BURGLARY the unlawful entry of a structure to commit a felony or theft. (13)

BURLS the large gnarly root at the base of walnut trees, sought after by tree "rustlers." (14)

BURN INDICATORS visible evidence of the effects of heating or partial burning. (16)

BURNING A SAFE opening a safe using a burn bar or an oxy-acetylene tank, a hose and a torch. (13)

BYTE the amount of space needed to store one character of information. (17)

C

CADAVERIC SPASM a condition occurring in certain muscle groups that can indicate suicide. Usually occurs when the victim is holding something at the time of death and the hand closes tightly around the object due to the stress and tension of dying. Does not disappear as rigor mortis does. (8)

CALIBER refers to the diameter of a weapon's bore as measured between lands, as well as the size of bullet intended to be used with a specific weapon. (5)

CAPITAL FLIGHT large-scale removal of funds or capital from a country; not to be confused with money laundering. (18)

CARJACKING taking of a motor vehicle from a person by force or the threat of force. A new category of robbery. (12)

***CARROLL* DECISION** established that vehicles may be searched without a warrant if there is probable cause for the search and if the vehicle would be gone before a search warrant could be obtained. (4)

CAST to make an impression using plaster of Paris or a similar substance. Also, the physical reproduction of such an impression. (5)

CHAIN OF CUSTODY *See chain of evidence.* (5)

CHAIN OF EVIDENCE documentation of what has happened to evidence from the time it was discovered until it is needed in court, including every person who has had custody of the evidence and why. (5)

CHICKEN HAWK a pedophile, often using the Internet using chat lines and member profiles to locate potential victims. (11)

CHILD MOLESTATION the violation of a child by lewd or lascivious acts, indecent exposure, incest or rape. Usually a felony. (10)

CHILD SEXUAL ABUSE includes sexually molesting a child, performing sexual acts with a child and statutory rape and seduction. (11)

***CHIMEL* DECISION** established that in a search incidental to a lawful arrest, the search must be made simultaneously with the arrest and must be confined to the area within the suspect's immediate control. (4)

CHOP SHOP an auto body shop that disassembles stolen vehicles and sells the parts. (15)

CHOPPING A SAFE opening a safe by chopping a hole in it. (13)

CHRONOLOGICAL ORDER in time sequence. (3)

CIRCLE SEARCH (PATTERN) begins at the center of the crime scene and then spreads out in ever-widening concentric circles. (4)

CIRCUMSTANTIAL EVIDENCE a fact or event that tends to incriminate a person in a crime; e.g., being seen running from a crime scene. (5)

CIVIL LIABILITY a person's risk of being sued. Any person acting under the authority of law who violates another person's constitutional rights can be sued. (1)

CLASS CHARACTERISTICS features that place an item into a specific category; e.g., the size and shape of a tool. (5)

CLOSE TAIL moving surveillance by which the subject is kept constantly within view. Also called a *tight tail*. (7)

CLUB DRUGS drugs commonly found at Raves (dance parties). (18)

COGNITIVE INTERVIEW interviewing technique that helps victims or witnesses put themselves mentally at the scene of the crime. (6)

COMMERCIAL BURGLARY one that involves churches, schools, barns, public buildings, shops, offices, stores, factories, warehouses, stables, ships and railroad cars. (13)

COMMERCIAL EXPLOITATION having as a direct or indirect goal monetary or other material gain. (11)

COMMUNITY POLICING a philosophy that the police must work with the community through partnerships and problem solving to address problems of crime and disorder; a belief that by working together, the police and the community can accomplish what neither can accomplish alone. (1)

COMPASS-POINT (PLOTTING) METHOD measures the angles between two lines. (2)

COMPETENT EVIDENCE evidence that has been properly collected, identified, filed and continuously secured. (5)

COMPETENT PHOTOGRAPH a photograph that accurately represents what it purports to represent, is properly identified and is properly placed in the chain of evidence and secured until court presentation. (2)

COMPLAINANT the person who requests an investigation or that action be taken. Is often the victim of a crime. (6)

COMPUTER CRIME that which involves the addition, deletion, change or theft of information. (17)

COMPUTER VIRUS a computer program created specifically to "infect" other programs with copies of itself; it attacks, attaches itself to and becomes part of another executable program. (17)

CONCISE avoiding wordiness; making every word count without leaving out important facts. (3)

CONCLUSIONARY LANGUAGE nonfactual; drawing inferences; for example, "The man was *nervous*"; to be avoided in police reports. (3)

CONFESSION information supporting the elements of a crime that is provided and attested to by any person involved in committing the crime. Can be oral or written. (6

CONFIDENCE GAME obtains money or property by a trick, device or swindle that takes advantage of a victim's trust in the swindler. The confidence game offers a get-rich-quick scheme. (14)

CONNOTATIVE adjective describing words that have an emotional effect, with meanings that impart either positive or negative overtones. (3)

CONTAGION EFFECT a phenomenon in which media publicity of an act or event inspires more such acts or events; for example, the belief that coverage of terrorism inspires more terrorism. (20)

CONTAMINATION the post-crime transfer of material to or from evidence. (5)

CONTENT *what* is said in a narrative, as opposed to form, which is *how* a narrative is written. The content of an effective report is factual, accurate, objective, and complete. (3)

COOK (METH) someone who produces methamphetamine. (18)

CORPORATE CRIME *see* **WHITE-COLLAR CRIME**. (14)

CORPUS DELICTI the elements of a specific crime. Evidence establishing that a specific crime has been committed. (5)

CORPUS DELICTI EVIDENCE all evidence establishing that a crime was committed. (5)

COVEN a group of witches or Satanists. (19

COVER assumed identity used while on an undercover assignment. (7)

CRACK cocaine mixed with baking soda and water, heated in a pan and then dried and split into pellet-size bits or chunks, which are smoked to produce effects reportedly ten times greater than cocaine at a tenth the cost. (18)

CRACKER a computer hacker in the negative sense; someone who cracks software protection and removes it, deliberately and maliciously intruding into a computer or network to cause damage. (17)

CRAMMING billing consumers for unauthorized, misleading, or deceptive charges, such as a personal 800 number, paging, and voice mail. (14)

CRANK a street name for methamphetamine, not to be confused with crack. (18)

CRAZING formation of irregular cracks in glass due to rapid, intense heat. Can indicate arson or the use of an accelerant. (16)

CREDIT CARD any credit plate, charge plate, courtesy card or other identification or device used to obtain a cash advance, a loan or credit or to purchase or lease property or services on the issuer's or holder's credit. (14)

CRIME an act or omission forbidden by law and punishable by a fine, imprisonment or even death. Crimes and their penalties are established and defined by state and federal statutes and local ordinances. (1)

CRIME MAPPING focuses on the location of crimes-the hot spots where most crimes occur-rather than on the criminal. (1)

CRIME PREVENTION THROUGH ENVIRONMENTAL DESIGN (CPTED) altering physical characteristics of a property so as to make it less attractive to criminals, e.g., removing dense shrubbery next to windows and doors, improving lighting, and closing garage doors. Also called *target hardening*. (13)

CRIMINAL ENTERPRISE by FBI definition, a group of individuals with an identified hierarchy, or comparable structure, engaged in significant criminal activity. While *organized crime* and *criminal enterprise* are often equated and used interchangeably, several federal statutes specifically delineate the elements of an *enterprise* that must be proven to convict individuals or groups under those statutes. (18)

CRIMINAL HOMICIDE includes murder and manslaughter and is a felony. (8)

CRIMINAL INTENT performing an unlawful act on purpose, knowing the act to be illegal. (1)

CRIMINAL INVESTIGATION seeking all facts associated with a crime to determine the truth: what happened and who is responsible. (1)

CRIMINAL NEGLIGENCE acts of commission or omission creating situations resulting in unreasonable risk of death or great bodily harm. (8)

CRIMINAL PROFILING method of suspect identification that attempts to identify the individual's mental, emotional and psychological characteristics. Also called *psychological profiling*. (7)

CRIMINAL STATUTE legislative act relating to crime and its punishment. (1)

CRIMINALIST a person who searches for, collects, and preserves physical evidence in the investigation of crime and suspected criminals. Also called a crime scene technician, examiner, or investigator. (1)

CRIMINALISTICS a branch of forensic science involved with the recording, identification, and interpretation of the minutiae (minute details) of physical evidence. (1)

CRIPS an African American gang; associated with the colors blue and purple. (19)

CROSS CONTAMINATION allowing items of evidence to touch one another and, thus, exchange matter. (5)

CROSS-EXAMINATION questioning by the opposite side in a trial that attempts to assess the validity of testimony given under direct examination. (21)

CROSS-PROJECTION SKETCH a sketch that presents the floor and walls of a room on the same surface. (2)

CULT a system of religious beliefs and rituals and its body of adherents. (19)

CULTURAL GANGS neighborhood-centered gangs that exist independently of criminal activity. (19)

CULTURALLY ADROIT skilled in interacting across gender, ethnic, generational, social, and political group lines. (1)

CUNNILINGUS sexual activity involving oral contact with the female genitals. (10)

CURTILAGE the portion of the residence that is not open to the public and is reserved for private owner or family use-in contrast to sidewalks and alleys, which are used by the public. (4)

CUSTODIAL ARREST *see* **IN CUSTODY.** (6)

CUSTODIAL INTERROGATION questioning by law enforcement officers after a person has been taken into custody or otherwise deprived of freedom in a significant way. Requires that the Miranda warning be given. (6)

CYBERCRIME part of the larger category of *computer crime*, a criminal act that is carried out using cybertechnology and that takes place in cyberspace. (17)

CYBERSPACE an intangible, virtual world existing in the network connections between two or more computers. Also called the *cyberrealm*. (17)

CYBERSTALKING preying on a victim via computer. (9)

CYBERTECHNOLOGY the spectrum of computing and information/communication technologies, from individual computers to computer networks to the Internet. (17)

CYBERTERRORISM a premeditated, politically motivated attack against information, computer systems, computer programs, and data that results in harm to noncombatant targets by subnational groups or clandestine agents. It also refers to the use of a computer system as a conduit for causing terror. (17,19)

D

DANGEROUS WEAPON any firearm, loaded or unloaded; any device designed as a weapon and capable of producing great bodily harm or death; or any other device or instrument that is used or intended to be used in a way likely to produce great bodily harm or death.

DATA MINING a process that uses powerful analytical tools to quickly and thoroughly explore mountains of data to discover new patterns or confirm suspected patterns or trends. (1)

DATA REMANENCE refers to the residual physical representation of data that has been erased from a computer's hard drive. (17)

DATE RAPE type of sexual assault, where the victim knows the suspect. (10)

DAUBERT STANDARD the two-pronged requirement that an expert's testimony be both reliable and relevant. (5)

DE FACTO **ARREST** the functional equivalent of an arrest; illegally bringing someone in for questioning without probable cause. Any evidence obtained through this method is inadmissible in court. (7)

DEBIT CARD a card presented to a merchant exactly as a credit card would be, with the amount instantly credited before verification of the existence of funds is established. Also called a *check card*. (14)

DECONFLICTION protocol or guidelines to avoid conflict; can be applied to declassified and confidential investigations. (20)

DEDUCTIVE REASONING a logical process in which a conclusion follows from specific facts; a reconstructive process based on specific pieces of evidence to establish proof that a suspect is guilty of an offense. (1)

DEFENSE WOUNDS nonfatal wounds incurred by victims as they attempt to ward off attackers. Indicative of murder. (8)

DEMINIMUS COMMUNICATION allowed or acceptable contact between a witness and juror, such as exchanging a simple hello or giving directions. (21)

DENIAL-OF-SERVICE (DoS) ATTACK a disruption or degradation of a computer or network's Internet connection or e-mail service that interrupts the regular flow of data. Using multiple agents to create a widespread interruption is a Distributed DoS, or DDoS. (17)

DENOTATIVE adjective describing words that have little emotional effect and are objective in their meaning. (3)

DEPRESSANT drug that reduces restlessness and emotional tension and induces sleep; most common are the barbiturates. (18)

DEPTH OF CHAR how deeply wood is burned. (16)

DESIGNER DRUGS substances created by adding to or taking something away from an existing drug. (18)

DIRECT EVIDENCE *see PRIMA FACIE* **EVIDENCE.** (5)

DIRECT EXAMINATION the initial questioning of a witness or defendant during a trial by the lawyer who is using the person's testimony to further his or her case. (21)

DIRECT QUESTION a question that is to the point with little chance of misinterpretation, for example, "What time did you leave?" (6)

DISCOVERY PROCESS the pretrial disclosure between prosecution and defense as to the evidence they intend to use at trial, thus avoiding "trial by surprise." (21)

DISK DRIVE physical location of disks on a computer (internal hard drives are usually labeled as C Drive; floppy drives are generally identified as A or B Drive). (17)

DISRUPTERS devices that use gunpowder to fire a jet of water or a projectile at a particular component of an explosive to make it safe. (16)

DNA deoxyribonucleic acid. An organic substance found in the nucleus of living cells that provides the genetic code determining a person's individual characteristics. (5)

DNA PROFILING forensic analysis of blood, hair, saliva, semen or cells from almost any part of the body to ascertain a positive identity or match. (5)

DOMAIN NAME the unique name of a computer system on the Internet that distinguishes it from all other online systems; associated with a specific IP address and easier to remember than a string of numbers. *Not* the same as a web address. (17)

DOMESTIC VIOLENCE (DV) a pattern of behaviors involving physical, sexual, economic and emotional abuse, alone or in combination, by an intimate partner often for the purpose of establishing and maintaining power and control over the other partner. (9)

DOS Disk Operating System. (17)

DOWNLOAD to receive data, files or pictures from another computer; opposite of *upload*. (17)

DRAGGING A SAFE *see* **PULLING.** (13)

DRUG ABUSE use of illegal drugs. (18)

DRUG ADDICT a person who habitually uses habit-forming narcotic drugs and thus endangers the public morals, health, safety or welfare; or who is or has been so far addicted to habit-forming narcotic drugs as to have lost self-control. (18)

DRUG GANGS smaller than other gangs; much more cohesive; focused on the drug business; strong, centralized leadership with market-defined roles. (19)

DYE PACK a bundle of currency containing a colored dye and tear gas. Taken during a robbery, it is activated when the robber crosses an electromagnetic field at the facility's exit, staining the money with brightly colored dye and emitting a cloud of colored smoke. (12)

DYER ACT made interstate transportation of a stolen motor vehicle a federal crime and allowed for federal assistance in prosecuting such cases. (15)

E

ECONOMIC CRIME *see* **WHITE-COLLAR CRIME.** (14)

ECOTERRORISM seeks to inflict economic damage to those who profit from the destruction of the natural environment. (20)

E-CRIME electronic crime. Any criminal violation in which a computer or electronic media is used in the commission of that crime. Also called *cybercrime.* (17)

ECSTASY (MDMA) a derivative of amphetamine or speed, a powerful stimulant; an increasingly popular club drug. (18)

ELDER ABUSE the physical or mental mistreatment of a senior citizen. May include fraud as well as assault, battery and even murder. (9)

ELECTRONIC SURVEILLANCE using wiretapping and/or bugging to obtain information. (7)

ELEMENTS OF THE CRIME conditions that must exist and be proven to exist for an act to be called a specific kind of crime. (1)

"ELEPHANT IN A MATCHBOX" DOCTRINE the doctrine requiring that searchers consider the probable size and shape of evidence they seek; e.g., large objects cannot be concealed in tiny areas. (4)

ELIMINATION PRINTS fingerprints taken of every individual whose prints are likely to be found at the crime scene but who is *not* a suspect. (5)

E-MAIL electronic mail. (17)

EMBEZZLEMENT fraudulent appropriation of property by a person to whom it was entrusted. (14)

EMOTIONAL ABUSE causing fear or feelings of unworthiness in others by such means as locking them in closets, ignoring them or constantly belittling them. (11)

ENCRYPTION a technique that puts information in code and thus obscures a normally comprehensible message. (17)

ENTRAPMENT tricking someone into committing a crime that they would not normally commit. (7)

EQUIVOCAL DEATH death inquiries that are open to interpretation investigations; there may be two or more meanings; the case may be presented as either a homicide or a suicide depending upon the circumstances. (8)

EVIDENCE data on which a judgment or conclusion may be based; used for determining the facts in a case, for later laboratory examination and for direct presentation in court. (5)

EXCEPTIONALLY CLEARED disposition of a case when circumstances outside the investigation result in no charges being filed (e.g., if the suspect dies). (21)

EXCESSIVE FORCE more than ordinary force, justified only when exceptional resistance occurs and there is no other way to make the arrest. (7)

EXCITED DELIRIUM a term used to describe the manifestations of extreme drug abuse. (18)

EXCLUSIONARY RULE established that the courts cannot accept evidence obtained by unreasonable searches and seizures, regardless of its relevance to the case (*Weeks v. United States*). (4)

EXIGENT CIRCUMSTANCES emergency situations; they do not require a warrant. (4)

EXCULPATORY EVIDENCE physical evidence favorable to the accused, that would clear one of blame; for example, having a blood type different from that found at a homicide. (1)

EXCUSABLE HOMICIDE unintentional, truly accidental killing of another person. (8)

EXHIBITIONISTS people who gain sexual satisfaction by exposing themselves. (10)

EXPERT WITNESS a person having special knowledge not known to persons of moderate education and/or experience in the same field. (21)

EXPLOITATION taking unfair advantage of people or using them illegally. (11)

EXPRESSIVE VIOLENCE that stemming from hurt feelings, anger, or rage, in contrast to instrumental violence, which is goal-directed predatory behavior used to exert control. (8)

F

FACT something known to be true. (1,3)

FELLATIO sexual activity involving oral contact with the male genitals. (10)

FELONIOUS ASSAULT *see* **AGGRAVATED ASSAULT.** (9)

FELONY a major crime such as homicide, aggravated assault or robbery. Usually carries a penalty of imprisonment in a state penitentiary or death. (1)

FEMICIDE the murder of a woman. (9)

FENCE a seller of stolen property. (13)

FIELD IDENTIFICATION on-the-scene identification of a suspect by the victim of or witnesses to a crime, conducted within minutes of the commission of the crime. (7)

FIELD INTERVIEW when questioning occurs spontaneously at the scene. (6)

FINISHED SCALE DRAWING *see* **SCALE DRAWING.** (2)

FIRE TRIANGLE the three elements necessary for a substance to burn: heat, fuel and air. (16)

FIREWALL a software or hardware protective measure that blocks ports of access to a computer or network to prevent unauthorized access and stop malicious programs from entering. (17)

FIRST PERSON the use of *I, me, we* and *us* in speaking and writing; in contrast to the second person (*you*) and the third person (*he* or *this officer*). (3)

FIRST-DEGREE MURDER premeditated killing of another person or killing someone while committing or attempting to commit a felony. (8)

FIXED SURVEILLANCE *see* **STATIONARY SURVEILLANCE.** (7)

FLAGGERS thieves who go around neighborhoods hitting mailboxes with their flags up, searching for envelopes containing checks and other forms of payment. (14)

FLASHROLL money used in an undercover drug buy. (18)

FLIPPING *see* **PROPERTY FLIPPING.** (14)

FLOOR-RELEASE LIMIT maximum dollar amount that may be paid with a check or credit card without authorization from the central office. (14)

FLOPPY DISK magnetic media capable of storing large amounts of information (a 3 ½" disk can hold as much as 470 sheets of paper). (17)

FLUFFING telephone rates are increased without notification. (14)

FORCE any non-negotiable use of police authority to influence citizen behavior. (7)

FORCIBLE RAPE sexual intercourse against a person's will by use or threat of force. (10)

FORENSIC ANTHROPOLOGY uses standard scientific techniques developed by physical anthropologists and archaeologists to identify human skeletal remains as they relate to criminal cases; a relatively new but rapidly expanding field of forensics. (5)

FORENSIC SCIENCE application of the physical sciences and their technology to examining physical evidence of crimes; includes the branch of criminalistics. (1)

FORGERY signing someone else's name to a document or altering the name or amount on a check or document with the intent to defraud. (14)

FORM *how* a narrative is written, in contrast to content, which is *what* is said in a narrative. The form of a well-written report is concise, clear, grammatically and mechanically correct, and written in standard English. (3)

FRAUD intentional deception to cause a person to give up property or some lawful right. (14)

FRISK an external search of an individual's clothing. Also called a *pat down*. (4)

FRUIT-OF-THE-POISONOUS-TREE DOCTRINE the doctrine that evidence obtained as a result of an earlier illegality must be excluded from trial. (4)

FULL FAITH AND CREDIT a legal status wherein a document, contract, license, or court order issued anywhere in the country is legally binding and enforceable nationwide. (9)

G

GANG a group of people who form an allegiance for a common purpose and engage in unlawful or criminal activity. (19)

GENETIC FINGERPRINT DNA analysis used to positively identify a person. (5)

GIGABYTE (GB) one billion bytes. (17)

GOOD-FAITH DOCTRINE a doctrine stating that illegally obtained evidence may be admitted into trial if the police were truly not aware that they were violating the suspect's Fourth Amendment rights. (4)

GOODS property, including anything that is tangible and has value; e.g., gas, clothing, money, food. (14)

GOUGING companies have undisclosed fees when calls are made from pay phones or hotel rooms. (14)

GRAFFITI wall writing; sometimes called the "newspaper of the street." (19)

GRAND LARCENY a felony based on the substantial value of the property stolen. (14)

GRID (SEARCH PATTERN) adaptation of the lane search pattern in which the lanes are traversed and then cross-traversed. *See also* **LANE SEARCH PATTERN.** (4)

H

HACKER a computer buff; one who intrudes into another's computer or network for the challenge and status; not necessarily a negative term. In contrast to a *cracker*, who is someone who intrudes to commit a crime. (17)

HACKTIVISM using cyberspace to harass or sabotage sites that conduct activities or advocate philosophies that hacktivists find unacceptable. (17)

HALLUCINOGEN a mind-expanding drug; e.g., LSD, DMT and PCP or angel dust. (18)

HAND OF GLORY the left hand of a person who has died. (19)

HARD DISK a non-removable means of data storage located inside a computer. (17)

HARDWARE (COMPUTER) computer equipment, including the keyboard, monitor and printer. (17)

HARDWARE DISABLER a device designed to ensure a self-destruct sequence of any potential evidence. It may be present on or around a computer, with a remote power switch being the most prevalent of the disabler hardware devices. (17)

HATE CRIME a crime in which the defendant intentionally selects a victim, or in the case of a property crime, the property that is the object of the crime, because of the actual or perceived race, color, national origin, ethnicity, gender, disability or sexual orientation of any person." Also called *bias crime*. (19)

HATE INCIDENTS behaviors that, though motivated by bias against a victim's race, religion, ethnic/national origin, gender, age, disability or sexual orientation, are *not* criminal acts, e.g., hostile or hateful speech, or other disrespectful/discriminatory behavior motivated by bias. (19)

HAWALA an informal banking system based on trust and often bartering, common throughout the Middle East and used to transfer billions of dollars every year. (20)

HEAT OF PASSION extremely volatile emotional condition. (8)

HEBEPHILE person who selects high-school-age youths as sex victims. (11)

HEDONISTIC/SOCIAL GANGS only moderate drug use and offending, involved mainly in using drugs and having a good time; little involvement in crime, especially violent crime. (19)

HESITATION WOUNDS less severe cutting marks caused by an individual's attempts to build up courage before making a fatal cutting wound. Indicates suicide. (8)

HIT-AND-RUN BURGLARY theft in which a window is smashed to steal merchandise. Also called smash-and-grab. (13)

HOLDER person to whom a credit or debit card is issued. (14)

HOMICIDE the killing of one person by another. (8)

HOT SPOTS geographic areas with a higher incidence rate of criminal activity. (1)

HYPNOSIS a trancelike condition, psychically induced, in which the subject loses consciousness but responds to the hypnotist's suggestions. (6)

I

IDENTIFYING FEATURES *see* **INDIVIDUAL CHARACTERISTICS.** (5)

IDENTITY THEFT the criminal act of assuming someone else's identity for some type of gain, normally financial. (14)

IGNITERS substances or devices used to start a fire. (16)

IMAGING making a byte-by-byte copy of everything on the hard drive. (17)

IMMEDIATE CONTROL within a person's reach. (4)

IMMERSIVE IMAGING a 360-degree photographic view of a crime scene that allows viewers to virtually "walk through it" as though they were there. (2)

IMPEACH to discredit testimony; to call into question the truth or accuracy of what a prosecution witness testified to under direct examination. (21)

IN CUSTODY (CUSTODIAL ARREST) that point at which an officer has decided a suspect is not free to leave, there has been considerable deprivation of the suspect's liberty, or the officer has, in fact, arrested the suspect. (6)

IN LOCO PARENTIS having the authority to take the place of the parent. Teachers usually have this right. (9)

INCANTATIONS verbal spells. (19)

INCEST sexual intercourse with another person known to be nearer of kin than first cousin, in some states whether biological or adopted. (10)

INDECENT EXPOSURE revealing oneself to such an extent as to shock others' sense of decency. (10)

INDIRECT EVIDENCE that which merely tends to incriminate a person, such as a suspect's footprints found near the crime scene; also called *circumstantial evidence.* (5)

INDICATOR CRIMES offenses that, in situations involving the same victim and suspect, can establish a pattern of events indicative of an abusive relationship. (9)

INDIRECT QUESTION question that skirts the issue, for example, "How do you and the victim get along?" Should be used sparingly if at all. (6)

INDIVIDUAL CHARACTERISTICS features that set one item apart from others of the same type. Also called *identifying characteristics.* (5)

INDUCTIVE REASONING making a generalization and establishing it by gathering specific facts. (1)

INEVITABLE DISCOVERY DOCTRINE the doctrine that if the evidence would in all likelihood eventually be discovered anyway, it may be used even if it was obtained illegally. (4)

INFERENCE a conclusion based on reasoning. (1,3)

INFORMANT any individual who can provide information related to a case and who is not a complainant, witness, victim or suspect. (6)

INFORMATION AGE period of time driven by information rather than by agriculture or industry as in the past. (6)

INKLESS FINGERPRINTS fingerprints created through a procedure that uses pretreated or special card stock or standard cards to retain nonsmearable, nonerasable fingerprints that can be read by a computer. (5)

INSTRUMENTAL GANGS formed for the express purpose of criminal activity, primarily drug trafficking. (19)

INSTRUMENTAL VIOLENCE goal-directed predatory behavior used to exert control, in contrast to expressive violence, which stems from hurt feelings, anger, or rage. (8)

INTEGRATION the third and final step in the money laundering cycle, where criminals repatriate their money through seemingly legitimate business transactions. (14)

INTEGRITY OF EVIDENCE referring to the requirement that any item introduced in court must be in the same condition as when it was found at the crime scene. (5)

INTERNET PROTOCOL (IP) ADDRESS a unique number, analogous to a phone number, needed to access the Internet; commonly issued by a user's Internet Service Provider (ISP). (17)

INTERROGATION questioning people suspected of direct or indirect involvement in the crime being investigated. (6)

INTERVIEW questioning people not suspected of being involved in a crime but who know about the crime or the individuals involved in it. (6)

INTIFADA an armed uprising of Palestinians against Israel's occupation of the West Bank and the Gaza strip.

INTIMATE PARTS usually refers to the primary genital areas, groin, inner thighs, buttocks and breasts. (10)

INTUITION a "sudden knowing" without any conscious reasoning or apparent logic. Based on knowledge and experience or what is commonly called "street sense." An intangible urge; a "gut feeling" developed by experience. (1)

INVESTIGATE to observe or study closely; to inquire into something systematically in a search for truthful information. (1)

INVISIBLE FINGERPRINTS those not readily seen but that can be developed through powders or chemicals. (5)

INVOLUNTARY MANSLAUGHTER killing someone through extreme, culpable negligence. Unintentional homicide. (8)

ISP Internet Service Provider; a company that offers access to the Internet for a fee. (17)

J

JAMMING setting up roadblocks to make it difficult to switch in-state long distance. (14)

JIHAD a holy war. (20)

JUSTIFIABLE HOMICIDE killing another person under authorization of the law. (8)

K

KEYLESS DOORS doors that are unlocked by entering a set combination by pushing numbered pads in a programmed sequence. Used on some newer automobiles. (15)

KEYSTROKE LOGGING a diagnostic technique that captures a user's keystrokes; used in espionage to bypass security measures and obtain passwords or encryption keys. Also called *keylogging.* (17)

KIDNAPPING taking a person to another location by force, often for ransom. (11)

KILOBYTE (KB) one thousand bytes. (17)

L

LANDS two opposing ridges in the barrel of a firearm. (5)

LANE a narrow passage or strip. (4)

LANE-SEARCH PATTERN a search pattern that divides a crime scene into lanes by using stakes and strings or by having officers walk shoulder to shoulder or at arm's length. (4)

LARCENY/THEFT the unlawful taking, carrying, leading or riding away of property from another's possession. (14)

LASER-BEAM PHOTOGRAPHY an imaging process that reveals evidence indiscernible to the naked eye, such as a footprint in a carpet. (2)

LATENT FINGERPRINTS print impressions caused by perspiration on the ridges of the fingers being transferred to a surface or occurring as residues of oil, dirt or grease. (5)

LAYERING the second step in the money laundering process, where the money is cleaned by moving it around through a series of elaborate transactions, often involving offshore bank accounts and International Business Companies or IBCs. (14)

LEADS avenues bearing clues or potential sources of information relevant to solving a crime. (1)

LEAKAGE the illegal or unauthorized removal of cargo from the supply chain; a concept similar to that of shrinkage. (14)

LEGEND that part of a crime scene sketch containing the case number, name of victim or complainant, location, date, time, investigator, person(s) assisting, scale, direction of north and any other identifying information required by the department. (2)

LETHAL PREDATOR a extremely dangerous subtype of lethal criminal who possesses the four elements of lethal violence, multiple acts of sexual predation, mental abnormality, and legal sanity. (8)

LEWDNESS (WITH MINOR) touching a minor so as to arouse, appeal to or gratify the perpetrator's sexual desires; the touching may be done by the perpetrator or by the minor under the perpetrator's direction. (11)

LINE OF DEMARCATION (FIRE) a boundary between charred and uncharred material. (16)

LINEUP IDENTIFICATION having victims or witnesses identify suspects from among at least five individuals presented before them. Used when the suspect is in custody. (7)

LIVOR MORTIS *see* **POSTMORTEM LIVIDITY.** (8)

LOAN-SHARKING the loaning of money at exorbitant rates. (18)

LOCARD'S PRINCIPLE OF EXCHANGE a basic forensic theory that objects that come in contact with each other always transfer material, however minute, to each other. (1)

LOGIC BOMB secretly attaches another program to a company's computer system. The attached program monitors the input data and waits for some type of error to occur. When this happens, the new program exploits the weakness to steal money or company secrets or to sabotage the system. (17)

LONG-CON GAMES schemes in which the victims are sent for whatever money they can raise. (14)

LUST MURDER a sex-related homicide involving a sadistic, deviant assault, where the killer depersonalizes the victim, sexually mutilates the body and may displace body parts. (8)

LOOSE TAIL moving surveillance in which it does not matter if the subject is temporarily lost. (7)

M

MACROPHOTOGRAPHY photographic enlargement of a subject to show details of evidence such as fingerprints or tool marks. (2)

MAGICK the glue that binds occult groups; the supernatural act or force that causes a change in the environment. (19)

MALICIOUS INTENT (MALICE) ill will, wickedness, cruelty or recklessness; an evil intent, wish or design to annoy or injure another person. Can be inferred from an act done in willful disregard for the rights of another, an act done without just cause or excuse or an omission of a duty by willful disregard. (8)

MALTREATMENT includes neglect, medical neglect, physical abuse, sexual abuse and psychological maltreatment. (11)

MALWARE a contraction of "malicious software." Software developed to cause harm. (17)

MANSLAUGHTER unlawful killing of another person with no prior malice. Can be voluntary or involuntary. (8)

MARKER (PHOTOGRAPHIC) an item included in a photograph to show accurate or relative size. (2)

MASS MURDER when multiple victims are killed in a single incident by one or a few suspects. (8)

MATERIAL EVIDENCE that which is relevant to the specific case and forms a substantive part of the case presented or that has a legitimate and effective influence on the decision of the case. (5)

MATERIAL PHOTOGRAPH an image that relates to the specific case and the subject being discussed. (2)

MDMA 3,4-methylenedioxymethylamphetamine, known more commonly as *Ecstasy*; a powerful stimulant derivative of amphetamine or speed. (18)

MECHANICS the use of spelling, capitalization and punctuation in written communication (3)

MEGABYTE (MB) one million bytes. (17)

MEGAPIXEL pixels are the dots making up a digital image; one megapixel is about a million dots. (2)

MICROPHOTOGRAPHY taking pictures through a microscope to help identify minute particles of evidence (e.g., hair or fiber). (2)

MINOR a person under the legal age for becoming an adult, the most common being under the age of 16 or 18. (11)

MIRANDA WARNING informs suspects of their right to remain silent, to have counsel present and to have the state appoint and pay counsel if they cannot afford one. It also warns suspects that anything they say can be used against them in court. (6)

MISDEMEANOR a minor crime such as shoplifting or pilferage. Usually carries a fine or a short sentence in a county or municipal jail. (1)

MISOPED a person who hates children, has sex with them and then brutally destroys them. (11)

MOBILITY a characteristic assigned to an object that can be easily moved. (4)

MODEM a device linking a computer to telephone lines so that messages can be sent between computers at different locations. (17)

MODUS OPERANDI (MO) the characteristic way a criminal commits a specific type of crime. (1)

MOLESTATION (SEXUAL) acts motivated by unnatural or abnormal sexual interest in another person that would reasonably be expected to disturb, irritate or offend the victim. No touching of the victim is necessary. (11)

MONEY LAUNDERING converting illegally earned (dirty) cash to one or more alternative forms (clean) to conceal its illegal origin and true ownership. (14)

MONIKER street name; nickname. (19)

MOTION IN LIMINE a request for the judge to issue a protective order against prejudicial questions or statements. (21)

MOTOR VEHICLE any self-propelled device for moving persons or property or pulling implements, whether operated on land, water or air. Includes automobiles, trucks, buses, motorcycles, snowmobiles, vans, construction equipment, self-propelled watercraft and aircraft. (15)

MOVING SURVEILLANCE following people or vehicles on foot or in a vehicle to observe their actions or destinations. Also called *tailing*. (7)

MUG SHOTS photographs of those who have been taken into custody and booked. (2)

MULES individuals who sell or transport drugs for a regular dealer in return for being assured of a personal drug supply. (18)

MUMMIFICATION complete dehydration of all body tissues that occurs when a cadaver is left in an extremely dry, hot area. (8)

MUNCHAUSEN SYNDROME involves self-induced or self-inflicted injuries. (11)

MUNCHAUSEN SYNDROME BY PROXY (MSBP) a form of child abuse where the parent or adult caregiver deliberately stimulates or causes medical distress in a child. (1)

MURDER *see* **FIRST-, SECOND-** and **THIRD-DEGREE MURDER.** (8)

N

NARCOTIC a drug that is physically and psychologically addicting; examples include heroin, morphine, codeine and cocaine. (18)

NARRATIVE a technical report structured in chronological order describing a sequence of investigative events. (3)

NATIONAL CRIME INFORMATION CENTER (NCIC) the FBI clearinghouse for criminal fingerprint records and information on wanted criminals, stolen property, and vehicle information. (6)

NEGLECT failure to properly care for a child, property or one's actions. (11)

NETWORK relationships, links between people, and between people and their beliefs. Two or more computers connected for the purpose of sharing data and resources. (6,17)

NIGHTCAP PROVISION court-approved stipulation that an arrest or search warrant may be carried out at night. (7)

NO-KNOCK WARRANT search warrant that contains a special provision permitting officers to execute the warrant without first announcing themselves. (4)

NONCRIMINAL HOMICIDE classification that includes excusable and justifiable homicide. (8)

NONVERBAL COMMUNICATION messages conveyed by dress, eye contact, posture, gestures, distance, mannerisms, rate of speech and tone of voice. (6)

O

OBJECTIVE nonopinionated, fair, and impartial. (3)

OCCULT secret knowledge of supernormal powers. Many cults claim to have such knowledge. (19)

OPEN TAIL no extraordinary means are used to remain undetected. Also called a *rough tail*. (7)

OPERATING SYSTEM (OS) the software installed in a computer responsible for the control and management of the hardware; it allows the computer to run various application software, such as word-processing programs, graphics programs, spreadsheets, etc. (17)

OPINION a personal belief. (1,3)

ORAL COPULATION the act of joining the mouth of one person with the sexual organ of another person. *See* **CUNNILINGUS** and **FELLATIO.** (10)

ORDINANCE an act of the legislative body of a municipality relating to all the rules governing the municipality, inclusive of misdemeanor crimes (1)

ORGANIZED CRIME two or more persons conspiring to commit crimes for profit and using fear and corruption to obtain immunity from the law. (18)

ORGANIZED/CORPORATE GANGS heavy involvement in all kinds of crime, heavy use and sale of drugs; may resemble major corporations, with separate divisions handling sales, marketing, discipline, and so on; discipline is strict, and promotion is based on merit. (19)

OTC DRUGS over-the-counter drugs. (18)

OSTEOGENESIS IMPERFECTA (OI) a genetic disorder characterized by bones that break easily, often from little or no apparent cause. Also called *brittle bone disease*. (11)

OVERLAPPING a photographic technique whereby the entire scene is photographed in a clockwise direction with the picture so that a specific object is on the right side of the first photograph, on the next photo the same object is on the left side of the photo and so on until the entire scene is photographed. (2)

P

PARALLEL PROCEEDINGS pursing civil and criminal sanctions at the same time. (14)

PARTY GANGS commonly called "party crews"; relatively high use and sale of drugs, but only one major form of delinquency—vandalism, may contain both genders or may be one gender; many have no specific dress style, but some dress in stylized clothing worn by street gang members, such as baseball caps and oversize clothing; some have tattoos and use hand signs; their flexible turf is called the "party scene"; crews compete over who throws the biggest party, with alcohol, marijuana, nitrous oxide, sex and music critical party elements. (19)

PAST TENSE use of verbs that indicate that the action has already occurred, for example, *lived* rather than *lives*. (3)

PATDOWN *see* **FRISK.** (4)

PC personal computer. (17)

PECULIARITY REQUIREMENT dictates that a search conducted with a warrant must be limited to the specific area and specific items named in the warrant, as held in *Stanford v Texas* (1965). (4)

PEDOPHILE a person who is sexually attracted to young children. (10,11)

PEELING A SAFE opening a safe using a breast drill, a set of graduate drills and a jimmy. (13)

PENETRATION *see* **SEXUAL PENETRATION.** (10)

PETTY (PETIT) LARCENY a misdemeanor based on the value of the property stolen. (14)

PHARMING an emerging cybercrime that involves the hijacking of a domain name for the purpose of redirecting online traffic away from a legitimate Web site toward a fake site, such as a bogus bank Web site. Also refers to the dangerous act of rifling through the family medicine cabinet for pills, both OTC and prescription, combining everything in a bowl, scooping out and ingesting a handful and waiting to see what happens. (17, 18)

PHISHING the use of unsolicited e-mails to deceive Internet users into providing sensitive information, such as social security number or credit card numbers, by pretending to be a legitimate and trustworthy business or individual. Sometimes called *spoofing*. (17)

PHOTOGRAMMETRY making 3-D measurements of the real world directly from two-dimensional photographs. (2)

PHOTOGRAPHIC IDENTIFICATION having victims or witnesses identify suspects from among pictures of people of comparable general description. Used when a suspect is not in custody or when a fair lineup cannot be conducted. (7)

PHREAKING exploiting the telephone system's vulnerabilities to acquire free access and usage. Considered a type of electronic hacking. (17)

PHYSICAL ABUSE beating, whipping, burning or otherwise inflicting physical harm. (11)

PHYSICAL EVIDENCE anything real—that has substance—and helps to establish the facts of a case. (5)

PICTOMETRY a high-tech application of aerial photography that uses computer technology to integrate various aerial shots of a land-based artifact taken straight down (orthogonal) and from numerous angles (oblique) to generate a high-resolution 3-D image of the object. (2)

PIRACY the copying and use of computer programs in violation of copyrights and trade secret laws. (17)

PIXEL the smallest unit of a digital image, also referred to as a dot. (2)

PLACEMENT the first step in the process of laundering money that inserts the ill-gotten funds into the legitimate U.S. market; common methods include *smurfing* (technically known as *structuring*) whereby large amounts of cash are broken into increments less than $10,000, to avoid federal reporting requirements, and deposited into various bank accounts. (14)

PLAIN FEEL/TOUCH EVIDENCE an object discovered by a police officer who is lawfully patting down a suspect's outer clothing and which is *immediately* identified, by touch, as contraband; a warrantless seizure is justified because there is no invasion of the suspect's privacy beyond that already authorized by the officer's search for weapons (*Minnesota v. Dickerson*, 1993). (4)

PLAIN-VIEW EVIDENCE unconcealed evidence that is seen by an officer engaged in a lawful activity. (4)

PLANT *see* **STATIONARY SURVEILLANCE.** (7)

PLASTIC FINGERPRINTS impressions left in soft substances such as putty, grease, tar, butter or soft soap. *See also* **VISIBLE PRINTS.** (5)

POACHING illegally taking or possessing fish, game or other wildlife, including deer, elk, bear, pheasant, ducks, wild turkeys and grouse. (14)

POLYGRAPH lie detector. Scientifically measures respiration and depth of breathing, changes in the skin's electrical resistance and blood pressure and pulse. (6)

PONZI SCHEME a pyramid-type fraud scheme, named after Charles Ponzi, that involves using capital from new investors to pay off earlier investors, requiring an ever expanding base of new investors to support the financial obligations to the existing "higher ups," which, eventually and inevitably, will collapse. (14)

PORT SCANNING Looking for access (open "doors") into a computer. (17)

POSTMORTEM LIVIDITY dark blue or purple discoloration of the body where blood has drained to the lowest level after death. Also called *livor mortis* or simply *lividity*. (8)

PPI pixels per inch. (2)

PREDATION an intentional act of selecting, pursuing, and overpowering a person and then inflicting harm on that person for the pleasure of the predator. (8)

PREDATORY GANGS heavily involved in serious crimes (robberies, muggings) and the abuse of addictive drugs such as crack cocaine; may engage in selling drugs but not in organized fashion. (19)

PREMEDITATION considering, planning or preparing for an act, no matter how briefly, before committing it. (8)

PRESUMPTIVE EVIDENCE that which provides a reasonable basis for belief. (13)

PRETEXTUAL TRAFFIC STOPS stops of vehicles when an officer's intent (pretext) was not the real reason for the stop; presence of an ulterior motive on an officer's part for the stop. (7)

PRIMA FACIE EVIDENCE that made so by law; e.g., the blood alcohol level for intoxication. Also called *direct evidence*. (5)

PROBABLE CAUSE evidence that warrants a person of reasonable caution to believe that a crime has been committed. (4)

PROBATIVE EVIDENCE evidence that is vital for the investigation or prosecution of a case. Tending to prove or actually proving guilt or innocence. (5)

PROCESSING EVIDENCE includes discovering, recognizing and examining it; collecting, recording and identifying it; packaging, conveying and storing it; exhibiting it in court; and disposing of it when the case is closed. (5)

PROFILING *see* **PSYCHOLOGICAL PROFILING.** (7)

PROGRAM a series of commands instructing a computer to perform a desired task. (17)

PROPERTY all forms of tangible property, real and personal, including valuable documents, electricity, gas, water, heat and animals. (14)

PROPERTY FLIPPING a practice whereby an offender buys a property near its estimated market value, artificially inflates the property value through a false appraisal, and then resells (flips) the property, often within days of the original purchase, for a greatly increased price. Although flipping *per se* is not illegal, it often involves mortgage fraud, which is illegal. (14)

PROSTITUTION soliciting sexual intercourse for pay. (10)

PROTECTIVE SWEEP authority for the police to search areas immediately adjoining the place of arrest, justified when reasonable suspicion exists that another person might be present who poses a danger to the arresting officers. (4)

PROXY DATA remnants of an interaction, transfer or exchange of material between two items (Locard's exchange principle); the evidence analyzed by forensic scientists to uncover the relationships between people, places, and objects. (5)

PSYCHOLINGUISTICS the study of the mental processes involved in the comprehension, production, and acquisition of language. (5)

PSYCHOLOGICAL PROFILING indicates the type of person most likely to have committed a crime having certain unique characteristics. Also called simply *profiling*. (7)

PUBLIC SAFETY EXCEPTION ruling that police may interrogate a suspect without first giving the Miranda warning if a public threat exists that might be removed by having the suspect talk. (6)

PULLING LEVERS pulling every legal lever available to stop gang activity. (19)

PULLING (DRAGGING) A SAFE opening a safe with a heavy plate of steel by using a V-cut and drilling holes in the corners in which to insert bolts. (13)

PUNCHING A SAFE opening a safe with a short-handled sledge, a steel chisel and a drift pin. (13)

R

RACIAL PROFILING occurs when an officer focuses on an individual as a suspect based solely on that person's race. This is unconstitutional. (7)

RAID a planned, organized invasion that uses the element of surprise to recover stolen property, seize evidence and/or arrest a suspect. (7)

RAPE having sexual intercourse with a person against his or her will. (10)

RAPPORT a harmonious relationship between individuals created by genuine interest and concern. (6)

RAVES dance parties that feature fast-paced, repetitive electronic music and accompanying light shows and usually entail the use of alcohol, tobacco and drugs. (18)

REASONABLE FORCE the amount of force a prudent person would use in similar circumstances. (7)

REBUTTAL testimony by a witness for the prosecution given to contradict the testimony (or evidence) presented by the defense. (21)

RECTANGULAR-COORDINATE (PLOTTING) METHOD uses two adjacent walls of a room as fixed points from which distances are measured at right angles from each wall. (2)

RELEVANT EVIDENCE evidence that applies to the matter in question. (5)

RELEVANT PHOTOGRAPH an image that assists or explains testimony regarding the matter in question. (2)

RETAILING forewarning gang members that violent crime will bring consequences and offering incentives, such as services, to reject crime. (19)

RES GESTAE **STATEMENTS** spontaneous statements made at the time a crime is committed. Considered more truthful than planned responses. (1)

RESIDENTIAL BURGLARY one that occurs in buildings, structures or attachments that are used as or are suitable for dwellings, even though they may be unoccupied at the time of the burglary. (13)

RESOLUTION the fineness of image detail either captured with a camera, displayed on a monitor or printed on paper, commonly quantified in terms of pixels. (2)

REVERSE BUY labor-intensive, logistically complex narcotics investigation tactic. Also called a *sting*. (18)

RIFLING the lands and grooves inside a weapon, which grip and spin the bullet as it passes through the bore, providing greater projectile control and accuracy. (5)

RIGOR MORTIS a stiffening of portions of the body after death, presumably due to enzyme breakdown. (8)

RITUAL prescribed form of religious or mystical ceremony. (19)

RITUALISTIC CRIME an unlawful act committed with or during a ceremony. (19)

ROBBERY the felonious taking of another's property, either directly from the person or in the person's presence, through force or intimidation. (12)

ROBOTRIPPING slang for the act of drinking bottles of cough syrup, such as Robitussin DM, to get high. (18)

ROGUES' GALLERY mug shots gathered in files and displayed in groups. (2)

ROHYPNOL the "date rape drug," a sedative that dissolves rapidly when placed in a carbonated drink and acts quickly (20 to 30 minutes) to produce physical as well as mental incapacitation. after ingestion. (10)

ROUGH SKETCH the first, pencil-drawn outline of the crime scene, which shows the location of objects and evidence. Basis for the finished *scale drawing*. (2)

ROUGH TAIL moving surveillance in which it does not matter if the surveillant is detected. (7)

ROUTINE ACTIVITY THEORY crime results from the convergence of three elements in time and space: a presence of likely or motivated offenders; a presence of suitable targets; and an absence of capable guardians to prevent the criminal act. (13)

RULE ON WITNESSES the common exclusion of witnesses from the courtroom during a trial, in an effort to keep witnesses from hearing each other's testimony. Also called the *witness sequestration rule*. (21)

S

SABBAT a gathering of witches. (19)

SADIST person who receives sexual gratification from causing pain to others, often through mutilation. (10)

SADOMASOCHISTIC ABUSE fettering, binding or otherwise physically restraining, whipping or torturing for sexual gratification. (10)

SAFE semiportable strongbox with combination lock. (13)

SCALE used in sketching, determined by taking the longest measurement at the scene and dividing it by the longest measurement of the paper. (2)

SCALE DRAWING (FINISHED DRAWING) the final drawing, drawn to scale using exact measurements, done in ink and usually on a better grade paper. (2)

SCANNER a device that can look at a typed page or photograph, convert it to digital format and copy it onto a disk. (17)

SCAVENGER GANGS loosely organized groups described as "urban survivors"; prey on the weak in inner cities; engage in rather petty crimes but sometimes violence, often just for fun; members have no greater bond than their impulsiveness and need to belong; lack goals and are low achievers; often illiterate with poor school performance. (19)

SCRIPT a text file containing a sequence of computer commands. (17)

SEARCH an examination of a person's house or other buildings or premises or of the person for the purpose of discovering contraband, illicit or stolen property or some evidence of guilt to be used in prosecuting a criminal action with which the person is charged. (4)

SEARCH PATTERNS systematic approaches to seeking evidence at a crime scene; e.g., by using lanes, concentric circles or zones. (4)

SECOND-DEGREE MURDER intent to cause the death of another, but without premeditation. (8)

SECTOR (SEARCH PATTERN) see **ZONE SEARCH PATTERN**. (4)

SERIAL MURDER the killing of three or more victims with emotional time breaks between the killings. (8)

SERIOUS DELINQUENT GANGS heavy involvement in both serious and minor crimes, but much lower involvement in drug use and drug sales than party gangs. (19)

SEXUAL CONTACT (ILLEGAL) any sexual act committed without the complainant's consent for the suspect's sexual or aggressive satisfaction. (10)

SEXUAL EXPLOITATION (OF MINOR) to employ, use, persuade, induce, entice or coerce a minor to engage or assist in engaging in any sexually explicit conduct; e.g., prostitution and pornography. (11)

SEXUAL PENETRATION includes sexual intercourse, cunnilingus, fellatio, anal intercourse or any other intrusion, no matter how slight, into the victim's genital, oral or anal openings by the suspect's body or by an object. An emission of semen is not required. (10)

SEXUAL SEDUCTION (OF MINOR) ordinary sexual intercourse, anal intercourse, cunnilingus or fellatio committed by a nonminor with a consenting minor. (11)

SEXUALLY EXPLICIT CONDUCT general term referring to any type of sexual intercourse between persons of the same or opposite sex, bestiality, sadomasochistic abuse, lewd exhibition or masturbation. (10)

SHOPLIFTING taking an item from a retail store without paying for it. (14)

SHORT-CON GAMES victims are taken for whatever money they have on their person at the time of the swindle. (14)

SHOW-UP IDENTIFICATION on-the-scene identification of a suspect by a victim of or witness to a crime. Also called *field identification*. (7)

SHRINKAGE the unexplained or unauthorized reduction of inventory from a retail establishment. (14)

SIMPLE ARSON intentional destruction by fire or explosives that does not create imminent danger to life or risk of great bodily harm. (16)

SIMPLE ASSAULT intentionally causing another person to fear immediate bodily harm or death or intentionally inflicting or attempting to inflict bodily harm on another. Usually a misdemeanor. (9)

SINSEMILLA homegrown marijuana. (18)

SKETCH a drawing (noun), or to create a drawing (verb). May be a rough or a finished sketch. (2)

SKITTLING ingesting high doses of Coricidin Cough and Cold ("Triple C") tablets to get high. (18)

SLAMMING the unauthorized switch of a long-distance carrier, representing the number one and fastest growing category of complaints to the FCC. (14)

SLANTING including only one side of a story or only facts that tend to prove or support one side's theory; result of a lack of objectivity (3)

SLEEPER CELL a group of terrorists who blend into a community. (20)

SLIDING occurs when an unauthorized carrier switches a specific call from the long-distance carrier. (14)

SMASH AND GRAB in burglary, breaking a window and taking items from the window display. (13)

SMURFING more technically known as *structuring*, it is a method of money laundering whereby large amounts of cash are broken into increments less than $10,000, to avoid federal reporting requirements, and deposited into various bank accounts. (14)

SNIFFING monitoring data traveling along a network. (17)

SODOMY any form of unnatural sex. (10)

SOFTWARE (COMPUTER) the programs run by a computer. (1)

SOLVABILITY FACTORS those crucial to resolving criminal investigations. (7)

SOURCES-OF-INFORMATION FILE a file that contains the name and location of persons, organizations and records that can assist in a criminal investigation. (6)

SPALLING the breaking off of surface pieces of concrete, cement or brick due to intense heat. (16)

SPAM unsolicited bulk e-mail messages, similar in concept to junk mail and commonly commercial in nature. Less commonly known by its formal designation as *unsolicited commercial email* (UCE). (17)

SPECTROGRAPHIC ANALYSIS using a laboratory instrument that rapidly analyzes color and coloring agents in small samples of material to determine what elements they contain. (5)

SPOOFING Acquiring unauthorized access to a computer or network through a message using an IP address that appears to be from a trusted host; often considered synonymous with phishing (17)

SPYWARE malicious, covert (difficult to detect) software that infects a computer in a manner similar to viruses, collecting information or executing other programs without the user's knowledge. Some programs can track which Web sites a user visits; some can track and capture personal user information. (17)

STAKE-IN-CONFORMITY a constellation of variables that, in effect, influence someone to take a particular course of action. For offenders, it comprises what they stand to lose if convicted, such as marital status, residential stability, or employment. (9)

STAKEOUT see **STATIONARY SURVEILLANCE**. (7)

STALKER a person who intentionally and repeatedly follows, attempts to contact, harasses, and/or intimidates another person. (9)

STALKING harassing or threatening behavior that an individual engages in repeatedly. (9)

STANDARD OF COMPARISON an object, measure or model with which evidence is compared to determine whether both originated from the same source. (5)

STATEMENT a legal narrative description of events related to a crime. (6)

STATIONARY SURVEILLANCE observing a location from a fixed location. Also called *fixed surveillance, plant* and *stakeout.* (7)

STATUTORY RAPE sexual intercourse with a minor, with or without consent. (10)

STEGANOGRAPHY Greek for "hidden writing," aims to keep everyone except the intended recipient of a message oblivious to its very existence by making the message appear as some type of "cover" message—a shopping list, a picture, etc. (17)

STING a complex operation organized and implemented by undercover agents to apprehend criminals, especially drug dealers. Also called a *reverse buy.*(18)

STOCKHOLM SYNDROME a psychological phenomenon where hostages bear no ill feelings toward the hostage takers and, in fact, fear the police more than their captors. (12)

STREET GANG a group of individuals who form a social allegiance and engage in unlawful or criminal activity. (19)

STRIATIONS highly individualized and characteristic scratches made on a projectile (bullet) as it passes through a weapon's rifling; provide valuable comparison evidence on recovered bullets. (5)

STRIKERS firefighters who set fires to become heroes in putting them out. (16)

STRIP-SEARCH-PATTERN an adaptation of the lane search pattern that is used when only one officer is available to search. (4)

STRUCTURING A common method of money laundering whereby large amounts of cash are broken into increments less than $10,000 to avoid federal reporting requirements and deposited into various bank accounts; also called *smurfing.* (14)

SUBJECT what is observed during surveillance; e.g., a person, place, property, vehicle, group of persons, organization, object. (7)

SUBPOENA a written order to appear before the court. (21)

SUDDEN INFANT DEATH SYNDROME (SIDS) a tragic condition, whose cause is uncertain, that takes the lives of young victims and for which parents may become suspected of child abuse. (11)

SUICIDE intentionally taking one's own life. (8)

SUICIDE BY POLICE a situation where a person decides he or she wants to die but doesn't want to pull the trigger and so, therefore, creates a situation where police are forced to shoot. (8)

SURREBUTTAL testimony by a witness for the defense given to contradict the testimony (or evidence) presented by the prosecution. (21)

SURVEILLANCE the covert, discrete observation of people, places or objects. (7)

SURVEILLANT an investigator assigned to surveillance. (7)

SUSPECT person considered to be directly or indirectly connected with a crime, either by overt act or by planning and/or directing it. If charged and brought to trial, is called a *defendant.* (6)

SWARMING a theft technique where a mass of individuals rapidly enter, steal from and exit an establishment, overwhelming employees' capabilities to do anything about the situation. (19)

T

TAIL *see* **MOVING SURVEILLANCE.** (7)

TARGET HARDENING altering physical characteristics of a property to make it less attractive to criminals; also called *crime prevention through environmental design* (CPTED). (13)

TECHNOLOGICAL TERRORISM attacking our sources of power or converting a power source into a weapon of destruction. (20)

TELEMATIC TECHNOLOGY the transfer of data between a remote vehicle and a host computer, such as with bait cars. (15)

TEMPORARY CUSTODY WITHOUT HEARING removing a child from the custody of parents or guardians for a brief period, usually 48 hours. (11)

TERRITORIAL GANGS gangs that are associated with a specific area or turf and, as a result, get involved in conflicts with other gangs over their respective turfs. (19)

TERRORISM the unlawful use of force or violence against persons or property to intimidate or coerce a government, the civilian population, or any segment thereof, in furtherance of political or social objectives (FBI). (20)

TERRY DECISION established that a patdown or frisk is a protective search for weapons and, as such, must be confined to a scope reasonably designed to discover guns, knives, clubs and other hidden instruments for the assault of a police officer or others. (4)

TERRY STOP the detaining, questioning, and possible frisking of an individual based on an officer's *reasonable suspicion* of that individual's involvement in criminal activity. (4)

TESTIMONIAL HEARSAY prior testimony or statements made as a result of police interrogation; a witness' statement obtained through "structured questioning" by police officers that is inadmissible in a criminal trial unless the witness is unavailable to testify and be cross-examined by the defendant. (6)

THE WELL the area within the courtroom that exists in front of the judge and between the judge and the attorney's tables; normally off-limits and to be entered only if the judge so directs or permission is granted. Traditionally, the area is a sword's length and was intended for the judge's protection. (21)

THEFT *see* **LARCENY.** (14)

THIRD DEGREE the use of physical force, threats of force or other physical, mental or psychological abuse to get a suspect to confess. (6)

THIRD-DEGREE MURDER death that results from an imminently dangerous act but does not involve premeditation or intent. (8)

TIGHT TAIL *see* **CLOSE TAIL.** (7)

TOOL MARK an impression left by a tool on a surface. (5)

TOTALITY-OF-THE-CIRCUMSTANCES TEST a principle upon which a number of legal assessments are made; refers to the sum total of factors leading a reasonable person to a course of action. (4)

TOXICOLOGY the study of poisons. Toxicologists are consulted if food or drink poisoning is suspected. (8)

TRACE EVIDENCE extremely small physical matter. (5)

TRAILER a path, consisting of paper, hay, flammable compounds or any other substance that burns, that is set down for a fire to follow. Indicates arson. (16)

TRAP PHOTOGRAPHY photos that prove an incident occurred, can assist in identifying suspects and the weapons used and can corroborate witness testimony and identification. Also called *surveillance photography.* (2)

TRASHING to scavenge through a business' garbage looking for useful information. Also called *dumpster diving.* (17)

TRIANGULATION (PLOTTING METHOD) uses straight-line measurements from two fixed objects to the location of the evidence, creating a triangle. The evidence is in the angle formed by the two straight lines. (2)

TROJAN HORSE a malicious program hidden inside an apparently harmless, legitimate program, intended to carry out unauthorized or illegal functions. (17)

TRUE (UNCONTAMINATED) SCENE crime scene where no evidence has been introduced or removed except by the person(s) committing the crime. (4)

TRUTH SERUMS fast-acting barbiturates used to produce sleep at the approximate level of surgical anesthesia for the purpose of releasing a person's inhibitions so that he or she will give information not available otherwise. Most commonly used are sodium amytol and sodium pentathol. (6)

TURF geographic area claimed by a gang. Often marked by graffiti. (19)

TWEAKER a methamphetamine addict. (18)

U

ULTRAVIOLET (UV) LIGHT the invisible energy at the violet end of the color spectrum that causes substances to emit visible light. Commonly called *fluorescence.* Used to detect secret inks, invisible laundry marks, seminal fluid stains, marked buy money or extortion packages. (5)

ULTRAVIOLET-LIGHT PHOTOGRAPHY uses the low end of the color spectrum, which is invisible to human sight, to make visible impressions of bruises and injuries long after their occurrence. In addition, the type of weapon used can often be determined by examining its impression developed using ultraviolet light. (2)

UNCONTAMINATED SCENE *see* **TRUE SCENE.** (5)

UNDERCOVER using an assumed identity to obtain information and/or evidence. (7)

UPLOAD to transfer data, files or pictures to another computer; opposite of *download.* (17)

URL Uniform Resource Locator; a Web address. (17)

V

VAULT stationary security chamber of reinforced concrete, often steel-lined, with a combination lock. (13)

VEHICLE IDENTIFICATION NUMBER *see* **VIN** (15)

VERIFIED RESPONSE POLICY a procedure implemented by some law enforcement agencies, whereby they will not respond to a burglary alarm unless criminal activity is first confirmed through either an onsite security officer or some method of electronic surveillance, such as CCTV. (13)

VICTIM the person injured by a crime. (6)

VICTIMLESS CRIME crime in which the victim is a willing participant in the illegal activity; e.g., a person who bets. (18)

VIN (VEHICLE IDENTIFICATION NUMBER) the primary nonduplicated, serialized number assigned by the manufacturer to each vehicle manufactured. Formerly called *serial number* or *motor vehicle identification number.* (15)

VIRTUAL REALITY an artificial, interactive world created by computer technology (usually involving some kind of immersion system such as a headset). (17)

VIRUS, COMPUTER a program created specifically to infect other programs with copies of itself. (17)

VISIBLE FINGERPRINTS prints made when fingers are dirty or stained when they leave their impression on a soft substance. (5)

VISUAL MEDIUM also called *visual print;* any film, photograph, negative, slide, book, magazine or other visual medium. (11)

VISUAL PRINT *see* **VISUAL MEDIUM.** (11)

VOICEPRINT graphic record of an individual's voice characteristics made by a sound spectrograph that records energy patterns emitted by speech. (5)

VOLUNTARY MANSLAUGHTER intentionally causing the death of another person in the heat of passion. (8)

VOYEURISM window peeking; Peeping Tom. (10)

W

WAIVER giving up of certain rights. (6)

WHITE-COLLAR CRIME business-related or occupational crime; e.g., embezzlement, computer crimes, bribery, pilferage. Also called *corporate crime* or *economic crime.* (14)

WIRETAPPING intercepting and recording telephone conversations by a mechanical device without the consent of either party in the conversation. (7)

WITNESS a person who saw a crime or some part of it being committed or who has relevant information. (6)

WITNESS SEQUESTRATION RULE the common practice of excluding witnesses from the courtroom during a trial to prevent one witness from hearing another witness's testimony. Also called the *rule on witnesses.* (21)

WORM (COMPUTER) a self-contained program that travels from machine to machine across network connections, often clogging networks and information systems as it spreads; need not become part of another program to propagate itself. (17)

X

X-RAY DIFFRACTION laboratory instrument that compares unknown crystalline substances and mixtures of crystals. (5)

Z

ZERO FLOOR RELEASE the requirement that all transactions by credit card be authorized. (14)

ZOMBIE a computer that has been taken over by another computer, typically through infection with hidden software (virus) that allows the zombie machine to be accessed and controlled remotely, often with the intention of perpetrating attacks on other computers. (17)

ZONE (SEARCH PATTERN) search pattern in which an area is divided into equal squares and numbered and then each square is searched individually. Also called *sector search pattern.* (4)

Photo Credits

Chapter 1

09: © Eric Liebowitz/CBS Photo Archive via Getty Images **14:** © Bob Daemmrich/PhotoEdit **18:** © AP/Wide World Photos **20:** © San Antonio Police Department **23:** © Michael Newman/PhotoEdit

Chapter 2

17: © Joel Gordon **42:** © Stockdisc/Getty Images **43:** © Crime Scene Virtual Tour **44:** © AP/Wide World Photos **48:** top, Images Courtesty of Pictometry International **48:** bottom, © Will Smith/Pictometry **49:** © Joel Gordon **52:** © AP/Wide World Photos **60:** Image created by CAD Zone, Inc. **61:** Created by VS Visual Statement, Inc. using Vista FX Software.

Chapter 3

68: © A. Ramey/PhotoEdit **82:** © Robert E. Daemmrich/Getty Images

Chapter 4

93: © Jonathan Kirn/Stock Connection **105:** © James Shaffer/PhotoEdit **107:** © Paul J.Richards/AFP/Getty Images

Chapter 5

114: center left, © Sean O'brien/Custom Medical Stock Photo **115:** bottom left, © AP/ Wide World Photos **118:** © BVDA America Inc. **119:** © Reuters/CORBIS **120:** © Mario Villafuerte/Getty Images **127:** bottom left, © Mauro Fermariello/Science Photo Library/Photo Researchers, Inc. **130:** © Mauro Fermariello/Science Photo Library/Photo Researchers, Inc. **136:** top, © Joel Gordon **137:** © Science VU/Visuals Unlimited **138:** © Spencer Grant/PhotoEdit **139:** top, Courtesy of the Lakewood Police Department Crime Lab **139:** bottom, © Stephen Ferry/ Liaison/ Getty Images **140:** © Clouds Hill Imaging Ltd./Corbis **141:** top right, © County of Westchester, New York. Used with Permission. **130:** © Mauro Fermariello/Science Photo Library/Photo Researchers, Inc. **148:** © AP/Wide World Photos **149:** © CDC/PHIL/CORBIS **151:** © Marco Di Lauro/ Getty Images **152:** © Reuters/CORBIS

Chapter 6

163: top, © Paul Conklin/PhotoEdit **167:** © Joel Gordon **185:** © AP/Wide World Photos **186:** © AP/Wide World Photos

Chapter 7

197: top, © Environmental Criminology Research Inc. **197:** bottom, © Environmental Criminology Research Inc. **202:** © Helen King/Corbis **210:** © TEK IMAGE/Science Photo Library/Photo Researchers, Inc. **212:** © Michael Newman/PhotoEdit **214:** © 911 Pictures

Chapter 8

243: © AP/Wide World Photos **245:** top, Courtesy of the Lakewood Police Department Crime Lab **245:** bottom, Courtesy of the Lakewood Police Department Crime Lab **248:** © Shepard Sherbell/CORBIS **250:** © 2000-2005 Custom Medical Stock Photo

Chapter 9

273: © Mark Burnett/Photo Researchers, Inc. **277:** Sonkin, Daniel J. (2000. rev. 2003) Domestic Violence: The Court Mandated Perpetrator Assessment and Treatment Handbook. Sausalito, CA: Daniel Sonkin (http://www.daniel-sonkin.com) **284:** © AP/Wide World Photos

Chapter 10

299: © Spencer Grant/PhotoEdit **303:** © Joel Gordon **311:** © State of Arizona, Department of Public Safety/Sex Offender Info Center

Chapter 11

319: © Jacques M. Chenet/CORBIS **325:** bottom, © Cynthia Harnest/www.teach-a-bodies.com **325:** top, © Michael Newman/PhotoEdit **327:** © Hill Creek Pictures/ Index Stock Imagery **329:** © AP/Wide World Photos **335:** © L. Clarke/CORBIS **343:** © AP/Wide World Photos **344:** © AP/Wide World Photos

Chapter 12

355: © Eleanor Bentall/CORBIS **358:** © AP/Wide World Photos

Chapter 13

377: © Digital Vision Ltd./SuperStock **378:** © 911 Pictures **383:** © Joel Gordon **384:** © James Shaffer **385:** bottom, United States Department of Justice/Bureau of Alcohol, Tobacco, Fire Arms and Explosives **385:** top, © Digital Vision Ltd./SuperStock

Chapter 14

395: © Bill Varie/CORBIS **398:** AP/WideWorld Photos **409:** bottom, © AP/WideWorld **409:** top, © Ingram Publishing/Alamy **413:** The United States Federal Trade Commission **416:** © Evening Chronicle, UK. **417:** © Stuart Ramson/Getty Images **421:** © OSF/CORDANO, MARTY/ Animals Animals

Chapter 15

429: © Robert Mecea/Newsmakers/Getty Images **430:** © Malcom Fife/zefa/Corbis **440:** © Joel Gordon **442:** © 2005 National Equipment Register, Inc. 1-866-FIND PIN, www.NERusa.com Reprinted by permission.

Chapter 16

456: © 911 Pictures **460:** © James Shaffer/ PhotoEdit **461:** top, © James Shaffer **461:** bottom, © 911 Pictures **462:** © Spencer Platt/Getty Images **468:** © 911 Pictures

Chapter 17

478: © AP/Wide World Photos **482:** © Roslan Rahman/AFP/Getty Images **484:** © US-CERT **487:** Modified with permission from artwork © BBC News **500:** © Getty Images **504:** © Getty Images

Chapter 18

518: © Mark Richards/PhotoEdit **519:** © Scott Houston/CORBIS **525:** © James Shaffer **527:** © Debbie Bragg/ Everynight Images/

Author Index

Subject Index